FINANCIAL ACCOUNTING

Tools for Business Decision-Making

Canadian Edition

Paul D. Kimmel PhD, CPA

Associate Professor of Accounting
University of Wisconsin—Milwaukee
Milwaukee, Wisconsin

Jerry J. Weygandt PhD, CPA

Arthur Andersen Alumni Professor of Accounting
University of Wisconsin
Madison, Wisconsin

Donald E. Kieso PhD, CPA

KPMG Peat Marwick Emeritus Professor of Accountancy
Northern Illinois University
DeKalb, Illinois

Barbara Trenholm MBA, FCA

Professor of Accounting
University of New Brunswick
Fredericton, New Brunswick

John Wiley & Sons Canada, Ltd.

Toronto • New York • Chichester • Weinheim • Brisbane • Singapore

Dedicated to our families,
most especially our spouses.

Canadian Cataloguing in Publication Data

Financial accounting: tools for business decision making

1st Canadian ed.
Includes index.
ISBN 0-471-64604-0

1. Accounting. I. Trenholm, Barbara A.

HF5635.F44 2000 657'.044 C00-932580-8

Production Credits

Acquisitions Editor: John Horne
Publishing Services Director: Karen Bryan
Managing Editor: Karen Staudinger
New Media Editor: Elsa Passera
Editorial Production Assistant: Michelle Love
Cover Illustration: Marcelle Faucher
Cover Design: Interrobang Graphic Design Inc.
Senior Graphic Designer: Ian J. Koo
Text Layout: Lakshmi Gosyne, Natalia Burobina
Printing and Binding: Tri-Graphic Printing Limited

Printed and Bound in Canada
10 9 8 7 6 5 4 3 2 1

John Wiley & Sons Canada, Ltd.
22 Worcester Road
Etobicoke, Ontario
M9W 1L1
Visit our website at: www.wiley.com/canada

ABOUT THE AUTHORS

CANADIAN EDITION

Barbara Trenholm, MBA, FCA is a professor of accounting at the University of New Brunswick. She is a recipient of the University of New Brunswick's Excellence in Teaching Award and has received international recognition for the quality of her teaching as a recipient of the Global Teaching Excellence Award.

Her experience in education has been widely recognized throughout Canada. She is the Chair of the Canadian Institute of Chartered Accountants (CICA) Academic Research Committee and member and past co-chair of the Canadian Institute of Chartered Accountants/Canadian Academic Accounting Association Liaison Committee. She is a past chair of the CICA Interprovincial Education Committee, past president of the New Brunswick Institute of Chartered Accountants, and has served on the CICA Board of Governors, the Education Reengineering Task Force, International Qualifications Appraisal Board, the Atlantic School of Chartered Accountancy Board of Governors, the American Accounting Association's Globalization Initiatives Task Force, and the National Post Leaders in Management Education awards panel. Within the University, she is the co-chair of the University's Pension Board, and has had responsibilities as Acting Dean of the Faculty of Administration and as a member of the University Senate, in addition to numerous other faculty and university committees.

She has published widely in the field of accounting standard setting and explored various director and auditor liability issues in journals including *Accounting Horizons, International Journal of Production Economics, CAmagazine, CGA Magazine,* and *CMA Magazine*. She is on the editorial board of the *Journal of Academy of Business Administration* and on the board of reviewers for the *Journal of Business Education*. She is also the Canadian author of the Weygandt, Kieso, Trenholm, *Accounting Principles*, published by John Wiley & Sons Canada, Ltd.

US EDITION

Paul D. Kimmel, PhD, CPA, is an Associate Professor at the University of Wisconsin—Milwaukee. He has public accounting experience with Deloitte & Touche (Minneapolis). He is the recipient of the UWM School of Business Advisory Council Teaching Award, the Reggie Taite Excellence in Teaching Award, a three-time winner of the Outstanding Teaching Assistant Award at the University of Wisconsin, and a recipient of the Elijah Watts Sells Award for Honourary Distinction for his results on the CPA exam. He is a member of the American Accounting Association and has published articles in the *Accounting Review, Accounting Horizons, Issues in Accounting Education*, and the *Journal of Accounting Education* as well as other journals. His research interests include accounting for financial instruments and innovation in accounting education. He has published papers and given numerous talks on incorporating critical thinking into accounting education, and helped prepare a catalogue of critical thinking resources for the Federated Schools of Accountancy.

Jerry J. Weygandt, PhD, CPA, is the Arthur Andersen Alumni Professor of Accounting at the University of Wisconsin-Madison. Articles by Professor Weygandt have appeared in the *Accounting Review, Journal of Accounting Research*, the *Journal of Accountancy*, and other professional journals. These articles have examined such financial reporting issues as accounting for price-level adjustments, pensions, convertible securities, stock option contracts, and interim reports. He is a member of the American Accounting Association, the American Institute of Certified Public Accountants, and the Wisconsin Society of Certified Public Accountants. He has served on numerous committees of the American Accounting Association and as a member of the editorial board of the *Accounting Review*. In addition, he is actively involved with the American Institute of Certified Public Accountants and has been a member of the Accounting Standards Executive Committee (AcSEC) of that organization. He has served on the FASB task force that examined the reporting issues related to "accounting for income taxes" and is presently a trustee of the Financial Accounting Foundation. Professor Weygandt has received the Chancellor's Award for Excellence in Teaching, the Wisconsin Institute of CPA's Outstanding Educator's Award and the Lifetime Achievement Award. He also has served as President and Secretary-Treasurer of the American Accounting Association.

Donald E. Kieso, PhD, CPA, is the KPMG Emeritus Professor of Accounting at Northern Illinois University. He has public accounting experience with Price Waterhouse & Co. (San Francisco and Chicago) and Arthur Andersen & Co. (Chicago) and research experience with the Research Division of the American Institute of Certified Public Accountants (New York). He is a recipient of NIU's Teaching Excellence Award and four Golden Apple Teaching Awards. He has served as a member of the Board of Directors of the Illinois CPA Society, the AACSB's Accounting Accreditation Committee, the State of Illinois Comptroller's Commission, as Secretary-Treasurer of the Federation of Schools of Accountancy, and as Secretary-Treasurer of the American Accounting Association. Professor Kieso is serving as Chairman of the Board of Trustees and Executive Committee of Aurora University, the Boards of Directors of Castle BancGroup Inc. and Valley West Community Hospital, and as Secretary-Treasurer of The Sandwich Hospital Resolution Board. From 1989 to 1993 he served as a charter member of the national Accounting Education Change Commission. In 1988 he received the Outstanding Accounting Educator Award from the Illinois CPA Society. In 1992 he received the FSA's Joseph A. Silvoso Award of Merit and the NIU Foundation's Humanitarian Award for Service to Higher Education. In 1995 he received a Distinguished Service Award from the Illinois CPA Society.

PREFACE

In recent years accounting education has seen numerous efforts to change the way accounting is taught. These efforts reflect the demands of an ever-changing business world, opportunities created by new instructional technologies, and an increased understanding of how students learn. In this book we have drawn from what we believe to be the most promising of these innovations. Our efforts were driven by a few key beliefs:

- **"Less is more."**
  Our instructional objective is to provide students with an understanding of those concepts that are fundamental to the use of accounting. Most students will forget procedural details within a short period of time. On the other hand, concepts, if well taught, should be remembered for a lifetime. Concepts are especially important in a world where the details are constantly changing.

- **"Don't just sit there—do something."**
  Students learn best when they are actively engaged. The overriding pedagogical objective of this book is to provide students with continual opportunities for active learning. One of the best tools for active learning is strategically placed questions. Our discussions are framed by questions, often beginning with rhetorical questions and ending with review questions. Even our selection of analytical devices, called Decision Tools, is referenced using key questions to emphasize the purpose of each.

- **"I'll believe it when I see it."**
  Students will be most willing to commit time and energy to a topic when they believe that it is relevant to their future career. There is no better way to demonstrate relevance than to ground discussion in the real world. Consistent with this, we adopted a macro-approach: Chapters 1 and 2 show students how to use financial statements of real companies. By using high-profile companies such as Loblaw, Sobeys, Chapters, Canadian Tire, Le Château, and Sears to frame our discussion of accounting issues, we demonstrate the relevance of accounting while teaching students about companies with which they have daily contact. As they become acquainted with the financial successes and failures of these companies many students will begin to follow business news more closely, making their learning a dynamic, ongoing process. We also discuss small companies to highlight the challenges they face as they try to grow.

- **"You need to make a decision."**
  All business people must make decisions. Decision-making involves critical evaluation and analysis of the information at hand, and this takes practice. We have integrated important analytical tools throughout the book. After each new decision tool is presented, we summarize the key features of that tool in a Decision Toolkit. At the end of each chapter we provide a comprehensive demonstration of an analysis of a real company using the decision tools presented in the chapter. The presentation of these tools throughout the book is sequenced to take full advantage of the tools presented in earlier chapters, culminating in a capstone analysis chapter.

- **"It's a small world."**
  Rapid improvements to both information technology and transportation are resulting in a single global economy. The Internet has made it possible for even small businesses to sell their products virtually anywhere in the world. Few business decisions can be made without consideration to international factors. In fact, a significant number of Canadian companies operate globally and have key US or non-North American competitors. To heighten student awareness of international issues, we reference non-Canadian companies and discuss how to compare financial statements of companies in other countries.

PROVEN PEDAGOGICAL FRAMEWORK

In this book we have used many proven pedagogical tools to help students learn accounting concepts and apply them to decision-making in the business world. This pedagogical framework emphasizes the processes students undergo as they learn.

Learning How to Use the Text

A Student Owner's Manual begins the text to help students understand the value of the pedagogical framework and how to use it. After becoming familiar with the pedagogy, students can take a learning styles quiz to help them identify how they learn best (visually, aurally, through reading and writing, kinesthetically, or through a combination of these styles). We then offer tips on in-class and out-of-class learning strategies, as well as help in identifying the text pedagogy that would be most useful to them for their learning style. Finally, Chapter 1 contains notes (printed in red) that explain each pedagogical element the first time it appears.

Understanding the Context

- **Study Objectives**, listed at the beginning of each chapter, form a learning framework throughout the text, with each objective repeated in the margin at the appropriate place in the main body of the chapter and again in the **Summary of Study Objectives**. Also, end-of-chapter assignment materials are linked to the Study Objectives.
- A **Chapter-Opening Vignette** presents a scenario that relates an actual business situation of a well-known company to the topic of the chapter. The vignette also serves as a recurrent example throughout the chapter. The vignettes include the Internet address of the company cited in the story to encourage students to go on-line to get more information about these companies.
- A chapter **Preview** links the chapter-opening vignette to the major topics of the chapter. First, an introductory paragraph explains how the vignette relates to the topics to be discussed, and then a graphic outline of the chapter provides a "visual road map," useful for seeing the big picture as well as the connections between subtopics.

Learning the Material

- This book emphasizes the accounting experiences of **real companies** throughout, from chapter-opening vignettes to the chapter's last item of assignment material. Details on these many features follow. In addition, every chapter uses financial statements from real companies. These specimen financial statements are easily identified by the company logo or related photo that appears near the statement heading.

  Our "focus companies" are **Loblaw** and **Sobeys**. They were chosen because they had high name recognition with students, they operate primarily in a single industry, and they have relatively simple financial statements. Selections from Loblaw's and Sobeys' annual reports are included in appendices to the text.

  To emphasize the **global** nature of today's business world, references to, and discussions about, non-Canadian companies have been incorporated.
- Continuing the real-world flavour of the book, **Business Insight** boxes in each chapter give students glimpses into how real companies make decisions using accounting information. The boxes, highlighted with striking photographs, focus on three different accounting perspectives—those of investors, managers, and international business.
- Colour **illustrations** support and reinforce the concepts of the text. **Infographics** are a special type of illustration that help students visualize and apply accounting concepts to the real world. The infographics often portray important concepts in entertaining and memorable ways.
- **Before You Go On** sections occur at the end of each key topic and consist of two parts: ***Review It*** serves as a learning check within the chapter by asking students to stop and answer knowledge and comprehension questions about the material just covered. ***Review It*** questions marked with the Loblaw symbol send students to find information in **Loblaw's** 1999 annual report, which is printed in Appendix A at the back of the book. These exercises help cement students' understanding of how topics covered in the chapter are reported in real-world financial statements. Answers appear at the end of the chapter. ***Do It*** is a brief demonstration problem that gives immediate practice using the material just covered. Solutions are provided to help students understand the reasoning involved in reaching an answer.
- **Accounting equation analyses** have been inserted in the margin next to key journal entries. This feature reinforces students' understanding of the impact of an accounting transaction on the financial statements.
- **Helpful Hints** in the margins expand upon or

DECISION TOOLKIT

Decision Checkpoints	Info Needed for Decision	Tool to Use for Decision	How to Evaluate Results
Are collections being made in a timely fashion?	Net credit sales and average receivables balance	$\text{Receivables turnover ratio} = \frac{\text{Net credit sales}}{\text{Average net receivables}}$ $\text{Average collection period} = \frac{\text{365 days}}{\text{Receivables turnover ratio}}$	Average collection period should be consistent with corporate credit policy. An increase may suggest a decline in financial health of customers.

help clarify concepts under discussion in the nearby text. This feature actually makes the book an Annotated Student Edition.

- **Alternative Terminology** notes in the margins present synonymous terms that students may come across in subsequent accounting courses and in business.
- Marginal **International Notes** provide a helpful and convenient way for instructors to begin to expose students to international issues in accounting, reporting, and decision-making.
- Each chapter presents **decision tools** that are useful for analysing the financial statement components discussed in that chapter. At the end of the text discussion relating to the decision tool, a **Decision Toolkit** summarizes the key features of that decision tool and reinforces its purpose. For example, Chapter 8 presents the receivables turnover ratio and average collection period as tools for use in analysing receivables. At the end of that discussion the Toolkit you see at the top of this page is shown.
- A **Using the Decision Toolkit** exercise, which follows the final Before You Go On section in the chapter, asks students to use the decision tools presented in that chapter. Students evaluate the financial situation of a real-world company, often using ratio analysis to do so. In many cases the company used in this analysis is a **competitor** of the example company in the chapter. For example, in Chapter 10, **Quebecor**, the world's largest commercial printer and Canada's second largest daily newspaper publisher, was analysed as the example company in the chapter discussion. **Hollinger**, Canada's largest daily newspaper publisher, was chosen to be analysed in the Using the Decision Toolkit at the end of the chapter. In chapter 13, both **Rogers Communications**, Canada's top cable company, and **Shaw Communications**, it's closest competitor, are compared in the Decision Tool Kit. Such comparisons expand and enrich the analysis and help focus student attention on comparative situations that flavour real-world decision-making.

Putting It Together

- At the end of each chapter, between the body of the text and the assignment materials, are several useful features for review and reference: a **Summary of Study Objectives** lists the main points of the chapter; the **Decision Toolkit—A Summary** presents in one place the decision tools used throughout the chapter; and a **Glossary** of important terms gives definitions with page references to the text. A complete summary of the Decision Toolkits found in each chapter is available on the website at www.wiley.com/canada/kimmel.
- Next, a **Demonstration Problem** gives students another opportunity to refer to a detailed solution to a representative problem before they do any of the end-of-chapter assignments. **Problem-solving Strategies** help establish a logic for approaching similar problems and assist students in understanding the solution.

Developing Skills Through Practice

Throughout the assignment material, certain questions, exercises, and problems make use of the decision tools presented in the chapter. These are marked with the icon . The financial results of real companies are included in many exercises and problems. These are indicated by the company name shown in red in the end of chapter material.

- **Self-Study Questions** comprise a practice test to enable students to check their understanding of important concepts. Answers to these questions appear at the end of the chapter. These questions are keyed to the Study Objectives, so students can go back and review sections of the chapter in which they find they need further work.

- **Questions** provide a full review of chapter content and help students prepare for class discussions and testing situations. These questions are also keyed to the Study Objectives.
- **Brief Exercises** build students' confidence and test their basic skills. Each exercise focuses on one of the Study Objectives.
- Each of the **Exercises** focuses on one or more of the Study Objectives. These tend to take a little longer to complete, and they present more of a challenge to students than Brief Exercises. The Exercises help instructors and students make a manageable transition to more challenging problems.
- **Problems** stress the applications of the concepts presented in the chapter, and are paired in sets **A** and **B**. Instructors have corresponding problems keyed to the same **Study Objectives**, thus giving greater flexibility in assigning problems. Certain problems, marked with the icon , help build business writing skills.
- Each Self-Study Question, Question, Brief Exercise, Exercise, and Problem has a **description of the concept** covered and is keyed to the Study Objectives.

Expanding and Applying Knowledge

Broadening Your Perspective is a unique section at the end of each chapter that offers a wealth of resources to help instructors and students pull together the learning for the chapter. This section offers problems and projects for those instructors who want to broaden the learning experience by bringing in more real-world decision-making and critical thinking activities.

- **Financial Reporting and Analysis** problems use financial statements of real-world companies for further practice in understanding and interpreting financial reporting. A ***Financial Reporting Problem*** in each chapter directs students to study various aspects of the financial statements of **Loblaw Companies Limited**, which are printed in Chapter 1 (in simplified form) and in Appendix A (in full). A ***Comparative Analysis Problem*** offers the opportunity to compare and contrast the financial reporting of Loblaw Companies Limited with a competitor, **Sobeys Inc.** Since the ability to read and understand business publications is an asset over the span of one's career, ***Research Cases*** direct students to articles published in popular business news sources and periodicals for further study and analysis of key topics. The ***Interpreting Financial Statements*** cases offer one or more minicases per chapter that ask students to read parts of financial statements of actual companies and use the decision tools presented in the chapter to interpret this information. A ***Global Focus*** asks students to apply concepts presented in the chapter to specific situations faced by international companies. ***Financial Analysis on the Web*** guide students to web sites from which they can mine and analyse information related to the chapter topic.
- **Critical Thinking** problems offer additional opportunities and activities. The ***Collaborative Learning Activities*** help students build decision-making skills by analysing accounting information in a less structured situation. These cases require teams of students to evaluate a manager's decision or lead to a decision among alternative courses of action. They also give practice in building business communication skills. ***Communication Activities*** provide practice in written communication—a skill much in demand among employers. ***Ethics Cases*** describe typical ethical dilemmas and ask students to analyse the situation, identify the ethical issues involved, and decide on an appropriate course of action.

ACKNOWLEDGMENTS

During the course of development of Financial Accounting, the author benefitted greatly from the input of manuscript reviewers, ancillary authors, and proofers. The constructive suggestions and innovative ideas of the reviewers and the creativity and accuracy of the ancillary authors, contributors, and proofers are greatly appreciated.

REVIEWERS

Cécile Ashman, *Algonquin College*
Rick Bates, *University of Guelph*
Ann Clarke-Okah, *Carleton University*
Judy Cumby, *Memorial University of Newfoundland*
Ian Feltmate, *Acadia University*
Gilbert Fick, *Langara College*
Leo Gallant, *St. Francis Xavier University*
Irene Griswold, *Douglas College*
Karen Touche Lightstone, *Saint Mary's University*
Dale Northey, *Sir Sanford Fleming College*
Sandra M. Robinson, *Concordia University*
Catherine Seguin, *University of Toronto*
Stuart B. Thomas, *University of Lethbridge*

ANCILLARY AUTHORS, CONTRIBUTORS, AND PROOFERS

Ann Clarke-Okah, *Carleton University*—Student Workbook author
Susan Cohlmeyer—Solutions Manual author
Judy Cumby, *Memorial University of Newfoundland*—Problem Material contributor
Elizabeth D'Anjou—Chapter Vignette author
Robin Hemmingsen, *Centennial College*—Computerized Test Bank author
Joanne Hinton, *University of New Brunwick*—Solutions Manual Proofreader
Majidul Islam and Lynn DeGrace, *Concordia University*—Instructor's Manual authors
Zofia Laubitz—Proofreader
Bob Maher, *University of New Brunswick*—Website Demonstration Problem contributor
David Schwinghamer, *Collège Ahuntsic*—Copyeditor
Barbara Trenholm, *University of New Brunswick*—PowerPoint Presentations author

This Canadian edition is based on the second US edition of *Financial Accounting: Tools for Business Decision-Making*, authored by Paul Kimmel, Jerry Weygandt, and Don Keiso. I would like to express my sincere appreciation to Paul, Jerry and Don for their willingness to work closely with me. Their extensive teaching and writing experiences provided valuable insights in the development of the Canadian edition.

I appreciate the exemplary support and professional commitment given me by Wiley Canada's president Diane Wood, acquisitions editor John Horne, managing editor Karen Staudinger, publishing services director Karen Bryan and her team of talented designers, marketing manager Janine Daoust, director of sales and marketing Maureen Talty, new media editor Elsa Passera, and review co-ordinator Michelle Harrington. I wish to also thank Wiley's dedicated sales representatives who work tirelessly to service your needs.

I thank Loblaw and Sobeys for permitting the use of their 1999 Annual Reports for the text's specimen financial statements and accompanying notes. I would also like to acknowledge the co-operation of many Canadian and international companies that allowed me to include extracts from their financial statements in the text and end-of-chapter material.

It would not have been possible to write this text without the understanding of my employer, colleagues, students, family, and friends. Together, they provided a creative and supportive environment for my work.

Suggestions and comments from users are encouraged and appreciated.

Barbara Trenholm
trenholm@unb.ca
Fredericton, New Brunswick
October 2000

CHAPTER 2

A Further Look at Financial Statements

After studying this chapter, you should be able to:

1. Describe the basic objective of financial reporting, and explain the meaning of generally accepted accounting principles.
2. Discuss the qualitative characteristics of accounting information.
3. Identify the two constraints in accounting.
4. Identify the sections of a classified balance sheet.
5. Identify and calculate ratios for analysing a company's profitability.
6. Explain the relationship between a statement of retained earnings, a statement of earnings, and a balance sheet.
7. Identify and calculate ratios for analysing a company's liquidity and solvency.

Just Fooling Around?

Few people could have predicted how dramatically the Internet would change the investment world. One of the most interesting results is how it has changed the way ordinary people invest their savings. Until recently, most individuals put their savings into mutual funds, relying on professionals to decide which shares to buy and sell. Now, more and more people are spurning investment professionals, choosing to strike out on their own and make their own investment decisions. In fact, a whole new breed of investors, known as "day traders," has arisen. These are people—from doctors to mechanics—who spend hours a day trading shares over the Internet. What has caused this change? The Internet has empowered individuals by providing instant access to information that was never available before.

Two early pioneers in this area were Tom and David Gardner. They created an on-line investor service called The Motley Fool. The name comes from Shakespeare's *As You Like It*. The brothers note that the fool in Shakespeare's plays was the only one who could speak unpleasant truths to kings and queens without being killed. Tom and David view themselves as twentieth century "fools," revealing the truths of the stock markets to the small investor, whom they feel insiders have taken advantage of. Their on-line bulletin board enables investors to exchange information and insights about companies.

Critics of these bulletin boards contend that they are nothing more than high-tech rumour mills that are largely

52

At the beginning of each chapter, **Study Objectives** provide you with a learning framework. Each Study Objective then reappears at the point within the chapter where the concept is discussed and is also summarized at the end of the chapter.

The **Chapter-Opening Vignette** is a brief story that helps you picture how the topics of the chapter relate to the real worlds of accounting and business. Throughout the chapter, references to the vignette will help you put new ideas in context, organize them, and remember them. Each vignette ends with the **Internet addresses** of the companies cited in the story.

The **Preview** begins by linking the vignette with the major topics of the chapter. It then gives a graphic outline of major topics and subtopics that will be discussed. This narrative and visual preview give you a mental framework upon which to arrange the information you are learning.

If you are thinking of purchasing shares on the Internet, or elsewhere, how can you decide what the shares are worth? If you own shares, how can you determine whether it is time to buy more shares—or time to bail out? Your decision will be influenced by a variety of considerations; one should be your careful analysis of a company's financial statements. The reason: financial statements offer relevant and reliable information which will help you in your share purchase decisions.

In this chapter we begin by looking at the objectives of financial reporting. We then take a closer look at the balance sheet and introduce some useful ways of evaluating the information provided by the statements. The content and organization of the chapter are as follows:

A FURTHER LOOK AT FINANCIAL STATEMENTS

- Objectives of Financial Reporting
  - Characteristics of Useful Information
  - Constraints in Accounting
- The Financial Statements Revisited
  - The Classified Balance Sheet
  - Using the Financial Statements

Objectives of Financial Reporting

STUDY OBJECTIVE 1

Describe the basic objective of financial reporting, and explain the meaning of generally accepted accounting principles.

Financial reporting is the term used to describe all of the financial information presented by a company—both in its financial statements and in additional disclosures provided in the annual report. For example, if you are deciding whether to invest in a company's shares, you need financial information to help make your decision. Such information should help you understand the company's past financial performance and current financial picture, and it should give you some idea of its future prospects. Although information found on electronic bulletin boards, like The Motley Fool, has its place, there is no substitute for careful study of the information available through traditional financial reporting channels.

The primary objective of financial reporting is to provide useful information for decision-making.

54

58 **CHAPTER 2** A Further Look at Financial Statements

The characteristics that make accounting information useful are summarized in Illustration 2-1.

Illustration 2-1
Characteristics of useful information

Colour illustrations, such as this infographic, help you visualize and apply the information as you study. They reinforce important concepts and therefore often contain material that may appear on exams.

CONSTRAINTS IN ACCOUNTING

STUDY OBJECTIVE 3
Identify the two constraints in accounting.

The goal of the characteristics we have discussed is to provide users of financial statements with the most useful information. Taken to the extreme, however, the pursuit of useful financial information could be far too costly for a company. Some constraints have therefore been agreed upon to ensure that accounting rules are applied in a reasonable fashion, from the perspectives of both the company and the user. **Constraints** permit a company to modify generally accepted accounting principles without jeopardizing the usefulness of the reported information. The constraints are cost-benefit and materiality.

Study Objectives reappear in the margins at the point where that topic is discussed. End-of-chapter exercises and problems are keyed to Study Objectives.

COST-BENEFIT

The cost-benefit constraint ensures that the value of the information exceeds the cost of providing it. Accountants could disclose every financial event that occurs and every contingency that exists. However, providing additional information entails a cost, and the benefits of providing this information, in some cases, may be less than the costs.

Key terms that represent essential concepts of the chapter topic are printed in blue where they are first explained in the text. They are listed and defined again in the end-of-chapter **Glossary.**

MATERIALITY

Materiality relates to a financial statement item's impact on a company's overall financial condition and operations. An item is **material** when its size makes it likely to influence the decision of an investor or creditor. It is **not material** if it is too small to affect a user's decision. In short, if the item does not make a difference, GAAP does not have to be followed. To determine the materiality of an amount—that is, to determine its financial significance—the item is compared to such items as total assets, total liabilities, sales revenue, and net earnings.

To illustrate how the constraint of materiality is applied, assume that Loblaw made a $100 error in recording revenue. Loblaw's total revenue exceeds $18 billion; thus, a $100 error is not material.

The two constraints are shown in Illustration 2-2.

Helpful Hint In fact, for Loblaw even a $100,000 difference is not material for most investment decisions.

Helpful Hints in the margins help clarify concepts being discussed.

Illustration 2-5 Current assets illustration

CANADA POST CORPORATION (in millions of dollars)	
Current Assets	
Cash and short-term investments	$411
Accounts receivable	346
Prepaid expenses	69
Total current assets	826

A company's current assets are important in assessing its short-term debt-paying ability, as is explained later in the chapter.

Financial statements appear regularly throughout the book. Often, numbers or categories are highlighted in red type to draw your attention to key information.

LONG-TERM INVESTMENTS

Long-term investments are generally investments in stocks and bonds of other corporations that are normally held for many years. Sears' long-term investments of $50.9 million in 1998 include bonds and loans. BCE, a global communications company, reported the following in a recent balance sheet:

Alternative Terminology *Long-term investments are often just referred to as investments.*

Illustration 2-6 Long-term investments section

BCE INC. (in millions of dollars)	
Assets	
Investments in associated and other companies	$9,536

Alternative terminology notes present synonymous terms that you may come across in practice.

BCE owns shares in telecommunications companies such as Teleglobe, Aliant, and Nortel Networks, to name but a few.

CAPITAL ASSETS

Capital assets are assets with relatively long useful lives that are used in operating the business. Capital assets can be tangible (with physical substance) or intangible (without physical substance). **Tangible capital assets** may include (1) property, plant and equipment, and (2) natural resources, such as mineral deposits, oil and gas reserves, and timber. **Intangible capital assets** provide future benefits through the special rights and privileges they convey, rather than through any physical characteristics. Patents, copyrights, trademarks, and franchises are some examples of intangible assets.

Alternative Terminology *Property, plant, and equipment are sometimes called fixed assets.*

Accounting equation analyses appear in the margin next to key journal entries. They will help you understand the impact of an accounting transaction on the financial statements.

124 CHAPTER 3 The Accounting Information System

Separate journal entries are made for each transaction. A complete entry consists of: (1) the date of the transaction, (2) the accounts and amounts to be debited and credited, and (3) a brief explanation of the transaction. These transactions would be recorded in the journal as in Illustration 3-17.

Illustration 3-17
Recording transactions in journal form

A	= L	+ SE
+10,000		+10,000

A	= L	+ SE
+5,000	+5,000	

A	= L	+ SE
+5,000		
−5,000		

GENERAL JOURNAL

Date		Account Titles and Explanation	Debit	Credit
2001				
Oct.	1	Cash	10,000	
		Common Shares		10,000
		(Invested cash in business)		
	1	Cash	5,000	
		Notes Payable		5,000
		(Issued three-month, 12% note payable for cash)		
	2	Office Equipment	5,000	
		Cash		5,000
		(Purchased office equipment for cash)		

Note the following features of the journal entries:

In the margins next to key journal entries are **equation analyses** that summarize the effect of the transaction on the three elements of the accounting equation.

1. The date of the transaction is entered in the Date column.
2. The account to be debited is entered first at the left. The account to be credited is then entered on the next line, indented under the line above. The indentation differentiates debits from credits and decreases the possibility of switching the debit and credit amounts.
3. The amounts for the debits are recorded in the Debit (left) column, and the amounts for the credits are recorded in the Credit (right) column.
4. A brief explanation of the transaction is given.

doing in this text; however, you will have to be careful to identify and interpret results that may only be due to the differing time periods.

Another factor that can complicate comparisons is the use of different currencies and different accounting standards when one compares companies from different countries. For example, one of Sears' primary competitors is U.S.-based Wal-Mart. Comparing the financial statements of these two competitors can be challenging. With no universally accepted set of international accounting standards, companies have responded with a variety of strategies, including preparing different sets of statements that report results in different languages, currencies, or accounting principles.

International Note
Accounting standards vary from country to country. Most countries have their own standard-setting body. One group, the International Accounting Standards Committee (IASC), has been working to reduce the differences in accounting practices and standards across countries.

International Notes introduce international issues and similarities and differences in accounting.

BUSINESS INSIGHT
Management Perspective

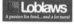

Canada is teeming with foreign culture and products—Microsoft, Samsung, Wal-Mart, The Gap, McDonald's, NIKE, and Toyota, just to name a few. Foreign controlled companies—mostly American, but also British and Japanese—accounted for 31.5% of the $1.3 trillion in corporate revenue generated in Canada in a recent year.

Canadians have also become increasingly global. More than 220 Canadian companies are listed on at least one stock exchange outside of Canada. Canadian companies are expanding foreign operations, selling to foreign interests, and/or merging with companies located in other countries in record numbers in order to compete in the global marketplace more effectively.

What does this mean to the users of financial information? One must understand not only the differences in reporting requirements, but also important economic, legal, political, and cultural issues, before well-informed business decisions can be made.

Source: Eric Reguly, "The Devouring of Corporate Canada," *Globe and Mail*, September 4, 1999, B4.

Business Insight examples give glimpses into how real companies make decisions using accounting information. Three different icons identify three different points of view—briefcase and newspapers for *investor perspectives*, a business meeting for *management perspectives*, and a globe for *international perspectives*.

Each chapter presents **decision tools** that help business decision makers use financial statements. At the end of the text discussion, a **Decision Toolkit** summarizes the key features of a decision tool and reviews why and how you would use it.

DECISION TOOLKIT

Decision Checkpoints	Info Needed for Decision	Tool to Use for Decision	How to Evaluate Results
Is the company using its assets effectively?	Net earnings and average assets	Return on assets ratio = Net earnings / Average assets	Higher value suggests favourable efficiency (use of assets).
Is the company maintaining an adequate margin between sales and expenses?	Net earnings and net sales	Profit margin ratio = Net earnings / Net sales	Higher value suggests favourable return on each dollar of sales.

Before You Go On sections follow each key topic. ***Review It*** questions (often relating to the Loblaw financial statements) prompt you to stop and review the key points you have just studied. If you cannot answer these questions, you should go back and read the section again. Brief ***Do It*** exercises ask you to put newly acquired knowledge to work in some form of financial statement preparation. They outline the ***Reasoning*** necessary to complete the exercise and show a ***Solution***.

BEFORE YOU GO ON . . .

● **Review It**

1. Identify three types of useful comparisons in ratio analysis.
2. What are the key features found in a statement of earnings?
3. What are the key features found in Loblaw's statement of earnings, reproduced in Appendix A to this textbook? The answer to this question is at the end of the chapter.
4. What are profitability ratios? Explain the return on assets ratio and the profit margin ratio.

Loblaws
A passion for food... and a lot more!

USING THE DECISION TOOLKIT

Using the Decision Toolkit exercises, which follow the final set of Review It questions in the chapter, ask you to use information from financial statements to make financial decisions. We encourage you to think through the questions related to the decision before you study the solution.

Sobeys originally began as a proprietorship, in 1907, when John William Sobey opened his first butcher shop in Stellarton, Nova Scotia. Today, Sobeys Inc. is Canada's second largest grocery chain, after Loblaw. It has grown to 1,400 stores, of which more than 900 are supermarkets, in 10 provinces. Late in the calendar year 1998, Sobeys bought The Oshawa Group Limited and combined about 700 Oshawa stores with the Sobeys chain. Synergies made possible by this combination are expected to result, annually, in over $11 billion of sales and $70 million of cost savings in future years. Imagine that you are considering purchasing some of Sobeys' shares, in order to capitalize on their anticipated future success.

A **Using the Decision Toolkit** exercise follows the final set of ***Review It*** questions in the chapter. It asks you to use information from financial statements to make financial decisions. You should think through the questions related to the decision before you study the printed ***Solution.***

Cash provided by (used for) financing			
Issue of debt	995,641	5,597	8,000
Repayment of debt	(264,032)	(7,811)	(30,345)
Issue of capital stock	580,406	—	—
Payment of dividends	(13,930)	(12,993)	(12,478)
Other	13,200	—	—
Total cash provided by (used for) financing	1,311,285	(15,207)	(34,823)
Increase (decrease) in cash	43,957	(3,237)	11,538
Cash, beginning of year	27,176	30,413	18,875
Cash, end of year	$ 71,133	$ 27,176	$ 30,413

Solution

1. Before you invest, you should investigate the statement of earnings, statement of retained earnings, statement of cash flows, balance sheet, and the accompanying notes. Note that Sobeys Inc. calls its statement of cash flows by its alternative name, "statement of changes in financial position."
2. You would probably be most interested in the statement of earnings because it shows past performance and thus gives an indication of future performance. The statement of retained earnings shows the impact current earnings (or losses), and any dividends paid, have on the company's accumulated retained earnings balance from prior years. The statement of cash flows reveals where the company is getting and spending its cash. This is especially important for a company that wants to grow. Finally, the balance sheet reveals the financial position of the company and the relationship between assets and liabilities.
3. You would want audited financial statements—statements that have been examined by an independent public accountant who has expressed an opinion that the statements present fairly the financial position and results of operations of the company. Grant Thornton is Sobeys' auditor and its unqualified audit opinion is attached to Sobeys' financial statements. Investors and creditors should not make decisions without studying audited financial statements.
4. Both financial statements cover a one-year period, with Loblaw's fiscal year overlapping Sobeys' for four months (January 3, 1999, through May 1, 1999). If there have been no substantial changes during the eight-month period that Loblaw's financial results cover but Sobeys' do not, it really doesn't matter when each company's fiscal year ends. It is more important that we compare what each company was able to achieve within an equivalent period of time—whether it be one year, six months, or a quarter. Note also that Sobeys presents three fiscal years of results in its financial statements, while Loblaw presents only two years. Three years allows trends to be more easily identified. Of course, prior period's annual reports allow you to access the same information for Loblaw.

   If, however, a substantial change does occur in the intervening period, such a change would likely reduce the usefulness of a comparison of the financial statements of the two companies. Say, for example, that the economy changed dramatically during the non-overlapping period. The impact of this change in the economy would be reflected in Loblaw's current statements, but not in Sobeys' until the following fiscal year. It is important for users to be aware of relevant non-financial information such as this before they commence their comparisons.

earnings per share and price-earning
to see the details of the company's s
ability to generate the funding requi
also want to read the management d
annual report to see management's a

SUMMARY OF STUDY OBJECTIVES

❶ ***Describe the basic objective of financial reporting, and explain the meaning of generally accepted accounting principles.*** The basic objective of financial reporting is to provide information that is useful for decision-making. Generally accepted accounting principles are a set of rules and practices recognized as a general guide for financial reporting purposes.

❷ ***Discuss the qualitative characteristics of accounting information.*** To be judged useful, information should possess these qualitative characteristics: understandability, relevance, reliability, and comparability.

❸ ***Identify the two constraints in accounting.*** The major constraints are cost-benefit and materiality.

❹ ***Identify the sections of a classified balance sheet.*** In a classified balance sheet, assets are classified as current assets, long-term investments, and capital assets. Liabilities are classified as either current or long-term. There is also a shareholders' equity section, which shows share capital and retained earnings.

❺ ***Identify and calculate ratios for analysing a company's profitability.*** Profitability ratios, such as profit margin and return on assets, measure different aspects of the operating success of an enterprise for a given period of time.

The **Summary of Study Objectives** gives a summary related to the Study Objectives located throughout the chapter. It provides you with another opportunity to review as well as to see how all the key topics within the chapter are related.

At the end of each chapter, **Decision Toolkit—A Summary** reviews the contexts and techniques useful for decision making that were covered in the chapter.

DECISION TOOLKIT—A SUMMARY

Decision Checkpoints	Info Needed for Decision	Tool to Use for Decision	How to Evaluate Results
Is the company using its assets effectively?	Net earnings and average assets	Return on assets ratio = Net earnings / Average assets	Higher value suggests favourable efficiency (use of assets).
Is the company maintaining an adequate margin between sales and expenses?	Net earnings and net sales	Profit margin ratio = Net earnings / Net sales	Higher value suggests favourable return on each dollar of sales.
Can the company meet its short-term obligations?	Current assets and current liabilities	Working capital = Current assets − Current liabilities	Higher amount indicates liquidity.
		Current ratio = Current assets / Current liabilities	Higher ratio suggests favourable liquidity.
	Current liabilities and cash provided (used) by operating activities	Cash current debt coverage ratio = Cash provided (used) by operating activities / Average current liabilities	A higher ratio indicates liquidity—that the company is generating cash sufficient to meet its short-term needs.
Can the company meet its	Total debt and total assets	Debt to total = Total liabilities	Lower value suggests

The **Glossary** defines all the **key terms** and concepts introduced in the chapter.

80 CHAPTER 2 A Further Look at Financial Statements

GLOSSARY

Capital assets Long-lived resources used in operating the business that are tangible (property, plant, and equipment, and natural resources) and intangible. (p. 61)

Cash current debt coverage ratio A measure of liquidity that is calculated as follows: cash provided by operating activities divided by average current liabilities. (p. 74)

Cash total debt coverage ratio A measure of solvency that is calculated as follows: cash provided by operating activities divided by average total liabilities. (p. 74)

usually issued every quarter, but may be of other time durations. (p. 56)

Liquidity The ability of a company to pay obligations that are expected to become due within the next year or operating cycle. (p. 69)

Liquidity ratios Measures of the short-term ability of the company to pay its maturing obligations and to meet unexpected needs for cash. (p. 69)

Long-term investments Investments in shares and bonds of other companies that are normally held for

Demonstration Problem 81

A **Demonstration Problem** is the final step before you begin homework. **Problem-Solving Strategies** in the margins give you tips about how to approach the problem, and the **Solution** demonstrates both the form and content of complete answers.

DEMONSTRATION PROBLEM

Listed here are items taken from the statement of earnings and balance sheet of Hudson's Bay Company for the year ended January 31, 1999. Certain items have been combined for simplification and all numbers are reported in millions.

Sales and revenue	$7,075
Cash	8
Receivables	950
Operating expenses	6,888
Long-term investments	59
Interest expense	97
Dividends	53
Short-term borrowings	190
Prepaid expenses	60
Long-term debt	1,290
Other long-term liabilities	25
Income tax expense	50
Capital assets, net	1,451
Other long-term assets	406
Accounts payable	928
Short-term deposits	14
Long-term debt due within one year	112
Share capital	1,531
Merchandise inventories	1,656
Retained earnings, February 1, 1998	541

Instructions

Prepare a statement of earnings and a classified balance sheet using the items listed. No item should be used more than once.

Solution to Demonstration Problem

HUDSON'S BAY COMPANY
Statement of Earnings
For the Year Ended January 31, 1999
(in millions)

Sales and revenue		$7,075
Expenses		
Operating expenses	6,888	
Interest expense	97	
Total expenses		6,985
Earnings before income taxes		90
Income taxes		50
Net earnings		$ 40

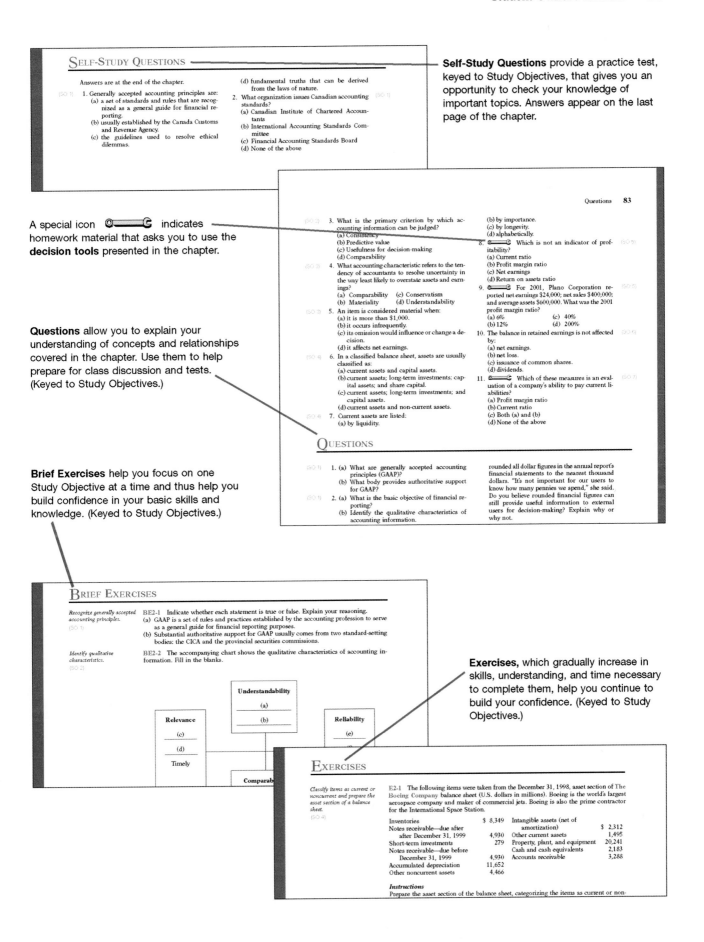

SELF-STUDY QUESTIONS

Answers are at the end of the chapter.

(SO 1) 1. Generally accepted accounting principles are:
(a) a set of standards and rules that are recognized as a general guide for financial reporting.
(b) usually established by the Canada Customs and Revenue Agency.
(c) the guidelines used to resolve ethical dilemmas.
(d) fundamental truths that can be derived from the laws of nature.

(SO 1) 2. What organization issues Canadian accounting standards?
(a) Canadian Institute of Chartered Accountants
(b) International Accounting Standards Committee
(c) Financial Accounting Standards Board
(d) None of the above

Self-Study Questions provide a practice test, keyed to Study Objectives, that gives you an opportunity to check your knowledge of important topics. Answers appear on the last page of the chapter.

(SO 2) 3. What is the primary criterion by which accounting information can be judged?
(a) Consistency
(b) Predictive value
(c) Usefulness for decision-making
(d) Comparability

(SO 2) 4. What accounting characteristic refers to the tendency of accountants to resolve uncertainty in the way least likely to overstate assets and earnings?
(a) Comparability (c) Conservatism
(b) Materiality (d) Understandability

(SO 3) 5. An item is considered material when:
(a) it is more than $1,000.
(b) it occurs infrequently.
(c) its omission would influence or change a decision.
(d) it affects net earnings.

(SO 4) 6. In a classified balance sheet, assets are usually classified as:
(a) current assets and capital assets.
(b) current assets; long-term investments; capital assets; and share capital.
(c) current assets; long-term investments; and capital assets.
(d) current assets and non-current assets.

(SO 4) 7. Current assets are listed:
(a) by liquidity.
(b) by importance.
(c) by longevity.
(d) alphabetically.

(SO 5) 8. Which is not an indicator of profitability?
(a) Current ratio
(b) Profit margin ratio
(c) Net earnings
(d) Return on assets ratio

(SO 5) 9. For 2001, Plano Corporation reported net earnings $24,000; net sales $400,000; and average assets $600,000. What was the 2001 profit margin ratio?
(a) 6% (c) 40%
(b) 12% (d) 200%

(SO 6) 10. The balance in retained earnings is not affected by:
(a) net earnings.
(b) net loss.
(c) issuance of common shares.
(d) dividends.

(SO 7) 11. Which of these measures is an evaluation of a company's ability to pay current liabilities?
(a) Profit margin ratio
(b) Current ratio
(c) Both (a) and (b)
(d) None of the above

A special icon indicates homework material that asks you to use the **decision tools** presented in the chapter.

Questions allow you to explain your understanding of concepts and relationships covered in the chapter. Use them to help prepare for class discussion and tests. (Keyed to Study Objectives.)

QUESTIONS

(SO 1) 1. (a) What are generally accepted accounting principles (GAAP)?
(b) What body provides authoritative support for GAAP?

(SO 1) 2. (a) What is the basic objective of financial reporting?
(b) Identify the qualitative characteristics of accounting information.

rounded all dollar figures in the annual report's financial statements to the nearest thousand dollars. "It's not important for our users to know how many pennies we spend," she said. Do you believe rounded financial figures can still provide useful information to external users for decision-making? Explain why or why not.

Brief Exercises help you focus on one Study Objective at a time and thus help you build confidence in your basic skills and knowledge. (Keyed to Study Objectives.)

BRIEF EXERCISES

Recognize generally accepted accounting principles. (SO 1)

BE2-1 Indicate whether each statement is true or false. Explain your reasoning.
(a) GAAP is a set of rules and practices established by the accounting profession to serve as a general guide for financial reporting purposes.
(b) Substantial authoritative support for GAAP usually comes from two standard-setting bodies: the CICA and the provincial securities commissions.

Identify qualitative characteristics. (SO 2)

BE2-2 The accompanying chart shows the qualitative characteristics of accounting information. Fill in the blanks.

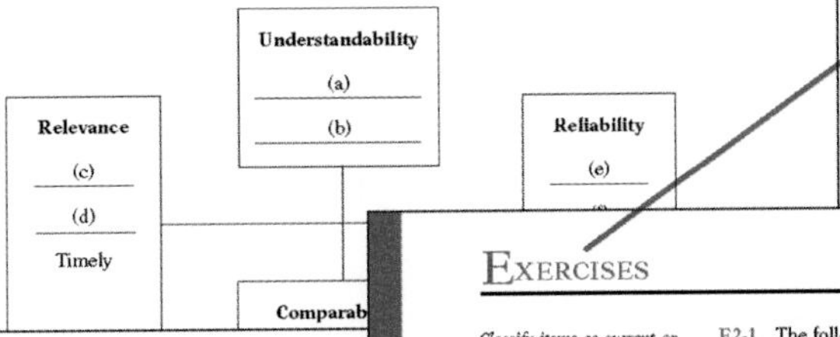

Exercises, which gradually increase in skills, understanding, and time necessary to complete them, help you continue to build your confidence. (Keyed to Study Objectives.)

EXERCISES

Classify items as current or noncurrent and prepare the asset section of a balance sheet. (SO 4)

E2-1 The following items were taken from the December 31, 1998, asset section of The Boeing Company balance sheet (U.S. dollars in millions). Boeing is the world's largest aerospace company and maker of commercial jets. Boeing is also the prime contractor for the International Space Station.

Inventories	$ 8,349	Intangible assets (net of amortization)	$ 2,312
Notes receivable—due after December 31, 1999	4,930	Other current assets	1,495
Short-term investments	279	Property, plant, and equipment	20,241
Notes receivable—due before December 31, 1999	4,930	Cash and cash equivalents	2,183
Accumulated depreciation	11,652	Accounts receivable	3,288
Other noncurrent assets	4,466		

Instructions
Prepare the asset section of the balance sheet, categorizing the items as current or non-

Certain exercises or problems marked with a pencil icon help you practice **written business communication,** a skill much in demand among employers.

Each **Problem** helps you pull together and apply several concepts of the chapter. (Keyed to one or more Study Objectives.)

Two sets of problems—**A** and **B**—provide additional opportunities to apply or expand concepts learned in the chapter. (Each problem in **Set B** is generally keyed to the same Study Objectives as its counterpart in the **Set A**.)

The financial results of real companies are included in the end of chapter material. These are indicated by the company name here in red.

Calculate and interpret solvency ratios.
(SO 7)

E2-7 The Québec Winter Carnival is recognized as the world's biggest winter celebration and is the third largest carnival (after those in Rio de Janeiro and New Orleans). The following data were taken from the 1999 and 1998 financial statements of the Carnaval de Québec Inc.:

	April 30, 1999	April 30, 1998
Current assets	$1,064,667	$726,484
Total assets	1,136,256	790,603
Current liabilities	401,111	315,589
Total liabilities	417,951	348,612
Total equity	718,305	441,991
Cash provided by operating activities	50,320	294,467
Cash used by investing activities	52,142	38,399

Instructions

Do each of the following:

(a) Calculate the debt to assets ratio for each year.

(b) Calculate the cash current debt coverage ratio and the cash total debt coverage ratio for 1999.

(c) Discuss the Carnival's solvency in 1999 versus 1998.

(d) Discuss the Carnival's ability to finance its investment activities with cash provided by operating activities, and how any deficiency would be met.

PROBLEMS: SET A

Comment on the qualitative characteristics of accounting information.
(SO 1, 2)

P2-1A Net Nanny Software International Inc., headquartered in Vancouver, specializes in Internet safety and computer security products for both the home and enterprise markets. Its balance sheet, as at June 30, 1999, reported a deficit (negative retained earnings) of US$5,678,288. It has only reported net losses since inception, June 30, 1996. In spite of these losses, Net Nanny's common shares have traded anywhere from a high of $3.70 to a low of $0.32 on the Canadian Venture Exchange.

Net Nanny's financial statements of the company have historically been prepared in Canadian dollars. As of June 30, 1998, the company adopted the U.S. dollar as its report ing currency.

Instructions

(a) What is the objective of financial reporting? How does this objective meet or not meet Net Nanny's investor's needs?

(b) Why would investors want to buy Net Nanny's shares if the company has consistently reported losses over the last few years? Include in your answer an assessment of the relevance and reliability of the information reported on Net Nanny's financial statements.

n how the change in reporting information from Canadian dollars to U.S. y affected the readers of Net Nanny's financial statements. Include in your ssessment of the comparability of the information.

d of yours, Ryan Konotopsky, has come to you looking for some answers statements. Ryan tells you that he is thinking about opening a movie the- e town. Before doing so, he wants to find out how much in sales he could from food concessions as opposed to ticket sales. He wants to know what t sales he could expect from children, youth and seniors versus adults who admission rate. He also wants to know how much profit he would make ersus sales at the concession stands; and the average wage per employee. that Empire Theatres operates in many cities and towns in Atlantic Canada ed the financial statements of Empire Company Limited from the Internet. the company's statement of earnings reported revenues for the year ended f $6,377,651,000 and cost of sales, selling and administrative expenses of He read through Empire Company's Limited's annual report and learned Theatres is just one part of the Investments division of the company. There ution and real estate divisions as well. Ryan discovers from reading the an- mpire Company Limited that the company reports segmented information. other operations to describe the results of Empire Theatres and reports r 1999:

PROBLEMS: SET B

Comment on the objective and qualitative characteristics of financial reporting.
(SO 1, 2)

P2-1B A friend of yours, Emily Collis, recently completed an undergraduate degree in science and has just started working with a Canadian biotechnology company. Emily tells you that the owners of the business are trying to secure new sources of financing which are needed in order for the company to proceed with development of a new health care product. Emily said that her boss told her that the company must put together a report to present to potential investors.

Emily thought that the company should include in this package the detailed scientific findings related to the Phase I clinical trials for this product. "I know that the biotech industry sometimes has only a 10% success rate with new products, but if we report all the scientific findings, everyone will see what a sure success this is going to be! The president was talking about the importance of following some set of accounting principles. Why do we need to look at some accounting rules? What they need to realize is that we have scientific results that are quite encouraging, some of the most talented employees around, and the start of some really great customer relationships. We haven't made any sales yet, but we will. We just need the funds to get through all the clinical testing and get government approval for our product. Then these investors will be quite happy that they bought in to our company early!"

Instructions

(a) What is financial reporting? Explain to Emily what is meant by generally accepted accounting principles.

(b) Comment on how Emily's suggestions for what should be reported to prospective investors conforms to the qualitative characteristics of accounting information. Do you think that the things that Emily wants to include in the information for investors will conform to financial reporting guidelines?

Comment on the constraints of accounting.
(SO 1, 3)

P2-2B No separate disclosure is required on the statement of earnings for the Cost of Goods Sold, the cost of merchandise sold to customers. Because this disclosure is not specifically required, less than half of reporting companies disclose their cost of goods sold separately on their statement of earnings. Most companies include it with other expenses in their reporting of this item, similar to that reported by Sears Canada Inc. in its statement of earnings for the year ended January 1, 2000:

Cost of merchandise sold, operating, administrative and selling expenses	$5,600.8 million

Instructions

(a) Why do you think Sears does not report it's cost of merchandise sold separately on its statement of earnings? Comment on how this disclosure meets the objective of financial reporting.

(b) What are the two constraints in accounting? Do either of these constraints likely have an impact on Sears's reporting policy with respect to cost of merchandise sold? Give an example of how each constraint might affect Sears's reporting of its financial information.

Prepare a classified balance sheet.
(SO 4)

P2-3B Headquartered in Vancouver, Intrawest Corporation is the number 2 ski resort operator in North America. The following items are taken from its March 31, 1999, quarterly balance sheet (in thousands of dollars):

Share capital	$ 495,526	Bank and other indebtedness, current portion	$263,971
Capital assets	1,456,228	Other current liabilities	80,422
Amounts payable	183,653	Retained earnings, March 31, 1999	236,200
Other noncurrent assets	141,510	Cash and short-term deposits	81,609
Other current assets	367,600	Long-term liabilities	892,293
Amounts receivable	105,118		

The **Broadening Your Perspective** section helps you pull together various concepts covered in the chapter and apply them to real-world business decisions.

In the **Financial Reporting Problem** you study various aspects of the financial statements of Loblaw Companies Limited, which are printed in Chapter 1 (in simplified form) and in Appendix A (in full).

A **Comparative Analysis Problem** offers the opportunity to compare and contrast the financial reporting of Loblaw with a competitor, Sobeys Inc., whose financial statements are printed in Chapter 1 (in simplified form) and in Appendix B (in full).

Research Cases ask students to find a source of data, and then study or analyse the data and evaluate it.

Interpreting Financial Statements offers minicases that ask you to read parts of financial statements of actual companies and use the decision tools presented in the chapter to interpret this information.

BROADENING YOUR PERSPECTIVE

Financial Reporting and Analysis

FINANCIAL REPORTING PROBLEM: ***Loblaw Companies Limited***

BYP2-1 The financial statements of **Loblaw Companies Limited** are presented in Appendix A at the end of this book.

Instructions

Answer the following questions using the Consolidated Balance Sheets and the Notes to Consolidated Financial Statements section:

(a) What were Loblaw's total current assets at January 1, 2000 (1999 fiscal year), and January 2, 1999 (1998 fiscal year)?
(b) Are the assets in current assets listed in the proper order? Explain.
(c) How are Loblaw's assets classified?
(d) What were Loblaw's total current liabilities at January 1, 2000, and January 2, 1999?

COMPARATIVE ANALYSIS PROBLEM: ***Loblaw and Sobeys***

BYP2-2 The financial statements of **Sobeys Inc.** are presented in Appendix B after the financial statements for **Loblaw**.

Instructions

(a) For each company, calculate the following values for fiscal 1999:
   1. Working capital
   2. Current ratio
   3. Debt to total assets ratio
   4. Profit margin ratio
   5. Return on assets ratio
(b) Based on your findings above, discuss the relative liquidity, solvency, and profitability of the two companies.

RESEARCH CASE

BYP2-3 Several commonly available indices help individuals find articles from business publications and periodicals. Articles can generally be searched for by company name or by subject matter. Two common indices are CBCA (Canadian Business and Current Affairs) Fulltext Business, which covers over 130 Canadian industry and professional periodicals and news sources, and Lexis-Nexis, which includes the full text of major newspapers from around the world, as well as company reports, marketing, and financial information.

Instructions

Use one of these resources, or others, to find a list of articles about Sears, Hudson's Bay, or Canadian Tire. Choose an article that you believe would be of interest to an investor or creditor of this company. Read the article and answer the following questions. (Note: Your library may have either print or electronic versions of these indices.)

(a) What is the article about?
(b) What information about the company is included in the article?
(c) Is the article related to anything you read in this chapter?
(d) Identify any accounting-related issues discussed in the article.

INTERPRETING FINANCIAL STATEMENTS

BYP2-4 **Ford Motor Company of Canada, Limited**, was incorporated on August 17, 1904. The event marked Ford Motor Company's first expansion outside of the U.S. and the beginning of the company's globalization. Headquartered in Detroit, Michigan, the Ford Motor Company is now the world's largest truck maker and the second largest maker of trucks and cars combined.

The following information was reported by Ford in its 1998 annual report.

A GLOBAL FOCUS

BYP2-6 Many Canadian companies have revenue and expenses from other countries. One such company is **Doman Industries Ltd.**, whose products are sold in 30 countries worldwide. Doman is an integrated Canadian forest products company, located in British Columbia.

The majority of Doman's lumber products are sold in the U.S. and a significant amount of its pulp products in Asia. In addition to earning revenue from these and 29 other countries, Doman also has loans from other countries. For example, on June 18, 1999, the company borrowed US$160 million at an annual interest rate of 12%. Doman must repay this loan and the accompanying interest in U.S. dollars.

One of the challenges global companies face is to make themselves attractive to investors from other countries. This is difficult to do when different accounting rules in other countries can blur the real impact of earnings. For example, in the statement of earnings—which is what most investors examine—Doman reported a loss of $2.3 million, using Canadian accounting rules. Had it reported under U.S. accounting rules, its loss would have been $12.1 million.

Many companies that want to be more easily compared with U.S. and other global competitors have switched to U.S. accounting principles. Canadian National Railway, Corel, Cott, Inco, and the Thomson Corporation are but a few examples of large Canadian companies whose financial statements are now presented in U.S. dollars, and which either are presented in accordance with U.S. GAAP or reconciled to it.

Instructions

(a) Identify any advantages and disadvantages that companies should consider when switching to U.S. reporting standards.
(b) Suppose you wish to compare Doman Industries to a U.S.-based competitor, such as the formerly Canadian-owned forestry giant MacMillan Bloedel. Do you believe the use of both countries' accounting policies would hinder your comparison? If so, explain how.
(c) Suppose you wish to compare Doman Industries to a Canadian-based competitor, such as Nexfor, formerly Noranda Forest. If they chose to use different generally acceptable Canadian accounting policies, how could this affect your comparison of their financial results?
(d) Do you see any significant distinction between comparing statements prepared in different countries and comparing statements prepared using different accounting policies within the same country?

FINANCIAL ANALYSIS ON THE WEB

BYP2-7 ***Purpose:*** To identify summary information about companies. This information includes a basic description of various industries and companies in Canada.

Instructions

Specific requirements of this web case can be found on the Kimmel website.

Critical Thinking

COLLABORATIVE LEARNING ACTIVITY

BYP2-8 As the accountant for Martinez Manufacturing Inc., you have been asked to develop some key ratios from the comparative financial statements. This information will be used to convince creditors that Martinez Manufacturing Inc. is liquid, solvent, and profitable, and therefore deserves their continued support. Lenders are particularly con-

A Global Focus asks you to apply concepts presented in the chapter to specific situations faced by actual international companies.

Financial Analysis on the Web exercises guide you to the Kimmel web site where you can find and analyse information related to the chapter topic.

Critical Thinking offers additional opportunities and activities.

Collaborative Learning Activities prepare you for the business world, where you will be working with many people, by giving you practice in solving less structured problems with colleagues.

cerned about the company's ability to continue as a going concern.

Here are the data and calculations you developed from the financial statements:

	2001	2000
Current ratio	3.1:1	2.1:1
Working capital	Up 22%	Down 7%
Debt to total assets ratio	60%	70%
Net earnings	Up 32%	Down 8%
Profit margin ratio	5%	1.5%
Return on assets ratio	9%	4%

Instructions

You have now been asked to prepare brief comments which explain how each of these items supports the argument that Martinez's financial health is improving. The company wishes to use these comments in a presentation of data to its creditors. Prepare the comments as requested, giving the implications and the limitations of each item separately, and then state what may be drawn from them as a whole about Martinez's financial well-being.

COMMUNICATION ACTIVITY

BYP2-9 L.R. Stanton is the chief executive officer of Hi-Tech Electronics. Stanton is an expert engineer but a novice in accounting.

Instructions

Write a letter to L.R. Stanton that explains (a) the three main types of ratios, (b) examples of each, how they are calculated, and what they mean, and (c) the bases for comparison in analysing Hi-Tech's financial statements.

ETHICS CASE

BYP2-10 As the controller of Breathless Perfume Co. Ltd., you discover a significant overstatement of net earnings in the prior year's financial statements. The misleading financial statements are contained in the company's annual report, which was issued to banks and other creditors less than a month ago. After much thought about the consequences of telling the president, Eddy Kadu, about this misstatement, you gather your courage to inform him. Eddy says, "Hey! What they don't know won't hurt them. But, just so we set the record straight, we'll adjust this year's financial statements for last year's misstatement. We can absorb that misstatement better this year than last year anyway! Just don't make that kind of mistake again."

Instructions

(a) Who are the stakeholders in this situation?
(b) What are the ethical issues?
(c) What would you do as the controller?

Answers to Self-Study Questions

1. a 2. a 3. c 4. c 5. c 6. c 7. a 8. a 9. a 10. c 11. b

Answer to Loblaw Review It Question 3

The key features of Loblaw's statement of earnings are sales, reduced by operating expenses to determine operating income. Operating income less interest expense results in earnings before income taxes. Income taxes are then deducted to find net earnings for the period. These earnings are expressed in total, and on a per share basis, in Loblaw's statement of earnings.

Communication Activities ask you to engage in real-world business situations via written communication.

Through the **Ethics Cases** you will reflect on typical ethical dilemmas and decide on an appropriate course of action.

Answers to Self-Study Questions provide feedback on your understanding of concepts.

Answers to Review It questions based on Loblaw's financial statements appear here.

HOW DO YOU LEARN BEST?

Now that you have looked at your Owner's Manual, take time to find out how you learn best. This quiz is designed to help you find out something about your preferred learning method. Research on left brain/right brain differences and also on learning and personality differences suggests that each person has preferred ways to receive and communicate information. After taking the quiz, we will help you pinpoint the study aids in this test that will help you learn the material based on your learning style.

Circle the letter of the answer that best explains your preferences. If a single answer does not match your perception, please circle two or more choices. Leave blank any question that does not apply.

1. You are about to give directions to a person. She is staying in a hotel in town and wants to visit your house. She has a rental car. Would you
   V) draw a map on paper?
   R) write down the directions (without a map)?
   A) tell her the directions?
   K) pick her up at the hotel in your car?
2. You are staying in a hotel and have a rental car. You would like to visit friends whose address/location you do not know. Would you like them to
   V) draw you a map on paper?
   R) write down the directions (without a map)?
   A) tell you the directions by phone?
   K) pick you up at the hotel in their car?
3. You have just received a copy of your itinerary for a world trip. This is of interest to a friend. Would you
   A) call her immediately and tell her about it?
   R) send her a copy of the printed itinerary?
   V) show her on a map of the world?
4. You are going to cook a dessert as a special treat for your family. Do you
   K) cook something familiar without need for instructions?
   V) thumb through the cookbook looking for ideas from the pictures?
   R) refer to a specific cookbook where there is a good recipe?
   A) ask for advice from others?
5. A group of tourists has been assigned to you to find out about national parks. Would you
   K) drive them to a national park?
   R) give them a book on national parks?
   V) show them slides and photographs?
   A) give them a talk on national parks?
6. You are about to purchase a new stereo. Other than price, what would most influence your decision?
   A) A friend talking about it.
   K) Listening to it.
   R) Reading the details about it.
   V) Its distinctive, upscale appearance.
7. Recall a time in your life when you learned how to do something like playing a new board game. (Try to avoid choosing a very physical skill, e.g., riding a bike.) How did you learn best? By
   V) visual clues—pictures, diagrams, charts?
   A) listening to somebody explaining it?
   R) written instructions?
   K) doing it?
8. Which of these games do you prefer?
   V) *Pictionary*
   R) *Scrabble*
   K) Charades
9. You are about to learn to use a new program on a computer. Would you
   K) ask a friend to show you?
   R) read the manual that comes with the program?
   A) telephone a friend and ask questions about it?
10. You are not sure whether a word should be spelled "dependent" or "dependant." Do you
    R) look it up in the dictionary?
    V) see the word in your mind and choose the best way it looks?
    A) sound it out in your mind?
    K) write both versions down?
11. Apart from price, what would most influence your decision to buy a particular book?
    K) Using a friend's copy.
    R) Skimming parts of it.
    A) A friend talking about it.
    V) It looks OK.
12. A new movie has arrived in town. What would most influence your decision to go or not to go?
    A) Friends talked about it.
    R) You read a review of it.
    V) You saw a preview of it.
13. Do you prefer a lecturer/teacher who likes to use
    R) handouts and/or a textbook?
    V) flow diagrams, charts, slides?
    K) field trips, labs, practical sessions?
    A) discussion, guest speakers?

Results: To determine your learning preference, add up the number of individual Vs, As, Rs, and Ks you have circled. Take the letter you have the greatest number of and match it to the same letter in the Learning Styles Chart. Next to each letter in the chart are suggestions that will refer you to different learning aids throughout this text.

LEARNING STYLES CHART

V VISUAL

WHAT TO DO IN CLASS	WHAT TO DO WHEN STUDYING	TEXT FEATURES THAT MAY HELP YOU THE MOST	WHAT TO DO PRIOR TO AND DURING EXAMS
Underline. Use different colours. Use symbols, charts, arrangements on the page.	Use the "In Class" strategies. Reconstruct images in different ways. Redraw pages from memory. Replace words with symbols and initials.	**Vignettes** **Previews** **Infographics/Illustrations** **Accounting Equation Analysis in margin** **Photos** **Business Insights** **Decision Toolkits** **Key Terms in blue** **Words in bold** **Questions/Exercises/ Problems** **Financial Reporting and Analysis**	Recall the "pictures of the pages." Draw, use diagrams where appropriate. Practise turning visuals back into words.

A AURAL

WHAT TO DO IN CLASS	WHAT TO DO WHEN STUDYING	TEXT FEATURES THAT MAY HELP YOU THE MOST	WHAT TO DO PRIOR TO AND DURING EXAMS
Attend lectures and tutorials. Discuss topics with students. Explain new ideas to other people. Use a tape recorder. Describe overheads, pictures, and visuals to somebody not there. Leave space in your notes for later recall.	You may take poor notes because you prefer to listen. Therefore: Expand your notes. Put summarized notes on tape and listen. Read summarized notes out loud. Explain notes to another "aural" person.	**Infographics/Illustrations** **Business Insights** **Review It/Do It** **Summary of Study Objectives** **Glossary** **Demonstration Problem** **Self-Study Questions** **Questions/Exercises/ Problems** **Financial Reporting and Analysis** **Critical Thinking**	Listen to your "voices" and write them down. Speak your answers. Practise writing answers to old exam questions.

R READING/WRITING

WHAT TO DO IN CLASS	WHAT TO DO WHEN STUDYING	TEXT FEATURES THAT MAY HELP YOU THE MOST	WHAT TO DO PRIOR TO AND DURING EXAMS
Use lists, headings. Use dictionaries and definitions. Use handouts and textbooks. Read. Use lecture notes.	Write out words again and again. Reread notes silently. Rewrite ideas into other words. Organize diagrams into statements.	**Study Objectives** **Previews** **Accounting Equation Analysis in margin** **Review It/Do It** **Using the Decision Toolkit** **Summary of Study** **Objectives** **Glossary** **Self-Study Questions** **Questions/Exercises/ Problems** **Writing Problems** **Financial Reporting and Analysis** **Critical Thinking**	Practise with multiple-choice questions. Write out lists. Write paragraphs, beginnings and endings.

K KINESTHETIC

WHAT TO DO IN CLASS	WHAT TO DO WHEN STUDYING	TEXT FEATURES THAT MAY HELP YOU THE MOST	WHAT TO DO PRIOR TO AND DURING EXAMS
Use all your senses. Go to labs, take field trips. Use trial-and-error methods. Listen to real-life examples. Use hands-on approach.	You may take notes poorly because topics do not seem relevant. Therefore: Put examples in note summaries. Use pictures and photos to illustrate. Talk about notes with another "kinesthetic" person.	**Vignettes** **Previews** **Infographics/Illustrations** **Decision Toolkits** **Review It/Do It** **Using the Decision Toolkit** **Summary of Study Objectives** **Demonstration Problem** **Self-Study Questions** **Questions/Exercises/ Problems** **Financial Reporting and Analysis** **Critical Thinking**	Write practice answers. Role-play the exam situation.

Source: Adapted from Neil D. Fleming and Colleen Mills, "Not Another Inventory, Rather a Catalyst for Reflections," *To Improve the Academy,* Volume II (1992), pp. 137–155. Used by permission.

BRIEF CONTENTS

CONTENTS

CHAPTER 1

Introduction to Financial Statements

STUDY OBJECTIVES

After studying this chapter, you should be able to:

1. Describe the primary forms of business organization.
2. Identify the users and uses of accounting.
3. Explain the three principal types of business activity.
4. Describe the content and purpose of each of the financial statements.
5. Explain the meaning of assets, liabilities, and shareholders' equity, and state the basic accounting equation.
6. Describe the components that supplement the financial statements in an annual report.
7. Explain the basic assumptions and principles underlying financial statements.

Need Milk?

Every time you pick up *President's Choice* chocolate-chip cookies, or buy milk at IGA, Dominion, Loblaws, Atlantic SaveEasy, Provigo, Zehrs—or one of several dozen other Canadian grocery chains—and every time you purchase food in bulk from No Frills, Valu-Mart, or SuperValu, you are shopping at Canada's #1 grocery retailer and wholesaler: Loblaw Companies Limited.

Loblaw, which boasted revenues of nearly $19 billion in 1999, is headed by CEO Galen Weston, a member of one of Canada's most established business families. His Toronto-born father, Garfield, was both a British member of parliament and CEO of Canadian-based George Weston Ltd., a multinational conglomerate that owns over 70% of Loblaw. Upon Garfield's death in 1978, Galen took over Weston's Canadian operations and his brother Garry headed foreign operations. Hilary Weston, Galen's wife, was named Lieutenant-Governor of Ontario in 1997.

How does an enterprise become one of the largest names in Canadian business? Largely through carefully planned acquisitions. During the 1940s, Garfield Weston, CEO of George Weston Limited—a baked-goods company his own father, George, had built from a small family biscuit business in England—began acquiring shares in the Chicago food wholesaling company Loblaw Groceterias. In 1956, he incorporated the business as Loblaw Companies Limited, and over the next two decades, he steadily acquired dozens of food distributors and wholesalers in both the U.S. and Canada.

When Garfield died in 1978, his son Galen set out to restructure and revitalize Loblaw, which had become an underperforming part of the Weston empire by then. In the 1980s, he acquired Golden Dawn Foods, Star Supermarkets, Wittington Leaseholds, and a number of Kroger stores in St. Louis, and he also expanded west to Winnipeg. In the early 1990s, Loblaw opened new Ontario stores and made inroads into New Brunswick.

In 1995 and 1996, Loblaw expanded to 50 new Canadian locations and moved into the

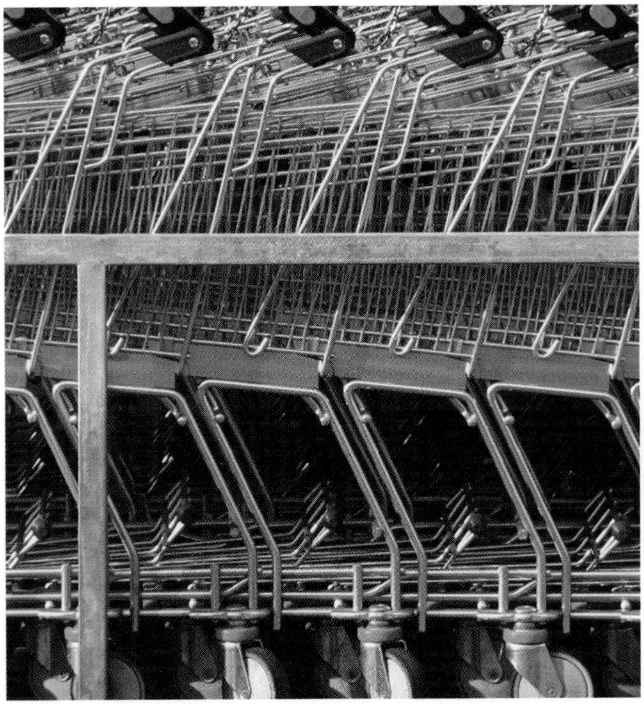

> *On the World Wide Web*
> Loblaw Companies Limited
> http://www.loblaw.com

Every **chapter-opening vignette** ends with the **Internet addresses** of the companies cited in the story to help you connect with these real businesses and explore them further.

Quebec market by buying the Montreal-based Provigo chain for $1.1 billion. It also expanded significantly in eastern Canada, buying over 80 stores from Oshawa Group.

Careful not to spread the company too thinly, however, Weston had divested Loblaw of its U.S. holdings in the mid-1990s to focus on this Canadian expansion. Furthermore, part of the deal to aquire Provigo involved selling or franchising some 90 stores in Ontario.

Another aspect of Loblaw's success was innovation at the retail level. Many of its new stores were unusually large, boasting extra amenities such as a flower shop, pharmacy, photo shop, financial services pavilion, and at Toronto's enormous Queen's Quay location, even an interior market and restaurant.

Loblaw also led the trend toward private labels in Canada—what Canadian doesn't recognize *President's Choice* brand, first developed as a Loblaw line, or *G-R-E-E-N* and *Too Good To Be True!* The high profitability of private labels makes them an expanding segment of today's grocery market.

Over time, the path of a huge corporation like this one naturally involves a myriad of decisions. Some are internal—should George Weston's bakery sell more bread and fewer biscuits? Should Loblaw purchase a particular distributing operation or introduce a new frozen entrée? Sell groceries on-line? Other decisions that affect the company are external—should investment company X purchase some of the shares being issued by Loblaw to finance a new acquisition? To make such financial decisions, both internal and external parties rely on their primary tool, accounting.

The **preview** describes the purpose of the chapter and outlines its major topics and subtopics.

How do you start a business? How do you make it grow into a widely recognized brand name like Loblaw? How do you determine whether your business is making or losing money? When you need to expand your operations, where do you get money to finance expansion—should you borrow or issue shares? How do you convince lenders to lend you money or investors to buy your shares? Success in business requires making countless decisions, and decisions require financial information.

The purpose of this chapter is to show you the role accounting plays in providing financial information. The content and organization of the chapter are as follows:

INTRODUCTION TO FINANCIAL STATEMENTS

- **Forms of Business Organization**
  - Proprietorship
  - Partnership
  - Corporation
- **Users and Uses of Financial Information**
  - Internal Users
  - External Users
- **Business Activities**
  - Financing
  - Investing
  - Operating
- **Communicating with Users**
  - Statement of Earnings
  - Statement of Retained Earnings
  - Balance Sheet
  - Statement of Cash Flows
  - Interrelationships of Statements
- **A Quick Look at Loblaw's Financial Statements**
  - Statement of Earnings
  - Statement of Retained Earnings
  - Balance Sheet
  - Statement of Cash Flows
  - Other Elements of an Annual Report
- **Assumptions and Principles in Financial Reporting**
  - Assumptions
  - Principles

Forms of Business Organization

STUDY OBJECTIVE 1

Describe the primary forms of business organization.

Suppose you graduate with a marketing major and open your own marketing agency. One of your initial decisions is what organizational form your business should take. You have three choices—proprietorship, partnership, or corporation. A business owned by one person is a **proprietorship.** A business owned by more than one person is a **partnership.** A business organized as a separate legal entity owned by shareholders is a **corporation.** Illustration 1-1 highlights these three types of organizations and the advantages of each.

Terms for essential concepts are printed in blue when they are first explained. They are defined again in the **glossary** at the end of the chapter.

You will probably choose the proprietorship form for your marketing agency. It is **simple to set up** and **gives you control** over the business. Small owner-operated businesses such as hair salons, service stations, and restaurants are often proprietorships, as are farms and small retail stores.

Another possibility is for you to join forces with other individuals to form a partnership. Partnerships are often formed because one individual does not have **enough economic resources** to initiate or expand the business, or because

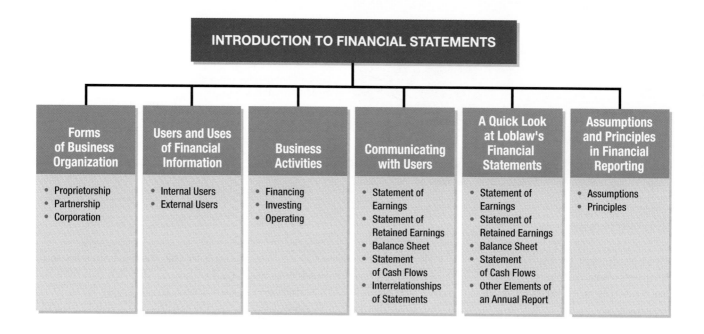

Illustrations like this one use pictures to help you visualize and apply the ideas, as you study.

Illustration 1-1 Forms of business organization

partners bring **unique skills or resources** to the partnership. You and your partners should formalize your duties and contributions in a written partnership agreement. Partnerships are often used to organize retail and service-type businesses, including professional practices (lawyers, doctors, architects, engineers, and accountants).

As a third alternative, you might start a corporation. As an investor in a corporation, you receive shares to indicate your ownership claim. Buying shares in a corporation is often more attractive than investing in a partnership because shares are **easy to sell** (to transfer ownership of). Selling a proprietorship or partnership interest is much more involved. Also, individuals can become shareholders by investing relatively small amounts of money. Therefore, it is easier for **corporations to raise funds**. Successful corporations often have thousands of shareholders, and their shares are traded on organized stock exchanges like the Toronto Stock Exchange. Many businesses start as proprietorships or partnerships and eventually incorporate.

Alternative Terminology *Shareholders* are sometimes called *stockholders.* In fact, the words *stock* and *shares* are often used interchangably.

Alternative Terminology notes present synonymous terms that you will likely come across in practice.

Other factors to consider in deciding which organizational form to choose are **legal liability** and **income taxes**. If you choose a proprietorship or partnership, you are personally liable for all debts of the business, whereas corporate shareholders are not. Proprietors and partners pay personal income tax on their respective share of the profits, while corporations pay income taxes as separate legal entities on any corporate profits. Corporations may also receive more favourable tax treatment than other forms of business organization. We will discuss these issues in more depth in a later chapter.

Helpful Hint You can usually tell whether a company is a corporation by looking at its name. The words *Limited* (Ltd.), *Incorporated* (Inc.), or *Corporation* (Corp.) normally follow its name.

Although the combined number of proprietorships and partnerships in Canada is more than the number of corporations, the revenue produced by corporations is far greater. Most of the largest enterprises in Canada—for example, General Motors of Canada Ltd., BCE Inc., Nortel Networks Corp., George Weston Ltd., Loblaw Companies. Ltd., and Bombardier Inc.—are corporations. Because the majority of Canadian business is transacted by corporations, the emphasis in this book is on the corporate form of organization.

Helpful Hints in the margins help clarify concepts being discussed.

Users and Uses of Financial Information

STUDY OBJECTIVE 2

Identify the users and uses of accounting.

The purpose of financial information is to provide data for decision-making. **Accounting** is the information system that identifies, records, and communicates the economic events of an organization to interested users. Many people have an interest in knowing about the ongoing activities of a business. These people are **users** of accounting information. Users can be divided broadly into two groups: internal users and external users.

INTERNAL USERS

Internal users of accounting information are managers who plan, organize, and run a business. These include **marketing managers, production supervisors, finance directors, and company officers**. In running a business, internal users must answer many important questions, as shown in Illustration 1-2.

Illustration 1-2
Questions asked by internal users

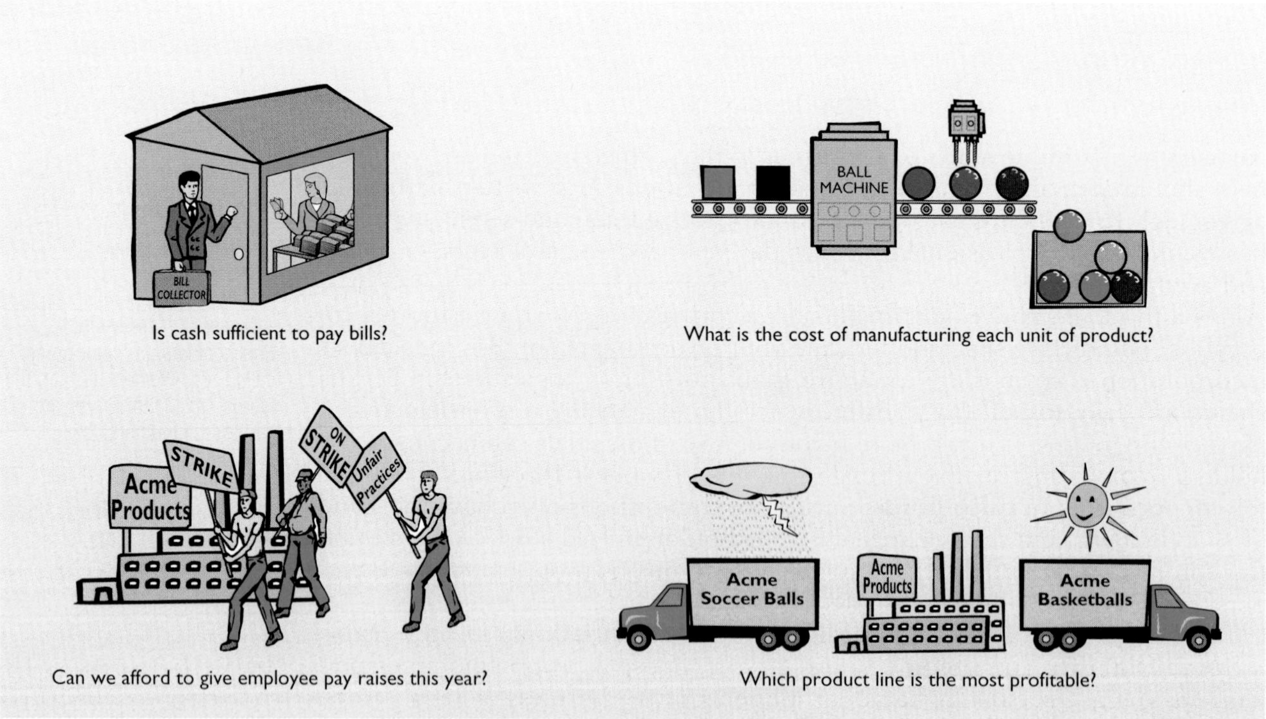

To answer these and other questions, users need detailed information on a timely basis. For internal users, accounting provides internal reports, such as financial comparisons of operating alternatives, projections of earnings from new sales campaigns, and forecasts of cash needs for the next year. In addition, summarized financial information is presented in financial statements.

EXTERNAL USERS

External users are those who do not work for the organization but who have an interest in, and need information about, its financial position and performance. There are several types of external users of accounting information. **Investors** (owners) use accounting information to make decisions to buy, hold, or sell their shares. **Creditors**, such as suppliers and bankers, use accounting information to evaluate the risks of granting credit or lending money. Some questions that may be asked by investors and creditors about a company are shown in Illustration 1-3.

Illustration 1-3
Questions asked by external users

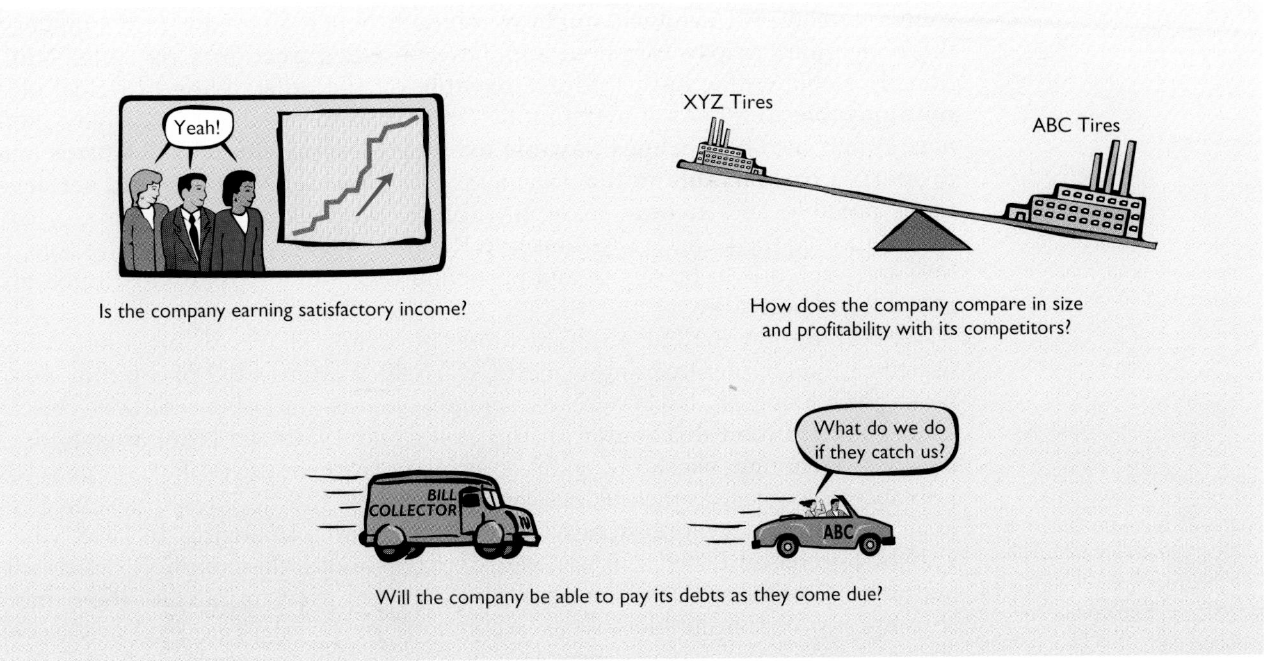
Yeah!
Is the company earning satisfactory income?
XYZ Tires
ABC Tires
How does the company compare in size and profitability with its competitors?
What do we do if they catch us?
BILL COLLECTOR
ABC
Will the company be able to pay its debts as they come due?

The information needs and questions of other external users vary considerably. **Taxing authorities**, such as the Canada Customs and Revenue Agency, want to know whether the company complies with the tax laws. **Regulatory agencies**, such as provincial securities commissions, want to know whether the company is operating within prescribed rules. **Customers** are interested in whether a company will continue to honour product warranties and support its product lines. **Labour unions** want to know whether the owners have the ability to pay increased wages and benefits. **Economic planners** use accounting information to analyse and forecast economic activity.

Business Activities

STUDY OBJECTIVE 3

Explain the three principal types of business activity.

All businesses are involved in three types of activity—**financing, investing, and operating**. For example, Loblaw needed financing to purchase Provigo. To finance the $860 million acquisition, Loblaw sold common shares to investors and borrowed money from outside sources like banks. The cash obtained was then invested in the Provigo line of Quebec and Ontario supermarkets. Once the acquisition was finalized, the new supermarkets helped increase Loblaw's operating activities of buying and selling food products.

The accounting information system keeps track of the results of each of the various business activities—financing, investing, and operating. Let's look in more detail at each type of business activity.

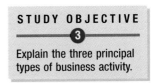

SHARE
BOND
Financing

FINANCING ACTIVITIES

It takes money to make money. The two primary ways of raising outside funds for corporations are borrowing money and selling shares.

For example, Loblaw may borrow money in a variety of ways. It can take out a loan at a bank, borrow directly from investors by issuing debt securities (bonds), or borrow money from its suppliers by purchasing goods on credit. The persons or entities to whom Loblaw owes money are its **creditors**. Amounts owed to creditors—in the form of debt and other obligations—are called **liabilities**. Specific names are given to different types of liabilities, depending on their source. Loblaw, for instance, might purchase produce on credit from suppliers; the obligations to pay for these supplies are called **accounts payable**. Additionally, Loblaw may have **interest payable** on the outstanding principal of a **note payable** to a bank, for the money borrowed to purchase its display cabinets. It may also have **wages payable** to employees, **provincial sales taxes** and **property taxes payable** to the provincial government, and **goods and services taxes payable** and **income taxes payable** to the federal government's collection authority, the Canada Customs and Revenue Agency. Debt securities sold to investors, and due to be repaid at a particular date some years in the future, are called **bonds payable**.

A corporation may also obtain funds by selling shares to investors. Mentioned in the chapter-opening vignette, Garfield Weston, CEO of a family business specializing in bakery goods, bought shares in Loblaw Groceterias, a Chicago-based food distributor, in the 1940s and 1950s. In 1956, after he had purchased enough shares to gain control, he incorporated the company as Loblaw Companies. As the business grew in the next five decades, it became necessary to sell shares more broadly to obtain additional financing. In 1998, when Loblaw purchased Provigo, it issued 28,715,059 additional common shares valued at $890 million. **Common shares** is the term used to indicate the ownership interest of shareholders when a company issues only one kind or class of shares. Loblaw also has another class of shares, called **preferred shares**. Preferred shares differ from common shares in that preferred shareholders have many preferential rights over the common shareholders. For example, preferred shareholders are entitled to receive certain payments before common shareholders are. **Share capital** is the total of all the different classes of shares issued by a company.

Alternative Terminology The word *issued* means *sold*, and is commonly used when speaking of share transactions.

The claims of creditors differ from those of shareholders. If you loan money to a company, you are one of its creditors. In loaning money, you specify a repayment schedule—for example, payment at the end of three months. As a creditor, you have a legal right to be paid at the agreed time. In the event of nonpayment, you may legally force the company to sell its property to pay its debts. The law requires that creditor claims be paid before ownership claims.

Owners, on the other hand, have no claim to corporate resources until the claims of creditors are satisfied. If you buy a company's shares instead of loaning it money, you have no right to expect any payments until all of its creditors are paid. Also, once shares are issued, the company has no obligation to buy it back, whereas debt obligations must be repaid. Many companies pay shareholders a return on their investment on a regular basis, as long as there is sufficient cash to cover expected payments to creditors. Payments to shareholders are called **dividends**. Loblaw paid its shareholders a cash dividend of $0.24 per share in 1999.

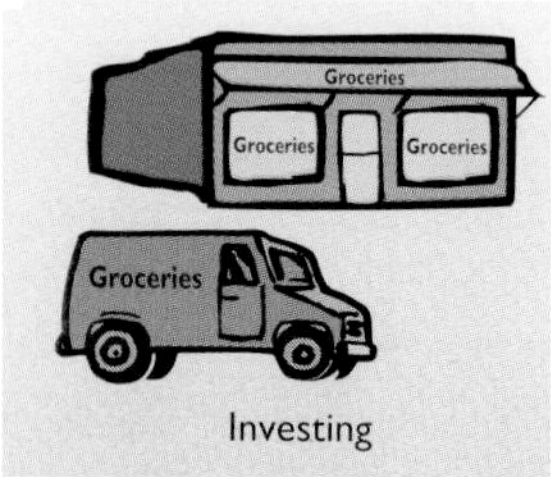

INVESTING ACTIVITIES

Once Loblaw obtained financing, it bought the resources it needed to operate. Resources owned by a business are called **assets**. For example, cash, accounts receivable, office supplies, inventory, computers, delivery trucks, buildings, and land are all assets.

Different types of assets are given different names. A very important asset to Loblaw or any other business is **cash**. If Loblaw sells goods to an affiliated store and does not receive cash immediately, then Loblaw has a right to expect payment from that customer in the future. This right to receive money in the future is called an **account receivable**. Goods available for future sales, like President's Choice merchandise, are assets called **inventory**. Longer-lived assets such as land, buildings, and other types of equipment are often just referred to as **capital assets**.

OPERATING ACTIVITIES

Operating

Once a business has the assets it needs to get started, it can begin its operations. Loblaw is in the business of selling food and household products. It sells its own brands of products, ranging from frozen entrees to gourmet cookies, under such labels as *President's Choice*, *Club Pack*, *no name*, *G-R-E-E-N*, and *TOO GOOD TO BE TRUE!*, in addition to others. Loblaw's also offers in-store pharmacies, film developing, dry-cleaning, and banking services. In short, if it has anything to do with one-stop shopping for everyday household needs, Loblaw sells it. We call the money from the sale of these products **revenues**. In accounting language, revenues are increases in economic resources—normally an increase in an asset but sometimes a decrease in a liability—resulting from a business's operating activities.

Revenues arise from different sources and are identified by various names, depending on the nature of the business. For instance, Loblaw's primary source of revenue is the money it earns from grocery sales to consumers. It also earns interest revenue on securities and commercial paper held as short-term investments. Sources of revenue common to many businesses are **sales revenue**, **service revenue**, and **interest revenue**.

BUSINESS INSIGHT

Management Perspective

Although the Vancouver Canucks earn revenue from many sources, by far the largest share—nearly 50%,—comes from regular season hockey game ticket sales. The sources of the Canucks, 1999 total revenue of $58 million are as follows:

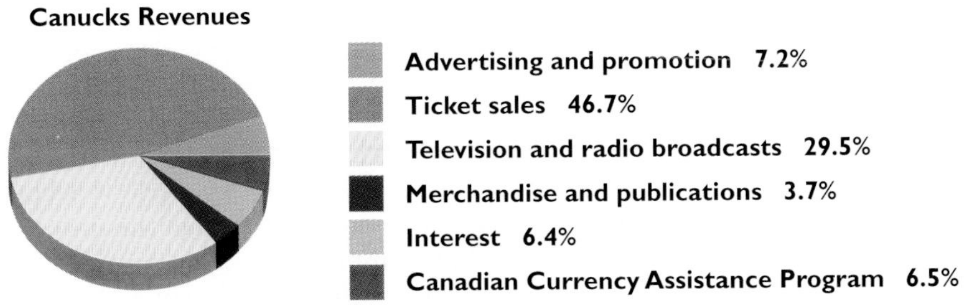

Source: Northwest Sports Enterprises Ltd. 1999 Annual Report.

Business Insight examples provide interesting information about actual accounting situations in business.

Before Loblaw can sell any food products, it must buy produce, meat, and other food supplies. It also incurs more mundane costs like salaries, utilities, and income taxes. All of these costs, referred to as expenses, are necessary to sell the product. In accounting language, **expenses** are the cost of assets consumed or services used in the process of generating revenues.

Expenses take many forms and are identified by various names, depending on the type of asset consumed or service used. For example, Loblaw keeps track of these types of expenses: **cost of sales**, **selling and administrative expenses** (such as cost of food products, wages of store employees, advertising costs, office supplies, utilities), **amortization expense** (allocation of the cost of using long-lived capital assets), **interest expense** (amounts of interest paid on various

Alternative Terminology
Amortization expense is also called *depreciation expense.*

debts), and **income taxes** (corporate income taxes paid to the provincial and federal governments).

Alternative Terminology *Net earnings* are also commonly known as *net income.*

To determine whether it earned a profit, Loblaw compares the revenues of a period with the expenses of that period. When revenues exceed expenses, **net earnings** result. When expenses exceed revenues, a **net loss** results.

BEFORE YOU GO ON . . .

Review It questions at the end of major text sections prompt you to stop and review the key points you have just studied. Sometimes Review It questions stand alone; other times they are accompanied by practice exercises. The **Do It** exercises, like the one here, ask you to put newly acquired knowledge to work in some form of financial statement preparation. They outline the reasoning necessary to complete the exercise and show a solution.

Review It

1. What are the three forms of business organization and the advantages of each?
2. What are the two primary categories of users of financial information? Give examples of each.
3. What are the three types of business activity?
4. What are assets, liabilities, share capital, revenues, and expenses?

Do It

Classify each item as an asset, liability, share capital, revenue, or expense:

(a) Cost of using truck
(b) Service revenue
(c) Notes payable
(d) Issuance of shares
(e) Truck purchased
(f) Amounts owed to suppliers

Reasoning: Accounting classifies items by their economic characteristics. Proper classification of items is critical if accounting is to provide useful information.

Solution:

(a) Cost of using truck is classified as expense.
(b) Service revenue is classified as revenue.
(c) Notes payable are classified as liabilities.
(d) Issuance of shares is classified as share capital, likely common shares if there is only one class of shares.
(e) Truck purchased is classified as an asset.
(f) Amounts owed to suppliers are classified as liabilities.

COMMUNICATING WITH USERS

STUDY OBJECTIVE 4
Describe the content and purpose of each of the financial statements.

Assets, liabilities, revenues, and expenses are of interest to users of accounting information. For business purposes, it is customary to arrange this information in the format of four different **financial statements**, which form the backbone of financial accounting. To present a picture of what your business owns (its assets) and what it owes (its liabilities) at a specific point in time, you would present a **balance sheet**. To show how successfully your business performed during a period of time, you would report its revenues and expenses in the **statement of earnings**. To indicate how much of net earnings (from the current period or prior periods) was distributed to you and the other owners of your business in the form of dividends, and how much was retained in the business to allow for future growth, you would present a **statement of retained earnings**. And finally, of particular interest to your bankers and other creditors, you would present a **statement of cash flows** to show where your business obtained cash during a period of time and how that cash was used.

Helpful Hint The heading of every statement identifies the company, the type of statement, and the time period covered by the statement. Sometimes another line is added to indicate the unit of measure. When it is used, this fourth line usually indicates that the data are presented in thousands or in millions.

To introduce you to these statements, we have prepared the financial statements for a marketing agency, Sierra Corporation, in Illustration 1-4. Take some time now to become familiar with their general form and categories in preparation for the more detailed discussion that follows.

Illustration 1-4 Sierra Corporation's financial statements

SIERRA CORPORATION
Statement of Earnings
For the Month Ended October 31, 2001

Revenues		
Service revenue		$10,600
Expenses		
Salaries expense	$5,200	
Supplies expense	1,500	
Rent expense	900	
Insurance expense	50	
Interest expense	50	
Amortization expense	40	
Total expenses		7,740
Earnings before income tax		2,860
Income tax expense		600
Net earnings		$ 2,260

SIERRA CORPORATION
Statement of Retained Earnings
For the Month Ended October 31, 2001

Retained earnings, October 1	$ 0
Add: Net earnings	2,260
	2,260
Less: Dividends	500
Retained earnings, October 31	$1,760

SIERRA CORPORATION
Balance Sheet
October 31, 2001

Assets	
Cash	$15,200
Accounts receivable	200
Advertising supplies	1,000
Prepaid insurance	550
Office equipment, net	4,960
Total assets	$21,910

Liabilities and Shareholders' Equity	
Liabilities	
Notes payable	$ 5,000
Accounts payable	2,500
Interest payable	50
Unearned revenue	800
Salaries payable	1,200
Income tax payable	600
Total liabilities	10,150
Shareholders' equity	
Common shares	10,000
Retained earnings	1,760
Total shareholders' equity	11,760
Total liabilities and shareholders' equity	$21,910

SIERRA CORPORATION
Statement of Cash Flows
For the Month Ended October 31, 2001

Cash flows from operating activities		
Cash receipts from operating activities	$11,200	
Cash payments for operating activities	(5,500)	
Net cash provided by operating activities		$ 5,700
Cash flows from investing activities		
Purchased office equipment	$(5,000)	
Net cash used by investing activities		(5,000)
Cash flows from financing activities		
Issuance of common shares	$10,000	
Issued note payable	5,000	
Payment of dividend	(500)	
Net cash provided by financing activities		14,500
Net increase in cash		15,200
Cash at beginning of period		0
Cash at end of period		$15,200

Helpful Hint Note that dollar signs ($) begin each new column and precede final sums. Note also that final sums are double-underlined and negative amounts are in parentheses.

Helpful Hint The arrows in this illustration show interrelationships of the four financial statements.

STATEMENT OF EARNINGS

The **statement of earnings** reports the success or failure of the company's operations for a period of time. This statement is also commonly known as the **income statement** or **statement of operations**. Although *earnings* and *income* are both often used terms in the title of this statement, *Financial Reporting in Canada* reports that *earnings* has predominated over the past decade, with nearly half of the companies they survey using the title "Statement of Earnings."

To indicate that Sierra's statement of earnings reports the results of operations for a **period of time**, the statement of earnings is dated "For the Month Ended October 31, 2001." The statement of earnings lists the company's revenues followed by its expenses. Expenses are deducted from revenues to determine earnings before income tax (commonly abbreviated as EBIT). Income tax expense is usually shown separately, immediately following earnings before income tax. Finally, the net earnings (or net loss) are determined by deducting income tax expense. The result is the famed "bottom line" often referred to in business.

Why are financial statement users interested in the bottom line? Investors buy and sell shares based on their beliefs about the future performance of a company. If you believe that Sierra will be even more successful in the future, and that this success will translate into a higher share price, you should buy Sierra's shares. Investors are interested in a company's past net earnings because they provide information which suggests future net earnings. Similarly, creditors also use the statement of earnings to predict the future. When a bank loans money to a company, it does so with the belief that it will be repaid in the future. If it didn't think it was going to be repaid, it wouldn't loan the money. Therefore, prior to making the loan, the bank loan officer must try to predict whether the company will be profitable enough to repay its loan.

Every chapter presents useful information about how decision-makers use financial statements. **Decision Toolkits** summarize discussions of key decision-making contexts and techniques.

Note that **the issuance of shares and dividend distributions are not used in determining net earnings**. For example, $10,000 of cash received from issuing new shares was not treated as revenue by Sierra Corporation, and dividends paid of $500 were not regarded as a business expense because they were not incurred to generate revenue.

DECISION TOOLKIT

Decision Checkpoints	Info Needed for Decision	Tool to Use for Decision	How to Evaluate Results
Are the company's operations profitable?	Statement of earnings	The statement of earnings reports on the success or failure of the company's operations by reporting its revenues and expenses.	If the company's revenue exceeds its expenses, it will report net earnings; otherwise it will report a net loss.

STATEMENT OF RETAINED EARNINGS

If Sierra is profitable, at the end of each period it must decide what portion of earnings to pay to shareholders in dividends. In theory it could pay all of its current period earnings, but few companies choose to do this. Why? Because they want to retain part of the earnings or profits in the business to allow for further expansion. High growth companies, for example, often choose to pay no dividends. **Retained earnings** are the cumulative earnings that have been retained in the corporation (that is, not paid out to shareholders).

The **statement of retained earnings** shows the amounts and causes of changes in retained earnings during the period. The time period is the same as that covered by the statement of earnings. The beginning retained earnings amount is shown on the first line of the statement. Then net earnings are added and dividends are deducted to calculate the retained earnings at the end of the period. If a company has a net loss, it is deducted (rather than added) in the statement of retained earnings.

By monitoring the statement of retained earnings, users of financial statements learn a great deal about management's dividend payment philosophy. Some investors seek companies that pay high dividends, whereas others seek companies that pay lower dividends, and instead reinvest to increase the share's growth potential. Lenders monitor their corporate customers' dividend payments, because any money paid in dividends reduces a company's ability to repay its debts.

DECISION TOOLKIT

Decision Checkpoints	Info Needed for Decision	Tool to Use for Decision	How to Evaluate Results
What is the company's policy toward dividends and growth?	Statement of retained earnings	How much of this year's earnings did the company pay out in dividends to shareholders?	A company striving for rapid growth will pay a low dividend.

BALANCE SHEET

STUDY OBJECTIVE 5

Explain the meaning of assets, liabilities, and shareholders' equity, and state the basic accounting equation.

The **balance sheet** reports assets and claims to those assets at a specific point in time. These claims are subdivided into two categories: claims of creditors and claims of owners (shareholders). As noted earlier, claims of creditors are called liabilities. Claims of owners are called **shareholders' equity**. This relationship is shown in equation form in Illustration 1-5. This equation is referred to as the **basic accounting equation**.

Illustration 1-5 Basic accounting equation

Assets = Liabilities + Shareholders' Equity

This relationship is where the name *balance sheet* comes from. Assets must be in balance with the claims to the assets. The right-hand side of the equation—the liabilities and equities—shows how the assets have been financed (borrowing from creditors, investing by shareholders, or self-financing through earnings retained in the company).

As you can see from looking at Sierra's balance sheet in Illustration 1-4, assets are listed first, followed by liabilities and shareholders' equity. Shareholders' equity comprises two parts: (1) share capital and (2) retained earnings. Share capital represents the shareholders' investments and includes all the classes of shares that a company has issued. If only one class of shares is issued, it is always common shares. As noted earlier, common (and preferred) shares result when the company sells new shares in exchange for cash or other assets. Retained earnings are the cumulative net earnings retained in the corporation. Sierra has common shares of $10,000 and retained earnings of $1,760, for total shareholders' equity of $11,760.

Helpful Hint Corporations may issue several classes of shares, but the shares that represents the primary ownership interest is **common shares**.

Creditors use the balance sheet as another source of information to determine the likelihood that they will be repaid. They carefully evaluate the nature of a company's assets and liabilities. For example, does the company have assets that could be easily sold to repay its debts? Managers use the balance sheet to determine whether inventory is adequate to support future sales and whether cash on hand is sufficient for immediate cash needs. Managers also look at the relationship between debt and shareholders' equity to determine whether they have the best proportion of debt and equity financing.

DECISION TOOLKIT

Decision Checkpoints	Info Needed for Decision	Tool to Use for Decision	How to Evaluate Results
Does the company rely primarily on debt or shareholders' equity to finance its assets?	Balance sheet	The balance sheet reports the company's resources and claims to those resources. There are two types of claims: liabilities and shareholders' equity.	Compare the amount of debt versus the amount of shareholders' equity to determine whether the company relies more on creditors or owners for its financing.

STATEMENT OF CASH FLOWS

Alternative Terminology The *statement of cash flows* is also sometimes called a *statement of changes in financial position.*

The primary function of a **statement of cash flows** is to provide financial information about the cash receipts and cash payments of a business for a specific period of time. To help investors, creditors, and others in their analysis of a company's cash position, the statement of cash flows reports the cash effects of a company's (1) operating activities, (2) investing activities, and (3) financing activities. In addition, the statement shows the net increase or decrease in cash during the period, and the cash amount at the end of the period.

Users are interested in the statement of cash flows because they want to know what is happening to a company's most important resource. The statement of cash flows provides answers to these simple but important questions:

1. Where did cash come from during the period?
2. How was cash used during the period?
3. What was the change in the cash balance during the period?

The statement of cash flows for Sierra, in Illustration 1-4, shows that cash increased by $15,200 during the year. This increase resulted because operating activities (services to clients) increased cash by $5,700, and financing activities increased cash by $14,500. Investing activities used $5,000 of cash for the purchase of office equipment.

DECISION TOOLKIT

Decision Checkpoints	Info Needed for Decision	Tool to Use for Decision	How to Evaluate Results
Does the company generate sufficient cash from operations to fund its investing activities?	Statement of cash flows	The statement of cash flows shows the amount of cash provided or used by operating activities, investing activities, and financing activities.	Compare the amount of cash provided by operating activities with the amount of cash used by investing activities. Any deficiency in cash from operating activities must be made up with cash provided by financing activities.

INTERRELATIONSHIPS OF STATEMENTS

Because the results on some statements are used as data for other statements, the statements are interrelated. These interrelationships are evident in Sierra's statements in Illustration 1-4:

1. The statement of retained earnings is dependent on the results of the statement of earnings. Sierra reported net earnings of $2,260 for the period. This amount is added to the beginning amount of retained earnings as part of the process of determining ending retained earnings.
2. The balance sheet and statement of retained earnings are interrelated because the ending amount of $1,760 on the statement of retained earnings is reported as the retained earnings amount on the balance sheet.
3. The statement of cash flows and the balance sheet are also interrelated. The statement of cash flows shows how the cash account changed during the period by stating the amount of cash at the beginning of the period, the sources and uses of cash during the period, and the amount of cash at the end of the period, $15,200. The ending amount of cash shown on the statement of cash flows must agree with the amount of cash on the balance sheet.

Study these interrelationships carefully. To prepare financial statements you must understand the sequence in which these amounts are determined and how each statement affects the next.

BEFORE YOU GO ON . . .

Review It

1. What questions that could be answered by financial information might each of the following decision-makers have: bank loan officer, investor, labour union, and government?
2. What are the content and purpose of each statement: statement of earnings, balance sheet, statement of retained earnings, and statement of cash flows?
3. The basic accounting equation is: assets = liabilities + shareholders' equity. Replacing words with dollar amounts, what is Loblaw's accounting equation as at January 1, 2000? The answer to this question is at the end of this chapter.

Review It questions marked with this Loblaw icon require that you use Loblaw's 1999 annual report in Appendix A at the end of this book.

Loblaws
A passion for food... *and a lot more!*

Do It

CSU Corporation began operations on January 1, 2001. The following information is available for CSU Corporation on December 31, 2001: service revenue $22,200; accounts receivable $4,000; accounts payable $2,000; building rental expense $9,000; notes payable $5,000; common shares $10,000; retained earnings ?; equipment $16,000; insurance expense $1,000; supplies $1,800; supplies expense $200; cash $2,000; income tax expense $5,200; and dividends $0. Using this information, prepare a statement of earnings, a statement of retained earnings, and a balance sheet.

Reasoning: A statement of earnings reports the success or failure of a company's operations for a period of time. A statement of retained earnings shows the amounts and causes of changes in retained earnings during the period. A balance sheet presents a company's assets and claims to those assets at a specific point in time.

Solution:

CSU CORPORATION
Statement of Earnings
For the Year Ended December 31, 2001

Revenues		
Service revenue		$22,200
Expenses		
Rent expense	$9,000	
Insurance expense	1,000	
Supplies expense	200	
Total expenses		10,200
Earnings before income tax		12,000
Income tax expense		5,200
Net earnings		$ 6,800

CSU CORPORATION
Statement of Retained Earnings
For the Year Ended December 31, 2001

Retained earnings, January 1	$ 0
Add: Net earnings	6,800
	6,800
Less: Dividends	0
Retained earnings, December 31	$6,800

CSU CORPORATION
Balance Sheet
December 31, 2001

Assets	
Cash	$ 2,000
Accounts receivable	4,000
Supplies	1,800
Equipment	16,000
Total assets	$23,800
Liabilities and Shareholders' Equity	
Liabilities	
Notes payable	$ 5,000
Accounts payable	2,000
Total liabilities	7,000
Shareholders' equity	
Common shares	10,000
Retained earnings	6,800
Total shareholders' equity	16,800
Total liabilities and shareholders' equity	$23,800

A QUICK LOOK AT LOBLAW'S FINANCIAL STATEMENTS

The same relationships that you observed among the financial statements of Sierra Corporation are evident in the 1999 simplified financial statements of Loblaw Companies Limited, which are presented in Illustrations 1-6 through 1-9. Loblaw's actual financial statements are presented in Appendix A at the end of the book. They may look complicated to you. Do not be alarmed by their seeming complexity. (If you could already read and understand them, there would be little reason to take this course, except possibly to add a high grade to your transcript—which we hope you'll do anyway.) By the end of the book, you'll have a great deal of experience in reading and understanding financial statements such as these.

Before examining them, we need to explain three points:

1. Note that numbers are reported in millions of dollars on Loblaw's financial statements—that is, the last six zeros (000,000) are omitted. Thus, Loblaw's net earnings in 1999 are $376,000,000 not $376.
2. Loblaw, like most companies, presents its financial statements for more than one year. Financial statements that report information for more than one period are called **comparative statements**. Comparative statements allow users to compare the financial position of a business at the end of one accounting period to that of previous periods.
3. Many companies choose December 31 as their accounting year end, although an increasing number of companies are choosing dates other than December 31. Loblaw's **fiscal year**, or accounting year end, ends on the Saturday nearest the end of the calendar year. Consequently, its year end does not fall on the same date each year. It was December 28, 1996, for the 1996 fiscal year; January 3, 1998, for the 1997 fiscal year; January 2, 1999, for the 1998 fiscal year; and January 1, 2000, for the 1999 fiscal year. As a consequence, for Loblaw, fiscal 1997 had 53 weeks, whereas fiscal 1999 and 1998 each had 52 weeks.

Helpful Hint An accounting time period that is one year long is called a ***fiscal year***.

Business Insight examples provide interesting information about actual accounting situations in business.

BUSINESS INSIGHT

Management Perspective

About 70% of Canadian companies use December 31 for their year end. Why do companies choose the particular year ends that they do? In other words, why doesn't every company use December 31 as the accounting year end? Many companies choose to end their accounting year when the inventory or operations are at a low. This is advantageous because compiling accounting information requires much time and effort by managers, so they would rather do it when they aren't too busy operating the business. Also, inventory is easier and less costly to count when it is low. Some companies whose year ends differ from December 31 are Mark's Work Wearhouse (last Saturday in January), Molson's (March 31), Intrawest (June 30), and Salter Street Films (October 31). Most universities and governments use March 31 for their fiscal year end.

Helpful Hint The percentage change in any amount from one year to the next is calculated as follows:

$$\frac{\text{Change during period}}{\text{Previous value}}$$

Thus, the percentage change in net earnings is

$$\frac{\text{Change in earnings}}{\text{Previous year's earnings}}$$

STATEMENT OF EARNINGS

A simplified version of Loblaw's statement of earnings is presented in Illustration 1-6. Sierra is a service company: it provides services to earn its revenue. Loblaw sells a product: its primary source of revenue is called sales. For 1999, Loblaw reports sales of $18,783 million. It then subtracts a variety of expenses related to operating the business. These operating expenses include the cost of sales, selling and administrative expenses and amortization—amortization is the cost of the capital assets allocated to each period. It also deducts interest expense (payment of interest on debt) of $112 million, to arrive at earnings before income taxes of $699 million. After subtracting income tax expense of $280 million and a nonrecurring expense for goodwill related to the Provigo acquisition, the company reports net earnings for the period of $376 million. The goodwill charge is unusual and seldom reported in this manner on statements. We will learn more about goodwill in Chapter 12. Net earnings represent a 144% increase over the results of the previous year.

Illustration 1-6
Loblaw statement of earnings

Loblaws
A passion for food... *and a lot more!*

LOBLAW COMPANIES LIMITED
Statements of Earnings
Year Ended January 1, 2000
(in millions of dollars)

	1999	1998
Revenues		
Sales	$ 18,783	$ 12,497
Expenses		
Cost of sales, selling and administrative expenses	17,699	11,785
Amortization	273	183
Interest expense	112	68
Total expenses	18,084	12,036
Earnings before income taxes	699	461
Income tax expense	280	199
Earnings before goodwill charges	419	262
Goodwill charges	43	1
Net earnings	$ 376	$ 261

Financial statements of real companies are accompanied by either a company logo or an associated photograph.

STATEMENT OF RETAINED EARNINGS

Loblaw presents information about its retained earnings in the Statement of Retained Earnings in Illustration 1-7. Unlike Loblaws, many companies use a single statement to present their earnings and retained earnings. Find the line "Retained earnings, beginning of period," in Illustration 1-7 and you will see that retained earnings at the beginning of the period (January 3, 1999) were $1,429 million. Note that this amount agrees with the end of period balance for 1998. As we proceed down the statement of retained earnings, the next figure for 1999 is net earnings of $376 million. Loblaw paid $61 million in dividends to its preferred and common shareholders. The 1999 ending balance of retained earnings, after adjustment for other items (cancelled shares and stock option plan payments), is $1,721 million. Find this amount of retained earnings near the bottom of Loblaw's 1999 balance sheet, presented in Illustration 1-8.

Illustration 1-7
Loblaw statement of retained earnings

LOBLAW COMPANIES LIMITED
Statements of Retained Earnings
Year Ended January 1, 2000
(in millions of dollars)

		1999	1998
Retained earnings, beginning of period		$1,429	$1,221
Add:	Net earnings for the period	376	261
Less:	Other adjustments	23	2
	Dividends	61	51
Retained earnings, end of period		$1,721	$1,429

Illustration 1-8
Loblaw balance sheet

LOBLAW COMPANIES LIMITED
Balance Sheets
As At January 1, 2000
(in millions of dollars)

	1999	1998
Assets		
Cash	$ 481	$ 624
Short-term investments	245	48
Accounts receivable	325	345
Inventories	1,222	1,141
Prepaid expenses and other	142	91
Capital assets, net	5,234	4,557
Other assets	330	299
Total assets	$ 7,979	$ 7,105
Liabilities and Shareholders' equity		
Liabilities		
Bank indebtedness	$ 296	$ 135
Notes payable	428	1,001
Accounts payable and accrued liabilities	2,066	1,806
Long-term debt	2,001	1,378
Other liabilities	284	190
Total liabilities	5,075	4,510
Shareholders' equity		
Share capital	1,183	1,166
Retained earnings	1,721	1,429
Total shareholders' equity	2,904	2,595
Total liabilities and shareholders' equity	$ 7,979	$ 7,105

BALANCE SHEET

As shown in Loblaw's balance sheet in Illustration 1-8, Loblaw's assets include the kinds mentioned in our discussion of Sierra Corporation, such as cash, accounts receivable, inventories, and capital assets, plus other types of assets that we will discuss in later chapters, such as prepaid expenses. Similarly, its liabilities include bank indebtedness (amounts owing to the bank), notes payable, accounts payable, as well as items not yet discussed, such as accrued liabilities. Loblaw's balance sheet shows that total assets increased from a 1998 balance of $7,105 million to a 1999 balance of $7,979 million. Not all categories increased at an equal rate, however. For instance, notes payable decreased, while accounts payable increased. As you learn more about financial statements, we will discuss how to interpret changes in financial statement items.

STATEMENT OF CASH FLOWS

Loblaw's cash (and cash equivalents, which we will examine in a later chapter) decreased by $304 million from 1998 to 1999 ($143 million decrease in cash and $161 million decrease in bank indebtedness). The reasons for this decrease can be determined by examining the statement of cash flows in Illustration 1-9. This statement presents Loblaw's sources and uses of cash during the period. Loblaw is in an expansion mode. Consequently, it spent considerable cash, $890 million, on investment activities. For example, it spent $802 million on new capital assets in order to expand. It also recovered $147 by selling 44 of its Loeb stores in Ontario. Note that its cash provided by operating activities, $656 million, was not sufficient to finance this expansion. These amounts are consistent with what might be expected of a company during a growth stage. In order to expand, the company needs to invest in property and equipment, but the cash provided by its current operations is not sufficient to support this growth. Thus, it must borrow, or issue shares. An examination of the financing activities shows that Loblaw received $799 million in cash from new financing. It also repaid short-term bank loans incurred to finance the Provigo and Agora Foods acquisition. The net result of the sources and uses of cash during the year was the cash decrease of $304 million.

Illustration 1-9
Loblaw statement of cash flows

Loblaws
A passion for food... *and a lot more!*

LOBLAW COMPANIES LIMITED
Statements of Cash Flows
Year Ended January 1, 2000
(in millions of dollars)

	1999	1998
Operating activities		
Cash receipts from operating activities	$ 18,803	$ 12,302
Cash payments from operating activities	(18,147)	(11,772)
Cash flows provided by operating activities	656	530
Investing activities		
Capital asset purchases	(802)	(599)
Proceeds from capital asset sales	21	17
Disposition (acquisition) of other businesses	147	(941)
Short-term investment purchases	(197)	54
Other	(59)	79
Cash flows used by investing activities	(890)	(1,390)
Financing activities		
Issue of debt	799	967
Retirement of debt	(784)	(141)
Issue of share capital	3	22
Retirement of share capital	(22)	(22)
Dividends	(61)	(51)
Other	(5)	
Cash flows provided by operating activities	(70)	775
Increase (decrease) in cash	(304)	(85)
Cash, beginning of period	489	574
Cash, end of period	$ 185	$ 489

Cash is defined as cash net of bank indebtedness.

OTHER ELEMENTS OF AN ANNUAL REPORT

STUDY OBJECTIVE 6

Describe the components that supplement the financial statements in an annual report.

Canadian companies that are publicly traded must provide their shareholders with an **annual report** each year. The annual report is a document that includes useful non-financial information about the company, as well as financial information. Non-financial information may include a management discussion of the company's mission, goals and objectives, market position, and people. Financial information may include a review of current operations and a summary of historical key financial figures and ratios, in addition to the comparative financial statements introduced in this chapter.

When **preparing the financial statements**, the statement of earnings must be prepared first, followed by the statement of retained earnings, balance sheet, and statement of cash flows. However, the financial statements are normally presented in the following order within the annual report: balance sheet, statement of earnings, statement of retained earnings, and statement of cash flows. Every set of financial statements is accompanied by explanatory notes and supporting schedules that are an integral part of the statements. The **notes to the financial statements** clarify information presented in the financial statements and expand upon it where additional detail is needed. Information in the notes does not always have to include quantifiable (numeric) data. Examples of notes include descriptions of the accounting policies and methods used in preparing the statements, explanations of uncertainties and contingencies, and statistics and details too voluminous to be included in the statements. The notes are essential to understanding a company's performance and position.

Public company financial statements are usually audited. An audit is an independent examination of the accounting data presented by a company. If the auditor is satisfied that the financial statements present the financial position, results of operations, and cash flows in accordance with prescribed accounting principles, then an **unqualified audit opinion** is expressed. If the auditor expresses anything other than an unqualified opinion, the financial statements should only be used with caution. That is, without an unqualified opinion, we cannot have complete confidence that the financial statements give a reliable picture of the company's financial health. Loblaw received an unqualified opinion from their auditors, KPMG.

You will find the audit opinion expressed in an **auditor's report** attached to the financial statements. A statement of management responsibility is also attached to the financial statements, usually immediately preceding the auditor's report. This statement is prepared by management and discusses their role in assuring the accuracy and integrity of the financial statements, as well as their responsibility for them.

Assumptions and Principles in Financial Reporting

STUDY OBJECTIVE 7

Explain the basic assumptions and principles underlying financial statements.

Preparation of financial statements relies on some key assumptions and principles. It is helpful to look at some of these now that we have begun to see how accounting can be used to convey financial information to decision-makers. These assumptions and principles underlie all financial reporting and will be referred to throughout the book.

ASSUMPTIONS

Monetary Unit Assumption

We begin with the assumptions. In looking at Loblaw's financial statements, you will notice that everything is stated in terms of dollars. The **monetary unit assumption** requires that only those things that can be expressed in money be included in the accounting records. This might seem so obvious that it doesn't bear mentioning, but it has important implications for financial reporting. Because the exchange of money is fundamental to business transactions, it makes sense that we measure a business in terms of money. However, it also means that certain important information needed by investors, creditors, and managers is not reported in the financial statements. For example, customer satisfaction is important to every business, but it is not easily quantified in dollar terms; thus it is not reported in the financial statements.

Economic Entity Assumption

The **economic entity assumption** states that every economic entity must be separately identified and accounted for. For example, suppose you are a shareholder in Loblaw. The amount of cash you have in your personal bank account and the balance owed on your personal car loan are not reported in Loblaw's balance sheet. The reason is that, for accounting purposes, you and Loblaw are separate accounting entities. In order to accurately assess Loblaw's performance and financial position, it is important to distinguish its activities from personal transactions, or the transactions of any other company, such as George Weston Limited.

BUSINESS INSIGHT

Management Perspective

A violation of the economic entity assumption contributed to the imprisonment of Bruce McNall, former co-owner of the Toronto Argonauts football team, Los Angeles Kings hockey team, and other interests in the entertainment and sports worlds. Creditors and investors were angered to learn that company invoices, inventories, other assets, and income tax returns were falsified to help support McNall's $300,000-a-month glamorous personal lifestyle that included a Maserati, Rolls-Royce, and Aston Martin.

Time Period Assumption

Next, notice that Loblaw's statement of earnings, statement of retained earnings, and statement of cash flows all cover periods of one year, and that the balance sheet is prepared at the end of each year. The **time period assumption** states that the life of a business can be divided into artificial time periods and that useful reports covering those periods can be prepared for the business. All companies report at least annually. Many also report at least every three months (quarterly) to shareholders and prepare monthly statements for internal purposes.

Going Concern Assumption

The **going concern assumption** states that the business will remain in operation for the foreseeable future. Of course businesses do fail, but in general, it is reasonable to assume that the business will continue operating. The going concern assumption underlies much of what we do in accounting. To give you just one example, if going concern is not assumed, capital assets should be stated at their liquidation value (selling price less cost of disposal), not at their cost. Only when liquidation of the business appears likely is the going concern assumption inappropriate.

These four accounting assumptions are shown graphically in Illustration 1-10.

Illustration 1-10
Accounting assumptions

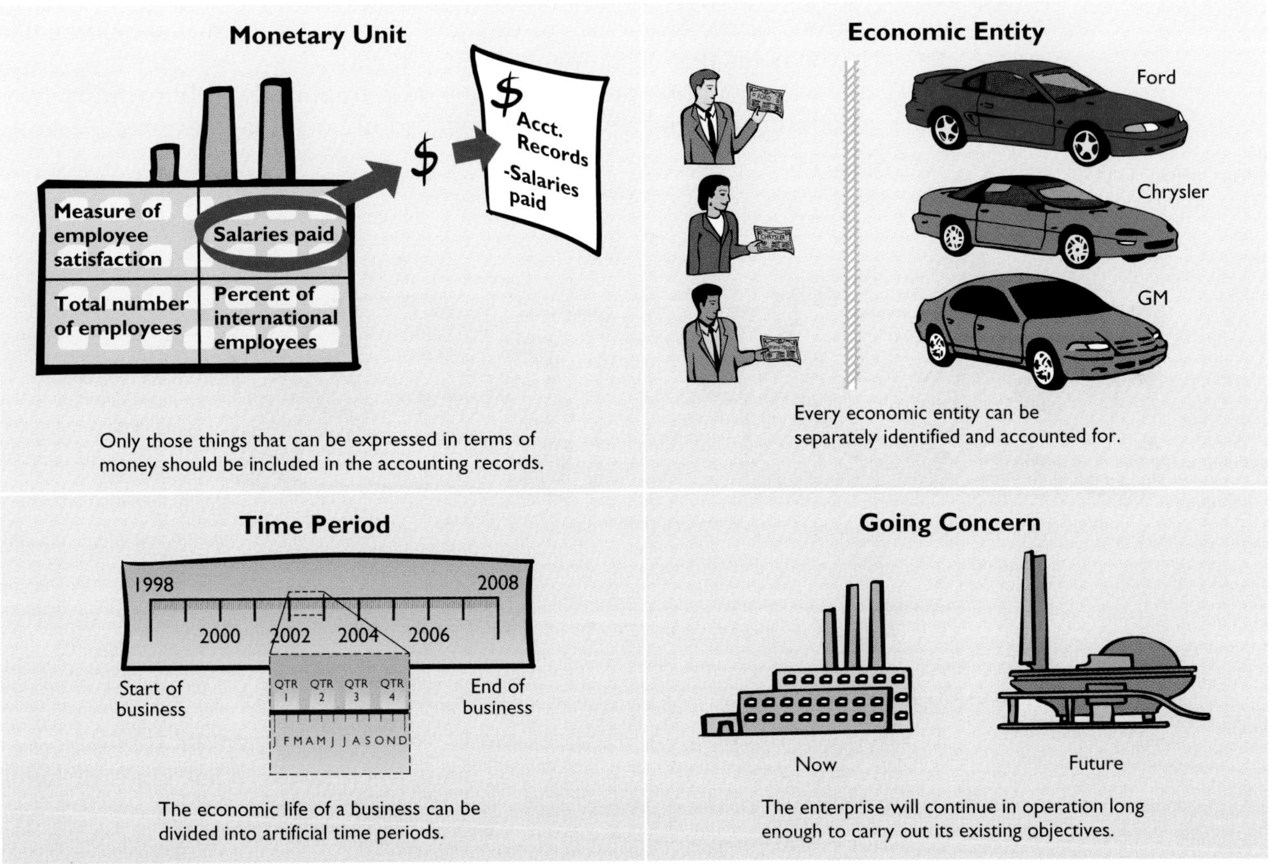

PRINCIPLES

Cost Principle

All of the assets on Loblaw's financial statements are recorded at the amount paid for them. The **cost principle** dictates that assets be recorded at their cost. This is true not only at the time the asset is purchased, but also over the time the asset is held. For example, if Loblaw were to purchase land for $30 million, it would initially be reported on the balance sheet at $30 million. But what would Loblaw do if, by the end of the next year, the land had increased in value to $40 million? The answer is that under the cost principle the land would continue to be reported at $30 million. This continues to be true even if the land decreases in value to $20 million. The land will continue to be reported at cost, until it is either sold or the going concern assumption is no longer valid.

The cost principle is often criticized as being irrelevant. Critics contend that market value would be more useful to financial decision-makers. Proponents of the cost principle counter that cost is the best measure because it can be easily verified from transactions between two parties, while market value is often subjective.

Full Disclosure Principle

There is important financial information that is not easily reported by the statements. For example, Loblaw has debt outstanding. Investors and creditors would like to know the terms of the debt; that is, when does it mature, what is its interest rate, and is it renewable? Or a customer might be suing Loblaw without investors and creditors knowing about it. The **full disclosure principle** requires that all circumstances and events which would make a difference to financial statement users be disclosed. If an important item cannot reasonably be reported directly in one of the four types of financial statements, then it should be discussed in the notes that accompany the statements.

These two accounting principles are shown graphically in Illustration 1-11. Other accounting principles will be introduced in later chapters.

Illustration 1-11
Accounting principles

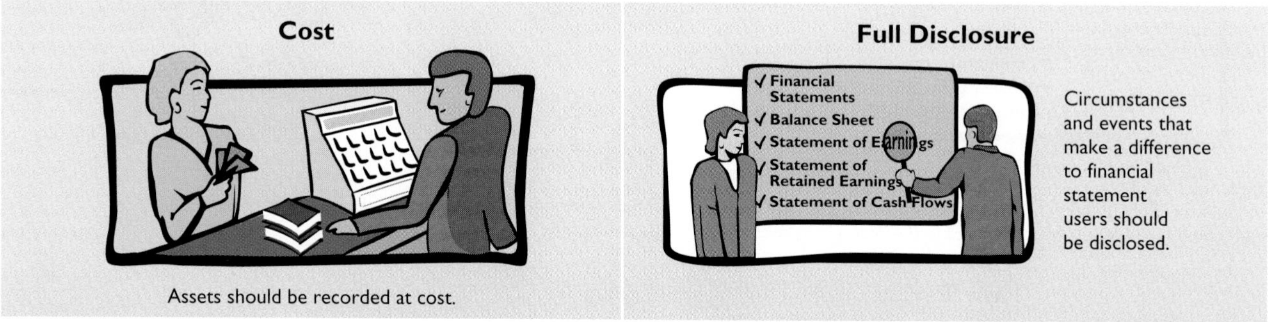

Cost
Assets should be recorded at cost.
Full Disclosure
√ Financial Statements
√ Balance Sheet
√ Statement of Earnings
√ Statement of Retained Earnings
√ Statement of Cash Flows
Circumstances and events that make a difference to financial statement users should be disclosed.

BEFORE YOU GO ON . . .

Review It

1. What non-financial information might you find in an annual report?
2. Why are notes to the financial statements necessary? What kinds of items are included in these notes?
3. What is the purpose of the auditor's report?
4. Describe the assumptions and principles of accounting addressed in this chapter.

USING THE DECISION TOOLKIT

Using the Decision Toolkit exercises, which follow the final set of Review It questions in the chapter, ask you to use information from financial statements to make financial decisions. We encourage you to think through the questions related to the decision before you study the solution.

Sobeys originally began as a proprietorship, in 1907, when John William Sobey opened his first butcher shop in Stellarton, Nova Scotia. Today, Sobeys Inc. is Canada's second largest grocery chain, after Loblaw. It has grown to 1,400 stores, of which more than 900 are supermarkets, in 10 provinces. Late in the calendar year 1998, Sobeys bought The Oshawa Group Limited and combined about 700 Oshawa stores with the Sobeys chain. Synergies made possible by this combination are expected to result, annually, in over $11 billion of sales and $70 million of cost savings in future years. Imagine that you are considering purchasing some of Sobeys' shares, in order to capitalize on their anticipated future success.

Instructions

Answer these questions related to your decision about whether to invest:

1. What financial statements should you request from the company?
2. What should each of these financial statements tell you?
3. Should you request audited financial statements? Explain.
4. Loblaw has a fiscal year end of January 1, 2000. Sobeys' fiscal year end is May 1, 1999. Is it possible to compare financial statements of these companies since they have different fiscal year ends?
5. Will the financial statements show the market value of Sobeys' assets? Explain.
6. Simplified financial statements for Sobeys Inc. are shown in Illustrations 1-12 through 1-15. What comparisons can you make between Sobeys and Loblaw in terms of their respective financial positions and results from operations?

Illustration 1-12 Sobeys statement of earnings

SOBEYS INC.
Statements of Earnings
Year Ended May 1
(in thousands)

	1999	1998	1997
Revenues			
Sales	$6,231,838	$3,155,084	$2,947,574
Investment income	1,074	4,409	2,031
Total revenues	6,232,912	3,159,493	2,949,605
Expenses			
Cost of sales, selling and administrative expenses	6,038,344	3,049,530	2,858,182
Amortization	81,817	45,408	42,963
Interest expense	46,301	10,831	12,031
Other expenses	85,143	10	7
Total expenses	6,251,605	3,105,779	2,913,183
Earnings (loss) before income taxes	(18,693)	53,714	36,422
Income tax expense (recovery)	(10,619)	16,375	9,552
Net earnings (loss)	$ (8,074)	$ 37,339	$ 26,870

Illustration 1-13 Sobeys statement of retained earnings

SOBEYS INC.
Statements of Retained Earnings
Year Ended May 1
(in thousands)

	1999	1998	1997
Balance, beginning of year	$125,016	$100,670	$86,278
Add (deduct): Net earnings (loss)	(8,074)	37,339	26,870
Less: Dividends paid	13,930	12,993	12,478
Balance, end of year	$103,012	$125,016	$100,670

Illustration 1-14 Sobeys balance sheet

SOBEYS INC.
Balance Sheets
May 1
(in thousands)

	1999	1998	1997
Assets			
Cash	$ 71,133	$ 27,176	$ 30,413
Marketable securities	4,546	315,205	215,205
Receivables	394,323	77,289	65,562
Income taxes recoverable	9,623		
Inventories	462,122	190,289	183,314
Prepaid expenses	31,284	8,446	8,454
Long-term investments	144,633	9,853	9,758
Capital assets, net	1,603,277	277,745	240,528
Other assets	157,876	16,910	17,293
Total assets	$2,878,817	$922,913	$770,527
Liabilities and Shareholders' Equity			
Liabilities			
Notes payable	$ 122,485	$ 90,500	$ 85,500
Accounts payable and accrued charges	1,013,017	292,531	265,040
Income taxes payable		5,467	3,145
Long-term debt	973,905	141,230	148,444
Other liabilities	19,421	200,000	100,171
Total liabilities	2,128,828	729,728	602,300
Shareholders' equity			
Share capital	647,207	66,801	66,801
Other	(230)	1,368	756
Retained earnings	103,012	125,016	100,670
Total shareholders' equity	749,989	193,185	168,227
Total liabilities and shareholders' equity	$2,878,817	$922,913	$770,527

Illustration 1-15 Sobeys statement of cash flows

SOBEYS INC.
Statements of Changes in Financial Position
Year Ended May 1
(in thousands)

	1999	1998	1997
Cash provided by (used for) operations			
Cash receipts from operating activities	$5,914,804	$3,143,357	detail N/A
Cash payments from operating activities	(5,654,854)	(3,051,628)	detail N/A
Total cash provided by operations	259,950	91,729	82,746
Cash provided by (used for) investments			
Purchase of capital assets	(265,839)	(109,197)	(73,838)
Proceeds on disposal of capital assets	69,213	27,672	22,640
Purchase of investments	(4,755)	—	(412)
Sale of investments	38,222	7	—
Acquisition of businesses	(1,461,945)	(1,176)	(15,279)
Other	97,826	2,935	30,504
Total cash used for investments	(1,527,278)	(79,759)	(36,385)

Cash provided by (used for) financing			
Issue of debt	995,641	5,597	8,000
Repayment of debt	(264,032)	(7,811)	(30,345)
Issue of capital stock	580,406	—	—
Payment of dividends	(13,930)	(12,993)	(12,478)
Other	13,200	—	—
Total cash provided by (used for) financing	1,311,285	(15,207)	(34,823)
Increase (decrease) in cash	43,957	(3,237)	11,538
Cash, beginning of year	27,176	30,413	18,875
Cash, end of year	$ 71,133	$ 27,176	$ 30,413

Solution

1. Before you invest, you should investigate the statement of earnings, statement of retained earnings, statement of cash flows, balance sheet, and the accompanying notes. Note that Sobeys Inc. calls its statement of cash flows by its alternative name, "statement of changes in financial position."
2. You would probably be most interested in the statement of earnings because it shows past performance and thus gives an indication of future performance. The statement of retained earnings shows the impact current earnings (or losses), and any dividends paid, have on the company's accumulated retained earnings balance from prior years. The statement of cash flows reveals where the company is getting and spending its cash. This is especially important for a company that wants to grow. Finally, the balance sheet reveals the financial position of the company and the relationship between assets and liabilities.
3. You would want audited financial statements—statements that have been examined by an independent public accountant who has expressed an opinion that the statements present fairly the financial position and results of operations of the company. Grant Thornton is Sobeys' auditor and its unqualified audit opinion is attached to Sobeys' financial statements. Investors and creditors should not make decisions without studying audited financial statements.
4. Both financial statements cover a one-year period, with Loblaw's fiscal year overlapping Sobeys' for four months (January 3, 1999, through May 1, 1999). If there have been no substantial changes during the eight-month period that Loblaw's financial results cover but Sobeys' do not, it really doesn't matter when each company's fiscal year ends. It is more important that we compare what each company was able to achieve within an equivalent period of time—whether it be one year, six months, or a quarter. Note also that Sobeys presents three fiscal years of results in its financial statements, while Loblaw presents only two years. Three years allows trends to be more easily identified. Of course, prior period's annual reports allow you to access the same information for Loblaw.

   If, however, a substantial change does occur in the intervening period, such a change would likely reduce the usefulness of a comparison of the financial statements of the two companies. Say, for example, that the economy changed dramatically during the non-overlapping period. The impact of this change in the economy would be reflected in Loblaw's current statements, but not in Sobeys' until the following fiscal year. It is important for users to be aware of relevant non-financial information such as this before they commence their comparisons.

5. The financial statements will not show the market value of the company. As indicated, one important principle of accounting is the cost principle, which states that assets should be recorded at cost. Cost has an important advantage over other valuations: it is objective and reliable.
6. Many interesting comparisons can be made between the two companies. Sobeys is much smaller, about one third the size of Loblaw. For example, Sobeys has total assets of $2,879 million versus $7,979 million for Loblaw. Also, Sobeys has lower revenue—sales of $6,232 million versus $18,783 million. Sobeys reported a net loss for its current fiscal year of $8 million, compared to Loblaw's net earnings of $376 million. However, Sobeys' net loss in fiscal 1999 was due in part to a comprehensive restructuring program to integrate Oshawa into Sobeys. This restructuring identified operating efficiencies, cost savings and revenue enhancements and is anticipated to result in future sales of $11 billion and cost savings of $70 million.

   Sobeys has a balance of $103 million of accumulated retained earnings, while Loblaw's retained earnings of $1,721 million are nearly 17 times this amount. In 1999, Loblaw generated cash from operating activities of $656 million versus $260 million for Sobeys. While these comparisons are useful, these basic measures are not enough to determine whether one company will be a better investment than the other. In later chapters, you will acquire more tools to help you compare the relative profitability and financial health of these, and other, companies.

Summary of Study Objectives

❶ ***Describe the primary forms of business organization.*** A proprietorship is a business owned by one person. A partnership is a business owned by two or more people. A corporation is a separate legal entity whose shares provide evidence of ownership.

❷ ***Identify the users and uses of accounting.*** Internal users work for the business and need accounting information to plan, organize, and run operations. The primary external users are investors and creditors. Investors (present and future shareholders) use accounting information to help decide whether to buy, hold, or sell shares. Creditors (suppliers and bankers) use accounting information to assess the risk of granting credit or loaning money to a business. Other groups who have an indirect interest in a business are taxing authorities, regulatory agencies, customers, labour unions, and economic planners.

❸ ***Explain the three principal types of business activity.*** Financing activities involve collecting the necessary funds to support the business. Investing activities involve acquiring the resources necessary to run the business. Operating activities involve putting the resources of the business into action to generate a profit.

❹ ***Describe the content and purpose of each of the financial statements.*** A statement of earnings presents the revenues and expenses of a company for a specific period of time. A statement of retained earnings summarizes the changes in retained earnings that have occurred for a specific period of time. Retained earnings are the cumulative earnings (less losses) over the company's life, less any dividends paid to shareholders. A balance sheet reports the assets, liabilities, and shareholders' equity of a business at a specific date. A statement of cash flows summarizes information concerning the cash inflows (receipts) and outflows (payments) for a specific period of time.

❺ ***Explain the meaning of assets, liabilities, and shareholders' equity, and state the basic accounting equation.*** Assets are resources owned by a business. Liabilities are the debts and obligations of the business. Liabilities represent claims of creditors on the assets of the business. Shareholders' equity represents the claims of owners on the assets of the business. It is composed of two parts: share capital and retained earnings. The basic accounting equation is: Assets = Liabilities + Shareholders' Equity.

❻ ***Describe the components that supplement the financial statements in an annual report.*** The annual report includes non-financial information, such as details about the operations of the company, management's interpretation of the company's results and financial position, as well as a discussion of plans for the future. Financial information that supplements the four financial statements includes management's statement of responsibility, the auditor's report, and the supporting notes to the financial statements.

❼ ***Explain the basic assumptions and principles underlying financial statements.*** The monetary unit assumption requires that only transaction data capable of being expressed in terms of money be included in the accounting records of the economic entity. The economic entity assumption states that economic events should be identified with a particular unit of accountability. The time period assumption states that the economic life of a business can be divided into artificial time periods and that meaningful accounting reports can be prepared for each period. The going concern assumption states that the enterprise will continue in operation long enough to carry out its existing objectives. The cost principle states that assets should be recorded at their cost. The full disclosure principle dictates that circumstances and events which matter to financial statement users be disclosed.

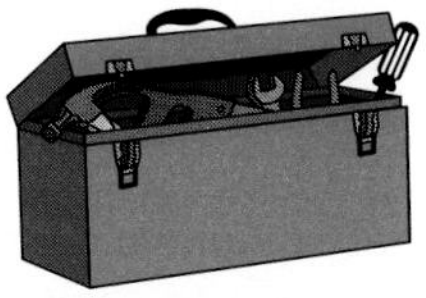

DECISION TOOLKIT—A SUMMARY

Decision Checkpoints	Info Needed for Decision	Tool to Use for Decision	How to Evaluate Results
Are the company's operations profitable?	Statement of earnings	The statement of earnings reports on the success or failure of the company's operations by reporting its revenues and expenses.	If the company's revenue exceeds its expenses, it will report net earnings; otherwise it will report a net loss.
What is the company's policy toward dividends and growth?	Statement of retained earnings	How much of this year's earnings did the company pay out in dividends to shareholders?	A company striving for rapid growth will pay a low dividend.
Does the company rely primarily on debt or shareholders' equity to finance its assets?	Balance sheet	The balance sheet reports the company's resources and claims to those resources. There are two types of claims: liabilities and shareholders' equity.	Compare the amount of debt versus the amount of shareholders' equity to determine whether the company relies more on creditors or owners for its financing.
Does the company generate sufficient cash from operating activities to fund its investing activities?	Statement of cash flows	The statement of cash flows shows the amount of cash provided or used by operating activities, investing activities, and financing activities.	Compare the amount of cash provided by operating activities with the amount of cash used by investing activities. Any deficiency in cash from operating activities must be made up with cash provided by financing activities.

GLOSSARY

Accounting The process of identifying, recording, and communicating the economic events of a business to interested users of the information. (p. 6)

Annual report A report, prepared by management, that presents financial and non-financial information about the company. (p. 21)

Assets Resources owned by a business. (p. 8)

Auditor's report A report prepared by an independent outside auditor stating the auditor's opinion as to the fairness of the presentation of the financial position and results of operations, as well as their conformance with generally accepted accounting principles and standards. (p. 21)

Balance sheet A financial statement that reports the assets, liabilities, and shareholders' equity at a specific date. (p. 13)

Basic accounting equation Assets = Liabilities + Shareholders' Equity. (p. 13)

Comparative statements A presentation of the financial statements of a company for multiple years. (p. 17)

Corporation A business organized as a separate legal entity having ownership divided into transferable shares. (p. 4)

Cost principle An accounting principle that states that assets should be recorded at their cost. (p. 23)

Dividends Distribution of retained earnings from a corporation to its shareholders in the form of cash or other assets. (p. 8)

Economic entity assumption An assumption that economic events can be identified with a particular unit of accountability. (p. 22)

Expenses The cost of assets consumed or services used in ongoing operations to generate resources. (p. 9)

Fiscal year An accounting period that is one year long. (p. 17)

Full disclosure principle An accounting principle that dictates that circumstances and events which make a difference to financial statement users be disclosed. (p. 24)

Going concern assumption The assumption that the enterprise will continue operating long enough to carry out its existing objectives and commitments. (p. 22)

Liabilities The debts and obligations of a business. Liabilities represent claims of creditors on the assets of a business. (p. 8)

Monetary unit assumption An assumption stating that only transaction data that can be expressed in terms of money should be included in the accounting records of the economic entity. (p. 22)

Net earnings (also known as net income) The amount by which revenues exceed expenses. (p. 10)

Net loss The amount by which expenses exceed revenues. (p. 10)

Notes to the financial statements Notes that clarify information presented in the financial statements and expand upon it where additional detail is needed. (p. 21)

Partnership A business owned by more than one person. (p. 4)

Proprietorship A business owned by one person. (p. 4)

Retained earnings The amount of accumulated net earnings (less losses, if any), from the prior and current periods, that has been kept in the corporation for future use and not distributed to shareholders as dividends. (p. 12)

Revenues The economic resources that result from the operating activities of a business, such as the sale of a product or rendering of a service. (p. 9)

Share capital Shares representing the ownership interest in a corporation. If only one class of shares exists, it is known as common shares. (p. 8)

Statement of cash flows A financial statement that provides information about the cash inflows (receipts) and cash outflows (payments) for a specific period of time. (p. 14)

Statement of earnings (also known as income statement) A financial statement that presents the revenues and expenses and resulting net earnings or net loss of a company for a specific period of time. (p. 12)

Statement of retained earnings A financial statement that summarizes the changes in retained earnings for a specific period of time. (p. 12)

Shareholders' equity The shareholders' claim on total assets, represented by the investments of the shareholders and undistributed earnings generated by the company. (p. 13)

Time period assumption An accounting assumption that the economic life of a business can be divided into artificial time periods. (p. 22)

DEMONSTRATION PROBLEM

Demonstration problems are a final review before you begin assignments.

Jeff Andringa, a former university hockey player, quit his job and started Ice Camp Ltd., a hockey camp for kids from ages 8 to 18. Eventually he would like to open hockey camps nationwide. Jeff has asked you to help him prepare financial statements at the end of his first year of operations. He relates the following facts about his business activities.

In order to get the business off the ground, he decided to incorporate. He sold common shares to a few close friends, and bought some of the shares himself. He initially raised $25,000 through the sale of these shares. In addition, the company took out a $10,000 loan at a local bank. A bus for transporting kids was purchased for $12,000 cash. Hockey goals and other miscellaneous equipment were purchased with $1,500 cash. The company earned camp tuition during the year of $100,000 but had collected only $80,000 of this amount. Thus, at the end of the year it was still owed $20,000. The company rents time at a local rink for $50 per hour. Total rink rental costs during the year were $8,000, insurance was $10,000, salary expense was $20,000, administrative expenses totalled $9,000, and income taxes amounted to $15,000—all of which were paid in cash. The company incurred $800 in interest expense on the bank loan, which it still owed at the end of the year.

The company paid dividends during the year of $5,000 cash. The balance in the corporate bank account at December 31, 2000, was $34,500.

Instructions

Using the format of the Sierra Corporation statements in this chapter, prepare a statement of earnings, statement of retained earnings, balance sheet, and statement of cash flows. [*Hint:* Prepare the statements in the order stated to take advantage of the flow of information from one statement to the next, as shown in Illustration 1-4.]

Solution to Demonstration Problem

ICE CAMP LTD.
Statement of Earnings
For the Year Ended December 31, 2000

Revenues		
Camp tuition revenue		$100,000
Expenses		
Salaries expense	$20,000	
Rink rental expense	8,000	
Insurance expense	10,000	
Administrative expense	9,000	
Interest expense	800	
Total expenses		47,800
Earnings before income taxes		52,200
Income tax expense		15,000
Net earnings		$ 37,200

ICE CAMP LTD.
Statement of Retained Earnings
For the Year Ended December 31, 2000

Retained earnings, January 1, 2000	$ 0
Add: Net earnings	37,200
	37,200
Less: Dividends	5,000
Retained earnings, December 31, 2000	$ 32,200

ICE CAMP LTD.
Balance Sheet
December 31, 2000

Assets

Cash	$ 34,500
Accounts receivable	20,000
Bus	12,000
Equipment	1,500
Total assets	$ 68,000

Liabilities and Shareholders' Equity

Liabilities	
Bank loan payable	$ 10,000
Interest payable	800
Total liabilities	10,800
Shareholders' equity	
Common shares	25,000
Retained earnings	32,200
Total shareholders' equity	57,200
Total liabilities and shareholders' equity	$ 68,000

Problem-Solving Strategies

1. The statement of earnings shows revenues and expenses for a period of time.
2. The statement of retained earnings shows the changes in retained earnings for a period of time.
3. The balance sheet reports assets, liabilities, and shareholders' equity at a specific date.
4. The statement of cash flows reports sources and uses of cash provided or used by operating, investing, and financing activities for a period of time.

Problem-solving strategies that appear in the margins give you tips about how to approach the problem, and the solution provided illustrates both the form and content of complete answers.

ICE CAMP LTD.
Statement of Cash Flows
For the Year Ended December 31, 2000

Cash flows from operating activities	
Cash receipts from operating activities	$80,000
Cash payments for operating activities	(62,000)
Net cash provided by operating activities	18,000
Cash flows from investing activities	
Purchase of bus	(12,000)
Purchase of equipment	(1,500)
Net cash used by investing activities	(13,500)
Cash flows from financing activities	
Issuance of bank loan payable	10,000
Issuance of common shares	25,000
Dividends paid	(5,000)
Net cash provided by financing activities	30,000
Net increase in cash	34,500
Cash at beginning of period	0
Cash at end of period	$34,500

This would be a good time to return to the **Student Owner's Manual** at the beginning of the book (or look at it for the first time if you skipped it before) to read about the various types of assignment materials that appear at the end of each chapter. Knowing the purpose of the different assignments will help you appreciate what each one contributes to your accounting skills and competencies.

The tool icon means that an activity uses one of the decision tools presented in the chapter.

The pencil icon means that an activity requires you to write a detailed answer.

Self-Study Questions

Answers are at the end of the chapter.

(SO 1) 1. Which is *not* one of the three forms of business organization?
(a) Proprietorship
(b) Creditorship
(c) Partnership
(d) Corporation

(SO 1) 2. Which is an advantage of corporations compared to partnerships and proprietorships?
(a) Harder to raise funds
(b) Harder to transfer ownership
(c) Harder to organize
(d) Reduced legal liability for investors

(SO 2) 3. Which statement about users of accounting information is *incorrect?*
(a) Management is an internal user.
(b) The Canada Customs and Revenue Agency is an external user.
(c) Present creditors are external users.
(d) Regulatory authorities are internal users.

(SO 3) 4. Which is *not* one of the three primary business activities?
(a) Financing
(b) Operating
(c) Selling
(d) Investing

5. Net earnings will result during a time period when: (SO 4)
(a) assets exceed liabilities.
(b) assets exceed revenues.
(c) expenses exceed revenues.
(d) revenues exceed expenses.

6. Which section of a statement of cash flows indicates the cash spent on new equipment during the past accounting period? (SO 4)
(a) The investing section
(b) The operating section
(c) The financing section
(d) The cash flow statement does not give this information.

7. Which financial statement reports assets, liabilities, and shareholders' equity? (SO 4)
(a) Statement of earnings
(b) Statement of retained earnings
(c) Balance sheet
(d) Statement of cash flows

8. As at December 31, 2001, Stoneland Corporation has assets of $3,500 and shareholders' equity of $2,000. What are the liabilities for Stoneland Corporation as at December 31, 2001? (SO 5)
(a) $1,500 (c) $2,500
(b) $1,000 (d) $2,000

(SO 6) 9. The segment of a corporation's annual report that describes the corporation's accounting methods is the:
(a) notes to the financial statements.
(b) management discussion and analysis.
(c) auditor's report.
(d) statement of earnings.

(SO 7) 10. The cost principle states that:
(a) assets should be recorded at cost and adjusted when the market value changes.
(b) activities of an entity should be kept separate and distinct from its owner.
(c) assets should be recorded at their cost.
(d) only transaction data capable of being expressed in terms of money should be included in the accounting records.

(SO 7) 11. Valuing assets at their market value rather than at their cost is inconsistent with the:
(a) time period assumption.
(b) economic entity assumption.
(c) cost principle.
(d) all of the above

12. The full disclosure principle dictates that: (SO 7)
(a) financial statements should disclose all assets at their cost.
(b) financial statements should disclose only those events that can be measured in dollars.
(c) financial statements should disclose all events and circumstances that would matter to users of financial statements.
(d) financial statements should not be relied on unless an auditor has expressed an unqualified opinion on them.

QUESTIONS

(SO 1) 1. What are the three basic forms of business organizations?

(SO 1) 2. What are the advantages of being a corporation? What are the advantages of being a partnership or proprietorship? What are the disadvantages of each?

(SO 2) 3. "Accounting is ingrained in our society and is vital to our economic system." Do you agree? Explain.

(SO 2) 4. Who are the internal users of accounting data? How does accounting provide relevant data to the internal users?

(SO 2) 5. Who are the external users of accounting data? Give examples.

(SO 3) 6. Name two primary sources of financing activities for a corporation.

(SO 4) 7. Why do you think a balance sheet is prepared *as at a specific point in time,* while the other statements cover *a period of time?*

(SO 4) 8. How are each of the following pairs of financial statements interrelated?
(a) Statement of earnings and statement of retained earnings
(b) Statement of retained earnings and balance sheet
(c) Balance sheet and statement of cash flows

(SO 5) 9. What is the basic accounting equation?

(SO 5) 10. Sue Leonard is president of Better Books Dot Com. She has no accounting background. Leonard cannot understand why market value is not used as the basis for accounting measurement and reporting. Explain what basis is used and why.

(SO 5) 11. (a) Define the terms *assets, liabilities,* and *shareholders' equity.*
(b) What items affect shareholders' equity?

12. Which of these items are liabilities for Kool-Jewellery Stores Inc.? (SO 5)
(a) Cash
(b) Accounts payable
(c) Dividends
(d) Accounts receivable
(e) Supplies
(f) Equipment
(g) Salaries payable
(h) Service revenue
(i) Rent expense

13. Here are some items found in the financial statements of Elizabeth D'Anjou, Inc. Indicate in which financial statement(s) each item would appear. (SO 5)
(a) Service revenue
(b) Equipment
(c) Advertising expense
(d) Accounts receivable
(e) Common shares
(f) Wages payable
(g) Cash provided from operating activities
(h) Dividends

14. What is the purpose of the statement of cash flows? (SO 5)

15. What are the three main categories of the statement of cash flows? Why do you think these categories were chosen? (SO 5)

16. What are retained earnings? What items increase the balance in retained earnings? What items decrease the balance in retained earnings? (SO 5)

17. **Loblaw's** year end is not a fixed date; rather, it can vary slightly from one year to the next. What possible problems does this pose for financial statement users? (SO 5)

18. Why is it important for financial statements to receive an unqualified auditor's opinion? (SO 6)

19. What types of information are presented in the notes to the financial statements? (SO 6)

20. What is the importance of the economic entity assumption? Give an example of its violation. (SO 7)

21. How does the going concern assumption influence the values reported on our financial statements? (SO 7)

Brief Exercises

Describe forms of business organization.
(SO 1)

BE1-1 Write the correct form of business organization—proprietorship (P), partnership (PP), or corporation (C)—beside each set of characteristics.
(a) _____ Simple to set up, founder retains control
(b) _____ Shared control, increased skills and resources
(c) _____ Easier to transfer ownership and raise funds, no personal liability

Identify users of accounting information.
(SO 2)

BE1-2 Write the number (lettered items) of the decision or type of evaluation beside the appropriate user of accounting information.
1. Trying to determine whether the company complied with income tax regulations
2. Trying to determine whether the company can pay its obligations
3. Trying to determine whether a marketing proposal will be cost-effective
4. Trying to determine whether the company's net earnings will result in a share price increase
5. Trying to determine whether the company should use debt or equity financing

(a) _____ Investors in common shares
(b) _____ Marketing managers
(c) _____ Creditors
(d) _____ Chief Financial Officer
(e) _____ Canada Customs and Revenue Agency

Classify items by activity.
(SO 3)

BE1-3 Indicate the part of the statement of cash flows—operating activities (O), investing activities (I), or financing activities (F)—in which each item would appear.
(a) _____ Cash received from customers
(b) _____ Cash paid to shareholders (dividends)
(c) _____ Cash received from issuing new common shares
(d) _____ Cash paid to suppliers
(e) _____ Cash paid to purchase a new office building

Classify statement of earnings items.
(SO 4)

BE1-4 Classify each of the following items as revenue (R), expense (E), or neither (N).
(a) _____ Costs incurred for advertising
(b) _____ Services performed
(c) _____ Costs incurred for income taxes
(d) _____ Amounts paid to employees
(e) _____ Cash distributed to shareholders
(f) _____ Rent received in exchange for allowing the use of a building

Determine effect of transactions on shareholders' equity.
(SO 4)

BE1-5 Presented below are three transactions. Determine whether each transaction affects common shares (C), dividends (D), revenue (R), expense (E), or does not affect shareholders' equity (NE).
(a) _____ Paid cash to purchase equipment
(b) _____ Received cash for services performed
(c) _____ Paid employee salaries

Prepare a balance sheet.
(SO 4)

BE1-6 In alphabetical order below are balance sheet items for the Harrington Corporation at December 31, 2001. Prepare a balance sheet following the format of Illustration 1-4.

Accounts payable	$90,000
Accounts receivable	81,000
Cash	40,500
Common shares	31,500

Determine where items appear on financial statements.
(SO 4)

The **financial results of real companies** are included in the end of chapter material; these are indicated by the company name being shown in red.

BE1-7 The **Calgary Exhibition and Stampede Limited** was established in 1886 to produce "The Greatest Outdoor Show on Earth." Today, the direct economic benefit of the stampede to the City of Calgary exceeds $235 million annually. The Company has the following selected accounts included in its financial statements. In each case, identify whether the item would appear on the balance sheet (BS) or statement of earnings (SE).
(a)_____ Accounts receivable
(b)_____ Inventories
(c)_____ Amortization expense
(d)_____ Capital stock
(e)_____ Building
(f) _____ Stampede revenue
(g)_____ Horse racing revenue
(h)_____ Accounts payable and accrued liabilities
(i) _____ Cash and short-term deposits
(j) _____ Administration, marketing, and park services expenses

BE1-8 Indicate which statement—statement of earnings (SE), balance sheet (BS), statement of retained earnings (RE), or statement of cash flows (CF)—you would examine to find each of the following items:

Determine proper financial statements. (SO 4)

(a) _____ Revenue during the period
(b) _____ Supplies on hand at the end of the year
(c) _____ Cash received from issuing new bonds during the period
(d) _____ Total debts outstanding at the end of the period

BE1-9 Use the basic accounting equation to determine the missing amounts.

Use basic accounting equation. (SO 5)

Assets	= Liabilities +	Shareholders' Equity
$90,000	$50,000	(a)
(b)	$48,000	$70,000
$94,000	(c)	$72,000

BE1-10 Use the basic accounting equation to answer these questions:

Use basic accounting equation. (SO 5)

(a) The liabilities of Houle Corporation are $90,000 and the shareholders' equity is $240,000. What is the amount of Houle's total assets?
(b) The total assets of Pitre Limited are $170,000 and its shareholders' equity is $90,000. What is the amount of its total liabilities?
(c) The total assets of Budovitch Inc. are $700,000 and its liabilities are equal to half of its total assets. What is the amount of Budovitch's shareholders' equity?

BE1-11 At the beginning of the year, Lamson Company had total assets of $700,000 and total liabilities of $500,000.

Use basic accounting equation. (SO 5)

(a) If total assets increased by $150,000 during the year and total liabilities decreased by $80,000, what is the amount of shareholders' equity at the end of the year?
(b) If total liabilities increased by $100,000 and shareholders' equity decreased by $70,000, what is the amount of total assets at the end of the year?
(c) If total assets decreased by $90,000 and shareholders' equity increased by $110,000 during the year, what is the amount of total liabilities at the end of the year?

BE1-12 Indicate whether each of these items is an asset (A), a liability (L), or part of shareholders' equity (SE):

Identify assets, liabilities, and shareholders' equity. (SO 5)

(a) _____ Accounts receivable
(b) _____ Salaries payable
(c) _____ Equipment
(d) _____ Office supplies
(e) _____ Common shares
(f) _____ Notes payable

EXERCISES

E1-1 Here is a list of words or phrases discussed in this chapter:

Match words with descriptions. (SO 1, 2, 4, 6)

1. Accounts payable
2. Creditor
3. Shareholder
4. Partnership
5. Corporation
6. Share capital
7. Accounts receivable
8. Auditor's opinion

Instructions

Match each word or phrase with the best description of it.

(a) _____ An expression about whether financial statements are presented in accordance with prescribed accounting principles
(b) _____ A business enterprise that raises money by issuing shares
(c) _____ The portion of shareholders' equity that results from receiving cash from investors
(d) _____ Obligations to suppliers of goods
(e) _____ Amounts due from customers
(f) _____ A party to whom a business owes money
(g) _____ A party that invests in common or preferred shares
(h) _____ A business that is owned jointly by two or more individuals but that does not issue shares

Prepare statements of earnings and retained earnings.
(SO 4)

E1-2 This information relates to Tone Kon Co. for the year 2001:

Retained earnings, January 1, 2001	$45,000
Advertising expense	1,800
Dividends paid during 2001	5,000
Rent expense	10,400
Service revenue	50,000
Utilities expense	3,100
Salaries expense	28,000
Income tax expense	2,000

Instructions

After analysing the data, prepare a statement of earnings and a statement of retained earnings for the year ending December 31, 2001.

Correct an incorrectly prepared balance sheet.
(SO 4)

E1-3 Kit Lucas is the bookkeeper for Aurora Co. Ltd. Kit has been trying to get the balance sheet of Aurora to balance. It finally balanced, as shown below, but he's not sure if it's correct.

AURORA COMPANY
Balance Sheet
December 31, 2001

Assets		Liabilities and Shareholders' Equity	
Cash	$16,500	Accounts payable	$20,000
Supplies	8,000	Accounts receivable	(10,000)
Equipment	46,000	Common shares	50,000
Dividends paid during year	7,000	Retained earnings	17,500
Total assets	$77,500	Total liabilities and shareholders' equity	$77,500

Instructions

Prepare a correct balance sheet.

Calculate net earnings and prepare a balance sheet.
(SO 4)

E1-4 Berry Hill Campground Inc. is a public camping ground in Gros Morne National Park. It has compiled the following financial information as at December 31, 2001:

Revenues during 2001: camping fees	$137,000	Dividends paid during 2001	$ 4,000
Revenues during 2001: general store	20,000	Notes payable	50,000
Accounts payable	11,000	Operating expenses during 2001	142,000
Cash on hand	37,500	Supplies on hand	2,500
Equipment	110,000	Common shares	40,000
Income tax expense	6,000	Retained earnings (1/1/2001)	44,000

Instructions

(a) Determine net earnings from Berry Hill Campground, Inc. for 2001.

(b) Prepare a statement of retained earnings and a balance sheet for Berry Hill Campground, Inc. as at December 31, 2001.

Identify financial statement components and prepare a statement of earnings.
(SO 4, 5)

E1-5 **Yogen Früz World-Wide Inc.** is headquartered in Markham, Ontario. It is one of the top frozen dessert companies in the world, operating in 80 countries. The following items were taken from its 1998 statement of earnings and balance sheet (all dollars are in thousands):

A	Cash and short-term investments	$37,538	E	Income tax expense	$ 3,282
SE	Retained earnings	31,156	R	Sales	77,463
E	Cost of goods sold	33,371	L	Income taxes payable	2,796
E	Selling, general and administrative expenses	27,415	L	Accounts payable	14,929
E	Store costs and expenses	12,970	R	Franchising revenues	8,475
A	Receivables	25,931	R	Rental and other income	4,041

Instructions

(a) In each case, identify on the blank line whether the item is an asset (A), liability (L), shareholders' equity (SE), revenue (R), or expense (E).

(b) Prepare a statement of earnings for Yogen Früz for the year ended August 31, 1998.

E1-6 Here is some information for Langille Inc.:

Prepare a statement of retained earnings. (SO 4)

Retained earnings, January 1, 2001	$150,000
Total revenues—2001	380,000
Total expenses—2001	205,000
Dividends paid—2001	76,000

Instructions

Prepare the statement of retained earnings for Langille Inc. for the year ended December 31, 2001.

E1-7 The summaries of data from the balance sheet and statements of earnings and retained earnings for two corporations, Chiasson Corporation and Maxim Enterprises, Ltd., are presented below for 2000:

Use financial statement relationships to determine missing amounts. (SO 4)

	Chiasson Corporation	Maxim Enterprises, Ltd.
Beginning of year:		
Total assets	$ 90,000	$130,000
Total liabilities	80,000	(c)
Total shareholders' equity	(a)	95,000
End of year:		
Total assets	160,000	180,000
Total liabilities	120,000	55,000
Total shareholders' equity	40,000	125,000
Changes during year in retained earnings:		
Dividends	(b)	5,000
Total revenues	215,000	(d)
Total expenses	165,000	80,000

Instructions

Two items are missing from each summary. Determine the missing amounts.

E1-8 Consider each of the following independent situations:

Interpret financial facts. (SO 4)

(a) The statement of retained earnings of Megan Corporation shows dividends of $70,000, while net earnings for the year were $75,000.

(b) The statement of cash flows for Surya Corporation shows that cash provided by operating activities was $10,000, cash used by investing activities was $110,000, and cash provided by financing activities was $130,000.

Instructions

For each company, write a brief interpretation of these financial facts. For example, you might discuss the company's financial health or its apparent growth philosophy.

E1-9 This information is for Dat Van Tran Corporation for 2001:

Prepare a statement of cash flows. (SO 4)

Cash received from customers	$50,000
Cash dividends paid	2,000
Cash paid to suppliers	20,000
Cash paid for new equipment	40,000
Cash received from lenders	20,000
Cash, January 1, 2001	10,000
Cash, December 31, 2001	18,000

Instructions

Prepare the statement of cash flows for Dat Van Tran Corporation for the year ended December 31, 2001.

E1-10 The following items were taken from the balance sheet of **NIKE, Inc.** NIKE is the world's number one shoe company, selling its products in 110 countries.

Classify items as assets, liabilities, and shareholders' equity and prepare accounting equation. (SO 5)

Instructions

(a) Classify each of these items as an asset (A), liability (L), or shareholders' equity (SE) item (all items are in millions of U.S. dollars).

_____	Cash	$ 108.6	_____	Inventories	$1,396.6
_____	Accounts receivable	1,674.4	_____	Income taxes payable	28.9
_____	Common stock	265.4	_____	Property, plant, and equipment	1,153.1
_____	Notes payable	480.2	_____	Retained earnings	2,996.2
_____	Other assets	1,064.7	_____	Accounts payable	584.6
_____	Other liabilities	1,042.1			

(b) Determine NIKE's accounting equation by calculating the value of total assets, total liabilities, and total shareholders' equity.

Classify various items in an annual report.
(SO 6)

E1-11 The annual report provides financial information in a variety of formats including the following:

Statement of management responsibility (SMR)
Financial statements (FS)
Notes to the financial statements (NFS)
Auditor's opinion (AO)

Instructions
For each of the following, state in what area of the annual report the item would be presented. If the item would probably not be found in an annual report, state "not disclosed" (ND).

(a) _____ Total revenue from operating activities
(b) _____ An independent assessment concerning whether the financial statements present a fair depiction of the company's results and financial position
(c) _____ Management's role in the reliability of the accounting records
(d) _____ The interest rate the company is being charged on all outstanding debts
(e) _____ The total amount received from shareholders in exchange for common shares
(f) _____ The names and positions of all employees hired in the last year

Identify accounting assumptions and principles.
(SO 7)

E1-12 Presented below are the assumptions and principles discussed in this chapter:

1. Full disclosure principle
2. Cost principle
3. Monetary unit assumption
4. Time period assumption
5. Going concern assumption
6. Economic entity assumption

Instructions
Use the numbers from the above list to identify the accounting assumption or principle that is described below. Do not use a number more than once.

(a) _____ States the rationale for why capital assets are not reported at liquidation value (*Note:* Do not use the cost principle.)
(b) _____ Indicates that personal and business record-keeping should be separately maintained
(c) _____ Assumes that the dollar is the measure used to report on financial performance
(d) _____ Separates financial information into time periods for reporting purposes
(e) _____ Indicates that market value changes subsequent to purchase are not recorded in the accounts
(f) _____ Dictates that all circumstances and events that make a difference to financial statement users be disclosed

Identify the assumption or principle that has been violated.
(SO 7)

E1-13 Marietta Corp. had three major business transactions during 2001:

(a) Merchandise inventory with a cost of $208,000 was reported at its market value of $260,000.
(b) The president of Marietta, George Winston, purchased a truck for personal use and charged it to his expense account.
(c) Marietta wanted to make its 2001 net earnings look better, so it added two more weeks to the year, creating a 54-week year. Previous years were 52 weeks.

Instructions
In each situation, identify the assumption or principle that has been violated, if any, and explain what should have been done.

Problems: Set A

Determine forms of business organization. (SO 1)

P1-1A Presented below are five independent situations:

(a) Three physics professors have formed a business to improve the speed of information transfer over the Internet for stock exchange transactions. Each has contributed an equal amount of cash and knowledge to the venture. While their approach looks promising, they are concerned about the legal liabilities that their business might confront.

(b) Joseph LeBlanc, a student looking for summer employment, opened a bait shop in a small shed on a local fishing dock.

(c) Robert Steven and Tom Cheng each owned separate shoe manufacturing businesses. They have decided to combine their businesses. They expect that within the coming year, they will need significant funds to expand their operations.

(d) Darcy Becker, Ellen Sweet, amd Meg Dwyer recently graduated with marketing degrees. Friends since childhood, they have decided to start a consulting business focused on marketing sporting goods over the Internet.

(e) Hervé Gaudet wants to rent CD players and CDs in airports across the country. His idea is that customers will be able to rent equipment and CDs at one airport, listen to the CDs on their flight, and return the equipment and CDs at their destination airport. Of course, this will require a substantial investment for equipment and CDs, as well as employees and locations in each airport. Hervé has no savings or personal assets. He wants to maintain control over the business.

Instructions

In each case, explain what form of organization the business is likely to take—proprietorship, partnership, or corporation. Give reasons for your choice.

Classify accounts. (SO 3)

P1-2A Canada's largest food processor is **Maple Leaf Foods Inc.** The following accounts have been selected from a recent annual report and placed in alphabetical order:

	(a)	(b)
Accounts payable	____	____
Accounts receivable	____	____
Income and other taxes payable	____	____
Interest expense	____	____
Inventories	____	____
Long-term debt	____	____
Property and equipment	____	____
Sales	____	____

Instructions

(a) Classify each of the above accounts as an asset (A), liability (L), revenue (R), or expense (E) item. Use column (a). If you believe a particular account doesn't fit in any of these activities, explain why.

(b) Classify each of the above accounts as a financing activity (F), investing activity (I), or operating activity (O). Use column (b).

Identify business activities. (SO 3)

P1-3A All business are involved in three types of activities—financing, investing, and operating. The names and description of companies in several different industries follow:

Indigo.ca—on-line book retailer
Highliner Foods Incorporated—processor and marketer of seafood products
Mountain Equipment Co-op—outdoor equipment supplier
Nortel Networks Corporation—maker of telecommunications products
Royal Bank—provider of banking and financial services
The Gap, Inc.—casual clothing retailer

Instructions

(a) For each of the above companies, provide examples of (i) a financing activity, (ii) an

investing activity, and (iii) an operating activity which the company likely engages in.
(b) Which of the activities you identified in (a) are common to most businesses? Which activities are different?

Identify users and uses of financial statements.
(SO 2, 4)

P1-4A Financial decisions often place heavier emphasis on one type of financial statement over the others. Consider each of the following independent hypothetical situations:

(a) The North Face Inc. is considering extending credit to a new customer. The terms of the credit would require the customer to pay within 30 days of receipt of goods.
(b) An investor is considering purchasing the common shares of Chapters Online. The investor plans on holding the investment for at least five years.
(c) Caisse d'Économie Base Montréal is thinking about extending a loan to a small company. The company would be required to make interest payments at the end of each year for five years, and to repay the loan at the end of the fifth year.
(d) The CEO of Ganong Bros. Limited, Canada's oldest candy company, is trying to determine if the company is generating enough cash to increase the amount of dividends paid to investors in this, and future, years. He needs to be sure that Ganong will still have enough cash to buy equipment when needed.

Instructions

For each situation, state whether the individual would pay most attention to the information provided by the statement of earnings, balance sheet, or statement of cash flows. Choose only one financial statement in each case, and provide a brief justification for your choice.

Prepare statements of earnings and retained earnings, and balance sheet.
(SO 4)

P1-5A On June 1, One Planet Cosmetics Corp. was started with an initial investment in the common shares of the company of $26,200 cash. Here are the assets and liabilities of the company at June 30, and the revenues and expenses for the month of June:

Cash	$11,000	Notes payable	$13,000
Accounts receivable	4,000	Accounts payable	1,200
Service revenue	6,500	Supplies expense	1,200
Cosmetic supplies	2,400	Gas and oil expense	800
Advertising expense	500	Utilities expense	300
Equipment	25,000	Income tax expense	1,500

The company issued no additional shares during June, but paid dividends of $200.

Instructions

Prepare a statement of earnings and a statement of retained earnings for the month of June, and a balance sheet at June 30, 2001.

Determine items included in a statement of cash flows and prepare.
(SO 4)

P1-6A Presented below is selected financial information for Maison Corporation at December 31, 2001:

Cash, December 31, 2000	$ 50,000
Cash, December 31, 2001	40,000
Inventory	25,000
Cash paid to suppliers	80,000
Building	200,000
Common shares	50,000
Cash dividends paid	5,000
Cash paid to purchase equipment	15,000
Equipment	40,000
Revenues	100,000
Cash received from customers	90,000

Instructions

First determine which items should be included in a statement of cash flows. Then prepare the statement for Maison Corporation for the year ended December 31, 2001.

P1-7A Here are incomplete financial statements for Baxter, Inc.:

Use financial statement relationships to calculate missing amounts.
(SO 4)

BAXTER, INC.
Balance Sheet

Assets		Liabilities and Shareholders' Equity	
Cash	$ 5,000	Liabilities	
Inventory	10,000	Accounts payable	$ 7,000
Building	50,000	Shareholders' equity	
Total assets	$65,000	Common shares	(i)
		Retained earnings	(ii)
		Total liabilities and shareholders' equity	$65,000

Statement of Earnings

Revenues	$80,000
Cost of goods sold	(iii)
Administrative expenses	10,000
Earnings before income tax	30,000
Income tax expense	10,000
Net earnings	$ (iv)

Statement of Retained Earnings

Beginning retained earnings	$10,000
Net earnings	(v)
Dividends	5,000
Ending retained earnings	$25,000

Instructions

(a) Calculate the missing amounts (i) to (v).

(b) Write a memo explaining (1) the sequence for preparing the financial statements, and (2) the interrelationships of the statement of retained earnings with the statement of earnings and balance sheet.

P1-8A GG Corporation was formed on January 1, 2001. At December 31, 2001, Guy Gélinas, the president and sole shareholder, decided to prepare a balance sheet, which appeared as follows:

Comment on proper accounting treatment and prepare a corrected balance sheet.
(SO 4)

GG CORPORATION
Balance Sheet
December 31, 2001

Assets		Liabilities and Shareholders' Equity	
Cash	$30,000	Accounts payable	$ 40,000
Accounts receivable	50,000	Notes payable	15,000
Inventory	20,000	Boat loan	10,000
Boat	15,000	Shareholders' equity	115,000

Guy willingly admits that he is not an accountant by training. He is concerned that his balance sheet might not be correct. He has provided you with the following additional information:

1. The boat actually belongs to Guy Gélinas, not to GG Corporation. However, because he thinks he might take customers out on the boat occasionally, he decided to list it as an asset of the corporation. To be consistent, he also listed as a liability of the corporation his personal loan that he took out at the bank to buy the boat.
2. The inventory was originally purchased for $10,000, but due to a surge in demand Guy now thinks he could sell it for $20,000. He thought it would be best to record it at $20,000.
3. Included in the accounts receivable balance is $5,000 that Guy Gélinas loaned to his brother five years ago. Guy included this in the receivables of GG Corporation, so he wouldn't forget that his brother owes him money.

Instructions

(a) Comment on the proper accounting treatment of the three items above.
(b) Provide a corrected balance sheet for GG Corporation. (Hint: To get the balance sheet to balance, adjust shareholders' equity.)

Discuss impact of accounting principle on auditor's report.
(SO 6, 7)

P1-9A The president of Martin Press Ltd. must present audited financial statements to its bank for a review of the company's application for an increased line of credit. However, the auditors advised the president that this year, they would have to attach a qualified opinion as their auditor's report on the financial statements. They identified two issues that they could not express an unqualified opinion on, regarding the financial statements being presented in accordance with generally accepted accounting principles:

1. *Investments*: The company had purchased short-term investments (shares of another company) with some excess cash. Martin paid $15,000 for these investments, but reported them as assets on the balance sheet at $20,000.
2. *Land*: The company owned a particularly valuable piece of land in the downtown core that they had originally paid $250,000 for. The land was recently appraised at $1,000,000, and Martin reported this land as an asset valued at $1,000,000 on the balance sheet.

The president was astonished by the auditors' attitude. These values are more relevant, she argued, for their primary external user—the bank. The short-term investments had already been sold, shortly after year end, for more than $20,000. The land, while not for sale, is worth $1,000,000 to the company as it is prime real estate location.

Instructions

(a) What is the implication for Martin Press of receiving a qualified audit opinion on its financial statements?
(b) What accounting principle (or principles) is involved here?
(c) Which amount do you think the investments and the land should be reported at in the year-end financial statements? Explain.

Discuss accounting assumptions and principles related to value.
(SO 7)

P1-10A The president of Richelieu Motors Co. Ltd. received a draft statement of earnings from his controller for the year ended December 31, 2001. "Suzanne," he said to the controller, "the statement indicates that a net earnings of $2 million was earned last year. You know the value of the company is more than $2 million greater than it was this time last year."

"You're probably right," replied Suzanne. "You see, there are factors in accounting that sometimes keep reported operating results from reflecting the change in the value of the company."

Instructions

Prepare a short memo explaining what accounting factors the controller is referring to.

Identify the assumption or principle violated.
(SO 7)

P1-11A A number of accounting reporting situations are described below:

(a) In preparing its financial statements, Seco Corporation omitted information about an ongoing lawsuit which its lawyers advised they could very well lose when it gets to court.
(b) Dot.com Corporation believes its people are its most significant assets. It estimates and records their value on its balance sheet.
(c) Barton, Inc. is carrying inventory at its current market value of $100,000. The inventory had an original cost of $75,000.
(d) Bonilla Corp. is in its fifth year of operation and has yet to issue financial statements.
(e) Steph Wolfson, president of the Classic CD Company Ltd., bought a computer for her personal use. She paid for the computer with company funds and debited the "Computers" account.

Instructions

For each of the above situations, list the assumption or principle that has been violated, and explain why the situation described violates this assumption or principle.

Problems: Set B

Determine forms of business organization. (SO 1)

P1-1B Presented below are five independent situations:

(a) Dawn Addington, a student looking for summer employment, opened a vegetable stand along a busy local highway. Each morning, she buys produce from local farmers, then sells it in the afternoon as people return home from work.

(b) Joseph Counsell and Sabra Surkis each own separate bike shops. They have decided to combine their businesses and try to expand their operations to include skis and snowboards. They expect that within the coming year, they will need significant funds to expand their operations.

(c) Three chemistry professors have formed a business which uses bacteria to clean up toxic waste sites. Each has contributed an equal amount of cash and knowledge to the venture. The use of bacteria in this situation is experimental, and legal obligations could result.

(d) Abdur Rahim has run a successful, but small, cooperative health and organic food store for over 20 years. The increased sales at his store have made him believe that the time is right to open a chain of health and organic food stores across the country. Of course, this will require a substantial investment for inventories and capital assets, as well as for employees and other resources. Abdur has no savings or personal assets.

(e) Mary Emery and Richard Goedde recently graduated with graduate degrees in economics. They have decided to start a consulting business focused on teaching the basics of international economics to small business owners interested in international trade.

Instructions

In each case, explain what form of organization the business is likely to take—proprietorship, partnership, or corporation. Give reasons for your choice.

Classify accounts. (SO 3)

P1-2B The **Mill Run Golf & Country Club**, located in Uxbridge, Ontario, details the following accounts in a recent annual report:

	(a)	(b)
Accounts payable	_____	_____
Accounts receivable	_____	_____
Capital assets	_____	_____
Cash	_____	_____
Food and beverage operations revenue	_____	_____
Golf course operations revenue	_____	_____
Inventory	_____	_____
Office expense	_____	_____
Professional fees expense	_____	_____
Wages and benefits expense	_____	_____

Instructions

(a) Classify each of the above accounts as an asset (A), liability (L), revenue (R), or expense (E) item. Use column (a).

(b) Classify each of the above accounts as a financing activity (F), investing activity (I), or operating activity (O). Use column (b). If you believe a particular account doesn't fit in any of these activities, explain why.

Identify business activities. (SO 3)

P1-3B All business are involved in three types of activities—financing, investing, and operating. The names and descriptions of companies in several different industries follow:

Abitibi Consolidated Inc.—manufactures and markets newsprint

Concordia Student Union Inc./L'Union des Étudiants et Étudiantes de Concordia Inc.—Concordia University student union

Corel Corporation—computer software developer and retailer
Northwest Sports Enterprises Ltd.—owner and operator of the Vancouver Canucks
Grant Thornton LLP—professional accounting and business advisory firm
WestJet Airlines Ltd.—discount airline

Instructions

(a) For each of the above companies, provide examples of (i) a financing activity, (ii) an investing activity, and (iii) an operating activity which the company likely engages in.
(b) Which of the activities you identified in (a) are common to most businesses? Which activities are different?

Identify users and uses of financial statements.
(SO 2, 4)

P1-4B Financial decisions often place heavier emphasis on one type of financial statement over the others. Consider each of the following independent hypothetical situations:

(a) An Ontario investor is considering purchasing the common shares of Bally Total Fitness Company, which operates 13 fitness centres in the Toronto area. The investor plans on holding the investment for at least three years.
(b) Bombardier is considering extending credit to a new customer. The terms of the credit would require the customer to pay within 60 days of receipt of the goods.
(c) The CEO of the Tommy Hilfiger Corporation is trying to determine whether the company is generating enough cash to increase the amount of dividends paid to investors in this, and future, years. He needs to ensure that there will still be enough cash to expand operations when needed.
(d) The Laurentian Bank is considering extending a loan to a small company. The company would be required to make interest payments at the end of each year for five years, and to repay the loan at the end of the fifth year.

Instructions

For each situation, state whether the individual would pay most attention to the information provided by the statement of earnings, balance sheet, or statement of cash flows. Choose only one financial statement in each case, and provide a brief justification for your choice.

Prepare statements of earnings and retained earnings, and balance sheet.
(SO 4)

P1-5B Aero Flying School Ltd. started on May 1 with cash of $45,000 and common shares of $45,000. Here are the assets and liabilities of the company on May 31, 2001, and the revenues and expenses for the month of May, its first month of operations:

Cash	$ 7,800	Notes payable	$30,000
Accounts receivable	7,200	Rent expense	1,200
Equipment	64,000	Repair expense	400
Service revenue	9,600	Fuel expense	2,200
Advertising expense	500	Insurance expense	400
Accounts payable	800	Income tax expense	1,500

Additional common shares of $1,800 were issued in May, and a dividend of $2,000 in cash was paid.

Instructions

Prepare a statement of earnings and a statement of retained earnings for the month of May, and a balance sheet at May 31, 2001.

Determine items included in a statement of cash flows and prepare.
(SO 4)

P1-6B Presented below are selected financial statement items for Kennedy Corporation for June 30, 2001:

Cash, July 1, 2000	$ 30,000
Cash, June 30, 2001	37,000
Inventory	55,000
Cash paid to suppliers	70,000
Building	400,000
Common shares	20,000
Cash paid to the Canada Customs and Revenue Agency (for income tax expense)	20,000
Cash dividends paid	8,000

Cash paid to purchase equipment	15,000
Equipment	40,000
Revenues	200,000
Cash received from customers	120,000

Instructions

Determine which items should be included in a statement of cash flows, and then prepare the statement for Kennedy Corporation for the year ended June 30, 2001.

P1-7B Here are incomplete financial statements for Wu, Inc.:

Use financial statement relationships to calculate missing amounts.
(SO 4)

WU, INC.
Balance Sheet

Assets		Liabilities and Shareholders' Equity	
Cash	$ (ii)	Liabilities	
Accounts receivable	20,000	Accounts payable	$10,000
Land, building and equipment	50,000	Shareholders' equity	
Total assets	$ (i)	Common shares	(vii)
		Retained earnings	(vi)
		Total liabilities and shareholders' equity	$85,000

Statement of Earnings

Service revenue	$75,000
Operating expenses	(iii)
Earnings before income tax	30,000
Income tax expense	10,000
Net earnings	$ (iv)

Statement of Retained Earnings

Beginning retained earnings	$10,000
Net earnings	(v)
Dividends	5,000
Ending retained earnings	$25,000

Instructions

(a) Calculate the missing amounts (i) to (vii).
(b) Write a memo explaining (1) the sequence for preparing and presenting the financial statements, and (2) the interrelationships of the statement of retained earnings with the statement of earnings and balance sheet.

P1-8B In 2001, Pam Bollinger formed Kettle Corporation. She is the president and sole shareholder. At December 31, 2001, Pam prepared a statement of earnings by looking at the financial statements of other companies. She is not an accountant, but thinks she did a reasonable job. She has asked you for advice. Pam's statement of earnings appears as follows:

Comment on proper accounting treatment and prepare a corrected statement of earnings.
(SO 4)

KETTLE CORPORATION
Statement of Earnings
For the Year Ended December 31, 2001

Accounts receivable	$10,000
Revenue	60,000
Rent expense	20,000
Insurance expense	3,000
Vacation expense	2,000
Net earnings	$45,000

Pam has also provided you with these facts:

1. Included in the revenue account is $5,000 of revenue that the company earned and received payment for in 2000. She forgot to include it in the 2000 statement of earn-

ings, so she put it in this year's statement.
2. Income tax expense for Kettle Corporation for the year ended December 31, 2001, was determined to be $15,000. However, the income tax payment is not due until March 31, 2002, so Pam decided not to record the income tax expense yet.
3. Pam operates her business out of the basement of her parents' home. They do not charge her anything, but she thinks that if she paid rent it would cost her about $20,000 per year. She therefore included $20,000 of rent expense in the statement.
4. To reward herself for a year of hard work, Pam went skiing for a week at Whistler. She did not use company funds to pay for the trip, but she reported it as an expense on the statement of earnings, since it was her job that made her need the vacation.

Instructions

(a) Comment on the proper accounting treatment of the four items above.
(b) Prepare a corrected statement of earnings for Kettle Corporation.

Discuss impact of accounting principle on auditor's report.
(SO 6,7)

P1-9B The Seah Kwee Ling Corporation has prepared financial statements but decided to exclude the statement of cash flows. Because of significant competitive pressures, Seah Kwee Ling does not want to disclose any of the details of its cash transactions. It also explains that the users of its financial statements are more interested in its bottom line than its cash flow.

The auditors issued a qualified opinion, and nothing the management of the Seah Kwee Ling Corporation said swayed the auditors' opinion.

Instructions

(a) What is the implication for the Seah Kwee Ling Corporation of receiving a qualified audit opinion on its financial statements?
(b) What accounting principle (or principles) is involved here?
(c) Why do you think the auditors believe that the disclosure of this information is essential to the financial statement readers?

Discuss accounting assumptions and principles related to value.
(SO 7)

P1-10B The president of Montiero Corporation received a draft balance sheet from her controller for the year ended December 31, 2001. "Sergio," she said to her controller, "the statement shows total assets of $2 million. You know the value of the company's assets is far more than $2 million."

"You're right," replied Sergio. "You see, there are factors in accounting that prohibit the recording of assets on the books at their market value."

Instructions

Prepare a short memo explaining what accounting factors the controller is referring to.

Identify the assumption or principle violated.
(SO 7)

P1-11B A number of accounting reporting situations are described below:

1. In preparing its financial statements, Karim Corporation tried to estimate and record the impact of the recent death of its president.
2. Topilynyckyj Co. Ltd. does not comply with generally accepted accounting principles when it prepares its financial statements because it is a small, not a large, business.
3. The Saint John Shipbuilding Co. Ltd. takes a very long time to build ships—sometimes up to five years. It is wondering if it would be appropriate to report its financial results once every two years.
4. Paradis Inc. recently purchased a power boat. It plans on inviting clients for outings occasionally, so the boat was paid for by the company and recorded in its records. Marc Paradis's family will use the boat whenever it is not being used to entertain clients. They estimate that the boat will be used by the family about 75% of the time.
5. Because of a "flood sale," equipment worth $300,000 was purchased for only $200,000. The equipment was recorded for $300,000 on the Bourque Corporation's books.

Instructions

For each of the above situations, list the assumption or principle that has been violated. Explain why the situation described violates this assumption or principle.

BROADENING YOUR PERSPECTIVE

FINANCIAL REPORTING AND ANALYSIS

FINANCIAL REPORTING PROBLEM: *Loblaw Companies Limited*

BYP1-1 Actual financial statements from **Loblaw Companies Limited's** 1999 annual report are presented in Appendix A, and simplified financial statements are given in Illustrations 1-6 through 1-9.

Instructions

Refer to Loblaw's financial statements to answer these questions:

(a) Loblaw's current financial statements are dated January 1, 2000. What is Loblaw's fiscal year end?
(b) Who are the auditors for Loblaw Companies Limited?
(c) What were Loblaw's total assets at January 1, 2000? Total liabilities and shareholders' equity at January 1, 2000?
(d) How much cash and short-term investments did Loblaw have on January 1, 2000?
(e) What amount of accounts payable and accrued liabilities did Loblaw report at the end of its 1999 fiscal year? 1998 fiscal year?
(f) What were Loblaw's sales in 1999? In 1998?
(g) What is the amount of the change in Loblaw's net earnings from 1997 to 1998? From 1998 to 1999?

COMPARATIVE ANALYSIS PROBLEM: *Loblaw and Sobeys*

BYP1-2 Simplified financial statements of **Sobeys** are presented in Illustrations 1-12 through 1-15, and **Loblaw's** simplified financial statements are presented in Illustrations 1-6 through 1-9. Actual financial statements from each company are presented in Appendices A and B.

Instructions

(a) Based on the information in these financial statements, determine the following for each company:
   1. Loblaw's total assets at January 1, 2000, and Sobeys' at May 1, 1999.
   2. Loblaw's accounts receivable at January 1, 2000, and Sobeys' receivables at May 1, 1999.
   3. Loblaw's and Sobeys' sales for fiscal 1999.
   4. Net earnings for Loblaws and Sobeys for fiscal 1999.
(b) What inferences concerning the two companies can you draw from these data?

RESEARCH CASES

BYP1-3 The *National Post* is a premier source of business information.

Instructions

Examine a recent copy and answer these questions:

(a) How many separate sections are there? What are the contents of each section?
(b) The *Financial Post*, found in section C of the *National Post*, includes information about what's going on in the corporate business world. Read one of the articles about a company that interests you. What is the article about? Identify any accounting-related issues discussed in the article.

BYP1-4 Most libraries have annual reports from companies on file or available on disk or microfiche. You can also access annual reports through company websites and sites such as SEDAR (System for Electronic Document Analysis and Retrieval).

Instructions

Obtain copies of the financial statements of two companies in the same industry and answer these questions:

(a) What two companies did you choose? Which industry do they operate in?
(b) What were the total assets, total liabilities, and total shareholders' equity at the most recent balance sheet date for each company?

(c) Use the appropriate amounts to demonstrate that the basic accounting equation is valid for each company.
(d) Who was the auditor of each company?
(e) What were the net sales (or net revenue) and net earnings in the most recent statement of earnings of each company?

INTERPRETING FINANCIAL STATEMENTS

BYP1-5 Clearly Canadian Beverage Corporation is a leading producer of premium beverages, including Clearly Canadian®, Clearly Canadian O+2™, REfresher, and Orbitz™—all of which are distributed extensively in Canada, the U.S., and numerous countries worldwide. Clearly Canadian holds the exclusive licence to manufacture and distribute Battery® in Canada and the U.S., and the distribution rights to distribute Jamaican Gold® in North America. Clearly Canadian also owns CC Beverage (U.S.) Corp., which produces a line of alternative beverages, including Cascade Clear Refresher, Mountain Spring Water, Premium Drinking Water, and Distilled Water for retail sale in North America and the Pacific Rim.

In its 1998 statement of cash flows, Clearly Canadian showed a $2,930,000 increase in cash from its operating activities, and decreases in cash from financing and investing activities of $1,166,000 and $1,881,000, respectively. The largest uses of cash were for the repayment of long-term debt and the purchase of property, plant, and equipment. Overall, the cash and short-term deposits at the end of 1998 were $1,004,000 less than the cash at the end of 1997, and $6,299,000 less than the cash at the end of 1996.

Instructions

Answer these questions:

(a) Would an investor view this decline in the overall cash position as negative or positive? Explain.
(b) Do you think creditors of Clearly Canadian might have concerns about this information reported in the statement of cash flows? If so, what additional information might a creditor seek in order to confirm or reduce these concerns?

BYP1-6 Corel Corporation is an innovative Canadian software company. The company's products, which include CorelDRAW®[1] and WordPerfect®, are used by more than 50 million people worldwide. Corel's 1998 annual report included the following excerpt from its corporate profile statement:

> With over 1,300 employees in two locations and sales offices worldwide, Corel is one of the world's top software developers. The Company's corporate headquarters in Ottawa, Canada, is home to its business and graphics development teams. Its Dublin, Ireland, office handles software localization, along with a portion of the Company's technical support and customer service. ... Recognized the world over, Corel's award-winning products ship in over 15 languages through a network of more than 160 distributors in over 60 countries.

In the financial statements section of its 1998 annual report, the following data were presented in the asset portion of Corel's balance sheet:

	As at November 30	
	1998	1997
	(in thousands of US$)	
Assets		
Current assets:		
Cash and short-term investments	$ 24,506	$ 30,629
Accounts receivable		
Trade	45,789	50,951
Other	877	2,310
Inventory	17,098	11,412
Deferred income taxes	2,495	2,353
Prepaid expenses	4,618	2,591
Capital assets	44,776	63,497
Total assets	$140,159	$163,743

[1]Corel, CorelDRAW, WordPerfect and the Corel logo are registered trademarks of Corel Corporation or Corel Corporation Limited.

Instructions

(a) For a software development company such as Corel, what do you think its most important economic resources (assets) would be? Where would these be recorded on the balance sheet? At what value (if any) should they be shown?

(b) Does the balance sheet tell you what Corel Corporation is worth? What information does the balance sheet give you regarding the value of the Company?

(c) Why do you think a Canadian company such as Corel would prepare its financial statements in U.S. dollars?

A GLOBAL FOCUS

BYP1-7 Today, companies must compete in a global economy. For example, Canada's oldest candy company, Ganong Bros. Limited, which has been making chocolates since 1873, must compete with **Nestlé S.A.**, among others. Nestlé, a Swiss company, best known for its chocolates and confections, is also the largest food company in the world. Comparing companies such as Ganong's and Nestlé's can pose some challenges. Consider the following excerpts from the notes to Nestlé's financial statements.

NESTLÉ S.A.

Notes to the Financial Statements (partial)

- The Group accounts comply with International Accounting Standards (IAS) issued by the International Accounting Standards Committee (IASC) and with the Standards Interpretations issued by the Standards Interpretation Committee of the IASC.
- The accounts have been prepared under the historical cost convention and on an accrual basis. All significant consolidated companies have a 31st December accounting year end. All disclosures required by the 4th and 7th European Union company law directives are provided.
- On consolidation, assets and liabilities of Group companies denominated in foreign currencies are translated into Swiss francs at year-end rates. Income and expense items are translated into Swiss francs at the annual average rates of exchange or, where known or determinable, at the rate on the date of the transaction for significant items.

Instructions

Discuss the effect each of these notes might have (positive or negative) on your ability to compare Nestlé's to Ganong's. (Hint: In preparing your answer, review the discussion of principles and assumptions in financial reporting.)

FINANCIAL ANALYSIS ON THE WEB

BYP1-8 ***Purpose:*** No financial decision-maker should ever rely solely on the financial information reported in the annual report to make decisions. It is important to keep abreast of financial news. This activity shows you how to search for financial news about Loblaw and Sobeys using CNEWS, the news section of the popular CANOE (Canadian Online Explorer) website.

www.wiley.com/canada/kimmel

Instructions

Specific requirements of this web case can be found on the Kimmel website.

BYP1-9 ***Purpose:*** This exercise is an introduction to the "Big Six" accounting firms.

Instructions

Specific requirements of this web case can be found on the Kimmel website.

CRITICAL THINKING

COLLABORATIVE LEARNING ACTIVITY

KELLY SERVICES

BYP1-10 In the late 1960s, William Russell Kelly opened the first international office of Kelly Services in Canada, the country of his birth. **Kelly Services (Canada), Ltd.**, has 52 offices across Canada that provide personnel for temporary positions. When a company requests assistance, Kelly matches the qualifications of its standby personnel with the requirements of the position. The companies pay Kelly Services, and Kelly Services, in turn, pays the employees.

In a recent annual report, Kelly Services chronicled its contributions to community services over the past 30 years or so. The following excerpts illustrate the variety of services provided:

1. During KellyWeek, a Saint Patrick's Day customer appreciation event, Kelly Services made donations of stationery, office decorations, and decals containing the company's name. KellyWeek was later expanded by making donations of temporary help.
2. In support of a country-wide beautification campaign in the 1960s, the company donated, and its employees planted, gladiolus gardens in cities across the country.
3. The company initiated a holiday drawing in which thousands of customers throughout North America nominate their favourite children's charities. Winning charities in the drawing receive a monetary donation from Kelly Services in the name of the customer.
4. Kelly executives regularly volunteer their time and resources to serve as role models and mentors to youth

Instructions

With the class divided into groups, answer the following:

(a) The economic entity assumption requires that a company keep the personal expenses of its employees separate from business expenses. Which of the activities listed above were expenses of the business, and which were personal expenses of the employees? Be specific. If part of the donation is business and part is personal, note which part is which.

(b) For those items that were company expenses, tell whether the expense was probably categorized as an advertising expense, employee wages expense, grounds maintenance expense, or charitable contribution expense. You may use any or all of the categories. Explain your answer.

COMMUNICATION ACTIVITY

BYP1-11 Amy Joan is the bookkeeper for Vermon Company, Inc. and has been trying to get the company's balance sheet to balance. She finally succeeded, but she still isn't sure that it is correct.

Instructions

In a memo, explain to Amy Joan the purpose of a balance sheet, why her balance sheet is incorrect, and what she should do to correct it.

VERMON COMPANY, INC.
Balance Sheet
For the Month Ended December 31, 2001

Assets		Liabilities and Shareholders' Equity	
Equipment	$20,500	Common shares	$11,000
Cash	9,000	Accounts receivable	(3,000)
Supplies	2,000	Dividends	(2,000)
Accounts payable	(5,000)	Notes payable	10,500
Total assets	$26,500	Retained earnings	10,000
		Total liabilities and shareholders' equity	$26,500

ETHICS CASE

BYP1-12 The December 14, 1998, issue of *Forbes* magazine includes an article by Michael Ozanian entitled "Selective Accounting." The article describes accounting practices by professional sports teams that result in lower reported earnings.

Instructions

Read the article and answer the following questions:

(a) What incentives do sports teams have to report lower earnings? Who is affected by their actions?

(b) What is the primary method used to report lower earnings—that is, what statement of earnings item is affected the most by their methods?

(c) Are sports teams required to make their financial results available to the public?

(d) You will learn in this course that accounting requires many subjective choices between accounting rules. These choices result in differing amounts being reported on a company's financial statements. Is it unethical to choose accounting methods that accomplish particular objectives like reporting higher, or in this case, lower net earnings?

Answers to Self-Study Questions

1. b 2. d 3. d 4. c 5. d 6. a 7. c 8. a 9. a 10. c
11. c 12. c

Answers to Loblaw Review It Question 3

Loblaw's accounting equation as at January 1, 2000 is (in millions of dollars):

Assets	=	Liabilities	+	Shareholders' Equity
$7,979	=	$5,075	+	$2,904

Loblaws
A passion for food... and a lot more!

C H A P T E R 2

A Further Look at Financial Statements

STUDY OBJECTIVES

After studying this chapter, you should be able to:

1. Describe the basic objective of financial reporting, and explain the meaning of generally accepted accounting principles.
2. Discuss the qualitative characteristics of accounting information.
3. Identify the two constraints in accounting.
4. Identify the sections of a classified balance sheet.
5. Identify and calculate ratios for analysing a company's profitability.
6. Explain the relationship between a statement of retained earnings, a statement of earnings, and a balance sheet.
7. Identify and calculate ratios for analysing a company's liquidity and solvency.

Just Fooling Around?

Few people could have predicted how dramatically the Internet would change the investment world. One of the most interesting results is how it has changed the way ordinary people invest their savings. Until recently, most individuals put their savings into mutual funds, relying on professionals to decide which shares to buy and sell. Now, more and more people are spurning investment professionals, choosing to strike out on their own and make their own investment decisions. In fact, a whole new breed of investors, known as "day traders," has arisen. These are people—from doctors to mechanics—who spend hours a day trading shares over the Internet. What has caused this change? The Internet has empowered individuals by providing instant access to information that was never available before.

Two early pioneers in this area were Tom and David Gardner. They created an on-line investor service called The Motley Fool. The name comes from Shakespeare's *As You Like It*. The brothers note that the fool in Shakespeare's plays was the only one who could speak unpleasant truths to kings and queens without being killed. Tom and David view themselves as twentieth century "fools," revealing the truths of the stock markets to the small investor, whom they feel insiders have taken advantage of. Their on-line bulletin board enables investors to exchange information and insights about companies.

Critics of these bulletin boards contend that they are nothing more than high-tech rumour mills that are largely responsible for building a speculative house of cards. They suggest that, because of the fervour created by the bulletin board chatter, share prices get bid up to unreasonable levels, and people often pay prices that are far higher than the underlying worth of the company. One potentially troubling aspect of bulletin boards is that participants on the board rarely give their real identities—instead using aliases. Consequently, there is little to stop people from putting misinformation on the board to influence a share's price in the direction they desire. Some observers are concerned that small investors—ironically, the very people the Gardner brothers were trying to help—will be hurt the most by misinformation and intentional scams.

One of the most notorious examples of misinformation and

On the World Wide Web
The Motley Fool
http://www.fool.com

scams occurred with Bre-X Minerals, Ltd., a Calgary-based mining exploration company. Bre-X Minerals drew worldwide attention in the 1990s, after it claimed to have discovered the largest gold find of the century in Busang, Indonesia, on the jungle island of Borneo. The share price skyrocketed in 1996 from pennies to about $280 per share based on the company's claims of massive gold deposits—claims which were never verified. It plunged to just 2.5 cents, before being delisted, after it was revealed that the Busang deposit contained only negligible amounts of gold. All told, less-than-cautious investors lost $6 billion on the Bre-X shares. With unfounded rumours and conspiracy theories abounding on the Internet, large and small buyers kept pouring money into the shares even as questions about the reliability of the find were being raised.

So, how should you decide what shares to buy? Rather than getting swept away by rumours, investors must sort out the good information from the bad. One thing is certain—as information services such as The Motley Fool increase in number, gathering information will become even easier, and evaluating it will become the harder task.

PREVIEW OF CHAPTER 2

If you are thinking of purchasing shares on the Internet, or elsewhere, how can you decide what the shares are worth? If you own shares, how can you determine whether it is time to buy more shares—or time to bail out? Your decision will be influenced by a variety of considerations; one should be your careful analysis of a company's financial statements. The reason: financial statements offer relevant and reliable information which will help you in your share purchase decisions.

In this chapter we begin by looking at the objectives of financial reporting. We then take a closer look at the balance sheet and introduce some useful ways of evaluating the information provided by the statements. The content and organization of the chapter are as follows:

A FURTHER LOOK AT FINANCIAL STATEMENTS

Objectives of Financial Reporting

- Characteristics of Useful Information
- Constraints in Accounting

The Financial Statements Revisited

- The Classified Balance Sheet
- Using the Financial Statements

SECTION 1

OBJECTIVES OF FINANCIAL REPORTING

STUDY OBJECTIVE 1

Describe the basic objective of financial reporting, and explain the meaning of generally accepted accounting principles.

Financial reporting is the term used to describe all of the financial information presented by a company—both in its financial statements and in additional disclosures provided in the annual report. For example, if you are deciding whether to invest in a company's shares, you need financial information to help make your decision. Such information should help you understand the company's past financial performance and current financial picture, and it should give you some idea of its future prospects. Although information found on electronic bulletin boards, like The Motley Fool, has its place, there is no substitute for careful study of the information available through traditional financial reporting channels.

The primary objective of financial reporting is to provide useful information for decision-making.

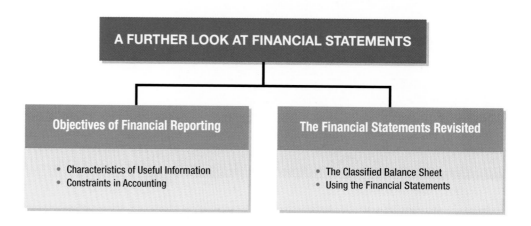

Characteristics of Useful Information

STUDY OBJECTIVE 2

Discuss the qualitative characteristics of accounting information.

How does a company decide on the amount of financial information to disclose? In what format should its financial information be presented? How should assets, liabilities, revenues, and expenses be measured? The answers to these questions are found in accounting rules that have substantial authoritative support and are recognized as a general guide for financial reporting purposes. These rules are referred to as **generally accepted accounting principles (GAAP)**.

The accounting standard-setting body in Canada is the Canadian Institute of Chartered Accountants (CICA). Federal and provincial incorporating acts, and provincial securities commissions, all recognize generally accepted accounting principles. This means that GAAP has the force of law for incorporated and publicly traded companies.

The CICA's overriding criterion is that the accounting rules should generate the most useful financial information for making business decisions. To be useful, information should possess these qualitative characteristics: **understandability, relevance, reliability, and comparability**.

UNDERSTANDABILITY

In order for information provided in financial statements to be useful, it must be understandable by all users. Users are defined primarily as investors and creditors, but include other interested decision-makers. These users may vary widely in the types of decisions they must make and in their level of interest in the information. At one extreme is a sophisticated financier who carefully scrutinizes all aspects of the financial information. At the other extreme is an unsophisticated shareholder who may only scan the text and not study the numbers.

It is quite simply impossible to satisfy all users' needs with one general purpose set of financial statements. It is therefore necessary to agree upon a basic level of **understandability** to assist both the preparer of financial information and its user. **The average user is assumed to have an understanding of accounting concepts and procedures, as well as of general business and economic conditions, to be able to study the statements intelligently.** If this level of understanding and ability does not exist, the user is expected to rely upon professionals with an appropriate level of expertise. With your study of this course, you are well on your way to becoming this average user!

RELEVANCE

Information of any sort is relevant if it would influence a decision. Accounting information is of **relevance** if it would influence a business decision. For example, when a company such as Bre-X issued financial statements, the information in the statements was considered relevant because it provided a basis for forecasting Bre-X's future earnings. Accounting information is also relevant to business decisions when it confirms or corrects prior expectations. Thus, Bre-X's financial statements should have both helped **predict** future events and **provided feedback** on prior expectations about the financial health of the company. Unfortunately, premature investors did not take the time to fully analyse the company's financial statements. Not only were Bre-X's earnings not growing, it didn't have any at all, as from 1993 through 1995 the company remained in the red. Admittedly, most gold and silver companies don't have earnings, but industry instability is just one more reason for investors to be cautious before investing.

For accounting information to be relevant, it must also be **timely**; that is, it must be available to decision-makers before it loses its capacity to influence decisions. If Bre-X reported its financial information only every five years, the information would not have been very useful. Many people believe that by the time annual financial statements are issued—sometimes up to six months after year end—the information is in fact of limited usefulness for decision-making. Timely **interim financial reporting** is therefore essential to relevant decision-making.

RELIABILITY

Reliability of information means that the information can be depended on. To be reliable, accounting information must be **verifiable**—we must be able to prove that it is free of error. Also, the information must be a **faithful representation** of what it says it is—it must be factual. When Bre-X reported that there were over 70 million ounces of gold in the Busang deposit when there was really very little gold, the statement was not a faithful representation. Accounting information must also be **neutral**—it cannot be selected, prepared, or presented to favour one set of interested users over another. Many accountants refer to information which is verifiable, a faithful representation, and neutral as **objective** information. That is, two or more people reviewing this information would reach the same basic conclusions about it. As noted in Chapter 1, to ensure reliability, objective public accountants audit financial statements.

In situations of uncertainty, neutrality is affected by the use of conservatism. **Conservatism** in accounting means that when preparing financial statements, a company should choose the accounting method that will be least likely to overstate assets and earnings. **It does not mean understating assets or earnings.** Conservatism provides a guide in difficult situations, and the guide is a reasonable one: do not overstate assets and earnings.

Conservatism is commonly applied when valuing inventories. Inventories are normally recorded at their cost. To be conservative, however, inventories are reported at market value if market value is below cost. This practice results in lower net earnings on the statement of earnings and a lower stated amount of inventory on the balance sheet.

COMPARABILITY

Let's say that you and a friend kept track of your height each year as you were growing up. If you measured your height in feet and your friend measured hers in metres, it would be difficult to compare your heights. A conversion would be necessary. In accounting, **comparability** results when companies with similar circumstances use the same accounting principles.

At one level, accounting standards are fairly comparable because they are based on certain basic principles and assumptions. These principles and assumptions, however, do allow for some variation in methods. For example, there are a variety of ways to report inventory. Often these different methods result in different amounts of net earnings. As we learned in Chapter 1, the **full disclosure principle** makes comparisons of companies easier, as each company must disclose the accounting methods used. From the disclosures, the external user can determine whether the financial information is comparable and can try to make adjustments. Unfortunately, converting the accounting numbers of companies that use different methods is not as easy as converting your height from feet to metres.

Users of accounting information also want to compare the same company's financial results over time. For example, to track a company's net earnings over several years, you'd need to know that the same principles have been used from year to year; otherwise, you might be comparing apples to oranges. **Consistency** means that a company uses the same accounting principles and methods from year to year. Thus, if a company selects one inventory accounting method in the first year of operations, it is expected to continue to use that same method in succeeding years. When financial information has been reported on a consistent basis, the financial statements permit meaningful analysis of trends within a company.

A company can change to a new method of accounting if management can show that the new method produces more meaningful financial information. In the year in which the change occurs, the change must be disclosed in the notes to the financial statements so that users of the statements are aware of the lack of consistency.

One factor that can affect the ability to compare two companies is their choice of accounting or fiscal year end. For example, Loblaw's current fiscal year end is January 1, 2000; Sobeys' May 1, 1999. This can create two problems for analysis. First, when you compare the companies, you are comparing neither performance over the same period of time nor financial position at the same point in time. Second, each company has chosen as its year end the nearest Saturday rather than a specific date. In doing so, the number of weeks in the fiscal year can change. Recall from Chapter 1 that Loblaw's 1997 fiscal year included 53 weeks. You can still compare companies with different fiscal year ends, as we are doing in this text; however, you will have to be careful to identify and interpret results that may only be due to the differing time periods.

Another factor that can complicate comparisons is the use of different currencies and different accounting standards when one compares companies from different countries. For example, one of Sears' primary competitors is U.S.-based Wal-Mart. Comparing the financial statements of these two competitors can be challenging. With no universally accepted set of international accounting standards, companies have responded with a variety of strategies, including preparing different sets of statements that report results in different languages, currencies, or accounting principles.

International Note

Accounting standards vary from country to country. Most countries have their own standard-setting body. One group, the International Accounting Standards Committee (IASC), has been working to reduce the differences in accounting practices and standards across countries.

BUSINESS INSIGHT
Management Perspective

Canada is teeming with foreign culture and products—Microsoft, Samsung, Wal-Mart, The Gap, McDonald's, NIKE, and Toyota, just to name a few. Foreign controlled companies—mostly American, but also British and Japanese—accounted for 31.5% of the $1.3 trillion in corporate revenue generated in Canada in a recent year.

Canadians have also become increasingly global. More than 220 Canadian companies are listed on at least one stock exchange outside of Canada. Canadian companies are expanding foreign operations, selling to foreign interests, and/or merging with companies located in other countries in record numbers in order to compete in the global marketplace more effectively.

What does this mean to the users of financial information? One must understand not only the differences in reporting requirements, but also important economic, legal, political, and cultural issues, before well-informed business decisions can be made.

Source: Eric Reguly, "The Devouring of Corporate Canada," *Globe and Mail*, September 4, 1999, B4.

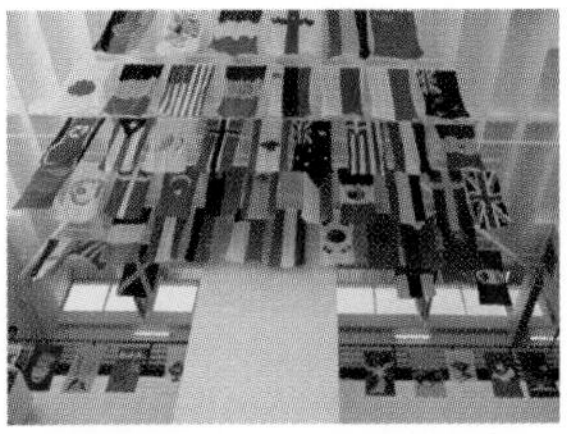

The characteristics that make accounting information useful are summarized in Illustration 2-1.

Illustration 2-1
Characteristics of useful information

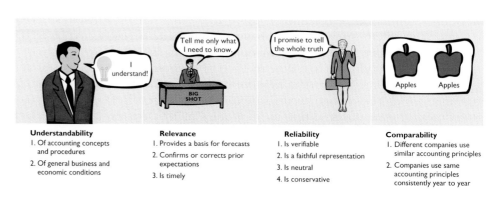

Understandability
1. Of accounting concepts and procedures
2. Of general business and economic conditions

Relevance
1. Provides a basis for forecasts
2. Confirms or corrects prior expectations
3. Is timely

Reliability
1. Is verifiable
2. Is a faithful representation
3. Is neutral
4. Is conservative

Comparability
1. Different companies use similar accounting principles
2. Companies use same accounting principles consistently year to year

CONSTRAINTS IN ACCOUNTING

STUDY OBJECTIVE 3
Identify the two constraints in accounting.

The goal of the characteristics we have discussed is to provide users of financial statements with the most useful information. Taken to the extreme, however, the pursuit of useful financial information could be far too costly for a company. Some constraints have therefore been agreed upon to ensure that accounting rules are applied in a reasonable fashion, from the perspectives of both the company and the user. **Constraints** permit a company to modify generally accepted accounting principles without jeopardizing the usefulness of the reported information. The constraints are cost-benefit and materiality.

COST-BENEFIT

The **cost-benefit** constraint ensures that the value of the information exceeds the cost of providing it. Accountants could disclose every financial event that occurs and every contingency that exists. However, providing additional information entails a cost, and the benefits of providing this information, in some cases, may be less than the costs.

MATERIALITY

Materiality relates to a financial statement item's impact on a company's overall financial condition and operations. An item is **material** when its size makes it likely to influence the decision of an investor or creditor. It is **not material** if it is too small to affect a user's decision. In short, if the item does not make a difference, GAAP does not have to be followed. To determine the materiality of an amount—that is, to determine its financial significance—the item is compared to such items as total assets, total liabilities, sales revenue, and net earnings.

Helpful Hint In fact, for Loblaw even a $100,000 difference is not material for most investment decisions.

To illustrate how the constraint of materiality is applied, assume that Loblaw made a $100 error in recording revenue. Loblaw's total revenue exceeds $18 billion; thus, a $100 error is not material.

The two constraints are shown in Illustration 2-2.

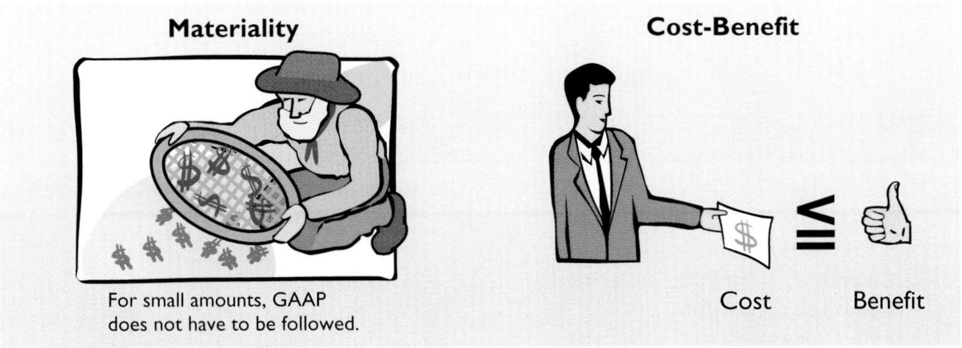
Materiality
Cost-Benefit
For small amounts, GAAP does not have to be followed.
Cost
≤
Benefit

Illustration 2-2
Accounting constraints

BEFORE YOU GO ON . . .

Review It

1. What is the basic objective of financial information?
2. What are generally accepted accounting principles?
3. What qualitative characteristics make accounting information useful?
4. What are the cost-benefit and materiality constraints?

SECTION 2

THE FINANCIAL STATEMENTS REVISITED

In Chapter 1, we introduced the four financial statements. In this section, we review the statements and illustrate how these statements accomplish their intended objectives. We begin by introducing the classified balance sheet and will use Sears, one of Canada's largest department stores, for illustrations.

THE CLASSIFIED BALANCE SHEET

STUDY OBJECTIVE 4
Identify the sections of a classified balance sheet.

The balance sheet presents a snapshot of a company's financial position at a point in time. To improve users' understanding of a company's financial position, companies often group similar assets and similar liabilities together. This is useful because it tells you that items within a group have similar economic characteristics. A **classified balance sheet** generally contains the standard classifications listed in Illustration 2-3.

Assets	Liabilities and Shareholders' Equity
Current assets	Current liabilities
Long-term investments	Long-term liabilities
Capital assets	Shareholders' equity

Illustration 2-3
Standard balance sheet classifications

These groupings help readers determine such things as (1) whether the company has enough assets to pay its debts as they come due and (2) the claims of short- and long-term creditors on the company's total assets. These groupings can be seen in the balance sheet of Sears shown in Illustration 2-4.

Illustration 2-4 Sears balance sheet

SEARS CANADA INC.
Statement of Financial Position
(in millions)

	January 2, 1999	January 3, 1998
Assets		
Current Assets		
Cash and short-term investments	$ 190.4	$ 68.3
Accounts receivable	595.0	690.1
Other receivables	505.4	534.5
Inventories	738.7	640.3
Prepaid expenses and other assets	119.0	90.8
Total current assets	2,148.5	2,024.0
Investments	50.9	22.8
Net capital assets	867.6	825.1
Other assets	131.0	135.4
Total assets	$3,198.0	$3,007.3
Liabilities and Shareholders' Equity		
Current Liabilities		
Accounts payable	$ 683.4	$ 560.2
Accrued liabilities	312.4	318.4
Income and other taxes payable	90.8	162.7
Principal payments on long-term obligations due within one year	163.4	11.6
Total current liabilities	1,250.0	1,052.9
Long-Term Obligations	783.7	912.0
Total liabilities	2,033.7	1,964.9
Shareholders' Equity		
Capital stock	451.8	450.9
Retained earnings	712.5	591.5
Total shareholders' equity	1,164.3	1,042.4
Total liabilities and shareholders' equity	$3,198.0	$3,007.3

Alternative Terminology
The *balance sheet* is sometimes called the *statement of financial position*, as Sears does.

Each of the groupings will now be explained.

CURRENT ASSETS

Current assets are assets that are expected to be converted to cash or used in the business within a relatively short period of time. Sears had current assets of $2,148.5 million as at January 2, 1999. For most businesses the cut-off for classification as current assets is 1 year from the balance sheet date. For example, accounts receivable are included in current assets because they will be converted to cash through collection within 1 year. Prepaid expenses are a current asset because we expect that these will be used in the business within 1 year.

Some companies use a period longer than one year to classify assets and liabilities as current, because they have an operating cycle longer than one year. The **operating cycle** of a company is the average time that it takes to go from cash to cash in producing revenues. For example, if your business sells in-line skates, your operating cycle would be the average length of time it would take for you to purchase your inventory, sell it, and then collect cash from your customers. For most businesses, this cycle takes less than a year, so they use a one-year cut-off. But, for some businesses, such as shipyards and vineyards, this period may be longer than a year. Except where noted, we will assume that one year is used to determine whether an asset or liability is current or long-term.

Common types of current assets are (1) **cash**, (2) short-term or temporary **investments**, such as treasury bills, investment certificates, shares, or bonds, (3) **receivables** such as notes receivable, accounts receivable, and interest receivable, (4) **inventories**, and (5) **prepaid expenses** such as rent, insurance, and supplies. On the balance sheet, these items are listed in the order in which they are expected to be converted into cash. This arrangement is shown in Illustration 2-5 for Canada Post. Note that, similar to Sears, Canada Post has combined the current assets cash and short-term investments together in one line, for reporting purposes. This is a common practice for many companies since short-term investments, if readily marketable, are considered to be *nearly cash*.

Illustration 2-5 Current assets illustration

CANADA POST CORPORATION (in millions of dollars)	
Current Assets	
Cash and short-term investments	$411
Accounts receivable	346
Prepaid expenses	69
Total current assets	826

A company's current assets are important in assessing its short-term debt-paying ability, as is explained later in the chapter.

LONG-TERM INVESTMENTS

Alternative Terminology *Long-term investments* are often just referred to as *investments.*

Long-term investments are generally investments in stocks and bonds of other corporations that are normally held for many years. Sears' long-term investments of $50.9 million in 1998 include bonds and loans. BCE, a global communications company, reported the following in a recent balance sheet:

Illustration 2-6 Long-term investments section

BCE INC. (in millions of dollars)	
Assets	
Investments in associated and other companies	$9,536

BCE owns shares in telecommunications companies such as Teleglobe, Aliant, and Nortel Networks, to name but a few.

CAPITAL ASSETS

Capital assets are assets with relatively long useful lives that are used in operating the business. Capital assets can be tangible (with physical substance) or intangible (without physical substance). **Tangible capital assets** may include (1) property, plant and equipment, and (2) natural resources, such as mineral deposits, oil and gas reserves, and timber. **Intangible capital assets** provide future benefits through the special rights and privileges they convey, rather than through any physical characteristics. Patents, copyrights, trademarks, and franchises are some examples of intangible assets.

Alternative Terminology *Property, plant, and equipment* are sometimes called *fixed assets.*

Although the order of listing capital assets can vary among companies, capital assets are normally listed in the balance sheet in order of permanency. That is, land is usually listed first, as it has an indefinite life, and is followed by the asset with the next longest useful life, normally buildings, and so on.

All capital assets, except land, have estimated useful lives over which they are expected to generate revenues. Because capital assets benefit future periods, their cost is matched to revenues over their *entire* estimated useful life through a process called **amortization**. This is preferable to simply expensing (recording as an expense) the full purchase price of the asset and matching the cost to revenues generated only in the year of acquisition. Land also generates revenue, but its estimated useful life is considered to be infinite as land does not usually wear out or lose its value. Consequently, the cost of land is never amortized.

Alternative Terminology *Amortization* is also commonly known as *depreciation.*

Assets subject to amortization should be reported at cost less accumulated amortization. Accumulated amortization shows the amount of amortization taken over the *life of the asset*. The difference between cost and accumulated amortization reported on the balance sheet is referred to as **net book value**.

Many companies, including Sears, report their capital assets at net book value on their balance sheet, and detail the cost and accumulated amortization in a note to the financial statements. Sears' gross capital assets total $1,720.4 million at the end of fiscal 1998, and its accumulated amortization totals $852.8 million. Capital assets ($1,720.4 million) less accumulated amortization ($852.8 million) equals a net book value of $867.6 million, as reported on Sears' balance sheet.

The Forzani Group Ltd., a sport and leisure company, details its net capital assets in note 2 to its financial statements, as shown in Illustration 2-7. Note that except for land, all other capital assets are amortized.

Illustration 2-7 Capital assets note disclosure

THE FORZANI GROUP LTD.
(in thousands of dollars)

Capital Assets	Cost	Accumulated Amortization	Net Book Value
Land	$ 638	—	$ 638
Building	4,900	$ 752	4,148
Building on leased land	3,136	481	2,655
Furniture, fixtures, equipment, and automotive	32,597	20,612	11,985
Leasehold improvements	42,264	21,122	21,142
Trademarks	259	194	65
Total	$83,794	$43,161	$40,633

CURRENT LIABILITIES

In the liabilities and shareholders' equity section of the balance sheet, the first grouping is current liabilities. **Current liabilities** are obligations that are to be paid within the coming year. Common examples are accounts payable, wages payable, bank loans payable, interest payable, taxes payable, and current maturities of long-term obligations (payments to be made within the next year on long-term obligations). Sears reported four different types of current liabilities, for a total of $1,250 million in 1998.

Within the current liabilities section, notes payable are usually listed first, followed by accounts payable. Other items are then listed in any order. The current liabilities section from the balance sheet of The Jean Coutu Group, a leader in Quebec and second in Canada in the number of pharmacy outlets, is shown in Illustration 2-8.

Illustration 2-8 Current liabilities section

THE JEAN COUTU GROUP INC. (in thousands of dollars)	
Current Liabilities	
Bank loans	$ 37,821
Accounts payable	181,060
Income taxes payables	2,930
Current portion of long-term debt	19,744
Total current liabilities	241,555

LONG-TERM LIABILITIES

Obligations expected to be paid after one year are classified as **long-term liabilities**. Liabilities in this category include bonds payable, mortgages payable, long-term notes payable, lease liabilities, and pension liabilities. Many companies report long-term debt maturing after one year as a single amount in the balance sheet and show the details of the debt in notes that accompany the financial statements. Others list the various types of long-term liabilities. Sears reported long-term liabilities related to bond and lease repayments, and future income tax liabilities of $783.7 million in 1998. In its balance sheet, Sleeman Breweries details its long-term obligations, as shown in Illustration 2-9.

Illustration 2-9 Long-term liabilities section

SLEEMAN BREWERIES LTD.	
Long-Term Obligations	
Bank of Nova Scotia – Non-revolving term loans	$34,209,901
Less amount due within one fiscal year	
(reported as a current liability)	4,744,880
Total long-term obligations	29,465,021

SHAREHOLDERS' EQUITY

Shareholders' equity is divided into two parts: share capital and retained earnings. Investments of assets in the business by the shareholders are recorded as either common or preferred shares. If preferred shares are issued in addition to common shares, the total of all classes of shares issued is classified as, or headed, **share capital**. Sears only has one class of shares outstanding, common shares. Earnings retained for use in the business is recorded as **retained earnings**. These two parts are combined and reported as **shareholders' equity** on the balance sheet. In its balance sheet, Sears reported total share capital (called capital stock) of $451.8 million and retained earnings of $712.5 million in 1998.

In its balance sheet, Le Château reported its shareholders' equity section as follows:

Illustration 2-10 Shareholders' equity section

CHÂTEAU STORES OF CANADA LTD. (in thousands of dollars)	
Shareholders' equity	
Capital stock	$13,169
Retained earnings	33,658
Total shareholders' equity	46,827

USING THE FINANCIAL STATEMENTS

In Chapter 1, we briefly discussed how the four financial statements provide information about a company's performance and financial position. In this chapter, we extend this discussion by showing you specific tools that can be used to analyse financial statements in order to make a more meaningful evaluation of a company.

RATIO ANALYSIS

Ratio analysis expresses the relationship among selected items of financial statement data. A **ratio** expresses the mathematical relationship between one quantity and another. The relationship is expressed as either a percentage, a rate, or a simple proportion. To illustrate, Sears recently had current assets of $2,148.5 million and current liabilities of $1,250 million. The relationship is determined by dividing current assets by current liabilities. The three means of expressing this ratio are:

Percentage: Current assets are 172% of current liabilities.
Rate: Current assets are 1.72 times greater than current liabilities.
Proportion: The relationship of current assets to liabilities is 1.72:1.

For analysis of the primary financial statements, ratios can be classified as shown in Illustration 2-11.

Illustration 2-11
Financial ratio classifications

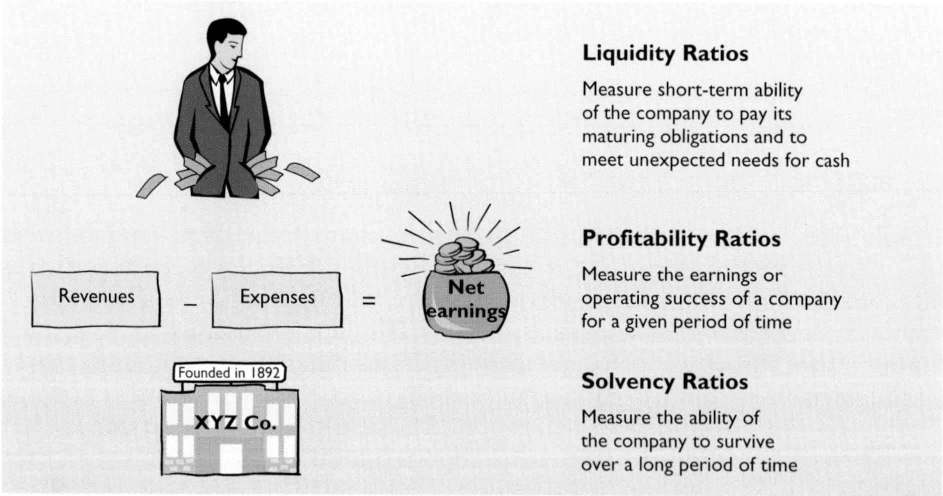

Liquidity Ratios
Measure short-term ability of the company to pay its maturing obligations and to meet unexpected needs for cash
Revenues
–
Expenses
=
Net earnings
Profitability Ratios
Measure the earnings or operating success of a company for a given period of time
Founded in 1892
XYZ Co.
Solvency Ratios
Measure the ability of the company to survive over a long period of time

Ratios can provide clues to underlying conditions that may not be apparent when components of a particular ratio are examined individually. Since a single ratio by itself is not very meaningful, in this and subsequent chapters, we will use:

1. **Intracompany comparisons** covering two years for the same company.
2. **Intercompany comparisons** based on comparisons with a competitor in the same industry.
3. **Industry average comparisons** based on average ratios for particular industries.

USING THE STATEMENT OF EARNINGS

STUDY OBJECTIVE 5

Identify and calculate ratios for analysing a company's profitability.

Sears tries to generate a profit for its shareholders by selling merchandise. The statement of earnings reports how successful it is at generating this profit. It reports the amount earned during the period (revenues) and the costs incurred during the same period (expenses). A statement of earnings for Sears is provided in Illustration 2-12.

Illustration 2-12 Sears statement of earnings

SEARS CANADA INC.
Statement of Earnings
For the 52 Weeks Ended
(in millions)

	January 2, 1999	January 3, 1998
Total revenues	$4,966.6	$4,583.5
Expenses		
Cost of merchandise sold, operating, administrative, and selling expenses	4,516.8	4,204.1
Amortization	95.5	78.1
Interest	85.6	86.1
Total expenses	4,697.9	4,368.3
Earnings before income taxes	268.7	215.2
Income taxes	122.3	98.7
Net earnings	$ 146.4	$ 116.5

From this statement of earnings, we can see that Sears' total revenues and net earnings both increased significantly during the year. Net earnings increased from $116.5 million to $146.4 million. In order to increase net earnings, the company needs its revenues to increase more than its expenses. While this was the case for Sears during this period, this is not as easy as it sounds. While consumer spending has been on the increase in recent years, most such spending has been directed to specialty boutique retailers, niche superstores, and electronic commerce on the Internet. Canadian department store sales have been relatively flat over the last decade, according to Statistics Canada.

Profitability

To evaluate the profitability of Sears (and later its liquidity and solvency), we will use ratio analysis for two fiscal years, 1997 and 1998. This will provide us with our **intracompany comparison**. We will then compare Sears' ratios to those of one of its primary competitors, Hudson's Bay Company, to broaden our analysis to include an **intercompany comparison**. Hudson's Bay, which includes the Zellers discount chain, is Canada's largest and oldest department store chain. Finally, we will compare our ratios to **industry average comparisons** for the retail department store industry.

We start with **profitability ratios**, which measure the income or operating success of a company for a given period of time. We will look at two examples of profitability ratios: **return on assets** and **profit margin**.

Return on Assets. An overall measure of profitability is the **return on assets ratio**. This ratio is computed by dividing net earnings by average assets. Average assets are usually calculated by adding the beginning and ending values of assets and dividing by 2. Whenever an end-of-period figure (e.g., assets on the balance sheet) is compared to a period figure (e.g., net earnings on the statement of earnings), the end-of-period figure must be averaged so that it approximates

Helpful Hint Ratios that use the phrase *return on* express net earnings as a percentage of something.

the same period of time as the period figure. Comparisons of end-of-period figures to end-of-period figures, or period figures to period figures, do not require averaging.

The return on assets ratio indicates the amount of net earnings generated by each dollar invested in assets. Thus, the higher the return on assets, the more profitable the company. Sears' net earnings were obtained from the statement of earnings presented in Illustration 2-12. Assets were obtained from its balance sheet, presented earlier in the chapter in Illustration 2-4. The 1998 and 1997 returns on assets of Sears, Hudson's Bay, and averages for the industry are presented in Illustration 2-13.

Illustration 2-13 Return on assets ratio

$$\text{RETURN ON ASSETS RATIO} = \frac{\text{NET EARNINGS}}{\text{AVERAGE ASSETS}}$$

(numbers in millions)	1998	1997
Sears*	$\frac{\$146.4}{(\$3,198.0 + \$3,007.3)/2} = 4.7\%$	$\frac{\$116.5}{(\$3,007.3 + \$2,734.0)/2} = 4.1\%$
Hudson's Bay	0.9%	(2.3%)
Industry average	1.6%	0.3%

*Amounts to calculate average assets are taken from Sears' balance sheet (Illustration 2-4). Also note that amounts in the ratio calculations have been rounded. Total assets in 1996 were $2,734.0 million.

We can evaluate Sears' 1998 and 1997 return on assets ratios in a number of ways. First, we can compare the ratio across time; that is, did its performance improve? The increase from 4.1% in 1997 to 4.7% in 1998 suggests improvement. The ratio tells us that in 1997, Sears generated 4.1 cents on every dollar invested in assets, while in 1998, it generated 4.7 cents on every dollar invested in assets. We can also compare Sears' ratios to those of its main rival, Hudson's Bay. In both years, Sears' return on assets ratio was substantially better than that of The Bay. Finally, we can compare Sears' performance to industry averages. Again, in each year Sears' return on assets ratio exceeds that of the average firm in the industry. Thus, based on the return on assets ratio, Sears' profitability appears strong.

Profit Margin. The **profit margin ratio** measures the percentage of each dollar of sales that results in net earnings. It is computed by dividing net earnings by net sales (revenue) for the period. Profit margins for Sears, Hudson's Bay, and averages for the industry are shown in Illustration 2-14. Businesses with high turnover, such as grocery stores (Loblaw) and discount stores (Wal-Mart), generally experience low profit margins; whereas low-turnover businesses, such as jewellery stores (Birks) or airplane manufacturers (Bombardier), have high profit margins.

Illustration 2-14 Profit margin ratio

$$\text{PROFIT MARGIN RATIO} = \frac{\text{NET EARNINGS}}{\text{NET SALES}}$$

(numbers in millions)	1998	1997
Sears	$\frac{\$146.4}{\$4,966.6} = 2.9\%$	$\frac{\$116.5}{\$4,583.5} = 2.5\%$
Hudson's Bay	0.6%	(1.4%)
Industry average	1.0%	(0.5%)

Sears' profit margin improved from 2.5% in 1997 to 2.9% in 1998. This means that in 1997, it generated 2.5 cents on each dollar of sales, while in 1998, it generated 2.9 cents on each dollar of sales—a remarkable improvement because it was during tight economic times for department store retailers. But how does it compare to that of its competitors? Sears' profit margin is substantially better than that of Hudson's Bay in both years. It also exceeded the industry average in both years. Thus, its profit margin ratio also supports our earlier observations that Sears's profitability is indeed strong.

DECISION TOOLKIT

Decision Checkpoints	Info Needed for Decision	Tool to Use for Decision	How to Evaluate Results
Is the company using its assets effectively?	Net earnings and average assets	$\text{Return on assets ratio} = \frac{\text{Net earnings}}{\text{Average assets}}$	Higher value suggests favourable efficiency (use of assets).
Is the company maintaining an adequate margin between sales and expenses?	Net earnings and net sales	$\text{Profit margin ratio} = \frac{\text{Net earnings}}{\text{Net sales}}$	Higher value suggests favourable return on each dollar of sales.

BEFORE YOU GO ON . . .

Review It

1. Identify three types of useful comparisons in ratio analysis.
2. What are the key features found in a statement of earnings?
3. What are the key features found in Loblaw's statement of earnings, reproduced in Appendix A to this textbook? The answer to this question is at the end of the chapter.
4. What are profitability ratios? Explain the return on assets ratio and the profit margin ratio.

Loblaws
A passion for food... *and a lot more!*

STUDY OBJECTIVE 6

Explain the relationship between a statement of retained earnings, a statement of earnings, and a balance sheet.

USING THE STATEMENT OF RETAINED EARNINGS

The beginning balance on the statement of retained earnings represents undistributed earnings that have accumulated from prior years. Of course, at the beginning of the very first year of a company's operations, this opening balance will be zero since the company has not had time to accumulate any earnings as yet. As discussed in Chapter 1, the statement of retained earnings describes the changes in retained earnings during the year. For the current period, the statement of retained earnings adds net earnings (or deducts net losses) and then subtracts dividends from the beginning retained earnings balance to arrive at ending retained earnings.

Dividends are distributions—normally by paying cash—of accumulated past and current period earnings (i.e., retained earnings) to shareholders. Even though dividends are included on the statement of retained earnings along with net earnings (revenues less expenses), it is important to remember that **dividends are not expenses**. They are not deducted on the statement of earnings because they are not incurred for the purpose of earning revenue. They are deducted instead on the statement of retained earnings and reduce the earnings retained in the business.

Illustration 2-15 is a simplified statement of retained earnings for Sears.

Illustration 2-15 Sears statement of retained earnings

SEARS CANADA INC.
Statement of Retained Earnings
(in millions)
For the 52 Weeks Ended

	January 2, 1999	January 3, 1998
Opening balance	$591.5	$500.4
Net earnings	146.4	116.5
	737.9	616.9
Dividends	25.4	25.4
Closing balance	$712.5	$591.5

Note that the closing balance for the year ended January 3, 1998, becomes the opening balance for the subsequent year. Note also that the net earnings figures agree with the net earnings reported on Sears' statement of earnings (see Illustration 2-12). Finally, ending retained earnings is presented on Sears' balance sheet (see Illustration 2-4) as one of the components of shareholders' equity. Recall, however, that shareholders' equity comprises two parts: share capital and retained earnings. Therefore, the shareholders' equity of most companies is affected by factors other than just changes in retained earnings. For example, the company may issue common shares. Information about changes in share capital during the period can usually be found in the notes to the financial statements.

One observation that we can learn from this financial statement is that Sears has paid the same total dollar amount of dividends in each of the last two years. In fact, the 11-year summary in Sears' annual report reveals that Sears has maintained the same dividend per share rate ($0.24) for the last 11 years. New investors would be particularly interested in this fact, as they decide whether or not to buy and sell Sears shares from other investors, for what it suggests about future earnings potential.

USING THE CLASSIFIED BALANCE SHEET

STUDY OBJECTIVE 7

Identify and calculate ratios for analysing a company's liquidity and solvency.

You can learn a lot about a company's financial health by evaluating the relationship between its various assets and its liabilities. A simplified balance sheet for Sears was provided earlier in this chapter in Illustration 2-4, when we introduced classifications within the balance sheet. You may wish to refer to this illustration as each of the following ratios is discussed.

Liquidity

Suppose you are a banker thinking of lending money to Sears, or you are a computer manufacturer interested in selling computers to Sears. You would be concerned about its **liquidity**—Sears' ability to pay obligations that are expected to become due within the next year or operating cycle. To have an idea of this, you would look closely at the relationship of its current assets to its current liabilities, using liquidity ratios. **Liquidity ratios** measure the short-term ability of the enterprise to pay its maturing obligations and to meet unexpected needs for cash.

Working Capital. One measure of liquidity is **working capital**, which is the excess of current assets over current liabilities. When working capital is positive, there is a greater likelihood that the company will pay its liabilities. When the reverse is true, short-term creditors may not be paid, and the company may ultimately be forced into bankruptcy.

Illustration 2-16 Working capital

WORKING CAPITAL = CURRENT ASSETS – CURRENT LIABILITIES

(numbers in millions)	1998	1997
Sears	\$2,148.5 – \$1,250.0 = \$898.5	\$2,024.0 – \$1,052.9 = \$971.1
Hudson's Bay	\$1,457.2	\$1,501.0
Industry average	n/a	n/a

Industry averages are not available for working capital and for some other ratios we compute in this text. These are denoted by "n/a" (not available). Industry averages are not very meaningful for working capital, since working capital is expressed in absolute dollars, rather than as a ratio.

Current Ratio. One liquidity ratio is the **current ratio**, which is calculated by dividing current assets by current liabilities. The current ratio is a more dependable indicator of liquidity than working capital. Two companies with the same amount of working capital may have significantly different current ratios. The 1998 and 1997 current ratios for Sears, for Hudson's Bay, and industry averages are shown in Illustration 2-17.

Illustration 2-17 Current ratio

$$\text{CURRENT RATIO} = \frac{\text{CURRENT ASSETS}}{\text{CURRENT LIABILITIES}}$$

(numbers in millions)	1998	1997
Sears	$\frac{\$2,148.5}{\$1,250.0} = 1.72:1$	$\frac{\$2,024.0}{\$1,052.9} = 1.92:1$
Hudson's Bay	2.18:1	2.73:1
Industry average	1.48:1	1.61:1

What does the ratio actually mean? The 1998 ratio of 1.72:1 means that for every dollar of current liabilities, Sears has $1.72 of current assets. Sears' current ratio has declined in the current year, as have Hudson's Bay's and the industry average. However, when compared to the industry average, Sears' short-term liquidity appears to be strong, even though its current ratio is below Hudson's Bay's in both years.

One drawback of the current ratio is that it does not take into account the **composition** of the current assets. For example, a satisfactory current ratio does not disclose the fact that a portion of the current assets may be tied up in slow-moving inventory. Suppose a company's cash balance declined while its merchandise inventory increased substantially. If inventory increased because the company is having difficulty selling its inventory, then the current ratio might not fully reflect the reduction in the company's liquidity.

During 1998, Sears' principal payments on long-term obligations due within one year increased substantially. Its current assets also increased, but not as significantly. Sears still has far more current assets than current liabilities, so it continues to hold an enviable liquidity position. However, sales must continue to provide sufficient cash flow to repay long-term debt and its related interest payments in the future. In a later chapter you will learn additional ways to analyse a company's liquidity position.

Solvency

Now suppose that instead of being a short-term creditor, you are interested in either buying Sears' shares or extending the company a long-term loan. Long-term creditors and shareholders are interested in a company's long-run **solvency**—its ability to pay interest as it comes due and to repay the face value of the debt at maturity. **Solvency ratios** measure the ability of the enterprise to survive over a long period of time. The debt to total assets ratio is one source of information about debt-paying ability.

Helpful Hint Some users evaluate solvency using a ratio of debt divided by shareholders' equity. The higher this ratio, the lower a company's solvency.

Debt to Total Assets Ratio. The **debt to total assets ratio** measures the percentage of assets financed by creditors rather than shareholders. Financing provided by creditors is riskier than financing provided by shareholders, because debt must be repaid at specific points in time, whether the company is performing well or not. Thus, the higher the percentage of debt financing, the riskier the company. The debt to total assets ratio is computed by dividing total debt (both current and long-term liabilities) by total assets. The higher the percentage of debt to total assets, the greater the risk that the company may be unable to pay its debts as they come due. The ratios of debt to total assets for Sears, for Hudson's Bay, and industry averages are presented in Illustration 2-18.

Illustration 2-18 Debt to total assets ratio

$$\text{DEBT TO TOTAL ASSETS RATIO} = \frac{\text{TOTAL LIABILITIES}}{\text{TOTAL ASSETS}}$$

(numbers in millions)	1998	1997
Sears	$\frac{\$2,033.7}{\$3,198.0} = 64\%$	$\frac{\$1,964.9}{\$3,007.3} = 65\%$
Hudson's Bay	55%	56%
Industry average	59%	65%

The 1998 ratio of 64% means that 64 cents of every dollar Sears invested in assets has been provided by Sears' creditors. Sears' ratio exceeds both Hudson's Bay's debt to total assets ratio of 55% and the industry average of 59%. The higher the ratio, the lower the equity "cushion" available to creditors if the company becomes insolvent. Thus, from the creditors' point of view, a high ratio of debt to total assets is undesirable. In other words, Sears' solvency appears lower than that of both Hudson's Bay and of the average company in the industry.

Helpful Hint Because total assets = total liabilities + shareholders' equity, this also means that 36% (100% − 64%) of every dollar invested in assets has been provided by Sears' shareholders.

The significance of this ratio is often judged in the light of the company's earnings. Generally, companies with relatively stable earnings have higher debt to total assets ratios than do cyclical companies with widely fluctuating earnings. In later chapters you will learn additional ways to evaluate solvency.

BUSINESS INSIGHT

Investor Perspective

Debt financing differs greatly across industries and companies. Here are some debt to total assets ratios for selected companies:

	Total Debt to Total Assets
Chapters Inc.	67%
Future Shop Ltd.	80%
Leon's Furniture Limited	30%
The Molson Companies Limited	57%
The Second Cup Ltd.	26%

DECISION TOOLKIT

Decision Checkpoints	Info Needed for Decision	Tool to Use for Decision	How to Evaluate Results
Can the company meet its short-term obligations?	Current assets and current liabilities	Working capital = Current assets − Current liabilities	Higher amount indicates liquidity.
		Current ratio = $\frac{\text{Current assets}}{\text{Current liabilities}}$	Higher ratio suggests favourable liquidity.
Can the company meet its long-term obligations?	Total debt and total assets	Debt to total assets ratio = $\frac{\text{Total liabilities}}{\text{Total assets}}$	Lower value suggests favourable solvency.

BEFORE YOU GO ON . . .

Review It

1. Explain how a statement of retained earnings relates to a statement of earnings and balance sheet.
2. What are the major sections in a classified balance sheet?
3. What is liquidity? How can it be measured?
4. What is solvency? How can it be measured?

Do It

Selected financial data for Drummond Company at December 31, 2001, are as follows: cash \$60,000; receivables (net) \$80,000; inventory \$70,000; capital assets \$100,000. Current liabilities are \$140,000 and long-term liabilities, \$50,000. Calculate working capital and the current ratio.

Reasoning: Current assets include cash, receivables, and inventory (\$60,000 + \$80,000 + \$70,000 = \$210,000). The formula for working capital is: Current assets − current liabilities. The current ratio is: Current assets ÷ current liabilities.

Solution: Working capital is \$70,000 (\$210,000 − \$140,000) and the current ratio is 1.5:1 (\$210,000 ÷ \$140,000).

USING THE STATEMENT OF CASH FLOWS

As you learned in Chapter 1, the statement of cash flows provides financial information about the sources and uses of a company's cash. Investors, creditors, and others want to know what is happening to a company's most liquid resource—its cash. In fact, many people think that "cash is king," since a company which can't generate cash won't survive. To aid in the analysis of cash, the statement of cash flows reports the cash effects of (1) a company's **operating activities**, (2) its **investing activities**, and (3) its **financing activities**.

Sources of cash matter. For example, you would feel much better about a company's health if you knew that its cash was generated from the operations of the business rather than from borrowing. A statement of cash flows provides this information. Similarly, net earnings do not tell you how much cash the firm generated from operations. The statement of cash flows, however, can tell you that. In summary, neither the statement of earnings nor the balance sheet can directly answer most of the important questions about cash, but the statement of cash flows does. A simplified statement of cash flows for Sears is provided in Illustration 2-19. Remember, as we learned in Chapter 1, the statement of cash flows is also sometimes called a statement of changes in financial position.

Illustration 2-19 Sears statement of cash flows

SEARS CANADA INC.
Statement of Changes in Financial Position
For the 52 Weeks Ended
(in millions)

	January 2, 1999	January 3, 1998
Cash Generated From (Used For) Operations		
Cash receipts from operating activities	$ 4,995.7	$ 4,474.7
Cash payments for operating activities	(4,771.6)	(4,375.8)
Net cash generated from (used for) operating activities	224.1	98.9
Cash Generated From (Used For) Investment Activities		
Purchases of capital assets	(142.2)	(160.4)
Proceeds from sale of capital assets	6.9	1.1
Investments and other assets	61.6	(77.9)
Net cash generated from (used for) investment activities	(73.7)	(237.2)
Cash Generated From (Used For) Financing Activities		
Issue of long-term obligations	7.8	134.9
Repayment of long-term obligations	(11.6)	(104.6)
Net proceeds from issue of capital stock	0.9	2.6
Cash used for dividends	(25.4)	(25.4)
Net cash generated from (used for) financing activities	(28.3)	7.5
Increase (decrease) in cash and short-term investments at end of year	122.1	(130.8)
Cash and short-term investments at beginning of year	68.3	199.1
Cash and short-term investments at end of year	$ 190.4	$ 68.3

Different users have different reasons for being interested in the statement of cash flows. If you were a creditor of Sears (either short-term or long-term), you would be interested in knowing the source of its cash in recent years. This information would give you some indication of where it might get cash to pay you. If you had a long-term interest in Sears as a shareholder, you would look to the statement of cash flows for information about the company's ability to generate cash over the long run to meet its cash needs for growth.

Companies get cash from two sources: operating activities and financing activities. In the early years of a company's life, it typically won't generate enough cash from operating activities to meet its investing needs, and so it will have to issue shares or borrow money. An established firm, however, will often be able to meet most of its cash needs with cash from operating activities. Sears' cash from operating activities last year was sufficient to meet its investing needs. The prior year, ended January 3, 1998, cash from operating activities was substantially less at $98.9 million and insufficient to cover its investments of $237.2 million. In 1997, the company started a planned program of major renovations to its department stores, which was completed in 1998. This was a nonrecurring cost intended to generate increased profitability in subsequent years, as it did. In order to finance its investing activities in fiscal 1997, Sears had to supplement its internally generated cash with cash from outside sources, by issuing new shares and by borrowing. Note that the bulk of Sears' cash from outside sources has come from borrowing. As noted earlier, the more a company borrows, the harder it is for the company to meet its debt obligations.

While investors and creditors can take some comfort from Sears' liquidity and profitability position, they would be wise to closely monitor its cash-generating ability to ensure that Sears will be able to continue meeting its obligations.

Earlier we introduced you to measures of liquidity and solvency. The statement of cash flows can be used to calculate additional measures of liquidity and solvency. The **cash current debt coverage ratio** is a measure of liquidity that is calculated as follows: cash provided by operating activities divided by average current liabilities. It indicates the company's ability to generate sufficient cash to meet its short-term needs. In general, a value below 0.40 times is cause for additional investigation of a company's liquidity. The **cash total debt coverage ratio** is also a measure of solvency and it is calculated in this manner: cash provided by operating activities divided by average total liabilities. The cash total debt coverage ratio indicates the company's ability to generate sufficient cash to meet its long-term needs.

Illustration 2-20 presents the cash current and total debt coverage ratios for Sears and Hudson's Bay. Industry measures are not available for these ratios.

Illustration 2-20 Cash current debt coverage ratio and cash total debt coverage ratio

$$\text{CASH CURRENT DEBT COVERAGE RATIO} = \frac{\text{CASH PROVIDED BY OPERATING ACTIVITIES}}{\text{AVERAGE CURRENT LIABILITIES}}$$

(numbers in millions)	1998	1997
Sears*	$\frac{\$224.1}{(\$1,250.0 + \$1,052.9)/2} = 0.19$ times	$\frac{\$98.9}{(\$1,052.9 + \$1,070.8)/2} = 0.09$ times
Hudson's Bay	0.15 times	(0.11) times
Industry average	n/a	n/a

$$\text{CASH TOTAL DEBT COVERAGE RATIO} = \frac{\text{CASH PROVIDED BY OPERATING ACTIVITIES}}{\text{AVERAGE TOTAL LIABILITIES}}$$

(numbers in millions)	1998	1997
Sears*	$\frac{\$224.1}{(\$2,033.7 + \$1,964.9)/2} = 0.11$ times	$\frac{\$98.9}{(\$1,964.9 + \$1,785.3)/2} = 0.05$ times
Hudson's Bay	0.07 times	(0.5) times
Industry average	n/a	n/a

* Amounts to calculate average current liabilities and average total liabilities are taken from Sears' balance sheet (Illustration 2-4). Also note that the amounts in the ratio calculations have been rounded. Current liabilities in 1996 were $1,070.8 million and total liabilities in 1996 were $1,785.3 million.

Using these measures of solvency and liquidity for 1998 and 1997, Sears appears to be more liquid and solvent than its larger rival, Hudson's Bay. Hudson's Bay had cash used by, rather than provided by, operating activities in 1997, and less cash than Sears in 1998. While a negative number should be investigated further, it is not cause for immediate alarm. Both of these companies have been growing rapidly in recent years, and it is not unusual for fast-growing companies to have cash used by operating activities. Still, this situation is not sustainable over the long term.

DECISION TOOLKIT

Decision Checkpoints	Info Needed for Decision	Tool to Use for Decision	How to Evaluate Results
Can the company meet its short-term obligations?	Current liabilities and cash provided (used) by operating activities	Cash current debt coverage ratio = Cash provided (used) by operating activities / Average current liabilities	A higher ratio indicates liquidity—that the company is generating cash sufficient to meet its short-term needs.
Can the company meet its long-term obligations?	Total liabilities and cash provided (used) by operating activities	Cash total debt coverage ratio = Cash provided (used) by operating activities / Average total liabilities	A higher ratio indicates solvency—that the company is generating cash sufficient to meet its long-term needs.

BEFORE YOU GO ON . . .

Review It

1. What information does the statement of cash flows provide that is not available in statement of earnings or a balance sheet?
2. What does the cash current debt coverage ratio measure? What does the cash total debt coverage ratio measure?

USING THE DECISION TOOLKIT

It may surprise you that Canadian Tire Corporation, Limited, is one of Sears' top competitors. Don't be fooled by the modest name; it sells a wide array of products, including home, car, sports, and leisure products.

Illustration 2-21
Canadian Tire balance sheet

CANADIAN TIRE CORPORATION, LIMITED
Balance Sheet
(dollars in thousands)

	January 2, 1999	January 3, 1998
Assets		
Current assets		
Cash and short-term investments	$ 308,392	$ 263,422
Accounts receivable	403,083	347,207
Other receivables	372,511	404,695
Merchandise inventories	411,696	409,058
Prepaid expenses and deposits	10,589	13,894
Total current assets	1,506,271	1,438,276
Long-term receivables and other assets	41,088	33,351
Property and equipment	1,618,521	1,403,413
Total assets	$3,165,880	$2,875,040
Liabilities		
Current liabilities		
Notes payable	$ 181,768	$ 362,905
Accounts payable and other	801,182	701,448
Income taxes payable	70,713	62,977
Current portion of long-term debt	951	40,000
Total current liabilities	1,054,614	1,167,330
Long-term debt	815,000	380,401
Other long-term liabilities	34,714	28,734
Total liabilities	1,904,328	1,576,465
Shareholders' Equity		
Share capital	318,558	318,558
Other	(375,244)	(196,881)
Retained earnings	1,318,238	1,176,898
Total shareholders' equity	1,261,552	1,298,575
Total liabilities and shareholders' equity	$3,165,880	$2,875,040

CANADIAN TIRE CORPORATION, LIMITED
Statement of Earnings
For the Years Ended
(dollars in thousands)

	January 2, 1999	January 3, 1998
Gross operating revenue	$4,347,283	$4,087,802
Operating expenses		
Cost of merchandise sold and all expenses except for the undernoted items	3,914,678	3,716,392
Interest	74,457	63,562
Amortization	86,720	79,862
Other	21,716	18,488
Total operating expenses	4,097,571	3,878,304
Earnings before income taxes	249,712	209,498
Income taxes	82,732	60,927
Net earnings	$ 166,980	$ 148,571

Additional information: Canadian Tire's net cash provided by operating activities was $313,116 (thousand).

Instructions

Using the above statements, answer the following questions:

1. Calculate Canadian Tire's current ratio for fiscal 1998 and 1997. Next calculate its cash current debt coverage ratio for 1998, and finally, discuss its liquidity position.
2. Calculate Canadian Tire's debt to total assets ratio for 1998 and 1997. Next calculate its cash current debt coverage ratio for 1998, and finally discuss its liquidity position.
3. Calculate the profit margin ratio for 1998 and 1997 and the return on assets ratio for Canadian Tire for 1998. Discuss Canadian Tire's profitability.
4. What other information would be useful in your analysis?

Solution

1. Current ratio:

   1998: ($1,506,271/$1,054,614) = 1.43:1

   1997: ($1,438,276/$1,167,330) = 1.23:1

   Canadian Tire's liquidity improved substantially from 1997 to 1998. Both current assets and current liabilities improved in fiscal 1998, as did working capital. Working capital in 1998 was $451,657 ($1,506,271 − $1,054,614); in 1997, $270,946 ($1,438,276 − $1,167,330). While the current ratio indicates that Canadian Tire is reasonably liquid, it is still not as good as that of either Sears or Hudson's Bay. It is also below its industry competitors, especially in 1997, but is drawing very close to the industry average in 1998.

   Cash current debt coverage ratio:

   1998 $\frac{\$313,116}{(\$1,054,614 + \$1,167,330)/2} = 0.28 \text{ times}$

   A value above 0.40 times for this ratio is generally considered acceptable. While low, this ratio is significantly stronger than that of Sears and Hudson's Bay.

2. Debt to total assets ratio:

   1998: ($1,904,328/$3,165,880) = 60%

   1997: ($1,576,465/$2,875,040) = 55%

   Based on the change in its ratio of debt to total assets, Canadian Tire's reliance on debt increased considerably from 1997 to 1998. Solvency reflects a company's ability to survive over the long term. While the ratios are comparable to those of Sears and Hudson's Bay, such a change might be cause for concern. In particular, even though Canadian Tire's 1998 debt to total assets ratio is quite close to the industry's, the direction of the change is troubling. Canadian Tire's reliance on debt increased while the industry's, in general, decreased, dropping from 65% in 1997 to 59% in 1998.

Cash total debt coverage ratio:

$$1998 \quad \frac{\$313{,}116}{(\$1{,}904{,}328 + \$1{,}576{,}465)/2} = 0.18 \text{ times}$$

Canadian Tire's value of 0.18 times is close to the generally acceptable level of 0.20 times and better than that of Sears or Hudson's Bay.

3. Profit margin ratio:

1998: ($166,980/$4,347,283) = 3.8%

1997: ($148,571/$4,087,802) = 3.6%

Return on assets ratio:

$$1998 \quad \frac{\$166{,}980}{(\$3{,}165{,}880 + \$2{,}875{,}050)/2} = 5.5\%$$

Canadian Tire's profit margin increased slightly in fiscal 1998, from 3.6% to 3.8%. It is stronger by far than that either of Sears or Hudson's Bay, or of its other industry counterparts. Its return on assets ratio is 5.5%, versus 4.7% for Sears, 0.9% for Hudson's Bay, and 1.6% for the industry. This means that Canadian Tire generated 5.5 cents of net earnings for every dollar invested in assets. Canadian Tire is more profitable than its competition on both measures of profitability.

4. The information gathered above is useful for learning about Canadian Tire, but it is very limited. In order to assess the performance of Canadian Tire more fully, we would want considerably more information, both financial and non-financial. First, we would want to calculate additional performance measures that you will learn about in later chapters (e.g., earnings per share and price-earnings ratios). In addition, we would want to see the details of the company's statement of cash flows to assess its ability to generate the funding required for continued growth. We would also want to read the management discussion and analysis section of the annual report to see management's assessment of its plans.

Summary of Study Objectives

❶ ***Describe the basic objective of financial reporting, and explain the meaning of generally accepted accounting principles.*** The basic objective of financial reporting is to provide information that is useful for decision-making. Generally accepted accounting principles are a set of rules and practices recognized as a general guide for financial reporting purposes.

❷ ***Discuss the qualitative characteristics of accounting information.*** To be judged useful, information should possess these qualitative characteristics: understandability, relevance, reliability, and comparability.

❸ ***Identify the two constraints in accounting.*** The major constraints are cost-benefit and materiality.

❹ ***Identify the sections of a classified balance sheet.*** In a classified balance sheet, assets are classified as current assets, long-term investments, and capital assets. Liabilities are classified as either current or long-term. There is also a shareholders' equity section, which shows share capital and retained earnings.

❺ ***Identify and calculate ratios for analysing a company's profitability.*** Profitability ratios, such as profit margin and return on assets, measure different aspects of the operating success of an enterprise for a given period of time.

6 ***Explain the relationship between a statement of retained earnings, a statement of earnings, and a balance sheet.*** The statement of retained earnings presents the factors that changed the retained earnings balance during the period. These include the net earnings (or loss), reported in more detail on the statement of earnings, and any dividends paid to shareholders during the period. The ending balance of retained earnings is reported in the shareholders' equity section of the balance sheet.

7 ***Identify and calculate ratios for analysing a company's liquidity and solvency.*** Liquidity ratios, such as working capital, the current ratio, and the cash current debt coverage ratio, measure the short-term ability of a company to pay its maturing obligations and to meet unexpected needs for cash. Solvency ratios, such as the debt to total assets ratio and cash total debt coverage ratio, measure the ability of a company to survive over a long period.

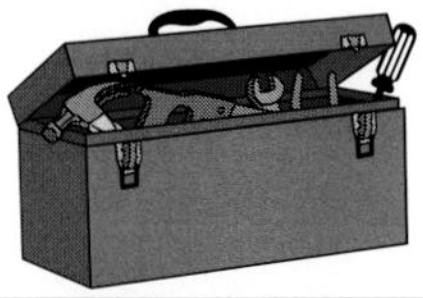

Decision Toolkit—A Summary

Decision Checkpoints	Info Needed for Decision	Tool to Use for Decision	How to Evaluate Results
Is the company using its assets effectively?	Net earnings and average assets	Return on assets ratio $= \frac{\text{Net earnings}}{\text{Average assets}}$	Higher value suggests favourable efficiency (use of assets).
Is the company maintaining an adequate margin between sales and expenses?	Net earnings and net sales	Profit margin ratio $= \frac{\text{Net earnings}}{\text{Net sales}}$	Higher value suggests favourable return on each dollar of sales.
Can the company meet its short-term obligations?	Current assets and current liabilities	Working capital $=$ Current assets $-$ Current liabilities	Higher amount indicates liquidity.
		Current ratio $= \frac{\text{Current assets}}{\text{Current liabilities}}$	Higher ratio suggests favourable liquidity.
	Current liabilities and cash provided (used) by operating activities	Cash current debt coverage ratio $= \frac{\text{Cash provided (used) by operating activities}}{\text{Average current liabilities}}$	A higher ratio indicates liquidity—that the company is generating cash sufficient to meet its short-term needs.
Can the company meet its long-term obligations?	Total debt and total assets	Debt to total assets ratio $= \frac{\text{Total liabilities}}{\text{Total assets}}$	Lower value suggests favourable solvency.
	Total liabilities and cash provided (used) by operating activities	Cash total debt coverage ratio $= \frac{\text{Cash provided (used) by operating activities}}{\text{Average total liabilities}}$	A higher ratio indicates solvency—that the company is generating cash sufficient to meet its long-term needs.

GLOSSARY

Capital assets Long-lived resources used in operating the business that are tangible (property, plant, and equipment, and natural resources) and intangible. (p. 61)

Cash current debt coverage ratio A measure of liquidity that is calculated as follows: cash provided by operating activities divided by average current liabilities. (p. 74)

Cash total debt coverage ratio A measure of solvency that is calculated as follows: cash provided by operating activities divided by average total liabilities. (p. 74)

Classified balance sheet A balance sheet that contains a number of standard classifications or sections. (p. 59)

Comparability The ability to compare the accounting information of companies in similar circumstances, because they use similar accounting principles. (p. 56)

Conservatism The approach of choosing an accounting method, when in doubt, that will be least likely to overstate assets and net earnings. (p. 56)

Consistency Use of the same accounting principles and methods from year to year within a company. (p. 57)

Cost-benefit The constraint that the costs of obtaining and providing information should not exceed the benefits gained. (p. 58)

Current assets Cash and other resources that it is reasonable to expect will be realized in cash, or sold, or consumed in the business, within one year or the operating cycle, whichever is longer. (p. 60)

Current liabilities Obligations that it is reasonable to expect will be paid from existing current assets or through the creation of other current liabilities, within the next year or operating cycle, whichever is longer. (p. 62)

Current ratio A measure used to evaluate a company's liquidity and short-term debt-paying ability; calculated by dividing current assets by current liabilities. (p. 69)

Debt to total assets ratio A measure showing the percentage of total financing provided by creditors; computed by dividing total debt by total assets. (p. 70)

Generally accepted accounting principles (GAAP) A set of rules and practices, having substantial authoritative support, that are recognized as a general guide for financial reporting purposes. (p. 55)

Interim financial reporting Financial reports issued periodically within the fiscal year. Interim reports are usually issued every quarter, but may be of other time durations. (p. 56)

Liquidity The ability of a company to pay obligations that are expected to become due within the next year or operating cycle. (p. 69)

Liquidity ratios Measures of the short-term ability of the company to pay its maturing obligations and to meet unexpected needs for cash. (p. 69)

Long-term investments Investments in shares and bonds of other companies that are normally held for many years. (p. 61)

Long-term liabilities (or long-term debt) Obligations not expected to be paid within one year or the operating cycle. (p. 63)

Materiality The constraint of determining whether an item is large enough to influence the decision of an investor or creditor. (p. 58)

Operating cycle The average time required to go from cash to cash in producing revenues. (p. 60)

Profit margin ratio A measure of the percentage of each dollar of sales that results in net earnings; computed by dividing net earnings by net sales. (p. 66)

Profitability ratios Measures of the earnings or operating success of an enterprise for a given period of time. (p. 65)

Relevance A quality for describing information that makes a difference in a decision. (p. 55)

Reliability A quality for describing information that is free of error and bias. (p. 56)

Return on assets ratio An overall measure of profitability; computed by dividing net earnings by average assets. (p. 65)

Solvency The ability of a company to pay interest as it comes due and to repay the face value of debt at maturity. (p. 70)

Solvency ratios Measures of the ability of the company to survive over a long period of time. (p. 70)

Understandability Information provided in the financial statements must be understandable for the users in order to be useful. (p. 55)

Working capital The excess of current assets over current liabilities. (p. 69)

DEMONSTRATION PROBLEM

Listed here are items taken from the statement of earnings and balance sheet of Hudson's Bay Company for the year ended January 31, 1999. Certain items have been combined for simplification and all numbers are reported in millions.

Sales and revenue	$7,075
Cash	8
Receivables	950
Operating expenses	6,888
Long-term investments	59
Interest expense	97
Dividends	53
Short-term borrowings	190
Prepaid expenses	60
Long-term debt	1,290
Other long-term liabilities	25
Income tax expense	50
Capital assets, net	1,451
Other long-term assets	406
Accounts payable	928
Short-term deposits	14
Long-term debt due within one year	112
Share capital	1,531
Merchandise inventories	1,656
Retained earnings, February 1, 1998	541

Instructions

Prepare a statement of earnings and a classified balance sheet using the items listed. No item should be used more than once.

Solution to Demonstration Problem

HUDSON'S BAY COMPANY
Statement of Earnings
For the Year Ended January 31, 1999
(in millions)

Sales and revenue	$7,075
Expenses	
Operating expenses	6,888
Interest expense	97
Total expenses	6,985
Earnings before income taxes	90
Income taxes	50
Net earnings	$ 40

HUDSON'S BAY COMPANY
Balance Sheet
January 31, 1999
(in millions)

Assets	
Current assets	
Cash	$ 8
Short-term deposits	14
Receivables	950
Merchandise inventories	1,656
Prepaid expenses	60
Total current assets	2,688
Long-term investments	59
Net capital assets	1,451
Other assets	406
Total assets	$4,604
Liabilities and Shareholders' Equity	
Current liabilities	
Short-term borrowings	$ 190
Accounts payable	928
Long-term debt due within one year	112
Total current liabilities	1,230
Long-term liabilities	
Long-term debt	1,290
Other long-term liabilities	25
Total long-term liabilities	1,315
Total liabilities	2,545
Shareholders' equity	
Share capital	1,531
Retained earnings	528*
Total shareholders' equity	2,059
Total liabilities and shareholders' equity	$4,604

* Note that ending retained earnings = beginning retained earnings + net earnings − dividends. $541 + $40 − $53 = $528.

SELF-STUDY QUESTIONS

Answers are at the end of the chapter.

(SO 1) 1. Generally accepted accounting principles are:
(a) a set of standards and rules that are recognized as a general guide for financial reporting.
(b) usually established by the Canada Customs and Revenue Agency.
(c) the guidelines used to resolve ethical dilemmas.
(d) fundamental truths that can be derived from the laws of nature.

2. What organization issues Canadian accounting standards? (SO 1)
(a) Canadian Institute of Chartered Accountants
(b) International Accounting Standards Committee
(c) Financial Accounting Standards Board
(d) None of the above

(SO 2) 3. What is the primary criterion by which accounting information can be judged?
(a) Consistency
(b) Predictive value
(c) Usefulness for decision-making
(d) Comparability

(SO 2) 4. What accounting characteristic refers to the tendency of accountants to resolve uncertainty in the way least likely to overstate assets and earnings?
(a) Comparability (c) Conservatism
(b) Materiality (d) Understandability

(SO 3) 5. An item is considered material when:
(a) it is more than $1,000.
(b) it occurs infrequently.
(c) its omission would influence or change a decision.
(d) it affects net earnings.

(SO 4) 6. In a classified balance sheet, assets are usually classified as:
(a) current assets and capital assets.
(b) current assets; long-term investments; capital assets; and share capital.
(c) current assets; long-term investments; and capital assets.
(d) current assets and non-current assets.

(SO 4) 7. Current assets are listed:
(a) by liquidity.
(b) by importance.
(c) by longevity.
(d) alphabetically.

8. Which is not an indicator of profitability? (SO 5)
(a) Current ratio
(b) Profit margin ratio
(c) Net earnings
(d) Return on assets ratio

9. For 2001, Plano Corporation reported net earnings $24,000; net sales $400,000; and average assets $600,000. What was the 2001 profit margin ratio? (SO 5)
(a) 6% (c) 40%
(b) 12% (d) 200%

10. The balance in retained earnings is not affected by: (SO 6)
(a) net earnings.
(b) net loss.
(c) issuance of common shares.
(d) dividends.

11. Which of these measures is an evaluation of a company's ability to pay current liabilities? (SO 7)
(a) Profit margin ratio
(b) Current ratio
(c) Both (a) and (b)
(d) None of the above

QUESTIONS

(SO 1) 1. (a) What are generally accepted accounting principles (GAAP)?
(b) What body provides authoritative support for GAAP?

(SO 1) 2. (a) What is the basic objective of financial reporting?
(b) Identify the qualitative characteristics of accounting information.

(SO 2) 3. Ray Aldag, the president of Raynard Corporation, is pleased. Raynard substantially increased its net earnings in 2001, while keeping its unit inventory almost the same. Chief accountant Tom Erhardt has cautioned Aldag, however. Erhardt says that since Raynard changed its method of inventory valuation, there is a consistency problem and it is difficult to determine whether Raynard is better off. Is Erhardt correct? Why or why not?

(SO 2) 4. What is the distinction between comparability and consistency?

(SO 2) 5. Your roommate believes that international accounting standards are uniform throughout the world. Is your roommate correct? Explain.

(SO 3) 6. Describe the two constraints in the presentation of accounting information.

(SO 3) 7. The newly hired accountant of a corporation rounded all dollar figures in the annual report's financial statements to the nearest thousand dollars. "It's not important for our users to know how many pennies we spend," she said. Do you believe rounded financial figures can still provide useful information to external users for decision-making? Explain why or why not.

8. What is meant by the term *operating cycle*? (SO 4)

9. Define current assets. What basis is used for ordering individual items within the current assets section? (SO 4)

10. Distinguish between long-term investments and capital assets. (SO 4)

11. How do current liabilities differ from long-term liabilities? (SO 4)

12. Identify the two parts of shareholders' equity in a corporation, and indicate the purpose of each. (SO 4)

13. Robins is puzzled. His company had a profit margin ratio of 10% in 2001. He feels that this indicates that the company is doing well. Amod Phatarpekar, his accountant, says that more information is needed to determine the firm's financial well-being. Who is correct? Why? (SO 5)

(SO 5, 7) 14.
(a) Tia Kim believes that the analysis of financial statements is directed at two characteristics of a company: liquidity and profitability. Is Tia correct? Explain.
(b) Are short-term creditors, long-term creditors, and shareholders primarily interested in the same characteristics of a company? Explain.

(SO 5, 7) 15. Name ratios that are useful in assessing (a) liquidity, (b) solvency, and (c) profitability.

(SO 5, 7) 16. What do these classes of ratios measure?
(a) Liquidity ratios
(b) Profitability ratios
(c) Solvency ratios

17. Keeping all other factors constant, indicate whether each of the following signals generally good or bad news about a company: (SO 5, 7)
(a) Increase in the profit margin ratio
(b) Increase in the current ratio
(c) Increase in the debt to total assets ratio
(d) Decrease in the return on assets ratio

18. In your opinion, which ratio or ratios from this chapter should be of greatest interest to: (SO 5, 7)
(a) a pension fund considering investing in a corporation's 20-year bonds?
(b) a bank contemplating a short-term loan?
(c) a common shareholder?

Brief Exercises

Recognize generally accepted accounting principles.
(SO 1)

BE2-1 Indicate whether each statement is true or false. Explain your reasoning.
(a) GAAP is a set of rules and practices established by the accounting profession to serve as a general guide for financial reporting purposes.
(b) Substantial authoritative support for GAAP usually comes from two standard-setting bodies: the CICA and the provincial securities commissions.

Identify qualitative characteristics.
(SO 2)

BE2-2 The accompanying chart shows the qualitative characteristics of accounting information. Fill in the blanks.

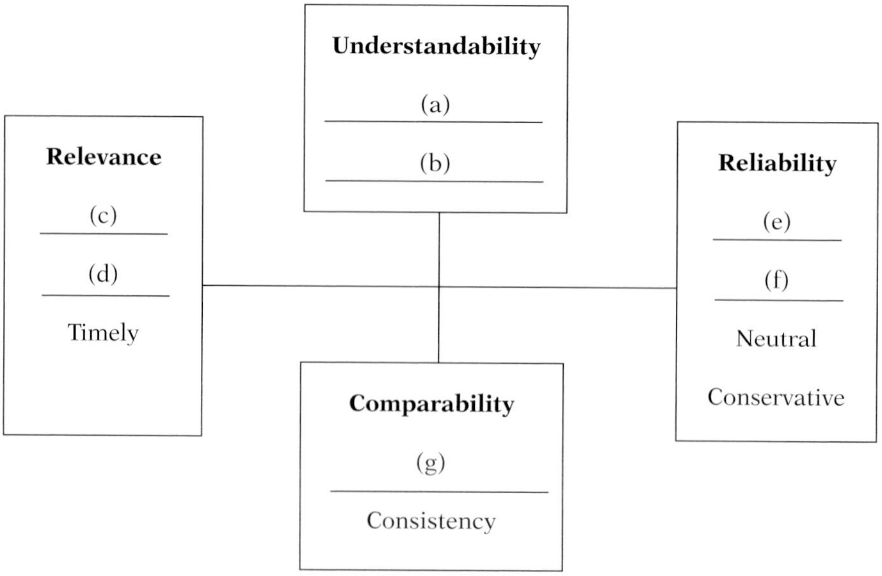

Identify qualitative characteristics.
(SO 2)

BE2-3 Given the qualitative characteristics of accounting established by the CICA's conceptual framework, complete each of the following statements.
(a) For information to be ______________, it should have predictive or feedback value, and it must be presented on a timely basis.
(b) ______________ is the quality of information that is free of error and bias; it can be depended on.
(c) ______________ means companies with similar circumstances use similar accounting principles.

Identify qualitative characteristics.
(SO 2)

BE2-4 Here are some qualitative characteristics of accounting information:

1. Predictive value
2. Neutral
3. Verifiable
4. Timely

Match each qualitative characteristic to one of the following statements.

(a) _____ Accounting information should help users make predictions about the outcome of past, present, and future events.
(b) _____ Accounting information cannot be selected, prepared, or presented to favour one set of interested users over another.
(c) _____ Accounting information must be proved free of error and bias.
(d) _____ Accounting information must be available to decision-makers before it loses its capacity to influence their decisions.

Identify constraints that have been violated.
(SO 3)

BE2-5 The Levesque Co. Inc. uses these accounting practices:
(a) Levesque currently records its accounting transactions and prepares its financial reports manually. The cost of implementing a new computerized accounting system to do these tasks is estimated to be $25,000. Annual savings are anticipated to be $10,000.
(b) Small tools are recorded as capital assets and amortized.
(c) The statement of earnings shows paper clips expense of $5.
Indicate the accounting constraint, if any, that has been violated by each practice.

Prepare the current assets section of a balance sheet.
(SO 4)

BE2-6 A list of financial statement items for Swann Limited includes the following: accounts receivable $16,500; prepaid insurance $3,600; cash $18,400; supplies $5,200; and marketable securities $8,200. Prepare the current assets section of the balance sheet listing the items in the proper sequence.

Calculate return on assets ratio and profit margin ratio.
(SO 5)

BE2-7 The following information is available for **Leon's Furniture Limited—Meubles Leon Ltée.** for the calendar year 1998 (all dollars in thousands):

	December 31, 1998	**December 31, 1997**
Sales	$336,895	$315,817
Cost of sales	199,369	187,680
Net earnings	26,406	21,635
Total assets	245,270	217,641
Total shareholders' equity	163,197	152,315

Calculate the return on assets ratio and profit margin ratio for Leon's for 1998.

Identify items affecting shareholders' equity.
(SO 6)

BE2-8 For each of the following events affecting the shareholders' equity of Wu Corporation, indicate whether the event would increase retained earnings (↑), decrease retained earnings (↓), increase share capital (↑), or decrease share capital (↓). Leave the line blank if there is no effect.

	Share Capital	Retained Earnings
(a) Issued additional common shares	_______	_______
(b) Paid a cash dividend to shareholders	_______	_______
(c) Reported net earnings of $75,000	_______	_______
(d) Paid cash to creditors	_______	_______
(e) Issued preferred shares	_______	_______

Calculate liquidity ratios.
(SO 7)

BE2-9 These selected and condensed data are taken from a recent balance sheet of **Bob Evans Farms**:

Cash	$ 8,241,000
Marketable securities	1,947,000
Accounts receivable	12,545,000
Inventories	14,814,000
Other current assets	5,371,000
Total current assets	$42,918,000
Total current liabilities	$44,844,000

Additional information: Current liabilities at the beginning of the year were $38,242,000, and cash provided by operating activities for the current year was $58,297,200.

Calculate (a) the working capital, (b) current ratio, and (c) the cash current debt coverage ratio.

EXERCISES

Classify items as current or noncurrent and prepare the asset section of a balance sheet.
(SO 4)

E2-1 The following items were taken from the December 31, 1998, asset section of **The Boeing Company** balance sheet (U.S. dollars in millions). Boeing is the world's largest aerospace company and maker of commercial jets. Boeing is also the prime contractor for the International Space Station.

Inventories	$ 8,349	Intangible assets (net of amortization)	$ 2,312
Notes receivable—due after after December 31, 1999	4,930	Other current assets	1,495
Short-term investments	279	Property, plant, and equipment	20,241
Notes receivable—due before December 31, 1999	4,930	Cash and cash equivalents	2,183
Accumulated depreciation	11,652	Accounts receivable	3,288
Other noncurrent assets	4,466		

Instructions
Prepare the asset section of the balance sheet, categorizing the items as current or noncurrent, and listing the current assets in order of their estimated liquidity.

Prepare a classified balance sheet.
(SO 4)

E2-2 These items are taken from the financial statements of Summit's Bowling Alley Ltd. at December 31, 2001:

Building	$125,800
Accounts receivable	14,520
Prepaid insurance	4,680
Cash	20,840
Equipment	62,400
Land	61,200
Insurance expense	780
Amortization expense	5,360
Interest expense	2,600
Common shares	80,000
Retained earnings	30,000
Accumulated amortization—building	45,600
Accounts payable	13,480
Mortgage payable	93,600
Accumulated amortization—equipment	18,720
Interest payable	2,600
Bowling revenues	14,180

Instructions
Prepare a classified balance sheet; assume that $13,600 of the mortgage payable will be paid in 2002.

Prepare a classified balance sheet.
(SO 4)

E2-3 Texas Instruments Incorporated is the world leader in digital signal processing and analog technologies—the semiconductor engines of the Internet age. The company has manufacturing or sales operations in more than 25 countries. The following items were taken from the 1998 financial statements of Texas Instruments Incorporated (U.S. dollars in millions):

Long-term debt	$1,027	Loans payable in 1999	$ 267
Common stock	1,436	Cash and cash equivalents	540
Prepaid expenses	75	Accumulated depreciation	3,006
Property, plant, and equipment	6,379	Accounts payable	1,582
Income taxes payable	193	Other noncurrent assets	467
Long-term investments	2,564	Other noncurrent liabilities	1,500
Short-term investments	1,709	Retained earnings, December 31, 1998	5,091
Accounts receivable	1,343	Inventories	596
Other current assets	583	Other current liabilities	154

Instructions
Prepare a classified balance sheet as at December 31, 1998.

E2-4 These financial statement items are for Batra Corporation at year end, July 31, 2001:

Prepare financial statements.
(SO 4, 6)

Salaries expense	$58,700
Utilities expense	14,900
Equipment	15,900
Accounts payable	6,220
Commission revenue	63,100
Rent revenue	6,500
Unearned rent revenue	1,800
Common shares	20,000
Cash	11,940
Accounts receivable	8,780
Accumulated amortization	5,400
Dividends	14,000
Amortization expense	4,000
Retained earnings (beginning of the year)	25,200

Instructions
(a) Prepare a statement of earnings and a statement of retained earnings for the year.
(b) Prepare a classified balance sheet at July 31.

E2-5 Selected statement data for Mighty Products Corporation are presented here for comparison. All balance sheet data are as at December 31.

Calculate profitability ratios.
(SO 5)

	2000	2001
Net sales	$800,000	$720,000
Cost of goods sold	480,000	40,000
Interest expense	7,000	5,000
Net earnings	56,000	42,000
Accounts receivable	120,000	100,000
Inventory	85,000	75,000
Total assets	600,000	500,000
Total shareholders' equity	450,000	310,000

Instructions
(a) What is the profit margin ratio for 2001?
(b) Calculate the return on assets ratio for 2001.

E2-6 For more than 130 years, until its closure in September 1999, the venerable **The T. Eaton Company Limited** name was one of the most recognized brand names in Canadian retailing. The company's department stores were located in major shopping centres and prime downtown locations in most Canadian provinces. Selected financial statement data for 1998 and 1997, are as follows (in thousands of dollars):

Calculate liquidity ratios and compare results.
(SO 7)

	1998	1997
Cash	$ 7,319	$ 7,514
Accounts receivable and prepaid expenses	45,966	56,737
Merchandise inventories	352,790	350,619
Discontinued operations	—	469,557
Total current assets	$406,075	$884,427
Total current liabilities	$304,003	$840,780

For 1998, revenue was $1,607,994 (thousand) and cost of merchandise sold was $1,107,342 (thousand).

Instructions
(a) Calculate the working capital and current ratio for 1998 and 1997.
(b) Did Eaton's liquidity improve or worsen during the year?
(c) Using the data in the chapter, compare Eaton's liquidity to Sears'.

Calculate and interpret solvency ratios.
(SO 7)

E2-7 The **Québec Winter Carnival** is recognized as the world's biggest winter celebration and is the third largest carnival (after those in Rio de Janeiro and New Orleans). The following data were taken from the 1999 and 1998 financial statements of the Carnaval de Québec Inc.:

	April 30, 1999	April 30, 1998
Current assets	$1,064,667	$726,484
Total assets	1,136,256	790,603
Current liabilities	401,111	315,589
Total liabilities	417,951	348,612
Total equity	718,305	441,991
Cash provided by operating activities	50,320	294,467
Cash used by investing activities	52,142	38,399

Instructions

Do each of the following:

(a) Calculate the debt to assets ratio for each year.
(b) Calculate the cash current debt coverage ratio and the cash total debt coverage ratio for 1999.
(c) Discuss the Carnival's solvency in 1999 versus 1998.
(d) Discuss the Carnival's ability to finance its investment activities with cash provided by operating activities, and how any deficiency would be met.

PROBLEMS: SET A

Comment on the qualitative characteristics of accounting information.
(SO 1, 2)

P2-1A **Net Nanny Software International Inc.**, headquartered in Vancouver, specializes in Internet safety and computer security products for both the home and enterprise markets. Its balance sheet, as at June 30, 1999, reported a deficit (negative retained earnings) of US$5,678,288. It has only reported net losses since inception, June 30, 1996. In spite of these losses, Net Nanny's common shares have traded anywhere from a high of $3.70 to a low of $0.32 on the Canadian Venture Exchange.

Net Nanny's financial statements of the company have historically been prepared in Canadian dollars. As of June 30, 1998, the company adopted the U.S. dollar as its reporting currency.

Instructions

(a) What is the objective of financial reporting? How does this objective meet or not meet Net Nanny's investor's needs?
(b) Why would investors want to buy Net Nanny's shares if the company has consistently reported losses over the last few years? Include in your answer an assessment of the relevance and reliability of the information reported on Net Nanny's financial statements.
(c) Comment on how the change in reporting information from Canadian dollars to U.S. dollars likely affected the readers of Net Nanny's financial statements. Include in your answer an assessment of the comparability of the information.

Comment on the constraints of accounting.
(SO 3)

P2-2A A friend of yours, Ryan Konotopsky, has come to you looking for some answers about financial statements. Ryan tells you that he is thinking about opening a movie theatre in his home town. Before doing so, he wants to find out how much in sales he could expect to make from food concessions as opposed to ticket sales. He wants to know what portion of ticket sales he could expect from children, youth and seniors versus adults who pay the highest admission rate. He also wants to know how much profit he would make on ticket sales versus sales at the concession stands; and the average wage per employee.

Ryan knows that Empire Theatres operates in many cities and towns in Atlantic Canada so he downloaded the financial statements of Empire Company Limited from the Internet. He noticed that the company's statement of earnings reported revenues for the year ended April 30, 1999 of $6,377,651,000 and cost of sales, selling and administrative expenses of $6,098,147,000. He read through Empire Company's Limited's annual report and learned that the Empire Theatres is just one part of the Investments division of the company. There are food distribution and real estate divisions as well. Ryan discovers from reading the annual report of Empire Company Limited that the company reports segmented information. It uses the term other operations to describe the results of Empire Theatres and reports the following for 1999:

Revenue: $38,063,000
Operating income: $4,455,000
Identifiable assets: $45,926,000

Ryan is disillusioned because he cannot find many details about Empire Theatres in the annual report. He has come to you looking for explanations.

Instructions
What are two constraints in accounting? What impact have these constraints had on the financial reporting by Empire Theatres?

Prepare a classified balance sheet.
(SO 4)

P2-3A For most of the web-surfing public, Yahoo! and the Internet are indistinguishable, and that's just the way the number 1 Internet portal would like to keep it. Yahoo! is also one of the few Internet players operating in the black. The following items are taken from the 1998 balance sheet of **Yahoo! Inc.** (in thousands of U.S. dollars):

Common stock	$523,020	Prepaid expenses and other current assets	$ 8,909
Property and equipment, net	15,189	Short-term investments	308,025
Accounts payable	6,302	Retained earnings, December 31, 1998	13,190
Other assets	49,190	Cash and cash equivalents	125,474
Long-term investments	90,266	Long-term liabilities	5,691
Accounts receivable	24,831	Other current liabilities	35,380
Unearned revenue—current	38,301		

Instructions
Prepare a classified balance sheet for Yahoo! Inc. as at December 31, 1998.

Classify balance sheet items.
(SO 4)

P2-4A You are provided with the following alphabetical list of balance sheet accounts for **Leon's Furniture Limited—Meubles Leon Ltée** as at December 31, 1999:

Accounts payable and accrued liabilities
Accounts receivable
Cash and cash equivalents
Common shares
Current portion of long-term debt
Customers' deposits
Dividends payable
Fixed assets, net
Income taxes payable
Inventory
Marketable securities
Retained earnings

Instructions
Identify the balance sheet category for classifying each account. For example, cash and cash equivalents should be classified as a current asset on the balance sheet.

Prepare financial statements.
(SO 4, 6)

P2-5A These items are taken from the financial statements of Melinda Corporation for 2001:

Retained earnings (beginning of year)	$16,000
Utilities expense	1,700
Equipment	26,000
Accounts payable	13,300
Cash	13,600
Salaries payable	3,000
Common shares	20,000
Dividends	12,000
Service revenue	54,000
Prepaid insurance	3,500
Repair expense	1,800
Amortization expense	2,600
Accounts receivable	13,500
Insurance expense	2,200
Salaries expense	35,000
Accumulated amortization	5,600

Instructions

Prepare a statement of earnings, a statement of retained earnings, and a classified balance sheet for December 31, 2001.

Prepare financial statements.
(SO 4, 6)

P2-6A You are provided with the following information for Cheung Corporation, effective as of their April 30, 2001 year end.

Accounts payable	5,972
Accounts receivable	7,840
Accumulated amortization	4,921
Amortization expense	671
Cash	18,052
Common shares	20,000
Dividends	3,650
Equipment	23,050
Fees earned	12,590
Income tax expense	1,135
Income taxes payable	1,135
Interest expense	57
Interest payable	57
Long-term notes payable	5,700
Prepaid rent	2,280
Rent expense	760
Retained earnings, beginning	13,960
Salaries expense	6,840

Instructions

(a) Prepare a statement of earnings and a statement of retained earnings for Cheung Corporation for the year ended April 30, 2001.
(b) Prepare a classified balance sheet for Cheung as of April 30, 2001.
(c) Explain how each financial statement interrelates with the others.

Calculate ratios and comment on relative profitability, liquidity, and solvency.
(SO 5, 7)

P2-7A Financial statement data for Chen Corporation and Caissie Corporation, two competitors, appear below. All balance sheet data are as at December 31, 2001, and December 31, 2000.

	Chen Corporation		Caissie Corporation	
	2001	**2000**	**2001**	**2000**
Net sales	$1,549,035		$339,038	
Cost of goods sold	1,080,490		238,006	
Operating expenses	302,275		79,000	
Interest expense	6,800		1,252	
Income tax expense	47,840		7,740	
Current assets	325,975	$312,410	83,336	$ 79,467
Capital assets (net)	521,310	500,000	139,728	125,812
Current liabilities	66,325	75,815	35,348	30,281
Long-term liabilities	108,500	90,000	29,620	25,000
Share capital	500,000	500,000	120,000	120,000
Retained earnings	172,460	146,595	38,096	29,998

Additional information: Cash provided by operating activities for 2001 was $162,594 for Chen, and $24,211 for Caissie.

Instructions

(a) Comment on the relative profitability of the companies by calculating the return on assets ratio and the profit margin ratio for both companies.
(b) Comment on the relative liquidity of the companies by calculating working capital, the current ratio, and the cash current debt coverage ratio for both companies.
(c) Comment on the relative solvency of each company by calculating its debt to total assets ratio and cash total debt coverage ratio.

P2-8A Here are the comparative statements of Johannsen Inc.:

Calculate liquidity, solvency, and profitability ratios.

(SO 5, 7)

JOHANNSEN INC.
Statement of Earnings
For the Years Ended December 31

	2001	2000
Net sales	$1,818,500	$1,750,500
Cost of goods sold	1,005,500	996,000
Selling and administrative expenses	506,000	479,000
Interest expense	18,000	19,000
Total expenses	1,529,500	1,494,000
Earnings before income taxes	289,000	256,500
Income tax expense	86,700	77,000
Net earnings	$ 202,300	$ 179,500

JOHANNSEN INC.
Balance Sheet
December 31

	2001	2000
Assets		
Current assets		
Cash	$ 60,100	$ 64,200
Marketable securities	54,000	50,000
Accounts receivable (net)	107,800	102,800
Inventory	123,000	115,500
Total current assets	344,900	332,500
Capital assets (net)	625,300	520,300
Total assets	$970,200	$852,800
Liabilities and Shareholders' Equity		
Current liabilities		
Accounts payable	$150,000	$145,400
Income taxes payable	43,500	42,000
Total current liabilities	193,500	187,400
Bonds payable	210,000	200,000
Total liabilities	403,500	387,400
Shareholders' equity		
Share capital	280,000	300,000
Retained earnings	286,700	165,400
Total shareholders' equity	566,700	465,400
Total liabilities and shareholders' equity	$970,200	$852,800

Additional information: The cash provided by operating activities for 2001 was $190,800.

Instructions

Calculate these values and ratios for 2001:

(a) Working capital
(b) Current ratio
(c) Cash current debt coverage ratio
(d) Debt to total assets ratio
(e) Cash total debt coverage ratio
(f) Profit margin ratio
(g) Return on assets ratio

Analyse ratios and discuss results.
(SO 5, 7)

P2-9A Condensed balance sheet and statement of earnings data for Pitka Corporation are presented here:

PITKA CORPORATION
Balance Sheet
December 31

	2001	2000	1999
Assets			
Cash	$ 25,000	$ 20,000	$ 18,000
Receivables (net)	50,000	45,000	48,000
Other current assets	90,000	85,000	64,000
Investments	75,000	70,000	45,000
Capital assets (net)	400,000	370,000	358,000
Total assets	$640,000	$590,000	$533,000
Liabilities and Shareholders' Equity			
Current liabilities	$ 75,000	$ 80,000	$ 70,000
Long-term debt	80,000	85,000	50,000
Share capital	340,000	300,000	300,000
Retained earnings	145,000	125,000	113,000
Total liabilities and shareholders' equity	$640,000	$590,000	$533,000

PITKA CORPORATION
Statement of Earnings
For the Years Ended December 31

	2001	2000
Sales	$700,000	$650,000
Operating expenses (including income taxes)	656,000	618,000
Net earnings	$ 44,000	$ 32,000

Instructions

(a) Calculate these values and ratios for 2000 and 2001:
1. Profit margin ratio
2. Return on assets ratio
3. Working capital
4. Current ratio
5. Debt to total assets ratio

(b) Based on the ratios calculated, briefly discuss Pitka Corporation's change in financial position and operating results from 2000 to 2001.

Calculate liquidity, solvency, and profitability ratios.
(SO 5, 7)

P2-10A The following financial information is for the Wells Corporation:

WELLS CORPORATION
Balance Sheet
December 31

Assets	2001	2000
Cash	$ 70,000	$ 65,000
Short-term investments	45,000	40,000
Receivables (net)	94,000	90,000
Inventories	130,000	125,000
Prepaid expenses	25,000	23,000
Land	130,000	130,000
Capital assets, net	190,000	175,000
Total assets	$684,000	$648,000

Liabilities and Shareholders' Equity		
Notes payable	$100,000	$100,000
Accounts payable	45,000	42,000
Accrued liabilities	40,000	40,000
Bonds payable, due 2003	150,000	150,000
Share capital	200,000	200,000
Retained earnings	149,000	116,000
Total liabilities and shareholders' equity	$684,000	$648,000

WELLS CORPORATION
Statement of Earnings
For the Year Ended December 31

	2001	2000
Sales	$850,000	$790,000
Operating expenses (including income taxes)	814,000	755,000
Net earnings	$ 36,000	$ 35,000

Additional information: Total assets at the beginning of 2000 were $630,000, current liabilities were $155,000, and total liabilities were $305,000. Cash provided by operating activities was $47,000 for 2001, and $32,000 for 2000.

Instructions

Indicate, by using ratios, the change in liquidity, solvency, and profitability of the Wells Corporation from 2000 to 2001.

P2-11A Selected financial data (in millions) from a recent year of two intense competitors, **Kmart** and **Walmart**, are presented here:

Analyse ratios and discuss results.

(SO 5, 7)

	Kmart	Wal-Mart
	Statement of Earnings Data for Year	
Total revenue	$34,597	$83,412
Cost of goods sold	25,992	65,586
Selling and administrative expenses	7,701	12,858
Interest expense	494	706
Income taxes	114	1,581
Net earnings	$ 296	$ 2,681
	Balance Sheet Data (End of Year)	
Current assets	$ 9,187	$15,338
Capital assets (net)	7,842	17,481
Total assets	$17,029	$32,819
Current liabilities	$ 5,626	$ 9,973
Long-term debt	5,371	10,120
Total shareholders' equity	6,032	12,726
Total liabilities and shareholders' equity	$17,029	$32,819
	Beginning-of-Year Balances	
Total assets	$17,504	$26,441

Instructions

(a) For each company, calculate these values and ratios:
   1. Working capital
   2. Current ratio
   3. Debt to total assets ratio
   4. Return on assets ratio
   5. Profit margin ratio

(b) Compare the liquidity, solvency, and profitability of the two companies.

Problems: Set B

Comment on the objective and qualitative characteristics of financial reporting.
(SO 1, 2)

P2-1B A friend of yours, Emily Collis, recently completed an undergraduate degree in science and has just started working with a Canadian biotechnology company. Emily tells you that the owners of the business are trying to secure new sources of financing which are needed in order for the company to proceed with development of a new health care product. Emily said that her boss told her that the company must put together a report to present to potential investors.

Emily thought that the company should include in this package the detailed scientific findings related to the Phase I clinical trials for this product. "I know that the biotech industry sometimes has only a 10% success rate with new products, but if we report all the scientific findings, everyone will see what a sure success this is going to be! The president was talking about the importance of following some set of accounting principles. Why do we need to look at some accounting rules? What they need to realize is that we have scientific results that are quite encouraging, some of the most talented employees around, and the start of some really great customer relationships. We haven't made any sales yet, but we will. We just need the funds to get through all the clinical testing and get government approval for our product. Then these investors will be quite happy that they bought in to our company early!"

Instructions

(a) What is financial reporting? Explain to Emily what is meant by generally accepted accounting principles.

(b) Comment on how Emily's suggestions for what should be reported to prospective investors conforms to the qualitative characteristics of accounting information. Do you think that the things that Emily wants to include in the information for investors will conform to financial reporting guidelines?

Comment on the constraints of accounting.
(SO 1, 3)

P2-2B No separate disclosure is required on the statement of earnings for the Cost of Goods Sold, the cost of merchandise sold to customers. Because this disclosure is not specifically required, less than half of reporting companies disclose their cost of goods sold separately on their statement of earnings. Most companies include it with other expenses in their reporting of this item, similar to that reported by **Sears Canada Inc.** in its statement of earnings for the year ended January 1, 2000:

Cost of merchandise sold, operating, administrative and selling expenses	$5,600.8 million

Instructions

(a) Why do you think Sears does not report it's cost of merchandise sold separately on its statement of earnings? Comment on how this disclosure meets the objective of financial reporting.

(b) What are the two constraints in accounting? Do either of these constraints likely have an impact on Sears's reporting policy with respect to cost of merchandise sold? Give an example of how each constraint might affect Sears's reporting of its financial information.

Prepare a classified balance sheet.
(SO 4)

P2-3B Headquartered in Vancouver, **Intrawest Corporation** is the number 2 ski resort operator in North America. The following items are taken from its March 31, 1999, quarterly balance sheet (in thousands of dollars):

Share capital	$ 495,526	Bank and other indebtedness, current portion	$263,971
Capital assets	1,456,228	Other current liabilities	80,422
Amounts payable	183,653	Retained earnings, March 31, 1999	236,200
Other noncurrent assets	141,510	Cash and short-term deposits	81,609
Other current assets	367,600	Long-term liabilities	892,293
Amounts receivable	105,118		

Instructions
Prepare a classified balance sheet for Intrawest as at March 31, 1999.

P2-4B You are provided with the following alphabetical list of accounts.

Classify financial statement items.
(SO 4)

Accounts payable
Accounts receivable
Accumulated amortization, building
Accumulated amortization, equipment
Amortization expense
Building
Cash
Common shares
Cost of merchandising
Current portion of long-term debt
Dividends paid during the year
Equipment
Income tax expense
Income taxes payable
Interest expense
Inventories
Land
Long-term debt
Prepaid expenses
Retained earnings, beginning
Revenues
Selling expenses
Short-term investments
Wages payable

Instructions
Identify the financial statement and category for classifying each account. For example, cash should be classified as a current asset on the balance sheet.

P2-5B These items are taken from the financial statements of Batavia Limited:

Prepare financial statements.
(SO 4, 6)

Cash	$ 8,200
Accounts receivable	7,500
Prepaid insurance	1,800
Equipment	28,000
Accumulated amortization	8,600
Accounts payable	12,000
Salaries payable	3,000
Common shares	20,000
Retained earnings (beginning)	14,000
Dividends	7,200
Service revenue	42,000
Repair expense	3,200
Amortization expense	2,800
Insurance expense	1,200
Salaries expense	36,000
Utilities expense	3,700

Instructions
Prepare a statement of earnings, a statement of retained earnings, and a classified balance sheet for December 31, 2001.

P2-6B You are provided with the following information for Commerce Crusaders, effective as of its April 30, 2001 year end.

Prepare financial statements.
(SO 4, 6)

Accounts payable	834
Accounts receivable	810
Amortization expense	335

Building, net of accumulated amortization	1,537
Cash	570
Common shares	900
Cost of merchandising	990
Current portion of long-term debt	450
Dividends paid during the year	325
Equipment, net of accumulated amortization	1,220
Income tax expense	135
Income taxes payable	135
Interest expense	400
Inventories	967
Land	1,400
Long-term debt	3,500
Prepaid expenses	12
Retained earnings, beginning	1,600
Revenues	3,400
Selling expenses	440
Short-term investments	1,200
Wages expense	700
Wages payable	222

Instructions

(a) Prepare a statement of earnings and a statement of retained earnings for Commerce Crusaders for the year ended April 30, 2001.

(b) Prepare a classified balance sheet for Commerce Crusaders as of April 30, 2001.

Calculate ratios and comment on relative profitability, liquidity, and solvency.
(SO 5, 7)

P2-7B Comparative statement data for Belliveau Corp. and Shields Corp., two competitors, are presented here. All balance sheet data are as at December 31, 2001, and December 31, 2000.

	Belliveau Corp.		Shields Corp.	
	2001	**2000**	**2001**	**2000**
Net sales	$250,000		$1,200,000	
Cost of goods sold	160,000		720,000	
Operating expenses	51,000		252,000	
Interest expense	3,000		10,000	
Income tax expense	11,000		65,000	
Current assets	130,000	$110,000	700,000	$650,000
Capital assets (net)	305,000	270,000	800,000	750,000
Current liabilities	60,000	52,000	250,000	275,000
Long-term liabilities	50,000	68,000	200,000	150,000
Share capital	260,000	210,000	750,000	700,000
Retained earnings	65,000	50,000	300,000	275,000

Additional information: Cash provided by operating activities for 2001 was $22,000 for Belliveau and $185,000 for Shields.

Instructions

(a) Comment on the relative profitability of the companies by calculating the return on assets ratio and the profit margin ratio of each one.

(b) Comment on the relative liquidity of the companies by calculating working capital, the current ratio, and the cash current debt coverage ratio for each one.

(c) Comment on the relative solvency of the companies by calculating the debt to total assets ratio and the cash total debt coverage ratio for each one.

Calculate liquidity, solvency, and profitability ratios.
(SO 5, 7)

P2-8B The comparative statements of the Fast Corporation are presented here:

FAST CORPORATION
Statement of Earnings
For the Years Ended December 31

	2001	2000
Sales	$660,000	$624,000
Expenses		
Cost of goods sold	440,000	405,600
Selling and administrative expense	143,880	149,760
Interest expense	7,920	7,200
Total expenses	591,800	562,560
Earnings before income taxes	68,200	61,440
Income tax expense	25,300	24,000
Net earnings	$ 42,900	$ 37,440

FAST CORPORATION
Balance Sheet
December 31

	2001	2000
Assets		
Current assets		
Cash	$ 23,100	$ 21,600
Marketable securities	34,800	33,000
Accounts receivable (net)	106,200	93,800
Inventory	72,400	64,000
Total current assets	236,500	212,400
Capital assets (net)	465,300	459,600
Total assets	$701,800	$672,000
Liabilities and Shareholders' Equity		
Current liabilities		
Accounts payable	$134,200	$132,000
Income taxes payable	25,300	24,000
Total current liabilities	159,500	156,000
Bonds payable	132,000	120,000
Total liabilities	291,500	276,000
Shareholders' equity		
Share capital	140,000	150,000
Retained earnings	270,300	246,000
Total shareholders' equity	410,300	396,000
Total liabilities and shareholders' equity	$701,800	$672,000

Additional information: Cash provided by operating activities was $64,600 for 2001.

Instructions

Calculate these values and ratios for 2001:

(a) Current ratio
(b) Working capital
(c) Cash current debt coverage ratio
(d) Debt to total assets ratio
(e) Cash total debt coverage ratio
(f) Profit margin ratio
(g) Return on assets ratio

Analyse ratios and discuss results.
(SO 5, 7)

P2-9B Condensed balance sheet and statement of earnings data for Giasson Corporation are presented next:

GIASSON CORPORATION
Balance Sheet
December 31

	2001	2000	1999
Assets			
Cash	$ 40,000	$ 24,000	$ 20,000
Receivables (net)	70,000	45,000	48,000
Other current assets	80,000	75,000	62,000
Investments	90,000	70,000	50,000
Capital assets (net)	450,000	400,000	360,000
Total assets	$730,000	$614,000	$540,000
Liabilities and Shareholders' Equity			
Current liabilities	$ 98,000	$ 75,000	$ 70,000
Long-term debt	97,000	75,000	65,000
Share capital	400,000	340,000	300,000
Retained earnings	135,000	124,000	105,000
Total liabilities and shareholders' equity	$730,000	$614,000	$540,000

GIASSON CORPORATION
Statement of Earnings
For the Years Ended December 31

	2001	2000
Sales	$660,000	$700,000
Operating expenses (including income taxes)	614,000	637,000
Net earnings	$ 46,000	$ 63,000

Instructions

(a) Calculate these values and ratios for 2000 and 2001:
1. Profit margin ratio
2. Return on assets ratio
3. Working capital
4. Current ratio
5. Debt to total assets ratio

(b) Based on the ratios calculated, briefly discuss Giasson's changes in financial position and operating results from 2000 to 2001.

Calculate liquidity, solvency, and profitability ratios.
(SO 5, 7)

P2-10B Financial information for Star Track Corporation is presented here:

STAR TRACK CORPORATION
Balance Sheet
December 31

	2001	2000
Assets		
Cash	$ 50,000	$ 42,000
Short-term investments	80,000	100,000
Receivables (net)	100,000	87,000
Inventories	440,000	400,000
Prepaid expenses	25,000	31,000
Land	75,000	75,000
Building and equipment (net)	570,000	500,000
Total assets	$1,340,000	$1,235,000

Liabilities and Shareholders' Equity		
Notes payable	$ 125,000	$ 125,000
Accounts payable	160,000	140,000
Accrued liabilities	50,000	50,000
Bonds payable, due 2003	200,000	200,000
Common shares	500,000	500,000
Retained earnings	305,000	220,000
Total liabilities and shareholders' equity	$1,340,000	$1,235,000

STAR TRACK CORPORATION
Statement of Earnings
For the Year Ended December 31

	2001	2000
Sales	$1,000,000	$ 940,000
Operating expenses (including income taxes)	885,000	850,000
Net earnings	$ 115,000	$ 90,000

Additional information: Total assets at the beginning of 2000 were $1,175,000, current liabilities were $300,000, and total liabilities were $500,000. Cash provided by operating activities was $125,000 in 2001, and $75,000 in 2000.

Instructions

Use ratios to indicate the change in liquidity, solvency, and profitability of Star Track Corporation from 2000 to 2001.

P2-11B Selected financial data (in millions) from a recent year of two Montreal-based producers of integrated forest products **Alliance Forest Products Inc.** and **Tembec Inc.**, are presented here:

Analyse ratios and discuss results.

(SO 5, 7)

	Alliance Forest Products Inc.	Tembec Inc.
	Statement of Earnings Data for Year	
Sales	$1,085.1	$1,422.9
Operating expenses	990.9	1,198.0
Interest expense	58.7	103.6
Income taxes	9.6	60.2
Net earnings	$ 25.9	$ 61.1
	Balance Sheet Data (End of Year)	
Current assets	$ 312.4	$ 696.8
Long-term investments	—	13.5
Capital assets	1,369.7	1,587.5
Other assets	89.7	199.1
Total assets	$1,771.8	$2,496.9
Current liabilities	$ 177.3	$ 233.4
Long-term debt	636.7	1,301.8
Total shareholders' equity	957.8	961.7
Total liabilities and shareholders' equity	$1,771.8	$2,496.9
	Beginning-of-Year Balances	
Total assets	$1,688.9	$3,436.0

Instructions

(a) For each company, calculate these values and ratios:
1. Working capital
2. Current ratio
3. Debt to total assets ratio
4. Return on assets ratio
5. Profit margin ratio

(b) Compare the liquidity, profitability, and solvency of the two companies.

BROADENING YOUR PERSPECTIVE

Financial Reporting and Analysis

FINANCIAL REPORTING PROBLEM: *Loblaw Companies Limited*

BYP2-1 The financial statements of **Loblaw Companies Limited** are presented in Appendix A at the end of this book.

Instructions

Answer the following questions using the Consolidated Balance Sheets and the Notes to Consolidated Financial Statements section:

(a) What were Loblaw's total current assets at January 1, 2000 (1999 fiscal year), and January 2, 1999 (1998 fiscal year)?
(b) Are the assets in current assets listed in the proper order? Explain.
(c) How are Loblaw's assets classified?
(d) What were Loblaw's total current liabilities at January 1, 2000, and January 2, 1999?

COMPARATIVE ANALYSIS PROBLEM: *Loblaw and Sobeys*

BYP2-2 The financial statements of **Sobeys Inc.** are presented in Appendix B after the financial statements for **Loblaw**.

Instructions

(a) For each company, calculate the following values for fiscal 1999:
  1. Working capital
  2. Current ratio
  3. Debt to total assets ratio
  4. Profit margin ratio
  5. Return on assets ratio

(b) Based on your findings above, discuss the relative liquidity, solvency, and profitability of the two companies.

RESEARCH CASE

BYP2-3 Several commonly available indices help individuals find articles from business publications and periodicals. Articles can generally be searched for by company name or by subject matter. Two common indices are CBCA (Canadian Business and Current Affairs) Fulltext Business, which covers over 130 Canadian industry and professional periodicals and news sources, and Lexis-Nexis, which includes the full text of major newspapers from around the world, as well as company reports, marketing, and financial information.

Instructions

Use one of these resources, or others, to find a list of articles about Sears, Hudson's Bay, or Canadian Tire. Choose an article that you believe would be of interest to an investor or creditor of this company. Read the article and answer the following questions. (Note: Your library may have either print or electronic versions of these indices.)

(a) What is the article about?
(b) What information about the company is included in the article?
(c) Is the article related to anything you read in this chapter?
(d) Identify any accounting-related issues discussed in the article.

INTERPRETING FINANCIAL STATEMENTS

BYP2-4 **Ford Motor Company of Canada, Limited**, was incorporated on August 17, 1904. The event marked Ford Motor Company's first expansion outside of the U.S. and the beginning of the company's globalization. Headquartered in Detroit, Michigan, the Ford Motor Company is now the world's largest truck maker and the second largest maker of trucks and cars combined.

The following information was reported by Ford in its 1998 annual report.

	1998	1997	1996	1995	1994	1993	1992
Total assets ($US millions)	$3,964	$3,338	$2,627	$2,343	$2,004	$1,763	$1,379
Working capital ($US millions)	$319	$839	$554	$728	$556	$494	$356
Current ratio	1.21:1	1.81:1	1.72:1	2.32:1	2.11:1	2.07:1	2.06:1
Debt to total assets ratio	13%	15%	0%	0%	0%	4%	5%
Return on assets ratio	23%	18%	18%	16%	17%	16%	17%

Instructions

(a) Determine the percentage of the overall increase in Ford's total assets from 1992 to 1998. What was the average increase per year?

(b) Comment on the change in Ford's liquidity. Does working capital or the current ratio appear to provide a better indication of Ford's liquidity? What might explain the change in Ford's liquidity during this period?

(c) Comment on the change in Ford's solvency during this period.

(d) Comment on the change in Ford's profitability during this period. What was the average value of Ford's return on assets ratio from 1992 to 1997? How might this affect your prediction about Ford's future profitability?

BYP2-5 Chapters Inc. is the largest book retailer in Canada, representing approximately 25% of the estimated $2 billion Canadian retail book market. It operates bookstores in all provinces, under the names *Chapters, Coles, SmithBooks, LibrairieSmith, The Book Company,* and *World's Biggest Bookstore*. Through Chapters Campus Bookstores, the company also manages several college and university bookstores.

Chapters www.chapters.ca

Chapters' balance sheet and statement of earnings for its fiscal years ended April 3, 1999, and March 28, 1998, are reproduced on the following pages.

CHAPTERS INC.
CONSOLIDATED BALANCE SHEETS
(thousands)

	April 3, 1999	March 28, 1998
Assets		
Current		
Cash	$ —	$ 6,128
Accounts receivable	7,636	6,117
Inventories	224,606	142,103
Prepaid expenses	5,333	3,087
Total current assets	237,575	157,435
Capital assets, net	107,235	58,998
Other assets	675	2,977
	$345,485	$219,410
Liabilities and Shareholders' Equity		
Current		
Bank indebtedness	$ 55,521	$ —
Accounts payable and accrued liabilities	154,936	95,461
Income taxes payable	1,884	1,430
Deferred revenue	4,670	2,961
Current portion of long-term debt	11,125	4,000
Total current liabilities	228,136	103,852
Long-term debt	—	11,125
Deferred income taxes	2,127	—
Total liabilities	230,263	114,977
Commitments and contingencies (notes 10 and 11)		
Shareholders' equity		
Share capital	99,288	98,800
Retained earnings	15,934	5,633
Total shareholders' equity	115,222	104,433
	$345,485	$219,410

CHAPTERS INC.
CONSOLIDATED STATEMENT OF EARNINGS
(thousands)

	53-week period ended April 3, 1999	52-week period ended March 28, 1998
Revenue		
Superstores	$296,917	$166,678
Traditional bookstores	253,204	278,839
Other	27,759	11,094
	577,880	456,611
Cost of product, purchasing, selling and administration	536,580	423,707
	41,300	32,904
Amortization expense	18,012	13,907
Earnings before interest and income taxes	23,288	18,997
Interest on long-term debt	886	1,752
Interest on current debt	2,899	875
Earnings before income taxes	19,503	16,370
Provision for income taxes	9,202	7,950
Net earnings for the period	$ 10,301	$ 8,420

To capitalize on the expanding e-commerce business in the book and related products industry, Chapters Inc. launched Chapters Online Inc. after its 1999 fiscal year end. Chapters Online's *www.Chapters.ca* website features millions of books, music, video, software, and video game titles, as well as consumer electronics from around the world at Canadian prices with a focus on products of interest to Canadians. "Given the explosive growth of the Internet, Chapters is committed to being the number 1 Internet retailer in Canada," said Larry Stevenson, President and CEO of Chapters Inc. and Chapters Online Inc. And it has become so—Chapters Online is Canada's premier e-retailer. In 1999, Chapters Online received Internet World Canada's "Site of the Year Award" for its positive impact on the lives of Canadians.

The following additional information excerpted from Chapters Inc.'s fiscal 1999 annual report details some of the risk factors faced by the company:

Risk Factors

INTERNET BOOKSTORE OPERATIONS

The success of these [Internet bookstore] initiatives is dependent on consumer acceptance of electronic commerce and the cost of building awareness of the websites at a national level.

COMPETITION

The retail bookselling business is highly competitive. Specialty bookstores, independents, other book superstores, regional multi-store operators, supermarkets, drug stores, warehouse clubs, mail order clubs, Internet booksellers, mass merchandisers, and other retailers offering books are all sources of competition for the Company.

ECONOMIC ENVIRONMENT

Traditionally, retail businesses are highly susceptible to downturns in consumer confidence in the economy. A decline in consumer spending could have an adverse effect on the Company's financial condition. However, Chapters believes that the general economic environment will remain positive and provide opportunities for growth in 2000.

Instructions
(a) Comment on Chapters' overall financial performance by calculating and evaluating the current ratio, the debt to total assets ratio, and the profit margin ratio.
(b) From the information given in the case, describe the performance you would expect from Chapters in the fiscal year 2000. Which events are likely to affect performance? Be specific. For example, which ratio(s) would you expect to improve or worsen?

A GLOBAL FOCUS

BYP2-6 Many Canadian companies have revenue and expenses from other countries. One such company is **Doman Industries Ltd.**, whose products are sold in 30 countries worldwide. Doman is an integrated Canadian forest products company, located in British Columbia.

The majority of Doman's lumber products are sold in the U.S. and a significant amount of its pulp products in Asia. In addition to earning revenue from these and 29 other countries, Doman also has loans from other countries. For example, on June 18, 1999, the company borrowed US$160 million at an annual interest rate of 12%. Doman must repay this loan and the accompanying interest in U.S. dollars.

One of the challenges global companies face is to make themselves attractive to investors from other countries. This is difficult to do when different accounting rules in other countries can blur the real impact of earnings. For example, in the statement of earnings—which is what most investors examine—Doman reported a loss of $2.3 million, using Canadian accounting rules. Had it reported under U.S. accounting rules, its loss would have been $12.1 million.

Many companies that want to be more easily compared with U.S. and other global competitors have switched to U.S. accounting principles. Canadian National Railway, Corel, Cott, Inco, and the Thomson Corporation are but a few examples of large Canadian companies whose financial statements are now presented in U.S. dollars, and which either are presented in accordance with U.S. GAAP or reconciled to it.

Instructions
(a) Identify any advantages and disadvantages that companies should consider when switching to U.S. reporting standards.
(b) Suppose you wish to compare Doman Industries to a U.S.-based competitor, such as the formerly Canadian-owned forestry giant MacMillan Bloedel. Do you believe the use of both countries' accounting policies would hinder your comparison? If so, explain how.
(c) Suppose you wish to compare Doman Industries to a Canadian-based competitor, such as Nexfor, formerly Noranda Forest. If they chose to use different generally acceptable Canadian accounting policies, how could this affect your comparison of their financial results?
(d) Do you see any significant distinction between comparing statements prepared in different countries and comparing statements prepared using different accounting policies within the same country?

FINANCIAL ANALYSIS ON THE WEB

BYP2-7 ***Purpose:*** To identify summary information about companies. This information includes a basic description of various industries and companies in Canada.

Instructions
Specific requirements of this web case can be found on the Kimmel website.

www.wiley.com/canada/kimmel

CRITICAL THINKING

COLLABORATIVE LEARNING ACTIVITY

BYP2-8 As the accountant for Martinez Manufacturing Inc., you have been asked to develop some key ratios from the comparative financial statements. This information will be used to convince creditors that Martinez Manufacturing Inc. is liquid, solvent, and profitable, and therefore deserves their continued support. Lenders are particularly concerned about the company's ability to continue as a going concern.

Here are the data and calculations you developed from the financial statements:

	2001	2000
Current ratio	3.1:1	2.1:1
Working capital	Up 22%	Down 7%
Debt to total assets ratio	60%	70%
Net earnings	Up 32%	Down 8%
Profit margin ratio	5%	1.5%
Return on assets ratio	9%	4%

Instructions

You have now been asked to prepare brief comments which explain how each of these items supports the argument that Martinez's financial health is improving. The company wishes to use these comments in a presentation of data to its creditors. Prepare the comments as requested, giving the implications and the limitations of each item separately, and then state what may be drawn from them as a whole about Martinez's financial well-being.

COMMUNICATION ACTIVITY

BYP2-9 L.R. Stanton is the chief executive officer of Hi-Tech Electronics. Stanton is an expert engineer but a novice in accounting.

Instructions

Write a letter to L.R. Stanton that explains (a) the three main types of ratios, (b) examples of each, how they are calculated, and what they mean, and (c) the bases for comparison in analysing Hi-Tech's financial statements.

ETHICS CASE

BYP2-10 As the controller of Breathless Perfume Co. Ltd., you discover a significant overstatement of net earnings in the prior year's financial statements. The misleading financial statements are contained in the company's annual report, which was issued to banks and other creditors less than a month ago. After much thought about the consequences of telling the president, Eddy Kadu, about this misstatement, you gather your courage to inform him. Eddy says, "Hey! What they don't know won't hurt them. But, just so we set the record straight, we'll adjust this year's financial statements for last year's misstatement. We can absorb that misstatement better this year than last year anyway! Just don't make that kind of mistake again."

Instructions

(a) Who are the stakeholders in this situation?
(b) What are the ethical issues?
(c) What would you do as the controller?

Answers to Self-Study Questions

1. a 2. a 3. c 4. c 5. c 6. c 7. a 8. a 9. a 10. c 11. b

Loblaws
A passion for food... *and a lot more!*

Answer to Loblaw Review It Question 3

The key features of Loblaw's statement of earnings are sales, reduced by operating expenses to determine operating income. Operating income less interest expense results in earnings before income taxes. Income taxes are then deducted to find net earnings for the period. These earnings are expressed in total, and on a per share basis, in Loblaw's statement of earnings.

CHAPTER 3

The Accounting Information System

STUDY OBJECTIVES

After studying this chapter, you should be able to:

1. Analyse the effect of business transactions on the basic accounting equation.
2. Explain what an account is and how it helps in the recording process.
3. Define debits and credits and explain how they are used to record business transactions.
4. Identify the basic steps in the recording process.
5. Explain what a journal is and how it helps in the recording process.
6. Explain what a ledger is and how it helps in the recording process.
7. Explain what posting is and how it helps in the recording process.
8. Explain the purposes of a trial balance.

Accidents Happen

How organized are you financially? Take a short quiz.

- Is your wallet so stuffed with ATM receipts, Interac transaction records, and Canadian Tire money that you've been declared a walking fire hazard?
- Do you often come across credit card bills for restaurants and gas stations from towns you barely remember visiting?
- Is your wallet such a mess that, rather than dig around in it for cash, you sometimes fish for loonies in the crack of your car seat?
- Was Wayne Gretzky still playing hockey the last time you balanced your cheque book?
- Are you tempted every spring to burn down your house to avoid looking for all the forms, receipts, and records that you need to fill out your tax returns?

If you think it's hard to keep track of the many transactions that make up your life, imagine what it is like for Fidelity Investments. Fidelity is the largest mutual fund management firm in the world, serving over 15 million investors.

Needless to say, corporations can ill afford to be disorganized about tracking money. If your life savings were part of the $25 billion of Canadian assets that Fidelity manages in this country, you would no doubt be a little distressed if, when you called to check your balance, the representative said, "You know, I kind of remember someone with a name like yours sending us some money—now what did we do with that?"

To ensure the accuracy of its clients' balances and the security of their funds, Fidelity, like many other companies large and small, relies on a sophisticated computerized accounting information system. But that's not to say that Fidelity—or anybody else—is error-free.

In fact, if you've ever really messed up your cheque book register, you may take some

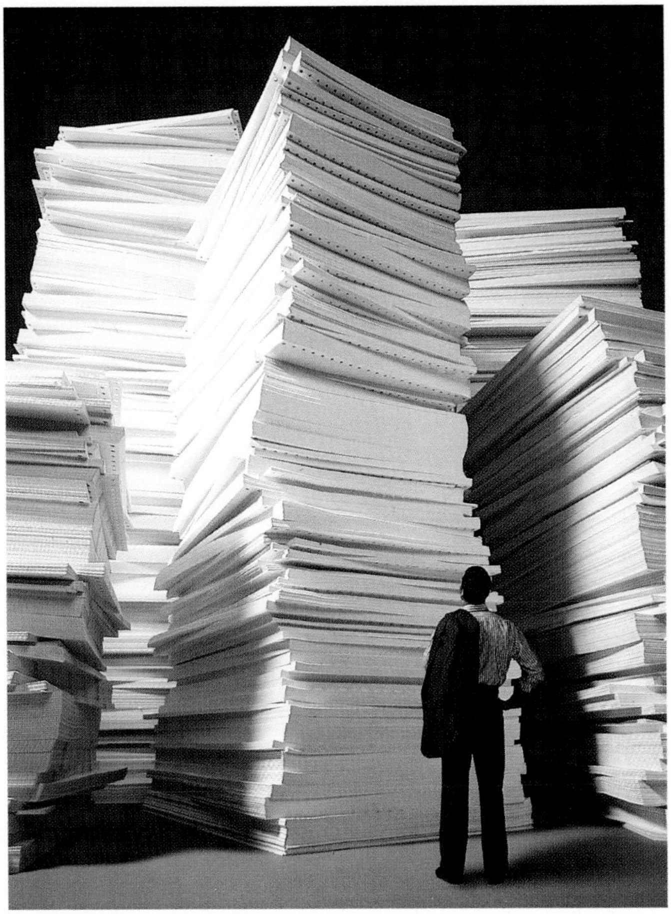

On the World Wide Web
Fidelity Investments
http://www.fidelity.ca

comfort from learning about a mistake once made at Fidelity Investments. An accountant failed to include a minus sign while doing a calculation, making what was actually a $1.9 billion loss look like a $1.9 billion gain. Yes, billion! Fortunately, like most accounting errors, this one was detected before any real harm was done.

This incident just proves that—even at a firm like Fidelity, which has up-to-date computer systems and is staffed by top professionals—perfection in accounting systems is unattainable. As a company spokesperson wrote, explaining the error to shareholders, "Some people have asked how, in this age of technology, such a mistake could be made. While many of our processes are computerized, accounting systems are complex and dictate that some steps must be handled manually by our managers and accountants, and people can make mistakes."

As indicated in the opening story, a reliable information system is a necessity for any company. The purpose of this chapter is to explain and illustrate the features of an accounting information system. The content and organization of the chapter are as follows:

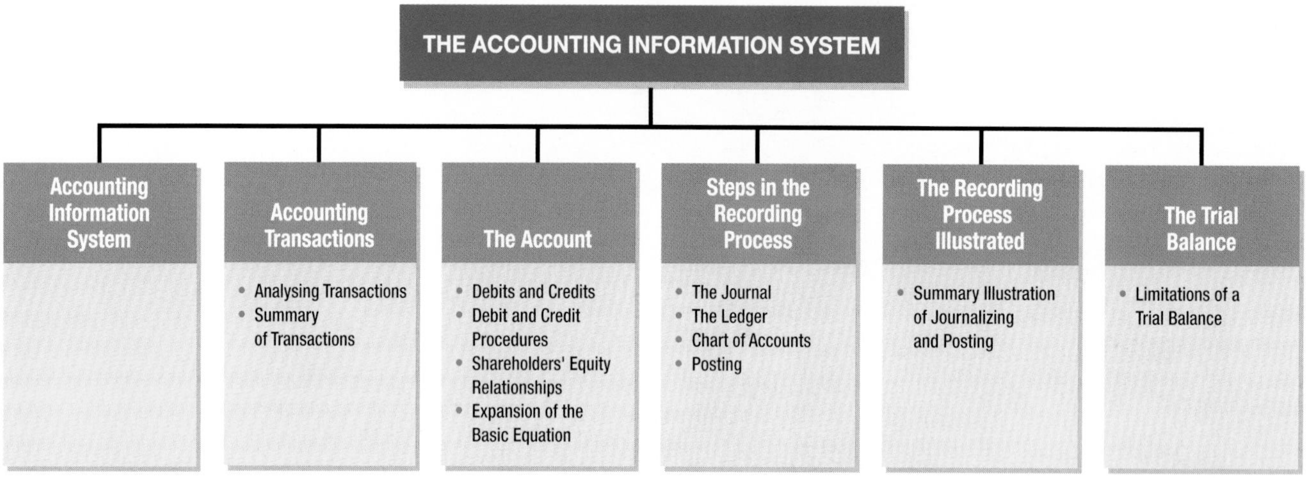

ACCOUNTING INFORMATION SYSTEM

The system of collecting and processing transaction data and communicating financial information to interested parties is known as the **accounting information system**. Accounting information systems vary widely from one business to another. Factors that shape these systems are the nature of the business and the transactions in which it engages, the size of the firm, the volume of data to be handled, and the information demands that management and others place on the system.

In reading this chapter, it is important to note that most businesses today, whatever their size, use computerized accounting systems—often referred to as electronic data processing (EDP) systems. These systems handle all the steps involved in the recording process, from initial data entry to preparation of the financial statements. In order to remain competitive, companies are continually updating and improving their accounting systems to provide accurate and timely data for decision-making. For example, in its annual report, Sobeys notes, under the caption "Working smarter every day," that "harnessing new technology has long been a key part of our approach."

In this chapter, we focus on a manual system, because the accounting concepts and principles do not change whether a system is computerized or manual. It is important to first have a good understanding of manual systems and then to progress to an understanding of computerized accounting systems.

ACCOUNTING TRANSACTIONS

To use the accounting information system to develop financial statements, you need to know what economic events to recognize (record). For example, suppose Bombardier hires a new employee or purchases a new computer. Are these events entered in its accounting records? Not all events are recorded and reported in the financial statements. We call economic events that require recording in the financial statements **accounting transactions**.

An accounting transaction occurs when assets, liabilities, or shareholders' equity items change as a result of some economic event. The purchase of a computer by Bombardier, the payment of salaries by Tim Hortons, and the sale of advertising space by Sierra Corporation are examples of events that change a company's assets, liabilities, or shareholders' equity. Illustration 3-1 summarizes the process used to decide whether or not to record economic events.

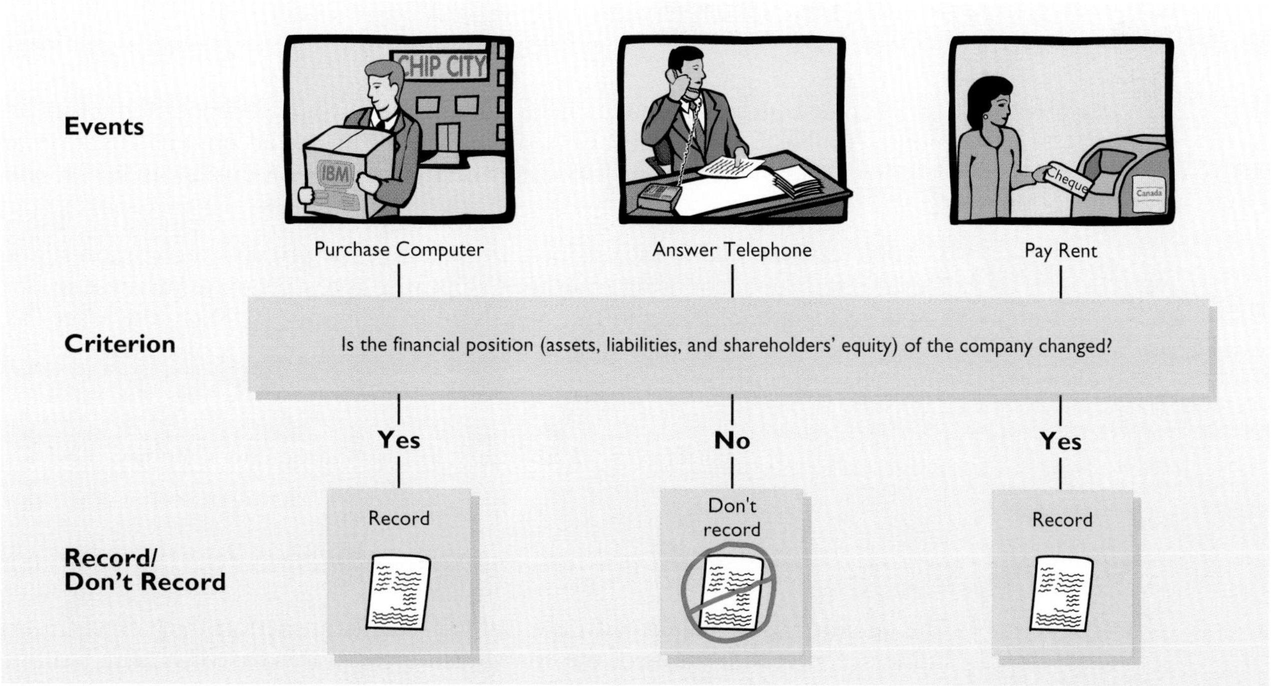

Illustration 3-1 Transaction identification process

ANALYSING TRANSACTIONS

In Chapter 1, you learned the basic accounting equation:

Assets = Liabilities + Shareholders' equity

STUDY OBJECTIVE 1

Analyse the effect of business transactions on the basic accounting equation.

In this chapter, you will learn how to analyse transactions in terms of their effect on assets, liabilities, and shareholders' equity. **Transaction analysis** is the process of identifying the specific effects of economic events on the accounting equation.

The accounting equation must always balance. Therefore, each transaction has a dual (double-sided) effect on the equation. For example, if an individual asset is increased, there must be a corresponding

decrease in another asset, *or*
increase in a specific liability, *or*
increase in shareholders' equity.

It is quite possible that two or more items could be affected when an asset is increased. For example, if a company purchases a computer for $10,000 by paying $6,000 in cash and signing a note for $4,000, one asset (Computer) increases by $10,000, another asset (Cash) decreases by $6,000, and a liability (Notes Payable) increases by $4,000. The result is that the accounting equation remains in balance—assets increased by a net $4,000 and liabilities also increased by $4,000.

Assets	=	Liabilities	+	Shareholders' Equity
+$10,000		+$4,000		
– 6,000				
$ 4,000	=	$4,000		

Chapter 1 presented the financial statements for Sierra Corporation for its first month. To illustrate the effect of economic events on the accounting equation, we will now examine the events affecting Sierra Corporation during its first month.

EVENT (1). INVESTMENT OF CASH BY SHAREHOLDERS. On October 1, cash of $10,000 was invested in the business in exchange for $10,000 of common shares. This event is an accounting transaction because it results in an increase in both assets and shareholders' equity. There is an increase of $10,000 in the asset Cash and an increase of $10,000 in Common Shares on the books of Sierra Corporation. The effect of this transaction on the basic equation is

	Assets	=	Liabilities	+	Shareholders' Equity	
	Cash	=			Common Shares	
(1)	+$10,000	=			+$10,000	Issued shares

The equation is in balance. To the right of each transaction that affects shareholders' equity the source of the change is noted; in this case it was an issuance of common shares. Keeping track of the source of each change in shareholders' equity is essential for later accounting activities.

EVENT (2). NOTE ISSUED IN EXCHANGE FOR CASH. On October 1, Sierra issued a three-month, 12%, $5,000 note payable to CIBC. This transaction results in an equal increase in assets and liabilities: Cash (an asset) increases by $5,000 and Notes Payable (a liability) increases by $5,000. The specific effect of this transaction and the cumulative effect of the first two transactions are

		Assets	=	Liabilities	+	Shareholders' Equity
		Cash	=	Notes Payable	+	Common Shares
	Old Balance	$10,000				$10,000
(2)		+5,000		+$5,000		
	New Balance	$15,000	=	$5,000	+	$10,000
				$15,000		

Observe that total assets are now $15,000 and shareholders' equity plus the new liability also total $15,000.

EVENT (3). PURCHASE OF OFFICE EQUIPMENT FOR CASH. On October 2, Sierra acquired office equipment by paying $5,000 cash to Superior Equipment Sales Corp. This event is a transaction because an equal increase and decrease in Sierra's assets occurs: Office Equipment (an asset) increases by $5,000 and Cash (an asset) decreases by $5,000

		Assets			=	Liabilities	+	Shareholders' Equity
		Cash	+	Office Equipment	=	Notes Payable	+	Common Shares
	Old Balance	$15,000				$5,000		$10,000
(3)		−5,000		+$5,000				
	New Balance	$10,000	+	$5,000	=	$5,000	+	$10,000
		$15,000				$15,000		

The total assets are now $15,000 and shareholders' equity plus the liability also total $15,000.

EVENT (4). RECEIPT OF CASH IN ADVANCE FROM CUSTOMER. On October 2, Sierra received a $1,200 cash advance from R. Knox, a client. This event is a transaction because cash (an asset) was received for advertising services that are expected to be completed by Sierra by December 31. However, revenue should not be recorded until the work has been performed. Since the cash was received prior to performance of the service, Sierra has a liability for the work due. Cash increases by $1,200 and a liability, Unearned Service Revenue (abbreviated as Unearned Revenue), increases by an equal amount.

		Assets			=	Liabilities			+	Shareholders' Equity
		Cash	+	Office Equipment	=	Notes Payable	+	Unearned Revenue	+	Common Shares
	Old Balance	$10,000		$5,000		$5,000				$10,000
(4)		+1,200						+$1,200		
	New Balance	$11,200	+	$5,000	=	$5,000	+	$1,200	+	$10,000
		$16,200				$16,200				

EVENT (5). SERVICES RENDERED FOR CASH. On October 3, Sierra received $10,000 in cash from Copa Company Ltd. for advertising services performed. This event is a transaction because Sierra received an asset, cash, in exchange for services. Advertising service is the principal revenue-producing activity of Sierra. **Revenue increases shareholders' equity.** Both assets and shareholders' equity are thus increased by this transaction. Cash is increased by $10,000, and Retained Earnings is increased by $10,000. The new balances in the equation are

		Assets			=	Liabilities			+	Shareholders' Equity			
		Cash	+	Office Equipment	=	Notes Payable	+	Unearned Revenue	+	Common Shares	+	Retained Earnings	
	Old Balance	$11,200		$5,000		$5,000		$1,200		$10,000			
(5)		+10,000										+$10,000	**Service revenue**
	New Balance	$21,200	+	$5,000	=	$5,000	+	$1,200	+	$10,000	+	$10,000	
		$26,200				$26,200							

Often companies provide services "on account." That is, they provide service for which they are paid at a later date. Revenue, however, is earned when services are performed. Therefore, shareholders' equity increases when services are performed, even though cash has not been received. Instead of receiving cash, the company receives a different type of asset, an account receivable. Accounts receivable represent the right to receive payment at a later date. Suppose that Sierra had provided these services on account rather than for cash. This event would be reported using the accounting equation as follows:

Assets	=	Liabilities	+	Shareholders' Equity	
Accounts Receivable				Retained Earnings	
+$10,000				+$10,000	**Service revenue**

Later, when the $10,000 is collected from the customer, Accounts Receivable would decline by $10,000, and Cash would increase by $10,000.

Assets		=	Liabilities	+	Shareholders' Equity
Cash	Accounts Receivable				
+$10,000	−$10,000				

Note that in this case, shareholders' equity is not affected by the collection of cash. Instead, we record an exchange of one asset (Accounts Receivable) for a different asset (Cash).

EVENT (6). PAYMENT OF RENT. On October 3, Sierra Corporation paid its office rent for the month of October in cash, $900. Rent is an expense incurred by Sierra Corporation in its effort to generate revenues. **Expenses decrease shareholders' equity.** This rent payment is a transaction because it results in a decrease in cash. It is recorded by decreasing cash and decreasing shareholders' equity (specifically, Retained Earnings) to maintain the balance of the accounting equation. To record this transaction, Cash is decreased by $900 and Retained Earnings is decreased by $900. The effect of these payments on the accounting equation is

	Assets		=	**Liabilities**		+	**Shareholders' Equity**		
	Cash	+ Office Equipment	=	Notes Payable	+ Unearned Revenue	+	Common Shares	+ Retained Earnings	
Old Balance	$21,200	$5,000		$5,000	$1,200		$10,000	$10,000	
(6)	−900							−900	**Rent expense**
New Balance	$20,300 +	$5,000	=	$5,000 +	$1,200	+	$10,000 +	$ 9,100	
	$25,300			$25,300					

EVENT (7). PURCHASE OF INSURANCE POLICY IN CASH. On October 4, Sierra paid $600 for a one-year insurance policy that will expire next year on September 30. This event is a transaction because one asset was exchanged for another. The asset Cash is decreased by $600. The asset Prepaid Insurance is increased by $600 because the payment extends to more than the current month; payments of expenses that will benefit more than one accounting period are identified as prepaid expenses or prepayments. Note that the balance in total assets did not change; one asset account decreased by the same amount that another increased.

		Assets			= Liabilities		+ Shareholders' Equity	
		Cash	Prepaid Insurance	Office Equipment	Notes Payable	Unearned Revenue	Common Shares	Retained Earnings
	Old Balance	$20,300		$5,000	$5,000	$1,200	$10,000	$9,100
(7)		−600	+$600					
	New Balance	$19,700	$600	$5,000	$5,000	$1,200	$10,000	$9,100
			$25,300			$25,300		

EVENT (8). PURCHASE OF SUPPLIES ON CREDIT. On October 5, Sierra purchased an estimated three-month supply of advertising materials on account from Aero Supply Corp. for $2,500. Assets are increased by this transaction because supplies represent a resource that will be used in the process of providing services to customers. Liabilities are increased by the amount due to Aero Supply. The asset Supplies is increased by $2,500, and the liability Accounts Payable is increased by the same amount. The effect on the equation is

		Assets				= Liabilities			+ Shareholders' Equity	
		Cash	Supplies	Prepaid Insurance	Office Equipment	Notes Payable	Accounts Payable	Unearned Revenue	Common Shares	Retained Earnings
	Old Balance	$19,700		$600	$5,000	$5,000		$1,200	$10,000	$9,100
(8)			+$2,500				+$2,500			
	New Balance	$19,700	$2,500	$600	$5,000	$5,000	$2,500	$1,200	$10,000	$9,100
				$27,800				$27,800		

EVENT (9). HIRING OF NEW EMPLOYEES. On October 9, Sierra hired four new employees to begin work on October 15. Each employee is to receive a weekly salary of $500 for a five-day work week, payable every two weeks. Employees are to receive their first paycheques on October 26. There is no effect on the accounting equation because the assets, liabilities, and shareholders' equity of the company have not changed. An accounting transaction has not occurred. At this point, there is only an agreement that the employees will begin work on October 15. (See Event (11) for the first payment.)

EVENT (10). PAYMENT OF CASH DIVIDEND. On October 20, Sierra paid a $500 dividend. Dividends are a distribution of retained earnings and not an expense. A cash dividend transaction affects assets and shareholders' equity: Cash and Retained Earnings are each decreased by $500.

		Assets				= Liabilities			+ Shareholders' Equity		
		Cash	Supplies	Prepaid Insurance	Office Equipment	Notes Payable	Accounts Payable	Unearned Revenue	Common Shares	Retained Earnings	
	Old Balance	$19,700	$2,500	$600	$5,000	$5,000	$2,500	$1,200	$10,000	$9,100	
(10)		−500								−500	Dividends
	New Balance	$19,200	$2,500	$600	$5,000	$5,000	$2,500	$1,200	$10,000	$8,600	
				$27,300				$27,300			

EVENT (11). PAYMENT OF CASH FOR EMPLOYEE SALARIES. Employees worked two weeks, earning $4,000 in salaries, and were paid on October 26. Salaries are an expense similar to rent because they are a cost of generating revenues. This event involving employees is a transaction because assets and shareholders' equity are affected, each by an equal amount. Thus, Cash and Retained Earnings are each decreased by $4,000.

	Assets				=	Liabilities			+	Shareholders' Equity		
	Cash	+ Supplies	+ Prepaid Insurance	+ Office Equipment	=	Notes Payable	+ Accounts Payable	+ Unearned Revenue	+	Common Shares	+ Retained Earnings	
Old Balance	$19,200	$2,500	$600	$5,000		$5,000	$2,500	$1,200		$10,000	$8,600	
(11)	−4,000										−4,000	Salaries expense
New Balance	$15,200	+ $2,500	+ $600	+ $5,000	=	$5,000	+ $2,500	+ $1,200	+	$10,000	+ $4,600	
	$23,300					$23,300						

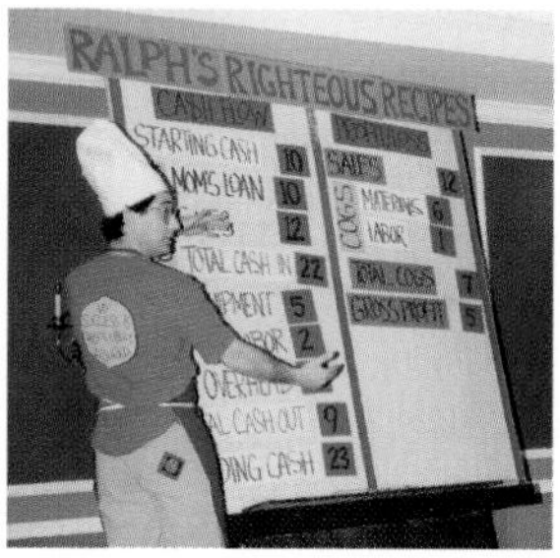

BUSINESS INSIGHT
Management Perspective

Many companies are finding that teaching their factory workers basic accounting skills can be a useful motivational tool. For example, Rhino Foods uses a financial reporting game to motivate its production line employees. Employees are taught the costs of each element of the production process, from raw materials to machinery malfunctions, so that they will make decisions that will benefit the company. The employees' bonus cheques (for managers as well as factory workers) are based on the results of the game. The owner, a former hockey coach, believes that his workers will work harder, and enjoy their work more, if they know what the score is.

SUMMARY OF TRANSACTIONS

The transactions of Sierra Corporation are summarized in Illustration 3-2 to show their cumulative effect on the basic accounting equation. The transaction number, the specific effects of the transaction, and the balances after each transaction are indicated. Remember that Event (9) did not result in a transaction, so no entry is included for that event. The illustration demonstrates three significant facts:

1. Each transaction is analysed in terms of its effect on assets, liabilities, and shareholders' equity.
2. The two sides of the equation must always be equal.
3. The cause of each change in shareholders' equity must be indicated.

	Assets				=	Liabilities			+ Shareholders' Equity		
	Cash	+ Supplies	+ Prepaid Insurance	+ Office Equipment	=	Notes Payable	+ Accounts Payable	+ Unearned Revenue	+ Common Shares	+ Retained Earnings	
(1)	+$10,000				=				+$10,000		Issued shares
(2)	+5,000					+$5,000					
	15,000					5,000			+ 10,000		
(3)	−5,000			+$5,000	=						
	10,000			+ 5,000	=	5,000			+ 10,000		
(4)	+1,200				=			+$1,200			
	11,200			+ 5,000	=	5,000		+ 1,200	+ 10,000		
(5)	+10,000									+$10,000	Service revenue
	21,200			+ 5,000	=	5,000		+ 1,200	+ 10,000	+ 10,000	
(6)	−900				=					−900	Rent expense
	20,300			+ 5,000	=	5,000		+ 1,200	+ 10,000	+ 9,100	
(7)	−600		+$600		=						
	19,700		+ 600	+ 5,000	=	5,000		+ 1,200	+ 10,000	+ 9,100	
(8)		+$2,500			=		+$2,500				
	19,700	+ 2,500	+ 600	+ 5,000	=	5,000	+ 2,500	+ 1,200	+ 10,000	+ 9,100	
(10)	−500									−500	Dividends
	19,200	+ 2,500	+ 600	+ 5,000	=	5,000	+ 2,500	+ 1,200	+ 10,000	+ 8,600	
(11)	−4,000									−4,000	Salaries expense
	$15,200	+ $2,500	+ $600	+ $5,000	=	$5,000	+ $2,500	+ $1,200	+ $10,000	+ $ 4,600	
	$23,300					$23,300					

Illustration 3-2
Summary of transactions

DECISION TOOLKIT

Decision Checkpoints	Info Needed for Decision	Tool to Use for Decision	How to Evaluate Results
Has an accounting transaction occurred?	Details of the event	Accounting equation	Determine the effect, if any, on assets, liabilities, and shareholders' equity.

The Account

STUDY OBJECTIVE 2

Explain what an account is and how it helps in the recording process.

Rather than use a tabular summary like the one in Illustration 3-2 for Sierra Corporation, an accounting information system uses accounts. An **account** is an individual accounting record of increases and decreases in a specific asset, liability, or shareholders' equity item. For example, Sierra Corporation has separate accounts for Cash, Accounts Receivable, Accounts Payable, Service Revenue, Salaries Expense, and so on. (Note that whenever we refer to a specific account, we capitalize the name.) In its simplest form, an account consists of three parts: (1) the title of the account, (2) a left or debit side, and (3) a right or credit side. Because the alignment of these parts of an account resembles the letter T, it is referred to as a **T account.** The basic form of an account is shown in Illustration 3-3.

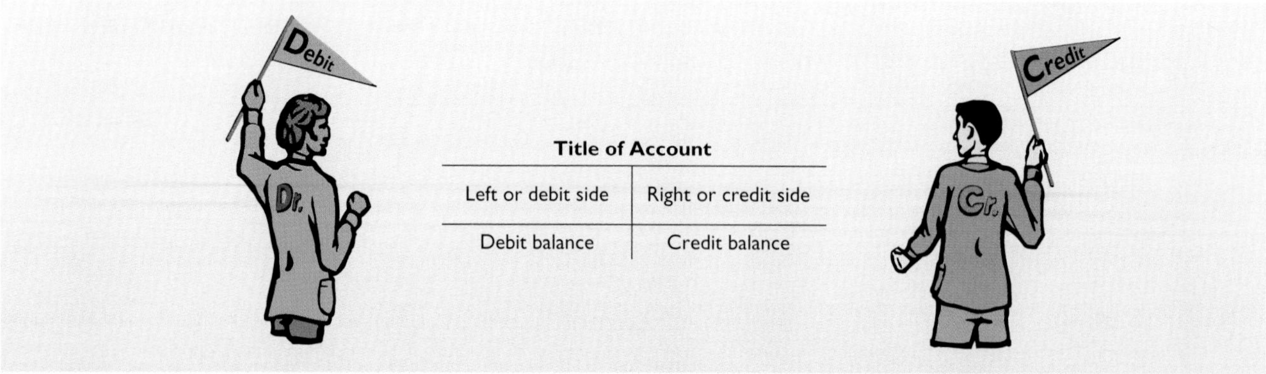

Illustration 3-3 Basic form of account

This form of account is used throughout this book to explain basic accounting relationships.

DEBITS AND CREDITS

STUDY OBJECTIVE 3

Define debits and credits and explain how they are used to record business transactions.

The terms "**debit**" and "**credit**" mean "left" and "right," respectively. They are commonly abbreviated as **Dr.** for debit and **Cr.** for credit. These terms **do not** mean "increase" or "decrease." The terms "debit" and "credit" are used repeatedly in the recording process to describe where entries are made in accounts. For example, the act of entering an amount on the left side of an account is called **debiting** the account, and making an entry on the right side is **crediting** the account. When the totals of the two sides are compared, an account will have a **debit balance** if the total of the debit amounts exceeds the credits. Conversely, an account will have a **credit balance** if the credit amounts exceed the debits. Note the position of the debit or credit balances in Illustration 3-3.

The procedure of recording debits and credits in an account is shown in Illustration 3-4 for the transactions affecting the Cash account of Sierra Corporation. The data are taken from the Cash column of the tabular summary in Illustration 3-2.

Illustration 3-4 Tabular summary and account form for Sierra Corporation's Cash account

Tabular Summary

Cash
$10,000
5,000
−5,000
1,200
10,000
−900
−600
−500
−4,000
$15,200

Account Form

Cash			
(Debits)	10,000	**(Credits)**	5,000
	5,000		900
	1,200		600
	10,000		500
			4,000
Balance **(Debit)**	15,200		

Every positive item in the tabular summary represents a receipt of cash; every negative amount represents a payment of cash. Notice that in the account form, the increases in cash are recorded as debits, and the decreases in cash are recorded as credits. Having increases on one side and decreases on the other reduces recording errors and helps in determining the totals of each side of the account as well as the balance in the account. The account balance, a debit of $15,200, indicates that Sierra Corporation had $15,200 more increases than decreases in cash (since it started with a balance of zero). That is, it has $15,200 in its Cash account.

DEBIT AND CREDIT PROCEDURES

Each transaction must affect two or more accounts to keep the basic accounting equation in balance. In other words, for each transaction, debits must equal credits. The equality of debits and credits provides the basis for the double-entry accounting system.

Under the universally used **double-entry system**, the dual (two-sided) effect of each transaction is recorded in appropriate accounts. This system provides a logical method for recording transactions. As was the case with discovering Fidelity's account error in the opening story, the double-entry system also offers a means of ensuring the accuracy of the recorded amounts. If every transaction is recorded with equal debits and credits, then the sum of all the debits to the accounts must equal the sum of all the credits. The double-entry system for determining the equality of the accounting equation is much more efficient than the plus/minus procedure used earlier. There, it was necessary after each transaction to compare total assets with total liabilities and shareholders' equity to determine the equality of the two sides of the accounting equation.

The following diagram provides you with an advance summary of the basic accounting equation, and the impact debits and credits have on it.

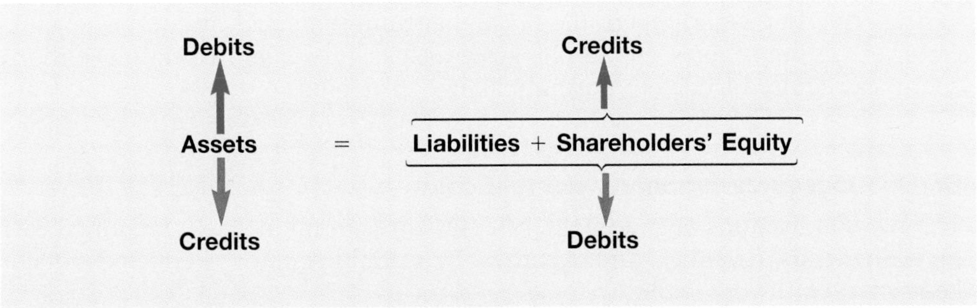

We will discuss each component of the accounting equation, with its debit and credit rules, in the following sections.

Dr./Cr. Procedures for Assets and Liabilities

In Illustration 3-4 for Sierra Corporation, increases in cash—an asset—were entered on the left side, and decreases in cash were entered on the right side. We know that both sides of the basic equation (Assets = Liabilities + Shareholders' Equity) must be equal; it therefore follows that increases and decreases in liabilities will have to be recorded *opposite from* increases and decreases in assets. Thus, increases in liabilities must be entered on the right or credit side, and decreases in liabilities must be entered on the left or debit side. The effects that debits and credits have on assets and liabilities are summarized in Illustration 3-5.

Illustration 3-5 Debit and credit effects—assets and liabilities

Debits	Credits
Increase assets	Decrease assets
Decrease liabilities	Increase liabilities

Asset accounts normally show debit balances; that is, debits to a specific asset account should exceed credits to that account. Likewise, liability accounts normally show credit balances; that is, credits to a liability account should exceed debits to that account. The normal balances may be diagrammed as in Illustration 3-6.

Illustration 3-6 Normal balances—assets and liabilities

Assets	
Increase Debit	Decrease Credit
Normal balance	

Liabilities	
Decrease Debit	Increase Credit
	Normal balance

Knowing which is the normal balance in an account may help when you are trying to trace errors. For example, a credit balance in an asset account such as Land or a debit balance in a liability account such as Wages Payable would indicate errors in recording. Occasionally, however, an abnormal balance may be correct. The Cash account, for example, will have a credit balance when a company has overdrawn its bank balance.

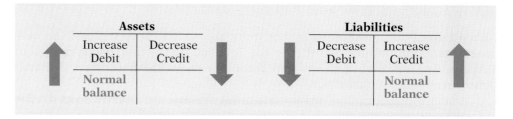

BUSINESS INSIGHT

Management Perspective

In automated accounting systems, the computer is programmed to flag violations of the normal account balances and to print out error or exception reports. In manual systems, careful visual inspection of the accounts is required to detect normal balance problems.

Dr./Cr. Procedures for Shareholders' Equity

The five subdivisions of shareholders' equity are common shares, retained earnings, dividends, revenues, and expenses. In a double-entry system, accounts are kept for each of these subdivisions.

Common Shares. Common shares are issued in exchange for the shareholders' investment. The Common Shares account is increased by credits and decreased by debits. For example, when cash is invested in the business, Cash is debited and Common Shares is credited. The effects of debits and credits on the Common Shares account are shown in Illustration 3-7.

Illustration 3-7 Debit and credit effects—Common Shares

Debits	Credits
Decrease Common Shares	Increase Common Shares

The normal balance in the Common Shares account may be diagrammed as in Illustration 3-8.

Illustration 3-8 Normal balance—Common Shares

Common Shares	
Decrease Debit	Increase Credit
	Normal balance

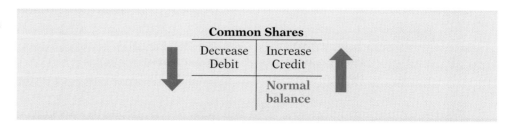

Sometimes another class of share capital, preferred shares, is issued. If so, the Preferred Shares account follows the same debit and credit rules illustrated here for the Common Shares account.

Retained Earnings. Retained Earnings is net earnings that are retained in the business. It represents the portion of shareholders' equity that has been accumulated through the profitable operation of the company and that has not been distributed to shareholders. Retained Earnings is increased by credits (for example, net earnings) and decreased by debits (for example, net losses), as shown in Illustration 3-9.

Illustration 3-9 Debit and credit effects—Retained Earnings

Debits	Credits
Decrease Retained Earnings	Increase Retained Earnings

The normal balance for Retained Earnings may be diagrammed as in Illustration 3-10.

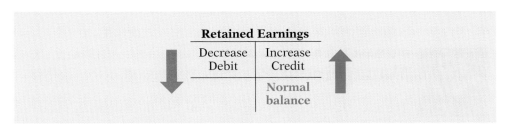

Illustration 3-10 Normal balance—Retained Earnings

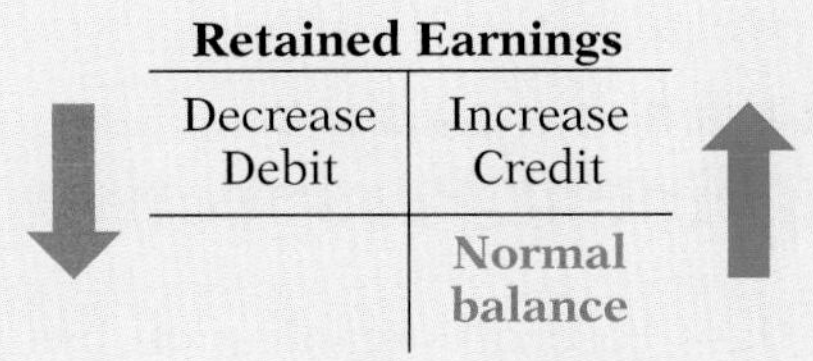

Dividends. A dividend is a distribution by a corporation to its shareholders of an amount proportional to each investor's percentage ownership. The most common form of distribution is a cash dividend. Dividends result in a reduction of the shareholders' claims on retained earnings. Because dividends reduce shareholders' equity, increases in the Dividends account are recorded with debits. Credits to the Dividends account are unusual, but might be used to correct a dividend recorded in error, for example. As shown in Illustration 3-11, the Dividends account normally has a debit balance.

Illustration 3-11 Normal balance—Dividends

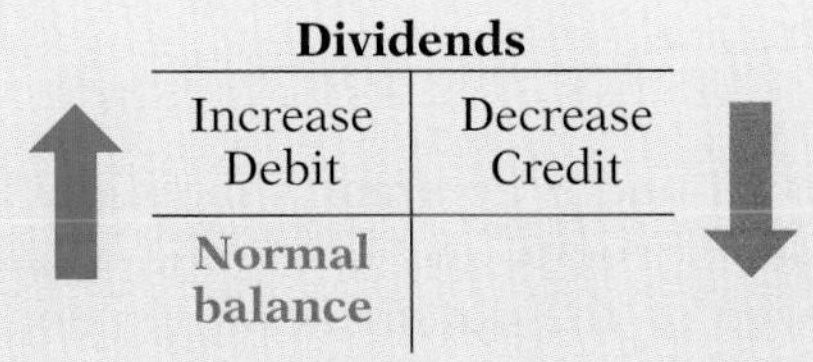

Revenues and Expenses. When revenues are earned, shareholders' equity is increased. Accordingly, **the effect of debits and credits on revenue accounts is identical to their effect on shareholders' equity**. Revenue accounts are increased by credits and decreased by debits.

On the other hand, **expenses decrease shareholders' equity**. As a result, expenses are recorded by debits. Since expenses are the negative factor in the calculation of earnings, and revenues are the positive factor, it is logical that the increase and decrease sides of expense accounts should be the reverse of revenue accounts. Thus, expense accounts are increased by debits and decreased by credits. The effects of debits and credits on revenues and expenses are shown in Illustration 3-12.

Illustration 3-12 Debit and credit effects—revenues and expenses

Debits	Credits
Decrease revenues	Increase revenues
Increase expenses	Decrease expenses

Credits to revenue accounts should exceed debits, and debits to expense accounts should exceed credits. Thus, revenue accounts normally show credit balances, and expense accounts normally show debit balances. The normal balances may be diagrammed as in Illustration 3-13.

Illustration 3-13 Normal balances—revenues and expenses

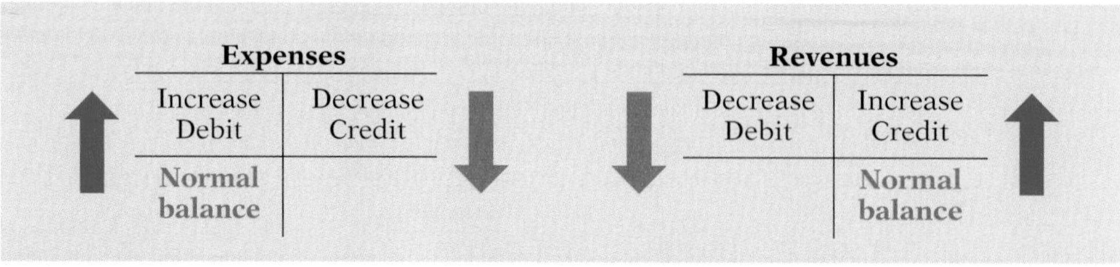

BUSINESS INSIGHT

Management Perspective

The Blue Jays baseball organization has the following major revenue and expense accounts:

Revenues	Expenses
Home admissions	Players' salaries
Radio, over-the-air television, and pay television	Team travel, lodging and meals
Concessions and publications	Team uniforms
Licensing royalties	Stadium rental
Stadium advertising	Game and other club promotions
Souvenir operations	Administration

SHAREHOLDERS' EQUITY RELATIONSHIPS

As indicated in Chapters 1 and 2, common shares and retained earnings are reported in the shareholders' equity section of the balance sheet. Dividends are reported and summarized on the statement of retained earnings. Revenues and expenses are summarized and reported on the statement of earnings as net earnings (or net loss), which is also reported on the statement of retained earnings. Dividends, revenues, and expenses are eventually transferred to retained earnings at the end of the period. As a result, a change in any one of these three items affects retained earnings, and ultimately shareholders' equity. The relationships among the accounts affecting shareholders' equity are shown in Illustration 3-14.

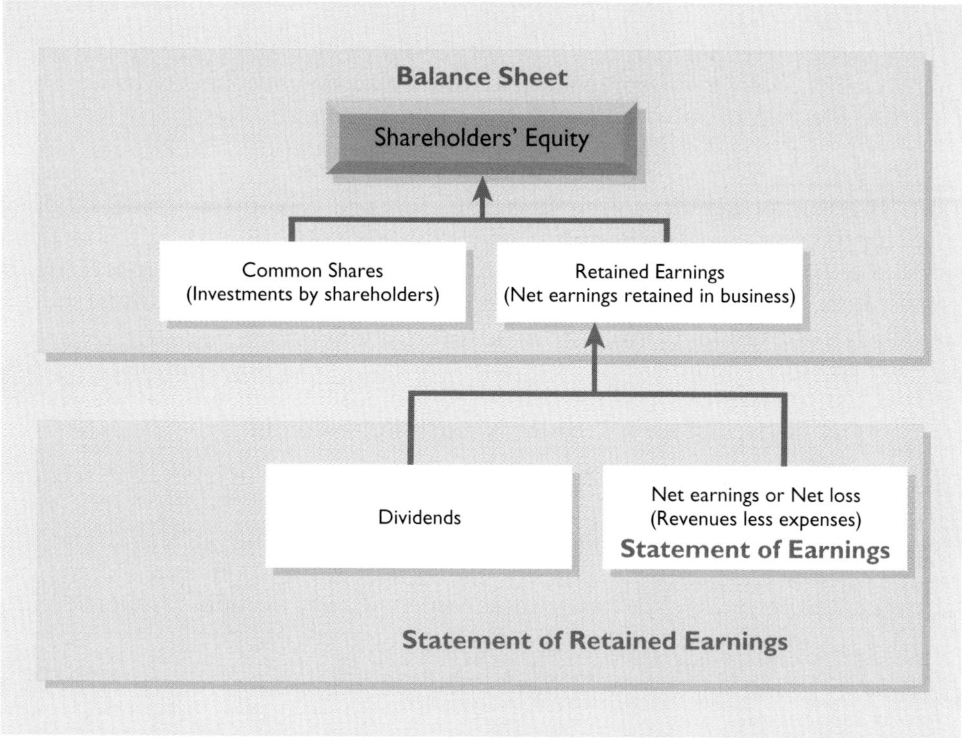

Illustration 3-14 Shareholders' equity relationships

EXPANSION OF THE BASIC EQUATION

You have already learned the basic accounting equation. Illustration 3-15 expands this equation to show the accounts that make up shareholders' equity. In addition, the debit/credit rules and effects on each type of account are illustrated. Study this diagram carefully. It will help you understand the fundamentals of the double-entry system. Like the basic equation, the expanded basic equation must be in balance: total debits must equal total credits.

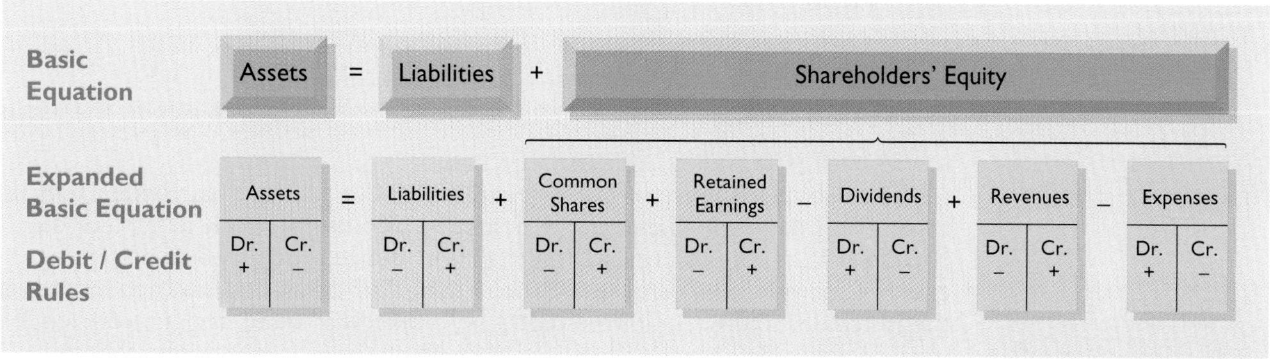

Illustration 3-15 Expansion of the basic accounting equation

BEFORE YOU GO ON . . .

Review It

1. What do the terms "debit" and "credit" mean?
2. What are the debit and credit effects on assets, liabilities, and shareholders' equity?

3. What are the debit and credit effects on revenues, expenses, and dividends?
4. What are the normal balances for Loblaw's Accounts Receivable, Taxes Payable, Sales, and Depreciation and Amortization accounts? The answer to this question is provided at the end of the chapter.

Loblaws
A passion for food... *and a lot more!*

Do It

Kate Browne, president of Hair It Is, Inc., has just rented space in a shopping mall for the purpose of opening and operating a beauty salon. Long before opening day and before purchasing equipment, hiring assistants, and remodelling the space, Kate is strongly advised to set up a double-entry set of accounting records in which to record all of her business transactions.

Identify the balance sheet accounts that Hair It Is, Inc. will likely need to record the transactions necessary to open for business. Also, indicate whether the normal balance of each account is a debit or a credit.

Reasoning: To start the business, Hair It Is, Inc. will need to have asset accounts for each different type of asset invested in the business. In addition, the corporation will need liability accounts for debts incurred by the business. Hair It Is, Inc. will need only one shareholders' equity account for common shares when it begins the business. The other shareholders' equity accounts (retained earnings) will be needed only after business has commenced.

Solution: Hair It Is, Inc. would likely need the following accounts in which to record the transactions that ready the beauty salon for opening day: Cash (debit balance); Equipment (debit balance); Supplies (debit balance); Accounts Payable (credit balance); Notes Payable (credit balance), if the business borrows money; and Common Shares (credit balance).

Steps in the Recording Process

STUDY OBJECTIVE 4

Identify the basic steps in the recording process.

Although it is possible to enter transaction information directly into the accounts, few businesses do so. Practically every business uses these basic steps in the recording process:

1. Analyse each transaction in terms of its effect on the accounts.
2. Enter the transaction information in a journal.
3. Transfer the journal information to the appropriate accounts in the ledger (book of accounts).

The actual sequence of events begins with the transaction. Evidence of the transaction comes in the form of a **source document**, such as a sales slip, a cheque, a bill, or a cash register tape. This evidence is analysed to determine the effect of the transaction on specific accounts. The transaction is then entered in the **journal**. Finally, the journal entry is transferred to the designated accounts in the **ledger**. The sequence of events in the recording process is shown in Illustration 3-16.

The Recording Process
JOURNAL
JOURNAL
LEDGER
Analyse each transaction
Enter transaction in a journal
Transfer journal information to ledger accounts

Illustration 3-16 The recording process

The basic steps in the recording process occur repeatedly in every business enterprise. While the analysis of transactions has already been illustrated, more examples of this step are given in this and later chapters. The other steps in the recording process are explained in the next sections.

THE JOURNAL

STUDY OBJECTIVE 5

Explain what a journal is and how it helps in the recording process.

Transactions are initially recorded in chronological order in a **journal** before they are transferred to the accounts. For each transaction, the journal shows the debit and credit effects on specific accounts. Companies may use various kinds of journals, but every company has the most basic form of journal, a **general journal**. The journal makes three significant contributions to the recording process:

1. It discloses the complete effect of a transaction in one place.
2. It provides a chronological record of transactions.
3. It helps to prevent or locate errors, because the debit and credit amounts for each entry can be readily compared.

Entering transaction data in the journal is known as **journalizing**. To illustrate the technique of journalizing, let's look at the first three transactions of Sierra Corporation. These transactions were (1) October 1, common shares were issued in exchange for $10,000 cash; (2) October 1, $5,000 was borrowed by signing a note; and (3) October 2, office equipment was purchased for $5,000. In equation form, these transactions appeared in our earlier discussion as follows:

Assets	=	**Liabilities**	+	**Shareholders' Equity**	
Cash	=			Common Shares	
+$10,000				+$10,000	Issued shares

Assets	=	**Liabilities**	+	**Shareholders' Equity**
Cash	=	Notes Payable		
+$5,000		+$5,000		

Assets		=	**Liabilities**	+	**Shareholders' Equity**
Cash	Office Equipment				
−$5,000	+$5,000				

Separate journal entries are made for each transaction. A complete entry consists of: (1) the date of the transaction, (2) the accounts and amounts to be debited and credited, and (3) a brief explanation of the transaction. These transactions would be recorded in the journal as in Illustration 3-17.

Illustration 3-17
Recording transactions in journal form

A = L + SE
+10,000 +10,000

A = L + SE
+5,000 +5,000

A = L + SE
+5,000
−5,000

GENERAL JOURNAL

Date		Account Titles and Explanation	Debit	Credit
2001				
Oct.	1	Cash	10,000	
		Common Shares		10,000
		(Invested cash in business)		
	1	Cash	5,000	
		Notes Payable		5,000
		(Issued three-month, 12% note payable for cash)		
	2	Office Equipment	5,000	
		Cash		5,000
		(Purchased office equipment for cash)		

Note the following features of the journal entries:

In the margins next to key journal entries are **equation analyses** that summarize the effect of the transaction on the three elements of the accounting equation.

1. The date of the transaction is entered in the Date column.
2. The account to be debited is entered first at the left. The account to be credited is then entered on the next line, indented under the line above. The indentation differentiates debits from credits and decreases the possibility of switching the debit and credit amounts.
3. The amounts for the debits are recorded in the Debit (left) column, and the amounts for the credits are recorded in the Credit (right) column.
4. A brief explanation of the transaction is given.

It is important to use correct and specific account titles in journalizing. Since most accounts appear later in the financial statements, erroneous account titles lead to incorrect financial statements. Some flexibility exists when first selecting account titles. The main criterion is that each title appropriately describes the content of the account. For example, a company could use any of these account titles for recording the cost of delivery trucks: Delivery Equipment, Delivery Trucks, or Trucks. Once the company chooses the specific title to use, however, all subsequent transactions involving the account should be recorded under that account title.

BEFORE YOU GO ON . . .

Review It

1. What is the correct sequence of steps in the recording process?
2. What contribution does the journal make to the recording process?
3. What are the standard form and content of a journal entry made in the general journal?

Do It

The following events occurred during the first month of business of Hair It Is, Inc., Kate Browne's beauty salon:

1. Issued common shares to shareholders in exchange for $20,000 cash
2. Purchased $4,800 of equipment on account (to be paid in 30 days)
3. Interviewed three people for the position of beautician

(a) In what document (type of record) should the company record these three activities?
(b) Prepare the entries to record the transactions.

Reasoning: Kate should record the transactions in a journal, which is a chronological record of the transactions. The record should be a complete and accurate representation of the transactions' effects on the assets, liabilities, and shareholders' equity of her business.

Solution:
(a) Each transaction that is recorded is entered in the general journal.
(b) The three activities are recorded as follows:

1. Cash	20,000	
Common Shares		20,000
(Invested cash in the business)		
2. Equipment	4,800	
Accounts Payable		4,800
(Purchased equipment on account)		
3. No entry because no transaction occurred		

THE LEDGER

STUDY OBJECTIVE 6
Explain what a ledger is and how it helps in the recording process.

The entire group of accounts maintained by a company is referred to collectively as the **ledger**. The ledger keeps all the information about changes in specific account balances in one place.

Companies may use various kinds of ledgers, but every company has a general ledger. A **general ledger** contains all the assets, liabilities, and shareholders' equity accounts, as shown in Illustration 3-18. A business can use a loose-leaf binder or card file for the ledger, with each account kept on a separate sheet or card. Most businesses today, however, use a computer disk or hard drive as the ledger. Whenever the term "ledger" is used in this textbook without additional specification, it will mean the general ledger.

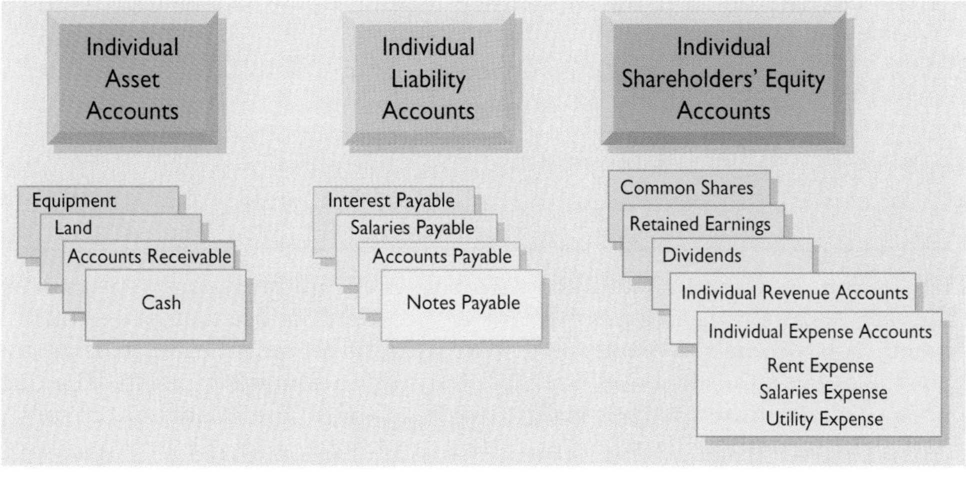

Illustration 3-18 The general ledger

CHART OF ACCOUNTS

The number and type of accounts used differ for each company, depending on the size, complexity, and type of business. For example, the number of accounts depends on the amount of detail desired by management. The management of one company may want one single account for all types of utility expense. Another may keep separate expense accounts for each type of utility expenditure, such as gas, electricity, and water. Similarly, a small corporation like Sierra Corporation will not have many accounts compared with a corporate giant like Magna International Inc. Sierra may be able to manage and report its activities in 20 to 30 accounts, whereas Magna requires thousands of accounts to keep track of its worldwide activities.

Most companies list the accounts in a **chart of accounts**. The chart of accounts for Sierra Corporation is shown in Illustration 3-19. Accounts shown in red are used in this chapter; accounts shown in black are explained in later chapters. New accounts may be created as needed during the life of the business.

SIERRA CORPORATION—CHART OF ACCOUNTS

Assets	Liabilities	Shareholders' Equity	Revenues	Expenses
Cash	**Notes Payable**	**Common Shares**	**Service Revenue**	**Salaries Expense**
Accounts Receivable	**Accounts Payable**	**Retained Earnings**		Supplies Expense
Supplies	Interest Payable	**Dividends**		**Rent Expense**
Prepaid Insurance	**Unearned Service Revenue**	Income Summary		Insurance Expense
Office Equipment	Salaries Payable			Interest Expense
Accumulated Amortization—Office Equipment				Amortization Expense

Illustration 3-19 Chart of accounts for Sierra Corporation

POSTING

The procedure of transferring journal entries to ledger accounts is called **posting**. **This phase of the recording process accumulates the effects of journalized transactions in the individual accounts.** Posting involves these steps:

1. In the ledger, enter in the appropriate columns of the debited account(s) the date and debit amount shown in the journal.
2. In the ledger, enter in the appropriate columns of the credited account(s) the date and credit amount shown in the journal.

THE RECORDING PROCESS ILLUSTRATED

STUDY OBJECTIVE 7

Explain what posting is and how it helps in the recording process.

Illustrations 3-20 through 3-30 show the basic steps in the recording process using the October transactions of Sierra Corporation. Its accounting period is a month. A basic analysis and a debit–credit analysis precede the journalizing and posting of each transaction. Study these transaction analyses carefully. **The purpose of transaction analysis is first to identify the type of account involved and then to determine whether a debit or a credit to the account is required.** You should always perform this type of analysis before preparing a journal entry. Doing so will help you understand the journal entries discussed in this chapter as well as more complex journal entries described in later chapters.

Illustration 3-20 Investment of cash by shareholders

Transaction

October 1: shareholders invest $10,000 cash in an advertising venture to be known as Sierra Corporation.

Basic Analysis

The asset Cash is increased by $10,000, and shareholders' equity (specifically Common Shares) is increased by $10,000.

Equation Analysis

	Assets	=	Liabilities	+	Shareholders' Equity
	Cash	=			Common Shares
(1)	+$10,000				+$10,000 Issued shares

Debit–Credit Analysis

Debits increase assets: debit Cash $10,000.
Credits increase shareholders' equity: credit Common Shares $10,000.

Journal Entry

Oct. 1	Cash		10,000	
	Common Shares			10,000
	(Invested cash in business)			

Posting

Cash	
Oct. 1 10,000	

Common Shares	
	Oct. 1 10,000

Illustration 3-21 Issue of note payable

Transaction

October 1: cash of $5,000 is received by signing a three-month, 12%, $5,000 note payable.

Basic Analysis

The asset Cash is increased by $5,000, and the liability Notes Payable is increased by $5,000.

Equation Analysis

	Assets	=	Liabilities	+	Shareholders' Equity
	Cash	=	Notes Payable		
(2)	+$5,000		+$5,000		

Debit–Credit Analysis

Debits increase assets: debit Cash $5,000.
Credits increase liabilities: credit Notes Payable $5,000.

Journal Entry

Oct. 1	Cash		5,000	
	Notes Payable			5,000
	(Issued three-month, 12% note payable for cash)			

Posting

Cash	
Oct. 1 10,000	
1 5,000	

Notes Payable	
	Oct. 1 5,000

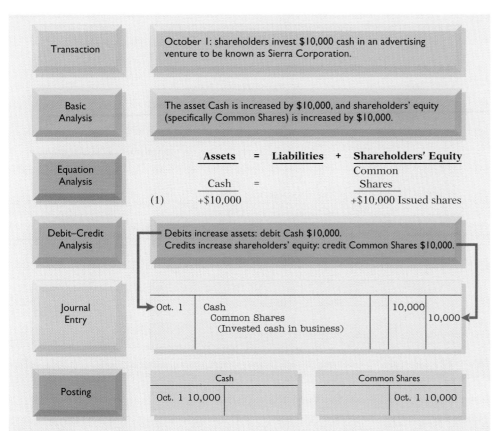

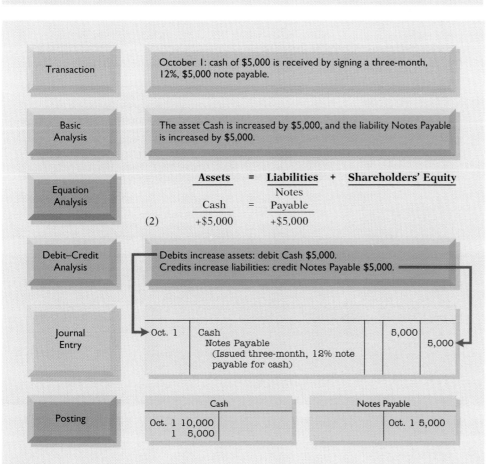

Illustration 3-22 Purchase of office equipment

Transaction

October 2: used $5,000 cash to purchase office equipment.

Basic Analysis

The asset Office Equipment is increased by $5,000; the asset Cash is decreased by $5,000.

Equation Analysis

	Assets		=	Liabilities	+	Shareholders' Equity
	Cash	+ Office Equipment				
(3)	−$5,000	+$5,000				

Debit–Credit Analysis

Debits increase assets: debit Office Equipment $5,000.
Credits decrease assets: credit Cash $5,000.

Journal Entry

Oct. 2	Office Equipment		5,000	
	Cash			5,000
	(Purchased office equipment for cash)			

Posting

Cash		Office Equipment	
Oct. 1 10,000	Oct. 2 5,000	Oct. 2 5,000	
1 5,000			

Illustration 3-23 Receipt of cash in advance from customer

Transaction

October 2: a $1,200 cash advance is received from R. Knox, a client, for advertising services that are expected to be completed by December 31.

Basic Analysis

The asset Cash is increased by $1,200; the liability Unearned Service Revenue is increased by $1,200 because the service has not been rendered yet. That is, when an advance payment is received, an unearned revenue (a liability) should be recorded in order to recognize the obligation that exists. Note also that although many liabilities have the word "payable" in their title, Unearned Service Revenue is considered a liability even though the word "payable" is not used.

Equation Analysis

	Assets	=	Liabilities	+	Shareholders' Equity
	Cash	=	Unearned Serv. Rev.		
(4)	+$1,200		+$1,200		

Debit–Credit Analysis

Debits increase assets: debit Cash $1,200.
Credits increase liabilities: credit Unearned Service Revenue $1,200.

Journal Entry

Oct. 2	Cash		1,200	
	Unearned Service Revenue			1,200
	(Received advance from R. Knox for future service)			

Posting

Cash		Unearned Service Revenue	
Oct. 1 10,000	Oct. 2 5,000		Oct. 2 1,200
1 5,000			
2 1,200			

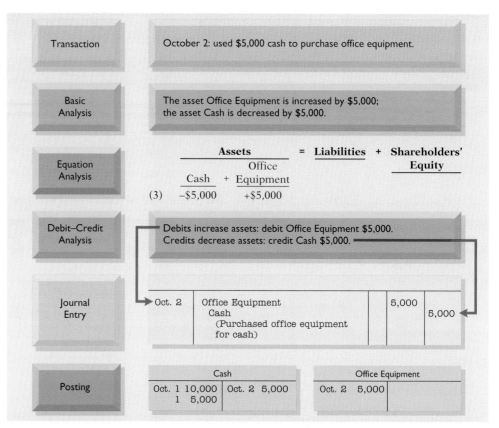

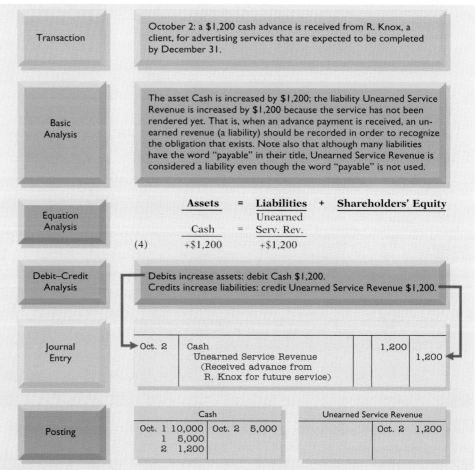

Illustration 3-24
Services rendered for cash

Transaction
October 3: received $10,000 in cash from Copa Company for advertising services rendered in October.

Basic Analysis
The asset Cash is increased $10,000; the revenue Service Revenue is increased $10,000.

Equation Analysis

	Assets	=	Liabilities	+	Shareholders' Equity
	Cash	=			Retained Earnings
(5)	+$10,000				+$10,000 Service revenue

Debit – Credit Analysis
Debits increase assets: debit Cash $10,000.
Credits increase revenues: credit Service Revenue $10,000.

Journal Entry

Oct. 3	Cash		10,000	
	Service Revenue			10,000
	(Received cash for services rendered)			

Posting

Cash

Oct. 1	10,000	Oct. 2	5,000
1	5,000		
2	1,200		
3	10,000		

Service Revenue

		Oct. 3	10,000

Illustration 3-25
Payment of rent in cash

Transaction
October 3: office rent for October is paid in cash, $900.

Basic Analysis
The expense Rent Expense is increased by $900 because the payment pertains only to the current month; the asset Cash is decreased by $900.

Equation Analysis

	Assets	=	Liabilities	+	Shareholders' Equity
	Cash	=			Retained Earnings
(6)	–$900				–$900 Rent expense

Debit–Credit Analysis
Debits increase expenses: debit Rent Expense $900.
Credits decrease assets: credit Cash $900.

Journal Entry

Oct. 3	Rent Expense		900	
	Cash			900
	(Paid cash for October office rent)			

Posting

Cash

Oct. 1	10,000	Oct. 2	5,000
1	5,000	3	900
2	1,200		
3	10,000		

Rent Expense

Oct. 3	900		

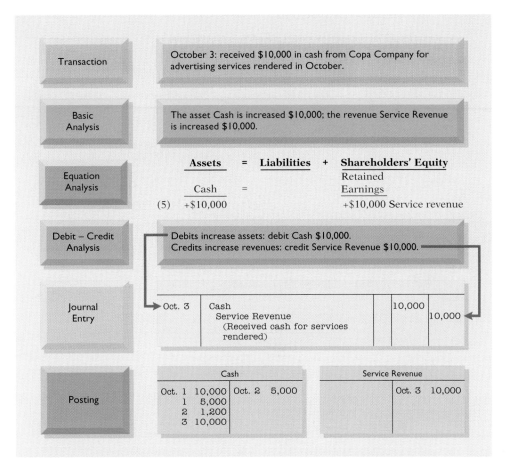

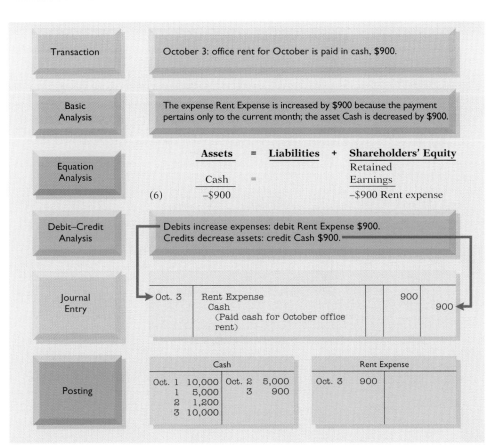

Illustration 3-26
Purchase of insurance policy in cash

Transaction

October 4: $600 is paid for a one-year insurance policy that will expire next year on September 30.

Basic Analysis

The asset Prepaid Insurance is increased by $600 because the payment extends to more than the current month; the asset Cash is decreased by $600. Note that payments of expenses that will benefit more than one accounting period are identified as prepaid expenses or prepayments. When a payment is made, an asset account is debited in order to show the service or benefit that will be received in the future

Equation Analysis

	Assets		= Liabilities	+ Shareholders' Equity
	Cash	+ Prepaid Insurance		
(7)	−$600	+$600		

Debit–Credit Analysis

Debits increase assets: debit Prepaid Insurance $600.
Credits decrease assets: credit Cash $600.

Journal Entry

Date	Account		Debit	Credit
Oct. 4	Prepaid Insurance		600	
	Cash			600
	(Paid one-year policy; effective date October 1)			

Posting

Cash			
Oct. 1	10,000	Oct. 2	5,000
1	5,000	3	900
2	1,200	4	600
3	10,000		

Prepaid Insurance			
Oct. 4	600		

Illustration 3-27
Purchase of supplies on credit

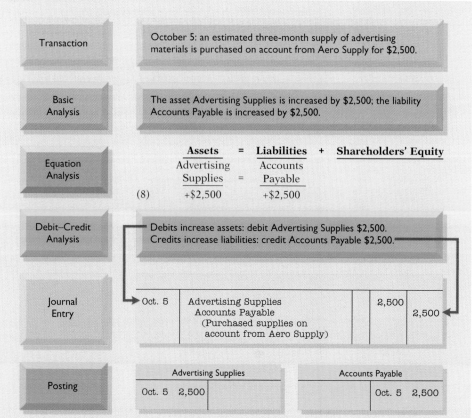

Transaction

October 5: an estimated three-month supply of advertising materials is purchased on account from Aero Supply for $2,500.

Basic Analysis

The asset Advertising Supplies is increased by $2,500; the liability Accounts Payable is increased by $2,500.

Equation Analysis

	Assets	=	Liabilities	+ Shareholders' Equity
	Advertising Supplies	=	Accounts Payable	
(8)	+$2,500		+$2,500	

Debit–Credit Analysis

Debits increase assets: debit Advertising Supplies $2,500.
Credits increase liabilities: credit Accounts Payable $2,500.

Journal Entry

Date	Account		Debit	Credit
Oct. 5	Advertising Supplies		2,500	
	Accounts Payable			2,500
	(Purchased supplies on account from Aero Supply)			

Posting

Advertising Supplies			
Oct. 5	2,500		

Accounts Payable			
		Oct. 5	2,500

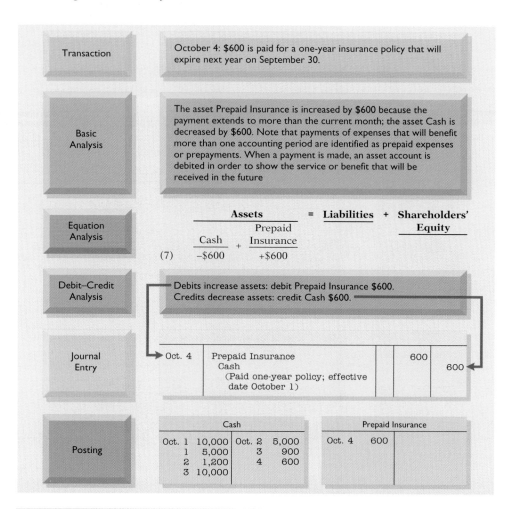

Illustration 3-28 Hiring of new employees

Transaction

October 9: hired four employees to begin work on October 15. Each employee is to receive a weekly salary of $500 for a five-day work week, payable every two weeks—first payment made on October 26.

Basic Analysis

An accounting transaction has not occurred. There is only an agreement that the employees will begin work on October 15. Thus, a debit–credit analysis is not needed because there is no accounting entry. (See transaction of October 26 for first entry.)

Illustration 3-29 Payment of dividend

Transaction

October 20: the board of directors declares and pays a $500 cash dividend to shareholders.

Basic Analysis

The Dividends account is increased by $500; the asset Cash is decreased by $500.

Equation Analysis

	Assets	=	Liabilities	+	Shareholders' Equity
	Cash	=			Retained Earnings
(10)	−$500				−$500 Dividends

Debit–Credit Analysis

Debits increase dividends: debit Dividends $500.
Credits decrease assets: credit Cash $500.

Journal Entry

Oct. 20	Dividends		500	
	Cash			500
	(Declared and paid a cash dividend)			

Posting

Cash			
Oct. 1	10,000	Oct. 2	5,000
1	5,000	3	900
2	1,200	4	600
3	10,000	20	500

Dividends		
Oct. 20	500	

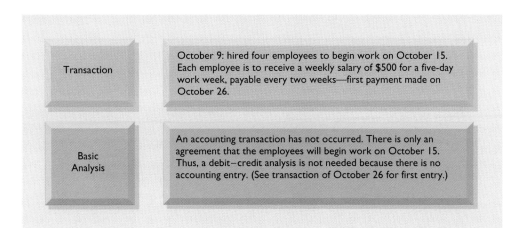

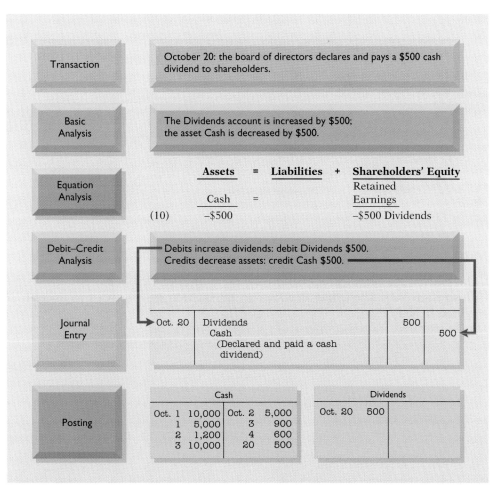

Illustration 3-30
Payment of cash for employee salaries

Transaction
October 26: employee salaries of $4,000 are paid in cash. (See October 9 transaction.)

Basic Analysis
The expense account Salaries Expense is increased by $4,000; the asset Cash is decreased by $4,000.

Equation Analysis

	Assets	=	Liabilities	+	Shareholders' Equity
	Cash	=			Retained Earnings
(11)	−$4,000				−$4,000 Salaries expense

Debit–Credit Analysis
Debits increase expenses: debit Salaries Expense $4,000.
Credits decrease assets: credit Cash $4,000.

Journal Entry

Oct. 26	Salaries Expense		4,000	
	Cash			4,000
	(Paid salaries to date)			

Posting

Cash

Oct. 1	10,000	Oct. 2	5,000
1	5,000	3	900
2	1,200	4	600
3	10,000	20	500
		26	4,000

Salaries Expense

Oct. 26	4,000	

SUMMARY ILLUSTRATION OF JOURNALIZING AND POSTING

The journal for Sierra Corporation for the month of October is summarized in Illustration 3-31. The ledger is shown in Illustration 3-32 with all balances highlighted in red.

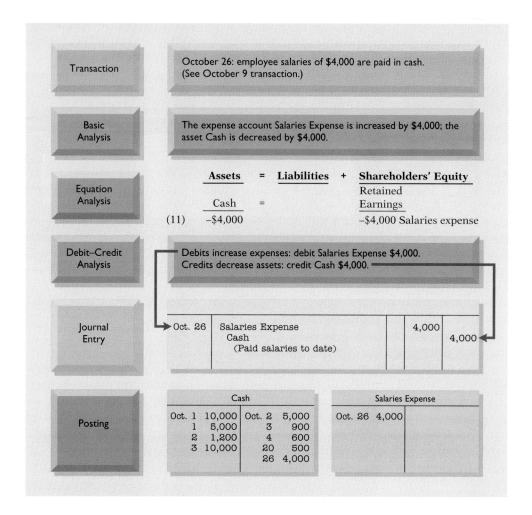

Illustration 3-31
General journal for Sierra Corporation

GENERAL JOURNAL

Date		Account Titles and Explanation	Debit	Credit
2001				
Oct.	1	Cash	10,000	
		Common Shares		10,000
		(Invested cash in business)		
	1	Cash	5,000	
		Notes Payable		5,000
		(Issued three-month, 12% note payable for cash)		
	2	Office Equipment	5,000	
		Cash		5,000
		(Purchased office equipment for cash)		
	2	Cash	1,200	
		Unearned Service Revenue		1,200
		(Received advance from R. Knox for future service)		
	3	Cash	10,000	
		Service Revenue		10,000
		(Received cash for services rendered)		
	3	Rent Expense	900	
		Cash		900
		(Paid cash for October office rent)		
	4	Prepaid Insurance	600	
		Cash		600
		(Paid one-year policy; effective date October 1)		
	5	Advertising Supplies	2,500	
		Accounts Payable		2,500
		(Purchased supplies on account from Aero Supply)		
	20	Dividends	500	
		Cash		500
		(Declared and paid a cash dividend)		
	26	Salaries Expense	4,000	
		Cash		4,000
		(Paid salaries to date)		

Illustration 3-32
General ledger for Sierra Corporation

GENERAL LEDGER

Cash

Oct. 1	10,000	Oct. 2	5,000
1	5,000	3	900
2	1,200	4	600
3	10,000	20	500
		26	4,000
Bal.	**15,200**		

Unearned Service Revenue

		Oct. 2	1,200
		Bal.	**1,200**

Advertising Supplies

Oct. 5	2,500		
Bal.	**2,500**		

Common Shares

		Oct. 1	10,000
		Bal.	**10,000**

Prepaid Insurance

Oct. 4	600		
Bal.	**600**		

Dividends

Oct. 20	500		
Bal.	**500**		

Office Equipment

Oct. 2	5,000		
Bal.	**5,000**		

Service Revenue

		Oct. 3	10,000
		Bal.	**10,000**

Notes Payable

		Oct. 1	5,000
		Bal.	**5,000**

Salaries Expense

Oct. 26	4,000		
Bal.	**4,000**		

Accounts Payable

		Oct. 5	2,500
		Bal.	**2,500**

Rent Expense

Oct. 3	900		
Bal.	**900**		

BEFORE YOU GO ON . . .

Review It

1. How does journalizing differ from posting?
2. What is the purpose of (a) the ledger and (b) a chart of accounts?

Do It

In the week following her successful grand opening of Hair It Is, Inc., Kate Browne collected $2,280 in cash for hair styling services, and she paid $400 in wages and $92 for utilities. Kate recorded these transactions in a general journal and posted the entries to the general ledger. Explain the purpose and process of journalizing and posting these transactions.

Reasoning: Every business must keep track of its financial activities (receipts, payments, receivables, payables, etc.); journalizing does this. However, just recording every transaction in chronological order does not make the entries useful. To be useful, the entries need to be classified and summarized; posting the entries to specific ledger accounts does this.

Solution: The purpose of journalizing is to record every transaction in chronological order. Journalizing involves dating every transaction, measuring the dollar amount of each transaction, identifying or labelling each amount with account titles, and recording in a standard format equal debits and credits. Posting involves transferring the journalized debits and credits to specific accounts in the ledger.

THE TRIAL BALANCE

STUDY OBJECTIVE 8

Explain the purposes of a trial balance.

A **trial balance** is a list of accounts and their balances at a given time. It is usually prepared at the end of an accounting period. The accounts are listed in the order in which they appear in the ledger, with debit balances listed in the left column and credit balances in the right column. The totals of the two columns must be equal.

The primary purpose of a trial balance is to prove the mathematical equality of debits and credits after posting. Under the double-entry system this equality will occur when the sum of the debit account balances equals the sum of the credit account balances. **A trial balance also uncovers errors in journalizing and posting.** For example, a trial balance may well have facilitated detection of the error at Fidelity Investments discussed in the opening story. **In addition, a trial balance is useful in the preparation of financial statements**, as explained in the next chapter. The procedure for preparing a trial balance follows:

International Note

In Canada, trial balances can vary in format. For example, some companies sequence accounts in financial statement order; others in alphabetical order. In some other countries, such as the Czech Republic and Luxembourg, the format of the trial balance is prescribed and must be strictly adhered to.

1. List the account titles and their balances.
2. Total the debit and credit columns.
3. Verify the equality of the two columns.

The trial balance prepared from the ledger of Sierra Corporation is presented in Illustration 3-33. Note that the total debits, \$28,700, equal the total credits, \$28,700.

Illustration 3-33 Sierra Corporation trial balance

SIERRA CORPORATION
Trial Balance
October 31, 2001

	Debit	Credit
Cash	\$15,200	
Advertising Supplies	2,500	
Prepaid Insurance	600	
Office Equipment	5,000	
Notes Payable		\$ 5,000
Accounts Payable		2,500
Unearned Service Revenue		1,200
Common Shares		10,000
Dividends	500	
Service Revenue		10,000
Salaries Expense	4,000	
Rent Expense	900	
	\$28,700	\$28,700

LIMITATIONS OF A TRIAL BALANCE

A trial balance does not prove that all transactions have been recorded or that the ledger is correct. Numerous errors may exist even though the trial balance columns agree. For example, the trial balance may balance even when (1) a transaction is not journalized, (2) a correct journal entry is not posted, (3) a journal entry is posted twice, (4) incorrect accounts are used in journalizing or posting, or (5) offsetting errors are made in recording the amount of a transaction. In other words, as long as equal debits and credits are posted, even to the wrong account or in the wrong amount, the total debits will equal the total credits. Nevertheless, despite its limitations, the trial balance is a useful screen for finding errors and is frequently used in practice.

BEFORE YOU GO ON . . .

Review It

1. What is a trial balance and how is it prepared?
2. What is the primary purpose of a trial balance?
3. What are the limitations of a trial balance?

DECISION TOOLKIT

Decision Checkpoints	Info Needed for Decision	Tool to Use for Decision	How to Evaluate Results
How do you determine that debits equal credits?	All account balances	Trial balance	List the account titles and their balances; total the debit and credit columns; verify equality.

USING THE DECISION TOOLKIT

Prairie Grain Growers (PGG) Limited is an agri-business company. PGG's trial balance (which should balance but doesn't) follows. Accounts are listed in alphabetical order.

PRAIRIE GRAIN GROWERS LIMITED
Trial Balance
For the Year Ended July 31, 2002

	Debit	Credit
Accounts payable and accrued expenses		$ 102,171
Accounts receivable and prepaid expenses	$ 92,548	
Amortization expense	25,787	
Bank and other loans		11,694
Capital assets	280,442	
Cash	26,421	
Cost of goods sold	1,623,088	
Current portion of long-term debt		64
Dividends	5,301	
Dividends payable		5,301
Income tax expense	4,492	
Interest expense	13,569	
Inventories	109,168	
Long-term debt		360,894
Operating, general, and administrative expenses	161,804	
Other assets	28,401	
Retained earnings		75,924
Sales and revenue from services		1,832,315
Short-term deposits—The Canadian Wheat Board	9,842	
Totals	$2,380,863	$2,388,363

After checking with various people responsible for entering accounting data, you discover the following:

1. The purchase of a forklift, costing $7,000 and paid for with cash, was not recorded.
2. A data entry clerk accidentally deleted the account name for an account with a credit balance of $158,984, so the amount was added to the Long-Term Debt account in the trial balance.
3. July sales revenue on account of $7,500 was credited to the Sales and Revenue from Services account, but the other half of the entry was not made.
4. $5,000 of operating expenses were mistakenly charged to Amortization Expense.

Instructions

(a) Which mistake or mistakes have caused the trial balance to be out of balance?

(b) Should all of the items be corrected? Explain.

(c) What is the likely name of the account the data entry clerk deleted?
(d) Make the necessary corrections and balance the trial balance.
(e) On your trial balance, write B beside the accounts that should be shown on the balance sheet, E beside those that should be shown on the statement of earnings, and RE beside those that should be shown on the statement of retained earnings.

Solution

(a) Only mistake 3 has caused the trial balance to be out of balance.
(b) All of the items should be corrected. The misclassification error (mistake 4) on the amortization expense would not affect bottom line net earnings, but it does affect the amounts reported in the two expense accounts.
(c) There is no Common Shares account, so that must be the account that was deleted by the data entry clerk.
(d) and (e). Note that the trial balance is dated "for the year ended July 31, 2002." Trial balances are normally dated as at a specific point in time, as shown in the solution. Also note that the Retained Earnings balance included in the trial balance is the beginning balance. Therefore, it would be included in the statement of retained earnings as part of the calculation of the ending Retained Earnings balance. The ending Retained Earnings balance is included in the balance sheet.

PRAIRIE GRAIN GROWERS LIMITED
Trial Balance
July 31, 2000

	Debit	Credit	
Accounts payable and accrued expenses		$ 102,171	B
Accounts receivable and prepaid expenses ($92,548 + $7,500)	$ 100,048		B
Amortization expense ($25,787 – $5,000)	20,787		E
Bank and other loans payable		11,694	B
Capital assets ($280,442 + $7,000)	287,442		B
Cash ($26,421 – $7,000)	19,421		B
Common shares		158,984	B
Cost of goods sold	1,623,088		E
Current portion of long-term debt		64	B
Dividends	5,301		RE
Dividends payable		5,301	B
Income tax expense	4,492		E
Interest expense	13,569		E
Inventories	109,168		B
Long-term debt ($360,894 – $158,984)		201,910	B
Operating, general, and administrative expenses ($161,804 + $5,000)	166,804		E
Other assets	28,401		B
Retained earnings		75,924	RE
Sales and revenue from services		1,832,315	E
Short-term deposits—The Canadian Wheat Board	9,842		B
Totals	$2,388,363	$2,388,363	

Summary of Study Objectives

❶ ***Analyse the effect of business transactions on the basic accounting equation.*** Each business transaction must have a dual effect on the accounting equation. For example, if an individual asset is increased, there must be a corresponding (a) decrease in another asset, or (b) increase in a specific liability, or (c) increase in shareholders' equity.

❷ ***Explain what an account is and how it helps in the recording process.*** An account is an individual accounting record of increases and decreases in specific asset, liability, and shareholders' equity items.

❸ ***Define debits and credits and explain how they are used to record business transactions.*** The terms "debit" and "credit" are synonymous with "left" and "right." Assets, dividends, and expenses are increased by debits and decreased by credits. Liabilities, common stock, retained earnings, and revenues are increased by credits and decreased by debits.

❹ ***Identify the basic steps in the recording process.*** The basic steps in the recording process are (a) analysing each transaction in terms of its effect on the accounts, (b) entering the transaction information in a journal, and (c) transferring the journal information to the appropriate accounts in the ledger.

❺ ***Explain what a journal is and how it helps in the recording process.*** The initial accounting record of a transaction is entered in a journal before the data are entered in the accounts. A journal (a) discloses the complete effect of a transaction in one place, (b) provides a chronological record of transactions, and (c) prevents or helps locate errors because the debit and credit amounts for each entry can be readily compared.

❻ ***Explain what a ledger is and how it helps in the recording process.*** The entire group of accounts maintained by a company is referred to collectively as a ledger. The ledger keeps all the information about changes in specific account balances in one place.

❼ ***Explain what posting is and how it helps in the recording process.*** Posting is the procedure of transferring journal entries to the ledger accounts. This step of the recording process accumulates the effects of journalized transactions in the individual accounts.

❽ ***Explain the purposes of a trial balance.*** A trial balance is a list of accounts and their balances at a given time. The primary purpose of the trial balance is to prove the mathematical equality of debits and credits after posting. A trial balance also uncovers errors in journalizing and posting and is useful in preparing financial statements.

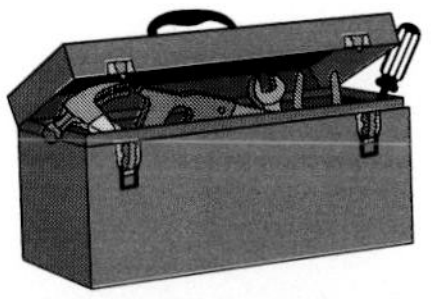

Decision Toolkit—A Summary

Decision Checkpoints	Info Needed for Decision	Tool to Use for Decision	How to Evaluate Results
Has an accounting transaction occurred?	Details of the event	Accounting equation	Determine the effect, if any, on assets, liabilities, and shareholders' equity.
How do you determine that debits equal credits?	All account balances	Trial balance	List the account titles and their balances; total the debit and credit columns; verify equality.

GLOSSARY

Account An individual accounting record of increases and decreases in specific asset, liability, and shareholders' equity items. (p. 115)

Accounting information system The system of collecting and processing transaction data and communicating financial information to interested parties. (p. 108)

Accounting transactions Events that require recording in the financial statements because they involve an exchange affecting assets, liabilities, or shareholders' equity (an external event) or because a reasonable estimate of value can be determined (an internal event). (p. 109)

Chart of accounts A list of a company's accounts. (p. 126)

Credit The right side of an account. (p. 116)

Debit The left side of an account. (p. 116)

Double-entry system A system that records the dual effect of each transaction in appropriate accounts. (p. 117)

General journal The most basic form of journal. (p. 123)

General ledger A ledger that contains all asset, liability, and shareholders' equity accounts. (p. 125)

Journal An accounting record in which transactions are initially recorded in chronological order. (p. 123)

Ledger The group of accounts maintained by a company. (p. 125)

Posting The procedure of transferring journal entries to the ledger accounts. (p. 126)

T account The basic form of an account. (p. 115)

Trial balance A list of accounts and their balances at a given time. (p. 135)

DEMONSTRATION PROBLEM

Paul Briffet and other student investors opened Campus Laundry Inc. on September 1, 2001. During the first month of operations the following transactions occurred:

Sept. 1 Shareholders invested $20,000 cash in the business.
2 Paid $1,000 cash for store rent for the month of September.
3 Purchased washers and dryers for $25,000, paying $10,000 in cash and signing a $15,000 six-month, 12% note payable.
4 Paid $1,200 for a one-year accident insurance policy.
10 Received a bill from the *Daily News* for advertising the opening of the laundromat, $200.
15 Performed services on account for $6,200.
20 Declared and paid a $700 cash dividend to shareholders.
30 Received $5,000 from customers billed on September 15.

The chart of accounts for the company is the same as for Sierra Corporation except for the following: Laundry Equipment and Advertising Expense.

Instructions

(a) Journalize the September transactions.
(b) Open ledger accounts and post the September transactions.
(c) Prepare a trial balance at September 30, 2001.

Problem-Solving Strategies

1. Make separate journal entries for each transaction.
2. Note that all debits precede all credit entries.
3. In journalizing, make sure debits equal credits.
4. In journalizing, use specific account titles taken from the chart of accounts.
5. Provide an appropriate explanation of the journal entry.
6. Arrange ledger in statement order, beginning with the balance sheet accounts.
7. Post in chronological order.
8. Prepare a trial balance which lists accounts in the order in which they appear in the ledger.
9. List debit balances in the left column and credit balances in the right column.

Solution to Demonstration Problem

(a) **GENERAL JOURNAL**

Date	Account Titles and Explanation	Debit	Credit
2001			
Sept. 1	Cash	20,000	
	Common Shares		20,000
	(Invested cash in business)		

2	Rent Expense	1,000	
	Cash		1,000
	(Paid September rent)		
3	Laundry Equipment	25,000	
	Cash		10,000
	Notes Payable		15,000
	(Purchased laundry equipment for cash and six-month, 12% note payable)		
4	Prepaid Insurance	1,200	
	Cash		1,200
	(Paid one-year insurance policy)		
10	Advertising Expense	200	
	Accounts Payable		200
	(Received bill from *Daily News* for advertising)		
15	Accounts Receivable	6,200	
	Service Revenue		6,200
	(Record revenue for laundry services rendered)		
20	Dividends	700	
	Cash		700
	(Declared and paid a cash dividend)		
30	Cash	5,000	
	Accounts Receivable		5,000
	(Record collection of cash on account)		

(b)

GENERAL LEDGER

Cash

Sept. 1	20,000	Sept. 2	1,000
30	5,000	3	10,000
		4	1,200
		20	700
Bal.	12,100		

Common Shares

	Sept. 1	20,000
	Bal.	20,000

Accounts Receivable

Sept. 15	6,200	Sept. 30	5,000
Bal.	1,200		

Dividends

Sept. 20	700	
Bal.	700	

Prepaid Insurance

Sept. 4	1,200	
Bal.	1,200	

Service Revenue

	Sept. 15	6,200
	Bal.	6,200

Laundry Equipment

Sept. 3	25,000	
Bal.	25,000	

Advertising Expense

Sept. 10	200	
Bal.	200	

Notes Payable

	Sept. 3	15,000
	Bal.	15,000

Rent Expense

Sept. 2	1,000	
Bal.	1,000	

Accounts Payable

	Sept. 10	200
	Bal.	200

(c)

CAMPUS LAUNDRY INC.
Trial Balance
September 30, 2001

	Debit	Credit
Cash	$12,100	
Accounts Receivable	1,200	
Prepaid Insurance	1,200	
Laundry Equipment	25,000	
Notes Payable		$15,000
Accounts Payable		200
Common Shares		20,000
Dividends	700	
Service Revenue		6,200
Advertising Expense	200	
Rent Expense	1,000	
	$41,400	$41,400

SELF-STUDY QUESTIONS

Answers are at the end of the chapter.

(SO 1) 1. The effects on the basic accounting equation of performing services for cash are to:
(a) increase assets and decrease shareholders' equity.
(b) increase assets and increase shareholders' equity.
(c) increase assets and increase liabilities.
(d) increase liabilities and increase shareholders' equity.

(SO 1) 2. Genesis Company buys a $900 machine on credit. This transaction will affect the:
(a) statement of earnings only.
(b) balance sheet only.
(c) statement of earnings and statement of retained earnings only.
(d) statement of earnings, statement of retained earnings, and balance sheet.

(SO 2) 3. Which statement about an account is *true?*
(a) In its simplest form, an account consists of two parts.
(b) An account is an individual accounting record of increases and decreases in specific asset, liability, and shareholders' equity items.
(c) There are separate accounts for specific assets and liabilities but only one account for shareholders' equity items.
(d) The left side of an account is the credit or decrease side.

(SO 3) 4. Debits:
(a) increase both assets and liabilities.
(b) decrease both assets and liabilities.
(c) increase assets and decrease liabilities.
(d) decrease assets and increase liabilities.

5. A revenue account: (SO 3)
(a) is increased by debits.
(b) is decreased by credits.
(c) has a normal balance of a debit.
(d) is increased by credits.

6. Which accounts normally have debit balances? (SO 3)
(a) Assets, expenses, and revenues
(b) Assets, expenses, and retained earnings
(c) Assets, liabilities, and dividends
(d) Assets, dividends, and expenses

7. Which is *not* part of the recording process? (SO 4)
(a) Analysing transactions
(b) Preparing a balance sheet
(c) Entering transactions in a journal
(d) Posting transactions

8. Which of these statements about a journal is *false?* (SO 5)
(a) It contains only revenue and expense accounts.
(b) It provides a chronological record of transactions.
(c) It helps to locate errors because the debit and credit amounts for each entry can be readily compared.
(d) It discloses the complete effect of a transaction in one place.

9. A ledger: (SO 6)
(a) contains only asset and liability accounts.
(b) should show accounts in alphabetical order.
(c) is a collection of the entire group of accounts maintained by a company.
(d) provides a chronological record of transactions.

(SO 7) 10. Posting:
   (a) normally occurs before journalizing.
   (b) transfers ledger transaction data to the journal.
   (c) is an optional step in the recording process.
   (d) transfers journal entries to ledger accounts.

(SO 8) 11. A trial balance:
   (a) is a list of accounts with their balances at a given time.
   (b) proves the mathematical accuracy of journalized transactions.
   (c) will not balance if a correct journal entry is posted twice.
   (d) proves that all transactions have been recorded.

12. A trial balance will not balance if: (SO 8)
   (a) a correct journal entry is posted twice.
   (b) the purchase of supplies on account is debited to Supplies and credited to Cash.
   (c) a \$100 cash dividend is debited to Dividends for \$1,000 and credited to Cash for \$100.
   (d) a \$450 payment on account is debited to Accounts Payable for \$45 and credited to Cash for \$45.

QUESTIONS

(SO 1) 1. Can a business enter into a transaction that affects only the left side of the basic accounting equation? If so, give an example.

(SO 1) 2. Are the following events recorded in the accounting records? Explain your answer in each case.
   (a) A major shareholder of the company dies.
   (b) Supplies are purchased on account.
   (c) An employee is fired.
   (d) The company pays a cash dividend to its shareholders.

(SO 1) 3. Indicate how each business transaction affects the basic accounting equation.
   (a) Paid cash for janitorial services
   (b) Purchased equipment for cash
   (c) Issued common shares to investors in exchange for cash
   (d) Paid an account payable in full

(SO 2) 4. Why is an account referred to as a T account?

(SO 3) 5. The terms "debit" and "credit" mean "increase" and "decrease," respectively. Do you agree? Explain.

(SO 3) 6. Charles Thon, a fellow student, contends that the double-entry system means each transaction must be recorded twice. Is Charles correct? Explain.

(SO 3) 7. Natalie Boudreau, a beginning accounting student, believes debit balances are favourable and credit balances are unfavourable. Is Natalie correct? Discuss.

(SO 3) 8. State the rules of debit and credit as applied to (a) asset accounts, (b) liability accounts, and (c) the Common Shares account.

(SO 3) 9. What is the normal balance for each of these accounts?
   (a) Accounts Receivable
   (b) Cash
   (c) Dividends
   (d) Accounts Payable
   (e) Service Revenue
   (f) Salaries Expense
   (g) Common Shares

10. Indicate whether each account below is an asset, a liability, or a shareholders' equity account and whether it would have a normal debit or credit balance: (SO 3)
   (a) Accounts Receivable
   (b) Accounts Payable
   (c) Equipment
   (d) Dividends
   (e) Supplies

11. For the following transactions, indicate the account debited and the account credited: (SO 3)
   (a) Supplies are purchased on account.
   (b) Cash is received on signing a note payable.
   (c) Employees are paid salaries in cash.

12. For each account listed here, indicate whether it generally will have debit entries only, credit entries only, or both debit and credit entries: (SO 3)
   (a) Cash
   (b) Accounts Receivable
   (c) Dividends
   (d) Accounts Payable
   (e) Salaries Expense
   (f) Service Revenue

13. Should the balance in total shareholder's equity equal the balance in the Cash account? Explain why or why not. (SO 3)

14. A company received cash from a customer. It debited the Cash account. Name two credit accounts that the company might have used to record a cash receipt from a customer. (SO 3)

15. Identify and describe the steps in the recording process. (SO 4)

(SO 5) 16. An efficiency expert who was reviewing the steps in the recording process suggested dropping the general journal and recording and summarizing transactions directly into the general ledger instead. Comment on this suggestion.

(SO 5) 17. What are the advantages of using the journal in the recording process?

(SO 5) 18. (a) When entering a transaction in the journal, should the debit or credit be written first?
(b) Which should be indented, the debit or the credit?

(SO 5) 19. Journalize these accounting transactions.
(a) Doris Wang invests $9,000 in the business in exchange for common shares.
(b) Insurance of $800 is paid for the year.
(c) Supplies of $1,500 are purchased on account.
(d) Cash of $7,500 is received for services rendered.

(SO 6) 20. (a) Can accounting transaction debits and credits be recorded directly in the ledger accounts?
(b) What are the advantages of first recording transactions in the journal and then posting to the ledger?

21. (a) What is a ledger? (SO 6)
(b) Why is a chart of accounts important?

22. What is a trial balance and what are its purposes? (SO 8)

23. Kap Shin is confused about how accounting information flows through the accounting system. He believes information flows in the following order: (SO 8)
1. Debits and credits are posted to the ledger.
2. Accounting transaction occurs.
3. Information is entered in the journal.
4. Financial statements are prepared.
5. Trial balance is prepared.

Indicate to Kap the proper flow of the information.

24. Two students are discussing the use of a trial balance. They wonder whether the following errors, each considered separately, would prevent the trial balance from balancing. What would you tell them? (SO 8)
(a) The bookkeeper debited Cash for $600 and credited Wages Expense for $600 for payment of wages.
(b) Cash collected on account was debited to Cash for $900, and Service Revenue was credited for $90.

BRIEF EXERCISES

Determine effect of transaction on basic accounting equation.
(SO 1)

BE3-1 Presented here are three economic events. On a sheet of paper, list the letters (a), (b), and (c) with columns for assets, liabilities, and shareholders' equity. In each column, indicate on the line of the appropriate letter whether the event increased (+), decreased (−), or had no effect (NE) on assets, liabilities, and shareholders' equity.
(a) Purchased supplies on account.
(b) Received cash for providing a service.
(c) Expenses paid in cash.

Determine effect of transaction on basic accounting equation.
(SO 1)

BE3-2 Follow the same format as in BE3-1. Determine the effect on assets, liabilities, and shareholders' equity of the following three events:
(a) Issued common shares to investors in exchange for cash.
(b) Paid cash dividend to shareholders.
(c) Received cash from a customer who had previously been billed for services provided.

Indicate debit and credit effects.
(SO 3)

BE3-3 For each of the following accounts, indicate the effect of a debit or credit on the account and the normal balance:

(a) Accounts Payable	(d) Accounts Receivable
(b) Advertising Expense	(e) Retained Earnings
(c) Service Revenue	(f) Dividends

Identify accounts to be debited and credited.
(SO 3)

BE3-4 Transactions for the H.J. Oslo Company Ltd. for the month of June are presented next. Identify the accounts to be debited and credited for each transaction.

June	1	Issues common shares to investors in exchange for $2,500 cash.
	2	Buys equipment on account for $900.
	3	Pays $500 to landlord for June rent.
	12	Bills J. Kronsnoble $300 for welding work done.
	30	Pays $100 for income taxes.

Journalize transactions.
(SO 5)

BE3-5 Use the data in BE3-4 and journalize the transactions. (You may omit explanations.)

BE3-6 Tage Shumway, a fellow student, is unclear about the basic steps in the recording process. Identify and briefly explain the steps in the order in which they occur.

Identify steps in the recording process.
(SO 4)

BE3-7 Norris Corporation has the following transactions during August of the current year. Indicate (a) the basic analysis and (b) the debit–credit analysis similar to that shown in Illustrations 3-20 to 3-30.

Indicate basic debit–credit analysis.
(SO 5)

Aug. 1 Issues common shares to investors in exchange for $5,000.
4 Pays insurance in advance for six months, $1,800.
16 Receives $900 from clients for services rendered.
27 Pays secretary $500 salary.

BE3-8 Use the data in BE3-7 and journalize the transactions. (You may omit explanations.)

Journalize transactions.
(SO 5)

BE3-9 Selected transactions for Paquin Company Limited are presented in journal form (without explanations). Post the transactions to T accounts.

Post journal entries to T accounts.
(SO 7)

Date		Account Title	Debit	Credit
May	5	Accounts Receivable	3,200	
		Service Revenue		3,200
	12	Cash	2,400	
		Accounts Receivable		2,400
	15	Cash	2,000	
		Service Revenue		2,000
	15	Income Tax Expense	1,000	
		Income Tax Payable		1,000

BE3-10 From the ledger balances given below, prepare a trial balance for Carland Company, Inc. at June 30, 2001. All account balances are normal.

Prepare a trial balance.
(SO 8)

Accounts Payable	$4,000	Service Revenue	$6,000
Cash	$3,800	Accounts Receivable	$3,000
Common Shares	$20,000	Salaries Expense	$4,000
Dividends	$1,200	Rent Expense	$1,000
Equipment	$17,000	Income Tax Expense	$250

BE3-11 An inexperienced bookkeeper prepared the following trial balance that does not balance. Prepare a correct trial balance, assuming all account balances are normal.

Prepare a corrected trial balance.
(SO 8)

GOMEZ COMPANY LIMITED
Trial Balance
December 31, 2001

	Debit	Credit
Cash	$18,800	
Prepaid Insurance		$ 3,500
Accounts Payable		3,000
Unearned Revenue	2,200	
Common Shares		10,000
Retained Earnings		7,000
Dividends		4,500
Service Revenue		25,600
Salaries Expense	18,600	
Rent Expense		2,400
	$39,600	$56,000

EXERCISES

Analyse the effect of transactions.
(SO 1)

E3-1 Selected transactions for Green Lawn Care Company, Inc. follow:

1. Issued common shares to investors in exchange for cash received from investors.
2. Paid monthly rent.
3. Purchased equipment on account.
4. Billed customers for services performed.
5. Paid dividend to shareholders.
6. Received cash from customers billed in (4).
7. Incurred advertising expense on account.
8. Purchased additional equipment for cash.
9. Received cash from customers when service was rendered.
10. Paid monthly income taxes.

Instructions

Describe the effect of each transaction on assets, liabilities, and shareholders' equity. For example, the first answer is "1. Increase in assets and increase in shareholders' equity."

Analyse the effect of transactions on assets, liabilities, and shareholders' equity.
(SO 1)

E3-2 Li Wang Computer Timeshare Corporation entered into these transactions during May 2001:

1. Purchased computer terminals for $19,000 from Digital Equipment on account.
2. Paid $4,000 cash for May rent on storage space.
3. Received $15,000 cash from customers for contracts billed in April.
4. Provided computer services to Brieske Construction Company for $3,000 cash.
5. Paid Southern States Power Co. $11,000 cash for energy usage in May.
6. Li Wang invested an additional $32,000 in the business in exchange for common shares of the company.
7. Paid Digital Equipment for the terminals purchased in (1).
8. Incurred advertising expense for May of $1,000 on account.

Instructions

Indicate with the appropriate letter whether each of the transactions above results in

(a) an increase in assets and a decrease in assets.
(b) an increase in assets and an increase in shareholders' equity.
(c) an increase in assets and an increase in liabilities.
(d) a decrease in assets and a decrease in shareholders' equity.
(e) a decrease in assets and a decrease in liabilities.
(f) an increase in liabilities and a decrease in shareholders' equity.
(g) an increase in shareholders' equity and a decrease in liabilities.

Analyse transactions and calculate net earnings.
(SO 1)

E3-3 A tabular analysis of the transactions made by Roberta Mendez & Co. Inc. for the month of August is shown below. Each increase and decrease in shareholders' equity is explained.

	Cash	+	Accounts Receivable	+	Supplies	+	Office Equipment	=	Accounts Payable	+	Shareholders' Equity	
1.	+$15,000										+$15,000	Issued common shares
2.	−2,000						+$5,000		+$3,000			
3.	−750				+$750							
4.	+4,600		+$3,400								+8,000	Service revenue
5.	−1,500								−1,500			
6.	−2,000										−2,000	Dividends
7.	−650										−650	Rent expense
8.	+450		−450									
9.	−2,900										−2,900	Salaries expense
10.									+500		−500	Utilities expense
11.	−1,500										−1,500	Increase tax expense

Instructions
(a) Describe each transaction.
(b) Determine how much shareholders' equity increased for the month.
(c) Calculate the net earnings for the month.

E3-4 The tabular analysis of transactions for Roberta Mendez & Co. is presented in E3-3.

Prepare a statement of earnings, statement of retained earnings, and a balance sheet.
(SO 1)

Instructions
Prepare a statement of earnings and a statement of retained earnings for the month of August and a balance sheet at August 31, 2001.

E3-5 Selected transactions for the Decorators Mill Ltd., an interior decorator corporation in its first month of business, are as follows:

Identify debits, credits, and normal balances.
(SO 3)

1. Issued shares to investors for $10,000 in cash.
2. Purchased used car for $4,000 cash for use in business.
3. Purchased supplies on account for $500.
4. Billed customers $1,800 for services performed.
5. Paid $200 cash for advertising start of business.
6. Received $700 cash from customers billed in transaction (4).
7. Paid creditor $300 cash on account.
8. Paid dividends of $500 cash to shareholders.

Instructions
For each transaction indicate (a) the basic type of account debited and credited (asset, liability, shareholders' equity); (b) the specific account debited and credited (Cash, Rent Expense, Service Revenue, etc.); (c) whether the specific account is increased or decreased; and (d) the normal balance of the specific account. Use the following format, in which transaction 1 is given as an example:

	Account Debited				Account Credited			
Trans-action	**(a) Basic Type**	**(b) Specific Account**	**(c) Effect**	**(d) Normal Balance**	**(a) Basic Type**	**(b) Specific Account**	**(c) Effect**	**(d) Normal Balance**
1.	Asset	Cash	Increase	Debit	Share-holders' equity	Common Shares	Increase	Credit

E3-6 Data for the Decorators Mill Ltd. are presented in E3-5.

Journalize transactions.
(SO 5)

Instructions
Journalize the transactions.

E3-7 This information relates to Marx Real Estate Agency Corporation:

Analyse transactions and determine their effect on accounts.
(SO 3)

Oct. 1 Lynn Marx begins business as a real estate agent with a cash investment of $13,000 in exchange for common shares of the corporation.
2 Hires an administrative assistant.
3 Buys office furniture for $1,900, on account.
6 Sells a house and lot for B. Rollins; commissions due from Rollins, $3,200 (not paid by Rollins at this time).
10 Receives cash of $140 as commission for renting an apartment for the owner.
27 Pays $700 on account for the office furniture purchased on October 3.
30 Pays the administrative assistant $960 in salary for October.

Instructions
Prepare the debit–credit analysis for each transaction as shown in Illustrations 3-20 to 3-30.

E3-8 Transaction data for Marx Real Estate Agency are presented in E3-7.

Journalize transactions.
(SO 5)

Instructions
Journalize the transactions.

Post journal entries and prepare a trial balance.
(SO 7, 8)

E3-9 The transaction data and journal entries for the Marx Real Estate Agency are presented in E3-7 and E3-8.

Instructions

(a) Post the transactions to T accounts.
(b) Prepare a trial balance at October 31, 2001.

Post journal entries and prepare a trial balance.
(SO 7, 8)

E3-10 Selected transactions from the journal of J.L. Kang, Inc., an investment brokerage corporation, are presented here:

Date	Account Titles	Debit	Credit
Aug. 1	Cash	1,600	
	Common Shares		1,600
10	Cash	2,400	
	Service Revenue		2,400
12	Office Equipment	4,000	
	Cash		1,000
	Notes Payable		3,000
25	Accounts Receivable	1,400	
	Service Revenue		1,400
31	Cash	900	
	Accounts Receivable		900

Instructions

(a) Post the transactions to T accounts.
(b) Prepare a trial balance at August 31, 2001.

Journalize transactions from T accounts and prepare a trial balance.
(SO 5, 7, 8)

E3-11 These T accounts summarize the ledger of Lush Landscaping Company, Inc. at the end of the first month of operations:

Cash

Apr. 1	9,000	Apr. 15	600
12	900	25	1,500
29	400		
30	800		

Unearned Revenue

		Apr. 30	800

Accounts Receivable

Apr. 7	3,200	Apr. 29	400

Common Shares

		Apr. 1	9,000

Supplies

Apr. 4	1,800		

Service Revenue

		Apr. 7	3,200
		12	900

Accounts Payable

Apr. 25	1,500	Apr. 4	1,800

Salaries Expense

Apr. 15	600		

Instructions

(a) Prepare, in the order they occurred, the journal entries (including explanations) that resulted in the amounts posted to the accounts.
(b) Prepare a trial balance at April 30, 2001.

E3-12 Here is the ledger for Holly Corp.:

Journalize transactions from T accounts and prepare a trial balance.
(SO 5, 7, 8)

Cash

Oct. 1	4,000	Oct. 4	400
10	650	12	1,500
10	5,000	15	250
20	500	30	300
25	2,000	31	500

Common Shares

		Oct. 1	4,000
		25	2,000

Accounts Receivable

Oct. 6	800	Oct 20	500
20	940		

Dividends

Oct. 30	300		

Supplies

Oct. 4	400	Oct. 31	180

Service Revenue

		Oct. 6	800
		10	650
		20	940

Furniture

Oct. 3	2,000		

Store Wages Expense

Oct. 31	500		

Notes Payable

		Oct. 10	5,000

Supplies Expense

Oct. 31	180		

Accounts Payable

Oct. 12	1,500	Oct. 3	2,000

Rent Expense

Oct. 15	250		

Instructions

(a) Reproduce the journal entries for the transactions that occurred on October 1, 10, and 20, and provide explanations for each.
(b) Prepare a trial balance at October 31, 2001.

E3-13 Selected transactions for the Basler Corporation during its first month in business are presented below:

Prepare journal entries and post transactions to T accounts.
(SO 5, 7)

Sept. 1 Issued common shares in exchange for $15,000 cash received from investors.
5 Purchased equipment for $10,000, paying $5,000 in cash and the balance on account.
25 Paid $3,000 cash on balance owed for equipment.
30 Paid $500 cash dividend.

Instructions

(a) Prepare a tabular analysis of the transactions. The headings over the three columns should be Cash + Equipment = Accounts Payable + Shareholder's Equity. For transactions affecting shareholders' equity, provide explanations in the right margin.
(b) Journalize the transactions.
(c) Post the transactions to T accounts.

E3-14 The bookkeeper for Castle's Equipment Repair Corporation made these errors in journalizing and posting:

Analyse errors and their effects on the trial balance.
(SO 8)

1. A credit posting of $400 to Accounts Receivable was omitted.
2. A debit posting of $750 for Prepaid Insurance was debited to Insurance Expense.
3. A collection on account of $100 was journalized and posted as a debit to Cash $100 and a credit to Service Revenue $100.
4. A credit posting of $300 to Property Taxes Payable was made twice.
5. A cash purchase of supplies for $250 was journalized and posted as a debit to Supplies $25 and a credit to Cash $25.
6. A debit of $465 to Advertising Expense was posted as $456.

Instructions

For each error, indicate (a) whether the trial balance will balance; (b) the amount of the difference if the trial balance will not balance; and (c) the trial balance column that will have the larger total. Consider each error separately. Use the following form, in which error 1 is given as an example:

Error	(a) In Balance	(b) Difference	(c) Larger Column
1.	No	$400	Debit

Prepare a trial balance.
(SO 8)

E3-15 The accounts in the ledger of Speedy Delivery Service, Inc. contain the following balances on July 31, 2001:

Accounts Receivable	$ 8,642	Prepaid Insurance	$ 1,968
Accounts Payable	7,396	Repair Expense	961
Cash	?	Service Revenue	10,610
Delivery Equipment	49,360	Dividends	700
Gas and Oil Expense	758	Common Shares	40,000
Insurance Expense	523	Salaries Expense	4,428
Notes Payable	18,450	Salaries Payable	815
		Retained Earnings	4,636

Instructions

Prepare a trial balance with the accounts arranged as illustrated in the chapter, and fill in the missing amount for Cash.

PROBLEMS: SET A

Prepare a statement of earnings and a statement of retained earnings.
(SO 1)

P3-1A These November 2001 transactions affected the Retained Earnings account of the Larsson Corporation:

Transaction	Amount	Description
(7)	$ 700	Property tax expense
(9)	6,000	Service revenue
(10)	350	Utilities expense
(13)	4,000	Wages expense
(16)	300	Utilities expense
(18)	1,250	Rent expense
(19)	450	Advertising expense
(22)	2,000	Service revenue
(23)	800	Dividends
(25)	600	Repair expense
(27)	400	Auto expense
(31)	9,000	Service revenue
(32)	1,600	Dividends
(33)	4,000	Wages expense
(34)	500	Utilities expense

In reviewing the account, Lars Larsson realized that the new bookkeeper had made the following error: transaction (27) was a payment for income tax expense.

Instructions

(a) Prepare a statement of earnings for the month of November.
(b) Prepare a statement of retained earnings for November, assuming that the beginning retained earnings balance was $9,500 on November 1.

P3-2A On April 1, Laura Seall established Seall Travel Agency, Inc. These transactions were completed during the month:

Analyse transactions and calculate net earnings.
(SO 1)

1. Laura Seall and other investors invested $20,000 cash in the company in exchange for common shares.
2. Paid $400 cash for April office rent.
3. Purchased office equipment for $2,500 cash.
4. Incurred $300 of advertising costs in the *Halifax Herald,* on account.
5. Paid $600 cash for office supplies.
6. Earned $9,000 for services rendered: cash of $1,000 is received from customers, and the balance of $8,000 is billed to customers on account.
7. Paid $200 cash dividends.
8. Paid *Halifax Herald* amount due in transaction (4).
9. Paid employees' salaries, $1,200.
10. Received $8,000 in cash from customers who had been billed in transaction (6).
11. Paid income tax of $2,000.

Instructions

(a) Prepare a tabular analysis of the transactions using these column headings: Cash, Accounts Receivable, Supplies, Office Equipment, Accounts Payable, Common Shares, and Retained Earnings.

(b) From an analysis of the Retained Earnings column, calculate the net earnings or net loss for April.

P3-3A Ivan Izo created a corporation providing legal services, Ivan Izo, Inc., on July 1, 2001. On July 31, the balance sheet showed Cash $4,000; Accounts Receivable $1,500; Supplies $500; Office Equipment $5,000; Accounts Payable $4,200; Common Shares $6,500; and Retained Earnings $300. During August the following transactions occurred:

Analyse transactions and prepare a statement of earnings, statement of retained earnings, and balance sheet.
(SO 1)

1. Collected $1,400 of accounts receivable.
2. Paid $2,700 cash on accounts payable.
3. Earned revenue of $6,400, of which $3,000 is collected in cash and the balance is due in September.
4. Purchased additional office equipment for $1,000, paying $400 in cash and the balance on account.
5. Paid salaries, $1,500; rent for August, $900; and advertising expenses, $350.
6. Declared and paid a cash dividend of $550.
7. Received $2,000 from Laurentian Bank; the money was borrowed on a note payable.
8. Incurred utility expenses for the month on account, $250.

Instructions

(a) Prepare a tabular analysis of the August transactions beginning with July 31 balances. The headings over the columns should be Cash + Accounts Receivable + Supplies + Office Equipment = Notes Payable + Accounts Payable + Common Shares + Retained Earnings.

(b) Prepare a statement of earnings for August, a statement of retained earnings for August, and a balance sheet at August 31.

P3-4A The bookkeeper for Katie Cater's dance studio made the following errors in journalizing and posting:

Analyse errors and their effects on the trial balance.
(SO 1, 8)

1. A credit to Supplies of $600 was omitted.
2. A debit posting of $300 to Accounts Payable was inadvertently debited to Accounts Receivable.
3. A purchase of supplies on account of $450 was debited to Supplies for $540 and credited to Accounts Payable for $540.
4. A credit to Wages Payable for $1,200 was credited to Wages Expense.
5. A credit posting of $250 to Wages Payable was posted twice.
6. A debit posting to Wages Payable for $250 and a credit posting to Cash for $250 were made twice.
7. A debit posting for $1,000 of Dividends was inadvertently posted to Travel Expenses instead.
8. A credit to Service Revenue for $400 was inadvertently posted as a debit to Service Revenue.

9. A credit to Accounts Receivable of $250 was omitted and was credited to Accounts Payable.
10. A credit to Common Shares of $3,000 was inadvertently debited to Service Revenue.

Instructions

For each error, indicate (a) whether the trial balance will balance; (b) the amount of the difference if the trial balance will not balance; and (c) the trial balance column that will have the larger total. Consider each error separately. Use the following form, in which error 1 is given as an example:

Error	(a) In Balance	(b) Difference	(c) Larger Column
1.	No	$600	Debit

Identify debits, credits, and normal balances; calculate cash flow and net earnings.

(SO 3)

P3-5A You are presented with the following transactions for Paddick Enterprises Ltd.

1. Purchased supplies on account at a cost of $600.
2. Purchased furniture for $10,000 by signing a note that is due in three months.
3. Earned fees of $90,000. Of this amount, $30,000 was received in cash. The balance was on account.
4. Paid $1,000 in cash dividends.
5. Paid $250 of the amount owing from transaction 1.
6. Collected $20,000 from the customers in transaction 3.
7. Paid operating expenses for the month of $12,000.
8. Recorded wages due to employees for work performed during the month, $4,000.

Instructions

(a) For each transaction indicate (1) the basic type of account debited and credited (asset, liability, shareholders' equity); (2) the specific account debited and credited (Cash, Fees Earned, etc.); (3) whether the specific account is increased or decreased; and (4) the normal balance of the specific account. Use the following format, in which transaction 1 is given as an example:

	Account Debited				Account Credited			
Transaction	(a) Basic Type	(b) Specific Account	(c) Effect	(d) Normal Balance	(a) Basic Type	(b) Specific Account	(c) Effect	(d) Normal Balance
1.	Asset	Supplies	Increase	Debit	Liability	Accounts Payable	Increase	Credit

(b) Calculate the cash flow and net earnings from these transactions.

P3-6A You are presented with the following alphabetical list of accounts for O'Laney's Welding Services Ltd.:

Identify the normal balance and financial statement for selected accounts.

(SO 3)

Account	(a) Normal Balance	(b) Financial Statement
Accounts receivable		
Amortization expense		
Common shares		
Cost of goods sold		
Equipment		
Income tax expense		
Income tax payable		
Insurance expense		
Interest expense		
Inventories		
Investment in shares of another company		
Long-term debt		
Notes payable		
Prepaid insurance		
Retained earnings		
Sales revenue		

Instructions

For each account, indicate (a) whether the normal balance is a debit or a credit and (b) the financial statement where the account should be classified: balance sheet or statement of earnings.

P3-7A Surepar Miniature Golf and Driving Range, Inc. was opened on March 1. These selected events and transactions occurred during March:

Journalize a series of transactions.

(SO 3, 5)

Mar. 1 Cash of $50,000 was invested in the business in exchange for common shares of the corporation.
3 Purchased Lee's Golf Land for $38,000 cash. The price consists of land $23,000, building $9,000, and equipment $6,000. (Record this in a single compound entry.)
5 Advertised the opening of the driving range and miniature golf course, paying advertising expenses of $1,600.
6 Paid $1,480 cash for a one-year insurance policy.
10 Purchased golf clubs and other equipment for $1,600 from Palmer Company, payable in 30 days.
18 Received golf fees of $800 in cash.
19 Sold 100 coupon books for $15.00 each. Each book contains 10 coupons that enable the holder to play one round of miniature golf or to hit one bucket of golf balls. (Hint: The revenue is not earned until the customers use the coupons.)
25 Declared and paid a $500 cash dividend.
30 Paid salaries of $600.
30 Paid Palmer Company in full.
31 Received $500 of fees in cash.

Instructions

Journalize the March transactions.

P3-8A Ashu Virmani incorporated as a licensed architect on April 1, 2001. During the first month, these events and transactions occurred:

Journalize transactions, post, and prepare a trial balance.

(SO 3, 5, 6, 7, 8)

Apr. 1 Cash of $13,000 was invested in exchange for common shares of the corporation.
1 Hired a secretary-receptionist at a salary of $300 per week, payable monthly.
2 Paid office rent for the month, $800.
3 Purchased architectural supplies on account from Halo Company, $1,500.
10 Completed blueprints on a carport and billed client $900 for services.
11 Received $500 cash advance from R. Welk for the design of a new home.

20 Received $1,500 cash for services completed and delivered to P. Donahue.
30 Paid secretary-receptionist for the month, $1,200.
30 Paid $600 to Halo Company on account.

Instructions

(a) Journalize the transactions.
(b) Post to the ledger T accounts.
(c) Prepare a trial balance at April 30, 2001.

Journalize transactions, post, and prepare a trial balance.
(SO 3, 5, 6, 7, 8)

P3-9A This is the trial balance of Dirty Laundry Corporation at September 30:

DIRTY LAUNDRY CORPORATION
Trial Balance
September 30, 2001

	Debit	Credit
Cash	$ 8,500	
Accounts Receivable	2,200	
Supplies	1,700	
Equipment	8,000	
Accounts Payable		$ 5,000
Unearned Revenue		700
Common Shares		14,700
	$20,400	$20,400

The October transactions were as follows:

Oct. 5 Received $900 cash from customers on account.
10 Billed customers for services performed, $5,500.
15 Paid employee salaries, $1,200.
17 Performed $400 of services for customers who paid in advance in August.
20 Paid $1,600 to creditors on account.
29 Paid a $500 cash dividend.
31 Paid utilities, $600.

Instructions

(a) Prepare a general ledger using T accounts. Enter the opening balances in the ledger accounts as at October 1. Provision should be made for these additional accounts: Dividends, Laundry Revenue, Salaries Expense, and Utilities Expense.
(b) Journalize the transactions.
(c) Post to the ledger accounts.
(d) Prepare a trial balance at October 31, 2001.

Prepare a trial balance and financial statements.
(SO 8)

P3-10A You are presented with the following alphabetical list of accounts and balances for Kia Taggar Enterprises Inc. at June 30, 2001:

Accounts receivable	$ 500
Amortization expense	150
Cash	180
Common shares	550
Cost of goods sold	870
Equipment	1,200
Income tax expense	160
Income tax payable	160
Insurance expense	130
Interest expense	225
Inventories	510
Investment in shares of another company	495
Land	800
Long-term debt	1,200
Notes payable, current	1,000
Prepaid insurance	90
Retained earnings, July 1, 2000	400
Sales revenue	2,000

Instructions

(a) Prepare a trial balance, sorting each account balance into the debit column or the credit column.

(b) Prepare a balance sheet as at June 30, 2001, and a statement of earnings for the year ended June 30, 2001, for Kia Taggar Enterprises Inc.

P3-11A This trial balance of Thom Wargo Co. does not balance:

Prepare a correct trial balance.
(SO 8)

THOM WARGO CO.
Trial Balance
June 30, 2001

	Debit	Credit
Cash		$ 2,840
Accounts Receivable	$ 3,231	
Supplies	800	
Equipment	3,000	
Accounts Payable		2,666
Unearned Revenue	1,200	
Common Shares		9,000
Dividends	800	
Service Revenue		2,380
Salaries Expense	3,400	
Office Expense	910	
	$13,341	$16,886

Each of the listed accounts has a normal balance per the general ledger. An examination of the ledger and journal reveals the following errors:

1. Cash received from a customer on account was debited for $570, and Accounts Receivable was credited for the same amount. The actual collection was for $750.
2. The purchase of a scanner on account for $340 was recorded as a debit to Supplies for $340 and a credit to Accounts Payable for $340.
3. Services were performed on account for a client for $890. Accounts Receivable was debited for $890 and Service Revenue was credited for $89.
4. A debit posting to Salaries Expense of $600 was omitted.
5. A payment on account for $206 was credited to Cash for $206 and credited to Accounts Payable for $260.
6. Payment of a $400 cash dividend to Wargo's shareholders was debited to Salaries Expense for $400 and credited to Cash for $400.

Instructions

Prepare the correct trial balance.

P3-12A Star Theatre, Inc. was recently formed and began operations in March. The Star will be unique in that it will show only triple features of sequential theme movies. As at February 28, Star's ledger showed Cash $16,000; Land $42,000; Buildings (concession stand, projection room, ticket booth, and screen) $18,000; Equipment $16,000; Accounts Payable $12,000; and Common Shares $80,000. During the month of March the following events and transactions occurred:

Journalize transactions, post, and prepare a trial balance.
(SO 3, 5, 6, 7, 8)

Mar. 2 Acquired three *Star Wars* movies (*Star Wars, The Empire Strikes Back,* and *The Return of the Jedi*) to be shown for the first three weeks of March. The film rental was $12,000; $4,000 was paid in cash and $8,000 will be paid on March 10.

3 Ordered the first three *Star Trek* movies, to be shown the last 10 days of March. They will cost $400 per night.

9 Received $6,500 cash from admissions.

10 Paid balance due on *Star Wars* movies rental and $3,000 on February 28 accounts payable.

11 Hired M. Brewer to operate concession stand. Brewer agrees to pay Star Theatre 15% of gross receipts, payable monthly.

12 Paid advertising expenses, $800.
20 Received $7,200 cash from admissions.
20 Received the *Star Trek* movies and paid rental fee of $4,000.
31 Paid salaries of $3,800.
31 Received statement from M. Brewer showing gross receipts from concessions of $8,000 and the balance due to Star Theatre of $1,200 for March. Brewer paid half the balance due and will remit the remainder on April 5.
31 Received $12,500 cash from admissions.

In addition to the accounts identified above, the chart of accounts includes Accounts Receivable, Admission Revenue, Concession Revenue, Advertising Expense, Film Rental Expense, and Salaries Expense.

Instructions

(a) Using T accounts, enter the beginning balances to the ledger.
(b) Journalize the March transactions.
(c) Post the March journal entries to the ledger.
(d) Prepare a trial balance at March 31, 2001.

Problems: Set B

Prepare statements of earnings and retained earnings.
(SO 1)

P3-1B Upton Consulting Corp. was started on March 1, 2001. The shareholders' equity column of the tabular summary for the month of March contained these recorded data:

Transaction	Amount	Description
(1)	$15,000	Investment
(4)	750	Rent expense
(6)	3,250	Service revenue
(8)	400	Advertising expense
(11)	1,000	Salaries expense
(12)	2,100	Service revenue
(15)	250	Utilities expense
(18)	500	Dividends
(20)	3,200	Service revenue
(22)	200	Repair expense
(24)	1,000	Advertising expense
(27)	300	Dividends
(29)	1,100	Service revenue
(32)	900	Salaries expense
(34)	200	Property tax expense
(36)	1,000	Income tax expense

All data were properly recorded except the following:

1. In transaction (22), $150 of the repair expense was applicable to Michael Upton's personal residence.
2. In transaction (36), $80 was applicable to repairs on business property.

Instructions

(a) Prepare a statement of earnings for the month of March.
(b) Prepare a statement of retained earnings for March.

Analyse transactions and calculate net earnings.
(SO 1)

P3-2B Tony's Repair Shop, Inc. was started on May 1. A summary of the May transactions follows:

1. Common shares were issued for $15,000 cash.
2. Purchased equipment for $5,000 cash.
3. Paid $400 cash for May office rent.
4. Paid $500 cash for supplies.

5. Incurred $250 of advertising costs in the *Beacon News*, on account.
6. Received $4,100 in cash from customers for repair service.
7. Declared and paid a $500 cash dividend.
8. Paid part-time employee salaries, $1,000.
9. Paid utility bills, $140.
10. Provided repair service on account to customers, $200.
11. Collected cash of $120 for services billed in transaction (10).

Instructions

(a) Prepare a tabular analysis of the transactions using these column headings: Cash, Accounts Receivable, Supplies, Equipment, Accounts Payable, Common Shares, and Retained Earnings. Revenue is called Service Revenue.

(b) From an analysis of the Retained Earnings column, calculate the net earnings or net loss for May.

Analyse transactions and prepare a statement of earnings, statement of retained earnings, and balance sheet.

(SO 1)

P3-3B Corso Care Corp. a veterinary business in Hills, Alberta, opened on August 1, 2001. On August 31, the balance sheet showed Cash $9,000; Accounts Receivable $1,700; Supplies $600; Office Equipment $6,000; Accounts Payable $3,600; Common Shares $13,000; and Retained Earnings $700. During September, the following transactions occurred:

1. Paid $3,100 cash on accounts payable.
2. Collected $1,300 of accounts receivable.
3. Purchased additional office equipment for $2,100, paying $800 in cash and the balance on account.
4. Earned revenue of $5,900, of which $2,500 is paid in cash and the balance is due in October.
5. Declared and paid a $600 cash dividend.
6. Paid salaries, $700; rent for September, $900; and advertising expense, $100.
7. Incurred utility expenses for the month on account, $170.
8. Received $7,000 from Canadian Western Bank; the money was borrowed on a note payable.

Instructions

(a) Prepare a tabular analysis of the September transactions beginning with August 31 balances. The headings over the columns should be Cash + Accounts Receivable + Supplies + Office Equipment = Notes Payable + Accounts Payable + Common Shares + Retained Earnings.

(b) Prepare a statement of earnings for September, a statement of retained earnings for September, and a balance sheet at September 30, 2001.

Analyse errors and their effects on the trial balance.

(SO 1, 8)

P3-4B A first year co-op student working for Insidz.com recorded the transactions for the month. He wasn't exactly sure how to journalize and post, but he did the best he could. He had a few questions, however, about the following transactions:

1. Cash received from a customer on account was recorded as a debit to Cash of $560 and a credit to Accounts Receivable of $650, instead of $560.
2. A cash service provided for cash was posted as a debit to Cash of $2,000 and a credit to Fees Earned of $2,000.
3. A debit of $750 for fees earned on account was neither recorded nor posted. The credit was recorded correctly.
4. The debit to record $1,000 of cash dividends was posted to the Salary Expense account.
5. The purchase, on account, of a computer that cost $2,500 was recorded as a debit to Supplies and a credit to Accounts Payable.
6. Insidz.com received advances from customers in the amount of $500 for work to be performed next month. The student debited Cash for $500 but didn't credit anything, as he wasn't sure what to credit.
7. A cash payment of $495 for salaries was recorded as a debit to Salary Expense and a credit to Salaries Payable.
8. Cash received from a customer on account was recorded as a debit to Cash and a credit to Accounts Payable, in the amount of $350.
9. Payment of rent for the month was debited to Rent Expense and credited to Cash, $850.
10. Issue of $5,000 of common shares was credited to the Common Shares account, but no debit was recorded.

Instructions

(a) Indicate which of the above transactions are correct, and which are incorrect.

(b) For each error identified in (a), indicate (1) whether the trial balance will balance; (2) the amount of the difference if the trial balance will not balance; and (3) the trial balance column that will have the larger total. Consider each error separately. Use the following form, in which transaction 1 is given as an example:

Error	(a) In Balance	(b) Difference	(c) Larger Column
1.	No	$90	Credit

Identify debits, credits, and normal balances; calculate cash flow and net earnings.
(SO 3)

P3-5B You are presented with the following transactions for Kailynn Corporation:

1. Issue $10,000 of common shares for cash.
2. Provide services for cash, $2,500.
3. Purchase a $35,000 truck for use in the business. Paid cash of $10,000 and recorded a note payable for the remainder.
4. Receive a $5,000 cash deposit from a customer for services to be provided in the future.
5. Pay $2,000 cash to employees on Friday for work done that week.
6. Bill customers $20,000 for services performed during month.
7. Purchase supplies of $500 on account.
8. Collect cash from transaction (6) above.
9. Pay rent for the month of $1,500.
10. Pay utilities for the month of $800.

Instructions

(a) For each transaction indicate (1) the basic type of account debited and credited (asset, liability, shareholders' equity); (2) the specific account debited and credited (Cash, Fees Earned, etc.); (3) whether the specific account is increased or decreased; and (4) the normal balance of the specific account. Use the following format, in which transaction 1 is given as an example:

(b) Calculate the cash flow and net earnings from these transactions.

	Account Debited				Account Credited			
Transaction	(a) Basic Type	(b) Specific Account	(c) Effect	(d) Normal Balance	(a) Basic Type	(b) Specific Account	(c) Effect	(d) Normal Balance
1.	Asset	Cash	Increase	Debit	Shareholders' Equity	Common Shares	Increase	Credit

Identify the normal balance and financial statement for selected accounts.
(SO 3)

P3-6B You are presented with the following alphabetical list of accounts selected from **Reitmans [Canada] Limited** 2000 financial statements:

Account	(a) Normal Balance	(b) Financial Statement
Accounts payable and accrued items		
Accounts receivable		
Capital assets		
Cash and short-term deposits		
Cost of goods sold and selling, general, and administrative expenses		
Depreciation and amortization expense		
Dividends		

Income tax expense
Income tax payable
Interest on long-term debt
Investments
Investment income
Merchandise inventories
Prepaid expenses
Retained earnings
Sales
Share capital

Instructions

For each account, indicate (a) whether the normal balance is a debit or a credit and (b) the financial statement where the account should be classified: balance sheet, statement of earnings, or statement of retained earnings.

P3-7B The Frontier Park Corp. was formed on April 1. These selected events and transactions occurred during April:

Journalize a series of transactions.
(SO 3, 5)

Apr.	1	Common shares were issued for $60,000 cash.
	4	Purchased land costing $30,000, for cash.
	8	Incurred advertising expense of $1,800 on account.
	11	Paid salaries to employees, $1,500.
	12	Hired park manager at a salary of $4,000 per month, effective May 1.
	13	Paid $1,500 for a one-year insurance policy.
	17	Paid $600 in cash dividends.
	20	Received $5,700 in cash for admission fees.
	25	Sold 100 coupon books for $25 each. Each book contains 10 coupons that entitle the holder to one admission to the park.
	30	Received $5,900 in cash admission fees.
	30	Paid $700 on account for advertising expense incurred on April 8.

Instructions

Journalize the April transactions.

P3-8B Iva Holz incorporated Skeptical Accountants Inc., an accounting practice, on May 1, 2001. During the first month of operations of her business, these events and transactions occurred:

Journalize transactions, post, and prepare a trial balance.
(SO 3, 5, 6, 7, 8)

May	1	Common shares were issued for $42,000 cash.
	2	Hired a secretary-receptionist at a salary of $1,000 per month.
	3	Purchased $1,200 of supplies on account from Read Supply Company.
	7	Paid office rent of $900 for the month.
	11	Completed a tax assignment and billed client $1,100 for services rendered.
	12	Received $3,500 advance on a management consulting engagement.
	17	Received cash of $1,200 for services completed for H. Arnold Co.
	31	Paid secretary-receptionist $1,000 salary for the month.
	31	Paid 40% of balance due to Read Supply Company.

Instructions

(a) Journalize the transactions.
(b) Post to the ledger T accounts.
(c) Prepare a trial balance at May 31, 2001.

Journalize transactions, post, and prepare a trial balance.
(SO 3, 5, 6, 7, 8)

P3-9B The trial balance of Sterling Dry Cleaners Ltd. at June 30 follows:

STERLING DRY CLEANERS LTD.
Trial Balance
June 30, 2001

	Debit	Credit
Cash	$12,532	
Accounts Receivable	10,536	
Supplies	4,844	
Equipment	25,950	
Accounts Payable		$15,878
Unearned Revenue		1,730
Common Shares		36,254
	$53,862	$53,862

The July transactions were as follows:

July 8 Collected $4,936 in cash on June 30 accounts receivable.
9 Paid employee salaries, $2,100.
11 Received $4,325 in cash for services rendered.
14 Paid June 30 creditors $10,750 on account.
17 Purchased supplies on account, $554.
22 Billed customers for services rendered, $4,700.
30 Paid employee salaries, $3,114; utilities, $1,384; repairs, $692; and income taxes, $500.
31 Paid $700 cash dividend.

Instructions

(a) Prepare a general ledger using T accounts. Enter the opening balances in the ledger accounts as at July 1. Provision should be made for the following additional accounts: Dividends, Dry Cleaning Revenue, Repair Expense, Salaries Expense, and Utilities Expense.
(b) Journalize the transactions.
(c) Post to the ledger accounts.
(d) Prepare a trial balance at July 31, 2001.

Prepare a trial balance and financial statements.
(SO 8)

P3-10B The **Hudson's Bay Company** has the following alphabetical list of accounts and balances (in thousands of dollars), as at January 31, 2000:

Capital assets	$1,447,200
Capital stock	1,521,917
Cash in stores	8,480
Credit card receivables	483,940
Dividends	35,521
Future income taxes payable	54,368
Income tax expense	96,369
Income taxes recoverable	25,445
Interest expense	79,140
Investments	49,264
Long-term debt	700,184
Long-term debt due within one year	151,695
Long-term receivables	29,348
Merchandise inventories	1,598,695
Operating expenses	7,024,207
Other accounts payable and accrued expenses	584,644
Other accounts receivable	127,522
Other assets	378,970
Other long-term liabilities	64,445
Other shareholders' equity items	198,799

Prepaid expenses	44,606
Retained earnings, February 1, 1999	484,295
Sales and revenue	7,295,751
Short-term borrowings	29,597
Short-term deposits	41,792
Trade accounts payable	384,804

Instructions

(a) Prepare a trial balance, sorting each account balance into the debit column or the credit column.

(b) Prepare a statement of earnings and a statement of retained earnings for the year ended January 31, 2000, and a balance sheet as at January 31, 2000, for Hudson's Bay.

P3-11B This trial balance of Saginaw Company Ltd. does not balance:

Prepare a correct trial balance.

(SO 8)

SAGINAW COMPANY LTD.
Trial Balance
May 31, 2001

	Debit	Credit
Cash	$ 5,850	
Accounts Receivable		$ 2,750
Prepaid Insurance	700	
Equipment	8,000	
Accounts Payable		4,500
Property Taxes Payable	560	
Common Shares		5,700
Retained Earnings		6,000
Service Revenue	6,690	
Salaries Expense	4,200	
Advertising Expense		1,100
Property Tax Expense	800	
	$26,800	$20,050

Your review of the ledger reveals that each account has a normal balance. You also discover the following errors:

1. The totals of the debit sides of Prepaid Insurance, Accounts Payable, and Property Tax Expense were each understated by $100.
2. Transposition errors were made in Accounts Receivable and Service Revenue. Based on postings made, the correct balances were $2,570 and $6,960, respectively.
3. A debit posting to Salaries Expense of $200 was omitted.
4. A $700 cash dividend was debited to Common Shares for $700 and credited to Cash for $700.
5. A $420 purchase of supplies on account was debited to Equipment for $420 and credited to Cash for $420.
6. A cash payment of $250 for advertising was debited to Advertising Expense for $25 and credited to Cash for $25.
7. A collection from a customer for $210 was debited to Cash for $210 and credited to Accounts Payable for $210.

Instructions

Prepare the correct trial balance. (Note: The chart of accounts also includes the following: Dividends, Supplies, and Supplies Expense.)

P3-12B Lake Theatre, Inc. was recently incorporated. All facilities were completed on March 31. At this time, the ledger showed Cash $6,000; Land $10,000; Buildings (concession stand, projection room, ticket booth, and screen) $8,000; Equipment $6,000; Accounts Payable $2,000; Mortgage Payable $8,000; and Common Shares $20,000. During April, the following events and transactions occurred:

Journalize transactions, post, and prepare a trial balance.

(SO 3, 5, 6, 7, 8)

Apr. 2 Paid film rental of $800 on first movie.
3 Ordered two additional films at $500 each.
9 Received $1,800 cash from admissions.
10 Made $2,000 payment on mortgage and $1,000 payment on accounts payable.
11 Hired R. Thoms to operate concession stand. Thoms agrees to pay the Lake Theatre 17% of gross receipts, payable monthly.
12 Paid advertising expenses, $300.
20 Received one of the films ordered on April 3 and was billed $500. The film will be shown in April.
25 Received $4,200 cash from admissions.
29 Paid salaries, $1,600.
30 Received statement from R. Thoms showing gross receipts of $1,000 and the balance due to the Lake Theatre of $170 for April. Thoms paid half of the balance due and will remit the remainder on May 5.
30 Prepaid $700 rental on special film to be run in May.

In addition to the accounts identified above, the chart of accounts shows Accounts Receivable, Prepaid Rentals, Admission Revenue, Concession Revenue, Advertising Expense, Film Rental Expense, and Salaries Expense.

Instructions

(a) Enter the beginning balances in the ledger T accounts as at April 1.
(b) Journalize the April transactions.
(c) Post the April journal entries to the ledger T accounts.
(d) Prepare a trial balance at April 30, 2001.

BROADENING YOUR PERSPECTIVE

FINANCIAL REPORTING AND ANALYSIS

FINANCIAL REPORTING PROBLEM: *Loblaw Companies Limited*

Loblaws
A passion for food... *and a lot more!*

BYP3-1 The financial statements of **Loblaw** in Appendix A at the back of this book contain the following selected accounts, all in millions of dollars:

Accounts payable and accrued liabilities	$1,806
Accounts receivable	345
Fixed assets	3,194
Income tax expense	198
Interest expense	96
Interest income	28

Instructions

(a) What is the increase and decrease side for each account? What is the normal balance for each account?
(b) Identify the probable other account in the transaction and the effect on that account when
1. Accounts Payable is decreased.
2. Accounts Receivable is decreased.
3. Fixed Assets is increased.
4. Income Tax Expense is increased.
5. Interest Expense is increased.
6. Interest Income is increased.

COMPARATIVE ANALYSIS PROBLEM: *Loblaw and Sobeys*

BYP3-2 The financial statements of **Sobeys Inc.** are presented in Appendix B, following the financial statements for **Loblaw** in Appendix A.

Instructions

(a) Using Loblaw's balance sheet, statement of retained earnings, and statement of earnings, recast the accounts and amounts provided into a trial balance format as at January 2, 2000.

(b) Using Sobeys balance sheet, statement of retained earnings, and statement of earnings, recast the accounts and amounts provided into a trial balance format as at May 1, 1999.

RESEARCH CASE

BYP3-3 The North American Industry Classification System (NAICS), a new classification system for organizing economic data, recently replaced the separate standard classification systems currently used by Canada, the United States, and Mexico. It provides a common standard framework for the collection of economic and financial data for all three nations.

NAICS Canada, the Canadian version of the classification, groups economic activity into 20 sectors and 921 industries.

Instructions

At your library, find *NAICS Canada* (published by Statistics Canada, Standards Division) and answer these questions:

(a) The NAICS numbering system uses five levels of detail to identify company activities. What do the first two digits identify? The fourth digit? The sixth digit?

(b) Identify the sector, subsector, industry group, NAICS industry, and Canadian industry represented by the code 513322.

(c) Identify the sector code (first two digits) for the following industries:

1. agriculture, forestry, fishing, and hunting.
2. information.
3. finance and insurance.
4. management of companies and enterprises.
5. arts, entertainment, and recreation.

(d) Suppose that you are interested in examining several companies in the arts, entertainment, and recreation industry. Determine the appropriate six-digit codes for each of your chosen companies.

INTERPRETING FINANCIAL STATEMENTS

BYP3-4 Irwin Toys Limited, established in 1926, is the largest Canadian-owned toy company. It manufactures and distributes over 1,800 toy products, such as dolls, games, Meccano construction sets, and crafts. The company also manufactures and distributes over 1,500 sporting goods, including the Cooper brand of baseball products and the Winnwell hockey line.

The following selected accounts have been extracted from Irwin Toys' general ledger:

	January 31	
	1998	**1997**
	(in thousands)	
Bank indebtedness	$ 22,944	$ 12,528
Capital stock	2,542	2,542
Cost of sales, selling, and administrative expenses	99,304	105,017
Dividends	1,061	1,061
Income and other taxes payable	42	
Inventories	27,445	24,552
Net sales	103,658	111,654
Prepaid expenses	3,629	2,650
Short-term investments		1,997

Instructions

(a) What is Irwin Toys' fiscal year end?

(b) Identify the accounts of Irwin Toys listed above that have normal debit balances in the trial balance.

(c) Are the accounts listed in the order in which they would likely appear in Irwin Toys' general ledger?

(d) Prepare the journal entries (you may omit explanations) necessary to record the following transactions for Irwin Toys. Use xxx for amounts.

1. sale of Katch games to Canadian Tire on account
2. record the cost of the sale of the above products
3. payment of cash dividends to junior shareholders
4. sale of short-term investment (you can ignore any gain or loss)
5. increase in prepaid expenses
6. record income and other taxes payable

BYP3-5 The Second Cup Ltd. was founded in 1988 by franchising entrepreneur Michael Bregman. Since that time, it has doubled its revenue and today is the largest specialty coffee retailer in Canada. A few years ago, the company's balance sheet reported $153 million in assets, with only $11 million in liabilities, all of which were current liabilities such as accounts payable and income taxes payable.

During the previous year, Second Cup had issued shares in response to growing investor interest and to finance the acquisition of the U.S.-based Gloria Jean's Coffee chain. The company generated $9 million cash from operating activities in 1997 and paid no dividends. It had a Cash and Short-Term Investment balance of $46 million at the end of the year.

Instructions

(a) Name at least two advantages for Second Cup which result from having no long-term debt. Can you think of any disadvantages?

(b) What are some of the advantages for Second Cup which result from having this large a cash balance? What is a disadvantage?

(c) Why do you suppose Second Cup has the $11 million balance in Current Liabilities, since it appears that it could have made all its purchases for cash?

A GLOBAL FOCUS

BYP3-6 Mo och Domsjo AB (MoDo) is one of Europe's largest forest products companies. It has production facilities in Sweden, France, and Great Britain and is headquartered in Stockholm, Sweden. Its accounts are prepared in conformity with the standards issued by the Swedish Standards Board. Its financial statements are harmonized (that is, there is a minimal difference in methods) with those of member countries of the European Union.

The following trial balance lists MoDo's general ledger accounts as at December 31, 1998. In Canada, and in this chapter, trial balances normally list accounts in financial statement order to facilitate later preparation of the financial statements. MoDo also lists its accounts in financial statement order—that is, the order in which they appear in MoDo's financial statements—but financial statements in the European Union are presented in a different order than in Canada. To assist you in understanding this trial balance, the normal classification of each account in Canada has also been included.

MoDo

MODO
Trial Balance
December 31, 1998
(Swedish krona, in millions)

Canadian Classification	Account	Debit	Credit
Capital assets	Goodwill, leases, and similar rights	32	
	Forest land	4,585	
	Buildings, other land, and land installations	2,565	
	Machinery and equipment	13,216	
	Fixed plants under construction and advance payments	341	
Other assets	Shares and participations	148	
	Other long-term receivables	44	
Current assets	Inventories	3,648	
	Current receivables	4,614	
	Short-term placements	780	
	Cash and bank	461	
Shareholders' Equity	Restricted equity (includes share capital)		12,262
	Non-restricted equity (includes retained earnings)		3,611
Minority interest Liabilities	Minority interests		5
	Interest-bearing (includes pension liabilities		135
	Interest-free (includes future income tax payable)		3,468
	Financial liabilities (includes current and long-term bank loans)		4,249
	Operating liabilities (includes current bills payable)		4,200
Revenues	Net turnover		22,676
	Other operating income		598
Expenses	Raw materials, goods for resale, and consumables	10,719	
	Personnel costs	3,592	
	Other external costs	4,987	
	Depreciation	1,507	
	Other	131	
	Income tax recovery		166
	Totals	51,370	51,370

Instructions
List all differences that you notice between MoDo's trial balance presentation (order and terminology) and the normal presentation of trial balances in Canada, as shown in the chapter.

FINANCIAL ANALYSIS ON THE WEB

BYP3-7 ***Purpose:*** Identify summary liquidity, solvency, and profitability information about companies, and compare this information across companies in the same industry.

Instructions
Specific requirements of this web case can be found on the Kimmel website.

Critical Thinking

COLLABORATIVE LEARNING ACTIVITY

BYP3-8 Lucy Lars operates Lucy Riding Academy, Inc. The academy's primary sources of revenue are riding fees and lesson fees, which are provided on a cash basis. Lucy also boards horses and bills their owners monthly for boarding fees. In a few cases, boarders pay in advance of expected use. For its revenue transactions, the academy maintains these accounts: Cash, Boarding Accounts Receivable, Unearned Revenue, Riding Revenue, Lesson Revenue, and Boarding Revenue.

The academy owns 10 horses, a stable, a riding corral, riding equipment, and office equipment. These assets are accounted for in the following accounts: Horses, Building, Riding Corral, Riding Equipment, and Office Equipment.

The academy employs stable helpers and an office employee who receive weekly salaries. At the end of each month, the mail usually brings bills for advertising, utilities, and veterinary service. Other expenses include feed for the horses and insurance. For its expenses, the academy maintains the following accounts: Hay and Feed Supplies, Prepaid Insurance, Accounts Payable, Salaries Expense, Advertising Expense, Utilities Expense, Veterinary Expense, Hay and Feed Expense, and Insurance Expense.

The corporation declares and pays periodic dividends. To record shareholders' equity in the business and dividends, two accounts are maintained: Common Shares and Dividends.

During the first month of operations an inexperienced bookkeeper was employed. Lucy Lars asks you to review the following eight entries of the 50 entries made during the month. In each case, the explanation for the entry is correct.

May 1	Cash	15,000	
	Common Shares		15,000
	(Issued common shares in exchange for $15,000 cash)		
5	Cash	250	
	Riding Revenue		250
	(Received $250 cash for lesson fees)		
7	Cash	500	
	Boarding Revenue		500
	(Received $500 for boarding of horses beginning June 1)		
9	Hay and Feed Expense	1,700	
	Cash		1,700
	(Purchased estimated five months' supply of feed and hay for $1,700 on account)		
14	Riding Equipment	80	
	Cash		800
	(Purchased desk and other office equipment for $800 cash)		
15	Salaries Expense	400	
	Cash		400
	(Paid dividend)		
20	Cash	145	
	Riding Revenue		154
	(Received $154 cash for riding fees)		
31	Veterinary Expense	75	
	Accounts Payable		75
	(Received bill of $75 from veterinarian for services rendered)		

Instructions

With the class divided into groups, answer the following:

(a) Indicate each journal entry that is correct. For each journal entry that is incorrect, prepare the entry that should have been made by the bookkeeper.
(b) Which of the incorrect entries would prevent the trial balance from balancing?
(c) What was the correct net earnings for May, assuming the bookkeeper reported net earnings of $4,500 after posting all 50 entries?
(d) What was the correct balance for Cash at May 31, assuming the bookkeeper reported a balance of $12,475 after posting all 50 entries?

COMMUNICATION ACTIVITY

BYP3-9 Milly Maid Company offers a home cleaning service. Two recurring transactions for the company are billing customers for services rendered and paying employee salaries. For example, on March 15, bills totalling $6,000 were sent to customers and $2,000 was paid in salaries to employees.

Instructions

Write a memorandum to your instructor that explains and illustrates the steps in the recording process for each of the March 15 transactions.

ETHICS CASE

BYP3-10 Mary Vonesh is the assistant chief accountant at Staples Corporation, a manufacturer of computer chips and cellular phones. The company presently has total sales of $20 million. It is the end of the first quarter and Mary is hurriedly trying to prepare a general ledger trial balance so that quarterly financial statements can be prepared and released to management and the regulatory agencies. To Mary's dismay, the total credits on the trial balance exceed the debits by $1,000. In order to meet the 4 p.m. deadline, Mary then decides to plug the difference! She believes that the difference is quite small and will not affect anyone's decisions, so she forces the debits and credits into balance by adding the amount of the difference to the Equipment account. She chose Equipment because it is one of the larger account balances; percentage-wise it will be the least misstated. She wishes that she had another few days to find the error but realizes that the financial statements are already late.

Instructions

(a) Who are the stakeholders in this situation?
(b) What ethical issues are involved?
(c) What are Mary's alternatives?

Answers to Self-Study Questions

1. b 2. b 3. b 4. c 5. d 6. d 7. b 8. a 9. c 10. d
11. a 12. c

Answer to Loblaw Review It Question 4

Accounts Receivable (Asset-Dr.), Taxes Payable (Liability-Cr.), Sales (Revenue-Cr.), and Depreciation and Amortization (Expense-Dr.).

Loblaws
A passion for food... *and a lot more!*

CHAPTER 4

Accrual Accounting Concepts

STUDY OBJECTIVES

After studying this chapter, you should be able to:

1. Explain the revenue recognition principle and the matching principle.
2. Differentiate between the cash basis and the accrual basis of accounting.
3. Explain why adjusting entries are needed and identify the major types of adjusting entries.
4. Prepare adjusting entries for prepayments.
5. Prepare adjusting entries for accruals.
6. Describe the nature and purpose of the adjusted trial balance.
7. Explain the purposes of closing entries.
8. Describe the required steps in the accounting cycle.

Timing Is Everything

You might not think accounting and comedy have much in common, but they share at least one important principle: Timing is everything. Like many rules, this one is perhaps best illustrated by an example of what happens when it is broken.

Livent Inc., the theatrical company founded by flamboyant Canadian businessmen Garth Drabinsky and Myron Gottlieb, was for years held up in Canadian business circles—and in textbooks—as a great Canadian success story. Considered one of the leading, and perhaps most original, theatre production houses in North America, it became known worldwide for its lavish musicals, including *Phantom of the Opera*, *Ragtime*, and *Beauty and the Beast*. Even its box-office failures, like *Sunset Boulevard*, were renowned. It also owned several of the venues in which its productions were shown, including Pantages Theatre in Toronto.

By 1998, however, a scandal erupted at Livent as the company became mired in debt. It first relegated Mr. Drabinsky and Mr. Gottlieb to non-financial roles in April, then, as talk of accounting irregularities grew, saw trading in its shares halted in August and its credit cut off by the CIBC in November. Finally, on November 18, it was forced to file for bankruptcy; and on the same day, the board voted to fire the two founders and file a civil lawsuit against them.

Early in 1999, Mr. Drabinsky and Mr. Gottlieb were indicted on criminal charges. They were accused of overseeing a scheme to manipulate the company's accounting practices in order to inflate earnings. Both the civil and criminal trials are still pending, but the allegations are very serious.

According to reports in the *Globe and Mail*, the civil lawsuit alleges several fraudulent practices, including the following:

- [hiding] expenses by transferring them to the account of a capital asset, so that the expenses were not deducted from revenue but were instead capitalized as an asset. The effect was to inflate revenue and overstate the net book value of the asset on the balance sheet.
- the understatement of expenses at the end of a quarter to ensure reported financial re-

sults met appropriate targets.

- transferring expenses and losses for shows which would have to be fully expensed in the quarter to the account of a different production that had not started its expense amortization. The suit claims that $12 million of such transfers were done in 1996 and 1997, relating to 27 different locations and seven different shows. The expenses were transferred to the accounts of 31 future locations and 10 shows in development.
- the manufacture of earnings at the end of a fiscal period. The lawsuit says there were 15 transactions where revenue was inappropriately recorded.

Each of these allegations involves the violation of accrual accounting concepts, particularly the revenue recognition and matching principles, with the result that Livent appeared to be much more profitable than it actually was.

As shareholders today are impatient for results, there is intense pressure on management to report higher earnings every year. When actual performance falls short of expectations, management is often tempted to bend the rules.

Garth Drabinsky claims that he is really a victim in this sad tale. He maintains that while the accounting practices used may be said to be "aggressive," they weren't adopted to manipulate the financial position of Livent to suit his interests.

As you are learning, these "rules" of accounting are not completely hard and fast. That is why we speak of generally accepted accounting principles. But the fact that accounting principles offer flexibility within an acceptable framework does not make these principles any less important. In the end, a failure to respect them, however great the temptation, rarely pays off.

Making adjustments properly is important and necessary, as indicated in the opening story. To do otherwise leads to a misstatement of revenues and expenses. In this chapter, we introduce you to the accrual accounting concepts that make such adjustments possible.

The content and organization of the chapter are as follows:

ACCRUAL ACCOUNTING CONCEPTS

- **Timing Issues**
  - Revenue Recognition Principle
  - Matching Principle
  - Accrual Versus Cash Basis of Accounting
- **The Basics of Adjusting Entries**
  - Types of Adjusting Entries
  - Adjusting Entries for Prepayments
  - Adjusting Entries for Accruals
  - Summary of Basic Relationships
  - Alternative Treatment of Prepaid Expenses and Unearned Revenues
  - Sierra Corporation Illustration
- **The Adjusted Trial Balance and Financial Statements**
  - Preparing the Adjusted Trial Balance
  - Preparing Financial Statements
- **Closing the Books**
  - Preparing Closing Entries
  - Preparing a Post-Closing Trial Balance
- **Summary of the Accounting Cycle**

TIMING ISSUES

STUDY OBJECTIVE 1

Explain the revenue recognition principle and the matching principle.

Consider this story:

> A grocery store owner from the old country kept his accounts payable on a spindle, accounts receivable on a notepad, and cash in a cigar box. His daughter, having just passed the CGA Professional Applications exam, chided her father: "I don't understand how you can run your business this way. How do you know what your profits are?"
>
> "Well," the father replied, "when I got off the boat 40 years ago, I had nothing but the pants I was wearing. Today your brother is a doctor, your sister is a professor, and you are a CGA. Your mother and I have a nice car, a well-furnished house, and a lake home. We have a good business and everything is paid for. So, you add all that together, subtract the pants, and there's your profit."

Although the old grocer may be correct in his evaluation of how to calculate earnings over his lifetime, most businesses need more immediate feedback about how well they are doing. For example, management usually wants monthly reports on financial results, most large corporations are required to present quarterly and annual financial statements to shareholders, and the Canada Customs and Revenue Agency requires all businesses to file annual tax returns. Consequently, **accounting divides the economic life of a business into artificial time periods**. As indicated in Chapter 1, this is the **time period assumption**. **Accounting time periods are generally a month, a quarter, or a year.**

Helpful Hint An accounting time period that is one year long is called a **fiscal year**.

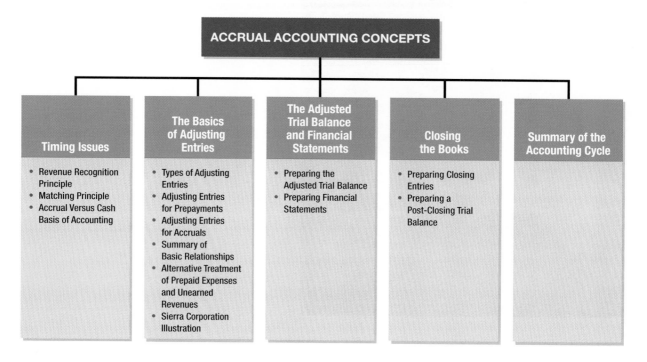

Many business transactions affect more than one of these arbitrary time periods. For example, a new building purchased by Sears or a new airplane purchased by Air Canada will be used for many years. It doesn't make sense to expense the full amount of the building or the airplane at the time it is purchased because each will be used for many subsequent periods. Therefore, it is necessary to determine the impact of each transaction on specific accounting periods.

Determining the amount of revenues and expenses to be reported in a given accounting period can be difficult. Proper reporting requires a thorough understanding of the nature of the company's business. Accountants have developed two principles to use as guidelines as part of generally accepted accounting principles: the revenue recognition principle and the matching principle.

REVENUE RECOGNITION PRINCIPLE

The **revenue recognition principle** dictates that revenue must be recognized in the accounting period in which it is earned. In a service company, revenue is considered to be earned at the time the service is performed. To illustrate, assume a dry cleaning business cleans clothing on June 30 but customers do not claim and pay for their clothes until the first week of July. Under the revenue recognition principle, revenue is earned in June when the service is performed, not in July when the cash is received. At June 30, the dry cleaning service would report a receivable on its balance sheet and revenue in its statement of earnings for the service performed.

Revenue Recognition

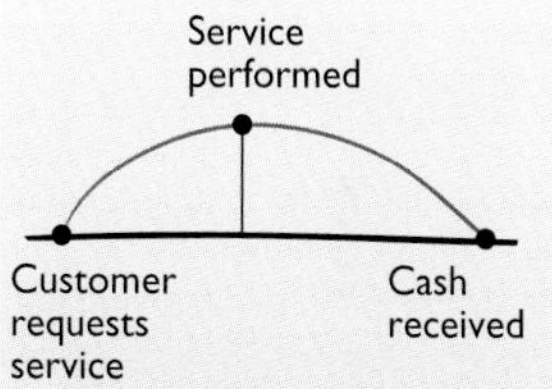

Revenue should be recognized in the accounting period in which it is earned (generally when the service is performed).

Improper application of the revenue recognition principle can have devastating consequences for investors. For example, the share price of the well-known outdoor clothing manufacturer North Face plunged when the company announced that $9 million of transactions that had been previously recorded as sales were reversed because North Face repurchased goods from a customer. This raised the question of whether a sale should have been recorded in the first place. And, as mentioned in the opening vignette, Mr. Drabinsky and Mr. Gottlieb have been sued by the new management of Livent Inc. for at least 15 violations of the revenue recognition principle, amongst other allegations. They are accused of representing certain transactions as "sales" for revenue recognition purposes which were, in substance, not earned, and indeed, in some cases, were something else altogether, such as loans.

DECISION TOOLKIT

Decision Checkpoints	Info Needed for Decision	Tool to Use for Decision	How to Evaluate Results
At what point should the company record revenue?	Need to understand the nature of the company's business	Revenue should be recorded when earned. For a service business, revenue is earned when a service is performed.	Recognizing revenue too early overstates current period revenue; recognizing it too late understates current period revenue.

MATCHING PRINCIPLE

In recognizing expenses, a simple rule is followed: "Let the expenses follow the revenues." Thus, expense recognition is tied to revenue recognition. With the preceding example, this means that the salary expense of performing the cleaning service on June 30 should be reported in the same period in which the service revenue is recognized. The critical issue in expense recognition is determining when the expense contributes to revenue. This may or may not be the same period in which the expense is paid. If the salary incurred on June 30 is not paid until July, the dry cleaner would report salaries payable on its June 30 balance sheet.

The practice of expense recognition is referred to as the **matching principle** because it dictates that efforts (expenses) must be matched with accomplishments (revenues). These relationships are shown in Illustration 4-1.

Illustration 4-1 GAAP relationships in revenue and expense recognition

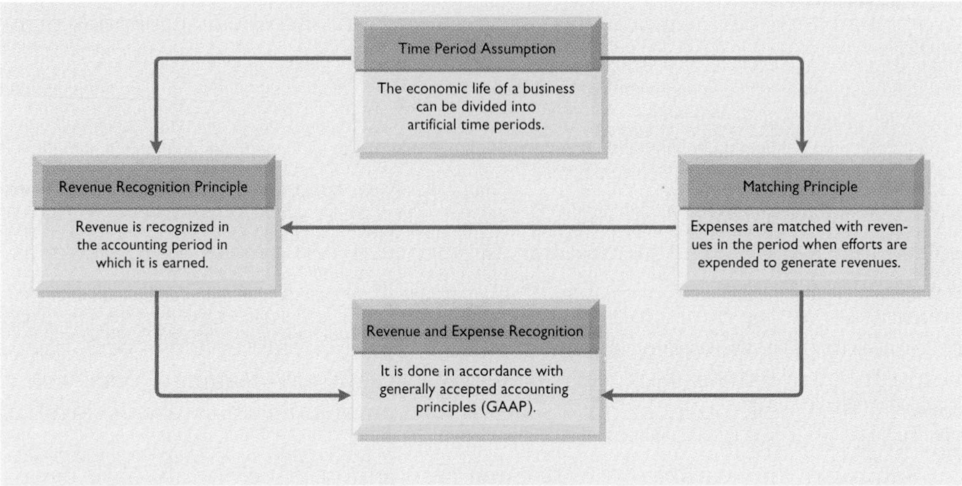

Time Period Assumption
The economic life of a business can be divided into artificial time periods.
Revenue Recognition Principle
Revenue is recognized in the accounting period in which it is earned.
Matching Principle
Expenses are matched with revenues in the period when efforts are expended to generate revenues.
Revenue and Expense Recognition
It is done in accordance with generally accepted accounting principles (GAAP).

B U S I N E S S I N S I G H T
Management Perspective

Suppose you are a filmmaker and spend $15 million to produce a film. Over what period should the $15 million be expensed? Yes, it should be expensed over the economic life of the film. But what is its economic life? The filmmaker must estimate how much revenue will be earned from box office sales, video sales, and television over a period that can easily stretch to 5 years or more. If a filmmaker allocates the cost over five years and the film produces revenue in the sixth year, then the matching is not correct. Furthermore, in some cases, a film flops and yet the costs are still spread out over five years in hopes that the film will eventually succeed. For example, Orion Pictures (now owned by MGM) earned $7.3 million in one year but lost $32 million the next year because it expensed 40 films that were not producing revenue. It was alleged that the company had overstated its earnings in earlier years because it did not expense these costs sooner. This case demonstrates the difficulty of properly matching expenses to revenues.

DECISION TOOLKIT

Decision Checkpoints	Info Needed for Decision	Tool to Use for Decision	How to Evaluate Results
At what point should the company record expenses?	Need to understand the nature of the company's business	Expenses should "follow" revenues—that is, the effort (expense) should be matched with the result (revenue).	Recognizing expenses too early overstates current period expense; recognizing them too late understates current period expense.

ACCRUAL VERSUS CASH BASIS OF ACCOUNTING

STUDY OBJECTIVE 2

Differentiate between the cash basis and the accrual basis of accounting.

Application of the revenue recognition and matching principles results in accrual basis accounting. **Accrual basis accounting** means that transactions that affect a company's financial statements are recorded **in the periods in which the events occur**, rather than in the periods in which the company receives or pays cash. For example, **using the accrual basis to determine net earnings means recognizing revenues when earned rather than when the cash is received, and recognizing expenses when incurred rather than when paid.**

In contrast, under **cash basis accounting**, **revenue is recorded only when the cash is received, and an expense is recorded only when cash is paid. A statement of earnings presented under the cash basis of accounting does not satisfy generally accepted accounting principles.** Why? Because it fails to record revenue that has been earned, but for which the cash has not been received, thus violating the revenue recognition principle. In addition, as expenses are also not matched with earned revenues, the matching principle is violated. Accountants are sometimes asked to convert cash-based records to the accrual basis. As you might expect, extensive adjustments to the accounting records are required for this task.

Illustration 4-2 shows the relationship between accrual-based numbers and cash-based numbers, using a simple example. Suppose that you own a painting company and you paint a large building during year 1. In year 1, you incur total expenses of $50,000, which includes the cost of the paint and your employees' salaries. Now assume that you bill your customer $80,000 at the end of year 1, but you aren't paid until year 2. On an accrual basis, you would report the revenue during the period earned—year 1—and the expenses would be matched to the period in which the revenues were earned. Thus, your net earnings for year 1 would be $30,000, and no revenue or expense from this project would be reported in year 2. The $30,000 of earnings reported for year 1 provides a useful indication of the profitability of your efforts during that period. If, instead, you were reporting on a cash basis, you would report expenses of $50,000 in year 1 and revenues of $80,000 in year 2. Net earnings for year 1 would be a loss of $50,000, while net earnings for year 2 would be $80,000. Cash basis measures are not very informative about the results of your efforts during year 1 or year 2.

International Note

Although different accounting standards are often used by companies in other industrialized countries, the accrual basis of accounting is central to all of these standards.

Illustration 4-2 Accrual versus cash basis accounting

	Year One	Year Two
Activity	 Purchased paint, painted building, paid employees	 Received payment for work done in year 1
Accrual basis	Revenue $80,000 Expense 50,000 Net earnings $30,000	Revenue $ 0 Expense 0 Net earnings $ 0
Cash basis	Revenue $ 0 Expense 50,000 Net loss ($50,000)	Revenue $80,000 Expense 0 Net earnings $80,000

Although most companies use the accrual basis of accounting, some small companies use the cash basis because they often have few receivables and payables.

BUSINESS INSIGHT

Management Perspective

You might wish to write to your Member of Parliament and suggest the government learn accrual accounting concepts. The 1997–98 federal accounts recorded a $2.5 billion expense for the Millennium Scholarship Fund—even though the first scholarships weren't awarded until the year 2000! The government—accused by the opposition of cooking the books to minimize the current budgetary surplus—staunchly maintained that it was appropriate to record these financial charges in the books in the year the program is announced. What do you think?

BEFORE YOU GO ON . . .

Review It

1. What are the revenue recognition and matching principles?
2. What are the differences between the cash and accrual bases of accounting?

The Basics of Adjusting Entries

STUDY OBJECTIVE 3

Explain why adjusting entries are needed and identify the major types of adjusting entries.

Adjusting entries are entries made to adjust or update accounts at the end of the accounting period. These entries enable revenues to be recorded in the period in which they are earned, and expenses to be recognized in the period in which they are incurred. **Adjusting entries are needed to ensure that the revenue recognition and matching principles are followed.**

The use of adjusting entries makes it possible to produce relevant financial statements at the end of the accounting period. Thus, the balance sheet reports appropriate assets, liabilities, and shareholders' equity at the statement date, and the statement of earnings shows the proper net earnings (or loss) for the period. However, the trial balance—the first pulling together of the transaction data—may not contain up-to-date and complete data. This is true for these reasons:

1. Some events are not journalized daily, because it would not be useful or efficient to do so. Examples are the use of supplies and the earning of wages by employees.
2. Some costs are not journalized during the accounting period, because these costs expire with the passage of time rather than as a result of recurring daily transactions. Examples of such costs are building and equipment amortization and rent and insurance.
3. Some items may be unrecorded. An example is a utility service bill that will not be received until the next accounting period.

Adjusting entries are required every time financial statements are prepared. An essential starting point is an analysis of each account in the trial balance to determine whether it is complete and up-to-date for financial statement purposes.

TYPES OF ADJUSTING ENTRIES

Adjusting entries can be classified as either prepayments or accruals. Each of these classes has two subcategories as shown in Illustration 4-3.

Prepayments:

1. **Prepaid expenses:** Expenses paid in cash and recorded as assets before they are used or consumed.
2. **Unearned revenues:** Cash received and recorded as liabilities before revenue is earned.

Accruals:

1. **Accrued revenues:** Revenues earned but not yet received in cash or recorded.
2. **Accrued expenses:** Expenses incurred but not yet paid in cash or recorded.

Illustration 4-3
Categories of adjusting entries

Specific examples and explanations of each type of adjustment are given in subsequent sections. Each example is based on the October 31 trial balance of Sierra Corporation, from Chapter 3, reproduced in Illustration 4-4. Note that Retained Earnings has been added to this trial balance with a zero balance. We will explain its use later.

Illustration 4-4
Trial balance

SIERRA CORPORATION
Trial Balance
October 31, 2001

	Debit	Credit
Cash	$15,200	
Advertising Supplies	2,500	
Prepaid Insurance	600	
Office Equipment	5,000	
Notes Payable		$ 5,000
Accounts Payable		2,500
Unearned Revenue		1,200
Common Shares		10,000
Retained Earnings		0
Dividends	500	
Service Revenue		10,000
Salaries Expense	4,000	
Rent Expense	900	
	$28,700	$28,700

It will be assumed that Sierra Corporation uses an accounting period of one month. Thus, monthly adjusting entries need to be made, and the current entries will be dated October 31.

ADJUSTING ENTRIES FOR PREPAYMENTS

STUDY OBJECTIVE 4

Prepare adjusting entries for prepayments.

Prepayments are either prepaid expenses or unearned revenues. Adjusting entries for prepayments are required at the statement date to record the portion of the prepayment that represents the expense incurred in the case of prepaid expenses, or the revenue earned in the case of unearned revenues, in the current accounting period. Adjusting entries for prepayments are shown in Illustration 4-5.

Illustration 4-5
Adjusting entries for prepayments

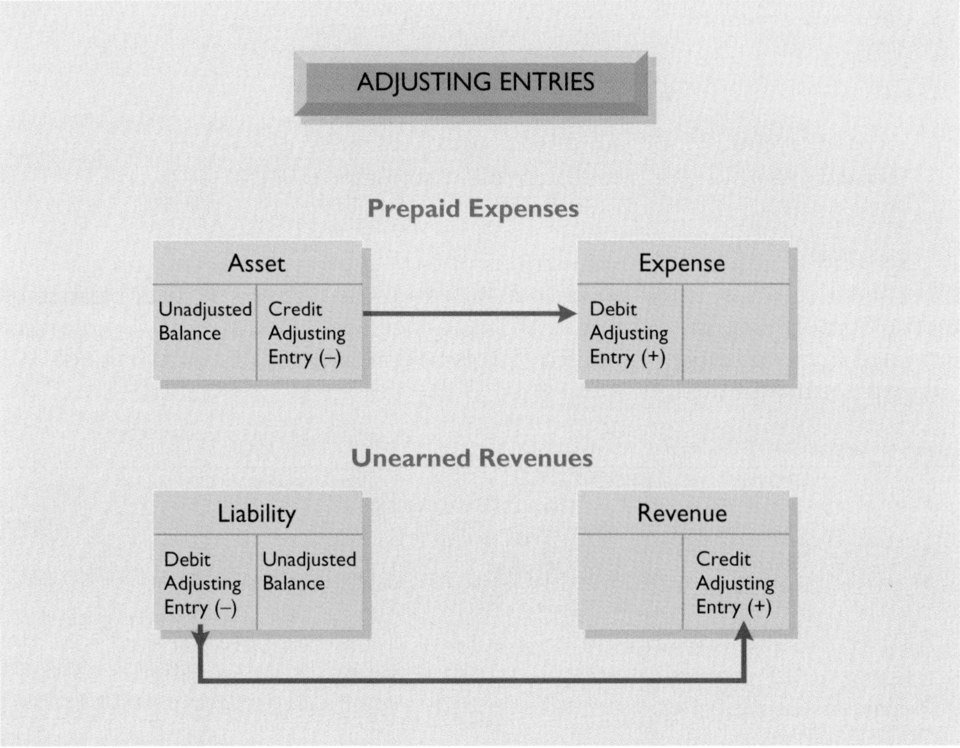

Prepaid Expenses

Payments of expenses that will benefit more than one accounting period are identified as **prepaid expenses** or **prepayments**. When such a cost is incurred, an asset account is debited to show the service or benefit that will be received in the future. Examples of common prepayments are insurance, supplies, advertising, and rent. In addition, prepayments are made when capital assets, such as buildings and equipment, are purchased.

Prepaid expenses expire either with the passage of time (e.g., rent and insurance) or through use (e.g., supplies). The expiration of these costs does not require daily entries, which would be impractical and unnecessary. Accordingly, we postpone the recognition of such cost expirations until financial statements are prepared. At each statement date, adjusting entries are made to record the expenses applicable to the current accounting period and to show the remaining amounts in the asset accounts. Prior to adjustment, assets are overstated and expenses are understated. Therefore, **an adjusting entry for prepaid expenses results in an increase (a debit) to an expense account and a decrease (a credit) to an asset account.**

Supplies. Supplies, such as paper, generally increase (debit) an asset account when they are acquired. During the accounting period, supplies are used. Rather than record supplies expense *as the supplies are used*, supplies expense is recognized at the *end* of the accounting period. At that time the company must count the remaining supplies. The difference between the balance in the Supplies (asset) account and the cost of supplies on hand represents the supplies used (expense) for that period.

Recall from the facts presented in Chapter 3 that Sierra Corporation purchased advertising supplies costing $2,500 on October 5. The debit was made to the asset Advertising Supplies, and this account shows a balance of $2,500 in the October 31 trial balance. An inventory count at the close of business on October 31 reveals that $1,000 of supplies are still on hand. Thus, the cost of supplies used is $1,500 ($2,500 − $1,000). This use of supplies decreases an asset, Advertising Supplies, and decreases shareholders' equity by increasing an expense account, Advertising Supplies Expense. The use of supplies affects the accounting equation in the following way:

Assets	=	Liabilities	+	Shareholders' Equity
−$1,500				−$1,500

Oct. 31	Advertising Supplies Expense	1,500	
	Advertising Supplies		1,500
	(To record supplies used)		

After the adjusting entry is posted, the two supplies accounts, in T account form, are as in Illustration 4-6.

Advertising Supplies		Advertising Supplies Expense	
Oct. 5 2,500	Oct. 31 Adj. 1,500	Oct. 31 Adj. 1,500	
Oct. 31 Bal. 1,000		Oct. 31 Bal. 1,500	

Illustration 4-6 Supplies accounts after adjustment

The asset account Advertising Supplies now shows a balance of $1,000, which is equal to the cost of supplies on hand at the statement date. In addition, Advertising Supplies Expense shows a balance of $1,500, which equals the cost of supplies used in October. **If the adjusting entry is not made, October expenses will be understated and net earnings overstated by $1,500. Moreover, both assets and shareholders' equity will be overstated by $1,500 on the October 31 balance sheet.**

BUSINESS INSIGHT

Management Perspective

The costs of advertising on radio, on television, and in magazines for burgers, bleaches, athletic shoes, and such products are normally considered an expense. Sometimes, however, they are considered prepayments. As a manager for Procter & Gamble noted, "If we run a long ad campaign for soap and bleach, we sometimes report the costs as prepayments if we think we'll receive sales benefits from the campaign down the road." Presently, whether these costs should be prepayments or expenses in the current period is a judgement call. The issue is important because the outlays for advertising can be substantial. As examples, General Motors of Canada, the biggest Canadian advertiser, spent $111 million in a recent year; Procter & Gamble, $84 million; and Hudson's Bay, $72 million.

Insurance

Oct. 4

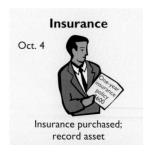

Insurance purchased; record asset

Insurance Policy			
Oct $50	Nov $50	Dec $50	Jan $50
Feb $50	March $50	April $50	May $50
June $50	July $50	Aug $50	Sept $50
I YEAR $600			

Oct. 31
Insurance expired; record insurance expense

Insurance. Companies purchase insurance to protect themselves from losses due to fire, theft, and unforeseen events. Insurance must be paid in advance, often for one year. Insurance payments (premiums) made in advance are normally recorded in the asset account Prepaid Insurance. At the financial statement date, it is necessary to increase (debit) Insurance Expense and decrease (credit) Prepaid Insurance for the cost of insurance that has expired during the period.

On October 4, Sierra Corporation paid $600 for a one-year fire insurance policy. Coverage began on October 1. The payment was recorded by increasing (debiting) Prepaid Insurance when it was paid, and this account shows a balance of $600 in the October 31 trial balance. An analysis of the policy reveals that $50 ($600/12 mos.) of insurance expires each month. The expiration of Prepaid Insurance would have the following impact on the accounting equation in October (and each of the next 11 months):

Assets	=	**Liabilities**	+	**Shareholders' Equity**
−$50				−$50

Thus, this adjusting entry is made:

Oct. 31	Insurance Expense	50	
	Prepaid Insurance		50
	(To record insurance expired)		

After the adjusting entry is posted, the accounts appear as in Illustration 4-7.

Illustration 4-7
Insurance accounts after adjustment

Prepaid Insurance		Insurance Expense	
Oct. 4 600	Oct. 31 **Adj. 50**	Oct. 31 **Adj. 50**	
Oct. 31 Bal. 550		Oct. 31 Bal. 50	

The asset Prepaid Insurance shows a balance of $550, which represents the cost that applies to the remaining 11 months of coverage. At the same time, the balance in Insurance Expense is equal to the insurance cost that was used in October. If this adjustment is not made, October expenses would be understated by $50 and net earnings overstated by $50. Moreover, as the accounting equation shows, both assets and shareholders' equity will be overstated by $50 on the October 31 balance sheet.

Amortization. A company typically owns a variety of assets that have long lives, such as buildings, equipment, and motor vehicles. The term of service is referred to as the **useful life** of the asset. Because a building is expected to provide service for many years, it is recorded as an asset, rather than an expense, on the date it is acquired. As explained in Chapter 1, such assets are recorded **at cost**, as required by the cost principle. According to the matching principle, a portion of this cost should then be reported as an expense during each period of the asset's useful life. **Amortization** is the process of allocating the cost of an asset to expense over its useful life.

Need for Adjustment. From an accounting standpoint, the acquisition of long-lived assets is essentially a long-term prepayment for services. The need for making periodic adjusting entries for amortization is therefore the same as described before for other prepaid expenses—that is, there is a need to recognize the cost that has been used (an expense) during the period and to report the unused cost (an asset) at the end of the period. One point is very important to understand: **Amortization is an allocation concept, not a valuation concept.** That is, we amortize an asset **to allocate its cost to the periods over which we use it. We are not attempting to reflect the actual change in the value of the asset.**

For Sierra Corporation, assume that amortization on office equipment is estimated to be $480 a year, or $40 per month. This would have the following impact on the accounting equation:

Assets	=	Liabilities	+	Shareholders' Equity
−$40				−$40

Accordingly, amortization for October is recognized by this adjusting entry:

Oct. 31	Amortization Expense	40	
	Accumulated Amortization—Office Equipment		40
	(To record monthly amortization)		

After the adjusting entry is posted, the accounts appear as in Illustration 4-8, which follows.

Amortization

Oct. 2

Office equipment purchased; record asset

Office Equipment			
Oct $40	Nov $40	Dec $40	Jan $40
Feb $40	March $40	April $40	May $40
June $40	July $40	Aug $40	Sept $40
Amortization = $480/year			

Oct. 31

Amortization recognized; record amortization expense

Office Equipment

Debit	Credit
Oct. 2 5,000	
Oct. 31 Bal. 5,000	

Accumulated Amortization—Office Equipment

Debit	Credit
	Oct. 31 **Adj. 40**
	Oct. 31 Bal. 40

Amortization Expense

Debit	Credit
Oct. 31 **Adj. 40**	
Oct. 31 Bal. 40	

Illustration 4-8 Accounts after adjustment for amortization

The balance in the Accumulated Amortization account will increase by $40 each month.

Statement Presentation. Accumulated Amortization—Office Equipment is a **contra asset account**, which means that it is offset against Office Equipment on the balance sheet, and its normal balance is a credit. This account is used instead of decreasing (crediting) Office Equipment in order to disclose *both* the original cost of the equipment and the total estimated cost that has expired to date. In the balance sheet, Accumulated Amortization—Office Equipment is deducted from the related asset account as shown in Illustration 4-9.

Helpful Hint All contra accounts have increases, decreases, and normal balances opposite to the account to which each one relates.

Office equipment	$5,000
Less: Accumulated amortization—office equipment	40
Book value	**$4,960**

Illustration 4-9 Balance sheet presentation of accumulated amortization

The difference between the cost of any asset requiring amortization and its related accumulated amortization is referred to as the **book value**, or **net book value**, of that asset. In Illustration 4-9, the book value of the equipment at the balance sheet date is $4,960. The book value and the market value of the asset are generally two different values. As noted earlier, amortization is not a matter of valuation, but a means of cost allocation.

Alternative Terminology *Book value* is also referred to as *carrying value.*

Note also that, in the example above, amortization expense identifies the portion of an asset's cost that has expired in October. The accounting equation shows that, as in the case of other prepaid adjustments, the omission of this adjusting entry would cause total assets, total shareholders' equity, and net earnings to be overstated and amortization expense to be understated.

You will recall from the opening vignette that Livent's past management was accused of capitalizing expenses as assets when they should have been expensed in the current period. This would have the effect of spreading the expense over multiple periods as the asset was amortized, thus overstating new earnings in the first period and understating net earnings in subsequent periods. In addition, as noted in the vignette, the book value of the asset (there shouldn't have been an asset!) was overstated on the balance sheet. Expenses were also allegedly transferred to preproduction assets that were not yet in use, and which consequently had not yet started their amortization process. Amortization of assets such as these is normally matched against the revenues the shows produce once the shows open.

Unearned Revenues

Cash received before revenue is earned is recorded by increasing (crediting) a liability account called **Unearned Revenues**. Items like rent, magazine subscriptions, and customer deposits for future service may result in unearned revenues. Airlines such as Air Canada, for instance, treat receipts from the sale of tickets as unearned revenue until the flight service is provided. Similarly, tuition fees received by universities and colleges prior to the academic session are considered unearned revenue. Unearned revenues are the opposite of prepaid expenses. Indeed, unearned revenue on the books of one company is likely to be a prepayment on the books of the company that has made the advance payment. For example, if identical accounting periods are assumed, a landlord will have unearned rent revenue when a tenant has prepaid rent.

Unearned Revenues

Oct. 2

Cash is received in advance; a liability is recorded

Oct. 31

Some service has been provided; some revenue is recorded

When the payment is received for services to be provided in a future accounting period, an unearned revenue (a liability) account should be credited to recognize the obligation that exists. Unearned revenues are subsequently earned by providing service to a customer. During the accounting period it is not practical to make daily entries as the revenue is earned. Instead, recognition of earned revenue is delayed until the adjustment process. Then an adjusting entry is made to record the revenue that has been earned during the period and to show the liability that remains at the end of the accounting period. Typically, prior to adjustment, liabilities are overstated and revenues are understated. Therefore, **the adjusting entry for unearned revenues results in a decrease (a debit) to a liability account and an increase (a credit) to a revenue account**.

Sierra Corporation received $1,200 on October 2 from R. Knox for advertising services expected to be completed by December 31. The payment was credited to Unearned Revenue, and this liability account shows a balance of $1,200 in the October 31 trial balance. From an evaluation of the work performed by Sierra for Knox during October, it is determined that $400 has been earned in October. This would affect the accounting equation in the following way:

Assets	=	Liabilities	+	Shareholders' Equity
		−$400		+$400

This adjusting entry is made:

Oct. 31	Unearned Service Revenue	400	
	Service Revenue		400
	(To record revenue earned)		

After the adjusting entry is posted, the accounts appear as in Illustration 4-10 below.

Illustration 4-10 Service revenue accounts after prepayment adjustment

Unearned Service Revenue

Debit		Credit	
Oct. 31	Adj. 400	Oct. 2	1,200
		Oct. 31 Bal.	800

Service Revenue

Debit		Credit	
		Oct. 3	10,000
		31	Adj. 400
		Oct. 31 Bal.	10,400

The liability Unearned Service Revenue now shows a balance of $800, which represents the remaining advertising services expected to be performed in the future. At the same time, Service Revenue shows total revenue earned in October of $10,400. **If this adjustment is not made, revenues and net earnings will be understated by $400 in the statement of earnings. Moreover, liabilities will be overstated and shareholders' equity will be understated by $400 on the October 31 balance sheet.**

BUSINESS INSIGHT

Investor Perspective

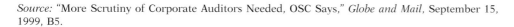

Companies would rather report steadily increasing profits than fluctuating profits. Sometimes, to "smooth" earnings, companies will shift the reporting of revenues or expenses between periods. Some analysts have suggested that Microsoft uses its Unearned Revenue account for this purpose. The company says that it reports a portion of some cash received for software sold as unearned revenue to reflect costs of delivering upgrades and customer support in future years for software that was shipped during the current year. But others contend that Microsoft intentionally overstates this amount—salting away unearned revenue that can be reported as revenue in some future period when the company's sales don't meet expectations.

In an effort to improve the reliability of financial information, the Ontario Securities Commission (OSC), regulator of Canada's largest capital market, has made the reduction of "earnings management" practices a priority. David Brown, Chair of the OSC, wryly noted recently that "more scrutiny is needed because companies are using creative accounting the way athletes use steroids to pump up earnings."

Source: "More Scrutiny of Corporate Auditors Needed, OSC Says," *Globe and Mail*, September 15, 1999, B5.

BEFORE YOU GO ON . . .

Review It

1. What are the four types of adjusting entries?
2. What is the effect on assets, shareholders' equity, expenses, and net earnings if a prepaid expense adjusting entry is not made?
3. What is the effect on liabilities, shareholders' equity, revenues, and net earnings if an unearned revenue adjusting entry is not made?

● **Do It**

The ledger of Hammond, Inc., on March 31, 2001, includes these selected accounts before adjusting entries are prepared:

	Debit	Credit
Prepaid Insurance	$ 3,600	
Office Supplies	2,800	
Office Equipment	25,000	
Accumulated Amortization—Office Equipment		$5,000
Unearned Service Revenue		9,200

An analysis of the accounts shows the following:

1. Insurance expires at the rate of $100 per month.
2. Supplies on hand total $800.
3. The office equipment is amortized at $200 a month.
4. Half of the unearned service revenue was earned in March.

Prepare the adjusting entries for the month of March.

Reasoning: For revenues to be recorded in the period in which they are earned and for expenses to be recognized in the period in which they are incurred, adjusting entries are made at the *end* of the accounting period. Adjusting entries for prepayments are required at the statement date to record the portion of the prepayment that represents the expense incurred or the revenue earned in the current accounting period. Not adjusting for the prepayment leads to an overstatement of the asset or liability and a related understatement of the expense or revenue.

Solution:

1. Insurance Expense	100	
Prepaid Insurance		100
(To record insurance expired)		
2. Office Supplies Expense	2,000	
Office Supplies		2,000
(To record supplies used ($2,800 − $800))		
3. Amortization Expense	200	
Accumulated Amortization		200
(To record monthly amortization)		
4. Unearned Service Revenue	4,600	
Service Revenue		4,600
(To record revenue earned ($9,200 × $\frac{1}{2}$))		

ADJUSTING ENTRIES FOR ACCRUALS

STUDY OBJECTIVE 5

Prepare adjusting entries for accruals.

The second category of adjusting entries is **accruals**. Adjusting entries for accruals are required in order to record revenues earned and expenses incurred in the current accounting period that have not been recognized through daily entries and thus are not yet reflected in the accounts. Prior to an accrual adjustment, the revenue account (and the related asset account), or the expense account (and the related liability account), is understated. Thus, adjusting entries for accruals will **increase both a balance sheet and statement of earnings account**. Adjusting entries for accruals are shown in Illustration 4-11.

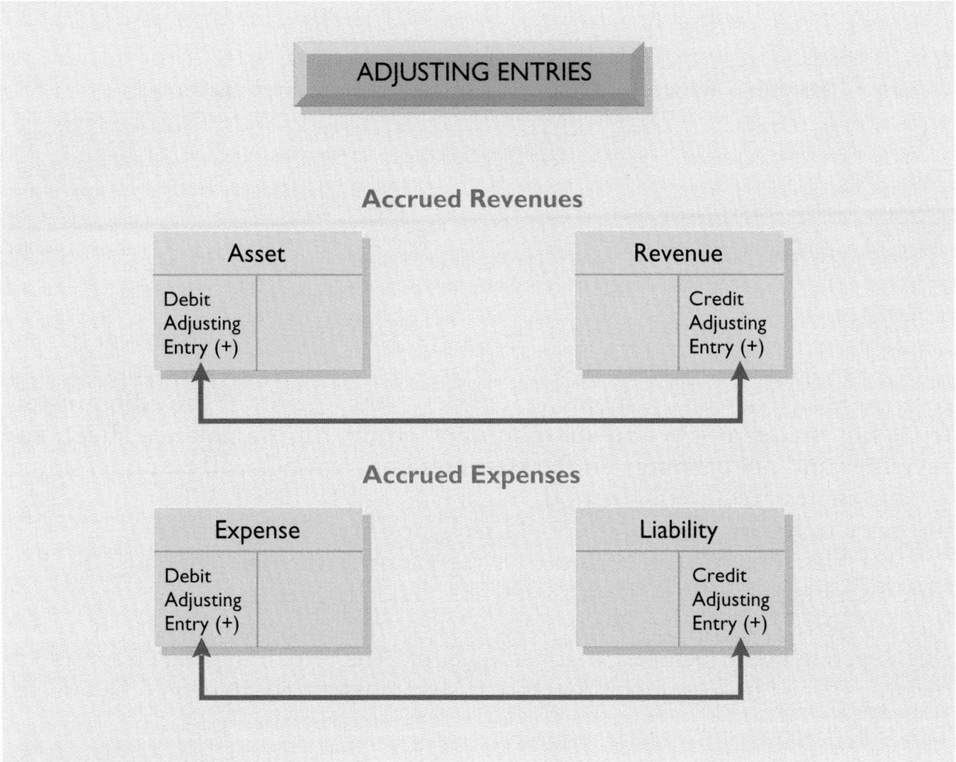

Illustration 4-11 Adjusting entries for accruals

ADJUSTING ENTRIES

Accrued Revenues

Asset	
Debit Adjusting Entry (+)	

Revenue	
	Credit Adjusting Entry (+)

Accrued Expenses

Expense	
Debit Adjusting Entry (+)	

Liability	
	Credit Adjusting Entry (+)

> **Helpful Hint** For accruals, there may be no prior entry and the accounts requiring adjustment may both have zero balances prior to adjustment.

Accrued Revenues

Revenues earned but not yet received in cash or recorded at the statement date are **accrued revenues**. Accrued revenues may accumulate (accrue) with the passing of time, as in the case of interest revenue. Or they may result from services that have been performed but neither billed nor collected, as in the case of commissions and fees. The former are unrecorded because the earning of interest does not involve daily transactions; the latter may be unrecorded because only a portion of the total service has been provided and the clients won't be billed until the service has been completed.

An adjusting entry is required to show the receivable that exists at the balance sheet date and to record the revenue that has been earned during the period. Prior to adjustment, both assets and revenues are understated. Accordingly, **an adjusting entry for accrued revenues results in an increase (a debit) to an asset account and an increase (a credit) to a revenue account**.

In October, Sierra Corporation earned $200 for advertising services that were not billed to clients before October 31. Because these services have not been billed, they have not been recorded. Assets and shareholders' equity would be affected as follows:

$$\underline{\text{Assets}} = \underline{\text{Liabilities}} + \underline{\text{Shareholders' Equity}}$$
$$+\$200 \qquad\qquad\qquad\qquad +\$200$$

Thus, this adjusting entry is made:

Oct. 31	Accounts Receivable	200	
	Service Revenue		200
	(To accrue revenue earned but not billed or collected)		

Accrued Revenues

Oct. 31

Revenue and receivable are recorded for unbilled services

Nov.

Cash is received; receivable is reduced

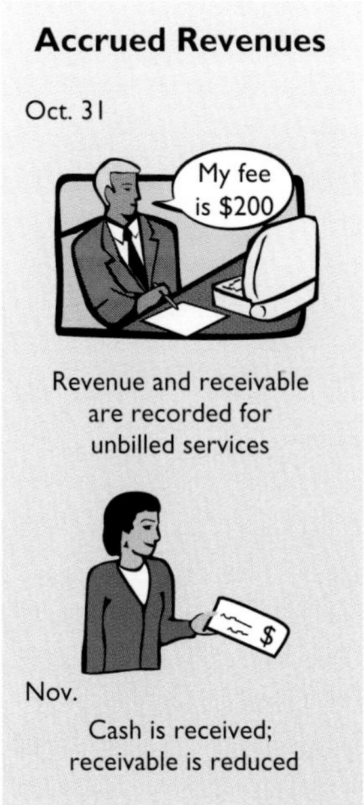

After the adjusting entry is posted, the accounts appear as in Illustration 4-12.

Illustration 4-12
Receivable and revenue accounts after accrual adjustments

Accounts Receivable		Service Revenue	
Oct. 31 **Adj. 200**			Oct. 3 10,000
			31 400
			31 **Adj. 200**
Oct. 31 Bal. 200			Oct. 31 Bal 10,600

The asset Accounts Receivable shows that $200 is owed by clients at the balance sheet date. The balance of $10,600 in Service Revenue represents the total revenue earned during the month ($10,000 + $400 + $200). **If the adjusting entry is not made, assets and shareholders' equity on the balance sheet, and revenues and net earnings on the statement of earnings will be understated.**

In the next accounting period, the clients will be billed. When this occurs, the entry to record the billing should recognize that $200 of revenue earned in October has already been recorded in the October 31 adjusting entry. To illustrate, assume that bills totaling $3,000 are mailed to clients on November 10. Of this amount, $200 represents revenue earned in October and recorded as Service Revenue in the October 31 adjusting entry. The remaining $2,800 represents revenue earned in November. Assets and shareholders' equity would be affected as follows:

Assets	=	Liabilities	+	Shareholders' Equity
+ $2,800				+ $2,800

Thus, the following entry is made:

Nov. 10	Accounts Receivable	2,800	
	Service Revenue		2,800
	(To record revenue earned)		

This entry records the amount of revenue earned between November 1 and November 10. The subsequent collection of cash from clients (including the $200 earned in October) will be recorded with an increase (a debit) to Cash and a decrease (a credit) to Accounts Receivable.

Accrued Expenses

Expenses incurred but not yet paid or recorded at the statement date are called **accrued expenses**. Interest, rent, taxes, and salaries are common examples of accrued expenses. Accrued expenses result from the same factors as accrued revenues. In fact, an accrued expense on the books of one company is an accrued revenue to another company. For example, the $200 accrual of service revenue by Sierra Corporation is an accrued expense to the client that received the service.

Adjustments for accrued expenses are necessary to record the obligations that exist at the balance sheet date and to recognize the expenses that apply to the current accounting period. Prior to adjustment, both liabilities and expenses are understated. Therefore, **an adjusting entry for accrued expenses results in an increase (a debit) to an expense account and an increase (a credit) to a liability account.**

Accrued Interest. Sierra Corporation signed a three-month note payable in the amount of $5,000 on October 1. The note requires interest at an annual rate of 12%. The amount of the interest accumulation is determined by three factors: (1) the face value of the note, (2) the interest rate, which is always expressed as an annual rate, and (3) the length of time the note is outstanding. In this instance, the total interest due on the $5,000 note at its due date, three months in the future, is $150 ($\$5,000 \times 12\% \times \frac{3}{12}$), or $50 for one month. Note that the time period is expressed as a fraction of a year. The formula for computing interest and its application to Sierra Corporation for the month of October are shown in Illustration 4-13.

Helpful Hint To make the illustration easier to understand, a simplified method of interest calculation is used. In reality, interest is calculated using the exact number of days in the interest period and year (365).

Illustration 4-13 Formula for computing interest

Face Value of Note	×	Annual Interest Rate	×	Time in Terms of One Year	=	Interest
$5,000	×	12%	×	$\frac{1}{12}$	=	**$50**

The accrual of interest at October 31 would have the following impact on the accounting equation:

Assets	=	Liabilities	+	Shareholders' Equity
		+$50		−$50

This would be reflected in an accrued expense adjusting entry at October 31 as follows:

Oct.	31	Interest Expense	50	
		Interest Payable		50
		(To accrue interest on note payable)		

After this adjusting entry is posted, the accounts appear as in Illustration 4-14.

Illustration 4-14 Interest accounts after adjustment

Interest Expense	
Oct. 31 **Adj. 50**	
Oct. 31 Bal. 50	

Interest Payable	
	Oct. 31 **Adj. 50**
	Oct. 31 Bal. 50

Interest Expense shows the interest charges for the month of October. The amount of interest owed at the statement date is shown in Interest Payable. It will not be paid until the note comes due at the end of three months. The Interest Payable account is used, instead of crediting Notes Payable, to disclose the two different types of obligations—interest and principal—in the accounts and statements. **If this adjusting entry is not made, liabilities and interest expense will be understated, and net earnings and shareholders' equity will be overstated.**

Accrued Salaries. Some types of expenses, such as employee salaries and commissions, are paid for after the services have been performed. At Sierra Corporation, salaries were last paid on October 26; the next payment of salaries will not occur until November 9. As shown in the calendar, three as yet unpaid working days remain in October (October 29–31).

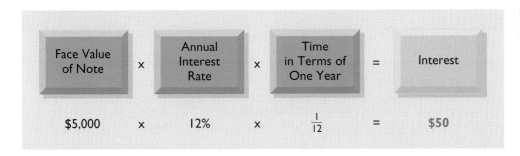

At October 31, the salaries for these days represent an accrued expense and a related liability to Sierra. The employees receive total salaries of $2,000 for a five-day work week, or $400 per day. Thus, accrued salaries at October 31 are $1,200 ($400 × 3). This accrual increases a liability, Salaries Payable, and an expense account, Salaries Expense, and has the following impact on the accounting equation:

Assets	=	Liabilities	+	Shareholders' Equity
		+ $1,200		− $1,200

The adjusting entry is:

Oct. 31	Salaries Expense	1,200	
	Salaries Payable		1,200
	(To record accrued salaries)		

After this adjusting entry is posted, the accounts are as in Illustration 4-15.

Illustration 4-15 Salary accounts after adjustment

Salaries Expense		Salaries Payable	
Oct. 26 4,000			Oct. 31 **Adj. 1,200**
31 **Adj. 1,200**			
Oct. 31 Bal. 5,200			Oct. 31 Bal. 1,200

After this adjustment, the balance in Salaries Expense of $5,200 (13 days × $400) is the actual salary expense for October. The balance in Salaries Payable of $1,200 is the amount of the liability for salaries owed as at October 31. **If the $1,200 adjustment for salaries is not recorded, Sierra's expenses will be understated $1,200 and its liabilities will be understated $1,200.**

At Sierra Corporation, salaries are payable every two weeks. Consequently, the next payday is November 9, when total salaries of $4,000 will again be paid. The payment consists of $1,200 of salaries payable at October 31 plus $2,800 of salaries expense for November (seven working days, as shown in the November calendar, × $400). Therefore, the following entry is made on November 9:

Nov. 9	Salaries Payable	1,200	
	Salaries Expense	2,800	
	Cash		4,000
	(To record November 9 payroll)		

A	=	L	+	SE
-4,000		-1,200		-2,800

This entry eliminates the liability for Salaries Payable that was recorded in the October 31 adjusting entry and records the proper amount of Salaries Expense for the period between November 1 and November 9.

Accrued Income Taxes. As discussed in Chapter 1, corporations pay income taxes on their net earnings. Just as individuals calculate the exact amount of income taxes owed annually, so must corporations. For interim periods, income taxes must be estimated and paid monthly in order to match what can be a significant expense with the earnings generated.

Alternative Terminology *Income tax expense* is also called *provision for income taxes* or just *income taxes* on the statement of earnings.

Assume that Sierra's monthly income taxes payable are estimated to be $600. This accrual increases a liability, Income Tax Payable, and an expense account, Income Tax Expense, and has the following impact on the accounting equation:

Assets	=	Liabilities	+	Shareholders' Equity
		+600		-600

The adjusting entry is:

Oct 31	Income Tax Expense	600	
	Income Tax Payable		600
	(To record accrued income taxes)		

After this adjusting entry is posted, the accounts are as in Illustration 4-16.

Illustration 4-16 Income tax accounts after adjustments

Income Tax Expense		Income Tax Payable	
Oct. 31 **Adj. 600**			Oct. 31 **Adj. 600**
Oct. 31 Bal. 600			Oct. 31 Bal. 600

As noted in Chapter 1, income tax expense is reported separately from other expenses, following the subtotal earnings before income tax in order to emphasize the earnings generated from operations. The income tax payable is reported as a current liability on the balance sheet as it is normally paid in monthly installments. Other taxes owning, such as sales and property taxes, must also be estimated and accrued in a similar manner.

BUSINESS INSIGHT

International Perspective

In Canada, the federal government, the 10 provinces, and the three territories all impose income taxes on corporate earnings. The combined federal and provincial income tax rate ranges from 16% for small businesses to 46% for large businesses. For national companies, income taxes include tax payable to every province in which the company operates, in addition to the tax payable to the federal government. International companies are taxed on their worldwide earnings, and their income taxes include tax payable to every country in which they operate. Canada's corporate income taxes are generally higher than those in the U.S. and lower than those in the United Kingdom.

BEFORE YOU GO ON . . .

Review It

1. What is the effect on assets, shareholders' equity, revenues, and net earnings if an accrued revenue adjusting entry is not made?
2. What is the effect on liabilities, shareholders' equity, expenses, and net earnings if an accrued expense adjusting entry is not made?
3. What was the amount of Loblaw's 1999 Depreciation and Amortization Expense? Its Accumulated Depreciation as at January 1, 2000? (Hint: This amount is reported in Note 5 to the financial statements.) The answer to these questions is provided at the end of this chapter.

Loblaws
A passion for food... *and a lot more!*

Do It

Micro Computer Services Inc. began operations on August 1, 2001. At the end of August 2001, management attempted to prepare monthly financial statements. This information relates to August:

1. Revenue earned but unrecorded for August totalled $1,100.
2. On August 1, the company borrowed $30,000 from a local bank on a 15-year mortgage. The annual interest rate is 10%.
3. At August 31, the company owed its employees $800 in salaries that will be paid on September 1.
4. Estimated income tax payable for August totalled $275.

Prepare the adjusting entries needed at August 31, 2001.

Reasoning: Adjusting entries for accruals are required to record revenues earned and expenses incurred in the current accounting period that have not been recognized through daily entries. An adjusting entry for accruals will increase both a balance sheet and a statement of earnings account.

Solution:

1. Accounts Receivable	1,100	
Service Revenue		1,100
(To accrue revenue earned but not billed or collected)		
2. Interest Expense	250	
Interest Payable		250
(To record accrued interest: $\$30,000 \times 10\% \times \frac{1}{12}$)		
3. Salaries Expense	800	
Salaries Payable		800
(To record accrued salaries)		
4. Income Tax Expense	275	
Income Tax Payable		275
(To record accrued income taxes)		

SUMMARY OF BASIC RELATIONSHIPS

Pertinent data on each of the four basic types of adjusting entries are summarized in Illustration 4-17. Take some time to study and analyse the adjusting entries. Be sure to note that **each adjusting entry affects one balance sheet account and one statement of earnings account**.

Illustration 4-17 Summary of adjusting entries

Type of Adjustment	Accounts Before Adjustment	Adjusting Entry
Prepaid expenses	Assets overstated Expenses understated	Dr. Expenses Cr. Assets
Unearned revenues	Liabilities overstated Revenues understated	Dr. Liabilities Cr. Revenues
Accrued revenues	Assets understated Revenues understated	Dr. Assets Cr. Revenues
Accrued expenses	Expenses understated Liabilities understated	Dr. Expenses Cr. Liabilities

ALTERNATIVE TREATMENT OF PREPAID EXPENSES AND UNEARNED REVENUES

In our discussion of adjusting entries for prepaid expenses and unearned revenues, we illustrated transactions for which the initial entries were made to balance sheet accounts. That is, in the case of prepaid expenses, the prepayment was debited to an asset account, and in the case of unearned revenue, the cash received was credited to a liability account. **Recording your initial entry to a balance sheet account facilitates internal control over assets and imitates the actual flow of costs (i.e., from asset to expense).** However, some businesses use an alternative treatment which is equally acceptable. At the time an expense is prepaid, it is debited to an expense account. At the time of a receipt for future services, it is credited to a revenue account. In such cases, the required adjusting journal entry differs from that illustrated in the summary of basic relationships since the original entry was different. **It is important to clearly identify the accounts debited or credited in the original transaction entry before planning your adjusting entry.** Even though the original and adjusting journal entries may differ from those described earlier in the chapter, the alternative treatment of prepaid expenses and unearned revenues will have exactly the same effect on the financial statements.

Alternative adjusting entries do not apply to accruals because no entries occur before these types of adjusting entries are made.

SIERRA CORPORATION ILLUSTRATION

The journalizing and posting of the adjusting entries described in this chapter for Sierra Corporation on October 31 are shown in Illustrations 4-18 and 4-19. When reviewing the general ledger in Illustration 4-19, note that the adjustments are highlighted in colour.

Illustration 4-18 General journal showing adjusting entries

GENERAL JOURNAL

Date	Account Titles and Explanation	Debit	Credit
2001	Adjusting Entries		
Oct. 31	Advertising Supplies Expense	1,500	
	Advertising Supplies		1,500
	(To record supplies used)		
31	Insurance Expense	50	
	Prepaid insurance		50
	(To record insurance expired)		
31	Amortization Expense	40	
	Accumulated Amortization—Office Equipment		40
	(To record monthly amortization)		
31	Unearned Service Revenue	400	
	Service Revenue		400
	(To record revenue earned)		
31	Accounts Receivable	200	
	Service Revenue		200
	(To accrue revenue earned but not billed or collected)		
31	Interest Expense	50	
	Interest Payable		50
	(To accrue interest on notes payable)		
31	Salaries Expense	1,200	
	Salaries Payable		1,200
	(To record accrued salaries)		
31	Income Tax Expense	600	
	Income Tax Payable		600
	(To record accrued income taxes)		

GENERAL LEDGER

Cash

Oct. 1	10,000	Oct. 2	5,000
1	5,000	3	900
2	1,200	4	600
3	10,000	20	500
		26	4,000
Oct. 31 Bal.	15,200		

Accounts Receivable

Oct. 31	**200**		
Oct. 31 Bal.	200		

Advertising Supplies

Oct. 5	2,500	Oct. 31	**1,500**
Oct. 31 Bal.	1,000		

Prepaid Insurance

Oct. 4	600	Oct. 31	**50**
Oct. 31 Bal.	550		

Office Equipment

Oct. 2	5,000		
Oct. 31 Bal.	5,000		

Accumulated Amortization—Office Equipment

		Oct. 31	**40**
		Oct. 31 Bal.	40

Notes Payable

		Oct. 1	5,000
		Oct. 31 Bal.	5,000

Accounts Payable

		Oct. 5	2,500
		Oct. 31 Bal.	2,500

Interest Payable

		Oct. 31	**50**
		Oct. 31 Bal.	50

Unearned Service Revenue

Oct. 31	**400**	Oct. 2	1,200
		Oct. 31 Bal.	800

Salaries Payable

		Oct. 31	**1,200**
		Oct. 31 Bal.	1,200

Income Tax Payable

		Oct. 31	**600**
		Oct. 31 Bal.	600

Common Shares

		Oct. 1	10,000
		Oct. 31 Bal.	10,000

Retained Earnings

		Oct. 1	0
		Oct. 31 Bal.	0

Dividends

Oct. 20	500		
Oct. 31 Bal.	500		

Service Revenue

		Oct. 3	10,000
		31	**400**
		31	**200**
		Oct. 31 Bal.	10,600

Salaries Expense

Oct. 26	4,000		
31	**1,200**		
Oct. 31 Bal.	5,200		

Advertising Supplies Expense

Oct. 31	**1,500**		
Oct. 31 Bal.	1,500		

Rent Expense

Oct. 3	900		
Oct. 31 Bal.	900		

Insurance Expense

Oct. 31	**50**		
Oct. 31 Bal.	50		

Interest Expense

Oct. 31	**50**		
Oct. 31 Bal.	50		

Amortization Expense

Oct. 31	**40**		
Oct. 31 Bal.	40		

Income Tax Expense

Oct. 31	**600**		
Oct. 31 Bal.	600		

Illustration 4-19 General ledger after adjustments

THE ADJUSTED TRIAL BALANCE AND FINANCIAL STATEMENTS

STUDY OBJECTIVE 6

Describe the nature and purpose of the adjusted trial balance.

After all adjusting entries have been journalized and posted, another trial balance is prepared from the ledger accounts. This trial balance is called an **adjusted trial balance.** It shows the balances of all accounts, including those that have been adjusted, at the end of the accounting period. The purpose of an adjusted trial balance is to **prove the equality** of the total debit balances and the total credit balances in the ledger after all adjustments have been made. Because the accounts contain all data that are needed for financial statements, the adjusted trial balance is the primary basis for the preparation of financial statements.

PREPARING THE ADJUSTED TRIAL BALANCE

The adjusted trial balance for Sierra Corporation presented in Illustration 4-20 has been prepared from the ledger accounts in Illustration 4-19. To facilitate the comparison of account balances, the trial balance data, labelled "Before Adjustment" (presented earlier in Illustration 4-4), are shown alongside the adjusted data, labelled "After Adjustment." In addition, the amounts affected by the adjusting entries are highlighted in colour in the "After Adjustment" columns.

Illustration 4-20 Trial balance and adjusted trial balance compared

SIERRA CORPORATION
Trial Balances
October 31, 2001

	Before Adjustment		After Adjustment	
	Dr.	Cr.	Dr.	Cr.
Cash	$15,200		$ 15,200	
Accounts Receivable			200	
Advertising Supplies	2,500		1,000	
Prepaid Insurance	600		550	
Office Equipment	5,000		5,000	
Accumulated Amortization—Office Equipment				$ 40
Notes Payable		$ 5,000		5,000
Accounts Payable		2,500		2,500
Interest Payable				50
Unearned Service Revenue		1,200		800
Salaries Payable				1,200
Income Tax Payable				600
Common Shares		10,000		10,000
Retained Earnings		0		0
Dividends	500		500	
Service Revenue		10,000		10,600
Salaries Expense	4,000		5,200	
Advertising Supplies Expense			1,500	
Rent Expense	900		900	
Insurance Expense			50	
Interest Expense			50	
Amortization Expense			40	
Income Tax Expense			600	
	$28,700	$28,700	$30,790	$30,790

PREPARING FINANCIAL STATEMENTS

Financial statements can be prepared directly from an adjusted trial balance. The interrelationships of data in the adjusted trial balance of Sierra Corporation are presented in Illustrations 4-21 and 4-22. As Illustration 4-21 shows, the statement of earnings is prepared from the revenue and expense accounts, and the statement of retained earnings is derived from the retained earnings account, dividends account, and the net earnings (or net loss) shown in the statement of earnings. As shown in Illustration 4-22, the balance sheet is then prepared from the asset and liability accounts and the ending retained earnings as reported in the statement of retained earnings.

Illustration 4-21
Preparation of the statement of earnings and statement of retained earnings from the adjusted trial balance

SIERRA CORPORATION
Adjusted Trial Balance
October 31, 2001

Account	Debit	Credit
Cash	$15,200	
Accounts Receivable	200	
Advertising Supplies	1,000	
Prepaid Insurance	550	
Office Equipment	5,000	
Accumulated Amortization— Office Equipment		$ 40
Notes Payable		5,000
Accounts Payable		2,500
Interest Payable		50
Unearned Service Revenue		800
Salaries Payable		1,200
Income Tax Payable		600
Common Shares		10,000
Retained Earnings		0
Dividends	500	
Service Revenue		10,600
Salaries Expense	5,200	
Advertising Supplies Expense	1,500	
Rent Expense	900	
Insurance Expense	50	
Interest Expense	50	
Amortization Expense	40	
Income Tax Expense	600	
	$30,790	$30,790

SIERRA CORPORATION
Statement of Earnings
For the Month Ended October 31, 2001

Revenues		
Service revenue		$10,600
Expenses		
Salaries expense	$5,200	
Advertising supplies expense	1,500	
Rent expense	900	
Insurance expense	50	
Interest expense	50	
Amortization expense	40	
Total expenses		7,740
Earnings before income taxes		2,860
Income tax expense		600
Net earnings		$ 2,260

SIERRA CORPORATION
Statement of Retained Earnings
For the Month Ended October 31, 2001

Retained earnings, October 1	$ 0
Add: Net earnings	2,260
	2,260
Less: Dividends	500
Retained earnings, October 31	$ 1,760

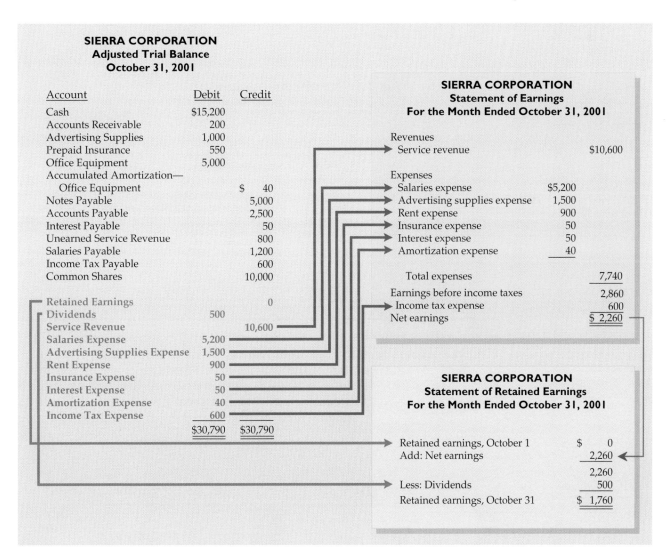

Illustration 4-22 Preparation of the balance sheet from the adjusted trial balance

SIERRA CORPORTAION
Adjusted Trial Balance
October 31, 2001

Account	Debit	Credit
Cash	$15,200	
Accounts Receivable	200	
Advertising Supplies	1,000	
Prepaid Insurance	550	
Office Equipment	5,000	
Accumulated Amortization—Office Equipment		$ 40
Notes Payable		5,000
Accounts Payable		2,500
Interest Payable		50
Unearned Service Revenue		800
Salaries Payable		1,200
Income Tax Payable		600
Common Shares		10,000
Retained Earnings		0
Dividends	500	
Service Revenue		10,600
Salaries Expense	5,200	
Advertising Supplies Expense	1,500	
Rent Expense	900	
Insurance Expense	50	
Interest Expense	50	
Amortization Expense	40	
Income Tax Expense	600	
	$30,790	$30,790

SIERRA CORPORATION
Balance Sheet
October 31, 2001

Assets		
Cash		$15,200
Accounts receivable		200
Advertising supplies		1,000
Prepaid insurance		550
Office equipment	$5,000	
Less: Accumulated amortization	40	4,960
Total assets		$21,910
Liabilities and Shareholders' Equity		
Liabilities		
Notes payable		$ 5,000
Accounts payable		2,500
Interest payable		50
Unearned service revenue		800
Salaries payable		1,200
Income tax payable		600
Total liabilities		10,150
Shareholders' equity		
Common shares		10,000
Retained earnings		1,760
Total shareholders' equity		11,760
Total liabilities and shareholders' equity		$21,910

Balance at Oct. 31 from Statement of Retained Earnings in Illustration 4-21

Closing the Books

Alternative Terminology
Temporary accounts are sometimes called *nominal accounts*, and *permanent accounts* are sometimes called *real accounts.*

In previous chapters, you learned that revenue and expense accounts and the dividends account are subdivisions of retained earnings, which is reported in the shareholders' equity section of the balance sheet. Because revenues, expenses, and dividends only relate to a given accounting period, they are considered **temporary accounts**. In contrast, all balance sheet accounts are considered **permanent accounts** because their balances are carried forward into future accounting periods. Illustration 4-23 identifies the accounts in each category.

Illustration 4-23 Temporary versus permanent accounts

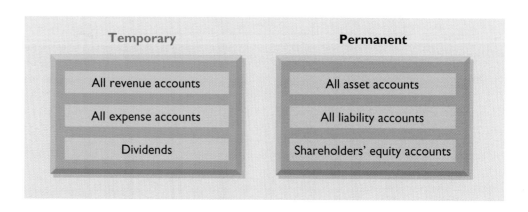

Temporary	Permanent
All revenue accounts	All asset accounts
All expense accounts	All liability accounts
Dividends	Shareholders' equity accounts

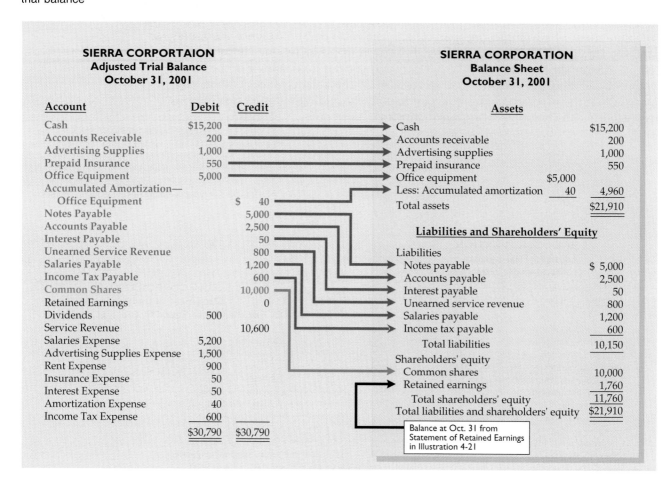

PREPARING CLOSING ENTRIES

STUDY OBJECTIVE 7

Explain the purposes of closing entries.

At the end of the accounting period, the temporary account balances are transferred to the permanent shareholders' equity account—Retained Earnings—through the preparation of closing entries. **Closing entries** formally recognize in the ledger the transfer of net earnings (or net loss) and dividends to retained earnings, which will be shown in the statement of retained earnings. For example, notice that in Illustration 4-22 Retained Earnings has an adjusted balance of zero. This is because it was Sierra's first year of operations. Retained Earnings started with a balance of zero, and net earnings has not yet been calculated and added (closed out) to Retained Earnings. Therefore, the adjusted balance is still zero. Similarly, the zero balance does not yet reflect dividends declared during the period, since that account has not yet been closed out either. In addition to updating Retained Earnings to its correct ending balance, closing entries produce a **zero balance in each temporary account**. As a result, these accounts are ready to accumulate data about revenues, expenses, and dividends in the next accounting period separate from the data in the prior periods. Permanent accounts are not closed.

When closing entries are prepared, each statement of earnings account could be closed directly to Retained Earnings. However, to do so would result in excessive detail in the Retained Earnings account. Accordingly, the revenue and expense accounts are closed to another temporary account, **Income Summary**, and only the resulting net earnings or net loss is transferred from this account to Retained Earnings. The closing entries for Sierra Corporation are shown in Illustration 4-24.

Helpful Hint Income Summary is a very descriptive title: total revenues are closed to Income Summary, total expenses are closed to Income Summary, and the balance in the Income Summary is the net earnings or net loss.

Illustration 4-24 Closing entries journalized

GENERAL JOURNAL

Date	Account Titles and Explanation	Debit	Credit
	Closing Entries		
	(1)		
Oct. 31	Service Revenue	10,600	
	Income Summary		10,600
	(To close revenue account)		
	(2)		
31	Income Summary	8,340	
	Salaries Expense		5,200
	Advertising Supplies Expense		1,500
	Rent Expense		900
	Insurance Expense		50
	Interest Expense		50
	Amortization Expense		40
	Income Tax Expense		600
	(To close expense accounts)		
	(3)		
31	Income Summary	2,260	
	Retained Earnings		2,260
	(To close net earnings to retained earnings)		
	(4)		
31	Retained Earnings	500	
	Dividends		500
	(To close dividends to retained earnings)		

The posting of Sierra Corporation's closing entries is shown in Illustration 4-25.

Illustration 4-25 Posting of closing entries

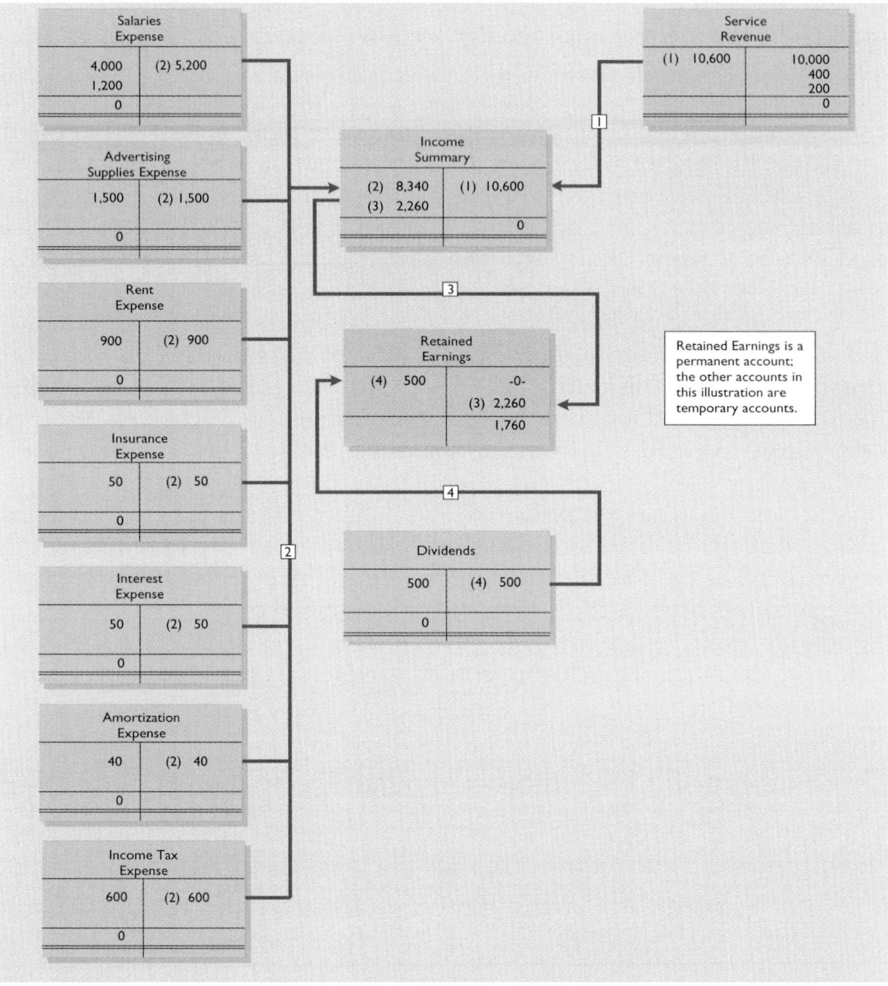

PREPARING A POST-CLOSING TRIAL BALANCE

After all closing entries are journalized and posted, another trial balance, called a **post-closing trial balance**, is prepared from the ledger. A post-closing trial balance is a list of all permanent accounts and their balances after closing entries are journalized and posted. **The purpose of this trial balance is to prove the equality of the permanent account balances that are carried forward into the next accounting period.** Since all temporary accounts will have zero balances, **the post-closing trial balance will contain only permanent—balance sheet—accounts.**

BUSINESS INSIGHT

Management Perspective

Until Sam Walton had opened 20 Wal-Mart stores, he used what he called the "ESP method" of closing the books. ESP was a pretty basic method: if the books didn't balance, Walton calculated the amount by which they were off and entered that amount under the heading ESP—which stood for "Error Some Place." As Walton noted, "It really sped things along when it came time to close those books."

Source: Sam Walton, *Made in America* (New York: Doubleday Publishing Company, 1992), 53.

Summary of the Accounting Cycle

The required steps in the accounting cycle are shown in Illustration 4-26. You can see that the cycle begins with the analysis of business transactions and ends with the preparation of a post-closing trial balance. The steps in the cycle are performed in sequence and are repeated in each accounting period.

Steps 1–3 may occur daily during the accounting period, as explained in Chapter 3. Steps 4–7 are performed on a periodic basis, such as monthly, quarterly, or annually. Steps 8 and 9, closing entries and a post-closing trial balance, are usually prepared only at the end of a company's **annual** accounting period.

STUDY OBJECTIVE 8

Describe the required steps in the accounting cycle.

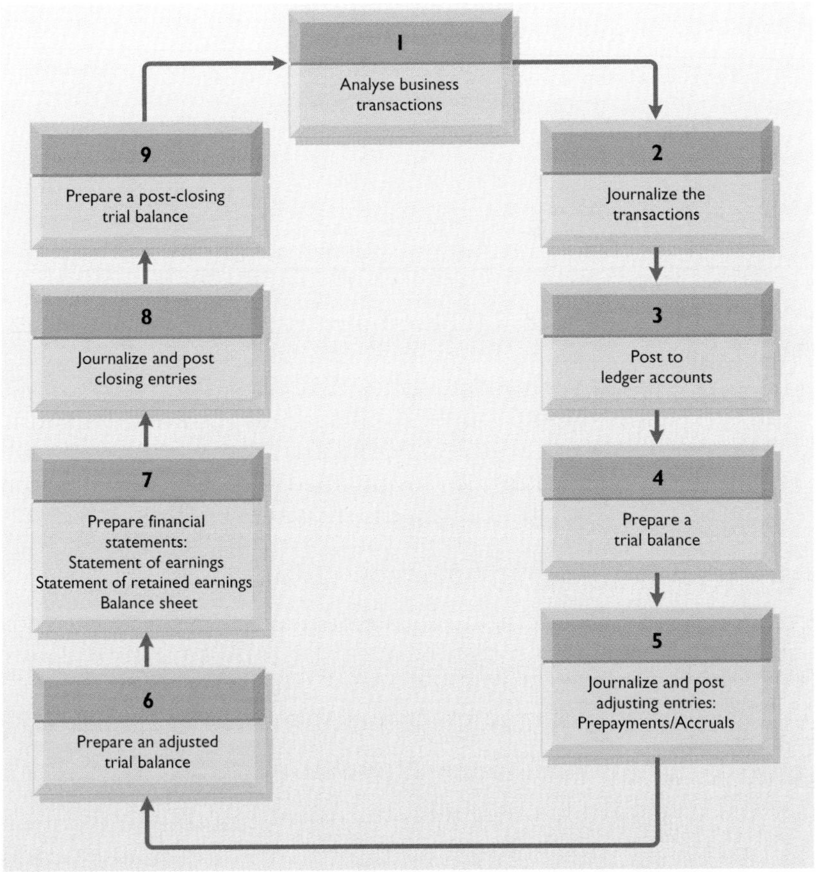

Illustration 4-26
Required steps in the accounting cycle

Helpful Hint Some accountants prefer to reverse certain adjusting entries at the beginning of a new accounting period to simplify the recording of later transactions related to the adjusting entries. A **reversing entry** is made at the beginning of the next accounting period and is the exact opposite of the adjusting entry made in the previous period.

BEFORE YOU GO ON . . .

Review It

1. How do permanent accounts differ from temporary accounts?
2. What are the two purposes of closing entries?
3. What four different types of entries are required in closing the books?
4. What financial statement amount will the balance in the Income Summary account equal immediately before it is closed into the Retained Earnings account?
5. What are the content and purpose of a post-closing trial balance?
6. What are the required steps in the accounting cycle?

BUSINESS INSIGHT

Management Perspective

Technology has dramatically changed the accounting process. When Larry Carter became chief financial officer of Cisco Systems, a worldwide leader in connecting Canadians and others on the Internet, closing the quarterly accounts would take up to 10 days. Within four years, he got it down to two days. Now, he is aiming at being able to do a "virtual close"—closing within a day on any day in the quarter. This is not just showing off. Knowing exactly where you are all of the time, says Mr. Carter, allows you to respond faster than your competitors. But it also means that the 600 people who used to spend 10 days a quarter tracking transactions can now be more usefully employed on things such as mining data for business intelligence.

Source: "Cisco @ Speed," Business and the Internet, *Economist*, June 26, 1999, 12.

USING THE DECISION TOOLKIT

Fishery Products International (FPI) Limited is the world's largest seafood supplier. Headquartered in St. John's, Newfoundland, FPI produces and markets a full range of seafood products, including shrimp, crab, scallops, cod, sole, redfish, pollock, turbot, haddock, salmon, tilapia, sea bass and many others. These products are acquired throughout North America, Southeast Asia, South America, and Europe. A simplified version of FPI's December 31, 1998, year-end adjusted trial balance is shown at the top of the next page.

Instructions

(a) From the trial balance, prepare a statement of earnings, statement of retained earnings, and classified balance sheet. **Be sure to prepare the statements in that order, since each statement depends on information determined in the preceding statement.**

(b) Using the appropriate financial statement amounts you determined in (a), calculate the following ratios for FPI for 1998: return on assets; profit margin; current ratio; and debt to total assets. Use year-end amounts instead of averages, where averages are called for. You may find it helpful to review the Decision Toolkit introduced in Chapter 2 before attempting these ratios.

(c) Comment briefly on FPI's liquidity, solvency and profitability.

FPI
FISHERY PRODUCTS INTERNATIONAL

FISHERY PRODUCTS INTERNATIONAL LIMITED
Trial Balance
December 31, 1998
(dollars in thousands)

Account	Dr.	Cr.
Cash	$ 933	
Accounts receivable	90,424	
Inventories	123,866	
Prepaid expenses	4,429	
Property, plant, and equipment	210,578	
Other long-term assets	16,782	
Accumulated amortization		$ 121,260
Short-term bank indebtedness		70,373
Accounts payable and accrued liabilities		31,739
Current portion of long-term debt		8,262
Long-term debt		57,471
Share capital		123,822
Retained earnings		25,659
Sales		681,213
Commission revenue		3,632
Cost of goods sold	615,367	
Administrative and marketing expenses	42,152	
Amortization expense	8,967	
Interest expense	7,467	
Other expenses	1,088	
Income tax expense	1,378	
Totals	$1,123,431	$1,123,431

Solution

(a)

FISHERY PRODUCTS INTERNATIONAL LIMITED
Statement of Earnings
Year Ended December 31, 1998
(dollars in thousands)

Revenues	
Sales	$681,213
Commission revenue	3,632
Total revenues	684,845
Expenses	
Cost of goods sold	615,367
Administrative and marketing expenses	42,152
Amortization expense	8,967
Interest expense	7,467
Other expenses	1,088
Total expenses	675,041
Earnings before income taxes	9,804
Income tax expense	1,378
Net earnings	$ 8,426

FISHERY PRODUCTS INTERNATIONAL

FISHERY PRODUCTS INTERNATIONAL LIMITED
Statement of Retained Earnings
Year Ended December 31, 1998
(dollars in thousands)

Retained earnings, beginning of year	$ 25,659
Net earnings	8,426
Retained earnings, end of year	$ 34,085

FISHERY PRODUCTS INTERNATIONAL LIMITED
Balance Sheet
December 31, 1998
(dollars in thousands)

Assets		
Current assets		
Cash		$ 933
Accounts receivable		90,424
Inventories		123,866
Prepaid expense		4,429
Total current assets		219,652
Capital assets		
Property, plant and equipment	$210,578	
Less: Accumulated amortization	121,260	89,318
Other assets		16,782
Total assets		$325,752
Liabilities and Shareholders' Equity		
Current liabilities		
Bank indebtedness		$ 70,373
Accounts payable and accrued liabilities		31,739
Current portion of long-term debt		8,262
Total current liabilities		110,374
Long-term debt		57,471
Total liabilities		167,845
Shareholders' equity		
Share capital		123,822
Retained earnings		34,085
Total shareholders' equity		157,907
Total liabilities and shareholders' equity		$325,752

(b) Return on assets	=	$\frac{\text{Net earnings}}{\text{Average total assets}}$	=	$\frac{\$8,426}{\$325,752}$	=	2.6%
Profit margin	=	$\frac{\text{Net earnings}}{\text{Net sales}}$	=	$\frac{\$8,426}{\$681,213}$	=	1.2%
Current ratio	=	$\frac{\text{Current assets}}{\text{Current liabilities}}$	=	$\frac{\$219,652}{\$110,374}$	=	2:1
Debt to total assets	=	$\frac{\text{Total debt}}{\text{Total assets}}$	=	$\frac{\$167,845}{\$325,752}$	=	52%

(c) FPI's short-term liquidity is strong, with twice as many current assets as current liabilities. It looks to be reasonably solvent, with slightly more than half of its assets financed by debt; the remainder by equity. The company's profitability appears positive, with a 2.6% return on assets and a 1.2% profit margin. However, one should compare these results to prior years' performance and industry averages in order to better assess performance.

SUMMARY OF STUDY OBJECTIVES

1 ***Explain the revenue recognition principle and the matching principle.*** The revenue recognition principle dictates that revenue must be recognized in the accounting period in which it is earned. The matching principle dictates that expenses must be recognized when they make their contribution to revenues.

2 ***Differentiate between the cash basis and the accrual basis of accounting.*** Accrual-based accounting means that events that change a company's financial statements are recorded in the periods in which the events occur. Under the cash basis, events are recorded only in the periods in which the company receives or pays cash.

3 ***Explain why adjusting entries are needed and identify the major types of adjusting entries.*** Adjusting entries are made at the end of an accounting period. They ensure that revenues are recorded in the period in which they are earned and that expenses are recognized in the period in which they are incurred. The major types of adjusting entries are prepaid expenses, unearned revenues, accrued revenues, and accrued expenses.

4 ***Prepare adjusting entries for prepayments.*** Prepayments are either prepaid expenses or unearned revenues. Adjusting entries for prepayments are required at the statement date to record the portion of the prepayment that represents the expense incurred or the revenue earned in the current accounting period.

5 ***Prepare adjusting entries for accruals.*** Accruals are either accrued revenues or accrued expenses. Adjusting entries for accruals are required to record revenues earned and expenses incurred in the current accounting period that have not been recognized through daily entries.

6 ***Describe the nature and purpose of the adjusted trial balance.*** An adjusted trial balance is a trial balance that shows the balances of all accounts, including those that have been adjusted, at the end of an accounting period. The purpose of an adjusted trial balance is to show the effects of all financial events that have occurred during the accounting period.

7 ***Explain the purposes of closing entries.*** One purpose of closing entries is to transfer the results of operations for the period to Retained Earnings. A second purpose is to enable all temporary accounts (revenue accounts, expense accounts, and dividends) to begin a new period with a zero balance. To accomplish this, all temporary accounts are "closed" at the end of an accounting period. Separate entries are made to close revenues and expenses to income summary, income summary to retained earnings, and dividends to retained earnings. Only temporary accounts are closed.

8 ***Describe the required steps in the accounting cycle.*** The required steps in the accounting cycle are: (a) analyse business transactions, (b) journalize the transactions, (c) post to ledger accounts, (d) prepare a trial balance, (e) journalize and post adjusting entries, (f) prepare an adjusted trial balance, (g) prepare financial statements, (h) journalize and post closing entries, and (i) prepare a post-closing trial balance.

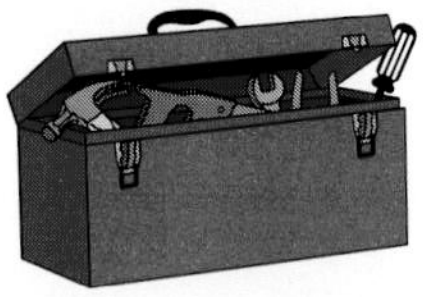

DECISION TOOLKIT—A SUMMARY

Decision Checkpoints	Info Needed for Decision	Tool to Use for Decision	How to Evaluate Results
At what point should the company record revenue?	Need to understand the nature of the company's business	Revenue should be recorded when earned. For a service business, revenue is earned when a service is performed.	Recognizing revenue too early overstates current period revenue; recognizing it too late understates current period revenue.
At what point should the company record expenses?	Need to understand the nature of the company's business	Expenses should "follow" revenues—that is, the effort (expense) should be matched with the result (revenue).	Recognizing expenses too early overstates current period expense; recognizing them too late understates current period expense.

APPENDIX 4A

ADJUSTING ENTRIES IN AN AUTOMATED WORLD—USING A WORK SHEET

STUDY OBJECTIVE 9

Describe the purpose and the basic form of a work sheet.

In the previous discussion, we used T accounts and trial balances to arrive at the amounts used to prepare financial statements. Accountants frequently use a device known as a work sheet to determine these amounts. A **work sheet** is a multiple-column form that may be used in the adjustment process and in preparing financial statements. Work sheets can be prepared manually, but today most are prepared on computer spreadsheets. As its name suggests, the work sheet is a working tool or a supplementary device for the accountant. **A work sheet is not a permanent accounting record**; it is neither a journal nor a part of the general ledger. The work sheet is merely a device used to make it easier to prepare adjusting entries and the financial statements. In small companies that have relatively few accounts and adjustments, a work sheet may not be needed. In large companies with numerous accounts and many adjustments, it is almost indispensable.

The basic form of a work sheet is shown in Illustration 4A-1. Note the headings. The work sheet starts with two columns for the trial balance. The next two columns record all adjustments, which are cross-referenced by letter. Next is the adjusted trial balance. The last two sets of columns correspond to the statement of earnings and the balance sheet. All items listed in the adjusted trial balance columns are recorded in either the statement of earnings or the balance sheet columns.

Illustration 4A-1 Form and procedure for a work sheet

SIERRA CORPORATION
Work Sheet
For the Month Ended October 31, 2001

Account Titles	Trial Balance		Adjustments		Adjusted Trial Balance		Statement of Earnings		Balance Sheet	
	Dr.	Cr.	Dr.	Cr.	Dr.	Cr.	Dr.	Cr.	Dr.	Cr.
Cash	15,200				15,200				15,200	
Advertising Supplies	2,500			(a) 1,500	1,000				1,000	
Prepaid Insurance	600			(b) 50	550				550	
Office Equipment	5,000				5,000				5,000	
Notes Payable		5,000				5,000				5,000
Accounts Payable		2,500				2,500				2,500
Unearned Service Revenue		1,200	(d) 400			800				800
Common Shares		10,000				10,000				10,000
Retained Earnings		0				0				0
Dividends	500				500				500	
Service Revenue		10,000		(d) 400 (e) 200		10,600		10,600		
Salaries Expense	4,000		(g) 1,200		5,200		5,200			
Rent Expense	900				900		900			
Totals	28,700	28,700								
Advertising Supplies Expense			(a) 1,500		1,500		1,500			
Insurance Expense			(b) 50		50		50			
Amortization Expense			(c) 40		40		40			
Accum. Amortization—Office Equipment				(c) 40		40				40
Accounts Receivable			(e) 200		200				200	
Interest Expense			(f) 50		50		50			
Interest Payable				(e) 50		50				50
Salaries Payable				(g) 1,200		1,200				1,200
Income Tax Expense			(h) 600		600		600			
Income Tax Payable				600		600				600
							8,340	10,600	22,450	20,190
Net Earnings							2,260			2,260
Totals			4,040	4,040	30,790	30,790	10,600	10,600	22,450	22,450

1. Prepare a trial balance on the work sheet.

2. Enter adjustment data.

3. Enter adjusted balances.

4. Extend adjusted balances to appropriate balance statement columns.

5. Total the statement columns, calculate net earnings (or net loss), and complete work sheet.

Summary of Study Objective for Appendix 4A

9 ***Describe the purpose and the basic form of a work sheet.*** The work sheet is a device used to make it easier to prepare adjusting entries and the financial statements. It is often prepared on a computer spreadsheet. The sets of columns of the work sheet are, from left to right, the unadjusted trial balance, adjustments, adjusted trial balance, statement of earnings, and balance sheet.

GLOSSARY

Accrual basis accounting Accounting basis in which transactions that change a company's financial statements are recorded in the periods in which the events occur, rather than in the periods in which the company receives or pays cash. (p. 173)

Accrued expenses Expenses incurred but not yet paid in cash or recorded. (p. 184)

Accrued revenues Revenues earned but not yet received in cash or recorded. (p. 183)

Adjusted trial balance A list of accounts and their balances after all adjustments have been made. (p. 192)

Adjusting entries Entries made at the end of an accounting period to ensure that the revenue recognition and matching principles are followed. (p. 174)

Amortization The process of allocating the cost of an asset to expense over its useful life. (p. 178)

Book value (net book value) The difference between the cost of an amortizable asset and its related accumulated amortization. (p. 179)

Cash basis accounting An accounting basis in which revenue is recorded only when cash is received, and an expense is recorded only when cash is paid. (p. 173)

Closing entries Entries at the end of an accounting period to transfer the balances of temporary accounts to a permanent shareholders' equity account, Retained Earnings. (p. 195)

Contra asset account An account that is offset against an asset account on the balance sheet. (p. 179)

Fiscal year An accounting period that is one year long. (p. 170)

Income summary A temporary account used in closing revenue and expense accounts. (p. 195)

Matching principle The principle that dictates that efforts (expenses) must be matched with accomplishments (revenues). (p. 172)

Permanent accounts Balance sheet accounts whose balances are carried forward to the next accounting period. (p. 194)

Post-closing trial balance A list of permanent accounts and their balances after closing entries have been journalized and posted. (p. 196)

Prepaid expenses (prepayments) Expenses paid in cash and recorded as assets before they are used or consumed. (p. 176)

Revenue recognition principle The principle that revenue must be recognized in the accounting period in which it is earned. (p. 171)

Temporary accounts Revenue, expense, and dividend accounts whose balances are transferred to Retained Earnings at the end of an accounting period. (p. 194)

Time period assumption An assumption that the economic life of a business can be divided into artificial time periods. (p. 170)

Unearned revenues Cash received before revenue is earned and recorded as a liability until it is earned. (p. 180)

Useful life The length of service of a productive facility. (p. 178)

Work sheet A multiple-column form that may be used in the adjustment process and in preparing financial statements. (p. 202)

DEMONSTRATION PROBLEM

Terry Thomas and a group of investors incorporate the Green Thumb Lawn Care Corporation on April 1. At April 30, the trial balance shows the following balances for selected accounts:

Prepaid Insurance	$ 3,600
Equipment	28,000
Income Tax Payable	0
Note Payable	20,000
Unearned Service Revenue	4,200
Service Revenue	1,800

Analysis reveals the following additional data pertaining to these accounts:

1. Prepaid insurance is the cost of a two-year insurance policy, effective April 1.
2. Amortization on the equipment is $500 per month.
3. The note payable is dated April 1. It is a six-month, 12% note.
4. Seven customers paid for the company's six-month lawn service package of $600 beginning in April. These customers were serviced in April.

5. Lawn services rendered to other customers but not billed at April 30 totalled $1,500.
6. Income tax expense for April is estimated to be $100.

Instructions

Prepare the adjusting entries for the month of April. Show calculations.

Solution to Demonstration Problem

GENERAL JOURNAL

Date	Account Titles and Explanation	Debit	Credit
	Adjusting Entries		
Apr. 30	Insurance Expense	150	
	Prepaid Insurance		150
	(To record insurance expired: $3,600 ÷ 24 mos. = $150 per month)		
30	Amortization Expense	500	
	Accumulated Amortization—Equipment		500
	(To record monthly amortization)		
30	Interest Expense	200	
	Interest Payable		200
	(To accrue interest on notes payable: $20,000 × 12% × $\frac{1}{12}$ = $200)		
30	Unearned Service Revenue	700	
	Service Revenue		700
	(To record revenue earned: $600 ÷ 6 mos.= $100; $100 per month × 7 = $700)		
30	Accounts Receivable	1,500	
	Service Revenue		1,500
	(To accrue revenue earned but not billed or collected)		
30	Income Tax Expense	100	
	Income Tax Payable		100
	(To accrue income taxes payable)		

Problem-Solving Strategies

1. Note that adjustments are being made for one month.
2. Make calculations carefully.
3. Select account titles carefully.
4. Make sure debits are made first and credits are indented.
5. Check that debits equal credits for each entry.

Self-Study Questions

Answers are at the end of the chapter.

(SO 1) 1. Which one of these statements about the accrual basis of accounting is *false*?
   (a) Events that change a company's financial statements are recorded in the periods in which the events occur.
   (b) Revenue is recognized in the period in which it is earned.
   (c) This basis is in accord with generally accepted accounting principles.
   (d) Revenue is recorded only when cash is received, and an expense is recorded only when cash is paid.

2. What is the time period assumption? (SO 1)
   (a) Revenue should be recognized in the accounting period in which it is earned.
   (b) Expenses should be matched with revenues.
   (c) The economic life of a business can be divided into artificial time periods.
   (d) The fiscal year should correspond with the calendar year.

3. Which principle dictates that efforts (expenses) must be recorded with accomplishments (revenues)? (SO 1)
   (a) Matching principle
   (b) Cost principle
   (c) Periodicity principle
   (d) Revenue recognition principle

(SO 3) 4. Adjusting entries are made to ensure that:
(a) expenses are recognized in the period in which they are incurred.
(b) revenues are recorded in the period in which they are earned.
(c) balance sheet and statement of earnings accounts have correct balances at the end of an accounting period.
(d) All of the above

(SO 4) 5. The trial balance shows Supplies $1,350 and Supplies Expense $0. If $600 of supplies are on hand at the end of the period, the adjusting entry is:

(a) Supplies	600	
Supplies Expense		600
(b) Supplies	750	
Supplies Expense		750
(c) Supplies Expense	750	
Supplies		750
(d) Supplies Expense	600	
Supplies		600

(SO 4) 6. Adjustments for unearned revenues:
(a) decrease liabilities and increase revenues.
(b) increase liabilities and increase revenues.
(c) increase assets and increase revenues.
(d) decrease revenues and decrease assets.

(SO 4, 5) 7. Each of the following is a major type (or category) of adjusting entry *except:*
(a) prepaid expenses.
(b) accrued revenues.
(c) accrued expenses.
(d) earned revenues.

(SO 5) 8. Adjustments for accrued revenues:
(a) increase assets and increase liabilities.
(b) increase assets and increase revenues.
(c) decrease assets and decrease revenues.
(d) decrease liabilities and increase revenues.

(SO 5) 9. Kathy Kiska earned a salary of $400 for the last week of September. She will be paid on October 1. The adjusting entry for Kathy's employer at September 30 is:

(a) No entry is required.

(b) Salaries Expense	400	
Salaries Payable		400
(c) Salaries Expense	400	
Cash		400
(d) Salaries Payable	400	
Cash		400

10. Which statement is *incorrect* concerning the adjusted trial balance? (SO 6)
(a) An adjusted trial balance proves the equality of the total debit balances and the total credit balances in the ledger after all adjustments are made.
(b) The adjusted trial balance provides the primary basis for the preparation of financial statements.
(c) The adjusted trial balance lists the account balances classified in financial statement format.
(d) The adjusted trial balance is prepared after the adjusting entries have been journalized and posted.

11. Which account will have a zero balance after closing entries have been journalized and posted? (SO 7)
(a) Service Revenue
(b) Advertising Supplies
(c) Prepaid Insurance
(d) Accumulated Amortization

12. Which types of accounts will appear in the post-closing trial balance? (SO 7)
(a) Permanent accounts
(b) Temporary accounts
(c) Accounts shown in the statement of earnings columns of a work sheet
(d) None of the above

13. All of the following are required steps in the accounting cycle *except:* (SO 8)
(a) journalizing and posting closing entries.
(b) preparing an adjusted trial balance.
(c) preparing a post-closing trial balance.
(d) preparing a work sheet.

Note: All questions and exercises marked with an asterisk relate to material in the appendix to this chapter.

QUESTIONS

(SO 1) 1. (a) How does the time period assumption affect an accountant's analysis of accounting transactions?
(b) Explain the term "fiscal year."

(SO 1) 2. Identify and state two generally accepted accounting principles that relate to adjusting the accounts.

3. Tony Galego, a lawyer, accepts a legal engagement in March, performs the work in April, and is paid in May. If Galego's law firm prepares monthly financial statements, when should it recognize revenue from this engagement? Why? (SO 1)

(SO 1) 4. In completing the engagement in question 3, Galego incurs $2,000 of expenses in March, $2,500 in April, and none in May. How much expense should be deducted from revenues in the month the revenue is recognized? Why?

(SO 2) 5. (a) What information do accrual basis financial statements provide that cash basis statements do not?
(b) What information do cash basis financial statements provide that accrual basis statements do not?

(SO 3) 6. "Adjusting entries are required by the cost principle of accounting." Do you agree? Explain.

(SO 3) 7. Why may the financial information in a trial balance not be up-to-date and complete?

(SO 3) 8. Distinguish between the two categories of adjusting entries and identify the types of adjustments applicable to each category.

(SO 4) 9. What accounts are debited and credited in a prepaid expense adjusting entry?

(SO 4) 10. "Amortization is a process of valuation that results in the reporting of the fair market value of the asset." Do you agree? Explain.

(SO 4) 11. Explain the difference between amortization expense and accumulated amortization.

(SO 4) 12. Cheung Company purchased equipment for $12,000. By the current balance sheet date, $7,000 had been amortized. Indicate the balance sheet presentation of the data.

(SO 4) 13. What accounts are debited and credited in an unearned revenue adjusting entry?

(SO 5) 14. A company fails to recognize revenue earned but not yet received. Which of the following accounts are involved in the adjusting entry: (a) asset, (b) liability, (c) revenue, or (d) expense? For the accounts selected, indicate whether they would be debited or credited in the entry.

(SO 5) 15. A company fails to recognize an expense incurred but not paid. Indicate which of the following accounts is debited and which is credited in the adjusting entry: (a) asset, (b) liability, (c) revenue, or (d) expense.

(SO 5) 16. A company makes an accrued revenue adjusting entry for $900 and an accrued expense adjusting entry for $600. How much was net earnings understated prior to these entries? Explain.

(SO 5) 17. On January 9, a company pays $5,000 for salaries, of which $1,700 was reported as Salaries Payable on December 31. Give the entry to record the payment.

18. For each of the following items before adjustment, indicate the type of adjusting entry—prepaid expense, unearned revenue, accrued revenue, and accrued expense—that is needed to correct the misstatement. If an item could result in more than one type of adjusting entry, indicate each of the types. (SO 4, 5)
(a) Assets are understated.
(b) Liabilities are overstated.
(c) Liabilities are understated.
(d) Expenses are understated.
(e) Assets are overstated.
(f) Revenue is understated.

19. Half of the adjusting entry is given below. Indicate the account title for the other half of the entry. (SO 4, 5)
(a) Salaries Expense is debited.
(b) Amortization Expense is debited.
(c) Interest Payable is credited.
(d) Supplies is credited.
(e) Accounts Receivable is debited.
(f) Unearned Service Revenue is debited.

20. "An adjusting entry may affect more than one balance sheet or statement of earnings account." Do you agree? Why or why not? (SO 4, 5)

21. Why is it possible to prepare financial statements directly from an adjusted trial balance? (SO 6)

22. What is the relationship, if any, between the amount shown in the adjusted trial balance column for an account and that account's ledger balance? (SO 6)

23. Identify the account(s) debited and credited in each of the four closing entries, assuming the company has net earnings for the year. (SO 7)

24. Describe the nature of the Income Summary account and identify the types of summary data that may be posted to this account. (SO 7)

25. What items are disclosed on a post-closing trial balance and what is the purpose of this trial balance? (SO 7)

26. Which of these accounts would not appear in the post-closing trial balance: Interest Payable, Equipment, Amortization Expense, Dividends, Unearned Service Revenue, Accumulated Amortization—Equipment, and Service Revenue? (SO 7)

27. Indicate, in the sequence in which they are made, the three required steps in the accounting cycle that involve journalizing. (SO 8)

28. Identify, in the sequence in which they are prepared, the three trial balances that are required in the accounting cycle. (SO 8)

*29. What is the purpose of a work sheet? (SO 9)

*30. What is the basic form of a work sheet? (SO 9)

Brief Exercises

Indicate impact of transaction on cash and earnings.
(SO 2)

BE4-1 Transactions that affect earnings do not necessarily affect cash. Identify the impact, if any, each of the following transactions would have upon cash and retained earnings. The first transaction has been completed for you as an example.

	Cash	Retained Earnings
(a) Purchased supplies for cash, $100.	$ −100	$0
(b) Recorded an adjusting entry to record use of $50 of the above supplies.		
(c) Made sales of $1,000, all on account.		
(d) Received $800 from customers in payment of their accounts.		
(e) Purchased capital asset for cash, $2,500.		
(f) Recorded amortization of capital asset for period used, $1,000.		

Indicate why adjusting entries are needed.
(SO 3)

BE4-2 The ledger of Lena Company Ltd. includes the following accounts. Explain why each account may require adjustment.

(a) Prepaid Insurance
(b) Amortization Expense
(c) Unearned Service Revenue
(d) Interest Payable

Identify the major types of adjusting entries.
(SO 3)

BE4-3 Riko Company Limited accumulates the following adjustment data at December 31. Indicate (1) the type of adjustment (prepaid expense, accrued revenues, and so on) and (2) the status of the accounts before adjustment (overstated or understated).

(a) Supplies of $600 are on hand.
(b) Service Revenues earned but unbilled total $900.
(c) Interest of $200 has accumulated on a note payable.
(d) Rent collected in advance totalling $800 has been earned.

Prepare adjusting entry for supplies.
(SO 4)

BE4-4 Sain Advertising Company's trial balance at December 31 shows Advertising Supplies $9,700 and Advertising Supplies Expense $0. On December 31, there is $1,500 worth of supplies on hand. Prepare the adjusting entry at December 31 and, using T accounts, enter the balances in the accounts, post the adjusting entry, and indicate the adjusted balance in each account.

Use an alternate method to prepare adjusting entry for supplies.
(SO 4)

BE4-5 Refer to BE4-4. Assume that instead of debiting purchases of advertising supplies to the Advertising Supplies account, Sain Advertising debits purchases of supplies to the Advertising Supplies Expense account. Sain Advertising Company's trial balance at December 31 shows Advertising Supplies $0 and Advertising Supplies Expense $9,700. On December 31, there is $1,500 worth of supplies on hand.

(a) Prepare the adjusting entry at December 31, and, using T accounts, enter the balances in the accounts, post the adjusting entry, and indicate the adjusted balance in each account.
(b) Compare the adjusted balances in BE4-3, when an asset account was originally debited, with the adjusted balances in BE4-4, when an expense account was originally debited. Does it matter whether an original entry is recorded to an asset account or an expense account?

Prepare adjusting entry for amortization.
(SO 4)

BE4-6 At the end of its first year, the trial balance of Shah Corporation shows Equipment $25,000 and zero balances for Accumulated Amortization—Equipment and Amortization Expense. Amortization for the year is estimated to be $3,000. Prepare the adjusting entry for amortization at December 31, post the adjustments to T accounts, and indicate the balance sheet presentation of the equipment at December 31.

BE4-7 On July 1, 2001, Bere Co. pays $15,000 to Marla Insurance Co. for a one-year insurance contract. Both companies have fiscal years ending December 31. Journalize and post Bere Co.'s entry on July 1 and the adjusting entry on December 31.

Prepare adjusting entry for prepaid expense.
(SO 4)

BE4-8 Using the data in BE4-7, journalize and post the entry on July 1 and the adjusting entry on December 31 for Marla Insurance Co.

Prepare adjusting entry for unearned revenue.
(SO 4)

BE4-9 The bookkeeper for DeVoe Company Ltd. asks you to prepare the following accrued adjusting entries at December 31:
(a) Interest on notes payable of $400 is accrued.
(b) Service revenue earned but unbilled totals $1,400.
(c) Salaries earned of $700 by employees have not been recorded.

Prepare adjusting entries for accruals.
(SO 5)

BE4-10 The trial balance of Hoi Company Inc. includes the following balance sheet accounts. Identify the accounts that might require adjustment. For each account that requires adjustment, indicate (1) the type of adjusting entry (prepaid expenses, unearned revenues, accrued revenues, and accrued expenses) and (2) the related account in the adjusting entry.
(a) Accounts Receivable
(b) Prepaid Insurance
(c) Equipment
(d) Accumulated Amortization—Equipment
(e) Notes Payable
(f) Interest Payable
(g) Unearned Service Revenue

Analyse accounts in an adjusted trial balance.
(SO 6)

BE4-11 The adjusted trial balance of Lumas Corporation at December 31, 2001, includes the following accounts: Retained Earnings $15,600; Dividends $6,000; Service Revenue $35,400; Salaries Expense $13,000; Insurance Expense $2,000; Rent Expense $4,000; Supplies Expense $1,500; Amortization Expense $1,000; and Income Tax Expense $5,500. Prepare a statement of earnings for the year.

Prepare a statement of earnings from an adjusted trial balance.
(SO 6)

BE4-12 Partial adjusted trial balance data for Lumas Corporation are presented in BE4-11. The balance in Retained Earnings is the balance as at January 1. Prepare a statement of retained earnings for the year assuming net earnings is $8,400.

Prepare a statement of retained earnings from an adjusted trial balance.
(SO 6)

BE4-13 The following selected accounts appear in the adjusted trial balance for Khanna Company Ltd. Indicate the financial statement on which each balance would be reported.
(a) Accumulated Amortization
(b) Amortization Expense
(c) Retained Earnings
(d) Dividends
(e) Service Revenue
(f) Supplies
(g) Accounts Payable
(h) Income Tax Expense

Identify financial statement for selected accounts.
(SO 6)

BE4-14 Using the data in BE4-13, identify the accounts that would be included in a post-closing trial balance.

Identify post-closing trial balance accounts.
(SO 7)

BE4-15 The required steps in the accounting cycle are listed in random order below. List the steps in proper sequence.
(a) Prepare a post-closing trial balance.
(b) Prepare an adjusted trial balance.
(c) Analyse business transactions.
(d) Prepare a trial balance.
(e) Journalize the transactions.
(f) Journalize and post closing entries.
(g) Prepare financial statements.
(h) Journalize and post adjusting entries.
(i) Post to ledger accounts.

List required steps in the accounting cycle in sequence.
(SO 8)

EXERCISES

Identify accounting assumptions, principles, and constraints.
(SO 1)

E4-1 These are the assumptions, principles, and constraints discussed in this and previous chapters:

1. Economic entity assumption
2. Going concern assumption
3. Monetary unit assumption
4. Time period assumption
5. Cost principle
6. Matching principle
7. Full disclosure principle
8. Revenue recognition principle
9. Materiality
10. Cost-benefit

Instructions

Write the number of the accounting assumption, principle, or constraint on the line beside the situation that it describes. Do not use a number more than once.

(a)_____ Is the rationale for why capital assets are not reported at liquidation value. (Do not use the cost principle.)
(b)_____ Indicates that personal and business record-keeping should be separately maintained.
(c)_____ Ensures that all relevant financial information is reported.
(d)_____ Assumes that the dollar is the "measuring stick" used to report on financial performance.
(e)_____ Requires that the operational guidelines be followed for all significant items.
(f)_____ Separates financial information into time periods for reporting purposes.
(g)_____ Requires recognition of expenses in the same period as related revenues.
(h)_____ Indicates that market value changes subsequent to purchase are not recorded in the accounts.

Identify the violated assumption, principle, or constraint.
(SO 1)

E4-2 Here are some accounting reporting situations:

(a) Tercek Company recognizes revenue at the end of the production cycle but before sale. The price of the product, as well as the amount that can be sold, is not certain.
(b) Ravine Hospital Supply Corporation reports only current assets and current liabilities on its balance sheet. Property, plant, and equipment and bonds payable are reported as current assets and current liabilities, respectively. Liquidation of the company is unlikely.
(c) Barton, Inc. is carrying inventory at its current market value of \$100,000. Inventory had an original cost of \$110,000.
(d) Bonilla Company is in its fifth year of operation and has yet to issue financial statements. (Do not use the full disclosure principle.)
(e) Watts Company has inventory on hand that cost \$400,000. Watts reports inventory on its balance sheet at its current market value of \$425,000.
(f) Steph Wolfson, president of the Classic Music Company, bought a computer for her personal use. She paid for the computer by using company funds and debited the Computers account.

Instructions

For each situation, list the assumption, principle, or constraint that has been violated, if any. Some of these were presented in earlier chapters. List only one answer for each situation.

Determine cash basis and accrual basis earnings.
(SO 2)

E4-3 In its first year of operations, Brisson Corp. earned \$26,000 in service revenue, of which \$4,000 was on account and the remainder, \$22,000, was received in cash from customers. The company incurred operating expenses of \$15,000, \$13,500 of which was paid in cash. Of this amount, \$1,500 was still owing on account at year end. In addition, Brisson prepaid \$2,500 for insurance coverage that would not be used until its second year of operations.

Instructions

(a) Calculate the first year's net earnings under the cash basis of accounting and calculate the first year's net earnings under the accrual basis of accounting.

(b) Which basis of accounting (cash or accrual) provides the most useful information for decision-makers?

Identify types of adjustments and accounts before adjustment.
(SO 3, 4, 5)

E4-4 Rafael Company Limited accumulates the following adjustment data at December 31:

(a) Service revenue earned but unbilled totals $600.
(b) Store supplies of $300 are on hand. The Supplies account shows an unadjusted account balance of $2,300.
(c) Utility expenses of $225 are unpaid.
(d) Service revenue of $260 collected in advance has been earned.
(e) Salaries of $800 are unpaid.
(f) Prepaid insurance totalling $350 has expired.

Instructions

For each item, indicate (1) the type of adjustment (prepaid expense, unearned revenue, accrued revenue, or accrued expense) and (2) the impact on the accounts before adjustment (overstatement or understatement).

Prepare adjusting entries from selected account data.
(SO 4, 5)

E4-5 On March 31 of the current year, the ledger of Easy Rental Agency Inc. includes these selected accounts before adjusting entries have been prepared:

	Debits	Credits
Prepaid Insurance	$ 3,600	
Supplies	2,800	
Equipment	25,000	
Accumulated Amortization—Equipment		$ 8,400
Notes Payable		20,000
Unearned Rent Revenue		9,300
Rent Revenue		60,000
Interest Expense	0	
Wage Expense	14,000	
Income Tax Expense	0	

An analysis of the accounts shows the following:

1. The equipment amortizes at $500 per month.
2. One-third of the unearned rent revenue was earned during the quarter.
3. Interest of $600 is accrued on the notes payable.
4. Supplies on hand total $850.
5. Insurance expires at the rate of $200 per month.
6. Income tax is estimated to be $15,000.

Instructions

Prepare the adjusting entries at March 31, assuming that adjusting entries are made quarterly.

Prepare adjusting entries.
(SO 4, 5)

E4-6 Kay Ong, D.D.S., opened an incorporated dental practice on January 1, 2001. During the first month of operations, the following transactions occurred:

1. Performed services for patients who had dental plan insurance. At January 31, $750 of such services were earned but not yet billed to the insurance companies.
2. Utility expenses incurred but not paid prior to January 31 totalled $650.
3. Purchased dental equipment on January 1 for $80,000, paying $20,000 in cash and signing a $60,000, three-year note payable. The equipment amortizes at $400 per month. Interest is $600 per month.
4. Purchased a one-year malpractice insurance policy on January 1 for $12,000.
5. Purchased $1,800 of dental supplies. On January 31, determined that $500 of supplies were on hand.

Instructions

Prepare the adjusting entries at January 31.

Prepare adjusting entries.
(SO 4, 5)

E4-7 The trial balance for Sierra Corporation is shown in Illustration 4-4. In lieu of the adjusting entries shown in the text at October 31, assume the following adjustment data:
1. Advertising supplies on hand at October 31 total $1,300.
2. Expired insurance for the month is $100.
3. Amortization for the month is $50.
4. Unearned revenue earned in October totals $500.
5. Revenue earned but unbilled at October 31 is $300.
6. Interest accrued at October 31 is $70.
7. Accrued salaries at October 31 are $1,600.
8. Accrued income taxes at October 31 are $750.

Instructions
Prepare the adjusting entries for these items.

Prepare a correct statement of earnings.
(SO 4, 5)

E4-8 The statement of earnings of Weller Co. for the month of July shows net earnings of $1,400 based on Service Revenue $5,500; Wages Expense $2,300; Supplies Expense $1,200; and Utilities Expense $600. In reviewing the statement, you discover the following:
1. Insurance expired during July of $300 was omitted.
2. Supplies expense includes $400 of supplies that are still on hand at July 31.
3. Amortization on equipment of $150 was omitted.
4. Accrued but unpaid wages at July 31 of $300 were not included.
5. Revenue earned but unrecorded totalled $750.
6. Income tax expense of $600 was not accrued.

Instructions
Prepare a correct statement of earnings for July 2001.

Analyse adjusted data.
(SO 4, 5, 6)

E4-9 This is a partial adjusted trial balance of Cordero Company Ltd.:

CORDERO COMPANY LTD.
Adjusted Trial Balance
January 31, 2001

	Debit	Credit
Supplies	$ 800	
Prepaid Insurance	2,400	
Salaries Payable		$ 700
Unearned Service Revenue		750
Supplies Expense	950	
Insurance Expense	400	
Salaries Expense	1,800	
Service Revenue		2,500

Instructions
Answer these questions, assuming the year begins January 1:
(a) If the amount in Supplies Expense is the January 31 adjusting entry, and $850 of supplies were purchased in January, what was the balance in Supplies on January 1?
(b) If the amount in Insurance Expense is the January 31 adjusting entry, and the original insurance premium was for one year, what was the total premium and when was the policy purchased?
(c) If $2,500 of salaries were paid in January, what was the balance in Salaries Payable at December 31, 2000?
(d) If $1,600 was received in January for services performed in January, what was the balance in Unearned Service Revenue at December 31, 2000?

E4-10 Selected accounts of Jasper Company Limited are shown here:

Re-create transactions and adjusting entries from adjusted data.
(SO 4, 5)

Supplies Expense

July 31 400	

Supplies

July 1 Bal. 1,100	July 31 400
10 300	

Salaries Payable

	July 31 1,200

Accounts Receivable

July 31 500	

Salaries Expense

July 15 1,200	
31 1,200	

Unearned Service Revenue

July 31 800	July 1 Bal. 1,500
	20 700

Service Revenue

	July 14 3,000
	31 800
	31 500

Instructions

After analysing the accounts, journalize (a) the July transactions and (b) the adjusting entries that were made on July 31. (Hint: July transactions were for cash.)

E4-11 Arseneault Corporation's annual income taxes are estimated to be $12,000. It pays its income taxes monthly, a few days after the end of each month. At year end, selected income tax accounts in the unadjusted trial balance are as follows:

Analyse income tax transactions and prepare adjusting entries.
(SO 5)

Income Tax Expense	$11,000	Income Tax Payable	$0

Belyea Corporation's annual income taxes are estimated to be $24,000. It pays its income taxes quarterly. At year end, selected income tax accounts in the unadjusted trial balance are as follows:

Income Tax Expense	$18,000	Income Tax Payable	$0

Instructions

(a) How much income tax did Arseneault and Belyea pay during the current year?
(b) How much income tax does each company owe at year end?
(c) Prepare the adjusting journal entry required to record any accrued income taxes for each company.

E4-12 The trial balances below are before and after adjustment for Inuit Company Inc. at the end of its fiscal year:

Prepare adjusting entries from analysis of trial balances.
(SO 4, 5, 6)

INUIT COMPANY INC.
Trial Balance
August 31, 2001

	Before Adjustment		After Adjustment	
	Dr.	Cr.	Dr.	Cr.
Cash	$10,400		$10,400	
Accounts Receivable	8,800		9,500	
Office Supplies	2,300		700	
Prepaid Insurance	4,000		2,500	
Office Equipment	14,000		14,000	
Accumulated Amortization—Office Equipment		$ 3,600		$ 4,800
Accounts Payable		5,800		5,800
Salaries Payable		0		1,000
Income Tax Payable		0		3,500
Unearned Rent Revenue		1,500		700
Common Shares		10,000		10,000
Retained Earnings		5,600		5,600
Service Revenue		34,000		34,700

Rent Revenue		11,000		11,800
Salaries Expense	17,000		18,000	
Office Supplies Expense	0		1,600	
Rent Expense	15,000		15,000	
Insurance Expense	0		1,500	
Amortization Expense	0		1,200	
Income Tax Expense	0		3,500	
	$71,500	$71,500	$77,900	$77,900

Instructions

Prepare the adjusting entries that were made.

Prepare financial statements from adjusted trial balance. (SO 6)

E4-13 The adjusted trial balance for Inuit Company is given in E4-12.

Instructions

Prepare the statements of earnings and retained earnings for the year ended August 31, 2001, and the balance sheet at August 31, 2001.

Prepare closing entries. (SO 7)

E4-14 The adjusted trial balance for Inuit company is given in E4-12 and the statements of earnings and retained earnings were prepared in E4-13.

Instructions

Prepare the closing entries for the temporary accounts at August 31.

Complete work sheet. (SO 9)

***E4-15** The adjusted trial balance columns of the work sheet for Wehring Company Ltd. are as follows:

WEHRING COMPANY LTD.
Work Sheet (Partial)
For the Month Ended April 30, 2001

	Adjusted Trial Balance		Statement of Earnings		Balance Sheet	
	Dr.	Cr.	Dr.	Cr.	Dr.	Cr.
Cash	$17,052					
Accounts Receivable	7,840					
Prepaid Rent	2,280					
Equipment	23,050					
Accumulated Amortization		$ 4,921				
Notes Payable		5,700				
Accounts Payable		5,972				
Common Shares		30,000				
Retained Earnings		3,960				
Dividends	3,650					
Service Revenue		12,590				
Salaries Expense	7,840					
Rent Expense	760					
Amortization Expense	671					
Interest Expense	57					
Interest Payable		57				
Totals	$63,200	$63,200				

Instructions

Complete the work sheet.

PROBLEMS: SET A

Identify accounting assumptions, principles, and constraints. (SO 1)

P4-1A Presented below are the assumptions, principles, and constraints used in this and previous chapters.

1. Economic entity assumption	6. Revenue recognition principle
2. Going concern assumption	7. Matching principle
3. Monetary unit assumption	8. Cost principle
4. Time period assumption	9. Materiality
5. Full disclosure principle	10. Cost-benefit

Instructions

In the space provided, write the number of the accounting assumption, principle, or constraint that describes each of these situations. Do not use a number more than once.

(a)_____ Repair tools are expensed when purchased. (Do not use cost-benefit.)
(b)_____ Allocates expenses to revenues in the proper period.
(c)_____ Assumes that the dollar is the measuring stick used to report financial information.
(d)_____ Separates financial information into time periods for reporting purposes.
(e)_____ Market value changes subsequent to purchase are not recorded in the accounts. (Do not use the revenue recognition principle.)
(f)_____ Indicates that personal and business record keeping should be separately maintained.
(g)_____ Ensures that all relevant financial information is reported.
(h)_____ Ensures that irrelevant financial information is not reported at a great expense.

Answer questions about cash position.
(SO 2)

P4-2A **Sleeman Breweries Ltd.** is the largest craft brewer in Canada and the country's leading brewer of premium beers. Founded in 1834, it produces all-natural bottled and draft beer marketed under its own name. In 1998, Sleeman's purchased the Upper Canada Brewery Company and West Coast Beverages Distributors for $25 million.

The 1998 balance sheet of Sleeman Breweries showed current assets of $24 million and current liabilities of $25 million, including a bank overdraft (negative cash balance) of close to $3 million. On a more positive note, Sleeman's nearly doubled its earnings in 1998, from $4 million in 1997 to $7 million in 1998. In addition, its statement of cash flows indicates that it generated $7 million of cash from operating activities in 1998.

Instructions

(a) Do you believe that Sleeman's creditors should be worried about the cash overdraft? Explain why or why not.
(b) If you were a creditor of Sleeman's, and noted that it did not have enough current assets to cover its current liabilities, what additional information might you request to help you assess its solvency?
(c) Why do you think Sleeman's generated $7 million cash from operating activities but has no cash?

Record transactions on accrual basis; convert revenue to cash receipts.
(SO 2, 4)

P4-3A The following data are taken from the comparative balance sheets of Breakers Billiards Club, which prepares its financial statements using the accrual basis of accounting:

December 31	2002	2001
Fees receivable from members	$12,000	$ 9,000
Unearned fees revenue	17,000	22,000

Fees are billed to members based upon their use of the club's facilities. Unearned fees arise from the sale of gift certificates, which members can apply to their future use of club facilities. The 2002 statement of earnings for the club showed that fee revenue of $153,000 was earned during the year.

Instructions

(Hint: You will find it helpful to use T accounts to analyse this data.)

(a) Prepare journal entries for each of the following events that took place during 2002:
  1. Fees receivable from 2001 were all collected.
  2. Gift certificates outstanding at the end of 2001 were all redeemed.
  3. An additional $30,000 worth of gift certificates were sold during 2002; a portion of these were used by the recipients during the year; the remainder were still outstanding at the end of 2002.
  4. Fees for 2002 were billed to members.
  5. Fees receivable for 2002 (i.e., those billed in item (4) above) were partially collected.
(b) Determine the amount of cash received by the club with respect to fees, during 2002.

Convert earnings from cash to accrual basis.
(SO 2, 4, 5)

P4-4A Your examination of the records of a company that follows the cash basis of accounting tells you that the company's reported cash basis earnings in 2002 are $35,190. If this firm had followed accrual basis accounting practices, it would have reported the following year-end balances:

	2001	2002
Accounts receivable	$2,500	$3,400
Supplies on hand	1,160	1,300
Unpaid wages owing	2,400	1,200
Other unpaid amounts	1,600	1,400

Instructions

Determine the company's net earnings on an accrual basis, for 2002. Show all your calculations in an orderly fashion.

Convert earnings from cash to accrual basis; prepare accrual-based financial statements.
(SO 2, 4, 5)

P4-5A During the first week of January 2002, Chantal Thériault began an office design business, Creative Designs Ltd. Although she kept no formal accounting records, she did maintain a record of cash receipts and disbursements. The business was an instant success. In fact, it was so successful that she required additional financing in order to expand during her second year of operations. She approached her bank for a $10,000 loan and was asked to submit a balance sheet and statement of earnings prepared on an accrual basis.

Knowing very little about accounting, she hires you to prepare the financial statements requested by the bank. She supplies you with the following information for the year ended December 31, 2002:

	Receipts	Disbursements
Investments by common shareholders	$30,000	
Equipment		$18,400
Supplies		12,200
Rent payments		9,600
Insurance		1,800
Advertising— all ads completed		3,600
Wages of assistant		18,400
Telephone		980
Dividend payments to shareholders		24,000
Design revenue received	61,500	
	91,500	88,980
Cash balance		2,520
	$91,500	$91,500

Additional information:

1. The equipment has an estimated 10-year life.
2. Supplies on hand on December 31, were $1,800.
3. Rent payments included $750 per month rental and a $600 deposit refundable at the end of the two-year lease.
4. The insurance was paid for a two-year period expiring on December 31, 2003.
5. Wages earned the last week in December to be paid in January 2003 amounted to $400.
6. Design revenue earned but not yet collected amounted to $3,800.
7. Chantal used her personal automobile for business purposes, 12,000 km at 30 cents per km. She was not paid for use of her car but would like to be paid for it.

Instructions:

(a) Prepare an accrual basis statement of earnings for the year ended December 31, 2002.
(b) Prepare the December 31, 2002, balance sheet.

Prepare original and adjusting journal entries for prepayments.
(SO 4, 5)

P4-6A Ouellette Corporation began operations on January 1, 2001. Its fiscal year end is December 31, and it prepares financial statements and adjusts it accounts only *annually*. Selected transactions during 2001 follow:

1. On January 1, 2001, bought office supplies for $4,500 cash. A physical count at December 31, 2001 revealed that $900 of supplies were still on hand.
2. Bought a $3,600 one-year insurance policy for cash on September 1, 2001. The policy came into effect on this date.
3. On November 15, Ouellette received a $1,200 advance cash payment from a client for accounting services expected to be provided in the future. As at December 31, all of these services had been performed and are now complete.
4. On December 15, the company rented out excess office space for a six-month period *starting on this date*, and received a $460 cheque for the first month's rent.

Instructions
Prepare the journal entry for the original transaction and any adjusting journal entry required at December 31, 2001, for each of the above situations. If no journal entry is required, state "**No journal entry required**."

Prepare original and adjusting journal entries for prepayments using an alternative treatment.
(SO 4, 5)

P4-7A In P4-6A, when journal entries were originally recorded, prepaid expenses were debited to an asset account, and unearned revenues were credited to a liability account. Although not specifically illustrated in the chapter, some companies prefer to debit an expense account rather than an asset account to record their original prepaid expense entry, and credit a revenue account rather than a liability account to record their original unearned revenue entry. This problem repeats P4-6A, assuming an alternative treatment of the original journal entry.

Instructions:
Prepare the journal entry for the original transaction and any adjusting journal entry required at December 31, 2001, for each of the situations outlined in P4-6A. If no journal entry is required, state "**No journal entry required**."

Prepare adjusting entries.
(SO 4, 5)

P4-8A A review of the ledger of Come-By-Chance Company Limited at December 31, 2001, produces these data pertaining to the preparation of annual adjusting entries:

1. Prepaid Insurance, $12,800. The company has separate insurance policies on its buildings and its motor vehicles. Policy B4564 on the building was purchased on July 1, 2000, for $9,600. The policy has a term of three years. Policy A2958 on the vehicles was purchased on January 1, 2001, for $4,800. This policy has a term of two years.
2. Unearned Subscription Revenue, $49,000. The company began selling magazine subscriptions in 2001 on an annual basis. The selling price of a subscription is $50. A review of subscription contracts reveals the following:

Subscription Date	Number of Subscriptions
October 1	200
November 1	300
December 1	480
	980

3. Notes Payable, $50,000. This balance consists of a note for six months at an annual interest rate of 9%, dated September 1.
4. Salaries Payable, $0. There are eight salaried employees. Salaries are paid every Friday for a 5-day week (M-F). Five employees receive a salary of $600 each per week, and three employees earn $700 each per week. December 31 is a Monday. All employees worked the last day of December.

Instructions
Prepare the adjusting entries at December 31, 2001.

Prepare original and adjusting journal entries.
(SO 4, 5)

P4-9A The following *independent* situations for Theatre New Brunswick during the year ended December 31, 2002, require either an original journal entry, or an adjusting journal entry, or both.

1. Office supplies on hand at Theatre New Brunswick amounted to $640 at the beginning of the year. During the year, additional office supplies were purchased for cash at a cost of $1,560.
   (a) Prepare the journal entry to record the purchase of the additional office supplies during the year.
   (b) At the end of the year, a physical count showed that supplies on hand amounted to $740. Prepare the year-end adjusting entry.
2. At the beginning of January, the Theatre borrowed $10,000 from the Bank of Montreal at an annual interest rate of 6%.
   (a) Prepare the journal entry the Theatre should make January 1 to record the borrowed funds.
   (b) The principal and interest are to be repaid in two years' time. Prepare the adjusting journal entry to accrue interest on December 31 for the year.

3. Upon reviewing its books on December 31, 2002, the Theatre's year end, it was noted that the telephone bill for the month of December had not yet been received. A call to NB Tel yielded the information that the telephone bill was $400. Prepare the December 31, 2002, adjusting entry.
4. On January 1, 2002, the Theatre purchased a used truck for use in its business for $8,000, paying cash in full.
   (a) Prepare the January 1, 2002, journal entry Theatre New Brunswick would make to record the purchase of the truck.
   (b) Prepare the December 31 adjusting entry to record the annual amortization of $1,600 on this truck at December 31, 2002.
5. The total payroll for the Theatre is $3,000 every Friday for employee wages earned during a five-day week (Monday through Friday, inclusive). This year, December 31 falls on a Wednesday.
   (a) Prepare the adjusting journal entry for the Theatre on Wednesday, December 31, 2002, with respect to wages.
   (b) Prepare the transaction journal entry the Theatre would make on the following Friday, January 2, to pay the weekly wages. Assume that no reversing entries were made on January 1.

Instructions:
Prepare the required journal entries as requested.

Prepare adjusting entries and a corrected statement of earnings.
(SO 4, 5)

P4-10A The Holiday Travel Court Ltd. was organized on April 1, 2001, by Alice Adare. Alice is a good manager but a poor accountant. From the trial balance prepared by a part-time bookkeeper, Alice prepared the following statement of earnings for her fourth quarter, which ended March 31, 2002:

HOLIDAY TRAVEL COURT LTD.
Statement of Earnings
For the Quarter Ended March 31, 2002

Revenues:		
Travel court rental fees		$95,000
Operating expenses:		
Advertising	$ 5,200	
Wages	29,800	
Utilities	900	
Amortization	800	
Repairs	4,000	
Total operating expenses		40,700
Net earnings		$54,300

Alice knew that something was wrong with the statement because net earnings had never exceeded $20,000 in any one quarter. Knowing that you are an experienced accountant, she asks you to review the statement of earnings and other data.

You first look at the trial balance. In addition to the account balances reported above in the statement of earnings, the ledger contains the following additional selected balances at March 31, 2002:

Supplies	$ 5,200
Prepaid Insurance	7,200
Note Payable	12,000

You then make inquiries and discover the following:
1. Travel court rental fees include advanced rentals for summer occupancy, in the amount of $28,000.
2. There were $1,300 of supplies on hand at March 31.
3. Prepaid insurance resulted from the payment of a one-year policy on January 1, 2002.
4. The mail in April 2002 brought the following bills: advertising for the week of March 24, $110; repairs made March 10, $4,260; and utilities for the month of March, $180.
5. There are four employees who receive wages that total $350 per day. At March 31, two days' wages have been incurred but not paid.
6. The note payable is a 10% note dated January 1, 2002, and due on June 30, 2002.
7. Income tax of $8,000 for the quarter is due in April but has not yet been recorded.

Instructions

(a) Prepare any adjusting journal entries required as at March 31, 2002.
(b) Prepare a correct statement of earnings for the quarter ended March 31, 2002.
(c) Explain to Alice the generally accepted accounting principles that she did not recognize in preparing her statement of earnings, and their effect on her results.

P4-11A The trial balance before adjustment of Scenic Tours Limited at the end of its first month of operations is presented here:

Prepare adjusting entries, post, and prepare adjusted trial balance.
(SO 4, 5, 6)

SCENIC TOURS LIMITED
Trial Balance
June 30, 2001

	Debit	Credit
Cash	$ 3,000	
Prepaid Insurance	7,200	
Office Equipment	1,800	
Buses	140,000	
Notes Payable		$ 62,000
Unearned Revenue		15,000
Common Shares		70,000
Tour Revenue		15,900
Salaries Expense	9,000	
Advertising Expense	800	
Gas and Oil Expense	1,100	
	$162,900	$162,900

Other data:

1. The insurance policy has a one-year term beginning June 1, 2001.
2. The monthly amortization is $50 on office equipment and $2,000 on buses.
3. Interest of $700 accrues on the notes payable each month.
4. Deposits of $1,500 each were received for advanced tour reservations from 10 school groups. At June 30, three of these deposits have been earned.
5. Bus drivers are paid a combined total of $400 per day. At June 30, three days' salaries are unpaid.
6. A senior citizens' organization that had not made an advance deposit took a tour on June 30 for $1,200. This group was not billed for the services rendered until July.
7. Income taxes payable are $1000.

Instructions

(a) Journalize the adjusting entries at June 30, 2001.
(b) Prepare a ledger using T accounts. Enter the trial balance amounts and post the adjusting entries.
(c) Prepare an adjusted trial balance at June 30, 2001.

P4-12A The River Run Motel Ltd. opened for business on May 1, 2001. Here is its trial balance before adjustment at May 31:

Prepare adjusting entries, adjusted trial balance, and financial statements.
(SO 4, 5, 6)

RIVER RUN MOTEL LTD.
Trial Balance
May 31, 2001

	Debit	Credit
Cash	$ 2,500	
Prepaid Insurance	1,800	
Supplies	1,900	
Land	15,000	
Lodge	70,000	
Furniture	16,800	
Accounts Payable		$ 4,700
Unearned Rent Revenue		3,600
Mortgage Payable		35,000
Common Shares		60,000
Rent Revenue		9,200
Salaries Expense	3,000	
Utilities Expense	1,000	
Advertising Expense	500	
	$112,500	$112,500

Other data:
1. Insurance expires at the rate of $200 per month.
2. An inventory of supplies shows $1,350 of unused supplies on May 31.
3. Annual amortization is $3,600 on the lodge and $3,000 on furniture.
4. The mortgage interest rate is 12%. (The mortgage was taken out on May 1.)
5. Unearned rent of $1,500 has been earned.
6. Salaries of $300 are accrued and unpaid at May 31.
7. Accrued income taxes are estimated to be $1,500.

Instructions

(a) Journalize the adjusting entries at May 31.
(b) Prepare a ledger using T accounts. Enter the trial balance amounts and post the adjusting entries.
(c) Prepare an adjusted trial balance at May 31.
(d) Prepare a statement of earnings and a statement of retained earnings for the month of May and a balance sheet at May 31.
(e) Identify which accounts should be closed on May 31, assuming that the company closes its books monthly.

Prepare adjusting entries and financial statements; identify accounts to be closed.
(SO 4, 5, 6, 7)

P4-13A Ozaki Corp. was organized on July 1, 2001. Quarterly financial statements are prepared. The trial balance and adjusted trial balance at September 30 are shown here:

OZAKI CORP.
Trial Balance
September 30, 2001

	Unadjusted		Adjusted	
	Dr.	Cr.	Dr.	Cr.
Cash	$ 6,700		$ 6,700	
Accounts Receivable	400		800	
Prepaid Rent	1,500		900	
Supplies	1,200		1,000	
Equipment	15,000		15,000	
Accumulated Amortization—Equipment				$ 350
Note Payable		$ 5,000		5,000
Accounts Payable		1,510		1,510
Salaries Payable				600
Interest Payable				50
Unearned Rent Revenue		900		600
Common Shares		14,000		14,000
Income Tax Payable		0		1,000
Retained Earnings		0		0
Dividends	600		600	
Commission Revenue		14,000		14,400
Rent Revenue		400		700
Salaries Expense	9,000		9,600	
Rent Expense	900		1,500	
Amortization Expense			350	
Supplies Expense			200	
Utilities Expense	510		510	
Interest Expense			50	
Income Tax Expense	0		1,000	
	$35,810	$35,810	$38,210	$38,210

Instructions

(a) Journalize the adjusting entries that were made.
(b) Prepare a statement of earnings and a statement of retained earnings for the three months ending September 30, and a balance sheet at September 30.
(c) Identify which accounts should be closed on September 30, if the books are closed quarterly.
(d) If the note bears interest at 12%, how many months has it been outstanding?

P4-14A On November 1, 2001, the following were the account balances of Alou Equipment Repair Corp.:

Journalize transactions and follow through accounting cycle to preparation of financial statements.

(SO 4, 5, 6, 8)

	Debits		Credits
Cash	$ 2,790	Accumulated Amortization	$ 500
Accounts Receivable	2,510	Accounts Payable	2,100
Supplies	1,000	Unearned Service Revenue	400
Store Equipment	10,000	Salaries Payable	500
		Common Shares	10,000
		Retained Earnings	2,800
	$16,300		$16,300

During November, the following summary transactions were completed:

Nov. 8 Paid $1,100 for salaries due employees, of which $600 is for November.
10 Received $1,200 cash from customers on account.
12 Received $1,400 cash for services performed in November.
15 Purchased store equipment on account, $3,000.
17 Purchased supplies on account, $1,500.
20 Paid creditors on account, $2,500.
22 Paid November rent, $300.
25 Paid salaries, $1,000.
27 Performed services on account and billed customers for services rendered, $700.
29 Received $550 from customers for future service.
30 Paid income tax instalment for the month, $250.

Adjustment data:
1. Supplies on hand are valued at $1,600.
2. Accrued salaries payable are $500.
3. Amortization for the month is $120.
4. Unearned service revenue of $300 is earned.

Instructions

(a) Enter the November 1 balances in the ledger accounts. (Use T accounts.)
(b) Journalize the November transactions.
(c) Post to the ledger accounts.
(d) Prepare a trial balance at November 30.
(e) Journalize and post adjusting entries.
(f) Prepare an adjusted trial balance.
(g) Prepare a statement of earnings and a statement of retained earnings for November, and a balance sheet at November 30.

P4-15A Brett Farve opened Corellian Window Washing Inc. on July 1, 2001. During July, the following transactions were completed:

Complete all steps in accounting cycle.

(SO 4, 5, 6, 7, 8)

July 1 Issued $9,000 of common shares for $9,000 cash.
1 Purchased used truck for $6,000, paying $3,000 cash and the balance on account.
3 Purchased cleaning supplies for $900 on account.
5 Paid $1,200 cash on one-year insurance policy effective July 1.
12 Billed customers $2,500 for cleaning services.
18 Paid $1,000 cash on amount owed on truck and $500 on amount owed on cleaning supplies.
20 Paid $1,200 cash for employee salaries.
21 Collected $1,400 cash from customers billed on July 12.
25 Billed customers $2,000 for cleaning services.
31 Paid gas and oil for month on truck, $200.
31 Paid monthly income taxes of $100.
31 Declared and paid $600 cash dividend.

Instructions

(a) Journalize the July transactions.
(b) Post to the ledger accounts. (Use T accounts.)
(c) Prepare a trial balance at July 31.
(d) Journalize the following adjustments:

1. Services provided but unbilled and uncollected at July 31 were $1,100.
2. Amortization on equipment for the month was $200.
3. One-twelfth of the insurance expired.
4. An inventory count shows $600 of cleaning supplies on hand at July 31.
5. Accrued but unpaid employee salaries were $400.

(e) Post adjusting entries to the T accounts.
(f) Prepare an adjusted trial balance.
(g) Prepare a statement of earnings and a statement of retained earnings for July and a classified balance sheet at July 31.
(h) Journalize and post closing entries and complete the closing process.
(i) Prepare a post-closing trial balance at July 31.

Prepare a work sheet, financial statements, and adjusting and closing entries.
(SO 4, 5, 6, 7, 9)

***P4-16A** The trial balance columns of the work sheet for Phantom Roofing Inc. at March 31, 2001, are as follows:

PHANTOM ROOFING INC.
Work Sheet
For the Month Ended March 31, 2001

	Trial Balance	
Account Titles	Dr.	Cr.
Cash	$ 2,700	
Accounts Receivable	1,600	
Roofing Supplies	1,100	
Equipment	6,000	
Accumulated Amortization—Equipment		$ 1,200
Accounts Payable		1,100
Unearned Revenue		300
Common Shares		5,000
Retained Earnings		2,000
Dividends	600	
Service Revenue		3,000
Salaries Expense	500	
Miscellaneous Expense	100	
	$12,600	$12,600

Additional facts:
1. A physical count reveals only $320 of roofing supplies on hand.
2. Amortization for March is $200.
3. Unearned revenue amounted to $200 after adjustment on March 31.
4. Accrued salaries are $400.

Instructions
(a) Enter the trial balance on a work sheet and complete the work sheet.
(b) Prepare a statement of earnings and a statement of retained earnings for the month of March, and a classified balance sheet at March 31.
(c) Journalize the adjusting entries from the adjustments columns of the work sheet.
(d) Journalize the closing entries from the financial statement columns of the work sheet, assuming closing entries are made monthly by the company.

PROBLEMS: SET B

Identify accounting assumptions, principles, and constraints.
(SO 1)

P4-1B Presented here are the assumptions, principles, and constraints used in this and previous chapters:

1. Economic entity assumption
2. Going concern assumption
3. Monetary unit assumption
4. Time period assumption
5. Full disclosure principle
6. Revenue recognition principle
7. Matching principle
8. Cost principle
9. Materiality
10. Cost-benefit

Instructions

In the space provided, write the number of the accounting assumption, principle, or constraint that describes each of these situations. Do not use a number more than once.

(a)_____ Assets are not stated at their liquidation value. (Do not use the cost principle.)
(b)_____ The death of the president is not recorded in the accounts.
(c)_____ Pencil sharpeners are expensed when purchased.
(d)_____ An allowance for doubtful accounts is established. (Do not use cost-benefit.)
(e)_____ Each entity is kept as a unit distinct from its owner or owners.
(f)_____ Reporting must be done at defined intervals.
(g)_____ Revenue is recorded at the point of sale.
(h)_____ Every financial event need not be disclosed if the cost is prohibitive.
(i)_____ All important information related to inventories is presented in the notes or in the financial statements.

Answer questions about cash position.
(SO 2)

P4-2B **Future Shop Ltd.** is one of North America's largest computer and electronics retailers. Established in 1982, the company has grown to over 83 stores in Canada. In addition, Future Shop sells its products on-line. In 1998, Future Shop bought seven Computer City stores in Canada from CompUSA, and it plans to use its Computer City chain as a platform for corporate and government sales.

The 1999 balance sheet of Future Shop showed current assets of $221.3 million and current liabilities of $253.9 million, including bank indebtedness (cash overdraft) of close to $24 million. Future Shop also recorded a net loss of $82.2 million in fiscal 1999, down from $4 million in reported net earnings in 1998. In addition, its statement of cash flows indicates that it used $49 million of cash for operating activities in 1999.

Instructions

(a) Do you believe that Future Shop's creditors should be worried about the cash overdraft? Explain why or why not.
(b) If you were a creditor of Future Shop, and noted that it did not have enough current assets to cover its current liabilities, what additional information might you request to help you assess its solvency?
(c) In spite of these results, Future Shop's stock price was around $12 a share at the end of its fiscal 1999 year. Why were investors willing to pay $12 a share for a company that had no cash?

Record transactions on accrual basis; convert revenue to cash receipts.
(SO 2, 4)

P4-3B The following selected data are taken from the comparative financial statements of Hammer Curling Club, which will be hosting the McCain TSN Skins Game in November 2001. The Club prepares its financial statements using the accrual basis of accounting:

September 30	2001	2000
Dues receivable from members	$ 15,000	$ 11,000
Unearned ticket revenue	20,000	25,000
Dues revenue	148,000	132,000

Dues are billed to members based upon their use of the Club's facilities. Unearned ticket revenues arise from the sale of tickets to events such as the Skins Game.

Instructions

(Hint: You will find it helpful to use T accounts to analyse the following data. You must analyse these data sequentially, as missing information must first be deduced before moving on. Post your journal entries as you progress, rather than waiting until the end.)

(a) Prepare journal entries for each of the following events that took place during 2001:
1. Dues receivable from members from 2000 were all collected.
2. Unearned ticket revenue at the end of 2000 was all earned.
3. Additional tickets were sold for $35,000 cash during 2001; a portion of these were used by the purchasers during the year. The entire balance remaining relates to the upcoming Skins Game in 2001.
4. Dues for the 2001–2002 fiscal year were billed to members.
5. Dues receivable for 2001 (i.e., those billed in item (4) above) were partially collected.

(b) Determine the amount of cash received by the Club from the above transactions during the year ended September 30, 2001.

Convert earnings from cash to accrual basis.
(SO 2, 4, 5)

P4-4B Your examination of the records of a company that follows the cash basis of accounting tells you that the company's reported cash basis earnings in 2002 are $43,900. If the company had followed accrual basis accounting practices, it would have reported the following year-end balances:

	2002	2001
Accounts receivable	$3,600	$2,700
Prepaid insurance	1,550	1,310
Accounts payable	1,500	2,200
Unearned revenues	1,360	1,500

Instructions

Determine the company's net earnings, on an accrual basis, for 2002. Show all your calculations.

Convert earnings from cash to accrual basis; prepare accrual-based financial statements.
(SO 2, 4, 5)

P4-5B During the first week of November 2001, Danielle Charron opened a ski tuning and repair shop, The Radical Edge Ltd., on a busy ski hill. She didn't do any bookkeeping, but she carefully kept track of all her cash receipts and cash payments. She supplies you with the following information at the end of the ski season, April 30, 2002:

	Cash Receipts	Cash Payments
Issue of common shares	$20,000	
Payment for repair equipment		$ 9,200
Rent payments		1,225
Newspaper advertising paid		375
Utility bills paid		970
Part-time helper's wages paid		2,600
Cash receipts from ski and snowboard repair services	32,150	
Subtotals	52,150	14,370
Cash balance		37,780
Totals	$52,150	$52,150

You learn that the repair equipment has an estimated useful life of eight years. The company rents space at a cost of $175 per month on a one-year lease. The lease contract requires payment of the first and last months' rent in advance, which was paid. The part-timer helper is owed $120 at April 30, 2002, for unpaid wages. At April 30, 2002, customers owe The Radical Edge $650 for services they have received but have not yet paid for.

Instructions

(a) Prepare an accrual basis statement of earnings for the six months ended April 30, 2002.
(b) Prepare the April 30, 2002, balance sheet.

Prepare original and adjusting journal entries for prepayments.
(SO 4, 5)

P4-6B Bourque Corporation began operations on January 1, 2001. Its fiscal year end is December 31, and it prepares financial statements and adjusts its accounts only *annually*. Selected transactions during 2001 follow:

1. On January 2, 2001, bought office supplies for $2,800 cash. A physical count at December 31, 2001, revealed $500 of supplies were still on hand.
2. Bought a $3,600 one-year insurance policy for cash on August 1, 2001. The policy came into effect on this date.
3. On December 15, the company paid $500 rent in advance for the month of January 2002.
4. On November 15, Bourque received a $1,200 advance cash payment from three clients for accounting services expected to be provided in the future. As at December 31, services had been performed for two of the clients ($400 each) and are now complete.

Instructions

Prepare the journal entry for the original transaction and any adjusting journal entry required at December 31, 2001, for each of the above situations.

P4-7B In P4-6B, when journal entries were originally recorded, prepaid expenses were debited to an asset account, and unearned revenues were credited to a liability account. Although not specifically illustrated in the chapter, some companies prefer to debit an expense account rather than an asset account to record their original prepaid expense entry, and credit a revenue account rather than a liability account to record their original unearned revenue entry. This problem repeats P4-6B, assuming an alternative treatment of the original journal entry.

Prepare original and adjusting journal entries for prepayments using an alternative treatment.
(SO 4, 5)

Instructions
Prepare the journal entry for the original transaction and any adjusting journal entry required at December 31, 2001, for each of the situations outlined in P4-6B.

P4-8B A review of the ledger of Greenberg Corporation at December 31, 2002, produces the following data pertaining to the preparation of annual adjusting entries:

Prepare adjusting entries.
(SO 4, 5)

1. Salaries Payable, $0. There are eight salaried employees. Salaries are paid every Friday for the current week. Five employees receive a salary of $600 each per week, and three employees earn $500 each per week. December 31 is a Tuesday. Employees do not work weekends. All employees worked the last two days of December.
2. Unearned Rent Revenue, $369,000. The company began subleasing office space in its new building on November 1. Each tenant is required to make a $5,000 security deposit that is not refundable until occupancy is terminated. At December 31 the company had the following rental contracts that are paid in full for the entire term of the lease:

Date	Term (in months)	Monthly Rent	Number of Leases
Nov. 1	6	$4,000	5
Dec. 1	6	8,500	4

3. Prepaid Advertising. $13,200. This balance consists of payments on two advertising contracts. The contracts provide for monthly advertising in two trade magazines and the first advertisement runs in the month in which the contract is signed. The terms of the contracts are as follows:

Contract	Date	Amount	Number of Magazine Issues
A650	May 1	$6,000	12
B974	Sept. 1	7,200	24

4. Notes Payable, $80,000. This balance consists of a note for one year at an annual interest rate of 12%, dated June 1.

Instructions
Prepare the adjusting entries at December 31, 2002. Show all calculations.

P4-9B The following *independent* situations for Repertory Theatre during 2000 may require either an original journal entry, or an adjusting journal entry, or both.

Prepare original and adjusting journal entries.
(SO 4, 5)

1. Office supplies on hand at Repertory Theatre amounted to $300 at the beginning of the year. During the year, additional office supplies were purchased for cash at a cost of $1,500.
   (a) Prepare the journal entry to record the purchase of the additional office supplies during the year.
   (b) At the end of the year, a physical count showed that supplies on hand amounted to $500. Prepare the year-end adjusting entry.
2. At the beginning of June, the Theatre borrowed $4,000 from La Caisse Populaire Desjardins at an annual interest rate of 8%.
   (a) Prepare the journal entry the Theatre should make June 1 to record the borrowed funds.
   (b) The principal and interest are to be repaid in a year's time. Prepare the adjusting journal entry to accrue interest on December 31 for the six months expired.
   (c) Prepare the journal entry to record the repayment of principal and the full year's interest in June 2001.

3. Upon reviewing its books on December 31, 2000, the Theatre's year end, it was noted that a utility bill for the month of December had not yet been received. A call to Hydro-Québec yielded the information that the electricity bill was $1,400. Prepare the December 31 adjusting entry.
4. On January 1, 2000, the Theatre purchased a truck for use in its business for $38,000, paying cash in full.
   (a) Prepare the January 1 journal entry the Theatre would make to record the purchase of the truck.
   (b) Prepare the December 31 adjusting entry to record the annual amortization of $10,000 on this truck at December 31, 2000.
5. Annual income taxes for the Theatre are estimated to be $13,000 for the year, $10,000 of which has been paid to date.
   (a) Prepare the adjusting journal entry for the Theatre to record accrued taxes.
   (b) Prepare the journal entry required on January 15, 2001, when the Theatre pays the $3,000 remaining income taxes due to the Canada Customs and Revenue Agency.

Instructions
Prepare the required journal entries as requested.

Prepare adjusting entries and a corrected statement of earnings.
(SO 4, 5)

P4-10B The Try-Us Travel Agency Ltd. was organized on January 1, 2002, by Paul Volpé. Paul is a good manager but a poor accountant. From the trial balance prepared by a part-time bookkeeper, Paul prepared the following statement of earnings for the quarter that ended March 31, 2002:

TRY-US TRAVEL AGENCY LTD.
Statement of Earnings
For the Quarter Ended March 31, 2002

Revenues:		
Travel service fees		$50,000
Operating expenses:		
Advertising	$2,600	
Amortization	400	
Income tax	1,500	
Salaries	6,000	
Utilities	400	10,900
Net earnings		$39,100

Paul knew that something was wrong with the statement because net earnings had never exceeded $5,000 in any one quarter. Knowing that you are an experienced accountant, he asks you to review the statement of earnings and other data.

You first look at the trial balance. In addition to the account balances reported above in the statement of earnings, the trial balance contains the following additional selected balances at March 31, 2002:

Supplies	$ 3,200
Prepaid insurance	1,200
Note payable	10,000

You then make inquiries and discover the following:
1. Travel service fees include advance payments for cruises, $30,000.
2. There were $800 of supplies on hand at March 31.
3. Prepaid insurance resulted from the payment of a one-year policy on February 1, 2002.
4. The mail on April 1, 2002, brought the utility bill for the month of March's heat, light, and power, $180.
5. There are two employees who receive salaries of $75 each per day. At March 31, three days' salaries have been incurred but not paid.
6. The note payable is a six-month, 10% note dated January 1, 2002.

Instructions
(a) Prepare any adjusting journal entries required as at March 31, 2002.
(b) Prepare a correct statement of earnings for the quarter ended March 31, 2002.
(c) Explain to Paul the generally accepted accounting principles that he did not recognize in preparing his statement of earnings, and their effect on his results.

P4-11B Ortega Limo Service Ltd. began operations on January 1, 2001. At the end of the first year of operations, this is the trial balance before adjustment:

Prepare adjusting entries, post, and prepare adjusted trial balance.

(SO 4, 5, 6)

ORTEGA LIMO SERVICE LTD.
Trial Balance
December 31, 2001

	Debit	Credit
Cash	$ 12,400	
Accounts Receivable	3,200	
Prepaid Insurance	3,600	
Automobiles	58,000	
Notes Payable		$ 45,000
Unearned Service Revenue		2,500
Common Shares		18,000
Service Revenue		84,000
Salaries Expense	57,000	
Repairs Expense	6,000	
Gas and Oil Expense	9,300	
	$149,500	$149,500

Other data:
1. Service revenue earned but unbilled is $1,500 at December 31.
2. Insurance coverage began on January 1, under a two-year policy.
3. Automobile amortization is $15,000 for the year.
4. Interest of $5,400 accrued on notes payable for the year.
5. An amount of $1,000 of the unearned service revenue has been earned.
6. Drivers' salaries total $500 per day. At December 31, four days' salaries are unpaid.
7. Repairs to automobiles of $650 have been incurred, but bills have not been received prior to December 31. (Use Accounts Payable.)
8. Income taxes accrued and unpaid for the year are $5,000.

Instructions

(a) Journalize the adjusting entries at December 31, 2001.
(b) Prepare a ledger using T accounts. Enter the trial balance amounts and post the adjusting entries.
(c) Prepare an adjusted trial balance at December 31, 2001.

P4-12B Highland Cove Resort Inc. opened for business on June 1 with eight air-conditioned units. Its trial balance before adjustment at August 31 is presented here:

Prepare adjusting entries, adjusted trial balance, and financial statements.

(SO 4, 5, 6)

HIGHLAND COVE RESORT INC.
Trial Balance
August 31, 2001

	Debit	Credit
Cash	$ 15,600	
Prepaid Insurance	5,400	
Supplies	3,300	
Land	25,000	
Cottages	125,000	
Furniture	26,000	
Accounts Payable		$ 6,500
Unearned Rent Revenue		6,800
Income Tax Payable		0
Mortgage Payable		80,000
Common Shares		100,000
Dividends	5,000	
Rent Revenue		80,000
Salaries Expense	51,000	
Utilities Expense	9,400	
Repair Expense	3,600	
Income Tax Expense	4,000	
	$273,300	$273,300

Other data:
1. Insurance expires at the rate of $300 per month.
2. An inventory count on August 31 shows $700 of supplies on hand.
3. Annual amortization is $4,800 on cottages and $2,400 on furniture.
4. Unearned rent of $5,000 was earned prior to August 31.
5. Salaries of $400 were unpaid at August 31.
6. Rentals of $800 were due from tenants at August 31. (Use Accounts Receivable.)
7. The mortgage interest rate is 12% per year. (The mortgage was taken out August 1.)
8. Income taxes owed are $1,000.

Instructions

(a) Journalize the adjusting entries at August 31 for the three-month period from June 1 to August 31.
(b) Prepare a ledger using T accounts. Enter the trial balance amounts and post the adjusting entries.
(c) Prepare an adjusted trial balance at August 31.
(d) Prepare a statement of earnings and a statement of retained earnings for the three months ended August 31, and a balance sheet as at August 31.
(e) Identify which accounts should be closed on August 31.

Prepare adjusting entries and financial statements; identify accounts to be closed.
(SO 4, 5, 6, 7)

P4-13B Grant Advertising Agency Limited was founded by Thomas Grant in January 1997. Presented here are both the adjusted and unadjusted trial balances as at December 31, 2001.

GRANT ADVERTISING AGENCY LIMITED
Trial Balance
December 31, 2001

	Unadjusted		Adjusted	
	Dr.	Cr.	Dr.	Cr.
Cash	$ 3,500		$ 3,500	
Accounts Receivable	20,000		21,000	
Art Supplies	8,400		5,000	
Prepaid Insurance	3,350		2,500	
Printing Equipment	60,000		60,000	
Accumulated Amortization		$ 28,000		$ 35,000
Accounts Payable		5,000		5,000
Interest Payable		0		150
Note Payable		5,000		5,000
Unearned Advertising Revenue		7,000		5,600
Salaries Payable		0		1,800
Income Tax Payable		0		2,500
Common Shares		20,000		20,000
Retained Earnings		5,500		5,500
Dividends	12,000		12,000	
Advertising Revenue		58,600		61,000
Salaries Expense	10,000		11,800	
Insurance Expense			850	
Interest Expense	350		500	
Amortization Expense			7,000	
Art Supplies Expense			3,400	
Rent Expense	4,000		4,000	
Income Tax Expense	7,500		10,000	
	$129,100	$129,100	$141,550	$141,550

Instructions

(a) Journalize the annual adjusting entries that were made.
(b) Prepare a statement of earnings and a statement of retained earnings for the year ended December 31, and a balance sheet at December 31.
(c) Identify which accounts should be closed on December 31.
(d) If the note has been outstanding three months, what is the annual interest rate on that note?
(e) If the company paid $13,500 in salaries in 2001, what was the balance in Salaries Payable on December 31, 2000?

Journalize transactions and follow through accounting cycle to preparation of financial statements.
(SO 4, 5, 6, 8)

P4-14B On September 1, 2001, the following were the account balances of Rijo Equipment Repair Corp.:

	Debits		Credits
Cash	$ 4,880	Accumulated Amortization	$ 1,500
Accounts Receivable	3,520	Accounts Payable	3,400
Supplies	1,000	Unearned Service Revenue	400
Store Equipment	15,000	Salaries Payable	500
	$24,400	Common Shares	10,000
		Retained Earnings	8,600
			$24,400

During September, the following summary transactions were completed:

Sept. 8 Paid $1,100 for salaries due employees, of which $600 is for September.
10 Received $1,200 cash from customers on account.
12 Received $3,400 cash for services performed in September.
15 Purchased store equipment on account, $3,000.
17 Purchased supplies on account, $1,500.
20 Paid creditors $4,500 on account.
22 Paid September rent, $500.
25 Paid salaries, $1,050.
27 Performed services on account and billed customers for services rendered, $900.
29 Received $650 from customers for future service.
30 Paid income tax for month, $750.

Adjustment data:
1. Supplies on hand, $1,800.
2. Accrued salaries payable, $400.
3. Amortization, $200 per month.
4. Unearned service revenue of $350 earned.

Instructions
(a) Enter the September 1 balances in the ledger T accounts.
(b) Journalize the September transactions.
(c) Post to the ledger T accounts.
(d) Prepare a trial balance at September 30.
(e) Journalize and post adjusting entries.
(f) Prepare an adjusted trial balance.
(g) Prepare a statement of earnings and a statement of retained earnings for September, and a balance sheet at September 30.

Complete all steps in accounting cycle.
(SO 4, 5, 6, 7, 8)

P4-15B Ewok-Ackbar opened Ewok's Carpet Cleaners Ltd. on March 1. During March, the following transactions were completed:

Mar. 1 Issued $10,000 of common shares for $10,000 cash.
1 Purchased used truck for $6,000, paying $4,000 cash and the balance on account.
3 Purchased cleaning supplies for $1,200 on account.
5 Paid $1,800 cash on one-year insurance policy effective March 1.
14 Billed customers $2,800 for cleaning services.
18 Paid $1,500 cash on amount owed on truck and $500 on amount owed on cleaning supplies.
20 Paid $1,500 cash for employee salaries.
21 Collected $1,600 cash from customers billed on July 14.
28 Billed customers $3,500 for cleaning services.
31 Paid gas and oil for month on truck, $200.
31 Paid income tax for month, $500.
31 Declared and paid a $900 cash dividend.

Instructions

(a) Journalize the March transactions.
(b) Post to the ledger accounts. (Use T accounts.)
(c) Prepare a trial balance at March 31.
(d) Journalize the following adjustments:
   1. Earned but unbilled revenue at March 31 was $600.
   2. Amortization equipment for the month was $250.
   3. One-twelfth of the insurance expired.
   4. An inventory count shows $400 of cleaning supplies on hand at March 31.
   5. Accrued but unpaid employee salaries were $500.
(e) Post adjusting entries to the T accounts.
(f) Prepare an adjusted trial balance.
(g) Prepare a statement of earnings and a statement of retained earnings for March, and a classified balance sheet at March 31.
(h) Journalize and post closing entries, and complete the closing process.
(i) Prepare a post-closing trial balance at March 31.

Prepare work sheet, financial statements and adjusting and closing entries.
(SO 4, 5, 6, 7, 9)

***P4-16B** Vader began operations as a private investigator on January 1, 2001. The trial balance columns of the work sheet for Vader P.I., Inc., at March 31, are as follows:

VADER P.I., INC.
Work Sheet
For the Quarter Ended March 31, 2001

	Trial Balance	
Account Titles	Dr.	Cr.
Cash	$13,700	
Accounts Receivable	5,620	
Supplies	1,050	
Prepaid Insurance	2,400	
Equipment	30,000	
Notes Payable		$10,000
Accounts Payable		12,350
Common Shares		20,000
Dividends	600	
Service Revenue		13,620
Salaries Expense	1,200	
Travel Expense	1,200	
Miscellaneous Expense	200	
	$55,970	$55,970

Other data:
1. Supplies on hand total $750.
2. Amortization is $400 per quarter.
3. Interest accrued on six-month note payable, issued January 1, $300.
4. Insurance expires at the rate of $150 per month.
5. Services provided but unbilled at March 31 total $750.
6. Accrued income taxes total $2,500.

Instructions

(a) Enter the trial balance on a work sheet and complete the work sheet.
(b) Prepare a statement of earnings and a statement of retained earnings for the quarter, and a classified balance sheet at March 31.
(c) Journalize the adjusting entries from the adjustments columns of the work sheet.
(d) Journalize the closing entries from the financial statement columns of the work sheet.

BROADENING YOUR PERSPECTIVE

FINANCIAL REPORTING AND ANALYSIS

FINANCIAL REPORTING PROBLEM: *Loblaw Companies Limited*

BYP4-1 The financial statements of **Loblaw** are presented in Appendix A at the end of this book.

Instructions

(a) Using the consolidated statement of earnings and the balance sheet, identify items that may result in adjusting entries for prepayments.
(b) Using the consolidated statement of earnings, identify two items that may result in adjusting entries for accruals.
(c) What was the amount of income tax expense for 1999 and 1998? Are there any taxes payable as at January 1, 2000?
(d) What has been the trend since 1997 for interest expense?
(e) What was the cash paid for interest during 1999? See the net interest paid amount reported at the bottom of the consolidated statement of cash flows. What was the net interest expense reported on the statement of earnings for 1999? Where is the remainder presumably reported in the balance sheet?

COMPARATIVE ANALYSIS PROBLEM: *Loblaw and Sobeys*

BYP4-2 The financial statements of **Sobeys Inc.** are presented in Appendix B, following the financial statements for **Loblaw** in Appendix A.

Instructions

(a) Identify two accounts on Sobeys' consolidated balance sheet that provide evidence that Sobeys uses accrual accounting. In each case, identify the statement of earnings account that would be affected by the adjustment process.
(b) Identify two accounts on Loblaw's balance sheet that provide evidence that Loblaw uses accrual accounting. In each case, identify the statement of earnings account that would be affected by the adjustment process.

RESEARCH CASE

BYP4-3 In Canada, electronics communication giant **Motorola** has 800 employees with sales of approximately $838 million. Worldwide, it conducts business on six continents and employs more than 133,000 people, with global sales of about $44 billion. The March 1995 issue of *Management Review* includes an article by Barbara Ettorre entitled "How Motorola Closes Its Books in Two Days."

Instructions

Read the article and answer these questions:

(a) How often does Motorola close its books? How long did the process formerly take?
(b) What was the major change Motorola initiated to shorten the closing process?
(c) What incentive does Motorola offer to ensure accurate and timely information?
(d) In a given year, how many journal entry lines does Motorola process?
(e) Provide an example of an external force that prevents Motorola from closing faster than a day-and-a-half.
(f) According to Motorola's corporate vice-president and controller, how do external users of financial statements perceive companies that release information early?

INTERPRETING FINANCIAL STATEMENTS

BYP4-4 **Cott Corporation**, headquartered in Pointe Claire, Quebec, is the fourth largest soft drink company in the world. It produces and distributes sports drinks, bottled water, and fruit-flavoured sparkling water in Canada, the U.S., the UK, Continental Europe, Japan, Australia, and Ireland.

Until October 31, 1998, Cott Corporation included on its balance sheet a non-current asset called Prepaid Contract Costs. An excerpt from the management discussion and analysis accompanying Cott's fiscal 1997 financial statements noted:

COTT CORPORATION
Prepaid Contract Costs
October 31, 1997

The Corporation has relatively few customers when compared with the customer bases of the national brand soft drink manufacturers, making it relatively more vulnerable to the loss of one or more customers. The risk that the Corporation will lose any single customer can be mitigated by entering into long-term contracts. With certain of its customers, the Corporation is able to obtain a long-term contract only with the payment of an up-front fixed amount of money. The contracts entered into generally provide: (i) that the Corporation will be the exclusive supplier of premium retailer brand soft drinks; and (ii) for minimum annual volume targets to be achieved by the customers. Since these amounts are paid with the objective of realizing a revenue stream over a period of more than one year, the Corporation elects to capitalize these amounts as prepaid contract costs and amortizes them over the term of the related contracts.

Effective October 31, 1998, Cott changed this accounting policy and is no longer capitalizing its prepaid contract costs. Instead, it is recording these costs as an expense when incurred.

Instructions

(a) Assume that the up-front contract payment costs paid by Cott for fiscal 1997 totalled $29,743,000. Prepare the journal entry Cott would have made to record this payment.
(b) Cott amortized its Prepaid Contract Costs in the same way it amortized its capital assets. Assume their amortization expense for fiscal 1997 was $26,349,000. Prepare the journal entry Cott would have made to record this amortization.
(c) Since the Prepaid Contract Costs were incurred to earn revenue, do you believe the amortization expense recorded above should be reported as a reduction of sales revenue or as an expense? Discuss your reasoning.
(d) In fiscal 1998 and subsequent years, Cott decided not to capitalize these costs any longer. It is now expensing these costs when incurred.
   1. Discuss the reasoning Cott might have used when making this change from capitalizing prepaid costs to expensing prepaid costs. Use the revenue recognition and matching principles to support your reasoning.
   2. Redraft the journal entries you made in (a) and (b) above now that Cott is expensing these contract costs rather than capitalizing them.

A GLOBAL FOCUS

BYP4-5 **Hoechst Marion Roussel (HMR)** is one of the world's largest research-based pharmaceutical companies. It is headquartered in Frankfurt, Germany, and operates in 160 countries. In Canada, it is based in Laval, Québec. Its financial statements are based on the accounting standards of the International Accounting Standards Committee.

Instructions

(a) The statement of cash flows reports interest paid during 1998 of $355 million, while the statement of earnings reports interest expense of $721 million. What might explain this difference?
(b) Among its liabilities, the company reports provisions for litigation and environmen-

tal protection. What types of litigation and environmental protection costs might this company incur? What are the possible points in time when litigation costs might be expensed? At what point do you think these costs should become expenses in the statement of earnings in order to provide a proper matching of revenues and expenses? What challenges to matching does litigation present?

(c) The notes to the company's financial statements state that the company records revenues "at the time of shipment of products or performance of services." Is this consistent with the revenue recognition practices described in this chapter? What considerations might you want to consider in determining whether this is the appropriate approach to recognize revenue?

FINANCIAL ANALYSIS ON THE WEB

BYP4-6 ***Purpose:*** SEDAR (System for Electronic Document Analysis and Retrieval) provides information about Canadian public companies and access to their documents. We will use SEDAR to locate and identify recent corporate filings for Loblaw and Sobeys.

Instructions

Specific requirements of this web case can be found on the Kimmel website.

www.wiley.com/canada/kimmel

CRITICAL THINKING

COLLABORATIVE LEARNING ACTIVITIES

BYP4-7 **Air Canada** is the country's largest airline, serving more than 540 destinations around the world. Air Canada sells tickets for airline flights to consumers at a number of different points of sale. For example, you can purchase a ticket in advance (seat sale fare) that may be non-refundable or include restrictions about making changes; you can purchase a fully refundable full fare ticket up to the time of flight departure; or you can fly standby at the last minute.

Air Canada's management team is brainstorming its options in terms of recognizing the revenue from its ticket sales. One person said they should record the revenue when they advertise the seat sale, because these were such great fares they just know that every seat will be sold. Another stated that revenue should be recognized when passengers pick up their tickets and pay for the flight. "What about when the boarding passes are collected at the gate?" a third asked. "Or when passengers get off the plane and kiss the ground because they arrived safely?" a fourth added.

Instructions

With the class divided into groups, do the following:

(a) Each group will be assigned, or should choose, one of the above revenue recognition options. Evaluate the effect of the option on recorded revenues, expenses, and net earnings for the period in question.

(b) Briefly review your option and compare it to the other options described in the above case. After doing so, determine the point at which you think Air Canada should recognize the revenue from flight ticket sales. Explain why you believe this point of revenue recognition to be the best, referring to relevant generally accepted accounting principles in your answer.

BYP4-8 Betsy and Bill Kite, local golf stars, opened Parmor Driving range on March 1, 2001, by investing $10,000 of their cash savings in the business. A caddy shack was constructed for cash at a cost of $4,000, and $800 was spent on golf balls and golf clubs. The shack was expected to last 10 years; the balls and clubs, five years. The Kites leased five acres of land at a cost of $1,000 per month and paid the first month's rent. During the first month, advertising costs totalled $750, of which $150 was unpaid at March 31; and $400 was paid to members of the high school golf team for retrieving golf balls. All fees from customers were deposited in the company's bank account. On March 15, a dividend of $800 in cash was paid. A $100 utility bill was received on March 31, but it was not paid. On March 31, the balance in the company's bank account was $8,550. Betsy and Bill thought they had a pretty good first month of operations. However, their estimates of profitability ranged from a loss of $1,450 to net earnings of $3,100.

Instructions

With the class divided into groups, answer the following questions:

(a) How could the Kites have concluded that the business operated at a loss of $1,450? Was this a valid basis on which to determine net earnings?

(b) How could the Kites have concluded that the business operated at a net earnings of $3,100? (Hint: Prepare a balance sheet at March 31.) Was this a valid basis on which to determine net earnings?

(c) Without preparing a statement of earnings, determine the actual net earnings for March.

(d) What were the fees earned in March?

COMMUNICATION ACTIVITY

BYP4-9 The federal government is making sweeping changes in the type of financial information it provides to decision-makers. By the year 2001, the Government of Canada will fully adopt accrual accounting. Government departments which have not yet made the change record transactions using the cash basis of accounting. For example, capital assets are expensed when purchased rather than capitalized and amortized, and many receivables and payables are not recorded.

Instructions

(a) What is the difference between accrual basis accounting and cash basis accounting?

(b) Comment on why politicians prefer a cash basis accounting system over an accrual basis system.

(c) Write a letter to your Member of Parliament explaining the benefits to the federal government of adopting the accrual basis of accounting.

ETHICS CASE

BYP4-10 Diamond Corporation is a pesticide manufacturer. Its sales declined greatly this year due to the passage of legislation outlawing the sale of several of Diamond's chemical pesticides. During the coming year, Diamond will have environmentally safe and competitive chemicals to replace these discontinued products. Sales in the next year are expected to greatly exceed those of any prior year. The decline in this year's sales and profits appears, therefore, to be a one-year aberration.

Even so, the company president believes that a large dip in the current year's profits could cause a significant drop in the market price of Diamond's stock and make it a takeover target. To avoid this possibility, he urges Carol Denton, controller, to accrue every possible revenue and to defer as many expenses as possible when making this period's year-end adjusting entries. The president says to Carol, "We need the revenues this year, and next year can easily absorb expenses deferred from this year. We can't let our stock price be hammered down!" Carol didn't get around to recording the adjusting entries until January 17, but she dated the entries December 31, as if they were recorded then. Carol also made every effort to comply with the president's request.

Instructions

(a) Who are the stakeholders in this situation?

(b) What are the ethical considerations of the president's request and Carol's dating the adjusting entries December 31?

(c) Can Carol accrue revenues and defer expenses and still be ethical?

Answers to Self-Study Questions

1. d 2. c 3. a 4. d 5. c 6. a 7. d 8. b 9. b 10. c
11. a 12. a 13. d

Answer to Loblaw Review It Question 3

Depreciation and Amortization Expense, $185 million (see Consolidated Statement of Earnings); Accumulated Depreciation, $1,195 million (see Note 5 in Notes to Consolidated Financial Statements)

CHAPTER 5

Merchandising Operations

STUDY OBJECTIVES

After studying this chapter, you should be able to:

1. Identify the differences between a service enterprise and a merchandising company.
2. Explain the recording of purchases under a perpetual inventory system.
3. Explain the recording of sales revenues under a perpetual inventory system.
4. Distinguish between a single-step and a multiple-step statement of earnings.
5. Explain the factors affecting profitability.

Who Doesn't Shop at Wal-Mart?

Until the twentieth century, the word "consumption" evoked negative images. To be labelled a "consumer" was an insult; in fact, one of the deadliest diseases in history, tuberculosis, was often referred to as "consumption."

Today, however, consumption describes the lifestyle of the Western world in a nutshell. Twentieth-century merchants realized that, in order to prosper, they had to convince people that it was good—even necessary—to buy things that had not previously been considered essential. For example, General Motors began making annual changes to the design of its cars so that people would be discontented with the cars they already owned.

North America was thus the birthplace of consumerism, and has led the world in its devotion to the concept ever since. As North Americans, we consume twice as much today per person as we did at the end of World War II. It appears that we live to shop.

The story of retail shopping in Canada began over three centuries ago with the Hudson's Bay Company. Founded in 1670 to trade European goods for furs in the vast Northern territories that would later become part of Canada, it is the oldest commercial organization in the world. Today, Hudson's Bay is Canada's largest department-store chain, accounting for 40% of all domestic department-store sales with its Bay, Zellers, and Kmart stores.

Another early retail giant in Canada was the T. Eaton Company, founded in 1869. Timothy Eaton revolutionized a fledgling retail industry with a simple guarantee that was then a new concept: "Goods satisfactory or money refunded." Eaton's expanded its operations to become a well-loved catalogue company, enabling people in rural areas to buy things by mail, and was for over a century a leader in Canadian merchandising and a household name. But in recent years Eaton's lost its edge, failing to recognize changes in consumer shopping patterns and tastes. After a decade of losses and unsuccessful restructuring attempts, Eaton's closed its doors in 1999.

Sears, another company that grew up on its catalogue business, joined the Canadian

On the World Wide Web
Hudson's Bay: http://www.hbc.com
Sears: http://www.sears.ca
Wal-Mart: http://www.walmart.com

landscape in 1953 and continues to be a major retailer of general merchandise in Canada. Over four million households receive the Sears Canada catalogue.

However, the undisputed king of the Canadian shopping cart today is the U.S.-based discount chain Wal-Mart, which is larger than Hudson's Bay and Sears combined. Wal-Mart opened its first store in the United States in 1950. In 1970, it had 18 stores and sales of US$44 million. In 1994, Wal-Mart entered Canada, acquiring 122 former Woolco stores and providing serious competition to Zellers, the Hudson's Bay discount chain. Today, it has 159 stores across the country, and is the number 1 retailer in Canada.

Wal-Mart also has operations in Mexico, South America, Asia, and Europe. It is the undisputed number one retailer in the world, with worldwide 1999 sales of US$138 billion from 3,600 Wal-Marts, Sam's Club warehouse stores, and Wal-Mart Supercentres (combination discount and grocery stores).

Wal-Mart has grown rapidly in recent years, with average annual increases in sales of 20%, and increases in earnings of 15% over the last decade. One key contributor to this success has been an amazing system of inventory control and distribution. Wal-Mart has a management information system that employs six satellite channels. Its computer system receives 8.4 million updates every minute on the items that customers take home and the relationship among the items in each basket. The result is an enormous database of purchasing information, transmitted by computer to its accounting systems, that enables Wal-Mart to keep its shelves stocked with exactly what customers want, while still keeping its inventory under tight control.

In 1998, Wal-Mart brought its huge selection and rock-bottom prices on-line. It now sells 80,000 products on-line—about the same number as are stocked in an average Wal-Mart store. Internet retailing has opened up a whole new way for people to meet their basic—and not-so-basic—needs. With its potential to connect sellers with consumers across the planet, 24 hours a day, who knows what changes it will bring to merchandising? One thing seems certain, however—the love affair between Canadians and shopping isn't likely to end any time soon.

Hudson's Bay, Sears, and Wal-Mart are called merchandising companies because they buy and sell merchandise, rather than perform services, as their primary source of revenue. Merchandising companies that purchase and sell directly to consumers are called **retailers**. Merchandising companies that sell to retailers are known as **wholesalers**. For example, retailer Future Shop might buy goods from wholesaler Canada Computer Paper, Inc.; retailer Toys "R" Us might buy toys from Valley Trading Company, a Canadian hobby and toy wholesaler.

As merchandising is one of the largest and most influential industries in Canada, understanding the financial statements of these companies is important. The content and organization of the chapter are as follows:

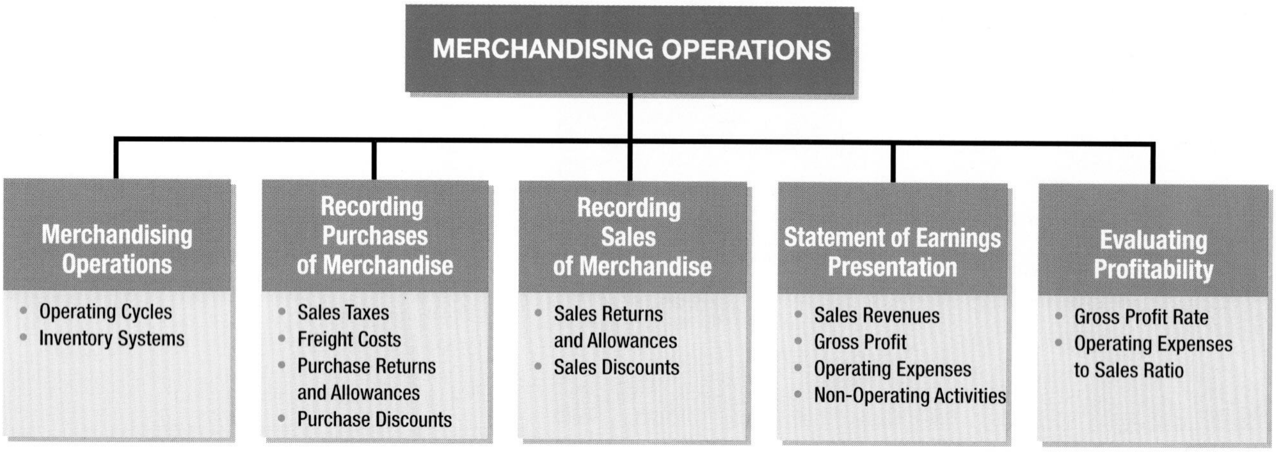

Merchandising Operations

STUDY OBJECTIVE 1

Identify the differences between a service enterprise and a merchandising company.

The primary source of revenues for merchandising companies is the sale of merchandise, often referred to simply as **sales revenue** or **sales**. Expenses for a merchandising company are divided into two categories: the cost of goods sold and operating expenses.

The **cost of goods sold** is the total cost of merchandise sold during the period. This expense is directly related to the revenue recognized from the sale of goods. The earnings measurement process for a merchandising company is shown in Illustration 5-1. The items in the two blue boxes are unique to a merchandising company; they are not used by a service company.

Illustration 5-1 Earnings measurement process for a merchandising company

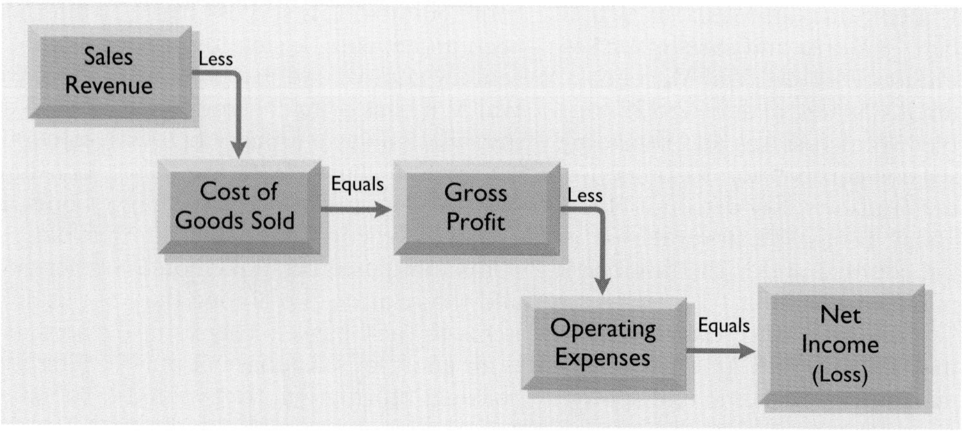

OPERATING CYCLES

The operating cycle—the time it takes to go from cash to cash in producing revenues—of a merchandising company ordinarily is longer than that of a service company. The purchase of merchandise inventory and its eventual sale lengthen the cycle. The operating cycles of service and merchandising companies can be contrasted as shown in Illustration 5-2. Note that the added asset account for a merchandising company is the Merchandise Inventory account.

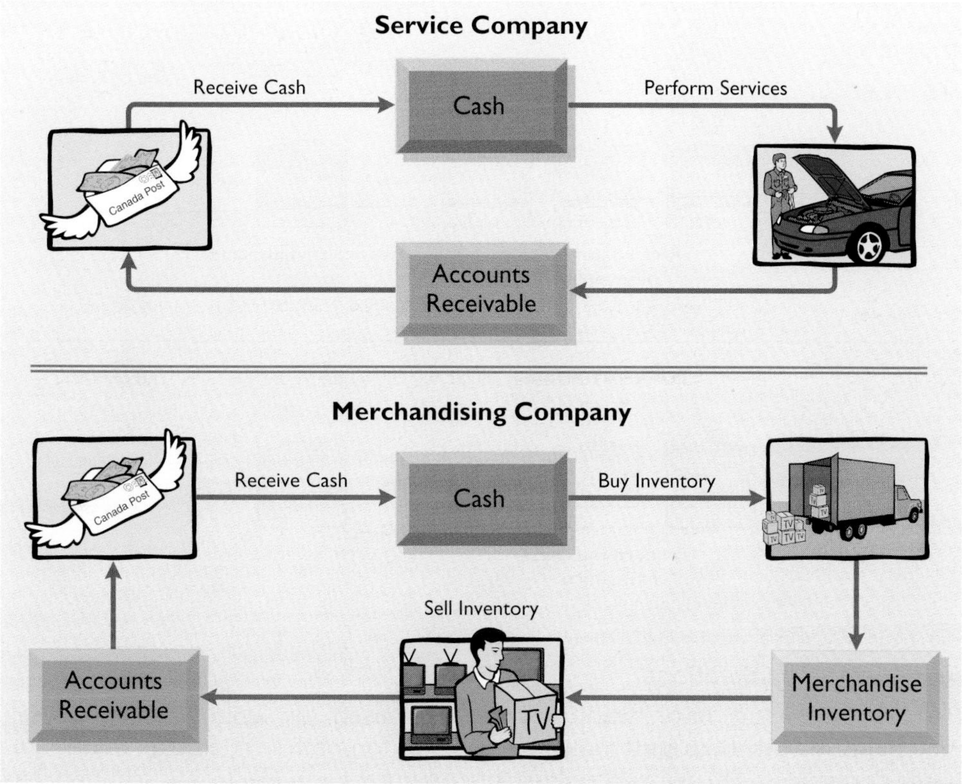

Illustration 5-2 Operating cycles for a service company and a merchandising company

INVENTORY SYSTEMS

A merchandising company keeps track of its inventory to determine what is available for sale and what has been sold. One of two systems is used to account for inventory: a **perpetual inventory system** or a **periodic inventory system**.

Perpetual System

In a **perpetual inventory system**, detailed records of the cost of each inventory purchase and sale are maintained and continuously—perpetually—show the inventory that should be on hand for every item. For example, a Ford dealership has separate inventory records for each automobile, truck, and van on its lot and showroom floor. Similarly, with the use of bar codes and optical scanners, a grocery store can keep a daily running record of every box of cereal and every jar of peanut butter that it buys and sells. Under a perpetual inventory system, the cost of goods sold is **determined each time a sale occurs**.

Helpful Hint For control purposes, a physical inventory count is also taken under the perpetual system to determine any discrepancies between the recorded inventory amount and that which is actually on hand.

Periodic System

In a **periodic inventory system**, detailed inventory records of the goods on hand are not kept throughout the period. The cost of goods sold is **determined only**

at the end of the accounting period—that is, periodically—when a physical inventory count is taken to determine the cost of goods on hand. To determine the cost of goods sold under a periodic inventory system, the following steps are necessary: (1) determine the cost of goods on hand at the beginning of the accounting period, (2) add to it the cost of goods purchased, and (3) subtract the cost of goods on hand at the end of the accounting period.

Illustration 5-3 compares the sequence of activities and the timing of the cost of goods sold calculation under the two inventory systems.

Illustration 5-3 Comparing periodic and perpetual inventory systems

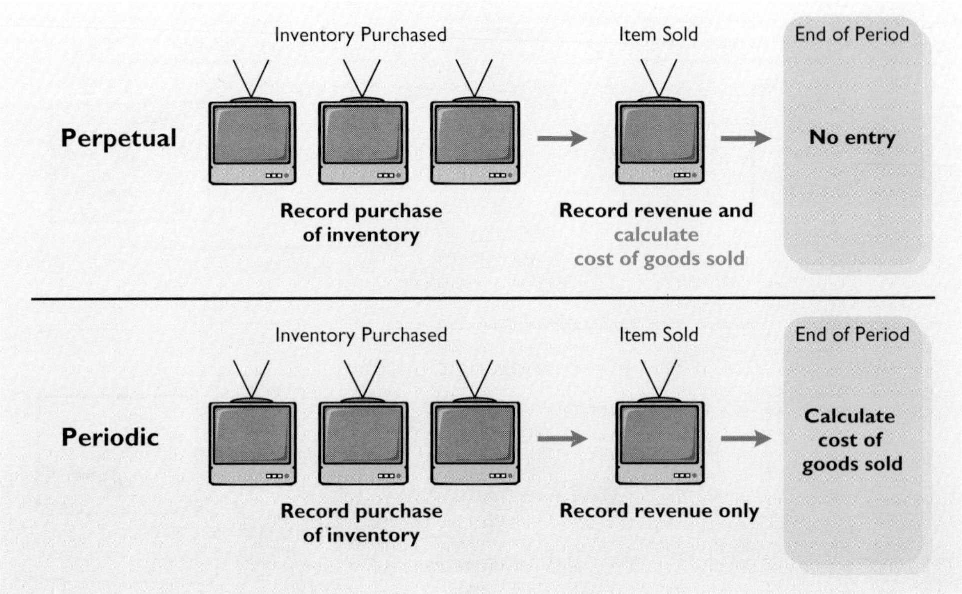

Additional Considerations

Perpetual systems have traditionally been used by companies that sell merchandise with high unit values, such as automobiles, furniture, and major home appliances. The widespread use of computers and electronic scanners has enabled many other companies to install perpetual inventory systems. The perpetual inventory system is so named because the accounting records perpetually show the quantity and cost of the inventory that should be on hand at any time.

A perpetual inventory system provides better control over inventories than a periodic system. Since the inventory records show the quantities that should be on hand, the goods can be counted at any time to see whether they actually exist. Any shortages uncovered can be investigated immediately. Although a perpetual inventory system requires additional clerical work and additional cost to maintain the subsidiary records, a computerized system can minimize this cost. As noted in the opening story, much of Wal-Mart's success is attributed to its sophisticated inventory system.

Some businesses find it either unnecessary or uneconomical to invest in a computerized perpetual inventory system. Many small merchandising businesses, in particular, find that a perpetual inventory system costs more than it is worth. By using a periodic inventory system, managers of these businesses can control their merchandise and manage day-to-day operations without detailed inventory records.

Because the perpetual inventory system is the most popular in use, we illustrate it in this chapter. The periodic system, still widely used, is described in the next chapter.

BUSINESS INSIGHT

Investor Perspective

Investors are often eager to invest in a company that has a hot new product. However, when snowboard maker Morrow Snowboards, Inc. issued shares of stock to the public for the first time, some investors expressed reluctance to invest in Morrow because of a number of accounting control problems. To reduce investor concerns, Morrow implemented a perpetual inventory system to improve its control over inventory. In addition, it stated that it would perform a physical inventory count every quarter until it felt that the perpetual inventory system was reliable.

Recording Purchases of Merchandise

STUDY OBJECTIVE 2

Explain the recording of purchases under a perpetual inventory system.

Purchases of inventory may be made for cash or on account (credit). Purchases are normally recorded when the goods are received from the seller. Every purchase should be supported by business documents that provide written evidence of the transaction. Each cash purchase should be supported by a cancelled cheque or a cash register receipt indicating the items purchased and amounts paid. Cash purchases are recorded by an increase in Merchandise Inventory and a decrease in Cash.

Each credit purchase should be supported by a **purchase invoice,** which indicates the total purchase price and other relevant information. However, the purchaser does not prepare a separate purchase invoice. Instead, the copy of the sales invoice sent by the seller is used by the buyer as a purchase invoice. In Illustration 5-4 on the following page, for example, the sales invoice prepared by PW Audio Supply, Inc. (the seller) is used as a purchase invoice by Sauk Stereo Ltd. (the buyer).

The associated entry for Sauk Stereo for the invoice from PW Audio Supply is:

May	4	Merchandise Inventory	3,800	
		Accounts Payable		3,800
		(To record goods purchased on account from PW Audio Supply)		

A	=	L	+	SE
+3,800		+3,800		

Under the perpetual inventory system, purchases of merchandise for sale are recorded in the Merchandise Inventory account. Thus, Wal-Mart Canada Inc. would increase (debit) Merchandise Inventory for clothing, sporting goods, and anything else purchased for resale to customers. Not all purchases are debited to Merchandise Inventory, however. Purchases of assets acquired for use and not for resale, such as supplies, equipment, and similar items, are recorded as increases to specific asset accounts rather than to Merchandise Inventory. For example, Wal-Mart would increase Supplies to record the purchase of materials used to make shelf signs or for cash register receipt paper.

Illustration 5-4 Sales invoice used as purchase invoice by Sauk Stereo

INVOICE NO. 731

PW AUDIO SUPPLY, INC.
277 WELLINGTON STREET, WEST
TORONTO, ONTARIO, M5V 3H2

SOLD TO
Firm Name: Sauk Stereo Ltd.
Attention of: James Hoover, Purchasing Agent
Address: 21 King Streeet, West
City: Hamilton Province: Ontario Postal Code: L8P 4W7

Date 5/4/01	Salesperson Malone	Terms 2/10, n/30	Freight Paid by Buyer	
Catalogue No.	**Description**	**Quantity**	**Price**	**Amount**
X572Y9820	Printed Circuit Board-prototype	1	2,300	$2,300
A2547Z45	Production Model Circuits	5	300	1,500

IMPORTANT: ALL RETURNS MUST BE MADE WITHIN 10 DAYS

TOTAL $3,800

Helpful Hint To better understand the contents of this invoice, identify these items:

1. Seller
2. Invoice date
3. Purchaser
4. Salesperson
5. Credit terms
6. Freight terms
7. Goods sold: catalogue number, description, quantity, price per unit
8. Total invoice amount

SALES TAXES

Sales taxes are collected by most service and merchandising enterprises on the services that they provide and the goods that they sell. Sales taxes may take the form of the goods and services tax (GST) and the provincial sales tax (PST). The federal GST is assessed at a rate of 7% across Canada. Provincial sales tax rates vary throughout the provinces and territories. In the Atlantic provinces (except for P.E.I.), GST and PST have been combined into one 15% tax, called the harmonized sales tax (HST).

Although a company collects these sales taxes in conjunction with a sale, sales taxes are not revenue to the company. These monies are collected on behalf of the federal and provincial governments and must be periodically remitted to the Receiver General, their collecting authority. Until then, they are a current liability of the company.

Sales taxes add much complexity to the accounting process. In addition, not all companies and their goods and services are taxable. Accounting transactions presented in this and other chapters are therefore presented without the added intricacies of sales taxes. That is why Invoice No. 731 depicted in Illustration 5-4 omitted sales taxes, which would normally be added to the invoice price. At this point in your studies, it is important that you have a good understanding of basic accounting concepts before you broaden your range to include detailed sales tax law.

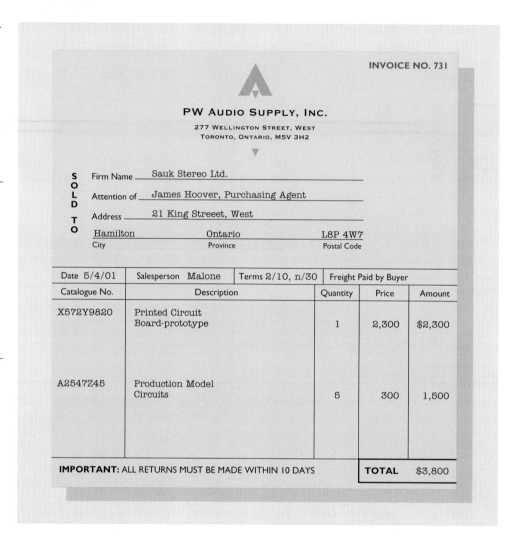

FREIGHT COSTS

The sales invoice indicates whether the seller or the buyer pays the cost of transporting the goods to the buyer's place of business. When the buyer pays the transportation costs, these costs are considered part of the cost of purchasing inventory. As a result, the account Merchandise Inventory is increased. For example, if upon delivery of the goods on May 4, Sauk Stereo pays Acme Freight Company $150 for freight charges, the entry on Sauk's books is:

May	4	Merchandise Inventory	150	
		Cash		150
		(To record payment of freight)		

A	=	L	+	SE
+150				
−150				

In contrast, **freight costs incurred by the seller on outgoing merchandise are an operating expense to the seller**. These costs increase an expense account titled Freight-out or Delivery Expense. For example, if the freight terms on the invoice in Illustration 5-4 had required that PW Audio Supply pay the $150 freight charges, the entry by PW Audio would be:

May	4	Freight-out	150	
		Cash		150
		(To record payment of freight on goods sold)		

A	=	L	+	SE
−150				−150

When the freight charges are paid by the seller, the seller will usually establish a higher invoice price for the goods to cover the expense of shipping.

PURCHASE RETURNS AND ALLOWANCES

A purchaser may be dissatisfied with the merchandise received because the goods are damaged or defective, of inferior quality, or do not meet the purchaser's specifications. In such cases, the purchaser may return the goods to the seller for credit if the sale was made on credit, or for a cash refund if the purchase was for cash. This transaction is known as a **purchase return**. Alternatively, the purchaser may choose to keep the merchandise if the seller is willing to grant an allowance (deduction) from the purchase price. This transaction is known as a **purchase allowance**.

Assume that Sauk Stereo returned goods costing $300 to PW Audio Supply on May 8. The entry by Sauk Stereo for the returned merchandise is:

May	8	Accounts Payable	300	
		Merchandise Inventory		300
		(To record return of goods received from PW Audio Supply)		

A	=	L	+	SE
−300		−300		

Because Sauk Stereo increased Merchandise Inventory when the goods were received, Merchandise Inventory is decreased when Sauk returns the goods.

PURCHASE DISCOUNTS

The credit terms of a purchase on account may permit the buyer to claim a cash discount for prompt payment. The buyer calls this cash discount a **purchase discount**. This incentive offers advantages to both parties: the purchaser saves money, and the seller is able to shorten the operating cycle by converting the accounts receivable into cash earlier.

The **credit terms** specify the amount of the cash discount and time period during which it is offered. They also indicate the length of time in which the purchaser is expected to pay the full invoice price. In the sales invoice in Illustration 5-4, credit terms are 2/10, n/30, which is read "two-ten, net thirty." This means that a 2% cash discount may be taken on the invoice price, less ("net of") any returns or allowances, if payment is made within 10 days of the invoice date (the **discount period**); otherwise, the invoice price, less any returns or allowances, is due 30 days from the invoice date. Alternatively, the discount period may extend to a specified number of days following the month in which the sale occurs. For example, 1/10 EOM (end of month) means that a 1% discount is available if the invoice is paid within the first 10 days of the next month.

Helpful Hint The term *net* in "net 30" means the remaining amount due after subtracting any sales returns and allowances and partial payments.

When the seller elects not to offer a cash discount for prompt payment, credit terms will specify only the maximum time period for paying the balance due. For example, the time period may be stated as n/30, n/60, or n/10 EOM, meaning, respectively, that the net amount must be paid in 30 days, 60 days, or within the first 10 days of the next month.

When an invoice is paid within the discount period, the amount of the discount decreases Merchandise Inventory because inventory is recorded at its cost and, by paying within the discount period, the merchandiser has reduced its cost. To illustrate, assume Sauk Stereo pays the balance due of $3,500 (gross invoice price of $3,800 less purchase returns and allowances of $300) on May 14, the last day of the discount period. The cash discount is $70 ($3,500 × 2%), and the amount of cash paid by Sauk Stereo is $3,430 ($3,500 − $70). The entry to record the May 14 payment by Sauk Stereo is:

A	=	L	+	SE
−3,430				−3,500
−70				

May 14	Accounts Payable	3,500	
	Cash		3,430
	Merchandise Inventory		70
	(To record payment within discount period)		

If Sauk Stereo fails to take the discount and instead makes full payment on June 3, Sauk's entry is:

A	=	L	+	SE
−3,500		−3,500		

June 3	Accounts Payable	3,500	
	Cash		3,500
	(To record payment with no discount taken)		

BUSINESS INSIGHT
Management Perspective

In the early 1990s, Sears wielded its retail clout by telling its suppliers that rather than pay its obligations in the standard 30-day period, it would now pay in 60 days. This practice is often adopted by firms that are experiencing financial distress from a shortage of cash. A Sears spokesperson insisted, however, that Sears did not have cash problems but, rather, was simply utilizing "vendor-financed inventory methods to improve its return on investment." Supplier trade groups have been outspoken critics of Sears' policy and have suggested that consumers are the ultimate victims, because the financing costs are eventually passed on to them.

A merchandising company should usually take all available discounts. Passing up the discount may be viewed as paying interest for use of the money. For example, if Sauk Stereo passed up the discount, it would be like paying an interest rate of 2% for the use of $3,500 for 20 days. This is the equivalent of an annual interest rate of 36.5% (2% × 365/20). Obviously, it would be better for Sauk Stereo to borrow at prevailing bank interest rates of 8% to 12% than to lose the discount.

Helpful Hint So as not to miss purchase discounts, unpaid invoices should be filed by due dates. This procedure helps the purchaser remember the discount date, prevents early payment of bills, and maximizes the time that cash can be used for other purposes.

BEFORE YOU GO ON . . .

Review It

1. How does the measurement of net earnings in a merchandising company differ from that in a service enterprise?
2. In what ways is a perpetual inventory system different from a periodic system?
3. Under the perpetual inventory system, what entries are made to record purchases, purchase returns and allowances, purchase discounts, and freight costs?

Recording Sales of Merchandise

STUDY OBJECTIVE 3

Explain the recording of sales revenues under a perpetual inventory system.

Sales revenues, like service revenues, are recorded when earned in order to comply with the revenue recognition principle. Typically, sales revenues are earned when the goods are transferred from the seller to the buyer. At this point the sales transaction is completed and the sales price is established.

Sales may be made on credit or for cash. Every sales transaction should be supported by a **business document** that provides written evidence of the sale. **Cash register tapes** provide evidence of cash sales. A **sales invoice**, like the one that was shown in Illustration 5-4, provides support for a credit sale. The original copy of the invoice goes to the customer, and a copy is kept by the seller for use in recording the sale. The invoice shows the date of sale, customer name, total sales price, and other relevant information.

Two entries are made for each sale. The first entry records the sale: assuming a cash sale, Cash is increased by a debit and Sales is increased by a credit at the selling (invoice) price of the goods. The second entry records the cost of the merchandise sold: Cost of Goods Sold is increased by a debit and Merchandise Inventory is decreased by a credit for the cost of those goods. For example, assume that on May 4, PW Audio Supply has cash sales of $2,200 from merchandise having a cost of $1,400. The entries to record the day's cash sales are as follows:

A	=	L	+	SE
+2,200				+2,200

May	4	Cash	2,200	
		Sales		2,200
		(To record daily cash sales)		

A	=	L	+	SE
-1,400				-1,400

	4	Cost of Goods Sold	1,400	
		Merchandise Inventory		1,400
		(To record cost of merchandise sold for cash)		

For credit sales, (1) Accounts Receivable is increased and Sales is increased, and (2) Cost of Goods Sold is increased and Merchandise Inventory is decreased. As a result, the Merchandise Inventory account will show at all times the amount of inventory that should be on hand. To illustrate a credit sales transaction, PW Audio Supply's sale of $3,800 on May 4 to Sauk Stereo (see Illustration 5-4) is recorded as follows (assume the merchandise cost PW Audio Supply $2,400):

A	=	L	+	SE
+3,800				+3,800

May	4	Accounts Receivable	3,800	
		Sales		3,800
		(To record credit sale to Sauk Stereo per invoice #731)		

A	=	L	+	SE
-2,400				-2,400

	4	Cost of Goods Sold	2,400	
		Merchandise Inventory		2,400
		(To record cost of merchandise sold on invoice #731 to Sauk Stereo)		

Helpful Hint The Sales account is only credited for sales of goods held for resale. Sales of assets not held for resale, such as equipment or land, are credited directly to the asset account.

For internal decision-making purposes, merchandising companies may use more than one sales account. For example, PW Audio Supply may decide to keep separate sales accounts for its sales of TV sets, videocassette recorders, and microwave ovens. By using separate sales accounts for major product lines, rather than a single combined sales account, company management can monitor sales trends more closely and respond in a more strategic fashion to changes in sales patterns. For example, if TV sales are increasing while microwave oven sales are decreasing, the company should re-evaluate both its advertising and pricing policies on each of these items to ensure they are optimal. On its statement of earnings presented to outside investors, a merchandising company would normally provide only a single sales figure—the sum of all of its individual sales accounts. This is done for two reasons. First, providing detail on all of its individual sales accounts would add considerable length to its statement of earnings. Second, companies do not want their competitors to know the details of their operating results.

SALES RETURNS AND ALLOWANCES

We now look at the "flip side" of purchase returns and allowances, which are recorded as **sales returns and allowances** on the books of the seller. PW Audio Supply's entries to record credit for returned goods involve (1) an increase in Sales Returns and Allowances and a decrease in Accounts Receivable at the $300 selling price, and (2) an increase in Merchandise Inventory (assume a $140 cost) and a decrease in Cost of Goods Sold. This second entry assumes that the merchandise is not damaged and is resaleable. Otherwise, a Loss account would be debited rather than an Inventory account.

May 8	Sales Returns and Allowances	300	
	Accounts Receivable		300
	(To record return of goods delivered to Sauk Stereo)		

A	=	L	+	SE
−300				−300

8	Merchandise Inventory	140	
	Cost of Goods Sold		140
	(To record cost of goods returned)		

A	=	L	+	SE
+140				+140

Sales Returns and Allowances is a **contra revenue account** to Sales. The normal balance of Sales Returns and Allowances is a debit. A contra account is used, instead of debiting Sales, to disclose in the accounts and in the statement of earnings the amount of sales returns and allowances. Disclosure of this information is important to management: excessive returns and allowances suggest inferior merchandise, inefficiencies in filling orders, errors in billing customers, and mistakes in delivery or shipment of goods. Moreover, a decrease (debit) recorded directly to Sales would obscure the relative importance of sales returns and allowances as a percentage of sales. It could also distort comparisons between total sales in different accounting periods.

Helpful Hint Remember that the increases, decreases, and normal balances of contra accounts are the opposite of the accounts to which they correspond.

BUSINESS INSIGHT

Investor Perspective

How high is too high? Returns can become so high that it is questionable whether sales revenue should have been recognized in the first place. An example of high returns is Florafax International Inc., a floral supply company, which was alleged to ship its product without customer authorization on ten holiday occasions, including 8,562 shipments of flowers to customers for Mother's Day and 6,575 for Secretary's Day. The return rate on these shipments went as high as 69% of sales. As one employee noted, "Products went out the front door and came in the back door."

SALES DISCOUNTS

As mentioned in our discussion of purchase transactions, the seller may offer the customer a cash discount—called a **sales discount** by the seller—for the prompt payment of the balance due. Like a purchase discount, a sales discount is based on the invoice price less returns and allowances, if any. The Sales Discounts account is increased (debited) for discounts that are taken. The entry by PW Audio Supply to record the cash receipt on May 14 from Sauk Stereo within the discount period is:

May 14	Cash	3,430	
	Sales Discounts	70	
	Accounts Receivable		3,500
	(To record collection within 2/10, n/30 discount period from Sauk Stereo)		

A	=	L	+	SE
+3,430				−70
−3,500				

Like Sales Returns and Allowances, Sales Discounts is a **contra revenue account** to Sales. Its normal balance is a debit. This account is used, instead of debiting Sales, to disclose the amount of cash discounts taken by customers. If the discount is not taken, PW Audio Supply increases Cash for $3,500 and decreases Accounts Receivable for the same amount at the date of collection.

BEFORE YOU GO ON . . .

Review It

1. Under a perpetual inventory system, what are the two entries that must be recorded for each sale?
2. Why is it important to use the Sales Returns and Allowances account, rather than simply reduce the Sales account, when goods are returned?
3. In what ways is a perpetual inventory system different from a periodic inventory system?

Do It

On September 5, Guerette Company buys merchandise on account from Lalonde Company. The selling price of the goods is $1,500, and the cost to Lalonde Company was $800. On September 8 goods with a selling price of $300 and a cost of $140 are returned and restored to inventory. Record the transaction on the books of both companies.

Reasoning: Under a perpetual inventory system, the purchaser records goods at cost. The seller records both the sale and the cost of goods sold at the time of the sale. When goods are returned, the purchaser directly reduces Merchandise Inventory, but the seller records the return in a contra account, Sales Returns and Allowances. In addition, assuming the goods are resaleable, the seller will return the goods to inventory and reduce the Cost of Goods Sold, since the goods were returned and not sold.

Solution:

Guerette Company (Purchaser)

Sept.	5	Merchandise Inventory	1,500	
		Accounts Payable		1,500
		(To record goods purchased on account)		
Sept.	8	Accounts Payable	300	
		Merchandise Inventory		300
		(To record return of goods)		

Lalonde Company (Seller)

Sept.	5	Accounts Receivable	1,500	
		Sales		1,500
		(To record credit sale)		
	5	Cost of Goods Sold	800	
		Merchandise Inventory		800
		(To record cost of goods sold on account)		
Sept.	8	Sales Returns and Allowances	300	
		Accounts Receivable		300
		(To record credit granted for receipt of returned goods)		
	8	Merchandise Inventory	140	
		Cost of Goods Sold		140
		(To record cost of goods returned)		

Statement of Earnings Presentation

STUDY OBJECTIVE 4

Distinguish between a single-step and a multiple-step statement of earnings.

Two forms of the statement of earnings are widely used by companies. One is the **single-step statement of earnings**. The statement is so named because only one step, subtracting total expenses from total revenues, is required in determining net earnings (or net loss). In a single-step statement, all data are classified into two categories: (1) **revenues**, which include both operating revenues and non-operating revenues and gains (for example, interest revenue and gain on sale of equipment); and (2) **expenses**, which include cost of goods sold, operating expenses, and non-operating expenses and losses (for example, interest expense and loss on sale of equipment). Sometimes income tax expense is listed with the expenses, but more often it is disclosed separately. A condensed single-step statement for Leon's Furniture is shown in Illustration 5-5.

Illustration 5-5
Single-step statement of earnings

LEON'S FURNITURE LIMITED
Earnings Statement
Years Ended December 31
($ in thousands)

	1998	1997
Revenues		
Sales	$336,895	$315,817
Interest earnings	4,440	2,847
Other earnings	9,352	7,622
Total revenues	350,687	326,286
Expenses		
Cost of sales	199,369	187,680
Salaries and commissions	49,870	46,105
Advertising	21,704	20,649
Depreciation and amortization	5,649	5,483
Rent and property taxes	6,518	5,207
Employee profit-sharing plan	1,770	1,339
Interest on long-term debt	19	33
Other operating expenses	17,852	20,051
Total expenses	302,751	286,547
Earnings before income taxes	47,936	39,739
Income tax expense	21,530	18,104
Net earnings	$ 26,406	$ 21,635

Alternative Terminology
Note that Leon's *statement of earnings* is entitled *earnings statement*.

The single-step statement of earnings is the form we have used thus far in the text. There are two primary reasons for using the single-step form: (1) a company does not realize any type of profit or earnings until total revenues exceed total expenses, so it makes sense to divide the statement into these two categories; and (2) the form is simple and easy to read.

A second form of the statement of earnings is the **multiple-step statement of earnings**. The multiple-step statement is often considered more useful because it highlights the components of net earnings. Leon's statement of earnings in Illustration 5-6 is an example.

Illustration 5-6
Multiple-step statement of earnings

LEON'S FURNITURE LIMITED
Earnings Statement
Years Ended December 31
($ in thousands)

	1998	1997
Sales	$336,895	$315,817
Cost of sales	199,369	187,680
Gross profit	**137,526**	**128,137**
Operating expenses		
Salaries and commissions	49,870	46,105
Advertising	21,704	20,649
Depreciation and amortization	5,649	5,483
Rent and property taxes	6,518	5,207
Employee profit-sharing plan	1,770	1,339
Other operating expenses	17,852	20,051
Total operating expenses	103,363	98,834
Earnings from operations	**34,163**	**29,303**
Other revenues and gains		
Interest earnings	4,440	2,847
Other earnings	9,352	7,622
Total other revenues and gains	13,792	10,469
Other expenses and losses		
Interest on long-term debt	19	33
Earnings before income taxes	47,936	39,739
Income tax expense	21,530	18,104
Net earnings	**$ 26,406**	**$ 21,635**

The multiple-step statement of earnings has three important line items: **gross profit**, **earnings from operations**, and **net earnings**. They are determined as follows: (1) cost of goods sold is subtracted from sales to determine gross profit; (2) operating expenses are deducted from gross profit to determine earnings from operations; and (3) the results of activities not related to operations are added (other revenue and gains) or subtracted (other expenses and losses) to determine net earnings. You should note that income tax expense is reported in a separate section of the statement of earnings before net earnings. The following discussion provides additional information about the components of a multiple-step statement of earnings.

SALES REVENUES

The statement of earnings for a merchandising company typically presents gross sales revenues for the period and provides details about deductions from that total amount. As contra revenue accounts, sales returns and allowances and sales discounts are deducted from sales in the statement of earnings to arrive at **net sales**. The sales revenues section of the statement of earnings for PW Audio Supply is shown in Illustration 5-7.

PW AUDIO SUPPLY, INC. Statement of Earnings (Partial)		
Sales revenues		
Sales		$ 480,000
Less: Sales returns and allowances	$12,000	
Sales discounts	8,000	20,000
Net sales		**$460,000**

Illustration 5-7
Statement presentation of sales revenues section

GROSS PROFIT

Cost of goods sold is deducted from sales revenue to determine gross profit. As shown in Illustration 5-6, Leon's had a gross profit of $137,526,000 in fiscal year 1998. Sales revenue used for this computation is **net sales**, which takes into account sales returns and allowances and sales discounts. On the basis of the sales data presented in Illustration 5-7 (net sales of $460,000) and the cost of goods sold (assume a balance of $316,000), the gross profit for PW Audio Supply is $144,000, determined as follows:

Net sales	$ 460,000
Cost of goods sold	316,000
Gross profit	**$144,000**

It is important to understand what gross profit is—and what it is not. Gross profit represents the **merchandising profit** of a company. It is *not* a measure of the overall profit of a company because operating expenses have not been deducted. Nevertheless, the amount and trend of gross profit are closely watched by management and other interested parties. Comparisons of current gross profit with past amounts and rates, and with those in the industry, indicate the effectiveness of a company's purchasing and pricing policies.

Alternative Terminology
Gross profit is sometimes referred to as *gross margin.*

OPERATING EXPENSES

Operating expenses are the next component in measuring net earnings for a merchandising company. At Leon's, operating expenses were $103,363,000 in fiscal year 1998. These expenses are similar in merchandising and service enterprises. At PW Audio Supply, operating expenses were $114,000. The firm's earnings from operations are determined by subtracting operating expenses from gross profit. Thus, earnings from operations are $30,000, as shown below:

Gross profit	$144,000
Operating expenses	**114,000**
Earnings from operations	$ 30,000

Subgrouping of Operating Expenses

Alternative Terminology *Administrative expenses* are sometimes called *general expenses.*

Sometimes, operating expenses are subdivided into selling expenses and administrative expenses (as shown in the statement of earnings in Illustration 5-9). **Selling expenses** are those associated with making sales. They include advertising expenses as well as the expenses of completing the sale, such as delivery and shipping expenses. **Administrative expenses** relate to general operating activities such as human resources management, accounting, and store security.

NON-OPERATING ACTIVITIES

Non-operating activities consist of various revenues and expenses, and gains and losses that are unrelated to the company's primary operations. When non-operating items are included, the label earnings from operations (or income from operations) precedes them. This clearly identifies the results of the company's normal operations, an amount determined by subtracting cost of goods sold and operating expenses from net sales. The results of non-operating activities are shown in **other revenues and gains** and **other expenses and losses**. Examples of each are listed in Illustration 5-8.

Illustration 5-8
Items reported in non-operating sections

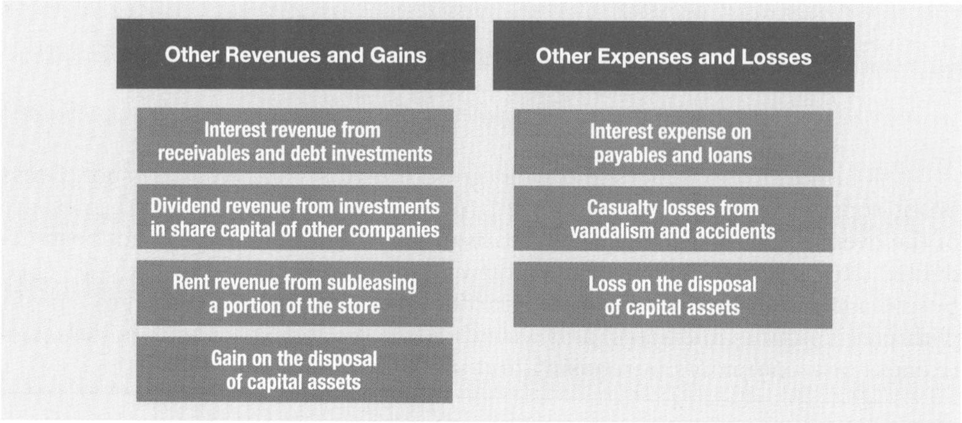
Other Revenues and Gains
Interest revenue from receivables and debt investments
Dividend revenue from investments in share capital of other companies
Rent revenue from subleasing a portion of the store
Gain on the disposal of capital assets
Other Expenses and Losses
Interest expense on payables and loans
Casualty losses from vandalism and accidents
Loss on the disposal of capital assets

The distinction between operating and non-operating activities is crucial to many external users of financial data. Earnings from operations are viewed as sustainable and therefore long-term, and non-operating activities are viewed as nonrecurring and therefore short-term.

BUSINESS INSIGHT

Investor Perspective

It was once reported that a large cinema chain in North America was selling some of its assets and counting the gains as part of earnings from operations. As a result, operating losses were being offset by these gains. Because of unfavourable press reaction to this practice, the company revised its financial statements. By not counting its nonrecurring items as part of earnings from operations, its first quarter results changed from \$35 million in earnings from operations to a \$32 million loss. Although the net earnings figure didn't change, investors were able to see that earnings were derived from selling assets rather than from selling movie tickets. Thus, with this new information, investors were able to make a more informed decision about the company's earnings.

The non-operating sections are reported in the statement of earnings immediately after the operating activities. Included among these activities in Illustration 5-6 for Leon's is other revenue earned from interest and other sources of $13,792,000 in 1998. Other expenses include interest on long-term debt of $19,000 for 1998. After adding the earnings (or income) from operations to nonoperating other revenues and gains and then deducting the non-operating other expenses and losses, as well as income tax expense, the amount remaining is Leon's net earnings of $26,406,000. Note that the net earnings in Illustrations 5-5 and 5-6 are the same. The differences in the two statements of earnings are the amount of detail displayed and the order presented.

In Illustration 5-9, we have provided the multiple-step statement of earnings for a hypothetical company. This statement provides more detail than that of Leon's.

For assignments, you should use the multiple-step form of the statement of earnings unless the requirements state otherwise.

Illustration 5-9
Multiple-step statement of earnings

PW AUDIO SUPPLY, INC.
Statement of Earnings
For the Year Ended December 31, 2001

Calculation of gross profit	**Sales revenues**		
	Sales		$480,000
	Less: Sales returns and allowances	$12,000	
	Sales discounts	8,000	20,000
	Net sales		460,000
	Cost of goods sold		316,000
	Gross profit		144,000
Calculation of earnings from operations	**Operating expenses**		
	Selling expenses		
	Store salaries expense	$45,000	
	Advertising expense	16,000	
	Amortization expense—store equipment	8,000	
	Freight-out	7,000	
	Total selling expenses	76,000	
	Administrative expenses		
	Salaries expense	$19,000	
	Utilities expense	17,000	
	Insurance expense	2,000	
	Total administrative expenses	38,000	
	Total operating expenses		114,000
	Earnings from operations		30,000
Calculation of activities not related to operations	**Other revenues and gains**		
	Interest revenue	$3,000	
	Gain on sale of equipment	600	
		3,600	
	Other expenses and losses		
	Interest expense	$1,800	
	Casualty loss from vandalism	200	
		2,000	
			1,600
	Earnings before income taxes		31,600
	Income tax expense		10,100
	Net earnings		$ 21,500

Helpful Hint Note the distinction between earnings from operations and the final figure on the statement of earnings, net earnings. Which figure should you use to assess the future profitability of the company?

BEFORE YOU GO ON . . .

● **Review It**

1. Under the perpetual inventory system, what entries are made to record sales, sales returns and allowances, and sales discounts?
2. How are sales and contra revenue accounts reported in the statement of earnings?
3. What is the significance of gross profit?
4. Does Loblaw use the single-step or multiple-step form of statement of earnings? The answer to this question is provided at the end of this chapter.

Loblaws
A passion for food... *and a lot more!*

EVALUATING PROFITABILITY

GROSS PROFIT RATE

STUDY OBJECTIVE 5

Explain the factors affecting profitability.

A company's gross profit may be expressed as a **percentage** by dividing the amount of gross profit by net sales; this is referred to as the **gross profit rate**. For PW Audio Supply the gross profit rate is 31.3% ($144,000 ÷ $460,000). The gross profit *rate* is generally considered to be more informative than the gross profit *amount* because it expresses a more meaningful relationship between gross profit and net sales. For example, a gross profit amount of $1,000,000 may sound impressive. But if it was the result of sales of $100,000,000, the company's gross profit rate was only 1%. A 1% gross profit rate is acceptable in only a few industries.

A decline in a company's gross profit rate might have several causes. The company may have begun to sell products with a lower "markup"—for example, budget blue jeans versus designer blue jeans. Increased competition may have resulted in a lower selling price. Or the company may be forced to pay higher prices to its suppliers without being able to pass these costs on to its customers. The gross profit rate for Leon's Furniture is presented in Illustration 5-10.

Illustration 5-10
Gross profit rate

$$\text{GROSS PROFIT RATE} = \frac{\text{GROSS PROFIT}}{\text{NET SALES}}$$

($ in thousands)	1998	1997
Leon's Furniture	$\frac{\$137,526}{\$336,895}$ = 40.8%	$\frac{\$128,137}{\$315,817}$ = 40.6%
Industry average	30.0%	30.0%

Leon's attributes some of its success to its "pin-point inventory accuracy." It takes particular pride in its product shipping and receiving efficiency.

Normally, we would compare Leon's gross profit rate to that of its nearest competitor, Sears Canada, which is the largest furniture and major appliance retailer in Canada. It currently has 18 Sears Whole Home Furnitures Stores across Canada, which offer triple the selection of furniture found in Sears department stores. However, Sears, like many companies in Canada, does not report gross profit separately on its statement of earnings. Rather, it combines cost of merchandise sold with its operating, administrative, and selling expenses for reporting purposes. Gross profit is considered sensitive information that some companies do not wish to make available to their competitors. In fact, only about 15% of companies in Canada report a separate cost of goods sold figure on their statement of earnings. Even if we had been able to calculate Sears' gross profit rate, it would not have provided a meaningful comparison to Leon's Furniture as Sears' rate would have included all of Sears' operations, not just its furniture and appliance sales. Companies often calculate and compare gross profit on each of their product lines, although this information is usually only reported internally.

BUSINESS INSIGHT

Management Perspective

Gross profit rates vary across retailers. In a recent year, Future Shop reported a gross profit rate of 22%; Mark's Work Wearhouse, 38%, Clearly Canadian Beverage, 40%; and Mitel, 50%. "If you don't have someone monitoring it," says one business consultant, "you are asking for instant death." A decline should trigger a search for the cause. The drop could be due to an increase in cost of goods sold or a decrease in sales revenue, either of which needs prompt attention. The change may be temporary and easily reversed, or it may signal the beginning of a bad trend.

DECISION TOOLKIT

Decision Checkpoints	Info Needed for Decision	Tool to Use for Decision	How to Evaluate Results
Is the price of goods keeping pace with changes in the cost of inventory?	Gross profit and net sales	Gross profit rate $= \frac{\text{Gross profit}}{\text{Net sales}}$	Higher ratio suggests the average margin between selling price and inventory cost is increasing. Too high a margin may result in lost sales.

OPERATING EXPENSES TO SALES RATIO

A useful measure of operating expenses is the ratio of **operating expenses to sales**. In recent years, many companies have improved the efficiency of their operations, thus reducing the ratio of operating expenses to sales. As a consequence, they have increased their profitability. The record profits of many companies in the 1990s were achieved as much by reducing costs as by increasing revenues. The use of computers and changes in organizational structure brought added efficiency. For example, one study of 1,000 companies that successfully reengineered their warehouse operations by employing new technologies found savings on labour costs averaging 25%. Epson Computers, for example, reported space savings of 50%, labour savings of 43%, and operating cost savings of 25% on its warehouses. Operating costs have been reduced to such low levels for so many companies that many investors believe further improvements in corporate profits from cost reductions will be difficult to accomplish.

The ratios of operating expenses to sales for Leon's are presented in Illustration 5-11. The ratios suggest that Leon's is not as good as the industry in controlling its operating costs. In its annual report, however, Leon's assures its shareholders that "we will continue to be ever vigilant, in terms of establishing new methods of becoming yet even more productive in all areas of our operations."

Illustration 5-11 Operating expenses to sales ratio

$$\text{OPERATING EXPENSES TO SALES RATIO} = \frac{\text{OPERATING EXPENSES}}{\text{NET SALES}}$$

($ in thousands)	1998	1997
Leon's Furniture	$\frac{\$103,363}{\$336,895} = 30.7\%$	$\frac{\$98,834}{\$315,817} = 31.3\%$
Industry average	20.0%	20.0%

BUSINESS INSIGHT

Management Perspective

A study entitled *How Business Buys* surveyed Canadian business purchasing practices. The authors calculated the average cost to prepare a purchase order to be $63, and the average cost to process an invoice to be $31. Businesses surveyed used an average of 531 suppliers. They also found that fewer than one in seven companies used information processing technology to reduce the costs of ordering from and paying these suppliers.

Source: "Purchasing Departments Fall Behind in IT," *CAmagazine*, April 1997, 12.

BEFORE YOU GO ON . . .

Review It

1. How is the gross profit rate calculated? What might cause it to decline?
2. What effect does improved efficiency of operations have on the operating expenses to sales ratio?

DECISION TOOLKIT

Decision Checkpoints	Info Needed for Decision	Tool to Use for Decision	How to Evaluate Results
Is management controlling operating costs?	Net sales and operating expenses	Operating expenses to sales ratio $= \frac{\text{Operating Expenses}}{\text{Net Sales}}$	Higher value should be investigated to determine whether cost cutting is necessary.

USING THE DECISION TOOLKIT

Zellers, owned by the Hudson's Bay Company, is currently the number 2 discount department store in Canada, behind Wal-Mart. The following financial data are available for **Zellers** and **Wal-Mart**:

	Zellers Year ended January 31 (C$ in thousands)		Wal-Mart Year ended January 31 (US$ in millions)	
	1999	1998	1999	1998
Beginning total assets	$1,577,930	$1,568,000	$ 45,384	$ 39,604
Ending total assets	1,957,645	1,577,930	49,996	45,384
Net earnings	133,839	72,472	4,430	3,526
Net sales	4,498,113	3,808,743	137,634	117,958
Cost of goods sold	2,968,755 [1]	2,628,033 [1]	108,725	93,438
Operating expenses	1,395,245 [1]	1,107,967 [1]	22,363	19,358

[1] The cost of goods sold and operating expense figures have been assumed for Zellers, since this information is not publicly disclosed.

Instructions

(a) Wal-Mart's financial figures are presented in U.S. dollars and Zellers' in Canadian dollars. Is it possible to compare these two companies meaningfully using ratio analysis?

(b) Using the data provided in the table, evaluate the following components of Zellers' and Wal-Mart's profitability for the years ended January 31, 1999 and 1998:

Return on assets ratio
Profit margin ratio
Gross profit rate
Operating expenses to sales ratio

(c) How does Zellers' profitability compare to Wal-Mart's?

Solution

(a) Ratio analysis puts both companies' financial information into the same perspective for comparison purposes. Once data is converted into a ratio, it doesn't matter what currency it was originally reported in. It also doesn't matter that Wal-Mart is more than 25 times larger than Zellers. It is the relationship between the figures that is meaningful.

(b) **Zellers** (Cdn$ in thousands)

	1999		1998	
Return on assets ratio	$\frac{\$133,839}{(\$1,957,645 + \$1,577,930) / 2}$	= 7.6%	$\frac{\$72,472}{(\$1,577,930 + \$1,568,000) / 2}$	= 4.6%
Profit margin ratio	$\frac{\$133,839}{\$4,498,113}$	= 3.0%	$\frac{\$72,472}{\$3,808,743}$	= 1.9%
Gross profit rate	$\frac{\$4,498,113 - \$2,968,755}{\$4,498,113}$	= 34.0%	$\frac{\$3,808,743 - \$2,628,033}{\$3,808,743}$	= 31.0%
Operating expenses to sales ratio	$\frac{\$1,395,245}{\$4,498,113}$	= 31.0%	$\frac{\$1,107,967}{\$3,808,743}$	= 29.1%

Wal-Mart (US$ in millions)

	1999		1998	
Return on assets ratio	$\frac{\$4,430}{(\$49,996 + \$45,384) / 2}$	= 9.3%	$\frac{\$3,526}{(\$45,384 + \$39,604) / 2}$	= 8.3%
Profit margin ratio	$\frac{\$4,430}{\$137,634}$	= 3.2%	$\frac{\$3,526}{\$117,958}$	= 3.0%
Gross profit rate	$\frac{\$137,634 - \$108,725}{\$137,634}$	= 21.0%	$\frac{\$117,958 - \$93,438}{\$117,958}$	= 20.8%
Operating expenses to sales ratio	$\frac{\$22,363}{\$137,634}$	= 16.2%	$\frac{\$19,358}{\$117,958}$	= 16.4%

(c) The return on assets ratio for Zellers improved between 1998 and 1999. Part of this improvement was attributable to former Kmart stores that were acquired in February 1998 and converted to the Zellers format. But, in addition to this, Zellers' retail store sales were up in nearly every category. The profit margin ratio (earnings per dollar of sales) increased from 1.9% to 3.0%. The gross profit rate also improved from 31% to 34%. Lower markdowns were the primary factor in the improvement at Zellers. Operating expenses incurred per dollar of sales marginally increased.

Wal-Mart's return on assets ratio also increased in 1999, from 8.3% to 9.3%, and exceeds Zellers' ratio. Wal-Mart's profit margin also increased but is roughly comparable to Zellers' in 1999. Zellers' gross profit rate, however, is much higher than Wal-Mart's. This implies that Zellers can command a higher markup on its goods. Wal-Mart's operating expenses to sales ratio is much better than Zellers', which suggests that it is able to control its operating costs better than Zellers.

Summary of Study Objectives

❶ ***Identify the differences between a service enterprise and a merchandising company.*** Because of the presence of inventory, a merchandising company has sales revenue, cost of goods sold, and gross profit. To account for inventory, a merchandising company must choose between a perpetual inventory system and a periodic inventory system.

❷ ***Explain the recording of purchases under a perpetual inventory system.*** The Merchandise Inventory account is debited for all purchases of merchandise and for freight costs, and it is credited for purchase discounts and purchase returns and allowances.

❸ ***Explain the recording of sales revenues under a perpetual inventory system.*** When inventory is sold, Accounts Receivable (or Cash) is debited and Sales is credited for the selling price of the merchandise. At the same time, Cost of Goods Sold is debited and Merchandise Inventory is credited for the cost of inventory items sold. When sales revenues are recorded, entries are required for (a) cash and credit sales, (b) sales returns and allowances, and (c) sales discounts.

❹ ***Distinguish between a single-step and a multiple-step statement of earnings.*** In a single-step statement of earnings, all data are classified under two categories, revenues or expenses, and net earnings are determined in one step. A modified single-step statement separates income tax expense from the other expenses and reports it separately after earnings before income taxes. A multiple-step statement of earnings shows numerous steps in determining net earnings, including results of non-operating activities.

❺ ***Explain the factors affecting profitability.*** Profitability is affected by gross profit, as measured by the gross profit rate, and by management's ability to control costs, as measured by the ratio of operating expenses to sales.

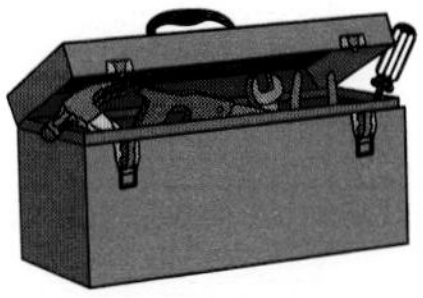

Decision Toolkit—A Summary

Decision Checkpoints	Info Needed for Decision	Tool to Use for Decision	How to Evaluate Results
Is the price of goods keeping pace with changes in the cost of inventory?	Gross profit and net sales	Gross profit rate $= \frac{\text{Gross profit}}{\text{Net sales}}$	Higher ratio suggests the average margin between selling price and inventory cost is increasing. Too high a margin may result in lost sales.
Is management controlling operating costs?	Net sales and operating expenses	Operating expenses to sales ratio $= \frac{\text{Operating expenses}}{\text{Net sales}}$	Higher value should be investigated to determine whether cost cutting is necessary.

GLOSSARY

Contra revenue account An account that is offset against a revenue account on the earnings statement. (p. 247)

Cost of goods sold The total cost of merchandise sold during the period. (p. 238)

Gross profit The excess of net sales over the cost of goods sold. (p. 251)

Gross profit rate Gross profit expressed as a percentage by dividing the amount of gross profit by net sales. (p. 254)

Net sales Sales less sales returns and allowances and sales discounts. (p. 250)

Operating expenses to sales ratio A measure that indicates whether a company is controlling operating expenses relative to each dollar of sales. (p. 255)

Periodic inventory system An inventory system in which detailed records are not maintained and the cost of goods sold is determined only at the end of an accounting period. (p. 239)

Perpetual inventory system A detailed inventory system in which the cost of each inventory item is maintained and the records continuously show the inventory that should be on hand. (p. 239)

Purchase discount A cash discount claimed by a buyer for prompt payment of a balance due. (p. 244)

Purchase invoice A document that supports each credit purchase. (p. 241)

Sales discount A reduction given by a seller for prompt payment of a credit sale. (p. 247)

Sales invoice A document that provides support for credit sales. (p. 245)

Sales revenue The primary source of revenue in a merchandising company. (p. 238)

DEMONSTRATION PROBLEM

The adjusted trial balance for the year ended December 31, 2001, for Dykstra Company Inc. follows:

DYKSTRA COMPANY INC.
Adjusted Trial Balance
For the Year Ended December 31, 2001

	Dr.	Cr.
Cash	$ 4,500	
Accounts Receivable	11,100	
Merchandise Inventory	29,000	
Prepaid Insurance	2,500	
Store Equipment	95,000	
Accumulated Amortization		$ 18,000
Notes Payable		25,000
Accounts Payable		10,600
Common Shares		70,000
Retained Earnings		11,000
Dividends	12,000	
Sales	536,800	
Sales Returns and Allowances	6,700	
Sales Discounts	5,000	
Cost of Goods Sold	363,400	
Freight-out	7,600	
Advertising Expense	12,000	
Store Salaries Expense	56,000	
Utilities Expense	18,000	
Rent Expense	24,000	
Amortization Expense	9,000	
Insurance Expense	4,500	
Interest Revenue	3,600	
Interest Revenue		2,500
Income Tax Expense	10,000	
	$673,900	$673,900

Instructions

Prepare statement of earnings assuming Dykstra Company does not use subgroupings for operating expenses.

Solution to Demonstration Problem

DYKSTRA COMPANY INC.
Statement of Earnings
For the Year Ended December 31, 2001

Sales Revenues		
Sales		$536,800
Less: Sale returns and allowances	$ 6,700	
Sales discounts	5,000	11,700
Net sales		525,100
Cost of goods sold		363,400
Gross profit		161,700
Operating expenses		
Store salaries expense	$56,000	
Rent expense	24,000	
Utilities expense	18,000	
Advertising expense	12,000	
Amortization expense	9,600	
Freight-out	7,600	
Insurance expenses	4,500	
Total operating expenses		131,100
Earnings from operations		30,600
Other revenues and gains		
Interest revenue	$ 2,500	
Other expenses and losses		
Interest expense	3,600	1,100
Earnings before income taxes		29,500
Income tax expense		10,000
Net earnings		$ 19,500

Problem-Solving Strategies

1. In preparing the statement of earnings, remember that the key components are net sales, cost of goods sold, gross profit, total operating expenses, and net earnings (loss). These components are reported in the right-hand column of the statement of earnings.
2. Nonoperating items follow earnings from operations.

SELF-STUDY QUESTIONS

Answers are at the end of the chapter.

(SO 1) 1. Which of the following statements about a periodic inventory system is true?
   (a) Cost of goods sold is only determined at the end of the accounting period.
   (b) Detailed records of the cost of each inventory purchase and sale are maintained continuously.
   (c) The periodic system provides better control over inventories than a perpetual system.
   (d) The widespread use of computerized systems has increased the use of the periodic system.

(SO 2) 2. Under a perpetual system, which of the following items does *not* result in an entry to the Merchandise Inventory account?
   (a) A purchase of merchandise
   (b) A return of merchandise inventory to the supplier
   (c) Payment of freight costs for goods shipped to a customer
   (d) Payment of freight costs for goods received from a supplier

(SO 3) 3. Which sales accounts normally have a debit balance?
   (a) Sales discounts
   (b) Sales returns and allowances
   (c) Both (a) and (b)
   (d) Neither (a) nor (b)

(SO 3) 4. A credit sale of $750 is made on June 13, terms 2/10, n/30, on which a return of $50 is granted on June 16. What amount is received as payment in full on June 23?
   (a) $700 (c) $685
   (b) $686 (d) $650

(SO 4) 5. Gross profit will result if:
   (a) operating expenses are less than net earnings.
   (b) sales revenues are greater than operating expenses.
   (c) sales revenues are greater than cost of goods sold.
   (d) operating expenses are greater than cost of goods sold.

6. If sales revenues are $400,000, cost of goods sold is $310,000, and operating expenses are $60,000, what is the gross profit? (SO 4)
   (a) $30,000 (c) $340,000
   (b) $90,000 (d) $400,000

7. The multiple-step statement of earnings for a merchandising company shows each of the following features *except:* (SO 4)
   (a) gross profit.
   (b) cost of goods sold.
   (c) a sales revenue section.
   (d) all of these are present.

8. Which of the following would *not* affect the operating expenses to sales ratio? (Assume sales remain constant.) (SO 5)
   (a) An increase in advertising expense
   (b) A decrease in amortization expense
   (c) An increase in cost of goods sold
   (d) A decrease in insurance expense

9. The gross profit *rate* is equal to: (SO 5)
   (a) net earnings divided by sales.
   (b) cost of goods sold divided by sales.
   (c) sales minus cost of goods sold, divided by net sales.
   (d) sales minus cost of goods sold, divided by cost of goods sold.

10. Which factor would *not* affect the gross profit rate? (SO 5)
   (a) An increase in the cost of heating the store
   (b) An increase in the sale of luxury items
   (c) An increase in the use of "discount pricing" to sell merchandise
   (d) An increase in the price of inventory items

QUESTIONS

(SO 1) 1. (a) Explain the earnings measurement process in a merchandising company.
(b) How does earnings measurement differ between a merchandising company and a service company?
(c) How is earnings measurement the same for a merchandising company and a service company?

(SO 1) 2. Why is the normal operating cycle for a merchandising company likely to be longer than that of a service company?

(SO 1) 3. Distinguish between a perpetual and a periodic inventory system.

(SO 1) 4. "A physical inventory count is taken only in periodic inventory systems." Do you agree or disagree? Explain.

(SO 2) 5. What types of businesses are most likely to use a perpetual inventory system?

(SO 2) 6. Goods costing \$1,600 are purchased on account on July 15 with credit terms of 2/10, n/30. On July 18 a \$100 credit memo is received from the supplier for damaged goods. Give the journal entry on July 24 to record payment of the balance due within the discount period.

(SO 2, 3) 7. (a) What is the primary source document for recording (1) cash sales, and (2) credit sales?
(b) Using Xs for amounts, give the journal entries for each of the transactions in part (a) for both the purchaser and the seller.

8. Joan Hollins believes revenues from credit sales must be collected in cash before they are earned. Do you agree? Explain. (SO 3)

9. A credit sale is made on July 10 for \$900, terms 2/10, n/30. On July 12, \$100 of goods are returned for credit. Give the journal entry on July 19 to record the receipt of the balance due within the discount period. (SO 3)

10. Identify the distinguishing features of a statement of earnings for a merchandising company. (SO 4)

11. Identify the sections of a multiple-step statement of earnings that relate to (a) operating activities, and (b) non-operating activities. (SO 4)

12. Distinguish between the types of groupings of operating expenses. What problem is created by these groupings? (SO 4)

13. Rudy Corp. has sales revenue of \$100,000, cost of goods sold of \$70,000, and operating expenses of \$20,000. What is its gross profit? (SO 4)

14. Ford Company Ltd. reports net sales of \$800,000, gross profit of \$580,000, and net earnings of \$300,000. What are its operating expenses? (SO 4)

15. What two ratios measure factors that affect profitability? (SO 5)

16. What factors affect a company's gross profit rate—that is, what can cause the gross profit rate to increase and what can cause it to decrease? (SO 5)

Brief Exercises

BE5-1 Prepare the journal entries to record the following transactions in Hunt Company Ltd.'s books using a perpetual inventory system.

Journalize sales transactions. (SO 3)

(a) On March 2, Hunt Company sold $900,000 of merchandise to Streisand Company, terms 2/10, n/30. The cost of the merchandise sold was $600,000.

(b) On March 6, Streisand Company returned $130,000 of the merchandise purchased on March 2 because it didn't need it. The cost of the merchandise returned was $80,000 and it was restored to inventory.

(c) On March 12, Hunt Company received the balance due from Streisand Company.

BE5-2 From the information in BE5-1, prepare the journal entries to record these transactions in Streisand Company Ltd.'s books under a perpetual inventory system.

Journalize purchase transactions.

BE5-3 Keo Company Ltd. buys merchandise on account from Mayo Company Inc. The selling price of the goods is $900 and the cost of goods is $600. Both companies use perpetual inventory systems. Journalize the transactions on the books of both companies.

Journalize perpetual inventory entries. (SO 2, 3)

BE5-4 Presented here are the components in Sang Nam Company Inc.'s statement of earnings. Determine the missing amounts.

Calculate missing amounts in determining net earnings. (SO 4)

Sales	Cost of Goods Sold	Gross Profit	Operating Expenses	Net Earnings
$ 75,000	(b)	$ 43,500	(d)	$10,800
$108,000	$65,000	(c)	(e)	$29,500
(a)	$71,900	$109,600	$39,500	(f)

BE5-5 Cosby Company Inc. provides this information for the month ended October 31, 2001: sales on credit $300,000; cash sales $100,000; sales discounts $5,000; and sales returns and allowances $20,000. Prepare the sales revenue section of the statement of earnings based on this information.

Prepare sales revenue section of statement of earnings. (SO 4)

BE5-6 Explain where each of these items would appear on a multiple-step statement of earnings: gain on sale of equipment, cost of goods sold, amortization expense, interest expense, and sales returns and allowances.

Identify placement of items on a multiple-step statement of earnings. (SO 4)

BE5-7 Paisley Corporation reported net sales of $250,000, cost of goods sold of $100,000, operating expenses of $50,000, net earnings of $80,000, beginning total assets of $500,000, and ending total assets of $600,000. Calculate each of these values:

Calculate profitability ratios. (SO 5)

(a) Return on assets ratio
(b) Profit margin ratio
(c) Gross profit rate
(d) Operating expenses to sales ratio

BE5-8 Ry Corporation reported net sales $550,000; cost of goods sold $300,000; operating expenses $150,000; and net earnings $70,000. Calculate these values:

Calculate profitability ratios. (SO 5)

(a) Profit margin ratio
(b) Gross profit rate
(c) Operating expenses to sales ratio

Exercises

Journalize purchase transactions.
(SO 2)

E5-1 This information relates to Hans Olaf Corp.:

1. On April 5, purchased merchandise from DeVito Company for $18,000, terms 2/10, n/30.
2. On April 6, paid freight costs of $900 on merchandise purchased from DeVito.
3. On April 7, purchased equipment on account for $26,000.
4. On April 8, returned damaged merchandise to DeVito Company and was granted a $3,000 allowance.
5. On April 15, paid the amount due to DeVito Company in full.

Instructions

(a) Prepare the journal entries to record the transactions listed above in the books of Hans Olaf Corp.

(b) Assume that Hans Olaf Corp. paid the balance due to DeVito Company on May 4 instead of April 15. Prepare the journal entry to record this payment.

Journalize sales and purchase transactions.
(SO 2, 3)

E5-2 On September 1, Campus Office Supply Ltd. had an inventory of 30 deluxe pocket calculators at a cost of $20 each. The company uses a perpetual inventory system. During September these transactions occurred:

Sept.	6	Purchased 60 calculators at $19 each from Digital Co. for cash.
	9	Paid freight of $60 on calculators purchased from Digital Co.
	10	Returned two calculators to Digital Co. for $40 credit because they did not meet specifications.
	12	Sold 26 calculators costing $20 (including freight) for $30 each to Campus Book Store, terms n/30.
	14	Granted credit of $30 to Campus Book Store for the return of one calculator that was not ordered.
	20	Sold 30 calculators costing $20 for $30 each to Varsity Card Shop, terms n/30.

Instructions

Journalize the September transactions.

Journalize sales transactions.
(SO 3)

E5-3 The following transactions are for C. Pippen Company Ltd.:

1. On December 3, C. Pippen Company sold $400,000 of merchandise to I. Thomas Co., terms 2/10, n/30. The cost of the merchandise sold was $320,000.
2. On December 8, I. Thomas Co. was granted an allowance of $20,000 for merchandise purchased on December 3.
3. On December 13, C. Pippen Company received the balance due from I. Thomas Co.

Instructions

(a) Prepare the journal entries to record these transactions in the books of C. Pippen Company Ltd.

(b) Assume that C. Pippen Company received the balance due from I. Thomas Co. on January 2 of the following year instead of December 13. Prepare the journal entry to record the receipt of payment on January 2.

Journalize sales and purchase transactions.
(SO 2, 3)

E5-4 On June 10, Pele Company Ltd. purchased $5,000 of merchandise from Duvall Company Ltd., terms 2/10, n/30. Pele pays the freight costs of $300 on June 11. Damaged goods totalling $300 are returned to Duvall for credit on June 12. On June 19, Pele Company pays Duvall Company in full, less the purchase discount.

Instructions

(a) Prepare separate entries for each transaction in the books of Pele Company Ltd.

(b) Prepare separate entries for each transaction for Duvall Company Ltd. The merchandise purchased by Pele on June 10 cost Duvall $3,000. The merchandise returned by Pele on June 12 cost Duvall $180. The merchandise was repaired and restored to inventory.

Prepare sales revenue section of statement of earnings.
(SO 4)

E5-5 The adjusted trial balance of Cecilie Company Ltd. shows these data pertaining to sales at the end of its fiscal year, October 31, 2001: Sales $900,000; Freight-out $12,000; Sales Returns and Allowances $24,000; and Sales Discounts $15,000.

Instructions

Prepare the sales revenue section of the statement of earnings.

Prepare multiple-step statement of earnings and calculate profitability ratios.
(SO 4, 5)

E5-6 Presented is information related to Baja Co. for the month of January 2001:

Cost of goods sold	$208,000	Rent expense	$ 20,000
Freight-out	7,000	Sales discounts	8,000
Insurance expense	12,000	Sales returns and allowances	13,000
Salary expense	61,000	Sales	342,000

Instructions

(a) Prepare a multiple-step statement of earnings. Operating expenses should not be segregated into selling and administrative expenses.
(b) Calculate these values: profit margin ratio, gross profit rate, and operating expenses to sales ratio.

Determine missing amounts and calculate profitability ratios.
(SO 4, 5)

E5-7 Financial information is presented here for two companies:

	Young Company	Rice Company
Sales	$90,000	?
Sales returns	?	$ 5,000
Net sales	81,000	95,000
Cost of goods sold	56,000	?
Gross profit	?	38,000
Operating expenses	15,000	?
Net earnings	?	15,000

Instructions

(a) Fill in the missing amounts. Show all calculations.
(b) Calculate the profit margin ratio, gross profit rate, and operating expenses to sales ratio for each company.

Prepare multiple-step statement of earnings and calculate profitability ratios.
(SO 4, 5)

E5-8 In its statement of earnings for the year ended December 31, 2001, Chevalier Company Ltd. reported the following condensed data:

Administrative expenses	$435,000	Selling expenses	$ 690,000
Cost of goods sold	989,000	Loss on sale of equipment	10,000
Interest expense	70,000	Net sales	2,359,000
Interest revenue	45,000		

Instructions

(a) Prepare a multiple-step statement of earnings.
(b) Calculate the profit margin ratio, gross profit rate, and operating expenses to sales ratio.

Prepare single-step and multiple-step statements of earnings and calculate profitability ratios.
(SO 4, 5)

E5-9 JetForm Corporation, headquartered in Ottawa, is a world leader in electronic forms. Winner of Microsoft's 1999 industry solutions award, JetForm's automated business processes enable companies to operate efficiently and effectively, to increase revenues, lower operating costs and reduce cycle times. JetForm has offices in more than ten countries throughout the world, and its clients include the U.S. government, Chase Manhattan, and Boeing, among others.

In its statement of earnings for the year ended April 30, 1998, JetForm reported the following condensed data (in thousands):

Revenues from products and services	$111,227	Interest expenses	$ 3,564
Sales and marketing expenses	40,214	Income tax expense	1,690
Cost of products and services	22,798	Amortization expense	47,285
General and administrative expenses	20,466		

Instructions

(a) Prepare a single-step statement of earnings.
(b) Prepare a multiple-step statement of earnings.
(c) Calculate the profit margin ratio, gross profit rate, and operating expenses to sales ratio.

Problems: Set A

P5-1A You are provided with the following list of accounts from the adjusted trial balance of Swirsky Inc.

Classify the accounts of a merchandising company.
(SO 1)

Accounts payable
Accounts receivable
Accumulated amortization, office building
Accumulated amortization, store equipment
Advertising expense
Amortization expense, office building
Amortization expense, store equipment
Cash
Common shares
Freight-out
Income tax expense
Income tax payable
Insurance expense
Interest expense
Interest payable
Merchandise inventory
Mortgage payable
Office building
Prepaid insurance
Property taxes payable
Retained earnings
Salaries expense, office staff
Salaries expense, store staff
Salaries payable
Sales
Sales discounts
Sales returns and allowances
Store equipment
Utilities expense, office
Utilities expense, store
Wages payable

Instructions

For each account, identify whether the account should be reported on the balance sheet or a multiple-step statement of earnings. Also, please specify where the account should be classified. For example, amortization expense on the office building would be classified under administrative expenses on the statement of earnings

P5-2A Presented here are selected transactions for the Norlan Company Inc. during September of the current year. Norlan Company uses the perpetual inventory system.

Journalize transactions.
(SO 2, 3)

Sept.	2	Purchased delivery equipment on account for $28,000.
	4	Purchased merchandise on account from Hillary Company at a cost of $60,000, terms 2/10, n/30.
	5	Paid freight charges of $2,000 on merchandise purchased from Hillary Company on September 4.
	5	Returned damaged goods costing $7,000 received from Hillary Company on September 4.
	6	Sold merchandise to Fischer Company costing $15,000 on account for $21,000, terms 1/10, n/30.
	14	Paid Hillary balance due related to September 4 transaction.
	15	Purchased supplies costing $4,000 for cash.
	16	Received balance due from Fischer Company.
	18	Purchased merchandise for cash $6,000.
	22	Sold to Waldo Company on account for $28,000 inventory costing $20,000, terms 1/10, n/30.

Instructions
Journalize the September transactions for Norlan Company.

Journalize, post, and prepare trial balance and partial statement of earnings.
(SO 2, 3, 4)

P5-3A Joe Weir, a former professional golf star, operates Weir's Pro Shop at Bay Golf Course. At the beginning of the current season, on April 1, the ledger of Weir's Pro Shop showed Cash $2,500; Merchandise Inventory $3,500; and Common Shares $6,000. The following transactions were completed during April:

Apr.	5	Purchased golf bags, clubs, and balls on account from Balata Co. $1,600, terms 2/10, n/60.
	7	Paid freight on Balata purchase $80.
	9	Received credit from Balata Co. for merchandise returned $100.
	10	Sold merchandise on account to members $900, terms n/30. The merchandise sold had a cost of $630.
	12	Purchased golf shoes, sweaters, and other accessories on account from Arrow Sportswear $660, terms 1/10, n/30.
	14	Paid Balata Co. in full.
	17	Received credit from Arrow Sportswear for merchandise returned $60.
	20	Made sales on account to members $700, terms n/30. The cost of the merchandise sold was $490.
	21	Paid Arrow Sportswear in full.
	27	Granted an allowance to members for clothing that did not fit properly $30.
	30	Received payments on account from members $1,100.

Instructions
(a) Journalize the April transactions.
(b) Using T accounts, enter the beginning balances in the ledger accounts and post the April transactions.
(c) Prepare a trial balance as at April 30, 2001.
(d) Prepare a multiple-step statement of earnings through gross profit.

Journalize, post, and prepare partial statement of earnings, and calculate ratios.
(SO 2, 3, 4, 5)

P5-4A Eagle Hardware Store Inc. completed the following merchandising transactions in the month of May. At the beginning of May, Eagle's ledger showed Cash of $5,000 and Common Shares of $5,000.

May	1	Purchased merchandise on account from Depot Wholesale Supply for $5,000, terms 2/10, n/30.
	2	Sold merchandise on account for $4,000, terms 2/10, n/30. The cost of the merchandise sold was $3,000.
	5	Received credit from Depot Wholesale Supply for merchandise returned $200.
	9	Received collections in full, less discounts, from customers billed on sales of $4,000 on May 2.

10 Paid Depot Wholesale Supply in full, less discount.
11 Purchased supplies for cash $900.
12 Purchased merchandise for cash $2,400.
15 Received refund for poor-quality merchandise from supplier on cash purchase $230.
17 Purchased merchandise from Harlow Distributors for $1,900, terms 2/10, n/30.
19 Paid freight on May 17 purchase $250.
24 Sold merchandise for cash $6,200. The cost of the merchandise sold was $4,340.
25 Purchased merchandise from Horicon Inc. for $1,000, terms 2/10, n/30.
27 Paid Harlow Distributors in full, less discount.
29 Made refunds to cash customers for returned merchandise $100. The returned merchandise had cost $70 and was restored to inventory.
31 Sold merchandise on account for $1,600, terms n/30. The cost of the merchandise sold was $1,120.

Instructions

(a) Journalize the transactions.
(b) Post the transactions to T accounts. Be sure to enter the beginning Cash and Common Share balances.
(c) Prepare a multiple-step statement of earnings through gross profit for the month of May.
(d) Calculate the profit margin ratio and the gross profit rate. (Assume operating expenses were $1,500.)

Journalize, post, and prepare adjusted trial balance and financial statements.
(SO 4)

P5-5A The trial balance of Mesa Wholesale Company Inc. at December 31, the end of the company's fiscal year, follows:

MESA WHOLESALE COMPANY INC.
Trial Balance
December 31, 2001

	Debit	Credit
Cash	$ 33,400	
Accounts Receivable	37,600	
Merchandise Inventory	90,000	
Land	92,000	
Buildings	197,000	
Accumulated Amortization—Buildings		$ 54,000
Equipment	83,500	
Accumulated Amortization—Equipment		42,400
Notes Payable		50,000
Accounts Payable		37,500
Common Shares		200,000
Retained Earnings		67,800
Dividends	10,000	
Sales		902,100
Sales Discounts	4,600	
Cost of Goods Sold	709,900	
Salaries Expense	69,800	
Utilities Expense	9,400	
Repair Expense	5,900	
Gas and Oil Expense	7,200	
Insurance Expense	3,500	
	$1,353,800	$1,353,800

Adjustment data:

1. Amortization is $10,000 on buildings and $9,000 on equipment. (Both are administrative expenses.)
2. Interest of $7,000 is due and unpaid on notes payable at December 31.
3. Income taxes of $20,000 are due and unpaid.

Other data: $15,000 of the notes payable are payable next year.

Instructions

(a) Journalize the adjusting entries.
(b) Create T accounts for all accounts used in part (a). Enter the trial balance into the T accounts and post the adjusting entries.
(c) Prepare an adjusted trial balance.
(d) Prepare a multiple-step statement of earnings and a statement of retained earnings for the year, and a classified balance sheet at December 31, 2001.

Prepare a correct multiple-step and single-step statement of earnings.
(SO 4)

P5-6A An inexperienced accountant prepared this condensed statement of earnings for Zambrana Company Ltd., a retail firm that has been in business for a number of years.

ZAMBRANA COMPANY LTD.
Statement of Earnings
For the Year Ended December 31, 2001

Revenues	
Net sales	$740,000
Other revenues	24,000
	764,000
Cost of goods sold	555,000
Gross profit	209,000
Operating expenses	
Selling expenses	104,000
Administrative expenses	72,000
	176,000
Net earnings	$ 33,000

As an experienced, knowledgeable accountant, you review the statement and determine the following facts:

1. Net sales consists of sales $800,000, less delivery expense on merchandise sold $30,000, and sales returns and allowances $30,000.
2. Other revenues consists of sales discounts $16,000 and rent revenue $8,000.
3. Selling expenses consists of salespersons' salaries $80,000; amortization on equipment $8,000; advertising $10,000; and sales commissions $6,000. The commissions represent commissions paid. At December 31, $4,000 of commissions have been earned by salespersons but have not been paid.
4. Administrative expenses consists of office salaries $27,000; dividends $4,000; utilities $12,000; interest expense $2,000; rent $24,000, which includes prepayments totalling $6,000 for the first quarter of 2002; and income tax expense $3000.

Instructions

(a) Prepare a correct, detailed, multiple-step statement of earnings.
(b) Prepare a correct, condensed, single-step statement of earnings

Prepare financial statements and calculate profitability ratios.
(SO 4, 5)

P5-7A Metro Department Store is located in midtown. During the past several years, net earnings have been declining because suburban shopping centres have been attracting business away from city areas. At the end of the company's fiscal year on November 30, 2001, these accounts appeared in its adjusted trial balance:

Accounts Payable	$ 37,310
Accounts Receivable	11,770
Accumulated Amortization—Delivery Equipment	19,680
Accumulated Amortization—Store Equipment	41,800
Amortization Expense—Delivery Equipment	4,000
Amortization Expense—Store Equipment	9,500
Cash	3,500
Common Shares	70,000
Cost of Goods Sold	633,220
Delivery Expense	8,200
Delivery Equipment	57,000
Dividends	12,000
Income Tax Expense	4,500
Insurance Expense	9,000
Interest Expense	8,000
Interest Revenue	5,000
Merchandise Inventory	36,200
Notes Payable, due 2005	46,000
Prepaid Insurance	4,500
Property Tax Expense	3,500
Property Taxes Payable	3,500
Rent Expense	19,000
Retained Earnings	14,200
Salaries Expense	120,000
Sales	860,000
Sales Commissions Expense	14,000
Sales Commissions Payable	6,000
Sales Returns and Allowances	10,000
Store Equipment	125,000
Utilities Expense	10,600

Instructions

(a) Prepare a multiple-step statement of earnings, a statement of retained earnings, and a classified balance sheet. (Do not separate operating expenses into selling and administrative categories.)

(b) Calculate the return on assets ratio, profit margin ratio, gross profit rate, and operating expenses to sales ratio. Assume that total assets at the beginning of the year were $160,000.

Calculate missing amounts and assess profitability.
(SO 2, 4, 5)

P5-8A Psang Inc. operates a retail operation that purchases and sells snowmobiles, amongst other outdoor products, in Regina, Saskatchewan. The company purchases all merchandise inventory on credit and uses a perpetual inventory system. The accounts payable account is used for recording inventory purchases only; all other current liabilities are accrued in separate accounts. You are provided with the following selected information for the fiscal years 1999 through 2002, inclusive:

	1999	2000	2001	2002
Income Statement Data				
Sales		$96,850	$ (e)	$82,220
Cost of goods sold		(a)	27,140	26,550
Gross profit		69,260	61,540	(i)
Operating expenses		63,500	(f)	52,060
Net earnings		$ (b)	$ 4,570	$ (j)
Balance Sheet Data				
Merchandise inventory	$13,000	$ (c)	$14,700	$ (k)
Accounts payable	5,000	6,500	4,600	(l)
Additional Information				
Purchases of merchandise inventory on account		$25,890	$ (g)	$24,050
Cash payments to suppliers		(d)	(h)	24,650

Instructions

(a) Calculate the missing amounts.

(b) Sales declined over the three-year fiscal period, 2000-2002. Does that mean that profitability necessarily also declined? Explain, computing the gross profit rate and operating expenses to sales ratios for each fiscal year to help support your answer.

Analyse impact of transactions on ratios.
(SO 2, 3, 5)

P5-9A Merchandise inventory transactions can sometimes have a significant impact on profitability ratios.

	Transaction	Gross profit rate (25%)	Operating expenses to sales ratio (15%)	Return on assets ratio (10%)	Profit margin ratio (5%)
(a)	Purchased merchandise inventory on account, $500.				
(b)	Paid freight, $100 cash, for merchandise inventory purchased above. Terms FOB shipping point.				
(c)	Returned merchandise for credit on account, $100.				
(d)	Sold merchandise inventory for $850 cash. Cost of sale, $600.				
(e)	Sale return of merchandise, $140. Customer's account credited and merchandise (cost, $100) returned to inventory.				
(f)	Incurred cash operating expenses of $1,200.				

Instructions

Indicate whether the above transactions will increase (I), decrease (D), or not affect (NA) each of the profitability ratios presented. Assume that the profitability ratios, before each transaction, were as follows: gross profit rate, 25%; operating expenses to sales ratio, 15%; return on assets ratio, 10%; and profit margin ratio, 5%. The company uses a perpetual inventory system to account for its merchandise transactions.

Evaluate profitability.
(SO 5)

P5-10A Perkins Papers Ltd. is a leading manufacturer and converter of Cascades tissue products in Quebec, the second largest in Canada, and the seventh largest in North America. For a recent three-year period, Perkins reported the following selected statement of earnings data (in thousands of dollars):

	1999	1998	1997
Net sales	$290,156	$267,478	$236,658
Cost of sales	205,283	181,800	155,377
Selling and administrative expenses	30,268	25,372	23,420
Net earnings	21,554	27,235	27,231

In her message to shareholders, Suzanne Blanchet, President and Chief Executive Officer, made the following comments:

> As forecast, our strategic investments and dynamic market development initiatives led to robust growth in shipments over the past year.... Unfortunately, growth and operating-efficiency gains in 1999 were temporarily held back by a sharp increase in the cost of recycled fibre, which could not be offset immediately by corresponding increases in selling prices.... We will take full advantage of the efficiency of our production infrastructure and the strength of our human resources to ensure sustained sales growth and to contain cost increases.

Instructions

(a) Calculate the percentage change in sales and in net earnings from 1997 to 1999.

(b) Calculate the company's gross profit rate for each of the three years. What contribution, if any, did the company's gross profit rate make to the declining earnings in 1999?

(c) Calculate the operating (selling and administrative expense) expenses to sales ratio for each year. Has this ratio improved or deteriorated since 1997?

(d) What was Perkins' profit margin in each of the three years? Comment on any trend in this percentage.

(e) Based on the trends in these ratios, are the President's comments appropriate? What steps do you think Perkins will be able to take to contain cost increases in future?

Consider how the timing of sales and purchases can affect profitability.
(SO 5)

P5-11A You are presented with the following information for Katie Inc. as at May 24, 2001. The company's year end is May 31.

KATIE INC.
Balance Sheet
May 24, 2001

Current assets	$ 80,000
Other assets	29,000
Total assets	$109,000
Current liabilities	$ 35,000
Long-term liabilities	30,000
Total liabilities	65,000
Shareholders' equity	44,000
Total liabilities and shareholders' equity	$109,000

KATIE INC.
Statement of Earnings
For the 51 Weeks Ended May 24, 2001

Sales	$ 24,000
Cost of goods sold	(16,000)
Operating expenses	(7,000)
Net earnings	$ 1,000

The company has debt covenants with the bank which require it to maintain a current ratio in excess of 2 to 1, at least $40,000 of working capital, a profit margin of 2% of sales and a debt to total assets ratio which cannot exceed 60%. The company wants to boost its financial performance by year end as it may be going back to the bank to finance the purchase of some equipment.

The sales manager has come to you with a proposal. She says that she can purchase some inventory on credit for $13,500. She has a customer who she can sell the inventory to, also on credit, for $16,000. "I know the gross profit on the deal is not as high as usual.

But the beauty of this is that we should be able to collect the cash from our customer early next month, in time to pay the supplier. And the bank will be impressed by the $2,500 increase in earnings! So we can boost our profit without having to pay out any cash, which I know that we are short on anyway!"

Instructions

(a) Calculate the following, based on the financial data presented as of May 24:
   1. Current ratio
   2. Working capital
   3. Debt to total assets ratio
   4. Profit margin ratio

(b) 1. What would be the impact on each of the ratios you calculated in (a) if you followed the sales manager's proposal? For purposes of simplicity, you can ignore the income tax consequences of the transactions.
   2. Make a recommendation with respect to proceeding with the sales manager's suggestion.

PROBLEMS: SET B

Classify the accounts of a merchandising company.
(SO 1)

P5-1B The following list of accounts has been selected from the financial statements of **Alcan Aluminium Limited**. Alcan, headquartered in Montreal, is involved in most aspects of the aluminum industry in more than 30 countries around the world.

Accumulated depreciation
Cash and time deposits
Common shares
Cost of sales
Depreciation expense
Dividends
Income taxes expense
Interest expense
Inventories—aluminum
Inventories—other supplies
Inventories—raw materials
Operating income
Other expenses
Payables
Property, plant, and equipment
Receivables
Retained earnings
Sales
Selling, administrative, and general expenses

Instructions

For each account listed above, indicate whether the account was likely reported on Alcan's balance sheet, statement of earnings, or statement of retained earnings. Specify where the account was most likely classified. For example, depreciation (amortization) expense is classified under Operating Expenses on the statement of earnings.

Journalize entries.
(SO 2, 3)

P5-2B Varsity Auto Sales Ltd. uses a perpetual inventory system. On April 1, the new car inventory records show total inventory of $230,000 consisting of the following:

Model	Units	Unit Cost
Custom sedans	4	$24,000
Convertibles	3	26,000
Recreational vans	2	28,000

During April the following purchases and sales were made on account:

Apr. 5 Purchased three custom sedans for $24,000 each.
7 Sold two custom sedans for $28,200 each.
13 Purchased two recreational vans for $28,000 each.
17 Sold one custom sedan for $28,500.
20 Purchased two convertibles for $26,000 each.
22 Returned one convertible purchased on April 20 for $26,000 credit.
24 Sold three recreational vans for $34,000 each.
28 Sold one convertible for $31,000.

Instructions
Journalize the transactions. Use separate accounts for each model.

Journalize, post, and prepare trial balance and partial statement of earnings.
(SO 2, 3, 4)

P5-3B Jana Nejedly, a former professional tennis star, operates J.'s Tennis Shop at the Ontario Racquet Club. At the beginning of the current season, the ledger of J.'s Tennis Shop showed Cash $2,500; Merchandise Inventory $1,700; and Common Shares $4,200. The following transactions were completed during April:

Apr. 4 Purchased racquets and balls from Robert Co. $640, terms 3/10, n/30.
6 Paid freight on Robert Co. purchase $40.
8 Sold merchandise to members $900, terms n/30. The merchandise sold cost $600.
10 Received credit of $40 from Robert Co. for a damaged racquet that was returned.
11 Purchased tennis shoes from Niki Sports for cash $300.
13 Paid Robert Co. in full.
14 Purchased tennis shirts and shorts from Martina's Sportswear $700, terms 2/10, n/60.
15 Received cash refund of $50 from Niki Sports for damaged merchandise that was returned.
17 Paid freight on Martina's Sportswear purchase $30.
18 Sold merchandise to members $800, terms n/30. The cost of the merchandise sold was $530.
20 Received $500 in cash from members in settlement of their accounts.
21 Paid Martina's Sportswear in full.
27 Granted an allowance of $30 to members for tennis clothing that did not fit properly.
30 Received cash payments on account from members $500.

Instructions
(a) Journalize the April transactions.
(b) Using T accounts, enter the beginning balances in the ledger accounts and post the April transactions.
(c) Prepare a trial balance as at April 30, 2001.
(d) Prepare a statement of earnings through gross profit.

Journalize, post, and prepare partial statement of earnings, and calculate ratios.
(SO 2, 3, 4, 5)

P5-4B Nisson Distributing Company Ltd. completed the following merchandising transactions in the month of April. At the beginning of April, Nisson's ledger showed Cash of $9,000 and Common Shares of $9,000.

Apr. 2 Purchased merchandise on account from Kai Supply Co. $4,900, terms 2/10, n/30.
4 Sold merchandise on account $5,000, terms 2/10, n/30. The cost of the merchandise sold was $4,000.
5 Paid $200 freight on April 4 sale.
6 Received credit from Kai Supply Co. for merchandise returned $300.
11 Paid Kai Supply Co. in full, less discount.
13 Received collections in full, less discounts, from customers billed on April 4.
14 Purchased merchandise for cash $4,400.
16 Received refund from supplier on cash purchase of April 14 $500.

18 Purchased merchandise from Pigeon Distributors $4,200, terms 2/10, n/30.
20 Paid freight on April 18 purchase $100.
23 Sold merchandise for cash $6,400. The cost of the merchandise sold was $5,120.
26 Purchased merchandise for cash $2,300.
27 Paid Pigeon Distributors in full, less discount.
29 Made refunds to cash customers for returned merchandise $90. The returned merchandise had a cost of $70 and was restored to inventory.
30 Sold merchandise on account $3,700, terms n/30. The cost of the merchandise sold was $3,000.

Instructions

(a) Journalize the transactions.
(b) Post the transactions to T accounts. Be sure to enter the beginning cash and common share balances.
(c) Prepare the statement of earnings through gross profit for the month of April.
(d) Calculate the profit margin ratio and the gross profit rate. (Assume operating expenses were $1,400.)

Journalize, post, and prepare adjusted trial balance and financial statements.
(SO 4)

P5-5B The trial balance of Ivanna Fashion Centre Ltd. contained the following accounts at November 30, the end of the company's fiscal year:

IVANNA FASHION CENTRE LTD.
Trial Balance
November 30, 2001

	Debit	Credit
Cash	$ 16,700	
Accounts Receivable	33,700	
Merchandise Inventory	45,000	
Store Supplies	5,500	
Store Equipment	85,000	
Accumulated Amortization—Store Equipment		$ 18,000
Delivery Equipment	48,000	
Accumulated Amortization—Delivery Equipment		6,000
Notes Payable		51,000
Accounts Payable		48,500
Common Shares		80,000
Retained Earnings		30,000
Dividends	12,000	
Sales		757,200
Sales Returns and Allowances	4,200	
Cost of Goods Sold	507,400	
Salaries Expense	140,000	
Advertising Expense	26,400	
Utilities Expense	14,000	
Repair Expense	12,100	
Delivery Expense	16,700	
Rent Expense	24,000	
	$990,700	$990,700

Adjustment data:

1. Store supplies on hand total $3,500.
2. Amortization expense for the period is $9,000 on the store equipment and $7,000 on the delivery equipment.
3. Interest of $11,000 is accrued on notes payable at November 30.

Other data: $30,000 of notes payable are due for payment next year. No income taxes are due.

Instructions

(a) Journalize the adjusting entries.
(b) Prepare T accounts for all accounts used in part (a). Enter the trial balance into the T accounts and post the adjusting entries.
(c) Prepare an adjusted trial balance.
(d) Prepare a multiple-step statement of earnings and a statement of retained earnings for the year, and a classified balance sheet at November 30, 2001.

Prepare a correct multiple-step and single-step statement of earnings.
(SO 4)

P5-6B A part-time bookkeeper prepared this statement of earnings for Tao Company Inc. for the year ending December 31, 2001:

TAO COMPANY INC.
Statement of Earnings
December 31, 2001

Revenues		
Sales		$702,000
Less: Freight-out	$10,000	
Sales discounts	11,300	21,300
Net sales		680,700
Other revenues (net)		1,300
Total revenues		682,000
Expenses		
Cost of goods sold		470,000
Selling expenses		110,000
Administrative expenses		50,000
Dividends		12,000
Total expenses		642,000
Net earnings		$ 40,000

As an experienced, knowledgeable accountant, you review the statement and determine the following facts:

1. Sales includes $10,000 of deposits from customers for future sales orders.
2. Other revenues contains two items: interest expense $4,000 and interest revenue $5,300.
3. Selling expenses consists of sales salaries $76,000; advertising $10,000; amortization on store equipment $7,500; sales commissions expense $6,500; and income taxes of $10,000.
4. Administrative expenses consists of office salaries $19,000; utilities expense $8,000; rent expense $16,000; and insurance expense $7,000. Insurance expense includes $1,200 of insurance applicable to 2002.

Instructions

(a) Prepare a correct, detailed, multiple-step statement of earnings.
(b) Prepare a correct, condensed, single-step statement of earnings.

Prepare financial statements and calculate profitability ratios.
(SO 4, 5)

P5-7B N-Mart Department Store Ltd. is located near the Village Shopping Mall. At the end of the company's fiscal year on December 31, 2001, the following accounts appeared in its adjusted trial balance:

Accounts Payable	$ 89,300
Accounts Receivable	50,300
Accumulated Amortization—Building	52,500
Accumulated Amortization—Equipment	42,900
Amortization Expense—Building	10,400
Amortization Expense—Equipment	13,300
Building	190,000
Cash	17,000
Common Shares	150,000
Cost of Goods Sold	412,700
Dividends	28,000
Equipment	110,000
Income Tax Expense	6,000

Insurance Expense	7,200
Interest Expense	11,000
Interest Payable	8,000
Interest Revenue	4,000
Merchandise Inventory	75,000
Mortgage Payable	80,000
Office Salaries Expense	32,000
Prepaid Insurance	2,400
Property Taxes Expense	4,800
Property Taxes Payable	4,800
Retained Earnings	26,600
Sales Salaries Expense	76,000
Sales	618,000
Sales Commissions Expense	14,500
Sales Commissions Payable	3,500
Sales Returns and Allowances	8,000
Utilities Expenses	11,000

Additional data: $20,000 of the mortgage payable is due for payment next year.

Instructions

(a) Prepare a multiple-step statement of earnings, a statement of retained earnings and a classified balance sheet.

(b) Calculate the return on assets ratio, profit margin ratio, gross profit rate, and operating expenses to sales ratio. Assume total assets at the beginning of the year were $320,000.

Calculate missing amounts and assess profitability.
(SO 2, 4, 5)

P5-8B Danielle MacLean operates a clothing retail operation in Bridgewater, Nova Scotia. She purchases all merchandise inventory on credit and uses a perpetual inventory system. The accounts payable account is used for recording inventory purchases only; all other current liabilities are accrued in separate accounts. You are provided with the following selected information for the fiscal years 1999, 2000, 2001, and 2002:

	1999	2000	2001	2002
Inventory (ending)	$13,000	$ 11,300	$ 14,700	$ 12,200
Accounts payable (ending)	20,000			
Sales		225,700	227,600	219,500
Purchases of merchandise inventory on account		141,000	150,000	132,000
Cash payments to suppliers		135,000	161,000	127,000

Instructions

(a) Calculate cost of goods sold for each of the 2000, 2001, and 2002 fiscal years.

(b) Calculate the gross profit for each of the 2000, 2001, and 2002 fiscal years.

(c) Calculate the ending balance of accounts payable for each of the 2000, 2001, and 2002 fiscal years.

(d) Sales declined in fiscal 2002. Does that mean that profitability, as measured by the gross profit rate, necessarily also declined? Explain, calculating the gross profit rate for each fiscal year to help support your answer.

Evaluate impact of transactions on ratios.
(SO 2, 3, 5)

P5-9B The following ratios were computed for Khalil Enterprise Ltd. at year end, December 31, 2002.

Gross profit rate	Gross profit / Sales	$17,200 / $39,200	43.88%
Operating expenses to sales ratio	Operating expenses / Sales	$12,600 / $39,200	32.14%
Return on assets ratio	Net earnings / Average assets	$2,550 / $440,000	0.58%
Profit margin ratio	Net earnings / Sales	$2,550 / $39,200	6.51%

It was recently discovered that the following transactions, which occurred on a day the bookkeeper was ill in December, were not recorded:

1. A credit sale for $10,000 needs to be recorded in December. The cost of the inventory items sold was $4,800.
2. A sale return for $3,000 needs to be recorded in December. The customer's account receivable was credited for the full amount. The cost of the inventory items that were returned in excellent condition was $1,700.
3. A $500 bill for advertising expense was paid in December. However, the amount was not recorded in any of the accounting records.
4. As a result of the preceding adjustments, income tax expense went up by another $850. Again, this amount was not recorded in any of the accounting records.

Instructions

(a) Prepare the correcting journal entries required to record each of the omitted transactions listed above.

(b) Recalculate the four ratios, after taking into account the impact the corrections recorded in (a) had on the components of each ratio.

Evaluate profitability.
(SO 5)

P5-10B Bob Evans Farms, Inc. operates more than 400 restaurants that serve home-style meals with country hospitality throughout Canada and the U.S. In addition to operating its own eateries, the company sells fresh and frozen food products to grocery stores. For a recent three-year period, Bob Evans Farms reported the following selected financial statement data:

(in millions of U.S. dollars)	1999	1998	1997
Net sales	$968.5	$886.8	$822.2
Cost of sales	275.9	271.4	265.5
Selling and administrative expenses	566.5	509.3	470.4
Net earnings	57.6	45.7	36.1
Total assets	590.4	579.9	564.1

In his letter to the shareholders, Bob Evans Farms' chief executive officer (CEO) expressed great enthusiasm for the company's future. Here is an excerpt from that letter:

> "Bob Evans Farms is uniquely positioned as a trusted brand name in both the restaurant and grocery store sectors, providing us with numerous growth opportunities. Our principal long-term goal is to capitalize on that potential for the benefit of our shareholders."

Instructions

(a) Calculate the percentage change in sales and in net earnings from 1997 to 1999.

(b) Calculate the company's gross profit rate for each of the three years. What contribution, if any, did the company's gross profit rate make to the improved earnings?

(c) Calculate the operating (selling and administrative expense) expenses to sales ratio for each year. Comment on any trend in this percentage.

(d) What was Bob Evans Farm's profit margin in each of the three years? Comment on any trend in this percentage.

(e) The CEO's letter also stated that the company's "same-store sales" have increased by 5% in each of the last two years. What effect would you expect this change to have on return on assets? Calculate the company's return on assets for 1998 and 1999 to see if it reflects the increase in same-store sales.

(f) Based on the trend in these ratios, does the CEO's optimism seem appropriate?

Consider impact of percentage changes on profitability.
(SO 5)

P5-11B You are presented with the following statement of earnings for Merigomish Mariners Inc. for the year ended July 31, 2001.

MERIGOMISH MARINERS INC.
Statement of Earnings
Year Ended July 31, 2001

Sales	$450,000
Cost of goods sold	(315,000)
Gross profit	135,000
Operating expenses:	
Administrative expenses:	
Amortization expense, office building	4,000
Insurance expense	1,200
Salaries, administrative staff	28,000
Utilities expense	12,000
Total administrative expenses	45,200
Selling expenses:	
Advertising expense	5,600
Amortization expense, selling equipment	2,700
Freight-out	1,500
Salaries, selling staff	37,000
Total selling expenses	46,800
Total operating expenses	92,000
Earnings from operations	43,000
Other expense:	
Interest expense	8,000
Earnings before income taxes	35,000
Income tax expense	8,750
Net earnings	$ 26,250

The sales manager has come to the company president with a proposal. He wants to increase advertising expense and the salaries for the selling staff by 10% each. He also wants to cut the gross profit rate by three percentage points (that is, if the gross profit rate is 25%, it would have to be cut to 22%). The sales manager says that marketing research shows that sales will increase by 12%! The sales manager is really pushing this new proposal: "This increase in sales will be great!"

Instructions

(a) Calculate the following ratios for Merigomish Mariners, using the financial data presented in the statement of earnings:
 1. Gross profit rate
 2. Operating expenses to sales ratio
 3. Profit margin ratio

(b) The president wants to make sure that the company's profit ratio will not deteriorate if she follows the sales manager's proposal. She knows that income tax expense is 25% of earnings before income taxes. To help the president make her decision,
 1. Prepare revised ratios for the ratios listed in part (a), and
 2. Comment on the revised numbers and whether or not the president should agree to follow the sales manager's proposal.

BROADENING YOUR PERSPECTIVE

FINANCIAL REPORTING AND ANALYSIS

FINANCIAL REPORTING PROBLEM: *Loblaw Companies Limited*

Loblaws
A passion for food... *and a lot more!*

BYP5-1 The financial statements for **Loblaw** are presented in Appendix A at the end of this book.

Instructions

Answer these questions using the consolidated statement of earnings:

(a) What was the percentage change in sales and in net earnings from 1998 to 1999?

(b) What was the profit margin in each of the two years presented in the annual report?

Comment on the trend.

(c) Is there sufficient information in the statement to determine Loblaw's gross profit rate? If so, calculate this rate for each of the two years.

(d) What was the operating expenses to sales ratio in each of the two years? While operating expenses do not normally include cost of sales, include the cost of sales in this calculation for comparison purposes. Comment on any trend in this percentage.

(e) Are any non-operating revenues and non-operating expenses included in Loblaw's statement of earnings? If so, identify the accounts included.

COMPARATIVE ANALYSIS PROBLEM: *Loblaw and Sobeys*

BYP5-2 The financial statements of **Sobeys Inc.** are presented in Appendix B following the financial statements for **Loblaw** in Appendix A.

Instructions

(a) Based on the information contained in these financial statements, determine the following values for each company for each of the two most recent years presented in their annual reports:

1. Profit margin ratio
2. Percentage change in sales
3. Percentage change in operating earnings
4. Operating expenses (including cost of sales) to sales ratio

(b) What conclusions concerning the relative profitability of the two companies can be drawn from these data?

RESEARCH CASE

BYP5-3 Online retailing has had a significant impact on pricing strategies and the resultant profitability of traditional "bricks and mortar" retailers. The article "Inflation-fighter.com" by Peter Verburg, published in the December 10, 1999, issue of *Canadian Business*, discusses the role of Internet retailing in pricing strategies and outlines the ways that Internet competition affects these bricks and mortar businesses.

Instructions

Read the article and answer the following questions:

(a) How is the use of the Internet affecting the pricing strategies of retailers?

(b) What percentage of North American households does Forrester Research Inc. predict will be on line by 2003?

(c) Why does the author predict that comparison price shopping using the Internet will have a deflationary (price-reducing) effect on the economy?

INTERPRETING FINANCIAL STATEMENTS

BYP5-4 **Chapters Inc.** is a Canadian retailer of a variety of entertainment items such as books, magazines, videos, DVDs, etc. **Chapters Online Inc.**, an e-commerce company, was established in April 1999 and operates *www.chapters.ca*. Chapters Online reported the following unaudited information for the quarters indicated:

CHAPTERS ONLINE INC.
Statement of Earnings
Quarter Ended

	Jan. 1, 2000	Oct. 2, 1999
Revenue	$ 12,169,315	$ 6,399,986
Cost of sales	(10,346,301)	(5,488,393)
Gross profit	1,823,014	911,593
Operating expenses	(13,343,512)	(8,281,093)
Amortization	(852,660)	(676,657)
Interest income	623,761	103,482
Net loss for the period	($11,749,397)	($7,942,675)

The majority of the shares of Chapters Online are owned by Chapters Inc. Chapters Inc. records revenue from sales in its superstores, traditional bookstores, Chapters Online, and other sources. Chapters Inc. reported the following unaudited information for the quarters indicated:

Chapters
www.chapters.ca

CHAPTERS INC.
Statement of Earnings
Quarter Ended

	Jan. 1, 2000	Oct. 2, 1999
Revenue	$ 234,695,000	$ 148,120,000
Cost of product, purchasing, selling and administration	(215,426,000)	(154,785,000)
	19,269,000	(6,665,000)
Amortization expense	(6,304,000)	(5,962,000)
Interest expense	(1,496,000)	(1,897,000)
Net gain on sale of Chapters Online and Pegasus Inc.	5,749,000	35,558,000
Other items, net	(7,485,000)	6,724,000
Net earnings for the period	$ 9,733,000	$ 27,758,000

Instructions

(a) Calculate the percentage increase in sales over the two quarters for Chapters Online. What factors do you think contributed to the increase in sales?

(b) Calculate the gross margin percentage for each quarter for Chapters Online. What impact did the change in gross profit percentage have on profitability for the second quarter?

(c) Why is it not possible to make a meaningful comparison of Chapters Online's gross profit percentages with those of Chapters Inc.?

(d) Calculate the sales for each quarter for Chapters Inc. with the sales for Chapters Online *excluded* from your numbers. What amount of sales each quarter are from sources other than Chapters Online? What was the percentage increase in these sales figure?

(e) What would be the impact on net earnings if Chapters Inc. had not recorded gains on the sales of Chapters Online and Pegasus Inc.?

BYP5-5 Mark's Work Wearhouse Ltd. (L'Equipeur in Quebec) is Canada's largest specialty apparel and footwear store. They carry 4,000 items in stock for sale in 140 stores across Canada. Mark's quantify their corporate financial goals and carefully monitor their progress in order to assess their success. Some of their profitability goals for fiscal 1999, expressed in conservative to optimistic ranges, included the following:

Gross margin	40.6% - 40.7%
Operating expenses as a percentage of sales	35.5% - 34.7%
Profit margin	2.7% - 3.2%
Sales (in thousands)	$288,616 - $297,871
Gross margin (in thousands)	$117,180 - $121,113
Net earnings (in thousands)	$7,805 - $9,450

Mark's Work Wearhouse's statement of earnings for the year ended January 30, 1999 is condensed and reproduced here:

MARK'S WORK WEARHOUSE LTD.
Statement of Earnings
52 Weeks Ended January 30, 1999
(thousands)

Corporate operations		
Sales		$283,401
Cost of sales		169,163
Gross margin		114,238
Front-line expenses	$85,102	
Back-line expenses	22,195	
Other	(4,055)	103,242
Earnings before income taxes		10,996
Income taxes		5,244
Net earnings		$ 5,752

Instructions

(a) The statement of earnings is shown in summary form. This means that each account title listed is a summary of several other accounts. For example, the Front-line Expenses include such things as staff and occupancy expenses. Back-line Expenses account includes computer services, maintenance expenses, and long-term interest, among other accounts. In which summary account from the statement of earnings would the following merchandising accounts be located:
   1. Sales returns and allowances
   2. Purchase discounts
   3. Freight-in

(b) Determine Mark's Work Wearhouse actual gross margin rate, operating expenses to sales ratio, and profit margin for the year ended January 30, 1999. Compare its actual profitability to its forecasted profitability goals.

A GLOBAL FOCUS

BYP5-6 In late August 1999, it was announced that two giant French retailers (**Carrefour SA** and **Promodes SA**) would merge. Both companies are primarily supermarkets, but they also operate hypermarkets, which sell everything from cheese to car batteries. Carrefour was present in 20 countries, in Asia, and especially in Latin America. Promodes was strong in Europe, especially Spain and Italy. It also had stores in Asia and Latin America.

The merger created the world's second largest retailer, second only to **Wal-Mart**. While Wal-Mart's total sales still exceed those of the combined company, Wal-Mart's international sales are far lower. This is a serious concern for Wal-Mart, since its primary opportunity for future growth lies outside of North America.

Below are basic financial data for the combined corporation (in French francs) and Wal-Mart (in U.S. dollars). Even though their results are presented in different currencies, by employing ratios, we can make some basic comparisons.

	Carrefour-Promodes (in billions)	Wal-Mart (in billions)
Sales	FF298.0	$137.6
Cost of goods sold	274.0	108.7
Operating expenses	9.6	22.4
Net earnings	5.5	4.4
Total assets	155.0	50.0
Average total assets	140.4	47.7
Current assets	63.5	21.1
Current liabilities	85.8	16.8
Total liabilities	114.2	28.9

Instructions

Compare the two companies by answering the following:

(a) Calculate the gross profit rate and operating expense to sales ratio for each company. Discuss their relative profitability.
(b) Calculate the return on assets ratio and profit margin ratio. Discuss their relative profitability.
(c) Calculate the current ratios and the debt to total assets ratios for the two companies. Discuss their relative liquidity and solvency.
(d) What concerns might you have in relying on this comparison?

FINANCIAL ANALYSIS ON THE WEB

www.wiley.com/canada/kimmel

BYP5-7 Identify profitability ratios for **Nortel Networks Corp.**, and compare this information to industry, sector and market indices.

Instructions

Specific requirements for this web case can be found on the Kimmel website.

CRITICAL THINKING

COLLABORATIVE LEARNING ACTIVITY

BYP5-8 Three years ago Kathy Webb and her brother-in-law John Utley opened FedCo Department Store. For the first two years, business was good, but the following condensed earnings results for 2001 were disappointing:

FEDCO DEPARTMENT STORE
Statement of Earnings
For the Year Ended December 31, 2001

Net sales	$700,000
Cost of goods sold	546,000
Gross profit	154,000
Operating expenses	
Selling expenses	100,000
Administrative expenses	25,000
	125,000
Net earnings	$ 29,000

Kathy believes the problem lies in the relatively low gross profit rate (gross profit divided by net sales) of 22%. John believes the problem is that operating expenses are too high. Kathy thinks the gross profit rate can be improved by making two changes: (1) increase average selling prices by 17%—this increase is expected to lower sales volume so that total sales will increase only 6%—and (2) buy merchandise in larger quantities and take all purchase discounts—these changes are expected to increase the gross profit rate by 3%. Kathy does not anticipate that these changes will have any effect on operating expenses.

John thinks expenses can be cut by making these two changes: (1) cut 2001 sales salaries of $60,000 in half and give sales personnel a commission of 2% of net sales, (2) reduce store deliveries to one day per week rather than twice a week—this change will reduce 2001 delivery expenses of $30,000 by 40%. John feels that these changes will not have any effect on net sales.

Kathy and John come to you for help in deciding the best way to improve net earnings.

Instructions

With the class divided into groups answer the following:

(a) Prepare a condensed statement of earnings for 2002 assuming (1) Kathy's changes are implemented and (2) John's ideas are adopted.
(b) What is your recommendation to Kathy and John?
(c) Prepare a condensed statement of earnings for 2002 assuming both sets of proposed changes are made.
(d) Discuss the impact that other factors might have. For example, would increasing the

quantity of inventory increase costs? Would a salary cut affect employee morale? Would decreased morale affect sales? Would decreased store deliveries decrease customer satisfaction? What other suggestions might be considered?

COMMUNICATION ACTIVITY

BYP5-9 Consider the following events, which are listed in chronological order:

1. Dexter Maersk decides to buy a custom-made snowboard and calls The Great Canadian Snowboard Company, Inc. to inquire about its products.
2. Dexter asks Great Canadian Snowboard to manufacture a custom board for him.
3. The company sends Dexter a purchase order to fill out, which he immediately completes, signs, and sends back.
4. Great Canadian Snowboard receives Dexter's purchase order and begins working on the board.
5. The Great Canadian Snowboard Company has its fiscal year end. At this time, Dexter's board is 75% completed.
6. The company completes the snowboard for Dexter and notifies him to take delivery.
7. Dexter picks up his snowboard from the company and carefully takes it home.
8. Dexter tries the snowboard out and likes it so much that he paints his initials on it.
9. The Great Canadian Snowboard Company bills Dexter for the cost of the snowboard.
10. The company receives partial payment from Dexter.
11. The company receives payment of the balance due from Dexter.

Instructions

In a memo to the president of The Great Canadian Snowboard Company, answer these questions:

(a) When should The Great Canadian Snowboard Company record the revenue and cost related to the snowboard? Refer to the revenue recognition principle in your answer.

(b) Suppose that with his purchase order Dexter was required to make a down payment. Would that change your answer to part (a)?

ETHICS CASE

BYP5-10 Rita Pelzer was just hired as the assistant treasurer of Yorkshire Stores, a specialty chain store company that has nine retail stores concentrated in one metropolitan area. Among other things, the payment of all invoices is centralized in one of the departments Rita will manage. Her primary responsibility is to maintain the company's high credit rating by paying all bills when due and to take advantage of all cash discounts.

Jamie Caterino, the former assistant treasurer, who has been promoted to treasurer, is training Rita in her new duties. He instructs Rita that she is to continue the practice of preparing all cheques "net of discount" and dating the cheques the last day of the discount period. "But," Jamie continues, "we always hold the cheques at least four days beyond the discount period before mailing them. That way we get another four days of interest on our money. Most of our creditors need our business and don't complain. And, if they scream about our missing the discount period, we blame it on the mailroom or the post office. We've only lost one discount out of every hundred we take that way. I think everybody does it. By the way, welcome to our team!"

Instructions

(a) What are the ethical considerations in this case?

(b) What stakeholders are harmed or benefited?

(c) Should Rita continue the practice started by Jamie? Does she have any choice?

Answers to Self-Study Questions

1. a 2. c 3. c 4. b 5. c 6. b 7. d 8. c 9. c 10. a

Answer to Loblaw Review It Question 4

Loblaw uses a multiple-step statement of earnings and reports its non-operating interest income and expense separate from operating earnings. However, the first portion of its statement of earnings are not the same as the multiple-step statements presented in this Chapter. Loblaw does not separately report its cost of sales, or its gross profit, for competitive reasons.

Loblaws
A passion for food... *and a lot more!*

CHAPTER 6

Reporting and Analysing Inventory

STUDY OBJECTIVES

After studying this chapter, you should be able to:

1. Explain the recording of purchases and sales of inventory under a periodic inventory system.
2. Explain how to determine cost of goods sold under a periodic inventory system.
3. Describe the steps in determining inventory quantities.
4. Identify the unique features of the statement of earnings for a merchandising company under a periodic inventory system.
5. Explain the basis of accounting for inventories and apply the inventory cost flow methods under a periodic inventory system.
6. Explain the financial statement effects of each of the inventory cost flow assumptions.
7. Explain the lower of cost and market basis of accounting for inventories.
8. Calculate and interpret the inventory turnover ratio.

How Many Dump Trucks Did You Want?

Let's talk inventory—BIG inventory. The world's largest dump truck, the Caterpillar 797, is as tall as a three-storey building and has a capacity of over 325 tonnes. The first 19 of these square behemoths rolled off the production line in 1999, and six were promptly sent to Fort McMurray, Alberta—no easy feat, since many highways and bridges can't take their weight— to be tested at Syncrude Canada's oil extraction project before Caterpillar goes into a full production cycle of up to 200 units per year.

A Cat 797 retails for about $4.5 million, depending on the options—and requires one heck of a big garage for storage. You can imagine, therefore, that the company wants to avoid having too much of this kind of inventory sitting around tying up its resources. Conversely, it has to have enough inventory to meet its customers' demands. In short, Caterpillar is a big company that makes big products—and has big inventory challenges.

Headquartered in Peoria, Illinois, Caterpillar, the world's largest manufacturer and retailer of construction and mining products, has manufacturing plants in 16 countries and sells products in nearly 200 countries. Already a global organization—exports account for some 50% of its sales—Caterpillar is investing in new markets such as China, the former Soviet republics, Central Europe, and a number of other developing nations. In Canada, it has a Montreal manufacturing plant and financial services locations in Calgary and Toronto.

After a difficult period in the 1980s, Caterpillar today enjoys record sales, profits, and growth; and a big part of this turnaround can be attributed to its effective management of inventory. Between 1991 and 1999, Caterpillar's sales increased by nearly 90%, while its inventory increased by only 40%. In the early 1990s, the average item went from 87 days in inventory to only 57 days.

To achieve this dramatic reduction in the amount of resources tied up in inventory, while continuing to meet its customers' needs, Caterpillar used a two-pronged approach. First, it

On the World Wide Web
Caterpillar Inc.
http://www.caterpillar.com

completed a factory modernization program in 1993, which dramatically increased its production efficiency: the time it takes to manufacture a part was reduced by an incredible 75%.

Second, Caterpillar vastly improved its distribution system. It ships 84,000 items daily from 25 distribution centres located around the world (centres which add up to nearly 1 million square metres of warehouse space—remember, we're talking dump trucks and bulldozers). The company guarantees that it can get any part to any customer, anywhere in the world, in 24 hours.

In fact, its distribution system is so advanced that Caterpillar has created a separate unit, Caterpillar Logistics Services, that warehouses and distributes other companies' products—from running shoes to software to auto parts.

The bottom line is that Caterpillar's inventory management and accounting practices make a crucial contribution to its own and other companies' profitability.

PREVIEW OF CHAPTER 6

In the previous chapter, we discussed the accounting for merchandise inventory using a perpetual inventory system. In this chapter, we explain the periodic inventory system and methods used to calculate the cost of inventory on hand at the balance sheet date. We conclude by illustrating methods for analysing inventory.

The content and organization of this chapter are as follows:

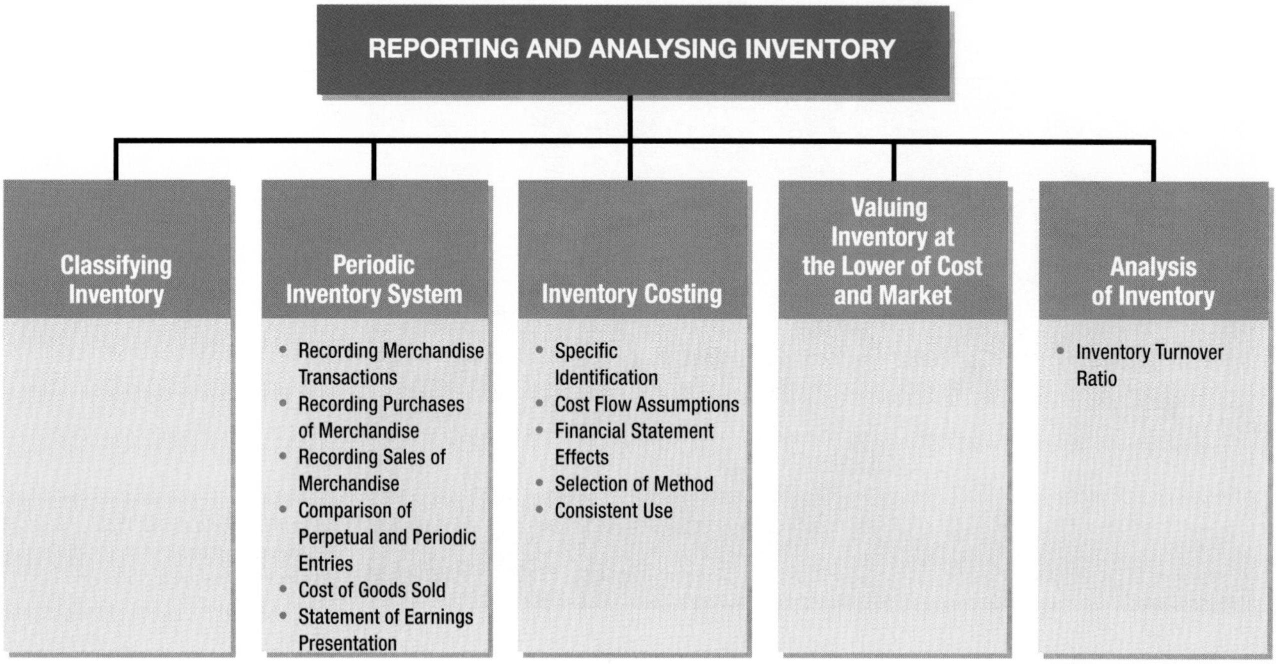

CLASSIFYING INVENTORY

How a company classifies its inventory depends on whether the firm is a merchandiser or a manufacturer. In a **merchandising** company, such as those described in Chapter 5, inventory consists of many different items. For example, in a grocery store, canned goods, dairy products, meats, and produce are just a few of the inventory items on hand. These items have two common characteristics: (1) they are owned by the company, and (2) they are in a form ready for sale to customers in the ordinary course of business. Thus, only one inventory classification, **merchandise inventory**, is needed to describe the many different items that make up the total inventory.

In a **manufacturing** company, some of its inventory may not yet be ready for sale. As a result, inventory is usually classified into three categories: finished goods, work in process, and raw materials. **Finished goods inventory** is manufactured items that are completed and ready for sale. **Work in process** is that portion of manufactured inventory that has been placed into the production process but is not yet complete. **Raw materials** are the basic goods that will be used in production but have not yet been sent into production. For example, Caterpillar classifies earth-moving trucks completed and ready for sale as **finished goods**. The trucks on the assembly line in various stages of production are classified as **work in process**. The steel, glass, tires, and other components that are on hand waiting to be used in the production of trucks are identified as **raw materials**.

By observing the levels and changes in the levels of these three inventory types, financial statement users can gain insight into management's production plans. For example, low levels of raw materials and high levels of finished goods could suggest that management believes it has enough inventory on hand and will slow down production—perhaps in anticipation of a recession. On the other hand, high levels of raw materials and low levels of finished goods probably indicate that management is planning to step up production.

The accounting concepts discussed in this chapter apply to the inventory classifications of both merchandising and manufacturing companies. Our focus here is primarily on merchandise inventory. Manufacturing inventories will be discussed in more detail in a managerial accounting course.

Periodic Inventory System

As described in Chapter 5, one of two basic systems of accounting for inventories may be used: (1) the perpetual inventory system or (2) the periodic inventory system. In Chapter 5 we focused on the characteristics of the perpetual inventory system. In this chapter we discuss and illustrate the periodic inventory system. One key difference between the two systems is the point at which cost of goods sold is calculated. For a visual reminder of this difference, you may want to refer back to Illustration 5-3.

RECORDING MERCHANDISE TRANSACTIONS

STUDY OBJECTIVE 1

Explain the recording of purchases and sales of inventory under a periodic inventory system.

In a **periodic inventory system**, revenues from the sale of merchandise are recorded when sales are made, just as in a perpetual system. Unlike the perpetual system, however, **no attempt is made on the date of sale to record the cost of the merchandise sold**. Instead, a physical inventory count is taken at the **end of the period** to determine (1) the cost of the merchandise then on hand and (2) the cost of the goods sold during the period. And, under a periodic system, purchases of merchandise are recorded in the Purchases account rather than the Merchandise Inventory account. Also, in a periodic system, purchase returns and allowances, purchase discounts, and freight costs on purchases are recorded in separate temporary accounts.

To show the recording of merchandise transactions under a periodic inventory system, we will use the purchase/sale transactions between PW Audio Supply and Sauk Stereo, Inc. which illustrated the perpetual inventory system in Chapter 5.

RECORDING PURCHASES OF MERCHANDISE

On the basis of the sales invoice (Illustration 5-4, shown on page 206) and receipt of the merchandise ordered from PW Audio Supply, Sauk Stereo records the $3,800 purchase as follows:

May	4	Purchases	3,800	
		Accounts Payable		3,800
		(To record goods purchased on account, terms 2/10, n/30)		

A	=	L	+	SE
		+3,800		-3,800

Purchases is a temporary account whose normal balance is a debit.

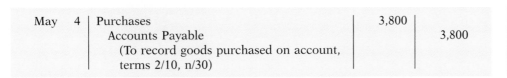

Freight Costs

When the purchaser directly incurs the freight costs, the account Freight-in (or Transportation-in) is debited. For example, if upon delivery of the goods on May 4, Sauk pays Acme Freight Company $150 for freight charges on its purchase from PW Audio Supply, the entry on Sauk's books is as follows:

A	=	L	+	SE
-150				-150

May	4	Freight-in (Transportation-in)	150	
		Cash		150
		(To record payment of freight)		

Like Purchases, Freight-in is a temporary account whose normal balance is a debit. In addition, **freight-in is part of cost of goods purchased**. The reason is that cost of goods purchased should include any freight charges necessary to bring the goods to the purchaser. Finally, freight costs are not subject to a purchase discount. Purchase discounts only apply to the invoice cost of the merchandise.

BUSINESS INSIGHT

Management Perspective

Many companies have invested large amounts of time and money in automated shipping systems. One such system is Air Canada's waybill database system. Until the mid-1990s, Air Canada drowned in a sea of paper as it tried to maintain waybill slips on file for seven years, for every piece of cargo it shipped throughout the world. It was often difficult for Air Canada employees to find a particular slip, but this difficulty was not appreciated by customers trying to track a missing shipment. Now, waybills are scanned into a database and indexed. Customers can call a 1-800 number to find the location of their shipment at any time of the day or night.

Purchase Returns and Allowances

Because $300 of merchandise received from PW Audio Supply is defective, Sauk Stereo returns the goods and prepares the following entry to recognize the return:

A	=	L	+	SE
		-300		+300

May	8	Accounts Payable	300	
		Purchase Returns and Allowances		300
		(To record return of defective goods purchased from PW Audio Supply)		

Purchase Returns and Allowances is a temporary account whose normal balance is a credit.

Purchase Discounts

On May 14, Sauk Stereo pays the balance due on account to PW Audio Supply, taking the 2% cash discount allowed by PW Audio for payment within 10 days. The payment and discount are recorded by Sauk Stereo as follows:

May 14	Accounts Payable ($3,800 − $300)	3,500	
	Purchase Discounts ($3,500 × .02)		70
	Cash		3,430
	(To record payment to PW Audio Supply within the discount period)		

A	=	L	+	SE
−3,430		−3,500		+70

Purchase Discounts is a temporary account whose normal balance is a credit.

RECORDING SALES OF MERCHANDISE

The sale of $3,800 of merchandise to Sauk Stereo on May 4 (sales invoice No. 731, Illustration 5-4) is recorded by the seller, PW Audio Supply, as follows:

May 4	Accounts Receivable	3,800	
	Sales		3,800
	(To record credit sales per invoice #731 to Sauk Stereo)		

A	=	L	+	SE
+3,800				+3,800

Sales Returns and Allowances

To record the returned goods received from Sauk Stereo on May 8, PW Audio Supply records the $300 sales return as follows:

May 8	Sales Returns and Allowances	300	
	Accounts Receivable		300
	(To record return of goods from Sauk Stereo)		

A	=	L	+	SE
−300				−300

Sales Discounts

On May 15, PW Audio Supply receives payment of $3,430 on account from Sauk Stereo. PW Audio honours the 2% cash discount and records the payment of Sauk's account receivable in full as follows:

May 15	Cash	3,430	
	Sales Discounts ($3,500 × .02)	70	
	Accounts Receivable ($3,800 − $300)		3,500
	(To record collection from Sauk Stereo within 2/10, n/30 discount period)		

A	=	L	+	SE
+3,430				−70
−3,500				

COMPARISON OF ENTRIES—PERPETUAL VS. PERIODIC

The periodic inventory system entries just seen are shown in Illustration 6-1 next to those that were illustrated in Chapter 5 (pages 241–247) under the perpetual inventory system for both Sauk Stereo and PW Audio Supply.

Illustration 6-1 Comparison of journal entries under perpetual and periodic inventory systems

ENTRIES ON SAUK STEREO'S BOOKS (PURCHASER)

Date	Transaction	Perpetual Inventory System			Periodic Inventory System		
May 4	Purchase of merchandise on credit.	Merchandise Inventory	3,800		Purchases	3,800	
		Accounts Payable		3,800	Accounts Payable		3,800
May 4	Freight costs on purchases.	Merchandise Inventory	150		Freight-In	150	
		Cash		150	Cash		150
May 8	Purchase returns and allowances.	Accounts Payable	300		Accounts Payable	300	
		Merchandise Inventory		300	Purchase Returns and Allowances		300
May 14	Payment on account with a discount.	Accounts Payable	3,500		Accounts Payable	3,500	
		Cash		3,430	Purchase Discounts		70
		Merchandise Inventory		70	Cash		3,430

ENTRIES ON PW AUDIO SUPPLY'S BOOKS (SELLER)

Date	Transaction	Perpetual Inventory System			Periodic Inventory System		
May 4	Sale of merchandise on credit.	Accounts Receivable	3,800		Accounts Receivable	3,800	
		Sales		3,800	Sales		3,800
		Cost of Goods Sold	2,400		No entry for cost of goods sold		
		Merchandise Inventory		2,400			
May 8	Return of merchandise sold.	Sales Returns and Allowances	300		Sales Returns and Allowances	300	
		Accounts Receivable		300	Accounts Receivable		300
		Merchandise Inventory	140		No entry		
		Cost of Goods Sold		140			
May 15	Cash received on account with a discount.	Cash	3,430		Cash	3,430	
		Sales Discounts	70		Sales Discounts	70	
		Accounts Receivable		3,500	Accounts Receivable		3,500

COST OF GOODS SOLD

STUDY OBJECTIVE 2

Explain how to determine cost of goods sold under a periodic inventory system.

Under a periodic inventory system, a running account of the changes in inventory is not recorded when either purchases or sales occur. Neither the daily amount of inventory of merchandise on hand nor the cost of goods sold is known. To determine the **cost of goods sold** under a periodic inventory system, it is necessary to (1) record purchases of merchandise, (2) determine the cost of goods purchased, and (3) determine the cost of goods on hand at the beginning and end of the accounting period. The cost of goods on hand must be determined by (a) counting physical inventory and (b) applying costs to the items counted in the inventory.

Determining Cost of Goods Purchased

Under a periodic inventory system, various accounts, such as purchases, freight-in, purchase discounts, and purchase returns and allowances, are used to record the cost of goods purchased. (A perpetual system uses only one account, Merchandise Inventory.) These accounts, with their impact on cost of goods purchased, are listed in Illustration 6-2.

Illustration 6-2 Accounts used to record purchases of inventory

Item	Periodic Inventory Account Title	Normal Balance	Effect on Cost of Goods Purchased
Invoice price	Purchases	Debit	Increase
Freight charges paid by purchaser	Freight-in	Debit	Increase
Purchase discounts taken by purchaser	Purchase Discounts	Credit	Decrease
Purchase returns and allowances granted by seller	Purchase Returns and Allowances	Credit	Decrease

To determine cost of goods purchased, we begin with **gross** purchases. From this amount, we subtract any savings resulting from purchase discounts and any reductions resulting from the return of unwanted goods. The result is **net purchases**. Because freight charges are a necessary cost incurred to acquire inventory, **freight-in** is added to net purchases to arrive at **cost of goods purchased**. To summarize:

1. The accounts with credit balances (Purchase Returns and Allowances and Purchase Discounts) are subtracted from Purchases to get **net purchases**.
2. Freight-in is added to net purchases to arrive at **cost of goods purchased**.

To illustrate, assume that PW Audio Supply shows these balances for the accounts above: purchases $325,000; purchase returns and allowances $10,400; purchase discounts $6,800; and freight-in $12,200. Net purchases and cost of goods purchased are $307,800 and $320,000, respectively, as calculated in Illustration 6-3.

Illustration 6-3 Calculation of net purchases and cost of goods purchased

	Purchases		$ 325,000
(1)	Less: Purchase returns and allowances	$10,400	
	Purchase discounts	6,800	17,200
	Net purchases		**307,800**
(2)	Add: Freight-in		12,200
	Cost of goods purchased		**$320,000**

All four of the accounts used in the periodic system are temporary accounts. They are used to determine cost of goods sold. Therefore, the balances in these accounts are reduced to zero at the end of each accounting period (i.e., annually).

Determining Inventory Quantities

STUDY OBJECTIVE 3

Describe the steps in determining inventory quantities.

Companies that use a periodic inventory system take a physical inventory to determine the inventory on hand at the balance sheet date and to calculate cost of goods sold. Even businesses that use a perpetual inventory system take a physical inventory. They do so to check the accuracy and quality of the "book inventory" and to determine the amount of inventory shortage or shrinkage due to wasted raw materials, shoplifting, or employee theft.

Determining inventory quantities involves two steps: (1) taking a physical inventory of goods on hand and (2) determining the ownership of goods.

Taking a Physical Inventory. Taking a physical inventory involves actually counting, weighing, or measuring each kind of inventory on hand. In many companies, taking an inventory is a formidable task. Retailers such as Caterpillar, Zellers, Canadian Tire, or Loblaw have thousands of different inventory items. An inventory count is generally more accurate when goods are not being sold or received during the counting. Consequently, companies often "take inventory" when the business is closed or when business is slow. Many retailers close early on a chosen day in January—after the holiday sales and returns, when inventories are at their lowest level—to count inventory. Recall from Chapter 5 that both Wal-Mart and Zellers have year ends at the end of January. Under a periodic inventory system, the physical inventory is taken at the end of the accounting period.

After the physical inventory is taken, the quantity of each kind of inventory is listed on **inventory summary sheets**. To assure the accuracy of the summary sheets, the listing should be verified by a second employee or supervisor. Subsequently, unit costs are applied to the quantities to determine a total cost of the inventory—which is the topic of later sections. Although taking the physical inventory may seem mechanical, an accurate inventory count is important to help companies avoid the negative consequences of poor inventory taking—incorrect financial statements and incorrect income tax returns. Inventory counts also provide a welcome opportunity for management to assess the condition and saleability of the inventory.

BUSINESS INSIGHT

Management Perspective

Failure to observe internal control procedures over inventory contributed to the Great Salad Oil Swindle. In this case, management intentionally overstated its salad oil inventory, which was stored in large holding tanks. Three procedures contributed to overstating the oil inventory. (1) Water added to the bottom of the holding tanks caused the oil to float to the top. Inventory-taking crews who viewed the holding tanks from the top observed only salad oil, when, in fact, as much as 11 out of 12 metres of many of the holding tanks contained water. (2) The company's inventory records listed more holding tanks than it actually had. The company repainted numbers on the tanks after inventory crews examined them, so the crews counted the same tanks twice. (3) Underground pipes pumped oil from one holding tank to another during the inventory taking; therefore, the same salad oil was counted more than once. Although the salad oil swindle was unusual, it demonstrates the complexities involved in assuring that inventory is properly counted.

Determining Ownership of Goods. To determine ownership of goods, two questions must be answered: (1) do all of the goods included in the count belong to the company? And (2) does the company own any goods that were not included in the count?

Goods in Transit. Goods in transit at the end of the period (on board a truck, train, ship, or plane) make determining ownership a bit more complex. The company may have purchased goods that have not yet been received, or it may have sold goods that have not yet been delivered. To arrive at an accurate count, ownership of these goods must be determined.

Goods in transit should be included in the inventory of the company that has legal title to the goods. Legal title is determined by the terms of the sale, as shown in Illustration 6-4 and described below:

Illustration 6-4 Terms of sale

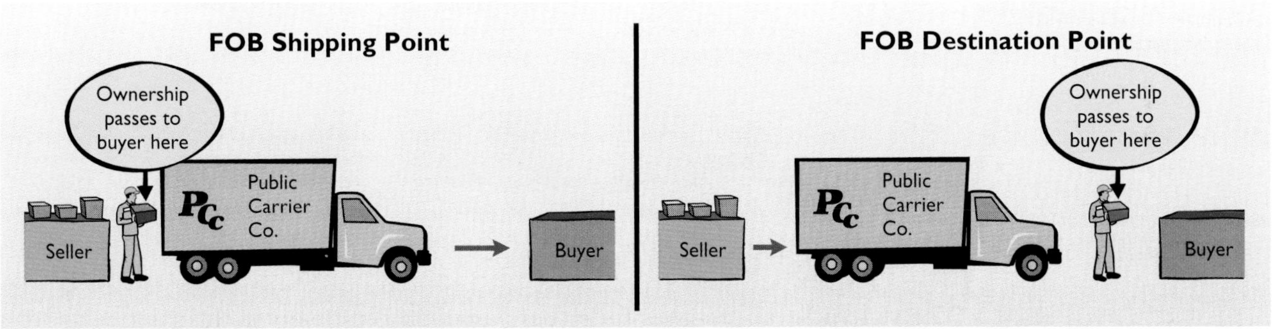

1. When the terms are **FOB (free on board) shipping point**, ownership of the goods passes to the buyer when the public carrier accepts the goods from the seller.
2. When the terms are **FOB destination**, ownership of the goods remains with the seller until the goods reach the buyer.

Alternative Terminology
Other common shipping terms of sale include *FCA* (free carrier), *CIF* (cost, insurance, freight), or *CPT* (carriage paid to).

Consigned Goods. In some lines of business, it is customary to receive a fee for holding the goods of other parties and selling the goods for them without ever taking ownership of the goods. These are called **consigned goods**. For example, you might have a used car that you would like to sell. If you take the item to a dealer, the dealer might be willing to put the car on a lot and charge you a commission if it is sold. But under this agreement the dealer **would not take ownership** of the car—it would still belong to you. Therefore, if an inventory count were taken, the car would not be included in the dealer's inventory. Many car, boat, craft, and antique dealers sell goods on consignment to keep their inventory costs down and to avoid the risk of purchasing an item they won't be able to sell.

The general rule to determine the ownership of goods is that goods belong to whoever has legal title at the inventory cut-off date (e.g., year end). It is very important not only to accurately determine the physical count of your inventory on hand, but to adjust the count for any other inventory located elsewhere or inventory located on your premises that may belong to someone else. As you will learn later in this chapter, errors in determining inventory quantities can have a significant effect on both your statement of earnings and balance sheet, and sometimes for more than one period.

Calculating Cost of Goods Sold

We have now reached the point where we can calculate cost of goods sold. Doing so involves two steps:

1. Add the cost of goods purchased to the cost of goods on hand at the beginning of the period (beginning inventory) to obtain the **cost of goods available for sale.**
2. Subtract the cost of goods on hand at the end of the period (ending inventory) from the cost of goods available for sale to arrive at the **cost of goods sold.**

For PW Audio Supply the cost of goods available for sale and the cost of goods sold are $356,000 and $316,000, respectively. The beginning and ending inventory are assumed to be $36,000 and $40,000, respectively.

Illustration 6-5 Calculation of (1) cost of goods available for sale and (2) cost of goods sold

(1)

Beginning Inventory	+	Cost of Goods Purchased	=	Cost of Goods Available for Sale
$36,000	+	$320,000	=	$356,000

(2)

Cost of Goods Available for Sale	−	Ending Inventory	=	Cost of Goods Sold
$356,000	−	$40,000	=	$316,000

STATEMENT OF EARNINGS PRESENTATION

STUDY OBJECTIVE 4

Identify the unique features of the statement of earnings for a merchandising company under a periodic inventory system.

The statement of earnings for a merchandising company is the same whether a periodic or perpetual inventory system is used, except for the cost of goods sold section. **Under a periodic inventory system, the cost of goods sold section generally contains more detail.** A statement of earnings for PW Audio Supply, using a periodic inventory system, is shown in Illustration 6-6.

Illustration 6-6 Statement of earnings for a merchandising company using a periodic inventory system

PW AUDIO SUPPLY, INC.
Statement of Earnings
For the Year Ended December 31, 2001

Sales revenues				
Sales				$480,000
Less: Sales returns and allowances			$ 12,000	
Sales discounts			8,000	20,000
Net sales				460,000
Cost of goods sold				
Inventory, January 1			36,000	
Purchases		$325,000		
Less: Purchase returns and allowances	$10,400			
Purchase discounts	6,800	17,200		
Net purchases		307,800		
Add: Freight-in		12,200		
Cost of goods purchased			320,000	
Cost of goods available for sale			356,000	
Inventory, December 31			40,000	
Cost of goods sold				316,000
Gross profit				144,000
Operating expenses				114,000
Earnings before income tax				30,000
Income tax expense				7,500
Net earnings				$ 22,500

Helpful Hint The far right column identifies the major subdivisions of the statement of earnings. The next column identifies the primary items that make up cost of goods sold of $316,000; in addition, contra revenue items of $20,000 are reported. The third column explains cost of goods purchased of $320,000. The fourth column reports contra purchase items of $17,200.

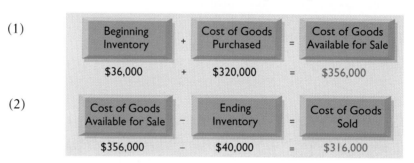

The use of the periodic inventory system does not affect the content of the balance sheet. As under the perpetual system, the ending merchandise inventory balance is reported at the same amount in the current assets section.

In the remainder of this chapter we address additional issues related to inventory costing. To simplify our presentation, we continue to assume a periodic inventory accounting system.

BEFORE YOU GO ON . . .

Review It

1. Discuss how cost of goods sold is determined in a periodic inventory system.
2. What accounts are used in determining the cost of goods purchased?
3. In what ways is a perpetual inventory system different from a periodic inventory system?

Do It

Aerosmith Company Ltd.'s accounting records show the following at year end: purchase discounts $3,400; freight-in $6,100; sales $240,000; purchases $162,500; beginning inventory $18,000; ending inventory $20,000; sales discounts $10,000; purchase returns $5,200; operating expenses $57,000; and income tax expense $4,000. Calculate the following amounts for Aerosmith Company:

(a) Net sales
(b) Cost of goods purchased
(c) Cost of goods sold
(d) Gross profit
(e) Net earnings

Reasoning: To determine the required amounts, it is important to understand the components used to measure net earnings for a merchandising company. For example, it is necessary to know the relationships between sales and net sales, goods available for sale and cost of goods sold, and gross profit and net earnings.

Solution:

(a) Net sales:
Sales − Sales discounts
$240,000 − $10,000 = $230,000

(b) Cost of goods purchased:
Purchases − Purchase returns − Purchase discounts = Net purchases + Freight-in
$162,500 − $5,200 − $3,400 = $153,900 + $6,100 = $160,000

(c) Cost of goods sold:
Beginning inventory + Cost of goods purchased = Cost of goods available for sale − Ending inventory
$18,000 + $160,000 = $178,000 − $20,000 = $158,000

(d) Gross profit:
Net sales − Cost of goods sold
$230,000 − $158,000 = $72,000

(e) Net earnings:
Gross profit − Operating expenses − Income tax expense
$72,000 − $57,000 − $4,000 = $11,000

Inventory Costing

STUDY OBJECTIVE 5

Explain the basis of accounting for inventories and apply the inventory cost flow methods under a periodic inventory system.

Purchases, purchase discounts, purchase returns and allowances, and freight-in are all costs included in the cost of goods available for sale. Cost of goods available for sale must be allocated between cost of goods sold and ending inventory at the end of the accounting period. First, the costs assignable to the ending inventory are determined. Second, the cost of the ending inventory is subtracted from the cost of goods available for sale to determine the cost of goods sold. (Refer back to Illustration 6-5 to see this calculation.)

Determining ending inventory can be complicated if the units on hand for a specific item of inventory have been purchased at different prices. Assume, for example, that Crivitz TV purchases three 32-inch TVs at costs of $700, $750, and $800. During the year, two sets are sold at $1,200 each. Ending inventory might be $700, $750, or $800, and corresponding cost of goods sold might be $1,550 ($750 + $800), $1,500 ($700 + $800), or $1,450 ($700 + $750), respectively, depending on how Crivitz measures the cost flows of the inventory purchased and sold. In this section we discuss alternative inventory costing methods.

SPECIFIC IDENTIFICATION

If we determine that the TV in Crivitz's inventory is the one originally purchased for $750, then the ending inventory is $750 and cost of goods sold is $1,500 for the two TVs sold ($700 + $800). If Crivitz can positively identify which particular units were sold and which are still in ending inventory, it can use the **specific identification method** of inventory costing. In this case ending inventory and cost of goods sold are easily and accurately determined.

Illustration 6-7 Specific identification

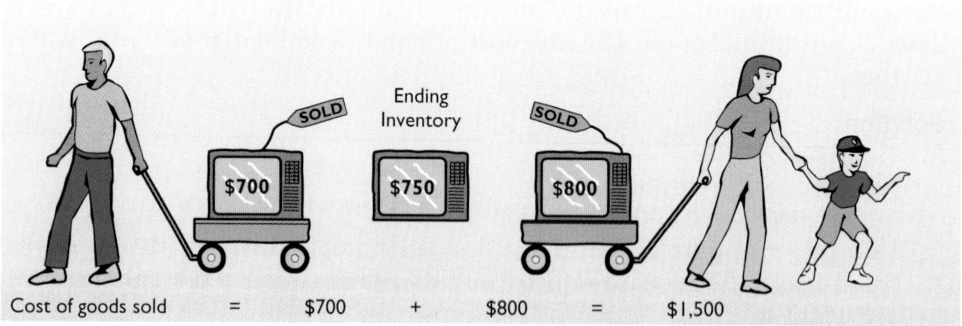

Helpful Hint A major disadvantage of the specific identification method is that management may be able to manipulate net earnings through the selection of specific items to be sold.

Specific identification is possible when a company sells a limited variety of high-unit-cost items that can be identified clearly from the time of purchase through the time of sale. Examples of such companies are automobile dealerships (cars, trucks, and vans), music stores (pianos and organs), and antique shops (tables and cabinets).

But what if we cannot specifically identify particular inventory units? For example, drug, grocery, and hardware stores sell thousands of relatively low-unit-cost items of inventory. These items are often indistinguishable from one another, making it impossible or impractical to track each item's cost. In that case, we must make assumptions, called **cost flow assumptions**, about which units were sold.

COST FLOW ASSUMPTIONS

Because specific identification is often impractical, other cost flow methods are allowed. These differ from specific identification as they assume flows of costs that may be unrelated to the physical flow of goods. There are three commonly assumed cost flow methods:

1. First-in, first-out (FIFO)
2. Average cost
3. Last-in, first-out (LIFO)

International Note

A survey of accounting standards in 21 major industrial countries found that all three methods were permissible. Even so, very few companies worldwide use LIFO, except in the U.S.

No accounting rule requires the cost flow assumption to be consistent with the physical movement of goods. The selection of the appropriate cost flow method is made by management and **should be the one which results in the fairest matching of costs against revenues** in the circumstances.

To illustrate these three inventory cost flow methods, we will assume that Wynneck Electronics Ltd. uses a periodic inventory system and has the information shown in Illustration 6-8 for its Astro condenser.

Illustration 6-8 Cost of goods available for sale

WYNNECK ELECTRONICS LTD.
Astro Condensers

Date	Explanation	Units	Unit Cost	Total Cost
Jan. 1	Beginning inventory	100	$10	$ 1,000
Apr. 15	Purchase	200	11	2,200
Aug. 24	Purchase	300	12	3,600
Nov. 27	Purchase	400	13	5,200
	Total	1,000		$12,000

The company had a total of 1,000 units available that it could have sold during the period. The total cost of these units was $12,000. A physical inventory at the end of the year determined that during the year 550 units were sold and 450 units were in inventory at December 31. The question then is how to determine what unit costs to use to value the goods sold and the ending inventory. The sum of the cost allocated to the units sold plus the cost of the units in inventory must add up to $12,000, the total cost of all goods available for sale.

First-In, First-Out (FIFO)

The **FIFO method** assumes that the **earliest goods** purchased are the first to be sold. FIFO often parallels the actual physical flow of merchandise because it generally is good business practice to sell the oldest units first. Under the FIFO method, therefore, the **costs** of the earliest goods purchased are the first to be recognized as cost of goods sold. (Note that this does not necessarily mean that the oldest units *are* sold first, but that the costs of the oldest units are recognized first. In a bin of picture hangers at the hardware store, for example, no one really knows, nor would it matter, which hangers are sold first.) The allocation of the cost of goods available for sale at Wynneck Electronics under FIFO is shown in Illustration 6-9.

Note that under FIFO, since it is assumed that the first goods sold were the first goods purchased, ending inventory is based on the prices of the most recent units purchased. That is, **under FIFO, the cost of the ending inventory is obtained by taking the unit cost of the most recent purchase and working backward until all units of inventory have been costed (LISH—last in, still here)**. In this example, the 450 units of ending inventory must be costed using the most recent purchase prices. The last purchase was 400 units at $13 on November 27. The remaining 50 units are costed at the price of the second most recent purchase, $12, on August 24. Next, cost of goods sold can be calculated by subtracting the cost of the units **not sold** (ending inventory) from the cost of all goods available for sale.

Illustration 6-9
Allocation of costs—FIFO method

POOL OF COSTS
COST OF GOODS AVAILABLE FOR SALE

Date	Explanation	Units	Unit Cost	Total Cost
Jan. 1	Beginning inventory	100	$10	$ 1,000
Apr. 15	Purchase	200	11	2,200
Aug. 24	Purchase	300	12	3,600
Nov. 27	Purchase	400	13	5,200
	Total	1,000		**$12,000**

STEP 1: ENDING INVENTORY

Date	Units	Unit Cost	Total Cost
Nov. 27	400	$13	$ 5,200
Aug. 24	50	12	600
Total	450		**$5,800**

STEP 2: COST OF GOODS SOLD

Cost of goods available for sale	$12,000
Less: Ending inventory	5,800
Cost of goods sold	**$ 6,200**

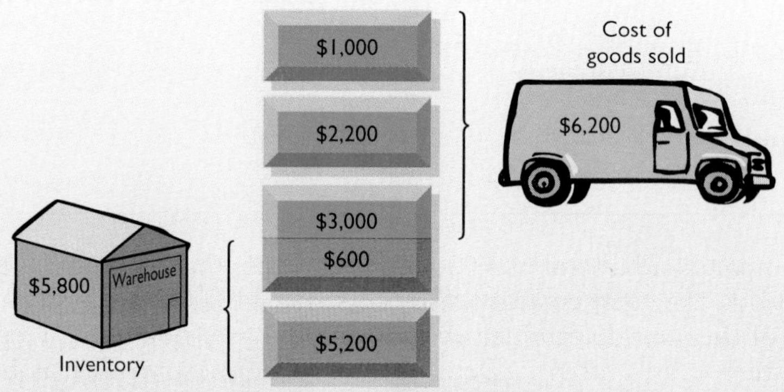

Helpful Hint The calculation of FIFO ending inventory is based on the LISH (last in, still here) assumption.

Illustration 6-10 demonstrates that cost of goods sold can also be calculated by costing the 550 units sold using the prices of the first 550 units acquired. Note that of the 300 units purchased on August 24, only 250 units are assumed sold. This agrees with our calculation of the cost of ending inventory, where 50 of these units were assumed unsold and thus included in ending inventory.

Illustration 6-10 Proof of cost of goods sold

Date	Units	Unit Cost	Total Cost
Jan. 1	100	$10	$1,000
Apr. 15	200	11	2,200
Aug. 24	250	12	3,000
Total	550		**$6,200**

Helpful Hint The calculation of the FIFO cost of goods sold is based on the FIFO (first-in, first-out) assumption.

Because of the potential for calculation errors, it is the authors' preference to calculate separately both the ending inventory and cost of goods sold amounts. The total of these two amounts can then be compared to the cost of goods available for sale amount to check the accuracy of the reported results.

Average Cost

The **average cost method** assumes that the goods available for sale are homogeneous. Under this method, the allocation of the cost of goods available for sale is made on the basis of the **weighted average unit cost** incurred. The formula and a sample calculation of the weighted average unit cost are given in Illustration 6-11.

Cost of Goods Available for Sale ÷ Total Units Available for Sale = Weighted Average Unit Cost

$12,000 ÷ 1,000 = $12.00

Illustration 6-11
Formula for weighted average unit cost

The weighted average unit cost is then applied to the units on hand to determine the cost of the ending inventory. The allocation of the cost of goods available for sale at Wynneck Electronics using weighted average cost is shown in Illustration 6-12.

Illustration 6-12
Allocation of costs—average cost method

POOL OF COSTS
COST OF GOODS AVAILABLE FOR SALE

Date	Explanation	Units	Unit Cost	Total Cost
Jan. 1	Beginning inventory	100	$10	$ 1,000
Apr. 15	Purchase	200	11	2,200
Aug. 24	Purchase	300	12	3,600
Nov. 27	Purchase	400	13	5,200
	Total	1,000		$12,000

STEP 1: ENDING INVENTORY

$12,000 ÷ 1,000 = $12.00

Units		Weighted Average Unit Cost		Total Cost
450	×	$12.00	=	$5,400

STEP 2: COST OF GOODS SOLD

Cost of goods available for sale	$12,000
Less: Ending inventory	5,400
Cost of goods sold	$ 6,600

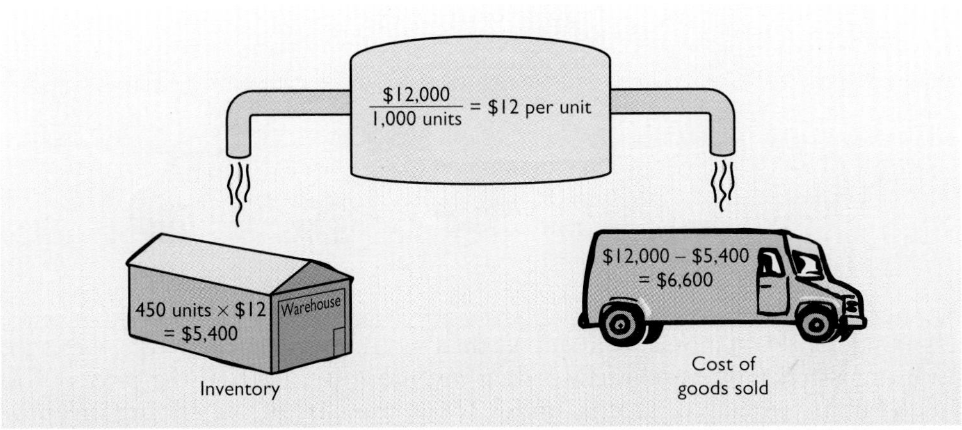

We can verify the cost of goods sold under this method by multiplying the units sold by the weighted average unit cost (550 × $12 = $6,600). Note that this method does not use the average of the unit costs. That average is $11.50 ($10 + $11 + $12 + $13 = $46; $46 ÷ 4 = $11.50). The average cost method instead uses the average **weighted** by the quantities purchased at each unit cost.

Last-In, First-Out (LIFO)

The **LIFO method** assumes that the **latest goods** purchased are the first to be sold. LIFO seldom coincides with the actual physical flow of inventory. (Exceptions include goods stored in piles, such as coal or hay, where goods are removed from the top of the pile as sold.) Under the LIFO method, the **costs** of the latest goods purchased are the first to be recognized as cost of goods sold. The allocation of the cost of goods available for sale at Wynneck Electronics under LIFO is shown in Illustration 6-13.

Illustration 6-13
Allocation of costs—LIFO method

POOL OF COSTS
COST OF GOODS AVAILABLE FOR SALE

Date	Explanation	Units	Unit Cost	Total Cost
Jan. 1	Beginning inventory	100	$10	$ 1,000
Apr. 15	Purchase	200	11	2,200
Aug. 24	Purchase	300	12	3,600
Nov. 27	Purchase	400	13	5,200
	Total	1,000		$12,000

STEP 1: ENDING INVENTORY

Date	Units	Unit Cost	Total Cost
Jan. 1	100	$10	$ 1,000
Apr. 15	200	11	2,200
Aug. 24	150	12	1,800
Total	450		$5,000

STEP 2: COST OF GOODS SOLD

Cost of goods available for sale	$12,000
Less: Ending inventory	5,000
Cost of goods sold	$ 7,000

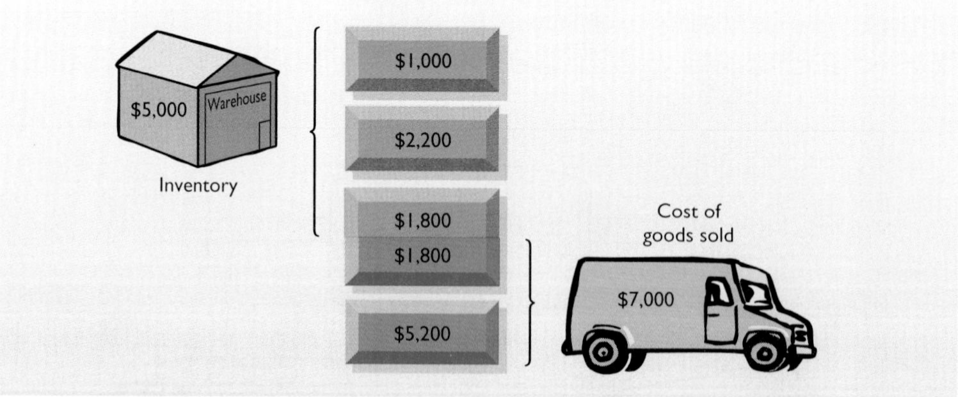

Helpful Hint The calculation of LIFO ending inventory is based on the FISH (first in, still here) assumption.

Under LIFO, since it is assumed that the first goods sold were those that were most recently purchased, ending inventory is based on the prices of the oldest units purchased. That is, **under LIFO, the cost of the ending inventory is obtained by taking the unit cost of the earliest goods available for sale and working forward until all units of inventory have been costed (FISH—first in, still here)**. In this example, the 450 units of ending inventory must be costed using the earliest purchase prices. The first purchase was 100 units at $10 in the January 1 beginning inventory. Then 200 units were purchased at $11. The remaining 150 units needed are costed at $12 per unit (August 24 purchase). Next, cost of goods sold is calculated by subtracting the cost of the units **not sold** (ending inventory) from the cost of all goods available for sale.

Illustration 6-14 demonstrates that cost of goods sold can also be calculated by costing the 550 units sold using the prices of the last 550 units acquired. Note that of the 300 units purchased on August 24, only 150 units are assumed sold. This agrees with our calculation of the cost of ending inventory, where 150 of these units were assumed unsold and thus included in ending inventory.

Date	Units	Unit Cost	Total Cost
Nov. 27	400	$13	$5,200
Aug. 24	150	12	1,800
Total	550		$7,000

Illustration 6-14 Proof of cost of goods sold

Helpful Hint The calculation of LIFO cost of goods sold is based on the LIFO (last-in, first-out) assumption.

Under a periodic inventory system, which we are using here, **all goods purchased during the period are assumed to be available for the first sale, regardless of the date of purchase.**

Perpetual Inventory Cost Flow Assumptions

We have just illustrated the periodic method of calculating cost of goods sold and ending inventory for the assumed cost flow methods. As noted in Chapter 5, companies can allocate their cost of goods available between cost of goods sold and ending inventory using two different systems. In a **periodic inventory system**, this allocation is performed at the end of the accounting period. In a **perpetual inventory system**, this allocation is done each time a sale occurs. Perpetual inventory system calculations are illustrated in Appendix 6A and follow the same general principles outlined in the periodic inventory system.

FINANCIAL STATEMENT EFFECTS OF COST FLOW METHODS

STUDY OBJECTIVE 6

Explain the financial statement effects of each of the inventory cost flow assumptions.

The specific identification method and each of the three assumed cost flow methods are all acceptable for use. For example, Ault Foods, Canadian Tire, and Sobeys currently use the FIFO method of inventory costing. Abitibi-Price, Andrés Wines, and Mountain Equipment Co-op use the average cost method. Alberta Natural Gas, Cominco, and Suncor use LIFO for part or all of their inventory. Indeed, a company may also use more than one cost flow method at the same time. Finning Tractor, for example, uses specific identification to account for its equipment inventory, FIFO to account for about 70% of its inventory of parts and supplies, and average cost to account for the remaining 30%. Illustration 6-15 shows the use of the three assumed cost flow methods in public companies surveyed by *Financial Reporting in Canada.*

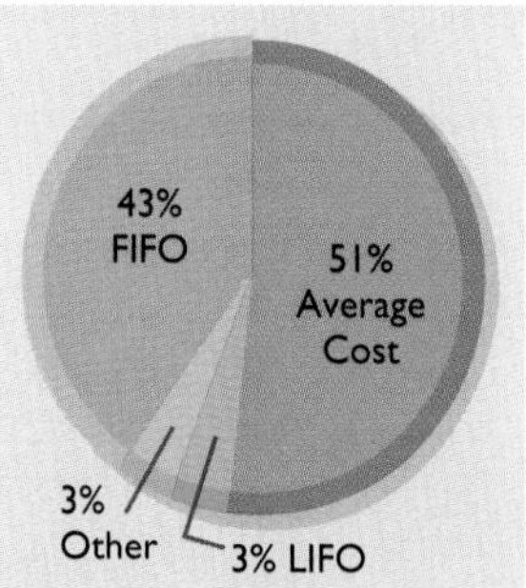

Illustration 6-15 Use of cost flow methods in Canadian public companies

The reasons companies have for adopting different inventory cost flow methods are varied, but they usually involve one of two factors:

1. Statement of earnings effects
2. Balance sheet effects

Statement of Earnings Effects

To understand why companies might choose a particular cost flow method, let's examine the effects of the different cost flow assumptions on the financial statements of Wynneck Electronics. The condensed statements of earnings in Illustration 6-16 assume that Wynneck sold its 550 units for $11,500, had operating expenses of $2,000, and is subject to an income tax rate of 30%.

Helpful Hint The management of companies in the same industry may reach different conclusions as to the most appropriate method for their respective companies.

Although the cost of goods available for sale ($12,000) is the same under each of the three inventory cost flow methods, both the ending inventories and costs of goods sold are different. This difference is due to the unit costs that are

Illustration 6-16 Comparative effects of cost flow methods

WYNNECK ELECTRONICS LTD.
Condensed Statements of Earnings

	FIFO	Average Cost	LIFO
Sales	$11,500	$11,500	$11,500
Beginning inventory	1,000	1,000	1,000
Purchases	11,000	11,000	11,000
Cost of goods available for sale	12,000	12,000	12,000
Ending inventory	5,800	5,400	5,000
Cost of goods sold	6,200	6,600	7,000
Gross profit	5,300	4,900	4,500
Operating expenses	2,000	2,000	2,000
Earnings before income tax	3,300	2,900	2,500
Income tax expense (30% except for LIFO)	990	870	990
Net earnings	$ 2,310	$ 2,030	$ 1,510

allocated to cost of goods sold and to ending inventory. Each dollar of difference in ending inventory results in a corresponding dollar difference in earnings before income tax. For Wynneck, an $800 difference exists between the FIFO and LIFO cost of goods sold.

In periods of changing prices, the cost flow assumption can have a significant impact on earnings and on evaluations based on earnings. In most instances, prices are rising (inflation). In a period of inflation, FIFO produces higher net earnings because the lower unit costs of the first units purchased are matched against revenues. In a period of rising prices (as is the case here for Wynneck), FIFO reports the highest net earnings ($2,310) and LIFO the lowest ($1,510); average cost falls roughly in the middle ($2,030). If prices are falling, the results from the use of FIFO and LIFO are reversed: FIFO will report the lowest net earnings and LIFO the highest. To management, higher net earnings are an advantage: they cause external users to view the company more favourably. In addition, if management bonuses are based on net earnings, FIFO will provide the basis for higher bonuses.

In spite of this, **LIFO does provide the best statement of earnings valuation**. It **matches** current costs with current revenues since, under LIFO, the cost of goods sold is assumed to be the cost of goods most recently acquired. However, even though LIFO may produce the best match of revenues and expenses, it is seldom used in Canada. The method is subject to manipulation, depending on the timing of purchases. The use of LIFO is also not permitted for income tax purposes and most firms do not wish to maintain two sets of inventory records—one for accounting purposes and another for income tax purposes. Companies can use FIFO or average cost to determine their income tax, but not LIFO. That is why, in Illustration 6-16, it was assumed that the income tax expense was the same under both FIFO and LIFO alternatives.

BUSINESS INSIGHT

International Perspective

In the U.S., contrary to Canadian practice, the use of LIFO is permitted for income tax purposes. Not surprisingly, many U.S. corporations choose LIFO because it reduces inventory profits and taxes. It also increases after-tax cash flow, since less income tax has to be paid in the short term.

The international community has considered a rule that would ban LIFO entirely and force corporations to use FIFO. This proposed rule was defeated. As John Wulff, controller for Union Carbide, noted, "We were in support of the international effort up until the proposal to eliminate LIFO." Wulff says that if Union Carbide had been suddenly forced to switch from LIFO to FIFO, its reported $632 million pretax earnings would have jumped by $300 million. That would have increased Carbide's income tax bill by as much as $120 million.

Balance Sheet Effects

A major advantage of the FIFO method is that in a period of inflation, the costs allocated to ending inventory will approximate their current cost. For example, for Wynneck, 400 of the 450 units in the ending inventory are costed under FIFO at the higher November 27 unit cost of $13.

Helpful Hint LIFO may provide the best income statement valuation, but FIFO provides the best balance sheet valuation.

Conversely, a major shortcoming of the LIFO method is that in a period of inflation, the costs allocated to ending inventory may be significantly understated in terms of current cost. This is true for Wynneck, where the cost of the ending inventory includes the $10 unit cost of the beginning inventory. The understatement becomes greater over prolonged periods of inflation if the inventory includes goods purchased in one or more prior accounting periods.

Summary of Effects

Illustration 6-17 summarizes the key differences that will result from the different choices of cost flow assumption during a period of rising prices. These effects will be the inverse if prices are falling, and equal if prices are constant.

	FIFO	Average	LIFO
Cost of goods sold	Lowest	Results will fall in between FIFO and LIFO	Highest
Gross profit/Net earnings	Highest	Results will fall in between FIFO and LIFO	Lowest
Pretax cash flow	Same	Same	Same
Ending inventory	Highest	Results will fall in between FIFO and LIFO	Lowest

Illustration 6-17
Financial statement effects of cost flow methods during a period of inflation

We have seen that both inventory on the balance sheet and net earnings on the statement of earnings are highest when FIFO is used in a period of inflation. Do not confuse this with cash flow. All three assumed cost flow methods produce exactly the same cash flow for corporations, before income taxes. Sales and purchases are not affected by the choice of cost flow assumption. The only thing affected is the allocation between ending inventory and cost of goods sold, which does not involve cash.

It is also worth remembering that all three cost flow assumptions will yield exactly the same results over the life cycle of the business or its product. That is, the allocation between cost of goods sold and ending inventory may vary annually, but will yield the same cumulative results over time. Although much has been written about the impact of the choice of inventory cost flow method on a variety of performance measures, in reality there is little real economic distinction between the methods over time.

DECISION TOOLKIT

Decision Checkpoints	Info Needed for Decision	Tool to Use for Decision	How to Evaluate Results
What is the impact of the choice of inventory costing method?	Are prices increasing, or are they decreasing?	Statement of earnings and balance sheet effects	Depends on objective. In a period of rising prices, earnings and inventory are higher under FIFO. LIFO provides opposite results. Average cost can moderate the impact of changing prices.

SELECTION OF COST FLOW METHOD

Accounting should provide information that is useful to decision-makers. We have learned that the choice of cost flow method can lead to substantially different financial statement effects, depending on the direction of prices. Is the useful information objective achieved if managers can select a method depending on its desired influence on their financial results? The answer to this is "No." While the accounting profession does permit a choice among acceptable methods, the reason they do so is to **accommodate differences in the particular circumstances of the company and the industry**. It is not to permit managers to manipulate their financial position at will. The CICA also recommends that in those cases "where the choice of method of inventory valuation is an important factor in determining income, the most suitable method for determining cost is that which results in charging against operations costs which **most fairly match** the sales revenue for the period."

USING INVENTORY COST FLOW METHODS CONSISTENTLY

Whatever cost flow method a company chooses, it should be used consistently from one accounting period to another. Consistent application enhances the comparability of financial statements over successive time periods. In contrast, using the FIFO method one year and the average method the next year would make it difficult to compare the net earnings of the two years.

Although consistent application is preferred, it does not mean that a company may *never* change its method of inventory costing. When a company adopts a different method, the change and its effects on prior periods should be disclosed in the financial statements. This conforms with the full disclosure principle, which requires all relevant information to be disclosed. The accounting procedure for changes in accounting principles, such as a change in the method of inventory costing, is illustrated in more detail in a later chapter.

Helpful Hint As you learned in Chapter 2, comparability is an important characteristic of accounting information.

Valuing Inventory at the Lower of Cost and Market

STUDY OBJECTIVE 7

Explain the lower of cost and market basis of accounting for inventories.

The value of the inventory of companies selling high-technology or fashion goods can drop very quickly due to changes in technology or changes in fashions. These circumstances sometimes call for inventory valuation methods other than those presented so far. For example, suppose you are the owner of a retail store that sells Dell computers. During the recent 12-month period, the cost of the computers dropped $1,800 (almost 50%). At the end of your fiscal year, you have some of these computers in inventory. Do you think your inventory should be stated at cost, in accordance with the cost principle, or at its lower net realizable value?

As you probably reasoned, this situation requires a departure from the cost basis of accounting. When the value of inventory is lower than its cost, the inventory is written down to its market value. This is done by valuing the inventory at the **lower of cost and market (LCM)** in the period in which the price decline occurs. LCM is an example of the accounting concept of conservatism, which means that the best choice among accounting alternatives is the method that is least likely to overstate assets and net earnings.

LCM is applied to the items in inventory after one of the cost flow methods (specific identification, FIFO, average cost, or LIFO) has been used to determine cost.

The term *market* in the phrase *lower of cost and market* is not specifically defined in Canada. It may include **replacement cost** or **net realizable value**, among other definitions. The majority of Canadian companies use net realizable value to define market for LCM purposes. **For a merchandising company, net realizable value is the selling price, less any costs required to make the goods ready for sale.**

International Note

Almost every country in the world applies the LCM rule; however, the definition of market can vary. The International Accounting Standards Committee defines market as net realizable value, as do the UK, France, and Germany. The U.S., Italy, and Japan define market as replacement cost.

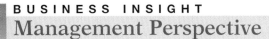

BUSINESS INSIGHT

Management Perspective

Some industries, such as the computer chip industry, have taken the application of the lower of cost and market rule into their own hands. A practice known as "ship and debit" is quite common in the volatile market of computer chip pricing. Ship and debit—or ship from stock and debit—refers to an accounting and sales practice where distributors purchase parts from suppliers and then receive credits or rebates from the suppliers when the market price of the product declines below the purchase cost.

While this practice is legal, it also opens the door for unscrupulous distributors to lie on point of sale reports to manufacturers about the price received for the chips. Future Electronics Inc. in Montreal is alleged by the FBI to have systematically altered its sales records on a massive scale, in order to take advantage of this ship and debit practice. The National Electronics Dealers Association says that the complicated, cumbersome, and common computer chip industry sales practice known as "ship and debit" should be eliminated. It is extremely difficult to regulate and "we'd do away with it completely if we could," said Robin Gray, President of the Association, which represents North America's major component suppliers.

Source: Michael Lewis, "Future, FBI Clash Over Sales Practices," *Financial Post,* November 11, 1999, C1.

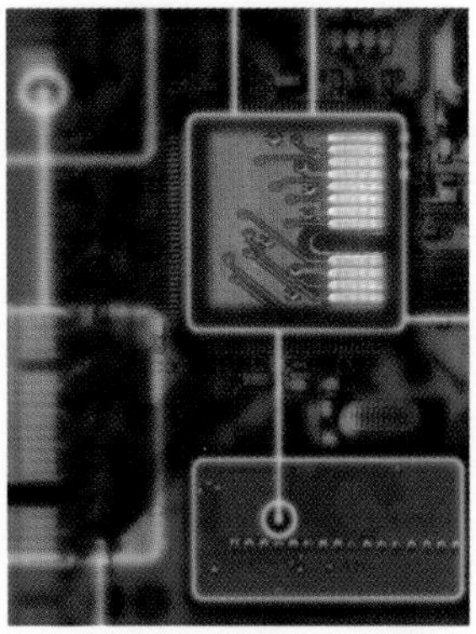

BEFORE YOU GO ON . . .

Review It

Loblaws
A passion for food... *and a lot more!*

1. What factors should be considered by management in selecting an inventory cost flow method?
2. What inventory cost flow method does Loblaw use to account for most of its inventories? Does Loblaw apply the lower of cost and market rule? If so, how does it define *market*? (Hint: You will have to look at Note 1 to the financial statements to find these answers.) The answer to this question is provided at the end of the chapter.
3. Which inventory cost flow method produces the highest net earnings in a period of rising prices? The lowest ending inventory valuation? The highest cash flow?
4. When should inventory be reported at a value other than cost?

Do It

The accounting records of Shumway Ag Implement Inc. show these data:

Beginning inventory	4,000 units at \$3
Purchases	6,000 units at \$4
Sales	5,000 units at \$12

Determine the cost of goods sold during the period under a periodic inventory system using (a) the FIFO method, (b) the average cost method, and (c) the LIFO method.

Reasoning: Because the units of inventory on hand and available for sale may have been purchased at different prices, a systematic method must be adopted to allocate the costs between the goods sold and the goods on hand (ending inventory).

Solution:

(a) FIFO: (4,000 @ \$3) + (1,000 @ \$4) = \$12,000 + \$4,000 = \$16,000
(b) Average cost: [(4,000 @ \$3) + (6,000 @ \$4)] ÷ 10,000
= (\$12,000 + \$24,000) ÷ 10,000
= \$3.60 per unit; 5,000 @ \$3.60 = \$18,000
(c) LIFO: 5,000 @ \$4 = \$20,000

ANALYSIS OF INVENTORY

For companies that sell goods, managing inventory levels can be one of the most critical tasks. Having too much inventory on hand can cost the company money in storage costs, interest costs (on funds tied up in inventory), and costs associated with the obsolescence of technology-driven goods (e.g., computer chips) or shifts in fashion for products like clothes. But having too little inventory on hand can result in lost sales. In this section we discuss some issues related to evaluating inventory levels.

INVENTORY TURNOVER RATIO

STUDY OBJECTIVE 8
Calculate and interpret the inventory turnover ratio.

The **inventory turnover ratio** is calculated as cost of goods sold divided by average inventory. Its complement, **days in inventory**, indicates the average age of the inventory; it is calculated as 365 days divided by the inventory turnover ratio. Both measures indicate how quickly a company sells its goods—how many times the inventory "turns over" (is sold) during the year. Low inventory turnover or high days in inventory could indicate that the company is incurring excessive carrying costs (e.g., interest, storage, insurance, taxes) as well as the possibility of inventory obsolescence. High inventory turnover or low days in inventory indicates the company is tying up little of its funds in inventory—that it has a minimal amount of inventory on hand at any one time. Although minimizing the funds tied up in inventory is efficient, too high an inventory turnover ratio may indicate that the company is losing sales opportunities because of inventory shortages. Thus, management should closely monitor this ratio to achieve the best balance between too much and too little inventory.

In Chapter 5 we discussed the increasingly competitive environment of retailers like Wal-Mart and Zellers. We noted that Wal-Mart has implemented many technological innovations to improve the efficiency of its operations. Illustration 6-18 presents the inventory turnover ratios and days in inventory for Wal-Mart and Zellers, using data from the financial statements of those corporations for 1999 and 1998. Some data had to be assumed for Zellers, since cost of goods sold and other data related to inventories were not disclosed in its annual report.

$$\text{INVENTORY TURNOVER RATIO} = \frac{\text{COST OF GOODS SOLD}}{\text{AVERAGE INVENTORY}}$$

$$\text{DAYS IN INVENTORY} = \frac{365}{\text{INVENTORY TURNOVER RATIO}}$$

($ in millions)		1999	1998
Wal-Mart	Inventory turnover ratio	$\frac{\$108,725}{(\$17,076 + \$16,497)/2} = 6.5$ times	$\frac{\$93,438}{(\$16,497 + \$15,897)/2} = 5.8$ times
	Days in inventory	$\frac{365 \text{ days}}{6.5} = 56$ days	$\frac{365 \text{ days}}{5.8} = 63$ days
Zellers	Inventory turnover ratio	3.1 times	3.2 times
	Days in inventory	118 days	114 days
Industry average	Inventory turnover ratio	4.9 times	n/a
	Days in inventory	73 days	n/a

Illustration 6-18 Inventory turnover ratio and days in inventory

The calculations in Illustration 6-18 show that Wal-Mart turns its inventory more frequently than both the industry and Zellers and, consequently, the average time an item spends on a Wal-Mart shelf is shorter. This suggests that Wal-Mart is more efficient in its inventory management. Wal-Mart's sophisticated inventory tracking and distribution system allows it to keep minimum amounts of inventory on hand, while still keeping the shelves full of what customers are looking for. Zellers' high ratios have been affected, no doubt, by the integration of the Kmart Canada stores. One would expect its ratios to improve in future years as duplication is eliminated. The CEO of Zellers notes in the annual report that "significant progress was achieved in logistics, with rapid improvement in distribution and transportation." He also notes that a new merchandising system, Retek, is scheduled for implementation at Zellers in early 2000.

Before one fully accepts the interpretation suggested in the above paragraph—that Wal-Mart's inventory management is more efficient than Zellers'—one must be very careful to make sure that the difference in ratios is not solely attributable to differences in choice of cost flow methods. For example, if one company used LIFO to cost its inventory, and the other FIFO, one would naturally expect the inventory turnover ratio to be higher in a period of inflation for the company using LIFO (higher cost of goods sold and lower ending inventory). This does not mean that one company is more efficient in managing its inventory. In fact, both companies could physically be holding inventory items for exactly the same number of days and it just appears that their inventory turnover is different because of the impact of the choice of cost flow assumption.

In reality, Wal-Mart and Zellers do use different cost flow assumptions—Wal-Mart uses the LIFO method, while Zellers uses the average method. While we do not know the exact impact on the inventory turnover ratio caused by the use of these two dissimilar cost flow assumptions, it is safe to speculate, in this particular case, that the difference between the inventory turnover ratios for Wal-Mart and Zellers is too great to be attributed only to the difference in inventory costing method. Therefore, the interpretation put forth above appears to be a reasonable one.

BUSINESS INSIGHT

Management Perspective

As noted in the opening story, in recent years many companies, including Caterpillar, have adopted inventory management techniques to reduce the amount of inventory they have on hand. These practices are referred to as "just-in-time" inventory, or JIT. A *Wall Street Journal* story noted, however, that sometimes these practices can cause hardship for companies. Drops in supply and surges in the prices of oil, natural gas, corn, wheat, and coffee have left many companies that are reliant on these raw materials scrambling to find enough goods to meet their needs. By having only small amounts of inventory on hand, these companies subject themselves to much more price and supply volatility than if they held large inventories.

To reduce such volatility, many companies enter into "hedges"—financial transactions that act as a sort of insurance against big price changes. Even with hedges such as futures contracts, companies often have to pass higher prices of commodities or raw materials on to the consumer.

Source: Aaron Lucchetti, "Low Inventories Add to Unpredictability," *Wall Street Journal,* March 10, 1997, C1.

BEFORE YOU GO ON . . .

Review It

1. What is the purpose of the inventory turnover ratio? What is the relationship between the inventory turnover ratio and days in inventory?

DECISION TOOLKIT

Decision Checkpoints	Info Needed for Decision	Tool to Use for Decision	How to Evaluate Results
How long is an item in inventory?	Cost of goods sold; beginning and ending inventory	$\text{Inventory turnover ratio} = \frac{\text{Cost of goods sold}}{\text{Average inventory}}$ $\text{Days in inventory} = \frac{\text{365 days}}{\text{Inventory turnover ratio}}$	A higher inventory turnover ratio or lower days in inventory suggests that management is reducing the amount of inventory on hand, relative to sales.

USING THE DECISION TOOLKIT

IPSCO Inc., headquartered in Regina, Saskatchewan, produces and sells steel mill and fabricated products for the oil and natural gas, manufacturing, agricultural, and transportation industries in Canada and the U.S. IPSCO has about 20 manufacturing and scrap-processing facilities throughout Canada and the U.S. Combined, these plants produce about 2.3 million tons of steel annually.

Selected financial information related to IPSCO's inventories from its December 31, 1998 consolidated financial statements (in thousands) follow:

IPSCO Inc.
Selected Financial Information

Balance Sheet (and Note 4)	1998	1997	1996
Inventories			
Finished goods	$ 85,976	$ 99,556	$ 57,424
Work in process	65,417	76,298	47,203
Raw materials and supplies	100,923	105,719	63,492
	$252,316	$281,573	$168,119
Statement of Income			
Sales	$1,099,320	$1,025,642	$804,898
Cost of sales	839,892	765,210	619,771
Selling, research, and administration expenses	54,732	44,458	42,082
Net earnings	113,241	132,173	83,298

Extract from the Notes to Financial Statements:

2. Significant Accounting Policies

INVENTORIES
Inventories are valued at the lowest of average cost, replacement cost, and net realizable value.

Selected industry data follow:

Inventory turnover	3.9 times
Days in inventory	94 days
Gross profit rate	15.6%
Profit margin rate	2.8%

Instructions

(a) Why does the company report its inventory on its balance sheet in three components?

(b) The steel industry is highly sensitive to general economic conditions. During recent years, steel prices have been dropping with an increase of steel imports into North America. If IPSCO had used the FIFO method of inventory cost instead of the average cost method, would you anticipate its earnings to be higher or lower than currently reported? What if it used the LIFO method instead of the average cost method?

(c) Perform each of the following:
1. Calculate the inventory turnover ratio and days in inventory for 1998 and 1997.
2. Calculate the gross profit rate, the profit margin rate, and the operating expenses to sales ratio for each of 1998 and 1997.
3. Evaluate IPSCO's performance with respect to inventories.

(d) Effective January 1, 1999, IPSCO announced that it will begin reporting its financial results in U.S. dollars. Speculate about what might have influenced this company decision.

Solution

(a) IPSCO is a manufacturer, so it purchases raw materials and makes them into finished products. At the end of each period, it has some goods that have been started but are not yet complete, referred to as work in process. By reporting all three components of inventory, the company reveals important information about its inventory position. For example, if amounts of raw materials have increased significantly compared to the previous year, as they have for IPSCO, we might safely assume that the company is planning to step up production. On the other hand, if levels of finished goods have increased relative to last year and raw materials have declined, we might conclude that sales are slowing down and that the company therefore has too much inventory on hand and is cutting back production.

(b) If IPSCO used the FIFO cost flow assumption instead of the average cost flow assumption during a period of declining prices, its cost of goods sold would be higher and its net earnings lower than currently reported. If IPSCO used LIFO instead of average, its cost of goods sold would be lower and its net earnings higher than currently reported.

(c) 1.

Ratio	1998	1997	Industry Average
Inventory turnover	$\frac{\$839,892}{(\$252,316 + \$281,573)/2}$ = 3.1 times	$\frac{\$765,210}{(\$281,573 + \$168,119)/2}$ = 3.4 times	3.9 times
Days in inventory	$\frac{365 \text{ days}}{3.1}$ = 118 days	$\frac{365 \text{ days}}{3.4}$ = 107 days	94 days

2.

Ratio	1998	1997	Industry Average
Gross profit	$\frac{\$1,099,320 - \$839,892}{\$1,099,320}$ = 23.6%	$\frac{\$1,025,642 - \$765,210}{\$1,025,642}$ = 25.4%	15.6%
Profit margin	$\frac{\$113,421}{\$1,099,320}$ = 10.3%	$\frac{\$132,173}{\$1,025,642}$ = 12.9%	2.8%
Operating expenses to sales	$\frac{\$54,732}{\$1,099,320}$ = 5.0%	$\frac{\$44,458}{\$1,025,642}$ = 4.3%	

3. IPSCO's inventory turnover ratio and days in inventory ratios deteriorated in 1998. In fact, they fell below the industry averages. That means that IPSCO has more inventory on hand and is not selling it as fast as its competitors. This is a result, no doubt, of the price erosion IPSCO suffered on many of its products. IPSCO was also affected by a less active oil and gas drilling sector, further reducing the demand for its products.

   IPSCO's profitability ratios also declined in 1998, but are far better than the industry averages. IPSCO is better able to cope with declining prices than its competitors. In fact, IPSCO was able to reduce steel purchases from third parties and use more of its own material to soften the blow caused by the market conditions.

(d) IPSCO will change its reporting from Canadian to U.S. dollars in 1999 for two reasons. The first is to reflect the company's growing American presence. Approximately 70% of the value of the company's capital assets is now located in the U.S. Secondly, in Canada, many of the company's input costs are substantially influenced by currency changes to the U.S. dollar.

Summary of Study Objectives

❶ ***Explain the recording of purchases and sales of inventory under a periodic inventory system.*** In records of purchases, entries are required for (a) cash and credit purchases, (b) purchase returns and allowances, (c) purchase discounts, and (d) freight-in costs. In records of sales, entries are required for (a) cash and credit sales, (b) sales returns and allowances, and (c) sales discounts.

2 ***Explain how to determine cost of goods sold under a periodic inventory system.*** The steps in determining cost of goods sold are (a) recording the purchase of merchandise, (b) determining the cost of goods purchased, and (c) determining the cost of goods on hand at the beginning and end of the accounting period. Beginning inventory + cost of goods purchased = cost of goods available for sale – ending inventory = cost of goods sold.

3 ***Describe the steps in determining inventory quantities.*** The steps are (1) taking a physical inventory of goods on hand and (2) determining the ownership of goods in transit or on consignment.

4 ***Identify the unique features of the statement of earnings for a merchandising company under a periodic inventory system.*** The statement of earnings for a merchandising company contains three features not found in a service enterprise's statement of earnings: sales revenue, cost of goods sold, and a gross profit line. The cost of goods sold section generally shows more detail under a periodic than a perpetual inventory system by reporting beginning and ending inventories, net purchases, and total goods available for sale.

5 ***Explain the basis of accounting for inventories and apply the inventory cost flow methods under a periodic inventory system.*** The primary basis of accounting for inventories is cost. Cost includes all expenditures necessary to acquire goods and make them ready for sale. Cost of goods available for sale includes (a) cost of beginning inventory and (b) cost of goods purchased. The inventory cost flow methods are: specific identification and three assumed cost flow methods—FIFO, average cost, and LIFO.

6 ***Explain the financial statement effects of each of the inventory cost flow assumptions.*** The cost of goods available for sale may be allocated to cost of goods sold and ending inventory by specific identification or by a method based on an assumed cost flow. When prices are rising, the first-in, first-out (FIFO) method results in lower cost of goods sold and higher net earnings than the average cost and the last-in, first-out (LIFO) methods. The reverse is true when prices are falling. In the balance sheet, FIFO results in an ending inventory that is closest to current (replacement) value, whereas the inventory under LIFO is the farthest from current value. All three methods result in the same cash flow before income taxes. LIFO is not permitted for income tax purposes in Canada.

7 ***Explain the lower of cost and market basis of accounting for inventories.*** The lower of cost and market (LCM) basis may be used when the net realizable value (market) is less than cost. Under LCM, the loss is recognized in the period in which the price decline occurs.

8 ***Calculate and interpret the inventory turnover ratio.*** The inventory turnover ratio is calculated as cost of goods sold divided by average inventory. It can be converted to days in inventory by dividing 365 days by the inventory turnover ratio. A higher turnover ratio or lower days in inventory suggests that management is trying to keep inventory levels low relative to its sales level.

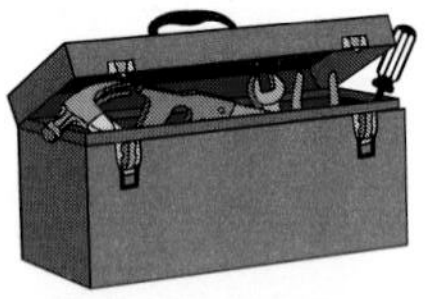

Decision Toolkit—A Summary

Decision Checkpoints	Info Needed for Decision	Tool to Use for Decision	How to Evaluate Results
What is the impact of the choice of inventory costing method?	Are prices increasing, or are they decreasing?	Statement of earnings and balance sheet effects	Depends on objective. In a period of rising prices, earnings and inventory are higher under FIFO. LIFO provides opposite results. Average cost can moderate the impact of changing prices.
How long is an item in inventory?	Cost of goods sold; beginning and ending inventory	$\text{Inventory turnover ratio} = \dfrac{\text{Cost of goods sold}}{\text{Average inventory}}$ $\text{Days in inventory} = \dfrac{\text{365 days}}{\text{Inventory turnover ratio}}$	A higher inventory turnover ratio or lower days in inventory suggests that management is reducing the amount of inventory on hand, relative to sales.

APPENDIX 6A

Inventory Cost Flow Methods in Perpetual Inventory Systems

STUDY OBJECTIVE 9

Apply the inventory cost flow methods to perpetual inventory records.

Each of the inventory cost flow methods described in the chapter for a periodic inventory system may be used in a perpetual inventory system. To illustrate the application of the three assumed cost flow methods (FIFO, average cost, and LIFO), we will use the data shown below and earlier in this chapter for Wynneck Electronics' Astro Condenser.

Illustration 6A-1
Inventoriable units and costs

WYNNECK ELECTRONICS LTD.
Astro Condensers

Date	Explanation	Units	Unit Cost	Total Cost	Balance in Units
1/1	Beginning inventory	100	$10	$ 1,000	100
4/15	Purchases	200	11	2,200	300
8/24	Purchases	300	12	3,600	600
9/10	Sale	550			50
11/27	Purchases	400	13	5,200	450
				$12,000	

First-In, First-Out (FIFO)

Under FIFO, the cost of the earliest goods on hand **prior to each sale** is charged to cost of goods sold. Therefore, the cost of goods sold on September 10 consists of the units on hand January 1 and the units purchased April 15 and August 24. The inventory on a FIFO method perpetual system is shown in Illustration 6A-2.

Illustration 6A-2
Perpetual system—FIFO

Date	Purchases	Sales	Balance
January 1			(100 @ $10) $1,000
April 15	(200 @ $11) $2,200		(100 @ $10) (200 @ $11) } $3,200
August 24	(300 @ $12) $3,600		(100 @ $10) (200 @ $11) (300 @ $12) } $6,800
September 10		(100 @ $10) (200 @ $11) (250 @ $12) $6,200	(50 @ $12) $ 600
November 27	(400 @ $13) $5,200		(50 @ $12) (400 @ $13) } $5,800

The ending inventory in this situation is $5,800, and the cost of goods sold is $6,200.

The results under FIFO in a perpetual system are the **same as in a periodic system** (see Illustration 6-9 where, similarly, the ending inventory is $5,800 and cost of goods sold is $6,200). Regardless of the system, the first costs in are the ones assigned to cost of goods sold.

Average Cost

The average cost method in a perpetual inventory system is called the **moving average method**. Under this method a new average is calculated **after each purchase**. The average cost is calculated by dividing the cost of goods available for sale by the units on hand. The average cost is then applied to: (1) the units sold, to determine the cost of goods sold, and (2) the remaining units on hand, to determine the ending inventory amount. The application of the average cost method by Wynneck Electronics is shown in Illustration 6A-3.

Illustration 6A-3
Perpetual system—average cost method

Date	Purchases		Sales	Balance	
January 1				(100 @ $10)	$1,000
April 15	(200 @ $11)	$2,200		(300 @ $10.667)	$3,200
August 24	(300 @ $12)	$3,600		(600 @ $11.333)	$6,800
September 10			(550 @ $11.333) $6,233	(50 @ $11.333)	$ 567
November 27	(400 @ $13)	$5,200		(450 @ $12.816)	$5,767

As indicated in Illustration 6A-3, **a new average is calculated each time a purchase (or purchase return) is made**. On April 15, after 200 units are purchased for $2,200, a total of 300 units costing $3,200 ($1,000 + $2,200) are on hand. The average unit cost is $10.667 ($3,200 ÷ 300). On August 24, after 300 units are purchased for $3,600, a total of 600 units costing $6,800 ($1,000 + $2,200 + $3,600) are on hand at an average cost per unit of $11.333 ($6,800 ÷ 600). This unit cost of $11.333 is used in costing sales until another purchase is made, when a new unit cost is computed. Accordingly, the unit cost of the 550 units sold on September 10 is $11.333, and the total cost of goods sold is $6,233. On November 27, following the purchase of 400 units for $5,200, there are 450 units on hand costing $5,767 ($567 + $5,200) with a new average cost of $12.816 ($5,767 ÷ 450).

This moving average cost under the perpetual inventory system should be compared to Illustration 6-12 (shown earlier in the chapter) which presents the weighted average method under a periodic inventory system.

Last-In, First-Out (LIFO)

Under the LIFO method using a perpetual system, the cost of the most recent purchase prior to sale is allocated to the units sold. Therefore, the cost of the goods sold on September 10 consists of all the units from the August 24 and April 15 purchases and 50 of the units in beginning inventory. The ending inventory on a LIFO method is computed in Illustration 6A-4.

Illustration 6A-4
Perpetual system—LIFO

Date	Purchases		Sales	Balance	
January 1				(100 @ $10)	$1,000
April 15	(200 @ $11)	$2,200		(100 @ $10) (200 @ $11)	$3,200
August 24	(300 @ $12)	$3,600		(100 @ $10) (200 @ $11) (300 @ $12)	$6,800
September 10			(300 @ $12) (200 @ $11) (50 @ $10) $6,300	(50 @ $10)	$ 500
November 27	(400 @ $13)	$5,200		(50 @ $10) (400 @ $13)	$5,700

The use of LIFO in a perpetual system will usually produce cost allocations that differ from using LIFO in a periodic system. In a perpetual system, the latest units incurred prior to each sale are allocated to cost of goods sold. In contrast, in a periodic system, the latest units incurred during the period are allocated to cost of goods sold. Thus, when a purchase is made after the last sale, the LIFO periodic system will apply this purchase to the previous sale. See Illustration 6-14 where the proof shows the 400 units at $13 purchased on November 27 applied to the sale of 550 units on September 10.

As shown above under the LIFO perpetual system, the 400 units at $13 purchased on November 27 are all applied to the ending inventory.

The ending inventory in this LIFO perpetual illustration is $5,700 and cost of goods sold is $6,300, as compared to the LIFO periodic example in Illustration 6-13, where the ending inventory is $5,000 and cost of goods sold is $7,000.

Comparison of the cost of goods sold and ending inventory figures for each of these perpetual cost flow assumptions yield the same proportionate outcomes that we saw in the application of periodic cost flow assumptions. That is, in a period of rising prices (prices rose from $4 to $5 in this problem), FIFO will always yield the highest ending inventory valuation and LIFO the lowest. On the other hand, LIFO will always result in the highest cost of goods sold figure (and lowest net earnings) and FIFO the lowest. Of course, if prices are falling, the inverse relationships will result. And, finally, remember that the sum of cost of goods sold and ending inventory always equals the cost of goods available for sale, which is the same regardless of the choice of cost flow assumption.

Illustration 6A-5 Financial statement effects of cost flow methods

	FIFO	Average	LIFO
Cost of goods sold	$ 6,200	$ 6,233	$ 6,300
Ending inventory	5,800	5,767	5,700
Cost of goods available for sale	$12,000	$12,000	$12,000

Demonstration Problem for Appendix 6A

The Demonstration Problem on page 322 shows cost of goods sold calculations under a periodic inventory system. Here, we assume that Englehart Company Ltd. uses a perpetual inventory system and has the same inventory, purchases, and sales data for the month of March as shown there:

Inventory, March 1	200 units @ $4.00	$ 800
Purchases		
March 10	500 units @ $4.50	2,250
March 20	400 units @ $4.75	1,900
March 30	300 units @ $5.00	1,500
Sales		
March 15	500 units @ $8.00	4,000
March 25	400 units @ $8.00	3,200

The physical inventory count on March 31 shows 500 units on hand.

Instructions

Under a **perpetual inventory system**, determine the cost of inventory on hand at March 31 and the cost of goods sold for March under (a) the first-in, first-out (FIFO) method; (b) the average cost method; and (c) the last-in, first-out (LIFO) method.

Problem-Solving Strategies

1. For FIFO, the latest costs are allocated to inventory at the time of each sale.
2. For average cost, use a weighted average for periodic and a moving average for perpetual.
3. For LIFO, the earliest costs are allocated to inventory at the time of each sale.
4. Total purchases and cost of goods available for sale are the same under all three cost flow methods.

Solution to Demonstration Problem

The cost of goods available for sale is $6,450:

Inventory	200 units @ $4.00	$ 800
Purchases		
March 10	500 units @ $4.50	2,250
March 20	400 units @ $4.75	1,900
March 30	300 units @ $5.00	1,500
Total cost of goods available for sale	1,400	$6,450

Under a **perpetual inventory system**, the cost of goods sold (1,400 – 500 = 900 units) under each cost flow method is as follows:

(a) **FIFO Method**

Date	Purchases	Sales	Balance
March 1			(200 @ $4.00) $ 800
March 10	(500 @ $4.50) $2,250		(200 @ $4.00) (500 @ $4.50) $3,050
March 15		(200 @ $4.00) (300 @ $4.50) $2,150	(200 @ $4.50) $ 900
March 20	(400 @ $4.75) $1,900		(200 @ $4.50) (400 @ $4.75) $2,800
March 25		(200 @ $4.50) (200 @ $4.75) $1,850	(200 @ $4.75) $ 950
March 30	(300 @ $5.00) $1,500		(200 @ $4.75) (300 @ $5.00) $2,450

Ending inventory $2,450. Cost of goods sold: $6,450 – $2,450 = $4,000 or $2,150 + $1,850 = $4,000.

(b) **Moving Average Cost Method**

Date	Purchases	Sales	Balance
March 1			(200 @ $4.00) $ 800
March 10	(500 @ $4.50) $2,250		(700 @ $4.357)$3,050
March 15		(500 @ $4.357) $2,179	(200 @ $4.357)$ 871
March 20	(400 @ $4.75) $1,900		(600 @ $4.618)$2,771
March 25		(400 @ $4.618) 1,847	(200 @ $4.618)$ 924
March 30	(300 @ $5.00) $1,500		(500 @ $4.848)$2,424

Ending inventory $2,424. Cost of goods sold: $6,450 – $2,424 = $4,026 or $2,179 + $1,847 = $4,026.

(c) **LIFO Method**

Date	Purchases	Sales	Balance
March 1			(200 @ $4.00) $ 800
March 10	(500 @ $4.50) $2,250		(200 @ $4.00) (500 @ $4.50) $3,050
March 15		(500 @ $4.50) $2,250	(200 @ $4.00) $ 800
March 20	(400 @ $4.75) $1,900		(200 @ $4.00) (200 @ $4.75) $2,700
March 25		(400 @ $4.75) $1,900	(200 @ $4.00) $ 800
March 30		(300 @ $5.00) $1,500	(200 @ $4.00) (300 @ $5.00) $2,300

Ending inventory $2,300. Cost of goods sold: $6,450 – $2,300 = $4,150 or $2,250 + $1,900 = $4,150.

SUMMARY OF STUDY OBJECTIVE FOR APPENDIX 6A

9 ***Apply the inventory cost flow methods to perpetual inventory records.*** Under FIFO, the cost of the earliest goods on hand prior to each sale is charged to cost of goods sold. Under the average cost method, a new average cost is calculated after each purchase. Under LIFO, the cost of the most recent purchase prior to sale is charged to cost of goods sold.

APPENDIX 6B

INVENTORY ERRORS

Unfortunately, errors occasionally occur in accounting for inventory. In some cases, errors are caused by failure to count or cost the inventory correctly. In other cases, errors occur because proper recognition is not given to the transfer of legal title to goods that are in transit. When errors occur, they affect both the statement of earnings and the balance sheet, as well as any ratios using inventory (or related) accounts.

STUDY OBJECTIVE 10

Indicate the effects of inventory errors on the financial statements.

STATEMENT OF EARNINGS EFFECTS

As you know, both the beginning and ending inventories appear in the statement of earnings. The ending inventory of one period automatically becomes the beginning inventory of the next period. Inventory errors can affect the determination of cost of goods sold and net earnings in two periods.

The effects on cost of goods sold can be determined by entering incorrect data in the formula in Illustration 6B-1 and then substituting the correct data.

Beginning Inventory + Cost of Goods Purchased = Cost of Goods Available for Sale − Ending Inventory = Cost of Goods Sold

Illustration 6B-1 Formula for cost of goods sold

If beginning inventory is understated, cost of goods sold will be understated. On the other hand, understating ending inventory will overstate cost of goods sold. The effects of inventory errors on the current year's statement of earnings are shown in Illustration 6B-2.

Inventory Error	Cost of Goods Sold	Net Earnings
Understate beginning inventory	Understated	Overstated
Overstate beginning inventory	Overstated	Understated
Understate cost of goods purchased	Understated	Overstated
Overstate cost of goods purchased	Overstated	Understated
Understate ending inventory	Overstated	Understated
Overstate ending inventory	Understated	Overstated

Illustration 6B-2 Effects of inventory errors on the current year's statement of earnings

An error in the *ending* inventory of the current period will have a **reverse effect on net earnings of the next accounting period**. This is shown in Illustration 6B-3. Note that the understatement of ending inventory in 2000 results in an understatement of beginning inventory in 2001 and an overstatement of net earnings in 2001.

Over the two years, total net earnings are correct because the errors offset each other. Notice that total earnings using incorrect data are $35,000 ($22,000 + $13,000), which is the same as the total earnings of $35,000 ($25,000 + $10,000) using correct data. Also note in this example that an error in the beginning

SAMPLE COMPANY
Condensed Statement of Earnings

	2000				2001			
	Incorrect		Correct		Incorrect		Correct	
Sales		$80,000		$80,000		$90,000		$90,000
Beginning inventory	$20,000		$20,000		**$12,000**		**$15,000**	
Cost of goods purchased	40,000		40,000		68,000		68,000	
Cost of goods available for sale	60,000		60,000		80,000		83,000	
Ending inventory	**12,000**		**15,000**		23,000		23,000	
Cost of goods sold		48,000		45,000		57,000		60,000
Gross profit		32,000		35,000		33,000		30,000
Operating expenses		10,000		10,000		20,000		20,000
Net earnings		$22,000		$25,000		$13,000		$10,000

($3,000) Net earnings understated | **$3,000** Net earnings overstated

The errors cancel. Thus the combined total earnings for the two-year period are correct.

Illustration 6B-3 Effects of inventory errors on statements of earnings for two years

inventory does not result in a corresponding error in the ending inventory for that period. The correctness of the ending inventory depends entirely on the accuracy of taking and costing the inventory at the balance sheet date under the periodic inventory system.

BUSINESS INSIGHT

Investor Perspective

The average amount of money lost to fraud by each of Canada's largest companies in 1998 was $958,927. Inventory fraud increases during recessions. Such fraud includes pricing inventory at amounts in excess of their actual value, or claiming to have inventory when no inventory exists. Inventory fraud is usually done to overstate ending inventory, thereby understating cost of goods sold and creating higher earnings.

Source: KPMG Canada, Investigation Security, *1999 Fraud Survey Report*.

Balance Sheet Effects

The effect of ending inventory errors on the balance sheet can be determined by using the basic accounting equation: Assets = Liabilities + Shareholders' Equity. Errors in the ending inventory have the effects shown in Illustration 6B-4.

Illustration 6B-4 Effects of ending inventory errors on balance sheet

Ending Inventory Error	Assets	=	Liabilities	+	Shareholders' Equity
Overstated	Overstated		No effect		Overstated
Understated	Understated		No effect		Understated

Recall from the previous section that errors in ending inventory affect net earnings. If net earnings are affected, then shareholders' equity will be affected by the same amount since net earnings is closed into the Retained Earnings account within the shareholders' equity classification. Consequently, an error in ending inventory will equally affect both the asset Inventory account and the shareholders' equity Retained Earnings account.

The effect of an error in ending inventory on the subsequent period was shown in Illustration 6B-3. Recall that if the error is not corrected, the combined total net earnings for the two periods would be correct. Thus, total shareholders' equity reported on the balance sheet at the end of 2001 will also be correct.

Summary of Study Objective for Appendix 6B

⑩ ***Indicate the effects of inventory errors on the financial statements.*** In the statement of earnings of the current year: (a) an error in beginning inventory will have a reverse effect on net earnings (overstatement of inventory results in understatement of net earnings, and vice versa) and (b) an error in ending inventory will have a similar effect on net earnings (e.g., overstatement of inventory results in overstatement of net earnings). If ending inventory errors are not corrected in the following period, their effect on net earnings for that period is reversed, and total net earnings for the two years will be correct. In the balance sheet, ending inventory errors will have the same effect on total assets and total shareholders' equity and no effect on liabilities.

Glossary

Average cost method An inventory costing method that assumes that the goods available for sale are homogeneous. (p. 300)

Consigned goods Goods held for sale by one party (the consignee) although ownership of the goods is retained by another party (the consignor). (p. 295)

Cost of goods available for sale The sum of the beginning merchandise inventory and the cost of goods purchased. (p. 296)

Cost of goods purchased The sum of net purchases and freight-in. (p. 293)

Cost of goods sold (CGS) The total cost of merchandise sold during the period, determined by subtracting ending inventory from the cost of goods available for sale. (p. 293)

Days in inventory Measure of the average number of days inventory is held; calculated as 365 divided by the inventory turnover ratio. (p. 308)

Finished goods inventory Manufactured items that are completed and ready for sale. (p. 288)

First-in, first-out (FIFO) method An inventory costing method that assumes that the costs of the earliest goods acquired are the first to be recognized as cost of goods sold. (p. 299)

FOB (free on board) destination Freight terms indicating that the goods are placed free on board at the buyer's place of business, and the seller pays the freight cost. Goods belong to the seller while in transit. (p. 295)

FOB (free on board) shipping point Freight terms indicating that the goods are placed free on board the carrier by the seller, and the buyer pays the freight cost. Goods belong to the buyer while in transit. (p. 295)

Inventory turnover ratio A ratio that measures the number of times on average the inventory is sold during the period; calculated by dividing cost of goods sold by the average inventory during the period. (p. 308)

Last-in, first-out (LIFO) method An inventory costing method that assumes that the costs of the latest units purchased are the first to be allocated to cost of goods sold. (p. 302)

Lower of cost and market (LCM) basis A basis whereby inventory is stated at the lower of cost and market (net realizable value). (p. 307)

Net purchases Purchases less purchase returns and allowances and purchase discounts. (p. 293)

Net realizable value The selling price of an inventory item, less any costs required to make the item saleable. (p. 307)

Periodic inventory system An inventory system in which inventoriable costs are allocated to ending inventory and cost of goods sold at the end of the period. Cost of goods sold is calculated at the end of the period by subtracting the ending inventory (costs are assigned to a physical count of items on hand) from the cost of goods available for sale. (p. 289)

Raw materials Basic goods that will be used in production but have not yet been sent into production. (p. 288)

Replacement cost The cost of replacing an asset with a similar asset. (p. 307)

Specific identification method An actual physical flow costing method in which items still in inventory are specifically costed to arrive at the total cost of the ending inventory. (p. 298)

Weighted average unit cost Average cost that is weighted by the number of units purchased at each unit cost. (p. 300)

Work in process That portion of manufactured inventory that has begun the production process but is not yet complete. (p. 288)

Demonstration Problem

Englehart Company Ltd. has the following inventory, purchases, and sales data for the month of March:

Inventory, March 1	200 units @ \$4.00	\$ 800
Purchases		
March 10	500 units @ \$4.50	2,250
March 20	400 units @ \$4.75	1,900
March 30	300 units @ \$5.00	1,500
Sales		
March 15	500 units @ \$8.00	4,000
March 25	400 units @ \$8.00	3,200

The physical inventory count on March 31 shows 500 units on hand.

Instructions

Under a **periodic inventory system**, determine the cost of inventory on hand at March 31 and the cost of goods sold for March under (a) the first-in, first-out (FIFO) method; (b) the average cost method; and (c) the last-in, first-out (LIFO) method.

Problem-Solving Strategies

1. For FIFO, the earliest costs are allocated to cost of goods sold and the latest costs are allocated to inventory.
2. For average cost, use a weighted average for periodic.
3. For LIFO, the latest costs are allocated to cost of goods sold and the earliest costs are allocated to inventory.
4. Remember, the costs allocated to cost of goods sold should be proved.
5. Total cost of goods available for sale is the same under all three cost flow assumptions.

Solution to Demonstration Problem

The cost of goods available for sale is \$6,450:

Inventory	200 units	@ \$4.00	\$ 800
Purchases			
March 10	500 units	@ 4.50	2,250
March 20	400 units	@ 4.75	1,900
March 30	300 units	@ 5.00	1,500
Total cost of goods available for sale	1,400		\$ 6,450

(a) **FIFO Method**

Ending inventory:

Date	Units	Unit Cost	Total Cost	
Mar. 30	300	\$5.00	\$1,500	
Mar. 20	200	4.75	950	\$2,450
	500			

Cost of goods sold:

Inventory	200	\$4.00	\$ 800	
March 10	500	4.50	2,250	
March 20	200	4.75	950	\$4,000
	900			

or

Cost of goods sold: \$6,450 − \$2,450 = \$4,000

(b) **Weighted Average Cost Method**

Weighted average unit cost: \$6,450 ÷ 1,400 = \$4.607

Ending inventory: 500 × \$4.607 = \$2,303.50

Cost of goods sold: 900 × \$4.607 = \$4,146.50 (rounded)

or

Cost of goods sold: \$6,450 − \$2,303.50 = \$4,146.50

(c)

LIFO Method

Ending inventory:

Date	Units	Unit Cost	Total Cost	
Mar. 1	200	$4.00	$ 800	
Mar. 10	300	4.50	1,350	$2,150
	500			

Cost of goods sold:

March 30	300	$5.00	$1,500	
March 20	400	$4.75	1,900	
March 10	200	4.50	900	$4,300
	900			

or

Cost of goods sold: $6,450 − $2,150 = $4,300

Note: All questions, exercises, and problems marked with an asterisk relate to material in chapter appendices.

Self-Study Questions

Answers are at the end of the chapter.

(SO 1) 1. When goods are purchased for resale by a company using a periodic inventory system:
(a) purchases on account are debited to Merchandise Inventory.
(b) purchases on account are debited to Purchases.
(c) purchase returns are debited to Purchase Returns and Allowances.
(d) freight costs are debited to Purchases.

(SO 2) 2. In determining the cost of goods purchased:
(a) purchase discounts are deducted from net purchases.
(b) freight-out is added to net purchases.
(c) purchase returns and allowances are deducted from net purchases.
(d) freight-in is added to net purchases.

(SO 2) 3. If beginning inventory is $60,000, cost of goods purchased is $380,000, and ending inventory is $50,000, what is cost of goods sold?
(a) $390,000 (c) $330,000
(b) $370,000 (d) $420,000

(SO 3) 4. Which of the following should *not* be included in the physical inventory of a company?
(a) Goods held on consignment from another company.
(b) Goods shipped on consignment to another company.
(c) Goods in transit purchased from another company shipped FOB shipping point.
(d) All of the above should be included.

(SO 5) 5. Kam Company Ltd. has the following units and costs:

	Units	Unit Cost
Inventory, Jan. 1	8,000	$11
Purchase, June 19	13,000	12
Purchase, Nov. 8	5,000	13

If 9,000 units are on hand at December 31, what is the cost of the ending inventory under FIFO?
(a) $99,000 (c) $113,000
(b) $108,000 (d) $117,000

6. From the data in question 5, what is the cost of the ending inventory under LIFO? (SO 5)
(a) $113,000 (c) $99,000
(b) $108,000 (d) $100,000

7. In periods of rising prices, weighted average cost will produce: (SO 6)
(a) higher net earnings than FIFO.
(b) the same net earnings as FIFO.
(c) lower net earnings than FIFO.
(d) lower net earnings than LIFO.

8. Considerations that affect the selection of an inventory costing method should include: (SO 6)
(a) tax effects.
(b) balance sheet effects.
(c) the particular circumstances of the company.
(d) perpetual versus periodic inventory system.

9. The lower of cost and market rule for inventory is an example of the application of: (SO 7)
(a) the conservatism concept.
(b) the historical cost principle.
(c) the materiality constraint.
(d) the economic entity assumption.

10. Which of these would cause the inventory turnover ratio to increase the most? (SO 8)

(a) Increasing the amount of inventory on hand.
(b) Keeping the amount of inventory on hand constant but increasing sales.
(c) Keeping the amount of inventory on hand constant but decreasing sales.
(d) Decreasing the amount of inventory on hand and increasing sales.

(SO 9) *11. In a perpetual inventory system:
(a) LIFO cost of goods sold will be the same as in a periodic inventory system.
(b) average costs are based entirely on straight unit cost averages.
(c) a new average is calculated under the moving average cost method after each purchase.
(d) FIFO cost of goods sold will be different than in a periodic inventory system.

*12. Fran Company Ltd.'s ending inventory is understated by $4,000. The effects of this error on the current year's cost of goods sold and net earnings, respectively, are: (SO 10)
(a) understated and overstated.
(b) overstated and understated.
(c) overstated and overstated.
(d) understated and understated.

QUESTIONS

(SO 1) 1. Goods costing $1,600 are purchased on account on July 15 with credit terms of 2/10, n/30. On July 18, a $100 credit memo is received from the supplier for damaged goods. Give the journal entry on July 24 to record payment of the balance due within the discount period assuming a periodic inventory system.

(SO 1) 2. An item must possess two characteristics to be classified as inventory. What are these two characteristics?

(SO 1) 3. What is the primary basis of accounting for inventories? What is the major objective in accounting for inventories?

(SO 2) 4. Identify the accounts that are added to or deducted from purchases to determine the cost of goods purchased. For each account, indicate (a) whether it is added or deducted and (b) its normal balance.

(SO 2) 5. In the following cases, use a periodic inventory system to identify the item(s) designated by the letters X and Y.
(a) Purchases $- X - Y =$ Net purchases
(b) Cost of goods purchased $-$ Net purchases $= X$
(c) Beginning inventory $+ X =$ Cost of goods available for sale
(d) Cost of goods available for sale $-$ Cost of goods sold $= X$

(SO 2) 6. Mary Ann's Hat Shop Ltd. received a shipment of hats for which it paid the wholesaler $2,940. The price of the hats was $3,000, but Mary Ann's was given a $60 cash discount and required to pay freight charges of $70. In addition, Mary Ann's paid $100 to cover the travel expenses of an employee who negotiated the purchase of the hats. What amount should Mary Ann's include in inventory? Why?

(SO 3) 7. Your friend Tom Wetzel has been hired to help take the physical inventory in Casey's Hardware Store. Explain to Tom Wetzel what this job will entail, with particular attention to determining the inventory quantities to which Casey's has legal title.

8. (a) Janine Company Ltd. ships merchandise to Laura Corporation on December 30. The merchandise reaches the buyer on January 5. Indicate the terms of sale that will result in the goods being included in (1) Janine's December 31 inventory and (2) Laura's December 31 inventory. (SO 3)
(b) Under what circumstances should Janine Company Ltd. include consigned goods in its inventory?

9. Identify the distinguishing features of a statement of earnings for a merchandising company. (SO 4)

10. Dave Wier believes that the allocation of cost of goods available for sale should be based on the actual physical flow of the goods. Explain to Dave why this may be both impractical and inappropriate. (SO 5)

11. Name a major advantage and a major disadvantage of the specific identification method of inventory costing. (SO 5)

12. "The selection of an inventory cost flow method is a decision made by accountants." Do you agree? Explain. Once a method has been selected, what accounting requirement applies? (SO 5)

13.(a) Which assumed inventory cost flow method assumes that goods available for sale during an accounting period are homogeneous? (SO 5)
(b) Which one assumes that the latest units purchased are the first to be sold?

14. In a period of rising prices, the inventory reported in Plato Company Ltd.'s balance sheet is close to the current cost of the inventory, whereas York Company Ltd.'s inventory is considerably below its current cost. Identify the inventory cost flow method used by each company. Which company probably has been reporting the higher gross profit? (SO 6)

(SO 6) 15. Shaunna Corporation has been using the FIFO cost flow method during a prolonged period of inflation. During the same time period, Shaunna has been paying out all of its net earnings as dividends. What adverse effects may result from this policy?

(SO 7) 16. Lucy Ritter is studying for the next accounting midterm examination. What should Lucy know about (a) departing from the cost basis of accounting for inventories and (b) the usual meaning of *market* in the lower of cost and market method in Canada?

(SO 7) 17. Rock Music Centre Inc. has five CD players on hand at the balance sheet date that cost $400 each. The net realizable value is $320 per unit. Under the lower of cost and market basis of accounting for inventories, what value should be reported for the CD players on the balance sheet? Why?

(SO 7) 18. What cost flow assumption(s) may be used under the lower of cost and market basis of accounting for inventories?

(SO 7) 19. Maureen Corporation's balance sheet shows Inventories $162,800. What additional disclosures should be made?

(SO 8) 20. "The key to successful business operations is effective inventory management." Do you agree? Explain.

21. Under what circumstances might the inventory turnover ratio be too high—that is, what possible negative consequences might occur? (SO 8)

22. Would an increase in the days in inventory ratio from one year to the next year be viewed as an improvement or a deterioration in the company's efficiency in managing their inventory? (SO 8)

*23. "When perpetual inventory records are kept, the results under the FIFO and LIFO methods are the same as they would be in a periodic inventory system." Do you agree? Explain. (SO 9)

*24. How does the average method of inventory costing differ between a perpetual inventory system and a periodic inventory system? (SO 9)

*25. Mila Company Ltd. discovers in 2001 that its ending inventory at December 31, 2000, was $5,000 understated. What effect will this error have on (a) 2000 net earnings, (b) 2001 net earnings, and (c) the combined net earnings for the two years? (SO 10)

Brief Exercises

Journalize purchase transactions in a periodic inventory system. (SO 1)

BE6-1 Prepare the journal entries to record these transactions on (1) Hunt Company Ltd.'s books and (2) Streisand Company Ltd.'s books, using a periodic inventory system.

(a) On March 2, Hunt Company purchased $900,000 of merchandise from Streisand Company, terms 2/10, n/30.

(b) On March 6, Hunt Company returned $130,000 of the merchandise purchased on March 2.

(c) On March 12, Hunt Company paid the balance due to Streisand Company.

Journalize merchandise transactions in a perpetual inventory system. (SO 9)

***BE6-2** Transactions for Hunt Company Ltd. and Streisand Company Ltd. are presented in BE6-1. Prepare the journal entries to record these transactions on (1) Hunt Company's books and (2) Streisand Company's books, assuming that each company uses a perpetual inventory system. The cost of goods sold by Streisand on March 2 was $600,000 and that of the goods returned on March 6 was $90,000. Assume that the merchandise returned was put back into inventory for future resale by Streisand.

Calculate net purchases and cost of goods purchased. (SO 2)

BE6-3 Assume that Bassing Company Ltd. uses a periodic inventory system and has these account balances: Purchases $400,000; Purchase Returns and Allowances $11,000; Purchase Discounts $8,000; and Freight-in $16,000. Determine net purchases and cost of goods purchased.

Calculate cost of goods sold and gross profit. (SO 2)

BE6-4 Assume the same information as in BE6-3 and also that Bassing Company Ltd. has beginning inventory of $60,000, ending inventory of $90,000, and net sales of $630,000. Determine the amounts to be reported for cost of goods sold and gross profit.

Identify items to be included in taking a physical inventory. (SO 3)

BE6-5 Helgeson Company Inc. identifies the following items for possible inclusion in the physical inventory. Indicate whether each item should be included in or excluded from the inventory.

(a) Goods shipped on consignment by Helgeson to another company.

(b) Goods in transit from a supplier shipped FOB destination.
(c) Goods sold but being held for customer pickup.
(d) Goods held on consignment from another company.

Identify the components of cost of goods available for sale. (SO 3)

BE6-6 The ledger of Wharton Company Ltd. includes these items: Freight-in, Purchase Returns and Allowances, Purchases, Sales Discounts, and Purchase Discounts. Identify which items are included in calculating cost of goods available for sale.

Calculate CGS and ending inventory using FIFO, average, and LIFO in a periodic inventory system. (SO 5)

BE6-7 In its first month of operations, Quilt Company Inc. made three purchases and two sales of merchandise in the following sequence: (1) 300 units purchased at $6, (2) 200 units sold at $9, (3) 400 units purchased at $7, (4) 400 units sold at $10, and (5) 300 units purchased at $8. Calculate the cost of goods sold and ending inventory under (a) the FIFO method, (b) the weighted average cost method, and (c) the LIFO method. Quilt uses a periodic inventory system.

Calculate CGS and ending inventory using FIFO, average and LIFO in a perpetual inventory system. (SO 9)

***BE6-8** Data for Quilt Company Inc. are presented in BE6-7. Calculate the cost of goods sold and ending inventory under (a) the FIFO method, (b) the moving average cost method, and (c) the LIFO method, assuming Quilt uses a perpetual inventory system.

Determine the LCM valuation. (SO 7)

BE6-9 Hawkeye Appliance Centre Corporation accumulates the following cost and market data at December 31:

Inventory Categories	Cost Data	Market Data
Cameras	$12,000	$10,200
Camcorders	9,000	9,500
VCRs	14,000	12,800

Calculate the lower of cost and market valuation for Hawkeye's total inventory.

Calculate inventory turnover ratio and days in inventory. (SO 8)

BE6-10 At December 31, 2001, the following information was available for Sauk Company: ending inventory $80,000; beginning inventory $60,000; cost of goods sold $210,000; and sales revenue $280,000. Calculate the inventory turnover ratio and days in inventory for Sauk Company.

Apply cost flow methods in a perpetual inventory system. (SO 9)

***BE6-11** Berthiaume Company Inc. uses a perpetual inventory system. Data for product E2-D2 include the following purchases:

Date	Number of Units	Unit Price
May 7	50	$10
July 28	30	$15

On June 1, Berthiaume sold 30 units for $20 each, and on August 27, 33 more units for $20 each. Compute the ending inventory and cost of goods sold using (1) FIFO, (2) average cost, and (3) LIFO.

Determine correct financial statement amount. (SO 10)

***BE6-12** Creole Company Ltd. reports net earnings of $90,000 in 2001. However, ending inventory was understated by $7,000. What is the correct net earnings for 2001? What effect, if any, will this error have on total assets as reported in the balance sheet at December 31, 2001?

Determine the effect of ending inventory error on balance sheet for two years. (SO 10)

***BE6-13** DuPlessis Corporation counted and recorded its ending inventory as at December 31, 2001 incorrectly, understating its correct value by $25,000. Assuming that this misstatement was not subsequently discovered and corrected, what is the impact of this error on assets, liabilities, and shareholders' equity at the end of 2001? At the end of 2002?

EXERCISES

Journalize purchase transactions in a periodic inventory system. (SO 1)

E6-1 This information for Hans Olaf Corp. relates to transactions with DeVito Company Ltd.:

1. On April 5, purchased merchandise from DeVito Company for $18,000, terms 2/10, net/30, FOB shipping point.
2. On April 6, paid freight costs of $900 on merchandise purchased from DeVito Company.

3. On April 7, purchased equipment on account for $26,000.
4. On April 8, returned damaged merchandise to DeVito Company and was granted a $3,000 allowance.
5. On April 15, paid the amount due to DeVito Company in full.

Instructions

(a) Prepare the journal entries to record these transactions on the books of (1) Hans Olaf Corp. and (2) DeVito Company Ltd., using a periodic inventory system.

(b) Assume that Hans Olaf Corp. paid the balance due to DeVito Company on May 4 instead of April 15. Prepare the journal entry to record this payment on each company's books.

Prepare cost of goods sold section.
(SO 2, 4)

E6-2 The trial balance of Garbo Company Inc. at the end of its fiscal year, August 31, 2001, includes these accounts: Merchandise Inventory $17,200; Purchases $142,400; Sales $190,000; Freight-in $4,000; Sales Returns and Allowances $3,000; Freight-out $1,000; and Purchase Returns and Allowances $2,000. The ending merchandise inventory is $26,000.

Instructions

Prepare a cost of goods sold section for the year ending August 31.

Determine missing amounts for cost of goods sold section.
(SO 2, 4)

E6-3 Below is a series of cost of goods sold sections for four companies:

	Co. 1	Co. 2	Co. 3	Co. 4
Beginning inventory	$ 250	$ 120	$1,000	$ (j)
Purchases	1,500	1,080	(g)	43,590
Purchase returns and allowances	40	(d)	290	(k)
Net purchases	(a)	1,020	7,210	44,330
Freight-in	110	(e)	(h)	2,240
Cost of goods purchased	(b)	1,230	7,940	(l)
Cost of goods available for sale	1,820	1,350	(i)	49,530
Ending inventory	310	(f)	1,450	6,230
Cost of goods sold	(c)	1,250	7,490	43,300

Instructions

Fill in the lettered blanks to complete the cost of goods sold sections.

Determine the correct inventory amount.
(SO 3)

E6-4 Gatineau Bank and Trust is considering giving Novotna Corporation a loan. Before doing so, it decides that further discussions with Novotna's accountant may be desirable. One area of particular concern is the inventory account, which has a year-end balance of $295,000. Discussions with the accountant reveal the following:

1. Novotna sold goods costing $35,000 to Moghul Company FOB shipping point on December 28. The goods are not expected to arrive in India until January 12. The goods were not included in the physical inventory because they were not in the warehouse.
2. The physical count of the inventory did not include goods costing $95,000 that were shipped to Novotna FOB destination on December 27 and were still in transit at year end.
3. Novotna received goods costing $25,000 on January 2. The goods were shipped FOB shipping point on December 26 by Cellar Co. The goods were not included in the physical count.
4. Novotna sold goods costing $40,000 to Sterling of Britain FOB destination on December 30. The goods were received in Britain on January 8. They were not included in Novotna's physical inventory.
5. Novotna received goods costing $44,000 on January 2 that were shipped FOB destination on December 29. The shipment was a rush order that was supposed to arrive December 31. This purchase was included in the ending inventory of $295,000.

Instructions

Determine the correct inventory amount on December 31.

Prepare a multiple-step statement of earnings.
(SO 4)

E6-5 Presented here is information related to Baja Corp. for the month of January 2001:

Freight-in	$ 10,000
Rent expense	20,000
Freight-out	7,000
Salary expense	61,000
Insurance expense	12,000
Income tax expense	4,000
Sales discounts	8,000
Purchases	200,000
Sales returns and allowances	13,000
Purchase discounts	3,000
Sales	312,000
Purchase returns and allowances	6,000

Beginning merchandise inventory was $42,000, and ending merchandise inventory was $63,000.

Instructions

Prepare a multiple-step statement of earnings. Operating expenses need not be divided into selling and administrative expenses.

Calculate cost of goods sold using specific identification and FIFO periodic.
(SO 5)

E6-6 On December 1, Discount Electronics Ltd. has three DVD players left in stock. All are identical, all are priced to sell at $750. Of the three DVD players left in stock, one with serial #1012 was purchased on June 1 at a cost of $500, another with serial #1045 was purchased on November 1 for $450. The last player, serial #1056, was purchased on November 30 for $400.

Instructions

(a) Calculate the cost of goods sold using the FIFO periodic inventory method assuming that two of the three players were sold by the end of December, Discount Electronic's year end.

(b) If Discount Electronics used the specific identification method instead of the FIFO method, how might it alter its earnings by "selectively choosing" which particular players to sell to the two customers? What would Discount's cost of goods sold be if the company wished to minimize earnings? Maximize earnings?

(c) Which inventory method do you recommend that Discount use? Explain why.

Calculate inventory and cost of goods sold using FIFO, average, and LIFO in a periodic inventory system.
(SO 5)

E6-7 Mawmey Inc. uses a periodic inventory system. Its records show the following for the month of May, in which 78 units were sold:

Date	Explanation	Units	Unit Cost	Total Cost
May 1	Inventory	30	$ 8	$240
15	Purchase	25	10	250
24	Purchase	35	12	420
	Total	90		$910

Instructions

Calculate the ending inventory at May 31 using the (a) FIFO, (b) average cost, and (c) LIFO methods. Prove the amount allocated to cost of goods sold under each method.

Calculate inventory and cost of goods sold using FIFO, average, and LIFO in a periodic inventory system and answer questions.
(SO 5, 6)

E6-8 At the end of June, Lakshmi Company Ltd. reports the following for the month:

Date	Explanation	Units	Unit Cost	Total Cost
June 1	Inventory	200	$5	$1,000
12	Purchase	300	6	1,800
23	Purchase	500	7	3,500
30	Inventory	180		

Instructions

(a) Calculate the cost of the ending inventory and the cost of goods sold under (1) FIFO, (2) average cost, and (3) LIFO.

(b) Which costing method gives the highest ending inventory? Why?

(c) Which method results in the highest cost of goods sold? Why?

(d) Which method results in the highest cash flow? Why?

Calculate inventory and cost of goods sold using three cost flow methods in a perpetual inventory system.
(SO 9)

* **E6-9** Inventory data for Lakshmi Company Ltd. are presented in E6-8.

Instructions

(a) Calculate the cost of the ending inventory and the cost of goods sold for each cost flow assumption, using a perpetual inventory system. Assume a sale of 400 units occurred on June 15 for a selling price of \$8 and a sale of 420 units on June 27 for \$9.
(b) How do the results differ from E6-8?
(c) Why is the average unit cost not \$6 ((\$5 + \$6 + \$7) ÷ 3 = \$6)?

Calculate inventory turnover ratio, days in inventory, and gross profit rate.
(SO 8)

E6-10 This information is available for **Future Shop Ltd.**, Canada's largest computer and electronic retailer, for the years ended March 31, 1998, 1997, and 1996 (in thousands):

	1998	1997	1996
Inventory	\$ 254,690	\$ 244,074	\$ 223,978
Sales	1,760,160	1,523,016	1,303,828
Cost of sales	1,370,773	1,170,801	1,021,452

Instructions

Calculate the inventory turnover ratio, days in inventory, and gross profit rate (from Chapter 5) for Future Shop for 1998 and 1997. Comment on any trends.

Calculate ending inventory and cost of goods sold in periodic and perpetual systems.
(SO 5, 9)

***E6-11** Powder! sells the Xpert snowboard that is popular with snowboard enthusiasts. Below is information relating to Powder!'s purchases and sales of Xpert snowboards during September:

Date	Transaction	Units	Unit Price	Total Sales Price	Total Purchase Cost
Sept. 1	Beginning inventory	26	\$ 97		\$ 2,522
Sept. 5	Sale	(12)	199	\$ 2,388	
Sept. 12	Purchase	45	102		4,590
Sept. 16	Sale	(50)	199	9,950	
Sept. 19	Purchase	28	104		2,912
Sept. 22	Purchase	40	105		4,200
Sept. 26	Sale	(62)	209	12,958	
	Totals	15		\$25,296	\$14,224

Instructions

(a) Calculate the ending inventory and the cost of goods sold using FIFO, average cost, and LIFO, assuming a perpetual inventory system is utilized by Powder!.
(b) What would the ending inventory and cost of goods sold be, if Powder! used each of these cost flow assumptions in a periodic inventory system?

Prepare journal entries for cost flow assumptions in perpetual and periodic inventory systems.
(SO 5, 9)

***E6-12** Refer to the data provided for Powder! in *E6-11.

Instructions

(a) Prepare journal entries to record purchases and sales for Powder! in a perpetual inventory system under each of the following cost flow assumptions: (1) FIFO, (2) Moving average cost, and (3) LIFO.
(b) Prepare journal entries to record purchases and sales for Powder! in a periodic inventory system under each of the following cost flow assumptions: (1) FIFO, (2) Weighted average cost, and (3) LIFO.

Determine effects of inventory errors.
(SO 10)

***E6-13** Seles Hardware Limited reported cost of goods sold as follows:

	2001	2002
Beginning inventory	\$ 20,000	\$ 30,000
Cost of goods purchased	150,000	175,000
Cost of goods available for sale	170,000	205,000
Ending inventory	30,000	35,000
Cost of goods sold	\$140,000	\$170,000

Seles made two errors:

1. 2001 ending inventory was overstated by $4,000.
2. 2002 ending inventory was understated by $3,000.

Instructions

Calculate the correct cost of goods sold for each year.

Prepare correct statements of earnings.
(SO 10)

***E6-14** Aruba Company Inc. reported these statement of earnings data for a two-year period:

	2001	2002
Sales	$210,000	$250,000
Beginning inventory	32,000	40,000
Cost of goods purchased	173,000	202,000
Cost of goods available for sale	205,000	242,000
Ending inventory	40,000	52,000
Cost of goods sold	165,000	190,000
Gross profit	$ 45,000	$ 60,000

Aruba Company uses a periodic inventory system. The inventories at January 1, 2001, and December 31, 2002, are correct. However, the ending inventory at December 31, 2001, is overstated by $6,000.

Instructions

(a) Prepare correct statement of earnings data for the two years.
(b) What is the cumulative effect of the inventory error on total gross profit for the two years?
(c) Calculate the gross profit rate for each of the two years, before and after the correction.
(d) Explain in a letter to the president of Aruba Company what has happened—that is, the nature of the error and its effect on the financial statements.

Prepare correcting entries for sales and purchases.
(SO 10)

***E6-15** An inexperienced accountant for Churchill Company Ltd. made the following errors in recording merchandising transactions:

1. A $150 refund to a customer for faulty merchandise was debited to Sales $150 and credited to Cash $150.
2. A $250 credit purchase of supplies was debited to Purchases $250 and credited to Cash $250.
3. An $80 sales discount was debited to Purchase Discounts.
4. A $50 purchase return was recorded as a debit to Accounts Payable $50 and a credit to Purchases $50.
5. A cash payment of $30 for freight on merchandise purchases was debited to Purchases $300 and credited to Cash $300.

Instructions

Prepare separate correcting entries for each error.

PROBLEMS: SET A

Journalize, post, and prepare trial balance and partial statement of earnings.
(SO 1, 2, 4)

P6-1A Joanie Kane, a former professional golfer, operates Kane's Pro Shop at Crowbush Golf Course. At the beginning of the current season on April 1, the ledger of Kane's Pro Shop showed Cash $2,500; Merchandise Inventory $3,500; and Common Shares $6,000. These transactions occurred during April 2001:

Apr. 5 Purchased golf bags, clubs, and balls on account from Balata Co. $1,600, FOB shipping point, terms 2/10, n/60.
7 Paid freight on Balata Co. purchases $80.
9 Received credit from Balata Co. for merchandise returned $100.
10 Sold merchandise on account to members $900, terms n/30.
12 Purchased golf shoes, sweaters, and other accessories on account from Arrow Sportswear $660, terms 1/10, n/30.
14 Paid Balata Co. in full.
17 Received $60 credit from Arrow Sportswear for merchandise returned.

20 Made sales on account to members $700, terms n/30.
21 Paid Arrow Sportswear in full.
27 Granted credit to members for clothing that did not fit $30.
30 Made cash sales $600.
30 Received payments on account from members $1,100.

Instructions

(a) Journalize the April transactions for Kane's Pro Shop using a periodic inventory system.
(b) Using T accounts, enter the beginning balances in the ledger accounts and post the April transactions.
(c) Prepare a trial balance as at April 30, 2001.
(d) Prepare a multiple-step statement of earnings through gross profit, assuming merchandise inventory on hand at April 30 is $4,200.

Prepare journal entries for purchaser and seller using average cost periodic method; apply lower of cost and market.
(SO 1, 7)

P6-2A You are provided with the following information concerning the transactions for Amelia Inc. Amelia purchases all items from Karina Inc. and makes sales to a variety of customers. All transactions are settled in cash. Returns are usually not damaged and are restored immediately to inventory for resale. Both Amelia and Karina use the periodic inventory method and the weighted average cost flow assumption. These transactions involve a high-tech product; increased competition has reduced the price of the product.

Date	Description	Quantity	Unit Dollar Amount
July 1	Beginning inventory	25	$10.00
July 5	Purchase	60	9.00
July 8	Sale	45	11.00
July 10	Sale return	10	11.00
July 15	Purchase	25	8.00
July 16	Purchase return	5	8.00
July 20	Sale	60	9.00
July 25	Purchase	10	6.50

Instructions

(a) Prepare all journal entries for the month of July for Amelia Inc.
(b) Prepare all journal entries for the month of July for Karina Inc.
(c) Determine the ending inventory amount, using the weighted average cost flow assumption, for Amelia Inc.
(d) By July 31, Amelia Inc. learns that the product has a net realizable value of $7 per unit. What amount should ending inventory be valued at on the July 31 balance sheet?

Prepare a multiple-step statement of earnings.
(SO 2, 4)

P6-3A Metro Department Store Ltd. is located in midtown Metropolis. During the past several years, net earnings have been declining because of competition from suburban shopping centres. At the end of the company's fiscal year on November 30, 2001, the following accounts appeared in alphabetical order in its adjusted trial balance:

Accounts Payable	$ 35,310
Accounts Receivable	13,770
Accumulated Amortization—Delivery Equipment	19,680
Accumulated Amortization—Store Equipment	41,800
Amortization Expense—Delivery Equipment	4,000
Amortization Expense—Store Equipment	9,500
Cash	8,000
Common Shares	70,000
Delivery Equipment	57,000
Delivery Expense	8,200
Dividends	12,000
Freight-in	5,060
Income Tax Expense	5,000
Income Tax Payable	4,500
Insurance Expense	9,000
Merchandise Inventory	34,360
Notes Payable	46,000

Prepaid Insurance	4,500
Property Tax Expense	3,500
Purchases	630,000
Purchase Discounts	7,000
Purchase Returns and Allowances	3,000
Rent Expense	19,000
Retained Earnings	17,200
Salaries Expense	140,000
Sales	860,000
Sales Commissions Expense	12,000
Sales Commissions Payable	8,000
Sales Returns and Allowances	10,000
Store Equipment	125,000
Utilities Expense	2,600

Additional facts:
1. Merchandise inventory at November 30, 2001, is $36,200.
2. Metro Department Store uses a periodic system.

Instructions

Prepare a multiple-step statement of earnings for the year ended November 30, 2001.

Determine items and amounts to be recorded in inventory.
(SO 3)

P6-4A Kananaskis Country Limited is trying to determine the value of its ending inventory as at February 28, 2001, the company's year end. The following transactions occurred, and the accountant asked your help in determining whether they should be recorded or not.

(a) On February 26, Kananaskis shipped goods costing $800 to a customer and charged the customer $1,000. The goods were shipped with terms FOB destination and the receiving report indicates that the customer received the goods on March 2.
(b) On February 26, Seller Inc. shipped goods to Kananaskis under terms FOB shipping point. The invoice price was $350 plus $25 for freight. The receiving report indicates that the goods were received by Kananaskis on March 2.
(c) Kananaskis had $500 of inventory isolated in the warehouse. The inventory is designated for a customer who has requested that the goods be shipped on March 10.
(d) Also included in Kananaskis' warehouse is $400 of inventory that Craft Producers shipped to Kananaskis on consignment.
(e) On February 26, Kananaskis issued a purchase order to acquire goods costing $750. The goods were shipped with terms FOB destination and the receiving report indicates that Kananaskis received the goods on March 2.
(f) On February 26, Kananaskis shipped goods to a customer under terms FOB shipping point. The invoice price was $350 plus $25 for freight; the cost of the items was $280. The receiving report indicates that the goods were received by the customer on March 2.

Instructions

For each of the above transactions, specify whether the item in question should be included in ending inventory, and if so, at what amount.

Determine cost of goods sold and ending inventory using FIFO, average cost, and LIFO in a periodic inventory system and assess financial statement effects.
(SO 5, 6)

P6-5A Kane Company Ltd. had a beginning inventory on January 1 of 100 units of Product SXL at a cost of $20 per unit. During the year, purchases were:

Mar. 15	300 units at $24	Sept. 4	300 units at $28
July 20	200 units at $25	Dec. 2	100 units at $30

Kane Company sold 850 units, and it uses a periodic inventory system.

Instructions

(a) Determine the cost of goods available for sale.
(b) Determine the ending inventory and the cost of goods sold under each of the assumed cost flow methods (FIFO, average cost, and LIFO). Prove the accuracy of the cost of goods sold under each method.
(c) Which cost flow method results in the highest inventory amount for the balance sheet? The highest cost of goods sold for the statement of earnings?

P6-6A The management of Tumatoe Inc. asks for your help in determining the comparative effects of the FIFO, average, and LIFO periodic inventory cost flow methods. For 2001 the accounting records show these data:

Calculate ending inventory, prepare statements of earnings, and answer questions using FIFO, average, and LIFO periodic inventory methods.

(SO 5, 6)

Inventory, January 1 (10,000 units)	$ 35,000
Cost of 110,000 units purchased	460,000
Selling price of 95,000 units sold	665,000
Operating expenses	120,000

Units purchased consisted of 40,000 units at $4.00 on May 10; 50,000 units at $4.20 on August 15; and 20,000 units at $4.50 on November 20. Income taxes are $48,300 under all three methods.

Instructions

(a) Prepare comparative condensed statements of earnings for 2001 under FIFO, average, and LIFO. (Show calculations of ending inventory.)

(b) Answer the following questions for management in the form of a business letter:

1. Which inventory cost flow method produces the most meaningful inventory amount for the balance sheet? Why?
2. Which inventory cost flow method produces the most meaningful net earnings? Why?
3. Which inventory cost flow method is most likely to approximate the actual physical flow of the goods? Why?
4. How much cash will be available for management under each method?
5. What factors should influence management's choice of method?

P6-7A This information is available for the Automotive and Electronics Divisions of **General Motors Corporation** for 1998.

Calculate inventory turnover ratio, days in inventory, and current ratio.

(SO 8)

(in millions of USD)	1998
Beginning inventory	$ 12,102
Ending inventory	12,207
Current assets	44,363
Current liabilities	47,806
Cost of goods sold	117,973
Sales	140,433

Instructions

Calculate the inventory turnover ratio, days in inventory, and current ratio for General Motors Corporation for 1998. Comment on GM's liquidity.

***P6-8A** You are provided with the following information for Danielle Inc. for the month ended June 30, 2002. Danielle uses the average cost flow assumption for inventory.

Calculate gross profit and ending inventory under average cost flow assumption for both periodic and perpetual methods.

(SO 5, 9)

Date	Description	Quantity	Unit Dollar Amount
June 1	Beginning inventory	25	$60
June 4	Purchase	85	64
June 10	Sale	70	90
June 11	Sale return	10	90
June 18	Purchase	35	68
June 18	Purchase return	5	68
June 25	Sale	50	95
June 28	Purchase	20	72

Instructions

Calculate gross profit and the value of ending inventory assuming:

(a) a perpetual inventory system.

(b) a periodic inventory system.

Prepare a multiple-step statement of earnings in a perpetual inventory system.
(SO 9)

***P6-9A** Refer to the data provided in P6-3A for Metro Department Store. Assume that instead of using a periodic inventory system, Metro uses a perpetual inventory system.

Instructions

(a) Which accounts and amounts, appearing in a periodic inventory system general ledger, would *not* appear on a perpetual inventory system general ledger?
(b) What would be the amount of the cost of goods sold reported for the period by Metro Department Store? How does this amount compare to that reported for cost of goods sold in a periodic inventory system?
(c) Using the accounts reported in P6-3A and the cost of goods sold amount determined in (b), prepare a multiple-step statement of earnings for the year ended November 30, 2001.

Determine cost of goods sold under FIFO and average perpetual inventory systems, and assess financial statement impact of each method.
(SO 6, 9)

***P6-10A** Save-Mart Centre Inc. began operations on July 1. It uses a perpetual inventory system. During July, the company had the following purchases and sales:

	Purchases		Sales
Date	**Units**	**Unit Cost**	**Units**
July 1	5	$ 90	
July 6			3
July 11	4	99	
July 14			3
July 21	3	106	
July 27			4

Instructions

(a) Determine the cost of goods sold under a perpetual inventory system using (1) FIFO, and (2) moving average cost.
(b) Which costing method produces the highest gross profit and net earnings?
(c) Which method produces the highest ending inventory valuation?

Prepare journal entries for FIFO and average under the perpetual system. Compare gross profit and cash flow under each assumption.
(SO 6, 9)

***P6-11A** Matthew Inc. is a retailer operating in Dartmouth, Nova Scotia. Matthew uses the perpetual inventory method. All sales returns from customers result in the goods being returned to inventory; the inventory is not damaged. Assume that there are no credit transactions; all amounts are settled in cash. You are provided with the following information for Matthew Inc. for the month of January 2001.

Date	Description	Quantity	Unit Dollar Amount
January 1	Beginning inventory	50	$12
January 5	Purchase	100	14
January 8	Sale	80	25
January 10	Sale return	10	25
January 15	Purchase	30	18
January 16	Purchase return	5	18
January 20	Sale	90	25
January 25	Purchase	10	20

Instructions

(a) For each of the following cost flow assumptions, prepare all required journal entries using the:
   1. FIFO cost flow assumption.
   2. moving average cost flow assumption.
(b) Compare the results of the FIFO assumption to the moving average cost assumption for
   1. the impact on net cash flow.
   2. the impact on gross profit.

Compare specific identification, FIFO, and LIFO under perpetual method; use of cost flow assumption to justify price increase.

(SO 6, 9)

***P6-12A** You are provided with the following information for Gas Guzzlers. Gas Guzzlers uses the perpetual method of accounting for its inventory transactions.

March 1	Opening inventory 1,500 litres at a cost of 40¢ per litre.
March 3	Purchased 2,000 litres at a cost of 45¢ per litre.
March 5	Sold 1,800 litres for 60¢ per litre.
March 10	Purchased 3,500 litres at a cost of 49¢ per litre.
March 20	Purchased 2,000 litres at a cost of 55¢ per litre.
March 30	Sold 5,000 litres for 70¢ per litre.

Instructions

(a) Prepare partial statements of earnings to gross profit and calculate the value of ending inventory that would be reported on the balance sheet, under each of the following cost flow assumptions:

1. Specific identification method assuming
   - the March 5 sale consisted of 900 litres from the March 1 beginning inventory and 900 litres from the March 3 purchase; and
   - the March 30 sale consisted of the following from each purchase: 400 litres from March 1; 500 litres from March 3; 2,600 litres from March 10; 1,500 litres from March 20.
2. FIFO.
3. LIFO.

(b) How can companies use a cost flow method to justify price increases? Which cost flow method would best support an argument to increase prices?

Illustrate impact of inventory error.

(SO 10)

***P6-13A** The records of Alyssa Inc. show the following data:

Account	2001	2002
Sales	$300,000	$320,000
Beginning inventory	30,000	22,000
Cost of goods purchased	200,000	240,000
Ending inventory	22,000	31,000
Operating expenses	60,000	64,000

Subsequent to the July 31, 2002 year end, Alyssa Inc. discovers that its inventory at the end of 2001 was actually $27,000 not $22,000.

Instructions

(a) Prepare both incorrect and corrected Statements of Earnings for Alyssa Inc. for 2001 and 2002.

(b) What is the impact of this error on retained earnings at July 31, 2002?

PROBLEMS: SET B

Journalize, post, and prepare trial balance and partial statement of earnings.

(SO 1, 2, 4)

P6-1B At the beginning of the current season, the ledger of Kicked-Back Tennis Shop showed Cash $2,500; Merchandise Inventory $1,700; and Common Shares $4,200. These transactions were completed during April 2001:

Apr.	4	Purchased racquets and balls from Robert Co. $640, FOB shipping point, terms 3/10, n/30.
	6	Paid freight on Robert Co. purchase $40.
	8	Sold merchandise to members $900, terms n/30.
	10	Received credit of $40 from Robert Co. for a damaged racquet that was returned.
	11	Purchased tennis shoes from Niki Sports for cash $300.
	13	Paid Robert Co. in full.
	14	Purchased tennis shirts and shorts from Martina's Sportswear $700, FOB shipping point, terms 2/10, n/60.

15 Received cash refund of $50 from Niki Sports for damaged merchandise that was returned.
17 Paid freight on Martina's Sportswear purchase $30.
18 Sold merchandise to members $800, terms n/30.
20 Received $500 in cash from members in settlement of their accounts.
21 Paid Martina's Sportswear in full.
27 Granted credit of $30 to members for tennis clothing that did not fit.
30 Sold merchandise to members $900, terms n/30.
30 Received cash payments on account from members, $500.

Instructions

(a) Journalize the April transactions for the Kicked-Back Tennis Shop using a periodic inventory system.
(b) Using T accounts, enter the beginning balances in the ledger accounts and post the April transactions.
(c) Prepare a trial balance as at April 30, 2001.
(d) Prepare a multiple-step statement of earnings through gross profit, assuming merchandise inventory on hand at April 30 is $1,800.

Prepare journal entries for purchaser and seller using FIFO periodic method; apply lower of cost and market.
(SO 1, 7)

P6-2B You are provided with the following information concerning the transactions for Schwinghamer Inc. Schwinghamer purchases all items from Pataki Inc. and makes sales to a variety of customers. All transactions are settled in cash. Returns are normally not damaged and are restored immediately to inventory for resale. Both companies use the periodic inventory method and the FIFO cost flow assumption. These transactions involve a high-tech product; increased competition has reduced the price of the product.

Item	Description	Units	Unit Dollar Amount
October 1	Beginning inventory	60	$15
October 9	Purchase	120	14
October 11	Sale	100	35
October 13	Sale return	10	35
October 17	Purchase	70	13
October 19	Purchase return	5	13
October 22	Sale	60	30
October 25	Purchase	80	12
October 29	Sale	50	30

Instructions

(a) Prepare all journal entries for the month of October for Schwinghamer Inc.
(b) Prepare all journal entries for the month of October for Pataki Inc.
(c) Determine the ending inventory amount, using the FIFO cost flow assumption, for Schwinghamer Inc.
(d) By October 31, Schwinghamer Inc. learns that the product has a replacement cost of $11 per unit. What amount should ending inventory be valued at on the October 31 balance sheet?
(e) What impact would the reduction of the ending inventory valuation due to the application of the lower of cost and market rule have on Schwinghamer's inventory turnover ratio?

Prepare a multiple-step statement of earnings.
(SO 2, 4)

P6-3B The N-Mart Department Store Ltd. is located near the Village Shopping Mall. At the end of the company's fiscal year on December 31, 2001, the following accounts appeared in alphabetical order in its adjusted trial balance:

Accounts Payable	$ 89,300
Accounts Receivable	50,300
Accumulated Amortization—Building	52,500
Accumulated Amortization—Equipment	42,900
Amortization Expense—Building	10,400
Amortization Expense—Equipment	13,300
Building	190,000
Cash	23,000

Common Shares	150,000
Dividends	28,000
Equipment	110,000
Freight-in	5,600
Income Tax Expense	7,000
Insurance Expense	7,200
Merchandise Inventory	40,500
Mortgage Payable	80,000
Office Salaries Expense	32,000
Prepaid Insurance	2,400
Property Tax Expense	4,800
Property Tax Payable	4,800
Purchases	442,000
Purchase Discounts	12,000
Purchase Returns and Allowances	6,400
Retained Earnings	16,600
Sales	618,000
Sales Commissions Expense	14,500
Sales Commissions Payable	3,500
Sales Returns and Allowances	8,000
Sales Salaries Expense	76,000
Utilities Expense	11,000

Additional facts:

1. Merchandise inventory on December 31, 2001, is $75,000.
2. Note that N-Mart Department Store uses a periodic system.

Instructions

Prepare a multiple-step statement of earnings for the year ended December 31, 2001.

Determine items and amounts to be recorded in inventory. (SO 3)

P6-4B Banff Limited is trying to determine the value of its ending inventory as at February 28, 2001, the company's year end. The accountant counted everything that was in the warehouse, as at February 28, which resulted in an ending inventory valuation of $48,000. However, she didn't know how to treat the following transactions so she didn't record them.

(a) On February 26, Banff shipped goods costing $800 to a customer. The goods were shipped FOB shipping point and the receiving report indicates that the customer received the goods on March 2.

(b) On February 26, Seller Inc. shipped goods to Banff FOB destination. The invoice price was $350 plus $25 for freight. The receiving report indicates that the goods were received by Banff on March 2.

(c) Banff had $500 of inventory at a customer's warehouse "on approval." The customer was going to let Banff know whether it wanted the merchandise by the end of the week, March 4.

(d) Banff also had $400 of inventory at a Jasper craft shop, on consignment from Banff.

(e) On February 26, Banff ordered goods costing $750. The goods were shipped FOB shipping point. The receiving report indicates that Banff received the goods on March 1.

(f) On February 28, Banff packaged goods and had them ready for shipping to a customer FOB destination. The invoice price was $350 plus $25 for freight; the cost of the items was $280. The receiving report indicates that the goods were received by the customer on March 2.

(g) Banff had damaged goods set aside in the warehouse because they were not saleable. These goods originally cost $400 and, originally, Banff expected to sell these items for $600.

Instructions

For each of the above transactions, specify whether the item in question should be included in ending inventory, and if so, at what amount. For each item that is not included in ending inventory, indicate who owns it and what account, if any, it should have been recorded in.

Determine cost of goods sold and ending inventory using FIFO, average cost, and LIFO in a periodic inventory system, and assess financial statement effect.
(SO 5, 6)

P6-5B Steward Company Inc. had a beginning inventory of 400 units of Product MLN at a cost of $8.00 per unit. During the year, purchases were:

Feb. 20	700 units at $9	Aug. 12	300 units at $11
May 5	500 units at $10	Dec. 8	100 units at $12

Steward Company uses a periodic inventory system. Sales totalled 1,550 units.

Instructions

(a) Determine the cost of goods available for sale.
(b) Determine the ending inventory and the cost of goods sold under each of the assumed cost flow methods (FIFO, average cost, and LIFO). Prove the accuracy of the cost of goods sold under the FIFO and LIFO methods.
(c) Which cost flow method results in the lowest inventory amount for the balance sheet? The lowest cost of goods sold for the statement of earnings?

Calculate ending inventory, prepare statements of earnings, and answer questions using FIFO, average, and LIFO periodic inventory methods.
(SO 5, 6)

P6-6B The management of Real Novelty Inc. is reevaluating the appropriateness of using its present inventory cost flow method, which is average cost. The company requests your help in determining the results of operations for 2001 if the FIFO, average cost, or LIFO periodic inventory method had been used. For 2001 the accounting records show these data:

Inventories		**Purchases and Sales**	
Beginning (15,000 units)	$34,000	Total net sales (225,000 units)	$865,000
Ending (20,000 units)	?	Total cost of goods purchased (230,000 units)	578,500

Purchases were made quarterly as follows:

Quarter	Units	Unit Cost	Total Cost
1	60,000	$2.30	$138,000
2	50,000	2.50	125,000
3	50,000	2.60	130,000
4	70,000	2.65	185,500
	230,000		$578,500

Operating expenses were $147,000, and the company's income tax was $45,000 under all three methods.

Instructions

(a) Prepare comparative condensed statements of earnings for 2001 under FIFO, average, and LIFO. (Show calculations of ending inventory.)
(b) Answer the following questions for management:
  1. Which cost flow method produces the more meaningful inventory amount for the balance sheet? Why?
  2. Which cost flow method produces the more meaningful net earnings? Why?
  3. Which cost flow method is more likely to approximate the actual physical flow of goods? Why?
  4. How much cash will be available for management under each method?
  5. Which method provides the most realistic gross profit figure?

Calculate inventory turnover ratio, days in inventory, and current ratio.
(SO 8)

P6-7B SAM Sports Systems™ Inc. is a software company, located throughout Western Canada, marketing high-quality sports education multimedia to help coaches and athletes improve performance. The following information is available for SAM for the year ended April 30, 1999. Fiscal 1999 was SAM's first full year of operations.

	1999
Beginning inventory	$ 0
Ending inventory	4,966
Current assets	298,499
Current liabilities	259,851
Sales	1,472
Cost of goods sold	631

Instructions

Calculate the inventory turnover ratio, days in inventory, and current ratio for SAM for 1999. Comment on SAM's liquidity.

***P6-8B** You are provided with the following information for Lahti Inc. for the month ended October 31, 2002.

Calculate gross profit and ending inventory under FIFO and average cost flow assumptions for both periodic and perpetual methods.

(SO 5, 9)

Date	Description	Units	Unit Dollar Amount
October 1	Beginning inventory	60	$25
October 9	Purchase	120	26
October 11	Sale	100	35
October 17	Purchase	70	27
October 22	Sale	60	40
October 25	Purchase	80	28
October 29	Sale	150	40

Instructions

Calculate the gross profit and ending inventory assuming:

(a) that Lahti uses the FIFO cost flow assumption and
   1. a periodic inventory system,
   2. a perpetual inventory system;

(b) that Lahti uses the average cost flow assumption and
   1. a periodic inventory system,
   2. a perpetual inventory system.

(c) Compare your results obtained in (a) and (b), commenting particularly on any differences or similarities between each cost flow assumption and inventory system.

***P6-9B** Refer to the data provided in P6-3B for the N-Mart Department Store. Assume that instead of using a periodic inventory system, N-Mart uses a perpetual inventory system.

Prepare a multiple-step statement of earnings in a perpetual inventory system.

(SO 9)

Instructions

(a) Which accounts and amounts, appearing in a periodic inventory system general ledger, would *not* appear on a perpetual inventory system general ledger?

(b) What would be the amount of the cost of goods sold reported for the period in a perpetual inventory system? How does this amount compare to that reported for cost of goods sold in a periodic inventory system?

(c) Using the accounts reported in P6-3B and the cost of goods sold amount determined in (b), prepare a multiple-step statement of earnings for the year ended December 31, 2001.

***P6-10B** The Family Home Appliance Mart Ltd. began operations on May 1 and uses a perpetual inventory system. During May, the company had the following purchases and sales for its Model 25 Sureshot camera:

Determine cost of goods sold under FIFO, average, and LIFO perpetual inventory systems, and assess financial statement impact of each method.

(SO 6, 9)

	Purchases		Sales
Date	**Units**	**Unit Cost**	**Units**
July 1	5	$ 90	
July 6			3
July 11	4	99	
July 14			5
July 21	3	103	
July 27			4
July 29	2	106	

Instructions

(a) Determine the cost of goods sold under a perpetual inventory system using (1) FIFO, (2) moving average cost, and (3) LIFO.

(b) Which costing method produces the highest gross profit and net earnings?

(c) Which method produces the highest ending inventory valuation?

Prepare journal entries for FIFO, average, and LIFO under the perpetual system. Compare ending inventory, gross profit, and cash flow under each assumption.
(SO 6, 9)

***P6-11B** Yuan Li Ltd. is a retailer operating in Edmonton, Alberta. Yuan Li uses the perpetual inventory method. All sales returns from customers result in the goods being returned to inventory; the inventory is not damaged. Assume that there are no credit transactions; all amounts are settled in cash. You are provided with the following information for Yuan Li Ltd. for the month of January 2001.

Date	Description	Quantity	Unit Dollar Amount
December 31	Ending inventory	150	$17
January 2	Purchase	100	21
January 6	Sale	150	40
January 9	Sale return	10	40
January 9	Purchase	75	24
January 10	Purchase return	15	24
January 10	Sale	50	45
January 23	Purchase	100	28
January 30	Sale	160	50

Instructions

(a) For each of the following cost flow assumptions, prepare all required journal entries using the:
  1. FIFO cost flow assumption.
  2. moving average cost flow assumption.
  3. LIFO cost flow assumption.

(b) Compare the results of each assumption for
  1. the impact on ending inventory reported in the balance sheet.
  2. the impact on net cash flow.
  3. the impact on gross profit.

Compare specific identification and FIFO under perpetual method; use of cost flow assumption to influence earnings.
(SO 6, 9)

***P6-12B** You are provided with the following information for Discount Diamonds. Discount Diamonds uses the perpetual method of accounting for its inventory transactions. Discount only carries one brand and size of diamonds—all are identical. Each batch of diamonds purchased is carefully coded and marked with its purchase cost.

March 1	Opening inventory 150 diamonds at a cost of $300 per diamond.
March 3	Purchased 200 diamonds at a cost of $350 each.
March 5	Sold 180 diamonds for $600 each.
March 10	Purchased 350 diamonds at a cost of $375 each.
March 25	Sold 500 diamonds for $650 each.

Instructions

(a) Assume that Discount Diamonds uses the specific identification cost flow method.
  1. Demonstrate how Discount Diamonds could maximize its gross profit for the month by specifically selecting which diamonds to sell on March 5 and March 25.
  2. Demonstrate how Discount Diamonds could minimize its gross profit for the month by selecting which diamonds to sell on March 5 and March 25.

(b) Assume that Discount Diamonds uses the FIFO cost flow assumption. How much gross profit would Discount Diamonds report under this cost flow assumption?

(c) Which cost flow method should Discount Diamonds select? Explain.

Illustrate impact of inventory errors.
(SO 8, 10)

***P6-13B** The records of Pelletier Inc. show the following data:

Account	2001	2002
Sales	$300,000	$320,000
Beginning inventory	30,000	22,000
Cost of goods purchased	200,000	240,000
Ending inventory	22,000	31,000
Operating expenses	60,000	64,000

Subsequent to the July 31, 2002, year end, Pelletier Inc. discovers two errors. Its ending inventory was understated by $3,000 in 2001, and its cost of goods purchased was understated by $25,000 in 2002.

Instructions
(a) Prepare both incorrect and corrected Statements of Earnings for Pelletier Inc. for 2001 and 2002.
(b) Calculate both the incorrect and corrected inventory turnover ratios for 2001 and 2002.

BROADENING YOUR PERSPECTIVE

Financial Reporting and Analysis

FINANCIAL REPORTING PROBLEM: *Loblaw Companies Limited*

BYP6-1 The notes that accompany a company's financial statements provide informative details that would clutter the amounts and descriptions presented in the statements. Refer to the financial statements of **Loblaw** in Appendix A.

Instructions
Answer the following questions. (Give the amounts in millions of dollars, as shown in Loblaw's annual report.)
(a) What did Loblaw report for the amount of inventories in its consolidated balance sheet at January 1, 2000? At January 2, 1999?
(b) Calculate the dollar amount of change and the percentage change in inventories between 1998 and 1999. Calculate inventory as a percentage of current assets for each of the two years presented.
(c) Does Loblaw report cost of sales separately on its consolidated statement of earnings? If not, what does it include with cost of sales? Why might Loblaw not wish to report its cost of sales separately?

COMPARATIVE ANALYSIS PROBLEM: *Loblaw and Sobeys*

BYP6-2 The financial statements of **Sobeys Inc.** are presented in Appendix B, following the financial statements for **Loblaw** in Appendix A.

Instructions
(a) Based on the information in these statements, calculate these values for Loblaw and for Sobeys for fiscal 1999 and 1998:
   1. Inventory turnover ratio, using cost of sales, selling, and administrative expenses instead of cost of sales.
   2. Days in inventory.
(b) What conclusions concerning the management of inventory, and selling and administrative expenses can be drawn from your results in (a)?

RESEARCH CASE

BYP6-3 The March 5, 1999, issue of *Industry Week* contains an article by Doug Bartholomew entitled "What's Really Driving Apple's Recovery." Apple Computer, Inc. changed the computing world forever in the late 1970s with its "for dummies" approach to personal computing, and the invention of such products as the Macintosh computer.

Instructions
Read the article and answer these inventory-related questions:
(a) What were Timothy D. Cook's twin goals upon being hired as senior vice-president at Apple Computer Inc.?
(b) What did Cook say was the primary cause of Apple Computer's huge $1 billion loss in 1997?
(c) What was Apple's inventory turnover ratio in 1997, and what were its competitors' inventory turnover ratios?
(d) What improvements relative to inventory turnover did Cook accomplish by the end of 1998 at Apple Computer?

INTERPRETING FINANCIAL STATEMENTS

BYP6-4 **Morrow Snowboards** is a leading designer, manufacturer, and marketer of premium snowboards. Morrow's sales total about 50% in North America, 40% in Japan, and 10% in Europe. In 1997, Morrow acquired Westbeach Snowboard Canada Ltd., a snowboard apparel company, in an effort to increase its growth rate and expand its product line. In addition, Blair Mullin, Westbeach's CEO, has become Morrow's CFO, a move that company officials believed would strengthen the financial end of Morrow's business.

A couple of years earlier, in 1995 when Morrow went public, it disclosed the following information in its prospectus. A prospectus is an information-filled document that must be provided by every publicly traded firm the first time it issues shares to the public.

MORROW SNOWBOARDS
Prospectus

Uncertain Ability to Manage Growth: Since inception, the Company has experienced rapid growth in its sales, production, and employee base. These increases have placed significant demands on the Company's management, working capital, and financial and management control systems. The Company's independent auditors used management letters in connection with their audit of the fiscal years ended December 31, 1993 and 1994, and the 9-month period ended September 30, 1995, that identified certain significant deficiencies in the Company's accounting systems, procedures, and controls. To address these growth issues, the Company has, in the past 18 months, relocated its facilities and expanded production capacity, implemented a number of financial accounting control systems, and hired experienced finance, accounting, manufacturing, and marketing personnel. In the accounting area, the Company has begun implementing or improving a perpetual inventory system, a cost accounting system, written accounting policies and procedures, and a comprehensive annual capital expenditure budget. Until the Company develops a reliable perpetual inventory system, it intends to perform physical inventories on a quarterly basis. Although the Company is continuously evaluating and improving its facilities, management, and financial control systems, there can be no assurance that such improvements will meet the demands of future growth. Any inadequacies in these areas could have a material adverse effect on the Company's business, financial condition, and results of operations.

Instructions

(a) What implications did this disclosure likely have for someone interested in investing in Morrow Snowboards?
(b) Do you think that the price of Morrow's shares suffered because of these admitted deficiencies in its internal controls, including its controls over inventory?
(c) Why do you think Morrow decided to disclose this negative information?
(d) List the steps that Morrow has taken to improve its control systems.
(e) Do you think that these weaknesses are unusual for a rapidly growing company?

BYP6-5 **Nike** and **Reebok** compete head-to-head in the sport shoe and sport apparel business. For both companies, inventory is a significant portion of total assets. The following information was taken from each company's financial statements and notes to those financial statements.

NIKE, INC.
Notes to the Financial Statements

Inventory. Inventories are stated at the lower of cost or market. Cost is determined using the last-in, first-out (LIFO) method for substantially all U.S. inventories. International inventories are valued on a first-in, first-out (FIFO) basis.

Inventories by major classification are as follows (in thousands of US$):

	May 31	
	1998	**1997**
Finished goods	$1,303.8	$1,248.4
Work in process	34.7	50.2
Raw materials	58.1	40.0

Other information for Nike (in thousands of US$):

	1998	1997
Inventory	$1,396.6	$1,338.6
Cost of goods sold	6,065.5	5,503.0

REEBOK INTERNATIONAL, LTD.
Notes to the Financial Statements

Inventory. Inventory, substantially all finished goods, is recorded at the lower of cost (first-in, first-out method) or market.

Other information for Reebok (in thousands of US$):

	1998	1997
Inventory	$ 535.5	$ 563.7
Cost of goods sold	2,037.5	2,294.0

Instructions

Address each of these questions on how these two companies manage inventory:

(a) What problems of inventory management face Nike and Reebok in the international sport apparel industry?

(b) What inventory cost flow assumptions does each company use? Why might Nike use a different approach for U.S. operations than for international operations? What are the implications of their respective cost flow assumptions for their financial statements?

(c) Nike provides more detail than does Reebok regarding the nature of its inventory (e.g., raw materials, work in process, and finished goods). How might this additional information be useful in evaluating Nike?

(d) Calculate and interpret the inventory turnover ratio and days in inventory for each company. Comment on how the use of different cost flow methods by the two companies affects your ability to compare their ratios.

A GLOBAL FOCUS

BYP6-6 Fuji Photo Film Co., Ltd. is a Japanese manufacturer of photographic products. Its counterpart, and arch rival, is U.S.-based **Eastman Kodak**. Together, the two dominate the global market for film. The following information was extracted from the financial statements of the two companies.

FUJI PHOTO FILM CO., LTD.
Notes to the Financial Statements

Summary of significant accounting policies

The Company and its domestic subsidiaries maintain their records and prepare their financial statements in accordance with accounting practices generally accepted in Japan...Certain reclassifications and adjustments...have been incorporated in the accompanying consolidated financial statements to conform with accounting principles generally accepted in the United States.

Inventories

Inventories are valued at the lower of cost or market, cost being determined generally by the moving average method, except that the cost of the principal raw materials is determined by the last-in, first-out method.

Note 6. Inventories

Inventories at March 31, 1998 and 1997 consisted of the following:

	(millions of yen)		(millions of U.S. dollars)	
	1998	1997	1998	1997
Finished goods	¥135,795	¥123,010	$1,028.8	
Work in process	51,001	48,867	386.4	
Raw materials and supplies	55,525	46,959	420.6	
	¥242,321	¥218,836	$1,835.8	$1,764.8

Additional information

1998 beginning total inventory was $1,764.8 million; 1998 cost of goods sold, $5,575 million.

Kodak

EASTMAN KODAK COMPANY
Notes to the Financial Statements

Inventories

Inventories are valued at cost, which is not in excess of market. The cost of most inventories in the U.S. is determined by the last-in, first-out (LIFO) method.

EASTMAN KODAK COMPANY
Notes to the Financial Statements

Authors' helpful hint: Using different inventory cost flow assumptions complicates attempts to compare the results of companies that use different inventory methods. Fortunately, in the U.S., companies using LIFO are required to also report their inventory using an alternate cost flow assumption. The following note presents Eastman Kodak Company's inventories at FIFO or average cost, in addition to LIFO.

Note 3. Inventories

	(millions of U.S. dollars)	
	1998	**1997**
At FIFO or average cost (approximates current cost)		
Finished goods	$ 907	$ 788
Work in process	569	538
Raw materials and supplies	439	460
Total inventories at FIFO or average	$ 1,915	$ 1,786
At LIFO		
Total inventories at LIFO	$ 1,424	$ 1,252

Additional information

1998 cost of goods sold, $7,293 million.

Instructions

(a) Why do you suppose Fuji makes reclassifications and adjustments to its accounts so that they conform with U.S. accounting principles and currency when it reports its results?

(b) Does Fuji use a perpetual or periodic inventory method to account for most of its inventories?

(c) Why do you think Fuji would use a different cost flow assumption to account for its inventory of raw materials than is used to account for finished goods and work in process?

(d) Using the FIFO/average cost flow assumptions, what are the 1998 inventory turnover ratios and days in inventory of the two companies in U.S. dollars? How does this comparison change when you use Eastman Kodak's inventory figures at LIFO to calculate the inventory turnover and days in inventory? Explain which comparison is the most relevant for decision-making purposes.

(e) Calculate, as a percentage of total inventory, the portion that each of the components of 1998 inventory (raw materials, work in process, and finished goods) represents. Comment on your findings.

FINANCIAL ANALYSIS ON THE WEB

BYP6-7 ***Purpose:*** Use a company's annual report to identify the inventory method used and analyse the effects on the statement of earnings and balance sheet.

Instructions

Specific requirements of this Web case can be found on the Kimmel website.

Critical Thinking

COLLABORATIVE LEARNING ACTIVITY

BYP6-8 Headquartered in Aurora, Ontario, **Magna International Inc.** makes everything you need for a car, van, or truck including instrument panels, seats, bumpers, engines, doors, chassis, and interior and exterior components. The company can even assemble the vehicle. Magna sells to manufacturers in Asia, Europe, and North and South America. Magna operates more than 162 plants and 29 development centres in 18 countries.

Magna's inventories, reported on its balance sheet at July 31, 1998, total $1,094.7 million. Assume that the following transactions occurred during July and August 1998.

1. Office supplies were shipped to Magna by Office Maxx, FOB destination. The goods were shipped July 31 and received August 3.
2. Magna purchased specialty plastic from DuPont Canada for use in the manufacture of door mouldings. The goods were shipped FOB shipping point July 31 and received August 3.
3. Ford Motor Company of Canada, Limited purchased 3,000 rear liftgate assemblies to be used in the manufacture of the Ford Windstar. They were shipped FOB shipping point July 29, and were received by Ford August 1.
4. Nadeau Furniture shipped office furniture to Magna, FOB destination, July 27. The furniture was received August 3.
5. Inland Specialty Chemical shipped Magna chemicals that Magna uses in the manufacture of door mouldings and other items. The goods were sent FOB shipping point July 30, and were received August 3.
6. Magna purchased new Cadillac Sevilles for its executives to drive. The cars were shipped FOB destination July 30, and were received August 5.
7. Magna purchased steel, to be used in expanding its manufacturing plant, from IPSCO, FOB Regina (shipping point). The steel was shipped July 30, arrived in Ontario August 2, and at Magna's plant in Aurora, August 3.
8. Magna shipped instrument panels to Jaguar, FOB destination Coventry, England. The panels were shipped July 31, arrived in England August 5, and at Jaguar's headquarters August 7.

Instructions
With the class divided into groups, answer the following:

(a) Which of the above items are owned by Magna International as at July 31, 1998?
(b) Determine which of the above transactions affect Magna's Inventory account, and whether the transaction would result in an increase or a decrease in the Inventory account.

COMMUNICATION ACTIVITIES

BYP6-9 In a discussion of dramatic increases in coffee bean prices, a recent newspaper article noted the following fact about **Starbucks:**

> Before this year's bean-price hike, Starbucks added several defences that analysts say could help it maintain earnings and revenue. The company last year began accounting for its coffee-bean purchases by taking the average price of all beans in inventory.
>
> *Source:* Aaron Lucchetti, "Crowded Coffee Market May Keep a Lid on Starbucks After Price Rise Hurt Stock," *The Wall Street Journal,* June 4, 1997, C1.

Prior to this change the company was using FIFO.

Instructions
Your client, the CEO of **The Second Cup Ltd.**, read this article and sent you an e-mail message requesting that you explain why Starbucks might have taken this action. The

Second Cup Ltd. currently uses FIFO to cost its inventories. Your response should explain what impact this change in accounting method has on earnings, why the company might want to do this, and any possible disadvantages of such a change.

*BYP6-10 You are the controller of Small Toys Inc. Joy Small, the president, recently mentioned to you that she found an error in the 2000 financial statements which she believes has corrected itself. She determined, in discussions with the purchasing department, that 2000 ending inventory was overstated by $1 million. Joy says that the 2001 ending inventory is correct, and she assumes that 2001 net earnings are correct. Joy says to you, "What happened has happened—there's no point in worrying about it anymore."

Instructions

You conclude that Joy is incorrect. Write a brief, tactful memo to her, clarifying the situation.

ETHICS CASE

BYP6-11 Lonergan Wholesale Corp. uses the average cost flow method. In the current year, profit at Lonergan is running unusually high. The corporate tax rate is also high this year, but it is scheduled to decline significantly next year. In an effort to lower the current year's net earnings and to take advantage of the changing income tax rate, the president of Lonergan Wholesale instructs the plant accountant to recommend to the purchasing department a large purchase of inventory for delivery three days before the end of the year. The price of the inventory to be purchased has doubled during the year, and the purchase will represent a major portion of the ending inventory value.

Instructions

(a) What is the effect of this transaction on this year's and next year's statement of earnings and income tax expense? Why?

(b) If Lonergan Wholesale had been using the FIFO method of inventory costing, would the president give the same directive?

(c) Should the plant accountant order the inventory purchase to lower earnings? What are the ethical implications of this order?

Answers to Self-Study Questions

1. b 2. d 3. a 4. a 5. c 6. d 7. c 8. c 9. a 10. d *11. c *12. b

Answer to Loblaw Review It Question 2

Loblaw uses the FIFO (first-in, first-out) method to account for its inventories. Loblaw does apply the LCM rule and values its inventories at the lower of FIFO cost and net realizable value.

Loblaws
A passion for food... and a lot more!

CHAPTER 7

Internal Control and Cash

STUDY OBJECTIVES

After studying this chapter, you should be able to:

1. Identify the principles of internal control.
2. Explain the applications of internal control to cash receipts.
3. Explain the applications of internal control to cash disbursements.
4. Prepare a bank reconciliation.
5. Explain the reporting of cash.
6. Discuss the basic principles of cash management.
7. Identify the primary elements of a cash budget.
8. Identify and interpret measures that evaluate the adequacy of cash.

Counting Out the Money

Couples, students, locals just finished work—on any given evening you can find them all hanging out at the Granite Brewery, enjoying traditional pub food and a range of international cuisine, not to mention quality ale brewed right on the premises. The Brewery, which seats about 120 diners on two floors and employs 25 people, has become something of a Halifax institution since it opened in 1987. "We're right downtown, but not in the bar core," explains general manager Denise Avery. "We have great music, but it's not so loud that you can't have a conversation. And our food is a little more upscale than in many bars—but with generous portions. You get a bang for your buck!"

These attractions bring in over $1 million in annual sales to the Brewery, all of which flows in one way or another through the hands of its wait staff. Ms. Avery has a detailed system in place to track it all.

"There are two cash registers—one upstairs and one down," explains Ms. Avery, "and up to three people might use each one on any given shift. Each server has a private code number that they punch into the register when they ring up a sale, and it tracks their totals separately." Everyone is given a float of $30 at the beginning of the shift to make change from, and is responsible for turning in that amount plus whatever his or her cash receipts total is at the end.

What if there's a discrepancy between the machine's total and the amount in the till? "The machine prints two tapes—one we can use as receipts and one that stays inside," says Ms. Avery, "so we can look for the error." The register is preprogrammed with the cost of each item, so the staff need not enter any numbers—they just press a button labelled "domestic beer" or "fish and chips." "That and the cash register codes eliminate a lot of problems," Ms. Avery says.

"With a good system, discrepancies just don't happen often," she continues. "If ever there is one, it's usually pretty easy to find the problem from looking at the cash tapes. Of course, theft is always the last thing you want to think of. The controls are there so that there is practically no opportunity for trouble. You assume your staff is

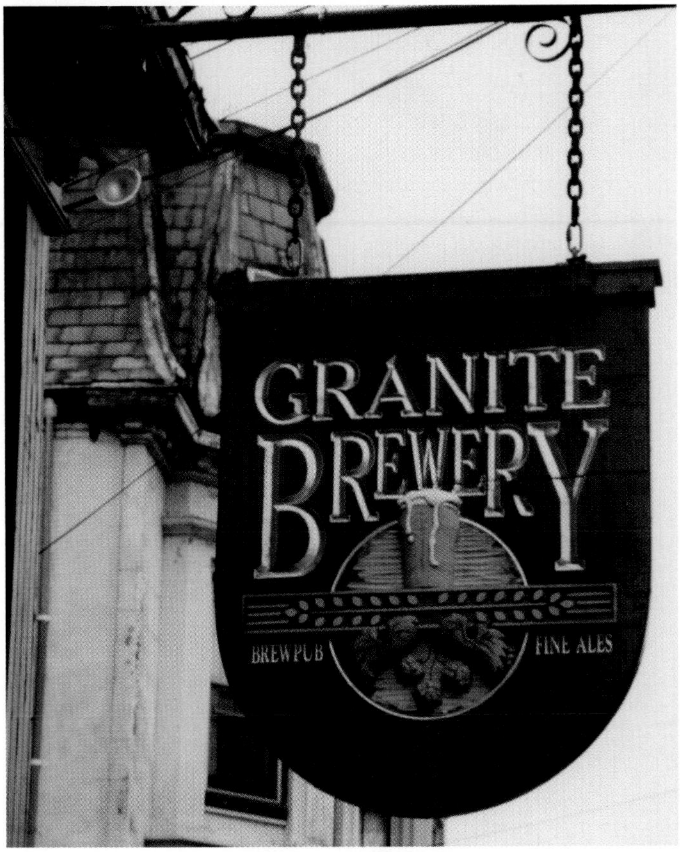

On the World Wide Web
Granite Brewery
http://www.granitebrewery.ca

honest, but you know there's such a thing as human nature, so you don't put temptation in their way."

Of course, these days, fewer and fewer customers pay with actual cash. Ms. Avery estimates that about 40% of sales are paid for by debit card, and another 20% by bank credit card, so that actual cash makes up less than half of a day's receipts. These amounts—considered cash for accounting purposes—are processed through the two debit/credit card machines (one by each cash) which also produce totals for each member of the wait staff at the end of the shift. Since the amounts are transferred electronically directly to the Granite Brewery's bank account, there's virtually no chance of discrepancies with these amounts.

"At the end of the day—or more realistically, the next morning," laughs Ms. Avery, "I prepare the deposit and take the cash to the bank." At the end of the month, "everything is reconciled on the computer—cash, sales, payables. We have ACC-PAC computerized accounting software, which works just fine."

Cash control is crucial to a business like the Granite Brewery. "A place like this is basically a cash business," says Ms. Avery. "We have almost no receivables." But with a carefully thought-out system and the help of modern automation, cash can be controlled reliably and fairly easily. The owner doesn't like to be bothered with daily problems, Ms. Avery explains; it's her job to keep things running smoothly so he can spend his time brewing great beer.

PREVIEW OF CHAPTER 7

Cash is the lifeblood of any company. Large and small companies alike must guard it carefully. Even companies that are in every other way successful can go bankrupt if they fail to manage cash. Managers must know both how to use cash efficiently and how to protect it, as described in the opening story. Due to its liquid nature, cash is the easiest asset to steal.

In this chapter, you will learn ways to reduce the risk of theft of cash and other assets, how to report cash in the financial statements, and how to manage cash through the course of the company's operating cycle. The content and organization of the chapter are as follows:

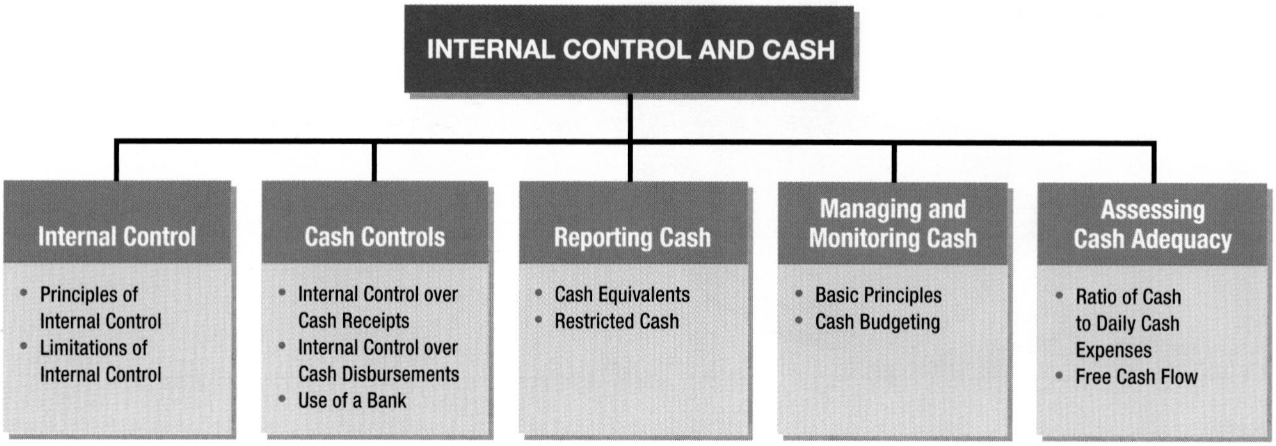

INTERNAL CONTROL

In KPMG's 1999 *Fraud Survey Report*, 57% of the respondents from Canada's 1,000 largest companies reported that fraud had occurred in their organization in 1998. The average amount of money lost to fraud in 1998 was $958,927. One company reported that it had been defrauded of $25 million. Survey findings such as these emphasize the need for a good system of internal control.

Internal control consists of all the related methods and measures adopted within a business to

1. **optimize the use of resources** to reduce inefficiencies and waste
2. **prevent and detect errors and irregularities** in the accounting process
3. **safeguard assets** from theft, robbery, and unauthorized use
4. **maintain reliable control systems** to enhance the accuracy and reliability of its accounting records

All federally incorporated companies are required, under the *Canada Business Corporations Act*, to maintain an adequate system of internal control. The CICA's Criteria of Control Board stresses that this internal control should address not only external financial reporting, but also the reliability of internal reporting.

BUSINESS INSIGHT

Investor Perspective

Poor internal controls can cost a company money even if no theft occurs. For example, it was once reported that the share prices of two companies, Morrow Snowboards and Home Theatre Products, suffered because their auditors said that the firms had inadequate internal controls. The prices fell because investors and creditors are uncomfortable investing in companies that don't have good internal controls. In addition, companies can even be fined for having poor internal controls. German multinational corporation Metallgesellschaft was fined by the Commodities Futures Trading Commission for material inadequacies in internal control systems.

PRINCIPLES OF INTERNAL CONTROL

STUDY OBJECTIVE 1

Identify the principles of internal control.

To optimize resources, prevent and detect errors and irregularities, safeguard assets, and maintain reliable systems, a company follows internal control principles. The specific control measures used vary with the size and nature of the business and with management's control philosophy. However, the six principles listed in Illustration 7-1 apply to most enterprises. Each principle is explained in the following sections.

Illustration 7-1 Principles of internal control

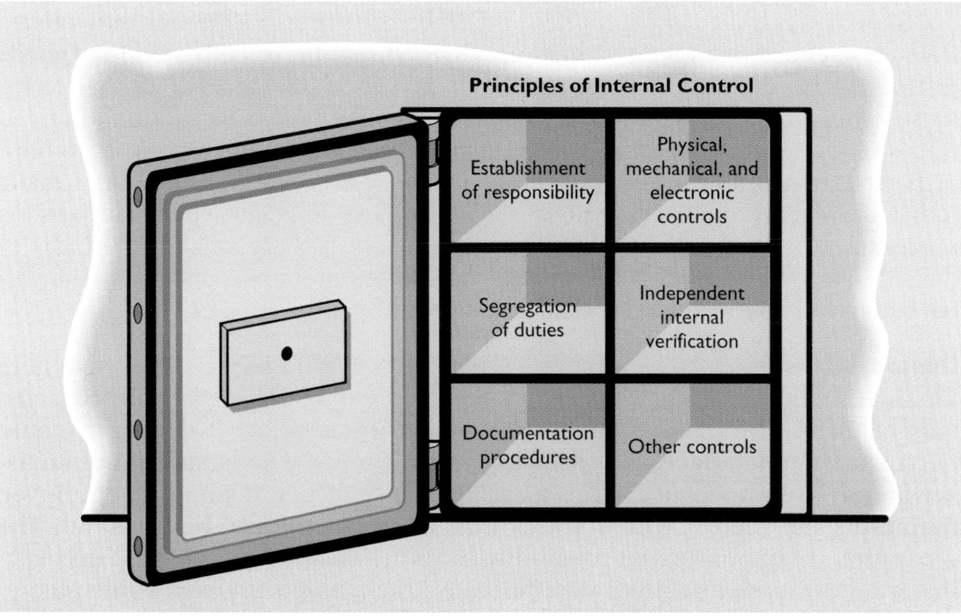

Establishment of Responsibility

An essential characteristic of internal control is the assignment of responsibility to specific individuals. **Control is most effective when only one person is responsible for a given task.** To illustrate, assume that the cash on hand at the end of the day in a Loblaw superstore is $10 short of the cash rung up on the cash register. If only one person has operated the register, responsibility for the shortage can be attributed quickly. If two or more individuals have worked the register, it may be impossible to determine who is responsible for the error unless each person is assigned a separate cash drawer or code number as used at the Granite Brewery, described in the opening story.

Transfer of cash drawers

Responsibility must also be assigned for the authorization and approval of transactions. The vice-president of sales should ordinarily have the authority to establish policies for making credit sales. Typically, these policies require written credit department approval of credit sales.

Segregation of Duties

Segregation of duties is indispensable in a system of internal control. There are two common applications of this principle:

1. The responsibility for related activities should be assigned to different individuals.
2. The responsibility for keeping the records for an asset should be separate from the responsibility for physical custody of that asset.

Segregation of duties is used as a measure of control because the work of one employee should, without a duplication of effort, provide a reliable basis for evaluating the work of another employee.

Related Activities. Related activities should be assigned to different individuals in both the purchasing and selling areas. **When one individual is responsible for all of the related activities, the potential for errors and irregularities is increased.** *Related purchasing activities* include ordering merchandise, receiving goods, and paying (or authorizing payment) for merchandise. In purchasing, for example, orders could be placed with friends or with suppliers who give kickbacks. In addition, payment might be authorized without a careful review of the invoice or, even worse, fictitious invoices might be approved for payment. When the responsibilities for ordering, receiving, and paying are assigned to different individuals, the risk of such abuses is minimized.

Similarly, *related sales activities* should be assigned to different individuals. Related sales activities include making a sale, shipping (or delivering) the goods to the customer, and billing the customer. When one person is responsible for these related sales transactions, a salesperson could make sales at unauthorized prices to increase sales commissions, a shipping clerk could ship goods to him- or herself, or a billing clerk could understate the amount billed for sales made to friends and relatives. These abuses are less likely to occur when salespersons make the sale, shipping department employees ship the goods on the basis of the sales order, and billing department employees prepare the sales invoice after comparing the sales order with the report of goods shipped.

Custody of Assets. If accounting is to provide a valid basis of accountability for an asset, the accountant (as record keeper) should have neither physical custody of the asset nor access to it. Moreover, the custodian of the asset should not maintain or have access to the accounting records. **The custodian of an asset is not likely to convert the asset to personal use if another employee maintains the record which states that the asset should be on hand.** The separation of accounting responsibility from the custody of assets is especially important for cash and inventories, because these assets are very vulnerable to unauthorized use or misappropriation.

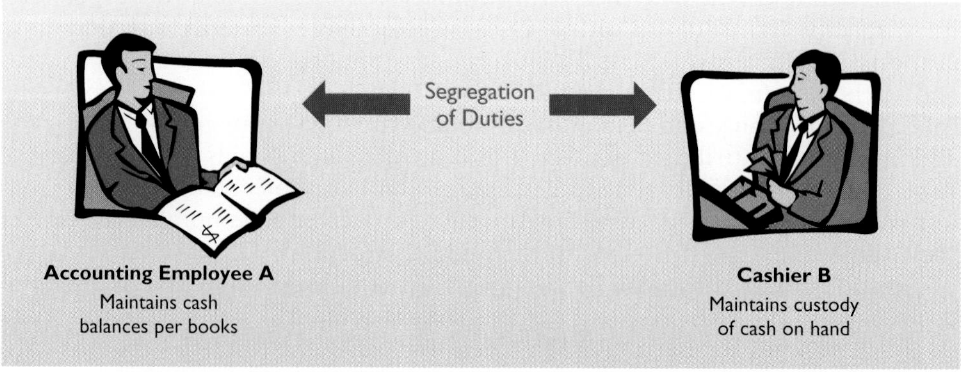

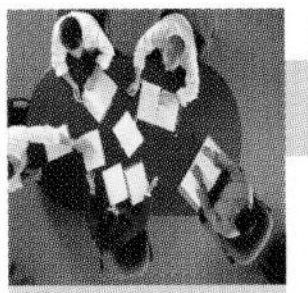

BUSINESS INSIGHT

Management Perspective

A senior administrator at the Hospital for Sick Children in Toronto, in charge of a $10.8 million budget, was recently accused of using hospital money and donations for her own benefit. An audit revealed that the administrator was reimbursed for purchases of CDs, food, and toys that allegedly never made it to the children's ward. In addition, the administrator convinced other employees at the hospital to file expenses in their own names, endorse their reimbursement cheques, and give them back to her. She then countersigned the cheques and deposited them in her own personal account. The audit also revealed that the now former administrator had a taste for the luxurious—spending $122,000 on computers, paintings, shoes, coats, and even liquor.

How did this happen? She had sole signing authority for purchases under $10,000. The lesson here is simple: the same person should not both authorize and pay for goods and services. Doing otherwise violates the segregation of duties principle of internal control.

Source: Krista Foss, "Sick Kids Audit Details Expense Abuse," *Globe and Mail*, October 23, 1999, A6.

Documentation Procedures

Documents provide evidence that transactions and events have occurred. For example, the shipping document indicates that the goods have been shipped, and the sales invoice indicates that the customer has been billed for the goods. By adding a signature (or initials) to the documents, the individual responsible for the transaction or event can be identified.

Procedures should be established for documents. First, whenever possible, **documents should be prenumbered and all documents should be accounted for**. Prenumbering helps to prevent a transaction from being recorded more than once or, conversely, to prevent the transaction from not being recorded. Second, documents that are **source documents for accounting entries should be promptly forwarded to the accounting department to help ensure timely recording of the transaction and event**. This control measure contributes directly to the accuracy and reliability of the accounting records.

Helpful Hint An important step in prenumbering is keeping voided documents until all documents are accounted for.

Physical, Mechanical, and Electronic Controls

Use of physical, mechanical, and electronic controls is essential. Physical controls relate primarily to the safeguarding of assets. Mechanical and electronic controls safeguard assets and enhance the accuracy and reliability of the accounting records. Examples of these controls are shown in Illustration 7-2.

Many books and movies have been produced with computer system tampering as a major theme. When computerized systems are being programmed, building in controls that limit unauthorized or unintentional tampering is a crucial consideration. Most programmers would agree that tamper proofing and debugging programs are the most difficult and time-consuming phases of their jobs. Program controls built into the computer prevent intentional or unintentional errors or unauthorized access. To prevent unauthorized access, the computer system may require that passwords be entered and random personal questions be correctly answered before system access is allowed. Once access has been allowed, other program controls identify data having a value higher or lower than a predetermined amount (limit checks), validate calculations (math checks), and detect improper processing orders (sequence checks).

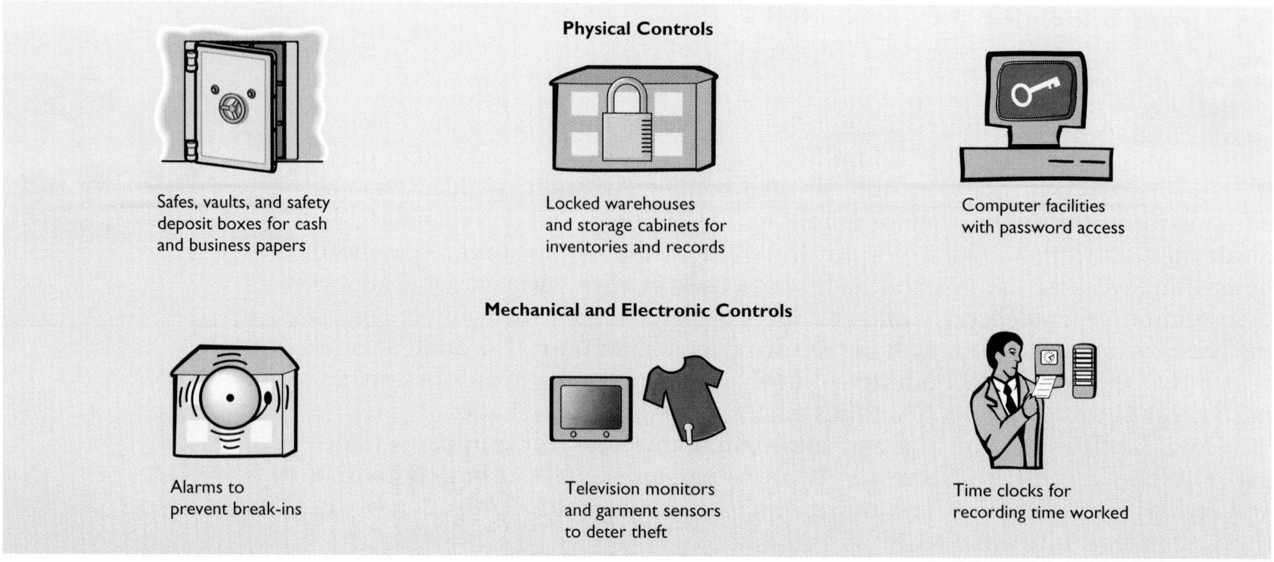

Illustration 7-2 Physical, mechanical, and electronic controls

Independent Internal Verification

Most systems of internal control provide for independent internal verification. This principle involves the review, comparison, and reconciliation of data prepared by employees. Three measures are recommended to obtain maximum benefit from independent internal verification:

1. The verification should be done periodically or on a surprise basis.
2. The verification should be done by an employee who is independent of the personnel responsible for the information.
3. Discrepancies and exceptions should be reported to a management level that can take appropriate corrective action.

Independent internal verification is especially useful in comparing accounting records with existing assets. The reconciliation of the cash register tape with the cash in the register at the Granite Brewery in the opening story is an example. Another common example is the reconciliation by an independent person of the cash balance per books with the cash balance per bank. The relationship between this principle and the segregation of duties principle is shown in Illustration 7-3.

Illustration 7-3 Relationship of segregation of duties principle to independent internal verification principle

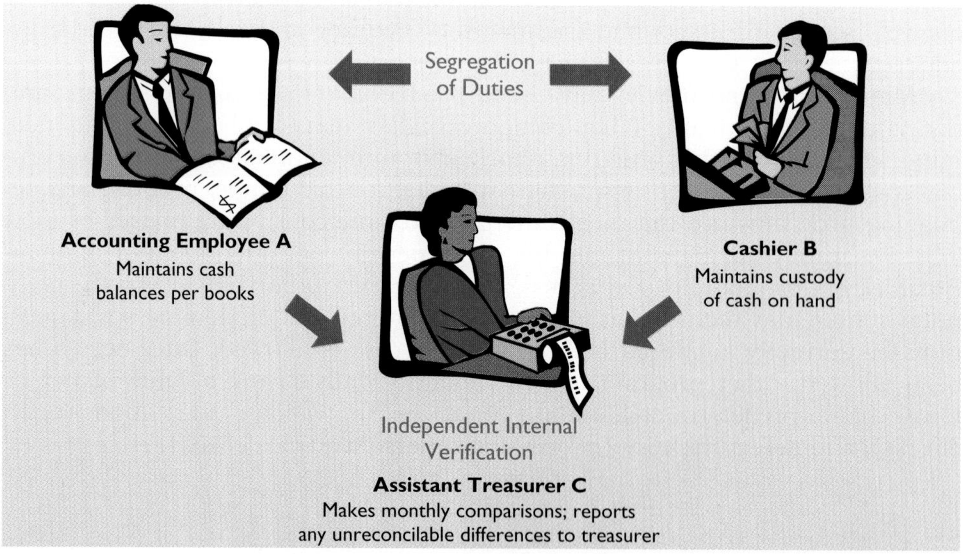

In large companies, independent internal verification is often assigned to internal auditors. **Internal auditors** are employees of the company who evaluate on a continuous basis the effectiveness of the company's system of internal control. They periodically review the activities of departments and individuals to determine whether prescribed internal controls are being followed. The importance of this function is illustrated by the fact that most fraud is discovered by the company through internal mechanisms, such as existing internal controls and internal audits. KPMG reports that only 5% of fraud is discovered by external auditors.

BUSINESS INSIGHT

International Perspective

In 1996, Sumitomo Corporation became the fifth Japanese company to announce a huge loss, this time a $1.8 billion copper trading loss. Some blamed Japanese culture, because it encourages group harmony over confrontation and thus may contribute to poor internal controls. For example, good controls require that both parties to a copper trade send a confirmation slip directly to management to verify all trades. In Japan, however, the counter-party to the trade often sends the confirmation slip to the trader, who then forwards it to management. It is thus possible for the trader to change the confirmation slip. An unethical trader could create fictitious trades to hide losses for an extended period of time or to conceal trades that are larger than allowed limits.

Source: Adapted from Sheryl Wudunn, "Big New Loss Makes Japan Look Inward," *New York Times*, June 17, 1996, D1.

Other Controls

Here are two other control measures:

1. **Bonding of employees who handle cash.** Bonding involves obtaining insurance protection against misappropriation of assets by dishonest employees. This measure contributes to the safeguarding of cash in two ways: first, the insurance company carefully screens all individuals before adding them to the policy and may reject risky applicants. Second, bonded employees know that the insurance company will vigorously prosecute all offenders.
2. **Rotating employees' duties and requiring employees to take vacations.** These measures are designed to deter employees from attempting any thefts, since they will not be able to permanently conceal their improper actions. Many bank embezzlements, for example, have been discovered when the perpetrator was on vacation or assigned to a new position.

DECISION TOOLKIT

Decision Checkpoints	Info Needed for Decision	Tool to Use for Decision	How to Evaluate Results
Are the company's financial statements supported by adequate internal controls?	Auditor's report, statement of management responsibility, management discussion and analysis, articles in financial press	The required measures of internal control are to (1) establish responsibility, (2) segregate duties, (3) document procedures, (4) employ physical or automated controls, and (5) use independent internal verification.	If any indication is given that these or other controls are lacking, the financial statements should be used with caution.

LIMITATIONS OF INTERNAL CONTROL

International Note

Other countries also have control problems. For example, a judge in France issued a 36-page "book" detailing many of the scams that are widespread, such as kickbacks in public works contracts, the skimming of development aid money to Africa, and bribes on arms sales.

A company's system of internal control is generally designed to provide **reasonable assurance** that assets are properly safeguarded and that the accounting records are reliable—in other words, that a reliable control system is maintained. **The concept of reasonable assurance rests on the premise that the costs of establishing control procedures should not exceed their expected benefit.** To illustrate, consider shoplifting losses in retail stores. Such losses could be completely eliminated by having a security guard stop and search customers as they leave the store. Store managers have concluded, however, that the negative effects of this procedure cannot be justified. Instead, stores have attempted to "control" shoplifting losses by using less costly procedures such as (1) posting signs saying, "We reserve the right to inspect all packages" and "All shoplifters will be prosecuted," (2) using hidden TV cameras and store detectives to monitor customer activity, and (3) using sensor equipment at exits.

The **human element** is an important factor in every system of internal control. A good system can become ineffective as a result of employee fatigue, carelessness, or indifference. For example, a receiving clerk may not bother to count goods received or may just "fudge" the counts. Occasionally, two or more individuals may work together to get around prescribed controls. Such **collusion** can significantly impair the effectiveness of a system because it eliminates the protection expected from segregation of duties. If a supervisor and a cashier collaborate to understate cash receipts, the system of internal control may be subverted (at least in the short run). This is what happened when the Sick Kids administrator and other employees worked together to allegedly abuse expense reimbursements. No system of internal control is perfect.

The size of the business may impose limitations on internal control. In a small company, for example, it may be difficult to apply the principles of segregation of duties and independent internal verification because of the small number of employees. In such instances, the owner usually assumes responsibility for, or oversees, incompatible functions and internal verification.

It has been suggested that the most important and inexpensive measure a business can take to reduce employee theft and fraud is to conduct thorough background checks. Two tips: (1) Check to see whether job applicants actually graduated from the schools they list. (2) Never use the telephone numbers for previous employers given on the reference sheet: always look them up yourself.

BEFORE YOU GO ON . . .

Review It

1. What are the four primary objectives of internal control?
2. Identify and describe the principles of internal control.
3. What are the limitations of internal control?

Do It

Li Song owns a small retail store. Li wants to establish good internal control procedures but is confused about the difference between segregation of duties and independent internal verification. Explain the differences to Li.

Reasoning: In order to help Li, you need to thoroughly understand each principle. From this knowledge and a study of Illustration 7-3, you should be able to explain the differences between the two principles.

Solution: Segregation of duties pertains to the assignment of responsibility so that (1) the work of one employee will evaluate the work of another employee and (2) the custody of assets is separated from the records that keep track of the assets. Segregation of duties occurs daily in using assets and in executing and recording transactions. In contrast, independent internal verification involves reviewing, comparing, and reconciling data prepared by one or several employees. Independent internal verification occurs after the fact, as in reconciling cash register totals at the end of the day with cash on hand.

CASH CONTROLS

Cash consists of coins, currency (paper money), cheques, money orders, and money on hand or on deposit in a bank or similar depository. The general rule is that if the bank will accept it for deposit, it is cash. Debit card transactions and bank credit card receipts, such as VISA and MasterCard, are considered to be cash but non-bank credit card receipts are not. (We will discuss the classification and accounting for these types of transactions in more detail in Chapter 8.) In addition, cash does *not* include postdated (payable in the future) or stale-dated (in excess of six months old) cheques, returned (NSF) cheques (receivables), postage stamps (office supplies), IOUs from employees (receivables), and the like, because these items are not the current medium of exchange, or acceptable at face value on deposit.

Just as cash is the beginning of a company's operating cycle, it is usually the starting point for a company's system of internal control. Cash is the one asset that is readily convertible into any other type of asset, easily concealed and transported, and highly desired. Because of these characteristics, cash is the asset most susceptible to improper diversion and use. Moreover, because of the large volume of cash transactions, numerous errors may occur in executing and recording such transactions. To safeguard cash and to ensure the accuracy of the accounting records, effective internal control over cash is imperative. The application of internal control principles to cash receipts and cash disbursements is explained in the next sections.

BUSINESS INSIGHT

Management Perspective

Counterfeiting is a growth business in Canada. In 1997 and 1998, the RCMP Central Bureau for Counterfeits reported more than a 90% increase in the face value of fake Bank of Canada notes. Counterfeit bills typically sell for 10% to 30% of the face value of the note. The face value of the notes seized by the RCMP exceeded \$5 million in 1998 and consisted primarily of \$10 bills. Bills of denominations over \$20 contain a metallic optical security device to deter counterfeiting.

"Developments in technology have a lot to do with the increase in counterfeiting," says Paul Laurin, head of the RCMP's counterfeiting squad. Colour copiers are technically more advanced, as well as cheaper, than the printing presses used in the past. An estimated 96% of forged currency is printed today on colour copiers. However, manufacturers of copiers have added hidden security features that may allow a copier to be connected with a particular crime.

Source: Margret Brady, "Spot the Fake", *Financial Post*, February 8, 1997, 25.

INTERNAL CONTROL OVER CASH RECEIPTS

STUDY OBJECTIVE 2

Explain the applications of internal control to cash receipts.

Cash receipts result from a variety of sources: cash sales; collections on account from customers; the receipt of interest, rents, and dividends; investments by shareholders; bank loans; and proceeds from the sale of noncurrent assets. A fundamental principle with respect to internal control over cash receipts is that **cash receipts should be deposited intact into the bank account on a daily basis**. The internal control principles explained earlier apply to cash receipt transactions as shown in Illustration 7-4. As might be expected, companies vary considerably in how they apply these principles.

Illustration 7-4 Application of internal control principles to cash receipts

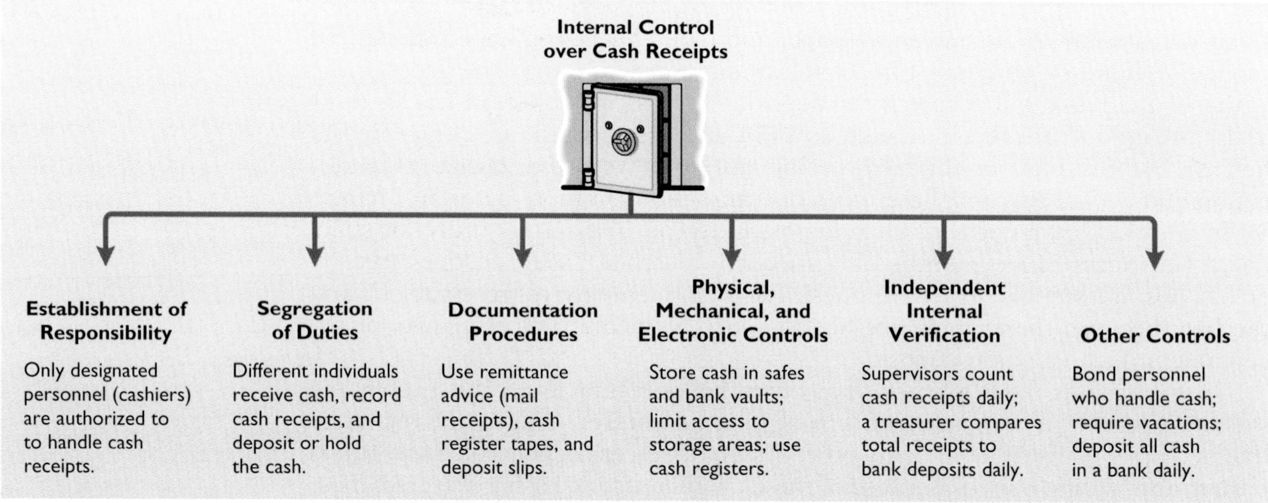

Internal Control over Cash Receipts
Establishment of Responsibility
Only designated personnel (cashiers) are authorized to to handle cash receipts.
Segregation of Duties
Different individuals receive cash, record cash receipts, and deposit or hold the cash.
Documentation Procedures
Use remittance advice (mail receipts), cash register tapes, and deposit slips.
Physical, Mechanical, and Electronic Controls
Store cash in safes and bank vaults; limit access to storage areas; use cash registers.
Independent Internal Verification
Supervisors count cash receipts daily; a treasurer compares total receipts to bank deposits daily.
Other Controls
Bond personnel who handle cash; require vacations; deposit all cash in a bank daily.

INTERNAL CONTROL OVER CASH DISBURSEMENTS

STUDY OBJECTIVE 3

Explain the applications of internal control to cash disbursements.

Cash is disbursed for a variety of reasons, such as to pay expenses and liabilities or to purchase assets. **Generally, internal control over cash disbursements is more effective when payments are made by cheque, rather than by cash, except for incidental amounts that are paid out of petty cash.** Payment is generally made by cheque only after specified control procedures have been followed. In addition, the "paid" cheque provides proof of payment. The principles of internal control apply to cash disbursements as shown in Illustration 7-5.

Illustration 7-5 Application of internal control principles to cash disbursements

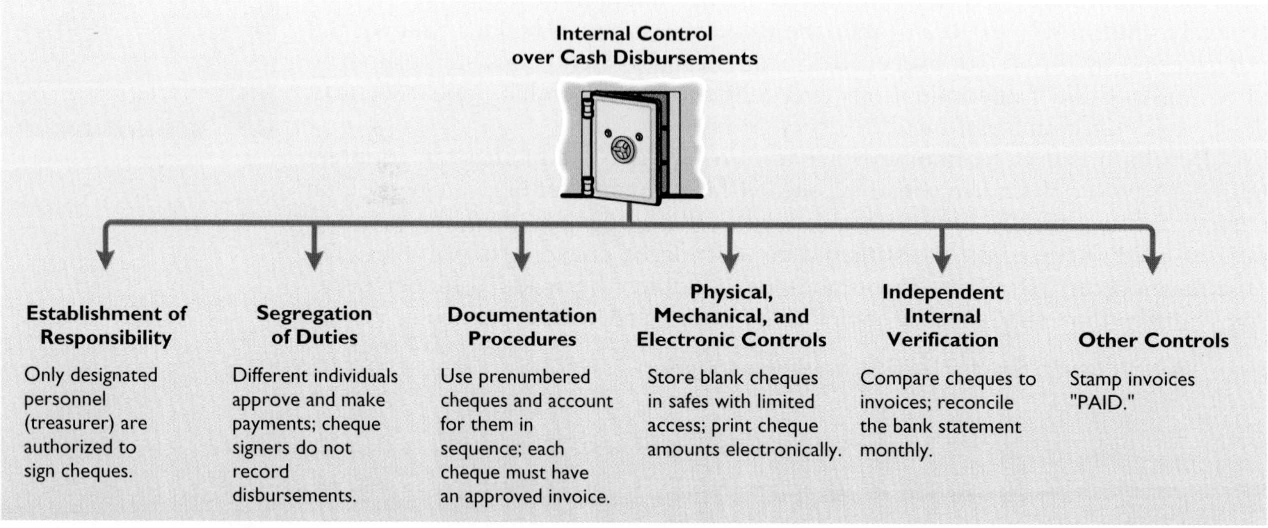

Internal Control over Cash Disbursements
Establishment of Responsibility
Only designated personnel (treasurer) are authorized to sign cheques.
Segregation of Duties
Different individuals approve and make payments; cheque signers do not record disbursements.
Documentation Procedures
Use prenumbered cheques and account for them in sequence; each cheque must have an approved invoice.
Physical, Mechanical, and Electronic Controls
Store blank cheques in safes with limited access; print cheque amounts electronically.
Independent Internal Verification
Compare cheques to invoices; reconcile the bank statement monthly.
Other Controls
Stamp invoices "PAID."

Electronic Funds Transfer (EFT) System

To account for and control cash is an expensive and time-consuming process. For example, the cost to process a cheque through a bank system is about $1.00 per cheque and is increasing. But it only costs 35¢ if the customer uses the telephone and 1¢ if the transaction is done through a computer. It is not surprising, therefore, that approaches have been developed to transfer funds among parties without the use of paper (deposit slips, cheques, etc.). Such procedures, called **electronic funds transfer (EFT)**, are disbursement systems that use a wire, telephone, or computer to transfer cash from one location to another. Use of EFT is quite common. For example, many employees receive no formal payroll cheques from their employers, which instead send information electronically to the appropriate banks for deposit. Regular payments such as those for house, car, or utilities are frequently made by EFT.

BUSINESS INSIGHT

Management Perspective

"A lot of people don't want to pay with cash anymore," says Bran Mladjenovic, a sales associate in a Toronto computer and software store. "Cash is still plentiful," he adds, "but a lot of people seem to be leaning toward debit." The electronic point-of-sale debit system allows consumers to pay for purchases at a store by swiping their card through a terminal at the cash register, which then deducts the money from their bank account and credits the retailer.

Debit cards have reached new heights of popularity. Canadians spent $58.5 billion through their debit cards in 1998 in nearly 1.5 billion transactions, buying everything from plane tickets to groceries. Canadians are a top user worldwide, second only to France, and way ahead of the U.S. Canadians, per capita, use their debit cards 10 times as much as Americans.

Source: Casey Mahood, "Canadians Embrace the Debit Card," *Globe and Mail,* June 14, 1999, B1.

Petty Cash Fund

As you learned earlier in the chapter, better internal control over cash disbursements is possible when payments are made by cheque. However, using cheques to pay such small amounts as those for postage due, employee working lunches, and taxi fares is both impractical and a nuisance. A common way of handling such payments, while maintaining satisfactory control, is to use a petty cash fund. A **petty cash fund** is a cash fund used to pay relatively small amounts. Information regarding the operation of a petty cash fund is provided in the appendix at the end of this chapter.

BEFORE YOU GO ON . . .

● **Review It**

1. How do the principles of internal control apply to cash receipts?

2. How do the principles of internal control apply to cash disbursements?
3. What is the purpose of a petty cash fund?

Do It

L. R. Lim is concerned about control over cash receipts in his fast-food restaurant, Big Cheese. The restaurant has two cash registers. At no time do more than two employees take customer orders and ring up sales. Work shifts for employees range from four to eight hours. Lim asks for your help in installing a good system of internal control over cash receipts.

Reasoning: Lim needs to understand the principles of internal control, especially establishing responsibility, the use of electronic controls, and independent internal verification. With this knowledge, an effective system of control over cash receipts can be designed and implemented.

Solution: Lim should assign a cash register to each employee at the start of each work shift, with register totals set at zero. Each employee should be instructed to use only the assigned register and to ring up all sales. At the end of each work shift, Lim or a supervisor/manager should total the register and make a cash count to see whether all cash is accounted for.

USE OF A BANK

The use of a bank contributes significantly to good internal control over cash. A company can safeguard its cash by using a bank as a depository and clearing house for cash and cheques received and cheques written. The use of a bank minimizes the amount of currency that must be kept on hand. In addition, it facilitates the control of cash because a double record is maintained of all bank transactions—one by the business and the other by the bank. The asset account Cash maintained by the company is the reciprocal of the bank's liability account for that company. It should be possible to **reconcile these accounts**—make them agree—at any time.

Many companies have more than one bank account. For efficiency of operations and better control, national retailers like Sears may have regional bank accounts. Similarly, a company such as Bell Canada, with more than 150,000 employees, may have a payroll bank account as well as one or more general bank accounts. In addition, a company may maintain several bank accounts in order to have more than one source for obtaining short-term loans when needed.

Bank Statements

Each month, the bank sends the company a **bank statement** showing the company's bank transactions and balances. For example, the statement for W.A. Laird Company Ltd., in Illustration 7-6, shows (1) cheques paid and other debits that reduce the balance in the depositor's account, (2) deposits and other credits that increase the balance in the depositor's account, and (3) the account balance after each day's transactions. Remember that bank statements are prepared from the *bank's* perspective. Therefore, every deposit received from W.A. Laird Company Ltd. by the Bank of Montreal is *credited* by the bank to W.A. Laird Company Ltd. The reverse occurs when the bank "pays" a cheque issued by W.A. Laird Company Ltd. on its chequing account balance: payment reduces the bank's liability and is therefore *debited* to Laird's account with the bank.

Helpful Hint

Bank	Company
Credit	*Debit*
Debit	*Credit*

All paid cheques are listed in chronological order on the bank statement along with the date the cheque was paid and its amount. Upon paying a cheque, the bank stamps the cheque "paid"; a paid cheque is sometimes referred to as a

Illustration 7-6 Bank statement

Bank of Montreal Banque de Montréal

505 King Street
Fredericton, NB
E3B 1E7

Transit No de dom	Date D/J M/M Y/A	Account Title Designation de comple	Account Type Type de comple	Account No. No de comple	Page
0123	30 04 01	Operating Account	FBOA	1050-800	58

TRANSACTION CODES *
CODES DE TRANSACTION *

- AD Adjustment — *Rectification*
- CB Cheque Posted By Branch — *Chèque inscrit par la succ*
- CC Certified Cheque — *Chèque certifié*
- CD Customer Deposit — *Dépôt*
- CK Cheque — *Chèque*
- CM Credit Memo — *Avis de crédit*
- CW Telephone Banking — *Services bancaires par téléphone*
- DC Other Charge — *Autres frais*
- DD Direct Deposit/Pre-authorized Debit — *Dépôt ou débit direct*
- DM Debit Memo — *Avis de débit*
- DN Not Service Chargeable — *Sans frais de gestion*
- DR Overdraft — *Découvert*
- DS Service Chargeable — *Avec frais de gestion*
- EC Error Correction — *Correction d'erreur*
- FX Foreign Exchange — *Change*
- GS Tax — *Taxe*
- IB Instabank — *Instabanque*
- IN Interest — *Intérêt*
- LI Loan Interest — *Intérêt sur prêt*
- LN Loan Payment — *Versement sur prêt*
- LP Loan Advance — *Avance sur prêt*
- LT Large Volume Account List Total — *Liste de chèque - compte superactif*
- MB Multi-Branch Banking — *Inter-Service*
- NR Non-Resident Tax — *Impôt de non-résident*
- NS Cheque returned NSF — *Chèque retourné - provision insuffisante*
- NT Nesbitt Burns Entry — *Transaction de Nesbitt Burns*
- OM Other Machine — *Autre machine*
- PR Purchase at Merchant — *Achat chez le commerçant*
- RC NSF Charge — *Frais pour provision insuffisante*
- RN Merchandise Return — *Retour de marchandise*
- RT Returned Item — *Article retourné*
- RV Merchant Reversal — *Correction - Commerçant*
- SC Service Charge — *Frais de gestion*
- SO Standing Order — *Ordre de virement*
- ST Merchant Deposit — *Dépôt du commerçant*
- TF Transfer of Funds — *Virement*
- TX Tax — *Taxe*
- WD Withdrawal — *Retrait*

Please see the reverse side for the Account Types.
Les types de compte figurent au verso.

W.A. Laird Company Ltd.
500 Queen Street
Fredericton, NB E3B 5C2

BALANCE FORWARD / SOLDE REPORTE — Date 03 31 — 13,256 90

CODE	Description/Message justificatif	Debits/Debits	Credits/Credits	Day Jour Mo.	Balance/Solde
CK	NO. 435	644.95		04 02	12,611.95
CK	NO. 438	776.65		04 03	11,835.30
CK	NO. 437	1,185.79		04 04	10,649.51
CK	NO. 436	3,260.00		04 05	7,389.51
CD			2,350.47	04 06	9,739.98
CK	NO. 440	1,487.90		04 09	8,252.08
CK	NO. 439	1,781.70		04 10	6,470.38
CK	NO. 441	2,420.00		04 10	4,050.38
CD			3,320.28	04 12	7,370.66
CM			1,035.00	04 13	8,405.66
CK	NO. 442	585.60		04 16	7,820.66
CD			2,720.00	04 18	10,540.06
CK	NO. 443	226.00		04 18	10,314.06
CD			757.41	04 20	11,071.47
CD			1,218.56	04 23	12,290.03
CD			715.42	04 25	13,005.45
RC		425.60		04 26	12,579.85
CK	NO. 444	1,080.30		04 26	11,499.55
CD			2,929.45	04 27	14,429.00
DM		30.00		04 30	14,399.00
CD			2,128.60	04 30	16,527.60
CK	NO. 448	620.15		04 30	15,907.45

cancelled cheque. In addition, the bank includes with the bank statement memoranda explaining other debits and credits made by the bank to the depositor's account.

A debit memorandum is used by the bank when a previously deposited customer's cheque "bounces" because of insufficient funds. In such a case, the cheque is marked **NSF (not sufficient funds)** or **RC (returned cheque)** by the customer's bank and is returned to the depositor's bank. The bank then debits (decreases) the depositor's account, as shown by the symbol RC on the bank statement in Illustration 7-6, and sends the NSF cheque and debit memorandum to the depositor as notification of the charge. The NSF cheque creates an account receivable for the depositor and reduces cash in the bank account.

Recording an account receivable assumes that the customer will honour the account due by replacing the "bounced" cheque with a valid cheque, or with cash. This happens in most cases. In the next chapter, we will discuss how to account for uncollectible accounts receivable when customers are unable to pay their accounts.

Reconciling the Bank Account

STUDY OBJECTIVE 4

Prepare a bank reconciliation.

Because the bank and the company maintain independent records of the company's chequing account, you might assume that the respective balances will always agree. In fact, the two balances are seldom the same at any given time. Therefore, it is necessary to make the balance per books agree with the balance per the bank—a process called **reconciling the bank account**. The lack of agreement between the balances has two causes:

1. **Time lags** that prevent one of the parties from recording the transaction in the same period as the other party
2. **Errors** by either party in recording transactions

Alternative Terminology When a cheque is paid by the bank, it is said to *clear* the bank.

Time lags occur frequently. For example, several days may elapse between the time a company pays by cheque and the date the cheque is presented to the bank for payment. Similarly, when a company uses the bank's night depository to make its deposits, there will be a difference of one day (or more, if holidays intervene) between the time the receipts are recorded by the company and the time they are recorded by the bank. A time lag also occurs whenever the bank mails a debit or credit memorandum to the company.

Helpful Hint Deposits in transit and outstanding cheques are reconciling items because of time lags.

The incidence of errors depends on the effectiveness of the internal controls maintained by the company and the bank. Bank errors are infrequent. However, either party could inadvertently record a $450 cheque as $45 or $540. In addition, the bank might mistakenly charge a cheque to the wrong account if the code is missing or if is not scannable.

BUSINESS INSIGHT

Management Perspective

Bank errors may be infrequent, but they can involve a story more suitable for Ripley's Believe It or Not than an accounting textbook. The Bank of Nova Scotia's discount brokerage arm accidentally put $17.1 million of somebody else's money into a Toronto doctor's Scotiabank account. It took four months to find and correct the error. Stories about banks misplacing customers' funds are a dime a dozen. But they usually involve misplaced debits, and rarely amounts as high as this.

Source: John Partridge, "Bank Error in Your Favour: Collect $17-Million," *Globe and Mail,* April 11, 2000, A1.

Reconciliation Procedure. In reconciling the bank account, it is customary to reconcile the balance per books and balance per bank to their adjusted (correct or true) cash balances. **To obtain maximum benefit from a bank reconciliation, the reconciliation should be prepared by an employee who has no other responsibilities pertaining to cash.** When the internal control principle of independent internal verification is not followed in preparing the reconciliation, cash embezzlements may escape unnoticed.

The reconciliation schedule is divided into two sections, as shown in Illustration 7-7.

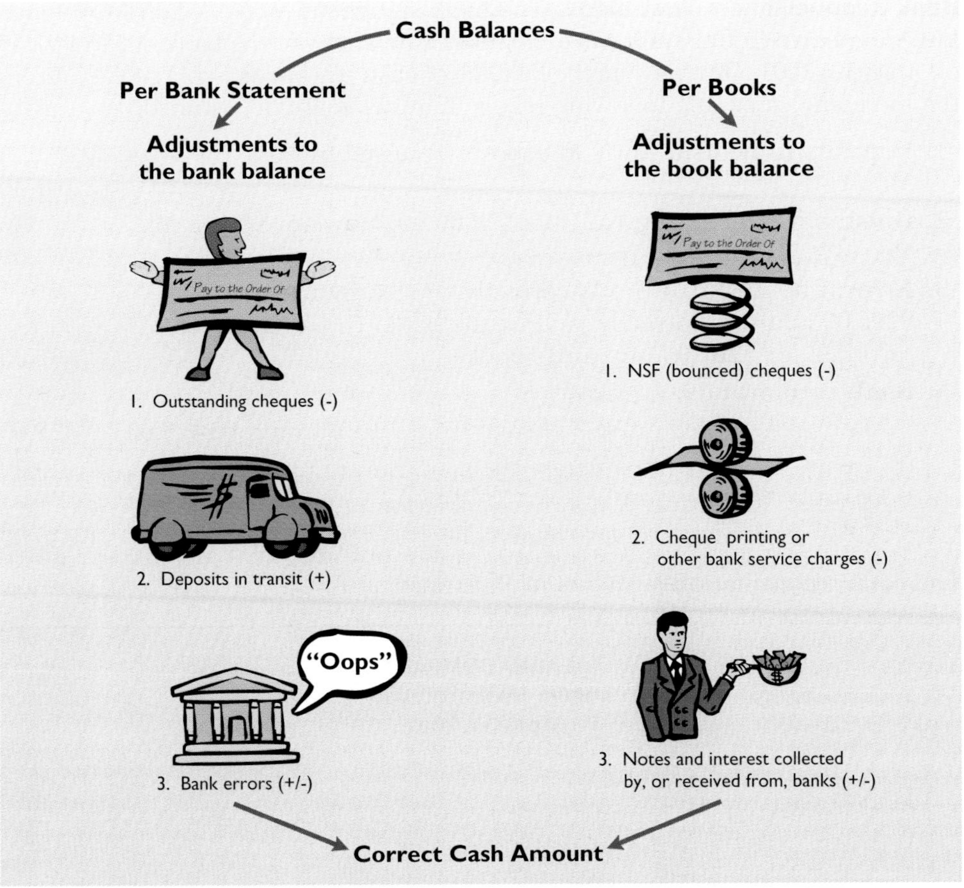

Illustration 7-7 Bank reconciliation procedures

The starting point in preparing the reconciliation is to enter the balance per bank statement and balance per books on the schedule. The following steps should reveal all the reconciling items that cause the difference between the two balances:

1. Compare the individual deposits on the bank statement with (a) the deposits in transit from the preceding bank reconciliation and (b) the deposits per company records or copies of duplicate deposit slips. Deposits recorded by the depositor that have not been recorded by the bank represent **deposits in transit** and are added to the balance per bank.
2. Compare the paid cheques shown on the bank statement or the paid cheques returned with the bank statement with (a) cheques outstanding from the preceding bank reconciliation and (b) cheques issued by the company as recorded in the cash payments journal. Issued cheques recorded by the company that have not been paid by the bank represent **outstanding cheques** that are deducted from the balance per the bank.
3. Note any **errors** discovered in the previous steps and list them in the appropriate section of the reconciliation schedule. For example, if a paid cheque correctly written by the company for $195 was mistakenly recorded by the company for $159, the error of $36 is deducted from the balance per books. All errors made by the depositor are reconciling items in determining the adjusted cash balance per books. In contrast, all errors made by the bank are reconciling items in determining the adjusted cash balance per the bank.
4. Trace **bank memoranda** to the depositor's records. Any unrecorded memoranda should be listed in the appropriate section of the reconciliation schedule. For example, a $5 debit memorandum for bank service charges is deducted from the balance per books, and a $32 credit memorandum for interest earned is added to the balance per books.

Bank Reconciliation Illustrated. The bank statement for W.A. Laird Company Ltd. was shown in Illustration 7-6. It shows a balance per the bank of $15,907.45 on April 30, 2001. On this date the balance of cash per books is $11,589.45. From the foregoing steps, the following reconciling items are determined:

Helpful Hint Note in the bank statement that cheque nos. 444 and 448 have been paid but cheque nos. 445, 446, and 447 are not listed. Thus, these cheques are outstanding. The amounts for these three cheques are obtained from the company's cash payments records.

1. **Deposits in transit:** April 30 deposit (received by bank on May 1).	$2,201.40
2. **Outstanding cheques:** No. 445: $3,000.00; No. 446: $1,401.30; No. 447: $1,502.70.	5,904.00
3. **Error:** Cheque No. 443 was correctly written by Laird for $226.00 and was correctly paid by the bank. However, it was recorded for $262.00 on Laird's books.	36.00
4. **Bank memoranda:**	
(a) Debit—Returned or NSF cheque from J.R. Baron for $425.60	425.60
(b) Debit—Printing of company cheques charge, $30.00	30.00
(c) Credit—Collection of note receivable for $1,000 plus interest earned $50, less bank collection fee $15.00	1,035.00

The bank reconciliation is shown in Illustration 7-8.

Illustration 7-8 Bank reconciliation

W. A. LAIRD COMPANY LTD.
Bank Reconciliation
April 30, 2001

Cash balance per bank statement		$15,907.45
Add: Deposits in transit		2,201.40
		18,108.85
Less: Outstanding cheques		
No. 445	$3,000.00	
No. 446	1,401.30	
No. 447	1,502.70	5,904.00
Adjusted cash balance per bank		**$12,204.85**
Cash balance per books		$11,589.45
Add: Collection of note receivable for $1,000 plus interest earned $50, less collection fee $15	$1,035.00	
Error in recording cheque No. 443	36.00	1,071.00
		12,660.45
Less: Returned (NSF) cheque	$ 425.60	
Bank service charge	30.00	455.60
Adjusted cash balance per books		**$12,204.85**

Helpful Hint The terms *adjusted balance, true cash balance,* and *correct cash balance* may be used interchangeably.

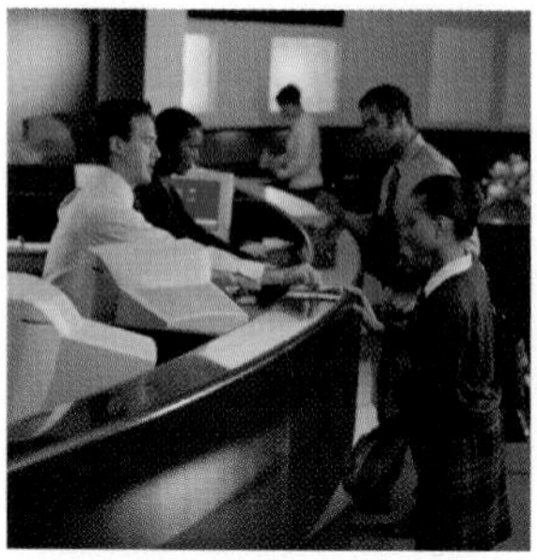

BUSINESS INSIGHT

Management Perspective

It would be easy to reconcile the bank statement for Mary Jane Lee, formerly of College Street, Toronto. Her account, with a balance of $14,007.60, was last touched in 1938! Mary Jane's inactive account is far from the only one. There are more than 770,000 unclaimed accounts at the Bank of Canada.

Chartered banks must transfer dormant accounts to the Bank of Canada if they have not been used in the last 10 years. Accounts with balances of less than $500 are written off; all other accounts remain with the Bank of Canada indefinitely until someone comes forward to claim the funds.

Entries from Bank Reconciliation. Each reconciling item which arises from determining the **adjusted cash balance per books** should be recorded by the depositor. If these items are not journalized and posted, the Cash account will not show the correct balance. The adjusting entries for the W.A. Laird Company Ltd. bank reconciliation on April 30 are as follows:

Helpful Hint These entries are adjusting entries. In prior chapters, Cash was an account that did not require adjustment because a bank reconciliation had not yet been explained.

Collection of Note Receivable. This entry involves four accounts. Assuming that the interest of $50 has not been recorded and the collection fee is charged to Bank Charges Expense, the entry is

Apr. 30	Cash	1,035.00	
	Bank Charges Expense	15.00	
	Notes Receivable		1,000.00
	Interest Revenue		50.00
	(To record collection of notes receivable by bank)		

A	=	L	+	SE
+1,035				−15
−1,000				+50

Book Error. An examination of the cash disbursements journal shows that cheque No. 443 was a payment on account to Andrea Corporation, a supplier. The correcting entry is

Apr. 30	Cash	36.00	
	Accounts Payable—Andrea Corporation		36.00
	(To correct error in recording cheque No. 443)		

A	=	L	+	SE
+36		+36		

NSF Cheque. As indicated earlier, an NSF cheque (RC) normally becomes an accounts receivable to the depositor. The entry is

Apr. 30	Accounts Receivable—J.R. Baron	425.60	
	Cash		425.60
	(To record returned cheque)		

A	=	L	+	SE
+425.60				
−425.60				

Bank Service Charges. Cheque printing charges (DM) and other bank service charges (SC) are debited to Bank Charges. Some companies use the account Interest Expense; others use Miscellaneous Expense if charges are nominal in amount. The entry is

Apr. 30	Bank Charges Expense	30.00	
	Cash		30.00
	(To record charge for printing cheques)		

A	=	L	+	SE
-30				-30

All of the entries above could also be combined into one compound entry.

After the entries are posted, the cash account will appear as in Illustration 7-9. The adjusted cash balance in the ledger should agree with the adjusted cash balance per books in the bank reconciliation in Illustration 7-8.

Illustration 7-9 Adjusted balance in cash account

Cash

Apr. 30 Bal.	11,589.45	Apr. 30	$425.60
30	1,035.00	30	30.00
30	36.00		
Apr. 30 Bal.	**12,204.85**		

What entries does the bank make? **The bank cannot correct your errors on their books and you cannot correct the bank's errors on your books.** If any bank errors are discovered in preparing the reconciliation, the bank should be notified so it can make the necessary corrections on its records. The bank does not make any entries for deposits in transit or outstanding cheques. Only when these items reach the bank will the bank record them.

BEFORE YOU GO ON . . .

Review It

1. Why is it necessary to reconcile a bank account in a timely fashion?
2. Who should reconcile the bank account?
3. What steps are involved in the reconciliation procedure?
4. What information is included in a bank reconciliation?

Do It

Sally Kist owns Linen Kist Fabrics Inc. Sally asks you to explain how the following reconciling items should be treated in reconciling the bank account at December 31: (1) a debit memorandum for an NSF cheque, (2) a credit memorandum for a note collected by the bank, (3) outstanding cheques from the prior period, (4) outstanding cheques from the current period, and (5) a deposit in transit.

Reasoning: Sally needs to understand that one cause of a reconciling item is time lags. Items (1) and (2) are reconciling items because Linen Kist Fabrics has not yet recorded the memoranda. Item (3) is a reconciling item if the cheque continues to be outstanding from a prior period. An outstanding cheque from a prior period means that the cheque was deducted from the company books last period, but not yet paid by the bank. If the cheque has been paid by the bank in the current month, both sides (company books and bank statements) are now reconciled and no further reconciliation of this item is required. If, however, the cheque continues to be outstanding, then it is still a reconciling item for the bank side of the reconciliation since the bank has not yet recorded the transaction. Items (4) and (5) are reconciling items because the bank has not recorded the transactions.

Solution: In reconciling the bank account, the reconciling items are treated by Linen Kist Fabrics as follows:

NSF cheque: deducted from balance per books
Collection of note: added to balance per books
Outstanding cheques: deducted from balance per bank
Deposit in transit: added to balance per bank

REPORTING CASH

STUDY OBJECTIVE 5

Explain the reporting of cash.

Cash is reported in two different statements: the balance sheet and the statement of cash flows. The balance sheet reports the amount of cash available at a given point in time. The statement of cash flows shows the sources and uses of cash during a period of time. The cash flow statement was introduced in Chapters 1 and 2 and will be discussed in detail in Chapter 13. In this section, we discuss some important points regarding the presentation of cash in the balance sheet.

When presented in a balance sheet, cash on hand, cash in banks, and petty cash are often combined and reported simply as **Cash**. Because it is the most liquid asset owned by the company, cash is listed first in the current asset section of the balance sheet.

CASH EQUIVALENTS

Many companies combine cash with temporary investments. These investments include short-term deposits, short-term investments such as treasury bills and money market funds, and short-term notes. If these investments are highly liquid (readily marketable with maturities of three months or less when purchased), and management intends to cash them if the need for cash arises, they are considered to be **cash equivalents**, or near cash items.

Over half of Canadian public companies present cash in this manner. Examples of companies that combine cash with temporary investments for reporting purposes include BCE, CBC, Canada Post, Canadian Pacific, Canadian Tire, George Weston, and Second Cup. As shown in Appendix A at the end of this textbook, Loblaw also combines its cash with short-term investments on its balance sheet.

A few companies use the term "cash and cash equivalents" in reporting cash. Cement group Lafarge Canada is one such example.

Some companies may be in a cash deficit or negative position at year end. This, hopefully, is a temporary situation and can occur when the company is in an overdraft position at the bank. Bank overdrafts occur when a cheque is written for more than the amount in the bank account. This, in effect, is a short-term loan from the bank. The cash account will show a credit balance in the general ledger and is reported as a current liability, as shown in a recent extract from Andrés Wines' balance sheet in Illustration 7-10.

Illustration 7-10
Presentation of a cash credit balance

ANDRÉS WINES LTD.
Balance Sheet (partial)
March 31, 1999
(in thousands of dollars)

LIABILITIES	
CURRENT LIABILITIES	
Bank indebtedness	$31,733

RESTRICTED CASH

A company may have cash that is not available for general use but, rather, is restricted for a special purpose. Examples include funds held on deposit until completion of an offer to purchase real estate and a plant expansion fund for financing new construction. Cash restricted in use should be reported separately on the balance sheet as **restricted cash**. If the restricted cash is expected to be used within the next year, the amount should be reported as a current asset. When this is not the case, the restricted funds should be reported as a noncurrent asset.

DECISION TOOLKIT

Decision Checkpoints	Info Needed for Decision	Tool to Use for Decision	How to Evaluate Results
Is all of the company's cash available for general use?	Balance sheet and notes to financial statements	Does the company report any cash as being restricted?	A restriction on the use of cash limits management's ability to use those resources for general obligations. This might be considered when assessing liquidity.

MANAGING AND MONITORING CASH

Many companies struggle, not because they can't generate sales, but because they can't manage their cash. A real-life example of this is a clothing manufacturing company owned by Sharon McCollick. McCollick gave up a stable, high-paying marketing job with Intel Corporation to start her own company. Soon she had more orders than she could fill. Yet she found herself on the brink of financial disaster, owing three mortgage payments on her house and $2,000 in taxes. Her company could generate sales, but it wasn't collecting cash fast enough to support its operations. The bottom line is that a business must have cash.

To understand cash management, consider the operating cycle of Sharon McCollick's clothing manufacturing company. To begin, it must purchase cloth. Let's assume that it purchases the cloth on credit provided by the supplier, so the company owes its supplier money. Next, employees convert the cloth to clothing. Now the company also owes its employees money. Next, it sells the clothing to retailers, on credit. McCollick's company has no money to repay suppliers or employees until its customers pay. In a manufacturing operation, there may be a significant lag between the original purchase of raw materials and the ultimate receipt of cash from customers. Managing the often precarious balance created by the ebb and flow of cash during the operating cycle is one of a company's greatest challenges. The objective is to ensure that a company has sufficient cash to meet payments as they come due, yet minimize the amount of non-revenue-generating cash on hand.

A merchandising company's operating cycle is generally shorter than a manufacturing company's, depending on how long the inventory is held for sale. The cash-to-cash operating cycle of a merchandising operation is shown in Illustration 7-11.

Illustration 7-11 Operating cycle of a merchandising company

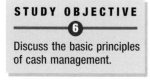

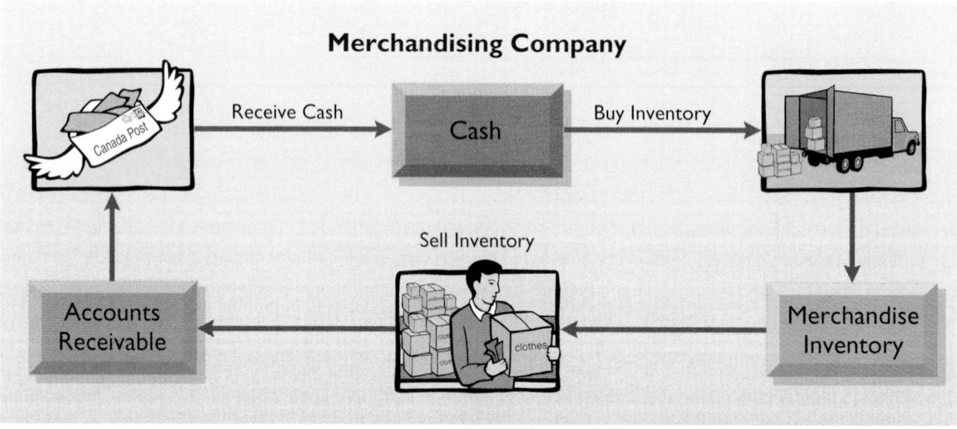

BASIC PRINCIPLES OF CASH MANAGEMENT

STUDY OBJECTIVE 6

Discuss the basic principles of cash management.

Any company can improve its chances of having adequate cash by following five basic principles of cash management:

1. **Increase the speed of collection on receivables.** Money owed to Sharon McCollick by her customers is money that she can't use. The more quickly customers pay her, the more quickly she can use those funds. Thus, rather than have an average collection period of 30 days, she may want an average collection period of 15 days. However, any attempt to force her customers to pay earlier must be carefully weighed against the possibility that she may anger or alienate customers. Perhaps her competitors are willing to provide a 30-day grace period. As noted in Chapter 5, one common way to encourage customers to pay more quickly is to offer cash discounts for early payments.
2. **Keep inventory levels low.** Maintaining a large inventory of cloth and finished clothing is costly. It requires that large amounts of cash be tied up, as well as warehouse space. Increasingly, firms are using techniques to reduce the inventory on hand, thus conserving their cash. Of course, if Sharon McCollick has inadequate inventory, she will lose sales. The proper level of inventory is an important decision.
3. **Delay payment of liabilities.** By keeping track of when her bills are due, Sharon McCollick's company can avoid paying bills too early. Let's say her supplier allows 30 days for payment. If she pays in 10 days, she has lost the use of cash for 20 days. Therefore, she should use the full payment period but should not "stretch" payment past the point that could damage her credit rating (and future borrowing ability). Sharon McCollick's company can also reduce its financing costs—real or opportunity—by taking cash discounts offered by suppliers, when possible.
4. **Plan the timing of major expenditures.** To maintain operations or to grow, all companies must make major expenditures, which normally require some form of outside financing. In order to increase the likelihood of obtaining outside financing, the timing of major expenditures should be carefully considered in light of the firm's operating cycle. If at all possible, the expenditure should be made when the firm normally has excess cash—usually during the off-season.
5. **Invest idle cash.** Cash on hand earns nothing. An important part of the treasurer's job is to ensure that any excess cash is invested, even if it is only overnight. Many businesses, such as Sharon McCollick's clothing company, are seasonal. During her slow season, when she has excess cash, she should invest it. To avoid a cash crisis, however, it is very important that these investments be highly liquid and risk-free. A *liquid investment* is one with a market in which someone is always willing to buy or sell the investment. A *risk-free investment* means there is no concern that the party will default on its promise to pay its principal and interest. For example, using excess cash to purchase shares in a small company because you heard that it was probably going to increase in value in the near term is inappropriate. First, the shares of small companies are often illiquid. Second, if the shares suddenly decrease in value, you might be forced to sell them at a loss in order to pay your bills as they come due. The most common form of liquid, risk-free investments are interest-paying government securities.

International Note

International sales complicate cash management. For example, if Nike must repay a Japanese supplier 30 days from today in Japanese yen, it will be concerned about how the exchange rate of Canadian dollars for yen might change during those 30 days. Often, corporate treasurers make investments known as *hedges* to lock in an exchange rate to reduce the company's exposure to exchange rate fluctuation.

These five principles of cash management are summarized in Illustration 7-12.

Illustration 7-12 Five principles of sound cash management

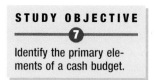

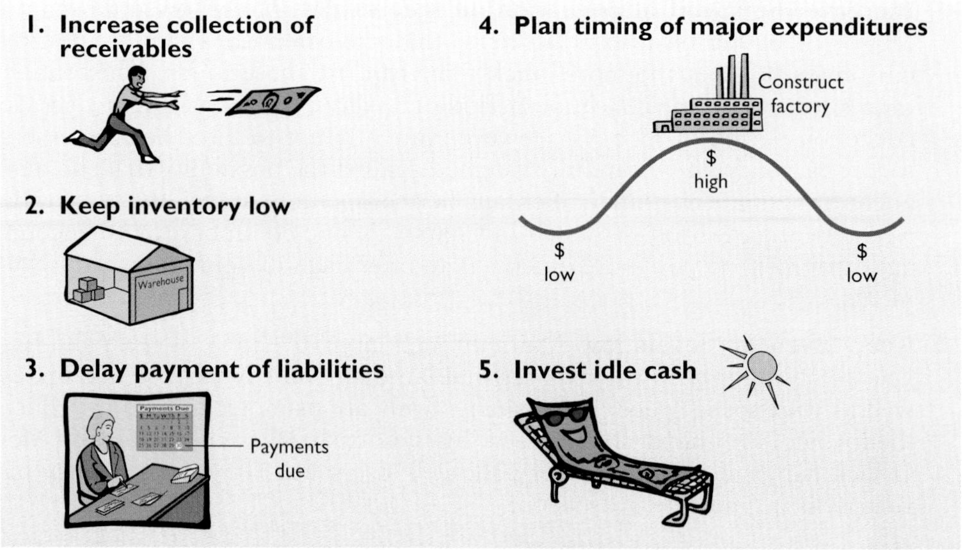
1. Increase collection of receivables
2. Keep inventory low
Warehouse
3. Delay payment of liabilities
Payments Due
Payments due
4. Plan timing of major expenditures
Construct factory
$ high
$ low
$ low
5. Invest idle cash

CASH BUDGETING

STUDY OBJECTIVE 7

Identify the primary elements of a cash budget.

Because cash is so vital to a company, **planning the company's cash needs** is a key business activity. It enables the company to plan ahead to cover possible cash shortfalls and to make investments of idle funds. The **cash budget** shows anticipated cash flows, usually over a one- to two-year period. In this section, we introduce the basics of cash budgeting. More advanced discussion of cash budgets and budgets in general is provided in managerial accounting texts.

As shown in Illustration 7-13, the cash budget contains three sections—cash receipts, cash disbursements, and financing—and the beginning and ending cash balances.

Illustration 7-13 Basic form of a cash budget

ANY COMPANY
Cash Budget

Beginning cash balance	$X,XXX
Add: **Cash receipts** (itemized)	X,XXX
Total available cash	X,XXX
Less: **Cash disbursements** (itemized)	X,XXX
Excess (deficiency) of available cash over cash disbursements	X,XXX
Financing needed	X,XXX
Ending cash balance	$X,XXX

The **cash receipts section** includes expected receipts from the company's principal source(s) of revenue, such as cash sales and collections from customers on credit sales. This section also shows anticipated receipts of interest and dividends, and proceeds from planned sales of investments, capital assets, and the company's share capital.

The **cash disbursements section** shows expected payments for purchases of merchandise, and selling and administrative expenses. This section also includes projected payments for income taxes, dividends, investments, and capital assets.

The **financing section** shows expected borrowings and the repayment of the borrowed funds plus interest. This is needed when there is a cash deficiency or when the cash balance is less than management's minimum required balance.

Data in the cash budget must be prepared in sequence, because the ending cash balance of one period becomes the beginning cash balance for the next period.

Data for preparing the cash budget are obtained from other budgets and from information provided by management. In practice, cash budgets are often prepared for the year, detailing cash receipts and disbursements by month or by quarter.

To minimize detail, we will assume that Hayes Company Ltd. prepares an annual cash budget by quarters. Preparing a cash budget requires making some assumptions. For example, the cash budget for Hayes Company is based on the company's assumptions regarding collection of accounts receivable, sales of securities, payments for merchandise and salaries, and purchases of capital assets. The accuracy of the cash budget is very dependent on the accuracy of these assumptions.

The cash budget for Hayes Company is shown in Illustration 7-14. The budget indicates that $23,000 of financing will be needed in the second quarter to maintain a minimum cash balance of $15,000. Since there is an excess of available cash over disbursements of $57,700 at the end of the third quarter, the borrowing is repaid in this quarter plus $300 interest.

In reality, few companies would borrow money ($23,000 – $8,000 = $15,000) just to increase the amount of cash on hand. Most companies would maintain an operating line of credit with the bank (discussed in Chapter 10) and borrow throughout the quarter only as they needed the additional cash. We have assumed here that Hayes needed to have access to the entire $15,000 minimum cash balance for the quarter.

A cash budget contributes to more effective cash management. For example, it can show when additional financing will be necessary well before the actual need arises. Conversely, it can indicate when excess cash will be available for repayment of debts, for investments, or for other purposes. Consequently, creditors find a cash budget to be a critical tool for assessing a company's ability to repay its debts.

Illustration 7-14 Cash budget

HAYES COMPANY LTD.
Cash Budget
For the Year Ending December 31, 2001

	Quarter			
	1	2	3	4
Beginning cash balance	$ 38,000	$ 25,500	$ 15,000	$ 34,400
Add: **Receipts**				
Collections from customers	168,000	198,000	263,200	258,000
Sale of securities	2,000	0	0	0
Total receipts	170,000	198,000	263,200	258,000
Total available cash	208,000	223,500	278,200	292,400
Less: **Disbursements**				
Purchases of merchandise	23,200	27,200	31,200	35,200
Salaries	62,000	72,000	82,000	92,000
Selling and administrative expenses (excluding amortization)	94,300	99,300	104,300	109,300
Purchase of truck	0	30,000	0	0
Income tax expense	3,000	3,000	3,000	3,000
Total disbursements	182,500	231,500	220,500	239,500
Excess (deficiency) of available cash over disbursements	25,500	(8,000)	57,700	52,900
Financing				
Borrowings	0	23,000	0	0
Repayments—plus $300 interest	0	0	23,300	0
Ending cash balance	$ 25,500	$ 15,000	$ 34,400	$ 52,900

DECISION TOOLKIT

Decision Checkpoints	Info Needed for Decision	Tool to Use for Decision	How to Evaluate Results
Will the company be able to meet its projected cash needs?	Cash budget (typically available only to management)	The cash budget shows projected sources and uses of cash. If cash uses exceed internal cash sources, then the company must look for outside sources.	Two issues: (1) Are management's projections reasonable? (2) If outside sources are needed, are they available?

BEFORE YOU GO ON . . .

Review It

1. What are the five principal elements of sound cash management?
2. What are the three sections of the cash budget?
3. What was Loblaw's balance in cash and cash equivalents as at January 1, 2000? How did Loblaw define cash equivalents? Refer to Note 4 and identify Loblaw's cash equivalents. Did Loblaw report any restricted cash? The answers to these questions are provided at the end of this chapter.

Loblaws
A passion for food... and a lot more!

Do It

Staudinger Company's management wants to maintain a minimum monthly cash balance of $5,000. At the beginning of March, the cash balance is $16,500; expected cash receipts for March are $210,000; and cash disbursements are expected to be $220,000. How much cash, if any, must be borrowed to maintain the desired minimum monthly balance?

Reasoning: The best way to answer this question is to insert the dollar data into the basic form of the cash budget.

Solution:

Beginning cash balance	$ 16,500
Add: Cash receipts for March	210,000
Total available cash	226,500
Less: Cash disbursements for March	220,000
Excess of available cash over cash disbursements	6,500
Financing	0
Ending cash balance	$ 6,500

To maintain the desired minimum cash balance of $5,000, Staudinger Company does not need to borrow any money, as its ending cash balance of $6,500 exceeds the minimum requirements.

ASSESSING CASH ADEQUACY

STUDY OBJECTIVE 8

Identify and interpret measures that evaluate the adequacy of cash.

In evaluating a company's cash management practices, we are interested in whether the amount of cash it has on hand is adequate. This can be evaluated using the ratio of cash to daily expenses. We also want to know whether the company can generate enough cash internally to meet its projected needs. This can be evaluated using a measure known as free cash flow.

BUSINESS INSIGHT

Investor Perspective

Is there such a thing as too much cash? Some Canadian companies are upsetting shareholders by not spending their excess cash. Unused cash hurts a company in a number of ways. Primarily, it is a lost opportunity—all that money sitting around is not producing the best return for shareholders. One Vancouver-based fund manager estimated that 70% of Canadian companies are sitting on excess cash. Cash-rich companies include George Weston Ltd., Brascan Ltd., Imperial Oil Ltd., DuPont Canada Inc., Molson Cos. Ltd., and PanCanadian Petroleum, Ltd. Companies argue that cash is needed to help them weather cyclical downturns or to be ready for strategic acquisitions. What do you think?

Source: David Thomas, "Socking Too Much Away for a Rainy Day," *Financial Post,* February 22, 1997, 5.

RATIO OF CASH TO DAILY CASH EXPENSES

Company managers as well as outside investors closely monitor a company's cash position. Announcement of a projected cash shortfall, such as that made by the former Canadian Airlines Corporation, can send shock waves through a company's share price.

One measure of the adequacy of cash is the **ratio of cash to daily cash expenses**. In this ratio, "cash" includes cash plus cash equivalents. It calculates the number of days of cash expenses that the cash on hand can cover. Cash expenses per day can be approximated by subtracting amortization (a non-cash expense) from total expenses and dividing by 365 days. (Note that this is a rough approximation that ignores many other accrual adjustments.) Dividing the balance in cash and cash equivalents by average daily cash expenses, as shown in Illustration 7-15, gives the number of days the company can operate without any additional infusion of cash.

$$\text{CASH TO DAILY CASH EXPENSES RATIO} = \frac{\text{CASH AND CASH EQUIVALENTS}}{\text{AVERAGE DAILY CASH EXPENSES}}$$

Illustration 7-15 Ratio of cash to daily cash expenses

FREE CASH FLOW

Another important analysis that helps investors and management understand a company's solvency and overall financial strength is free cash flow analysis. **Free cash flow is defined as the amount of discretionary cash flow a company has for purchasing additional investments, paying its debts, or adding to its liquidity.** To determine **free cash flow**, the calculation is net cash provided by operating activities less capital expenditures and dividends.

$$\text{FREE CASH FLOW} = \text{NET CASH PROVIDED BY OPERATING ACTIVITIES} - \left(\text{CAPITAL EXPENDITURES} + \text{CASH DIVIDENDS}\right)$$

Illustration 7-16 Free cash flow

A calculation of free cash flow for the Horne Company Inc. is shown below:

HORNE COMPANY INC.
Free Cash Flow Analysis

Cash provided by operating activities		$250,000
Less: Capital expenditures	$80,000	
Dividends paid	50,000	130,000
Free cash flow		$120,000

The information for Horne Company shows that it has a positive and substantial net cash provided by operating activities balance of $250,000. Capital spending is deducted first in the free cash flow analysis to indicate that it is the least discretionary expenditure a company makes. Dividends are then deducted to arrive at free cash flow. Although a company can cut its dividends, it will do so only in a financial emergency. Horne has more than sufficient cash flow to meet its dividend payments and, therefore, appears to have satisfactory solvency. In other words, Horne has discretionary cash flow to add to its liquidity, retire debt, or increase capital spending.

Horne Company also has financial flexibility. If it finds additional investments that are profitable, it can increase its spending without putting its dividend or basic capital spending in jeopardy. Companies that have substantial free cash flow can take advantage of profitable investments, even in tough times. In addition, companies with substantial free cash flow do not have to worry about survival in poor economic times. In fact, they often fare better in poor economic times because they can take advantage of opportunities that other companies cannot.

DECISION TOOLKIT

Decision Checkpoints	Info Needed for Decision	Tool to Use for Decision	How to Evaluate Results
Does the company have adequate cash to meet its daily needs?	Cash and cash equivalents, average daily expenses	Cash to daily cash expenses ratio = Cash and cash equivalents / Average daily cash expenses	A low measure should be investigated. If this measure is low, additional financing may be necessary.
Does the company have any discretionary cash available?	Net cash provided by operating activities, capital expenditures, and cash dividends	Free cash flow = Net cash provided by operating activities minus capital expenditures and cash dividends	Free cash flow allows a company to buy additional investments, reduce its debts, or add to its liquidity. The greater the free cash flow, the greater its options

The following financial information for Rothmans Inc., a North York, Ontario-based manufacturer of tobacco products, was provided in its 1999 financial statements.

ROTHMANS INC.
Selected Financial Information
($ in thousands)

	1999	1998
Sales	$532,883	$522,063
Total expenses (including amortization)	427,888	412,706
Amortization expense	13	3,800
Cash and short-term investments	38,068	99,275
Cash from operating activities	110,375	120,092
Cash paid for capital expenditures	14,841	4,175
Cash paid for dividends	166,631	78,886

Using the preceding information, it is possible to calculate the two cash adequacy measures discussed above, for Rothmans. The results appear in Illustration 7-17.

($ in thousands)	1999	1998	Industry average
Cash to daily cash expenses ratio	$\frac{\$38,068}{(\$427,888 - \$13)/365}$ = 32 days	$\frac{\$99,275}{(\$412,706 - \$3,800)/365}$ = 89 days	n/a
Free cash flow	$110,375 − $14,841 − $166,631 = ($71,097)	$120,092 − $4,175 − $78,886 = $37,031	n/a

Illustration 7-17
Rothmans' cash adequacy measures

Rothmans had a much stronger cash balance in 1998 than in 1999. The ratio of cash to daily cash expenses indicates that at the end of 1998, its cash was sufficient to meet the needs of nearly three months (89 days) of normal activity. In 1999, however, its cash balance covered about one third as much, or 32 days.

The calculation of Rothmans' free cash flow shows that, in 1998, a positive free cash flow of $37,031,000 was generated. This gave management the additional flexibility to increase capital expenditures or dividend payments or to retire its own shares or debt. And, indeed, Rothmans did pay a special dividend of $17 per share, over and above its normal dividend of $6 per share, in 1998. In contrast, in 1999, while cash flow from operations was sufficient to cover capital expenditures, it was not sufficient to cover the additional dividend payment. Since the current free cash flow was insufficient to cover payments, the remainder was drawn from the accumulated balance of cash and short-term investments. Note that this balance declined in 1999, from $99,275,000 to $38,068,000.

BEFORE YOU GO ON . . .

Review It

1. What is the formula for the cash to daily cash expenses ratio? What does it tell management about the company's cash position?
2. How is free cash flow calculated?

USING THE DECISION TOOLKIT

Presented below is financial information for **Mattel, Inc.**, the number one toy maker in the world. Included in this information is financial statement data from the year ended December 31, 1998, which can be used to calculate free cash flow and the cash to daily cash expenses ratio.

MATTEL, INC. Selected Financial Information Year Ended December 31, 1998 (in millions of US $)	
Cash provided by operating activities	$ 547.5
Capital expenditures	1,058.8
Dividends paid	98.0
Total expenses (including amortization)	4,449.6
Amortization expense	214.9
Cash balance	212.5

Also provided are hypothetical data which represent management's best estimate of its projected sources and uses of cash during 1999. This information is needed to prepare a cash budget for 1999.

MATTEL, INC. Projected Sources and Uses of Cash (in millions)	
Beginning cash balance	$ 694.9
Cash collected from sales	4,922.1
Cash received from marketable securities sold	20.0
Cash disbursed for inventory	2,371.1
Cash disbursed for selling and administrative expense	1,695.4
Cash paid for property, plant, and equipment	257.6
Cash paid for taxes	135.9

Mattel's management believes it should maintain a balance of $400 million cash.

Instructions

(a) Using the hypothetical projected sources and uses of cash information presented above, prepare a cash budget for 1999 for Mattel.
(b) Using the 1998 selected financial information presented above, calculate the cash to daily cash expenses ratio and free cash flow.
(c) Comment on Mattel's cash adequacy, and discuss steps that might be taken to improve its cash position.

Solution

(a)

MATTEL INC. Cash Budget For the Year 1999 (in millions)		
Beginning cash balance		$ 694.9
Add: Cash receipts during 1999		
From sales of product	$ 4,922.1	
From sale of marketable securities	20.0	4,942.1
Total cash available		5,637.0
Less: Cash disbursements during 1999		
Cash paid for inventory	$ 2,371.1	
Cash paid for selling and administrative costs	1,695.4	
Cash paid for taxes	135.9	
Cash paid for property, plant and equipment	257.6	4,460.0
Excess of available cash over cash disbursements		1,177.0
Financing needed		0.0
Ending cash balance		$1,177.0

(b) To calculate the cash to daily cash expenses ratio, first approximate average daily cash expenses as follows: total expenses minus amortization expense divided by 365. The average daily cash expenses (in millions) is calculated as: ($4,449.6 – $214.9)/365 = $11.60. Next, the cash to daily cash expenses ratio is calculated as: $212.5/$11.60 = 18 days. This ratio suggests the company will have cash sufficient to cover 18 days of normal expenses.

The company's free cash flow is calculated by subtracting cash paid for dividends and capital expenditures from cash provided by operating activities:

MATTEL INC. Free Cash Flow Analysis (in millions)		
Cash provided by operating activities		$ 547.5
Less: Capital expenditures	$1,058.8	
Dividends paid	98.0	1,156.8
Free cash flow in 1998		($ 609.3)

(c) Mattel's cash position appears to have been inadequate in 1998. It had enough cash on hand to cover 18 days, and its 1998 free cash flow was insufficient to cover its needs. In 1999, it was projecting a cash surplus, an improvement over 1998. This is not necessarily of concern, but it should be investigated. Given that its primary line of business is toys, and that most toys are sold at Christmas, we would expect Mattel's cash position to vary significantly during the course of the year. Early in the new year, it probably has a lot of excess cash, and later in the year, when it is making and selling its product but has not yet been paid, it may need to borrow to meet any temporary cash shortfalls, as it did in 1998.

In the event that Mattel's management is concerned with its cash position, as it was in 1998, it could take the following steps: (1) offer its customers cash discounts for early payment, such as 2/10, n/30; (2) implement inventory management techniques to reduce the need for large inventories of such things as the plastics used to make its toys; (3) carefully time payments to suppliers by keeping track of when payments are due, so as not to pay too early; and (4) if it has plans for major expenditures, time those expenditures to coincide with its seasonal period of excess cash.

Summary of Study Objectives

1 ***Identify the principles of internal control.*** The principles of internal control are establishment of responsibility; segregation of duties; documentation procedures; physical, mechanical, and electronic controls; independent internal verification; and other controls.

2 ***Explain the applications of internal control to cash receipts.*** Internal controls over cash receipts include (a) designating only personnel such as cashiers to handle cash; (b) assigning the duties of receiving cash, recording cash, and having custody of cash to different individuals; (c) obtaining remittance advices for mail receipts, cash register tapes for over-the-counter receipts, and deposit slips for bank deposits; (d) using company safes and bank vaults to store cash, with access limited to authorized personnel, and using cash registers in executing over-the-counter receipts; (e) making independent daily counts of register receipts and daily comparisons of total receipts with total deposits; and (f) bonding personnel who handle cash and requiring them to take vacations.

3 ***Explain the applications of internal control to cash disbursements.*** Internal controls over cash disbursements include (a) having only specified individuals authorized to sign cheques; (b) assigning the duties of approving items for payment, paying the items, and recording the payments to different individuals; (c) using prenumbered cheques and accounting for all cheques; (d) storing each cheque in a safe or vault with access restricted to authorized personnel, and using electronic means to imprint amounts on cheques; (e) comparing each cheque with the approved invoice before issuing the cheque, and making monthly reconciliations of bank and book balances; and (f) after payment, stamping each approved invoice "paid."

4 ***Prepare a bank reconciliation.*** In reconciling the bank account, it is customary to reconcile the balance per books and the balance per the bank to their adjusted balances. The steps in determining the reconciling items are done to detect deposits in transit, outstanding cheques, errors by the depositor or the bank, and unrecorded bank memoranda.

5 ***Explain the reporting of cash.*** Cash is listed first in the current assets section of the balance sheet. Cash is often reported together with temporary investments, called cash equivalents. Cash restricted for a special purpose is reported separately as a current asset or as a noncurrent asset depending on when the cash is expected to be used.

6 ***Discuss the basic principles of cash management.*** (a) Increase collection of receivables, (b) keep inventory levels low, (c) delay payment of liabilities, (d) plan timing of major expenditures, and (e) invest idle cash.

7 ***Identify the primary elements of a cash budget.*** The three main elements of a cash budget are the cash receipts section, cash disbursements section, and financing section.

8 ***Identify and interpret measures that evaluate the adequacy of cash.*** The cash to daily cash expenses ratio indicates how many days of expenditures the current cash resources will cover. The calculation of free cash flow reveals the amount of discretionary cash available.

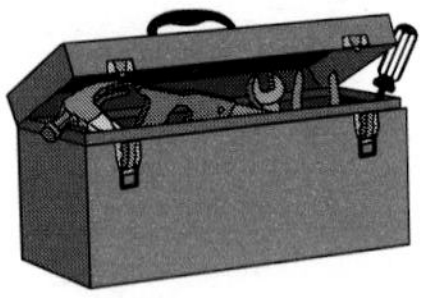

Decision Toolkit—A Summary

Decision Checkpoints	Info Needed for Decision	Tool to Use for Decision	How to Evaluate Results
Are the company's financial statements supported by adequate internal controls?	Auditor's report, statement of management responsibility, management discussion and analysis, articles in financial press	The required measures of internal control are to (1) establish responsibility, (2) segregate duties, (3) document procedures, (4) employ physical or automated controls, and (5) use independent internal verification.	If any indication is given that these or other controls are lacking, the financial statements should be used with caution.
Is all of the company's cash available for general use?	Balance sheet and notes to financial statements	Does the company report any cash as being restricted?	A restriction on the use of cash limits management's ability to use those resources for general obligations. This might be considered when assessing liquidity.
Will the company be able to meet its projected cash needs?	Cash budget (typically available only to management)	The cash budget shows projected sources and uses of cash. If cash uses exceed internal cash sources, then the company must look for outside sources.	Two issues: (1) Are management's projections reasonable? (2) If outside sources are needed, are they available?
Does the company have adequate cash to meet its daily needs?	Cash and cash equivalents, average daily expenses	$\text{Cash to daily cash expenses ratio} = \dfrac{\text{Cash and cash equivalents}}{\text{Average daily cash expenses}}$	A low measure should be investigated. If this measure is low, additional financing may be necessary.
Does the company have any discretionary cash available?	Net cash provided by operating activities, capital expenditures, and cash dividends	Free cash flow = Cash provided by operating activities minus capital expenditures minus cash dividends	Free cash flow allows a company to buy additional investments, reduce its debts, or add to its liquidity. The greater the free cash flow, the greater its options.

APPENDIX 7A

OPERATION OF THE PETTY CASH FUND

The operation of a petty cash fund involves (1) establishing the fund, (2) making payments from the fund, and (3) replenishing the fund.

STUDY OBJECTIVE 9

Explain the operation of a petty cash fund.

ESTABLISHING THE PETTY CASH FUND

Two essential steps in establishing a petty cash fund are appointing a petty cash custodian who will be responsible for the fund and determining the size of the fund. Ordinarily, the amount is expected to cover anticipated disbursements for a three- to four-week period. When the fund is established, a cheque payable to the petty cash custodian is issued for the stipulated amount. If the W.A. Laird Company decides to establish a $100 fund on March 1, the entry in general journal form is

Mar. 1	Petty Cash	100	
	Cash		100
	(To establish a petty cash fund)		

A	=	L	+	SE
+100				
- 100				

The cheque is then cashed and the proceeds are placed in a locked petty cash box or drawer. Most petty cash funds are established on a fixed amount or **imprest** basis. Moreover, no additional entries will be made to the Petty Cash account unless the stipulated amount of the fund is changed. For example, if W.A. Laird Company decides on July 1 to increase the size of the fund to $250, it would debit Petty Cash $150 and credit Cash $150.

MAKING PAYMENTS FROM PETTY CASH

The custodian of the petty cash fund has the authority to make payments from the fund that conform to prescribed management policies. Usually management limits the size of expenditures that may be made and does not permit use of the fund for certain types of transactions (such as making short-term loans to employees). Each payment from the fund must be documented on a prenumbered petty cash receipt (or petty cash voucher). Note that the signatures of both the custodian and the individual receiving payment are required on the receipt. If other supporting documents such as a freight bill or invoice are available, they should be attached to the petty cash receipt.

Helpful Hint From the standpoint of internal control, the receipt satisfies two principles: (1) establishment of responsibility (signature of custodian) and (2) documentation procedures.

The receipts are kept in the petty cash box until the fund is replenished. As a result, the sum of the petty cash receipts and money in the fund should equal the established total at all times. This means that surprise counts can be made at any time by an independent person, such as an internal auditor, to determine whether the fund is being maintained intact.

No accounting entry is made to record a payment at the time it is taken from petty cash. It is considered both inexpedient and unnecessary to do so. Instead, the accounting effects of each payment are recognized when the fund is replenished.

Replenishing the Petty Cash Fund

Helpful Hint Replenishing involves three internal control procedures: segregation of duties, documentation procedures, and independent internal verification.

When the money in the petty cash fund reaches a minimum level, the fund is replenished. The request for reimbursement is initiated by the petty cash custodian. This individual prepares a schedule (or summary) of the payments that have been made and sends the schedule, supported by petty cash receipts and other documentation, to the treasurer's office. The receipts and supporting documents are examined in the treasurer's office to verify that they were proper payments from the fund. The treasurer then approves the request and a cheque is prepared to restore the fund to its established amount. At the same time, all supporting documentation is stamped "paid" so that it cannot be submitted again for payment.

To illustrate, assume that on March 15, the petty cash custodian requests a cheque for $87. The fund contains $13 cash and petty cash receipts for postage $44, supplies (not used yet) $38, and miscellaneous expenses $5. The entry, in general journal form, to record the cheque is

A	=	L	+	SE
+38				−44
−87				−5

Mar. 15	Postage Expense	44	
	Supplies	38	
	Miscellaneous Expense	5	
	Cash		87
	(To replenish petty cash fund)		

Note that the Petty Cash account is not affected by the reimbursement entry. Replenishment changes the composition of the fund by replacing the petty cash receipts with cash, but it does not change the balance in the fund.

Occasionally, in replenishing a petty cash fund, it may be necessary to recognize a cash shortage or overage. To illustrate, assume in the preceding example that the custodian had only $12 in cash in the fund plus the receipts as listed. The request for reimbursement would therefore be for $88, and the following entry would be made:

A	=	L	+	SE
+38				−44
−88				−5
				−1

Mar. 15	Postage Expense	44	
	Supplies	38	
	Miscellaneous Expense	5	
	Cash Over and Short	1	
	Cash		88
	(To replenish petty cash fund)		

Conversely, if the custodian had $14 in cash, the reimbursement request would be for $86 and Cash Over and Short would be credited for $1. A debit balance in Cash Over and Short is reported in the statement of earnings as miscellaneous expense; a credit balance is reported as miscellaneous revenue. Cash Over and Short is closed to Income Summary at the end of the year.

A petty cash fund should be replenished **at the end of the accounting period, regardless of the cash in the fund**. Replenishment at this time is necessary in order to recognize the effects of the petty cash payments on the financial statements.

Internal control over a petty cash fund is strengthened by (1) having a supervisor make surprise counts of the fund to ascertain whether the paid vouchers and fund cash equal the designated amount and (2) cancelling or mutilating the paid vouchers so they cannot be resubmitted for reimbursement.

Summary of Study Objective for Appendix 7A

9 ***Explain the operation of a petty cash fund.*** In operating a petty cash fund, a company must establish the fund by appointing a custodian and determining the size of the fund, make payments from the fund for documented expenditures, and replenish the fund. The fund is replenished at least at the end of each accounting period, and accounting entries to record payments are made at that time.

Glossary

Bank statement A statement received monthly from the bank that shows the depositor's bank transactions and balances. (p. 360)

Cash Resources that consist of coins, currency, cheques, money orders, and money on hand or on deposit in a bank or similar depository. (p. 357)

Cash budget A projection of anticipated cash flows, usually over a one-to two-year period. (p. 370)

Cash equivalents Highly liquid investments, with maturities of three months or less when purchased, that can be converted to a specific amount of cash. (p. 367)

Deposits in transit Deposits recorded by the depositor that have not been recorded by the bank. (p. 363)

Electronic funds transfer (EFT) A disbursement system that uses a wire, telephone, or computer to transfer cash from one location to another. (p. 359)

Free cash flow A measure that calculates the amount of discretionary cash available by subtracting capital expenditures and cash dividends from net cash provided by operating activities. (p. 373)

Internal auditors Company employees who evaluate on a continuous basis the effectiveness of the company's system of internal control. (p. 355)

Internal control All the related methods and measures adopted within a business to (1) optimize resourses, (2) prevent and detect errors and irregularities, (3) safeguard its assets, and (4) maintain reliable control systems. (p. 350)

NSF (not sufficient funds) cheque A cheque that is not paid by a bank because of insufficient funds in a customer's bank account. (p. 361)

Outstanding cheques Cheques issued and recorded by a company that have not been paid by the bank. (p. 363)

Petty cash fund A cash fund used to pay relatively small amounts. (p. 359)

Ratio of cash to daily cash expenses A measure that indicates the number of days of expenses that available cash can cover. It is calculated as cash and cash equivalents divided by average daily expenses. (p. 373)

Restricted cash Cash that is not available for general use, but instead is restricted for a particular purpose. (p. 367)

Demonstration Problem

Trillo Company Ltd.'s bank statement for May 2001 shows these data:

Balance May 1	$12,650	Balance May 31	$14,280
Debit memorandum:		Credit memorandum:	
NSF cheque	175	Collection of note receivable	505

The cash balance per books at May 31 is $13,319. Your review of the data reveals the following:

1. The NSF cheque was from Hup Corp., a customer.
2. The note collected by the bank was a $500, three-month, 12% note, plus interest. The bank charged a $10 collection fee.
3. Outstanding cheques at May 31 total $2,410, including a cheque for $300 that was also outstanding at April 30.
4. Deposits in transit at May 31 total $1,752.
5. A Trillo Company cheque for $352 dated May 10 cleared the bank on May 25. This cheque, which was a payment on account, was journalized for $325.

Instructions

(a) Prepare a bank reconciliation at May 31.
(b) Journalize the entries required by the reconciliation.

Problem-Solving Strategies

1. Follow the four steps used in reconciling items (p. 301).
2. Work carefully to minimize mathematical errors in the reconciliation.
3. All entries are based on reconciling items per books.
4. Make sure the cash ledger balance after posting the reconciling entries agrees with the adjusted cash balance per books.

Solution to Demonstration Problem

(a)

Cash balance per bank statement		$14,280
Add: Deposits in transit		1,752
		16,032
Less: Outstanding cheques		2,410
Adjusted cash balance per bank		$13,622
Cash balance per books		$13,319
Add: Collection of note receivable $500, plus $15 interest less collection fee $10		505
		13,824
Less: NSF cheque	$175	
Error in recording cheque	27	202
Adjusted cash balance per books		$13,622

(b)

May 31	Cash	505	
	Bank Charges Expense	10	
	Notes Receivable		500
	Interest Revenue ($500 x 12% x 3/12)		15
	(To record collection of note by bank)		
31	Accounts Receivable—Hup Corp.	175	
	Cash		175
	(To record NSF cheque from Hup Corp.)		
31	Accounts Payable	27	
	Cash		27
	(To correct error in recording cheque)		

Note: All of the following questions, exercises, and problems marked with an asterisk relate to material in the appendix to the chapter.

SELF-STUDY QUESTIONS

Answers are at the end of the chapter.

(SO 1) 1. Internal control is used in a business to enhance the accuracy and reliability of its accounting records and to:
(a) safeguard its assets.
(b) prevent fraud.
(c) produce correct financial statements.
(d) eliminate employee dishonesty.

(SO 1) 2. The principles of internal control do *not* include:
(a) establishment of responsibility.
(b) documentation procedures.
(c) management responsibility.
(d) independent internal verification.

(SO 1) 3. Physical controls do *not* include:
(a) safes and vaults to store cash.
(b) independent bank reconciliations.
(c) locked warehouses for inventories.
(d) bank safety deposit boxes for important papers.

4. Permitting only designated personnel, such as cashiers, to handle cash receipts is an application of the principle of: (SO 2)
(a) segregation of duties.
(b) establishment of responsibility.
(c) independent internal verification.
(d) other controls.

5. The use of prenumbered cheques in disbursing cash is an application of the principle of: (SO 3)
(a) establishment of responsibility.
(b) segregation of duties.
(c) physical, mechanical, and electronic controls.
(d) documentation procedures.

6. The control features of a bank account do *not* include: (SO 3)
(a) having bank auditors verify the correctness of the bank balance per books.
(b) minimizing the amount of cash that must be kept on hand.

(c) providing a double record of all bank transactions.
(d) safeguarding cash by using a bank as a depository.

(SO 4) 7. In a bank reconciliation, deposits in transit are:
(a) deducted from the book balance.
(b) added to the book balance
(c) added to the bank balance.
(d) deducted from the bank balance.

(SO 5) 8. Which of the following items in a cash drawer at November 30 is *not* cash?
(a) Money orders
(b) Coins and currency
(c) A customer cheque dated December 1
(d) A customer cheque dated November 28

(SO 5) 9. Which statement correctly describes the reporting of cash?
(a) Cash cannot be combined with cash equivalents.
(b) Restricted cash funds may be combined with Cash.
(c) Cash is listed first in the current asset section.
(d) Restricted cash funds are always reported as a current asset.

10. Which of the following is *not* one of the sections of a cash budget? (SO 7)
(a) Cash receipts section
(b) Cash disbursements section
(c) Financing section
(d) Cash from operations section

*11. A cheque is written to replenish a $100 petty cash fund when the fund contains receipts of $94 and $3 in cash. In recording the cheque: (SO 9)
(a) Cash Over and Short should be debited for $3.
(b) Petty Cash should be debited for $94.
(c) Cash should be credited for $94.
(d) Petty Cash should be credited for $3.

QUESTIONS

(SO 1) 1. "Internal control is only concerned with enhancing the accuracy of the accounting records." Do you agree? Explain.

(SO 1) 2. What principles of internal control apply to most business enterprises?

(SO 1) 3. In the corner grocery store, all sales clerks make change out of one cash register drawer using the same password. Is this a violation of internal control? Why?

(SO 1) 4. J. Duma is reviewing the principle of segregation of duties. What are the two common applications of this principle?

(SO 1) 5. How do documentation procedures contribute to good internal control?

(SO 1) 6. What internal control objectives are met by physical, mechanical, and electronic controls?

(SO 1) 7. (a) Explain the control principle of independent internal verification.
(b) What practices are important in applying this principle?

(SO 1) 8. As the company accountant, explain these ideas to the management of Cobo Corporation:
(a) the concept of reasonable assurance in internal control
(b) the importance of the human factor in internal control

(SO 2) 9. What principle(s) of internal control is (are) involved in making daily cash counts and deposits of over-the-counter receipts?

(SO 2) 10. Dent Department Stores Ltd. has just installed new electronic cash registers with scanners in its stores. How do these cash registers improve internal control over cash receipts?

(SO 2) 11. At Allen Wholesale Company Ltd., two mail clerks open all mail receipts. How does this strengthen internal control?

12. "To have maximum internal control over cash disbursements, all payments should be made by cheque." Is this true? Explain. (SO 3)

13. Handy Company Inc.'s internal controls over cash disbursements require the treasurer to sign cheques imprinted by a computer after comparing the cheque with the approved invoice. Identify the internal control principles that are present in these controls. (SO 3)

14. How do these principles apply to cash disbursements? (SO 3)
(a) Physical, mechanical, and electronic controls
(b) Other controls

15. What is the essential feature of an electronic funds transfer (EFT) procedure? (SO 3)

16. "The use of a bank contributes significantly to good internal control over cash." Is this true? Why? (SO 4)

17. Paul Pascal is confused about the lack of agreement between the cash balance per books and the balance per the bank. Explain the causes for the lack of agreement to Paul, and give an example of each cause. (SO 4)

18. Mary Mora asks for your help concerning an NSF cheque. Explain to Mary (a) what an NSF cheque is, (b) how it is treated in a bank reconciliation, and (c) whether it will require an adjusting entry. (SO 4)

19. Midwest Inc. owns these assets at the balance sheet date: (SO 5)

Cash in bank—savings account	$ 5,000
Cash on hand	850
Cash refund due from Canada Customs and Revenue Agency	1,000

Chequing account balance	12,000
Postdated cheques	500

What amount should be reported as Cash in the balance sheet?

(SO 5) 20. (a) "Cash equivalents are the same as cash." Do you agree? Explain.
(b) How should restricted cash funds be reported on the balance sheet?

(SO 6) 21. Describe the basic principles of cash management.

22. (a) What is a cash budget? (SO 7)
(b) How does a cash budget contribute to effective cash management?

23. What measures may be calculated to evaluate the adequacy of cash? (SO 8)

*24. (a) Identify the three activities that pertain to a petty cash fund, and indicate an internal control principle that is applicable to each activity. (SO 9)
(b) When are journal entries required in the operation of a petty cash fund?

Brief Exercises

Explain the importance of internal control.
(SO 1)

BE7-1 Gina Milan is the new owner of Liberty Parking Ltd. She has heard about internal control but is not clear about its importance for her business. Explain to Gina the four purposes of internal control, and give her one application of each purpose for Liberty Parking.

Identify internal control principles.
(SO 1)

BE7-2 The internal control procedures in Marion Company Ltd. make the following provisions. Identify the principles of internal control that are being followed in each case.
(a) Employees who have physical custody of assets do not have access to the accounting records.
(b) Each month, the assets on hand are compared to the accounting records by an internal auditor.
(c) A prenumbered shipping document is prepared for each shipment of goods to customers.

Identify the internal control principles applicable to cash receipts.
(SO 2)

BE7-3 Tene Company Ltd. has the following internal control procedures over cash receipts. Identify the internal control principle that is applicable to each procedure.
(a) All over-the-counter receipts are recorded on cash registers.
(b) All cashiers are bonded.
(c) Daily cash counts are made by cashier department supervisors.
(d) The duties of receiving cash, recording cash, and having custody of cash are assigned to different individuals.
(e) Only cashiers may operate cash registers.
(f) All cash is deposited intact in the bank account every day.

Identify the internal control principles applicable to cash disbursements.
(SO 3)

BE7-4 Hills Company Ltd. has the following internal control procedures over cash disbursements. Identify the internal control principle that is applicable to each procedure.
(a) Company cheques are prenumbered.
(b) The bank statement is reconciled monthly by an internal auditor.
(c) Blank cheques are stored in a safe in the treasurer's office.
(d) Only the treasurer or assistant treasurer may sign cheques.
(e) Cheque signers are not allowed to record cash disbursement transactions.
(f) All payments, other than petty cash amounts, are made by cheque.

Identify the control features of a bank account.
(SO 3)

BE7-5 T.J. Boad is uncertain about the control features of a bank account. Explain the control benefits of (a) a cheque and (b) a bank statement.

Indicate location of reconciling items in a bank reconciliation.
(SO 4)

BE7-6 The following reconciling items are applicable to the bank reconciliation for Ashley Corp. Indicate how each item should be shown on a bank reconciliation.
(a) Outstanding cheques
(b) Bank debit memorandum for a service charge
(c) Bank credit memorandum for collecting a note for the depositor
(d) Deposit in transit

Identify reconciling items that require adjusting entries.
(SO 4)

BE7-7 Using the data in BE7-6, indicate (a) the items that will result in an adjustment to the depositor's records and (b) why the other items do not require adjustment.

Prepare partial bank reconciliation.
(SO 4)

BE7-8 At July 31, Dana Company Limited has this bank information: cash balance per bank, $7,420; outstanding cheques, $762; deposits in transit, $1,700; and a bank service charge, $20. Determine the adjusted cash balance per the bank at July 31.

BE7-9 In the month of November, Jayasinghe Company Inc. wrote cheques in the amount of $9,250. In December, cheques in the amount of $12,716 were written. In November, $8,578 of these cheques were presented to the bank for payment; $10,889, in December. What is the amount of outstanding cheques at the end of November? At the end of December?

Analyse outstanding cheques. (SO 4)

BE7-10 Ouellette Company Ltée has these cash balances: Cash in Bank, $12,742; Payroll Bank Account, $6,000; and Plant Expansion Fund Cash, $25,000. Explain how each balance should be reported on the balance sheet.

Explain the statement presentation of cash balances. (SO 5)

BE7-11 The following information is available for Marais Company Limited for the month of January: expected cash receipts, $60,000; expected cash disbursements, $65,000; cash balance on January 1, $12,000. Management wishes to maintain a minimum cash balance of $10,000. Prepare a basic cash budget for the month of January.

Prepare a cash budget. (SO 7)

BE7-12 **Clearnet Communications Inc.**, a leading Canadian wireless communications company, disclosed the following information in its 1998 annual report (all numbers in thouands): cash and short-term investments, $16,075; cash used in operations, $265,802; capital expenditures, $282,042; and a net loss of $544,000. No cash dividends were paid during the year. Clearnet notes in its annual report that it "expects to continue to incur significant net losses during the next several years and to generate negative cash flow from operating activities in 1999 as a result of the implementation and operation of its ... networks and from marketing expenses as the Company expands its subscriber base."

Calculate free cash flow. (SO 8)

(a) Clearnet has both a negative cash flow from operations and a net loss. Will companies that have net losses always have a negative cash flow from operations?
(b) Calculate Clearnet's free cash flow for 1998.
(c) As an investor in Clearnet, comment on whether or not you should be concerned with the adequacy of its cash.

BE7-13 Conor Pacific Environmental Technologies, Inc., a leading Canadian environmental company, disclosed the following financial information in its 1998 financial statements: total expenses, $32,692,346; depreciation and amortization, $1,151,939; and cash, $1,351,845. Calculate the company's cash to daily cash expenses ratio.

Calculate cash to daily cash expenses ratio. (SO 8)

***BE7-14** On March 20, Gimbal's petty cash fund of $100 is replenished when the fund contains $12 in cash and receipts for postage, $52; supplies, $26; and travel expenses, $10. Prepare the journal entry to record the replenishment of the petty cash fund.

Prepare entry to replenish a petty cash fund. (SO 9)

EXERCISES

E7-1 Bank employees use a system known as the "maker-checker" system. An employee will record an entry in the appropriate journal and then a supervisor will verify and approve the entry. These days, as all of a bank's accounts are computerized, the employee first enters a batch of entries into the computer and, then, the entries are posted automatically to the general ledger account after the supervisor approves them on the system.

Identify the principles of internal control. (SO 1)

Access to the computer system is password-protected and task-specific, which means that the computer system will not allow the employee to approve a transaction, or the supervisor to record a transaction.

Instructions

Identify the principles of internal control inherent in the "maker-checker" procedure used by banks.

E7-2 Joe Marino is the owner of Marino's Pizza. Marino's operates strictly on a carry-out basis. Customers pick up their orders at a counter where a clerk exchanges the pizza

Identify the principles of internal control. (SO 1)

for cash. While at the counter, the customer can see other employees making the pizzas and the large ovens in which the pizzas are baked.

Instructions
Identify the six principles of internal control and give an example of each principle that you might observe when picking up your pizza. (Note: It may not be possible to observe all the principles.)

List internal control weaknesses for cash receipts and suggest improvements.
(SO 1, 2)

E7-3 The following control procedures are used in Tolan Company Ltd. for over-the-counter cash receipts:

1. Cashiers are experienced; thus they are not bonded.
2. All over-the-counter receipts are registered by three clerks who use a cash register with a single cash drawer.
3. To minimize the risk of robbery, cash in excess of $100 is stored in an unlocked attaché case in the stock room until it is deposited in the bank.
4. At the end of each day, the total receipts are counted by the cashier on duty and reconciled to the cash register total.
5. The company accountant makes the bank deposit and then records the day's receipts.

Instructions
(a) For each procedure, explain the weakness in internal control and identify the control principle that is violated.
(b) For each weakness, suggest a change in procedure that will result in good internal control.

List internal control weaknesses for cash disbursements and suggest improvements.
(SO 3)

E7-4 The following control procedures are used in Ann's Boutique Shoppe Ltd. for cash disbursements:

1. Each week, Ann leaves 100 company cheques in an unmarked envelope on a shelf behind the cash register.
2. The store manager personally approves all payments before signing and issuing cheques.
3. When the store manager has to go away for extended periods of time, he pre-signs a number of cheques to be used in his absence.
4. The company cheques are unnumbered.
5. After payment, bills are "filed" in a paid invoice folder.
6. The company accountant prepares the bank reconciliation and reports any discrepancies to the owner.

Instructions
(a) For each procedure, explain the weakness in internal control and identify the internal control principle that is violated.
(b) For each weakness, suggest a change in procedure that will result in good internal control.

Identify internal control weaknesses for cash disbursements and suggest improvements.
(SO 3)

E7-5 At O'Malley Company Inc., cheques are not prenumbered, because both the purchasing agent and the treasurer are authorized to issue cheques. Each signer has access to unissued cheques kept in an unlocked file cabinet. The purchasing agent pays all bills pertaining to goods purchased for resale. Prior to payment, the purchasing agent determines that the goods have been received and verifies the mathematical accuracy of the vendor's invoice. After payment, the invoice is filed by the vendor and the purchasing agent records the payment in the cash disbursements journal. The treasurer pays all other bills after approval by authorized employees. After payment, the treasurer stamps all bills "paid," files them by payment date, and records the cheques in the cash disbursements journal. O'Malley Company Inc. maintains one chequing account that is reconciled by the treasurer.

Instructions
(a) List the weaknesses in internal control over cash disbursements.
(b) Write a memo indicating your recommendations for improving company procedures.

Prepare bank reconciliation and adjusting entries.
(SO 4)

E7-6 Ono LoKo is unable to reconcile the bank balance at January 31. Ono's reconciliation is shown here:

Cash balance per bank	$3,560.20
Add: NSF cheque	530.00
Less: Bank service charge	25.00
Adjusted balance per bank	$4,065.20

Cash balance per books	$3,875.20
Less: Deposits in transit	490.00
Add: Outstanding cheques	730.00
Adjusted balance per books	$4,115.20

Instructions

(a) Prepare a correct bank reconciliation.

(b) Journalize the entries required by the reconciliation.

E7-7 At April 30, the bank reconciliation of Drofo Company Limited shows three outstanding cheques: No. 254, $650; No. 255, $820; and No. 257, $410. The May bank statement and the May cash payments journal are given here:

Determine outstanding cheques. (SO 4)

Bank Statement Cheques Paid

Date	Cheque No.	Amount
5/4	254	$650
5/2	257	410
5/17	258	159
5/12	259	275
5/20	261	500
5/29	263	480
5/30	262	750

Cash Payments Journal Cheques Issued

Date	Cheque No.	Amount
5/2	258	$159
5/5	259	275
5/10	260	925
5/15	261	500
5/22	262	750
5/24	263	480
5/29	264	360

Instructions

List the outstanding cheques at May 31.

E7-8 The following information pertains to Mohammed Company Ltd.:

Prepare bank reconciliation and adjusting entries. (SO 4)

1. Cash balance per bank, July 31, $7,463.
2. July bank service charge not recorded by the depositor, $15.
3. Cash balance per books, July 31, $7,190.
4. Deposits in transit, July 31, $1,700.
5. Note for $1,200 collected for Mohammed in July by the bank, plus interest of $36, less fee of $20. The collection has not been recorded by Mohammed, and no interest has been accrued.
6. Outstanding cheques, July 31, $772.

Instructions

(a) Prepare a bank reconciliation at July 31.

(b) Journalize the adjusting entries at July 31 on the books of Mohammed Company Ltd.

E7-9 This information relates to the Cash account in the ledger of Reston Company Ltd.:

Prepare bank reconciliation and adjusting entries. (SO 4)

September 1—balance, $17,150; cash deposited, $64,000
September 30—balance, $17,404; cheques written, $63,746

The September bank statement shows a balance of $16,422 at September 30 and the following memoranda:

Credits		Debits	
Collection of $1,500 note plus interest, $30	$1,530	NSF cheque: J. Hower	$410
Interest earned on chequing account	45	Safety deposit box rent	30

At September 30, deposits in transit were $4,500 and outstanding cheques totalled $2,383.

Instructions

(a) Prepare the bank reconciliation at September 30.

(b) Prepare the adjusting entries at September 30, assuming (1) the NSF cheque was from a customer on account, and (2) no interest had been accrued on the note.

E7-10 The cash records of Lejeune Company Inc. show the following:

Calculate deposits in transit and outstanding cheques for two bank reconciliations. (SO 4)

1. The June 30 bank reconciliation indicated that deposits in transit total $850. During July, the general ledger account, Cash, shows deposits of $15,750, but the bank statement indicates that only $15,600 in deposits were received during the month.

2. The June 30 bank reconciliation also reported outstanding cheques of \$920. During the month of July, the Lejeune books show that \$17,200 of cheques were issued, yet the bank statement showed that \$16,400 of cheques cleared the bank in July.
3. In September, deposits per the bank statement totalled \$26,700, deposits per books were \$25,400, and deposits in transit at September 30 were \$2,400.
4. In September, cash disbursements per books were \$23,700, cheques clearing the bank were \$25,000, and outstanding cheques at September 30 were \$2,100.

There were no bank debit or credit memoranda, and no errors were made by either the bank or Lejeune Company Inc.

Instructions

Answer these questions:

(a) In situation 1, what were the deposits in transit at July 31?
(b) In situation 2, what were the outstanding cheques at July 31?
(c) In situation 3, what were the deposits in transit at August 31?
(d) In situation 4, what were the outstanding cheques at August 31?

Identify the reporting of cash and cash equivalents and other items.
(SO 5)

E7-11 A new accountant at La Maison is trying to identify which of the following amounts should be reported as the current asset "Cash and Cash Equivalents" in the year-end balance sheet, as at April 30, 2001:

1. \$57 of currency and coin in a locked box used for petty cash transactions
2. A \$10,000 guaranteed investment certificate, due May 31, 2001
3. \$300 of April-dated cheques that La Maison has received from customers but not yet deposited
4. An \$85 cheque received from a customer in payment of its April account, but post-dated May 1
5. \$2,500 in the company's Royal Bank chequing account
6. \$4,000 in its Royal Bank savings account
7. \$75 of prepaid postage in its postage meter
8. A \$100 IOU from the company receptionist

Instructions

(a) What balance should La Maison report as its "Cash and Cash Equivalents" balance at April 30, 2001?
(b) In what financial statement and in what account should the items not included in "Cash and Cash Equivalents" be reported?

Review cash management practices.
(SO 6)

E7-12 Tory, Hachey, and Wedunn, three law students who have joined together to open a law practice, are struggling to manage their cash flow. They haven't yet built up sufficient clientele and revenues to support their legal practice's ongoing costs. Initial costs, such as advertising, renovations to their premises, and the like, all result in outgoing cash flow at a time when little is coming in! Tory, Hachey, and Wedunn haven't had time to establish a billing system since most of their clients' cases haven't yet reached the courts and the lawyers didn't think it would be right to bill them until "results were achieved." Unfortunately, Tory, Hachey, and Wedunn's suppliers don't feel the same way. Their suppliers expect them to pay their accounts payable within a few days of receiving their bills. So far, there hasn't even been enough money to pay the three lawyers, and they are not sure how long they can keep practising law without getting some money into their pockets!

Instructions

Can you provide any suggestions for Tory, Hachey, and Wedunn to improve their cash management practices?

Prepare a cash budget for two months.
(SO 7)

E7-13 Hanover Company Limited expects to have a cash balance of \$46,000 on January 1, 2001. These are the relevant monthly budget data for the first two months of 2001:

1. Collections from customers: January, \$70,000; February, \$150,000
2. Payments to suppliers: January, \$40,000; February, \$75,000
3. Wages: January, \$30,000; February, \$40,000. Wages are paid in the month they are incurred.
4. Administrative expenses: January, \$21,000; February, \$30,000. These costs include amortization of \$1,000 per month. All other costs are paid as incurred.

5. Selling expenses: January, $14,000; February, $20,000. These costs are exclusive of amortization. They are paid as incurred.
6. Sales of marketable securities in January are expected to realize $10,000 in cash. Hanover has a line of credit at a local bank that enables it to borrow up to $25,000. The company wants to maintain a minimum monthly cash balance of $20,000.

Instructions
Prepare a cash budget for January and February.

Calculate and comment on cash to daily cash expenses ratio and free cash flow.
(SO 8)

E7-14 **Nortel Networks Corporation**, of Brampton, Ontario, is a global leader and maker of telecommunications products. It reported the following financial data in its 1998 financial statements (in millions of U.S. dollars): net loss, $537; total expenses, $15,879 (excluding amortization); cash provided from operating activities, $1,586; cash and cash equivalents, $2,281; capital expenditures, $615; and dividends paid, $210.

Instructions
Calculate and comment on the following two measures of cash adequacy:
(1) cash to daily cash expenses ratio, and (2) free cash flow.

Prepare journal entries for a petty cash fund.
(SO 9)

***E7-15** During October, Kadloc Company Ltd. has the following transactions for a petty cash fund:

Oct. 1 An imprest fund is established with a cheque for $100 issued to the petty cash custodian.

Oct. 31 A count of the petty cash fund disclosed the following items:

Currency	$ 6.00
Coins	0.40
Expenditure receipts:	
Office supplies	28.20
Telephone, Internet, and fax	16.40
Postage	41.30
Freight-out	6.80

Oct. 31 A cheque was written to reimburse the fund and increase the fund to $200.

Instructions
Journalize the entries in October that pertain to the petty cash fund.

Prepare journal entries for a petty cash fund.
(SO 9)

***E7-16** Ramona Company Ltd. uses a petty cash system. The fund was established on March 1 with a balance of $100. During March, the following petty cash receipts were found in the petty cash box:

Date	Receipt No.	For	Amount
Mar. 5	1	Stamp Inventory	$38
7	2	Supplies	19
9	3	Miscellaneous Expense	12
11	4	Travel Expense	24
14	5	Miscellaneous Expense	5

There was no cash over or short. The fund was replenished on March 15. On March 20, the amount in the fund was increased to $150.

Instructions
Journalize the entries in March that pertain to the operation of the petty cash fund.

PROBLEMS: SET A

Identify internal control weaknesses for cash receipts.
(SO 1, 2)

P7-1A Red River Theatre is in the Red River Mall. A cashier's booth is located near the entrance to the theatre and two cashiers are employed. One works from 1:00 p.m. to 5:00 p.m., the other from 5:00 p.m. to 9:00 p.m. Each cashier is bonded. The cashiers receive cash from customers and operate a machine that ejects serially numbered tickets. The rolls of tickets are inserted and locked into the machine by the theatre manager at the beginning of each cashier's shift.

After purchasing a ticket which may be at different prices depending on the day or age group, the customer takes the ticket to a doorperson stationed at the entrance to the theatre lobby, some 60 feet from the cashier's booth. The doorperson tears the ticket in half, admits the customer, and returns the ticket stub to the customer. The other half of the ticket is dropped into a locked box by the doorperson.

At the end of each cashier's shift, the theatre manager removes the ticket rolls from the machine and makes a cash count. The cash count sheet is initialled by the cashier. At the end of the day, the manager deposits the total receipts in a bank night deposit vault located in the mall. In addition, the manager sends copies of the deposit slip and the initialled cash count sheets to the theatre company treasurer for verification and to the company's accounting department. Receipts from the first shift are stored in a safe located in the manager's office.

Instructions

(a) Identify the internal control principles and their application to the cash receipts transactions of Red River Theatre.

(b) If the doorperson and cashier decided to collaborate to misappropriate cash, what actions might they take?

Identify internal control weaknesses for cash receipts and cash disbursements.

(SO 1, 2, 3)

P7-2A Cedar Grove School wants to raise money for a new sound system for its auditorium. The primary fundraising event is a dance at which the famous disc jockey Obnoxious Al will play pop music. Roger DeMaster, the music and theatre instructor, has been given the responsibility for coordinating the fundraising efforts. This is Roger's first experience with fundraising. He decides to put the Student Representative Council (SRC) in charge of the event; he will be a relatively passive observer.

Roger had 500 unnumbered tickets printed for the dance. He left the tickets in a box on his desk and told the SRC students to take as many tickets as they thought they could sell for $5 each. In order to ensure that no extra tickets would be floating around, he told them to dispose of any unsold tickets. When the students received payment for the tickets, they were to bring the cash back to Roger, and he would put it in a locked box in this desk drawer.

Some of the students were responsible for decorating the gymnasium for the dance. Roger gave each of them a key to the money box and told them that if they took money out to purchase materials, they should put a note in the box saying how much they took and what it was used for. After two weeks, the money box appeared to be getting full, so Roger asked Steve Stevens to count the money, prepare a deposit slip, and deposit the money in a bank account Roger had opened.

The day of the dance, Roger wrote a cheque from the account to pay Obnoxious Al. However, Al said that he accepted only cash and did not give receipts. So Roger took $200 out of the cash box and gave it to Al. At the dance, Roger had Sara Billings working at the entrance to the gymnasium, collecting tickets from students and selling tickets to those who had not prepurchased them. Roger estimated that 400 students attended the dance.

The following day Roger closed out the bank account, which had $250 in it, and gave that amount plus the $180 in the cash box to Principal Skinner. Principal Skinner seemed surprised that, after generating roughly $2,000 in sales, the dance netted only $430 in cash. Roger did not know how to respond.

Instructions

Identify as many internal control weaknesses as you can in this scenario, and suggest how each could be addressed.

Prepare bank reconciliation with internal control deficiencies.

(SO 1, 2, 3, 4)

P7-3A Acura Company Ltd. is a very profitable small business. It has not, however, given much consideration to internal control. For example, in an attempt to keep clerical and office expenses to a minimum, the company has combined the jobs of cashier and bookkeeper. As a result, Rob Rowe handles all cash receipts, keeps the accounting records, and prepares the monthly bank reconciliations.

The balance per the bank statement on October 31, 2001, was $18,380. Outstanding cheques were No. 62 for $126.75, No. 183 for $150, No. 284 for $253.25, No. 862 for $190.71, No. 863 for $226.80, and No. 864 for $165.28. Included with the statement was a credit memorandum of $200 indicating the collection of a note receivable for Acura

Company by the bank on October 25. This memorandum has not been recorded by Acura Company.

The company's ledger showed one cash account with a balance of $21,892.72. The balance included undeposited cash on hand. Because of the lack of internal controls, Rowe took for personal use all of the undeposited receipts in excess of $3,795.51. He then prepared the following bank reconciliation in an effort to conceal his theft of cash:

Cash balance per books, October 31		$21,892.72
Add: Outstanding cheques		
No. 862	$190.71	
No. 863	226.80	
No. 864	165.28	482.79
		22,375.51
Less: Undeposited receipts		3,795.51
Unadjusted balance per bank, October 31		18,580.00
Less: Bank credit memorandum		200.00
Cash balance per bank statement, October 31		$18,380.00

Instructions

(a) Prepare a correct bank reconciliation. (Hint: Deduct the amount of the theft from the adjusted balance per books.)
(b) Indicate the three ways that Rowe attempted to conceal the theft and the dollar amount involved in each method.
(c) What principles of internal control were violated in this case?

Prepare bank reconciliation and adjusting entries. (SO 4)

P7-4A On July 31, 2001, Dubeau Company Ltd. had a cash balance per books of $6,815.30. The statement from the Caisse Populaire on that date showed a balance of $7,075.80. A comparison of the bank statement with the cash account revealed the following facts:

1. The bank service charge for July was $25.
2. The bank collected a note receivable of $1,200 for Dubeau Company on July 15, plus $48 of interest. The bank made a $10 charge for the collection. Dubeau has not accrued any interest on the note.
3. The July 31 receipts of $1,819.60 were not included in the bank deposits for July. These receipts were deposited by the company in a night deposit vault on July 31.
4. Company cheque No. 2480 issued to J. Brokaw, a creditor, for $492, cleared the bank in July and was incorrectly entered in the cash payments journal on July 10 for $429.
5. Cheques outstanding on July 31 totalled $1,480.10.
6. On July 31, the bank statement showed an NSF charge of $550 for a cheque received by the company from R. Chiasson, a customer, on account.

Instructions

(a) Prepare the bank reconciliation as at July 31.
(b) Prepare the necessary adjusting entries at July 31.

Prepare a bank reconciliation and adjusting entries. (SO 4)

P7-5A Selected banking and books documents required to reconcile the bank account for the Yap Co. Ltd. as at March 31, 2002 are reproduced below:

BANK

The March bank statement showed the following:

Bank Statement
March 31, 2002

	Deposits	Cheques and Other Debits		
Date	**Amount**	**Number**	**Amount**	**Balance**
Feb. 28				$14,368
March 1	$2,530	#3451	$2,260	14,638
March 2		#3471	845	13,793

March 5	1,212			15,005
March 7		#3472	1,427	13,578
March 10		NSF - Jordan	550	13,028
March 15		#3473	1,641	11,387
March 22		#3474	2,130	9,257
March 27	2,567			11,824
March 30		SC	49	11,775

Additional information:

1. The bank statement contained two debit memoranda:
   (a) An NSF cheque in the amount of $550 that had been previously deposited by Yap had been returned due to insufficient funds in the payor's bank account. This cheque was originally given to Yap by Mr. Jordan, a customer, in payment of his account. Yap believes it will be able to recollect this amount from Mr. Jordan in the future, and
   (b) A service charge (SC) of $49 for bank services provided throughout the month.
2. No errors were made by the bank.

BOOKS

The cash records on the books of the company for the month of March showed the following:

Cash Receipts

Date	Amount
March 4	$1,221
March 26	2,567
March 30	1,025
	$4,813

Cash Payments

Date	Cheque Number	Amount
March 7	#3472	$1,427
March 15	#3473	1,641
March 22	#3474	2,130
March 29	#3475	600
		$5,798

Additional information:

1. All cash receipts were deposited daily in the bank, using the night deposit slot. All cash payments were made by cheque.
2. A $9 error was made by Yap in recording cash receipts from cash sales on March 4.

BANK RECONCILIATION

The bank portion of **last month's** bank reconciliation for the Yap Co. Ltd. at **February 28, 2002**, was as follows:

YAP CO. LTD.
Bank Reconciliation
February 28, 2002

Cash balance per bank			$14,368
Add: Deposits in transit			2,530
			16,898
Less: Outstanding cheques			
	Cheque Number	Cheque Amount	
	#3451	$2,260	
	#3470	720	
	#3471	845	3,825
Reconciled / adjusted cash balance			$13,073

Instructions

(a) Determine Yap Co. Ltd.'s unadjusted cash balance in its general ledger, on March 31.
(b) What is the amount of the deposits in transit, if any, at March 31?
(c) What is the amount of the outstanding cheques, if any, at March 31?
(d) Prepare a bank reconciliation for the Yap Co. Ltd. for the month of March 2002.
(e) Prepare any journal entries required to adjust the accounts at March 31, 2002.

P7-6A The bank portion of the bank reconciliation for London Company Inc. at October 31, 2001, is shown here:

Prepare bank reconciliation and adjusting entries.

(SO 4)

LONDON COMPANY INC.
Bank Reconciliation
October 31, 2001

Cash balance per the bank			$12,367.90
Add: Deposits in transit			1,530.20
			13,898.10
Less: Outstanding cheques			
	Cheque Number	Cheque Amount	
	2451	$1,260.40	
	2470	720.10	
	2471	844.50	
	2472	426.80	
	2474	1,050.00	4,301.80
Adjusted cash balance the per bank			$ 9,596.30

The adjusted cash balance per the bank agreed with the cash balance per books at October 31. The November bank statement showed the following cheques and deposits:

Bank Statement

Cheques			Deposits	
Date	Number	Amount	Date	Amount
11-1	2470	$ 720.10	11-1	$ 1,530.20
11-2	2471	844.50	11-4	1,211.60
11-5	2474	1,050.00	11-8	990.10
11-4	2475	1,640.70	11-13	2,575.00
11-8	2476	2,830.00	11-18	1,472.70
11-10	2477	600.00	11-21	2,945.00
11-15	2479	1,750.00	11-25	2,567.30
11-18	2480	1,330.00	11-28	1,650.00
11-27	2481	695.40	11-30	1,186.00
11-30	2483	575.50	Total	$16,127.90
11-29	2486	900.00		
	Total	$12,936.20		

The cash records per books for November showed the following:

Cash Payments Journal

Date	Number	Amount	Date	Number	Amount
11-1	2475	$1,640.70	11-20	2483	$ 575.50
11-2	2476	2,830.00	11-22	2484	829.50
11-2	2477	600.00	11-23	2485	974.80
11-4	2478	538.20	11-24	2486	900.00
11-8	2479	1,570.00	11-29	2487	398.00
11-10	2480	1,330.00	11-30	2488	800.00
11-15	2481	695.40	Total		$14,294.10
11-18	2482	612.00			

Cash Receipts Journal

Date	Amount
11-3	$ 1,211.60
11-7	990.10
11-12	2,575.00
11-17	1,472.70
11-20	2,954.00
11-24	2,567.30
11-27	1,650.00
11-29	1,186.00
11-30	1,225.00
Total	$15,831.70

The bank statement contained two bank memoranda:

1. A credit of $2,105.00 for the collection of a $2,000 note for London Company Inc., plus interest of $120, and less a collection fee of $15. London Company Inc. has not accrued any interest on the note.
2. A debit for the printing of additional company cheques, $50.00.

At November 30, the cash balance per books was $11,133.90 and the cash balance per the bank statement was $17,614.60. The bank did not make any errors, but two errors were made by London Company Inc.

Instructions

(a) Prepare a bank reconciliation at November 30.

(b) Prepare the adjusting entries based on the reconciliation. (Note: The correction of any errors pertaining to recording cheques should be made to Accounts Payable. The correction of any errors pertaining to recording cash receipts should be made to Accounts Receivable.)

Prepare bank reconciliation and adjusting entries.
(SO 4)

P7-7A Mayo Company Ltd.'s bank statement from Canadian Western Bank at August 31, 2001, gives this information:

Balance, August 1	$17,400	Bank debit memorandum:	
August deposits	73,000	Safety deposit box rent	$ 25
Cheques cleared in August	68,660	Balance, August 31	24,850
Bank credit memoranda:			
Collection of note receivable, $3,000 plus $90 interest	3,090		
Interest earned	45		

A summary of the Cash account in the ledger for August shows: balance, August 1, $16,900; receipts, $77,000; disbursements, $73,570; and balance, August 31, $20,330. Analysis reveals that the only reconciling items on the July 31 bank reconciliation were a deposit in transit for $4,000 and outstanding cheques of $4,500. The deposit in transit was the first deposit recorded by the bank in August. In addition, you determine that there were two errors involving company cheques drawn in August: (1) a cheque for $400 to a creditor on account that cleared the bank in August was journalized and posted for $420, and (2) a salary cheque to an employee for $275 was recorded by the bank as $285.

Instructions

(a) Prepare a bank reconciliation at August 31.

(b) Journalize the adjusting entries to be made by Mayo Company Ltd. at August 31. Assume the interest on the note has been accrued by the company.

Calculate cash balance.
(SO 5)

P7-8A A first year co-op student is trying to determine the amount of cash that should be reported on a company's balance sheet. The following information was provided to the student at year end:

1. Cash on hand in the cash registers totals $5,000.
2. The petty cash fund is $500.
3. The balance in the commercial bank savings account was $100,000 and in the commercial bank chequing account, $25,000. The company also has $45,000 Canadian dollars in a U.S. bank account.
4. A special bank account holds cash that is restricted in the amount of $150,000 for capital asset replacement.
5. A line of credit in the amount of $50,000 is available at the bank on demand.
6. Amounts due from employees (travel advances) total $12,000.
7. Short-term investments held by the company include: $32,000 in a money market fund; $25,000 in shares of Nortel Networks; and $75,000 in long-term bonds of BCE Inc.
8. The company has a supply of unused postage stamps totalling $150.
9. The company has NSF cheques that were returned by the bank totalling $2,500.
10. The company has cash deposits (advances) paid by customers held in a special bank account in the amount of $7,500.

Instructions

(a) Calculate the Cash balance that should be reported on the year-end balance sheet.
(b) Would your answer in (a) change if the company combines its Cash and Cash Equivalents?
(c) Identify where any items that were not reported in the Cash balance in (a) should be reported.

Prepare a cash budget.
(SO 7)

P7-9A Hanover Co. Ltd. expects to have a cash balance of $46,000 on January 1, 2002. Relevant monthly budget data for the first two months of 2002 are as follows:

Collections from customers: January $70,000; February, $150,000

Payments to suppliers: January, $40,000; February, $75,000

Salaries: January, $30,000; February, $40,000. Salaries are paid in the month they are incurred.

Selling and administrative expenses: January, $34,000; February, $49,000. These costs are exclusive of amortization and are paid as incurred.

Sales of short-term investments in January are expected to realize $10,000 in cash.

Hanover has a line of credit at a local bank that enables it to borrow up to $25,000. The company wants to maintain a minimum monthly cash balance of $20,000.

Instructions

(a) Prepare a cash budget for January, and February.
(b) Explain how a cash budget contributes to effective management.

Prepare cash budget.
(SO 7)

P7-10A Joplin Inc. prepares monthly cash budgets. Here are relevant data from operating budgets for 2001:

	January	**February**
Sales	$360,000	$400,000
Purchases	100,000	110,000
Salaries	80,000	95,000
Selling and administrative expenses	135,000	160,000

All sales are on account. Collections are expected to be 50% in the month of sale, 30% in the first month following the sale, and 20% in the second month following the sale. Forty percent (40%) of purchases are paid in cash in the month of purchase, and the balance due is paid in the month following the purchase. All other items above are paid in the month incurred. Amortization has been excluded from selling and administrative expenses.

Other data are listed here:

1. Credit sales—November 2000, $200,000; December 2000, $280,000
2. Purchases—December 2000, $90,000
3. Other receipts—January: collection of December 31, 2000, interest receivable, $3,000; February: proceeds from sale of securities, $5,000
4. Other disbursements—February: payment of $20,000 for land

The company's cash balance on January 1, 2001, is expected to be $60,000. The company wants to maintain a minimum cash balance of $50,000.

Instructions

(a) Prepare schedules for (1) expected collections from customers and (2) expected payments for purchases.
(b) Prepare a cash budget for January and February.

Assess cash adequacy.
(SO 8)

P7-11A Sherritt International Corporation, headquartered in Toronto, is facing a problem its chair described at the company's May 2000 annual meeting as "too much cash and a ton of earnings" after experiencing sustained high prices for nickel and oil and gas.

The following selected information is available for Sherritt for the year ended December 31, 1999:

(in thousands)	1999	1998
Cash and short-term investments	$386,018	$510,391
Net earnings (loss)	42,987	(70,687)
Average daily cash expenses	661	601
Net cash provided by operating activities	89,979	113,779
Capital expenditures	87,818	156,609
Dividends	1,957	

Instructions

(a) Why is too much cash considered to be a problem?
(b) Calculate the cash adequacy for Sherritt using the cash to daily expenses ratio and free cash flow for 1999 and 1998. Is the chair correct—does Sherritt really have too much cash?

Journalize and post petty cash fund transactions.
(SO 9)

***P7-12A** MTR Company Ltd. maintains a petty cash fund for small expenditures. These transactions occurred over a two-month period:

July 1	Established the petty cash fund by writing a cheque on the Royal Bank for $200.
15	Replenished the petty cash fund by writing a cheque for $194.30. On this date, the fund consisted of $5.70 in cash and these petty cash receipts: freight-out, $94.00; postage expense, $42.40; entertainment expense, $46.60; and miscellaneous expense, $10.70.
31	Replenished the petty cash fund by writing a cheque for $192.00. At this date, the fund consisted of $8.00 in cash and these petty cash receipts: freight-out, $82.10; charitable contributions expense, $30.00; postage expense, $47.80; and miscellaneous expense, $32.10.
Aug. 15	Replenished the petty cash fund by writing a cheque for $188.00. On this date, the fund consisted of $12.00 in cash and these petty cash receipts: freight-out, $74.40; entertainment expense, $43.00; postage expense, $33.00; and miscellaneous expense, $38.00.
16	Increased the amount of the petty cash fund to $300 by writing a cheque for $100.
31	Replenished the petty cash fund by writing a cheque for $283.00. On this date, the fund consisted of $17 in cash and these petty cash receipts: postage expense, $145.00; entertainment expense, $90.60; and freight-out, $45.40.

Instructions

(a) Journalize the petty cash transactions.
(b) Post to the Petty Cash account.
(c) What internal control features exist in a petty cash fund?

PROBLEMS: SET B

Identify internal control weaknesses for cash receipts.

(SO 1, 2)

P7-1B The board of trustees of a local church is concerned about the internal accounting controls pertaining to the offering collections made at weekly services. They ask you to serve on a three-person audit team with the internal auditor of the university and a CA who has just joined the church. At a meeting of the audit team and the board of trustees, you learn the following:

1. The church's board of trustees has delegated responsibility for the financial management and audit of the financial records to the finance committee. This group prepares the annual budget and approves major disbursements but is not involved in collections or record keeping. No audit has been done in recent years, because the same trusted employee has kept church records and served as financial secretary for 15 years. The church does not carry any fidelity insurance.
2. The collection at the weekly service is taken by a team of ushers who volunteer to serve for one month. The ushers take the collection plates to a basement office at the rear of the church. They hand their plates to the head usher and return to the church service. After all plates have been turned in, the head usher counts the cash received. The head usher then places the cash in the church safe along with a notation of the amount counted. The head usher volunteers to serve for three months.
3. The next morning, the financial secretary opens the safe and recounts the collection. The secretary withholds \$150–\$200 in cash, depending on the cash expenditures expected for the week, and deposits the remainder of the collections in the bank. To facilitate the deposit, church members who contribute by cheque are asked to make their cheques payable to "Cash."
4. Each month the financial secretary reconciles the bank statement and submits a copy of the reconciliation to the board of trustees. The reconciliations have rarely contained any bank errors and have never shown any errors per books.

Instructions

(a) Indicate the weaknesses in internal accounting control in the handling of collections.
(b) List the improvements in internal control procedures that you plan to make at the next meeting of the audit team for (1) the ushers, (2) the head usher, (3) the financial secretary, and (4) the finance committee.
(c) What church policies should be changed to improve internal control?

Identify internal control principles for cash disbursements.

(SO 1, 3)

P7-2B Segal Office Supply Company Limited recently changed its system of internal control over cash disbursements. The system includes the following features:

1. Instead of being unnumbered and manually prepared, all cheques must now be prenumbered and written by a new computerized cheque-writing system purchased by the company.
2. Before a cheque can be issued, each invoice must have the approval of Cindy Morris, the purchasing agent, and Ray Mills, the receiving department supervisor.
3. Cheques must be signed by either Frank Malone, the treasurer, or Mary Arno, the assistant treasurer. Before signing a cheque, the signer is expected to compare the amount of the cheque with the amount on the invoice.
4. After signing a cheque, the signer stamps the invoice "paid" and writes in the date, cheque number, and amount of the cheque. The "paid" invoice is then sent to the accounting department for recording.
5. Blank cheques are stored in a safe in the treasurer's office. The combination to the safe is known by only the treasurer and assistant treasurer.
6. Each month the bank statement is reconciled with the bank balance per books by the assistant chief accountant.

Instructions

Identify the internal control principles and their application to cash disbursements of Segal Office Supply Company Limited.

Prepare bank reconciliation with internal control deficiencies.
(SO 1, 2, 3, 4)

P7-3B Giant Company Inc. is a very profitable small business. It has not, however, given much consideration to internal control. For example, in an attempt to keep clerical and office expenses to a minimum, the company has combined the jobs of cashier and bookkeeper. As a result, K. Kilgora handles all cash receipts, keeps the accounting records, and prepares the monthly bank reconciliations.

The balance per the bank statement on November 30, 2001, was $19,460. Outstanding cheques were: No. 62 for $113.90, No. 183 for $160, No. 284 for $266.90, No. 862 for $170.73, No. 863 for $325.40, and No. 864 for $173.10. Included with the statement was a credit memorandum of $250 indicating the collection of a note receivable for the Giant Company by the bank on November 25. This memorandum has not been recorded by Giant Company.

The company's ledger showed one cash account with a balance of $23,756.78. The balance included undeposited cash on hand. Because of the lack of internal controls, Kilgora took for personal use all of the undeposited receipts in excess of $4,616.01. He then prepared the following bank reconciliation in an effort to conceal his theft of cash:

Cash balance per books, November 30		$23,756.78
Add: Outstanding cheques		
No. 862	$170.73	
No. 863	325.40	
No. 864	173.10	569.23
		24,326.01
Less: Undeposited receipts		4,616.01
Unadjusted balance per bank, November 30		19,710.00
Less: Bank credit memorandum		250.00
Cash balance per bank statement, November 30		$19,460.00

Instructions

(a) Prepare a correct bank reconciliation. (Hint: Deduct the amount of the theft from the adjusted balance per books.)

(b) Indicate the three ways that Kilgora attempted to conceal the theft and the dollar amount pertaining to each method.

(c) What principles of internal control were violated in this case?

Prepare bank reconciliation and adjusting entries from detailed data.
(SO 4)

P7-4B On May 31, 2001, Maloney Company Inc. had a cash balance per books of $5,781.50. The bank statement from Community Bank on that date showed a balance of $6,804.60. A comparison of the statement with the cash account revealed the following facts:

1. The statement included a debit memo of $40 for the printing of additional company cheques.
2. Cash sales of $836.15 on May 12 were deposited in the bank. The cash receipts journal entry and the deposit slip were incorrectly made for $846.15. The bank credited Maloney for the correct amount.
3. Outstanding cheques at May 31 totalled $1,276.25, and deposits in transit were $936.15.
4. On May 18, the company issued cheque No. 1181 for $685 to M. Helms, on account. The cheque, which cleared the bank in May, was incorrectly journalized and posted by Maloney for $658.
5. A $2,000 note receivable was collected by the bank for Maloney Company Inc. on May 31, plus $80 interest. The bank charged a collection fee of $20. No interest has been accrued on the note.
6. Included with the cancelled cheques was a cheque issued by Teller Company to P. Jonet for $600 that was incorrectly charged to Maloney by the bank.
7. On May 31, the bank statement showed an NSF charge of $700 for a cheque issued by W. Hoad, a customer, to Maloney on account.

Instructions

(a) Prepare the bank reconciliation as at May 31, 2001.
(b) Prepare the necessary adjusting entries at May 31, 2001.

P7-5B You are provided with the following information for Exploits River Adventures Ltd.

Prepare a bank reconciliation and adjusting entries.

(SO 4)

EXPLOITS RIVER ADVENTURES LTD.
Bank Reconciliation
April 30, 2001

Cash balance per the bank			$8,008.53
Add: deposits in transit			846.33
			8,854.86
Less: Outstanding cheques			
	Cheque Number	Cheque Amount	
	526	$1,357.99	
	533	89.78	
	541	363.44	
	555	78.82	
			(1,890.03)
Adjusted cash balance per the bank			$6,964.83

The adjusted cash balance per the bank agreed with the cash balance per books at April 30, 2001.

The May bank statement showed the following:

Date	Cheque Number	Cheque Amount	Deposit Amount	Balance
30-Apr.				$8,008.53
3-May	526	1,357.99	846.33	7,496.87
4-May	541	363.44		7,133.43
6-May	556	223.46		6,909.97
6-May	557	1,800.00	1,250.00	6,359.97
10-May			980.00	7,339.97
10-May	559	1,650.00		5,689.97
13-May			426.00	6,115.97
13-May			(a) 1,650.00	7,765.97
14-May	561	799.00		6,966.97
18-May	562	2,045.00		4,921.97
18-May			222.00	5,143.97
19-May	563	2,487.00		2,656.97
21-May	564	603.00		2,053.97
25-May	565	1,033.00		1,020.97
26-May			980.00	2,000.97
28-May			1,771.00	3,771.97
31-May		(b) 25.00		3,746.97
		$12,386.89	$8,125.33	

(a) Proceeds of $1,500 note plus interest
(b) Service charges

Cash Disbursements Journal

Date	Name	Amount
4-May	556	$ 223.46
5-May	557	1,800.00
7-May	558	943.00
7-May	559	1,650.00
8-May	560	890.00
10-May	561	799.00
15-May	562	2,045.00
18-May	563	2,487.00
20-May	564	603.00
25-May	565	1,033.00
31-May	566	750.00
Total		$13,223.46

Cash Receipts Journal

Date	Amount
5-May	$1,250.00
8-May	980.00
12-May	426.00
18-May	222.00
25-May	980.00
28-May	1,771.00
31-May	1,086.00
Total	$6,715.00

Instructions

(a) Calculate the balance of cash at May 31, 2001 according to Exploits River Adventures Ltd.'s general ledger.

(b) Prepare a bank reconciliation and necessary journal entries for Exploits River Adventures Ltd. as at May 31, 2001. The company has not accrued interest on the note.

Prepare bank reconciliation and adjusting entries.

(SO 4)

P7-6B The bank portion of the bank reconciliation for Sandra Company Limited at November 30, 2001, is shown here:

SANDRA COMPANY LIMITED
Bank Reconciliation
November 30, 2001

	Cheque Number	Cheque Amount	
Cash balance per the bank			$14,367.90
Add: Deposits in transit			2,530.20
			16,898.10
Less: Outstanding cheques			
	3451	$2,260.40	
	3470	720.10	
	3471	844.50	
	3472	1,426.80	
	3474	1,050.00	6,301.80
Adjusted cash balance per the bank			$10,596.30

The adjusted cash balance per the bank agreed with the cash balance per books at November 30. The December bank statement showed the following cheques and deposits:

Bank Statement

Cheques			Deposits	
Date	Number	Amount	Date	Amount
12-1	3451	$ 2,260.40	12-1	$ 2,530.20
12-2	3471	844.50	12-4	1,211.60
12-7	3472	1,426.80	12-8	2,365.10
12-4	3475	1,640.70	12-16	2,672.70
12-8	3476	1,300.00	12-21	2,945.00
12-10	3477	2,130.00	12-26	2,567.30
12-15	3479	3,080.00	12-29	2,836.00
12-27	3480	600.00	12-30	1,025.00
12-30	3482	475.50	Total	$18,152.90
12-29	3483	1,140.00		
12-31	3485	540.80		
	Total	$15,438.70		

The cash records per books for December showed the following:

Cash Payments Journal

Date	Number	Amount	Date	Number	Amount
12-1	3475	$1,640.70	12-20	3482	$ 475.50
12-2	3476	1,300.00	12-22	3483	1,140.00
12-2	3477	2,130.00	12-23	3484	832.00
12-4	3478	538.20	12-24	3485	450.80
12-8	3479	3,080.00	12-30	3486	1,389.50
12-10	3480	600.00	Total		$14,384.10
12-17	3481	807.40			

Cash Receipts Journal

Date	Amount
12-3	$ 1,211.60
12-7	2,365.10
12-15	2,672.70
12-20	2,954.00
12-25	2,567.30
12-28	2,836.00
12-30	1,025.00
12-31	1,190.40
Total	$16,822.10

The bank statement contained two memoranda:

1. A credit of $2,145 for the collection of a $2,000 note for Sandra Company, plus interest of $160, and less a collection fee of $15. Sandra Company has not accrued any interest on the note.
2. A debit of $547.10 for an NSF cheque written by A. Jordan, a customer. At December 31, the cheque had not been redeposited in the bank.

At December 31, the cash balance per books was $13,034.30, and the cash balance per the bank statement was $18,680.00. The bank did not make any errors, but two errors were made by Sandra Company.

Instructions

(a) Prepare a bank reconciliation at December 31.

(b) Prepare the adjusting entries based on the reconciliation. (Note: The correction of any errors pertaining to recording cheques should be made to Accounts Payable. The correction of any errors pertaining to recording cash receipts should be made to Accounts Receivable.)

Prepare bank reconciliation and adjusting entries.
(SO 4)

P7-7B Palmeiro Company Ltd. maintains a chequing account at ScotiaBank. At July 31, selected data from the ledger balance and the bank statement are as follows:

	Cash in Bank	
	Per Books	**Per Bank**
Balance, July 1	$17,600	$19,200
July receipts	82,000	
July credits		80,070
July disbursements	76,900	
July debits		74,740
Balance, July 31	$22,700	$24,530

Analysis of the bank data reveals that the credits consist of $78,000 of July deposits and a credit memorandum of $2,070 for the collection of a $2,000 note plus interest revenue of $70. The July debits per the bank consist of cheques cleared, $74,700, and a debit memorandum of $40 for printing additional company cheques. You also discover the following errors involving July cheques: (1) a cheque for $230 to a creditor on account that cleared the bank in July was journalized and posted as $320, and (2) a salary cheque to an employee for $255 was recorded by the bank as $155. The June 30 bank reconciliation contained only two reconciling items: deposits in transit, $5,000, and outstanding cheques of $6,600.

Instructions

(a) Prepare a bank reconciliation at July 31.
(b) Journalize the adjusting entries to be made by Palmeiro Company Ltd. at July 31. Assume the interest on the note has been accrued.

Calculate cash balance; prepare a bank reconciliation and adjusting entries.
(SO 4, 5)

P7-8B On August 31, 2001, Dublin Ltd. had a cash balance per the general ledger (books) of $780.97. The statement from the Royal Bank showed a balance of $1,250.47. A comparison of the bank statement with the cash account revealed the following facts:

1. The company had $150.00 of traveller's cheques on hand. This amount was included in the book amount of cash, but had already been subtracted from the bank records. The traveller's cheques will be charged to travel expense by the company as they have been used. There was a bank service charge of $16 related to the traveller's cheques which has not been recorded in the company's books.
2. The cash balance in the company's books includes $293 for Visa receipts, net of related charges, that have been submitted to the bank, but not yet included in the bank balance.
3. The bank collected a note receivable of $1,300 from Byrd Company on August 23, plus $52 of interest. The bank made a $15 charge for the collection. Dublin Ltd. has not accrued interest on the note.
4. The August 31 bank deposits of $2,607.61 were deposited by the company in the night deposit on August 31, but were not included in the bank deposits for the month of August.
5. The bank had processed cheque number 630 as $1,957 when the cheque was made out for $1,597.
6. A comparison of the bank statement to the book balance at August 31, 2001 showed the following cheques were still outstanding:
   - Cheque 628 $ 781.25
   - Cheque 635 1,333.33
   - Cheque 636 250.00
   - Cheque 637 224.53
7. Other bank service charges for the month were $30.

Instructions

(a) Prepare the bank reconciliation as at August 31, 2001.
(b) Prepare the necessary adjusting entries at August 31, 2001.
(c) What balance would Dublin report as cash in the current assets section of its balance sheet on August 31, 2001?

P7-9B You are provided with the following information taken from New Bay Inc.'s March 31, 2001 balance sheet:

Prepare cash budget.
(SO 7)

Cash	$ 8,000
Accounts receivable	20,000
Inventory	36,000
Capital assets, net of accumulated amortization	120,000
Accounts payable	21,750
Common shares	150,000
Retained earnings	12,250

Additional information concerning New Bay Inc. is as follows:

1. Gross margin is 25% of sales.
2. Actual and budgeted sales data:

March (actual)	$50,000
April (budgeted)	60,000

3. Sales are 60% for cash and 40% on credit. There are no sales discounts and credit sales are collected in the month following the sale.
4. Half of a month's purchases are paid for in the month of purchase and half in the following month. Purchases of inventory totalled $43,500 for the month of March and are anticipated to total $52,200 for the month of April. Ending inventory is expected to be $43,200 at the end of April.
5. Cash operating expenses are anticipated to be $13,300 for the month of April.
6. Equipment costing $2,500 will be purchased for cash in April.
7. The company wishes to maintain a minimum cash balance of $8,000. (Although this is not always a wise cash management practice, it is a policy used by some organizations.) An open line of credit is available at the bank. All borrowing is done at the beginning of the month and all repayments are made at the end of the month. The interest rate is 12% per annum and interest expense is accrued at the end of the month and paid in the following month.

Instructions

(a) Calculate cash collections in April for March and April sales.
(b) Calculate the cash disbursements in April related to March and April purchases.
(c) Prepare a cash budget for the month of April. Determine how much cash New Bay Inc. must borrow, or can repay, in April.

P7-10B Badger Corporation prepares monthly cash budgets. Here are relevant data from operating budgets for 2001:

Prepare cash budget.
(SO 7)

	January	February
Sales	$350,000	$400,000
Purchases	120,000	130,000
Salaries	80,000	95,000
Administrative expenses	70,000	75,000
Selling expenses	79,000	86,000

All sales are on account. Collections are expected to be 50% in the month of sale, 40% in the first month following the sale, and 10% in the second month following the sale. Fifty percent (50%) of purchases are paid in cash in the month of purchase, and the balance due is paid in the month following the purchase. All other items above are paid in the month incurred except for administrative expenses, which include $1,000 of amortization per month.

Other data are listed here:

1. Credit sales—November 2000, $260,000; December 2000, $300,000
2. Purchases—December 2000, $100,000
3. Other receipts—January: collection of December 31, 2000, notes receivable, $15,000; February: proceeds from sale of securities, $6,000
4. Other disbursements—February: $5,000 cash dividend

The company's cash balance on January 1, 2001, is expected to be $55,000. The company wants to maintain a minimum cash balance of $50,000.

Instructions

(a) Prepare schedules for (1) expected collections from customers and (2) expected payments for purchases.

(b) Prepare a cash budget for January and February.

Assess cash adequacy. (SO 8)

P7-11B You are presented with the following information taken from the 1999 financial statements of **BCE Inc.** and **Aliant Inc.**:

	BCE INC. (in thousands of dollars)		ALIANT INC. (in thousands of dollars)	
	31-Dec-99	**31-Dec-98**	**31-Dec-99**	**31-Dec-98**
Cash	$ 2,395,000	$ 370,000	$ 26,954	$ 20,019
Cash provided by operating activities	2,598,000	3,506,000	434,975	450,051
Capital expenditures	3,588,000	3,774,000	365,619	305,055
Cash dividends	968,000	961,000	106,305	95,216
Operating expenses	11,522,000	23,719,000	434,975	450,051
Amortization expense, included in the operating expenses (Aliant's amortization is reported separately.)	3,001,000	3,501,000	0	0

Instructions

(a) Calculate the cash to daily cash expenses ratios and free cash flow for each company.

(b) Compare the cash adequacy of each company.

Journalize and post petty cash fund transactions. (SO 9)

***P7-12B** Dockers Company Ltd. maintains a petty cash fund for small expenditures. The following transactions occurred over a two-month period:

July 1 Established the petty cash fund by writing a cheque on the CIBC for $200.

15 Replenished the petty cash fund by writing a cheque for $195.00. On this date, the fund consisted of $5.00 in cash and these petty cash receipts: freight-out, $94.00; postage expense, $42.40; entertainment expense, $46.60; and miscellaneous expense, $11.90.

31 Replenished the petty cash fund by writing a cheque for $192.00. At this date, the fund consisted of $8.00 in cash and these petty cash receipts: freight-out, $82.10; charitable contributions expense, $40.00; postage expense, $27.80; and miscellaneous expense, $42.10.

Aug. 15 Replenished the petty cash fund by writing a cheque for $187.00. On this date, the fund consisted of $13.00 in cash and these petty cash receipts: freight-out, $74.60; entertainment expense, $43.00; postage expense, $33.00; and miscellaneous expense, $37.00.

16 Increased the amount of the petty cash fund to $300 by writing a cheque for $100.

31 Replenished the petty cash fund by writing a cheque for $283.00. On this date, the fund consisted of $17 in cash and these petty cash receipts: postage expense, $140.00; travel expense, $95.60; and freight-out, $46.40.

Instructions

(a) Journalize the petty cash transactions.

(b) Post to the Petty Cash account.

(c) What internal control features exist in a petty cash fund?

BROADENING YOUR PERSPECTIVE

Financial Reporting and Analysis

FINANCIAL REPORTING PROBLEM: *Loblaw Companies Limited*

BYP7-1 **Loblaw Companies Limited's** annual report is presented in Appendix A of this book. This report includes two reports attached to its financial statements: (1) Management's Statement of Responsibility; and (2) the Auditors' Report. Another report, the Management Discussion and Analysis, is also found within the annual report.

Instructions

Using the annual report, answer these questions about Loblaw's internal controls and cash:

(a) What comments, if any, concerning the company's system of internal control are included in Management's Statement of Responsibility? In the Auditors' Report?
(b) What reference, if any, is made to internal auditors in each of the above reports?
(c) Did cash flows from operating activities increase or decrease in 1999 over 1998? What reason did management identify for this change in the Management Discussion and Analysis?
(d) What activities are identified as the major cash flow components in the Management Discussion and Analysis? Trace each of these amounts to the consolidated statement of cash flows.

COMPARATIVE ANALYSIS PROBLEM: *Loblaw and Sobeys*

BYP7-2 The financial statements of **Sobeys Inc.** are presented in Appendix B, following the financial statements for **Loblaw** in Appendix A.

Instructions

Answer the following questions for each company:

(a) What is the balance in cash and cash equivalents for the current fiscal year?
(b) How much cash was provided by operating activities for the current year?
(c) Calculate the ratio of cash to daily cash expenses.
(d) Calculate free cash flow.
(e) What conclusions regarding the ability to generate cash and the companies' cash management can be made from the comparison of these results?

RESEARCH CASE

BYP7-3 The *Globe and Mail* included an article by Allan Robinson in its October 25, 1999, newspaper entitled "Ottawa Plans Curb on Money Laundering."

Instructions

Read the article and answer these questions:

(a) What is money laundering?
(b) How much money does the Department of Finance estimate is laundered illegally in Canada each year?
(c) How many countries does the Financial Action Task Force on Money Laundering include?
(d) What is the purpose of the proposed legislation, Bill C-81, reintroduced by the federal government?
(e) Can you think of any other possible ways that the pace of money laundering could be slowed? What potential dilemmas do these solutions present?

INTERPRETING FINANCIAL STATEMENTS

BYP7-4 **Microsoft** is the leading developer of software in the world. To continue to be successful, Microsoft must generate new products, and generating new products requires significant amounts of cash. Selected information from Microsoft is shown below. Following the Microsoft data, selected financial information from **Corel**, another major software developer is shown.

MICROSOFT, INC. AND COREL CORPORATION
Selected Financial Statement Information

	Microsoft, Inc. June 30, 1998 (in millions)	Corel Corporation November 30, 1998 (in thousands)
Net earnings (loss)	$ 4,490	($ 30,448)
Cash and short-term investments	30,629	24,506
Total expenses	10,697	277,417
Depreciation and amortization	1,024	12,368
Cash provided by operations	6,880	14,368
Capital expenditures	494	10,054
Cash dividends	0	0

Instructions

(a) What is the definition of a cash equivalent? Give some examples of cash equivalents. How do cash equivalents differ from other types of short-term investments?
(b) Calculate (1) the ratio of cash to daily cash expenses and (2) free cash flow for each company. Discuss your results.
(c) Is it possible to have too much cash?
(d) Do you think Corel can effectively compete with Microsoft, given its more precarious financial situation?

A GLOBAL FOCUS

BYP7-5 The world's number 1 food company, **Nestlé S.A.**, dominates in several food areas. The Vevey, Switzerland-based company makes the world's number 1 coffee (Nescafé), the world's number 1 bottled water (Perrier, Poland Spring), as well as milk products (Carnation), cereals, ice cream, prepared dishes (Stouffers), pet food (Alpo), chocolate, and eye care products (Alcon). The company sells over 8,500 products worldwide and has more than 500 factories in over 80 countries.

The following information has been selected from Nestlé's 1998 financial statements:

NESTLÉ S. A.
Selected Financial Information
December 31, 1998
(in millions of Swiss francs)

	1998	1997
Cash and cash equivalents	Fr. 4,984	Fr. 3,412
Total expenses	67,817	65,839
Depreciation and amortization	2,910	2,817
Operating cash flow	6,372	7,401
Capital expenditures	2,574	891
Dividends	1,376	1,180
Net earnings	4,119	4,096

Instructions

(a) Calculate Nestlé's cash to daily cash expenses ratio and free cash flow for each year. Comment on the company's cash adequacy.

(b) As an international company, Nestlé is affected by economic and financial conditions in each of the countries where it operates. For example, when currencies devalue substantially, as they did in 1998, Nestlé's cash position is hit hard. In fact, Nestlé notes in its letter to shareholders that "evolution of foreign currencies against the Swiss franc... penalized our sales by 5.6%." Explain how Nestlé's operating cash flow is affected by devaluation of a foreign currency.

FINANCIAL ANALYSIS ON THE WEB

BYP7-6 KPMG Canada annually produces a *Fraud Survey Report*, comprising responses from the top 1,000 public and private Canadian companies. In this case, we review this report and examine e-commerce and the incidence and source of e-fraud in Canada.

Instructions
Specific requirements of this web case can be found on the Kimmel website.

BYP7-7 CICA's Criteria of Control Board, commonly known as CoCo, was established in 1995 to broaden the traditional definition of internal control. It recognizes that the approach to control should change in the face of re-engineering processes, delayered organizations, downsizing and outsourcing, employee empowerment, and the demands for enhanced and effective governance. This case reviews CoCo's mandate and its recommendations for designing, assessing and reporting on the control systems of organizations.

Instructions
Specific requirements of this web case can be found on the Kimmel website.

CRITICAL THINKING

COLLABORATIVE LEARNING ACTIVITY

BYP7-8 Alternative Distributor Corp., a distributor of groceries and related products, was founded in 1980 and today has seven employees and total sales of $7 million.

During its audit, Alternative Distributor Corp. was advised that existing internal controls necessary for the company to develop reliable financial statements were inadequate. The audit report stated that the current system of accounting for sales, receivables, and cash receipts constituted a material weakness. Among other items, the report focused on nontimely deposit of cash receipts, exposing Alternative Distributor to potential loss or misappropriation; excessive past due accounts receivable due to lack of collection efforts; disregard of advantages offered by vendors for prompt payment of invoices; absence of appropriate segregation of duties by personnel consistent with appropriate control objectives; inadequate procedures for applying accounting principles; lack of qualified management personnel; lack of supervision by an outside board of directors; and overall poor record keeping.

Instructions
With the class divided into groups, do the following:
(a) Identify the principles of internal control violated by Alternative Distributor Corp.
(b) Write a memo to the company's management. The memo should address the following points:
1. which principles of internal control were violated by Alternative Distributor Corp.
2. why these controls are important
3. steps that could be taken to improve the situation

COMMUNICATION ACTIVITY

BYP7-9 As a new auditor for the CA firm of Rawls, Keoto, and Landry, you have been assigned to review the internal controls over mail cash receipts of Laurentian Company Inc. Your review reveals that cheques are promptly endorsed "For Deposit Only," but no list of the cheques is prepared by the person opening the mail. The mail is opened either by the cashier or by the employee who maintains the accounts receivable records. Mail receipts are deposited in the bank by the cashier weekly.

Instructions

Write a letter to L.S. Osman, owner of the Laurentian Company Inc., explaining the weaknesses in internal control and your recommendations for improving the system.

ETHICS CASE

BYP7-10 Banks charge fees of up to $25 for "bounced" cheques—that is, cheques that exceed the balance in the account. It has been estimated that processing bounced cheques costs a bank roughly $1.50 per cheque. Thus, the profit margin on bounced cheques is very high. Recognizing this, some banks have started to process cheques from largest to smallest. By doing this, they maximize the number of cheques that bounce if a customer overdraws an account. One bank projected a $14 million increase in fee revenue as a result of processing largest cheques first. In response to criticism, banks have responded that their customers prefer to have large cheques processed first, because those tend to be the most important. At the other extreme, some banks will cover their customers' bounced cheques, effectively extending them overdraft protection.

Instructions

Answer each of the following questions:

(a) Antonio Freeman had a balance of $1,500 dollars in his chequing account on a day when the bank received the following five cheques for processing against his account:

Cheque Number	Amount	Cheque Number	Amount
3150	$ 35	3165	$550
3158	1,510	3169	180
3162	400		

Assuming a $25 fee assessed by the bank, how much fee revenue would the bank generate if it processed cheques from largest to smallest, (2) from smallest to largest, and (3) in the order of the cheque numbers?

(b) Do you think that processing cheques from largest to smallest is an ethical business practice?

(c) Besides ethical issues, what other considerations must a bank make in deciding whether to process cheques from largest to smallest?

(d) If you were managing a bank, what policy would you adopt on bounced cheques?

Answers to Self-Study Questions

1. a 2. c 3. b 4. b 5. d 6. a 7. c 8. c 9. c 10. d
*11. a

Answer to Loblaw's Review It Question 3

Loblaws
A passion for food... *and a lot more!*

Loblaw reported $672 million of cash and short-term investments as at January 1, 2000. Loblaw's cash equivalents included short-term investments, consisting of government securities, commercial paper, bank deposits, and repurchase agreements. Loblaw did not report any restricted cash for fiscal 1999.

CHAPTER 8

Reporting and Analysing Receivables

STUDY OBJECTIVES

After studying this chapter, you should be able to:

1. Identify the different types of receivables.
2. Explain how accounts receivable are recognized in the accounts.
3. Describe the method used to account for bad debts.
4. Explain how notes receivable are recognized and valued in the accounts.
5. Describe the entries to record the disposition of notes receivable.
6. Explain the statement presentation of receivables.
7. Describe the principles of sound accounts receivable management.
8. Identify ratios used to analyse a company's receivables.
9. Describe methods used to accelerate the receipt of cash from receivables.

A Dose of Careful Management Keeps Receivables Healthy

"Sometimes you have to know when to be very tough, and sometimes you can give them a bit of a break," says Vivi Su. She's not talking about her children, but about the customers of the Mississauga-based Canadian subsidiary of pharmaceutical company Whitehall-Robins, where she works as supervisor of credit and collections.

This kind of judgement call comes into play all the time in her job. For example, while the company's regular terms are 1/15, n/30 (1% discount if paid within 15 days), a customer might ask for and receive a few days of grace and still get the discount. "Or if a customer pays several invoices with one cheque, and some are under 15 days and some are over, we might allow the discount for them all," says Ms. Su. "After all, some smaller customers only write cheques once a week, or even once a month." Or a customer might place orders above its credit limit, in which case, depending on their payment history and the circumstances, Ms. Su might authorize the goods to be shipped anyway.

"It's not about drawing a line in the sand, and that's all," she explains. "You want a good relationship with your customers—but you also need to bring the money in."

"The money," in Whitehall-Robins' case amounts to some $170 million in sales a year, nearly all of which comes in through the credit accounts Ms. Su manages. The process starts with the decision to grant a customer an account in the first place, Ms. Su explains. (The company's customers are mostly drug wholesalers—a more profitable market than selling directly to pharmacies, since the distributors buy in bulk). "The sales rep approaches the customer, and if they agree to carry our product, he or she gives them a credit application. My department reviews this application very carefully; a customer needs to supply three good references, and we also run a check with a credit firm like Equifax. If we accept them, then based on their size and history, we assign a credit limit."

Once accounts are established, they are supervised very carefully. "I get an aging report every single day," says Ms. Su.

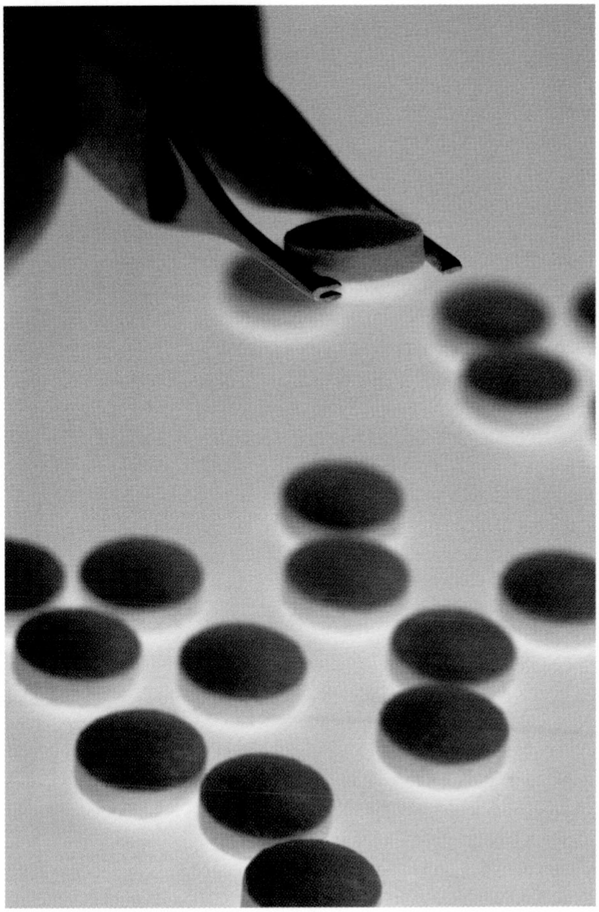

On the World Wide Web
Whitehall-Robins Healthcare, Inc.
http://www.whitehall-robins.com

"The rule of thumb is that we should always have at least 85% of receivables current—meaning they were billed less than 30 days ago," she continues. "But we try to do even better than that—I like to see 90%." Similarly, her guideline is never to have more than 5% of receivables at over 90 days. But long before that figure is reached, "we jump on it," she says firmly.

At 15 days overdue, the client gets a phone call. Often there's a reasonable explanation for the delay—an invoice may have gone astray, or the payables clerk is away. "But if a customer keeps on delaying, and tells us several times that it'll only be a few more days, we know there's a problem," says Ms. Su. After 45 days, "I send a letter. Then a second notice in writing. After the third and final notice, the client has 10 days to pay, and then I hand it over to a collection agency, and it's out of my hands."

This is the last resort, however, and it doesn't happen often. "So far, we've been lucky," says Ms. Su. "I sent only two accounts for collection last year." It helps, she says, when you choose carefully where to extend your credit in the first place. "Besides, our products are good, so people want to remain our customers!"

Ms. Su's boss, Terry Norton, records an estimate for bad debts every year, based on a percentage of receivables. What percentage depends on the current aging history. He also watches the company's receivables turnover ratio, which is reported in the financial statements. "I think of it in terms of collection period or DSO—days of sales outstanding," he explains. "You want to keep that number as close to your terms as possible. But it varies over the year. In the fall, for example, we often extend more favourable terms to customers to allow them to do special promotions, and our DSO might reach 60-odd days."

Ms. Su knows that she and Mr. Norton are crucial to Whitehall-Robins, profitability. "Receivables are generally the second-largest asset of any company (after its capital assets)," she points out. "So it's no wonder we keep a very close eye on them."

PREVIEW OF CHAPTER 8

In this chapter, we discuss some of the decisions related to reporting and analysing receivables. As indicated in the opening story, receivables are a significant asset on the books of many pharmaceutical companies. Receivables are significant to companies in other industries as well, because a significant portion of sales are made on credit in Canada. Companies must therefore pay close attention to their receivables balances and manage them carefully.

The content and organization of the chapter are as follows:

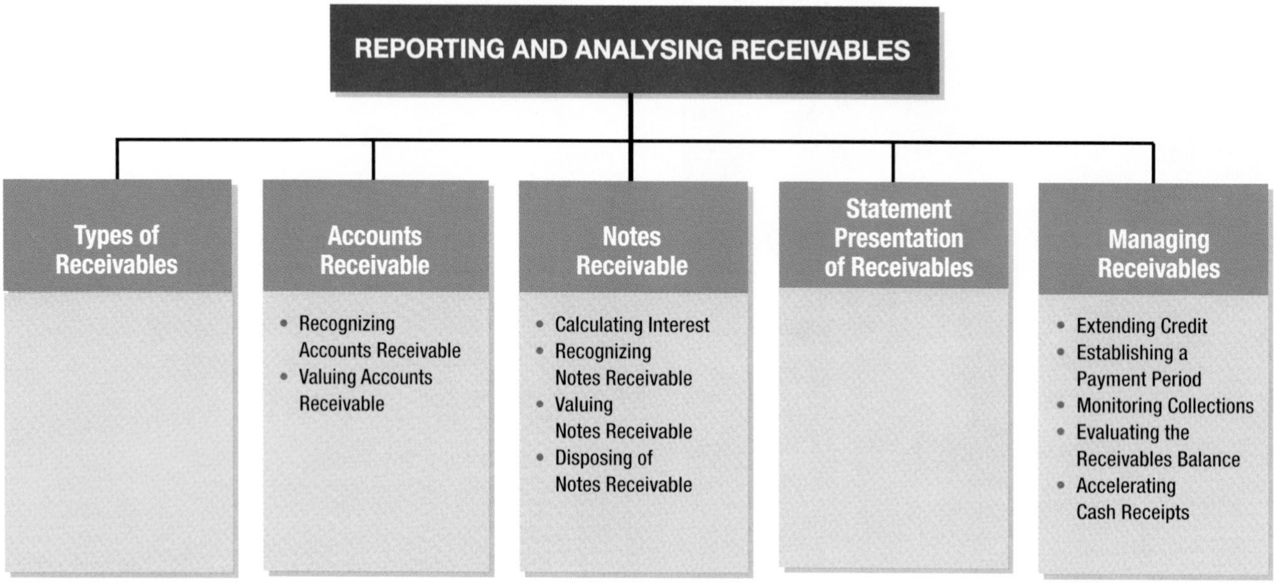

Types of Receivables

STUDY OBJECTIVE 1
Identify the different types of receivables.

The term **receivables** refers to amounts due from individuals and companies. Receivables are claims that are expected to be collected in cash. The management of receivables is a very important activity for any company that sells goods on credit. Receivables are important because they represent one of a company's most liquid assets. For many companies, receivables are also one of the largest assets. Illustration 8-1 lists receivables as a percentage of total assets for five well-known organizations in a recent year.

Illustration 8-1
Receivables as a percentage of assets

Company	Receivables as a Percentage of Total Assets
Canadian Tire Corporation, Limited	13%
Student Centre of McGill University	16
Jean Coutu Group (PJC) Inc.	30
Sears Canada Inc.	34
Royal LePage Limited	45

The relative significance of a company's receivables as a percentage of its assets differs depending on its industry, the time of year, whether it extends long-term financing, and its credit policies. To reflect important differences among receivables, they are frequently classified as (1) accounts, (2) notes, and (3) other.

Accounts receivable are amounts owed by customers on account. They result from the sale of goods and services. These receivables generally are expected to be collected within 30 days or so. They are usually the most significant type of claim held by a company.

Notes receivable represent claims for which formal instruments of credit are issued as evidence of the debt. The credit instrument normally requires the debtor to pay interest and extends for time periods of 60 to 90 days or longer. Notes and accounts receivable that result from sales transactions are often called **trade receivables**.

Other receivables include nontrade receivables such as interest receivable, loans to company officers, advances to employees, and recoverable sales and income taxes. As these are unusual, they are generally classified and reported as separate items in the balance sheet.

Accounts Receivable

Two accounting problems associated with accounts receivable are

1. Recognizing accounts receivable
2. Valuing accounts receivable

A third issue, accelerating cash receipts from receivables, is discussed later in the chapter.

RECOGNIZING ACCOUNTS RECEIVABLE

STUDY OBJECTIVE 2

Explain how accounts receivable are recognized in the accounts.

Initial recognition of accounts receivable is relatively straightforward. For a service organization, a receivable is recorded when service is provided on account. For a merchandiser, accounts receivable are recorded at the point of sale of merchandise on account. When a merchandiser sells goods, both accounts receivable and sales are increased.

Receivables are reduced as a result of sales discounts and sales returns. The seller may offer terms that encourage early payment by providing a discount. For example, terms of 2/10, n/30 provide the buyer with a 2% discount if paid within 10 days. If the buyer chooses to pay within the discount period, the seller's accounts receivable are reduced. Also, the buyer might find some of the goods unacceptable and choose to return the unwanted goods. For example, if merchandise with a selling price of $100 is returned, the seller reduces accounts receivable by $100 upon receipt of the returned merchandise.

Illustration 8-2 contains an excerpt from the notes to the financial statements of Del Laboratories, Inc. that describes its revenue recognition procedures. Del manufactures and distributes cosmetics, including the Sally Hansen nail care line, and over-the-counter pharmaceuticals, including Orajel toothache products.

Illustration 8-2 Disclosure of revenue recognition policy

DEL LABORATORIES, INC.
Notes to the Financial Statements

Revenues are recognized and product discounts are recorded when merchandise is shipped. Net sales are comprised of gross revenues less returns, trade discounts, and customer allowances. Merchandise returns are accrued at the earlier of customer deduction or receipt of goods.

VALUING ACCOUNTS RECEIVABLE

STUDY OBJECTIVE 3

Describe the method used to account for bad debts.

Once receivables are recorded in the accounts, the next question is: How should receivables be reported in the financial statements? They are reported on the balance sheet as an asset, but **determining the amount to report** is sometimes difficult because some receivables will become uncollectible.

Although each customer must satisfy the credit requirements of the seller before the credit sale is approved, inevitably some accounts receivable become uncollectible. For example, one of your customers may not be able to pay because of a decline in sales due to a downturn in the economy. Similarly, individuals may be laid off from their jobs or faced with unexpected dental bills. Credit losses are debited to the Bad Debts Expense (or Uncollectible Accounts Expense) account. Such losses are considered a normal and necessary risk of doing business on a credit basis.

The key issue in valuing accounts receivable is when to recognize these credit losses. If we wait until we know for sure that the specific account will not be collected, we could end up recording the bad debts expense in a period different than the period in which the revenue was recorded.

Consider the following example. In 2001, Quick Buck Computer Company decides it could increase its revenues by offering computers to students without requiring any money down, and with no credit approval process. It goes on campuses across the country and distributes 1 million computers with a selling price of $1,200 each. This increases Quick Buck's revenues and receivables by $1,200 million. The promotion is a huge success! The 2001 balance sheet and statement of earnings look wonderful. Unfortunately, during 2002, nearly 40% of the student customers default on their accounts. This makes the year 2002 statement of earnings and balance sheet look terrible. Illustration 8-3 shows that the promotion in 2001 is not such a great success after all.

Illustration 8-3 Effects of mismatching bad debts

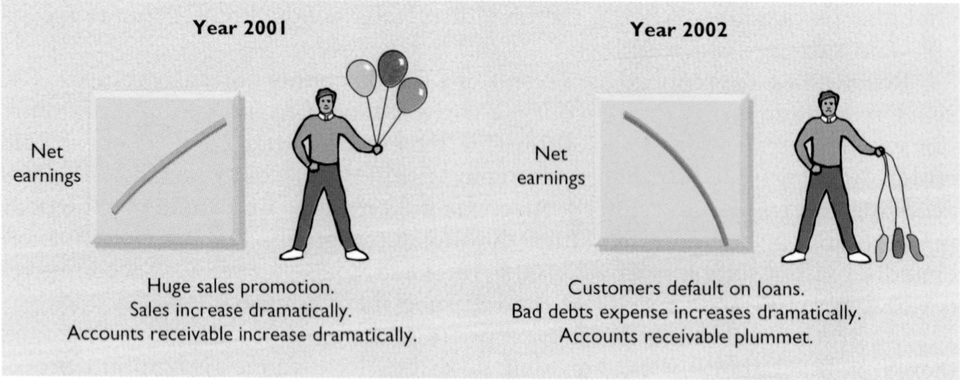
Year 2001
Net earnings
Huge sales promotion.
Sales increase dramatically.
Accounts receivable increase dramatically.
Year 2002
Net earnings
Customers default on loans.
Bad debts expense increases dramatically.
Accounts receivable plummet.

If we wait to record credit losses until they occur, no attempt is made to match bad debts expense to sales revenues in the statement of earnings or to show the accounts receivable in the balance sheet at the amount actually expected to be received. This does not provide useful information for decision-makers and is not acceptable for financial reporting purposes. Consequently, we need a method that will estimate uncollectible accounts receivable and match any anticipated credit losses against sales in the accounting period in which the sales occur. This method is known as the **allowance method**.

Helpful Hint Waiting to record credit losses until they occur is known as the **direct write-off method**. It is *not* acceptable under GAAP.

Allowance Method for Uncollectible Accounts

The **allowance method** of accounting for bad debts involves estimating uncollectible accounts at the end of each period. This provides better matching on the statement of earnings and ensures that receivables are stated at the net realizable value on the balance sheet. **Net realizable value** is the net amount expected to be received in cash. It excludes amounts that the company estimates it will not collect. Receivables are therefore reduced by estimated uncollectible receivables on the balance sheet through the use of the allowance method.

The allowance method is required for financial reporting purposes when bad debts are material in amount. It has three essential features:

1. Uncollectible accounts receivable are **estimated** and **matched against sales** in the same accounting period in which the sales occur.
2. Estimated uncollectibles are recorded as an increase (a debit) to Bad Debts Expense and an increase (a credit) to Allowance for Doubtful Accounts (a contra asset account) through an adjusting entry at the end of each period.
3. Actual uncollectibles are debited to Allowance for Doubtful Accounts and credited to Accounts Receivable at the time the specific account is written off as uncollectible.

Recording Estimated Uncollectibles. To illustrate the allowance method, assume that Abrams Furniture Ltd. has credit sales of $1,200,000 in 2001, of which $200,000 remains uncollected at December 31. The credit manager estimates that $12,000 of these accounts receivable will prove uncollectible. The adjusting entry to record the estimated uncollectibles is:

Dec. 31	Bad Debts Expense	12,000	
	Allowance for Doubtful Accounts		12,000
	(To record estimate of uncollectible accounts)		

A	=	L	+	SE
-12,000				-12,000

Bad Debts Expense is reported in the statement of earnings as an operating expense (usually as a selling expense). Thus, the estimated uncollectibles are matched with sales in 2001 because the expense is recorded in the same year the sales are made.

Allowance for doubtful accounts shows the estimated amount of claims on customers that are expected to become uncollectible in the future. A contra account is used instead of a direct credit to accounts receivable because we do not know which customers will not pay. The credit balance in the allowance account will absorb the specific write-offs when they occur. It is deducted from accounts receivable in the current asset section of the balance sheet as shown in Illustration 8-4.

Illustration 8-4
Presentation of allowance for doubtful accounts

ABRAMS FURNITURE LTD.
Balance Sheet (partial)

Current assets		
Cash		$ 14,800
Accounts receivable	**$200,000**	
Less: Allowance for doubtful accounts	**12,000**	**188,000**
Merchandise inventory		310,000
Prepaid expense		25,000
Total current assets		$537,800

International Note

The Finance Ministry in Japan recently noted that financial institutions should make better disclosure of bad loans. This disclosure would help depositors pick healthy banks.

The amount of $188,000 in Illustration 8-4 represents the expected **net (cash) realizable value** of the accounts receivable at the statement date.

Recording the Write-off of an Uncollectible Account. Companies use various methods of collecting past-due accounts, such as letters, calls, collection agencies, and legal action. When all means of collecting a past-due account have been exhausted and collection appears impossible, the account should be written off. In the credit card industry, it is standard practice to write off accounts that are 210 days past due. To prevent premature or unauthorized write-offs, each write-off should be formally approved in writing by authorized management personnel. To maintain good internal control, authorization to write off accounts should not be given to someone who also has daily responsibilities related to cash or receivables.

BUSINESS INSIGHT

International Perspective

Many investors are eager to buy shares of Chinese companies. Analysts advise caution, however, because tight credit in China is making it hard for many companies to collect their receivables. Thus, a significant number of transactions booked as sales will never be collected. Under Chinese accounting practices, bad debt write-offs are rare, and so some companies have two-year-old receivables on their books. Even those Chinese companies that follow international standards are not required to write off an account until it is one year old.

To illustrate a receivables write-off, assume that the vice-president of finance of Abrams Furniture authorizes a write-off of the $500 balance owed by R.A. Ware on March 1, 2002. The entry to record the write-off is:

Mar. 1	Allowance for Doubtful Accounts	500	
	Accounts Receivable—R.A. Ware		500
	(Write-off of R.A. Ware account)		

A	=	L	+	SE
+500				
-500				

Bad Debts Expense is not increased when the write-off occurs. **Under the allowance method, every bad debt write-off is debited to the allowance account and not to Bad Debts Expense.** A debit to Bad Debts Expense would be incorrect because the expense was already recognized when the adjusting entry was made for estimated bad debts. Instead, the entry to record the write-off of an uncollectible account reduces both Accounts Receivable and the Allowance for Doubtful Accounts. After posting, the general ledger accounts will appear as in Illustration 8-5.

Illustration 8-5 General ledger balances after write-off

Accounts Receivable		Allowance for Doubtful Accounts	
Jan. 1 Bal. 200,000	Mar. 1 **500**	Mar. 1 **500**	Jan. 1 Bal. 12,000
Mar. 1 Bal. 199,500			Mar. 1 11,500

A write-off affects only balance sheet accounts. Net realizable value in the balance sheet, therefore, remains the same, as shown in Illustration 8-6.

Illustration 8-6 Net realizable value comparison

	Before Write-off	**After Write-off**
Accounts receivable	$ 200,000	$ 199,500
Less: Allowance for doubtful accounts	12,000	11,500
Net realizable value	**$188,000**	**$188,000**

Recovery of an Uncollectible Account. Occasionally, a company collects from a customer after the account has been written off as uncollectible. Two entries are required to record the recovery of a bad debt: (1) the entry made in writing off the account is reversed to reinstate the customer's account; and (2) the collection is journalized in the usual manner. To illustrate, assume that on July 1, R.A. Ware pays the $500 amount that had been written off on March 1. These are the entries:

(1)

July 1	Accounts Receivable—R.A. Ware	500	
	Allowance for Doubtful Accounts		500
	(To reverse write-off of R.A. Ware account)		

A	=	L	+	SE
+500				
-500				

(2)

July 1	Cash	500	
	Accounts Receivable—R.A. Ware		500
	(To record collection from R.A. Ware)		

A	=	L	+	SE
+500				
-500				

Note that the recovery of a bad debt, like the write-off of a bad debt, affects only balance sheet accounts. The net effect of the two entries above is an increase in cash and an increase in allowance for doubtful accounts of $500. Accounts receivable and the allowance for doubtful accounts both increase in entry (1) for two reasons: first, the account receivable and allowance should not be written off after all. Second, R.A. Ware did pay, and therefore the accounts receivable account should show this collection for possible future credit purposes.

Estimating the Allowance. For Abrams Furniture in Illustration 8-4, the amount of the expected uncollectibles was given. However, in "real life," companies must estimate that amount if they use the allowance method. There are two bases that can be used to estimate that amount: (1) percentage of sales, and (2) percentage of receivables. While either method is acceptable for financial reporting, most companies use the percentage of receivables basis, which estimates uncollectible accounts using a percentage of the outstanding receivables. Most companies monitor their accounts receivable closely to reduce losses, and the percentage of receivables method lends itself to regular evaluation of the collectibility of the accounts receivable. Because of its frequency of use, we have chosen to illustrate only the percentage of receivables basis here.

Helpful Hint A few companies use a *percentage of sales basis* to estimate uncollectibles, establishing a relationship between the amount of sales and expected losses from uncollectible accounts.

Under the **percentage of receivables basis**, management establishes a percentage relationship between the amount of receivables and expected losses from uncollectible accounts. Sometimes a percentage is applied to total receivables, but more often a range of percentages are applied to subtotals or groupings of receivables. A schedule is prepared in which customer balances are classified by the length of time they have been unpaid. Because of its emphasis on time, this schedule is often called an aging schedule, and its completion is often called **aging the accounts receivable**.

After the accounts are arranged by age, the expected bad debt losses are determined by applying percentages based on past experience to the totals of each category. The longer a receivable is past due, the less likely it is to be collected. As a result, the estimated percentage of uncollectible debts increases as the number of days past due increases. An aging schedule for Dubé Company Lteé is shown in Illustration 8-7. Note the increasing uncollectible percentages from 2% to 40%.

Illustration 8-7 Aging schedule

		Number of Days Outstanding				
Customer	**Total**	**0–30**	**31–60**	**61–90**	**91–120**	**Over 120**
T. E. Adert	$ 600		$ 300		$ 200	$ 100
R. C. Bortz	300	$ 300				
B. A. Carl	450		200	$ 250		
O. L. Diker	700	500			200	
T. O. Ebbet	600			300		300
Others	36,950	26,200	5,200	2,450	1,600	1,500
	$39,600	$27,000	$5,700	$3,000	$2,000	$1,900
Estimated percentage uncollectible		2%	4%	10%	20%	40%
Total estimated bad debts	$ 2,228	$ 540	$ 228	$ 300	$ 400	$ 760

Total estimated bad debts for Dubé Company ($2,228) represents the existing customer claims expected to become uncollectible in the future. Thus, this amount represents the **required balance** in allowance for doubtful accounts at the balance sheet date. Accordingly, **the amount of the bad debt adjusting entry is the difference between the required balance and the existing balance in the allowance account.** If the trial balance shows Allowance for Doubtful Accounts with a credit balance of $528, then an adjusting entry for $1,700 ($2,228 – $528) is necessary:

Dec. 31	Bad Debts Expense	1,700	
	Allowance for Doubtful Accounts		1,700
	(To adjust allowance account to total estimated uncollectibles)		

A	=	L	+	SE
-1,700				-1,700

After the adjusting entry is posted, the accounts of Dubé Company will appear as in Illustration 8-8.

Illustration 8-8
Bad debt accounts after posting

Bad Debts Expense		Allowance for Doubtful Accounts	
Dec. 31 Adj. **1,700**			Bal. 528
			Dec. 31 Adj. **1,700**
			Bal. 2,228

An important aspect of accounts receivable management is simply maintaining a close watch on the accounts. Studies have shown that accounts more than 60 days past due lose approximately 50% of their value if no payment activity occurs within the next 30 days. For each additional 30 days that pass, the collectible value halves once again.

Occasionally, the allowance account will have a **debit balance** prior to adjustment because write-offs during the year have **exceeded** previous provisions for bad debts. In such cases, **the debit balance is added to the required balance** when the adjusting entry is made. Thus, if there had been a $500 debit balance in the allowance account before adjustment, the adjusting entry would have been for $2,728 ($2,228 + $500) to arrive at a credit balance of $2,228.

The percentage of receivables basis used with an aging schedule provides an estimate of the net realizable value of the receivables. It also provides a reasonable matching of expense to revenue. An accounts receivable aging schedule should be prepared at least monthly. In addition to estimating the allowance for bad debts, the aging schedule has other uses to management. It aids estimation of the timing of future cash inflows, which is very important to the treasurer's efforts to prepare a cash budget. It provides information about the overall collection experience of the company and identifies problem accounts. Problem accounts need to be pursued with phone calls, letters, collection agencies, and occasionally legal action.

BUSINESS INSIGHT

Management Perspective

Nearly half of the goods sold by Sears are puchased with a Sears credit card. This means that how Sears accounts for its uncollectible accounts can have a very significant effect on its net earnings. In one quarter, Sears reduced its bad debt expense by 61% compared to the same quarter in the previous year. In so doing, it was able to report earnings that slightly exceeded analysts' forecasts. Some analysts expressed concern because the number of delinquent accounts receivable had actually increased. Sears should probably have increased its bad debt expense, rather than reducing it. While Sears management defended its actions, analysts appeared to be unimpressed, and Sears' share price declined.

DECISION TOOLKIT

Decision Checkpoints	Info Needed for Decision	Tool to Use for Decision	How to Evaluate Results
Is the amount of past due accounts increasing? Which accounts require management's attention?	List of outstanding receivables and their due dates	Prepare an aging schedule showing the receivables in various stages: outstanding 0–30 days, 31–60 days, 61–90 days, 91–120 days, and over 120 days.	Accounts in the older categories require follow-up: letters, phone calls, e-mails, and possible renegotiation of terms.

BEFORE YOU GO ON . . .

Review It

1. What type of receivables does Loblaw report on its balance sheet? The answer to this question is provided at the end of this chapter.
2. To maintain adequate internal controls over receivables, who should authorize receivables write-offs?
3. What are the essential features of the allowance method?

Do It

Brule Corporation has been in business for five years. The ledger at the end of the current year shows: Accounts Receivable, $30,000; Sales, $180,000; and Allowance for Doubtful Accounts with a debit balance of $2,000. Bad debts are estimated to be 10% of accounts receivable. Prepare the entry necessary to adjust the Allowance for Doubtful Accounts.

Reasoning: Receivables are reported at their net realizable value—that is, the amount the company expects to collect in cash. This amount excludes any amount the company does not expect it will collect. The estimated uncollectible amount should be recorded in an allowance account.

Solution: The following entry should be made to bring the balance in the Allowance for Doubtful Accounts up to a credit balance of $3,000 (10% × $30,000):

Bad Debts Expense	5,000	
Allowance for Doubtful Accounts		5,000
(To record estimate of uncollectible accounts)		

Helpful Hint The debit to Bad Debts Expense is calculated as follows:

Allowance for Doubtful Accounts

2,000	**5,000**
	3,000

NOTES RECEIVABLE

Credit may also be granted in exchange for a formal credit instrument known as a promissory note. A **promissory note** is a written promise to pay a specified amount of money on demand or at a definite time. Promissory notes may be used (1) when individuals and companies lend or borrow money, (2) when the amount of the transaction and the credit period exceed normal limits, and (3) in settlement of accounts receivable.

In a promissory note, the party making the promise to pay is called the **maker**; the party to whom payment is to be made is called the **payee**. The payee may be specifically identified by name or may be designated simply as the bearer of the note.

In the note shown in Illustration 8-9, Brent Company Ltd. is the maker and Wilma Company Inc. is the payee. For Wilma Company, the promissory note is a note receivable; for Brent Company, the note is a note payable.

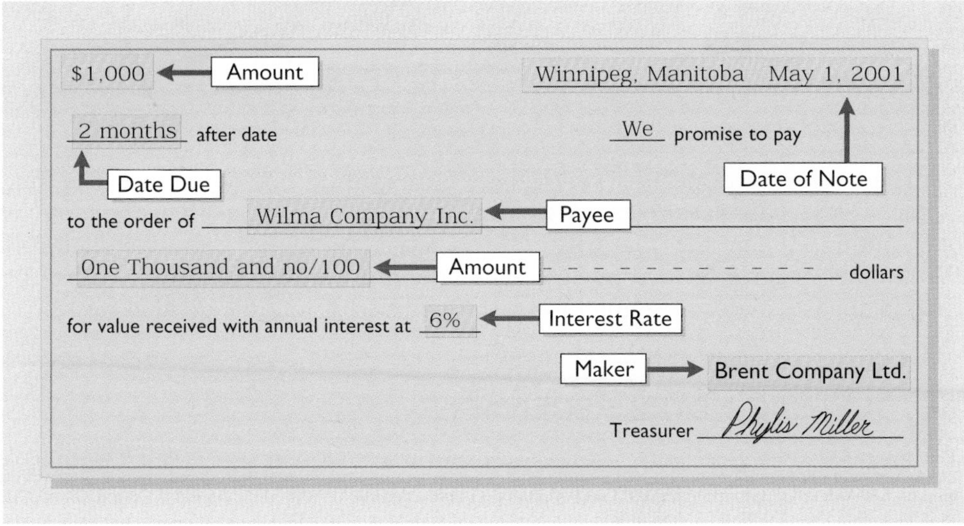

Illustration 8-9
Promissory note

Helpful Hint Who are the two key parties to a note, and what entry does each party make when the note is issued?
Answer:
1. The maker credits Notes Payable.
2. The payee debits Notes Receivable.

Notes receivable give the holder a stronger legal claim to assets than accounts receivable. Like accounts receivable, notes receivable can be readily sold to another party. Promissory notes are negotiable instruments (as are cheques), which means that, when sold, they can be transferred to another party by endorsement.

Notes receivable are frequently accepted from customers who need to extend the payment of an outstanding account receivable and are often required from high-risk customers. For example, it was recently reported that Intel Corporation (a major manufacturer of computer chips) required that Packard Bell NEC, Inc. (a manufacturer of personal computers) give it an interest-bearing note receivable in exchange for its past-due account receivable owed to Intel. This was cause for concern within the investment community. First because it suggested that Packard Bell NEC was in trouble, and second because of the impact on Intel's accounts receivable, since Packard Bell NEC is one of its largest customers.

In some industries (e.g., the pleasure and sport boat industry), all credit sales are supported by notes. The majority of notes, however, originate from lending transactions. There are three basic issues in accounting for notes receivable:

1. **Recognizing** notes receivable
2. **Valuing** notes receivable
3. **Disposing of** notes receivable

We will look at each of these issues, but first we need to consider an issue that did not apply to accounts receivable—at least those paid within the period due—calculating interest.

CALCULATING INTEREST

The basic formula for calculating interest on an interest-bearing note is given in Illustration 8-10.

Illustration 8-10 Formula for calculating interest

Face Value of Note × Annual Interest Rate × Time in Terms of One Year = Interest

The interest rate specified on the note is an **annual** rate of interest. The time factor in the calculation expresses the fraction of a year that the note is outstanding. When the maturity date is stated in days, the time factor is the number of days divided by 365. When the due date is stated in months, the time factor is usually simplified to be the number of months divided by 12.

RECOGNIZING NOTES RECEIVABLE

STUDY OBJECTIVE 4

Explain how notes receivable are recognized and valued in the accounts.

To illustrate the basic entry for notes receivable, we will use Brent Company's $1,000, two-month, 6% promissory note dated May 1. Assuming that the note was written to settle an open account, we record this entry for the receipt of the note by Wilma Company:

A	=	L	+	SE
+1,000				
-1,000				

May 1	Notes Receivable—Brent Company	1,000	
	Accounts Receivable—Brent Company		1,000
	(To record acceptance of Brent Company note)		

The note receivable is recorded at its **face value**, the value shown on the face of the note. No interest revenue is reported when the note is accepted because the revenue recognition principle does not recognize revenue until earned. Interest is earned (accrued) as time passes.

If a note is exchanged for cash, the entry is a debit to Notes Receivable and a credit to Cash in the amount of the loan.

VALUING NOTES RECEIVABLE

Like accounts receivable, short-term notes receivable are reported at their **net realizable value**. The notes receivable allowance account is Allowance for Doubtful Notes. Valuing short-term notes receivable is the same as valuing accounts receivable. The calculations and estimations involved in determining net (or cash) realizable value and in recording the proper amount of bad debts expense and related allowance are similar.

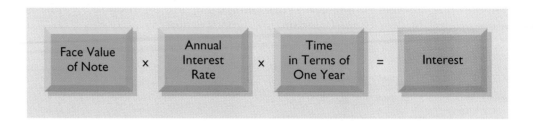

Long-term notes receivable, however, pose additional estimation problems. As an example, we need only look at the problems a number of large banks are having in collecting their receivables. Loans to less-developed countries are particularly worrisome. Developing countries, or countries in economic crisis, need loans but often find repayment difficult. The Royal Bank, at the end of 1999, had loans of $3.9 billion outstanding in Asia, $2.2 billion in Latin America, and $2.9 billion in the Caribbean. All banks are facing significant write-offs on loans such as these, ranging from 30% in Hong Kong to 80% or more in Indonesia. Determining the proper allowance is understandably difficult for these types of long-term receivables.

DISPOSING OF NOTES RECEIVABLE

STUDY OBJECTIVE 5

Describe the entries to record the disposition of notes receivable.

Notes may be held to their maturity date, at which time the face value plus accrued interest is due. In some situations, the maker of the note defaults and appropriate adjustment must be made. In other situations, similar to accounts receivable, the holder of the note speeds up the conversion to cash by selling the receivables. The entries for honouring and dishonouring notes are illustrated next.

Honour of Notes Receivable

A note is **honoured** when it is paid in full at its maturity date. For each interest-bearing note, the amount due at maturity is the face value of the note plus interest for the length of time specified on the note.

To illustrate, assume that Wolder Co. lends Higley Inc. $10,000 on June 1, accepting a four-month, 9% interest note. In this situation, interest is $300 ($\$10,000 \times 9\% \times \frac{4}{12}$) and payable at maturity. The amount due, the maturity value, is $10,300. To obtain payment, Wolder (the payee) must present the note either to Higley Inc. (the maker) or to the maker's agent, such as a bank. If Wolder presents the note to Higley Inc. on October 1, the maturity date, the entry by Wolder to record the collection is:

Oct. 1	Cash	10,300	
	Notes Receivable—Higley Inc.		10,000
	Interest Revenue		300
	(To record collection of Higley Inc. note and interest)		

A	=	L	+	SE
+10,300				+300
-10,000				

If Wolder Co. prepares financial statements as at September 30, it is necessary to accrue interest. In this case, the adjusting entry by Wolder is for four months, or $300, as shown below:

Sept. 30	Interest Receivable	300	
	Interest Revenue		300
	(To accrue four months' interest on Higley note)		

A	=	L	+	SE
+300				+300

When interest has been accrued, it is necessary to credit Interest Receivable at maturity. The entry by Wolder to record the honouring of the Higley note on October 1 is:

Oct. 1	Cash	10,300	
	Notes Receivable—Higley Inc.		10,000
	Interest Receivable		300
	(To record collection of Higley Inc. note and interest)		

A	=	L	+	SE
+10,300				
-10,000				
-300				

In this case, Interest Receivable is credited because the receivable was established in the adjusting entry.

Dishonour of Notes Receivable

A **dishonoured note** is a note that is not paid in full at maturity. A dishonoured note receivable is no longer negotiable; however, the payee still has a claim against the maker of the note. Therefore, the Notes Receivable account is usually transferred to an Account Receivable.

To illustrate, assume that Higley Inc. on October 1 indicates that it cannot pay at the present time. The entry to record the dishonour of the note depends on whether eventual collection is expected. If Wolder Co. expects eventual collection, the amount due (face value and interest) on the note is recorded as an increase (a debit) to Accounts Receivable. Wolder Co. would make the following entry at the time the note is dishonoured (assuming no previous accrual of interest):

A	= L +	SE
+10,300		+300
-10,000		

Oct. 1	Accounts Receivable—Higley Inc.	10,300	
	Notes Receivable—Higley Inc.		10,000
	Interest Revenue		300
	(To record the dishonour of Higley Inc. note)		

If there is no hope of collection, the face value of the note should be written off by decreasing (debiting) the Allowance for Doubtful Notes. No interest revenue would be recorded because collection will not occur.

BEFORE YOU GO ON . . .

Review It

1. What is the basic formula for calculating interest?
2. At what value are notes receivable reported on the balance sheet?
3. Explain the difference between honouring and dishonouring a note receivable.

Do It

Gambit Stores Ltd. accepts from Leonard Corp. a \$3,400, 90-day, 12% note dated May 10 in settlement of Leonard's overdue open account. What entry is made by Gambit at the maturity date, assuming Leonard pays the note and interest in full at that time?

Reasoning: When the maturity date is expressed in days, it is usual to calculate interest using the exact number of days. The entry to record interest at maturity in this solution assumes that no interest is previously accrued on the note.

Solution: The interest payable at the maturity date is \$101, calculated as follows:

$$\underline{\text{Face} \times \text{Rate} \times \text{Time} = \text{Interest}}$$

$$\$3,400 \times 12\% \times \frac{90}{365} = \$101 \text{ (rounded)}$$

The following entry is recorded by Gambit Stores at the maturity date:

Cash	3,501	
Notes Receivable—Leonard Corp.		3,400
Interest Revenue		101
(To record collection of Leonard note and interest)		

STATEMENT PRESENTATION OF RECEIVABLES

STUDY OBJECTIVE 6

Explain the statement presentation of receivables.

Each of the major types of receivables should be identified in the balance sheet or in the notes to the financial statements. Short-term receivables are reported in the current asset section of the balance sheet below temporary investments. Temporary investments appear before short-term receivables because these investments are nearer to cash. Although only the net amount of receivables less any allowance for doubtful accounts must be disclosed, it is helpful to report both the gross amount of receivables and the allowance for doubtful accounts either in the statement or notes supporting the statements. Illustration 8-11 shows the current asset presentation of receivables for Bell Canada International Inc. Note that notes receivable are often listed before accounts receivable because notes are more easily converted to cash.

Illustration 8-11
Balance sheet presentation of receivables

BELL CANADA INTERNATIONAL INC.
Balance Sheet
(partial; some information extracted from notes)
December 31, 1998
(in thousands)

Current assets		
Cash and cash equivalents		$ 98,232
Notes receivable		5,036
Accounts receivable	$275,354	
Less: Allowance for doubtful accounts	11,752	263,602
Receivables from related parties		14,758
Inventory		43,386
Prepaid expenses and other current assets		55,620
		480,634

BELL CANADA INTERNATIONAL

In the statement of earnings, bad debts expense is reported as selling expenses in the operating expenses section. Interest revenue is shown under other revenues and gains in the non-operating section of the statement of earnings.

If a company has significant risk of uncollectible accounts or other problems with its receivables, it is required to discuss this possibility in the notes to the financial statements.

BEFORE YOU GO ON . . .

Review It

1. Explain where receivables are reported on the balance sheet and in what order.
2. Where are bad debts expense and interest revenue reported on the statement of earnings?

MANAGING RECEIVABLES

STUDY OBJECTIVE 7

Describe the principles of sound accounts receivable management.

Managing accounts receivable involves five steps:

1. Determine whom to extend credit to
2. Establish a payment period
3. Monitor collections
4. Evaluate the receivables balance
5. Accelerate cash receipts from receivables when necessary

EXTENDING CREDIT

Determine whom to extend credit to

A critical part of managing receivables is determining who should be extended credit and who should not. Many companies increase sales by being generous with their credit policy, but they may end up extending credit to risky customers who do not pay. If the credit policy is too tight, you will lose sales; if it is too loose, you may sell to "deadbeats" who will pay either very late or not at all. One CEO noted that prior to getting his credit and collection department in order, his salespeople had 30 square metres of office space per person, while the people in credit and collections had six people crammed into a single 30-square-metre space. Although this arrangement boosted sales, it had very expensive consequences in bad debts expense.

Certain steps can be taken to help minimize losses as credit standards are relaxed. Risky customers might be required to provide letters of credit or bank guarantees. Then if the customer does not pay, the bank that provided the guarantee will. Particularly risky customers might be required to pay cash on delivery. In addition, you should ask potential customers for references from banks and suppliers to determine their payment history. It is important to check these references on potential new customers as well as periodically to check the financial health of continuing customers. Many resources are available for investigating customers. For example, companies such as Canadian Credit Reporting Limited provide credit opinions on companies around the world to aid in lending decisions.

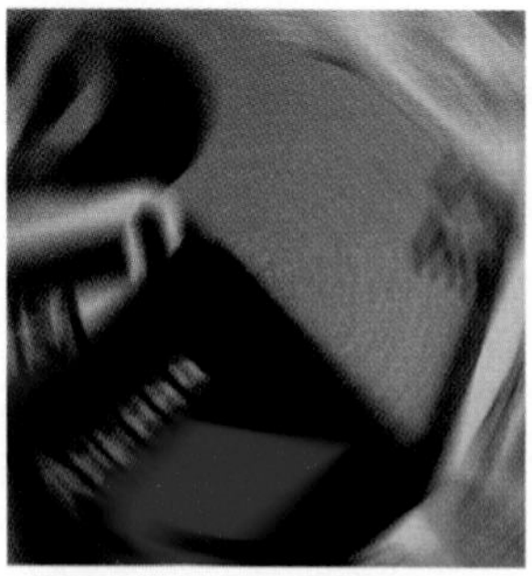

BUSINESS INSIGHT

Management Perspective

Give the man credit. Like most of us, John Galbreath receives piles of unsolicited, "pre-approved" credit card applications in the mail. Galbreath doesn't just toss them out, though. In April he filled out a credit card application on which he stated he was 97 years old and had no income and no telephone. In a space inviting him to let the credit card company pay off his other credit card balances, Galbreath said he owed money to the Mafia.

Back came a credit card and a letter welcoming John to the fold with a $1,500 credit limit. Galbreath had requested the card under a false name, John C. Reath, an alias under which he had received two other credit cards—earning exemplary credit. John C. Reath might be a bit "long in the tooth," but it seems he paid his bills on time.

Source: "Forbes Informer," edited by Kate Bohner Lewis, *Forbes*, August 14, 1995, 19.

ESTABLISHING A PAYMENT PERIOD

Companies that extend credit should determine a required payment period and communicate that policy to their customers. It is important to make sure that your company's payment period is consistent with that of your competitors. For example, if you decide to require payment within 15 days, but your competitors require payment within 45 days, you may lose sales to your competitors. However, as noted in Chapter 5, you might allow up to 45 days to pay but offer a sales discount for people paying within 15 days to match competitors' terms but encourage prompt payment of accounts.

Establish a payment period

MONITORING COLLECTIONS

One initial step that can be taken to monitor receivables is to calculate a company's **credit risk ratio**, which is determined by dividing the allowance for doubtful accounts by accounts receivable, as shown in Illustration 8-12:

Illustration 8-12 Credit risk ratio

$$\text{CREDIT RISK RATIO} = \frac{\text{ALLOWANCE FOR DOUBTFUL ACCOUNTS}}{\text{ACCOUNTS RECEIVABLE}}$$

Changes in this ratio over time may suggest that a company's overall credit risk is increasing or decreasing, and differences across companies may suggest differences in each company's overall credit risk. A high credit risk ratio indicates that a company is extending credit to questionable customers.

Monitor collections

To illustrate the use of the credit risk ratio, we will evaluate the receivables of McKesson HBOC, Inc. McKesson HBOC was formed when McKesson, North America's top distributor of pharmaceuticals and health care products, bought HBO & Company (HBOC), the world leader in health care information systems and technology. It has grown very rapidly in recent years, with total sales more than doubling during a four-year period. When evaluating a rapidly growing company, one concern would be whether the company has lowered its credit standards to increase sales. The following data are available for McKesson:

(in millions of U.S. dollars)	March 31, 1999	March 31, 1998
Accounts receivable, gross	\$2,765.2	\$2,043.7
Allowance for doubtful accounts	181.5	83.7
Accounts receivable, net	\$2,583.7	\$1,960.0

The credit risk ratio for McKesson and comparative industry data are shown in Illustration 8-13.

Illustration 8-13 Credit risk ratio comparison

(\$ in millions)	1999	1998
McKesson HBOC	$\frac{\$181.5}{\$2,765.2} = 6.6\%$	$\frac{\$83.7}{\$2,043.7} = 4.1\%$
Industry average	3.5%	3.8%

McKesson's credit risk ratio increased substantially from 4.1% in fiscal 1998 to 6.6% in fiscal 1999. We also note that in both years, its credit risk ratio is substantially higher than the industry average, especially in 1999. This would be of concern to analysts because it might suggest that McKesson's growth is being fueled by overly aggressive credit-granting practices. Since McKesson's growth was, in part, due to some major acquisitions and mergers, we might also question the quality of the receivables practices of the acquired companies.

DECISION TOOLKIT

Decision Checkpoints	Info Needed for Decision	Tool to Use for Decision	How to Evaluate Results
Is the company's credit risk increasing?	Allowance for doubtful accounts and accounts receivable	$\text{Credit risk ratio} = \frac{\text{Allowance for doubtful accounts}}{\text{Accounts receivable}}$	Increase in ratio may suggest increased credit risk, requiring evaluation of credit policies.

If a company has significant concentrations of credit risk, it is required to discuss this risk in the notes to its financial statements. A **concentration of credit risk** is a threat of non-payment from a single customer or class of customers that could adversely affect the financial health of the company. An excerpt from the credit risk note from the annual report of McKesson HBOC, Inc. is shown in Illustration 8-14.

Illustration 8-14 Note on concentration of credit risk

McKESSON HBOC, INC.
Notes to the Financial Statements

Concentrations of Credit Risk: Trade receivables subject the Company to a concentration of credit risk with customers in the retail and institutional sectors. This risk is spread over a large number of geographically dispersed customers.

This note to McKesson's financial statements suggests that, although the company extends significant amounts of credit, its exposure to any individual customer, or group of customers, is limited.

DECISION TOOLKIT

Decision Checkpoints	Info Needed for Decision	Tool to Use for Decision	How to Evaluate Results
Does the company have significant concentrations of credit risk?	Note to the financial statements on concentrations of credit risk	If risky credit customers are identified, the financial health of those customers should be evaluated to gain an independent assessment of the potential for a material credit loss.	If a material loss appears likely, the potential negative impact of that loss on the company should be carefully evaluated, along with the adequacy of the allowance for doubtful accounts.

STUDY OBJECTIVE 8
Identify ratios used to analyse a company's receivables.

EVALUATING THE RECEIVABLES BALANCE

Investors and managers keep a watchful eye on the relationship between sales, accounts receivable, and cash collections. If sales increase, then accounts receivable are also expected to increase. But a disproportionate increase in accounts receivable might signal trouble. Perhaps the company increased its sales by loosening its credit policy, and these receivables may be difficult or impossible to collect. Such receivables are considered less liquid. Recall that liquidity is measured by how quickly certain assets can be converted to cash. The ratio used to assess the liquidity of the receivables is the **receivables turnover ratio**. This ratio measures the number of times, on average, receivables are collected during the period. The receivables turnover ratio is calculated by dividing net credit sales (net sales less cash sales) by the average net receivables during the year. Unless seasonal factors are significant, **average** receivables outstanding can be calculated from the beginning and ending balances of the net receivables.[1]

Evaluate the receivables balance

A popular variant of the receivables turnover ratio its conversion to an **average collection period** in terms of days. This is done by dividing the receivables turnover ratio into 365 days. The average collection period is frequently used to assess the effectiveness of a company's credit and collection policies. The general rule is that the collection period should not greatly exceed the credit term period (i.e., the time allowed for payment).

The following data (in millions of U.S. dollars) are available for McKesson HBOC, Inc. and assume that all sales are credit sales.

	For the Year Ended March 31		
	1999	**1998**	**1997**
Sales	$30,382.3	$22,419.3	$16,914.3
Accounts receivable (net)	2,583.7	1,960.0	1,612.2

The receivables turnover ratio and average collection period for McKesson HBOC are shown in Illustration 8-15, along with comparative industry data.

Illustration 8-15 Receivables turnover ratio

$$\text{RECEIVABLES TURNOVER RATIO} = \frac{\text{NET CREDIT SALES}}{\text{AVERAGE NET RECEIVABLES}}$$

$$\text{AVERAGE COLLECTION PERIOD} = \frac{\text{365 DAYS}}{\text{RECEIVABLES TURNOVER RATIO}}$$

($ in millions)	Ratio	1999	1998
McKesson HBOC	Receivables turnover	$\frac{\$30,382.3}{(\$2,583.7 + \$1,960.0) / 2} = 13.4$ times	$\frac{\$22,419.3}{(\$1,960.0 + \$1,612.2) / 2} = 12.6$ times
	Average collection period	$\frac{365}{13.4} = 27$ days	$\frac{365}{12.6} = 29$ days
Industry average	Receivables turnover	10.5 times	10.1 times
	Average collection period	35 days	36 days

[1]If seasonal factors are significant, the average receivables balance might be determined by using monthly amounts.

McKesson's receivables turnover was 13.4 times in 1999, with a corresponding average collection period of 27 days. This was an improvement over its 1998 collection period of 29 days. It also compares very favourably with the industry average collection period of 35 days. What this means is that McKesson is able to turn its receivables into cash more quickly than most of its competitors. McKesson is also more liquid, meaning that it has a better likelihood of paying its current obligations than a company with a slower receivables turnover.

BUSINESS INSIGHT

Management Perspective

In some cases, receivables turnover may be misleading. Some companies, especially large retail chains, encourage credit and revolving charge sales, and they slow collections in order to earn a healthy return on the outstanding receivables in the form of interest at rates of up to 28.8%. This may explain why Sears Canada's turnover is only 8 times, for example. In general, however, the faster the turnover, the greater the reliance that can be placed on the current ratio for assessing liquidity.

DECISION TOOLKIT

Decision Checkpoints	Info Needed for Decision	Tool to Use for Decision	How to Evaluate Results
Are collections being made in a timely fashion?	Net credit sales and average receivables balance	$\text{Receivables turnover ratio} = \frac{\text{Net credit sales}}{\text{Average net receivables}}$ $\text{Average collection period} = \frac{\text{365 days}}{\text{Receivables turnover ratio}}$	Average collection period should be consistent with corporate credit policy. An increase may suggest a decline in financial health of customers.

ACCELERATING CASH RECEIPTS

STUDY OBJECTIVE 9

Describe methods used to accelerate the receipt of cash from receivables.

In the normal course of events, accounts receivable are collected in cash and removed from the books. However, as credit sales and receivables have grown in size and significance, the "normal course of events" has changed. Two common expressions apply to the collection of receivables: (1) Time is money—that is, waiting for the normal collection process costs money. (2) A bird in the hand is worth two in the bush—that is, getting the cash now is better than getting it later. Two typical ways to accelerate the receipt of cash from receivables include borrowing money on your receivables and selling your receivables.

Loans Secured by Receivables

One of the most common ways to speed up cash flow from accounts receivable is to go to a bank and borrow money using accounts receivable as collateral. While this does have a cost (interest has to be paid to the bank on your loan), you get the use of your cash sooner, and can repay the loan as you collect the receivables. Generally, banks are willing to provide financing for up to 75% of receivables that are less than 90 days old. Quite often, these arrangements occur through an **operating line of credit**, which is discussed in a later chapter.

Sale of Receivables

Accelerate cash receipts from receivables

Companies also frequently sell their receivables to another company for cash, thereby shortening the cash-to-cash operating cycle.

There are three reasons for the sale of receivables. The first is their size. In recent years, **for competitive reasons, sellers (retailers, wholesalers, and manufacturers) often have provided financing to purchasers of their goods**. For example, many major companies in the automobile, truck, industrial and farm equipment, computer, and appliance industries have created companies that accept responsibility for accounts receivable financing. Ford has Ford Credit Canada, Sears has Sears Acceptance Company Inc., and Bombardier has Bombardier Capital. These companies are referred to as **captive finance companies** because they are wholly owned by the company making the product. The purpose of captive finance companies is to encourage the sale of the product by assuring financing to buyers without the parent companies involved having to hold large amounts of receivables.

Second, **receivables may be sold because they may be the only reasonable source of cash**. When money is tight, companies may not be able to borrow money in the usual credit markets. If money is available, the cost of borrowing may be prohibitive.

A final reason for selling receivables is that **billing and collection are often time-consuming and costly**. As a result, it is often easier for a retailer to sell the receivable to another party that has expertise in billing and collection matters. Credit card companies such as MasterCard, VISA, American Express, and Diners Club specialize in billing and collecting accounts receivable.

Sale of Receivables to a Factor. A common way to accelerate receivables collection is by sale to a factor. A **factor** is a finance company or bank that buys receivables from businesses for a fee and then collects the payments directly from the customers. Factoring was traditionally associated with the textiles, apparel, footwear, furniture, and home furnishing industries but has now spread to other types of businesses and is a multibillion-dollar business. For example, Bell Canada and Nortel once sold their accounts receivable for $1.5 billion. McKesson sold accounts receivable of $299.9 million at March 31, 1999, and $147.7 million at the previous year end. McKesson's sale of receivables may explain why its receivables turnover ratio exceeds the industry average.

BUSINESS INSIGHT
Management Perspective

TCE Capital is one of a growing number of companies who help companies with their cash crunch by purchasing, at a discount, outstanding receivables. They don't call themselves factors; they prefer to be called invoice discounters and transaction financiers. "It seems that almost everyone takes at least 30 days to pay, and many companies are edging up through 60 days to 90 days," says Jim Shoniker, TCE's vice-president of business development. "By discounting invoices, businesses get the money today, when it's needed. That makes it possible for them to take on orders or projects they simply couldn't have done otherwise because of a lack of financing." In 1999, TCE provided Canadian businesses with short-term financing of $100 million, earning a base rate of $1 per $1,000 per day. That works out to 3% for 30 days, or about 36% per year.

Source: Terrence Belford, "Sell Your Invoices," *CAmagazine*, May 1999, 25.

Factoring arrangements vary widely, but typically the factor will advance up to 90% of the net realizable value of approved invoices, less the factor's fee. Fees are negotiable and can range from 16% to 36% of the amount of receivables purchased.

Credit Card Sales. Approximately 54 million credit cards were estimated to be in use in Canada recently—more than 2.3 credit cards for every adult over 18 years of age. Of these, about half are VISA or MasterCard; the other half are cards issued by large department stores, gasoline companies, and other issuers such as American Express and Diner's Club/enRoute. Three parties are involved when credit cards are used in making retail sales: (1) the credit card issuer, who is independent of the retailer, (2) the retailer, and (3) the customer. **A retailer's acceptance of a national credit card is another form of selling (factoring) the receivable by the retailer.**

The use of credit cards translates to more sales with zero bad debts for the retailer. Both are powerful reasons for a retailer to accept such cards. The major advantages of national credit cards to the retailer are shown in Illustration 8-16. In exchange for these advantages, the retailer pays the credit card issuer a fee of 2% to 6% of the invoice price for its services.

Illustration 8-16 Advantages of credit cards to the retailer

Issuer does credit investigation of customer
Issuer maintains customer accounts
E-Z Credit
shop-mart
Credit card issuer
Customer
Retailer
Issuer undertakes collection process and absorbs any losses
Retailer receives cash more quickly from credit card issuer

Sales resulting from the use of bank cards, such as VISA and MasterCard, are considered cash sales by the retailer. These cards are issued by banks. Upon receipt of credit card sales slips from a retailer, the bank immediately adds the amount to the seller's bank balance. These credit card sales slips are therefore recorded in the same manner as cheques deposited from a cash sale. To illustrate, Anita Ferreri purchases $1,000 of compact discs for her restaurant from Karen Kerr Music Co., and she charges this amount on her Royal Bank Financial Group VISA Card. The service fee that Royal Bank charges Karen Kerr Music is 3%. The entry by Karen Kerr Music to record this transaction is:

	Cash	970	
	Service Charge Expense	30	
	Sales		1,000
	(To record VISA credit card sales)		

A	=	L	+	SE
+970				-30
				+1,000

Non-bank cards, such as American Express, Diner's Club/enRoute, and Petro-Canada, are reported as credit sales, not cash sales. Conversion into cash does not occur until the financing company remits the net amount to the seller.

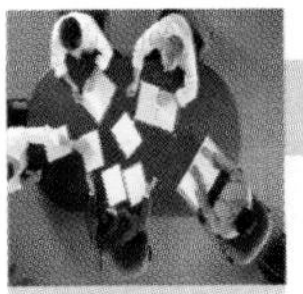

BUSINESS INSIGHT

Management Perspective

There are more than 600 different types of credit cards in Canada. Interest rates on most credit cards are quite high, ranging between 17.5% and 19.5% for bank cards, such as VISA and MasterCard. Even more significant is the spread between the Bank of Canada interest rate and the credit card interest rate—nearly 14% for most bank cards. As a result, consumers are looking for companies that charge lower interest rates. Low rate or discount credit cards, with interest rates between 9.5% and 14% and a spread ranging from 4% to 9%, are flourishing. But, be careful. The true cost of any credit card is really a function of four factors: (1) interest rate, (2) annual fee, (3) service charge, and (4) grace period. Industry Canada's Consumer Connection offers a useful credit card cost calculator on its website to assist consumers who want to identify the lowest cost credit card.

The basic principles of managing accounts receivable are summarized in Illustration 8-17.

Illustration 8-17 Managing receivables

BEFORE YOU GO ON . . .

Review It

1. What is meant by a concentration of credit risk?
2. What is the interpretation of the receivables turnover ratio and the average collection period?
3. Why do companies accelerate cash receipts from receivables?
4. For whom is the service charge on a credit card sale an expense?

Do It

Dell Wholesalers Corp. has been expanding faster than it can raise capital. According to its local banker, the company has reached its debt ceiling. Dell's customers are slow in paying (60–90 days), but its suppliers (creditors) are demanding 30-day payment. Dell has a cash flow problem.

Dell needs to raise $120,000 in cash to safely cover next Friday's employee payroll. Dell's present balance of outstanding receivables totals $750,000. What might Dell do to alleviate this cash crunch?

Reasoning: One source of immediate cash at a competitive cost is the sale of receivables to a factor. Rather than waiting until it can collect receivables, Dell may raise immediate cash by selling its receivables. The last thing Dell (or any employer) wants to do is miss a payroll.

Solution: If Dell wishes to raise $120,000 it would have to sell (discount) nearly $139,000 of its receivables to a factor. This assumes the company would receive 90% of the net realizable value factored ($139,000 × 90% = $125,100). The amount of receivables sold must also include the factor's fee, which is usually taken off the net proceeds immediately. Assuming the fee was 20% and that the period the receivables were outstanding before being collected was 60 days, $4,438 ($135,000 × 20% × 60/365 = $4,438) would also be deducted from the proceeds of $125,100 to net Dell $120,662 ($125,100 – $4,438).

USING THE DECISION TOOLKIT

BioChem Pharma Inc., an international biopharmaceutical company, is dedicated to the research, development and commercialization of innovative products, mainly for the prevention and treatment of human diseases, and with a focus on cancer and infectious diseases. The company has developed 3TC, the world's bestselling HIV treatment. BioChem Pharma, although much larger than McKesson HBOC, has also enjoyed exceptional growth. The following information was taken from the December 31, 1998, financial statements of BioChem Pharma.

BIOCHEM PHARMA INC.
Selected Financial Information
(in thousands)

	1998	1997
Total revenue	$347,368	$280,782
Net earnings	114,774	79,838
Trade accounts receivable (gross)	76,434	59,186
Allowance for doubtful trade accounts	3,219	2,635
Trade accounts receivable (net)	73,215	56,551
Current assets	363,952	447,187
Current liabilities	92,869	81,904

Credit risk: There is a geographic concentration of credit risk with regard to operations conducted in Italy.

Instructions

Comment on BioChem Pharma's accounts receivable management and liquidity relative to that of McKesson for the current year, with consideration given to (1) the credit risk ratio, (2) the current ratio, and (3) the receivables turnover ratio and the average collection period. McKesson's current ratio (current assets ÷ current liabilities) was 1.35:1; the industry average, 1.49:1. The other ratios were calculated earlier in the chapter.

Solution

1. Credit Risk Ratio

BioChem Pharma	McKesson	Industry
$\frac{\$3,219}{\$76,434} = 4.2\%$	6.6%	3.5%

This suggests that BioChem Pharma's credit risk is lower than McKesson's and higher than the industry.

2. Current Ratio

BioChem Pharma	McKesson	Industry
$\frac{\$363,952}{\$92,869} = 3.9:1$	1.35:1	1.49:1

This also suggests that BioChem Pharma is substantially more liquid than both McKesson and the industry. However, a high current ratio does not always mean that a company has excellent liquidity. The current ratio could be artificially high because of slow-moving receivables or inventory. So, further investigation is warranted before concluding on BioChem Pharma's liquidity.

3. Receivables Turnover Ratio and Average Collection Period

	BioChem Pharma	McKesson	Industry
Receivables Turnover	$\frac{\$347,368}{(\$73,215 + \$56,551)/2} = 5.4$ times	13.4 times	10.5 times

Average Collection Period	$\frac{365 \text{ days}}{5.4}$	= 68 days	27 days	35 days

BioChem Pharma's receivables turnover ratio and average collection period suggests that BioChem Pharma is collecting its receivables from its customers significantly more slowly than McKesson, which outperforms the industry. BioChem Pharma did note that it had increased credit risk from receivables in Italy. This may be part of the issue. However, trade accounts receivable increased at a faster rate than did BioChem Pharma's sales. It must monitor its collection policy very carefully as it appears BioChem Pharma's collections are lagging behind where they should be, depending upon their due dates. The low receivables turnover ratio is one of the factors driving BioChem Pharma's high current ratio, which is much higher than both McKesson's and the industry's. This means that BioChem Pharma's current ratio is not really as liquid as it appears. However, the low receivables turnover ratio is not likely the only reason for a high current ratio; we would have to investigate BioChem Pharma's inventory turnover ratio, in addition to other factors, before determining whether or not its liquidity is as strong as it appears from its current ratio.

Summary of Study Objectives

1 ***Identify the different types of receivables.*** Receivables are frequently classified as accounts, notes, and other. Accounts receivable are amounts owed by customers on account. Notes receivable represent claims that are evidenced by formal instruments of credit. Other receivables include nontrade receivables such as interest receivable, loans to company officers, advances to employees, and recoverable sales and income taxes.

2 ***Explain how accounts receivable are recognized in the accounts.*** Accounts receivable are recorded at invoice price. They are reduced by sales returns and allowances. Cash discounts reduce the amount received on accounts receivable.

3 ***Describe the method used to account for bad debts.*** The percentage of receivables basis is used to match anticipated credit losses against sales, in the period in which the sales occurred, and to estimate uncollectible accounts in the allowance method. It emphasizes the net realizable value of the accounts receivable. An aging schedule is frequently used with this basis.

4 ***Explain how notes receivable are recognized and valued in the accounts.*** Notes receivable are recorded at their face value. Interest is earned from the date the note is issued until it matures. Like accounts receivable, notes receivable are reported at their net realizable value. The notes receivable allowance account is Allowance for Doubtful Notes. The calculation and estimations involved in recording the proper amount of bad debt expense and related allowance are similar to those required for accounts receivable.

5 ***Describe the entries to record the disposition of notes receivable.*** Notes can be held to maturity, at which time the face value plus accrued interest is due and the note is removed from the accounts. In many cases, however, similar to accounts receivable, the holder of the note speeds up the conversion by selling the receivable to another party. In some situations, the maker of the note dishonours the note (defaults), and the note is written off.

6 ***Explain the statement presentation of receivables.*** Each major type of receivable should be identified in the balance sheet or in the notes to the financial statements. Short-term receivables are considered current assets. The gross amount of receivables and allowance for doubtful accounts should be reported. Bad debts and service charge expenses are reported in the statement of earnings as operating (selling) expenses, and interest revenue is shown as other revenues and gains in the non-operating section of the statement. Accounts receivable may be evaluated for liquidity by calculating the receivables turnover ratio and the average collection period.

7 ***Describe the principles of sound accounts receivable management.*** To properly manage receivables, management must (a) determine to whom to extend credit, (b) establish a payment period, (c) monitor collections, (d) evaluate the receivables balance, and (e) accelerate cash receipts from receivables when necessary.

❽ ***Identify ratios used to analyse a company's receivables.*** The receivables turnover ratio and the average collection period are both useful for analysing management's effectiveness in managing receivables. The accounts receivable aging schedule also provides useful information.

❾ ***Describe methods used to accelerate the receipt of cash from receivables.*** If the company needs additional cash resources, management can accelerate the collection of cash from receivables by borrowing money from a bank, and using the receivables as collateral for the loan, or by selling (factoring or discounting) its receivables.

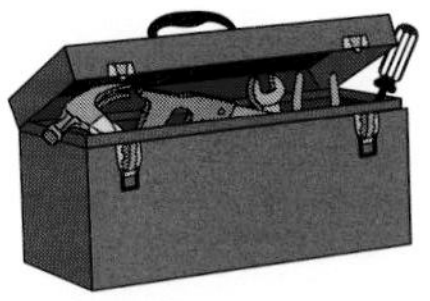

Decision Toolkit—A Summary

Decision Checkpoints	Info Needed for Decision	Tool to Use for Decision	How to Evaluate Results
Is the amount of past due accounts increasing? Which accounts require management's attention?	List of outstanding receivables and their due dates	Prepare an aging schedule showing the receivables in various stages: outstanding 0–30 days, 31–60 days, 61–90 days, 91–120 days, and over 120 days.	Accounts in the older categories require follow-up: letters, phone calls, e-mails, and possible renegotiation of terms.
Is the company's credit risk increasing?	Allowance for doubtful accounts and accounts receivable	$\text{Credit risk ratio} = \dfrac{\text{Allowance for doubtful accounts}}{\text{Accounts receivable}}$	Increase in ratio may suggest increased credit risk, requiring evaluation of credit policies.
Does the company have significant concentrations of credit risk?	Note to the financial statements on concentrations of credit risk	If risky credit customers are identified, the financial health of those customers should be evaluated to gain an independent assessment of the potential for a material credit loss.	If a material loss appears likely, the potential negative impact of that loss on the company should be carefully evaluated, along with the adequacy of the allowance for doubtful accounts.
Are collections being made in a timely fashion?	Net credit sales and average receivables balance	$\text{Receivables turnover ratio} = \dfrac{\text{Net credit sales}}{\text{Average net receivables}}$ $\text{Average collection period} = \dfrac{\text{365 days}}{\text{Receivables turnover ratio}}$	Average collection period should be consistent with corporate credit policy. An increase may suggest a decline in financial health of customers.

Glossary

Accounts receivable Amounts owed by customers on account. (p. 413)

Aging the accounts receivable The analysis of customer balances by the length of time they have been unpaid. (p. 418)

Allowance method A method of accounting for bad debts that involves estimating uncollectible accounts at the end of each period. (p. 415)

Average collection period The average amount of time that a receivable is outstanding, calculated by dividing 365 days by the receivables turnover ratio. (p. 429)

Concentration of credit risk The threat of non-payment from a single customer or class of customers that could adversely affect the financial health of the company. (p. 428)

Credit risk ratio A measure of the risk that a company's customers may not pay their accounts, calculated as the allowance for doubtful accounts divided by accounts receivable. (p. 427)

Dishonoured note A note that is not paid in full at maturity. (p. 424)

Factor A finance company or bank that buys receivables from businesses for a fee and then collects the payments directly from the customers. (p. 431)

Maker The party in a promissory note who is making the promise to pay. (p. 421)

Net realizable value The net amount expected to be received in cash. (p. 415)

Notes receivable Claims for which formal instruments of credit are issued as evidence of the debt. (p. 413)

Payee The party to whom payment of a promissory note is to be made. (p. 421)

Percentage of receivables basis A percentage relationship established by management between the amount of receivables and the expected losses from uncollectible accounts. (p. 418)

Promissory note A written promise to pay a specified amount of money on demand or at a definite time. (p. 420)

Receivables Amounts due from individuals and companies that are expected to be collected in cash. (p. 412)

Receivables turnover ratio A measure of the liquidity of receivables, calculated by dividing net credit sales by average net receivables. (p. 429)

Trade receivables Notes and accounts receivable that result from sales transactions. (p. 413)

Demonstration Problem

Presented here are selected transactions related to O'Reilly Corp:

Mar.	1	Sold $20,000 of merchandise to Potter Company, terms 2/10, n/30.
	11	Received payment in full from Potter Company for balance due.
	12	Accepted Juno Company's $20,000, six-month, 12% note for balance due.
	13	Made O'Reilly Corp. credit card sales for $13,200.
	15	Made VISA credit sales totalling $6,700. A 5% service fee is charged by VISA.
Apr.	13	Received collections of $8,200 on O'Reilly Corp. credit card sales and added interest charges of 1.5% to the remaining balances.
May	10	Wrote off as uncollectible $16,000 of accounts receivable. O'Reilly Corp. uses the percentage of receivables basis to estimate bad debts.
June	30	The balance in accounts receivable at the end of the first six months is $200,000. Using an aging schedule, estimated uncollectible accounts are determined to be $20,000. At June 30, the credit balance in the allowance account prior to adjustment is $3,500.
July	16	One of the accounts receivable written off in May pays the amount due, $4,000, in full.

Instructions

Prepare the journal entries for the transactions.

Problem-Solving Strategies

1. Accounts receivable are generally recorded at invoice price.
2. Sales returns and allowances and cash discounts reduce the amount received on accounts receivable.
3. Bad debts expense is an adjusting entry.
4. The percentage of receivables basis considers any existing balance in the allowance account.
5. Write-offs of accounts receivable affect only balance sheet accounts.

Solution to Demonstration Problem

Mar.	1	Accounts Receivable—Potter Company	20,000	
		Sales		20,000
		(To record sales on account)		
	11	Cash	19,600	
		Sales Discounts (2% × $20,000)	400	
		Accounts Receivable—Potter Company		20,000
		(To record collection of accounts receivable)		
	12	Notes Receivable—Juno Company	20,000	
		Accounts Receivable—Juno Company		20,000
		(To record acceptance of Juno Company note)		

	13	Accounts Receivable
		  Sales
		    (To record company credit card sales)
			13,200	
				13,200

	15	Cash
		Service Charge Expense (5% × $6,700)
		  Sales
		    (To record credit card sales)
			6,365
			335
				
				6,700

Apr.	13	Cash
		  Accounts Receivable
		    (To record collection of accounts receivable)
		Accounts Receivable
		[($13,200 − $8,200) × 1.5%]
		  Interest Revenue
		    (To record interest charges on overdue receivables)
			8,200
			
			75
				
				8,200
				
				75

May	10	Allowance for Doubtful Accounts
		  Accounts Receivable
		    (To record write-off of accounts receivable)
			16,000	
				16,000

June	30	Bad Debts Expense
		($20,000 − $3,500)
		  Allowance for Doubtful Accounts
		    (To record estimate of uncollectible accounts)
			
			16,500
				
				16,500

July	16	Accounts Receivable
		  Allowance for Doubtful Accounts
		    (To reverse write-off of accounts receivable)
		Cash
		  Accounts Receivable
		    (To record collection of accounts receivable)
			4,000
			
			4,000
				
				4,000
				
				4,000

SELF-STUDY QUESTIONS

Answers are at the end of the chapter.

(SO 2) 1. On June 15, Jones Company Ltd. sells merchandise on account to Bullock Co. for $1,000, terms 2/10, n/30. On June 20, Bullock Co. returns merchandise worth $300 to Jones Company. On June 24, payment is received from Bullock Co. for the balance due. What is the amount of cash received?
(a) $700 (c) $686
(b) $680 (d) None of the above

(SO 3) 2. Net credit sales for the month are $800,000. The accounts receivable balance is $160,000. The allowance is calculated as 7.5% of the total receivables balance using the percentage of receivables basis. If the Allowance for Doubtful Accounts has a credit balance of $5,000 before adjustment, what is the balance after adjustment?
(a) $12,000 (c) $17,000
(b) $7,000 (d) $31,000

3. In 2001 D.H. Lawrence Company Inc. had net credit sales of $750,000. On January 1, 2001, Allowance for Doubtful Accounts had a credit balance of $18,000. During 2001, $30,000 of uncollectible accounts receivable were written off. Aging indicates that the allowance should be $20,000 (percentage of receivables basis). What is the required adjustment to the Allowance for Doubtful Accounts at December 31, 2001? (SO 3)

(a) $20,000 (c) $32,000
(b) $75,000 (d) $30,000

(SO 3) 4. An analysis and aging of the accounts receivable of Machiavelli Corporation at December 31 reveal these data:

Accounts Receivable	$800,000
Allowance for Doubtful Accounts per books before adjustment (credit)	50,000
Amounts expected to become uncollectible	65,000

What is the net realizable value of the accounts receivable at December 31, after adjustment?
(a) $685,000 (c) $800,000
(b) $750,000 (d) $735,000

(SO 4) 5. Which of these statements about promissory notes is *incorrect?*
(a) The party making the promise to pay is called the maker.
(b) The party to whom payment is to be made is called the payee.
(c) A promissory note is not a negotiable instrument.
(d) A promissory note is sometimes more liquid than an account receivable.

(SO 4) 6. Sorenson Corp. accepts a $1,000, three-month, 12% promissory note in settlement of an account with Parton Co. The entry to record this transaction is:

(a) Notes Receivable	1,030	
Accounts Receivable		1,030
(b) Notes Receivable	1,000	
Accounts Receivable		1,000
(c) Notes Receivable	1,000	
Sales		1,000
(d) Notes Receivable	1,020	
Accounts Receivable		1,020

(SO 5) 7. Schlicht Corp. holds Osgrove Inc.'s $10,000, 120-day, 9% note. The entry made by Schlicht Corp. when the note is collected, assuming no interest has been accrued, and 365 days are used, is (rounded to the nearest dollar):

(a) Cash	10,296	
Notes Receivable		10,296
(b) Cash	10,000	
Notes Receivable		10,000
(c) Accounts Receivable	10,296	
Notes Receivable		10,000
Interest Revenue		296
(d) Cash	10,296	
Notes Receivable		10,000
Interest Revenue		296

8. Moore Corporation had net credit sales during the year of $800,000 and cost of goods sold of $500,000. The balance in receivables at the beginning of the year was $100,000 and at the end of the year was $150,000. What was the receivables turnover ratio? (SO 8)
(a) 6.4 (b) 8.0 (c) 5.3 (d) 4.0

9. Hoffman Corporation sells its goods on terms of 2/10, n/30. It has a receivables turnover ratio of 7. What is its average collection period (days)? (SO 8)
(a) 2,555 (b) 30 (c) 52 (d) 210

10. Which of these statements about VISA credit card sales is *incorrect?* (SO 9)
(a) The credit card issuer conducts the credit investigation of the customer.
(b) The retailer is not involved in the collection process.
(c) The retailer must wait to receive payment from the issuer.
(d) The retailer receives cash more quickly than it would from individual customers.

11. Morgan Retailers accepted $50,000 of Bank One VISA credit card charges for merchandise sold on July 1. Bank One charges 4% for its credit card use. The entry to record this transaction by Morgan Retailers will include a credit to Sales of $50,000 and a debit(s) to: (SO 9)
(a) Cash $48,000 and Service Charge Expense $2,000.
(b) Accounts Receivable $48,000 and Service Charge Expense $2,000.
(c) Cash $50,000.
(d) Accounts Receivable $50,000.

QUESTIONS

(SO 1) 1. What is the difference between an account receivable and a note receivable?

(SO 1) 2. What are some common types of receivables other than accounts receivable or notes receivable?

(SO 2) 3. On December 29, you sell $10,000 of merchandise to a company, terms of sale 1/10, n/30. The company, a frequent customer, always takes the discount. However, you won't know for sure in this instance until January 8. Should you record the receivable and sale at $10,000, or at $9,900 ($10,000 – $100 discount), on December 29?

4. What are the essential features of the allowance method of accounting for bad debts? (SO 3)

5. Soo Eng cannot understand why the net realizable value does not decrease when an uncollectible account is written off under the allowance method. Clarify this point for Soo Eng. (SO 3)

(SO 3) 6. Kersee Company Ltd. has a credit balance of \$3,200 in Allowance for Doubtful Accounts. The total estimated uncollectibles under the percentage of receivables basis is \$5,800. Prepare the adjusting entry.

(SO 3) 7. Should a company's attempts to collect a specific account receivable stop when it writes off the account as uncollectible? Explain why or why not.

(SO 4) 8. Your roommate is uncertain about the advantages of a promissory note. Compare the advantages of a note receivable to those of an account receivable.

(SO 4) 9. Danielle doesn't understand why a note receivable isn't originally recorded at its maturity value (face plus interest), rather than its face value. After all, you know you are going to collect both the face value and the interest when the note matures and you know how much each will be. Explain to Danielle why notes are not recorded at their maturity value.

(SO 4) 10. If a \$30,000 note is issued on May 1 with a 5% interest rate, maturing 10 months later, how much interest will the note earn in total? If financial statements are prepared at the company's year end, December 31, how much interest will be recorded for the year ended December 31?

(SO 4) 11. Explain how using the allowance method to estimate uncollectible notes receivable satisfies the matching principle.

(SO 5) 12. May Company Ltd. dishonours a note at maturity. Assuming eventual payment is intended, what entries should the payee and the maker (May Company) of the note make on their respective books?

13. Saucier Company Ltd. has accounts receivable, notes receivable, allowance for doubful accounts, and allowance for doubtful notes. How should the receivables be reported on the balance sheet? (SO 6)

14. What are the steps to good receivables management? (SO 7)

15. How might a company monitor the risk related to its accounts receivable? (SO 7)

16. What is meant by a concentration of credit risk? (SO 7)

17. The President of Ho Inc. proudly announces her company's improved liquidity since its current ratio has increased substantially from one year to the next. Does an increase in the current ratio always indicate improved liquidity? What other ratio or ratios might you review to determine whether or not the increase in the current ratio is an improvement in financial health? (SO 8)

18. If **Coca-Cola Company**'s receivables turnover ratio was 11.4 in 1998 and average net receivables during the period was \$1.652 million, what is the amount of net credit sales for the period? (SO 8)

19. Sears accepts both its own credit cards and bank credit cards. What are the advantages of accepting both types of cards? (SO 9)

20. An article recently indicated that companies are selling their receivables at a record rate. Why are companies selling their receivables? (SO 9)

BRIEF EXERCISES

Identify different types of receivables. (SO 1)

BE8-1 Presented below are three receivables transactions. Indicate whether these receivables are reported as accounts receivable, notes receivable, or other receivables on a balance sheet.
(a) Advanced \$10,000 to an employee.
(b) Received a promissory note of \$57,000 for services performed.
(c) Sold merchandise on account to a customer for \$60,000.

Record basic accounts receivable transactions. (SO 2)

BE8-2 Record the following transactions on the books of Essex Corp., which uses a perpetual inventory system:
(a) On July 1, Essex Corp. sold merchandise on account to Cambridge Inc. for \$14,000, terms 2/10, n/30. The cost of the merchandise sold was \$10,000.
(b) On July 8, Cambridge Inc. returned merchandise worth \$3,800 to Essex Corp. Its original cost was \$2,700. The merchandise was restored to inventory.
(c) On July 11, Cambridge Inc. paid for the merchandise.

Prepare entry for write-off, and determine net realizable value. (SO 3)

BE8-3 At the end of 2001, Searcy Corp. has accounts receivable of \$700,000 and an allowance for doubtful accounts of \$54,000. On January 24, 2002, it is learned that the company's receivable from Hutley Inc. is not collectible and management therefore authorizes a write-off of \$8,000.
(a) Prepare the journal entry to record the write-off.

(b) What is the net realizable value of the accounts receivable (1) before the write-off and (2) after the write-off?

Prepare entries for collection of bad debt writtten off.
(SO 3)

BE8-4 Assume the same information as BE8-3 and that on March 4, 2002, Searcy Corp. receives payment of $8,000 in full from Hutley Inc., subsequent to the write-off. Prepare the journal entries to record this transaction.

Prepare entry using percentage of receivables method.
(SO 3)

BE8-5 Massey Corp. uses the percentage of receivables basis to record bad debts expense and concludes that 1% of total accounts receivable will become uncollectible. Accounts receivable are $500,000 at the end of the year, and the allowance for doubtful accounts has a credit balance of $3,000.
(a) Prepare the adjusting journal entry to record bad debts expense for the year.
(b) If the allowance for doubtful accounts had a debit balance of $800 instead of a credit balance of $3,000, determine the amount to be reported for bad debts expense.

Calculate interest on note.
(SO 4)

BE8-6 Presented below are three promissory notes. Determine the missing amounts.

Date of Note	Terms	Principal	Annual Interest Rate	Total Interest
April 1	60 days	$900,000	10%	(b)
July 2	30 days	79,000	(a)	$390 (rounded)
March 7	6 months	56,000	12%	(c)

Prepare entry for note receivable exchanged for accounts receivable.
(SO 4)

BE8-7 On January 10, 2000, Raja Corp. sold merchandise on account to R. Opal for $12,000, terms n/30, costing $8,000. On February 9, R. Opal gave Raja Corp. a 10% promissory note in settlement of this account. Prepare the journal entry to record the sale and the settlement of the accounts receivable on Raja's books. Raja utilizes a perpetual inventory system.

Prepare entry for estimated uncollectibles and classifications, and calculate ratios.
(SO 3, 6, 7, 8)

BE8-8 During its first year of operations, Wendy Company Ltd. had credit sales of $3,000,000, of which $600,000 remained uncollected at year end. The credit manager estimates that $40,000 of these receivables will become uncollectible.
(a) Prepare the journal entry to record the estimated uncollectibles.
(b) Prepare the current asset section of the balance sheet for Wendy Company Ltd., assuming that in addition to the receivables it has cash of $90,000, merchandise inventory of $130,000, and prepaid expenses of $13,000.
(c) Calculate the credit risk ratio, receivables turnover ratio, and average collection period. Assume net receivables one year before were $500,000.

Analyse accounts receivable.
(SO 8)

BE8-9 The financial statements of **Maple Leaf Foods Inc.** report net sales of $3,281,464 for the year ended December 31, 1998. Net accounts receivable are $268,820 at the beginning of the year, and $181,626 at the end of the year. Compute Maple Leaf's receivables turnover ratio and average collection period.

Prepare entry for credit card sale.
(SO 9)

BE8-10 St. Pierre Restaurant accepted a VISA card in payment of a $100 lunch bill. The bank charges a 3% fee. What entry should St. Pierre make to record the sale? How would this entry differ if a non-bank card had been used in payment of the bill?

EXERCISES

Prepare entries for recognizing accounts receivable.
(SO 2)

E8-1 On January 6, Nicklaus Corp. sells merchandise on account to Watson Inc. for $4,000, terms 2/10, n/30. The merchandise originally cost Nicklaus $2,500. On January 16, Watson pays the amount due.

Instructions
Prepare the entries on Nicklaus Corp.'s books to record the sale and related collection. Nicklaus uses a perpetual inventory system.

Prepare entries for recognizing accounts receivable.
(SO 2)

E8-2 On January 10, Margaret Giger uses her Salizar Corp. credit card to purchase merchandise from Salizar Corp. for $11,000 that cost Salizar $9,000. On February 10, Giger is billed for the amount due of $11,000. On February 12, Giger pays $5,000 on the balance due. On March 10, Giger is billed for the amount due, including interest at 2% per month on the unpaid balance as of February 12.

Instructions
Prepare the entries on Salizar Corp.'s books related to the transactions that occurred on January 10, February 12, and March 10.

Prepare entries to record allowance for doubtful accounts.
(SO 3)

E8-3 The ledger of the Patillo Company Inc. at the end of the current year shows Accounts Receivable $80,000; Sales $940,000; and Sales Returns and Allowances $40,000.

Instructions
(a) If Allowance for Doubtful Accounts has a credit balance of $800 in the trial balance, journalize the adjusting entry at December 31, assuming bad debts are expected to be 10% of accounts receivable.
(b) If Allowance for Doubtful Accounts has a debit balance of $500 in the trial balance, journalize the adjusting entry at December 31, assuming bad debts are expected to be 8% of accounts receivable.

Determine bad debt expense, and prepare the adjusting entry.
(SO 3)

E8-4 Grevina Company Ltd. has accounts receivable of $92,500 at March 31, 2001. An analysis of the accounts shows these amounts:

	Balance, March 31	
Month of Sale	**2001**	**2000**
March	$65,000	$75,000
February	12,600	8,000
December and January	8,500	2,400
November and October	6,400	1,100
	$92,500	$86,500

Credit terms are 2/10, n/30. At March 31, 2001, there is a $1,600 credit balance in Allowance for Doubtful Accounts prior to adjustment. The company uses the percentage of receivables basis and an aging schedule for estimating uncollectible accounts. The company's estimates of bad debts are as follows:

Age of Accounts	Estimated Percentage Uncollectible
0–30	2.0%
31–60 days	10.0
61–90 days	30.0
Over 90 days	50.0

Instructions
(a) Determine the total estimated uncollectibles.
(b) Prepare the adjusting entry at March 31, 2001, to record bad debts expense.
(c) Discuss the implications of the changes in the aging schedule from 2000 to 2001.

Prepare entry for estimated uncollectibles, write-off, and recovery.
(SO 3)

E8-5 On December 31, 2001, when its Allowance for Doubtful Accounts had a debit balance of $1,000, Ceja Corp. estimates that 12% of its accounts receivable balance of $60,000 will become uncollectible and records the necessary adjustment to the Allowance for Doubtful Accounts. On May 11, 2002, Ceja Corp. determined that Robert Worthy's account was uncollectible and wrote off $900. On June 12, 2002, Worthy paid the amount previously written off.

Instructions
Prepare the journal entries on December 31, 2001, May 11, 2002, and June 12, 2002.

Prepare entries for notes receivable transactions.
(SO 4)

E8-6 Passara Supply Corp. has the following transactions related to notes receivable during the last two months of the year:

Nov.	1	Loaned $24,000 cash to A. Bouchard on a one-year, 10% note.
Dec.	11	Sold goods to Wright, Inc., receiving a $3,600, three-month, 12% note. These goods cost $2,500. Passara uses a perpetual inventory system to record sales of merchandise.
	16	Received a $4,000, six-month, 12% note on account from B. Barnes.
	31	Accrued interest revenue on all notes receivable.

Instructions
Journalize the transactions for Passara Supply Corp.

Journalize notes receivable transactions.
(SO 4, 5)

E8-7 These transactions took place for Rather Corp.:

2000

May 1	Received a $6,000, one-year, 10% note on account from T. Jones.
Dec. 31	Accrued interest revenue on the T. Jones note.

2001

May 1	Received principal plus interest on the T. Jones note.

Instructions
Record the transactions in the general journal.

Prepare entries for dishonour of notes receivable.
(SO 5)

E8-8 On May 2, Brey Company Ltd. lends $4,000 to Feingold Inc., issuing a six-month, 10% note. At the maturity date, November 2, Feingold indicates that it cannot pay.

Instructions
(a) Prepare the entry to record the dishonour of the note on Brey's books, assuming that Brey Company Ltd. expects collection will occur.
(b) Prepare the entry to record the dishonour of the note on Brey's books, assuming that Brey Company does not expect collection in the future.

Prepare a balance sheet presentation of receivables.
(SO 6)

E8-9 **Deere and Company** is the world's largest maker of farm and grounds care equipment. In addition, its Langley, B.C., plant manufactures forestry equipment. Deere had the following balances in receivable accounts at October 31, 1998 (in millions): Allowance for Doubtful Accounts, $31; Accounts Receivable, $2,907; Other Receivables, $228; and Notes Receivable, $955.

Instructions
Prepare the balance sheet presentation of Deere and Company's receivables in good form as at October 31, 1998.

Identify the principles of receivables management.
(SO 7)

E8-10 The following is a list of activities that companies perform in relation to their receivables:
(1) Selling (factoring or discounting) receivables
(2) Reviewing company credit ratings provided by Canadian Credit Reporting Limited
(3) Collecting information about competitors' payment period policies
(4) Preparing the accounts receivable aging schedule and calculating the credit risk ratio
(5) Calculating the receivables turnover ratio and average collection period

Instructions
Match each of the activities listed above with a purpose of the activity listed below:
(a) Determine whom to extend credit to
(b) Establish a payment period
(c) Monitor collections
(d) Evaluate the receivables balance
(e) Accelerate cash receipts from receivables when necessary

Calculate ratios to evaluate a company's receivables balance.
(SO 7, 8)

E8-11 The following information was taken from the 1998 and 1997 financial statements of the **Canadian National Railway Company**:

(in millions)	**1998**	**1997**	**1996**
Accounts receivable, gross	$ 440	$ 711	$ 724
Allowance for doubtful accounts	41	44	30
Accounts receivable, net	399	667	694
Revenues	4,121	4,322	3,995
Total current assets	1,038	1,533	1,243

Instructions
(a) Calculate the receivables turnover ratio and average collection period for each of 1998 and 1997.

(b) Calculate the 1998 and 1997 credit risk ratios.
(c) Are accounts receivable a material component of the company's current assets?
(d) Comment upon any improvement or deterioration in CN's management of its receivables.

Identify reason for sale of receivables.
(SO 9)

E8-12 The 1998 annual report of CN, the **Canadian National Railway Company**, notes that it entered into a revolving agreement to sell eligible freight trade receivables on June 25, 1998. It received $219 million cash from the sale of these receivables in 1998.

Instructions
Explain why CN, a financially stable company with positive cash flow, chose to sell its receivables.

Prepare entry for credit card sale.
(SO 9)

E8-13 On May 10, Monee Company Ltd. sold merchandise for $3,000, costing the company $2,000, and accepted the customer's Bank of Montreal MasterCard. At the end of the day, the MasterCard receipts were deposited in the company's bank account. Bank of Montreal charges a 4% service charge for credit card sales and uses a perpetual inventory system.

Instructions
(a) Prepare the entry on Monee Company Ltd.'s books to record the sale of merchandise.
(b) Prepare the entry on Monee Company Ltd.'s books to record the sale of merchandise assuming a non-bank credit card was used.

Prepare entry for credit card sale.
(SO 9)

E8-14 On July 4 Robyn's Restaurant accepts a VISA card for a $300 dinner bill. VISA charges a 3% service fee.

Instructions
Prepare the entries on Robyn's books related to the transaction.

PROBLEMS: SET A

Journalize transactions related to bad debts.
(SO 2, 3)

P8-1A The following represents selected information taken from a company's aging schedule to estimate uncollectible accounts receivable at year end:

		Number of Days Outstanding				
	Total	0-30	31-60	61-90	91-120	Over 120
Accounts receivable	$260,000	$100,000	$60,000	$50,000	$30,000	$20,000
% uncollectible		1%	5%	7.5%	10%	12%
Estimated bad debts						

Instructions
(a) Calculate the total estimated bad debts based on the above information.
(b) Prepare the year-end adjusting journal entry to record the bad debts using the allowance method and the aged uncollectible accounts receivable determined in (a). Assume the opening balance in the Allowance for Doubtful Accounts account is a $10,000 credit.
(c) Of the above accounts, $2,000 is determined to be specifically uncollectible. Prepare the journal entry to write off the uncollectible accounts.
(d) The company collects $1,000 subsequently on a specific account that had previously been determined to be uncollectible in (c). Prepare the journal entry(ies) necessary to restore the account and record the cash collection.
(e) Explain how establishing an allowance satisfies the matching principle.

Journalize transactions related to bad debts.
(SO 3)

P8-2A This is an aging schedule for Stoiko Company Ltd.:

		Number of Days Outstanding				
Customer	**Total**	**0–30**	**31–60**	**61–90**	**91-120**	**Over 120**
Aber	$ 20,000		$ 9,000	$11,000		
Bohr	30,000	$ 30,000				
Case	50,000	15,000	5,000		$30,000	
Datz	38,000					$38,000
Others	120,000	92,000	15,000	13,000		
	$258,000	$137,000	$29,000	$24,000	$30,000	$38,000
Estimated percentage uncollectible		3%	6%	12%	24%	50%
Total estimated bad debts	$ 34,930	$ 4,110	$ 1,740	$ 2,880	$ 7,200	$19,000

At December 31, 2001, the unadjusted balance in Allowance for Doubtful Accounts is a credit of $9,000.

Instructions

(a) Journalize and post the adjusting entry for bad debts at December 31, 2001. (Use T accounts.)
(b) Journalize and post to the allowance account these 2002 events and transactions:
1. March 1, an $800 customer balance originating in 2002 is judged uncollectible.
2. May 1, a cheque for $800 is received from the customer whose account was written off as uncollectible on March 1.
(c) Journalize the adjusting entry for bad debts at December 31, 2002, assuming that the unadjusted balance in Allowance for Doubtful Accounts is a debit of $1,100 and the aging schedule indicates that total estimated bad debts will be $27,100.

Calculate bad debt amounts.
(SO 3)

P8-3A Here is information related to Aris Company Ltd. for 2001:

Total credit sales	$1,800,000
Accounts receivable at December 31	600,000
Bad debts written off	26,000

Instructions

(a) What amount of bad debts expense will Aris Company report if it does not use the allowance method of accounting for bad debts?
(b) Assume that Aris Company decides to estimate its bad debts expense based on 4% of total accounts receivable. What amount of bad debts expense will Aris Company record if the Allowance for Doubtful Accounts has a credit balance of $4,000?
(c) Assume the same facts as in part (b), except that there is a $2,000 debit balance in Allowance for Doubtful Accounts. What amount of bad debts expense will Aris record?
(d) What are the advantages of using the allowance method of reporting bad debts expense?

Prepare entries to record transactions related to bad debts.
(SO 3)

P8-4A Carlo Fassi Co. uses 8% of the total accounts receivable balance to determine its allowance for bad debts for the period. At the beginning of the current period, Fassi had Allowance for Doubtful Accounts of $10,000 (credit). During the period, it had net credit sales of $900,000 and wrote off as uncollectible accounts receivable of $6,000. However, one of the accounts written off as uncollectible in the amount of $3,000 was recovered before the end of the current period. At the end of the period it had a balance in its accounts receivable account of $225,000.

Instructions

(a) Prepare the entry to record bad debts expense for the current period.
(b) Prepare the entry to record the write-off of uncollectible accounts during the current period.
(c) Prepare the entries to record the recovery of the uncollectible accounts during the current period.
(d) Determine the ending balance in Allowance for Doubtful Accounts.

P8-5A At December 31, 2001, the trial balance of Charron Company Ltd. contained the following amounts before adjustment:

Journalize entries to record transactions related to bad debts.

(SO 3)

	Debits	Credits
Accounts Receivable	$350,000	
Allowance for Doubtful Accounts		$ 1,500
Sales		875,000

Instructions

(a) Prepare the adjusting entry at December 31, 2001, to record bad debt expense assuming that the aging schedule indicates that $16,750 of accounts receivable will be uncollectible.

(b) Repeat part (a), assuming that instead of a credit balance, there is a $1,500 debit balance in the Allowance for Doubtful Accounts.

(c) During the next month, January 2002, a $4,500 account receivable is written off as uncollectible. Prepare the journal entry to record the write-off.

(d) Repeat part (c), assuming that Charron Company did not use the allowance method in accounting for uncollectible accounts receivable.

(e) What are the advantages of using the allowance method in accounting for uncollectible accounts?

P8-6A You are provided with the following information for Willow Brook Merchandisers Inc.:

Determine the missing amounts for sales and accounts receivable.

(SO 2, 3)

Merchandise inventory at the end of the year	$18,000
Accounts receivable at the beginning of the year	14,350
Cash sales made during the year	100,000
Gross profit on sales	27,600
Accounts receivable written off during the year	2,280
Purchases of merchandise made during the year	131,200
Accounts receivable collected during the year	58,320
Merchandise inventory at the beginning of the year	14,500

Instructions

Based on the information in this chapter and in Chapter 5, calculate the following amounts. (Hint: You will need to use the statement of earnings relationships introduced in Chapter 5.)

(a) cost of goods sold,

(b) credit sales, and

(c) the balance of accounts receivable at the end of the year.

P8-7A The balance sheets of Wilton Corporation at December 31, Year 1 and Year 2, showed credit balances in the Allowance for Doubtful Accounts at the end of Year 1 and Year 2—after adjusting entries—of $750,000 and $930,000, respectively.

Analyse accounts and prepare journal entries for receivables and bad debts.

(SO 2, 3)

The statements of earnings for Year 1 and Year 2 showed Sales of $25,000,000 and $30,000,000 and Bad Debts Expense of $249,000 and $285,000, respectively. Bad debts expense was 3% of gross ending accounts receivable. All sales were on account.

Instructions

Prepare summary journal entries for Year 2 to record the sales, collections, write-offs, and bad debts expense. (Hint: You may find the use of T accounts helpful in determining the amounts involved.)

P8-8A On January 1, 2000, Comaneci Company Ltd. had Accounts Receivable of $54,200 and Allowance for Doubtful Accounts of $4,700. Comaneci Company prepares financial statements annually and uses a perpetual inventory system. During the year the following selected transactions occurred:

Journalize various receivables transactions.

(SO 2, 4, 5)

Jan. 5 Sold $6,000 of merchandise to Brooks Company, terms n/30. Cost of merchandise sold, $4,000.

Feb. 2 Accepted a $6,000, four-month, 12% promissory note from Brooks Company for balance due.

	12	Sold $7,200 of merchandise costing $5,000 to Gage Company and accepted Gage's $7,200, two-month, 10% note for the balance due.
	26	Sold $5,000 of merchandise to Mathias Co., terms n/10. Cost of merchandise sold was $3,300.
Apr.	5	Accepted a $5,000, three-month, 8% note from Mathias Co. for balance due.
	12	Collected Gage Company note in full.
June	2	Collected Brooks Company note in full.
July	5	Mathias Co. dishonours its note of April 5. It is expected that Mathias will eventually pay the amount owed.
	15	Sold $3,000 of merchandise to Tritt Inc. costing $2,000, and accepted Tritt's $3,000, three-month, 12% note for the amount due.
Oct.	15	The Tritt Inc. note was dishonoured. Tritt Inc. is bankrupt, and there is no hope of future settlement.

Instructions
Journalize the transactions.

Prepare journal entries related to bad debt expense, and calculate ratios.
(SO 2, 3, 8)

P8-9A At December 31, 2001, Underwood Imports Inc. reported this information on its balance sheet:

Accounts receivable	$1,000,000
Less: Allowance for doubtful accounts	60,000

During 2002 the company had the following transactions related to receivables:

1. Sales on account	$2,600,000
2. Sales returns and allowances	40,000
3. Collections of accounts receivable	2,300,000
4. Write-offs of accounts receivable deemed uncollectible	80,000
5. Recovery of bad debts previously written off as uncollectible	25,000

Instructions
(a) Prepare the journal entries to record each of these five transactions. Assume that no cash discounts were taken on the collections of accounts receivable.
(b) Enter the January 1, 2002, balances in Accounts Receivable and Allowance for Doubtful Accounts, post the entries to the two accounts (use T accounts), and determine the balances.
(c) Prepare the journal entry to record bad debts expense for 2002, assuming that aging the accounts receivable indicates that estimated bad debts are $70,000.
(d) Calculate the receivables turnover ratio and average collection period.

Calculate maturity date, interest and gain or loss associated with a note.
(SO 4, 5)

P8-10A On November 1, 2001, a company accepted a three-month, $20,000, 8% note from a customer in settlement of the customer's account. The company's year-end is December 31 and the note is due February 1, 2002. The company bases interest calculations using months, rather than days, and makes adjusting entries at the end of each month.

Instructions
(a) Prepare all journal entries for the company over the life of the note. You are to assume that the customer settles the note in full on the maturity date. Round your answers to the nearest dollar.
(b) Assume that instead of honouring the note at maturity, the customer dishonours the note. Assuming that the entries made in part (a) for November, December, and January have already been recorded, record the necessary entry at the maturity date, February 1, 2002. We expect eventual collection of the note.

Prepare entries for various credit card and notes receivable transactions.
(SO 2, 4, 5, 6, 9)

P8-11A The Bon Ton Company Ltd. closes its books on July 31. On June 30, the Interest Receivable balance is $132.80, and the Notes Receivable account balance is $19,800. Notes Receivable include the following:

Date	Maker	Face Value	Term	Interest Rate
May 21	Alder Inc.	$ 6,000	2 months	12%
May 25	Dorn Co.	4,800	2 months	11%
June 30	MJH Corp.	9,000	6 months	9%
		$19,800		

During July the following transactions were completed:

July	5	Made sales of $6,200 on Bon Ton credit cards.
	14	Made sales of $700 on VISA credit cards. The credit card service charge is 3%.
	20	Received payment in full from Alder Inc. on the amount due.
	25	Received notice that Dorn Co. note has been dishonoured. (Assume that Dorn Co. is expected to pay in the future.)

Instructions

(a) Journalize the July transactions and the July 31 adjusting entry for accrued interest receivable.

(b) Enter the balances at July 1 in the receivable accounts and post the entries to all of the receivable accounts. (Use T accounts.)

(c) Show the balance sheet presentation of the receivable accounts at July 31.

Calculate and interpret various ratios.
(SO 7, 8)

P8-12A Presented here is basic financial information (in millions) from the 1998 annual reports of **Nike** and **Reebok**:

	Nike	Reebok
Sales	$9,553.1	$3,224.6
Allowance for doubtful accounts, Jan. 1	57.2	44.0
Allowance for doubtful accounts, Dec. 31	71.4	47.4
Accounts receivable balance (gross), Jan. 1	1,811.3	605.7
Accounts receivable balance (gross), Dec. 31	1,745.8	565.2

Instructions

(a) Calculate the receivables turnover ratio and average collection period for both companies. Comment on the difference in their collection experiences.

(b) Calculate the January 1 and December 31 credit risk ratio for each company. Comment on any apparent differences in their credit-granting practices.

Explain the impact of transactions on ratios; discuss acceleration of receipt of cash from receivables.
(SO 8, 9)

P8-13A The president of Hanlon Enterprises Ltd., Renée Hanlon, is considering the impact certain transactions have on its credit risk, receivables turnover, and average collection period ratios. Prior to the following transactions, Hanlon's credit risk ratio was 3%, its receivables turnover, 6 times, and its collection period, 61 days.

Transaction	Credit Risk Ratio (3%)	Receivables Turnover (6x)	Average Collection Period (61 days)
1. Recorded sales on account, $100,000.			
2. Collected $25,000 owing from customers.			
3. Recorded bad debt expense for the year, $7,500, using the allowance method.			
4. Recorded sales returns of $1,500 and credited the customers' accounts.			
5. Wrote off a $2,500 account from a customer as uncollectible.			

Instructions

(a) Complete the table, indicating whether each transaction will increase (I), decrease (D) or have no effect (NE) on the ratios.

(b) Renee Hanlon was reading through the financial statements for some publicly traded companies and noticed that they had recorded a loss on sale of receivables. She would like you to explain why companies would record such a loss.

Problems: Set B

Journalize transaction related to bad debts.
(SO 2, 3)

P8-1B Image.com uses the allowance method to estimate uncollectible accounts receivable. The computer produced the following aging of the accounts receivable at year end:

		Number of Days Outstanding				
	Total	**0–30**	**31–60**	**61–90**	**91-120**	**Over 120**
Accounts receivable	$375,000	$220,000	$90,000	$40,000	$10,000	$15,000
% uncollectible		1%	4%	5%	6%	10%
Estimated bad debts						

Instructions

(a) Calculate the total estimated bad debts based on the above information.

(b) Prepare the year-end adjusting journal entry to record the bad debts using the aged uncollectible accounts receivable determined in (a). Assume the opening balance in the Allowance for Doubtful Accounts account is a $10,000 debit.

(c) Of the above accounts, $5,000 is determined to be specifically uncollectible. Prepare the journal entry to write off the uncollectible accounts.

(d) The company collects $5,000 subsequently on a specific account that had previously been determined to be uncollectible in (c). Prepare the journal entry(ies) necessary to restore the account and record the cash collection.

(e) Comment on how your answers to (a)–(d) would change if Image.com used 3% of *total* accounts receivable, rather than aging the accounts receivable. What are the advantages to the company of aging the accounts receivable rather than applying a percentage to total accounts receivable?

Journalize transactions related to bad debts.
(SO 3)

P8-2B Presented here is an aging schedule for Deep Woods Company Ltd.:

		Number of Days Outstanding				
Customer	**Total**	**0–30**	**31–60**	**61–90**	**91-120**	**Over 120**
Anita	$ 22,000		$ 10,000	$ 12,000		
Barry	40,000	$ 40,000				
Chagnon	57,000	16,000	6,000		$ 35,000	
David	34,000					$ 34,000
Others	126,000	96,000	16,000	14,000		
	$279,000	$152,000	$ 32,000	$ 26,000	$ 35,000	$ 34,000
Estimated percentage uncollectible		4%	7%	13%	25%	50%
Total estimated bad debts	$ 37,450	$ 6,080	$ 2,240	$ 3,380	$ 8,750	$ 17,000

At December 31, 2001, the unadjusted balance in Allowance for Doubtful Accounts is a credit of $10,000.

Instructions

(a) Journalize and post the adjusting entry for bad debts at December 31, 2001. (Use T accounts.)

(b) Journalize and post to the allowance account these 2002 events and transactions:
1. March 31, an $800 customer balance originating in 2001 is judged uncollectible.
2. May 31, a cheque for $800 is received from the customer whose account was written off as uncollectible on March 31.

(c) Journalize the adjusting entry for bad debts on December 31, 2002, assuming that the unadjusted balance in Allowance for Doubtful Accounts is a debit of $800 and the aging schedule indicates that total estimated bad debts will be $28,300.

P8-3B Here is information related to Volkov Company Ltd. for 2001:

Calculate bad debt amounts.
(SO 3)

Total credit sales	$2,000,000
Accounts receivable at December 31	800,000
Bad debts written off	36,000

Instructions

(a) What amount of bad debts expense will Volkov Company report if it does not use the allowance method of accounting for bad debts?
(b) Assume that Volkov Company decides to estimate its bad debts expense based on 5% of total accounts receivable. What amount of bad debts expense will Volkov Company record if it has an Allowance for Doubtful Accounts credit balance of $3,000?
(c) Assume the same facts as in part (b) except that there is a $3,000 debit balance in Allowance for Doubtful Accounts. What amount of bad debts expense will Volkov record?
(d) What are the advantages of using the allowance method of reporting bad debts expense?

P8-4B Huang Corp. uses 8% of the total accounts receivable balance to determine its bad debts expense for the period. At the beginning of the current period, Huang had an Allowance for Doubtful Accounts of $9,000 (credit). During the period, it had net sales of $800,000 and wrote off as uncollectible accounts receivable of $7,000. However, one of the accounts written off as uncollectible in the amount of $4,000 was recovered before the end of the current period. At the end of the period, it had a balance in its accounts receivable account of $250,000.

Prepare entries to record transactions related to bad debts.
(SO 3)

Instructions

(a) Prepare the entry to record bad debts expense for the current period.
(b) Prepare the entry to record the write-off of uncollectible accounts during the current period.
(c) Prepare the entries to record the recovery of the uncollectible account during the current period.
(d) Determine the ending balance in Allowance for Doubtful Accounts.

P8-5B At December 31, 2001, the trial balance of Lexington Company Inc. contained the following amounts before adjustment:

Journalize entries to record transactions related to bad debts.
(SO 3)

	Debits	Credits
Accounts Receivable	$400,000	
Allowance for Doubtful Accounts		$ 1,000
Sales		950,000

Instructions

(a) Based on the information provided, can you tell if Lexington Company is using the allowance method? How can you tell?
(b) Prepare the adjusting entry at December 31, 2001, to record bad debt expense assuming that the aging schedule indicates that $11,750 of accounts receivable will be uncollectible.
(c) Repeat part (b), assuming that instead of a credit balance there is a $1,000 debit balance in the Allowance for Doubtful Accounts.
(d) During the next month, January 2002, a $5,000 account receivable is written off as uncollectible. Prepare the journal entry to record the write-off.
(e) Repeat part (d), assuming that Lexington Company does not use the allowance method in accounting for uncollectible accounts receivable.
(f) What type of account is the allowance for doubtful accounts? How does it affect how accounts receivable are reported on the balance sheet at the end of the accounting period?

P8-6B The following information pertains to the Moosa Merchandising Corporation:

Determine the missing amounts for sales and accounts receivable.
(SO 2, 3)

Merchandise inventory at the end of the year	$33,000
Accounts receivable at the beginning of the year	24,000
Cash sales made during the year	15,000
Gross profit on sales	27,000
Accounts receivable written off during the year	1,000

Purchases of merchandise made during the year	60,000
Accounts receivable collected during the year	78,000
Merchandise inventory at beginning of year	36,000

Instructions

(a) Calculate the amount of credit sales made during the year. (Hint: You will need to use the statement of earnings relationships introduced in Chapter 5.)

(b) Calculate the balance of Accounts Receivable at the end of the year.

Analyse accounts and prepare journal entries for receivables and bad debts.
(SO 2, 3)

P8-7B The balance sheet of Beancounter Corporation at December 31, Year 1, showed gross Accounts Receivable of $4,100,000. The credit balances in the Allowance for Doubtful Accounts at the end of Year 1 and Year 2—after adjusting entries—were $350,000 and $425,000, respectively. Accounts receivable written off amounted to $125,000 during Year 1 and $150,000 during Year 2.

All sales were made on account. The statements of earnings for Year 1 and Year 2 showed Sales of $30,000,000 and $45,000,000. Bad debts expense is estimated to be 5% of gross ending accounts receivable.

Instructions

Prepare summary journal entries for Year 2 for all transactions that had an effect on Accounts Receivable or the Allowance for Doubtful Accounts. (Hint: You may find the use of T accounts helpful in determining the amounts involved.)

Journalize various receivables transactions.
(SO 2, 4, 5)

P8-8B On January 1, 2001, Ricardo Company Ltd. had Accounts Receivable $146,000; Notes Receivable $15,000; and Allowance for Doubtful Accounts $13,200. The note receivable is from Annabelle Company. It is a four-month, 12% note dated December 31, 2000. Ricardo Company prepares financial statements annually and uses a perpetual inventory system. During the year, the following selected transactions occurred:

Jan.	5	Sold $12,000 of merchandise to George Company, terms n/15. The merchandise cost $8,000.
	20	Accepted George Company's $12,000, three-month, 9% note for balance due.
Feb.	18	Sold $8,000 of merchandise to Swaim Company costing $5,000, and accepted Swaim's $8,000, six-month, 10% note for the amount due.
Apr.	20	Collected George Company note in full.
	30	Received payment in full from Annabelle Company on the amount due.
May	25	Accepted Avery Inc.'s $7,000, three-month, 8% note in settlement of a past-due balance on account.
Aug.	18	Received payment in full from Swaim Company on note due.
	25	The Avery Inc. note was dishonoured. Avery Inc. is not bankrupt and future payment is anticipated.
Sept.	1	Sold $10,000 of merchandise to Young Company costing $6,500, and accepted a $10,000, six-month, 10% note for the amount due.

Instructions

Journalize the transactions.

Prepare journal entries related to bad debt expense, and calculate ratios.
(SO 2, 3, 8)

P8-9B At December 31, 2001, Bordeaux Inc. reported this information on its balance sheet:

Accounts receivable	$960,000
Less: Allowance for doubtful accounts	70,000

During 2002 the company had the following transactions related to receivables:

1. Sales on account	$3,200,000
2. Sales returns and allowances	50,000
3. Collections of accounts receivable	2,800,000
4. Write-offs of accounts receivable deemed uncollectible	90,000
5. Recovery of bad debts previously written off as uncollectible	35,000

Instructions

(a) Prepare the journal entries to record each of these five transactions. Assume that no cash discounts were taken on the collections of accounts receivable.

(b) Enter the January 1, 2002, balances in accounts receivable and allowance for doubtful accounts, post the entries to the two accounts (use T accounts), and determine the balances.
(c) Prepare the journal entry to record bad debts expense for 2002, assuming that aging the accounts receivable indicates that expected bad debts are $100,000.
(d) Calculate the receivables turnover ratio and average collection period.

Calculate maturity date, interest and gain or loss associated with a note.

(SO 4, 5)

P8-10B On July 26, 2001, a company accepted a 60-day, $50,000, 14% note from a customer in settlement of the customer's account. The company bases interest calculations on 365 days and makes adjusting entries at the end of each month.

Instructions

(a) What is the maturity date of the note? Prepare all journal entries for the company over the life of the note. You are to assume that the customer settles the note in full on the maturity date. Round your answers to the nearest dollar.
(b) Assume that instead of holding the note to maturity, the company sells it on September 2, 2001, for $49,000, which includes accrued interest. Assuming that the entries made in part (a) for July and August have already been recorded, record the necessary entry for September 2, 2001.

Prepare entries for various credit card and notes receivable transactions.

(SO 2, 4, 5, 6, 9)

P8-11B Selica Company Inc. closes its books on October 31. On September 30, the Notes Receivable account balance is $23,400. Notes Receivable include the following:

Date	Maker	Face Value	Term	Interest Rate
Aug. 16	Foran Inc.	$ 8,000	2 months	12%
Aug. 25	Drexler Co.	5,200	2 months	12%
Sept. 30	MGH Corp.	10,200	6 months	9%
		$ 23,400		

During October the following transactions were completed:

Oct. 7	Made sales of $6,900 on Selica credit cards.
12	Made sales of $750 on VISA credit cards. The credit card service charge is 4%.
15	Received payment in full from Foran Inc. on the amount due.
25	Received notice that Drexler Co. note has been dishonoured. (Assume that Drexler Co. is expected to pay in the future.)

Instructions

(a) Journalize the October transactions and the October 31 adjusting entry for accrued interest receivable. Assume interest is accrued only annually.
(b) Enter the balances at October 1 in the receivable accounts and post the entries to all of the receivable accounts. (Use T accounts.)
(c) Show the balance sheet presentation of the receivable accounts at October 31.

Calculate and interpret various ratios.

(SO 7, 8)

P8-12B Presented here is basic financial information from the 1998 annual reports of two primary manufacturers of silicon chips for personal computers: **Intel** and **Advanced Micro Devices (AMD)**.

(in millions)	Intel	AMD
Sales	$26,273.0	$2,542.0
Allowance for doubtful accounts, Jan. 1	65.0	11.2
Allowance for doubtful accounts, Dec. 31	62.0	12.7
Accounts receivable balance (gross), Jan. 1	3,503.0	340.3
Accounts receivable balance (gross), Dec. 31	3,589.0	428.2

Instructions

(a) Calculate the receivables turnover ratio and average collection period for both companies. Comment on the difference in their collection experiences.
(b) Calculate the January 1 and December 31 credit risk ratio for each company. Comment on any apparent differences in their credit-granting practices.

Explain the impact of transactions on ratios.
(SO 8)

P8-13B The president of Fort McMurray Enterprises Ltd. asks if you could indicate the impact certain transactions have on the following ratios.

Transaction	Current Ratio (2:1)	Receivables Turnover (10X)	Average Collection Period (36.5 days)	Credit Risk Ratio (5%)
1. Recorded $2,500 sales on account. Cost of sale was $1,500.				
2. Collected $1,500 of short-term notes receivable, including $100 of interest not previously accrued.				
3. Recorded bad debt expense of $500.				
4. Wrote off a $100 account receivable as uncollectible.				
5. Recorded the subsequent recovery and collection of the account in (4).				
6. Accrued interest on note receivable.				

Instructions
Complete the table, indicating whether each transaction will increase (I), decrease (D) or have no effect (NE) on the specific ratios provided for Fort McMurray Enterprises.

BROADENING YOUR PERSPECTIVE

FINANCIAL REPORTING AND ANALYSIS

FINANCIAL REPORTING PROBLEM: *Loblaw Companies Limited*

BYP8-1 Refer to the financial statements of **Loblaw** and the accompanying notes to its financial statements in Appendix A.

Instructions
(a) Assuming that all sales are credit sales, calculate the receivables turnover ratio and average collection period for 1999. What conclusions can you draw from these calculations?
(b) Is sufficient information provided to calculate the credit risk ratio? If so, calculate this ratio. If not, explain why Loblaw might choose not to separately report its allowance for doubtful accounts.
(c) Did Loblaw report any significant credit risks in 1999?

COMPARATIVE ANALYSIS PROBLEM: *Loblaw and Sobeys*

BYP8-2 The financial statements of **Sobeys Inc.** are presented in Appendix B, following the financial statements for **Loblaw** in Appendix A.

Instructions
(a) Based on the information contained in the financial statements and supporting notes, calculate the following 1999 values for each company:
1. Current ratio
2. Receivables turnover ratio (assume all sales were credit sales)

3. Average collection period for receivables

(b) The industry averages for each of the above ratios is provided below:

Receivables turnover	36.5 times
Average collection period	10 days
Current ratio	0.8:1

What conclusions concerning each company's liquidity, and the management of accounts receivable, can be drawn from your calculations in (a) and these data?

RESEARCH CASE

BYP8-3 The May 1999 issue of *CAmagazine* includes an article by Terrence Belford entitled "Sell Your Invoices & Save the Store." Read the article and answer the questions below.

Instructions

(a) Advanced Information Technology (AIT) Corp. needed short-term financing urgently. How much financing was it able to arrange by discounting its receivables with TCE Capital Corp.? What was the immediate discount percentage that TCE took on these receivables?

(b) Explain exactly how discounting your invoices works.

(c) How much short-term financing did discounters such as TCE and Montcap Financial Services Corp. provide to their customers in 1999?

(d) How much did Eaton's receive from the discounting of its receivables when it first went into receivership in 1997?

(e) Why is the number of companies seeking out this type of financing growing?

(f) In what circumstances are the costs attached to invoice discounting reasonable?

INTERPRETING FINANCIAL STATEMENTS

BYP8-4 High Liner Foods Incorporated, formerly known as National Sea Products Limited, processes and markets quality seafood products. It is one of the largest Canadian deep sea fishing companies, harvesting over 10 million kilograms of seafood annually from Georges Bank to Northern Labrador.

The following information (in thousands) was available in High Liner Foods' financial statements:

	Jan. 2, 1999	**Jan. 3, 1998**	**Dec. 28, 1996**
Accounts receivable, gross	$ 31,345	$ 23,814	$ 22,876
Allowance for doubtful accounts	569	435	416
Accounts receivable, net	30,776	23,379	22,460
Sales (assume all credit)	291,655	277,770	252,798

Additional detail about High Liner's receivables (in thousands) includes the following:

Accounts receivable	**Jan. 2, 1999**	**Jan. 3, 1998**	**Dec. 28, 1996**
Canada Trade	$10,353	$ 9,915	$ 8,350
U.S. Trade	17,026	10,737	11,742
Japan Trade	483	678	287
Affiliates	47	125	210
Other	2,867	1,924	1,871
	$30,776	$23,379	$22,460

Terms range from seven to 30 days, with most accounts being collected in 28 days. No one customer represents more than 10% of outstanding amounts. The company has experienced a bad debt expense of less than 0.1% of sales over the past five years.

Instructions

(a) Calculate the credit risk ratio, receivables turnover ratio, and average collection period for fiscal 1998 (January 2, 1999) and 1997 (January 3, 1998).

(b) Comment on High Liner Foods' management of its receivables.

(c) High Liner did not comment specifically upon credit risk, other than to detail the locations of its receivables. In addition, High Liner provides the same allowance for doubtful accounts (2%) of trade receivables, regardless of their location. Comment on the reasonableness of this policy.

A GLOBAL FOCUS

BYP8-5 Sears, Roebuck & Co. is one of the world's largest retailers. Sears, Roebuck owns about 55% of Sears Canada. It is also a huge provider of credit through its Sears credit card. Revenue generated from credit operations was $4.6 billion in 1998, from 30 million cardholders. The rate of interest Sears earns on outstanding receivables is 28% in Canada and 10% to 21% in the United States. In some instances, to acquire cash when needed, the company will sell its receivables. At December 31, 1998, Sears had sold $6.63 billion of its receivables.

The following information (in millions of U.S. dollars) was available in Sears' 1998 financial statements:

	1998	1997	1996
Accounts receivable (gross)	$18,946	$20,956	$22,371
Allowance for doubtful accounts	974	1,113	808
Merchandise sales	36,704	36,371	33,751
Credit revenues	4,618	4,925	4,313
Bad debts expense	1,287	1,532	971

Instructions

(a) Discuss whether the sale of receivables by Sears represents a significant portion of its receivables. Why might Sears have sold these receivables? As an investor, what concerns might you have about these sales?

(b) Calculate and discuss the receivables turnover ratio and average collection period for Sears for 1998 and 1997.

(c) Do you think Sears provides credit as a revenue-generating activity or as a convenience for its customers?

(d) Calculate the ratio of bad debts expense to merchandise sales for 1998 and 1997. Did this ratio improve or worsen? What considerations should Sears use in deciding whether it wants to have liberal or conservative credit-granting policies?

FINANCIAL ANALYSIS ON THE WEB

www.wiley.com/canada/kimmel

BYP8-6 This case examines the Credit Card Costs Calculator, provided by the Office of Consumer Affairs, Industry Canada. Based on how a credit card is used, we will determine which cards cost the least in interest and fees over a year. The cost of borrowing from a bank is then compared to the cost of using a credit card.

Instructions

Specific requirements of this web case can be found on the Kimmel website.

CRITICAL THINKING

COLLABORATIVE LEARNING ACTIVITIES

BYP8-7 Johanna and Jake Berkvom own Campus Fashions. From its inception, Campus Fashions has sold merchandise on either a cash or credit basis, but no credit cards have been accepted. During the past several months, the Berkvoms have begun to question their credit-sales policies. First, they have lost some sales because they refuse to accept credit cards. Second, representatives of two banks have convinced them to accept their national credit cards. One bank, CIBC, has stated that (1) its credit card fee is 4% and (2) it pays the retailer 96 cents on each $1 of sales within three days of receiving the credit card billings.

The Berkvoms decide that they should determine the cost of carrying their own credit sales. From the accounting records of the past three years, they accumulate these data:

	2001	2000	1999
Net credit sales	$500,000	$600,000	$400,000
Collection agency fees for slow-paying customers	2,450	2,500	1,600
Salary of part-time accounts receivable clerk	3,800	3,800	3,800

Credit and collection expenses as a percentage of net credit sales are as follows: uncollectible accounts 1.6%; billing and mailing costs 0.5%; and credit investigation fee on new customers 0.15%.

Johanna and Jake also determine that the average accounts receivable balance outstanding during the year is 5% of net credit sales. The Berkvoms estimate that they could earn an average of 10% annually on cash invested in other business opportunities.

Instructions

With the class divided into groups, perform the following:

(a) Prepare a tabulation for each year showing total credit and collection expenses in dollars and as a percentage of net credit sales.

(b) Determine the net credit and collection expenses in dollars and as a percentage of sales after considering the revenue not earned from other investment opportunities. [Note: The income lost on the cash held by the bank for three days is considered immaterial.]

(c) Discuss both the financial and non-financial factors that are relevant to the decision.

BYP8-8 Arvada Company Ltd. sells office equipment and supplies to many organizations in the city and surrounding area on contract terms of 2/10, n/30. In the past, more than 75% of the credit customers have taken advantage of the discount by paying within 10 days of the invoice date.

The number of customers taking the full 30 days to pay has increased within the last year. Current indications are that less than 60% of the customers are now taking the discount. Bad debts as a percentage of gross credit sales have risen from the 1.5% provided in past years to about 4% in the current year.

The controller has responded to a request from the finance committee for more information on the collections of accounts receivable with the report reproduced here.

ARVADA COMPANY LTD.
Accounts Receivable Collections
May 31, 2002

The fact that some credit accounts will prove uncollectible is normal. Annual bad debt write-offs have been 1.5% of gross credit sales over the past five years. During the last fiscal year, this percentage increased to slightly less than 4%. The current Accounts Receivable balance is $1,400,000. The condition of this balance in terms of age and probability of collection is as follows:

Proportion of Total	Age Categories	Probability of Collection
66%	0-30 days	99%
16	31-60 days	96
9	61-90 days	95
5	91 to 120 days	91
3	121 to 180 days	75
1	Over 180 days	20

The allowance for doubtful accounts had a credit balance of $29,500 on June 1, 2001. Total gross credit sales for the 2001–2002 fiscal year amounted to $2,800,000. Write-offs of bad accounts during the year totalled $96,000.

Instructions

With the class divided into groups, perform the following:

(a) Prepare an accounts receivable aging schedule for Arvada Company using the age categories identified in the controller's report to the finance committee showing:

1. The amount of accounts receivable outstanding for each age category and in total.

2. The estimated amount that is uncollectible for each category and in total.

(b) Calculate the amount of the year-end adjustment required to bring Allowance for Doubtful Accounts to the balance indicated by the age analysis. Then prepare the necessary journal entry to adjust the accounting records.

(c) Assume a recessionary environment with tight credit and high interest rates. Then:
1. Identify steps Arvada Company might take to improve the accounts receivable situation.
2. Evaluate each step identified in terms of the risks and costs involved.

COMMUNICATION ACTIVITY

BYP8-9 Sara Joy Corporation is a recently formed business selling the "World's Best Doormat." The corporation is selling doormats faster than Sara Joy can make them. It has been selling the product on a credit basis, telling customers to "pay when they can." Oddly, even though sales are tremendous, the company is having trouble paying its bills.

Instructions

Write a memo to the president of Sara Joy Corporation discussing these questions:

(a) What steps should be taken to improve its ability to pay its bills?

(b) What accounting steps should be taken to measure its success in improving collections, and in recording its collection success?

(c) If the corporation is still unable to pay its bills, what additional steps can be taken with its receivables to ease its liquidity problems?

ETHICS CASE

BYP8-10 The controller of Shirt Corporation believes that the company's yearly allowance for doubtful accounts should be 2% of total accounts receivable. The president of Shirt Corporation, nervous that the shareholders might expect the company to sustain its 10% sales growth rate, suggests that the controller increase the allowance for doubtful accounts to 4%. The president thinks that the lower net earnings, which reflect a 6% growth rate, will be more sustainable for Shirt Corporation.

Instructions

(a) Who are the stakeholders in this case?

(b) Does the president's request pose an ethical dilemma for the controller?

(c) Should the controller be concerned with Shirt Corporation's growth rate in estimating the allowance? Explain your answer.

Answers to Self-Study Questions

1. c 2. a 3. c 4. d 5. c 6. b 7. d 8. a 9. c 10. c 11. a

Loblaws
A passion for food... *and a lot more!*

Answer to Loblaw Review It Question 1

Loblaw reports only accounts receivable on its balance sheet.

CHAPTER 9

Reporting and Analysing Long-Lived Assets

STUDY OBJECTIVES

After studying this chapter, you should be able to:

1. Describe how the cost principle applies to tangible capital assets.
2. Explain the concept of amortization.
3. Calculate periodic amortization using the straight-line method, and contrast its expense pattern with those of other methods.
4. Describe the procedure for revising periodic amortization.
5. Explain how to account for the disposal of tangible capital assets.
6. Describe methods for evaluating the use of tangible capital assets.
7. Identify the basic issues related to reporting intangible capital assets.
8. Indicate how capital assets are reported on the balance sheet.

Tumult in the Skies

Nineteen ninety-nine was a year of turbulence in the Canadian airline industry.

At the beginning of the year, Canada had two major national carriers. Montreal-based Air Canada, which had started life as a Crown corporation that was generally considered to be poorly managed, had done well since it was privatized in the early 1990s. It was by far the more profitable of the two.

Canadian Airlines, headquartered in Calgary, had been mired in debt for a decade. CEO Kevin Benson instituted a four-year recovery plan when he took command in 1996—a combination of pay cuts, overhead savings, and negotiated reductions in fuel taxes and fees. These were not enough to overcome the company's constant cash crush. Generous labour agreements—particularly regarding layoffs—made it hard to shrink the labour force. Planned revenue gains from expanding into the Asian market disappeared when the bottom fell out of the Asian economy in 1998. The only year Canadian turned a profit in the 1990s was 1997, when it pocketed $5.4 million—only half the already modest $9 million it had predicted. With its deficit reaching $568 million, this profit wasn't even a drop in the bucket!

It was clear that the situation was not sustainable. While many marvelled at the ability of Mr. Benson and his team to run the cash-starved Canadian Airlines seemingly on fuel vapour, something was going to have to change.

And so it did. In fact, the next year brought nothing but changes.

In August, Air Canada proposed purchasing Canadian Airlines' international routes. Canadian rejected the offer, saying those routes were the most profitable. Shortly thereafter, Onex Corporation announced a plan to buy both Air Canada and Canadian Airlines and merge them in a bid backed by American Airlines parent AMR Corporation. Canadian (in which AMR had a 25% voting interest) backed the bid. Air Canada denounced it.

Air Canada challenged the legality of Onex's takeover plan, which would give more than the legal 10% individual limit of Canadian's shares to one shareholder. The 10% share rule was introduced when Air Canada was privatized to ensure broad ownership in the industry. While the case was pending, Air Canada offered a counterbid for Canadian,

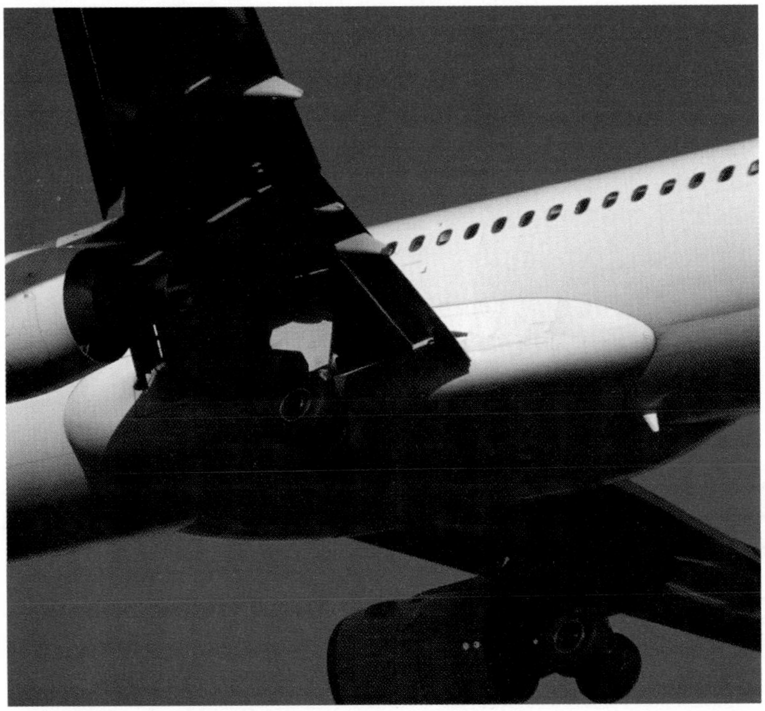

On the World Wide Web
Air Canada
http://www.aircanada.ca

backed by the CIBC and its Star Alliance airline partners. As the autumn progressed, first Onex, then Air Canada, raised their bids.

In early November, the Quebec Superior Court ruled that the Onex bid was in fact illegal, and Onex backed out of the bidding. Canadian looked around for other solutions, but in the end was forced to recommend that its shareholders accept the Air Canada bid, which was for $92 million. The deal was completed late in December, and will create the world's tenth largest air carrier when the integration of the two airlines is complete.

Much of the credit for Air Canada's triumph is given to the cool handling of the deal by CEO Robert Milton. Promoted from chief operating officer in the summer of 1999, Mr. Milton is an aviation nut—he spent the $15,000 his father gave him to buy his first car on an airplane instead, and started his own courier airline. He seems to have a particular flair for the management of assets. He is known to pop into an office and ask, "Why is that plane on the Florida route? Why isn't it on its way to Phoenix?" One of his first moves as CEO was to institute a late-night flight to the Bahamas that made use of a brand new 767 that was otherwise sitting in the hangar all night.

At the time of writing, the combining of Canada's two flying behemoths is still underway, and the new organization is evolving in all kinds of interesting ways. In March 2000, an Alberta court granted Canadian Airlines protection from its creditors, a move that allowed the airline to stay afloat while it works out the restructuring of its $3.5 billion debt and aircraft leases. Merging routes and reducing duplication of schedules has resulted in the two formerly independent airline unions bargaining together on such key issues as seniority, job security, and work ownership.

The new airline will need fewer planes than the two separate ones. Since Canadian's aircraft fleet is significantly older, on average, than Air Canada's, integrating, updating, and replacing the fleet provides the two companies with some interesting issues related to managing their newly combined capital assets.

Meanwhile, consumers and shareholders are keeping their eyes on the skies to see what happens next.

PREVIEW OF CHAPTER 9

For airlines and many other companies, making the right decisions regarding long-lived assets is critical, because these assets represent huge investments. Management must make many ongoing decisions—what to acquire and when, how to finance the acquisition of assets, how to account for them, and when to dispose of them.

In this chapter, we address these and other issues surrounding long-lived assets. Our discussion of long-lived assets is presented in two parts: tangible capital assets and intangible capital assets. *Tangible capital assets* are the property, plant, and equipment (physical assets) that commonly come to mind when we think of a company. Tangible capital assets can also include *natural resources*, such as mineral deposits, oil and gas reserves, and timber. In addition, a company may have many important *intangible capital assets*. These are assets, such as copyrights and patents, that lack physical substance but can be extremely valuable and vital to a company's success.

The content and organization of this chapter are as follows:

REPORTING AND ANALYSING LONG-LIVED ASSETS

Tangible Capital Assets
- Determining the Cost of Tangible Capital Assets
- Accounting for Tangible Capital Assets
- Analysing Tangible Capital Assets

Intangible Capital Assets
- Accounting for Intangible Capital Assets
- Types of Intangible Capital Assets

Financial Statement Presentation of Capital Assets

SECTION 1

TANGIBLE CAPITAL ASSETS

Tangible capital assets are resources that have physical substance (a definite size and shape), are used in the operations of a business, and are not intended for sale to customers. They are called by various names—property, plant, and equipment; plant and equipment; and fixed assets—but the term we use most often in this chapter is "property, plant, and equipment." By whatever name, these assets are generally long-lived and are expected to provide services to the company for a number of years. Property, plant, and equipment decline in service potential (value) over their useful lives; the only exception to this is land, which usually retains its value.

The acquisition of property, plant, and equipment is critical to the success of nearly all businesses, because these resources determine the company's capacity and therefore its ability to satisfy customers. With too few planes, for example, Air Canada may lose customers to its competitors (where competition exists), but with too many planes, it will be flying with a lot of empty seats. Management must constantly monitor its needs and acquire assets accordingly. Failure to do so results in lost business opportunities, or inefficient use of existing assets, and is likely to eventually show up in poor financial results, problems for management, and declining interest among investors.

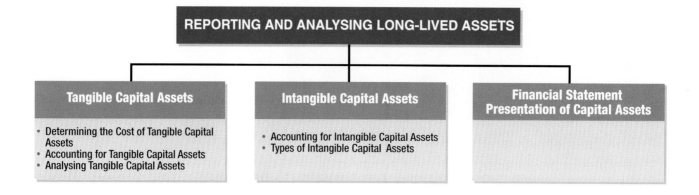

It is also important for a business enterprise to (1) keep assets in good operating condition, (2) replace worn-out or outdated facilities, and (3) expand its productive resources as needed. The decline of rail travel in Canada can be traced in part to the failure of railway companies to perform the first two operations. Conversely, the growth of air travel in this country can be attributed in part to the general willingness of airline companies to follow these essential guidelines.

Many companies have substantial investments in property, plant, and equipment. In public utility and telecommunication companies, for example, property, plant, and equipment can represent more than 75% of total assets. Recently, net property, plant, and equipment (property, plant, and equipment less accumulated amortization) accounted for more than 88% of Canadian Utilities Limited's assets. Illustration 9-1 shows the percentages of net property, plant, and equipment in relation to total assets in some other companies.

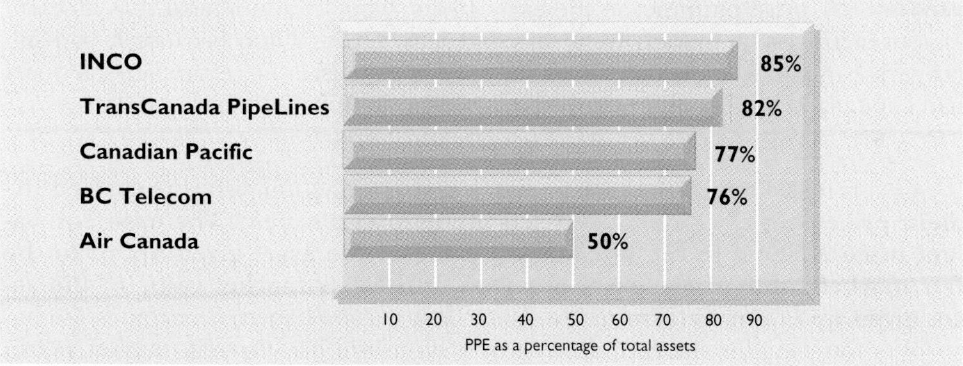

Illustration 9-1
Percentages of net property, plant, and equipment (PPE) to total assets

Property, plant, and equipment are often subdivided into four classes:

1. Land, such as a building site
2. Land improvements, such as driveways, parking lots, fences, and underground sprinkler systems
3. Buildings, such as stores, offices, factories, and warehouses
4. Equipment, such as store check-out counters, cash registers, coolers, office furniture, factory machinery, and delivery equipment

Determining the Cost of Tangible Capital Assets

STUDY OBJECTIVE 1
Describe how the cost principle applies to tangible capital assets.

Tangible capital assets are recorded at cost in accordance with the **cost principle** of accounting. Thus, the planes at Air Canada are recorded at cost. **Cost consists of all expenditures necessary to acquire the asset and make it ready for its intended use.** For example, the purchase price, freight costs paid by the purchaser, and installation costs are all considered part of the cost of factory machinery.

Determining which costs to include in a capital asset account and which costs not to include is very important. If a cost is not included in a capital asset account, then it must be expensed immediately. Such costs are referred to as **revenue (or operating) expenditures**. On the other hand, costs that are not expensed immediately, but are instead included in a capital asset account, are referred to as **capital expenditures**. This distinction is important, because it has immediate, and often material, implications for the statement of earnings. Some companies, in order to boost current earnings, have been known to improperly capitalize expenditures that should have been expensed. For example, suppose that $10,000 of maintenance costs incurred at the end of the year are improperly capitalized to a building account; that is, they are included in the asset account Buildings rather than being expensed immediately. If the cost of the building is being allocated as an expense (amortized) over a 40-year life, then the maintenance cost of $10,000 will be incorrectly spread across 40 years instead of being expensed in the current year. Current-year expenses will be understated by $10,000 (maintenance costs will be understated), and amortization expense will be overstated by about $250 ($10,000 ÷ 40). Significantly, expenses will therefore be overstated by the amount of the amortization for the remaining 39-year amortization period. Thus, determining which costs to capitalize and which to expense is very important.

BUSINESS INSIGHT

Investor Perspective

Chambers Development, a waste management company, saw its share price plummet in the early 1990s, when it announced that its earnings over a five-year period were overstated by $362 million because it had improperly capitalized costs that should have been expensed. For example, Chambers had capitalized $162 million that it had paid in dumping fees at landfill sites.

Cost is measured by the cash paid in a cash transaction or by the **cash equivalent price** paid when noncash assets are used in payment. **The cash equivalent price is equal to the fair market value of the asset given up, or to the fair market value of the asset received, if the fair market value of the asset given up is not determinable.** Once cost is established, it becomes the basis of accounting for the capital asset over its useful life. Current market values are not used after acquisition, unless there is a permanent decline or impairment in the value of the asset. The application of the cost principle to each of the major classes of property, plant, and equipment is explained in the following sections.

International Note

The United Kingdom is flexible regarding asset valuation. Companies revalue to fair value when they believe this information is more relevant. Switzerland and the Netherlands also permit revaluations.

LAND

The cost of land includes (1) the cash purchase price, (2) closing costs such as title and legal fees, (3) real estate brokers' commissions, and (4) accrued property taxes and other liens on the land assumed by the purchaser. For example, if the cash price is $50,000 and the purchaser agrees to pay accrued taxes of $5,000, the cost of the land is $55,000.

All necessary costs incurred in making land **ready for its intended use** increase (debit) the Land account. When vacant land is acquired, its cost includes expenditures for clearing, draining, filling, and grading. If the land has a building on it that must be removed to make the site suitable for construction of a new building, all demolition and removal costs, less any proceeds from salvaged materials, are chargeable to the Land account. To illustrate, assume that Hayes Manufacturing Corporation acquires real estate at a cash cost of $100,000. The property contains an old warehouse that is razed at a net cost of $6,000 ($7,500 in costs less $1,500 in proceeds from salvaged materials). Additional expenditures are for the legal fee, $1,000, and the real estate broker's commission, $8,000. Given these factors, the cost of the land is $115,000, calculated as shown in Illustration 9-2.

Illustration 9-2
Calculation of cost of land

Land	
Cash price of property	$ 100,000
Net removal cost of warehouse	6,000
Legal fee	1,000
Real estate broker's commission	8,000
Cost of land	**$115,000**

When the acquisition is recorded, Land is debited for $115,000 and Cash is credited for $115,000.

LAND IMPROVEMENTS

The cost of land improvements includes all expenditures necessary to make the improvements ready for their intended use. For example, the cost of a new company parking lot includes the amounts paid for paving, fencing, and lighting. These improvements have limited useful lives, and their maintenance and replacement are the responsibility of the company.

BUILDINGS

All necessary expenditures related to the purchase or construction of a building are charged to the Buildings account. When a building is purchased, such costs include the purchase price, closing costs (legal fees, title, interim insurance, etc.), and the real estate broker's commission. Costs to make the building ready for its intended use consist of expenditures for remodelling rooms and offices, and for replacing or repairing the roof, floors, electrical wiring, and plumbing.

When a new building is constructed, its cost consists of the contract price plus payments made by the owner for architects' fees, building permits, and excavation costs. In addition, interest costs incurred to finance the project are included in the cost of the asset when a significant period of time is required to get the asset ready for use. In these circumstances, interest costs are considered as necessary as materials and labour. However, the inclusion of interest costs in the cost of a constructed building is **limited to the construction period**. When construction has been completed, subsequent interest payments on funds borrowed to finance the construction are recorded as increases (debits) to Interest Expense.

EQUIPMENT

The cost of equipment consists of the cash purchase price and the provincial sales tax (where applicable). Unlike other capital assets, provincial sales tax is normally charged on equipment purchases. Any GST (or HST) paid is not a capital cost, as it is normally recoverable. As mentioned in Chapter 5, sales tax regulations are complicated and are ignored in this textbook in order to remain focused on fundamental concepts. The cost of equipment also includes freight charges, insurance during transit paid by the purchaser, and expenditures required in assembling, installing, and testing the unit. However, motor vehicle licences, and accident insurance on company trucks and cars, are treated as expenses as they are incurred, because they represent annual recurring expenditures and do not benefit future periods. Two criteria apply in determining the cost of equipment: (1) the frequency of the cost—one time or recurring and (2) the benefit period—the life of the asset or one year.

To illustrate, assume that Lenard Company Ltd. purchases a delivery truck at a cash price of $22,000. Related expenditures are for painting and lettering, $500, motor vehicle licence, $80, and a one-year accident insurance policy, $1,600. The cost of the delivery truck is $22,500, calculated as shown in Illustration 9-3.

Illustration 9-3
Calculation of cost of delivery truck

Delivery Truck	
Cash price	$ 22,000
Painting and lettering	500
Cost of delivery truck	**$22,500**

The cost of a motor vehicle licence is treated as an expense, and the cost of an insurance policy is considered a prepaid asset. Thus, the entry to record the purchase of the truck and related expenditures is as follows:

A	=	L	+	SE
+22,500				-80
+1,600				
-24,180				

Delivery Truck	22,500	
Licence Expense	80	
Prepaid Insurance	1,600	
Cash		24,180
(To record purchase of delivery truck and related expenditures)		

For another example, assume Unger Company Ltd. purchases factory machinery at a cash price of $50,000. Related expenditures are for insurance during shipping, $500, and installation and testing, $1,000. The cost of the factory machinery is $51,500, calculated as in Illustration 9-4.

Illustration 9-4
Calculation of cost of factory machinery

Factory Machinery	
Cash price	$ 50,000
Insurance during shipping	500
Installation and testing	1,000
Cost of factory machinery	**$51,500**

Thus, the entry to record the purchase and related expenditures is as follows:

A	=	L	+	SE
+51,500				
-51,500				

Factory Machinery	51,500	
Cash		51,500
(To record purchase of factory machinery and related expenditures)		

TO BUY OR LEASE?

In this chapter, we focus on assets that are purchased, but we would like to give you a brief look at an alternative to purchasing—leasing. In a lease, a party that owns an asset (the **lessor**) agrees to allow another party (the **lessee**) to use the asset for an agreed period of time at an agreed price. Here are some advantages of leasing an asset versus purchasing it:

1. **Reduced risk of obsolescence.** Frequently, lease terms allow the party using the asset (the lessee) to exchange the asset for a more modern one if it becomes outdated. This is much easier than trying to sell an obsolete asset.
2. **Little or no down payment.** To purchase an asset, most companies must borrow money, which usually requires a down payment of at least 20%. Leasing an asset requires little or no down payment.
3. **Shared tax advantages.** Startup companies typically do not make much money in their early years, and so they have little need for the tax deductions available from owning an asset. In a lease, the lessor gets the tax advantage because it owns the asset. It will often pass these tax savings on to the lessee in the form of lower lease payments.
4. **Assets and liabilities not reported.** Many companies prefer to keep assets and, especially, liabilities off their books. Certain types of leases, called **operating leases**, allow the lessee to account for the transaction as a rental with neither an asset nor a liability recorded.

Airlines often choose to lease many of their airplanes in long-term lease agreements. Air Canada, for example, leases 57% of its fleet. In 1999, it leased 88 of its 154 planes under operating leases. Because operating leases are accounted for as a rental, these 88 planes did not show up on its balance sheet.

Under another type of lease, a **capital lease**, both the asset and the liability are shown on the balance sheet. Under a capital lease, for the lessee, long-term lease agreements are accounted for in a way that is very similar to purchases: on the lessee's balance sheet, the leased item is shown as an asset and the obligation owed to the lessor is shown as a liability. The leased asset is amortized by the lessee in a manner similar to purchased assets. None of the 66 planes that are listed as assets on Air Canada's balance sheet are leased planes accounted for as capital leases. There will be additional discussion of leasing in Chapter 10 with regard to liabilities.

BUSINESS INSIGHT

Management Perspective

Leasing is big business in Canada. The Canadian Finance & Leasing Association estimated that nearly 25% of new property, plant, and equipment purchased in a recent year was financed by lease. The combined equipment and vehicle leasing industry is estimated to total between 60 and 80 billion dollars. The reasons often stated for leasing include favourable tax treatment, increased flexibility, keeping pace with technological improvements, driving down expense ratios, and increased cash flow.

BEFORE YOU GO ON . . .

Review It

1. What are tangible capital assets? What are the major classes of tangible capital assets? At what value should tangible capital assets be recorded?
2. What are revenue (or current) expenditures? What are capital expenditures?
3. What are the primary advantages of leasing?

Do It

Assume that a delivery truck is purchased for $45,000 cash plus sales taxes of $900 and delivery costs to the dealer of $500. The buyer also pays $200 for painting and lettering, $600 for an annual insurance policy, and $80 for a motor vehicle licence. Explain how each of these costs is accounted for.

Reasoning: The cost principle applies to all expenditures made in order to get delivery equipment ready for its intended use. The principle does not apply to operating costs incurred during the useful life of the equipment, such as gas and oil, motor tune-ups, licences, and insurance.

Solution: The first four payments ($45,000, $900, $500, and $200) are considered expenditures necessary to make the truck ready for its intended use. Thus, the cost of the truck is $46,600. The payments for the insurance and licence are considered operating expenses incurred during the useful life of the asset.

ACCOUNTING FOR TANGIBLE CAPITAL ASSETS

STUDY OBJECTIVE 2

Explain the concept of amortization.

AMORTIZATION

The use of the word "amortization" for tangible capital assets is quite recent in Canada. Before 1990, the commonly used term was "depreciation." This term is still widely used in practice, and you will see it in extracts from financial statements included in this chapter.

As explained in Chapter 4, **amortization is the process of allocating to expense the cost of a capital asset over its useful (service) life in a rational and systematic manner**. Such cost allocation is designed to properly match expenses with revenues in accordance with the matching principle.

Illustration 9-5
Amortization as an allocation concept

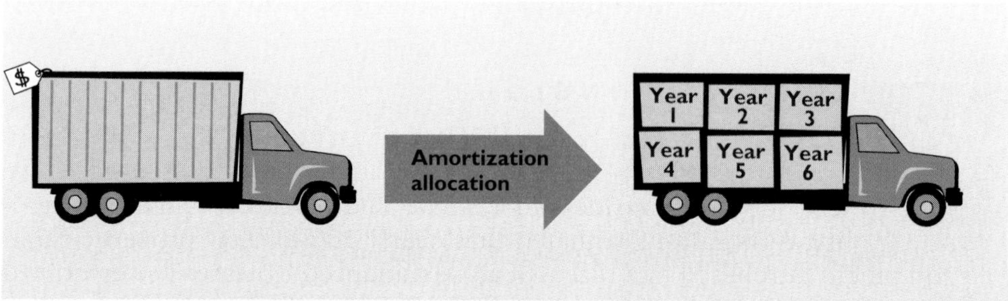

As we learned in Chapter 4, the adjusting journal entry to record periodic amortization is a debit to Amortization Expense and a credit to Accumulated Amortization. Amortization Expense is a statement of earnings account; Accumulated Amortization appears on the balance sheet as a contra account to the related capital asset account. This contra asset account is similar in purpose to the one used in Chapter 8 for the allowance for doubtful accounts. Both contra accounts reduce assets to their respective carrying values (termed "net realizable value" for accounts receivable and "net book value" for capital assets).

Helpful Hint Remember that amortization is the process of allocating cost over the useful life of an asset. It is not a measure of value.

Recognizing amortization for an asset does not result in the accumulation of cash for replacement of the asset. The balance in Accumulated Amortization represents the total amount of the asset's cost that has been charged to expense to date; **it is not a cash fund**.

It is important to understand that **amortization is a process of cost allocation, not a process of asset valuation**. No attempt is made to measure the change in an asset's market value during ownership because capital assets are not held for resale. Thus, the **net book value**—cost less accumulated amortization—of a capital asset may differ significantly from its **market value**. In fact, if an asset is fully amortized, it can have zero book value but still have a significant market value.

Amortization applies to three classes of property, plant, and equipment: land improvements, buildings, and equipment. Each of these classes is considered an **amortizable asset** because the usefulness to the company and the revenue-producing ability of each class declines over the asset's useful life. Amortization does not apply to land because its usefulness and revenue-producing ability generally remain intact as long as the land is owned. In fact, in many cases, the usefulness of land increases over time because of the scarcity of good sites. Thus, **land is not an amortizable asset**.

Helpful Hint Land does not amortize because it does not wear out.

During an amortizable asset's useful life, its revenue-producing ability declines because of **wear and tear**. A delivery truck that has been driven 100,000 kilometres will be less useful to a company than one driven only 800 kilometres. Similarly, trucks and cars exposed to snow and salt deteriorate faster than vehicles that are not exposed to these elements.

A decline in revenue-producing ability may also occur because of **obsolescence**. Obsolescence is the process by which an asset becomes out of date before it physically wears out. For example, many companies replace their computers long before they originally planned to, because improvements in hardware and software make their old computers obsolete.

Factors in Calculating Amortization

Three factors affect the calculation of amortization, as shown in Illustration 9-6:

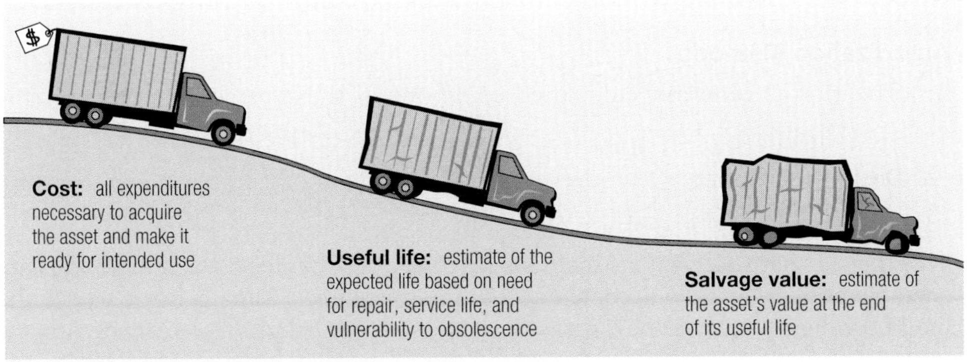

$
Cost: all expenditures necessary to acquire the asset and make it ready for intended use
Useful life: estimate of the expected life based on need for repair, service life, and vulnerability to obsolescence
Salvage value: estimate of the asset's value at the end of its useful life

Illustration 9-6
Three factors in calculating amortization

1. **Cost.** Considerations that affect the cost of an amortizable asset were explained earlier in this chapter. Remember that tangible capital assets are recorded at cost, in accordance with the cost principle.
2. **Useful life.** Useful life is an estimate of the expected productive life, also called "service life," of the asset. Useful life may be expressed in terms of time, units of activity (such as machine hours), or units of output. Useful life is an estimate. In making the estimate, management considers such factors as the intended use of the asset, repair and maintenance policies, and vulnerability of the asset to obsolescence. The company's past experience with similar assets is often helpful in determining expected useful life.
3. **Salvage value.** Salvage value is an estimate of the asset's value at the end of its useful life. The value may be based on the asset's worth as scrap or salvage, or on its expected trade-in value. Like useful life, salvage value is an estimate. In making the estimate, management considers how it plans to dispose of the asset and its experience with similar assets.

Alternative Terminology
Salvage value is also known as *residual value*.

BUSINESS INSIGHT

International Perspective

Willamette Industries, Inc. owns more than 100 pulp, paper, and other wood-product manufacturing plants in France, Ireland, Mexico, and the U.S. It said, in March 1999, that it would change its accounting estimates relating to amortization of certain assets, beginning with the first quarter of 1999. The company said the changes were due to advances in technology that have increased the service life on its equipment an extra five years. Willamette expected the accounting changes to increase its 1999 annual earnings by about $57 million, or $0.52 more per share than in 1998. Its 1998 earnings were $89 million, or $0.80 per share. Imagine a 56% improvement in earnings from a mere change in the estimated life of equipment!

BEFORE YOU GO ON . . .

Review It

1. What is the relationship, if any, of amortization to (a) cost allocation, (b) asset valuation, and (c) cash accumulation?
2. Explain the factors that affect the calculation of amortization.
3. What does Loblaw use as its estimated useful life range for its buildings? For its equipment and fixtures? For its leasehold improvements? The answer to these questions is provided at the end of this chapter.

Loblaws
A passion for food... *and a lot more!*

STUDY OBJECTIVE 3

Calculate periodic amortization using the straight-line method, and contrast its expense pattern with those of other methods.

Amortization Methods

Amortization is generally calculated using one of these three methods:

1. Straight-line
2. Declining-balance
3. Units-of-activity

Like the alternative inventory methods discussed in Chapter 6, each method is acceptable under generally accepted accounting principles. Management selects the method which it believes best measures an asset's contribution to revenue over its useful life. Once a method is chosen, it should be applied consistently over the useful life of the asset. Consistency enhances the comparability of financial statements.

Financial Reporting in Canada reports that straight-line amortization is the dominant method of amortization used in the companies it has surveyed over the past decade. Nearly 92% of companies disclosing the use of a single method of amortization in 1998 used straight-line amortization. Among those companies that disclosed the use of more than one method of amortization, 90% included the use of the straight-line method. For this reason, we illustrate procedures for straight-line amortization but only discuss the alternative approaches at a conceptual level. In this manner, we introduce you to the basic idea of amortization as an allocation concept without entangling you in too much procedural detail. (Also, note that many calculators and computers are programmed to perform the basic amortization methods.) Details on the alternative approaches are presented in the appendix to this chapter.

Our illustration of amortization methods, both here and in the appendix, is based on the following data relating to a small used delivery truck purchased by Bill's Pizzas Ltd. on January 1, 2001:

Cost	$13,000
Expected salvage value	$1,000
Estimated useful life (in years)	5
Estimated useful life (in kilometres)	100,000

Straight-Line. Under the **straight-line method**, amortization is the same for each year of the asset's useful life. It is measured solely by the passage of time. Management must choose the useful life of an asset based on its own expectations and experience. To calculate the annual amortization expense, we need to determine the amortizable cost, which represents the total amount subject to amortization. The **amortizable cost** is calculated as the cost of the asset less its salvage value. The amortizable cost is then divided by the asset's useful life to determine **amortization expense**. The calculation of amortization expense in the first year for Bill's Pizzas' delivery truck is shown in Illustration 9-7.

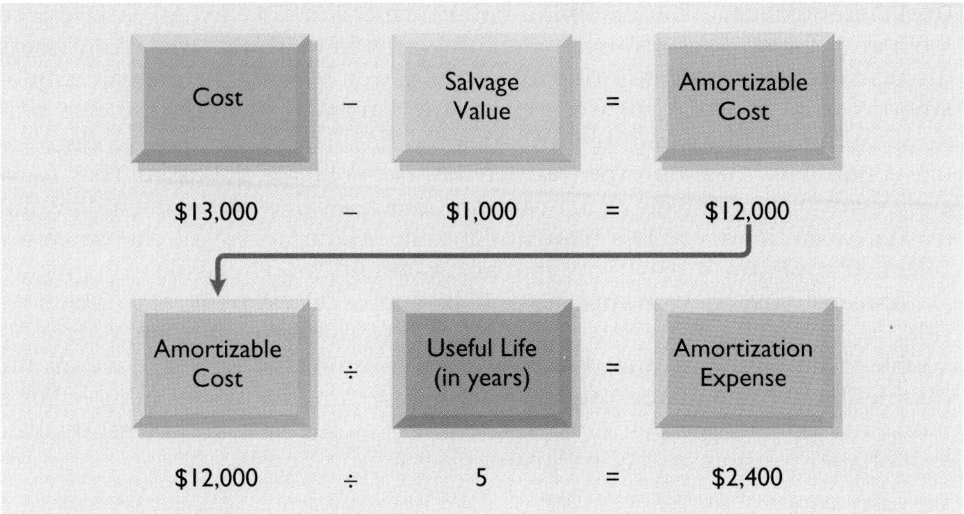

Illustration 9-7
Formula for straight-line method

Alternatively, we can calculate an annual *rate* at which the delivery truck is to be amortized. In this case, the rate is 20% (100% ÷ 5 years). When an annual rate is used under the straight-line method, the percentage rate is applied to the amortizable cost of the asset, as shown in the **amortization schedule** in Illustration 9-8.

Illustration 9-8
Straight-line amortization schedule

BILL'S PIZZAS LTD.

Year	Amortizable Cost	Amortization Rate	Annual Amortization Expense	End of Year: Accumulated Amortization	End of Year: Book Value
					$13,000
2001	$12,000	20%	$2,400	$ 2,400	10,600*
2002	12,000	20	2,400	4,800	8,200
2003	12,000	20	2,400	7,200	5,800
2004	12,000	20	2,400	9,600	3,400
2005	12,000	20	2,400	12,000	1,000
		Total	$12,000		

*$13,000 − $2,400 = $10,600

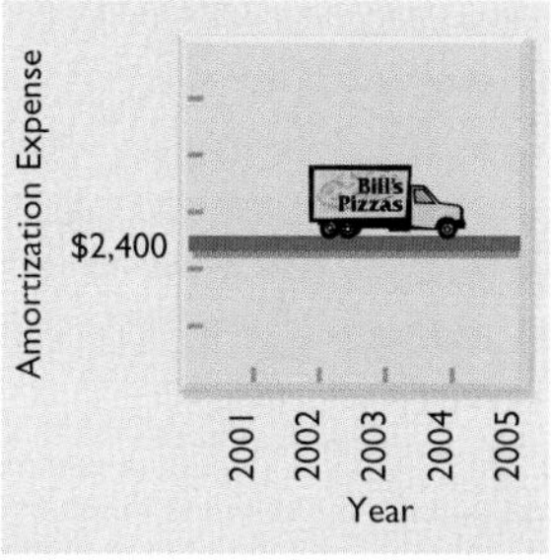

Note that the amortization expense of $2,400 is the same each year, and that the book value at the end of the useful life is equal to the estimated $1,000 salvage value.

What happens when an asset is purchased **during** the year, rather than on January 1, as in our example? In that case, it is necessary to **prorate the annual amortization** for the proportion of a year used. If Bill's Pizzas had purchased the delivery truck on April 1, 2001, the amortization for 2001 would be $1,800 ($12,000 × 20% × $\frac{9}{12}$ of a year).

As indicated earlier, the straight-line method predominates in practice. For example, such large companies as Bell Canada, Bombardier, Canadian Pacific, Domtar, Loblaw, and Northern Telecom use the straight-line method. It is simple to apply, and it matches expenses with revenues appropriately when the use of the asset is reasonably uniform throughout the service life. The types of assets that give equal benefits over useful life generally are those for which daily use does not affect productivity. Examples are office furniture and fixtures, buildings, warehouses, and garages for motor vehicles.

Alternative Terminology
The *declining-balance method* is also known as the *diminishing-balance method.*

Declining-Balance. The **declining-balance method** is called an "accelerated method" because it results in more amortization in the early years of an asset's life than does the straight-line approach. However, because the total amount of amortization (the amortizable cost) taken over an asset's life is the same no matter what approach is used, the declining-balance method produces a decreasing annual amortization expense over the useful life of the asset. That is, in early years, declining-balance amortization expense will exceed straight-line, but in later years, it will be less than straight-line. Managers might choose an accelerated approach if they think that an asset's utility will decline very quickly.

The declining-balance approach can be applied at different rates, which result in varying speeds of amortization. One declining-balance rate is double the straight-line rate. As a result, the method is often referred to as the **double-declining-balance method**. If we apply the double-declining-balance method to Bill's Pizzas' delivery truck, assuming a five-year life, we get the pattern of amortization shown in Illustration 9-9.

Illustration 9-9
Double-declining-balance amortization schedule

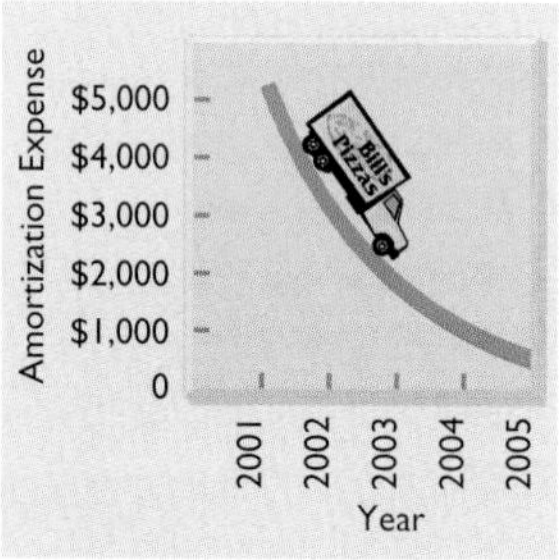

BILL'S PIZZAS LTD.

Year	Annual Amortization Expense	End of Year Accumulated Amortization	End of Year Book Value
			$13,000
2001	$ 5,200	$ 5,200	7,800
2002	3,120	8,320	4,680
2003	1,872	10,192	2,808
2004	1,123	11,315	1,685
2005	685	12,000	1,000
Total	$12,000		

The chapter's appendix presents the calculations behind these numbers. Again, note that total amortization over the life of the truck is $12,000, the amortizable cost.

Alternative Terminology
The *units-of-activity method* is also known as the *units-of-production method.*

Units-of-Activity. Under the **units-of-activity method**, instead of expressing the asset's life as a time period, useful life is expressed in terms of the total units of production or the use expected from the asset. The units-of-activity method is ideally suited to factory machinery: production can be measured in terms of units of output or in terms of machine hours used in operating the machinery. It is also possible to use the method for such items as delivery equipment (kilometres driven) and airplanes (hours in use). The units-of-activity method is generally not suitable for such assets as buildings or furniture, because amortization for these assets is a function more of time than of use.

Applying the units-of-activity method to the delivery truck owned by Bill's Pizzas, we first must know some basic information. Bill's expects to be able to drive the truck a total of 100,000 kilometres, with ongoing repairs and maintenance. Assuming that the mileage occurs in the pattern given over its five-year life, amortization in each year is shown in Illustration 9-10. The calculations used to arrive at these results are presented in the chapter's appendix.

Illustration 9-10
Units-of-activity amortization schedule

BILL'S PIZZAS LTD.				
			End of Year	
Year	Units of Activity (km)	Annual Amortization Expense	Accumulated Amortization	Book Value
				$13,000
2001	15,000	$ 1,800	$ 1,800	11,200
2002	30,000	3,600	5,400	7,600
2003	20,000	2,400	7,800	5,200
2004	25,000	3,000	10,800	2,200
2005	10,000	1,200	12,000	1,000
Total	100,000	$12,000		

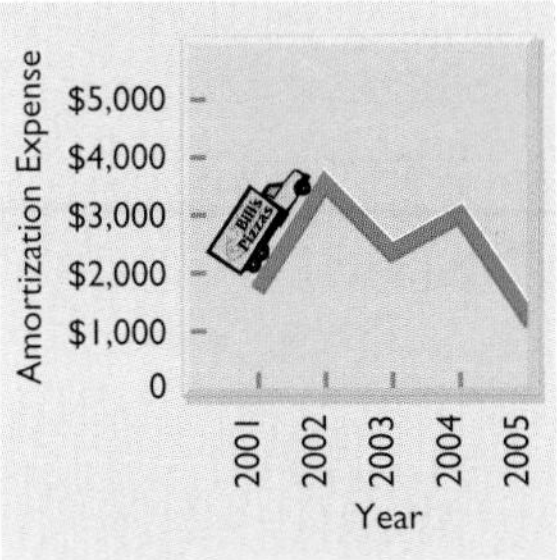

As the name implies, under units-of-activity amortization, the amount of amortization is proportional to the activity that took place during that period. For example, the delivery truck was driven twice as many kilometres in 2002 as in 2001, and amortization was exactly twice as much in 2002 as it was in 2001.

Management's Choice: Comparison of Methods. Illustration 9-11 presents a comparison of annual and total amortization expense for Bill's Pizzas under the three methods. In addition, if we assume (as we have in the illustration) that net earnings, prior to deducting amortization expense, were $25,000 for each of the five years, we can clearly see the impact the choice of method has on net earnings.

Illustration 9-11
Comparison of amortization methods and effects on earnings

	Straight-Line		Double-Declining-Balance		Unit-of-Activity	
Year	Amortization Expense	Net Earnings	Amortization Expense	Net Earnings	Amortization Expense	Net Earnings
2001	$ 2,400	$ 22,600	$ 5,200	$ 19,800	$ 1,800	$ 23,200
2002	2,400	22,600	3,120	21,880	3,600	21,400
2003	2,400	22,600	1,872	23,128	2,400	22,600
2004	2,400	22,600	1,123	23,877	3,000	22,000
2005	2,400	22,600	685	24,315	1,200	23,800
	$12,000	$113,000	$12,000	$113,000	$12,000	$113,000

As discussed earlier, straight-line amortization results in a constant amount of expense and earnings impact each year. Declining-balance results in a higher expense in the early years, and correspondingly lower earnings, and a lower expense in later years, with correspondingly higher earnings. The units-of-activity method results vary depending on actual usage each year. While periodic amortization and net earnings vary considerably each year among methods, *total* amortization and *total* net earnings are the same for a five-year period.

Each method is acceptable in accounting because each recognizes the decline in service potential of the asset in a rational and systematic manner. The amortization expense pattern under each method is presented in Illustration 9-12. The net earnings pattern (not shown) is inverted.

Illustration 9-12
Patterns of amortization

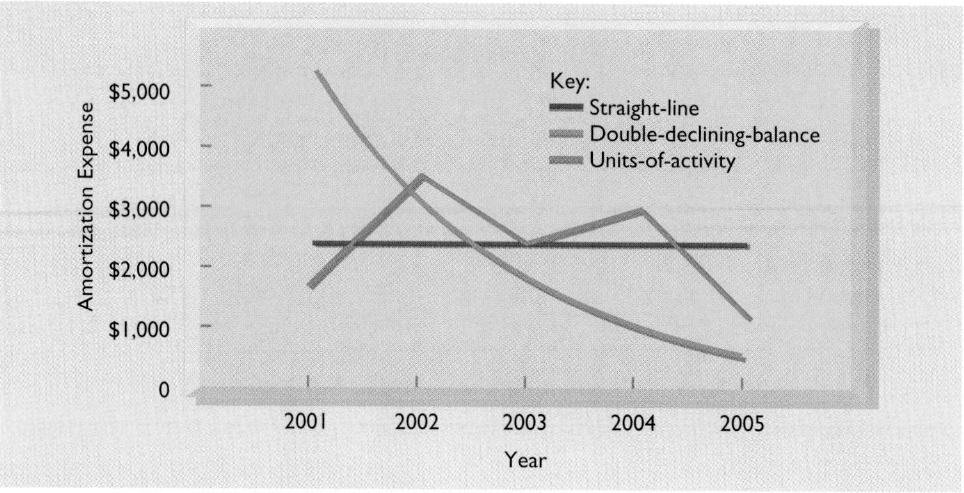

Helpful Hint Amortization per GAAP is usually different from amortization per tax regulations.

International Note

In Germany, tax laws have a strong influence on financial accounting. Amortization expense determined by the tax code must also be used for preparing financial statements.

Amortization and Income Taxes

The Canada Customs and Revenue Agency allows corporate taxpayers to deduct a specified amount of amortization expense when calculating taxable income. For accounting purposes, a company should choose the amortization method that best matches revenue to expense. Tax regulations have different objectives. Income tax regulations require the taxpayer to use a defined amortization method—single-declining-balance—on the tax return, regardless of which method is used in preparing financial statements.

The Canada Customs and Revenue Agency also does not permit corporations to estimate the useful lives, or amortization rates, of assets. It groups assets into various classes and provides maximum amortization rates for each class of capital assets. Amortization allowed for income tax purposes is calculated on a class (group) basis, and is termed capital cost allowance (CCA). Capital cost allowance is an optional deduction from taxable income, so you may see some businesses deducting amortization for accounting purposes (required to fulfill the matching principle) while deducting no CCA for tax purposes.

Amortization Disclosure in the Notes

The choice of amortization method must be disclosed in a company's financial statements or in the related notes that accompany the statements. Illustration 9-13 shows the "property and equipment" notes from the financial statements of Air Canada and the former Canadian Airlines.

Illustration 9-13
Disclosure of amortization policies

AIR CANADA
Notes to the Financial Statements

Depreciation and Amortization Operating property and equipment are depreciated or amortized to estimated residual values based on the straight-line method over their estimated service lives.

	Period of Amortization
Air Canada	20 years
Subsidiaries	12–20 years

Significant aircraft reconfiguration costs are amortized over 3 years. Aircraft introduction costs are amortized over 4 years. Betterments to aircraft on operating leases are amortized over the term of the lease.

CANADIAN AIRLINES CORPORATION
Notes to the Financial Statements

Property and equipment Amortization is provided at straight-line rates to estimated residual values based on the following estimated useful lives:

Asset	Basis
Flight equipment	5–20 years
Buildings	10–40 years
Ground equipment	5–10 years

From these notes, we learn that both companies use the straight-line method to amortize their planes, and other capital assets. At first glance, Canadian Airlines appears to be more conservative than Air Canada, because it is amortizing its planes over a shorter average life. However, Canadian has an older fleet than Air Canada, so it is not surprising that the company is using a shorter estimated life.

Revising Periodic Amortization

STUDY OBJECTIVE 4

Describe the procedure for revising periodic amortization.

Annual amortization expense should be reviewed periodically by management. If wear and tear or obsolescence indicates that annual amortization is inadequate or excessive, the amortization expense amount should be changed.

When a change in an estimate is required, the change is made in **current and future years but not to prior periods**. Thus, when a change is made, (1) there is no correction of previously recorded amortization expense, and (2) amortization expense for current and future years is revised. The rationale for this treatment is that continual restatement of prior periods would adversely affect the user's confidence in financial statements. The revised amortization is calculated using the net book value at the time of the change in estimate, the revised salvage value, and the remaining useful life.

Significant changes in estimates must be disclosed in the financial statements. Although a company may have a legitimate reason for changing an estimated life, financial statement users should be aware that some companies might change an estimate simply to achieve financial statement goals. For example, extending an asset's estimated life reduces amortization expense and increases current period earnings.

BEFORE YOU GO ON . . .

Review It

1. Why is amortization an allocation concept rather than a valuation concept?
2. What is the formula for calculating annual amortization under the straight-line method?
3. How do the amortization methods differ in their effects on annual amortization over the useful life of an asset?
4. Are revisions of periodic amortization made to prior periods? Explain.

Do It

On January 1, 2001, Iron Mountain Ski Corporation purchased a new snow grooming machine for $50,000. The machine is estimated to have a 10-year life with a $2,000 salvage value.

(a) What journal entry would Iron Mountain Ski Corporation make at December 31, 2001, if it uses the straight-line method of amortization?

(b) What journal entry would Iron Mountain Ski Corporation make at December 31, 2003, if it was decided on January 1, 2003, that the machine only had a five-year life remaining at that time with no salvage value?

Reasoning:

(a) Amortization is an allocation concept. Under straight-line amortization an equal amount of the amortizable cost is allocated to each period.

(b) The amortization expense for 2001 and 2002 was estimated on the basis of the best information available at the time. So we revise amortization for the current and future periods, not the past. Consequently, we must commence our calculation with the net book value in order to recognize the amortization that has already been deducted. No journal entry is made on January 1, 2003 but the December 31 journal entry reflects the revised amortization.

Solution:

(a)

$$\text{Amortization expense} = \frac{\text{Cost} - \text{Salvage value}}{\text{Useful life}} = \frac{\$50{,}000 - \$2{,}000}{10} = \$4{,}800$$

The entry to record the first year's amortization would be:

Dec. 31, 2001	Amortization Expense	4,800	
	Accumulated Amortization		4,800
	(To record annual amortization on snow grooming machine)		

(b) At January 1, 2003, the net book value of the grooming machine was $40,400 and the revised annual amortization, $8,080, calculated as follows:

Cost	$50,000
Accumulated amortization ($4,800 x 2 years)	9,600
Net book value	40,400
Less: Revised salvage value	0
Revised amortizable cost	40,400
Remaining useful life (7 years revised total life – 2 years passed)	5 years
Revised annual amortization	$ 8,080

The journal entry to record amortization at December 31, 2003 would be:

Dec. 31, 2003	Amortization Expense	8,080	
	Accumulated Amortization		8,080
	(To record annual amortization on snow grooming machine)		

Note below that the total amortization over the life of the machine equals its net book value at the end of its useful life ($50,000 cost – $0 salvage value):

Year	Amortization Expense
2001	$ 4,800
2002	4,800
2003	8,080
2004	8,080
2005	8,080
2006	8,080
2007	8,080
	$50,000

EXPENDITURES DURING USEFUL LIFE

During the useful life of a capital asset, a company may incur costs for ordinary repairs, additions, and improvements. **Ordinary repairs** are expenditures to maintain the operating efficiency and expected productive life of the unit. They are usually fairly small amounts that occur frequently throughout the service life. Motor tune-ups and oil changes, the painting of buildings, and the replacing of worn-out gears on factory machinery are examples. They are debited to Repair (or Maintenance) Expense as incurred. Because they are immediately charged against revenues as an expense, these costs are **revenue or operating expenditures**.

Additions and improvements are costs incurred to increase the operating efficiency, productive capacity, or expected useful life of the capital asset. These expenditures are usually material in amount and occur infrequently during the period of ownership. Expenditures for additions and improvements increase the company's investment in productive facilities and are generally debited to the plant asset affected. Accordingly, they are **capital expenditures**. The accounting for capital expenditures varies, depending on the nature of the expenditure.

Helpful Hint These expenditures occur after all costs have been incurred to make the asset ready for its intended use when it was acquired.

In order to comply with noise abatement regulations, Air Canada must either replace certain aircraft or install "hushkits" before April 1, 2002. Air Canada's entire operating fleet, except its DC-9s and the aircraft it acquired from Canadian Airlines, currently meets the noise standards. Air Canada does not intend to install hushkits on its DC-9 fleet. For the former Canadian Airlines' fleet, hushkitting is a reasonably priced alternative to purchasing new aircraft. Any costs incurred to install these hushkits would be treated as capital expenditures. Other recurring costs, such as maintenance and repairs, including major flight overhauls, are charged to expense as incurred.

IMPAIRMENTS

As noted earlier, the book value of capital assets is rarely the same as the market value. In instances where the market value of a capital asset declines substantially, its market value may be materially below book value. This may happen because a machine has become obsolete, or the market for the product made by the machine has dried up or has become very competitive. A **permanent decline** in the market value of an asset is referred to as an **impairment**. To prevent the asset from being overstated on the books, it is written down to its new market value during the year in which the decline in value occurs. In the past, some companies delayed recording losses on impairments until a year when it was "convenient" to do so—when the impact on the firm's reported results was minimized. For example, if a firm has record profits in one year, it can then afford to write down some of its bad assets without hurting its reported results too much. The practice of timing the recognition of gains and losses to achieve certain income results is known as **earnings management**. Immediate recognition of these write-downs is now required in order to reduce the practice of earnings management. Thirteen percent of the 200 companies sampled by *Financial Reporting in Canada* reported write-downs of tangible capital assets in a recent year.

BUSINESS INSIGHT

Investor Perspective

In recent years, companies such as IBM, 3M, Westinghouse, and Digital Equipment Corporation have reported huge write-downs. These companies are quick to emphasize that these are "nonrecurring events"; that is, they are one-time charges and thus do not represent a recurring drag on future earnings. However, a number of large firms have reported large write-downs in multiple years, which makes analysts suspicious. After one of IBM's recent write-downs, one analyst recommended not buying IBM shares because, with such frequent write-downs, "What confidence do we have the same will not happen again?"

STUDY OBJECTIVE 5

Explain how to account for the disposal of tangible capital assets.

TANGIBLE CAPITAL ASSET DISPOSALS

Companies dispose of tangible capital assets that are no longer useful to them. Illustration 9-14 shows the three ways in which tangible capital assets are disposed of.

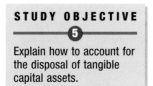

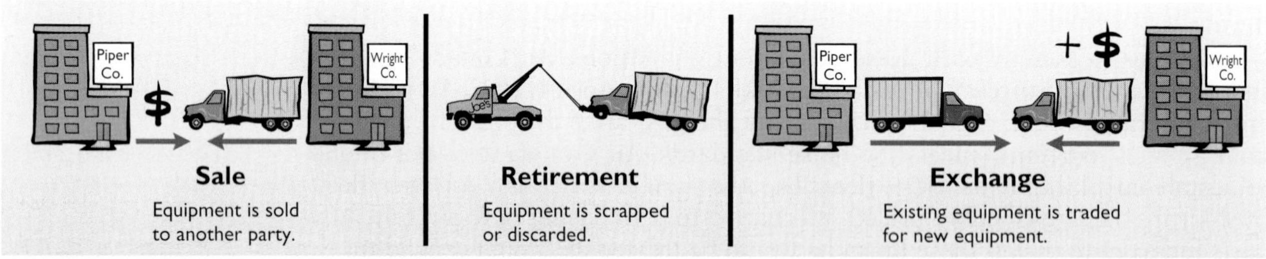
Piper Co.
Wright Co.
$
Sale
Equipment is sold to another party.
Retirement
Equipment is scrapped or discarded.
Piper Co.
+ $
Wright Co.
Exchange
Existing equipment is traded for new equipment.

Illustration 9-14
Methods of capital asset disposal

Whatever the disposal method, the company must determine the book value of the asset at the time of disposal. Recall that the book value is the difference between the cost of the asset and the accumulated amortization to date. If the disposal occurs at any time during the year, amortization for the fraction of the year to the date of disposal must be recorded. The book value is then eliminated by reducing (debiting) Accumulated Amortization for the total amortization associated with that asset to the date of disposal, and reducing (crediting) the asset account for the cost of the asset.

Sale of Property, Plant, and Equipment

In a disposal by sale, the book value of the asset is compared with the proceeds received from the sale. If the proceeds from the sale exceed the book value of the capital asset, a **gain on disposal** occurs. If the proceeds from the sale are less than the book value of the asset sold, a **loss on disposal** occurs.

Only by coincidence will the book value and the fair market value of the asset be the same at the time the asset is sold. Gains and losses on sales of capital assets are therefore quite common. As an example, Canadian Pacific reported a $37 million loss on the sale of its CP Trucks.

Gain on Sale. To illustrate a gain on sale of property, plant, and equipment, assume that on July 1, 2001, Wright Company Ltd. sells office furniture for $16,000 cash. The office furniture originally cost $60,000 and as at January 1, 2001, had accumulated amortization of $41,000. Amortization for the first six months of 2001 is $8,000. The entry to record amortization expense and update accumulated amortization to July 1 is as follows:

July 1	Amortization Expense	8,000	
	Accumulated Amortization—Office Furniture		8,000
	(To record amortization expense for the first six months of 2001)		

A	=	L	+	SE
-8,000				-8,000

After the accumulated amortization balance is updated, a gain on disposal of $5,000 is calculated as shown in Illustration 9-15.

Illustration 9-15
Calculation of gain on disposal

Cost of office furniture	$60,000
Less: Accumulated amortization ($41,000 + $8,000)	49,000
Book value at date of disposal	11,000
Proceeds from sale	16,000
Gain on disposal of capital asset	**$ 5,000**

The entry to record the sale and the gain on sale of the capital asset is as follows:

July 1	Cash	16,000	
	Accumulated Amortization—Office Furniture	49,000	
	Office Furniture		60,000
	Gain on Disposal		5,000
	(To record sale of office furniture at a gain)		

A	=	L	+	SE
+16,000				+5,000
+49,000				
-60,000				

The gain on disposal of the capital asset is usually reported in the Other Revenues and Gains section of the statement of earnings.

Loss on Sale. Assume that instead of selling the office furniture for $16,000, Wright sells it for $9,000. In this case, a loss of $2,000 is calculated as in Illustration 9-16.

Illustration 9-16
Calculation of loss on disposal

Cost of office furniture	$60,000
Less: Accumulated amortization	49,000
Book value at date of disposal	11,000
Proceeds from sale	9,000
Loss on disposal of capital asset	**$ 2,000**

The entry to record the sale and the loss on sale of the capital asset is as follows:

A	=	L	+	SE
+9,000				-2,000
+49,000				
-60,000				

July 1	Cash	9,000	
	Accumulated Amortization—Office Furniture	49,000	
	Loss on Disposal	2,000	
	Office Furniture		60,000
	(To record sale of office furniture at a loss)		

The loss on disposal of the capital asset is usually reported in the Other Expenses and Losses section of the statement of earnings.

Retirement of Property, Plant, and Equipment

Some assets are simply retired by the company at the end of their useful life rather than sold. For example, some productive assets used in manufacturing may have very specific uses and consequently have no ready market when the company no longer needs them. In this case, the asset is simply retired.

Retirement of an asset is recorded as a special case of a sale where no cash is received. Accumulated Amortization is decreased (debited) for the full amount of amortization taken over the life of the asset. The asset account is reduced (credited) for the original cost of the asset. The loss (a gain is not possible on a retirement) is equal to the asset's book value on the date of retirement.

The accounting for exchanges, the third method of disposal of property, plant, and equipment, is discussed in more advanced courses.

BEFORE YOU GO ON . . .

Review It

1. What is the difference between an ordinary repair and an addition or improvement? Why is this distinction important to financial reporting?
2. What is an impairment? Can companies manage their earnings through the write-downs associated with impairments?
3. What is the proper accounting for sales and retirements of property, plant, and equipment?

Do It

Overland Trucking Ltd. has an old truck that cost $30,000 and has accumulated amortization of $16,000. Assume two different situations: (1) the company sells the old truck for $17,000 cash, and (2) the truck is worthless, so the company simply retires it. What entry should Overland use to record each scenario?

Reasoning: Gains and losses on the sale or retirement of property, plant, and equipment are determined by the difference between the book value and the proceeds (fair market value) received from selling the company's asset.

Solution:

1. Sale of truck for cash:

Cash	17,000	
Accumulated Amortization—Truck	16,000	
Truck		30,000
Gain on Disposal [$17,000 – ($30,000 – $16,000)]		3,000
(To record sale of truck at a gain)		

2. Retirement of truck:

Accumulated Amortization—Truck	16,000	
Loss on Disposal	14,000	
Truck		30,000
(To record retirement of truck at a loss)		

Analysing Tangible Capital Assets

The presentation of financial statement information about tangible capital assets enables decision-makers to analyse the company's use of its property, plant, and equipment. We will use three ratios to analyse tangible capital assets: average useful life of property, plant, and equipment; average age of property, plant, and equipment; and the asset turnover ratio.

AVERAGE USEFUL LIFE OF PROPERTY, PLANT, AND EQUIPMENT

STUDY OBJECTIVE 6

Describe methods for evaluating the use of tangible capital assets.

By selecting a longer estimated useful life, a company spreads the cost of its capital assets over a longer period of time. As a result, the amount of amortization expense reported in each period is lower and net earnings are higher. A more conservative company will choose a shorter estimated useful life and will have a lower reported net income.

In the notes to financial statements, many companies are not very precise about the estimated useful life of specific assets. For example, a common disclosure might read, "Property, plant, and equipment are amortized using the straight-line method over estimated useful lives ranging from 5 to 40 years." This statement makes it difficult to determine whether a company is using a conservative approach for amortization. It is unclear, for example, how many assets are being amortized using short lives and how many using long lives. To overcome this problem, we can estimate the **average useful life** of tangible capital assets for a company and compare it to that of its competitors. The average useful life is estimated by dividing the average cost of property, plant, and equipment by the amortization expense.

The following data are for Air Canada and Canadian Airlines, prior to Air Canada's acquisition of Canadian Airlines.

($ in millions)	Air Canada	Canadian Airlines
Total cost of property and equipment—1998	$4,807	$1,448
Total cost of property and equipment—1997	4,369	1,512
Amortization expense—1998	292	120

Illustration 9-17 presents a calculation of the average useful life used by Air Canada and Canadian Airlines.

Illustration 9-17
Average useful life of property, plant, and equipment

$$\text{AVERAGE USEFUL LIFE OF PROPERTY, PLANT, AND EQUIPMENT} = \frac{\text{AVERAGE COST OF PROPERTY, PLANT, AND EQUIPMENT}}{\text{AMORTIZATION EXPENSE}}$$

Air Canada ($ in millions)	Canadian Airlines ($ in millions)
$\frac{(\$4,807 + \$4,369)/2}{\$292} = 15.7 \text{ years}$	$\frac{(\$1,448 + \$1,512)/2}{\$120} = 12.3 \text{ years}$

We estimate an average useful life of nearly 16 years for Air Canada and 12 years for Canadian. These estimates are consistent with the information published in their notes, shown earlier in this chapter.

We recommend that, when analysing a company, you use the estimate of the average useful life only as a check on the company's published amortizable lives. It is a rough approximation at best but can be useful when a company does not provide detailed disclosure for specific assets.

DECISION TOOLKIT

Decision Checkpoints	Info Needed for Decision	Tool to Use for Decision	How to Evaluate Results
Is the company's estimated useful life for amortization reasonable?	Estimated useful life of capital assets from notes to financial statements of this company and its competitors	If the company's estimated useful life significantly exceeds that of competitors, or does not seem reasonable in light of the circumstances, the reason for the difference should be investigated. If notes do not provide sufficient detail, average useful life can be estimated as follows: $\text{Average useful life} = \frac{\text{Average cost of property, plant, and equipment}}{\text{Amortization expense}}$	Too high an estimated useful life will result in understating amortization expense and overstating net earnings.

AVERAGE AGE OF PROPERTY, PLANT, AND EQUIPMENT

Consider the importance of new planes to an airline. Not only are newer planes more fuel efficient, they also require less maintenance and are safer—key features for an airline. Comparing the average age of tangible capital assets gives an indication of the potential effectiveness of a company's capital assets relative to the assets of competitors in the industry. Air Canada reports information about its fleet utilization and fleet renewal plans in its annual report. Although most companies do not report the age of their assets, because most companies use straight-line amortization, the **average age** of their capital assets can be approximated by dividing accumulated amortization by amortization expense. For example, if deVos Corp. has accumulated amortization of \$30,000 and amortization expense of \$10,000, the average age of its capital assets is three years (\$30,000 ÷ \$10,000).

The following 1998 data are for Air Canada and Canadian Airlines, again prior to the acquisition and combination of the two airlines:

($ in millions)	Air Canada	Canadian Airlines
Accumulated amortization	$1,925	$423
Amortization expense	292	120

The average age of property and equipment for Air Canada and Canadian is estimated in Illustration 9-18.

Illustration 9-18
Average age of property, plant, and equipment

$$\text{AVERAGE AGE OF PROPERTY, PLANT, AND EQUIPMENT} = \frac{\text{ACCUMULATED AMORTIZATION}}{\text{AMORTIZATION EXPENSE}}$$

Air Canada ($ in millions)	Canadian Airlines ($ in millions)
$\frac{\$1,925}{\$292} = 6.6$ years	$\frac{\$423}{\$120} = 3.5$ years

As neither airline provides information about amortization by major class of asset, we cannot refine our estimate. If, for example, they provided information on planes and buildings separately, we could calculate each and have a more precise estimate of the average age of planes and of buildings. Given the information available, we can only calculate the average age of property and equipment in general.

With that in mind, these numbers suggest that the average age of an Air Canada plane was 6.6 years, and the average age of a Canadian Airlines plane was 3.5 years. From this, one might conclude that Canadian's planes were substantially newer than those of Air Canada. But we know from information presented earlier in the chapter that Canadian has an older fleet than Air Canada—with an average useful life of 12 years. So what is wrong with our estimate?

Our estimate of average age is wrong because the ratio does not work when a company purchases used assets. The figure of 3.5 years tells us that Canadian has owned these assets for 3.5 years. If they had been purchased new, they would be 3.5 years old. However, if they were 24 years old when purchased, they would now be 27.5 years old. This is an important lesson: Never use ratios unless you fully understand their strengths and weaknesses. Ratios can be very informative but also very misleading.

DECISION TOOLKIT

Decision Checkpoints	Info Needed for Decision	Tool to Use for Decision	How to Evaluate Results
Are the company's capital assets possibly outdated or in need of replacement?	Amortization expense and accumulated amortization	$\text{Average age} = \frac{\text{Accumulated amortization}}{\text{Amortization expense}}$	A high average age relative to competitors might suggest that the company's assets are not as efficient, or that they may be in need of replacement.

ASSET TURNOVER RATIO

The **asset turnover ratio** indicates how efficiently a company is able to generate sales with a given amount of assets—that is, how many dollars of sales are generated by each dollar invested in assets. It is calculated by dividing net sales by average total assets. When we compare two firms in the same industry, the one with the higher asset turnover ratio is operating more efficiently. It is generating more sales per dollar invested in assets.

The following data are for Air Canada and the former Canadian Airlines. We will use operating revenues as a proxy for net sales.

($ in millions)	Air Canada	Canadian Airlines
Total assets—1998	$6,422	$2,099
Total assets—1997	5,991	1,911
Operating revenues—1998	5,932	3,171

The asset turnover ratios for Air Canada and Canadian for 1998 are calculated in Illustration 9-19.

Illustration 9-19
Asset turnover ratio

$$\text{ASSET TURNOVER RATIO} = \frac{\text{NET SALES}}{\text{AVERAGE TOTAL ASSETS}}$$

Air Canada ($ in millions)	Canadian Airlines ($ in millions)
$\frac{\$5,932}{(\$6,422 + \$5,991)/2} = 0.96$ times	$\frac{\$3,171}{(\$2,099 + \$1,911)/2} = 1.58$ times

The asset turnover ratios mean that for each dollar invested in assets, Air Canada generates sales of $0.96 and Canadian, $1.58. Canadian was more successful in generating sales per dollar invested in assets, perhaps due in part to its decision to buy older planes. The average asset turnover ratio for the airline industry is 1.01 times.

Asset turnover ratios vary considerably across industries. The average asset turnover for utility companies is 0.45, and the grocery store industry has an average asset turnover of 3.49. Asset turnover ratios, therefore, are only comparable within—not between—industries.

For a complete picture, one would want to also look at the companies' profit margin ratios. Canadian's decision to keep its planes longer might mean that it incurs more costs per dollar of sales (for things like repairs and additional fuel), which would result in a lower profit per dollar of sales, as measured by the profit margin ratio. And, indeed that's exactly what happened. Canadian Airlines' rapidly deteriorating profit picture made it an easy takeover candidate for Air Canada.

DECISION TOOLKIT

Decision Checkpoints	Info Needed for Decision	Tool to Use for Decision	How to Evaluate Results
How effective is the company at generating sales from its assets?	Net sales and average total assets	Asset turnover ratio $= \frac{\text{Net sales}}{\text{Average total assets}}$	Indicates the sales dollars generated per dollar of assets. A high value suggests the company is effective in using its resources to generate sales.

BEFORE YOU GO ON . . .

Review It

1. How can we estimate the average useful life of property, plant, and equipment?
2. What is the purpose of the calculation of the average age of property, plant, and equipment? How is it calculated?
3. What is the purpose of the asset turnover ratio? How is it calculated?

SECTION 2

INTANGIBLE CAPITAL ASSETS

Intangible capital assets are rights, privileges, and competitive advantages that result from ownership of long-lived assets that do not possess physical substance. Many companies' most valuable assets are intangible. Some widely known intangibles are Alexander Graham Bell's patent on the telephone, the franchises of Second Cup, the trade name of Canadian Beverages, and the trademark CBC.

As you will learn in this section, although financial statements do report many intangibles, many other financially significant intangibles are not reported. To give an example, according to its 1999 opening financial statements, Chapters Online Inc. had a net book value of less than \$9 million. However, it raised more than \$45 million with the initial public offering of its common shares. Thus, its actual market value was nearly \$37 million greater than what its balance sheet said the company was worth at that time. It is not uncommon for a company's reported book value to differ from its market value, because balance sheets are reported at historical cost. But such an extreme difference seriously diminishes the usefulness of the balance sheet to decision-makers. In the case of Chapters Online, some of the difference is due to unrecorded intangibles. For many high-tech or intellectual property companies, some of their value is from intangibles, many of which are not reported under current accounting rules.

Intangibles may be evidenced by contracts, licences, and other documents. Intangibles may arise from the following sources:

1. Government grants such as patents, copyrights, franchises, trademarks, and trade names
2. Acquisition of another business in which the purchase price includes a payment for goodwill
3. Private monopolistic arrangements arising from contractual agreements, such as franchises and leases

ACCOUNTING FOR INTANGIBLE CAPITAL ASSETS

STUDY OBJECTIVE 7

Identify the basic issues related to reporting intangible capital assets.

Intangible capital assets are recorded at cost, and this cost is expensed **over the useful life of the intangible asset in a rational and systematic manner**. The term used to describe the allocation of the cost of an intangible asset to expense is also called amortization, as with tangible capital assets. To record amortization of an intangible, amortization expense is increased (debited) and the specific intangible asset account is decreased (credited). Unlike tangible capital assets, no contra account, such as Accumulated Amortization, is used. Amortization expense is classified as an **operating expense** in the statement of earnings. At disposal, the book value of the intangible asset is eliminated, and a gain or loss, if any, is recorded.

As time, including legal life, is usually the most relevant factor for the pattern of use of intangible assets, intangibles are typically amortized on a straight-line basis over the shorter of their useful life or legal life. **In no case can the amortization period be longer than 40 years.** Normally, the useful life of the intangible asset is the shortest period, and so it is the one used as the amortization period. However, where the useful life and legal life (if any) exceed 40 years, the 40-year maximum applies. This rule helps ensure that all intangibles, especially those with indeterminate lives, will be written off in a reasonable period of time.

When analysing a company that has significant intangibles, the reasonableness of the estimated useful life should be evaluated. In determining useful life, the company should consider obsolescence, inadequacy, and other factors; these may cause an intangible to become economically ineffective before the end of its legal life. For example, suppose a computer hardware manufacturer obtained a patent on a new computer chip that it had developed. The legal life of the patent is 20 years (we will discuss patents in the next section). From experience, we know that the useful life of a computer chip is not more than four to five years, and often less—because new, superior chips are developed so rapidly, existing chips quickly become obsolete. Consequently, we would question the amortization expense of a company if it amortized its patent on a computer chip for longer than a five-year period. Amortizing an intangible over a period that is too long will understate amortization expense, overstate the company's net earnings, and overstate its assets.

DECISION TOOLKIT

Decision Checkpoints	Info Needed for Decision	Tool to Use for Decision	How to Evaluate Results
Is the company's amortization of intangibles reasonable?	Estimated useful life of intangibles from notes to financial statements of this company and its competitors	If the company's estimated useful life significantly exceeds that of competitors, or does not seem reasonable in light of the circumstances, the reason for the difference should be investigated.	Too high an estimated useful life will result in understating amortization expense and overstating net earnings.

TYPES OF INTANGIBLE CAPITAL ASSETS

PATENTS

A **patent** is an exclusive right issued by the Canadian Intellectual Property Office of Industry Canada that enables the recipient to manufacture, sell, or otherwise control an invention for a period of 20 years from the date of the application. **The initial cost of a patent is the cash or cash equivalent price paid to acquire the patent.**

The cost of a patent should be amortized over its 20-year legal life or its useful life, whichever is shorter. To illustrate the calculation of patent amortization, assume that National Labs purchases a patent at a cost of $60,000. If the useful life of the patent is estimated to be eight years, the annual amortization expense is $7,500 ($60,000 ÷ 8). The following entry records the annual amortization:

Dec. 31	Amortization Expense	7,500	
	Patent		7,500
	(To record patent amortization)		

A	=	L	+	SE
-7,500				-7,500

The saying "A patent is only as good as the money you're prepared to spend defending it" is very true. Most patents are subject to some type of litigation by competitors. A well-known example is the patent infringement suit won by Polaroid against Eastman Kodak in protecting its patent on instant cameras. If the owner incurs legal costs in successfully defending the patent in an infringement suit, such costs are considered necessary to establish the validity of the patent. Thus, **they are added to the Patent account and amortized over the remaining life of the patent**.

BUSINESS INSIGHT

Management Perspective

Other Canadian inventions have done more to change people's lives—Pablum, basketball, the Canadarm on the space shuttle—but the giant screen Imax film format ranks as one of this country's more memorable contributions to world culture. Five Canadians founded Imax and pioneered the giant screen, large format film medium, first introduced at Expo '70 in Osaka. Imax was subsequently sold to three U.S. investment bankers and a U.S. filmmaker for US$100 million. Although the carrying value of the invention was much smaller on the prior owners' books—essentially the cost of registering the patent—it now sits at a substantially higher amount on its new owners' books—the US$100 million which was spent to acquire Imax.

RESEARCH AND DEVELOPMENT COSTS

International Note

Accounting for R&D differs dramatically across nations. U.S. GAAP, as well as German, does not allow any R&D expenses to be capitalized, while other nations such as Canada, Great Britain, Japan, and Korea permit limited capitalization of some development costs. Still other countries, such as Italy, Sweden, and Brazil, have much more liberal R&D policies allowing full capitalization.

Helpful Hint Research and development costs are not intangible costs, but because these expenditures may lead to patents and copyrights, we discuss them in this section.

Research and development (R&D) costs are expenditures that may lead to patents, copyrights, new processes, and new products. Many companies spend considerable sums of money on research and development in an ongoing effort to develop new products or processes. For example, in a recent year Northern Telecom spent over $3 billion on research and development. There are many uncertainties in identifying the extent and timing of the future benefits of these expenditures. As a result, research costs are **always recorded as an expense when incurred**, whether the research and development is successful or not. Certain development costs with reasonable assured future benefits can be capitalized; otherwise, they must also be expensed.

To illustrate, assume that Laser Scanner Inc. spent $3 million on research and $2 million on development that resulted in two highly successful patents. The $3-million research cost cannot be included in the cost of the patent. Rather, it is recorded as an expense when incurred. The development cost of $2 million would be capitalized and included in the cost of the patent, since the development was successful.

Many disagree with this accounting approach. They argue that to expense research and some development costs leads to understated assets and net earnings. Others, however, argue that capitalizing these costs would lead to highly speculative assets on the balance sheet. Who is right is difficult to determine.

COPYRIGHTS

Copyrights are granted by the Canadian Intellectual Property Office, giving the owner the exclusive right to reproduce and sell an artistic or published work. Copyrights extend for the life of the creator plus 50 years. The cost of the copyright consists of the **cost of acquiring and defending it**. The cost may be only the fee paid, or it may amount to a great deal more if a copyright infringement suit is involved. Generally, the useful life of a copyright is significantly shorter than its legal life, and the copyright is therefore amortized over its useful life (not to exceed 40 years).

TRADEMARKS AND TRADE NAMES

A **trademark** or **trade name** is a word, phrase, jingle, or symbol that distinguishes or identifies a particular enterprise or product. Trade names like the Blue Jays, Swoosh, Kleenex, Coca-Cola, President's Choice, the Habs, and TSN create immediate product identification and generally enhance the sale of the product. The creator or original user may obtain the exclusive legal right to the trademark or trade name by registering it with the Canadian Intellectual Property Office. Such registration provides continuous protection and may be renewed every 15 years as long as the trademark or trade name is in use.

If the trademark or trade name is purchased, the cost is the purchase price. If it is developed by the enterprise itself, the cost includes legal fees, registration fees, design costs, successful legal defence costs, and other expenditures directly related to securing it.

As with other intangibles, the cost of trademarks and trade names must be amortized over the shorter of their useful life or 40 years. Because of the uncertainty involved in estimating the useful life, the cost is frequently amortized over a much shorter period.

BUSINESS INSIGHT

Management Perspective

Domain names are a good example of a trade name. Buying domain names is a hot market these days. Canada's domain name system has strict regulations to ensure that dot.ca Web addresses are granted to legitimate organizations and holders of registered trademarks. While the cost of registration is negligible, if a company has to purchase its name from a cybersquatter—people who register names in the hopes of reselling them for a profit—the cost can rise quickly.

When eBay Inc., the world's largest on-line auction house, recently tried to register <www.ebay.ca>, it discovered that the name had been registered previously by a Dartmouth, N.S., entrepreneur. eBay then had two options to consider. Since eBay is a registered trademark around the world, the company could take legal action, or it could negotiate to buy the name from the current registrant. In the meantime, eBay is using the domain name <www.ebaycanada.ca>, which had also been registered previously by a self-described "Internet entrepreneur." This Kelowna, B.C., entrepreneur said he hoped to make some quick money when he registered <www.ebaycanada.ca> last year. He eventually gave up the name without a fight rather than going to court and facing huge legal bills.

FRANCHISES AND LICENCES

When you drive down the street in your Protegé purchased from a Mazda dealer, fill up your tank at the corner Petro-Canada station, eat lunch at Wendy's, and buy coffee from Tim Hortons, you are dealing with franchises. A **franchise** is a contractual arrangement under which the franchisor grants the franchisee the right to sell certain products, to render specific services, or to use certain trademarks or trade names, usually within a designated geographic area.

Another type of franchise, granted by a governmental body, permits the enterprise to use public property in performing its services. Examples are the use of city streets for a bus line or taxi service; the use of public land for telephone, electric, and cable television lines; and the use of airwaves for radio or TV broadcasting. Such operating rights are referred to as **licences**.

Franchises and licences may be granted for a definite period of time, an indefinite period, or perpetually. **When costs can be identified with the acquisition of the franchise or licence, an intangible asset should be recognized.** Annual payments made under a franchise agreement should be recorded as **operating expenses** in the period in which they are incurred. In the case of a limited life, the cost of a franchise (or licence) should be amortized over the useful life. If the life is indefinite or perpetual, the cost may be amortized over a reasonable period not to exceed 40 years.

BUSINESS INSIGHT

Investor Perspective

Alliance Atlantis Communications Inc. is Canada's largest producer and distributor of films and TV shows. The Motion Picture Group has exclusive agreements to distribute New Line and Miramax's motion pictures, which have included hits such as *Austin Powers: The Spy Who Shagged Me* and *Shakespeare in Love*. Its Television Group produces and distributes shows such as *Traders*, *Due South*, and *Power Play*. The company's Broadcast Group has licences that include specialty channels, like Showcase Television and History Television, in both official languages. One of the company's most valuable assets is its broadcasting licences and rights to film and television programs. The value of Alliance Atlantis's broadcast licences was $78 million, and its broadcast rights, $41 million, as at March 31, 1999. The company amortizes these licences over 40 years, and amortizes its rights over the contracted exhibition period.

GOODWILL

Usually the largest intangible asset that appears on a company's balance sheet is goodwill. **Goodwill** represents the value of all favourable attributes that relate to a business enterprise. These include exceptional management, a desirable location, good customer relations, skilled employees, high-quality products, fair pricing policies, and harmonious relations with labour unions. Goodwill is therefore unusual: unlike other assets such as investments, property, plant, and equipment, and even other intangibles, which can all be sold *individually* in the marketplace, goodwill can be identified only with the business *as a whole*.

If goodwill can only be identified with the business as a whole, how can it be determined? Certainly, many business enterprises have many of the factors cited above (exceptional management, a desirable location, and so on). However, to determine the amount of goodwill in these situations would be difficult and very subjective. In other words, to recognize goodwill without an exchange transaction that puts a value on the goodwill would lead to subjective valuations that do not contribute to the reliability of financial statements. **Therefore, goodwill is recorded only when there is an exchange transaction that involves the purchase of an entire business. When an entire business is purchased, goodwill is the excess of cost over the fair market value of the net assets (assets less liabilities) acquired.**

In recording the purchase of a business, the net assets are shown at their fair market values, cash is credited for the purchase price, and the difference is recorded as the cost of goodwill. Goodwill is amortized over its useful life, not to exceed 40 years.

Air Canada reported $35 million of goodwill, net of amortization, on its 1999 financial statements. This goodwill will increase by the difference between Air Canada's cost to acquire Canadian Airlines and Canadian's fair market value when Air Canada completes its acquisition of Canadian, estimated to occur no later than May 1, 2001.

FINANCIAL STATEMENT PRESENTATION OF CAPITAL ASSETS

STUDY OBJECTIVE 8

Indicate how capital assets are reported on the balance sheet.

Both tangible capital assets (property, plant, and equipment and natural resources, if any) and intangible capital assets may be combined under the heading Capital Assets or disclosed under each individual group heading. Either on the balance sheet or in the notes, there should be disclosure of the balances of the major classes of assets, and accumulated amortization by major classes or in total. In addition, the amortization methods used should be described and the amount of amortization expense for the period disclosed.

Illustration 9-20 is an excerpt from Andrés Wines Ltd.'s 1999 financial statements. Capital assets are summarized in the balance sheet and detailed in Note 2. The accounting policy note to the financial statements reports that amortization is calculated on the straight-line basis using the following rates or useful lives: buildings, 2.5% per year; vineyards, 5% per year; machinery and equipment, 7.5%–20% per year; and goodwill, up to 40 years.

Illustration 9-20
Presentation of capital assets

ANDRÉS WINES LTD.
Balance Sheet (Partial)
March 31, 1999
(thousands of dollars)

Capital Assets	Cost	Accumulated Amortization	Net
Land	$ 2,411	$ —	$ 2,411
Vineyards	4,375	—	4,375
Buildings	17,201	5,318	11,883
Machinery and equipment	39,044	22,348	16,696
Goodwill	25,000	2,135	22,865
	$88,031	$29,801	$58,230

BEFORE YOU GO ON . . .

Review It

1. Identify the major types of intangible assets and the proper accounting for them.
2. How are intangible assets presented on the balance sheet?

USING THE DECISION TOOLKIT

Founded in 1983, Roberts Pharmaceuticals Corporation is a fully integrated pharmaceutical company with operating subsidiaries in Canada, the United States, and the United Kingdom. It is a rapidly growing company that acquires, develops, and markets specialty pharmaceuticals. In 1998, it reported a substantial increase in net earnings, after reporting a loss in 1996 and a small profit in 1997. The company has acquired, rather than developed internally, a number of existing products from other companies. It reports significant intangible capital assets related to these acquisitions. Suppose that you have noticed the improvement in Roberts' operating results and are considering investing in Roberts.

Instructions

Review the excerpts below from the company's 1998 financial statements.

ROBERTS PHARMACEUTICALS CORPORATION
Consolidated Balance Sheets (Assets Only)
(in thousands of U.S. dollars)

Assets	Dec. 31, 1998	Dec. 31, 1997
Total current assets	$157,234	$137,987
Property, plant, and equipment and other	53,137	39,144
Intangible assets	315,865	190,724
Total assets	$526,236	$367,855

ROBERTS PHARMACEUTICALS CORPORATION
Consolidated Statement of Operations
Years ended December 31
(in thousands of U.S. dollars)

	1998	1997
Total sales and revenue	$175,445	$122,508
Total operating costs and expenses	148,067	123,270
Operating earnings (loss)	27,378	(762)
Other revenues, expenses, gains, and losses	(10,591)	3,279
Net earnings	$ 16,787	$ 2,517

ROBERTS PHARMACEUTICALS CORPORATION
Selected Notes to the Financial Statements
December 31, 1998

Summary of Significant Accounting Policies

Intangible assets: Intangible assets are stated at cost less accumulated amortization. Amortization is determined using the straight-line method over the estimated useful lives of the related assets which are estimated to range from five to forty years. It is the Company's policy to review periodically and evaluate whether there has been impairment in the value of intangibles.

Intangible Assets

Intangible assets consist of (in thousands of U.S. dollars)

	Dec. 31	
	1998	1997
Product rights acquired	$349,282	$217,919
Less: Accumulated amortization	33,417	27,195
	$315,865	$190,724

In the fourth quarter of 1996, the Company recorded a charge to earnings for an impairment of intangible assets and to expense purchased development products totalling $25.4 million.

Answer the following questions:

1. What percentage of total assets are intangibles as at December 31, 1998?
2. What method does the company use to amortize intangibles, and over what period are they amortized?
3. Calculate the average useful life that the company is using to amortize its intangible assets. (Hint: Use the same formula as that shown in Illustration 9-17, substituting intangible assets for property, plant and equipment.)
4. Comment on whether, in your opinion, the company's intangibles amortization policy is reasonable.
5. What would 1998 earnings have been if the company had used a 15-year useful life for amortization? (Hint: Base your calculation on the average intangible assets in 1998.)
6. How might the company's sensitivity to the amortization of its intangbles affect your decision on whether to invest?

Solution

1. As a percentage of the company's total assets, intangibles represented 60% in 1998 ($315,865,000 ÷ $526,236,000).
2. The company uses the straight-line method to amortize intangibles. The notes state that they are amortized over a 5- to 40-year period.
3. The average useful life being used to amortize intangible assets can be estimated by dividing the average cost of the intangible assets by the amortization expense.

$$\frac{(\$349{,}282{,}000 + \$217{,}919{,}000) / 2}{\$9{,}815{,}000} = 29 \text{ years}$$

4. This is a matter of opinion. However, one factor to consider is that Roberts is purchasing the rights to existing products, so part of their useful life may already be gone. Additionally, because of rapidly changing technology, new drugs appear to be developed at a relatively rapid rate. Thus, it seems unlikely that on average, drugs would have a useful life of 40 years. Also, the notes state that the company took a $25.4 million write-down in 1996 due to the impairment of its intangibles. This suggests they were not being amortized fast enough. A 15-year life may be more appropriate.
5. In order to estimate amortization expense using a 15-year life, we would first need to calculate average intangibles for the year to approximate the amortization:

   Average intangibles = ($349,282,000 + $217,919,000) / 2 = $283,600,500

   Amortization over a 15-year period would be

$$\frac{\$283{,}600{,}500}{15 \text{ years}} = \$18{,}906{,}700$$

   The reduction in earnings from the increased amortization would be

   $18,906,700 – $9,815,000 = $9,091,700

   Therefore, with amortization over a 15-year period, the resulting ear ings for the year would have been $7,695,300 ($16,787,000 – $9,091,700).

6. The calculations above make it clear the company's earnings are very sensitive to the assumed useful life. Therefore, before investing, you would want to investigate further the reasonableness of the 5- to 40-year assumption currently being used.

Summary of Study Objectives

❶ ***Describe how the cost principle applies to tangible capital assets.*** The cost of tangible capital assets includes all expenditures necessary to acquire the assets and make them ready for their intended use. Cost is measured by the cash or cash equivalent price paid.

❷ ***Explain the concept of amortization.*** Amortization is the process of allocating to expense the cost of a capital asset over its useful (service) life in a rational and systematic manner. Amortization is not a process of valuation, and it is not a process that results in an accumulation of cash. Amortization is caused by wear and tear and by obsolescence.

❸ ***Calculate periodic amortization using the straight-line method, and contrast its expense pattern with those of other methods.*** The formula for straight-line amortization is

$$\frac{\text{Cost} - \text{Salvage value}}{\text{Useful life (in years)}}$$

The expense patterns of the three amortization methods are as follows:

Method	Annual Amortization Pattern
Straight-line	Constant amount
Declining-balance	Decreasing amount
Units-of-activity	Varying amount

❹ ***Describe the procedure for revising periodic amortization.*** Revisions of periodic amortization are made in present and future periods, not retroactively. The new annual amortization is determined by dividing the amortizable cost at the time of the revision (net book value less any revised salvage value) by the remaining useful life.

❺ ***Explain how to account for the disposal of tangible capital assets.*** The procedure for accounting for the disposal of tangible capital assets through sale or retirement is (a) eliminate the book value at the date of disposal, (b) record cash proceeds, if any, and (c) account for the difference between the book value and the cash proceeds as a gain or a loss on disposal.

❻ ***Describe methods for evaluating the use of tangible capital assets.*** These assets may be analysed using average useful life, average age, and the asset turnover ratio.

❼ ***Identify the basic issues related to reporting intangible capital assets.*** Intangible capital assets are reported at their cost less any amortized amounts. Amortization is done over the shortest of the useful life, legal life, or 40 years—usually on a straight-line basis.

❽ ***Indicate how capital assets are reported on the balance sheet.*** All classes of long-lived assets are often summarized under the heading Capital Assets. It is also common for property, plant, and equipment and natural resources to be combined under the heading Property, Plant, and Equipment, while intangible capital assets are listed separately as Intangible Assets. Either on the balance sheet or in the notes, the balances of the major classes of assets—such as land, buildings, and equipment—and accumulated amortization by major classes, or in total, are disclosed. The amortization methods used should be described, and the amount of amortization expense for the period should be disclosed.

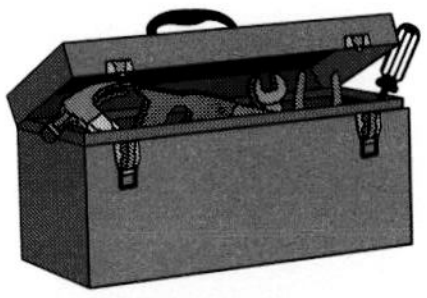

DECISION TOOLKIT—A SUMMARY

Decision Checkpoints	Info Needed for Decision	Tool to Use for Decision	How to Evaluate Results
Is the company's estimated useful life for amortization reasonable?	Estimated useful life of capital assets from notes to financial statements of this company and its competitors	If the company's estimated useful life significantly exceeds that of competitors, or does not seem reasonable in light of the circumstances, the reason for the difference should be investigated. If notes do not provide sufficient detail, average useful life can be estimated as follows $\text{Average useful life} = \frac{\text{Average cost of property, plant, and equipment}}{\text{Amortization expense}}$ This tool can also be used to assess the average age of intangible assets, substituting the average cost of intangible assets for property, plant, and equipment in the formula.	Too high an estimated useful life will result in understating amortization expense and overstating net earnings.
Are the company's capital assets possibly outdated or in need of replacement?	Amortization expense and accumulated amortization	$\text{Average age} = \frac{\text{Accumulated amortization}}{\text{Amortization expense}}$	A high average age relative to competitors might suggest that the company's assets are not as efficient, or that they may be in need of replacement.
How effective is the company at generating sales from its assets?	Net sales and average total assets	$\text{Asset turnover ratio} = \frac{\text{Net sales}}{\text{Average total assets}}$	Indicates the sales dollars generated per dollar of assets. A high value suggests the company is effective in using its resources to generate sales.
Is the company's amortization of intangibles reasonable?	Estimated useful life of intangibles from notes to financial statements of this company and its competitors	If the company's estimated useful life significantly exceeds that of competitors or does not seem reasonable in light of the circumstances, the reason for the difference should be investigated.	Too high an estimated useful life will result in understating amortization expense and overstating net earnings.

APPENDIX 9A

CALCULATION OF AMORTIZATION USING OTHER METHODS

STUDY OBJECTIVE 9

Calculate periodic amortization using the declining-balance method and the units-of-activity method.

In this appendix, we show the calculations of the amortization expense amounts used in the chapter for the declining-balance and units-of-activity methods.

DECLINING-BALANCE

The **declining-balance method** produces a decreasing annual amortization expense over the useful life of the asset. The method is so named because the calculation of periodic amortization is based on a **declining book value** (cost less accumulated amortization) of the asset. Annual amortization expense is calculated by multiplying the book value at the beginning of the year by the declining-balance amortization rate. **The amortization rate remains constant from year to year, but the book value to which the rate is applied declines each year.**

Book value for the first year is the cost of the asset, because the balance in accumulated amortization at the beginning of the asset's useful life is zero. In subsequent years, book value is the difference between cost and accumulated amortization at the beginning of the year. **Unlike other amortization methods, salvage value is ignored in determining the amount to which the declining-balance rate is applied.** Salvage value, however, does limit the total amortization that can be taken. Amortization stops when the asset's book value equals its expected salvage value.

Helpful Hint The straight-line rate is determined by dividing 100% by the estimated useful life. In this case, it is 100% ÷ 5 = 20%.

As noted in the chapter, one declining-balance rate is double the straight-line rate—a method often referred to as the **double-declining-balance method**. If Bill's Pizzas uses the double-declining-balance method, the amortization rate is 40% (2 × the straight-line rate of 20%). Illustration 9A-1 presents the formula and calculation of amortization for the first year on the delivery truck.

Illustration 9A-1
Formula for declining-balance method

Book Value at Beginning of Year	×	Declining-Balance Rate	=	Amortization Expense
$13,000	×	40%	=	$5,200

The amortization schedule under this method is given in Illustration 9A-2.

Illustration 9A-2
Double-declining-balance amortization schedule

BILL'S PIZZAS LTD.

Year	Book Value, Beginning of Year	×	Amortization Rate	=	Annual Amortization Expense	End of Year: Accumulated Amortization	End of Year: Book Value
							$13,000
2001	$13,000		40%		**$5,200**	$ 5,200	7,800*
2002	7,800		40		**3,120**	8,320	4,680
2003	4,680		40		**1,872**	10,192	2,808
2004	2,808		40		**1,123**	11,315	1,685
2005	1,685		40		**685****	12,000	**1,000**

* $13,000 − $5,200 = $7,800

**Calculation of $674 ($1,685 × 40%) is adjusted to $685 so book value will equal salvage value.

Helpful Hint Amortization stops when the asset's book value equals its expected salvage value.

You can see that the delivery equipment is 64% amortized ($8,320 ÷ $13,000) at the end of the second year. Under the straight-line method, it would be amortized 37% ($4,800 ÷ $13,000) at that time. Because the declining-balance method produces higher amortization expense in the early years than in the later years, it is considered an **accelerated amortization method**. The declining-balance method is compatible with the matching principle. The higher amortization expense in early years is matched with the higher benefits received in these years. Conversely, lower amortization expense is recognized in later years when the asset's contribution to revenue is less. Also, some assets lose their usefulness rapidly because of obsolescence. In these cases, the declining-balance method provides a more appropriate amortization amount.

Helpful Hint The method to be used for an asset that is expected to be more productive in the first half of its useful life is the declining-balance method.

When an asset is purchased during the year, it is necessary to prorate the declining-balance amortization in the first year on a time basis. For example, if Bill's Pizzas had purchased the delivery equipment on April 1, 2001, amortization for 2001 would be $3,900 ($13,000 × 40% × $\frac{9}{12}$). The book value for calculating amortization in 2002 then becomes $9,100 ($13,000 − $3,900), and the 2001 amortization is $3,640 ($9,100 × 40%).

UNITS-OF-ACTIVITY

Under the **units-of-activity method**, useful life is expressed in terms of the total units of production or use expected from the asset. The units-of-activity method is ideally suited to equipment whose activity can be measured in units of output, kilometres driven, and hours in use. The units-of-activity method is generally not suitable for assets for which amortization is a function more of time than of use.

To use this method, the total units of activity for the entire useful life are estimated and that amount is divided into the amortizable cost to determine the amortization cost per unit. The amortization cost per unit is then multiplied by the units of activity during the year to give the annual amortization. To illustrate, assume that the delivery truck of Bill's Pizzas is driven 15,000 kilometres in the first year. Illustration 9A-3 presents the formula and calculation of amortization expense in the first year.

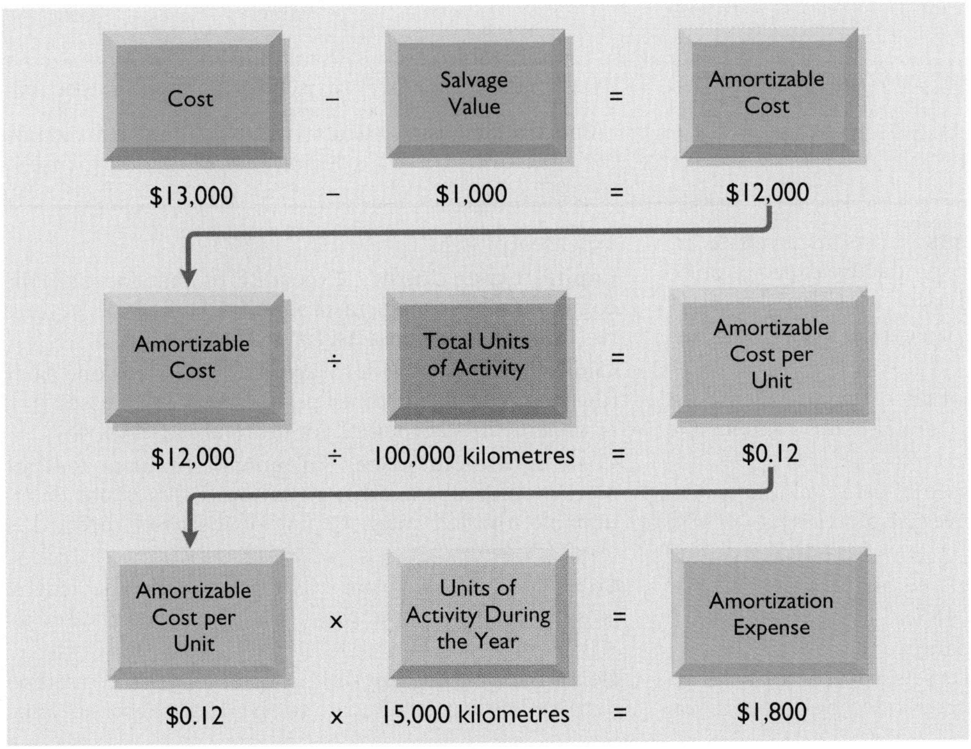

Cost
−
Salvage Value
=
Amortizable Cost
$13,000
−
$1,000
=
$12,000
Amortizable Cost
÷
Total Units of Activity
=
Amortizable Cost per Unit
$12,000
÷
100,000 kilometres
=
$0.12
Amortizable Cost per Unit
x
Units of Activity During the Year
=
Amortization Expense
$0.12
x
15,000 kilometres
=
$1,800

Illustration 9A-3
Formula for units-of-activity method

The amortization schedule, using assumed distance data, is shown in Illustration 9A-4.

Illustration 9A-4
Units-of-activity amortization schedule

BILL'S PIZZAS LTD.

Year	Units of Activity	×	Amortizable Cost/Unit	=	Annual Amortization Expense	End of Year: Accumulated Amortization	End of Year: Book Value
							$13,000
2001	15,000		$0.12		$1,800	$ 1,800	11,200*
2002	30,000		0.12		3,600	5,400	7,600
2003	20,000		0.12		2,400	7,800	5,200
2004	25,000		0.12		3,000	10,800	2,200
2005	10,000		0.12		1,200	12,000	1,000

*$13,000 − $1,800 = $11,200

The units-of-activity method is not nearly as popular as the straight-line method, primarily because it is often difficult to make a reasonable estimate of total activity. However, this method is used by some very large companies, such as Imperial Metals, Imperial Oil, and Pan-American. When the productivity of the asset varies significantly from one period to another, the units-of-activity method results in the best matching of expenses with revenues. This method is easy to apply when assets are purchased during the year. In such a case, the productivity of the asset for the partial year is used in calculating the amortization.

Summary of Study Objective for Appendix 9A

9 ***Calculate periodic amortization using the declining-balance method and the units-of-activity method.*** The calculation for each of these methods is shown here:

Declining-balance:

Book value at beginning of year × Declining-balance rate = Amortizable expense

Units-of-activity:

Cost − Salvage value = Amortizable cost

Amortizable cost ÷ Total units of activity = Amortizable cost per unit

Amortizable cost per unit × Units of activity during year = Amortization expense

Glossary

Additions and improvements Costs incurred to increase the operating efficiency, productive capacity, or expected useful life of a capital asset. (p. 477)

Amortizable cost The cost of a capital asset less its salvage value. (p. 470)

Amortization The process of allocating to expense the cost of a capital asset over its useful life in a rational and systematic manner. (p. 468)

Asset turnover ratio Measure of sales volume, calculated as net sales divided by average total assets. (p. 484)

Average age Measure of the age of a company's capital assets, calculated as accumulated amortization divided by amortization expense. (p. 483)

Average useful life A comparative measure of the useful life of a company's capital assets, calculated as the average cost of the capital assets divided by amortization expense. (p. 481)

Capital expenditures Expenditures that increase the company's investment in productive facilities. They are recorded as capital assets. (p. 463)

Capital lease A long-term agreement allowing one party (the lessee) to use another party's (the lessor) asset. The arrangement is accounted for as a purchase. (p. 467)

Cash equivalent price An amount equal to the fair market value of the asset given up. If this is not determinable, the fair market value of the asset received is used. (p. 464)

Copyright An exclusive right granted by the federal government allowing the owner to reproduce and sell an artistic or published work. (p. 488)

Declining-balance method An amortization method that applies a constant rate to the declining book value of the asset and produces a decreasing annual amortization expense over the useful life of the asset. (p. 472)

Franchise A contractual arrangement under which the franchisor grants the franchisee the right to sell certain products, to render specific services, or to use certain trademarks or trade names, usually within a designated geographic area. (p. 489)

Goodwill The value of all favourable attributes that relate to a business enterprise. (p. 490)

Impairment A permanent decline in the market value of an asset. (p. 477)

Intangible capital assets Rights, privileges, and competitive advantages that result from the ownership of long-lived assets that do not possess physical substance. (p. 485)

Lessee A party that has made contractual arrangements to use another party's asset without purchasing it. (p. 466)

Lessor A party that has agreed contractually to let another party use its asset. (p. 466)

Licences Operating rights to use public property, granted by a governmental agency to a business enterprise. (p. 489)

Net book value Cost less accumulated amortization of a capital asset. (p. 468)

Operating lease An arrangement allowing one party (the lessee) to use the asset of another party (the lessor). The arrangement is accounted for as a rental. (p. 466)

Ordinary repairs Expenditures to maintain the operating efficiency and expected productive life of the asset. (p. 477)

Patent An exclusive right issued by the federal government that enables the recipient to manufacture, sell, or otherwise control an invention for a period of 20 years from the date of the grant. (p. 487)

Research and development (R&D) costs Expenditures that may lead to patents, copyrights, new processes, and new products. (p. 488)

Revenue (operating) expenditures Expenditures that are immediately matched against revenues as an expense. (p. 463)

Straight-line method A method in which periodic amortization is the same for each year of the asset's useful life. (p. 470)

Tangible capital assets Tangible resources that have physical substance, are used in the operations of the business, and are not intended for sale to customers. (p. 462)

Trademark (trade name) A word, phrase, jingle, or symbol that distinguishes or identifies a particular enterprise or product. (p. 489)

Units-of-activity method An amortization method in which useful life is expressed in terms of the total units of production or use expected from the asset. (p. 472)

DEMONSTRATION PROBLEM 1

DuPage Company Ltd. purchased a factory machine at a cost of $18,000 on January 1, 2001. The machine was expected to have a salvage value of $2,000 at the end of its four-year useful life. During its useful life, the machine was expected to be used 160,000 hours. Actual annual hourly use was: 2001, 40,000 hours; 2002, 60,000 hours; 2003, 35,000 hours; and 2004, 25,000 hours.

Instructions

(a) Prepare an amortization schedule using the straight-line method.

*(b) Prepare amortization schedules for the following methods: (1) units-of-activity and (2) declining-balance using double the straight-line rate.

(a)

DUPAGE COMPANY LTD.
Amortization Schedule—Straight-Line Method

Year	Amortizable Cost	×	Amortization Rate	=	Annual Amortization Expense	End of Year Accumulated Amortization	End of Year Book Value
							$18,000
2001	$16,000*		25%**		$4,000	$ 4,000	14,000***
2002	16,000		25		4,000	8,000	10,000
2003	16,000		25		4,000	12,000	6,000
2004	16,000		25		4,000	16,000	2,000

* $18,000 − $2,000 = $16,000
** 1 ÷ 4 years = 25%
*** $18,000 − $4,000 = $14,000

Problem-Solving Strategy
Under the straight-line method, the amortization rate is applied to amortizable cost.

Problem-Solving Strategies

1. Under the units-of-activity method, amortizable cost per unit is calculated by dividing amortizable cost (cost less salvage value) by total units of activity.
2. Under the declining-balance method, the amortization rate is applied to the net book value at the beginning of the year. Do not deduct salvage value.

*(b)

DUPAGE COMPANY LTD.
Amortization Schedule—Units-of-Activity Method

						End of Year	
Year	Units of Activity	×	Amortizable Cost/Unit	=	Annual Amortization Expense	Accumulated Amortization	Book Value
							$18,000
2001	40,000		$0.10*		$4,000	$ 4,000	14,000
2002	60,000		0.10		6,000	10,000	8,000
2003	35,000		0.10		3,500	13,500	4,500
2004	25,000		0.10		2,500	16,000	2,000

*$18,000 − $2,000 = $16,000 ÷ 160,000 hours = $0.10

DUPAGE COMPANY LTD.
Amortization Schedule—Double-Declining-Balance Method

Year	Book Value, Beginning of Year	×	Amortization Rate	=	Amortization Expense	Accumulated Amortization	Book Value
							$18,000
2001	$18,000		50%*		$9,000	$ 9,000	9,000
2002	9,000		50		4,500	13,500	4,500
2003	4,500		50		2,250	15,750	2,250
2004	2,250		50		250**	16,000	2,000

* 25% × 2 = 50%
** Adjusted to $250 because ending book value should not be less than expected value.

DEMONSTRATION PROBLEM 2

On January 1, 2002, Skyline Limousine Corp. purchased a used limousine at an acquisition cost of $28,000. The vehicle has been amortized by the straight-line method using a four-year service life and a $4,000 salvage value. The company's fiscal year ends on December 31.

Instructions

Prepare the journal entry or entries to record the disposal of the limousine assuming that it was:
(a) Retired and scrapped with no salvage value on January 1, 2006.
(b) Sold for $8,000 on July 1, 2005.

Problem-Solving Strategies

1. Update any unrecorded amortization for the period.
2. Remove the asset and its accumulated amortization from the books. (Accumulated amortization is equal to amortization expense per year times the number of years or months of use.) Record cash, if any, and gain or loss on disposal.

Solution to Demonstration Problem

(a) Jan. 1, 2006	Accumulated Amortization—Limousine	24,000	
	Loss on Disposal	4,000	
	Limousine		28,000
	(To record retirement of limousine)		
(b) July 1, 2005	Amortization Expense (($28,000 − $4,000) ÷ 4 = $6000 × 6/12)	3,000	
	Accumulated Amortization—Limousine		3,000
	(To record amortization to date of disposal)		
	Cash	8,000	
	Accumulated Amortization—Limousine ($6,000 × 3.5 yrs)	21,000	
	Gain on Disposal		1,000
	Limousine		28,000
	(To record sale of limousine)		

Note: All of the following questions, exercises, and problems marked with an asterisk relate to material in the appendix to the chapter.

SELF-STUDY QUESTIONS

Answers are at the end of the chapter.

(SO 1) 1. Corrieten Company Ltd. purchased equipment and these costs were incurred:

Cash price	$24,000
Insurance during transit	200
Installation and testing	400
Total costs	$24,600

What amount should be recorded as the cost of the equipment?
(a) $0 (c) $24,200
(b) $24,000 (d) $24,600

(SO 1) 2. Harrington Corporation recently leased a number of trucks from André Corporation. In inspecting the books of Harrington Corporation, you notice that the trucks have not been recorded as assets on its balance sheet. From this you can conclude that Harrington is accounting for this transaction as a(n):
(a) operating lease. (c) purchase.
(b) capital lease. (d) None of the above

(SO 2) 3. Amortization is a process of:
(a) valuation. (c) cash accumulation.
(b) cost allocation. (d) appraisal.

(SO 3) 4. Cuso Company Ltd. purchased equipment on January 1, 2000, at a total invoice cost of $400,000. The equipment has an estimated salvage value of $10,000 and an estimated useful life of five years. What is the amount of accumulated amortization at December 31, 2001, if the straight-line method of amortization is used?
(a) $80,000 (c) $78,000
(b) $160,000 (d) $156,000

(SO 3) 5. A company would minimize its amortization expense in the first year of owning an asset if it:
(a) used a high estimated life, a high salvage value, and declining-balance amortization.
(b) used a low estimated life, a high salvage value, and straight-line amortization.
(c) used a high estimated life, a high salvage value, and straight-line amortization.
(d) used a low estimated life, a low salvage value, and declining-balance amortization.

(SO 4) 6. When there is a change in estimated amortization:
(a) previous amortization should be corrected.
(b) current and future years' amortization should be revised.
(c) only future years' amortization should be revised.
(d) None of the above

7. Additions to property, plant, and equipment: (SO 4)
(a) are revenue expenditures.
(b) increase a repair expense account.
(c) increase a purchases account.
(d) are capital expenditures.

8. Which of the following measures provides an indication of how efficient a company is in employing its assets? (SO 6)
(a) Current ratio
(b) Average useful life
(c) Average age
(d) Asset turnover ratio

9. Pierce Inc. incurred $150,000 of research costs in its laboratory to develop a new product. It spent $20,000 in legal fees for a patent granted on January 2, 2001. On July 31, 2001, Pierce paid $15,000 for legal fees in a successful defence of the patent. What is the total amount that should be debited to Patents through July 31, 2001? (SO 7)
(a) $35,000 (c) $185,000
(b) $150,000 (d) Some other amount

10. Indicate which one of these statements is *true:* (SO 7)
(a) Since intangible assets lack physical substance, they need to be disclosed only in the notes to the financial statements.
(b) Goodwill should be reported as a contra account in the Shareholders' Equity section of the balance sheet.
(c) Totals of major classes of assets can be shown in the balance sheet, with asset details disclosed in the notes to the financial statements.
(d) Intangible assets are typically combined with property, plant, and equipment and natural resources and then shown in the Property, Plant, and Equipment section of the balance sheet.

11. If a company reports goodwill as an intangible asset on its books, what is the one thing you know with certainty? (SO 7)
(a) The company is a valuable company worth investing in.
(b) The company has a well-established brand name.
(c) The company purchased another business.
(d) The goodwill will generate a lot of positive business for the company for many years to come.

*12. Kant Enterprises purchased a truck for $11,000 on January 1, 2000. The truck will have an estimated salvage value of $1,000 at the end of five years. If you use the units-of-activity (SO 9)

method, the balance in accumulated amortization at December 31, 2001, can be calculated by the following formula:
(a) ($11,000 ÷ Total estimated activity) × Units of activity for 2001.
(b) ($10,000 ÷ Total estimated activity) × Units of activity for 2001.
(c) ($11,000 ÷ Total estimated activity) × Units of activity for 2000 and 2001.
(d) ($10,000 ÷ Total estimated activity) × Units of activity for 2000 and 2001.

QUESTIONS

(SO 1) 1. Susan Leung is uncertain about how the cost principle applies to tangible capital assets. Explain the principle to Susan.

(SO 1) 2. Market values of capital assets are more relevant than historical cost for decisions made by users, including creditors, investors, and managers. Why do you suppose the cost principle has persisted, in spite of its perceived lack of usefulness?

(SO 1) 3. How is the cost of a tangible capital asset measured in a cash transaction? In a noncash transaction?

(SO 1) 4. What are the primary advantages of leasing?

(SO 1) 5. Jamie Company Ltd. acquires the land and building owned by Smitt Company Ltd. What types of costs may be incurred to make the asset ready for its intended use if Jamie wants to use only the land? Both the land and the building?

(SO 2) 6. In a recent newspaper release, the president of Lawsuit Inc. asserted that something has to be done about amortization. The president said, "Amortization does not come close to accumulating the cash needed to replace the asset at the end of its useful life." What is your response to the president?

(SO 3) 7. Contrast the straight-line method and the units-of-activity method in relation to (a) useful life and (b) the pattern of periodic amortization over useful life.

(SO 3) 8. Contrast the effects of the three amortization methods on annual amortization expense and net earnings.

(SO 3) 9. Morgan Corporation and Fairchild Corporation both operate in the same industry. Morgan uses the straight-line method to account for amortization, whereas Fairchild uses an accelerated method. Explain what complications might arise in trying to compare the results of these two companies.

(SO 3) 10. Lucille Corporation uses straight-line amortization for financial reporting purposes but an accelerated method for tax purposes. Is it acceptable to use different methods for the two purposes? What is Lucille Corporation's motivation for doing this?

(SO 3) 11. Distinguish between revenue expenditures and capital expenditures during an asset's useful life.

12. In the fourth year of an asset's five-year useful life, the company decides that the asset will have a six-year total service life. How should the revision of amortization be recorded? Why? (SO 4

13. How is a gain or a loss on the sale of property, plant, or equipment calculated? (SO 5

14. Rashid Corporation owns a machine that is fully amortized but is still being used. How should Rashid account for this asset and report it in the financial statements? (SO 5

15. You are comparing two companies in the same industry. You have determined that Betty Corp. amortizes its capital assets over a 40-year life, whereas Herb Corp. amortizes its capital assets over a 20-year life. Discuss the implications this has for comparing the results of the two companies. (SO 6

16. Give an example of an industry that would be characterized by (a) a high asset turnover ratio and a low profit margin ratio, and (b) a low asset turnover ratio and a high profit margin ratio. (SO 6

17. **Salter Street Films Limited** of Halifax, Nova Scotia, is an integrated entertainment company that develops, produces, and distributes original film and television programming. Salter Street's television programs include the award-winning top-rated comedy series *This Hour Has 22 Minutes* and the family drama series *Emily of New Moon*. It reported average total assets of $50,165,865 and total revenues (assume equal to net sales) of $28,493,461 in 1998. What is Salter Street's asset turnover ratio? (SO 6

18. Heflin Corporation hires an accounting student who says that intangible assets should always be amortized over their legal lives. Is the student correct? Explain. (SO 7

19. Goodwill has been defined as the value of all favourable attributes that relate to a business enterprise. What types of attributes could result in goodwill? (SO 7

20. Bob Leno, a business major, is working on a case problem for one of his classes. In this case problem, the company needs to raise cash to market a new product it developed. Saul Cain, an engineering major, takes one look at the company's balance sheet and says, "This company has an awful lot of goodwill. Why don't (SO 7

you recommend that they sell some of it to raise cash?" How should Bob respond to Saul?

(SO 7) 21. Often research and development costs provide companies with benefits that last a number of years. (For example, these costs can lead to the development of a patent that will increase the company's earnings for many years.) However, generally accepted accounting principles require that research costs be recorded as an expense when incurred and development costs expensed except in certain circumstances. Why?

22. Explain how capital assets should be reported on the balance sheet. Are any transactions related to capital assets reported on the statement of earnings? (SO 8)

23. What information should be disclosed in the notes to the financial statements related to capital assets? (SO 8)

*24. Cecile is studying for the next accounting examination. She asks for your help on two questions: (a) what is salvage value? and (b) is salvage value used in determining amortizable cost under each amortization method? Answer Cecile's questions. (SO 3, 9)

BRIEF EXERCISES

Determine the cost of land. (SO 1)

BE9-1 These expenditures were incurred by Shumway Company Ltd. in purchasing land: cash price, \$50,000; accrued property taxes, \$3,000; legal fees, \$2,500; real estate broker's commission, \$2,000; and clearing and grading, \$3,500. What is the cost of the land?

Determine the cost of a truck. (SO 1)

BE9-2 Basler Company Ltd. incurs these expenditures in purchasing a truck: cash price, \$18,000; accident insurance, \$2,000; motor vehicle licence, \$100; and painting and lettering, \$400. What is the cost of the truck?

Calculate straight-line amortization. (SO 3)

BE9-3 Cunningham Company Ltd. acquires a delivery truck at a cost of \$42,000. The truck is expected to have a salvage value of \$2,000 at the end of its four-year useful life. Calculate annual amortization for the first and second years using the straight-line method.

Calculate revised amortization. (SO 4)

BE9-4 On January 1, 2001, the Asler Corporation ledger shows Equipment, \$32,000, and Accumulated Amortization, \$12,000. The amortization resulted from using the straight-line method with a useful life of 10 years and a salvage value of \$2,000. On this date, the company concludes that the equipment has a remaining useful life of only four years with the same salvage value. Calculate the revised annual amortization.

Journalize entries for disposal of tangible capital assets. (SO 5)

BE9-5 Ruiz Company Ltd. retires its delivery equipment, which cost \$41,000. Prepare journal entries to record the transaction if (a) accumulated amortization is also \$41,000 on this delivery equipment and no salvage value is received; and (b) the accumulated amortization for Ruiz Company Ltd. is \$35,000 instead of \$41,000.

Journalize entries for sale of tangible capital assets. (SO 5)

BE9-6 Wiley Inc. sells office equipment on September 30, 2001, for \$21,000 cash. The office equipment originally cost \$72,000 and as at January 1, 2001, had accumulated amortization of \$42,000. Amortization for the first nine months of 2001 is \$6,250. Prepare the journal entries to (a) update amortization to September 30, 2001, and (b) record the sale of the equipment.

Calculate average life, average age of long-lived assets, and asset turnover ratios. (SO 6)

BE9-7 In its 1998 annual report, **McDonald's Corporation** reports beginning total assets of \$18.2 billion; ending total assets of \$19.8 billion; beginning property, plant, and equipment (at cost) of \$20.1 billion; ending property, plant, and equipment (at cost) of \$21.8 billion; accumulated amortization of \$5.7 billion; amortization expense of \$808 million; and net sales of \$12.4 billion.
(a) Calculate the average useful life of McDonald's Corp.'s property, plant, and equipment.
(b) Calculate the average age of McDonald's Corp.'s property, plant, and equipment.
(c) Calculate McDonald's Corp.'s asset turnover ratio.

Account for intangibles—patents. (SO 7)

BE9-8 Popper Company Ltd. purchases a patent for \$180,000 on January 2, 2001. Its estimated useful life is 10 years.
(a) Prepare the journal entry to record amortization expense for the first year.
(b) Show how this patent is reported on the balance sheet at the end of the first year.

Classify long-lived assets on balance sheet. (SO 8)

BE9-9 This information relates to capital assets, and research and development costs at April 30, 2001 for Joker Company Ltd.: buildings, \$800,000; accumulated amortization—buildings, $650,000; goodwill, net, $410,000; and patent, net, $200,000. It also spent $108,000 during the year on research and unproductive development. Prepare a partial balance sheet of Joker Company Ltd. for these items.

Calculate declining-balance amortization.
(SO 9)

***BE9-10** Amortization information for Cunningham Company Ltd. is given in BE9-3. Assuming the declining-balance amortization rate is double the straight-line rate, calculate annual amortization for the first and second years under the declining-balance method.

Calculate amortization using units-of-activity method.
(SO 9)

***BE9-11** Englehart Taxi Service uses the units-of-activity method in calculate amortization on its taxicabs. Each cab is expected to be driven 120,000 km. Taxi 10 cost $24,500 and is expected to have a salvage value of $500. Taxi 10 was driven 30,000 km in 2000 and 20,000 km in 2001. Calculate the amortization for each year.

EXERCISES

Determine cost of asset acquisitions.
(SO 1)

E9-1 The following expenditures relating to property, plant, and equipment were made by Kosinki Company Ltd. during the first two months of 2001:

1. Paid $250 to have company name and advertising slogan painted on new delivery truck.
2. Paid $75 motor vehicle licence fee on new truck.
3. Paid $850 for winter tires for the delivery truck.
4. Paid $17,500 for parking lots and driveways on new plant site.
5. Paid $5,000 of accrued property taxes when plant site was acquired.
6. Paid $8,000 for installation of new factory machinery.
7. Paid $900 for a one-year accident insurance policy on new delivery truck.
8. Paid $200 insurance to cover possible accident loss on new factory machinery while the machinery was in transit.

Instructions

(a) Explain the application of the cost principle in determining the acquisition cost of property, plant, and equipment.
(b) List the numbers of the foregoing transactions, and opposite each number indicate the account title to which the expenditure should be debited.

Determine acquisition costs of land.
(SO 1)

E9-2 On March 1, 2001, Orbis Company Inc. acquired real estate on which it planned to construct a small office building, by paying $100,000 in cash. An old warehouse on the property was razed at a cost of $6,600; the salvaged materials were sold for $1,700. Additional expenditures before construction began included a $1,100 legal fee for work concerning the land purchase, a $4,000 real estate broker's fee, a $7,800 architect's fee, and $14,000 to put in driveways and a parking lot.

Instructions

(a) Determine the amount to be reported as the cost of the land.
(b) For each cost not used in part (a), indicate the account to be debited.

Determine straight-line amortization for partial period.
(SO 3)

E9-3 Costello Company Limited purchased a new machine on October 1, 2001, at a cost of $96,000. The company estimated that the machine has a salvage value of $12,000. The machine is expected to be used for 84,000 working hours during its six-year life.

Instructions

Calculate the amortization expense under the straight-line method for 2001 and 2002, assuming a December 31 year end.

Calculate revised annual amortization.
(SO 3, 4)

E9-4 Lindy Weink, the new controller of Waterloo Company Inc., has reviewed the expected useful lives and salvage values of selected amortizable assets at the beginning of 2001. Here are her findings:

Type of Asset	Date Acquired	Cost	Accumulated Amortization, Jan. 1, 2001	Useful Life (in years)		Salvage Value	
				Old	Proposed	Old	Proposed
Building	Jan. 1, 1995	$800,000	$114,000	40	45	$40,000	$62,000
Warehouse	Jan. 1, 1998	100,000	11,400	25	20	5,000	3,600

All assets are amortized by the straight-line method. Waterloo Company uses a calendar year in preparing annual financial statements. After discussion, management has agreed to accept Lindy's proposed changes. (The "Proposed" useful life is total life, not remaining life.)

Instructions

(a) Calculate the revised annual amortization on each asset in 2001. (Show calculations.)
(b) Prepare the entry (or entries) to record amortization on the building in 2001.

Journalize entries for disposal of capital assets.
(SO 5)

E9-5 Presented here are selected transactions for Beck Corporation for 2001:

Jan. 1	Retired a piece of machinery that was purchased on January 1, 1991. The machine cost $62,000 and had a useful life of 10 years with no salvage value.
June 30	Sold a computer that was purchased on January 1, 1998. The computer cost $35,000 and had a useful life of seven years with no salvage value. The computer was sold for $28,000.
Dec. 31	Discarded a delivery truck that was purchased on January 1, 1997. The truck cost $27,000 and was amortized based on an eight-year useful life with a $3,000 salvage value.

Instructions

Journalize all entries required on the above dates, including entries to update amortization on assets disposed of, where applicable. Beck Corporation uses straight-line amortization.

Calculate average useful life, average age, and asset turnover ratios.
(SO 6)

E9-6 **Imax Corporation** of Mississauga, makes and leases projection and sound systems for about 200 giant-screen IMAX theatres in 25 countries. During 1998, it reported total revenue (assume equal to net sales) of $190,355,000, net earnings of $1,800,000, and amortization expense of $22,677,000. Its balance sheet also showed average total assets of $417,225,000, average tangible capital assets of $65,042,500, and accumulated amortization of $25,372,000.

Instructions

(a) Calculate (1) average useful life of property, plant, and equipment; (2) average age of property, plant, and equipment; and (3) the asset turnover ratio.
(b) The average asset turnover rate for Imax's industry is 0.5. Comment on how Imax's management of its assets compares to its industry.

Prepare adjusting entries for amortization of intangibles.
(SO 7)

E9-7 These are selected transactions for Graf Corporation in 2001:

Jan. 1	Purchased a small company and recorded goodwill of $120,000. The goodwill has a useful life of 55 years.
May 1	Purchased a patent with an estimated useful life of five years and a legal life of 20 years for $15,000.

Instructions

Prepare all adjusting entries at December 31 to record amortization required by the events.

Prepare entries to set up appropriate accounts for different intangibles; calculate amortization.
(SO 7)

E9-8 Collins Company Ltd., organized in 2001, has these transactions related to intangible assets in that year:

Jan. 2	Purchased patent (seven-year life), $350,000.
Apr. 1	Goodwill purchased (indefinite life), $360,000.
July 1	Acquired 10-year franchise (expiration date July 1, 2006), $450,000.
Sept. 1	Incurred research costs, $185,000.

Instructions

Prepare the necessary entries to record these intangibles. All costs incurred were for cash. Make the entries as at December 31, 2001, recording any necessary amortization and indicating what the balances should be on December 31, 2001.

Answer questions about amortization and intangibles.
(SO 2, 7)

E9-9 The questions listed below are independent of one another.

Instructions
Provide a brief answer to each question:

(a) Why should a company amortize its buildings and not its land?
(b) How can a company have a building that has a zero reported book value but substantial market value?
(c) What are some examples of intangibles that you might find on your university campus?

Discuss implications of amortization period.
(SO 7)

E9-10 **Alliance Atlantis Communications Inc.** noted in its 1999 annual report that, effective January 1, 1999, the company had changed its accounting policy to amortize broadcast rights over the contracted exhibition period, which is based on the estimated useful life of the program. Previously, the company amortized broadcast rights over the lesser of two years or the contracted exhibition period.

Instructions
Write a short memo to your client explaining the implications this has for the analysis of Alliance Atlantis's results. Also, discuss whether this change in amortization period appears reasonable.

Classify long-lived assets on balance sheet.
(SO 8)

E9-11 **Bell Canada Enterprises**, a leading communications services company, reported the following selected information as at December 31, 1999 (in millions):

Accounts	Amounts
Accumulated amortization—buildings	$ 16,964
Accumulated amortization—machinery and equipment	3,621
Accumulated amortization—other capital assets	74
Amortization expense	2,725
Buildings	52,324
Cash and cash equivalents	2,395
Common shares	6,789
Goodwill, net of accumulated amortization, $462	1,909
Land	94
Licences, net of accumulated amortization, $145	783
Machinery and equipment	6,448
Other capital assets	176
Plant	26,162
Plant under construction	1,561

Instructions
(a) Identify on which financial statement (balance sheet or statement of earnings) and which section (e.g., current assets) each of the above items should be reported.
(b) Prepare the Capital Assets section of the balance sheet, as at December 31, 1999.

Calculate amortization under units-of-activity method.
(SO 9)

***E9-12** Galactic Bus Lines uses the units-of-activity method in amortizing its buses. One bus was purchased on January 1, 2001, at a cost of $108,000. Over its four-year useful life, the bus is expected to be driven 100,000 km. Salvage value is expected to be $8,000.

Instructions
(a) Calculate the amortization cost per unit.
(b) Prepare an amortization schedule assuming actual mileage was: 2001, 28,000 km; 2002, 30,000 km; 2003, 25,000 km; and 2004, 17,000 km.

Calculate declining-balance and units-of-activity amortization.
(SO 9)

***E9-13** Basic information relating to a new machine purchased by Costello Company Limited is presented in E9-3.

Instructions
Using the facts presented in E9-3, calculate amortization using the following methods in the year indicated:
(a) Declining-balance using one times the straight-line rate for 2001 and 2002.
(b) Units-of-activity for 2001, assuming machine usage was 1,700 hours.

*E9-14 The Rahim Corporation purchased a computer for $10,000. The company planned to keep it for four years, after which it hoped to sell it for $2,000.

Determine effect of choice of amortization method over life of asset. (SO 9)

Instructions

(a) Calculate the amortization expense for each of the three years under the (1) straight-line method, and (2) double-declining-balance method.
(b) Assuming Rahim sold the computer for $2,500 at the end of the third year, calculate the loss on disposal under each amortization method.
(c) Determine the impact on earnings (total amortization plus loss on disposal) each method had for use of the computer for the three-year period.

PROBLEMS: SET A

P9-1A Weiseman Company Ltd. was organized on January 1. During the first year of operations, the following tangible capital asset expenditures and receipts were recorded in random order:

Determine acquisition costs of land and building. (SO 1)

Debits

1. Cost of real estate purchased as a plant site (land, $100,000, and building, $25,000)	$125,000
2. Installation cost of fences around property	4,000
3. Cost of demolishing building to make land suitable for construction of new building	13,000
4. Excavation costs for new building	20,000
5. Accrued real estate taxes paid at time of purchase of real estate	2,000
6. Cost of parking lots and driveways	12,000
7. Architect's fees on building plans	10,000
8. Real estate taxes paid for the current year on land	3,000
9. Full payment to building contractor	600,000
	$789,000

Credits

10. Proceeds from salvage of demolished building	$ 2,500

Instructions

Analyse the foregoing transactions using the following four table column headings Item; Land; Building; Other Accounts. Enter the number of each transaction in the Item column, and enter the amounts in the appropriate columns. For amounts in the Other Accounts column, also indicate the account title.

P9-2A Cumby Inc. incurred the following expenditures in a recent year:

Classify expenditures. (SO 1, 7)

Expenditure	Account Title
1. Architect fees	
2. Cost to demolish an old building that is on a piece of land intended for a new building	
3. Lawyer's fees associated with a successful patent application	
4. Lawyer's fees associated with an unsuccessful patent application	
5. Cost of a grease and oil change on the company's truck	
6. Cost of installing a new roof on the company's building	

Expenditure	Account Title
7. Cost of painting the president's office	
8. Cost of CDs and printer ink for the office computer	
9. Payment to a celebrity for endorsement of a product. The celebrity's endorsement is featured in television advertisements which have been airing for the past three months and will continue to be televised for another six months after year end.	
10. Cost of four new tires for the company delivery van	
11. Cost to rebuild the engine on the company delivery van	
12. Cost to pave the company parking lot	
13. Cost of painting the corporate logo on the sides of the company delivery van	

Instructions

For each of the above expenditures, indicate the account title to which the expenditure should be recorded.

Journalize equipment transactions related to purchase, sale, and retirement; prepare partial balance sheet.
(SO 1, 3, 5, 8)

P9-3A At December 31, 2001, Hamsmith Corporation reported these tangible capital assets:

Land		$ 3,000,000
Buildings	$26,500,000	
Less: Accumulated amortization—buildings	12,100,000	14,400,000
Equipment:	$40,000,000	
Less: Accumulated amortization—equipment	5,000,000	35,000,000
Total capital assets		$52,400,000

During 2002, the following selected cash transactions occurred:

Apr. 1	Purchased land for $2,200,000.
May 1	Sold equipment that cost $600,000 when purchased on January 1, 1998. The equipment was sold for $350,000.
June 1	Sold land for $1,800,000. The land cost $500,000.
July 1	Purchased equipment for $1,200,000.
Dec. 31	Retired equipment that cost $500,000 when purchased on December 31, 1992. No salvage value was received.

Instructions

(a) Journalize the transactions. (Hint: You may wish to set up T accounts, post beginning balances, and then post transactions for 2002.) Hamsmith uses straight-line amortization for buildings and equipment. The buildings are estimated to have a 40-year useful life and no salvage value; the equipment is estimated to have a 10-year useful life and no salvage value. Update amortization on assets disposed of at the time of sale or retirement.

(b) Record adjusting entries for amortization for 2002.

(c) Prepare the capital assets section of Hamsmith's balance sheet at December 31, 2002.

Revise amortization.
(SO 4)

P9-4A On January 1, 2000, Harrington Corporation acquired equipment costing $40,000. It was estimated at that time that this equipment would have a useful life of six years and a salvage value of $4,000. The straight-line method of amortization is used by Harrington for its equipment; and its fiscal year end is December 31.

At the beginning of 2002 (the beginning of the third year of the equipment's life), the company's engineers reconsidered their expectations, and estimated that the equipment's useful life would more likely be seven years in total, instead of the previously estimated six years. The estimated salvage value was also reduced to $2,400.

Instructions

(a) Indicate how much amortization expense should be recorded each year for this equipment by completing the following table. (Hint: Don't forget to revise amortization in 2002.)

Year	Amortization Expense	Accumulated Amortization
2000		
2001		
2002		
2003		
2004		
2005		
2006		

(b) What is the net book value of the asset at the end of its useful life, on December 31, 2006?

(c) If Harrington Corporation had *not* revised the equipment's remaining useful life, what would its total amortization expense and accumulated amortization have been? The net book value of the asset on December 31, 2006?

Journalize transactions related to disposals of tangible capital assets.

(SO 5)

P9-5A Express Corp. has delivery equipment that cost $48,000 and accumulated amortization of $20,000.

Instructions

Record entries for the disposal under the following assumptions:

(a) It was scrapped as having no value.

(b) It was sold for $31,000.

(c) It was sold for $18,000.

Show how capital assets are reported on the balance sheet; prepare journal entries for disposal of capital assets.

(SO 5, 7, 8)

P9-6A You are presented with the following list of accounts for the capital assets of Byrd Barracudas Ltd. as at October 31, 2001:

Accounts	Amount
Accumulated amortization—automobiles	$ 32,000
Accumulated amortization—equipment	11,000
Accumulated amortization—goodwill	21,000
Accumulated amortization—office building	30,000
Accumulated amortization—patent	15,000
Automobiles	45,000
Equipment	36,000
Goodwill	37,000
Land	65,000
Office building	120,000
Patent	25,000

Instructions

(a) Prepare the capital assets section for Byrd Barracudas as at October 31, 2001, in proper format.

(b) On November 1, 2001, the automobiles are sold for $15,000. Also on that date, the patents are written off as they are deemed to be worthless because of a technological breakthrough made by a competitor. Prepare journal entries to record these transactions.

Calculate and comment on average age, average useful life, and asset turnover ratios.

(SO 6)

P9-7A Croix Corporation and Rye Corporation, two corporations of roughly the same size, are both involved in the manufacturing of canoes and sea kayaks. Each company amortizes its capital assets using the straight-line approach. An investigation of their financial statements reveals this information:

	Croix Corp.	Rye Corp.
Net earnings	$ 400,000	$ 600,000
Sales	1,400,000	1,200,000
Total assets	2,000,000	1,500,000
Property, plant, and equipment	1,500,000	800,000
Accumulated amortization	300,000	625,000
Amortization expense	135,000	25,000

Instructions

(a) For each company, calculate these values:
   1. Average age of property, plant, and equipment
   2. Average useful life of property, plant, and equipment
   3. Asset turnover ratio

(b) Based on your calculations in part (a), comment on the relative effectiveness of the two companies in using their assets to generate sales and produce net earnings. What factors complicate your ability to compare the two companies?

Prepare entries to correct errors in recording and amortizing intangible capital assets.
(SO 7)

P9-8A Due to rapid employee turnover in the accounting department, the following transactions involving intangible capital assets were improperly recorded by Riley Corporation in 2001:

1. Riley developed a new manufacturing process, incurring research costs of $102,000. The company also purchased a patent for $37,400. In early January, Riley capitalized $139,400 as the cost of the patent. Patent amortization expense of $8,200 was recorded based on a 20-year useful life.
2. On July 1, 2001, Riley purchased a small company and as a result acquired goodwill of $60,000. Riley recorded a half year's amortization in 2001, based on a 50-year life ($600 amortization).

Instructions

Prepare all journal entries necessary to correct any errors made during 2001. Assume the books have not yet been closed for 2001.

Prepare entries to record transactions related to acquisition and amortization of intangibles; prepare the intangible capital assets section.
(SO 7, 8)

P9-9A The intangible capital asset section of Ghani Corporation's balance sheet at December 31, 2000, is presented here:

Patent ($60,000 cost less $6,000 amortization)	$54,000
Copyright ($36,000 cost less $14,400 amortization)	21,600
Total	$75,600

The patent was acquired in January 2000 and has a useful life of 10 years. The copyright was acquired in January 1997 and also has a useful life of 10 years. The following cash transactions may have affected intangible assets during 2001:

Jan. 2	Paid $9,000 legal costs to successfully defend the patent against infringement by another company.
Jan.–June	Developed a new product, incurring $140,000 in research and $50,000 in development costs. A patent was granted for the product on July 1, and its useful life is equal to its legal life.
Sept. 1	Paid $60,000 to a popular hockey player to appear in commercials advertising the company's products. The commercials will air in September and October.
Oct. 1	Acquired a copyright for $100,000. The copyright has a useful life of 50 years.

Instructions

(a) Prepare journal entries to record the transactions.
(b) Prepare journal entries to record the 2001 amortization expense for intangible assets.
(c) Prepare the intangible capital assets section of the balance sheet at December 31, 2001.

Calculate amortization under different methods.
(SO 3, 9)

***P9-10A** In recent years, Wind Corporation has purchased three machines. Because of frequent employee turnover in the accounting department, a different accountant was in charge of selecting the amortization method for each machine, and various methods have been used. Information concerning the machines is summarized in the table:

Machine	Acquired	Cost	Salvage Value	Useful Life (in years)	Amortization Method
1	Jan. 1, 1998	$ 86,000	$ 6,000	10	Straight-line
2	Jan. 1, 1999	100,000	10,000	8	Declining-balance
3	Nov. 1, 2001	78,000	6,000	6	Units-of-activity

For the declining-balance method, Wind Corporation uses the double-declining rate. For the units-of-activity method, total machine hours are expected to be 24,000. Actual hours of use in the first three years were: 2001, 4,000 hours; 2002, 4,500 hours; and 2003, 5,000 hours.

Instructions

(a) Calculate the amount of accumulated amortization on each machine at December 31, 2001.

(b) If machine 2 had been purchased on April 1 instead of January 1, what would be the amortization expense for this machine in 1999? In 2000? In 2001?

***P9-11A** Whitley Corporation purchased machinery on January 1, 2001, at a cost of $100,000. The estimated useful life of the machinery is four years, with an estimated residual value at the end of that period of $10,000. The company is considering different amortization methods that could be used for financial reporting purposes.

Calculate amortization under different methods.
(SO 3, 9)

Instructions

(a) Prepare separate amortization schedules for the machinery using the straight-line method and the declining-balance method using double the straight-line rate. Round to the nearest dollar.

(b) Which method would result in the higher reported 2001 earnings? In the highest total reported earnings over the four-year period?

(c) Which method would result in the higher reported 2001 cash flow? In the highest total reported cash flow over the four-year period?

***P9-12A** Forristal Farmers Inc. purchased a piece of equipment at a cost of $21,000. The equipment has an estimated useful life of four years with an estimated residual value at the end of the four years of $1,000. The president is debating the merits of using the single (*not* double) declining-balance method of amortization as opposed to the straight-line method of amortization. The president feels that the straight-line method will have a more favourable impact on the statement of earnings.

Calculate amortization under straight-line and declining-balance methods; calculate gain or loss on disposal and total expense over life of asset.
(SO 3, 5, 9)

Instructions

(a) Prepare a schedule comparing the amortization expense and net book values for each of the four years, and in total for the four years, under
  1. the straight-line method
  2. the declining-balance method

(b) Assume that the equipment is sold at the end of the third year for $7,000.
  1. Calculate the gain or loss on the sale of the equipment, under
     i. the straight-line method
     ii. the declining-balance method
  2. Prepare a schedule to show the overall impact of the total amortization expense combined with the gain or loss on sale for the three-year period under each method of amortization (consider the total effect on net earnings over the three-year period). Comment on your results.

Problems: Set B

P9-1B Kadlec Company Inc. was organized on January 1. During the first year of operations, the following asset expenditures and receipts were recorded in random order:

Determine acquisition costs of land and building.
(SO 1)

Debits	
1. Cost of real estate purchased as a plant site (land, $100,000, and building, $45,000)	$145,000
2. Accrued real estate taxes paid at time of purchase of real estate	2,000
3. Cost of demolishing building to make land suitable for construction of new building	12,000
4. Cost of filling and grading the land	4,000
5. Excavation costs for new building	20,000
6. Architect's fees on building plans	10,000
7. Full payment to building contractor	700,000
8. Cost of parking lots and driveways	14,000
9. Real estate taxes paid for the current year on land	5,000
	$912,000

Credits

10. Proceeds for salvage of demolished building	$ 3,500

Instructions

Analyse the transactions using the following four table column headings: Item; Land; Building; Other Accounts. Enter the number of each transaction in the Item column, and enter the amounts in the appropriate columns. For amounts in the Other Accounts column, also indicate the account titles.

Classify expenditures and report capital assets on balance sheet.
(SO 1, 7, 8)

P9-2B The following expenditures were made for Cohlmeyer Corporation, as it was getting ready to commence its first year of operations:

Jan. 10	Land was purchased for $65,000.
Jan. 15	The land was surveyed at a cost of $3,000.
Feb. 1	An existing building on the land was razed at a cost of $5,500 to provide room for the new structure.
Feb. 10	A security fence was built around the land for $2,500.
Feb. 23	$10,500 was paid to an architectural firm for plans for the new building.
Mar. 15	$3,500 was spent to remove trees and level the land in preparation for construction of the new building.
Mar. 17	A building permit was acquired for $1,000.
Apr. 10	Paid $5,000 in legal and application costs for a patent on a newly developed product that will be sold by Cohlmeyer.
May 1	$460,000 was spent to construct the building.
May 15	$4,000 was spent on landscaping.
May 20	A parking lot was constructed for $8,000.
May 25	The company's domain name, <www.cohlmeyer.ca>, was registered for $150.
May 28	Paid $4,000 to the lawyer for organizing costs of the new company.
June 1	The building was occupied and business commenced.

Instructions

(a) For each of the above expenditures, indicate the account title to which the expenditure should be recorded (debited).

(b) Prepare the capital assets section of the balance sheet for Cohlmeyer Corporation on June 1.

Journalize equipment transactions related to purchase, sale, and retirement; prepare partial balance sheet.
(SO 1, 3, 5, 8)

P9-3B At December 31, 2000, Yount Corporation reported these tangible capital assets:

Land		$ 4,000,000
Buildings	$28,500,000	
Less: Accumulated amortization—buildings	12,100,000	16,400,000
Equipment	$48,000,000	
Less: Accumulated amortization—equipment	5,000,000	43,000,000
Total tangible capital assets		$63,400,000

During 2001, the following selected cash transactions occurred:

Apr. 1	Purchased land for $2,630,000.
May 1	Sold equipment that cost $600,000 when purchased on January 1, 1997. The equipment was sold for $370,000.
June 1	Sold land purchased on June 1, 1991, for $1,800,000. The land cost $200,000.
July 1	Purchased equipment for $1,200,000.
Dec. 31	Retired equipment that cost $500,000 when purchased on December 31, 1991. No salvage value was received.

Instructions

(a) Journalize the transactions. (Hint: You may wish to set up T accounts, post beginning balances, and then post transactions for 2001.) Yount uses straight-line amortization for buildings and equipment. The buildings are estimated to have a 40-year life and no salvage value; the equipment is estimated to have a 10-year useful life and no salvage value. Update amortization on assets disposed of at the time of sale or retirement.

(b) Record adjusting entries for amortization for 2001.
(c) Prepare the tangible capital asset section of Yount's balance sheet at December 31, 2001.

P9-4B Tashia's Interior Decorators Ltd. operates out of an office building that it purchased 25 years ago for $85,000. Tashia estimates that the building has a useful life of 50 years and no salvage value. Tashia has been using straight-line amortization for the 25 years that the building has been in use.

Revise amortization; calculate gain or loss on disposal. (SO 4, 5)

At the beginning of the current year, Tashia installed an air conditioning system for the building. The air conditioning unit cost $19,125 and is embedded in the structure of the building; it cannot be easily removed. The air conditioning unit has a 30-year useful life.

Instructions

(a) What was the book value of the building at the beginning of the current year?
(b) How much amortization expense should be recorded in the current year, which is the twenty-sixth year of using the building?
(c) What is the book value of the capital asset at the end of the thirtieth year?
(d) Assume that the building is disposed of at the end of the thirtieth year for $40,000. What is the gain or loss on disposal?

P9-5B Walker Corp. has office furniture that cost $80,000 and has been amortized $47,000.

Journalize transactions related to disposals of tangible capital assets. (SO 5)

Instructions

Record entries for the disposal under these assumptions:
(a) It was scrapped as having no value.
(b) It was sold for $21,000.
(c) It was sold for $61,000.

P9-6B The following selected information, presented in alphabetical order, was extracted from the financial statements of **Northwest Sports Enterprises Ltd.**, owner of the Vancouver Canucks National Hockey League team, as at June 30, 1999:

Show how capital assets are reported on the balance sheet and determine average age and average useful life. (SO 6, 7, 8)

Accounts	Amount
Accumulated amortization—equipment	$ 710,146
Accumulated amortization—hockey franchise and rights to players	1,505,644
Accumulated amortization—leasehold improvements	160,454
Amortization expense—equipment	157,963
Amortization expense—hockey franchise and rights to players	188,206
Amortization expense—leasehold improvements	46,546
Equipment	1,003,764
Hockey franchise and rights to players	7,528,235
Leasehold improvements	1,049,516

Instructions

(a) Prepare the capital assets section of the balance sheet, in good format, as at June 30, 1999.
(b) Northwest Sports uses the straight-line method of amortization. Determine the average age and average useful life (using year-end balances) of the equipment, leasehold improvements, and hockey franchise and rights to players.

P9-7B Reggie Corporation and Newman Corporation, two corporations of roughly the same size, are both involved in the manufacturing of in-line skates. Each company amortizes its capital assets using the straight-line approach. An investigation of their financial statements reveals the information:

Calculate and comment on average age, average useful life, and asset turnover ratios. (SO 6)

	Reggie Corp.	Newman Corp.
Net earnings	$ 800,000	$1,000,000
Sales	1,600,000	1,300,000
Total assets	2,500,000	1,700,000
Property, plant, and equipment	1,800,000	1,000,000
Accumulated amortization	500,000	825,000
Amortization expense	180,000	31,250

Instructions

(a) For each company, calculate these values:
    1. Average age of property, plant, and equipment
    2. Average useful life of property, plant, and equipment
    3. Asset turnover ratio
(b) Based on your calculations in part (a), comment on the relative effectiveness of the two companies in using their assets to generate sales and produce net earnings. What factors complicate your ability to compare the two companies?

Prepare entries to correct errors in recording and amortizing intangible capital assets.
(SO 7)

P9-8B Due to rapid employee turnover in the accounting department, the following transactions involving intangible capital assets were improperly recorded by the Glover Company Ltd. in 2001:

1. Glover developed a new manufacturing process, incurring research costs of $136,000. The company also purchased a patent for $39,100. In early January, Glover capitalized $175,100 as the cost of the patents. Patent amortization expense of $10,300 was recorded based on a 20-year useful life.
2. On July 1, 2001, Glover purchased a small company and, as a result, acquired goodwill of $76,000. Glover recorded a half year's amortization in 2001 based on a 50-year life ($760 amortization).

Instructions

Prepare all journal entries necessary to correct any errors made during 2001. Assume the books have not yet been closed for 2001.

Prepare entries to record transactions related to acquisition and amortization of intangibles; prepare the intangible capital asset section and notes.
(SO 7, 8)

P9-9B The intangible capital asset section of the balance sheet for Eikel Company Inc. at December 31, 2000, is presented here:

Patent ($70,000 cost less $7,000 amortization)	$63,000
Copyright ($48,000 cost less $19,200 amortization)	28,800
Total	$91,800

The patent was acquired in January 2000 and has a useful life of 10 years. The copyright was acquired in January 1997 and also has a useful life of 10 years. The following cash transactions may have affected intangible assets during 2001:

Jan. 2	Paid $9,000 legal costs to successfully defend the patent against infringement by another company.
Jan.–June	Developed a new product, incurring $140,000 in research costs and $60,000 in development costs. A patent was granted for the product on July 1, and its useful life is equal to its legal life.
Sept. 1	Paid $80,000 to a successful rugby player to appear in commercials advertising the company's products. The commercials will air in September and October.
Oct. 1	Acquired a copyright for $80,000. The copyright has a useful life of 50 years.

Instructions

(a) Prepare journal entries to record the transactions.
(b) Prepare journal entries to record the 2001 amortization expense.
(c) Prepare the intangible capital assets section of the balance sheet at December 31, 2001.
(d) Prepare the notes to the financial statements on Eikel Company's intangible assets as at December 31, 2001.

Calculate amortization under different methods.
(SO 3, 9)

***P9-10B** Rapid Transportation purchased three used buses on January 1, 2000. Because of frequent employee turnover in the accounting department, a different accountant selected the amortization method for each bus and various methods have been used. Information concerning the buses is summarized in the table:

Bus	Acquired	Cost	Salvage Value	Useful Life (in years)	Amortization Method
1	Jan. 1, 2000	$ 96,000	$ 6,000	5	Straight-line
2	Jan. 1, 2000	120,000	10,000	4	Declining-balance
3	Jan. 1, 2000	80,000	8,000	5	Units-of-activity

For the declining-balance method, Rapid Transportation uses the double-declining rate. For the units-of-activity method, total kilometres are expected to be 120,000. Actual kilometres of use in the first three years were: 2000, 24,000 km; 2001, 34,000 km; and 2002, 30,000 km.

Instructions

(a) Calculate the amount of accumulated amortization on each bus at December 31, 2002.
(b) If Bus 2 was purchased on April 1 instead of January 1, what would be the amortization expense for this bus in 2000? In 2001? In 2002?

Calculate amortization under different methods.
(SO 3, 9)

***P9-11B** Scott Piper Corporation purchased machinery on January 1, 2001, at a cost of $243,000. The estimated useful life of the machinery is five years, with an estimated residual value at the end of that period of $12,000. The company is considering different amortization methods that could be used for financial reporting purposes.

Instructions

(a) Prepare separate amortization schedules for the machinery using the straight-line method, and the declining-balance method using one times the straight-line rate.
(b) Which method would result in the higher reported 2001 earnings? In the highest total reported earnings over the five-year period?
(c) Which method would result in the higher reported 2001 cash flow? In the highest total reported cash flow over the five-year period?

Calculate gain or loss on disposal and total expense over life of asset.
(SO 5, 9)

***P9-12B** Refer to Demonstration Problem 1 and its solution, on pages 497 and 498. Assume that rather than keeping the machine until the end of its useful life, DuPage Company Ltd. sells it at the end of 2003 for $4,400. Note that since the disposal occurs at the end of the year, the full amount of amortization is charged for 2003.

Instructions

(a) Calculate the gain or loss on the sale of the machine, under each of the three methods of amortization (straight-line, units-of-activity, and declining-balance) used in the Demonstration Problem.
(b) Comment on the results obtained in part (a). Can you say which of the amortization methods was the best, in this particular situation?
(c) For each of the three methods of amortization, calculate the overall impact of the amortization expense combined with the gain or loss on the sale of the machine. Consider the total effect on net earnings over the three-year period.
(d) Comment on the results obtained in part (c). What do they tell you about the relationship between the amount of amortization expense that is recorded during the asset's life and the gain or loss that is recorded on its disposal?

BROADENING YOUR PERSPECTIVE

FINANCIAL REPORTING AND ANALYSIS

FINANCIAL REPORTING PROBLEM: *Loblaw Corporation Limited*

BYP9-1 Refer to the financial statements and the Notes to Consolidated Financial Statements of **Loblaw**, in Appendix A.

Instructions

Answer the following questions:
(a) What were the total cost and net book value of fixed assets at January 1, 2000?
(b) What method or methods of amortization are used by Loblaw for financial reporting purposes?
(c) What was the amount of amortization expense and accumulated amortization for each of the two fiscal years 1998 and 1999?
(d) Using the statement of cash flows, what are the amounts of fixed assets purchased in 1999 and 1998?

(e) Read Loblaw's "Note 6. Fixed Assets" and "Note 10. Other Information" about contingent liabilities and commitments. Does the company primarily engage in capital leases or operating leases? What are the implications for analysis of its financial statements?

COMPARATIVE ANALYSIS PROBLEM: *Loblaw and Sobeys*

Loblaws
A passion for food... *and a lot more!*

Sobeys

BYP9-2 The financial statements of **Sobeys Inc.** are presented in Appendix B, following the financial statements for **Loblaw** in Appendix A.

Instructions

(a) Based on the information in these financial statements, calculate the following values for each company in 1999:
  1. Average useful life of fixed assets for Loblaw; property and equipment for Sobeys
  2. Average age of fixed assets for Loblaw; property and equipment for Sobeys
  3. Asset turnover ratio

(b) What conclusions concerning the management of tangible capital assets can be drawn from these data?

RESEARCH CASE

BYP9-3 Volume 18 of the 1999 issue of the *International Journal of Technology Management* includes an article by Morina Rennie entitled "Accounting for Knowledge Assets: Do We Need a New Financial Statement?" This article discusses the difficulty of accounting for intellectual assets and proposes a method to measure and include these assets in the financial statements.

Instructions

Read the article and answer these questions:

(a) What are knowledge assets?
(b) Where are the costs of creating knowledge currently recorded?
(c) Why do knowledge-based companies have more difficulty in obtaining financing than other companies?
(d) What financial statement does the author recommend creating to record knowledge assets on? Why does she not recommend including these "assets" in the balance sheet?

INTERPRETING FINANCIAL STATEMENTS

BYP9-4 Maple Leaf Foods Inc. is Canada's largest food processor. The company produces fresh and processed pork, poultry, and seafood for retailers and wholesalers, along with pet and livestock feeds. Its bakery groups produce fresh and frozen baked goods and fresh pasta and pasta sauces. Maple Leaf Foods also has operations in the U.S., Asia, and Europe.

Early in 1998, labour disputes occurred at three of Maple Leaf's meat products plants—one of which was a fresh pork facility. Prior to the labour dispute, the fresh pork facility in Burlington processed about 32,000 hogs per week on a single shift. Following resolution of the dispute, the facility initially processed only about 18,000 hogs per week. The hog supply was gradually increased over the balance of the year, to process 44,000 hogs per week.

This dispute had an adverse financial impact on Maple Leaf's financial results. Maple Leaf paid $37 million of labour dispute–related costs and payments to employees upon settlement of the strike at the Burlington fresh pork facility.

On a more positive note, late in 1998, Maple Leaf announced a $40-million investment that would be made over the next few years to add second shift capacity to the facility. When this is complete, it anticipates that it will be able to process 85,000 hogs per week on a double shift.

Instructions

(a) Identify and discuss the advantages and disadvantages of each amortization method for Maple Leaf Foods' pork facilities. Which method would you recommend Maple Leaf use to amortize the capital assets associated with its Burlington plant? Explain why you chose the method you did.

week on a double shift.

Instructions

(a) Identify and discuss the advantages and disadvantages of each amortization method for Maple Leaf Foods' pork facilities. Which method would you recommend Maple Leaf use to amortize the capital assets associated with its Burlington plant? Explain why you chose the method you did.
(b) How should Maple Leaf account for the $37 million of labour dispute–related costs? Determine which financial statement this amount should be reported on, and where.
(c) How should Maple Leaf account for the $40 million investment it will spend to create a world-class prepared meats facility? Discuss whether these costs should be treated as revenue expenditures or capital expenditures.

BYP9-5 Boeing and McDonnell Douglas were two leaders in the manufacturing of aircraft. In 1996, Boeing acquired McDonnell Douglas and created one huge corporation. Today, the **Boeing Company** is the world's largest maker of commercial jets and the number one aerospace company. Competitors, primarily Airbus of Europe, were very concerned that they would not be able to compete with such a huge rival. In addition, customers were concerned that this merger would reduce the number of suppliers to a point where Boeing could dictate prices. Provided below are figures taken from the 1995 financial statements of Boeing and McDonnell Douglas, which allow a comparison of the operations of the two corporations prior to their merger:

(US $ in millions)	**Boeing**	**McDonnell Douglas**
Total revenue	$19,515	$14,322
Net earnings (loss)	393	(416)
Total assets	22,098	10,466
Land	404	91
Buildings and fixtures	5,791	1,647
Machinery and equipment	7,251	2,161
Total property, plant, and equipment (at cost)	13,744	3,899
Accumulated amortization	7,288	2,541
Amortization expense	976	196

Instructions

(a) Which company had older assets?
(b) Which company used a longer average estimated useful life for its assets?
(c) Based on the asset turnover ratio, which company used its assets more effectively to generate sales?
(d) Besides an increase in size, what other factors might have motivated this merger?

J SAINSBURY PLC
Accounting Policies
April 1, 2000

Consolidation
Goodwill arising in connection with the acquisition of shares in subsidiaries and associated undertakings is calculated as the excess of the purchase price over the fair value of the net assets acquired. Under the transitional arrangements of FRS10, goodwill arising on acquisitions prior to 8 March 1998 has been set off against reserves [shareholders' equity]. For subsequent acquisitions, goodwill is recognised as an asset on the Group's balance sheet in the year in which it arises and amortised on a straight line basis over a finite life of a maximum of 20 years and, only under specific circumstances, will it be assumed that goodwill has an indefinite life.

Sainsbury's
making life taste better.

Instructions

(a) How does Sainsbury's current determination and recording of goodwill compare with that in Canada? That is, is goodwill initially calculated, recorded, and amortized in the same manner in both Britain and Canada?
(b) Prior to adoption of the new financial reporting standard (FRS10) in Great Britain, how did Sainsbury account for its goodwill? What were the implications for the balance sheet and statement of earnings?
(c) Similar to the new financial reporting standard in Great Britain, an International Accounting Standard (IAS22) imposes a 20 year ceiling on the amortization of goodwill, unless there is persuasive evidence that the useful life will exceed 20 years. How does this differ from the current practice in Canada? What are the implications of these differences when comparing Sainsbury's financial statements to those of a Canadian company?

FINANCIAL ANALYSIS ON THE WEB

BYP9-7 SEDAR (System for Electronic Document Analysis and Retrieval) provides information about Canadian public companies and access to some of their documents. We will use SEDAR to select a public company, examine its annual report, and identify the company's capital assets, profitability, amortization method, and current year expenditures on capital assets.

Instructions

Specific requirements of this web case can be found on the Kimmel website.

CRITICAL THINKING

COLLABORATIVE LEARNING ACTIVITY

*__BYP9-8__ Tammy Corporation and Hamline Corporation are two companies that are similar in many respects except that Tammy uses the straight-line method and Hamline uses the declining-balance method at double the straight-line rate. On January 2, 1999, both companies acquired the amortizable assets listed in the table.

Asset	Cost	Salvage Value	Useful Life
Building	$320,000	$20,000	40 years
Equipment	110,000	10,000	10 years

Hamline's amortization expense was $38,000 in 1999, $32,800 in 2000, and $28,520 in 2001. Including the appropriate amortization charges, annual net earnings for the companies in the years 1999, 2000, and 2001 and total earnings for the three years were as follows:

	1999	2000	2001	Total
Tammy Corporation	$84,000	$88,400	$90,000	$262,400
Hamline Corporation	68,000	76,000	85,000	229,000

At December 31, 2001, the balance sheets of the two companies are similar except that Hamline has lower assets and retained earnings than Tammy.

Dawna Tucci is interested in investing in one of the companies, and she comes to you for advice.

Instructions

With the class divided into groups, answer the following:
(a) Determine the annual and total amortization recorded by Tammy during the three years.
(b) Assuming that Hamline Company also uses the straight-line method of amortization instead of the declining-balance method (that is, Hamline's amortization expense would equal Tammy's), prepare comparative earnings data for the three years.
(c) Which company should Dawna Tucci buy? Why?

COMMUNICATION ACTIVITY

BYP9-9 The chapter presented some concerns regarding the current accounting standards for research and development expenditures.

Instructions

Pretend that you are either (a) the president of a company that is very dependent on ongoing research and development, and that you are writing a memo to the CICA complaining about the current accounting standards regarding research and development, or (b) the CICA member defending the current standards regarding research and development. Your letter should address these questions:

1. By requiring expensing of research costs, do you think companies will spend less on R&D? Why or why not? What are the possible implications for the competitiveness of Canadian companies?
2. If a company makes a commitment to spend money for R&D, it must believe it has future benefits. Shouldn't these costs all be capitalized just like the purchase of any long-lived asset that you believe will have future benefits?

ETHICS CASE

BYP9-10 Imporia Container Company Ltd. is suffering declining sales of its principal product, nonbiodegradable plastic cartons. The president, Benny Benson, instructs his controller, John Straight, to lengthen asset lives to reduce amortization expense. A processing line of automated plastic extruding equipment, purchased for $2.7 million in January 1999, was originally estimated to have a useful life of eight years and a salvage value of $300,000. Amortization has been recorded for two years on that basis. Benny wants the estimated life changed to 12 years total and the straight-line method continued. John is hesitant to make the change, believing it is unethical to increase net earnings in this manner. Benny says, "Hey, the life is only an estimate, and I've heard that our competition uses a 12-year life on their production equipment."

Instructions

(a) Who are the stakeholders in this situation?
(b) Is the proposed change in asset life unethical or simply a good business practice by an astute president?
(c) What is the effect of Benny Benson's proposed change on earnings before taxes in the year of change?

Answers to Self-Study Questions

1. d 2. a 3. b 4. d 5. c 6. b 7. d 8. d 9. a 10. c
11. c *12. d

Answers to Loblaw Review It Question 3

Loblaw amortizes its buildings over a period of 20 to 40 years and its equipment and fixtures over a period of 3 to 10 years. It amortizes its leasehold improvements over the lesser of the asset's useful life and the lease term.

Loblaws
A passion for food... *and a lot more!*

CHAPTER 10

Reporting and Analysing Liabilities

STUDY OBJECTIVES

After studying this chapter, you should be able to:

1. Explain what a current liability is and identify the major types of current liabilities.
2. Describe the accounting for notes payable.
3. Explain the accounting for other current liabilities.
4. Identify the requirements for the financial statement presentation and analysis of current liabilities.
5. Explain why bonds are issued and identify the types of bonds.
6. Prepare the entries for the issuance of bonds and interest expense.
7. Describe the entries when bonds are redeemed.
8. Identify the requirements for the financial statement presentation and analysis of long-term liabilities.

Borrowing Money to Make Money

"Neither a borrower nor a lender be," says Polonius in Shakespeare's *Hamlet*. But such a philosophy wouldn't get him far in the world of modern business! Take, for example, the case of Pierre Péladeau, who borrowed $1,500 in 1950 to start a small newspaper business. At the time of Mr. Péladeau's death 47 years later, he had turned this small business, through shrewd management and aggressive acquisitions, into one of the largest and most respected companies in Canada—a conglomerate operating on five continents, with over 60,000 employees worldwide and yearly sales counted in the billions.

Mr. Péladeau was often referred to by colleagues as "le grand bâtisseur"—the great builder. The first stone of his company, Quebecor Inc., was laid when he purchased the financially troubled *Le Journal de Rosemont* with that first loan money. Fifteen hundred dollars was a large sum for a 25-year-old law student in 1950. Mr. Péladeau borrowed it from his mother, who had her doubts about the wisdom of the loan. However, Mr. Péladeau was able to turn the neighbourhood weekly's finances around, and soon purchased several others. The next step was to acquire a printing firm, which printed his papers—and others—at a profit. In 1964, when the major Montreal daily was on strike, he founded *Le Journal de Montréal*, which grew to become one of the largest newspapers in the country and the "jewel" in Quebecor's crown.

Shortly thereafter, Quebecor began to grow more rapidly. In the 1970s, it expanded beyond newspapers and printing into other communications media.
In the 1980s, it grew beyond the Canadian border, purchasing several U.S. printing plants in 1985 and then the international printing group BCE PubliTech in 1988.

In the 1990s, Quebecor's growth became exponential. By then in his seventies, Mr. Péladeau continued to preside over a dizzying series of aquisitions. The company continued on this path after his death in 1997 and, by 1999, Quebecor was the largest commercial printer in the world, with

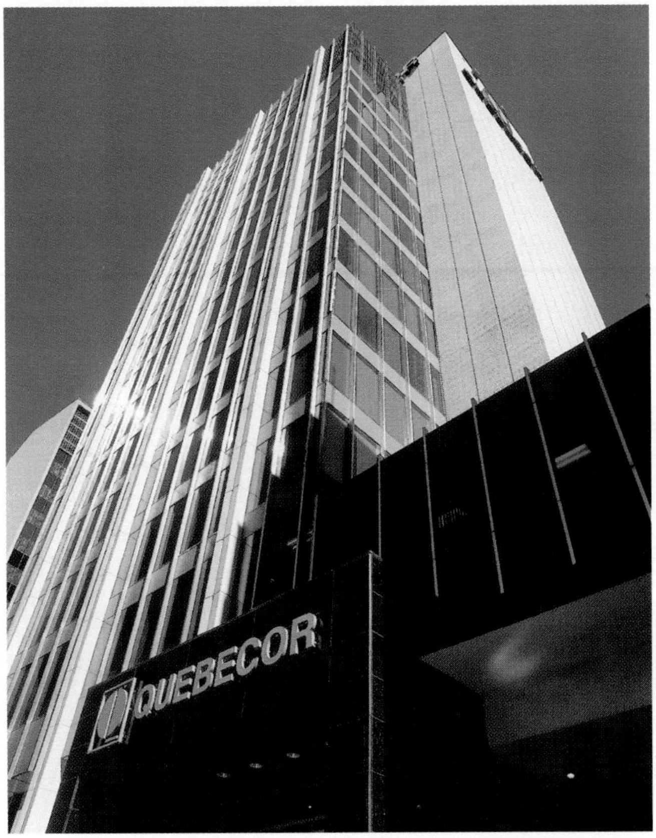

On the World Wide Web
Quebecor Inc.
http://www.quebecor.com

major subsidiaries in several related markets: lumber, pulp, and newsprint marketing; publications for CD-ROM and the Internet; TV networks; magazine and book publication; music retail; and, of course, newspaper publishing (Sun Media, the second-largest newspaper publisher in Canada, is 70% owned by Quebecor).

Clearly, that first loan was a smart move. Mr. Péladeau learned early that borrowing money can make good business sense. As the story of Quebecor shows, strategic acquisitions can be a wildly successful way of making a business grow quickly—and going into debt is one of the ways to finance such acquisitions.

Too much debt, of course, can be dangerous. The return on the investment made with the debt must be enough to cover the cost of the debt. Measures of immediate liquidity, in addition to measures of longer-term solvency, help test a company's strength in this area.

But too little debt can also be a problem. If you can invest only the cash you currently have on hand, you may be missing out on significant opportunities for profit. Pierre Péladeau knew this at age 25, and turned this knowledge into an empire that is envied worldwide.

The opening story suggests that Quebecor has grown rapidly. It is unlikely that it could have grown so large without debt, but at times debt can threaten a company's very existence. Given this risk, why do companies borrow money? Why do they sometimes borrow short-term and other times long-term? Besides bank borrowings, what other kinds of debts does a company incur? In this chapter, we answer these questions.

The content and organization of the chapter are as follows:

REPORTING AND ANALYSING LIABILITIES

Current Liabilities

- What is a Current Liability?
- Types of Current Liabilities
- Financial Statement Presentation and Analysis

Long-Term Liabilities

- Bond Basics
- Accounting for Bond Issues
- Accounting for Bond Retirements
- Financial Statement Presentation and Analysis
- Other Issues in Analysis

SECTION 1

CURRENT LIABILITIES

WHAT IS A CURRENT LIABILITY?

STUDY OBJECTIVE 1

Explain what a current liability is and identify the major types of current liabilities.

You have learned that liabilities are defined as "creditors' claims on total assets" and as "existing debts and obligations." These claims, debts, and obligations must be settled or paid at some time in the future by the transfer of assets or services. The future date on which they are due or payable (the maturity date) is a significant feature of liabilities.

As explained in Chapter 2, a **current liability** is a debt that will be paid (1) from existing current assets or through the creation of other current liabilities, and (2) within one year or the operating cycle, whichever is longer. Debts that do not meet both criteria are classified as **long-term liabilities**.

Financial statement users want to know whether a company's obligations are current or long-term. A company, for example, that has more current liabilities than current assets often lacks liquidity, or short-term debt-paying ability. In addition, users want to know the types of liabilities a company has. If a company declares bankruptcy, a specific, predetermined order of payment to creditors exists. Thus, the amount and type of liabilities are of critical importance.

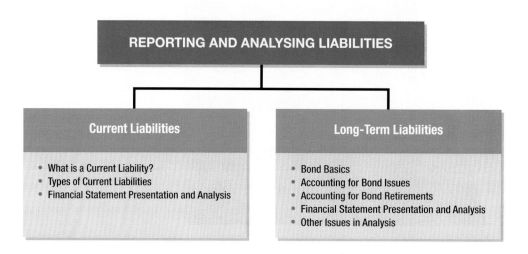

Types of Current Liabilities

The different types of current liabilities include notes payable, accounts payable, unearned revenues, the current portion of long-term debt, and accrued liabilities such as taxes, salaries and wages, and interest. In this section we discuss a few of the common and more important types of current liabilities. All current liabilities that are material should be reported in a company's balance sheet.

Helpful Hint The entries for accounts payable and the adjusting entries for some current liabilities have been explained in previous chapters.

NOTES PAYABLE

Obligations in the form of written notes are recorded as **notes payable**. Notes payable are often used instead of accounts payable because they give the lender written documentation of the obligation, which helps if legal remedies are needed to collect the debt. Notes payable are frequently issued to meet short-term financing needs and usually require the borrower to pay interest.

STUDY OBJECTIVE 2

Describe the accounting for notes payable.

Notes are issued for varying periods of time. **Those due for payment within one year of the balance sheet date are usually classified as current liabilities**. For example, recently, Southam Inc., the largest daily newspaper publisher in Canada, reported $147 million of short-term notes payable. Most notes are interest-bearing, and Southam's averaged an annual interest rate of 5.2%.

To illustrate the accounting for notes payable, assume that the HSBC Bank agrees to lend $100,000 on March 1, 2001, if Williams Co. Ltd. signs a $100,000, 12%, four-month note. With an interest-bearing note, the amount of assets received when the note is issued generally equals the note's face value. Williams, therefore, will receive $100,000 cash and will make the following journal entry:

Mar. 1	Cash	100,000	
	Notes Payable		100,000
	(To record issuance of 12%, four-month note to the HSBC Bank)		

A	=	L	+	SE
+100,000		+100,000		

Interest accrues over the life of the note and must be recorded periodically. If Williams has a March 31 year end, an adjusting entry is required to recognize interest expense and interest payable of $1,000 ($\$100,000 \times 12\% \times \frac{1}{12}$) at March 31. The adjusting entry is

Mar. 31	Interest Expense	1,000	
	Interest Payable		1,000
	(To accrue interest for one month on the HSBC Bank note)		

A	=	L	+	SE
		+1,000		−1,000

In the March 31 financial statements, the current liability section of the balance sheet will show notes payable, $100,000, and interest payable, $1,000. In addition, interest expense of $1,000 will be reported separately in the statement of earnings.

At maturity (July 1), Williams Co. Ltd. must pay the face value of the note ($100,000) plus $4,000 interest ($\$100,000 \times 12\% \times \frac{4}{12}$), $1,000 of which has already been accrued. The entry to record payment of the note and interest is

A	=	L	+	SE
−104,000		−100,000		−3,000
		−1,000		

July 1	Notes Payable	100,000	
	Interest Payable	1,000	
	Interest Expense ($100,000 × 12% × $\frac{3}{12}$)	3,000	
	Cash		104,000
	(To record payment of Hong Kong Bank interest-bearing note and accrued interest at maturity)		

SALES TAXES PAYABLE

STUDY OBJECTIVE 3

Explain the accounting for other current liabilities.

As consumers, we are well aware that many of the products we purchase at retail stores are subject to sales taxes. The taxes are expressed as a percentage of the sales price. As discussed in Chapter 5, sales taxes may take the form of the Goods and Services Tax (GST), Provincial Sales Tax (PST), or Harmonized Sales Tax (HST). In Quebec, the PST is known as the Quebec Sales Tax (QST). Federal GST is assessed at 7%. Provincial sales tax rates vary from 0% to 10% across Canada, and are subject to change. In Newfoundland and Labrador, Nova Scotia, and New Brunswick, the PST and GST have been combined into one 15% Harmonized Sales Tax.

The retailer (or selling company) collects the tax from the customer, when the sale occurs, and periodically (monthly or quarterly) remits the GST (or HST) collected to the Receiver General, and PST collected to the provincial Minister of Finance or Treasurer, as the case may be. In the case of GST and HST, collections may be offset against payments and only the net amount owing must be remitted.

The amount of the sale and the amount of the sales tax collected are usually rung up separately on the cash register. The cash register readings are then used to credit the Sales and Sales Taxes Payable accounts. For example, assuming that the March 25 cash register readings for the Setthawiwat Corporation show sales of $10,000, federal sales taxes of $700 (7% GST rate), and provincial sales taxes of $800 (PST rate of 8%), the entry is

A	=	L	+	SE
+11,500		+700		+10,000
		+800		

Mar. 25	Cash	11,500	
	Sales		10,000
	GST Payable ($10,000 × 7%)		700
	PST Payable ($10,000 × 8%)		800
	(To record daily sales and sales taxes)		

When the taxes are remitted to the Receiver General and/or Minister of Finance/Treasurer, GST and PST (or HST) Payable is debited and Cash is credited. The company does not report sales taxes as an expense; it simply forwards the amount paid by the customer to the government. Thus, Setthawiwat Corporation serves only as a collection agent for the respective government.

Helpful Hint Watch how sales are rung up at local retailers to see whether the sales tax is calculated separately.

Some businesses account for their sales on a tax inclusive basis, not separating sales taxes from their sales price. When this occurs, sales taxes must still be recorded apart from sales revenues. Total receipts can be divided by 100% plus the sales tax percentage to determine sales. To illustrate, assume in the above example that Setthawiwat records total receipts, which are $11,500. Because the amount received from the sale is equal to the sales price, 100%, plus 15% (7% + 8%) of sales, or 1.15 times the sales total, we can calculate sales as follows:

$$\$11,500 \div 1.15 = \$10,000$$

Thus, the total sales tax amount of $1,500 ($700 + $800) can be found by subtracting sales from total receipts ($11,500 – $10,000). The components of this total can be found by multiplying sales by the respective sales tax rates ($10,000 x 7% and $10,000 x 8%).

In some provinces, PST is charged on GST. For example, in P.E.I. a $100 sale would result in $7 GST (7%) and $10.70 PST [($100 + $7) x 10%] being paid. The escalated sales tax rate is 17.7% [($7 + $10.70) ÷ $100] rather than the 17% (7% GST + 10% PST). Caution must be exercised when extracting sales tax amounts from total receipts because of the varying rate combinations that may be in use.

BUSINESS INSIGHT

Management Perspective

The extent and complexity of sales taxes has increased so much over the past years that Canada now has the dubious distinction of having one of the world's most complicated sales tax systems. Some movement was made to embrace the principles of a single rate, a common base, and one administration with the institution of the HST in three Atlantic Canadian provinces in 1997. However, much more work needs to be done. Catherine McCutcheon, Tax Partner and Head of Arthur Andersen's Commodity Tax Practice, comments: "We have a patchwork of complex sales tax systems in Canada. What we need is consistency across the country. Only with uniformity and simplicity will we be able to realize the projected cost savings of $100 million for provincial governments and between $400 and $700 million for business."

PAYROLL AND EMPLOYEE BENEFITS PAYABLE

Every employer incurs liabilities relating to employees' salaries or wages. One is the amount of salary or wages owed to employees—Salaries and Wages Payable. Another is the amount required by law to be withheld from employees' gross pay. Until these withholdings—federal and provincial income taxes, Canada Pension Plan (CPP) contributions, and employment insurance (EI) premiums—are remitted to governmental taxing authorities, they are recorded as increases (credited) to appropriate liability accounts. Employees may also voluntarily authorize withholdings for charitable, retirement, medical, and other purposes. Illustration 10-1 summarizes the types of payroll deductions that normally occur.

Illustration 10-1
Payroll deductions

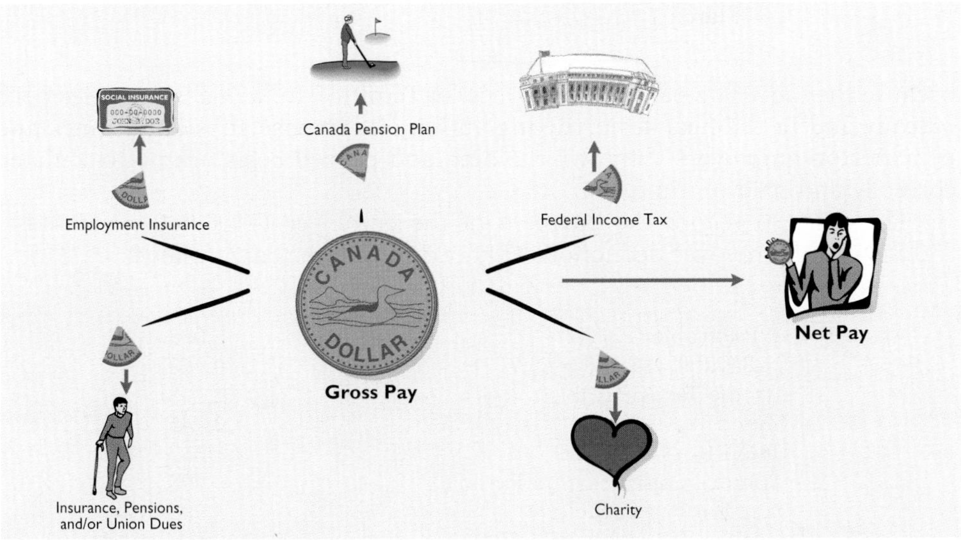

The following entry illustrates accrual and payment of a $100,000 payroll on which a corporation withholds deductions from its employees' wages and salaries. These entries could also be combined into one compound journal entry.

A	=	L	+	SE
		+2,544		−100,000
		+2,695		
		+22,238		
		+2,445		
		+667		
		+69,411		

Mar. 7	Salaries and Wages Expense	100,000	
	CPP Payable		2,544
	EI Payable		2,695
	Income Taxes Payable		22,238
	United Way Payable		2,445
	Union Dues Payable		667
	Salaries and Wages Payable		69,411
	(To record payroll and withholding taxes for the week ending March 7)		

A	=	L	+	SE
−69,411		−69,411		

7	Salaries and Wages Payable	69,411	
	Cash		69,411
	(To record payment of the March 7 payroll)		

While employee payroll deductions do not create an expense for their employers, employer payroll contributions do. With every payroll, the employer incurs liabilities to pay various payroll costs, such as the employer's share of CPP and EI, that are levied upon it. In addition, the provincial governments mandate employer funding of a Workplace Health, Safety and Compensation Plan. Each of these contributions, plus items such as paid vacations and employer-sponsored pensions, are collectively referred to as employee benefits.

Based on the $100,000 payroll in our example, the following entry would be made to record the employer's expense and liability for these payroll costs:
The payroll and payroll liability accounts are classified as current liabilities

A	=	L	+	SE
		+2,544		−11,308
		+3,773		
		+998		
		+3,993		

Mar. 7	Employee Benefits Expense	11,308	
	CPP Payable		2,544
	EI Payable		3,773
	Worker's Compensation Payable		998
	Vacation Pay Payable		3,993
	(To record employer's payroll costs on March 7 payroll)		

because they must be paid to employees, or remitted to taxing authorities periodically and in the near term. Taxing authorities impose substantial fines and penalties on employers if the withholding and payroll costs are not calculated correctly and paid on time.

The entry to record the payment of the employee ($100,000 − $69,411 = $30,589), and employer deductions ($11,308) at a later date, follows:

A	=	L	+	SE
−41,897		−5,088		
		−6,468		
		−22,238		
		−2,445		
		−667		
		−998		
		−3,993		

Mar. 15	CPP Payable ($2,544 + $2,544)	5,088	
	EI Payable ($2,695 + $3,773)	6,468	
	Income Taxes Payable	22,238	
	United Way Payable	2,445	
	Union Dues Payable	667	
	Worker's Compensation Payable	998	
	Vacation Pay Payable	3,993	
	Cash ($30,589 + $11,308)		41,897
	(To record payment of employee and employer deductions)		

CORPORATE INCOME TAXES PAYABLE

For many corporations, income tax can be a significant cash outflow. The combined federal and provincial income tax rate averages 45% of income for large businesses and 20% for small businesses. Income taxes are calculated annually on the earnings of the corporation, but must be estimated and remitted monthly. Therefore, the year-end current liability on the balance sheet is usually much less than the income tax expense reported for the period on the statement of earnings. Most small businesses have three months (two months for larger companies) after year end to remit any balance due without penalty, and six months after their fiscal year end to file their completed income tax return.

International Note

Canadian corporations face income tax rates—about 43%—that are second only to Japan (51%), of all the OECD countries. The U.S. corporate tax rate averages 39%, the UK, 30%, and Hungary, 18%.

UNEARNED REVENUES

A magazine publisher, such as Maclean's, may receive a customer's cheque when magazines are ordered, and an airline company, such as Air Canada, often receives cash when it sells tickets for future flights. How do these companies account for unearned revenues that are received before goods are delivered or services are rendered?

Alternative Terminology
Unearned revenues are also referred to as *deferred revenues* or simply as *advances.*

1. When the advance is received, Cash is increased (debited), and a current liability account identifying the source of the unearned revenue is also increased (credited).
2. When the revenue is earned, the unearned revenue account is decreased (debited), and an earned revenue account is increased (credited).

To illustrate, assume that Superior University sells 1,000 season hockey tickets at $50 each for its five-game home schedule. The entry for the sales of season tickets is

Sept. 6	Cash	50,000	
	Unearned Hockey Ticket Revenue		50,000
	(To record sale of 1,000 season tickets)		

A	=	L	+	SE
+50,000		+50,000		

As each game is completed, this entry is made:

Oct. 7	Unearned Hockey Ticket Revenue	10,000	
	Hockey Ticket Revenue		10,000
	(To record hockey ticket revenues earned)		

A	=	L	+	SE
		-10,000		+10,000

The account Unearned Hockey Ticket Revenue represents unearned revenue and is reported as a current liability in the balance sheet. As revenue is earned, a transfer from unearned revenue to earned revenue occurs. Unearned revenue is material for some companies: in the airline industry, tickets sold for future flights represent almost 50% of total current liabilities. At Air Canada, unearned ticket revenue is the second largest current liability, recently amounting to more than $349 million.

Illustration 10-2 shows specific unearned and earned revenue accounts used in selected types of businesses.

Illustration 10-2
Unearned and earned revenue accounts

Type of Business	Account Title	
	Unearned Revenue	**Earned Revenue**
Airline	Unearned Passenger Ticket Revenue	Passenger Ticket Revenue
Magazine publisher	Unearned Subscription Revenue	Subscription Revenue
Hotel	Unearned Rental Revenue	Rental Revenue

CURRENT MATURITIES OF LONG-TERM DEBT

Companies often have a portion of long-term debt that comes due in the current year. As an example, assume that Wendy Construction issues a five-year, interest-bearing, $25,000 note on January 1, 2001. This note specifies that each January 1, starting January 1, 2002, $5,000 of the note should be repaid. When financial statements are prepared on December 31, 2001, $5,000 should be reported as a current liability and $20,000 as a long-term liability. Current maturities of long-term debt are often identified on the balance sheet as **long-term debt due within one year**. Illustration 10-3 shows that at December 31, 1998, Quebecor had $174.2 million of such debt.

Illustration 10-3
Balance sheets for Quebecor Inc.

QUEBECOR INC.

QUEBECOR INC.
Consolidated Balance Sheets
December 31
(in millions)

Assets	1998	1997
Current assets		
Cash	$ 136.8	$ 38.3
Accounts receivable	1,493.8	1,247.6
Inventories	795.4	754.3
Other current assets	74.8	56.2
Total current assets	2,500.8	2,096.4
Noncurrent assets	7,340.6	5,788.8
Total assets	$9,841.4	$7,885.2
Liabilities and Shareholders' Equity		
Current liabilities		
Bank indebtedness	**$ 134.2**	**$ 61.9**
Accounts payable and accrued liabilities	**1,451.3**	**1,259.6**
Income and other taxes	**131.4**	**71.6**
Current portion of long-term debt	**174.2**	**195.9**
Total current liabilities	**1,891.1**	**1,589.0**
Long-term liabilities		
Long-term debt	3,003.5	2,022.6
Convertible debentures	90.3	86.1
Other liabilities	227.3	190.0
Total long-term liabilities	3,321.1	2,298.7
Total liabilities	5,212.2	3,887.7
Non-controlling interest and deferred taxes	3,204.7	2,773.4
Total shareholders' equity	1,424.5	1,224.1
Total liabilities and shareholders' equity	$9,841.4	$7,885.2

It is not necessary to prepare an adjusting entry to recognize the current maturity of long-term debt. The proper statement classification of each balance sheet account is recognized when the balance sheet is prepared.

BEFORE YOU GO ON . . .

Review It

1. What are the two criteria for classifying a debt as a current liability?
2. What are some examples of current liabilities?
3. What are three items generally withheld from employees' wages or salaries?
4. Identify three examples of unearned revenues.

Do It

A local not-for-profit organization has asked you to act as its treasurer. Each fall, the club holds a fundraiser at which it offers space to craftspeople who bring their wares for sale. The organization charges these vendors a commission on sales and uses these collections to raise scholarship money to donate to local universities. The cash register total of \$256,000 for the four-day event includes sales taxes. The GST tax rate is 7%, and PST is also 7%. Assuming that all sales were taxable, what amount of sales taxes must the organization collect from the vendors and remit to government? How should you, as treasurer, show that tax liability in the organization's financial statements?

Reasoning: To answer the first question, you must separate the sales taxes from the total sales amount. To answer the second question, you must know how sales taxes are reported in the financial statements and whether statements will be issued before you pay the sales taxes.

Solution: First divide the total proceeds by 100% plus the sales tax percentage to find the sales amount. Then, to determine the sales taxes, subtract the sales amount from the total proceeds, *or* multiply the sales amount by the tax rate:

Sales amount = \$256,000 ÷ 1.14 = \$224,561.40
Sales taxes due = \$256,000 − \$224,561.40 = \$31,438.60
or
= \$224,561.40 × .07 = \$15,719.30 PST
\$224,561.40 × .07 = \$15,719.30 GST
\$31,438.60

If financial statements are issued before you remit the sales taxes payable, you should show GST payable of \$15,719 and PST payable of \$15,719, both as current liabilities. It is unlikely that you would show the sales tax liability, however, because the sales taxes are normally remitted quickly. You would not show the sales tax as an expense because your organization was simply a collection agent.

FINANCIAL STATEMENT PRESENTATION AND ANALYSIS

PRESENTATION

STUDY OBJECTIVE 4

Identify the requirements for the financial statement presentation and analysis of current liabilities.

Current liabilities are the first category under liabilities on the balance sheet. Each of the principal types of current liabilities is listed separately within the category. In addition, the terms of notes payable and other pertinent information concerning the individual items are disclosed in the notes to the financial statements. The adapted balance sheet of Quebecor Inc. in Illustration 10-3 shows its presentation of current liabilities.

Current liabilities are seldom listed in their order of maturity because of the varying maturity dates that may exist for specific obligations, such as notes payable. A more common, and entirely satisfactory, method of presenting current liabilities is to list them by **order of magnitude**, with the largest obligations first.

ANALYSIS

Liquidity ratios measure the short-term ability of a company to pay its maturing obligations and to meet unexpected needs for cash. Two measures of liquidity were examined in Chapter 2: working capital (Current assets − Current liabilities) and the current ratio (Current assets ÷ Current liabilities). In this section, we add a third useful measure of liquidity, the acid-test ratio.

The current ratio is a frequently used ratio, but it can be misleading. Consider the current ratio's numerator, which can include some items in current assets that are not very liquid. For example, when a company is having a difficult time selling its merchandise, its inventory and current ratio increase, even though its liquidity has actually declined. Similarly, prepaid expenses increase assets, but generally cannot be sold and therefore do not contribute to liquidity. Consequently, the current ratio is often supplemented with the acid-test ratio.

Alternative Terminology
The *acid-test ratio* is often referred to as the *quick ratio.*

The **acid-test ratio** is a measure of a company's immediate short-term liquidity. It is calculated by dividing the sum of cash, short-term investments, and net receivables by current liabilities. Short-term investments, also called marketable securities, are investments that are readily convertible into cash. Cash, short-term investments, and net receivables are usually highly liquid compared to inventory and prepaid expenses. Thus, because it measures **immediate** liquidity, the acid-test ratio should be calculated along with the current ratio. Working capital, current ratios, and acid-test ratios for Quebecor are provided in Illustration 10-4. Industry averages are provided where available.

Illustration 10-4
Liquidity measures

$$\text{WORKING CAPITAL} = \text{CURRENT ASSETS} - \text{CURRENT LIABILITIES}$$

$$\text{CURRENT RATIO} = \frac{\text{CURRENT ASSETS}}{\text{CURRENT LIABILITIES}}$$

$$\text{ACID-TEST RATIO} = \frac{\text{CASH + SHORT-TERM INVESTMENTS + NET RECEIVABLES}}{\text{CURRENT LIABILITIES}}$$

($ in millions)	Quebecor 1998	Quebecor 1997	Industry Average 1998
Working Capital	$2,500.8 − $1,891.1 = $609.7	$2,096.4 − $1,589.0 = $507.4	n/a
Current Ratio	$\frac{\$2,500.8}{\$1,891.1}$ = 1.32:1	$\frac{\$2,096.4}{\$1,589.0}$ = 1.32:1	1.18:1
Acid-Test Ratio	$\frac{\$136.8 + \$1,493.8}{\$1,891.1}$ = 0.86:1	$\frac{\$38.3 + \$1,247.6}{\$1,589.0}$ = 0.81:1	0.70:1

Quebecor's working capital increased from 1997 to 1998, even though its current ratio remained relatively constant in both years at a ratio of 1.32 to 1. How can this happen? This means that current assets and current liabilities each increased in exactly the same proportion (119%) from 1997 to 1998.

Its acid-test ratio improved slightly, from 0.81 to 0.86 to 1. Both of Quebecor's current and acid-test ratios are better than the industry average.

DECISION TOOLKIT

Decision Checkpoints	Info Needed for Decision	Tool to Use for Decision	How to Evaluate Results
Can the company meet its current obligations?	Cash, accounts receivable, short-term investments, and other highly liquid assets, and current liabilities	$\text{Acid-test ratio} = \frac{\text{(Cash + Short-term investments + Net receivables)}}{\text{Current liabilities}}$	Ratio should be compared to others in the same industry. High ratio indicates good liquidity.

Many companies have reduced their liquid assets, because they cost too much to hold. Companies that keep fewer liquid assets on hand must rely on other sources of liquidity. One such source is a bank **line of credit**. A line of credit is a prearranged agreement between a company and a lender that permits a company to borrow up to an agreed-upon amount, should it be necessary. To the extent that its low amount of liquid assets causes a cash shortfall, a company may borrow money on its available short-term lines of credit. The debt footnote to Quebecor's 1998 financial statements discusses its available line of credit agreements. The note, in Illustration 10-5, discusses both Quebecor and two of its subsidiaries, Quebecor Printing (now known as Quebecor World) Inc. and Donahue Inc.

Illustration 10-5
Line of credit note

QUEBECOR INC.

QUEBECOR INC.
Notes to the Financial Statements

Quebecor Printing Inc.: As at December 31, 1998, these represented borrowings under long-term reducing revolving bank credits totalling $1,551.2 million. The agreements governing these bank credits contain certain covenants among which is the obligation to maintain certain financial ratios. The revolving bank credits bear interest at floating rates based on LIBOR [the London InterBank Offered Rate, the rate on Eurodollars traded between banks in London] or the banker's acceptance rate.

Donahue Inc.: In connection with the acquisition of the Champion International Corporations mills, subsidiaries of Donahue Inc. negotiated a new bank credit facility of $1,326.3 million. These credits bear interest at floating rates based on banker's acceptance rates, bank prime rate or LIBOR. The credit agreement contains the usual covenants such as the obligation to maintain certain financial ratios.

Quebecor Printing had utilized $1,028.0 million of its $1,551.2 million line of credit, and Donahue, $722.0 million, as at December 31, 1998, at interest rates ranging from 5.79% to 6.18%. Note the requirement in the above note to maintain certain financial ratios. This requirement may include ratios such as the dividend payout ratio (discussed in Chapter 11)—intended to protect creditors by ensuring that a company does not pay out all of its excess cash as dividends to shareholders before satisfying its debts. Note also that Quebecor's lines of credit, which total $2,877.5 million, amount to more than the sum of its existing cash, short-term investments, and net receivables. Thus, Quebecor's available lines of credit appear adequate to meet any short-term cash deficiency or bank indebtedness it might experience as it continues on its acquisition spree.

DECISION TOOLKIT

Decision Checkpoints	Info Needed for Decision	Tool to Use for Decision	How to Evaluate Results
Can the company obtain short-term financing when necessary?	Available lines of credit from notes to the financial statements	Compare available lines of credit to current liabilities. Also, evaluate liquidity ratios.	If liquidity ratios are low, then lines of credit should be high to compensate.

BEFORE YOU GO ON . . .

Review It

1. In what order are current liabilities usually presented?
2. Identify the liabilities classified as current by Loblaw. The answer to this question is provided at the end of the chapter.
3. What does the acid-test ratio measure and how is it calculated?
4. What is a line of credit?

SECTION 2

LONG-TERM LIABILITIES

Long-term liabilities are obligations that are expected to be paid after one year. In this section, we explain the accounting for the principal types of obligations reported in the long-term liability section of the balance sheet. These obligations are often in the form of bonds or long-term notes. Bonds are explained in the next sections; long-term notes in Appendix 10B to this chapter.

BOND BASICS

STUDY OBJECTIVE 5

Explain why bonds are issued and identify the types of bonds.

Bonds are a form of interest-bearing note payable issued by corporations, universities, and government agencies. Bonds, like common shares, are sold in small denominations (usually $1,000 or multiples of $1,000). As a result, bonds attract many investors.

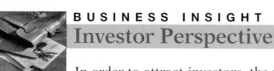

BUSINESS INSIGHT Investor Perspective

In order to attract investors, the type and range of bond financing opportunities is infinite. A New Democratic Party MP once proposed a motion in the House of Commons to create a special hockey savings bond. "The viability of hockey is ebbing in the country," he said. "We need to invest more as a society in this particular sport." Soccer bonds are popular in England and Ireland, with weekly prizes donated by corporations to encourage consumers to buy the bonds. Similar to these, Nelson Riis suggested that the interest on these hockey bonds should be directed to Canadian hockey.

Source: Mark Stevenson, "New Democrat Also Proposed Motion for Hockey Savings Bond," *National Post*, October 30, 1999, A8.

WHY ISSUE BONDS?

A corporation may use long-term financing other than bonds, such as notes payable and leasing. However, these other forms of financing involve an agreement between the corporation and one individual, one company, or a financial institution. Notes payable and leasing are therefore seldom sufficient to furnish the funds needed for plant expansion and major projects like new buildings. To obtain **large amounts of long-term capital**, corporate management usually must decide whether to issue bonds or sell common shares.

From the standpoint of the corporation seeking long-term financing, bonds offer advantages over common shares, as shown in Illustration 10-6.

International Note

The priority of bondholders' versus shareholders' rights varies across countries. In Japan, Germany, and France, shareholders and employees are given priority, with liquidation of the firm to pay creditors seen as a last resort. In Britain, creditors' interests are put first: the courts are quick to give control of the firm to creditors.

Illustration 10-6 Advantages of bond financing over common shares

Bond Financing	Advantages
	1. **Shareholder control is not affected.** Bondholders do not have voting rights, so current owners (shareholders) retain full control of the company.
	2. **Tax savings result.** Bond interest is deductible for tax purposes; dividends on shares are not.
	3. **Earnings per share may be higher.** Although bond interest expense reduces net earnings, earnings per share are often higher under bond financing because no additional common shares are issued.

One commonly reported measure of corporate performance is **earnings per share** (Net earnings ÷ Average common shares outstanding). We will discuss the pros and cons of earnings per share as a performance measure in Chapter 11. Now we focus on how earnings per share can be increased by the effective use of debt.

To illustrate the potential effect of debt on earnings per share, assume that Microsystems, Inc. is considering two plans for financing the construction of a new $5-million plant. Plan A involves issuing 200,000 common shares at the current market price of $25 per share. Plan B involves issuing $5 million of 12% bonds at face value. Earnings before interest and taxes on the new plant will be $1.5 million; income taxes are expected to be 30%. Microsystems currently has 100,000 common shares outstanding. The alternative effects on earnings per share are shown in Illustration 10-7.

Illustration 10-7 Effects on earnings per share—common shares vs. bonds

	Plan A: Issue Shares	Plan B: Issue Bonds
Earnings before interest and taxes	$1,500,000	$1,500,000
Interest (12% × $5,000,000)	—	600,000
Earnings before income taxes	1,500,000	900,000
Income tax expense (30%)	450,000	270,000
Net earnings	$1,050,000	$ 630,000
Outstanding shares	300,000	100,000
Earnings per share	**$ 3.50**	**$ 6.30**

Note that with long-term debt financing (bonds), net earnings are $420,000 less ($1,050,000 – $630,000). However, earnings per share are higher because there are 200,000 fewer common shares outstanding.

The major disadvantage resulting from the use of bonds is that the company locks in fixed payments that must be made in good times and bad. Interest must be paid on a periodic basis, and the principal (face value) of the bonds must be paid at maturity. A company with fluctuating earnings and a relatively weak cash position may experience great difficulty in meeting interest requirements in periods of low earnings. In the extreme, this can result in bankruptcy. With common share financing, on the other hand, the company can decide to pay low (or no) dividends if earnings are low.

TYPES OF BONDS

Bonds may have many different features. Some types of bonds commonly issued are described in the following sections.

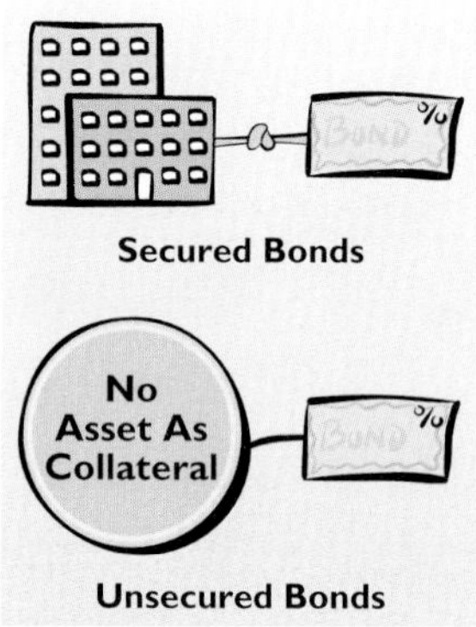

Secured and Unsecured Bonds

Secured bonds have specific assets of the issuer pledged as collateral for the bonds. A bond secured by real estate, for example, is called a **mortgage bond**. A bond secured by specific assets set aside to retire the bonds is called a **sinking fund bond**.

Unsecured bonds are issued against the general credit of the borrower. These bonds, called **debenture bonds**, are used extensively by large corporations with good credit ratings. For example, in Quebecor's financial statements, its subsidiary Quebecor Printing reported more than $465.4 million of debenture bonds outstanding, due in 2007.

BUSINESS INSIGHT

Investor Perspective

Although bonds are generally secured by solid, substantial assets like land, buildings, and equipment, exceptions occur. For example, Air Canada once issued junk (unsecured) bonds to finance the purchase of seven new Airbuses. Bond rating agencies, such as the Canadian Bond Rating Service and Dominion Bond Rating Service, help investors assess the risk level or creditworthiness of bonds. The highest quality bonds are graded as AAA bonds; superior quality, AA; good quality, A; medium grade, BBB. Bonds rated below BBB are commonly referred to as "junk bonds." They are considered to be of higher credit risk; that is, the chance of default is higher for them than for other bonds of better credit quality.

Term and Serial Bonds

Bonds that are due for payment—that are mature—at a single specified future date are called **term bonds**. In contrast, bonds that mature in installments are called **serial bonds**. For example, Quebec Printing debentures due in 2007 are term bonds.

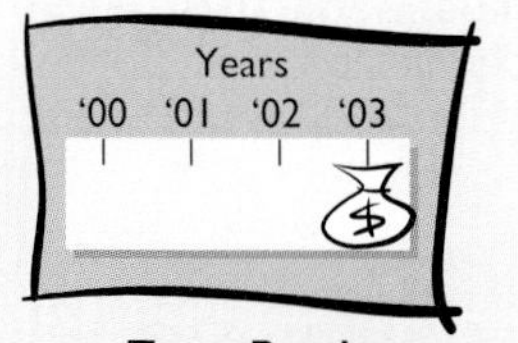

Term Bonds

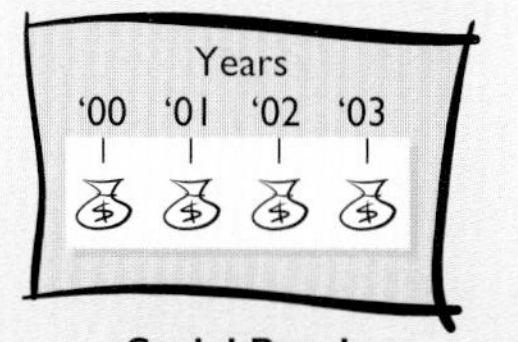

Serial Bonds

Convertible and Redeemable/Retractable Bonds

Bonds that can be converted into common shares at the bondholder's option are called **convertible bonds**. Bonds subject to retirement at a stated dollar amount prior to maturity at the option of the issuer are known as **redeemable (callable) bonds**. **Retractable bonds** are bonds which can be redeemed prior to maturity at the option of the bondholder.

Convertible bonds have features that are attractive both to bondholders and to the issuer. The conversion often gives bondholders an opportunity to benefit if the market price of the common shares increases substantially. Furthermore, until conversion, the bondholder receives interest on the bond. For the issuer, the bonds sell at a higher price and pay a lower rate of interest than comparable debt securities that do not have a conversion option. Quebecor reported $90.3 million of convertible debentures in its 1998 financial statements. These debentures are redeemable at the option of Quebecor Printing Inc.

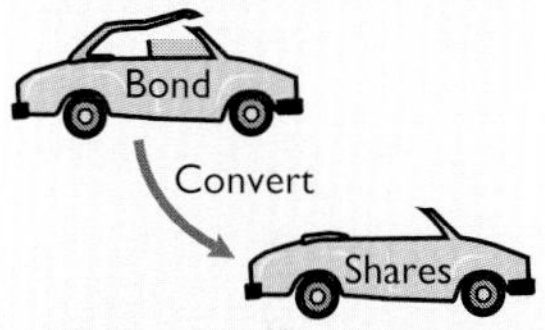

Convertible Bonds

Redeemable (Callable) Bonds

ISSUING PROCEDURES

Within the corporation, formal approval by both the board of directors and the shareholders is usually required before bonds can be issued. **In authorizing the bond issue, the board of directors must stipulate the total number of bonds to be authorized, the total face value, and the contractual interest rate.** The total bond authorization often exceeds the number of bonds originally issued. This is done intentionally to help ensure that the corporation will have the flexibility it needs to meet future cash requirements by selling more bonds.

The **face value** is the amount of principal due at the maturity date. The **contractual interest rate** is the rate used to determine the amount of cash interest the borrower pays and the investor receives. Usually, the contractual rate is stated as an annual rate, and interest is generally paid semi-annually.

Alternative Terminology
Face value is often referred to as the *par value;* and the contractual rate is often referred to as the *stated rate.*

The terms of the bond issue are set forth in a legal document called a **bond indenture**.

After the bond indenture is prepared, **bond certificates** are printed. The indenture and the certificate are separate documents. Bombardier Inc., a world leader in transportation, motorized consumer products, and aerospace, uses bonds to help finance its operations on five continents. As shown in Illustration 10-8, Bombardier's **bond certificate** provides information such as the name of the issuer, and the bond's face value, contractual interest rate, and maturity date. Bonds are generally sold through an investment company that specializes in selling securities. In most cases, the issue is **underwritten** by the investment company: the company sells the bonds to the investment company, which, in turn, sells the bonds to individual investors.

Illustration 10-8 Bond certificate

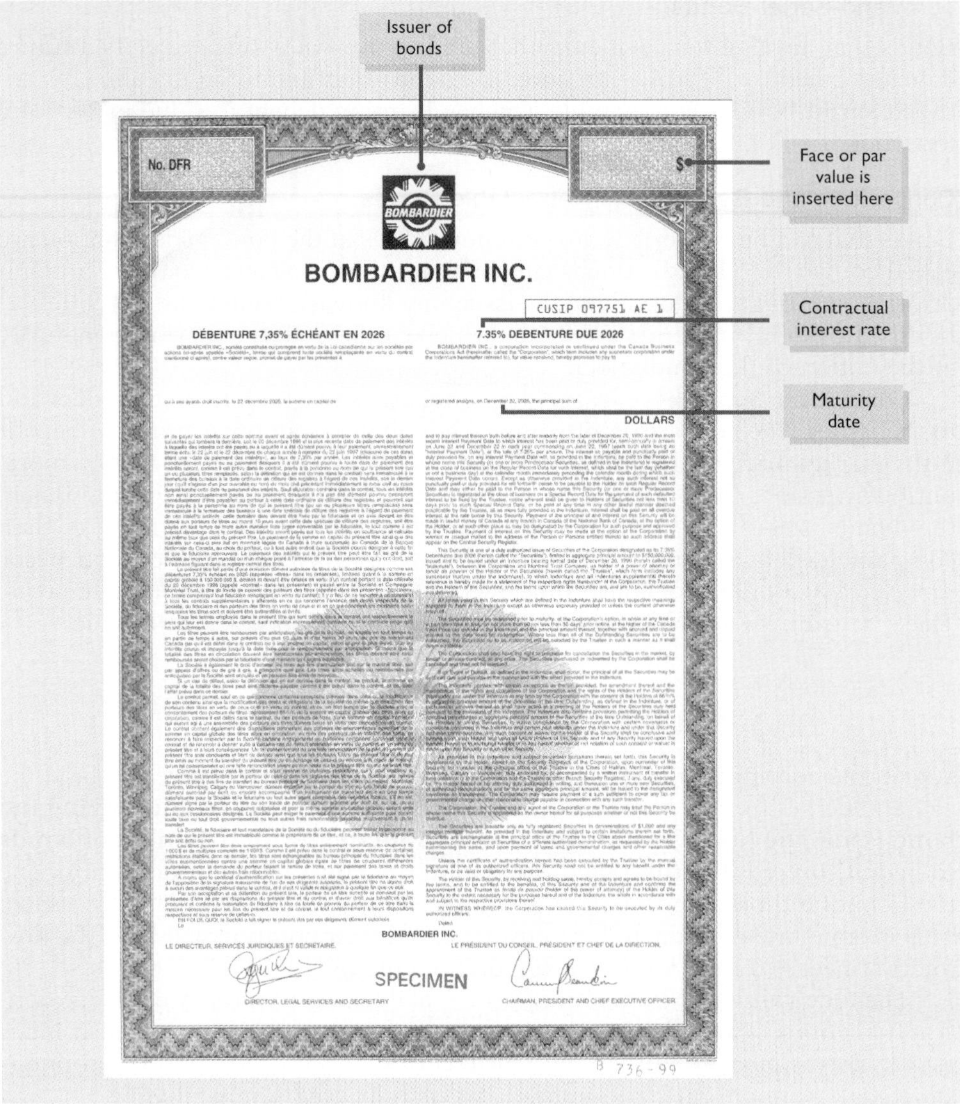

Same dollars at different times are not equal.

DETERMINING THE MARKET VALUE OF BONDS

If you were an investor interested in purchasing a bond, how would you determine how much to pay? To be more specific, assume that Coronet, Inc. issues a zero-interest bond (pays no interest) with a face value of $1,000,000 due in 20 years. For this bond, the only cash you receive is $1 million at the end of 20 years. Would you pay $1 million for this bond? We hope not, because $1 million received 20 years from now is not the same as $1 million received today. The reason you should not pay $1 million relates to what is called the **time value of money**. If you had $1 million today, you would invest it and earn interest such that at the end of 20 years, your investment would be worth much more than $1 million. Thus, if someone is going to pay you $1 million 20 years from now, you would want to find its equivalent today, or its **present value**. In other words, you would want to determine how much must be invested today at current interest rates to have $1 million in 20 years.

The current market value (present value) of a bond is therefore a function of three factors: (1) the dollar amounts to be received, (2) the length of time until the amounts are received, and (3) the market rate of interest. The **market interest rate** is the rate investors demand for loaning funds to the corporation. The process of finding the present value is referred to as **discounting** the future amounts.

Alternative Terminology The *market interest rate* is also known as the *effective interest rate.*

To illustrate, assume that Acropolis Company Ltd. on January 1, 2001, issues $100,000 of 9% bonds, due in five years, with interest payable annually at year end. The purchaser of the bonds would receive the following two cash payments: (1) **principal** of $100,000 to be paid at maturity, and (2) five $9,000 **interest payments** ($100,000 × 9%) over the term of the bonds. A time diagram depicting both cash flows is shown in Illustration 10-9.

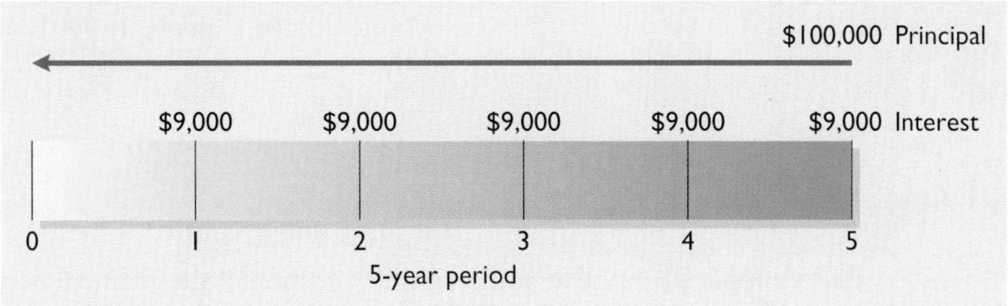

Illustration 10-9 Time diagram depicting cash flows

The current market value of a bond is equal to the present value of all the future cash payments promised by the bond. The present values of these amounts are listed in Illustration 10-10.

Present value of $100,000 received in five years	$ 64,993
Present value of $9,000 received annually for five years	35,007
Market price of bonds	**$100,000**

Illustration 10-10 Calculating the market price of bonds

Tables are available to provide the present value numbers to be used, or these values can be determined mathematically.[1] Further discussion of the concepts and the mechanics of the time value of money calculations is provided in Appendix C at the end of the book.

BEFORE YOU GO ON . . .

Review It

1. What are the advantages of bond versus common share financing?
2. What are secured versus unsecured bonds, term versus serial bonds, and redeemable versus retractable bonds?
3. Explain the terms "face value," "contractual interest rate," and "market interest rate."
4. Explain why you would prefer to receive $1 million today rather than five years from now.

ACCOUNTING FOR BOND ISSUES

A corporation receives payments for its bonds (and makes journal entries to record their sale) only when it issues or buys back bonds, or when bondholders convert bonds into common shares. If a bondholder sells a bond to another in-

[1] For those knowledgeable in the use of present value tables, the calculations in this example are as follows: $100,000 × 0.64993 = $64,993 and $9,000 × 3.88965 = $35,007 (rounded).

vestor, the issuing firm receives no further money on the transaction, **nor is the transaction journalized by the issuing corporation** (although it does keep records of the names of bondholders in some cases). Bonds may be issued at face value, below face value (discount), or above face value (premium). Bond prices for both new issues and existing bonds are quoted as a **percentage of the face value of the bond, which is usually $1,000**. Thus, a $1,000 bond with a quoted price of 97 means that the selling price of the bond is 97% of face value or $970 in this case.

STUDY OBJECTIVE 6

Prepare the entries for the issuance of bonds and interest expense.

ISSUING BONDS AT FACE VALUE

To illustrate the accounting for bonds issued at face value, assume that Devor Corporation issues 1,000 10-year, 9%, $1,000 bonds dated January 1, 2001, at 100 (100% of face value). The entry to record the sale is

A	=	L	+	SE
+1,000,000		+1,000,000		

Date	Account	Debit	Credit
Jan. 1	Cash	1,000,000	
	Bonds Payable		1,000,000
	(To record sale of bonds at face value)		

Bonds Payable are reported in the long-term liability section of the balance sheet because the maturity date is January 1, 2011 (more than one year away).

Over the term (life) of the bonds, entries are required for bond interest. Interest on bonds payable is calculated in the same manner as interest on notes payable, explained earlier. If it is assumed that interest is payable semi-annually on January 1 and July 1 on the bonds described above, interest of $45,000 ($1,000,000 $\times$ 9% $\times \frac{6}{12}$) must be paid on July 1, 2001. The entry for the payment, assuming no previous accrual of interest, is

A	=	L	+	SE
-45,000				-45,000

Date	Account	Debit	Credit
July 1	Bond Interest Expense	45,000	
	Cash		45,000
	(To record payment of bond interest)		

At December 31, an adjusting entry is required to recognize the $45,000 of interest expense incurred since July 1. The entry is

A	=	L	+	SE
		+45,000		-45,000

Date	Account	Debit	Credit
Dec. 31	Bond Interest Expense	45,000	
	Bond Interest Payable		45,000
	(To accrue bond interest)		

Bond Interest Payable is classified as a current liability because it is scheduled for payment within the next year. When the interest is paid on January 1, 2002, Bond Interest Payable is decreased (debited) and Cash is also decreased (credited) for $45,000.

DISCOUNT OR PREMIUM ON BONDS

The previous illustrations assumed that the interest rate paid on the bonds, often referred to as the contractual interest rate, and the market interest rate were the same. Recall that the contractual interest rate is the rate applied to the face value to arrive at the interest paid in a year. The market interest rate is the rate investors demand for loaning funds to the corporation. When the contractual interest rate and the market interest rate are the same, bonds sell at face value, as illustrated above.

However, market interest rates change daily. They are influenced by the type of bond issued, the state of the economy, current industry conditions, and the company's individual performance. As a result, the contractual and market interest rates often differ, and bonds therefore sell below or above face value.

To illustrate, suppose that investors have one of two options: purchase bonds that have a market interest rate of 10% or purchase bonds that have a contractual interest rate of 8%. Assuming that the bonds are of equal risk, investors will select the 10% investment. To make the investments equal, investors will demand a rate of return higher than the contractual interest rate on the 8% bonds. But the contractual interest rate cannot be changed, so investors will make up the difference by paying less than the face value for the bonds. In these cases, **bonds sell at a discount**. Without this discount, the 8% bonds would not be marketable until the market interest rate fell to that level.

Conversely, if the market interest rate is **lower** than the contractual interest rate, investors will have to pay more than face value for the bonds. That is, if the market interest rate is 8% but the contractual interest rate on the bonds is 9%, the issuer will require more funds from the investor. In these cases, **bonds sell at a premium**. These relationships are shown in Illustration 10-11.

Helpful Hint Bond prices vary inversely with changes in the market interest rate. As market interest rates decline, bond prices increase. When a bond is issued, if the market interest rate is below the contractual rate, the price will be higher than the face value.

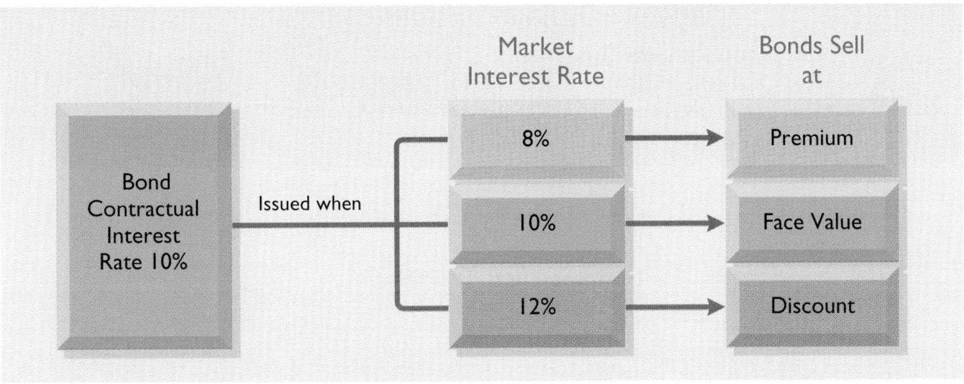

Illustration 10-11 Interest rates and bond prices

Issuance of bonds at an amount different from face value is quite common. By the time a company prints the bond certificates and markets the bonds, it will be a coincidence if the market rate and the contractual rate are the same. Thus, the issuance of bonds at a discount does not mean that the financial strength of the issuer is suspect. Conversely, the sale of bonds at a premium does not indicate that the financial strength of the issuer is exceptional.

Helpful Hint Some bonds are sold at a discount by design. "Zero-coupon" bonds, which pay no interest, sell at a deep discount to face value.

ISSUING BONDS AT A DISCOUNT

To illustrate the issuance of bonds at a discount, assume that on January 1, 2001, Candlestick, Inc., sells $1 million of five-year, 10% bonds at 98 (98% of face value) with interest payable on July 1 and January 1. The entry to record the issuance is

Jan. 1	Cash	980,000	
	Discount on Bonds Payable	20,000	
	Bonds Payable		1,000,000
	(To record sale of bonds at a discount)		

A	=	L	+	SE
+980,000		-20,000		
		+1,000,000		

Although Discount on Bonds Payable has a debit balance, **it is not an asset.** Rather, it is a **contra account**, which is **deducted from Bonds Payable** on the balance sheet as in Illustration 10-12.

Illustration 10-12 Statement presentation of discount on bonds payable

CANDLESTICK INC.
Balance Sheet (partial)
January 1, 2001

Long-term liabilities		
Bonds payable	$1,000,000	
Less: Discount on bonds payable	20,000	$980,000

The $980,000 represents the **carrying (or book) value** of the bonds. On the date of issue, this amount equals the market price of the bonds.

The issuance of bonds below face value causes the total cost of borrowing to differ from the bond interest paid. That is, at maturity, the issuing corporation must pay not only the contractual interest rate over the term of the bonds, but also the face value (rather than the issuance price). Therefore, the difference between the issuance price and the face value of the bonds—the discount—is an **additional cost of borrowing** that should be recorded as **bond interest expense** over the life of the bonds. The total cost of borrowing $980,000 for Candlestick, Inc. is $520,000, calculated as in Illustration 10-13.

Illustration 10-13 Calculation of total cost of borrowing—bonds issued at discount

Bonds Issued at a Discount

Semi-annual interest payments	
($1,000,000 × 10% × $\frac{1}{2}$ = $50,000; $50,000 × 10)	$ 500,000
Add: Bond discount ($1,000,000 − $980,000)	20,000
Total cost of borrowing	**$520,000**

Alternatively, the total cost of borrowing can be determined as in Illustration 10-14.

Illustration 10-14 Alternative calculation of total cost of borrowing—bonds issued at discount

Bonds Issued at a Discount

Principal at maturity	$1,000,000
Semi-annual interest payments ($50,000 × 10)	500,000
Cash to be paid to bondholders	1,500,000
Cash received from bondholders	980,000
Total cost of borrowing	**$ 520,000**

AMORTIZING A BOND DISCOUNT

To comply with the matching principle, the bond discount should be allocated systematically to each accounting period that benefits from the use of the cash proceeds. There are two methods to allocate this discount to interest expense: the straight-line and effective interest methods of amortization. The straight-line method is the simpler of the two methods. It allocates the same *dollar amount* to interest expense each interest period. The effective interest method determines interest expense by multiplying the carrying value of the bond by the same *percentage*, using the market (effective) interest rate, each interest period. The difference between the effective interest expense and the cash interest payment is the amount of amortization for the period. The effective interest method is considered conceptually superior to the straight-line method, because it better matches or measures the cost of borrowing. In spite of this, the straight-line method of bond amortization is the most widely used method in Canada. The effective interest method of amortization is, however, used for other types of liabilities, such as mortgage notes payable, leases, and pensions. The effective interest method of amortization is illustrated in Appendix 10A to this chapter.

The **straight-line method of amortization** is determined as shown in Illustration 10-15.

Bond Discount ÷ Number of Interest Periods = Bond Discount Amortization

Illustration 10-15 Formula for straight-line method of bond discount amortization

Continuing our Candlestick example, the bond discount amortization using the straight-line method of amortization is \$2,000 (\$20,000 ÷ 10). The entry to record the payment of bond interest and the amortization of the bond discount on the first interest date (July 1, 2001) is

July 1	Bond Interest Expense	52,000	
	Discount on Bonds Payable		2,000
	Cash		50,000
	(To record payment of bond interest and amortization of bond discount)		

A = L + SE
-50,000 +2,000 -52,000

At December 31, the adjusting entry is

Dec. 31	Bond Interest Expense	52,000	
	Discount on Bonds Payable		2,000
	Bond Interest Payable		50,000
	(To record accrued bond interest and amortization of bond discount)		

A = L + SE
+2,000 -52,000
+50,000

Over the term of the bonds, the balance in Discount on Bonds Payable will decrease annually by the same amount until it has a zero balance at the maturity date of the bonds. Thus, the carrying value of the bonds at maturity will be equal to their face value.

Preparing a bond discount amortization schedule, as shown in Illustration 10-16, is useful to determine interest expense, discount amortization, and the carrying value of the bond. As indicated, the interest expense recorded each period is \$52,000. Also note that the carrying value of the bond increases \$2,000 each period until it reaches its face value of \$1,000,000 at the end of period 10.

Illustration 10-16 Bond discount amortization schedule

Semi-annual Interest Periods	(A) Interest To Be Paid (5% × \$1,000,000)	(B) Interest Expense To Be Recorded (A) + (C)	(C) Discount Amortization (\$20,000 ÷ 10)	(D) Unamortized Discount (D) − (C)	(E) Bond Carrying Value (\$1,000,000 − (D))
Issue date				\$20,000	\$ 980,000
1	\$ 50,000	\$ 52,000	\$ 2,000	18,000	982,000
2	50,000	52,000	2,000	16,000	984,000
3	50,000	52,000	2,000	14,000	986,000
4	50,000	52,000	2,000	12,000	988,000
5	50,000	52,000	2,000	10,000	990,000
6	50,000	52,000	2,000	8,000	992,000
7	50,000	52,000	2,000	6,000	994,000
8	50,000	52,000	2,000	4,000	996,000
9	50,000	52,000	2,000	2,000	998,000
10	50,000	52,000	2,000	0	1,000,000
	\$500,000	\$520,000	\$20,000		

Column **(A)** remains constant because the face value of the bonds (\$1,000,000) is multiplied by the semi-annual contractual interest rate ($10\% \times \frac{6}{12} = 5\%$) each period.
Column **(B)** is calculated as the interest paid (Column A) plus the discount amortization (Column C).
Column **(C)** indicates the discount amortization each period.
Column **(D)** decreases each period by the same amount until it reaches zero at maturity.
Column **(E)** increases each period by the amount of discount amortization until it equals the face value at maturity.

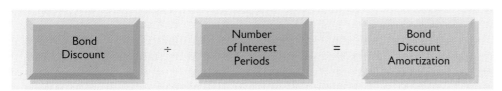

ISSUING BONDS AT A PREMIUM

The issuance of bonds at a premium can be illustrated by assuming the Candlestick, Inc. bonds described earlier are sold at 102 (102% of face value) rather than at 98. The entry to record the sale is

A	=	L	+	SE
+1,020,000		+1,000,000		
		+20,000		

Jan. 1	Cash	1,020,000	
	Bonds Payable		1,000,000
	Premium on Bonds Payable		20,000
	(To record sale of bonds at a premium)		

Premium on Bonds Payable is **added to Bonds Payable** on the balance sheet, as shown in Illustration 10-17.

Illustration 10-17 Statement presentation of bond premium

CANDLESTICK INC.
Balance Sheet (partial)
January 1, 2001

Long-term liabilities		
Bonds payable	$1,000,000	
Less: Discount on bonds payable	20,000	$1020,000

The sale of bonds above face value causes the total cost of borrowing to be **less than the bond interest paid**, because the borrower is not required to pay the bond premium at the maturity date of the bonds. Thus, the premium is considered to be **a reduction in the cost of borrowing** that reduces bond interest expense over the life of the bonds. The total cost of borrowing $1,020,000 for Candlestick, Inc. is $480,000, calculated as in Illustration 10-18.

Illustration 10-18 Calculation of total cost of borrowing—bonds issued at a premium

Bonds Issued at a Premium

Semi-annual interest payments	
($1,000,000 × 10% × $\frac{1}{2}$ = $50,000; $50,000 × 10)	$ 500,000
Less: Bond premium ($1,020,000 − $1,000,000)	20,000
Total cost of borrowing	**$480,000**

Alternatively, the cost of borrowing can be calculated as in Illustration 10-19.

Illustration 10-19 Alternative calculation of total cost of borrowing—bonds issued at a premium

Bonds Issued at a Premium

Principal at maturity	$1,000,000
Semi-annual interest payments ($50,000 × 10)	500,000
Cash to be paid to bondholders	1,500,000
Cash received from bondholders	1,020,000
Total cost of borrowing	**$ 480,000**

AMORTIZING A BOND PREMIUM

The formula for determining bond premium amortization under the straight-line method is presented in Illustration 10-20.

Illustration 10-20 Formula for straight-line method of bond premium amortization

Bond Premium	÷	Number of Interest Periods	=	Bond Premium Amortization

Thus, in our example, the premium amortization for each interest period is $2,000 ($20,000 ÷ 10). The entry to record the first payment of interest on July 1 is

July 1	Bond Interest Expense	48,000	
	Premium on Bonds Payable	2,000	
	Cash		50,000
	(To record payment of bond interest and amortization of bond premium)		

A	=	L	+	SE
−50,000		−2,000		−48,000

At December 31, the adjusting entry is

Dec. 31	Bond Interest Expense	48,000	
	Premium on Bonds Payable	2,000	
	Bond Interest Payable		50,000
	(To record accrued bond interest and amortization of bond premium)		

A	=	L	+	SE
		−2,000 +50,000		−48,000

Over the term of the bonds, the balance in Premium on Bonds Payable will decrease annually by the same amount until it has a zero balance at maturity.

Preparing a bond premium amortization schedule, as shown in Illustration 10-21, is useful to determine interest expense, premium amortization, and the carrying value of the bond. As indicated, the interest expense recorded each period is $48,000. Also note that the carrying value of the bond decreases by $2,000 each period until it reaches its face value $1,000,000 at the end of period 10.

Illustration 10-21 Bond premium amortization schedule

Semi-annual Interest Periods	(A) Interest To Be Paid (5% × $1,000,000)	(B) Interest Expense To Be Recorded (A) − (C)	(C) Premium Amortization ($20,000 ÷ 10)	(D) Unamortized Premium (D) − (C)	(E) Bond Carrying Value ($1,000,000 + (D))
Issue date				$20,000	$1,020,000
1	$ 50,000	$ 48,000	$ 2,000	18,000	1,018,000
2	50,000	48,000	2,000	16,000	1,016,000
3	50,000	48,000	2,000	14,000	1,014,000
4	50,000	48,000	2,000	12,000	1,012,000
5	50,000	48,000	2,000	10,000	1,010,000
6	50,000	48,000	2,000	8,000	1,008,000
7	50,000	48,000	2,000	6,000	1,006,000
8	50,000	48,000	2,000	4,000	1,004,000
9	50,000	48,000	2,000	2,000	1,002,000
10	50,000	48,000	2,000	0	1,000,000
	$500,000	$480,000	$20,000		

Column (A) remains constant because the face value of the bonds ($1,000,000) is multiplied by the semi-annual contractual interest rate (10% × $\frac{6}{12}$ = 5%) each period.
Column (B) is calculated as the interest paid (Column A) less the premium amortization (Column C).
Column (C) indicates the premium amortization each period.
Column (D) decreases each period by the same amount until it reaches zero at maturity.
Column (E) decreases each period by the amount of premium amortization until it equals the face value at maturity.

Accounting for Bond Retirements

Bonds are retired when they are purchased (redeemed) by the issuing corporation. The appropriate entries for these transactions are explained next.

REDEEMING BONDS AT MATURITY

STUDY OBJECTIVE 7

Describe the entries when bonds are redeemed.

Regardless of the issue price of bonds, the book value of the bonds at maturity will equal their face value. Assuming that the interest for the last interest period is paid and recorded separately, the entry to record the redemption of the Candlestick bonds at maturity is

A	=	L	+	SE
−1,000,000		−1,000,000		

Bonds Payable	1,000,000	
Cash		1,000,000
(To record redemption of bonds at maturity)		

REDEEMING BONDS BEFORE MATURITY

Bonds may be redeemed before maturity. A company may decide to retire bonds before maturity to reduce interest costs and remove debt from its balance sheet. A company should only retire debt early if it has sufficient cash resources. When bonds are retired before maturity, it is necessary to (1) eliminate the carrying value of the bonds at the redemption date, (2) record the cash paid, and (3) recognize the gain or loss on redemption. The carrying value of the bonds is the face value of the bonds less the unamortized bond discount, or plus the unamortized bond premium, at the redemption date.

To illustrate, assume at the end of the eighth period, Candlestick, Inc., having sold its bonds at a premium, retires its bonds at 103 after paying the semi-annual interest. The carrying value of the bonds at the redemption date is $1,004,000. (The calculation of this value is shown in Illustration 10-21.) The entry to record the redemption at the end of the eighth interest period (January 1, 2005) is

A	=	L	+	SE
−1,030,000		−1,000,000		−26,000
		−4,000		

Jan. 1	Bonds Payable	1,000,000	
	Premium on Bonds Payable	4,000	
	Loss on Bond Redemption	26,000	
	Cash		1,030,000
	(To record redemption of bonds at 103)		

Note that the loss of $26,000 is the difference between the cash paid of $1,030,000 and the carrying value of the bonds of $1,004,000.

This is very similar to the calculation of a loss or gain on the sale of capital assets where cash is also compared to carrying value. However, the determination of whether a loss or a gain results naturally differs, depending on whether you are selling capital assets (assets) or purchasing bonds (liabilities).

Illustration 10-22
Comparison of asset and liability gain and loss

Capital Assets	Bonds Payable
Sale price	Purchase price
− Carrying (book) value	− Carrying value
Gain (loss)	Loss (gain)

As with capital assets, losses (gains) on bond redemption are reported separately in the statement of earnings, often as Other Losses or Gains.

BUSINESS INSIGHT

International Perspective

A dramatic example of the importance of bond financing—which literally changed the course of history—is seen in Britain's struggle for supremacy in the 18th and 19th centuries. With only a fraction of the population and wealth of France, Britain ultimately humbled its mightier foe through the use of bonds. Because of its effective central bank and a fair system of collecting taxes, Britain developed the capital markets that enabled its government to issue bonds. Britain was able to borrow money at almost half the cost paid by France and was able to incur more debt as a proportion of the economy than could France. Britain thus could more than match the French navy, raise an army of its own, and lavishly subsidize other armies, eventually destroying Napoleon and his threat to Europe.

Source: "How British Bonds Beat Back Bigger France," *Forbes*, March 13, 1995, 26.

BEFORE YOU GO ON . . .

Review It

1. What entry is made to record the issuance of bonds payable of $1 million at 100? At 96? At 102?
2. Why do bonds sell at a discount? At a premium? At face value?
3. Explain the accounting for redemption of bonds at maturity and before maturity by payment in cash.

Do It

A bond amortization table shows (a) interest to be paid, $50,000, (b) interest expense to be recorded, $52,000, and (c) amortization, $2,000. Answer the following questions: (1) Were the bonds sold at a premium or a discount? (2) After recording the interest expense, will the bond carrying value increase or decrease?

Reasoning: To answer the questions, you need to know the effects that the amortization of bond discounts and bond premiums have on bond interest expense and on the carrying value of the bonds. Bond discount amortization increases both bond interest expense and the carrying value of the bonds. Bond premium amortization has the reverse effect.

Solution: The bond amortization table indicates that interest expense is $2,000 greater than the interest paid. This difference is equal to the amortization amount. Thus, the bonds were sold at a discount. The interest entry will decrease Discount on Bonds Payable and increase the carrying value of the bonds.

STUDY OBJECTIVE 8

Identify the requirements for the financial statement presentation and analysis of long-term liabilities.

Financial Statement Presentation and Analysis

PRESENTATION

Long-term liabilities are reported in a separate section of the balance sheet immediately following current liabilities, as shown in Illustration 10-23.

Illustration 10-23 Balance sheet presentation of long-term liabilities

ANY COMPANY LTD.
Balance Sheet (partial)

Long-term liabilities		
Bonds payable 10% due in 2009	$1,000,000	
Less: Discount on bonds payable	80,000	$ 920,000
Notes payable, 11%, due in 2015 and secured by capital assets		500,000
Lease liability		540,000
Total long-term liabilities		$1,960,000

Detailed data (such as interest rates, maturity dates, conversion privileges, and assets pledged as collateral) are usually shown in the notes to the financial statements. The current maturities of long-term debt should be reported as current liabilities if they are to be paid from current assets. This is evident on the Quebecor balance sheets in Illustration 10-3, presented earlier in this chapter.

ANALYSIS

International Note

The use of debt financing varies considerably across countries. The amount of debt borrowed by governments can affect a country's ability to borrow funds. One measure of the degree of debt financing is the ratio of national debt to gross national product. In a recent survey, this ratio was 69% in Canada, 100% in Japan, and 107% in Italy. Ratios for the U.S., Germany, France and Britain are close together, ranging from 40% to 50%.

In the area of print media, there are more than 107 daily newspapers published in Canada. Over 85% are English, 10% French, and the remainder are other languages. Trade magazines and other communication media also serve Canada from coast to coast. In order to survive in such a competitive industry, companies such as Quebecor must ensure that they do not impair their solvency when making a long-term loan or purchasing another company's share capital. Solvency ratios measure the ability of a company to repay its long-term debt and survive over a long period of time.

Debt to Total Assets

In an earlier chapter, you learned that one measure of a company's solvency is the **debt to total assets ratio**, calculated by dividing total debt by total assets. This ratio indicates the extent to which a company's debt could be repaid by liquidating its assets.

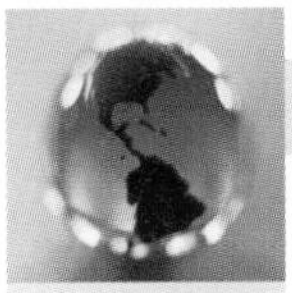

BUSINESS INSIGHT

International Perspective

The debt to total assets ratio isn't the only ratio we can use to assess our ability to handle debt. Another measure used by governments is the debt to net earnings ratio. This ratio compares debt as a percentage of net earnings. Canada's debt level, which stood at just over 76% of our after-tax pay in 1985, had skyrocketed to 112% just 13 years later. Canada now has the dubious distinction of increasing its debt level faster than any other country in the Group of Eight industrial nations. Germany increased its debt levels least, by maintaining its debt to net earnings ratio relatively constant at 60%.

Source: Mark MacKinnon, "Debt Pressure Mounts for Canadians," *Globe and Mail,* November 9, 1998, B8.

Times Interest Earned

Other measures besides the debt to total assets, or debt to net earnings, can also be useful. One such measure is the **times interest earned ratio**, which provides an indication of a company's ability to meet interest payments as they come due. It is calculated as follows: earnings before interest expense and income tax expense divided by interest expense. It uses earnings before interest and taxes (often abbreviated as **EBIT**) because this number best represents the amount available to cover interest.

Alternative Terminology
The *times interest earned ratio* is also known as the *interest coverage ratio.*

Cash Interest Coverage

The times interest earned ratio is based on earnings before interest and taxes, which does not necessarily indicate whether the company has cash available to pay the interest. By also deducting amortization from EBIT, we can use a cash flow–based measure, known as the **cash interest coverage ratio**. The numerator in this ratio is known as **EBITDA**, which is abbreviated for earnings before interest (expense), tax (expense), and depreciation and amortization (expense). EBITDA is a basic measure of a company's ability to generate cash from operations, and is frequently used as a solvency measure of cash flow available to meet obligations. The cash interest coverage ratio is calculated by dividing EBITDA by interest expense.

BUSINESS INSIGHT

Investor Perspective

Many capital-intensive companies report low or no earnings for years due to the huge capital costs of building their business, even though their cash flow is increasing. For example, communications and cable company Rogers Communications Inc. reported a net loss, before non recurring items, of $115 million for fiscal 1999. Yet, its EBITDA is a positive $615 million for the same period! No wonder creditors, and even investors, want to look at the EBITDA.

We can use the balance sheet information in Illustration 10-3 and the additional information below to calculate solvency ratios for Quebecor:

($ in millions)	1998	1997
Amortization expense	$573.5	$478.4
Interest expense	190.3	173.4
Income tax expense	270.0	213.7
Net earnings	172.7	143.3

The debt to total assets, times interest earned, and cash interest coverage ratios for Quebecor, and averages for the industry, where available, are shown in Illustration 10-24.

Illustration 10-24
Solvency ratios

$$\text{DEBT TO TOTAL ASSETS RATIO} = \frac{\text{TOTAL DEBT}}{\text{TOTAL ASSETS}}$$

$$\text{TIMES INTEREST EARNED RATIO} = \frac{\text{EBIT}}{\text{INTEREST EXPENSE}}$$

$$\text{CASH INTEREST COVERAGE RATIO} = \frac{\text{EBITDA}}{\text{INTEREST EXPENSE}}$$

	Quebecor		Industry Average
($ in millions)	1998	1997	1998
Debt to Total Assets Ratio	$\frac{\$5,212.2}{\$9,841.4} = 53\%$	$\frac{\$3,887.7}{\$7,885.2} = 49\%$	58%
Times Interest Earned Ratio	$\frac{\$172.7 + \$190.3 + \$270.0}{\$190.3} = 3.3$ times	$\frac{\$143.3 + \$173.4 + \$213.7}{\$173.4} = 3.1$ times	8.2 times
Cash Interest Coverage Ratio	$\frac{\$172.7 + \$190.3 + \$270.0 + \$573.5}{\$190.3} = 6.3$ times	$\frac{\$143.3 + \$173.4 + \$213.7 + \$478.4}{\$173.4} = 5.8$ times	n/a

The debt to total assets ratio varies across industries, because different capital structures are appropriate for different industries. The debt to assets ratio for the communications and media industry is 58%. Quebecor's ratio increased from 1997 to 1998, reflecting higher debt incurred to finance business acquisitions during 1998. One should be very careful when interpreting debt to assets ratios. In Quebecor's case, its consolidated financial statements include 100% of its subsidiaries' debt, which Quebecor is not responsible for in the event of default.

Quebecor appears to be equipped to handle the additional debt created by its acquisitions, as its improving times interest earned ratio indicates. These acquisitions led to increased earnings, which help to cover the additional finance costs. Yet, Quebecor is still below the industry average in its ability to cover its interest charges. Management is of the opinion that future cash flows generated by the combined operations will be more than adequate to cover debt reimbursement and interest payments. Quebecor's cash interest coverage ratio reinforces this opinion. Note that the cash interest coverage ratio is increasing faster than the times interest earned ratio. This is because higher amortization charges (resulting from acquisitions) had a larger impact on earnings in 1998 than in 1997 for the times interest earned ratio. Removing this expense gives a better signal about the company's ability to handle its interest repayments.

DECISION TOOLKIT

Decision Checkpoints	Info Needed for Decision	Tool to Use for Decision	How to Evaluate Results
Is the company generating sufficient earnings to cover annual interest payments?	EBIT and interest expense	Times interest earned ratio = $\frac{\text{EBIT}}{\text{Interest expense}}$	High ratio indicates sufficient earnings available to cover annual interest payments.
Is the company generating sufficient cash to repay its interest?	EBITDA and interest expense	Cash interest coverage ratio = $\frac{\text{EBITDA}}{\text{Interest expense}}$	High ratio indicates sufficient cash available to cover annual interest payments.

OTHER ISSUES IN ANALYSIS

CONTINGENT LIABILITIES

Contingencies are events with uncertain outcomes. For users of financial statements, contingencies are often very important to understanding a company's financial position. Although contingent gains exist, contingent losses are far more common. A common type of contingency is lawsuits. Suppose, for example, that you were analysing the financial statements of a cigarette manufacturer and did not consider the possible negative implications of existing unsettled lawsuits. Your analysis of the company's financial position would certainly be misleading. Other common types of contingencies are product warranties and environmental problems.

Accounting rules require that contingencies be disclosed in the notes; in some cases they must be accrued as liabilities. For example, suppose that Waterford Inc. is sued by a customer for $1 million due to an injury caused by a defective product. If at December 31 (the company's year end) the lawsuit has not yet been resolved, how should the company account for this event? If the company can determine **a reasonable estimate** of the expected loss, and if it is **likely** it will lose the suit, then the company should accrue for the loss. The loss is recorded by increasing (debiting) a loss account and increasing (crediting) a liability such as Lawsuit Liability. If *both* of these conditions are not met, then the company discloses the basic facts regarding this suit in the notes to its financial statements.

Helpful Hint Recognition of contingent losses is an application of **conservatism**.

The liabilities associated with contingencies can be material. For example, Exxon was ordered to pay billions of dollars as a result of an Alaskan oil spill, and the cigarette companies have been negotiating a settlement of all their lawsuits with total payments of hundreds of billions of dollars. The notes to recent financial statements of Imperial Tobacco Canada, contained more than a page of discussion regarding litigation. *Financial Reporting in Canada 1999* reported that 66% of the 200 companies surveyed disclosed contingencies. Of these, 57% were for lawsuits, 8% for environmental matters, 15% for guarantees of the debts of others, and 10% for possible tax reassessments and other items.

DECISION TOOLKIT

Decision Checkpoints	Info Needed for Decision	Tool to Use for Decision	How to Evaluate Results
Does the company have any contingent liabilities?	Knowledge of events with uncertain negative outcomes	Notes to financial statements and financial statements	If negative outcomes are possible, determine the probability, the amount of loss, and the potential impact on financial statements.

LEASE LIABILITIES

In most lease contracts, a periodic payment is made by the lessee and is recorded as rent expense in the statement of earnings. The renting of an apartment and the rental of a car at an airport are examples of these types of leases, often referred to as **operating leases**. **In an operating lease, the intent is temporary use of the property** by the lessee with continued ownership of the property by the lessor. In some cases, however, **the lease contract transfers substantially all the benefits and risks of ownership to the lessee, so that the lease is in effect a purchase of the property**. This type of lease is called a **capital lease** because the fair value of the leased asset is *capitalized* on the lessee's balance sheet.

International Note

Different countries use different criteria to determine whether a lease should be recorded as operating or capital. Brazil, Italy, and Japan classify all leases as operating. France, Spain, and Sweden require a purchase option to exist or to be exercised before capitalization occurs.

Accounting standards have precise criteria that determine whether or not a lease should be accounted for as a capital lease. We won't review the precise criteria here, but the goal is to determine whether the lease transaction more closely resembles a purchase transaction or a rental transaction. This is determined by asking these questions:

- Is it likely that the lessee will end up with the asset at the end of the lease?
- Will the lessee use the asset for most of its useful life?
- Will the payments made by the lessee be approximately the same as the payments that would be made to purchase the asset?

If the answer to any of these questions is yes, the lease should be accounted for as a capital lease. That is, the lessee's books must contain entries to record the asset and a related liability for the lease payments. Otherwise, the lessee can account for the transaction as an operating lease, meaning that neither an asset nor a liability is shown on the books.

Some lessees do not like to report leases on their balance sheets because the lease liability increases the company's total liabilities. This, in turn, may make it more difficult for the company to obtain needed funds from lenders.

As a result, companies may attempt to keep leased assets and lease liabilities off the balance sheet by structuring the lease agreement to avoid meeting the criteria of a capital lease. They then account for most of their leases as operating leases. Recall from Chapter 9, for example, that Air Canada leased more than half of its planes, and nearly all of these were accounted for as operating leases. Consequently, more than half of the planes used by Air Canada do not show up on its balance sheet, nor do the liabilities related to those planes. This procedure of keeping liabilities off the balance sheet is often referred to as **off–balance sheet financing**.

Critics of off–balance sheet financing contend that many operating leases represent unavoidable obligations that meet the definition of a liability, and they should therefore be reported as liabilities on the balance sheet. To reduce these concerns, companies are required to report their operating lease obligations for subsequent years in a note. This allows analysts and other financial statement users to adjust a company's financial statements by adding leased assets and lease liabilities if they feel that this treatment is more appropriate. The financial statement note describing Quebecor's obligations under operating leases in a recent year is presented in Illustration 10-25.

QUEBECOR INC.
Notes to the Financial Statements

COMMITMENTS AND CONTINGENCIES
Leases The Company rents premises and equipment under operating leases which expire at various dates up to 2010 and for which minimum lease payments total $367.9 million. Minimum payments (in millions) under these leases for each of the next five years are as follows: 1999, $94.6; 2000, $73.7; 2001, $58.3; 2002, $38.0; 2003, $25.9.

Illustration 10-25
Operating lease note

QUEBECOR INC.

The total increase in assets and liabilities that would result if these leases were recorded on the balance sheet is $367.9 million. However, this amount is not very significant relative to Quebecor's total assets of $9.8 billion or total liabilities of $5.2 billion. Thus, the potential unrecorded off–balance sheet assets and liabilities resulting from Quebecor's leases do not appear to be a concern.

DECISION TOOLKIT

Decision Checkpoints	Info Needed for Decision	Tool to Use for Decision	How to Evaluate Results
Does the company have significant unrecorded lease obligations?	Schedule of minimum lease payments from lease note	Compare liquidity and solvency ratios with and without unrecorded obligations included.	If ratios differ significantly after including unrecorded obligations, these obligations should not be ignored in analysis.

BEFORE YOU GO ON . . .

Review It

1. What is meant by solvency?
2. What information does the times interest earned ratio provide, and how is the ratio calculated?
3. What information does the cash interest coverage ratio provide that the times interest earned ratio does not?
4. Where should long-term capital lease obligations be reported in the balance sheet?
5. What are contingent liabilities?

USING THE DECISION TOOLKIT

Hollinger Inc. publishes newspapers, magazines, and other publications in Canada, Israel, the UK, and the U.S. Through its subsidiary Southam Inc., it is Canada's largest daily newspaper publisher (Quebecor is number two). In 1998, the company gained its first national newspaper by swapping four regional papers for the *National Post*. The company has been working towards restructuring its debt and equity in order to strengthen its balance sheet. It has subsequently sold its community newspapers in order to generate cash to reduce debt and retire shares. The balance sheet provides financial information for Hollinger, as at December 31, 1998, and 1997.

Instructions

1. Evaluate Hollinger's liquidity using appropriate ratios, and compare them to those of Quebecor and to the industry averages.
2. Evaluate Hollinger's solvency using appropriate ratios, and compare them to those of Quebecor and to industry averages.
3. Comment on Hollinger's available lines of credit.

HOLLINGER INC.
Consolidated Balance Sheets
December 31
(in thousands)

Assets	1998	1997
Current assets		
Cash	$ 128,061	$ 158,868
Accounts receivable	584,503	519,123
Inventories	56,294	48,713
Total current assets	768,858	726,704
Noncurrent assets	4,935,643	4,249,692
Total assets	$5,704,501	$4,976,396
Liabilities and Shareholders' Equity		
Current liabilities		
Bank indebtedness	$ 232,128	$ 48,839
Accounts payable and accrued expenses	792,669	525,238
Income taxes payable	2,465	38,897
Other current liabilities	496,766	146,547
Current portion of long-term debt	183,150	77,002
Total current liabilities	1,707,178	836,523
Long-term liabilities		
Long-term debt	2,229,599	2,079,646
Other noncurrent liabilities	51,038	711,357
Total long-term liabilities	2,280,637	2,791,003
Total liabilities	3,987,815	3,627,526
Minority interest and deferred credits	1,783,854	1,440,730
Total shareholders' equity (deficit)	(67,168)	(91,860)
Total liabilities and shareholders' equity	$5,704,501	$4,976,396
Other information		
Net earnings	$ 111,485	$ 171,286
Amortization expense	209,498	209,843
Income tax expense	300,929	163,307
Interest expense	246,268	194,968

Available lines of credit: $250 million. The Company's credit arrangements provide for up to $250 million in borrowings comprising an operating line of $10 million, a $90-million, 364-day revolving commitment, and a $150-million term commitment expiring June 2000.

Solution

1. Hollinger's liquidity can be measured using the current ratio and acid-test ratio:

Ratio	1998	1997	Industry Average
Current	$\frac{\$768,858}{\$1,707,178} = 0.45:1$	$\frac{\$726,704}{\$836,523} = 0.87:1$	1.18:1
Acid-test ratio	$\frac{\$128,061 + \$584,503}{\$1,707,178} = 0.42:1$	$\frac{\$158,868 + \$519,123}{\$836,523} = 0.81:1$	0.70:1

Hollinger's current ratio and acid-test ratio are low, both compared to Quebecor and to the industry (recall that Quebecor's current ratio in both 1998 and 1997 was 1.32:1; and that its acid-test ratio in 1998 was 0.86:1; and in 1997, 0.81:1). In fact, Hollinger's acid-test ratio is nearly the same as its current ratio and both these ratios declined nearly 50% between 1997 and 1998. The company's bank indebtedness and accounts payable rose in 1998, because it used some of its working capital to finance its acquisitions and restructuring. Hollinger must carefully monitor its liquidity, and must also make sure to have other short-term financing options available, such as lines of credit.

2. Hollinger's solvency can be measured with the debt to total assets ratio, the times interest earned ratio, and the cash interest coverage ratio:

Ratio	1998	1997	Industry Average
Debt to total assets ratio	$\frac{\$3,987,815}{\$5,704,501} = 69.9\%$	$\frac{\$3,627,526}{\$4,976,396} = 72.9\%$	58%
Times interest earned ratio	$\frac{\$111,485 + \$246,268 + \$300,929}{\$194,968}$ = 2.7 times	$\frac{\$171,286 + \$194,968 + \$163,307}{\$194,968}$ = 2.7 times	8.2 times
Cash interest coverage ratio	$\frac{\$111,485 + \$246,268 + \$300,929 + \$209,498}{\$246,268}$ = 3.5 times	$\frac{\$171,286 + \$194,968 + \$163,307 + \$209,843}{\$194,968}$ = 3.8 times	n/a

Hollinger's debt to total assets ratio is not as good as Quebecor's (recall that Quebecor's debt to assets ratio was 53% in 1998 and 49% in 1997). Hollinger's times interest earned ratio was also lower than Quebecor's (3.3 times in 1998, 3.1 times in 1997), and lower than the industry's. Hollinger's cash interest coverage ratio declined in 1998, with the decline of its amortization expense. It is also much lower than Quebecor's (6.3 times in 1998, 5.8 times in 1997). Still, in spite of its high debt to assets ratio and low times interest earned and cash coverage ratios, its earnings and cash are still positive and sufficient to handle its debt charges.

3. Hollinger has available lines of credit of up to $250 million. This significantly improves its liquidity. The company has tremendous resources available to it, should it face a liquidity crunch.

Summary of Study Objectives

1 ***Explain what a current liability is and identify the major types of current liabilities.*** A current liability is a debt that will be paid (1) from existing current assets or through the creation of other current liabilities, and (2) within one year or the operating cycle, whichever is longer. The major types of current liabilities are notes payable, accounts payable, sales taxes payable, unearned revenues, the current portion of long-term debt and accrued liabilities such as taxes, salaries and wages, and interest payable.

2 ***Describe the accounting for notes payable.*** When a note is interest-bearing, the amount of assets received upon the issuance of the note is generally equal to the face value of the note, and interest expense is accrued over the life of the note. At maturity, the amount paid is equal to the face value of the note plus interest.

3 ***Explain the accounting for other current liabilities.*** Sales taxes payable (GST, PST or HST) are recorded at the time the related sales occur. The company serves as a collection agent for the taxing authority. Sales taxes are not an expense to the company. Until employee withholding taxes are remitted to the taxing authorities, they are credited to appropriate liability accounts. Unearned revenues are initially recorded in an unearned revenue account. As the revenue is earned, a transfer from unearned revenue to earned revenue occurs. The current portion of long-term debt should be reported as a current liability in the balance sheet.

4 ***Identify the requirements for the financial statement presentation and analysis of current liabilities.*** The nature and amount of each current liability should be reported in the balance sheet or in the notes accompanying the statements. The liquidity of a company may be analysed by calculating working capital, the current ratio, and the acid-test ratio.

5 ***Explain why bonds are issued and identify the types of bonds.*** Bonds may be sold to many investors, and they offer the following advantages over common shares: (1) shareholder control is not affected, (2) tax savings result, and (3) earnings per common share may be higher. The following different types of bonds may be issued: secured and unsecured bonds, term and serial bonds, convertible bonds, and redeemable or retractable bonds.

6 ***Prepare the entries for the issuance of bonds and interest expense.*** When bonds are issued, Cash is debited for the cash proceeds and Bonds Payable is credited for the face value of the bonds. In addition, the accounts Premium on Bonds Payable and Discount on Bonds Payable are used to show the bond premium and bond discount, respectively. Bond discounts and bond premiums are amortized over the life of the bond.

7 ***Describe the entries when bonds are redeemed.*** When bonds are redeemed at maturity, Cash is credited and Bonds Payable is debited for the face value of the bonds. When bonds are redeemed before maturity, it is necessary to (a) eliminate the carrying value of the bonds at the redemption date, (b) record the cash paid, and (c) recognize the gain or loss on redemption.

8 ***Identify the requirements for the financial statement presentation and analysis of long-term liabilities.*** The nature and amount of each long-term debt should be reported in the balance sheet or in schedules in the notes accompanying the statements. The long-run solvency of a company may be analysed by calculating the debt to total assets ratio, the times interest earned ratio, and the cash interest coverage ratio. Other factors to consider are contingent liabilities and lease obligations.

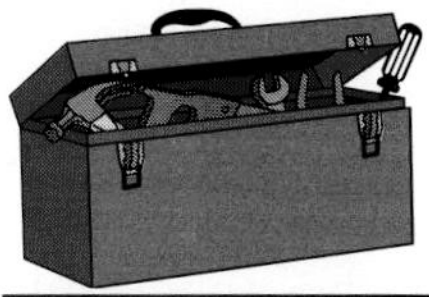

Decision Toolkit—A Summary

Decision Checkpoints	Info Needed for Decision	Tool to Use for Decision	How to Evaluate Results
Can the company meet its current obligations?	Cash, accounts receivable, short-term investments, and other highly liquid assets, and current liabilities	$\text{Acid-test ratio} = \frac{\text{(Cash + Short-term investments + Net receivables)}}{\text{Current liabilities}}$	Ratio should be compared to others in the same industry. High ratio indicates good liquidity.
Can the company obtain short-term financing when necessary?	Available lines of credit from notes to the financial statements	Compare available lines of credit to current liabilities. Also, evaluate liquidity ratios.	If liquidity ratios are low, then lines of credit should be high to compensate.
Is the company generating sufficient earnings to cover annual interest payments?	EBIT and interest expense	$\text{Times interest earned ratio} = \frac{\text{EBIT}}{\text{Interest expense}}$	High ratio indicates sufficient earnings available to cover annual interest payments.
Is the company generating sufficient cash to repay its interest?	EBITDA and interest expense	$\text{Cash interest coverage ratio} = \frac{\text{EBITDA}}{\text{Interest expense}}$	High ratio indicates sufficient cash available to cover annual interest payments.
Does the company have any contingent liabilities?	Knowledge of events with uncertain negative outcomes	Notes to financial statements and financial statements	If negative outcomes are possible, determine the probability, the amount of loss, and the potential impact on financial statements.
Does the company have significant unrecorded lease obligations?	Schedule of minimum lease payments from lease note	Compare liquidity and solvency ratios with and without unrecorded obligations included.	If ratios differ significantly after including unrecorded obligations, these obligations should not be ignored in analysis.

APPENDIX 10A

EFFECTIVE INTEREST AMORTIZATION

STUDY OBJECTIVE 9

Contrast the effects of the straight-line and effective interest methods of amortizing bond discounts and bond premiums.

The straight-line method of amortization that you studied in the chapter has a conceptual deficiency: it does not completely satisfy the matching principle. Under the straight-line method, interest expense as a percentage of the carrying value of the bonds varies each interest period. This can be seen by using data from the first three interest periods of the bond amortization schedule that was shown in Illustration 10-16, earlier in this chapter:

Illustration 10A-1
Interest percentage rates under straight-line method

Semi-annual Interest Period	Interest Expense to be Recorded	Bond Carrying Value	Interest Expense as a Percentage of Carrying Value
1	$52,000	$980,000	5.31%
2	52,000	982,000	5.30%
3	52,000	984,000	5.28%
10	52,000	998,000	5.21%

Note that interest expense as a percentage of carrying value declines in each interest period. However, to completely comply with the matching principle, interest expense as a percentage of carrying value should not change over the life of the bonds. This percentage, referred to as the **effective interest rate**, is established when the bonds are issued and remains constant in each interest period. The effective interest method of amortization accomplishes this result.

Under the **effective interest method**, the amortization of a bond discount or bond premium results in periodic interest expense equal to a constant percentage of the carrying value of the bonds. The effective interest method results in varying amounts of amortization and interest expense per period but a constant percentage rate. The straight-line method results in constant amounts of amortization and interest expense per period but a varying percentage rate.

Illustration 10A-2
Impact of straight-line and effective interest methods

Interest Expense	Straight-Line Method	Effective Interest Method
Dollar amount per period	Constant amount	Changing amount: Increases (discount); Decreases (premium)
As a percentage of carrying value	Changing amount: Increases (premium) Decreases (discount)	Constant %
Total dollar amount over bond term	Same as effective interest total	Same as straight-line total

As Illustration 10A-2 illustrates, **both the straight-line and effective interest methods of amortization result in the same total amount of interest expense over the term of the bonds**. However, **when the amounts are materially different each interest period, the effective interest method is required under generally accepted accounting principles (GAAP)**.

The following steps are required under the effective interest method:

1. Calculate the **bond interest expense** by multiplying the carrying value of the bonds at the beginning of the interest period by the effective interest rate.
2. Calculate the **bond interest paid** (or accrued) by multiplying the face value of the bonds by the contractual interest rate.
3. Calculate the **amortization amount** by determining the difference between the amounts calculated in steps (1) and (2).

These steps are shown in Illustration 10A-3.

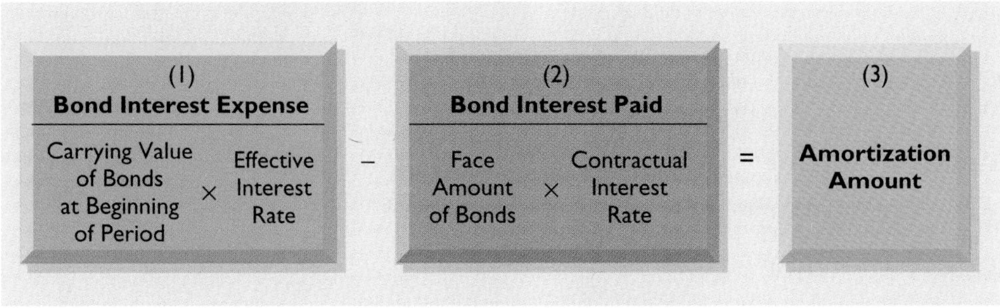

Illustration 10A-3
Calculation of amortization using effective interest method

AMORTIZING A BOND DISCOUNT

To illustrate the effective interest method of bond discount amortization, assume that Britton Corporation issues $100,000 of 10%, five-year bonds on January 1, 2001, with interest payable each July 1 and January 1. The bonds sell for $92,639 (92.639% of face value), which results in a bond discount of $7,361 ($100,000 − $92,639) and an effective interest rate of 12%. (Note that the $92,639 can be proven as shown in Appendix C at the end of this book.) Preparing a bond discount amortization schedule as shown in Illustration 10A-4 facilitates the recording of interest expense and the discount amortization. Note that interest expense as a percentage of carrying value remains constant at 6%.

BRITTON CORPORATION
Bond Discount Amortization
Effective Interest Method—Semi-annual Interest Payments
10% Bonds Issued at 12%

Semi-annual Interest Periods	(A) Interest To Be Paid (5% × $100,000)	(B) Interest Expense To Be Recorded (6% × Preceding Bond Carrying Value)	(C) Discount Amortization (B) – (A)	(D) Unamortized Discount (D) – (C)	(E) Bond Carrying Value ($100,000 – (D))
Issue date				$7,361	$ 92,639
1	$ 5,000	$ 5,558 (6% × $92,639)	$ 558	6,803	93,197
2	5,000	5,592 (6% × $93,197)	592	6,211	93,789
3	5,000	5,627 (6% × $93,789)	627	5,584	94,416
4	5,000	5,665 (6% × $94,416)	665	4,919	95,081
5	5,000	5,705 (6% × $95,081)	705	4,214	95,786
6	5,000	5,747 (6% × $95,786)	747	3,467	96,533
7	5,000	5,792 (6% × $96,533)	792	2,675	97,325
8	5,000	5,840 (6% × $97,325)	840	1,835	98,165
9	5,000	5,890 (6% × $98,165)	890	945	99,055
10	5,000	5,945* (6% × $99,055)	945	0	100,000
	$50,000	$57,361	$7,361		

Column **(A)** remains constant because the face value of the bonds ($100,000) is multiplied by the semi-annual contractual interest rate (10% × $\frac{6}{12}$ = 5%) each period.
Column **(B)** is calculated as the preceding bond carrying value times the semi-annual effective interest rate (12% × $\frac{6}{12}$ = 6%).
Column **(C)** indicates the discount amortization each period.
Column **(D)** decreases each period until it reaches zero at maturity.
Column **(E)** increases each period until it equals face value at maturity.

*$2 difference is due to rounding.

Illustration 10A-4 Bond discount amortization schedule

For the first interest period, the calculations of bond interest expense and the bond discount amortization are as follows:

Illustration 10A-5 Calculation of bond discount amortization

Bond interest expense ($92,639 × 6%)	$5,558
Bond interest paid ($100,000 × 5%)	5,000
Bond discount amortization	**$ 558**

As a result, the entry to record the payment of interest and amortization of bond discount by Britton Corporation on July 1, 2001, is

A	=	L	+	SE
−5,000		+558		−5,558

July 1	Bond Interest Expense	5,558	
	Discount on Bonds Payable		558
	Cash		5,000
	(To record payment of bond interest and amortization of bond discount)		

For the second interest period, bond interest expense will be $5,592 ($93,197 × 6%), and the discount amortization will be $592. At December 31, the following adjusting entry is made:

Dec. 31	Bond Interest Expense	5,592	
	Discount on Bonds Payable		592
	Bond Interest Payable		5,000
	(To record accrued interest and amortization of bond discount)		

A = L + SE

+592 −5,592
+5,000

On January 1, payment of the interest is recorded by a debit to Bond Interest Payable and a credit to Cash.

AMORTIZING A BOND PREMIUM

Helpful Hint When a $100,000 bond sells for $108,111, it is quoted as 108.111% of face value. Note that $108,111 can be proven as shown in Appendix C of the book.

The amortization of a bond premium by the effective interest method is similar to the procedures described for a bond discount. As an example, assume that Wrightway Corporation issues $100,000 of 10%, five-year bonds on January 1, 2001, with interest payable on July 1 and January 1. In this case, the bonds sell for $108,111, which results in a bond premium of $8,111 and an effective interest rate of 8%.

The bond premium amortization schedule is shown in Illustration 10A-6.

Illustration 10A-6 Bond premium amortization schedule

WRIGHTWAY CORPORATION
Bond Premium Amortization
Effective Interest Method—Semi-annual Interest Payments
10% Bonds Issued at 8%

Semi-annual Interest Periods	(A) Interest To Be Paid (5% × $100,000)	(B) Interest Expense To Be Recorded (4% × Preceding Bond Carrying Value)	(C) Premium Amortization (A) − (B)	(D) Unamortized Premium (D) − (C)	(E) Bond Carrying Value ($100,000 + (D))
Issue date				$8,111	$108,111
1	$ 5,000	$ 4,324 (4% × $108,111)	$ 676	7,435	107,435
2	5,000	4,297 (4% × $107,435)	703	6,732	106,732
3	5,000	4,269 (4% × $106,732)	731	6,001	106,001
4	5,000	4,240 (4% × $106,001)	760	5,241	105,241
5	5,000	4,210 (4% × $105,241)	790	4,451	104,451
6	5,000	4,178 (4% × $104,451)	822	3,629	103,629
7	5,000	4,145 (4% × $103,629)	855	2,774	102,774
8	5,000	4,111 (4% × $102,774)	889	1,885	101,885
9	5,000	4,075 (4% × $101,885)	925	960	100,960
10	5,000	4,040* (4% × $100,960)	960	0	100,000
	$50,000	$41,889	$8,111		

Column (A) remains constant because the face value of the bonds ($100,000) is multiplied by the semi-annual contractual interest rate ($10\% \times \frac{6}{12} = 5\%$) each period.
Column (B) is calculated as the carrying value of the bonds times the semi-annual effective interest rate ($8\% \times \frac{6}{12} = 4\%$).
Column (C) indicates the premium amortization each period.
Column (D) decreases each period until it reaches zero at maturity.
Column (E) decreases each period until it equals face value at maturity.

*$2 difference is due to rounding.

For the first interest period, the calculations of bond interest expense and the bond premium amortization are

Illustration 10A-7
Calculation of bond premium amortization

Bond interest paid ($100,000 × 5%)	$5,000
Bond interest expense ($108,111 × 4%)	4,324
Bond premium amortization	**$ 676**

The entry on the first interest date is

A	=	L	+	SE
−5,000		−676		−4,324

July 1	Bond Interest Expense	4,324	
	Premium on Bonds Payable	676	
	Cash		5,000
	(To record payment of bond interest and amortization of bond premium)		

For the second interest period, interest expense will be $4,297, and the premium amortization will be $703. Note that the amount of periodic interest expense decreases over the life of the bond when the effective interest method is applied to bonds issued at a premium. The reason is that a constant percentage is applied to a decreasing bond carrying value to calculate interest expense. The carrying value is decreasing because of the amortization of the premium.

SUMMARY OF STUDY OBJECTIVE FOR APPENDIX 10A

9 ***Contrast the effects of the straight-line and effective interest methods of amortizing bond discount and bond premium.*** The straight-line method of amortization results in a constant amount of amortization and interest expense per period but a varying percentage rate. In contrast, the effective interest method results in varying amounts of amortization and interest expense per period but a constant percentage rate of interest. The effective interest method generally results in a better matching of expenses with revenues. When the difference between the straight-line and effective interest method is material, the use of the effective interest method is required under GAAP.

DEMONSTRATION PROBLEM FOR APPENDIX 10A

Problem-Solving Strategies

1. Bond carrying value at beginning of period times effective interest rate equals interest expense.
2. Credit to Cash (or Bond Interest Payable) is calculated by multiplying the face value of the bonds by the contractual interest rate.
3. Don't forget to halve the effective and contractual interest rates when the bond interest is paid semi-annually.
4. Bond premium or discount amortization is the difference between (1) and (2).

Gardner Corporation issues $1,750,000 of 10-year, 12% bonds on January 1, 2001, at $1,968,090 to yield 10%. The bonds pay semi-annual interest July 1 and January 1. Gardner uses the effective interest method of amortization.

Instructions

(a) Prove the present value of the bonds, $1,968,090, using the present value tables provided in Appendix C.
(b) Prepare the journal entry to record the issuance of the bonds.
(c) Prepare the journal entry to record the payment of interest on July 1, 2001.

Solution to Demonstration Problem for Appendix 10A

(a) Present value of principal to be received at maturity	
$1,750,000 × PV of 1 due in 20 periods at 5%	
$1,750,000 × .37689 (Table 3)	$ 659,558
Present value of interest to be received periodically over the term of the bonds	
$1,750,000 × 6% = $105,000 × PV of 1 due periodically for 20 periods at 5%	
$105,000 × 12.46221 (Table 4)	1,308,532
Present value	$1,968,090

(b)

2001			
Jan. 1	Cash	1,968,090	
	Bonds Payable		1,750,000
	Premium on Bonds Payable		218,090
	(To record issuance of bonds at a premium)		

(c)

2001			
July 1	Bond Interest Expense	98,405*	
	Premium on Bonds Payable	6,595**	
	Cash		105,000
	(To record payment of semi-annual interest and amortization of bond premium)		
	*($1,968,090 × 5% = $98,405)		
	**($105,000 − $98,405 = $6,595)		

APPENDIX 10B

ACCOUNTING FOR LONG-TERM NOTES PAYABLE

STUDY OBJECTIVE 10

Describe the accounting for long-term notes payable.

The use of notes payable in long-term debt financing is quite common. Long-term notes payable are similar to short-term interest-bearing notes payable except that the terms of the notes exceed one year. In periods of unstable interest rates, the interest rate on long-term notes may be tied to changes in the market rate for comparable loans. Examples are Quebecor's revolving bank credits, which bear interest at floating rates.

A long-term note may be secured by a document called a **mortgage** that pledges title to specific assets as security for a loan. **Mortgage notes payable** are widely used in the purchase of homes by individuals and in the acquisition of capital assets by many small and some large companies. For example, approximately 18% of McDonald's Corporation's long-term debt relates to mortgage notes on land, buildings, and improvements. Like other long-term notes payable, the mortgage loan terms may stipulate either a fixed or an adjustable interest rate. Typically, the terms require the borrower to make instalment payments over the term of the loan. Each payment consists of (1) interest on the unpaid balance of the loan, and (2) a reduction of loan principal. The interest decreases each period, while the portion applied to the loan principal increases.

Helpful Hint Electronic spreadsheet programs can create a schedule of instalment loan payments. This allows you to put in the data for your own mortgage loan and get an illustration that really hits home.

Mortgage notes payable are recorded initially at face value, and entries are required subsequently for each instalment payment. To illustrate, assume that Porter Technology Inc. issues a $500,000, 12%, 20-year mortgage note on December 31, 2001, to obtain needed financing for the construction of a new research laboratory. The terms provide for semi-annual instalment payments of $33,231. The instalment payment schedule for the first two years is as follows:

Illustration 10B-1
Mortgage instalment payment schedule

Semi-annual Interest Period	(A) Cash Payment	(B) Interest Expense (D) × 6%	(C) Reduction of Principal (A) − (B)	(D) Principal Balance (D) − (C)
Issue date				$500,000
1	$33,231	$30,000	$3,231	496,769
2	33,231	29,806	3,425	493,344
3	33,231	29,601	3,630	489,714
4	33,231	29,383	3,848	485,866

The entries to record the mortgage loan and first instalment payment are as follows:

A =	L +	SE
+500,000	+500,000	

Date	Account	Debit	Credit
Dec. 31	Cash	500,000	
	Mortgage Notes Payable		500,000
	(To record mortgage loan)		

A =	L +	SE
−33,231	−3,231	−30,000

Date	Account	Debit	Credit
June 30	Interest Expense	30,000	
	Mortgage Notes Payable	3,231	
	Cash		33,231
	(To record semi-annual payment on mortgage)		

In the balance sheet, the reduction in principal for the next year is reported as a current liability, and the remaining unpaid principal balance is classified as a long-term liability. At December 31, 2002, the total liability is $493,344, of which $7,478 ($3,630 + $3,848) is current, and $485,866 ($493,344 − $7,478) is long-term.

Summary of Study Objective for Appendix 10B

1 ***Describe the accounting for long-term notes payable.*** Each payment consists of (1) interest on the unpaid balance of the loan, and (2) a reduction of loan principal. The interest decreases each period, while the portion applied to the loan principal increases each period.

Glossary

Acid-test (quick) ratio A measure of a company's immediate short-term liquidity, calculated by dividing the sum of cash, short-term investments, and net receivables by current liabilities. (p. 530)

Bond certificate A legal document that indicates the name of the issuer, the face value of the bonds, and such other data as the contractual interest rate and the maturity date of the bonds. (p. 535)

Bond indenture A legal document that sets forth the terms of the bond issue. (p. 535)

Bonds A form of interest-bearing notes payable issued by corporations, universities, and government entities. (p. 532)

Capital lease A type of lease whose characteristics make it similar to a debt-financed purchase, which is consequently accounted for in that fashion. (p. 550)

Cash interest coverage ratio A measure of a company's solvency, assessing cash available to pay annual interest obligations, calculated by dividing EBITDA by interest expense. (p. 547)

Contingencies Events with uncertain outcomes, such as a potential liability that may become an actual liability sometime in the future. (p. 549)

Contractual (stated) interest rate Rate used to determine the amount of interest the borrower pays and the investor receives. (p. 535)

Convertible bonds Bonds that permit bondholders to convert them into common shares at their option. (p. 535)

Current liability A debt that will be paid (1) from existing current assets or through the creation of other current liabilities, and (2) within one year or the operating cycle, whichever is longer. (p. 522)

Debenture bonds Bonds issued against the general credit of the borrower; also called unsecured bonds. (p. 534)

Discount (on a bond) The difference between the face value of a bond and its selling price, when a bond is sold for less than its face value. (p. 539)

EBIT Earnings before interest expense and income tax expense. (p. 547)

EBITDA Earnings before interest expense, income tax expense, and depreciation and amortization expense. (p. 547)

Effective interest method of amortization A method of amortizing a bond discount or premium that results in periodic interest expense equal to a constant percentage of the carrying value of the bonds. (p. 556)

Effective interest rate Market rate established when

bonds are issued that remains constant in each interest period. (p. 556)

Face (par) value Amount of principal due at the maturity date of the bond. (p. 535)

Line of credit A prearranged agreement between a company and a lender that allows a company to borrow up to an agreed-upon amount. (p. 531)

Long-term liabilities Obligations expected to be paid more than one year in the future. (p. 532)

Market (effective) interest rate The rate investors demand for loaning funds to the corporation. (p. 537)

Mortgage bond A bond secured by real estate. (p. 534)

Mortgage note payable A long-term note secured by a mortgage that pledges title to specific units of property as security for the loan. (p. 561)

Notes payable Obligations in the form of written notes. (p. 523)

Off–balance sheet financing The intentional effort by a company to structure its financing arrangements so as to avoid showing liabilities on its books. (p. 551)

Operating lease A contractual arrangement giving the lessee temporary use of the property with continued ownership of the property by the lessor, and accounted for as a rental. (p. 550)

Premium (on a bond) The difference between the selling price and the face value of a bond when a bond is sold for more than its face value. (p. 539)

Present value The value today of an amount to be received at some date in the future after taking into account current interest rates. (p. 536)

Redeemable (callable) bonds Bonds that are subject to retirement at a stated dollar amount prior to maturity at the option of the issuer. (p. 535)

Retractable bonds Bonds that are subject to retirement at a stated dollar amount prior to maturity at the option of the bondholder. (p. 535)

Secured bonds Bonds that have specific assets of the issuer pledged as collateral. (p. 534)

Serial bonds Bonds that mature in instalments. (p. 535)

Sinking fund bonds Bonds secured by specific assets set aside to retire them. (p. 534)

Straight-line method of amortization A method of amortizing a bond discount or bond premium that allocates the same amount to interest expense in each interest period. (p. 540)

Term bonds Bonds that mature at a single specified future date. (p. 535)

Times interest earned ratio A measure of a company's solvency, calculated by dividing earnings before interest expense and taxes by interest expense. (p. 547)

Unsecured bonds Bonds issued against the general credit of the borrower; also called debenture bonds. (p. 534)

Demonstration Problem

Snyder Software Inc. successfully developed a new spreadsheet program. However, to produce and market the program, the company needed $2.0 million of additional financing. On January 1, 2001, Snyder borrowed money as follows:

1. Snyder issued $500,000 of 11%, 10-year bonds. The bonds sold at face value and pay semi-annual interest on January 1 and July 1.
2. Snyder issued $1.0 million of 10%, 10-year bonds for $885,301. Interest is payable semi-annually on January 1 and July 1.

Snyder uses the straight-line method of amortization and its year end is December 31.

Instructions

(a) For the 11% bonds, prepare journal entries for these items:
   1. The issuance of the bonds on January 1, 2001
   2. Interest expense on July 1 and December 31, 2001
   3. The payment of interest on January 1, 2002

(b) For the 10% bonds do the following:
   1. Journalize the issuance of the bonds on January 1, 2001.
   2. Prepare the entry for the redemption of the bonds at 101 on January 1, 2004, after paying the interest due on this date. The carrying value of the bonds at the redemption date was $919,711.

Solution to Demonstration Problem

(a) 1. 2001

Jan. 1	Cash	500,000	
	Bonds Payable		500,000
	(To record issue of 11%, 10-year bonds at face value)		

2. 2001

July 1	Bond Interest Expense	27,500	
	Cash ($500,000 × 11% × $\frac{6}{12}$)		27,500
	(To record payment of semi-annual interest)		
Dec. 31	Bond Interest Expense	27,500	
	Bond Interest Payable		27,500
	(To record accrual of semi-annual bond interest)		

3. 2002

Jan. 1	Bond Interest Payable	27,500	
	Cash		27,500
	(To record payment of accrued interest)		

(b) 1. 2001

Jan. 1	Cash	885,301	
	Discount on Bonds Payable	114,699	
	Bonds Payable		1,000,000
	(To record issue of 10%, 10-year bonds at a discount)		

2. 2004

Jan. 1	Bonds Payable	1,000,000	
	Loss on Bond Redemption ($1,010,000 – $919,711)	90,289	
	Discount on Bonds Payable ($1,000,000 – $919,711)		80,289
	Cash ($1,000,000 × 101%)		1,010,000
	(To record redemption of bonds at 101)		

Note: All of the following questions, exercises, and problems marked with an asterisk relate to material in the appendices to the chapter.

Self-Study Questions

Answers are at the end of the chapter.

(SO 1) 1. The time period for classifying a liability as current is one year or the operating cycle, whichever is:
(a) longer.
(b) shorter.
(c) probable.
(d) possible.

(SO 1) 2. To be classified as a current liability, a debt must be expected to be paid:
(a) out of existing current assets.
(b) by creating other current liabilities.
(c) within two years.
(d) Either (a) or (b)

(SO 2) 3. Gilbert Company Ltd. borrows $88,500 on September 1, 2001, from TD Bank by signing an $88,500, 12%, one-year note. What is the accrued interest at December 31, 2001?
(a) $2,655
(b) $3,540
(c) $4,425
(d) $10,620

(SO 3) 4. Reeves Company Ltd. has total proceeds from sales of $4,515. If the proceeds include HST of 15%, what is the amount to be credited to Sales?
(a) $677
(b) $3,926
(c) $4,515
(d) The correct answer is not given.

(SO 4) 5. Which of the following would *not* be included in the numerator of the acid-test ratio?
(a) Accounts receivable
(b) Cash
(c) Short-term investments
(d) Inventory

(SO 4) 6. Which of the following is *not* a measure of liquidity?
(a) Debt to total assets ratio
(b) Working capital
(c) Current ratio
(d) Acid-test ratio

(SO 5) 7. What term is used for bonds that are unsecured?
(a) Callable bonds
(b) Indenture bonds
(c) Debenture bonds
(d) Sinking fund bonds

(SO 6) 8. Karson Inc. issues 10-year bonds with a maturity value of $200,000. If the bonds are issued at a premium, this indicates that:
(a) the contractual interest rate exceeds the market interest rate.
(b) the market interest rate exceeds the contractual interest rate.
(c) the contractual interest rate and the market interest rate are the same.
(d) no relationship exists between the two rates.

(SO 6) 9. On January 1, Hurley Corporation issues $500,000 of five-year, 12% bonds at 96 with interest payable on July 1 and January 1. The entry on July 1 to record payment of bond interest and the amortization of a bond discount using the straight-line method will include a:
(a) debit to Interest Expense, $10,000.
(b) debit to Interest Expense, $20,000.
(c) credit to Discount on Bonds Payable, $4,000.
(d) credit to Discount on Bonds Payable, $2,000.

10. For the bonds issued in question 9, what is the carrying value of the bonds at the end of the third interest period? (SO 6)
(a) $468,000
(b) $474,000
(c) $486,000
(d) $492,000

11. Gester Corporation retires its $100,000 face value bonds at 105 on January 1, following the payment of semi-annual interest. The carrying value of the bonds at the redemption date is $103,745. The entry to record the redemption will include a: (SO 7)
(a) credit of $3,745 to Loss on Bond Redemption.
(b) debit of $3,745 to Premium on Bonds Payable.
(c) credit of $1,255 to Gain on Bond Redemption.
(d) debit of $5,000 to Premium on Bonds Payable.

12. In a recent year, Kennedy Corporation had net earnings of $150,000, amortization expense of $50,000, interest expense of $30,000, and income tax expense of $20,000. What was Kennedy Corporation's times interest earned ratio for the year? (SO 8)
(a) 5.00
(b) 4.00
(c) 6.66
(d) 8.33

* 13. On January 1, Loptein Inc. issued $1,000,000 of 9%, five-year bonds. The market rate of interest for these bonds is 10%. Interest is payable annually on December 31. How much cash will Loptein receive from the sale of these bonds on January 1? (Hint: Use Appendix C.) (SO 9)
(a) $938,551
(b) $962,091
(c) $1,000,000
(d) $1,038,895

* 14. If Loptein uses the effective interest method of amortizing the bond discount on the bonds issued in question 13, how much interest expense will Loptein report at the end of the first year? (SO 9)
(a) $86,588
(b) $93,855
(c) $96,209
(d) $100,00

* 15. Assume that you take out a $100,000, 10-year mortgage on your first building. The mortgage has an annual interest rate of 6%, and is repayable monthly, in the amount of $1,110. How much will the first cash payment reduce the principal by? (SO 10)
(a) $500
(b) $600
(c) $610
(d) $1,110

QUESTIONS

(SO 1) 1. Li Feng believes a current liability is a debt that can be expected to be paid in one year. Is Li correct? Explain.

(SO 2) 2. What is the difference between accounts payable and notes payable?

(SO 3) 3. (a) Your roommate says, "Sales taxes are reported as an expense in the statement of earnings." Do you agree? Explain.
(b) Hard Walk Café has cash proceeds from sales of $11,500. This amount includes $1,500 of HST. Give the entry to record the proceeds.

(SO 3) 4. Aurora University sold 10,000 season soccer tickets at $90 each for its five-game home schedule. What entries should be made (a) when the tickets are sold and (b) after each game?

(SO 3) 5. Identify three payroll costs commonly withheld by an employer from an employee's gross pay.

(SO 3) 6. (a) Identify three payroll costs commonly paid by employers on employees' salaries and wages.
(b) Where in the financial statements does the employer report costs withheld from employees' pay that are paid by the employees? The employer?

(SO 4) 7. The Fraiser Riner Corporation obtains $25,000 in cash by signing a 9%, six-month, $25,000 note payable to First Bank on July 1. Fraiser's fiscal year ends on September 30. What information should be reported for the note payable in the annual financial statements?

(SO 4) 8. Lincoln Corporation has a current ratio of 1.1. Joe Investor has always been told that a corporation's current ratio should exceed 2.0. Lincoln argues that its ratio is low because it has a minimal amount of inventory on hand so as to reduce operating costs. Lincoln also points out that it has significant available lines of credit. Is Joe still correct? What other measures might he check?

(SO 5) 9. (a) What are long-term liabilities? Give two examples.
(b) What is a bond?

(SO 5) 10. (a) As a source of long-term financing, what are the major advantages of bonds over common shares?
(b) What are the major disadvantages in using bonds for long-term financing?

(SO 5) 11. Contrast these types of bonds:
(a) secured and unsecured
(b) term and serial
(c) retractable and redeemable

(SO 5) 12. Explain each of these important terms in issuing bonds:
(a) face value
(b) contractual interest rate
(c) bond indenture
(d) bond certificate

13. (a) What is a convertible bond? (SO 5)
(b) Discuss the advantages of a convertible bond from the standpoint of the bondholders and of the issuing corporation.

14. Describe the two major obligations incurred by a company when bonds are issued. (SO 6)

15. Assume that Stoney Inc. sold bonds with a face value of $100,000 for $104,000. Was the market interest rate equal to, less than, or greater than the bonds' contractual interest rate? Explain. (SO 6)

16. Barbara Secord and Jack Dalton are discussing how the market price of a bond is determined. Barbara believes that the market price of a bond is solely a function of the amount of the principal payment at the end of the term of a bond. Is she right? Discuss. (SO 6)

17. If a 10%, 10-year, $600,000 bond is issued at its face value and interest is paid semi-annually, what is the amount of the interest payment at the end of the first semi-annual period? (SO 6)

18. Distinguish between the effective interest and the straight-line method of amortizing discounts and premiums on bonds payable. (SO 6)

19. Brent Corporation issues $200,000 of 8%, five-year bonds on January 1, 2001, at 104. Assuming that the straight-line method is used to amortize the premium, what is the total amount of interest expense for 2001? (SO 6)

20. If the Bonds Payable account has a balance of $900,000 and the Discount on Bonds Payable account has a balance of $40,000, what is the carrying value of the bonds? (SO 7)

21. Which accounts are debited and which are credited if a bond issue originally sold at a premium is redeemed before maturity at 97, immediately following the payment of interest? (SO 7)

22. (SO 4, 8
(a) In general, what are the requirements for the financial statement presentation of current liabilities?
(b) In general, what are the requirements for the financial statement presentation of long-term liabilities?
(c) What ratios may be calculated to evaluate a company's liquidity and solvency?

(SO 4, 8) 23. Michael Feldman says that liquidity and solvency are the same thing. Is he correct? If not, how do they differ?

(SO 4, 8) 24. Tom Dodge needs a few new trucks for his business. He is considering buying the trucks but is concerned that the additional debt he will need to borrow will make his liquidity and solvency ratios look bad. What options does he have other than purchasing the assets, and how will these options affect his financial statements?

(SO 8) 25. Why is the cash interest coverage ratio considered by some to provide a superior measure of a company's ability to pay interest than the times interest earned ratio?

(SO 8) 26. What criteria must be met before a contingency has to be recorded as a liability? How should the contingency be disclosed if the criteria are not met?

(SO 8) 27. What is the primary difference between the nature of an operating lease and a capital lease? What is the difference in how they are recorded?

28. What are the implications for analysis if a company has significant operating leases? (SO 8)

*29. Summit Corporation issues $400,000 of 9%, five-year bonds on January 1, 2001 at 104. If Summit uses the effective interest method in amortizing the premium, will the annual interest expense increase or decrease over the life of the bonds? Explain. (SO 9)

*30. Doug Bareak, a friend of yours, has recently purchased a building for $125,000. He paid $25,000 down and financed the remainder with a 10.5%, 20-year mortgage, payable at $998 per month. At the end of the first month, Doug received a statement from the bank indicating that only $123 of principal was paid during the month. At this rate, he calculated that it would take over 67 years to pay off the mortgage. Explain why this is not the case. (SO 10)

BRIEF EXERCISES

Identify whether obligations are current liabilities.
(SO 1)

BE10-1 Fresno Company Ltd. has these obligations at December 31: (a) a note payable for $100,000 due in two years, (b) a 10-year mortgage payable of $200,000, payable in 10 $20,000 annual payments, (c) interest payable of $15,000 on the mortgage, and (d) accounts payable of $60,000. For each obligation, indicate whether it should be classified as a current liability.

Prepare entries for an interest-bearing note payable.
(SO 2)

BE10-2 Romez Company Limited borrows $60,000 on July 1 from the bank by signing a $60,000, 10%, one-year note payable. Prepare the journal entries to record (a) the proceeds of the note and (b) accrued interest at December 31, assuming adjusting entries are made only at the end of the year.

Calculate and record sales taxes payable.
(SO 3)

BE10-3 Grandy Auto Supply Inc. does not segregate sales and sales taxes at the time of sale. The register total for March 16 is $9,975. All sales are subject to GST of 7% and PST of 7%. PST is *not* charged on GST. Calculate sales taxes payable and make the entry to record sales taxes payable and sales.

Prepare entries for unearned revenues.
(SO 3)

BE10-4 Outstanding University sells 3,000 season basketball tickets at $60 each for its 12-game home schedule. Give the entry to record (a) the sale of the season tickets and (b) the revenue earned by playing the first home game.

Compare bond financing to share financing.
(SO 5)

BE10-5 Olga Inc. is considering these two alternatives to finance its construction of a new $2-million plant:
(a) issuance of 200,000 common shares at the market price of $10 per share
(b) issuance of $2 million of 8% bonds at face value
Complete the table and indicate which alternative is preferable.

	Issue Shares	Issue Bond
Earnings before interest and taxes	$1,000,000	$1,000,000
Interest expense from bonds	______	______
Earnings before income taxes		
Income tax expense (30%)	______	______
Net earnings	$	$
Outstanding shares	______	700,000
Earnings per share	$	$

Prepare journal entries for bonds issued at face value.
(SO 6)

BE10-6 Keystone Corporation issued 1,000 9%, five-year, $1,000 bonds dated March 1, 2001, at 100.
(a) Prepare the journal entry to record the sale of these bonds on March 1, 2001.
(b) Prepare the journal entry to record the first interest payment on September 1, 2001 (interest payable semi-annually).
(c) Prepare the adjusting journal entry on December 31, 2001, Keystone's year end, to record interest expense.

Prepare journal entries for bonds issued at a discount and a premium.
(SO 6)

BE10-7 Repeat the requirements of BE10-6 assuming (a) that the bonds were issued at 98, rather than 100, then (b) that the bonds were issued at 102, rather than 100. The straight-line method of amortization is used.

Prepare journal entries for bonds issued at a discount.
(SO 6)

BE10-8 Dominic Company Ltd. issues $2 million of 10-year, 9% bonds at 96, with interest payable on July 1 and January 1. The straight-line method is used to amortize the bond discount.
(a) Prepare the journal entry to record the sale of these bonds on January 1, 2001.
(b) Prepare the journal entry to record interest expense and bond discount amortization on July 1, 2001, assuming no previous accrual of interest.

Prepare journal entries for bonds issued at a premium.
(SO 6)

BE10-9 Hercules Inc. issues $5 million of five-year, 10% bonds at 103, with interest payable on July 1 and January 1. The straight-line method is used to amortize the bond premium.
(a) Prepare the journal entry to record the sale of these bonds on January 1, 2001.
(b) Prepare the journal entry to record interest expense and bond premium amortization on July 1, 2001, assuming no previous accrual of interest.

Prepare journal entry for redemption of bonds.
(SO 7)

BE10-10 The balance sheet for Hathaway Company Ltd. reports the following information:

HATHAWAY COMPANY LTD.
Balance Sheet (partial)
November 30, 2001

Long-term liabilities		
Bonds payable	$1,000,000	
Less: Discount on bonds payable	60,000	$940,000

Hathaway decides to redeem these bonds at 102 after paying semi-annual interest. Prepare the journal entry to record the redemption on November 30, 2001.

Prepare statement presentation of long-term liabilities.
(SO 8)

BE10-11 Presented here are liability items for Warner Company Ltd. at December 31, 2001. Prepare the long-term liabilities section of the balance sheet for Warner Company.

Interest payable	$ 40,000
Bonds payable, due 2003	900,000
Notes payable, due 2005	80,000
Discount on bonds payable	45,000

Analyse liquidity and solvency.
(SO 4, 8)

BE10-12 The **Molson Companies Limited**'s 1999 financial statements contain the following selected data (in thousands):

Cash and short-term investments	$ 43,934	Total liabilities	$2,331,497
Accounts receivable	163,962	Amortization expense	54,329
Total current assets	535,877	Interest expense	79,390
Total assets	3,439,577	Income tax expense	36,100
Total current liabilities	656,028	Net earnings	169,914

Calculate these values:
(a) working capital
(b) current ratio
(c) acid-test ratio
(d) debt to total assets ratio
(e) times interest earned ratio
(f) cash interest coverage ratio

Analyse liquidity and solvency.
(SO 4, 8)

BE10-13 The **Canadian National Railway Company**'s (CN) total assets in 1998 were $10,864 million and total liabilities were $6,573 million. That year, CN reported $216 million in required payments for operating equipment leases. If these assets had been recorded as a capital lease, assume that assets and liabilities would have risen by approximately $1,394 million.

(a) Calculate CN's debt to total assets ratio, first using the figures reported, and then after increasing assets and liabilities for the assumed value of the unrecorded operating leases.
(b) Discuss the potential effect of these operating leases on your assessment of CN's solvency.

* **BE10-14** Presented below is the partial bond amortization schedule for Chiasson Corporation, which uses the effective interest method of amortization.

Use effective interest method of bond amortization.
(SO 9)

Semi-annual Interest Periods	Interest To Be Paid	Interest Expense To Be Recorded	Discount Amortization	Unamortized Discount	Bond Carrying Value
Issue date				$62,311	$937,689
1	$45,000	$46,884	$1,884	60,427	939,573
2	45,000	46,979	1,979	58,448	941,552

(a) Prepare a journal entry to record the sale of the bond at the issue date.
(b) Prepare the journal entry to record the payment of interest and the discount amortization at the end of period 1.
(c) Explain why interest expense is greater than interest paid.
(d) Explain why interest expense will increase each period.
(e) What will be the carrying value of the bond on its maturity date?

* **BE10-15** You qualify for a $10,000 loan from the Canada Student Loans Program to help finance your education. Once you graduate, you start repaying this note payable at an interest rate of 10% and with a monthly cash payment of $132.15, principal and interest, for 120 payments (10 years). Prepare an instalment payment schedule, as shown in Illustration 10B-1, for the first three payments.

Do accounting for long-term notes payable.
(SO 10)

EXERCISES

E10-1 On June 1, Cairo Company Ltd. borrows $50,000 from First Bank on a six-month, $50,000, 12% note.

Prepare entries for interest-bearing notes.
(SO 2)

Instructions
(a) Prepare the entry on June 1.
(b) Prepare the adjusting entry on June 30.
(c) Prepare the entry at maturity (December 1), assuming monthly adjusting entries have been made through November 30.
(d) What was the total financing cost (interest expense)?

E10-2 On May 15, Maranga's Outback Clothiers Ltd. borrowed some money on a four-month note to provide cash during the slow season of the year. The interest rate of the note was 7%. At the time the note was due, the amount of interest owed was $294.

Prepare entries for interest-bearing notes.
(SO 2)

Instructions
(a) Determine the amount borrowed by Maranga's.
(b) Assume the amount borrowed was $18,500. What was the interest rate if the amount of interest owed was $740?
(c) Prepare the entry for the initial borrowing and the repayment using the facts in part (a).

E10-3 In providing accounting services to small businesses, you encounter the following situations pertaining to cash sales. Assume in both situations that PST is *not* charged on GST.

Journalize sales and related taxes.
(SO 3)

1. Nash Company Ltd. rings up sales and sales taxes separately on its cash register. On April 10, the register totals are sales, $25,000, GST, $1,750, and PST, $2,500.
2. Pontiac Company Ltd. does not segregate sales and sales taxes. Its register total for April 15 is $11,700, which includes a 7% GST and a 10% PST.

Instructions
Prepare the entries to record the sales transactions and related taxes for (a) Nash Company and (b) Pontiac Company.

Journalize unearned subscription revenue.
(SO 3)

E10-4 Westland Company Ltd. publishes a monthly sports magazine, *Fishing Preview*. Subscriptions to the magazine cost $24 per year. During November 2001, Westwood sells 6,000 subscriptions for cash beginning with the December issue. Westwood prepares financial statements quarterly and recognizes subscription revenue earned at the end of the quarter. The company uses the accounts Unearned Subscription Revenue and Subscription Revenue.

Instructions

(a) Prepare the entry in November for the receipt of the subscriptions.
(b) Prepare the adjusting entry at December 31, 2001, to record subscription revenue earned in December 2001.
(c) Prepare the adjusting entry at March 31, 2002, to record subscription revenue earned in the first quarter of 2002.

Journalize unearned revenue transactions.
(SO 3)

E10-5 The Bundoora Cats' season tickets are priced at $230 and include 23 games. Revenue is recognized after each game is played. When the season began, the amount credited to Unearned Season Ticket Revenue was $1,023,500. By the end of October, $756,500 of the Unearned Season Ticket Revenue had been recorded as earned.

Instructions

(a) How many season tickets did Bundoora sell?
(b) How many home games had Bundoora played by the end of October?
(c) Prepare the entry for the initial recording of the Unearned Season Ticket Revenue.
(d) Prepare the entry to recognize the revenue after the first home game had been played.

Calculate current and acid-test ratios before and after paying accounts payable.
(SO 4)

E10-6 The following financial data were reported by the **Calgary Exhibition & Stampede** for 1998 and 1997:

CALGARY EXHIBITION AND STAMPEDE LIMITED
Balance Sheet (partial)
September 30 (in thousands)

	1998	1997
Current assets		
Cash and short-term deposits	$ 574	$ 1,021
Accounts receivable	3,347	1,575
Inventories	1,201	1,010
Other current assets	322	192
Total current assets	5,444	3,798
Current liabilities	9,003	12,108

Instructions

(a) Calculate the current and acid-test ratios for the Calgary Stampede for 1998 and 1997.
(b) Suppose that at the end of 1998, the Stampede used $500 million cash to pay off $500 million of accounts payable. How would its current ratio and acid-test ratio change?
(c) At September 30, the Stampede has an undrawn operating line of credit of $12.5 million. Would this affect any assessment that you might make of the Stampede's short-term liquidity? Explain.

Compare issuance of share capital financing to issuance of bond financing.
(SO 5)

E10-7 Sundown Airlines is considering these two alternatives for financing the purchase of a fleet of airplanes:

1. Issue 60,000 common shares at $45 per share. (Cash dividends have not been paid; nor is the payment of any contemplated.)
2. Issue 13%, 10-year bonds at face value for $2,700,000.

It is estimated that the company will earn $900,000 before interest and taxes as a result of this purchase. The company has an estimated tax rate of 30% and has 90,000 common shares outstanding prior to the new financing.

Instructions
Determine the effect on net earnings and earnings per share for (a) issuing shares and (b) issuing bonds.

E10-8 On February 1, Laramie Company Ltd. issued $90,000 of 10%, 10-year bonds at face value. Interest is payable semi-annually on February 1 and August 1.

Prepare journal entries for issuance of bonds, and payment and accrual of interest.
(SO 6)

Instructions
Prepare journal entries to record these events:
(a) the issuance of the bonds
(b) the payment of interest on August 1
(c) the accrual of interest on December 31, Laramie's year end

E10-9 Pueblo Company Limited issued $240,000 of 9%, 20-year bonds on January 1, 2001, at 103. Interest is payable semi-annually on July 1 and January 1. Pueblo uses straight-line amortization for bond premiums or discounts and has a December 31 year end.

Prepare journal entries to record issuance of bonds, payment of interest, amortization of premium, and redemption at maturity.
(SO 6, 7)

Instructions
Prepare the journal entries to record these events:
(a) the issuance of the bonds
(b) the payment of interest and the premium amortization on July 1, 2001
(c) the accrual of interest and the premium amortization on December 31, 2001
(d) the redemption of the bonds at maturity, assuming interest for the last interest period has been paid and recorded

E10-10 Cotter Company Ltd. issued $180,000 of 11%, 10-year bonds on December 31, 2000, for $172,000. Interest is payable semi-annually on June 30 and December 31. Cotter uses the straight-line method to amortize bond premiums or discounts and has a December 31 year end.

Prepare journal entries to record issuance of bonds, payment of interest, amortization of discount, and redemption at maturity.
(SO 6, 7)

Instructions
Prepare the journal entries to record these events:
(a) the issuance of the bonds
(b) the payment of interest and the discount amortization on June 30, 2001
(c) the payment of interest and the discount amortization on December 31, 2001
(d) the redemption of the bonds at maturity, assuming interest for the last interest period has been paid and recorded

E10-11 The situations presented here are independent.

Prepare journal entries for redemption of bonds.
(SO 7)

Instructions
For each situation prepare the appropriate journal entry for the redemption of the bonds.
(a) Ernst Corporation retired $120,000 of face value, 12% bonds on June 30, 2001, at 102. The carrying value of the bonds at the redemption date was $107,500. The bonds pay semi-annual interest, and the interest payment due on June 30, 2001, has been made and recorded.
(b) Young, Inc., retired $150,000 of face value, 12.5% bonds on June 30, 2001, at 98. The carrying value of the bonds at the redemption date was $151,000. The bonds pay semi-annual interest, and the interest payment due on June 30, 2001, has been made and recorded.

E10-12 The adjusted trial balance for Montreal Corporation at the end of the current year contained these accounts:

Prepare statement presentation of long-term liabilities.
(SO 4, 8)

Bond Interest Payable	$ 9,000
Note Payable, due 2005	59,500
Bonds Payable, due 2010	120,000
Premium on Bonds Payable	32,000

Instructions

(a) Prepare the long-term liabilities section of the balance sheet.
(b) Indicate the proper balance sheet classification for the account(s) listed above that do not belong in the long-term liabilities section.

Calculate liquidity and solvency ratios; discuss impact of unrecorded obligations on liquidity and solvency.
(SO 4, 8)

E10-13 **McDonald's Corporation**'s 1998 financial statements contain the following selected data (in millions of US$):

Current assets	$ 1,309	Depreciation and amortization	$ 881
Total assets	19,784	Interest expense	414
Current liabilities	2,497	Income taxes	757
Total liabilities	10,260	Net income	1,550
Cash	299		
Accounts receivable	609		

Instructions

(a) Calculate these values:
1. working capital
2. current ratio
3. acid-test ratio
4. debt to total assets ratio
5. times interest earned ratio
6. cash interest coverage ratio

(b) The notes to McDonald's financial statements show that, subsequent to 1998, the company will have future minimum lease payments under operating leases of $7,366.9 million. Discuss the implications of these unrecorded obligations for the analysis of McDonald's liquidity and solvency.

Compare the straight-line and effective interest methods of amortization.
(SO 6, 9)

***E10-14** Villeneuve Inc. issues $1 million of 6% bonds for proceeds of $864,100, at a time when the market rate of interest is 8%. The bonds pay interest semi-annually and mature in 10 years.

Instructions

(a) Prepare the journal entry to record the issue of bonds.
(b) Prepare the journal entry to record the payment of interest and discount amortization at period 1 (the first period) and at period 20 (the last period) assuming that Villeneuve uses: (1) the straight-line method of amortization, and (2) the effective interest method of amortization. (Hint: Use present value tables to determine the carrying value of the bond at the end of period 19 (beginning of period 20).)
(c) Based on question (b), calculate the effective rate of interest by dividing the interest expense by the carrying value of the bond for options (1) and (2) for periods 1 and 20.
(d) Discuss which method of amortization provides the best measure of the effective cost of borrowing.

Prepare entries to record mortgage note and instalment payments.
(SO 10)

***E10-15** Pereira Corp. receives $110,000 when it issues a $110,000, 10% mortgage note payable to finance the construction of a building at December 31, 2001. The terms provide for semi-annual instalment payments of $7,500 on June 30 and December 31.

Instructions

Prepare the journal entries to record the mortgage loan and the first two instalment payments.

PROBLEMS: SET A

Prepare current liability entries, adjusting entries, and current liability section.
(SO 2, 3, 4)

P10-1A On January 1, 2001, the ledger of Cartier Company Inc., headquartered in the province of Quebec, contained these liability accounts:

Accounts Payable	$42,500
GST Payable	5,600
QST Payable	6,420
Unearned Service Revenue	15,000

During January, the following selected transactions occurred:

Jan. 1 Borrowed $15,000 in cash from the Caisse Populaire on a four-month, 10%, $15,000 note.
5 Sold merchandise for cash totalling $6,800, plus 7% GST and 7.5% QST. Note

that in Quebec, the QST is changed on sales plus GST.

12 Provided services for customers who had made advance payments of $8,000.

20 Sold 500 units of a new product on credit at $52 per unit, plus 7% GST and 7.5% QST.

25 Sold merchandise for cash totalling $9,950, plus 7% GST and 7.5% QST.

Instructions

(a) Journalize the January transactions. Round amounts to the nearest dollar.
(b) Journalize the adjusting entries at January 31 for the outstanding note payable.
(c) Prepare the current liabilities section of the balance sheet at January 31, 2001.

P10-2A Cling-on Company Ltd. sells rock-climbing products and also operates an indoor climbing facility for climbing enthusiasts. During the last part of 2001, Cling-on had the following transactions related to notes payable:

Journalize and post note transactions; show balance sheet presentation.
(SO 2, 4)

Sept. 1	Issued a $16,000 note to Black Diamond to purchase inventory. The note payable bears interest of 9% and is due in three months.
Sept. 30	Recorded accrued interest for the Black Diamond note.
Oct. 2	Issued a $10,000, 12%, two-month note to Montpelier Bank to finance the building of a new climbing area for advanced climbers.
Oct. 31	Recorded accrued interest for the Black Diamond note and the Montpelier Bank note.
Nov. 2	Issued an $18,000 note and paid $8,000 in cash to purchase a vehicle to transport clients to nearby climbing sites as part of a new series of climbing classes. This note bears interest of 14% and matures in 12 months.
Nov. 30	Recorded accrued interest for the Black Diamond note, the Montpelier Bank note and the vehicle note.
Dec. 1	Paid principal and interest on the Black Diamond note.
Dec. 31	Recorded accrued interest for the Montpelier Bank note and the vehicle note.

Instructions

(a) Prepare journal entries for the transactions above.
(b) Post the above entries to the Notes Payable, Interest Payable, and Interest Expense T accounts.
(c) Show the balance sheet presentation of notes payable and interest payable at December 31.
(d) How much interest expense relating to notes payable did Cling-on incur during the year?

P10-3A Beatrice Corporation sold $1,500,000 of 8%, 10-year bonds on April 1, 2001. The bonds were dated April 1, 2001, and pay interest on April 1 and October 1. Beatrice Corporation uses the straight-line method to amortize bond premiums or discounts and has a December 31 year end.

Prepare journal entries to record issuance of bonds, interest, and amortization of bond premium and discount.
(SO 6, 8)

Instructions

(a) Prepare all the necessary journal entries to record the issuance of the bonds and bond interest expense for 2001, assuming that the bonds sold at 102.
(b) Prepare journal entries as in part (a) assuming that the bonds sold at 97.
(c) Show the balance sheet presentation for each bond issue under the assumptions in (a) and (b) at December 31, 2001.

Prepare journal entries to record interest payments, discount amortization, and redemption of bonds.
(SO 6, 7)

P10-4A The following section is taken from Bermuda Corp.'s balance sheet:

BERMUDA CORPORATION
Balance Sheet (partial)
December 31, 2001

Current liabilities		
Bond interest payable (for 6 months from July 1 to December 31)		$ 132,000
Long-term liabilities		
Bonds payable, 11%, due January 1, 2012	$2,400,000	
Less: Discount on bonds payable	84,000	2,316,000

Interest is payable semi-annually on January 1 and July 1. The bonds are callable on any semi-annual interest date. Bermuda uses straight-line amortization for any bond premium or discount. From December 31, 2001, the bonds will be outstanding for an additional 10 years (120 months). Assume no interest is accrued on June 30.

Instructions

Round all calculations to the nearest dollar.

(a) Journalize the payment of bond interest on January 1, 2002.
(b) Prepare the entry to amortize bond discount and to pay the interest due on July 1, 2002.
(c) Assume on July 1, 2002, after paying interest, that Bermuda Corp. calls bonds having a face value of $800,000. The call price is 102. Record the redemption of the bonds.
(d) Prepare the adjusting entry at December 31, 2002, to amortize bond discount and to accrue interest on the remaining bonds.

Prepare journal entries to record issuance of bonds, interest accrual, and amortization of bond premium and discount. Show balance sheet presentation.
(SO 6, 8)

P10-5A Downey Corp. sold $5,000,000 of 9%, five-year bonds on January 1, 2002. The bonds were dated January 1, 2002, and pay interest on July 1 and January 1. The company uses straight-line amortization on bond premiums and discounts. Financial statements are prepared annually, each December 31.

Instructions

(a) Prepare the journal entry to record the issuance of the bonds assuming they sold at
 1. 103
 2. 98
(b) Prepare amortization tables for both assumed sales for the first three interest payments.
(c) Prepare the journal entries to record interest expense for 2002 under both assumed sales.
(d) Show balance sheet presentation for both assumed sales at December 31, 2002.

Prepare journal entries to record issuance of bonds. Show balance sheet presentation, and record bond redemption.
(SO 6, 7, 8)

P10-6A Moriarty Company Ltd. sold $4,000,000 of 9%, 20-year bonds on January 1, 2001. The bonds were dated January 1, 2001, and pay interest on December 31 and June 30. The bonds were sold at 97.

Instructions

(a) Prepare the journal entry to record the issuance of the bonds on January 1, 2001.
(b) At December 31, 2001, $6,000 of the bond discount had been amortized. Show the balance sheet presentation of the bond liability at December 31, 2001. (Assume that interest has been paid.)
(c) At December 31, 2002, when the carrying value of the bonds was $3,892,000, the company redeemed the bonds at 101. Record the redemption of the bonds assuming that interest for the year had already been paid.

P10-7A You have been presented with the following selected information taken from the financial statements of **Air Canada**:

Calculate and comment on ratios.

(SO 4, 8)

AIR CANADA
Balance Sheet
December 31
(in thousands)

Selected information:

	1999	1998	1997
Current assets			
Cash and short-term investments	$ 521	$ 366	$ 650
Accounts receivable	443	405	467
Spare parts, materials and supplies	228	258	225
Prepaid expenses	18	21	17
Deferred income taxes	48	42	35
Total current assets	1,258	1,092	1,394
Current liabilities	$1,405	$1,279	$1,139
Long-term liabilities	4,575	3,686	3,417
Total liabilities	5,980	4,965	4,556
Shareholders' equity	725	1,457	1,435
Total liabilities and shareholders' equity	$6,705	$6,422	$5,991

AIR CANADA
Statement of Earnings
Year Ended December 31
(in thousands)

Selected information:

	1999	1998	1997
Net (loss) earnings	$213	$ (16)	$427
Amortization expense	311	292	258
Income tax (recovery) expense	174	(13)	39
Interest expense	154	242	203

Instructions

(a) Calculate each of the following ratios for 1999, 1998 and 1997:
1. current ratio
2. acid-test ratio
3. debt to total assets
4. times interest earned
5. cash interest coverage

(b) Comment on the trend in ratios.

(c) In 1998, there was a pilots' strike at Air Canada. In the Management Discussion and Analysis filed with the 1999 financial statements, management estimates that the pilots' strike "lowered operating income by $250 million ($155 million after tax)." The 1997 results included a $57 million unfavourable operating income impact from a regional pilots' strike ($32 million after tax).

Calculate estimated times interest earned and cash interest coverage ratios for 1997 as if the strike had not taken place. That is, take the actual results and adjust them for management's estimates for the impact of strikes.

P10-8A Debt transactions can sometimes have an interesting impact on liquidity and solvency ratios.

Analyse impact of transactions on ratios.

(SO 4, 8)

Transaction	Current ratio (1:1)	Acid-test ratio (0.7:1)	Debt to total assets ratio (70%)	Times interest earned ratio (6.6x)	Cash interest coverage ratio (10.5x)
(a) Issue short-term notes payable for $1,000 cash.					

(b) Accrue $100 interest on note payable.

(c) Record $250 unearned subscription revenue as earned.

(d) Issue $50,000 of long-term bonds payable for cash.

(e) Redeem $50,000 of bonds payable (current liability) at maturity.

Instructions

Indicate whether the above transactions will increase (I), decrease (D), or not affect (NA) each of the liquidity and solvency ratios presented.

Prepare journal entries to record issuance of bonds, payment of interest, and amortization of bond discount using effective interest method.

(SO 6, 9)

***P10-9A** On July 1, 2001, Global Satellites Corporation issued $1,200,000 of face value, 9%, 10-year bonds at $1,125,227. This price resulted in an effective interest rate of 10% on the bonds. Global uses the effective-interest method to amortize a bond premium or discount. The bonds pay semi-annual interest July 1 and January 1.

Instructions

Round all calculations to the nearest dollar.

(a) Prepare the journal entry to record the issuance of the bonds on July 1, 2001.

(b) Prepare an amortization table through December 31, 2002 (three interest periods) for this bond issue.

(c) Prepare the journal entry to record the accrual of interest and the amortization of the discount on December 31, 2001.

(d) Prepare the journal entry to record the payment of interest and the amortization of the discount on July 1, 2002.

(e) Prepare the journal entry to record the accrual of interest and the amortization of the discount on December 31, 2002.

Prepare journal entries to record issuance of bonds, payment of interest, and amortization of premium using effective interest method. In addition, answer questions.

(SO 6, 9)

***P10-10A** On July 1, 2001, Amoco Imperial Company Ltd. issued $2,000,000 of face value, 12%, 10-year bonds at $2,249,245. This price resulted in a 10% effective interest rate on the bonds. Amoco Imperial uses the effective interest method to amortize a bond premium or discount. The bonds pay semi-annual interest on each of July 1 and January 1.

Instructions

(a) Prepare the journal entries for the following transactions:
   1. The issuance of the bond on July 1, 2001
   2. The accrual of interest and the amortization of the premium on December 31, 2001
   3. The payment of interest and the amortization of the premium on July 1, 2002
   4. The accrual of interest and the amortization of the premium on December 31, 2002

(b) Show the proper balance sheet presentation for the liability for bonds payable on December 31, 2002.

(c) Answer the following questions:
   1. What amount of interest expense is reported for 2002?
   2. Would the bond interest expense reported in 2002 be the same as, greater than, or less than the amount that would be reported if the straight-line method of amortization were used?

Prepare journal entries to record issuance of bonds, and interest; prepare instalment payments schedule and journal entries for a mortgage note payable.

(SO 6, 7, 8, 10)

***P10-11A** Atwater Corporation is building a new, state-of-the-art production and assembly facility for $10,000,000. To finance the facility, it is using $2,000,000 it received from the issuance of common shares, and the balance is being funded from the issuance of bonds. The $8,000,000 of 11%, five-year bonds were sold on August 1, 2001. They are dated August 1, 2001, and pay interest August 1 and February 1. Atwater uses the straight-line method to amortize bond premium or discount and has a December 31 year end.

Atwater also purchased a new piece of equipment to be used in its new facility. The $550,000 piece of equipment was purchased with a $50,000 down payment and with cash received through the issuance of a $500,000, 8%, three-year mortgage note payable issued on October 1, 2001. The terms provide for quarterly instalment payments of $47,280 on December 31, March 31, June 30, and September 30.

Instructions

Round all calculations to the nearest dollar.

(a) Prepare all necessary journal entries to record the issuance of the bonds and the bond interest expense for 2001, assuming the bonds sold at 101.

(b) Prepare an instalment payments schedule for the first five payments of the notes payable.

(c) Prepare all necessary journal entries related to the notes payable at December 31, 2001.

(d) Show balance sheet presentation for these obligations for December 31, 2001. (Hint: Be sure to distinguish between the current and long-term portions of the note.)

* **P10-12A** Peter Furlong has just approached a venture capitalist for financing for his sailing school. The lenders are willing to loan Peter $50,000 at a high-risk annual interest rate of 24%. The loan is payable over three years in instalments, blended as to principal and interest. Payments are due every other month (that is, six times per year). Peter uses the effective interest method for amortizing debt. You are to assume that Peter receives the loan on May 1, 2001, which is the first day of his fiscal year. Peter makes the first payment on June 30, 2001.

Calculate payments for long-term note payable; illustrate first year entries.
(SO 10)

Instructions

(a) Calculate the payments to be made by Peter bi-monthly. (Hint: Use Table 4 in Appendix C to determine the present value interest factor of an annuity that will be used to calculate the payments based on $i = 4\%$ and $n = 18$.)

(b) Prepare an amortization schedule for the fiscal year from May 1, 2001 to April 30, 2002. Round all calculations to the nearest dollar.

(c) Prepare all journal entries for Peter Furlong for the first six months of the fiscal year beginning May 1, 2001. Round all calculations to the nearest dollar.

* **P10-13A** Daniel Carol is the lead drummer in a band that tours around Prince Edward Island. He is in the process of leasing a van for the band to use. The van costs $25,000, and will be financed over three years at an annual interest rate of 8%. You are to assume that the lease will be settled with a payment of $9,701 due at the end of each year.

Prepare amortization schedule and compare operating and capital leases.
(SO 8, 10)

Daniel is wondering what the impact will be on the statement of earnings each year if he structures the lease as an operating lease instead of a capital lease. The operating lease would have the same annual payment of $9,701. He knows that with a capital lease, the asset is set up at its cost of $25,000 and amortized over the three years of use. The van is estimated to have no residual value at the end of the three years: the band plans on racking up a serious number of kilometres. Daniel uses a straight-line method of amortization.

Instructions

(a) Prepare a schedule to amortize the lease liability over three years using the effective interest method.

(b) Prepare a schedule to compare the impact on the statement of earnings of structuring the lease as a capital lease as compared with an operating lease.

PROBLEMS: SET B

Prepare current liability entries, adjusting entries, and current liability section.
(SO 2, 3, 4)

P10-1B On January 1, 2001, the ledger of Burlington Company Ltd. contained these liability accounts:

Accounts Payable	$52,000
GST Payable	7,500
PST Payable	8,570
Unearned Service Revenue	16,000

During January, the following selected transactions occurred:

Jan. 5 Sold merchandise for cash totalling $16,632, which includes 7% GST and 8% PST.
12 Provided services for customers who had made advance payments of $9,000. (Credit Service Revenue.)
14 Paid Receiver General and Minister of Finance for sales taxes collected in December 2000 ($7,500 and $8,570, respectively).
20 Sold 500 units of a new product on credit at $50 per unit, plus 7% GST and 8% PST.
21 Borrowed $18,000 from HSBC Bank on a three-month, 10%, $18,000 note.
25 Sold merchandise for cash totalling $11,340, which includes 7% GST and 8% PST.

Instructions

(a) Journalize the January transactions. Round all amounts to the nearest dollar.
(b) Journalize the adjusting entries at January 31 for the outstanding notes payable.
(c) Prepare the current liability section of the balance sheet at January 31, 2001.

Journalize and post note transactions; show balance sheet presentation.
(SO 2, 4)

P10-2B MileHi Mountain Bikes markets mountain-bike tours to clients vacationing in various locations in the mountains of British Columbia. In preparation for the upcoming summer biking season, MileHi entered into the following transactions related to notes payable.

Mar. 2 Purchased Mongoose bikes for use as rentals by issuing an $8,000, 9% note payable that is due in three months.
31 Recorded accrued interest for the Mongoose note.
Apr. 1 Issued a $20,000 note for the purchase of mountain property on which to build bike trails. The note bears 12% interest and is due in nine months.
30 Recorded accrued interest for the Mongoose and land notes.
May 2 Issued a note to Western Bank for $15,000 at 6%. The funds will be used for working capital for the beginning of the season; the note is due in four months.
31 Recorded accrued interest for all three notes.
June 1 Paid principal and interest on the Mongoose note.
30 Recorded accrued interest for the land note and the Western Bank note.

Instructions

(a) Prepare journal entries for the transactions above.
(b) Post the above entries to the Notes Payable, Interest Payable, and Interest Expense accounts.
(c) Assuming that MileHi's year end is June 30, show the balance sheet presentation of notes payable and interest payable at that date.
(d) How much interest expense relating to notes payable did MileHi incur during the year?

Prepare journal entries to record issuance of bonds, interest, and amortization of bond premium and discount.
(SO 6, 8)

P10-3B Diego Company Ltd. sold $1,500,000 of 12%, 10-year bonds on July 1, 2001. The bonds were dated July 1, 2001, and pay interest July 1 and January 1. Diego Company uses the straight-line method to amortize a bond premium or discount and has a December 31 year end.

Instructions

(a) Prepare all the necessary journal entries to record the issuance of the bonds and bond interest expense for 2001, assuming that the bonds sold at 102.
(b) Prepare journal entries as in part (a) assuming that the bonds sold at 94.
(c) Show the balance sheet presentation for each bond issue at November 30, 2001.

P10-4B The following section is taken from Walenda Oil Company Ltd.'s balance sheet:

Prepare journal entries to record interest payments, premium amortization, and redemption of bonds.
(SO 6, 7)

WALENDA OIL COMPANY LTD.
Balance Sheet (partial)
December 31, 2001

Current liabilities		
Bond interest payable (for 6 months from July 1 to December 31)		$ 216,000
Long-term liabilities		
Bonds payable, 12% due January 1, 2012	$3,600,000	
Add: Premium on bonds payable	300,000	3,900,000

Interest is payable semi-annually on January 1 and July 1. The bonds are callable on any semi-annual interest date. Walenda uses straight-line amortization for any bond premium or discount and has a December 31 year end. From December 31, 2001, the bonds will be outstanding for an additional 10 years (120 months).

Instructions

Round all calculations to the nearest dollar.
(a) Journalize the payment of bond interest on January 1, 2002.
(b) Prepare the entry to amortize the bond premium and to pay the interest due on July 1, 2002.
(c) Assume on July 1, 2002, after paying interest, that Walenda Company calls bonds having a face value of $1,800,000. The call price is 101. Record the redemption of the bonds.
(d) Prepare the adjusting entry at December 31, 2002, to amortize the bond premium and to accrue interest on the remaining bonds.

P10-5B Chula Vista Corporation sold $3,500,000 of 7%, 20-year bonds on June 30, 2001. The bonds were dated June 30, 2001, and pay interest on June 30 and December 31. The compnay uses straight-line amortization for premiums and discounts. Financial statements are prepared annually, each December 31.

Prepare journal entries to record issuance of bonds, interest, and amortization of bond discount and premium. Show balance sheet presentation.
(SO 6, 8)

Instructions

(a) Prepare the journal entry to record the issuance of the bonds assuming they sold at
1. 96 1/2
2. 104.
(b) Prepare amortization tables for both of the assumed sales for the first three interest payments.
(c) Prepare the journal entries to record interest expense for 2001 under both assumed sales.
(d) Show the balance sheet presentation for both assumed sales at December 31, 2001.

P10-6B Montego Electric Ltd. sold $3,000,000 of 10%, 20-year bonds on January 1, 2001. The bonds were dated January 1 and pay interest on July 1 and January 1. The bonds were sold at 104. Montego uses a calendar year end.

Prepare journal entries to record issuance of bonds. Show balance sheet presentation and record bond redemption.
(SO 6, 7, 8)

Instructions

(a) Prepare the journal entry to record the issuance of the bonds on January 1, 2001.
(b) At December 31, 2001, $6,000 of the bond premium had been amortized. Show the balance sheet presentation of the bond liability at December 31, 2001. (Assume that interest has been paid.)

(c) At December 31, 2003, when the carrying value of the bonds was $3,102,000, the company redeemed the bonds at 101. Record the redemption of the bonds assuming that interest for the year had already been paid.

Calculate and comment on ratios.

(SO 4, 8)

P10-7B The year 1999 saw unprecedented change and restructuring in the airline industry in Canada, offering a window of opportunity for **WestJet Airlines Ltd.** to extend its successful low fare strategy across Canada. The following selected information was taken from WestJet's financial statements:

WESTJET AIRLINES LTD.
Balance Sheet
December 31
(in thousands)

	1999	1998
Current assets		
Cash and short-term investments	$ 50,740	$ 13,500
Accounts receivable	5,168	5,240
Prepaid expenses and deposits	4,123	3,479
Inventory	462	500
Total current assets	60,493	22,719
Capital assets and other long-term assets	126,105	85,523
	$186,598	$108,242
Current liabilities	$ 49,926	$ 28,950
Long-term liabilities	42,185	29,931
Total liabilities	92,111	58,881
Shareholders' equity	94,487	49,361
Total liabilities and shareholders' equity	$186,598	$108,242

Commitments (see note 5)

WESTJET AIRLINES LTD.
Statement of Earnings (partial)
Year Ended December 31
(in thousands)

	1999	1998
Interest expense	$ 2,871	$ 1,137
EBIT	32,219	13,568
EBITDA	40,491	18,655

WESTJET AIRLINES LTD.
Notes to Financial Statements (partial)
Years Ended December 31, 1999 and 1998
(in thousands)

5. Leases

The Corporation has entered into operating leases for aircraft, buildings, computer hardware, and software licences. The obligations on a calendar-year basis, are as follows: 2000, $7,506; 2001, $7,196; 2002, $7,148; 2003, $5,155; 2004 and thereafter, $3,600.

Instructions

(a) Calculate each of the following ratios for 1999 and 1998:
1. current ratio
2. acid-test ratio
3. debt to total assets ratio
4. times interest earned ratio
5. cash interest coverage ratio

(b) Comment on WestJet's short- and long-run solvency.

(c) Discuss the implications of WestJet's operating leases for the analysis of WestJet's short- and long-run solvency assessed above.

P10-8B Debt transactions can sometimes have an interesting impact on liquidity and solvency ratios.

Analyse impact of transactions on ratios.
(SO 4, 8)

Transaction	Current ratio (1:1)	Acid-test ratio (0.6:1)	Debt to total assets ratio (60%)	Times interest earned ratio (5x)	Cash interest coverage ratio (8x)
(a) Purchase $1,000 of merchandise on account. (Perpetual inventory system used.)					
(b) Record $1,000 on account, for services rendered, plus $150 HST payable.					
(c) Enter into a $5,000-a-year operating lease. Make the first lease payment.					
(d) Make $500 principal payment on non-interest-bearing note payable					
(e) Sell $50,000 common shares for cash.					
(f) Pay annual interest expense of $5,000 on bonds. Interest not previously accrued.					

Instructions
Indicate whether the above transactions will increase (I), decrease (D), or not affect (NA) each of the liquidity and solvency ratios presented.

* **P10-9B** On July 1, 2001, Cleopatra Corporation issued $1,500,000 of face value, 12%, 10-year bonds at $1,686,934. This price resulted in an effective interest rate of 10% on the bonds. Cleopatra uses the effective interest method to amortize a bond premium or discount. The bonds pay semi-annual interest July 1 and January 1. Cleopatra has a December 31 year end.

Prepare journal entries to record issuance of bonds, payment of interest, and amortization of bond premium using effective interest method.
(SO 6, 9)

Instructions
Round all calculations to the nearest dollar.
(a) Prepare the journal entry to record the issuance of the bonds on July 1, 2001.
(b) Prepare an amortization table through December 31, 2002 (three interest periods) for this bond issue.
(c) Prepare the journal entry to record the accrual of interest and the amortization of the premium on December 31, 2001.
(d) Prepare the journal entry to record the accrual of interest and the amortization of the premium on July 1, 2002.
(e) Prepare the journal entry to record the accrual of interest and the amortization of the premium on December 31, 2002.

* **P10-10B** On July 1, 2001, Waubonsee Company Ltd. issued $2,200,000 of face value, 10%, 10-year bonds at $1,947,651. This price resulted in an effective interest rate of 12% on the bonds. Waubonsee uses the effective interest method to amortize a bond premium or discount. The bonds pay semi-annual interest July 1 and January 1. Waubonsee has a December 31 year end.

Prepare journal entries to record issuance of bonds, payment of interest, and amortization of discount using effective interest method. In addition, answer questions.
(SO 6, 9)

Instructions
(a) Prepare the journal entries to record the following transactions:
1. The issuance of the bonds on July 1, 2001
2. The accrual of interest and the amortization of the discount on December 31, 2001

3. The payment of interest and the amortization of the discount on July 1, 2002
4. The accrual of interest and the amortization of the discount on December 31, 2002

(b) Show the proper balance sheet presentation for the liability for the bonds payable on the December 31, 2002, balance sheet.

(c) Answer the following questions:
1. What amount of interest expense is reported for 2002?
2. Would the bond interest expense reported in 2002 be the same as, greater than, or less than the amount that would be reported if the straight-line method of amortization were used?
3. Determine the total cost of borrowing over the life of the bond.
4. Would the total bond interest expense be greater than, the same as, or less than the total interest expense that would be reported if the straight-line method of amortization were used?

Prepare journal entries for issuance of bonds, and interest; prepare instalment payments schedule and journal entries for a mortgage note payable.
(SO 6, 7, 8, 10)

* **P10-11B** Myron Corporation is building a new, state-of-the-art production and assembly facility for $15,000,000. To finance the facility, it is using $3,000,000 it received from the issuance of common shares, and the balance is being funded from the issuance of bonds. The $12,000,000 of 9%, 10-year bonds were sold on August 1, 2001. They are dated August 1, 2001, and pay interest August 1 and February 1. Myron uses the straight-line method to amortize a bond premium or discount and has a December 31 year end.

Myron also purchased a new piece of equipment to be used in its new facility. The $750,000 piece of equipment was purchased with a $50,000 down payment and with cash received through the issuance of a $700,000, 6%, four-year mortgage note payable issued on October 1, 2001. The terms provide for quarterly instalment payments of $49,536 on December 31, March 31, June 30, and September 30.

Instructions

Round all calculations to the nearest dollar

(a) Prepare all necessary journal entries to record the issuance of the bonds and bond interest expense for 2001, assuming the bonds sold at 98.

(b) Prepare an instalment payments schedule for the first five payments of the note payable.

(c) Prepare all necessary journal entries related to the notes payable at December 31, 2001.

(d) Show a balance sheet presentation for these obligations for December 31, 2001. (Hint: Be sure to distinguish between the current and long-term portions of the note.)

Calculate payments for long-term note payable; illustrate first year entries.
(SO 10)

* **P10-12B** Franca Cudini has just approached a venture capitalist for financing for her new business venture, the development of a local ski hill. On July 1, 2001, the lenders loaned Franca $100,000 at an annual interest rate of 10%. The loan is repayable over five years in annual instalments of $26,380, principal and interest, due each June 30. The first payment is due June 30, 2002. Franca uses the effective interest method for amortizing debt; and her ski hill company's year end will be June 30.

Instructions

(a) Prove the calculation of the annual payments to be made by Franca. (Hint: Use Table 4 in Appendix C to determine the present value interest factor of an annuity that will be used to calculate the payments based on $i = 10\%$ and $n = 5$.)

(b) Prepare an amortization schedule for the five years, 2001–2006. Round all calculations to the nearest dollar.

(c) Prepare all journal entries for Franca Cudini for the first two fiscal years ended June 30, 2002 and June 30, 2003. Round all calculations to the nearest dollar.

(d) Show the balance sheet presentation of the note payable as at June 30, 2003. (Hint: Don't forget to distinguish between the current and long-term portions of the note).

Prepare amortization schedule and compare operating and capital leases.
(SO 8, 10)

* **P10-13B** The Matthew Street Band are in the process of leasing a bus to transport the band on their road trips. The bus costs $100,000, and will be financed over five years at an annual interest rate of 8%, with an annual payment of $25,046 due at the end of each year.

The band is wondering what the impact will be on the statement of earnings each year if they structure the acquisition of the bus as an operating lease with the same payments, instead of a capital lease. They know that with a capital lease, the capital asset would be recorded at its cost of $100,000 and amortized, using the straight-line method of amortization, over the five years of use. The bus is estimated to have no residual value at the end of the five years: the band plans on racking up a serious number of kilometres.

Instructions
(a) Prepare a schedule to amortize the lease liability over five years using the effective interest method.
(b) Prepare a schedule to compare the impact on the statement of earnings of structuring the lease as a capital lease as compared with an operating lease. Comment on which choice—capital or operating—is more beneficial to the band.

BROADENING YOUR PERSPECTIVE

FINANCIAL REPORTING AND ANALYSIS

FINANCIAL REPORTING PROBLEM: *Loblaw Companies Limited*

BYP10-1 Refer to the financial statements of **Loblaw Companies Limited** and the Notes to Consolidated Financial Statements in Appendix A.

Instructions
Answer these questions about current and contingent liabilities and payroll costs:
(a) What were Loblaw's total current liabilities at January 1, 2000? What was the increase (decrease) in Loblaw's total current liabilities from the prior year?
(b) What were Loblaw's total long-term liabilities at January 1, 2000? What was the increase (decrease) in Loblaw's total long-term liabilities from the prior year?
(c) Identify the due date and interest rate of (1) one of Loblaw's debentures, and (2) one of Loblaw's notes payable.
(d) Does Loblaw have any contingent liabilities that are expected to have a material impact on its financial position?
(e) Does Loblaw have any operating leases? If so, how much do its commitments for net operating lease payments total?

COMPARATIVE ANALYSIS PROBLEM: *Loblaw and Sobeys*

BYP10-2 The financial statements of **Sobeys Inc.** are presented in Appendix B, following the financial statements of **Loblaw Companies Limited** in Appendix A.

Instructions
(a) Based on the information contained in the financial statements, calculate the following 1999 ratios for each company:
1. Current ratio.
2. Acid-test ratio
3. Debt to total assets
4. Times interest earned
5. Cash interest coverage
(b) What conclusions concerning the companies' liquidity can be drawn from the current and acid-test ratios?
(c) What conclusions concerning the companies' long-run solvency can be drawn from the ratios in (a)?
(d) Loblaw reports EBITDA in its annual report but Sobeys does not. How much was the EBITDA for 1999 reported by Loblaws? Calculate the EBITDA for Sobeys. Does Loblaw use EBITDA in conjunction with other figures to produce ratios? Explain what ratios are calculated using EBITDA and what they likely measure.

RESEARCH CASE

BYP10-3 The June 22, 1998, issue of *Fortune* magazine contains an article by Herb Greenberg entitled "EBITDA: Never Trust Anything That You Can't Pronounce."

Instructions

Read the article and answer these questions:

(a) What does EBITDA stand for?

(b) Coca-Cola uses EBITDA as a key measure of its operating performance. At what multiple of earnings do Coke's shares trade? At what multiple of EBITDA?

(c) The article states that EBITDA can make a company look as though it has more money to make interest payments. Explain why this might not be the case.

(d) Is EBITDA determined in accordance with GAAP?

INTERPRETING FINANCIAL STATEMENTS

BYP10-4 Reitmans (Canada) Limited and **Suzy Shier Limited** are two specialty women's clothing store merchandisers. Reitmans is Canada's largest ladies' apparel retailer with 598 stores, which include Reitmans, Smart Set/Dalmys, and Penningtons. Suzy Shier has 442 stores, which include Suzy Shier, L.A. Express, La Senza, and Silk & Satin.

Here are financial data for both companies at their most recent year ends (in thousands):

	Reitmans (Canada) Limited January 30, 1999	Suzy Shier Limited January 30, 1999
Cash	$ 19,416	$ 9,749
Accounts receivable	2,619	5,068
Short-term investments	44,560	25,859
Total current assets	100,607	89,955
Beginning total assets	212,185	229,857
Ending total assets	220,997	213,914
Beginning current liabilities	38,462	86,272
Ending current liabilities	71,650	47,006
Beginning total liabilities	67,462	132,423
Ending total liabilities	71,650	104,373
Net sales	456,674	335,373
Amortization expense	11,626	13,477
Interest expense	1,505	605
Income tax expense	5,227	3,748
Net earnings	13,872	13,486
Cash provided by operations	25,870	24,581
Total operating lease commitments for next five years and subsequent	140,375	205,775

Instructions

Using the data, perform the following analysis:

(a) Calculate working capital, the current ratio, the acid-test ratio, and the cash current debt coverage ratio for each company. Discuss their relative liquidity.

(b) Calculate the debt to total assets ratio, times interest earned ratio, cash total debt coverage ratio, and cash interest coverage ratio for each company. Discuss their relative solvency.

(c) The notes to the financial statements indicate that many of the retail stores' furniture and fixtures, and the like, are leased using operating leases. Discuss the implications of these operating leases for each company's solvency.

(d) Calculate the return on assets ratio and profit margin ratio for each company. Comment on their relative profitability.

A GLOBAL FOCUS

BYP10-5 SAirGroup, formerly Swissair, headquartered in Zurich, Switzerland, operates a diversified airline, aviation service, air cargo, and catering company with operating profits of about 700 million Swiss francs, or $700 million. On September 2, 1998, Swissair flight 111, en route to Geneva, Switzerland, plunged into the Atlantic Ocean near Peggy's Cove, Nova Scotia, while trying to make an emergency landing at the Halifax airport after the pilots reported smoke in the cockpit. There were no survivors.

Lawsuits against Swissair and its co-defendants total $24 billion. Analysts say that this figure is unrealistic and inflated on purpose to keep the plaintiffs' option open. Recently, SAirGroup offered compensatory damages to the families of the 229 people who died in the crash, totalling more than $8 million. SAirGroup is well insured and a company spokesperson has stated that the accident, while tragic, is unlikely to have financial repercussions for the company.

Instructions

(a) Do you think that a contingent loss such as the compensatory damages estimated above is relevant to users of SAirGroup's financial statements?

(b) How reliable do you think the estimate of the loss is? What information should the company use to estimate the loss?

(c) SAirGroup has recorded an estimated loss and a liability (less anticipated insurance recoveries) related to this lawsuit. Where in its financial statements would you expect to find these two amounts—that is, in what part of the statement of earnings would the loss be presented and in what part of the balance sheet would the liability be presented? What type of note disclosure would you anticipate would be provided for this event?

FINANCIAL ANALYSIS ON THE WEB

BYP10-6 Bonds have complex terminology associated with them. Bonds Online is a useful site that provides a glossary of bond terms to explore.

www.wiley.com/canada/kimmel

Instructions

Specific requirements of this web case can be found on the Kimmel website.

BYP10-7 Bond or debt securities pay a stated rate of interest. This rate of interest is dependent on the risk associated with the investment. The Dominion Bond Rating Service Limited provides ratings for companies that issue debt securities. We explore this site to familiarize ourselves with bond ratings.

Instructions

Specific requirements of this web case can be found on the Kimmel website.

CRITICAL THINKING

COLLABORATIVE LEARNING ACTIVITY

BYP10-8 On January 1, 1999, Landry Corporation issued $1,200,000 of five-year, 8% bonds at 97; the bonds pay interest semi-annually on July 1 and January 1. By January 1, 2001, the market rate of interest for bonds of risk similar to those of Landry Corporation had risen. As a result, the market value of these bonds was $1,000,000 on January 1, 2001—below their carrying value. Barbara Landry, president of the company, suggests repurchasing all of these bonds in the open market at the $1,000,000 price. But to do so, the company will have to issue $1,000,000 (face value) of new 10-year, 6% bonds. The president asks you as controller, "What is the feasibility of my proposed repurchase plan?"

Instructions

With the class divided into groups, answer the following:

(a) What is the carrying value of the outstanding Landry Corporation five-year bonds on January 1, 2001 (assume straight-line amortization)?

(b) Prepare the journal entry to retire the five-year bonds on January 1, 2001. Prepare the journal entry to issue the new 10-year bonds.

(c) Prepare a short memo to the president in response to her request for advice. List the economic factors that you believe should be considered for her repurchase proposal.

COMMUNICATION ACTIVITY

BYP10-9 Finn Berge, president of the Blue Marlin, is considering the issuance of bonds to finance an expansion of his business. He has asked you to (1) discuss the advantages of bonds over common share financing, (2) indicate the type of bonds he might issue, and (3) explain the issuing procedures used in bond transactions.

Instructions

Write a memorandum to the president, answering his request.

ETHICS CASE

BYP10-10 The July 10, 1998, issue of *Inc.* magazine includes an article by Jeffrey L. Seglin entitled "Would You Lie to Save Your Company?" It recounts the following true situation:

> A Chief Executive Officer (CEO) of a $20-million company that repairs aircraft engines received notice from a number of customers that engines that had recently been repaired had failed, and that the company's parts were to blame. The CEO had not yet determined whether the parts were, in fact, the cause of the problem. The Federal Aviation Administration (FAA), responsible for air transportation and safety in the U.S., had been notified and was investigating the matter.
>
> What complicated the situation was that the company was in the midst of its year-end audit. As part of the audit, the CEO was required to sign a letter saying that he was not aware of any significant outstanding circumstances that could negatively impact the company—in accounting terms, any contingent liabilities. The auditor was not aware of the problem.
>
> The company relied heavily on short-term loans from a number of banks. The CEO feared that if these lenders learned of the situation, they would pull their loans. The loss of these loans would force the company into bankruptcy, leaving hundreds of people without jobs. Prior to this problem, the company had a stellar performance record.

Instructions

(a) Who are the stakeholders in this situation?
(b) What are the CEO's possible courses of action? What are the potential results of each course of action? (Take into account the two alternatives: the FAA determines the company was not at fault, and the FAA determines the company was at fault.)
(c) What would you do and why?
(d) Suppose the CEO decides to conceal the situation, and that during the next year the company is found to be at fault and is forced into bankruptcy. What losses are incurred by the stakeholders in this situation? Do you think the CEO should suffer the legal consequences if he decides to conceal the situation?

Answers to Self-Study Questions

1. a 2. d 3. b 4. b 5. d 6. a 7. c 8. a 9. d 10. c
11. b 12. c *13. b *14. c *15. c

Loblaws
A passion for food... *and a lot more!*

Answer to Loblaw Review Question 2

Loblaw has the following current liabilities, totalling $2,812 million as at January 1, 2000: bank indebtedness; commercial paper; accounts payable and accrued liabilities; short-term bank loans; and long-term debt due within one year.

CHAPTER 11

Reporting and Analysing Shareholders' Equity

STUDY OBJECTIVES

After studying this chapter, you should be able to:

1. Identify and discuss the major characteristics of a corporation.
2. Record the issuance of common shares.
3. Differentiate preferred shares from common shares.
4. Prepare the entries for cash dividends and stock dividends.
5. Identify the items that affect retained earnings.
6. Prepare a comprehensive shareholders' equity section.
7. Evaluate a corporation's dividend and earnings performance from a shareholder's perspective.

Race You to the Corner

Here's a riddle for you: What major world corporation had its first big breakthrough in the 1970s with a waffle iron? Hint: It doesn't sell food. Another hint: Swoosh. Final hint: "Just do it."

That's right—Nike Inc. In 1971 Nike co-founder Bill Bowerman put a piece of rubber in a kitchen waffle iron, and the Waffle™ sole was born. The rest, as they say, was history.

Nike was founded by Bowerman and Phil Knight, a member of Bowerman's university track team. Each got into the shoe business independently during the early 1960s. Bowerman made hand-crafted running shoes for his university track team, and Knight, after completing graduate school, started a small business importing low-cost, high-quality shoes from Japan. In 1964 the two each contributed $500 and became partners in Blue Ribbon Sports.

At first the pair marketed Japanese shoes. It wasn't until 1971 that the company began manufacturing its own line. With these new shoes—and their waffle-textured soles—came a new corporate name: Nike, the Greek goddess of victory.

Today Nike is a household name, across North America and worldwide. It now boasts a stable full of world-class athletes as promoters. But, at one time it had part-time employees selling shoes out of car trunks at track meets. The company's success has been achieved through continual innovation combined with relentless promotion.

By 1980 Nike was sufficiently established to issue its first shares to the public. From the beginning, it offered a share ownership program for its employees, allowing them to take part in the company's success. Since then Nike has enjoyed phenomenal growth, with 1998 sales reaching US$9.5 billion throughout the world. The dividend paid to shareholders has increased every year for the last 11 years. Today, Nike is the world's number 1 shoe company, selling its products in 111 countries, and on-line.

Nike is not alone in its quest for the top spot in the sport shoe world. Reebok International Ltd. pushes Nike every step of the way. It was clearly outstripped by its giant rival in

On the World Wide Web
Nike: http://www.nike.com
Reebok: http://www.reebok.com

the 1990s—Reebok's 1998 sales of US$3.2 billion are only about a third of Nike's, and Reebok has issued no dividends for two years. But its unwillingness to give up the race is boldly symbolized in its recent ad campaign: "This is my planet." Reebok recently revamped its mission statement around the core value of "delighting our customers."

The race is far from over. Nike has seen revenues in South America and, especially, Canada drop recently. It is facing new PR challenges in the face of increasing awareness of globalization-related labour issues among its prime youth market.

The shoe market is notoriously fickle, with new styles becoming popular almost daily. And there is still plenty of room for expansion in international markets. As these two Olympians thunder down the track of the marketplace, shareholders sit anxiously in the stands. But in business, as in life, as another famed Nike ad proclaims, "There is no finish line."

PREVIEW OF CHAPTER 11

Corporations like Nike and Reebok have substantial resources at their disposal. In fact, the corporation is the dominant form of business organization in terms of sales, earnings, and number of employees. All of the largest Canadian companies are corporations. In this chapter, we look at the essential features of a corporation and explain the accounting for a corporation's share capital transactions.

The content and organization of this chapter are as follows:

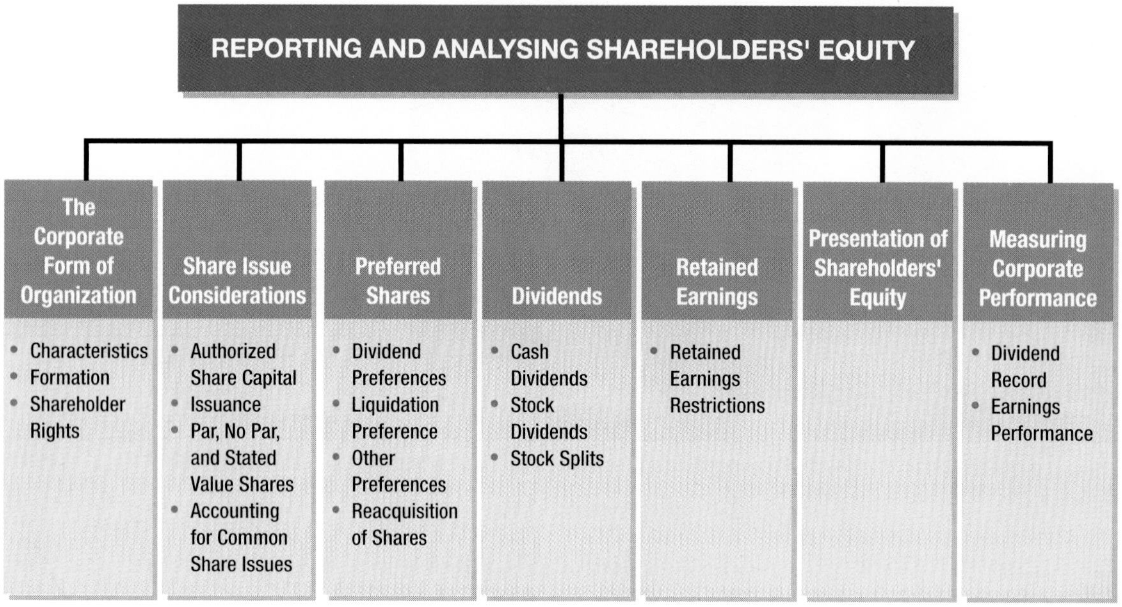

The Corporate Form of Organization

A corporation is created by law. As a legal entity, a **corporation** has most of the rights and privileges of a person. The major exceptions relate to privileges that can be exercised only by a living person, such as the right to vote or to hold public office. Similarly, a corporation is subject to the same duties and responsibilities as a person; for example, it must abide by the laws and it must pay taxes.

Corporations may be classified in a variety of ways. Two common classifications are **by purpose** and **by ownership**. A corporation may be organized for the purpose of making a profit (such as Nike), or it may be a not-for-profit, charitable, medical, or educational corporation (such as the Salvation Army, Canadian Cancer Society, or Queen's University).

Classification by ownership differentiates public and private corporations. A **public corporation** may have thousands of shareholders, and its shares are regularly traded on a securities market such as the Toronto Stock Exchange. Examples are BCE, Canadian Pacific, and Sears Canada. In contrast, a **private corporation**, often referred to as a closely held corporation, usually has only a few shareholders, and it does not offer its shares for sale to the general public. Private companies are generally much smaller than public companies, although some notable exceptions exist. Irving Oil Limited, a private corporation that refines and sells gasoline and oil, among other things, is one of the largest companies in Canada.

CHARACTERISTICS OF A CORPORATION

STUDY OBJECTIVE 1

Identify and discuss the major characteristics of a corporation.

In 1964, when Nike's founders, Knight and Bowerman, were just getting started in the running shoe business, they formed their original organization as a partnership. In 1968, they reorganized the company as a corporation. A number of characteristics distinguish a corporation from proprietorships and partnerships. The most important of these characteristics are explained below.

Separate Legal Existence

As an entity separate and distinct from its owners, the corporation acts under its own name rather than in the name of its shareholders. Nike, for example, may buy, own, and sell property, borrow money, and enter into legally binding contracts in its own name. It may also sue or be sued, and it pays its own taxes.

In contrast to a partnership, in which the acts of the owners (partners) bind the partnership, the acts of a corporation's owners (shareholders) do not bind the corporation unless such owners are agents of the corporation. For example, if you owned Nike shares, you would not have the right to purchase inventory for the company unless you were designated as an agent of the corporation.

Legal existence separate from owners

Limited Liability of Shareholders

Since a corporation is a separate legal entity, creditors ordinarily only have recourse to corporate assets to satisfy their claims. The liability of shareholders is normally limited to their investment in the corporation, and creditors have no legal claim on the personal assets of the shareholders unless fraud has occurred. Thus, even in the event of bankruptcy of the corporation, shareholders' losses are generally limited to the amount of capital they have invested in the corporation.

Limited liability of shareholders

Transferable Ownership Rights

Ownership of a corporation is shown in shares of capital, which are transferable units. Shareholders may dispose of part or all of their interest in a corporation simply by selling their shares. In contrast to the transfer of an ownership interest in a partnership, which requires the consent of each partner, the transfer of shares is entirely at the discretion of the shareholder. It does not require the approval of either the corporation or other shareholders.

The transfer of ownership rights among shareholders normally has no effect on the operating activities of the corporation or on a corporation's assets, liabilities, and total shareholders' equity. That is, the corporation does not participate in the transfer of these ownership rights after the original sale of the share capital.

Transferable ownership rights

Ability to Acquire Capital

It is generally relatively easy for a corporation to obtain capital through the issuance of shares. Buying shares in a corporation is often more attractive to an investor than investing in a partnership, because a shareholder has limited liability and because shares are readily transferable. Moreover, many individuals can become shareholders by investing small amounts of money. In sum, the ability of a successful corporation to obtain capital is virtually unlimited.

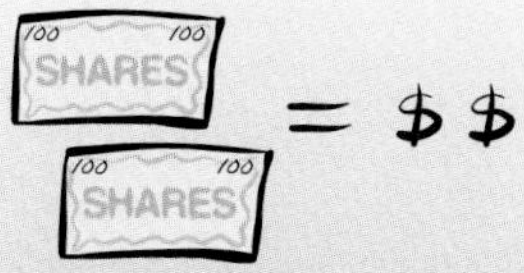

Ability to acquire capital

Continuous life

Continuous Life

The life of a corporation is stated in its **charter**—a written description of an organization's functions. The life may be perpetual or it may be limited to a specific number of years. If it is limited, the period of existence can be extended through renewal of the charter. Since a corporation is a separate legal entity, the life of a corporation as a going concern is separate from its owners; it is not affected by the withdrawal, death, or incapacity of a shareholder, employee, or officer. As a result, a successful corporation can have a continuous and perpetual life.

Corporation Management

Although shareholders legally own the corporation, they manage it indirectly through a board of directors they elect. Philip Knight is the chair of Nike's board of directors. Nike's board, in turn, formulates the operating policies for the company and selects officers, such as a president and one or more vice-presidents, to execute policy and to perform daily management functions.

The organizational structure of a corporation enables a company to hire professional managers to run the business. On the other hand, some view this separation as a weakness. The separation of ownership and management prevents owners from having an active role in managing the company, which some owners like to have.

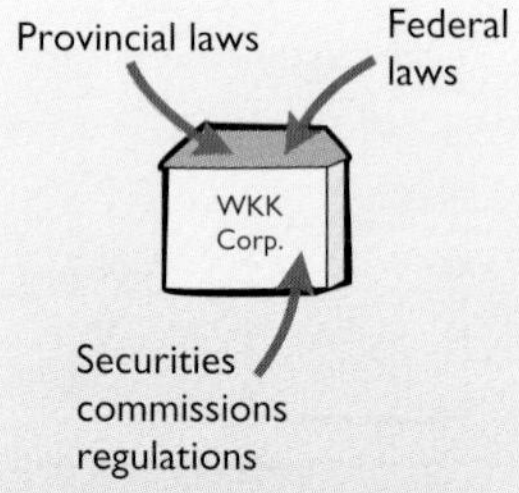

Government regulations

Government Regulations

Canadian companies may be incorporated federally, under the terms of the *Canada Business Corporations Act*, or provincially, under the terms of a provincial business corporations act. Federal and provincial laws usually prescribe the requirements for issuing shares, the distributions of earnings permitted to shareholders, and the effects of retiring shares. Similarly, provincial securities commissions regulations govern the sale of share capital to the general public. Also, most publicly held corporations are required to make extensive disclosure of their financial affairs to these commissions through quarterly and annual reports. Finally, when a corporation's shares are listed and traded on foreign securities markets, the corporation must comply with the reporting requirements of these exchanges. Compliance with federal, provincial, and securities regulations increases the cost and complexity for the corporate form of organization.

Additional Taxes

For proprietorships and partnerships, the owner's share of earnings is reported on his or her personal income tax return. Taxes are then paid by the individual on this amount. Corporations, on the other hand, must pay federal and provincial income taxes as a separate legal entity. These taxes are substantial as they can amount to as much as 50% of taxable income. There are, however, tax deductions available to some corporations. With eligible deductions, or other corporate tax incentives, a corporation's tax rate may be reduced to 20% to 25%, which is much lower than the tax rate for the same amount of income earned personally.

As shareholders are required to pay taxes on cash dividends, many argue that corporate income is **taxed twice (double taxation)**: once at the corporate level and again at the individual level. This is not exactly true, however, as individuals receive a dividend tax credit to relieve some of the tax burden.

The advantages and disadvantages of a corporation compared to a proprietorship and partnership are shown in Illustration 11-1.

Advantages	Disadvantages
• Corporation management—professional managers • Separate legal existence • Limited liability of shareholders • Deferral or reduction of taxes • Transferable ownership rights • Ability to acquire capital • Continuous life	• Corporation management—separation of ownership and management • Increased costs and complexity to adhere to government regulations • Additional taxes

Illustration 11-1 Advantages and disadvantages of a corporation

DECISION TOOLKIT

Decision Checkpoints	Info Needed for Decision	Tool to Use for Decision	How to Evaluate Results
Should the company incorporate?	Capital needs, growth expectations, type of business, tax status	Corporations have limited liability, easier capital raising ability, and professional managers; but they may suffer from additional taxes, government regulations, and separation of ownership from management.	Must carefully weigh the costs and benefits in light of the particular circumstances.

FORMING A CORPORATION

As previously mentioned, a company can incorporate federally, under the *Canada Business Corporations Act*, or provincially. The federal government and the majority of provinces file articles of incorporation, although other methods of incorporation also exist. Upon receipt of its articles of incorporation—essentially the constitution of the corporation—the corporation establishes by-laws for conducting its day-to-day affairs. Corporations engaged in interprovincial commerce must also obtain a licence from each province in which they do business. The licence subjects the corporation's operating activities to the general corporation laws of the province.

BUSINESS INSIGHT

International Perspective

Corporations in Canada are identified by (spelled out or abbreviated) "Ltd.," "Inc.," "Corp.," or in some cases, "Co.," following their names. In Brazil and France, the letters used are "SA" (Sôciedade Anonima, Société Anonyme); in Japan, "KK" (Kabushiki Kaisha); in the Netherlands, "NV" (Naamloze Vennootschap); in Italy, "SpA" (Società per Azioni); and in Sweden, "AB" (Aktiebolag).

In the UK, public corporations are identified by "Plc" (public limited company), while private corporations are denoted by "Ltd." The parallel designations in Germany are "AG" (Aktiengesellschaft) for public corporations and "GmbH" (Gesellschaft mit beschränkter Haftung) for private corporations.

SHAREHOLDER RIGHTS

Alternative Terminology *Shares* are also commonly known as *stock*.

When chartered, a corporation may begin selling ownership rights in the form of shares. When a corporation has only one class of shares, they are identified as **common shares**. Each common share gives the shareholder the ownership rights pictured in Illustration 11-2. The share ownership rights are stated in the articles of incorporation or in the by-laws.

Illustration 11-2 Ownership rights of shareholders

Shareholders have these rights:

1. To vote in election of board of directors at annual meeting. To vote on actions that require shareholder approval.

2. To share the corporate earnings through receipt of dividends.

3. To keep the same percentage ownership when new shares are issued (**preemptive right**[1]).

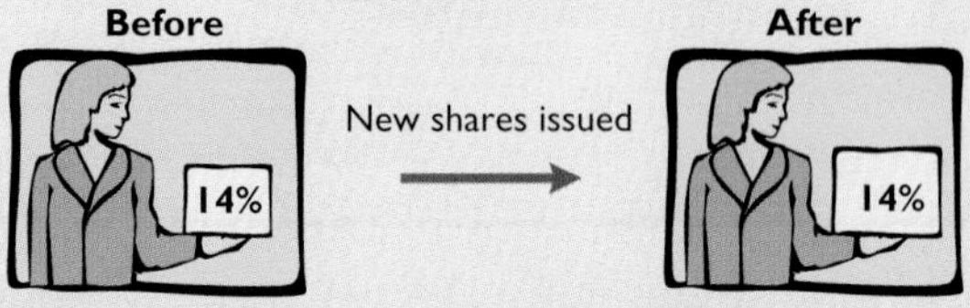

4. To share in assets upon liquidation in proportion to their holdings. This is called a **residual claim** because owners are paid with assets that remain after all claims have been paid.

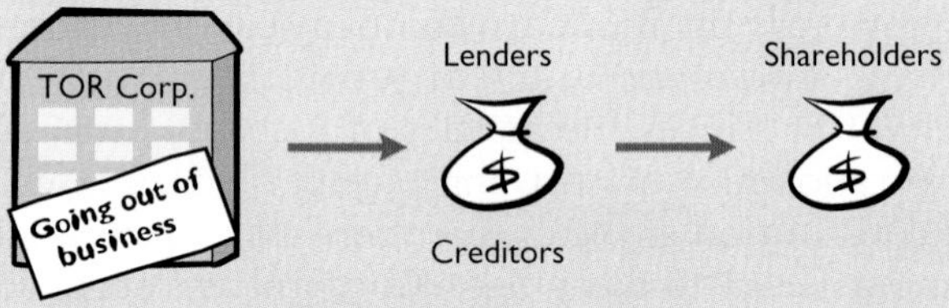

[1]A number of companies have eliminated the preemptive right because they believe it makes an unnecessary and cumbersome demand on management.

Proof of ownership is evidenced by a printed or engraved form known as a **share certificate**. As shown in Illustration 11-3, the face of the certificate has spaces for the number of shares owned, the name of the corporation, the shareholder's name, the date, the corporate seal, and signatures of authorized corporate officials. The share certificate also specifies the class and special features of the share—common in this case. Certificates are prenumbered to facilitate their accountability; they may be issued for any quantity of shares.

NUMBER SHARES

INCORPORATED IN THE PROVINCE OF NEW BRUNSWICK

AUTHORIZED CAPITAL

This is to Certify that ....

is the registered owner of ....

fully paid and non-assessable Common shares of

COMMON

transferable only on the books of the Company, by the holder hereof in person or by duly authorized attorney upon surrender of this Certificate properly endorsed.

IN WITNESS WHEREOF the Company has caused this Certificate to be signed by its duly authorized officers and to be sealed with the seal of the Company this .... day of ...., 19.....

SHARES EACH

Illustration 11-3 A share certificate

BUSINESS INSIGHT

International Perspective

In Japan, shareholders are considered to be far less important to a corporation than employees, customers, and suppliers. Shareholders are rarely asked to vote on an issue, and the notion of bending corporate policy to favour shareholders borders on heresy. This attitude toward shareholders appears to be slowly changing, however, as influential Japanese are advocating listening to investors, raising the extremely low dividends paid by Japanese corporations, and improving disclosure of financial information.

BEFORE YOU GO ON . . .

Review It

1. What are the advantages and disadvantages of a corporation compared to a proprietorship and a partnership?
2. Identify the principal steps in forming a corporation.
3. What rights are inherent in owning common shares of a corporation?

SHARE ISSUE CONSIDERATIONS

Although Nike incorporated in 1968, it did not sell shares to the public until 1980. At that time, Nike evidently decided it would benefit from the infusion of cash that a public sale of its shares would bring. When a corporation decides to issue share capital, it must resolve a number of basic questions: How many shares should be authorized for sale? How should the shares be issued? At what price should the shares be issued? What value should be assigned to the shares? These questions are answered in the following sections.

AUTHORIZED SHARE CAPITAL

The amount of share capital that a corporation is authorized to sell is indicated in its charter. If all **authorized shares** are sold, then a corporation must obtain consent to amend its charter before it can issue additional shares.

The authorization of common shares does not result in a formal accounting entry because the event has no immediate effect on either corporate assets or shareholders' equity. However, disclosure of the number of shares authorized is required in the shareholders' equity section of the balance sheet.

ISSUANCE OF SHARES

International Note

Canadian, U.S., and UK corporations raise most of their capital through millions of outside shareholders and bondholders. In contrast, companies in Germany, France, and Japan acquire financing from large banks or other institutions. Consequently, in the latter environment, shareholders are less important, and external reporting and auditing receive less emphasis.

A corporation has the choice of issuing common shares directly to investors or indirectly through an investment banking firm that specializes in bringing securities to the attention of prospective investors. Direct issue is typical in closely held companies, whereas indirect issue is customary for a public corporation. In Canada, new issues of shares may be offered for sale to the public through various organized securities exchanges: the Toronto Stock Exchange, Montreal Stock Exchange, Winnipeg Stock Exchange, Vancouver Stock Exchange, and the Canadian Venture Exchange. Stock may also be traded on the "over-the-counter" market, the Canadian Dealing Network (CDN).

How does a corporation set the price for a new issue of share capital? Among the factors to be considered are (1) the company's anticipated future earnings, (2) its expected dividend rate per share, (3) its current financial position, (4) the current state of the economy, and (5) the current state of the securities market. The calculation can be complex and is best approached through a finance course.

PAR, NO PAR, AND STATED VALUE SHARES

Par value shares are share capital that has been assigned a value per share in the corporate charter. The par value may be any amount selected by the corporation. Generally, the par value is quite low because provinces often levy fees on the corporation based on its par value. For example, Reebok's common shares have a par value of 1 cent.

The significance of par value is a legal matter. Par value represents the **legal capital** per share that must be retained in the business for the protection of corporate creditors; that is, it is not available for withdrawal by shareholders. Thus, in the past, most provinces required the corporation to sell its shares at par or above. Today, many provinces do not require a par value and, in fact, some provinces (e.g., Ontario) and the federal goverment prohibit the use of par value shares. Their usefulness as a protective device to creditors is questionable, because par value was often immaterial relative to the value of the company's shares—even at the time of issue. For example, Reebok's par value is $0.01 per share, yet a new issue in 2000 would have sold at a **market value** in the $15 per share range. Thus, par has no relationship with market value and, in the vast majority of cases, is an immaterial amount.

No par value shares are share capital that has not been assigned a value in the corporate charter. No par value shares are often issued because some confusion still exists concerning par value and fair market value. If shares have no par value, then the questionable treatment of using par value as a basis for fair market value never arises.

In many provinces, the board of directors is permitted to assign a **stated value** to the no par shares, which then becomes the legal capital per share. The stated value of no par shares may be changed at any time by action of the directors. Stated value, like par value, does not indicate or correspond to the market value of the stock.

Less than 15% of Canadian public companies surveyed by *Financial Reporting in Canada* reported a par or stated value for any of their shares. Because the use of par or stated values is either not required or prohibited in most jurisdictions, this text concentrates on the accounting for no par value shares.

ACCOUNTING FOR COMMON SHARE ISSUES

The shareholders' equity section of a corporation's balance sheet includes: (1) **share capital (contributed capital)** and (2) **retained earnings (earned capital)**. The distinction between share capital and retained earnings is important from both a legal and an economic point of view. **Share capital** is the amount contributed to the corporation by shareholders in exchange for shares of ownership. *Retained earnings* is earned capital held for future use in the business. In this section, we discuss the accounting for share capital. In a later section, we discuss retained earnings.

STUDY OBJECTIVE 2

Record the issuance of common shares.

Let's now look at how to account for new issues of common shares. The primary objectives in accounting for the issuance of common shares are to (1) identify the specific sources of share capital and (2) maintain the distinction between share capital and retained earnings. As shown below, **the issuance of no par value common shares affects only share capital accounts and all of the proceeds received upon issuance are considered to be legal capital of the no par value shares**.

To illustrate, assume that Hydro-Slide, Inc. issues 1,000 shares of no par value common shares for cash at $1 per share. The entry to record this transaction is

Cash	1,000	
Common Shares		1,000
(To record issuance of 1,000 common shares of no par value)		

A	=	L	+	SE
+1,000				+1,000

If Hydro-Slide, Inc. issues an additional 1,000 shares of the no par value common shares for cash at $5 per share, the entry is

Cash	5,000	
Common Shares		5,000
(To record issuance of 1,000 common shares of no par value)		

A	=	L	+	SE
+5,000				+5,000

If Hydro-Slide, Inc. has retained earnings of $27,000, the shareholders' equity section of the balance sheet is as shown in Illustration 11-4.

Illustration 11-4 Shareholders' equity

HYDRO-SLIDE, INC.
Balance Sheet (Partial)

Shareholders' equity	
Share capital	
Common shares	$ 6,000
Retained earnings	27,000
Total shareholders' equity	$33,000

Common shares may also be issued for considerations other than cash, such as services (e.g., compensation to lawyers, consultants) or noncash assets (e.g., land, buildings, equipment). To comply with the **cost principle** in a noncash transaction, **cost is the cash equivalent price**. Thus, cost is the **fair market value of the consideration (common shares) given up**. If the common shares do not have a ready market, we then look to the **fair market value of the consideration received** to determine cost.

BUSINESS INSIGHT

Investor Perspective

The shares of public companies are traded on organized exchanges at dollar prices per share established by the interaction between buyers and sellers. For each listed security, the financial press reports the high and low prices of the shares during the year, the total volume of shares traded on a given day, the high and low prices for the day, and the closing market price with the net change for the day. Chapters Online Inc. is listed on the Toronto Stock Exchange. Here is a recent listing for Chapters Online:

	52 Weeks		Volume				
Stock	High	Low	00s	High	Low	Close	Net change
ChaptOnln	28.00	3.00	253	5.00	4.70	5.00	+0.25

These numbers indicate that the high and low market prices for the last 52 weeks have been $28.00 and $3.00, respectively; the trading volume was 25,300 shares; the high, low, and closing prices for that date were $5.00, $4.70, and $5.00, respectively; and the net change for the day was an increase of $0.25 per share over the previous day's closing price.

The trading of common shares on securities exchanges involves the transfer of already issued shares from an existing shareholder to another investor. Consequently, these transactions have no impact on a corporation's shareholders' equity section.

BEFORE YOU GO ON . . .

Review It

1. To a corporation, what is the significance of the amount of authorized shares?
2. What alternative approaches may a corporation use to sell new shares to investors?
3. Distinguish between no par value and market value.
4. Explain the accounting for no par value common shares issued for cash.

Do It

Cayman Corporation begins operations on March 1 by issuing 100,000 shares of no par value common shares for cash at $12 per share. Journalize the issuance of the shares.

Reasoning: In issuing no par value shares for cash, the Common Shares account is credited.

Solution:

Mar. 1	Cash	1,200,000	
	Common Shares		1,200,000
	(To record issuance of 100,000 shares at $12 per share)		

PREFERRED SHARES

STUDY OBJECTIVE 3
Differentiate preferred shares from common shares.

To appeal to a larger segment of potential investors, a corporation may issue a class of shares in addition to common shares, called preferred shares. **Preferred shares** have contractual provisions that give them preference or priority over common shares in certain areas. Typically, preferred shareholders have a priority in relation to (1) dividends and (2) assets in the event of liquidation. However, they often do not have voting rights. Reebok has no outstanding preferred shares, while Nike has a very minor amount outstanding. A recent survey of 200 Canadian companies indicated that 40% have one or more classes of preferred shares.

Like common shares, preferred shares may be issued for cash or for noncash considerations. The entries for these transactions are similar to the entries for common shares. When a corporation has more than one class of shares, each capital account title should identify the shares to which it relates (e.g., Preferred Shares, Common Shares). Assume that Stine Corporation issues 10,000 shares of no par value preferred shares for $12 cash per share. The entry to record the issuance is

Helpful Hint The shares of the company are usually divided into different classes—class A, class B, and so on. These are differentiated by their generic terms "common" and "preferred," indicating the rights and privileges of each class.

Cash	120,000	
Preferred Shares		120,000
(To record the issuance of preferred 10,000 shares of no par value)		

A	=	L	+	SE
+120,000				+120,000

In the shareholders' equity section of the balance sheet, preferred shares are shown first because of their dividend and liquidation preferences over common shares.

DIVIDEND PREFERENCES

As indicated before, **preferred shareholders have the right to share in the distribution of dividends before common shareholders**. For example, if the dividend rate on preferred shares is $5 per share, common shareholders will not receive any dividends in the current year until preferred shareholders have received $5 per share. The first claim to dividends does not, however, **guarantee** dividends. Dividends depend on many factors, such as adequate retained earnings and availability of cash.

Cumulative Dividend

Preferred shares often contain a **cumulative dividend** feature. This right means that preferred shareholders must be paid both current-year dividends and any unpaid prior-year dividends before common shareholders receive dividends. When preferred shares are cumulative, preferred dividends not declared in a given period are called **dividends in arrears**. To illustrate, assume that Scientific-Leasing has 5,000 shares outstanding of no par value cumulative preferred shares. The annual dividend is $35,000 (5,000 × $7 per share). If dividends are two years in arrears, preferred shareholders are entitled to receive the dividends, as shown in Illustration 11-5, in the current year before any distribution may be made to common shareholders.

Illustration 11-5 Calculation of total dividends to preferred shares

Dividends in arrears ($35,000 × 2)	$ 70,000
Current-year dividends	35,000
Total preferred dividends	**$105,000**

Dividends in arrears are not considered a liability. No obligation exists until a dividend is declared by the board of directors. However, the amount of dividends in arrears should be disclosed in the notes to the financial statements. Doing so enables investors to assess the potential impact of this commitment on the corporation's financial position.

Dividends cannot be paid on common shares while any dividend on preferred shares is in arrears. The cumulative feature is often critical in selling a preferred share issue to investors. When preferred shares are noncumulative, a dividend passed over in any year is lost forever. Companies that are unable to meet their dividend obligations are not looked upon favourably by the investment community. As a financial officer noted in discussing one company's failure to pay its cumulative preferred dividend for a period of time, "Not meeting your obligations on something like that is a major black mark on your record."

LIQUIDATION PREFERENCE

Most preferred shares have a preference on corporate assets if the corporation fails. This feature provides security for the preferred shareholder. The preference to assets may be for the legal value of the shares or for a specified liquidating value. The liquidation preference is used in bankruptcy lawsuits involving the respective claims of creditors and preferred shareholders.

OTHER PREFERENCES

The attractiveness of preferred shares as an investment is sometimes enhanced by adding a conversion privilege. **Convertible preferred shares** allow the exchange of preferred shares for common shares at a specified ratio, at the shareholder's option. Convertible preferred shares are purchased by investors who want the greater security of preferred shares, but who also desire the added option of conversion if the market value of the common shares increases significantly.

Many preferred shares are also issued with a redemption or call feature. **Redeemable (or callable) preferred shares** grant the issuing corporation the right to purchase the shares from shareholders at specified future dates and prices. The redemption feature offers some flexibility to a corporation by enabling it to eliminate this type of equity security when it is advantageous to do so. When preferred shares are redeemable, the call price tends to set a ceiling on the market price of the shares.

Retractable preferred shares are similar to redeemable or callable preferred shares, except that it is at the *shareholder's* option rather than the corporation's option that the shares are redeemed. This usually occurs at an arranged price and date.

When preferred shares are retractable, the distinction between equity and debt begins to blur. Preferred shares and debt have many similarities. They both offer a rate of return to the investor, and with the redemption of the shares, they both offer a repayment of principal. These, and an increase in the use of other innovative **financial instruments**, have led the CICA to require companies to present these issues in accordance with their economic substance rather than their form. That is, retractable preferred shares would be presented in the *liability* section of the balance sheet, rather than the equity section, because they have more of the features of debt than of equity. Accounting for such financial instruments presents unique challenges for accountants.

REACQUISITION OF SHARES

Companies can purchase their own shares—whether common or preferred—on the open market. A corporation may acquire shares to meet any of these objectives:

1. Increase trading of the company's shares in the securities market in the hopes of enhancing its market value
2. Reduce the number of shares issued and thereby increase earnings per share
3. Have additional shares available to reissue to officers and employees under bonus and stock compensation plans
4. Have additional shares available for use in the acquisition of other companies

Another infrequent reason for purchasing one's own shares is that management may want to eliminate hostile shareholders by buying them out. Canadian Occidental Petroleum Ltd. (CanOxy) repurchased nearly half, roughly $600 million, of its shares held by Los Angeles–based Occidental Petroleum Corp. in 2000 to stop Occidental from taking over its huge Syncrude oil sands project in northern Alberta. Compliance reasons may also necessitate reacquisition of shares. For example, Section 55 of the *Canada Transportation Act* limits the level of ownership by non-Canadians of an airline licensed in Canada to 25% of the total voting shares. Canadian airlines have procedures in place to monitor the Canadian ownership level of their shares. If changes in the share ownership cause a problem in this area, an airline would have to repurchase shares from non-Canadians in order to ensure that the 25% level was not breached.

Helpful Hint *Financial Reporting in Canada* reported that 24% of the companies they surveyed in 1998 disclosed the repurchase and cancellation of shares.

When a federally incorporated company reacquires its own shares, the repurchased shares must be retired and cancelled. This effectively restores the shares to the status of authorized but unissued shares. Some provincially incorporated companies are also allowed to hold reacquired shares for future use. Shares for this purpose are called **treasury shares**. Treasury share transactions are extremely rare in Canada and only permitted in restricted circumstances.

If a company has treasury shares, this will result in a difference between the number of shares *issued*, and the number of shares *outstanding*. **Issued shares** are those that have been sold. **Outstanding shares** are those that have been sold and are held outside the company. In most circumstances, issued and outstanding shares are the same.

BUSINESS INSIGHT

Investor Perspective

Late in 1998, CHUM Limited, owner of MuchMusic, was considered by investors to be a "hot" share. One year later, investors were bored and CHUM's Class B non-voting share price had fallen to around $38, from a peak of $60. That's why CHUM bought back 5% of its shares on the Toronto Stock Exchange the next year.

Why do companies buy back their own shares? A share repurchase reduces the number of shares, and fewer shares mean increased earnings per share. As investors are attracted to higher earnings per share, the company's share price rises with the increased demand for its shares. A recent study confirmed that buyback shares outperform the markets by an average of 7% in each of the three years following their repurchase announcement.

Source: "They Take It Back," *Canadian Business*, October 8, 1999, 29.

BEFORE YOU GO ON . . .

Review It

1. Compare the normal rights and privileges of common and preferred shares.
2. Distinguish between convertible, redeemable, and retractable preferred shares.
3. Why might a company wish to repurchase its own shares on the open market?

DIVIDENDS

STUDY OBJECTIVE 4

Prepare the entries for cash dividends and stock dividends.

As noted earlier, a **dividend is a distribution by a corporation to its shareholders on a pro rata basis**. "Pro rata" means that if you own, say, 10% of the common shares, you will receive 10% of the dividend. Dividends can take four forms: cash, property, script (note payable to pay cash), or shares. Cash dividends, which predominate in practice, and stock dividends, which are declared with some frequency, are the focus of our discussion.

Investors are very interested in a company's dividend practices. In the financial press, **dividends are generally reported quarterly as a dollar amount per share**, although sometimes they are reported on an annual basis. For example, Nike's **annual** dividend rate recently was 48 cents per share, whereas BC Tel's dividend rate on one of its preferred shares was $6.

CASH DIVIDENDS

A **cash dividend** is a pro rata distribution of cash to shareholders. For a corporation to pay a cash dividend, it must have the following:

1. **Retained earnings.** In many jurisdictions, payment of dividends from legal capital is illegal. **Payment of dividends from retained earnings is legal in all provinces.**
2. **Adequate cash.** Recently, Nike had a balance in retained earnings of $3,043 million but a cash balance of only $109 million. Thus, in order to pay a dividend equal to its retained earnings, Nike would have to raise $2,934 mil-

lion more in cash. It is unlikely it would do this because a dividend of this size would not be sustainable in the future (that is, Nike would not be able to pay this much in dividends in future years). In addition, such a dividend would completely deplete Nike's balance in retained earnings, so it would not be able to pay a dividend in the next year unless it had positive net earnings.

3. **Declared dividends.** The board of directors has full authority to determine the amount of earnings to be distributed in the form of dividends and the amount to be retained in the business. Dividends do not accrue like interest on a note payable, and they are not a liability until declared.

The amount and timing of a dividend are important issues for management to consider. The payment of a large cash dividend could lead to liquidity problems for the enterprise. Conversely, a small dividend or a missed dividend may cause unhappiness among shareholders who expect to receive a reasonable cash payment from the company on a periodic basis. Many companies declare and pay cash dividends quarterly. On the other hand, a number of high-growth companies pay no dividends, preferring to retain earnings and use them to finance capital expenditures.

In order to remain in business, companies must honour their interest payments to creditors, bankers, and bondholders. But the payment of dividends to shareholders is another matter. Many companies can survive, and even thrive, without such payouts. "Why give money to those strangers?" is the response of one company president. Investors must keep an eye on the company's dividend policy and understand what it may mean. For most companies, for example, regular dividend boosts in the face of irregular earnings can be a warning signal. Companies with high dividends and rising debt may be borrowing money to pay shareholders. On the other hand, low dividends may not be a negative sign, because they may mean high returns through market appreciation. Presumably, investors for whom regular dividends are important tend to buy shares in companies that pay periodic dividends, and those for whom growth in the share price (capital gains) is more important tend to buy shares in companies that retain earnings.

Entries for Cash Dividends

Three dates are important in connection with dividends: (1) the declaration date, (2) the record date, and (3) the payment date. Normally, there is a time span between each date. Accounting entries are required on two of the dates: the declaration date and the payment date.

On the **declaration date**, the board of directors formally declares (authorizes) the cash dividend and announces it to shareholders. The declaration of a cash dividend **commits the corporation to a binding legal obligation** that cannot be rescinded. Thus, an entry is required to recognize the decrease in Retained Earnings and the increase in the liability Dividends Payable. To illustrate, assume that on December 1, 2001, the directors of Media General declare a \$0.50 per share cash dividend on 100,000 shares of no par value common shares. The dividend is \$50,000 (100,000 × \$0.50), and the entry to record the declaration is

Declaration Date

Dec. 1	Cash Dividends (or Retained Earnings)	50,000	
	Dividends Payable		50,000
	(To record declaration of cash dividend)		

A	=	L	+	SE
		+50,000		−50,000

Dividends Payable is a current liability, because it will normally be paid within the next month. You may recall that in Chapter 3, instead of decreasing Retained Earnings, the account Dividends was used. This account provides additional information in the ledger. For example, a company may have separate dividend accounts for each class of shares or each type of dividend. When a separate dividend account is used, its balance is transferred to Retained Earnings at the end of the year by a closing entry. Consequently, the effect of the declaration is the same: Retained Earnings is decreased and a current liability is increased.

Helpful Hint The record date is important in determining the dividend to be paid to each shareholder but not the total dividend.

The record date marks the time when ownership of the outstanding shares is determined for dividend purposes. The shareholders' records maintained by the corporation supply this information. The time interval between the declaration date and the record date enables the corporation to update its share ownership records. Between the declaration date and the record date, the number of shares outstanding should remain the same. Thus, the purpose of the record date is to identify the persons or entities that will receive the dividend, not to determine the amount of the dividend liability. For Media General, the record date is December 22. No entry is required on this date because the corporation's liability recognized on the declaration date is unchanged:

Record Date

Dec. 22	No entry necessary		

On the payment date, dividend cheques are mailed to the shareholders and the payment of the dividend is recorded. If January 20 is the payment date for Media General, the entry on that date is

A	=	L	+	SE
-50,000		-50,000		

Payment Date

Jan. 20	Dividends Payable	50,000	
	Cash		50,000
	(To record payment of cash dividend)		

Note that payment of the dividend reduces both current assets and current liabilities but has no effect on shareholders' equity. The cumulative effect of the **declaration and payment** of a cash dividend on a company's financial statements is to **decrease both shareholders' equity and total assets**.

STOCK DIVIDENDS

A stock dividend is a pro rata distribution of the corporation's own shares to shareholders. Whereas a cash dividend is paid in cash, a stock dividend is distributed in shares. **A stock dividend results in a decrease in retained earnings and an increase in share capital.** Unlike a cash dividend, a stock dividend does not decrease total shareholders' equity or total assets.

Because a stock dividend does not result in a distribution of assets, some view it as nothing more than a publicity gesture. Stock dividends are often issued by companies that do not have adequate cash to issue a cash dividend. These companies may not want to announce that they are not going to be issuing a dividend at their normal time to do so. By issuing a stock dividend, they "save face" by giving the appearance of distributing a dividend. Note that since a stock dividend neither increases nor decreases the assets in the company, investors are not receiving anything they didn't already own. In a sense, it is like ordering two pieces of pie and having the host take one piece of pie and cut it into two smaller pieces. You are not initially better off, but you have your two pieces of pie.

To illustrate a stock dividend, assume that you have a 2% ownership interest in Cetus Inc. by virtue of owning 20 of its 1,000 common shares. In a 10% stock dividend, 100 shares (1,000 × 10%) would be issued. You would receive two shares (2% × 100), but your ownership interest would remain at 2% (22 ÷ 1,100). **You now own more shares, but your ownership interest has not changed.** Moreover, no cash is disbursed, and no liabilities have been assumed by the corporation.

What then are the purposes and benefits of a stock dividend? Corporations generally issue stock dividends for one of the following reasons:

1. To satisfy shareholders' dividend expectations without spending cash
2. To increase the marketability of their shares by increasing the number of shares outstanding and thereby decreasing the market price per share. Decreasing the market price of the shares makes it easier for smaller investors to purchase them
3. To emphasize that a portion of shareholders' equity has been permanently reinvested in the business and is therefore unavailable for cash dividends

Helpful Hint Because of its effects, "issuing a stock dividend" is also referred to as "capitalizing retained earnings."

The size of the stock dividend and the value to be assigned to each dividend share are determined by the board of directors when the dividend is declared. The *Canada Business Corporations Act* recommends that directors of federally incorporated companies assign the **fair market value per share** for stock dividends, and it is widespread practice to do so. This directive is based on the assumption that a stock dividend will have little effect on the market price of the shares previously outstanding. Thus, many shareholders consider stock dividends to be a distribution of earnings equal to the fair market value of the shares distributed.

Entries for Stock Dividends

To illustrate the accounting for stock dividends, assume that Medland Corporation has a balance of $300,000 in retained earnings and declares a 10% stock dividend on its 50,000 no par value common shares. The current fair market value of its shares is $15 per share. The number of shares to be issued is 5,000 (10% × 50,000), and the total amount to be debited to Retained Earnings is $75,000 (5,000 × $15). The entry to record this transaction at the declaration date is

Stock Dividends (or Retained Earnings)	75,000	
Common Stock Dividends Distributable		75,000
(To record declaration of 10% stock dividend)		

A	=	L	+	SE
				−75,000
				+75,000

Note that at the declaration date Retained Earnings via the Stock Dividends account is decreased (debited) for the fair market value of the shares issued; Common Stock Dividends Distributable is increased for the same amount.

Common Stock Dividends Distributable is a shareholders' equity account; it is not a liability, because assets will not be used to pay the dividend. If a balance sheet is prepared before the dividend shares are issued, the distributable account is reported in Share Capital, as shown in Illustration 11-6.

MEDLAND CORPORATION
Balance Sheet (Partial)

Share capital		
Common shares	$500,000	
Common stock dividends distributable	75,000	$575,000

Illustration 11-6 Statement presentation of common stock dividends distributable

Helpful Hint Note that the dividend account title is "Distributable" not "Payable."

When the dividend shares are issued, Common Stock Dividends Distributable is decreased and Common Shares is increased as follows:

A	=	L	+	SE
				-75,000
				+75,000

Common Stock Dividends Distributable	75,000	
Common Shares		75,000
(To record issuance of 5,000 shares in a stock dividend)		

Effects of Stock Dividends

How do stock dividends affect shareholders' equity? They **change the composition of shareholders' equity**, because a portion of retained earnings is transferred to share capital. However, **total shareholders' equity remains the same**. Stock dividends also have no effect on the legal value per share, but the number of shares outstanding increases. These effects are shown in Illustration 11-7 for Medland Corporation.

Illustration 11-7 Stock dividend effects

	Before Stock Dividend	After Stock Dividend
Shareholders' equity		
Share capital		
Common shares	$ 500,000	$ 575,000
Retained earnings	300,000	225,000
Total shareholders' equity	**$800,000**	**$800,000**
Outstanding shares	**50,000**	**55,000**

In this example, total share capital is increased by $75,000 and retained earnings is decreased by the same amount. Note also that total shareholders' equity remains unchanged at $800,000.

STOCK SPLITS

Helpful Hint Some companies with penny shares do a ***reverse stock split***, i.e., one-for-two, to increase the market value per share.

A **stock split**, like a stock dividend, involves the issuance of additional shares to shareholders according to their percentage ownership. However, **a stock split results in a reduction in the legal capital per share and is usually much larger than a stock dividend**. The purpose of a stock split is to increase the marketability of the shares by lowering the market value per share. This, in turn, makes it easier for the corporation to issue additional shares.

The effect of a split on market value is generally inversely proportional to the size of the split. For example, after a two-for-one stock split, the market value of Scotiabank common shares fell from $70 to $35. In announcing the split, Robert Chisholm, Scotiabank Vice-Chair, said, "This share split makes the Bank's shares more affordable for the average Canadian investor."

Helpful Hint A stock split changes the legal capital per share but does not affect any balances in shareholders' equity.

In a stock split, the number of shares is increased in the same proportion that the legal capital per share is decreased. For example, in a two-for-one split, one share of no par value shares is exchanged for two shares of no par value shares. **A stock split does not have any effect on total share capital, retained earnings, or total shareholders' equity.** However, the number of shares outstanding increases. These effects are shown in Illustration 11-8, assuming that instead of issuing a 10% stock dividend, Medland splits its 50,000 common shares on a two-for-one basis.

Illustration 11-8 Stock split effects

	Before Stock Split	After Stock Split
Shareholders' equity		
Share capital		
Common shares	$ 500,000	$ 500,000
Retained earnings	300,000	300,000
Total shareholders' equity	**$800,000**	**$800,000**
Outstanding shares	**50,000**	**100,000**

Because a stock split does not affect the balances in any shareholders' equity accounts, **it is not necessary to journalize a stock split**. Significant differences between the effects of stock splits and stock dividends are shown in Illustration 11-9.

Illustration 11-9 Effects of stock splits and stock dividends differentiated

Item	Stock Split	Stock Dividend
Total share capital	No change	Increase
Total retained earnings	No change	Decrease
Total shareholders' equity	No change	No change
Legal capital per share	Decrease	No change

BUSINESS INSIGHT

Management Perspective

A handful of companies have no intention of keeping their share trading in a range accessible to mere mortals. These companies never split their shares, no matter how high their share price gets. The king of these is U.S. investment company Berkshire Hathaway's Class A shares, which go for a pricey US$58,000—per share! The highest Canadian share price is London Life Insurance Company's, at $5,500 per share.

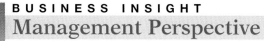

BEFORE YOU GO ON . . .

Review It

1. What factors affect the size of a company's cash dividend?
2. Why do companies issue stock dividends? Why do companies declare stock splits?
3. Did Loblaw repurchase any common shares in 1999? Did it declare any dividends? Stock splits? The answers to these questions are provided at the end of this chapter.
4. Contrast the effects of a stock dividend and a two-for-one stock split on (a) shareholders' equity and (b) outstanding shares.

Loblaws
A passion for food... *and a lot more!*

Do It

Due to five years of record earnings at Sing CD Corporation, the market price of its 500,000 no par value common shares tripled from $15 per share to $45. During this period, share capital remained the same at $2,000,000, but retained earnings increased from $1,500,000 to $10,000,000. President Joan Elbert is considering either a 10% stock dividend or a two-for-one stock split. She asks you to show the before- and after-effects of each option on retained earnings.

Reasoning: A stock dividend decreases retained earnings and increases share capital, but total shareholders' equity remains the same. A stock split changes only the legal capital per share and the number of shares outstanding. Thus, a stock split has no effect on the retained earnings balance.

Solution: The stock dividend amount is $2,250,000 [(500,000 × 10%) × $45]. The new balance in retained earnings is $7,750,000 ($10,000,000 – $2,250,000). The retained earnings balance after the stock split is the same as it was before the split: $10,000,000. The effects in the shareholders' equity accounts are as follows:

	Original Balances	After Stock Dividend	After Stock Split
Share capital	$ 2,000,000	$ 4,250,000	$ 2,000,000
Retained earnings	10,000,000	7,750,000	10,000,000
Total shareholders' equity	$12,000,000	$12,000,000	$12,000,000
Shares outstanding	500,000	550,000	1,000,000

Retained Earnings

STUDY OBJECTIVE 5

Identify the items that affect retained earnings.

Retained earnings are net earnings that are retained in the business. The balance in retained earnings is part of the shareholders' claim on the total assets of the corporation. It does not, however, represent a claim on any specific asset. Nor can the amount of retained earnings be associated with the balance of any asset account. For example, a $100,000 balance in retained earnings does not mean that there should be $100,000 in cash. The reason is that the cash resulting from the excess of revenues over expenses may have been used to purchase buildings, equipment, and other assets. Illustration 11-10 shows the amounts of retained earnings and cash in selected companies.

Illustration 11-10
Retained earnings and cash balances

	(in millions)	
Company	**Retained Earnings**	**Cash**
Canadian Tire Corporation Ltd.	$1,318	$ 308
Imasco Ltd.	2,789	6,226
Noranda Inc.	1,309	1,296
Corel Corporation	(176)	25

When expenses exceed revenues, a **net loss** results. In contrast to net earnings, a net loss decreases retained earnings. In closing entries, a net loss is debited to the Retained Earnings account. **Net losses are not debited to share capital accounts.** To do so would destroy the distinction between contributed and earned capital. If cumulative losses exceed cumulative earnings, over a company's life, a debit balance in Retained Earnings results. A debit balance in retained earnings, such as that of Corel Corporation, is identified as a **deficit** and is reported as a deduction in the shareholders' equity section of the balance sheet, as shown in Illustration 11-11.

Illustration 11-11
Shareholders' equity with deficit

COREL CORPORATION Balance Sheet (Partial) November 30, 1999 (in thousands)	
Shareholders' equity	
Share capital	$222,155
Contributed surplus	1,099
Deficit	**(158,888)**
Total shareholders' equity	$ 64,366

The term "contributed surplus" used in Corel's balance sheet indicates additional contributed capital when a corporation's shares have a par or stated value. The portion of the proceeds for these share issues above the par or stated value is recorded in a separate shareholders' equity category, known as **contributed surplus** or **additional contributed capital**. This additional contributed capital doesn't result when a corporation has no par value shares since all the proceeds of the share issue are credited to the share capital account.

RETAINED EARNINGS RESTRICTIONS

The balance in retained earnings is generally available for dividend declarations. In some cases, however, there may be **retained earnings restrictions** that make a portion of the balance currently unavailable for dividends. Restrictions result from one or more of these types of causes: legal, contractual, or voluntary. Retained earnings restrictions are generally disclosed in the notes to the financial statements. For example, Norcen Energy Resources Limited, an oil and gas company headquartered in Calgary, once disclosed the following dividend restriction in a note to its financial statements:

Illustration 11-12
Disclosure of retained earnings restriction

NORCEN ENERGY RESOURCES LIMITED
Notes to the Financial Statements

Covenants respecting certain of Norcen's non-convertible long-term debt impose a limit on dividend payments by Norcen, such limit being related in part to consolidated net earnings, as defined. Under the most restrictive of these covenants, retained earnings in the amount of $86 million were available for the payment of dividends at December 31.

FINANCIAL STATEMENT PRESENTATION OF SHAREHOLDERS' EQUITY

STUDY OBJECTIVE 6
Prepare a comprehensive shareholders' equity section.

In the shareholders' equity section of the balance sheet, **contributed capital** and **retained earnings** are reported, and the specific sources of contributed capital are identified if multiple sources exist. Within contributed capital, share capital is normally the only classification disclosed, unless additional contributed capital is present, as shown for Corel in Illustration 11-11. **Share capital** consists of preferred and common shares. Preferred shares are shown before common shares because of their preferential rights. Information about the legal capital, shares authorized, shares issued, and shares outstanding is reported for each class of shares.

The shareholders' equity section of the balance sheet of Graber Inc. is presented in Illustration 11-13. Note that Common Stock Dividends Distributable is shown under Share Capital, and a retained earnings restriction is disclosed. No additional contributed capital exists in this instance.

The shareholders' equity section for Graber Inc. includes most of the accounts discussed in this chapter. The disclosures pertaining to Graber's common shares indicate that 400,000 shares are issued and outstanding, and 100,000 shares are unissued (500,000 authorized less 400,000 issued).

Illustration 11-13 Comprehensive shareholders' equity section

GRABER INC.
Balance Sheet (Partial)

Shareholders' equity		
Share capital		
$9 preferred shares, no par value, cumulative, redeemable at $120, 10,000 shares authorized, 6,000 shares issued and outstanding		$ 630,000
Common shares, no par value, 500,000 shares authorized, 400,000 shares issued and outstanding	$2,000,000	
Common stock dividends distributable	**50,000**	2,050,000
Total share capital		2,680,000
Retained earnings (Note R)		1,160,000
Total shareholders' equity		$3,840,000

Note R: Loan agreements contain, among other covenants, a restriction on the payment of dividends, which limits future dividend payments to 75% of net earnings.

International Note

In Switzerland, there are no specific disclosure requirements for shareholders' equity. However, companies typically disclose separate categories of capital on the balance sheet.

In published annual reports, subclassifications within the shareholders' equity section are seldom presented.

BEFORE YOU GO ON . . .

Review It

1. Identify the classifications within the shareholders' equity section of a balance sheet.
2. How are stock dividends distributable reported in the shareholders' equity section?

MEASURING CORPORATE PERFORMANCE

Investors are interested in both a company's dividend record and its earnings performance. Although they are often parallel, that is not always the case. Thus, each should be investigated separately.

DIVIDEND RECORD

STUDY OBJECTIVE 7

Evaluate a corporation's dividend and earnings performance from a shareholder's perspective.

One way that companies reward investors for their investment is to pay them dividends. The **payout ratio** measures the percentage of earnings distributed in the form of cash dividends declared to common shareholders. It is calculated by **dividing total cash dividends to common shareholders by net earnings**. Another measure, the **dividend yield**, reports the rate of return an investor earned from dividends during the year. It is calculated by **dividing cash dividends declared per common share during the year by the share price at the end of the year**. From the information shown below, the payout ratios and dividend yields for Nike in 1997 and 1998 are calculated in Illustration 11-14:

	1998	1997
Dividends (in millions)	$132.90	$108.20
Dividends per share	0.46	0.38
Net earnings (in millions)	399.60	795.80
Share price at end of year	46.00	57.50

$$\text{PAYOUT RATIO} = \frac{\text{TOTAL CASH DIVIDENDS DECLARED ON COMMON SHARES}}{\text{NET EARNINGS}}$$

$$\text{DIVIDEND YIELD} = \frac{\text{DIVIDENDS DECLARED PER SHARE}}{\text{SHARE PRICE AT END OF YEAR}}$$

($ in millions except per share data)	1998	1997
Payout Ratio	$\frac{\$132.9}{\$399.6} = 33.3\%$	$\frac{\$108.2}{\$795.8} = 13.6\%$
Dividend Yield	$\frac{\$0.46}{\$46.00} = 1.0\%$	$\frac{\$0.38}{\$57.50} = 0.7\%$

Illustration 11-14 Nike dividend ratios

Companies that have high growth rates are characterized by low payout ratios and dividend yields because they reinvest most of their net earnings in the business. Thus, a low payout ratio or dividend yield is not necessarily bad news. Companies, such as Nike and Reebok, that believe they have many good opportunities for growth will reinvest those funds in the company rather than pay high dividends. However, low dividend payments, or a cut in dividend payments, might also signal that a company has liquidity or solvency problems and is trying to free up cash by not paying dividends. Thus, the reason for low dividend payments should always be investigated.

Listed in Illustration 11-15 are dividend ratios in recent years of four well-known companies.

Company	Payout Ratio	Dividend Yield
Bank of Montreal	9.6%	2.5%
Corel Corporation	0.0%	0.0%
Molson Inc.	23.8%	3.0%
Sears Canada Inc.	17.3%	1.1%

Illustration 11-15 Variability of dividend ratios among companies

DECISION TOOLKIT

Decision Checkpoints ✔	Info Needed for Decision	Tool to Use for Decision	How to Evaluate Results 👍👎
What portion of its earnings does the company pay out in dividends?	Net earnings and total cash dividends paid on common shares	Payout ratio $=$ $\dfrac{\text{Total cash dividends declared on common shares}}{\text{Net earnings}}$	A low ratio suggests that the company is retaining its earnings for investment in future growth.
What level of return can be earned on the company's dividends?	Market price and dividends paid per common share	Dividend yield $=$ $\dfrac{\text{Cash dividends declared per common share}}{\text{Share price at year end}}$	A high yield is attractive to investors looking for a steady investment earnings stream rather than share price appreciation.

EARNINGS PERFORMANCE

Earnings per share measures the net earnings for each common share. It is calculated by dividing **net earnings** by the **average number of common shares outstanding during the year**. Shareholders usually think in terms of the number of shares they own or plan to buy or sell, so reducing net earnings to a per share amount provides a useful perspective for determining the investment return. Advanced accounting courses present more refined techniques for calculating earnings per share. For now, a basic approach is to divide earnings available to common shareholders (net earnings − preferred share dividends) by average common shares outstanding during the year. By comparing earnings per share of a single company over time, one can evaluate its relative earnings performance from the perspective of a shareholder—that is, on a per share basis.

It is very important to note that comparisons of earnings per share across companies are **not meaningful** because of the wide variations in the numbers of outstanding shares among companies and in the share prices. Instead, in order to make a meaningful comparison of earnings across firms, we calculate the **price-earnings ratio**. The price-earnings ratio is an oft-quoted statistic that measures **the ratio of the market price of each common share to the earnings per share**. It is calculated by dividing the market price per share by earnings per share. The price-earnings (P-E) ratio reflects the investors' assessment of a company's future earnings. The ratio of price to earnings will be higher if investors think that current earnings levels will persist or increase rather than decline. A high price-earnings ratio might also indicate that the share price is too high and is likely to come down. From the information presented on the following page, the earnings per share and price-earnings ratios for Nike in 1997 and 1998 are calculated in Illustration 11-16. (Note that to simplify our calculations, we assumed that any change in shares for Nike occurred in the middle of the year.)

(in thousands except per share data)	1998	1997
Net earnings	$399,600	$795,800
Preferred share dividends	$30	$30
Shares outstanding at beginning of year	287,000	287,200
Shares outstanding at end of year	289,300	287,000
Market price of shares at end of year	$46.00	$57.50

$$\text{EARNINGS PER SHARE} = \frac{\text{NET EARNINGS} - \text{PREFERRED SHARE DIVIDENDS}}{\text{AVERAGE COMMON SHARES OUTSTANDING}}$$

$$\text{PRICE-EARNINGS RATIO} = \frac{\text{MARKET PRICE PER SHARE}}{\text{EARNINGS PER SHARE}}$$

($ in thousands except per share data)	1998	1997
Earnings per Share	$\frac{\$399{,}600 - \$30}{(287{,}000 + 289{,}300)/2} = \$1.39$	$\frac{\$795{,}800 - \$30}{(287{,}200 + 287{,}000)/2} = \$2.77$
Price-Earnings Ratio	$\frac{\$46.00}{\$1.39} = 33.1$ times	$\frac{\$57.50}{\$2.77} = 20.8$ times

Illustration 11-16 Nike earnings per share and price-earnings ratio

From 1997 to 1998, Nike's earnings per share decreased substantially on approximately the same number of shares. Its price-earnings ratio increased. This increase might reflect a belief that Nike will be able to return to its usual profitability and growth.

As noted, earnings per share cannot be meaningfully compared across companies. Price-earnings ratios, however, can be compared. Illustration 11-17 lists four companies and their earnings per share and price-earnings ratios for 1998 (calculated at the end of each company's fiscal year).

Company	Earnings per Share	Price-Earnings Ratio
Bank of Montreal	$4.72	18.2
Corel Corporation	0.40	52.8
Molson Inc.	1.89	14.6
Sears Canada Inc.	1.38	21.0

Illustration 11-17 Variability of earnings performance ratios among companies

DECISION TOOLKIT

Decision Checkpoints	Info Needed for Decision	Tool to Use for Decision	How to Evaluate Results
How does the company's earnings performance compare with that of previous years?	Net earnings available to common shareholders and average common shares outstanding	$\text{Earnings per share} = \frac{\text{Net earnings} - \text{Preferred share dividends}}{\text{Average common shares outstanding}}$	A higher measure suggests improved performance, although the number is subject to manipulation. Values should not be compared across companies.
How does the market perceive the company's prospects for future earnings?	Earnings per share and market price per share	$\text{Price-earnings ratio} = \frac{\text{Market price per share}}{\text{Earnings per share}}$	A high ratio suggests the market has favourable expectations, although it also may suggest shares are overvalued.

Another widely used ratio that measures profitability from the common shareholders' viewpoint is **return on common shareholders' equity**. This ratio shows how many dollars were earned for each dollar invested by common shareholders. It is calculated by dividing net earnings available to common shareholders (net earnings − preferred share dividends) by average common shareholders' equity. Common shareholders' equity is total shareholders' equity less the legal capital of any preferred shares. From the additional information presented below, Nike's return on common shareholders' equity ratios are calculated for 1997 and 1998 in Illustration 11-18.

($ in thousands)	1998	1997	1996
Net earnings	$ 399,600	$ 795,800	$ 553,200
Preferred share dividends	30	30	30
Common shareholders' equity	3,261,600	3,155,900	2,431,400

$$\text{RETURN ON COMMON SHAREHOLDERS' EQUITY RATIO} = \frac{\text{NET EARNINGS} - \text{PREFERRED SHARE DIVIDENDS}}{\text{AVERAGE COMMON SHAREHOLDERS' EQUITY}}$$

($ in thousands)	1998	1997
Return on Common Shareholders' Equity Ratio	$\frac{\$399,600 - \$30}{(\$3,261,600 + \$3,155,900)/2} = 12.5\%$	$\frac{\$795,800 - \$30}{(\$3,155,900 + \$2,431,400)/2} = 28.5\%$

Illustration 11-18 Nike return on common shareholders' equity

From 1997 to 1998, Nike's return on common shareholders' equity decreased from 28.5% to 12.5%. As a company grows larger, it becomes increasingly hard to sustain a high return. In Nike's case, since many believe the North American market for expensive sports shoes is saturated, Nike will need to grow either along new product lines, such as hiking shoes, or in new markets, such as Europe and Asia. We will talk more about factors that affect the return on common shareholders' equity in Chapter 14.

DECISION TOOLKIT

Decision Checkpoints	Info Needed for Decision	Tool to Use for Decision	How to Evaluate Results
What is the company's return on common shareholders' investment?	Earnings available to common shareholders and average common shareholders' equity	Return on common shareholders' equity ratio $= \frac{\text{Net earnings} - \text{Preferred share dividends}}{\text{Average common shareholders' equity}}$	A high measure suggests strong earnings performance from the common shareholders' perspective.

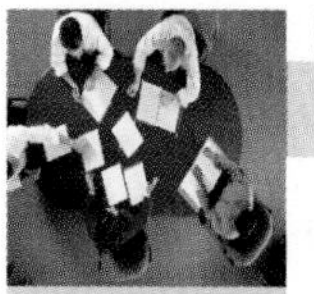

BUSINESS INSIGHT

Management Perspective

Nike's advertising success, envied throughout the business world, was recently spoofed in the humour magazine *The Onion*. The article blared, "Nike to Cease Manufacturing Products: 'From now on, we'll focus on just making ads,' says a spokesman." Another "quote" attributed to Phil Knight, Nike co-founder and CEO, was "The last few years, it became impossible to maintain our high standards of advertising while faced with the daily distractions of making sneakers. By discontinuing our entire product line, we will ensure that Nike remains the world's leader in the field of incredibly cool TV commercials well into the 21st century." Based on your understanding of accounting, how would this strategy affect Nike's return on common shareholders' equity?

Source: "Nike to Cease Manufacturing Products," *The Onion,* September 11, 1996, 1.

BEFORE YOU GO ON . . .

Review It

1. What measures can be used to evaluate a company's dividend record, and how are they calculated?
2. Why should earnings per share not be compared across companies?
3. What does a high price-earnings ratio suggest about a company's future earnings potential?

Using the Decision Toolkit

During 1998, Reebok hit difficult times in which both its profits and market share declined. As a result, its share price sagged and investors became impatient.

Instructions

The following facts are available for Reebok. Using this information, evaluate its (1) dividend record and (2) earnings performance, and contrast them with those of Nike for 1997 and 1998:

(in thousands except per share data)	1998	1997	1996
Dividends declared	0	0	$15,180
Dividends declared per share	0	0	$0.164
Net earnings	$23,927	$135,119	$138,950
Preferred share dividends	0	0	0
Common shares outstanding at end of year	56,590	56,400	55,840
Share price at end of year	$14.88	$28.81	$42.00
Common shareholders' equity	$524,377	$507,157	$381,234

Solution

1. *Dividend record:* Two measures to evaluate dividend record are the payout ratio and the dividend yield. For Reebok, these measures in 1997 and 1998 are calculated as shown here:

	1998	1997
Payout ratio	$\frac{\$0}{\$23,927} = 0\%$	$\frac{\$0}{\$135,119} = 0\%$
Dividend yield	$\frac{\$0}{\$14.88} = 0\%$	$\frac{\$0}{\$28.81} = 0\%$

   Nike's dividends paid per share increased 8 cents from 1997 to 1998, while Reebok's went from $0.164 in 1996 to zero in 1997 and 1998. Elimination of a dividend is generally perceived as bad news about a company's future prospects.

2. *Earnings performance:* There are many measures of earnings performance. Those presented in the chapter were earnings per share, the price-earnings ratio, and the return on common shareholders' equity ratio. These measures for Reebok in 1998 and 1997 are calculated as shown here:

	1998	1997
Earnings per share	$\frac{\$23,927 - 0}{(56,590 + 56,400)/2} = \$0.42$	$\frac{\$135,119 - 0}{(56,400 + 55,840)/2} = \$2.41$
Price-earnings ratio	$\frac{\$14.88}{\$0.42} = 35.4$	$\frac{\$28.81}{\$2.41} = 12.0$
Return on common shareholders' equity ratio	$\frac{\$23,927 - 0}{(\$524,377 + \$507,157)/2} = 4.6\%$	$\frac{\$135,119 - 0}{(\$507,157 + \$381,234)/2} = 30.4\%$

From 1997 to 1998, Reebok's earnings declined on both a total and per share basis. This decline was significant and would be of obvious concern to both management and shareholders. Reebok's price-earnings ratio increased, perhaps hinting that investors believe earnings will rebound somewhat in coming years. Also, compared to Nike's P-E ratio of 33.1, Reebok seems to be higher-priced; that is, Reebok's shareholders are paying more per dollar of earnings than are Nike's.

Reebok's return on common shareholders' equity declined from 30.4% to 4.6%. This is an alarming drop, which would be of great concern to shareholders.

Summary of Study Objectives

❶ ***Identify and discuss the major characteristics of a corporation.*** The major characteristics of a corporation are separate legal existence, limited liability of shareholders, transferable ownership rights, ability to acquire capital, continuous life, corporation management, government regulations, and corporate income taxes.

❷ ***Record the issuance of common shares.*** When the issuance of no par value common shares for cash is recorded, the entire proceeds from the issue become legal capital and are credited to the Common Shares account.

❸ ***Differentiate preferred shares from common shares.*** Preferred shares have contractual provisions that give them priority over common shares in certain areas. Typically, preferred shareholders have a preference as to (a) dividends and (b) assets in the event of liquidation. However, they often do not have voting rights.

In addition, preferred shares may be convertible, redeemable, and/or retractable. Convertible preferred shares entitle the holder to convert those shares to common shares at a specified ratio. The redemption feature grants the issuing corporation the right to purchase these shares from shareholders at specified future dates and prices. Retractable preferred shares give the shareholder the option of selling the shares to the corporation at specified future dates and prices.

❹ ***Prepare the entries for cash dividends and stock dividends.*** Entries for both cash and stock dividends are required at the declaration date and the payment date. At the declaration date, the entries are as follows: for a *cash dividend*—debit Cash Dividends (or Retained Earnings) and credit Dividends Payable; for a *stock dividend*—debit Stock Dividends (or Retained Earnings), and credit Common Stock Dividends Distributable. At the payment (distribution) date, the entries for cash and stock dividends, respectively, are debit Dividends Payable and credit Cash, and debit Common Stock Dividends Distributable and credit Common Shares.

❺ ***Identify the items that affect retained earnings.*** Additions to retained earnings consist of net earnings. Deductions consist of net loss, and cash and stock dividends. In some instances, portions of retained earnings are restricted, making that portion unavailable for the payment of dividends.

❻ ***Prepare a comprehensive shareholders' equity section.*** In the shareholders' equity section of the balance sheet, contributed capital and retained earnings are reported separately and specific sources of contributed capital (e.g., share capital) are identified.

❼ ***Evaluate a corporation's dividend and earnings performance from a shareholder's perspective.*** A company's dividend record can be evaluated by looking at what percentage of net earnings it chooses to pay out in dividends, as measured by the dividend payout ratio (dividends divided by net earnings), or it can be evaluated from the perspective of a rate of return on shareholders' investment through the dividend yield (dividends divided by share price). Earnings performance is measured with earnings per share (net earnings available to common shareholders divided by average number of shares). In order to compare the relative amounts that investors are currently paying per dollar of reported earnings, the price-earnings ratio is calculated (share price divided by earnings per share). Another measure of earnings performance is the return on common shareholders' equity ratio (earnings available to common shareholders divided by average common shareholders' equity).

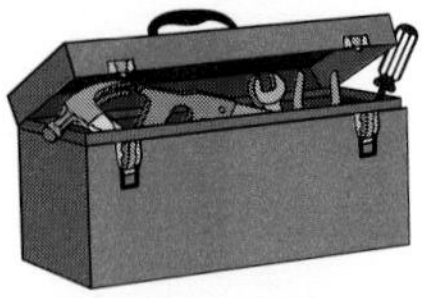

Decision Toolkit—A Summary

Decision Checkpoints	Info Needed for Decision	Tool to Use for Decision	How to Evaluate Results
Should the company incorporate?	Capital needs, growth expectations, type of business, tax status	Corporations have limited liability, easier capital raising ability, and professional managers; but they may suffer from additional taxes, government regulations, and separation of ownership from management.	Must carefully weigh the costs and benefits in light of the particular circumstances.
What portion of its earnings does the company pay out in dividends?	Net earnings and total cash dividends paid on common shares	$\text{Payout ratio} = \frac{\text{Total cash dividends declared on common shares}}{\text{Net earnings}}$	A low ratio suggests that the company is retaining its earnings for investment in future growth.
What level of return can be earned on the company's dividends?	Market price and dividends paid per common share	$\text{Dividend yield} = \frac{\text{Cash dividends declared per common share}}{\text{Share price at year end}}$	A high yield is attractive to investors looking for a steady investment earnings stream rather than share price appreciation.
How does the company's earnings performance compare with that of previous years?	Net earnings available to common shareholders and average common shares outstanding	$\text{Earnings per share} = \frac{\text{Net earnings} - \text{Preferred share dividends}}{\text{Average common shares outstanding}}$	A higher measure suggests improved performance, although the number is subject to manipulation. Values should not be compared across companies.
How does the market perceive the company's prospects for future earnings?	Earnings per share and market price per share	$\text{Price-earnings ratio} = \frac{\text{Market price per share}}{\text{Earnings per share}}$	A high ratio suggests the market has favourable expectations, although it may also suggest shares are overvalued.
What is the company's return on common shareholders' investment?	Earnings available to common shareholders and average common shareholders' equity	$\text{Return on common shareholders' equity ratio} = \frac{\text{Net earnings} - \text{Preferred share dividends}}{\text{Average common shareholders' equity}}$	A high measure suggests strong earnings performance from the common shareholders' perspective.

GLOSSARY

Authorized shares The amount of share capital that a corporation is authorized to sell as indicated in its charter. (p. 596)

Cash dividend A pro rata distribution of cash to shareholders. (p. 602)

Corporation A company organized as a separate legal entity, with most of the rights and privileges of a person. Evidence of ownership is shares. (p. 590)

Cumulative dividend A feature of preferred shares entitling the shareholder to receive current and unpaid prior-year dividends before common shareholders receive any dividends. (p. 600)

Convertible preferred shares Preferred shares that the shareholder can convert into common shares at a specifed ratio. (p. 600)

Declaration date The date the board of directors formally declares a dividend and announces it to shareholders. (p. 603)

Deficit A debit balance in retained earnings. (p. 608)

Dividend A distribution by a corporation to its shareholders on a pro rata (equal) basis. (p. 602)

Dividend yield A measure of the rate of return an investor earned from dividends during the year. (p. 611)

Dividends in arrears Preferred dividends that were scheduled to be declared but were not declared during a given period. (p. 600)

Earnings per share A measure of the net earnings on each common share; calculated by dividing net earnings minus preferred dividends by the average number of common shares outstanding during the year. (p. 612)

Issued shares Share capital that has been sold. (p. 601)

Legal capital The amount per share that must be retained in the business for the protection of corporate creditors. (p. 596)

No par value shares Share capital that has not been assigned a value in the corporate charter. (p. 597)

Outstanding shares Share capital that has been issued and is being held by shareholders. (p. 601)

Par value shares Share capital that has been assigned a value per share in the corporate charter. (p. 596)

Payment date The date dividend cheques are mailed to shareholders. (p. 604)

Payout ratio A measure of the percentage of earnings distributed in the form of cash dividends to common shareholders. (p. 611)

Preferred shares Share capital that has contractual preferences over common shares in certain areas. (p. 599)

Price-earnings ratio A measure of the ratio of the market price of each common share to the earnings per share; it reflects the stock market's belief about a company's future earnings potential. (p. 612)

Private corporation A corporation that has only a few shareholders and whose shares are not available for sale to the general public. (p. 590)

Public corporation A corporation that may have thousands of shareholders and whose shares are regularly traded on a national securities market. (p. 590)

Record date The date when ownership of outstanding shares is determined for dividend purposes. (p. 604)

Redeemable (callable) preferred shares Preferred shares that grant the issuer the right to purchase the shares from shareholders at specified future dates and prices. (p. 600)

Retained earnings Net earnings that are retained in the business. (p. 608)

Retained earnings restrictions Circumstances that make a portion of retained earnings currently unavailable for dividends. (p. 609)

Retractable preferred shares Preferred shares that grant the shareholder the right to redeem the shares at specified future dates and prices. (p. 601)

Return on common shareholders' equity ratio A measure of profitability from the shareholders' point of view; calculated by dividing net earnings minus preferred dividends by average common shareholders' equity. (p. 614)

Share capital The amount paid to the corporation by shareholders in exchange for shares of ownership. (p. 597)

Stated value The amount per share assigned by the board of directors to no par value shares that becomes legal capital per share. (p. 597)

Stock dividend A pro rata distribution of the corporation's own shares to shareholders. (p. 604)

Stock split The issuance of additional shares to shareholders accompanied by a reduction in the legal capital per share. (p. 606)

DEMONSTRATION PROBLEM

Rolman Corporation is authorized to issue 1,000,000 common shares. In its first year, the company has these share transactions:

Jan. 10	Issued 400,000 shares at $8 per share.
Dec. 24	Declared a cash dividend of 10 cents per share.

Instructions

(a) Journalize the transactions.
(b) Prepare the shareholders' equity section of the balance sheet assuming the company had retained earnings of $150,600 at December 31.

Solution to Demonstration Problem

Problem-Solving Strategies

When common shares have no par value, the Common Shares account is credited for all the proceeds received.

(a)

Jan.	10	Cash (400,000 × $8)	3,200,000	
		Common Shares		3,200,000
		(To record issuance of 400,000 common shares)		
Dec.	24	Cash Dividends (or Retained Earnings)	40,000	
		Dividends Payable		40,000
		(To record declaration of 10 cents per share cash dividend)		

(b)

ROLMAN CORPORATION
Balance Sheet (Partial)

Shareholders' equity	
Share capital	
Common shares, no par value, 1,000,000 shares authorized, 400,000 shares issued and outstanding	$3,200,000
Retained earnings	150,600
Total shareholders' equity	$3,350,600

SELF-STUDY QUESTIONS

Answers are at the end of the chapter.

(SO 1) 1. Which of these is a major advantage of a corporation?
(a) Separate legal existence
(b) Separation of ownership and management
(c) Government regulations
(d) Additional taxes

(SO 1) 2. A major disadvantage of a corporation is:
(a) limited liability of shareholders.
(b) government regulations.
(c) transferable ownership rights.
(d) None of the above

(SO 1) 3. Which of these statements is *false?*
(a) Ownership of common shares gives the owner a voting right.
(b) The shareholders' equity section begins with share capital.
(c) The authorization of share capital results in a formal accounting entry.
(d) Legal capital per share applies to no par value shares.

(SO 2) 4. ABC Corporation issues 1,000 no par value common shares at $12 per share. When the transaction is recorded, credits are made to:
(a) Share Capital, $12,000.
(b) Common Shares, $12,000.
(c) Retained Earnings, $12,000.
(d) Common Shares, $10,000, and Retained Earnings, $2,000.

5. Preferred shares may have priority over common shares *except* in: (SO 3)
(a) dividends.
(b) assets in the event of liquidation.
(c) conversion.
(d) voting.

6. A company will buy back its own shares: (SO 3)
(a) to force the share price up.
(b) to force the share price down.
(c) to increase the number of shares available for dividends.
(d) to save cash.

7. Entries for cash dividends are required on the: (SO 4)
(a) declaration date and record date.
(b) record date and payment date.
(c) declaration date, record date, and payment date.
(d) declaration date and payment date.

(SO 4) 8. Which of these statements about stock dividends is *true?*
   (a) A debit should be made to Cash Dividends (or Retained Earnings) for the market value of the shares issued.
   (b) Market value per share should be assigned to the dividend shares.
   (c) A stock dividend decreases total shareholders' equity.
   (d) A stock dividend ordinarily will have no effect on total share capital.

(SO 7) 9. A high price-earnings ratio indicates:
   (a) a company has strong future earnings potential.
   (b) a company's shares are priced too low and are likely to come up.
   (c) either (a) or (b).
   (d) neither (a) nor (b).

10. Herb Fischer is nearing retirement and would like to invest in shares that will provide a good steady earnings supply. Herb should choose shares with a: (SO 7)
   (a) high current ratio.
   (b) high dividend yield.
   (c) high earnings per share.
   (d) high price-earnings ratio.

QUESTIONS

(SO 1) 1. Pat Kabza, a student, asks for your help in understanding some characteristics of a corporation. Explain each of these to Pat:
   (a) separate legal existence
   (b) limited liability of shareholders
   (c) transferable ownership rights

(SO 1) 2. (a) Your friend T.R. Cedras cannot understand how the characteristic of corporation management is both an advantage and a disadvantage. Clarify this problem for T.R.
   (b) Identify and explain two other disadvantages of a corporation.

(SO 1) 3. Cary Brant believes a corporation must be incorporated in the province in which its office is located. Is Cary correct? Explain.

(SO 1) 4. What are the basic ownership rights of common shareholders?

(SO 1) 5. A corporation has been defined as an entity separate and distinct from its owners. In what ways is a corporation a separate legal entity?

(SO 1) 6. What factors help determine the market value of shares?

(SO 2) 7. WAT Inc.'s common shares have no par value and a current market value of $15. Explain why these amounts are different.

(SO 2) 8. Land with a fair market value of $125,000 is acquired by issuing common shares with a fair market value of $100,000. What value would this land be recorded at in the company's records?

(SO 2, 3) 9. The corporate charter of Letterman Corporation allows the issuance of a maximum of 100,000 common shares. During its first two years of operation, Letterman sold 60,000 shares to shareholders and reacquired and cancelled 7,000 of these shares. After these transactions, how many shares are authorized and issued?

(SO 3) 10. (a) What are the principal differences between common shares and preferred shares?
   (b) Preferred shares may be cumulative. Discuss this feature.
   (c) How are dividends in arrears presented in the financial statements?
   (d) Preferred shares may be redeemable. Discuss the feature.

11. For what reasons might a company repurchase some of its shares? (SO 3)

12. What three conditions must be met before a cash dividend is paid? (SO 4)

13. Three dates associated with Galena Company Ltd.'s cash dividend are May 1, May 15, and May 31. Discuss the significance of each date and give the entry at each date. (SO 4)

14. Contrast the effects of a cash dividend and a stock dividend on (a) a corporation's balance sheet and (b) an individual shareholder's personal financial position. (SO 4)

15. Jill Sims asks, "Since stock dividends don't change anything, why declare them?" What is your answer to Jill? (SO 4)

16. Bella Corporation has 10,000 common shares of no par value outstanding, when it announces a two-for-one split. Before the split, the shares had a market price of $140 per share. After the split, how many shares will be outstanding, and what will be the approximate market price per share? (SO 4)

17. The board of directors is considering a stock split or a stock dividend. They understand that total shareholders' equity will remain the same under either action. However, they are not sure of the different effects of the two actions on other aspects of shareholders' equity. Explain the differences to the directors. (SO 4)

18. Identify the events that result in credits and debits to retained earnings. (SO 5)

19. (a) What is the purpose of a retained earnings restriction? (SO 5)
   (b) Identify the possible causes of retained earnings restrictions.

20. What are the two principal components of shareholders' equity? (SO 6)

(SO 5) 21. Indicate how each of these accounts should be classified in the shareholders' equity section of the balance sheet:
(a) Common Shares
(b) Retained Earnings
(c) Stock Dividends Distributable
(d) Preferred Shares

(SO 7) 22. What are the formulas for the dividend yield and the payout ratio, and what does each indicate?

23. Matthew Dodge notes that TID Industries has an earnings per share that is double that of Derauf Inc. Therefore, he concludes that TID is a better investment. Is he correct? (SO 7)

24. Some investors like to buy shares that have low price-earnings ratios. What might their logic be in doing this? (SO 7)

BRIEF EXERCISES

Cite advantages and disadvantages of a corporation. (SO 1)

BE11-1 Tracy Bono is studying for her accounting mid-term examination. Identify for Tracy the advantages and disadvantages of the corporate form of business organization.

Journalize issuance of common shares. (SO 2)

BE11-2 On May 10, Armada Corporation issues 1,000 no par value common shares for cash at $14 per share. Journalize the issuance of the shares.

Journalize issuance of common shares. (SO 2)

BE11-3 On June 1, Eagle Inc. issues 2,000 no par value common shares at a cash price of $7 per share. Journalize the issuance of the shares.

Analyse a noncash share issue. (SO 2)

BE11-4 **Intrawest Corporation** issued 325,000 common shares with no par value to acquire the Raven golf resorts and Alpine Helicopters in 1999. The fair market value of these common shares at the time of acquisition was $9.1 million. If the fair market value of Raven and Alpine was $10 million at the time of acquisition, at what value did Intrawest record these assets, and the issue of common shares?

Journalize issuance of preferred shares. (SO 3)

BE11-5 Ozark Inc. issues 5,000 no par value preferred shares for cash at $112 per share. Journalize the issuance of the preferred shares.

Prepare entries for a cash dividend. (SO 4)

BE11-6 The Seabee Corporation has 10,000 common shares outstanding. It declares a $1 per share cash dividend on November 1 to shareholders of record on December 1. The dividend is paid on December 31. Prepare the entries on the appropriate dates to record the declaration and payment of the cash dividend.

Prepare entries for a stock dividend. (SO 4)

BE11-7 Satina Corporation has 100,000 no par value common shares outstanding. It declares a 10% stock dividend on December 1, when the market value per share is $12. The dividend shares are issued on December 31. Prepare the entries for the declaration and payment of the stock dividend.

Show before- and after-effects of a stock dividend. (SO 4)

BE11-8 The shareholders' equity section of Satina Corporation's balance sheet consists of common shares (no par), $1,000,000, and retained earnings, $400,000. A 10% stock dividend (10,000 shares) is declared when the market value per share is $12. Show the before- and after-effects of the dividend on (1) the components of shareholders' equity and (2) the shares outstanding.

Analyse the impact of a stock split. (SO 4)

BE11-9 North Vancouver–based **CyPost Corp.** is a hot share with a hot e-mail encryption product. On October 12, CyPost split its shares three-for-two. Prior to the split, its share price was $12. Assuming the markets are efficient, what would you anticipate its share price to be immediately after the split? Explain why CyPost, a relatively new company, might want to split its shares.

Prepare a shareholders' equity section. (SO 6)

BE11-10 Anita Corporation has these accounts at December 31: Common Shares, no par value, 5,000 shares issued, $50,000; and Retained Earnings, $29,000. Prepare the shareholders' equity section of the balance sheet.

BE11-11 Abdella Corporation had a share price of $25 per share at the beginning of the year and $20 per share at the end of the year. Its dividend has remained a constant $1 per share for the last three years. Calculate the dividend yield at the beginning and end of the year and comment on its implications for an investor interested in dividend income.

Calculate dividend yield at beginning and end of year; comment on implications.
(SO 7)

BE11-12 Paul Schwartz, president of Schwartz Corporation, believes that it is a good practice to maintain a constant payout of dividends relative to earnings. Last year, net earnings were $500,000, and the corporation paid $200,000 in dividends. This year, due to some unusual circumstances, the corporation had earnings of $2,000,000. Paul expects next year's net earnings to be about $600,000. What was Schwartz Corporation's payout ratio last year? If it is to maintain the same payout ratio, what amount of dividends would it pay this year? Is this necessarily a good idea—that is, what are the pros and cons of maintaining a constant payout ratio in this scenario?

Evaluate a company's dividend record.
(SO 7)

BE11-13 The share prices of dozens of high-tech companies soared in 1999. Take, for example, **JDS Uniphase Canada Ltd.**, which makes fibre-optic equipment in Nepean, Ontario. Its share price went from a low of $16 to a high of $210, an increase of 1,312%! Yet JDS reported no dividend payments and a loss per share of $2.14 in this same period. Why do you think shareholders are so anxious to pay increasing amounts for JDS's shares?

Evaluate factors affecting a company's share price.
(SO 7)

EXERCISES

E11-1 During its first year of operations, Bevis Corporation had these transactions pertaining to its common shares:

Journalize issuance of common shares.
(SO 2)

Jan. 10	Issued 80,000 shares for cash at $5 per share.
July 1	Issued 30,000 shares for cash at $7 per share.

Instructions
Journalize the transactions.

E11-2 Santiago Corp. had these transactions during a recent period:

Journalize issuance of common shares and preferred shares.
(SO 2, 3)

June 12	Issued 60,000 no par value common shares for cash of $375,000.
July 11	Issued 1,000 no par value preferred shares for cash at $105 per share.

Instructions
Prepare the journal entries for the transactions.

E11-3 Ferreri Corporation recently hired a new accountant with extensive experience in accounting for partnerships. Because of the pressure of the new job, the accountant was unable to review what he had learned earlier about corporation accounting. During the first month, he made the following entries for the corporation's share capital:

Prepare correct entries for share capital transactions.
(SO 2, 3)

May 2	Cash	144,000	
	Share Capital		144,000
	(Issued 12,000 no par value common shares at $12 per share)		
10	Cash	600,000	
	Share Capital		600,000
	(Issued 10,000 no par value preferred shares at $60 per share)		

Instructions
On the basis of the explanation for each entry, prepare the entries that should have been made for the share capital transactions.

E11-4 On January 1, Tarow Corporation had 75,000 shares of no par common shares issued and outstanding. During the year, the following transactions occurred:

Journalize cash dividends and indicate statement presentation.
(SO 2, 4, 6)

Apr. 1	Issued 5,000 additional common shares at $10 per share.
June 15	Declared a cash dividend of $1 per share to shareholders of record on June 30.
July 10	Paid the $1 cash dividend.
Dec. 1	Issued 2,000 additional common shares at $12 per share.
15	Declared a cash dividend on outstanding shares of $1.20 per share to shareholders of record on December 31.

Instructions
(a) Prepare the entries, if any, to record the above transactions.
(b) How are dividends and dividends payable reported in the financial statements prepared at December 31?

Answer questions about shareholders' equity section
(SO 2, 3, 4, 7)

E11-5 The shareholders' equity section of Kimbria Shumway Corporation's balance sheet at December 31 is presented here:

KIMBRIA SHUMWAY CORPORATION
Balance Sheet (Partial)

Shareholders' equity	
Share capital	
Preferred shares, cumulative, no par, 10,000 shares authorized, issued, and outstanding	$ 600,000
Common shares, no par, 750,000 shares authorized, 600,000 shares issued and outstanding	1,800,000
Total share capital	2,400,000
Retained earnings	1,158,000
Total shareholders' equity	$3,558,000

Instructions
From a review of the shareholders' equity section, answer these questions:
(a) Assuming that the preferred shares were sold at an average price of $100 per share, how many preferred shares are issued and outstanding?
(b) What was the average per share selling price of the common shares?
(c) How many additional common shares will Kimbria Shumway be able to sell if it wishes to raise additional equity financing?
(d) If the annual dividend on preferred shares is $48,000, what is the dividend per share on the preferred shares?
(e) If dividends of $96,000 were in arrears on the preferred shares, what would be the balance reported for retained earnings?

Identify reasons for share repurchase.
(SO 3)

E11-6 After an unsuccessful takeover attempt by **Onex** in 1999, **Air Canada** spent $1.1 million to buy back its shares to improve its share value.

Instructions
(a) Explain how a buyback of shares affects the number of shares issued and outstanding, the Share Capital account, earnings per share, and the market value of the shares.
(b) Why do you think Air Canada repurchased $1.1 million of shares late in 1999?

Journalize preferred share transactions and indicate statement presentation.
(SO 3, 6)

E11-7 Talley Corporation is authorized to issue both preferred and common shares. The preferred shares have no par value. During the first year of operations, the company had the following events and transactions pertaining to its preferred shares:

Feb. 1	Issued 30,000 shares for cash at $53 per share.
July 1	Issued 10,000 shares for cash at $57 per share.

Instructions
(a) Journalize the transactions.
(b) Post to the shareholders' equity accounts. (Use T accounts.)
(c) Describe the statement presentation of the accounts.

Journalize stock dividend.
(SO 4)

E11-8 On January 1, 2001, Keyes Corporation had 50,000 common shares outstanding that were issued at no par value for $1,500,000 and retained earnings of $750,000.

Instructions
Journalize the declaration of a 10% stock dividend on December 10, 2001, assuming the market value is $30.

Compare effects of a stock dividend and a stock split.
(SO 4)

E11-9 On October 31, the shareholders' equity section of Sarah Lane Company's balance sheet consists of common shares, $800,000, and retained earnings, $400,000. Sarah is considering the following two courses of action: (1) declaring a 10% stock dividend on the 80,000 no par value shares outstanding or (2) effecting a two-for-one stock split. The current market price is $15 per share.

Instructions

Prepare a tabular summary of the effects of the alternative actions on these components: shareholders' equity, outstanding shares, and book value per share. Use these column headings: "Before Action," "After Stock Dividend," and "After Stock Split."

Prepare correcting entries for dividends and a stock split.
(SO 4)

E11-10 Before preparing financial statements for the current year, the chief accountant for Koo Company Ltd. discovered the following errors in the accounts:

1. The declaration and payment of a $25,000 cash dividend was recorded as a debit to Interest Expense, $25,000, and a credit to Cash, $25,000.
2. A 10% stock dividend (1,000 shares) was declared on the no par value shares when the market value per share was $17. The only entry made was Retained Earnings (Dr.), $10,000, and Dividend Payable (Cr.), $10,000. The shares have not been issued.
3. A four-for-one stock split involving the issue of 400,000 no par value common shares for 100,000 no par value common shares was recorded as a debit to Retained Earnings, $2,000,000, and a credit to Common Shares, $2,000,000.

Instructions

Prepare the correcting entries at December 31.

Prepare a statement of retained earnings and a shareholders' equity section.
(SO 6)

E11-11 **Intrawest Corporation**, headquartered in Vancouver, is a leading developer and operator of resorts in North America. It reported the following selected accounts and information, as at June 30, 1999:

	(in thousands)
Cash dividends	$ 6,626
Common shares, 200,000,000 shares without par value authorized, 43,254,386 shares issued	527,255
Net earnings	51,447
NRP* common shares, 200,000,000 shares without par value authorized, 16,726,586 shares issued	60,076
Retained earnings, July 1, 1998	146,859

*The NRP shares are a special class of common shares related to non-resort real estate assets.

Instructions

Prepare a statement of retained earnings and the shareholders' equity section of the balance sheet for Intrawest, as at June 30, 1999.

Prepare a shareholders' equity section.
(SO 6)

E11-12 The following accounts appear in the ledger of Ozabal Inc. after the books are closed at December 31, 2002:

Common Shares (no par value, 400,000 shares authorized, 300,000 shares issued)	$300,000
Common Stock Dividends Distributable	75,000
Preferred Shares (no par value, $8, 40,000 shares authorized, 30,000 shares issued)	150,000
Retained Earnings	900,000

Instructions

Prepare the shareholders' equity section at December 31, 2002, assuming $100,000 of retained earnings is restricted for plant expansion.

Calculate ratios to evaluate dividend and earnings performance.
(SO 7)

E11-13 This financial information is available for **CIBC** at October 31, 1998 and 1997.

(in millions, except for market price)	**1998**	**1997**
Average common shareholders' equity	$8,952	$8,199.5
Dividends paid to common shareholders	$498	$434
Dividends paid to preferred shareholders	$116	$98
Net earnings	$1,056	$1,551
Average number of common shares outstanding	415.03	413.545
Market price of common shares	$30.70	$41.20

Instructions

Calculate the dividend yield, payout ratio, earnings per share, price-earnings ratio, and return on common shareholders' equity ratio for 1998 and 1997.

Calculate ratios to evaluate dividend and earnings performance.
(SO 7)

E11-14 This financial information is available for **Nortel Networks Corporation** as at December 31, 1998 and 1997:

(in millions, except for market price)	1998	1997
Average common shareholders' equity	$7,878	$4,655
Dividends paid to common shareholders	$178	$150
Dividends paid to preferred shareholders	$32	$17
Net earnings (loss)	($537)	$829
Average number of common shares outstanding	572	522
Market price of common shares	$38.30	$31.80

Instructions

Calculate the dividend yield, payout ratio, earnings per share, price-earnings ratio, and return on common shareholders' equity ratio for 1998 and 1997.

Problems: Set A

Journalize share transactions, post, and prepare share capital section.
(SO 2, 3, 6)

P11-1A Remmers Corporation was organized on January 1, 2001. It is authorized to issue 20,000, $3, no par value preferred shares and 500,000 no par value common shares. The following share transactions were completed during the first year:

Jan. 10	Issued 100,000 common shares for cash at $3 per share.
Mar. 1	Issued 10,000 preferred shares for cash at $51 per share.
May 1	Issued 75,000 common shares for cash at $4 per share.
Sept. 1	Issued 5,000 common shares for cash at $6 per share.
Nov. 1	Issued 2,000 preferred shares for cash at $53 per share.

Instructions

(a) Journalize the transactions.
(b) Post to the shareholders' equity accounts. (Use T accounts.)
(c) Prepare the share capital portion of the shareholders' equity section at December 31, 2001.
(d) Explain why Remmers may have chosen to finance its operations by issuing share capital rather than debt.

Journalize transactions, post, and prepare a shareholders' equity section; calculate ratios.
(SO 2, 3, 4, 6, 7)

P11-2A The shareholders' equity accounts of Chung Corporation on January 1, 2001, were as follows:

Preferred Shares ($10, no par value, noncumulative, 5,000 shares authorized, 3,000 shares issued)	$ 300,000
Common Shares (300,000 shares, no par value, authorized, 200,000 shares issued)	1,000,000
Retained Earnings	488,000

During 2001, the corporation had these transactions and events pertaining to its shareholders' equity:

Feb. 1	Issued 4,000 common shares for $25,000.
Oct. 1	Declared a $10 cash dividend on preferred shares, payable November 1.
Dec. 1	Declared a $0.40 per share cash dividend to common shareholders of record on December 15, payable December 31, 2001.
31	Determined that net earnings for the year were $215,000. At December 31, the market price of the common shares was $10 per share.

Instructions

(a) Journalize the transactions.
(b) Enter the beginning balances in the accounts and post the journal entries to the shareholders' equity accounts. (Use T accounts.)
(c) Prepare the shareholders' equity section of the balance sheet at December 31, 2001.
(d) Calculate the dividend yield, payout ratio, earnings per share, price-earnings ratio, and return on common shareholders' equity ratio for the common shareholders.

Prepare entries for share transactions, and prepare a shareholders' equity section.
(SO 2, 3, 6)

P11-3A Largent Corporation has been authorized to issue 20,000, no par value, $8, cumulative preferred shares and 1,000,000 no par value common shares. During the first year of operations, ended December 31, 2001, the following transactions occurred:

1. Issued 1,000 preferred shares for $144,000 cash.
2. Issued 400,000 common shares for $3,850,000 cash.
3. Issued 10,000 common shares in exchange for a building. At the time of the exchange, the building was valued at $110,000 and the common shares at $100,000.
4. Declared and paid annual preferred dividend.
5. Net earnings for the year were $90,000.

Instructions

(a) Prepare journal entries to record the above transactions.
(b) Prepare the shareholders' equity section of the balance sheet at December 31, 2001.

Compare the impact of cash and stock dividends on the company and the shareholder.
(SO 4)

P11-4A The condensed balance sheet of Laporte Corporation reports the following amounts:

LAPORTE CORPORATION
Balance Sheet (Partial)

Assets		$13,500,000
Liabilities and shareholders' equity		
Liabilities		$ 1,500,000
Shareholders' equity		
Share capital		
Common shares, 50,000 authorized, 40,000 issued, no par value	$ 2,000,000	
Retained earnings	10,000,000	12,000,000
Total liabilities and shareholders' equity		$13,500,000

Laporte Corporation wishes to assess the impact of two possible dividend alternatives on the corporation and its shareholders:

1. Payment of a $2 per share cash dividend.
2. Distribution of a 5% stock dividend. The market price of the common shares is currently $40 per share.

Instructions

(a) Determine the impact on assets, liabilities, shareholders' equity (common shares and retained earnings), and the number of shares of each of the two alternatives for Laporte Corporation.

(b) 1. Assess the impact of each alternative from a shareholder's perspective. Which alternative is most beneficial for the shareholder? Assume the shareholder currently owns 1,000 common shares, at a cost of $35,000.

2. How would a shareholder record receipt of the cash dividend or stock dividend on their own records?

Answer questions about shareholders' equity section.
(SO 4, 5)

P11-5A The shareholders' equity section of Maple Corporation, after closing on December 31, 2001, presented the following information:

MAPLE CORPORATION
Balance Sheet (Partial)
December 31, 2001

Shareholders' equity		
Share capital		
8% cumulative preferred shares, $100 par value, 25,000 shares authorized, ? shares issued		$1,200,000
Common shares, no par value, 500,000 shares authorized, 100,000 shares issued		1,000,000
Total share capital		2,200,000
Retained earnings		
January 1, 2001	$500,000	
Net earnings, 2001	175,000	675,000
Total shareholders' equity		$2,875,000

Instructions

(a) How many preferred shares were issued as at December 31, 2001?
(b) What was the average selling price of the preferred shares, expressed on a per share basis?
(c) What is the annual total preferred share dividend requirement, stated in dollars?
(d) What was the total amount of dividends, if any, declared by Maple Corporation in 2001?
(e) Assuming that there were no dividends in arrears at the beginning of 2001, are there any dividends in arrears now at the end of 2001? If so, worth how much?

P11-6A The ledger of Robichaud Corporation at December 31, 2001, after the books have been closed, contains the following shareholders' equity accounts:

Reproduce retained earnings account, and prepare a shareholders' equity section.
(SO 4, 5, 6)

Preferred Shares (10,000 shares issued)	$1,000,000
Common Shares (400,000 shares issued)	3,200,000
Common Stock Dividends Distributable	100,000
Retained Earnings	2,540,000

A review of the accounting records reveals this information:

1. Preferred shares are $10, no par value, noncumulative, and redeemable at $125. Since January 1, 2000, 10,000 shares have been outstanding; 20,000 shares are authorized.
2. Common shares are no par; 600,000 shares are authorized.
3. The January 1 balance in Retained Earnings was $2,200,000.
4. On October 1, 100,000 common shares were sold for cash at $8 per share.
5. A cash dividend of $400,000 was declared and allocated to preferred and common shares on November 1. No dividends were paid to preferred shareholders in 2000.
6. On December 31, a 5% common stock dividend was declared out of retained earnings on common shares when the market price per share was $7.
7. Net earnings for the year were $880,000.
8. On December 31, 2001, the directors authorized disclosure of a $100,000 restriction on retained earnings for plant expansion.

Instructions

(a) Reproduce the retained earnings account (T account) for the year.

(b) Prepare the shareholders' equity section of the balance sheet at December 31, including any required note disclosure.

P11-7A Investors sometimes pay close attention to ratios without questioning what caused the shareholders' equity ratios to change. You are provided with the following ratios and independent transactions for Val David Inc.:

Show the impact of transactions on various ratios.
(SO 4, 5, 7)

Transactions	**Payout ratio (20%)**	**Dividend yield (1%)**	**Earnings per share ($0.30)**	**Price-earnings ratio (10x)**	**Return on common shareholders' equity (3%)**
(a) $2,500 of cash dividends were declared, but not paid, to common shareholders.					
(b) Paid cash dividends declared to common shareholders in preceding transaction.					
(c) The company lost a major lawsuit and immediately recorded a $25,000 loss on the statement of earnings and accrued liability on the balance sheet.					
(d) A press release was issued detailing the lost lawsuit from the previous transaction. The price of the company's common shares dropped 8%.					

Transactions	Payout ratio (20%)	Dividend yield (1%)	Earnings per share ($0.30)	Price-earnings ratio (10x)	Return on common shareholders' equity (3%)
(e) The company effected a two-for-one stock split for common shareholders. Their share price dropped 50%.					

Instructions

Indicate whether the above transactions will increase (I), decrease (D), or not affect (NA) each of the ratios presented. Unless you are given specific information to the contrary, you are to assume that the transactions do not affect the market price of the shares.

Prepare dividend entries, prepare a shareholders' equity section, and calculate ratios.
(SO 4, 6, 7)

P11-8A On January 1, 2001, Wirth Corporation had these shareholders' equity accounts:

Common Shares (no par value, 80,000 shares issued and outstanding)	$800,000
Retained Earnings	540,000

During the year, the following transactions occurred:

Jan. 15	Declared a $1 per share cash dividend to shareholders of record on January 31, payable February 15.
Feb. 15	Paid the dividend declared in January.
Apr. 15	Declared a 10% stock dividend to shareholders of record on April 30, distributable May 15. On April 15, the market price of the shares was $13 per share.
May 15	Issued the shares for the stock dividend.
Dec. 1	Declared a $1 per share cash dividend to shareholders of record on December 15, payable January 10, 2002.
31	Determined that net earnings for the year were $220,000. On December 31, the market price of the shares was $15 per share.

Instructions

(a) Journalize the transactions.
(b) Enter the beginning balances and post the entries to the shareholders' equity T accounts. (Note: Open additional shareholders' equity accounts as needed.)
(c) Prepare the shareholders' equity section of the balance sheet at December 31.
(d) Calculate the dividend yield, payout ratio, earnings per share, price-earnings ratio, and return on common shareholders' equity ratio.

Prepare a shareholders' equity section.
(SO 6)

P11-9A The following shareholders' equity accounts, arranged alphabetically, are in the ledger of Dublin Corporation at December 31, 2001

Common Shares (no par value, unlimited number of shares authorized, 500,000 shares issued)	$1,500,000
Preferred Shares ($8, no par value, noncumulative, 4,000 shares issued and authorized)	400,000
Retained Earnings	1,134,000

Instructions

Prepare the shareholders' equity section of the balance sheet at December 31, 2001.

Prepare a shareholders' equity section.
(SO 6)

P11-10A On December 31, 2000, Conway Company Ltd. had 1,500,000 no par value common shares issued and outstanding. The shareholders' equity accounts at December 31, 2000, had the balances listed here:

Common Shares	$16,500,000
Retained Earnings	900,000

Transactions during 2001 and other information related to shareholders' equity accounts were as follows:

1. On January 10, 2001, Conway issued, at $110 per share, 100,000 shares of no par value, $8, cumulative preferred stock.
2. On June 8, 2001, Conway declared a cash dividend of $1 per share on the common shares outstanding, payable on July 10, 2001, to shareholders of record on July 1, 2001.
3. On December 15, 2001, Conway declared the yearly cash dividend on the preferred shares, payable January 10, 2002, to shareholders of record on December 31, 2001.
4. Net earnings for the year were $3,600,000. At December 31, 2001, the market price of the common shares was $18 per share.

Instructions

Prepare the shareholders' equity section of Conway's balance sheet at December 31, 2001.

Prepare a shareholders' equity section.
(SO 6)

P11-11A On January 1, 2001, Cedeno Inc. had these shareholders' equity balances:

Common Shares (500,000 shares issued)	$1,000,000
Stock Dividends Distributable	100,000
Retained Earnings	600,000

During 2001, the following transactions and events occurred:
1. Issued 50,000 no par value common shares as a result of a 10% stock dividend declared on December 15, 2000.
2. Issued 30,000 common shares for cash at $5 per share.
3. Issued 400 common shares to a consultant who performed advisory services for Cedeno and was interested in owning some shares. The market value of the shares was $5 per share. The consultant felt her services were worth $1,800.
4. Declared and paid a cash dividend of $100,000.
5. Reported net earnings of $300,000.

Instructions

Prepare the shareholders' equity section of the balance sheet at December 31, 2001.

Prepare ratios related to shareholders' equity and comment.
(SO 7)

P11-12A The following selected information is available for the **Canadian National Railway Company** (CN):

(in millions, except for market price)	December 31, 1999	December 31, 1998
Weighted average number of common shares outstanding	197.3	183.1
Net earnings	$602	$109
Common cash dividends	$118	$99
Preferred cash dividends	$9	$0
Average common shareholders' equity	$4,898.5	$3,854
Market price per common share	$38.20	$39.875

Industry averages for selected ratios (where available) in 1999 are as follows:

Payout ratio	32.9%
Dividend yield	n/a
Earnings per share	$1.70
Price-earnings ratio	15.23
Return on common shareholders' equity	5.0%

Instructions

(a) Calculate the following ratios for CN for 1999 and 1998:
 1. Payout ratio
 2. Dividend yield
 3. Earnings per share
 4. Price-earnings ratio
 5. Return on common shareholders' equity

(b) Comment on the above ratios for 1999 in comparison to the prior year, 1998, and in comparison to the industry.

PROBLEMS: SET B

Journalize share transactions, post, and prepare share capital section.
(SO 2, 3, 6)

P11-1B Wetland Corporation was organized on January 1, 2001. It is authorized to issue 10,000, $8, no par value preferred shares and 500,000 no par value common shares. The following share transactions were completed during the first year:

Jan. 10	Issued 80,000 common shares for cash at $3 per share.
Mar. 1	Issued 5,000 preferred shares for cash at $104 per share.
May 1	Issued 80,000 common shares for cash at $4 per share.
Sept. 1	Issued 10,000 common shares for cash at $5 per share.
Nov. 1	Issued 1,000 preferred shares for cash at $108 per share.

Instructions
(a) Journalize the transactions.
(b) Post to the shareholders' equity accounts. (Use T accounts.)
(c) Prepare the share capital section of shareholders' equity at December 31, 2001.
(d) Explain why Wetland may have chosen to finance its operations by issuing share capital rather than debt.

Journalize transactions, post, and prepare a shareholders' equity section; calculate ratios.
(SO 2, 3, 4, 6, 7)

P11-2B The shareholders' equity accounts of Capozza Corporation on January 1, 2001, were as follows:

Preferred Shares ($12, no par value, cumulative, 10,000 shares authorized, 4,000 shares issued)	$ 400,000
Common Shares (no par value, 2,000,000 shares authorized, 480,000 shares issued)	2,400,000
Retained Earnings	1,816,000

During 2001, the corporation had these transactions and events pertaining to its shareholders' equity:

Feb. 1	Issued 20,000 common shares for $100,000.
Nov. 15	Declared a $12 cash dividend on preferred shares, payable December 15.
Dec. 1	Declared a $0.20 per share cash dividend to common shareholders of record on December 15, payable December 31, 2001.
31	Determined that net earnings for the year were $377,000. The market price of the common shares on this date was $9 per share.

Instructions
(a) Journalize the transactions.
(b) Enter the beginning balances in the accounts, and post the journal entries to the shareholders' equity accounts. (Use T accounts.)
(c) Prepare the shareholders' equity section of the balance sheet at December 31, 2001, including the disclosure of the preferred dividends in arrears.
(d) Calculate the dividend yield, payout ratio, earnings per share, price-earnings ratio, and return on common shareholders' equity ratio for the common shareholder.

Prepare entries for share transactions, and prepare a shareholders' equity section.
(SO 2, 3, 6)

P11-3B Cattrall Corporation has been authorized to issue 20,000, no par value, $10, noncumulative preferred shares and 1,000,000 no par value common shares. During the first year of operations, ended December 31, 2001, the following transactions occurred:

1. Issued 1,200 preferred shares for $144,000 cash.
2. Issued 200,000 common shares for $1,000,000 cash.
3. Issued 5,000 common shares in exchange for land. At the time of the exchange, the land was valued at $30,000 and the common shares at $25,000.
4. No dividends were declared.
5. Net earnings were $412,000.

Instructions
(a) Prepare journal entries to record the above transactions.
(b) Prepare the shareholders' equity section of the balance sheet at December 31, 2001.

Show the impact of equity transactions on the company and a shareholder.
(SO 2, 4, 5)

P11-4B Gull Lake Enterprises Inc. has 100,000 no par value common shares outstanding at July 1, 2001, the beginning of the current fiscal year. Mark Bradbury is the president and largest shareholder of Gull Lake Enterprises and owns 18% of the common shares. On July 1, the common shares were trading on the Canadian venture (CDNX) stock exchange for $25 per share. On July 1, 2001, Gull Lake Enterprises' retained earnings were $120,000 and the Common Share account had a balance of $2,000,000.

You are provided with the following information about selected events and transactions that occurred during the year:

1. On August 1, Mark issued a press release stating that the company was coming very close to striking a lucrative deal to supply products to two provinces. The company's share price immediately jumped by 6%.
2. On August 31, Gull Lake declared and issued a 4% stock dividend. The shares were trading at $28.00 per share on that day.
3. On November 1, 2001, Mark issued another press release concerning the imminent deal with the provinces. The company's shares were now trading at $32 per share.
4. On December 1, 2001 the company issued another 20,000 of its no par value common shares. This issue was needed in order to finance the new product development. Mark Bradbury acquired 3,600 of these shares in order to maintain his 18% interest in the shares of the company. The market value of the shares was $30 per share.
5. By March 31, 2002, investors were growing weary of waiting for the company to close the deal that Mark had discussed in the press releases. On that date, the company's shares were trading at $26 per share and the company effected a two-for-one stock split. After the stock split, each share was trading at $13.
6. By June 30, 2002, the products were still in development. The company's statement of earnings for the year showed considerable expenses related to product development; this contributed to the company's net loss for the fiscal year of $42,000. The share price at the close of business June 30, 2002, was $10.50.

Instructions

(a) Prepare a schedule illustrating the impact of each transaction on:
  1. The balance of retained earnings (deficit)
  2. The number of shares outstanding
  3. The number of shares held by Mark Bradbury
  4. The market value of Mark Bradbury's portfolio of common shares

(b) Comment on the change in retained earnings and the change in the market value of Mark Bradbury's portfolio during the 2002 fiscal year.

Answer questions about shareholders' equity section.
(SO 1, 4, 5)

P11-5B The shareholders' equity section of Moreau Corporation, after closing on December 31, 2001, presented the following information:

MOREAU CORPORATION
Balance Sheet (Partial)
December 31, 2001

Shareholders' equity		
Share capital		
$4 cumulative preferred shares, no par value, 100,000 shares authorized, ? shares issued		$3,125,000
Common shares, no par value, 500,000 shares authorized, 250,000 shares issued		1,000,000
Total share capital		4,125,000
Retained earnings		
January 1, 2001	$500,000	
Net earnings		175,000
Preferred dividends	(75,000)	600,000
Total shareholders' equity		$4,725,000

Instructions

(a) How many preferred shares were issued as at December 31, 2001? Preferred shares were outstanding the entire year.

(b) What was the average selling price of the preferred shares, expressed on a per share basis?

(c) What is the annual *total* preferred share dividend requirement, stated in dollars?
(d) Assuming that there were no dividends in arrears at the beginning of 2001, are there any dividends in arrears now at the end of 2001? If so, worth how much?
(e) In terms of the limited liability characteristic of a corporation, what is the dollar amount of the investment subject to liability (legal capital) for the preferred shareholders?

Reproduce retained earnings account, and prepare a shareholders' equity section.
(SO 4, 5, 6)

P11-6B The post-closing trial balance of Maggio Corporation at December 31, 2001, contains these shareholders' equity accounts:

Preferred Shares (15,000 shares issued)	$1,000,000
Common Shares (250,000 shares issued)	2,500,000
Common Stock Dividends Distributable	200,000
Retained Earnings	743,000

A review of the accounting records reveals this information:
1. Preferred shares are no par value, $10, cumulative shares. 15,000 shares have been outstanding since January 1, 2000.
2. Authorized share capital is 20,000 preferred shares and 500,000 common shares with no par value.
3. The January 1 balance in Retained Earnings was $920,000.
4. On July 1, 20,000 common shares were sold for cash at $16 per share.
5. A cash dividend of $250,000 was declared and allocated to preferred shares on October 1. No dividends were paid to preferred shareholders in 2000.
6. On December 31, an 8% common stock dividend was declared out of retained earnings when the market price per share was $16.
7. Net earnings for the year were $418,600.
8. On December 31, 2001, the directors authorized disclosure of a $200,000 restriction on retained earnings for plant expansion.

Instructions
(a) Reproduce the retained earnings account (T account) for the year.
(b) Prepare the shareholders' equity section of the balance sheet at December 31, including any required note disclosure.

Show the impact of transactions on various ratios.
(SO 2, 4, 5, 7)

P11-7B Investors sometimes pay close attention to ratios without questioning what caused the shareholders' equity ratios to change. You are provided with the following independent transactions for Talty Inc.

Transactions	**Payout ratio (30%)**	**Dividend yield (2%)**	**Earnings per share ($0.50)**	**Price-earnings ratio (10x)**	**Return on common shareholders' equity (5%)**
(a) Talty Inc. issued 1,000 no par value common shares for $25 per share.					
(b) Declared and paid $25,000 cash dividends to common shareholders.					
(c) The company reacquired and cancelled 4,000 no par value common shares, for $100,000 cash.					

Transactions	Payout ratio (30%)	Dividend yield (2%)	Earnings per share ($0.50)	Price-earnings ratio (10x)	Return on common shareholders' equity (5%)
(d) The company effected a one-for-three reverse stock split for common shareholders. The share rose by $^1/_3$.					
(e) The company issued a 5% stock dividend to all common shareholders.					

Instructions

Indicate whether the above transactions will increase (I), decrease (D), or not affect (NA) each of the ratios presented. Unless you are given specific information to the contrary, you are to assume that the transactions do not affect the market price of the shares.

Prepare dividend entries, prepare a shareholders' equity section, and calculate ratios.
(SO 4, 6, 7)

P11-8B On January 1, 2001, Stengel Corporation had these shareholders' equity accounts:

Common Shares (no par value, 75,000 shares authorized, 60,000 shares issued and outstanding)	$1,200,000
Retained Earnings	500,000

During the year, the following transactions occurred:

Feb. 1	Declared a $1 per share cash dividend to shareholders of record on February 15, payable March 1.
Mar. 1	Paid the dividend declared in February.
July 1	Declared a 5% stock dividend to shareholders of record on July 15, distributable July 31. On July 1, the market price was $40 per share.
31	Issued the shares for the stock dividend.
Dec. 1	Declared a $2 per share cash dividend to shareholders of record on December 15, payable January 5, 2002.
31	Determined that net earnings for the year were $325,000. The market price of the common shares on this date was $48.

Instructions

(a) Journalize the transactions.
(b) Enter the beginning balances and post the entries to the shareholders' equity T accounts. (Note: Open additional shareholders' equity accounts as needed.)
(c) Prepare the shareholders' equity section of the balance sheet at December 31.
(d) Calculate the dividend yield, payout ratio, earnings per share, price-earnings ratio, and return on common shareholders' equity ratio.

Prepare a shareholders' equity section.
(SO 6)

P11-9B The following shareholders' equity accounts, arranged alphabetically, are in the ledger of Denson Corporation at December 31, 2001:

Common Shares (no par value, 1,000,000 shares authorized, 500,000 shares issued)	$4,000,000
Preferred Shares ($8, no par value, noncumulative, 10,000 shares authorized, 4,000 shares issued)	800,000
Retained Earnings	1,958,000

Instructions

Prepare the shareholders' equity section of the balance sheet at December 31, 2001.

Prepare a shareholders' equity section.
(SO 6)

P11-10B On December 31, 2000, Schipper Company Ltd. had 1,000,000 no par value common shares issued and outstanding. The shareholders' equity accounts at December 31, 2000, had the balances listed here:

Common Shares	$1,000,000
Retained Earnings	700,000

Transactions during 2001 and other information related to shareholders' equity accounts were as follows:

1. On January 9, 2001, Schipper issued, at $6 per share, 100,000 $4.50, cumulative preferred shares of no par value.
2. On June 10, 2001, Schipper declared a cash dividend of $1 per share on the common shares outstanding, payable on July 10, 2001, to shareholders of record on July 1, 2001.
3. On December 15, 2001, Schipper declared the yearly cash dividend on the preferred shares, payable December 28, 2001, to shareholders of record on December 15, 2001.
4. Net earnings for the year are $2,400,000. At December 31, 2001, the market price of the common shares was $15 per share.

Instructions

Prepare the shareholders' equity section of Schipper's balance sheet at December 31, 2001.

Prepare a shareholders' equity section.
(SO 6)

P11-11B On January 1, 2001, Anthony Inc. had these shareholder equity balances:

Common Shares (500,000 no par value shares issued)	$1,500,000
Common Stock Dividends Distributable	100,000
Retained Earnings	600,000

During 2001, the following transactions and events occurred:

1. Issued 50,000 common shares for $100,000 as a result of a 10% stock dividend declared on December 15, 2000.
2. Issued 30,000 common shares for cash at $5 per share.
3. Paid a lawyer for services rendered with 500 common shares. At the time, the common shares were worth $5. The lawyer's bill was for $3,000.
4. Declared and paid a cash dividend of $100,000.
5. Reported net earnings of $300,000.

Instructions

Prepare the shareholders' equity section of the balance sheet at December 31, 2001.

Prepare ratios related to shareholders' equity and comment.
(SO 7)

P11-12B You are presented with the following selected information for **BCE Inc.** and **BCT.Telus Communications Inc.** All numbers except year-end closing price per common share are in millions:

BCE Inc. data	**1999**	**1998**
Cash dividends to preferred shareholders	$93.0	$93.0
Cash dividends to common shareholders	$875.0	$868.0
Net earnings	$5,459.0	$4,598.0
Average number of common shares outstanding	642.8	637.6
Year-end closing price per common share	$131.15	$57.85

BCT.Telus Communications Inc. data	**1999**	**1998**
Cash dividends to preferred shareholders	$3.5	$3.5
Cash dividends to common shareholders	$331.4	$306.0
Net earnings	$349.7	$66.9
Average number of common shares outstanding	236.6	237.0
Year-end closing price per common share	$35.15	n/a*

*On January 31, 1999, the operations of BC TELECOM Inc. and TELUS Corporation were merged to form BCT.TELUS Communications Inc. As such, a comparable share price for December 31, 1998, is not presented.

Instructions

(a) Prepare the following for BCE Inc. and BCT.TELUS Communications for 1999 and 1998 (where there is sufficient information available to do so):
 1. Payout ratio
 2. Cash dividend per common share
 3. Dividend yield
 4. Earnings per share
 5. Price-earnings ratio

(b) Compare and comment on the results obtained in (a).

BROADENING YOUR PERSPECTIVE

Financial Reporting and Analysis

FINANCIAL REPORTING PROBLEM: *Loblaw Companies Limited*

BYP11-1 The shareholders' equity section of **Loblaw**'s balance sheet is shown in the Consolidated Balance Sheet in Appendix A. You will also find data relative to this problem in the Notes to the Consolidated Financial Statements and in other pages of the appendix.

Instructions

Answer these questions:

(a) How many common shares has Loblaw authorized? How many common shares were issued and outstanding at the end of the 1999 and 1998 fiscal years?

(b) Does Loblaws have any preferred shares?

(c) What is the company's dividend policy, as described in the Shareholder Information section of the report?

(d) Calculate or find the dividend yield, payout ratio, earnings per share (reported in the Eleven Year Summary), price-earnings ratio (reported in the Eleven Year Summary), and return on average common equity (reported in the Eleven Year Summary) for 1999 and 1998. Loblaw's share price at the end of 1999 was $35.25, and it was $37.40 at the end of 1998.

COMPARATIVE ANALYSIS PROBLEM: *Loblaw and Sobeys*

BYP11-2 The financial statements of **Sobeys Inc.** are presented in Appendix B, following the financial statements for **Loblaw** in Appendix A.

Instructions

(a) Based on the information in these financial statements, calculate the 1999 return on common shareholders' equity ratio for each company. Determine the earnings per share (disclosed on the Statement of Earnings) and calculate the price-earnings ratio for each company for 1999. Loblaw's year-end share price was $35.25; Sobeys' was $18.80.

(b) What conclusions concerning the companies' profitability can be drawn from these ratios?

RESEARCH CASE

BYP11-3 The June 1999 issue of *Money* magazine includes an article by David Futrelle entitled "Stock Splits: How the Dumb Get Rich."

Instructions

Read the article and answer the following questions:

(a) What is a stock split?

(b) How do anxious traders and investors obtain timely information about stock splits?

(c) What are the statistics relative to market price reactions for shares of companies that have split their stocks?

(d) Is there a downside to buying the shares of companies that announce stock splits?

INTERPRETING FINANCIAL STATEMENTS

BYP11-4 In January 1995, Vancouver-based **Net Nanny Software International Inc.** introduced the first filtering software product of its kind. Today, Net Nanny develops and sells the world's most recognized Internet filtering and personal computer security products. Net

Nanny continues to be the preferred choice for parents, schools, and businesses that want flexible, editable software tools and free databases for protecting their families, their organizations and their digital data.

Net Nanny has 100,000,000 no par value common shares authorized. The following information about issued share capital is provided for Net Nanny for the years ended June 30, 1999, 1998, and 1997:

	1999		1998		1997	
	Shares	Amount	Shares	Amount	Shares	Amount
Balance, beginning of year	11,686,883	$5,975,679	7,819,794	$3,784,760	5,869,974	$2,865,178
Issued during year	821,115	278,772	3,867,089	2,190,919	2,587,320	919,582
Cancelled during year	—	—	—	—	(637,500)	—
Balance, end of year	12,507,998	$6,254,451	11,686,883	$5,975,679	7,819,794	$3,784,760

The following additional information is also available:

	1999	1998
Total debt (all current)	$ 145,957	$ 154,168
Total assets	709,710	1,549,686
Net loss	(1,089,966)	(757,395)
Loss per common share	(0.09)	(0.07)
Dividends	0	0
Average common shareholders' equity	979,635	804,121
Market price per share	0.93	0.90

Instructions

(a) In 2000, Net Nanny cancelled 637,500 shares. What are some of the reasons why management repurchases and cancels its own shares?

(b) Calculate the debt to total assets and return on common shareholders' equity ratios for 1999 and 1998.

(c) Net Nanny reported a loss in both 1999 and 1998. Yet its market price per share is positive, and increasing. Can you explain why investors might be willing to pay an increasing price for a Net Nanny share despite its apparent poor operating performance?

(d) Speculate as to why Net Nanny is financing its operations by issuing additional common shares, rather than long-term debt.

BYP11-5 Toronto-based **Club Monaco Inc.** is an international specialty retailer of women's, men's, and children's clothing. In 1998, after hitting a 52-week low share price of $3, the stock seemed to turn around and gain momentum, peaking at $16.50.

The following table reflects the changes during fiscal 1998 to the company's shares, which consist of an unlimited number of common shares:

	Number of Shares	Amount (in thousands)
Outstanding common shares at February 1, 1997	4,171,503	$10,339
Stock split (4,171,503 common shares to 4,493,882 common shares)	322,379	—
Common shares issued for cash	1,818,182	19,286
Common shares issued for a stock option plan	750	8
Outstanding common shares at January 31, 1998	6,312,814	$29,633

The company also announced that it intends to repurchase 400,000 common shares in the upcoming fiscal year. Other relevant information includes the following:

	January 31, 1998	February 1, 1997
Earnings per share	$ 0.60	$ 0.68
Market price per share	11.38	12.88

One year later, in March 1999, Polo Ralph Lauren Corporation made a takeover bid of $13 per share for Club Monaco's shares, and was subsequently successful.

Instructions

(a) Calculate the company's price-earnings ratio for 1998 and 1997.
(b) Why is there no amount recorded for the stock split?
(c) Explain why Club Monaco likely split its stock.
(d) Explain why Club Monaco was likely considering repurchasing some of its shares.
(e) Why was Club Monaco a good candidate for takeover?

A GLOBAL FOCUS

BYP11-6 Littlehampton, UK–based cosmetics retailer **The Body Shop International plc** sells skin and hair care products so natural they sound edible (e.g., Peppermint Foot Lotion, Banana Shampoo). The Body Shop operates nearly 1,700 stores in 47 countries. In 1999, the company underwent a massive restructuring, eliminating its manufacturing operations to focus on its retail operations.

The Body Shop has 240 million authorized ordinary (common) shares of 5 pence (about 11 cents) each which trade on the London Stock Exchange. It has no preferred shares. Additional information about its shares, and other relevant financial information, follows:

	(£ million, except share price)	
	February 27, 1999	February 28, 1998
Average number of common shares outstanding	192.5	194.4
Average common shareholders' equity	£122.3	£130.2
Dividends declared	£10.9	£10.8
Net earnings (loss)	£(4.6)	£22.8
Closing share price	£1.40	£0.88

Instructions

Calculate the payout ratio, dividend yield, earnings per share, price-earnings ratio, and return on common shareholders' equity for each year. Comment on The Body Shop's common share performance.

FINANCIAL ANALYSIS ON THE WEB

BYP11-7 Incorporated in 1978, the Toronto Stock Exchange (TSE) is the second largest stock exchange in North America and among the top ten in the world. The TSE is Canada's largest capital market, accounting for over 80% of the value of shares traded on Canadian exchanges. This case explores the features and services available on this website.

www.wiley.com/canada/kimmel

Instructions

Specific requirements of this web case can be found on the Kimmel website.

CRITICAL THINKING

COLLABORATIVE LEARNING ACTIVITY

BYP11-8 The shareholders' meeting for Mantle Corporation has been in progress for some time. The chief financial officer for Mantle is presently reviewing the company's financial statements and is explaining the items that make up the shareholders' equity section of the balance sheet for the current year. The shareholders' equity section for Mantle Corporation is presented here:

MANTLE CORPORATION
Balance Sheet (Partial)
December 31, 2001

Shareholders' equity	
Share capital	
Preferred shares, authorized 1,000,000 shares, cumulative, no par value, $8 per share, 6,000 shares issued and outstanding	$ 650,000
Common shares, authorized 5,000,000 shares, no par value, 3,000,000 shares issued and outstanding	28,000,000
Total share capital	28,650,000
Retained earnings	900,000
Total shareholders' equity	$29,550,000

A number of questions regarding the shareholders' equity section of Mantle Corporation's balance sheet have been raised at the meeting.

Instructions

With the class divided into groups, answer the following questions as if your group were the chief financial officer for Mantle Corporation:

(a) "What does the cumulative provision related to the preferred shares mean?"

(b) "I thought the common shares were presently selling at $29.75, and yet the company has an average share price of $9.33 ($28,000,000 ÷ 3,000,000). How can that be?"

(c) The CFO mentions that the company repurchased 300,000 common shares during 2001. "Why is the company buying back its common shares?"

COMMUNICATION ACTIVITY

BYP11-9 Louis P. Brady, your uncle, is an inventor who has decided to incorporate. Uncle Lou knows that you are an accounting major at U.N.O. In a recent e-mail to you, he ends with the question, "I'm filling out an incorporation application. Can you tell me the difference between the following terms: (1) authorized shares, (2) issued shares, (3) outstanding shares, (4) preferred shares, and (5) common shares?"

Instructions

In a brief e-mail, differentiate for Uncle Lou the four different share terms. Write the e-mail to be friendly, yet professional.

ETHICS CASES

BYP11-10 The R&D division of Simplex Chemical Corp. has just developed a chemical for sterilizing the voracious Asian long-horned beetles that are invading North America. The president of Simplex is anxious to get the chemical on the market because Simplex's profits need a boost—and his job is in jeopardy because of decreasing sales and profits. Simplex has an opportunity to sell this chemical in Mexico, where the laws are much more relaxed than in Canada and the United States.

The director of Simplex's R&D division strongly recommends further research in the laboratory to test the side effects of this chemical on other insects, birds, animals, plants, and even humans. He cautions the president, "We could be sued from all sides if the chemical has tragic side effects that we didn't even test for in the lab." The president answers, "We can't wait an additional year for your lab tests. We can avoid losses from such lawsuits by establishing a separate wholly owned corporation to shield Simplex Chemical Corp. from such lawsuits. We can't lose any more than our investment in the new corporation, and we'll invest just the patent covering this chemical. We'll reap the benefits if the chemical works and is safe, and avoid the losses from lawsuits if it's a disaster." The following week, Simplex creates a new wholly owned corporation called Zoebeetle Inc., sells the chemical patent to it for $10, and watches the spraying begin.

Instructions

(a) Who are the stakeholders in this situation?
(b) Are the president's motives and actions ethical?
(c) Can Simplex shield itself against losses of Zoebeetle Inc.?

BYP11-11 Flambeau Corporation has paid 60 consecutive quarterly cash dividends (15 years' worth). The last six months have been a real cash drain on the company, however, as profit margins have been greatly narrowed by increasing competition. With a cash balance sufficient to meet only day-to-day operating needs, the president, Vince Ramsey, has decided that a stock dividend instead of a cash dividend should be declared. He tells Flambeau's financial vice-president, Janice Rahn, to issue a press release stating that the company is extending its consecutive dividend record with the issuance of a 5% stock dividend. "Write the press release convincing the shareholders that the stock dividend is just as good as a cash dividend," he orders. "Just watch our share price rise when we announce the stock dividend; it must be a good thing if that happens."

Instructions

(a) Who are the stakeholders in this situation?
(b) Is there anything unethical about President Ramsey's intentions or actions?
(c) What is the effect of a stock dividend on a corporation's shareholders' equity accounts? Which would you rather receive as a shareholder—a cash dividend or a stock dividend? Why?

Answers to Self-Study Questions

1. a 2. b 3. c 4. b 5. d 6. a 7. d 8. b 9. a 10. b

Answer to Loblaw Review Question 3

Loblaw repurchased 630,200 of its common shares in 1999. It did not declare any stock splits, but it did declare a $61 million (22 cents per share) dividend to its common shareholders.

CHAPTER 12

Reporting and Analysing Investments

STUDY OBJECTIVES

After studying this chapter, you should be able to:

1. Identify the reasons corporations invest in debt and equity securities.
2. Explain the accounting for debt investments.
3. Explain the accounting for equity investments.
4. Describe the purpose and usefulness of consolidated financial statements.
5. Distinguish between short-term and long-term investments.
6. Indicate how debt and equity investments are valued and reported in the financial statements.

Buy or Be Bought

What did MCA Records, Universal Studios theme park, Deutsche Grammophon, the movie *Gladiator*, Curious George lunch boxes, *Jerry Springer*, Chivas Regal 12-year-old scotch, Grolsch beer, *The Mummy* home video, and Wild Kiwi Strawberry cooler have in common?

All were part of the portfolio of brands held, until recently, by The Seagram Company Ltd. Most Canadians associated this Montreal-based company with the liquor business. But in today's business climate, a large corporation can rarely afford to have its fingers in just one pie. In a rapidly changing world, you must change rapidly or suffer the consequences.

Clearly this is not an environment for the timid. And the investment philosophy of Seagram, headed by the near-legendary Bronfman family, was anything but timid over the years.

In 1916, Sam Bronfman started selling liquor by mail order—the only legal way during Canadian Prohibition. In 1928, Seagram went public, and when Prohibition ended in 1933, the company had the world's largest supply of aged rye and sour mash whiskeys. Its first big purchase was an Indiana distillery that same year; seven decades of careful investing later, Seagram was one of the world's largest distillers.

But it was also much more than that. As early as the 1950s, the Bronfman family had diversified, buying into everything from Israeli supermarkets to Texas gas fields. The majority of sales at Seagram in the 1990s, under the leadership of Sam's grandson Edgar Bronfman, Jr., were from its entertainment holdings. In 1995, Seagram acquired 80% of entertainment conglomerate MCA from Japan's Matsushita Electric for $5.7 billion, changing its name to Universal Studios. In addition to its well-known Hollywood studio, Universal operates music labels and theme parks, and has holdings in home video and television as well.

Universal became the world's largest music company following Seagram's 1998 purchase of PolyGram. At least they were until the Warner Music Group/EMI Group merger created an even larger music powerhouse in 2000. Seagram also plunged into

On the World Wide Web
The Seagram Company Ltd.
http://www.seagram.com
Vivendi SA
http://www.vivendi.com

the exploding digital music industry, combining with BMG Entertainment to form the Internet service GetMusic in 1999, and joining with America Online and MTV in early 2000 to launch an Internet-based record label, FarmClub.com.

Change requires investment. If you guess (and invest) wrong, you could lose out in a big way. (Who remembers eight-track tape decks?) But with the right decisions, you can win very big indeed. After first transforming Seagram from a liquor giant into an entertainment giant, the company realized that it lacked the clout to go head-to-head with competitors that were more than twice its size.

Later in 2000, Seagram sold to a stronger international entertainment heavyweight. In a three-way merger with the French conglomerate Vivendi SA and its entertainment arm, Canal+ SA, one of the world's leading media and communications giants was born. The Bronfman family has an 8% stake in the resulting entity, Vivendi Universal, which is expected to produce revenue of a staggering US$65 billion. Seagram is selling off its investment in the drinks business that gave it its start: Vivendi's primary interest is apparently in the music holdings, which it wants to sell via its multilingual Web portal, Vizzavi.com.

Vivendi's history is as colourful as Seagram's, and even longer—the company started as a French water utility in the mid-1800s. It is now well on its way to becoming a global communications empire, sending entertainment streaming through today's "pipelines": televisions, cell phones, computers, and handheld devices. How will a Canadian distiller fit into this picture? For the answer, as they used to say in the quaint medium of radio, stay tuned.

Seagram's and Vivendi's management believe in a policy of aggressive growth through investing in the equity securities (shares) of other companies. In addition to purchasing equity securities, companies also purchase other securities, such as debt securities issued by corporations or by governments. Investments can be purchased for a short or long period of time, and as a passive investment or with the intent to control another company. As you will see later in the chapter, the way in which a company accounts for its investments is determined by a number of factors.

The content and organization of this chapter are as follows:

REPORTING AND ANALYSING INVESTMENTS

Why Corporations Invest

Accounting for Debt Investments
- Recording Acquisition of Bonds
- Recording Bond Interest
- Recording Sale of Bonds

Accounting for Equity Investments
- Holdings of Less Than 20%
- Holdings of Between 20% and 50%
- Holdings of More Than 50%

Short- and Long-Term Investments
- Short-Term Investments
- Long-Term Investments

Valuation and Reporting of Investments
- Short-Term Investments
- Long-Term Investments
- Evaluating Investment Portfolio Performance
- Balance Sheet Presentation
- Statement of Earnings Presentation
- Complete Balance Sheet

WHY CORPORATIONS INVEST

STUDY OBJECTIVE 1

Identify the reasons corporations invest in debt and equity securities.

Corporations purchase investments in debt or equity securities generally for one of three reasons. First, a corporation may **have excess cash** that it does not need for the immediate purchase of operating assets. For example, many companies experience seasonal fluctuations in sales. A Vancouver marina has more sales in the spring and summer than in the fall and winter, whereas the reverse is true for a ski shop. Thus, at the end of an operating cycle, many companies may have cash on hand that is idle until the start of another operating cycle. Until the cash is needed, these companies may invest the excess funds to earn, through interest and dividends, a greater return than they would get by just holding the funds in the bank. The role played by such short-term investments in the operating cycle is shown in Illustration 12-1.

Illustration 12-1 Short-term investments and the operating cycle

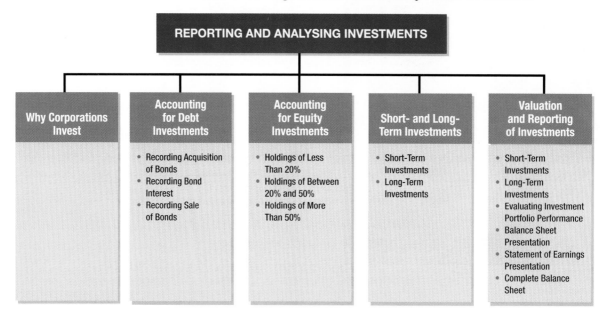

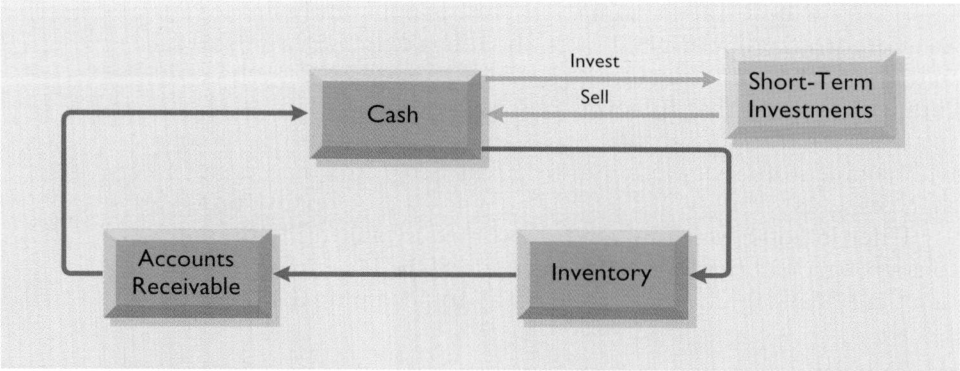

Excess cash may also result from economic cycles. For example, when the economy was booming, Seagram generated considerable excess cash. Although it used some of this cash to purchase new capital assets and paid out some of the cash in dividends, it also invested excess cash in liquid assets in anticipation of a future downturn in the economy. It could then liquidate these investments during a recession, when sales slow down and cash is scarce.

When investing excess cash for short periods of time, corporations invest in low-risk, highly liquid securities—most often short-term government securities. Generally, it is unwise to invest short-term excess cash in shares, because equity investments such as these can experience rapid price changes. If you do invest your short-term excess cash in shares and the price of the shares declines significantly just before you need the cash again, you will be forced to sell your investment at a loss.

A second reason some companies, such as banks, purchase investments is because they generate a **significant portion of their earnings from investment income**. Although banks make most of their earnings by lending money, they also generate earnings by investing in debt and equity securities. Banks purchase investment securities because loan demand varies both seasonally and with changes in the economic climate. Thus, when loan demand is low, a bank must find other uses for its cash. Investing in securities also allows banks to diversify some of their risk. As bank regulators severely limit the ability of banks to invest in shares, most bank investments are debt securities.

Pension funds and mutual funds are corporations that also regularly invest to generate earnings. They do so for *speculative reasons*; that is, they speculate that the investment will increase in value and thus result in positive returns. To attain this goal, they invest primarily in the common shares of other corporations. These investments are passive in nature, as the pension fund or mutual fund does not usually take an active role in controlling the affairs of the companies in which it invests.

A third reason why companies invest is for **strategic reasons**. A company may purchase a non-controlling interest in another firm in a related industry in which it wishes to establish a presence. For example, Universal purchased a significant interest in Port Aventura, a 2,000-acre theme park located south of Barcelona, Spain, drawing approximately 3 million visitors annually. Alternatively, a company can exercise some influence over one of its customers or suppliers by purchasing a significant, but not controlling, interest in that company.

A corporation may also choose to purchase a controlling interest in the common shares of another company. This might be done to enter a new industry without incurring the tremendous costs and risks associated with starting from scratch. Or a company might purchase another company in its industry as Vivendi did in acquiring Seagram's entertainment business. The purchase of a company that is in the industry, but involved in a different activity, is called a **vertical acquisition**. In a **horizontal acquisition**, the purchase is of a company that does the same activity as the purchasing company.

In summary, businesses invest in other companies for the reasons shown in Illustration 12-2.

Illustration 12-2 Why corporations invest

Reason	Typical Investment
To house excess cash until needed 	Low-risk, high-liquidity, short-term securities such as government-issued securities
To generate earnings 	Debt securities (money market instruments and bonds) and equity securities (preferred and common shares)
To meet strategic goals 	Common shares of companies in a related industry or an unrelated industry that the company wishes to enter

BUSINESS INSIGHT

Management Perspective

The number of strategic investments in the Canadian business community reached a record 600 acquisitions in 1999. Giant deals were commonplace in the late 1990s as mature companies found fewer opportunities for internal cost cutting. Reducing expenses rose near the top of the list of reasons to form large conglomerates. Alcan Aluminium Ltd., Pechiney SA, and the Alusuisse Lonze Group AG told investors that their mega-merger would allow them to cut US$600 million. "We will be eliminating overheads, we will be saving on the sales side because of overlapping of our sales organization, and there will be streamlining of our production facilities," Pechiney's CEO commented.

Other strategic investments included giant U.S. forestry company Weyerhaeuser's acquisition of B.C.'s MacMillan Bloedel, BAT's purchase of Montreal-based Imasco, and Toronto Dominion Bank's takeover of Canada Trust.

Source: Janet McFarland, "Mega-Mergers, Mega-Savings," *Globe and Mail*, August 14, 1999, B1.

ACCOUNTING FOR DEBT INVESTMENTS

STUDY OBJECTIVE 2
Explain the accounting for debt investments.

Debt investments include investments in money market instruments,[1] as well as investments in government and corporation bonds. In accounting for debt investments, entries are required to record (1) the acquisition, (2) the interest revenue, and (3) the sale. Although we will focus our attention in this section on entries for bonds, the entries for money market instruments are similar.

RECORDING ACQUISITION OF BONDS

At acquisition, the cost principle applies. Cost includes all expenditures made to acquire these investments, such as the price paid plus brokerage fees (commissions), if any. If, for example, Kuhl Corporation acquires 50 Doan Inc. 12%, 10-year, $1,000 bonds on January 1, 2001, for $54,000, including brokerage fees of $1,000, the entry to record the investment is

Jan. 1	Debt Investments—Doan Bonds	54,000	
	Cash		54,000
	(To record purchase of 50 Doan Inc. bonds)		

A	= L	+ SE
+54,000		
-54,000		

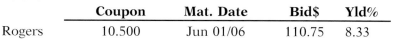

BUSINESS INSIGHT
Investor Perspective

Corporate bonds, like share capital, are traded on securities exchanges. They can be bought and sold at any time. Bond prices and trading activity are published daily in newspapers and the financial press, in the form shown below.

	Coupon	Mat. Date	Bid$	Yld%
Rogers	10.500	Jun 01/06	110.75	8.33

This information indicates that Rogers Communications Inc. has outstanding 10.5%, $1,000 bonds (default amount), maturing June 1, 2006. These bonds currently are yielding an 8.33% effective return, and investors are willing to pay 110.75% of face value, or $1,107.50 for each bond, on this particular day. Note that since the coupon rate is higher than the effective market rate, Rogers's bonds are trading at a premium.

RECORDING BOND INTEREST

Kuhl Corporation's investment in Doan bonds pays interest of $3,000 semi-annually on July 1 and January 1 ($50,000 × 12% × $\frac{6}{12}$). The entry for the receipt of interest on July 1 is

July 1	Cash	3,000	
	Interest Revenue		3,000
	(To record receipt of interest on Doan Inc. bonds)		

A	= L	+ SE
+3,000		+3,000

If Kuhl Corporation's fiscal year ends on December 31, it is necessary to accrue the interest of $3,000 earned since July 1. The adjusting entry is

[1]Money market instruments include (1) certificates of deposit issued by banks, (2) money market certificates issued by banks and savings and loan associations, (3) treasury bills issued by the government, and (4) commercial paper issued by corporations with good credit ratings.

A	=	L	+	SE
+3,000				+3,000

Dec. 31	Interest Receivable	3,000	
	Interest Revenue		3,000
	(To accrue interest on Doan Inc. bonds)		

Interest Receivable is reported as a current asset in the balance sheet; Interest Revenue is reported separately in the statement of earnings. When the interest is received on January 1, the entry is

A	=	L	+	SE
+3,000				
-3,000				

Jan. 1	Cash	3,000	
	Interest Receivable		3,000
	(To record receipt of accrued interest)		

A credit to the Interest Revenue account at this time is incorrect because the interest revenue was earned and accrued in the preceding accounting period.

RECORDING SALE OF BONDS

Helpful Hint The accounting for short-term debt investments and long-term debt investments is similar. Exceptions are discussed in more advanced courses.

When a bondholder sells bonds, it is necessary to decrease the investment account by the amount of the cost of the bonds. Any difference between the net proceeds from sale (sales price less brokerage fees) and the cost of the bonds is recorded as a gain or loss. Assume, for example, that Kuhl Corporation receives net proceeds of $58,000 on the sale of the Doan Inc. bonds on January 1, 2002, after receiving the interest due. Since the securities cost $54,000, a gain of $4,000 has been realized. The entry to record the sale is

A	=	L	+	SE
+58,000				+4,000
-54,000				

Jan. 1	Cash	58,000	
	Debt Investments—Doan Bonds		54,000
	Gain on Sale of Debt Investments		4,000
	(To record sale of Doan Inc. bonds)		

The gain on the sale of debt investments is reported separately in the statement of earnings, often as other revenues and gains.

BEFORE YOU GO ON . . .

Review It

1. What are the reasons corporations invest in debt and equity securities?
2. What entries are required in accounting for debt investments?

Do It

Waldo Corporation had these transactions pertaining to debt investments:

Jan. 1	Purchased 30 $1,000, 10% Hillary Co. bonds for $30,000 plus brokerage fees of $900. Interest is payable semi-annually on July 1 and January 1.
July 1	Received semi-annual interest on Hillary Co. bonds.
July 1	Sold 15 Hillary Co. bonds for $15,000, less $400 brokerage fees.

(a) Journalize the transactions.
(b) Prepare the adjusting entry for the accrual of interest on December 31.

Reasoning: Bond investments are recorded at cost by the investor, Waldo. Interest is recorded when received, accrued, or both. When bonds are sold, the investment account is credited for the cost of the bonds. Any difference between the cost and the net proceeds is recorded as a gain or loss.

Solution:

(a)

Date	Account	Debit	Credit
Jan. 1	Debt Investments—Hillary Bonds	30,900	
	Cash ($30,000 + $900)		30,900
	(To record purchase of 30 Hillary Co. bonds)		
July 1	Cash	1,500	
	Interest Revenue ($\$30,000 \times 0.10 \times \frac{6}{12}$)		1,500
	(To record receipt of interest on Hillary Co. bonds)		
July 1	Cash ($15,000 – $400)	14,600	
	Loss on Sale of Debt Investments	850	
	Debt Investments—Hillary Bonds ($\$30,900 \times \frac{15}{30}$)		15,450
	(To record sale of 15 Hillary Co. bonds)		

(b)

Date	Account	Debit	Credit
Dec. 31	Interest Receivable	750	
	Interest Revenue ($\$15,000 \times 0.10 \times \frac{6}{12}$)		750
	(To accrue interest on Hillary Co. bonds)		

Accounting for Equity Investments

STUDY OBJECTIVE 3

Explain the accounting for equity investments.

Equity investments are investments in the share capital—common and/or preferred—of corporations. When a company holds shares and/or debt of several different corporations, the group of securities is identified as an **investment portfolio**. The accounting for investments in common shares is based on the extent of the investor's influence over the operating and financial affairs of the issuing corporation (the **investee**) as shown in Illustration 12-3.

Illustration 12-3
Accounting guidelines for equity investments

	Investor's Ownership Interest in Investee's Common Shares	Presumed Influence on Investee	Accounting Guidelines
	Less than 20%	Insignificant	Cost method
	Between 20% and 50%	Significant	Equity method
	More than 50%	Controlling	Equity method for accounting; consolidated financial statements for reporting

In some cases, depending on the degree of investor influence, net earnings of the investee are considered to be earnings to the investor. The presumed influence may be negated by extenuating circumstances. For example, a company that acquires a 25% interest in another company in a "hostile" takeover may not have any significant influence over the investee.[2] In other words, companies are required to use judgment instead of blindly following the guidelines. We explain and illustrate the application of each guideline next.

HOLDINGS OF LESS THAN 20%

In accounting for equity investments of less than 20%, the cost method is used. Under the **cost method**, the investment is recorded at cost, and revenue is only recognized when cash dividends are received.

Recording Acquisition of Shares

At acquisition, the cost principle applies. Cost includes all expenditures made to acquire these investments, such as the price paid plus brokerage fees (commissions), if any. Assume, for example, that on July 1, 2001, Passera Corporation (the investor) acquires 1,000 common shares (10% ownership) of Beal Corporation (the investee) at $40 per share plus brokerage fees of $500. The entry for the purchase is

A	= L	+ SE
+40,500		
-40,500		

July 1	Equity Investments—Beal Common	40,500	
	Cash		40,500
	(To record purchase of 1,000 common shares of Beal)		

Recording Dividends

During the time the shares are held, entries are required for any cash dividends received. Thus, if a $2.00 per share dividend is received by Passera Corporation on December 31, the entry is

A	= L	+ SE
+2,000		+2,000

Dec. 31	Cash (1,000 × $2)	2,000	
	Dividend Revenue		2,000
	(To record receipt of a cash dividend)		

Dividend Revenue is reported separately in the statement of earnings, often as other revenues and gains.

Recording Sale of Shares

When shares are sold, the difference between the net proceeds from the sale (sales price less brokerage fees) and the cost of the shares is recognized as a gain or a loss. Assume, for instance, that Passera Corporation receives net proceeds of $39,500 on the sale of its Beal Corporation shares on February 10, 2002. Because the shares cost $40,500, there has been a loss of $1,000. The entry to record the sale is

A	= L	+ SE
+39,500		-1,000
-40,500		

Feb. 10	Cash	39,500	
	Loss on Sale of Equity Investments	1,000	
	Equity Investments—Beal Common		40,500
	(To record sale of Beal common shares)		

The loss is reported separately in the statement of earnings, often under other expenses and losses, whereas a gain on sale is shown as other revenues and gains.

[2]Among the factors that should be considered in determining an investor's influence are whether (1) the investor has representation on the investee's board of directors, (2) the investor participates in the investee's policy-making process, (3) there are material transactions between the investor and the investee, and (4) the common shares held by other shareholders are concentrated or dispersed.

HOLDINGS OF BETWEEN 20% AND 50%

When an investor company owns only a small portion of the common shares of another company (the investee), the investor cannot exercise control over the company. When an investor owns more than 20% of the common shares of a corporation, it is generally presumed that the investor has **significant influence** over the financial and operating activities of the investee. The investor probably has a representative on the investee's board of directors. With a representative on the board, the investor begins to exercise some control over the investee—and the timing of the distribution of earnings.

Helpful Hint Remember that common shareholders have the right to vote. They are often called the "owners" of the corporation.

Seagram had a 45% equity interest in USA Networks, Inc., the fourth largest cable group in the United States. Because it exercised significant control over major decisions made by USA Networks, Seagram used an approach called the equity method. Under the equity method, **the investor records its share of the net earnings of the investee in the year when it is earned**. To delay recognizing the investor's share of net earnings until a cash dividend is declared ignores the fact that the investor and investee are, in some sense, one company.

Under the **equity method**, the investment in common shares is initially recorded at cost, and the appropriate investment account is **adjusted annually** to show the investor's equity in the investee. Each year, the investor (1) increases (debits) the investment account and increases (credits) revenue for its share of the investee's net earnings[3]; and (2) decreases (credits) the investment account for the amount of dividends received. The investment account is reduced for dividends received because the net assets of the investee are decreased when a dividend is paid.

Recording Acquisition of Shares

Assume that Milar Corporation (the investor) acquires 30% of the common shares of Beck Company (the investee) for $120,000 on January 1, 2001. The entry to record this transaction is

Jan. 1	Equity Investments—Beck Common	120,000	
	Cash		120,000
	(To record purchase of Beck common shares)		

A	=	L	+	SE
+120,000				
-120,000				

Recording Revenue and Dividends

For 2001, Beck reports net earnings of $100,000 and declares and pays a $40,000 cash dividend. Milar is required to record (1) its share of Beck's earnings, $30,000 (30% × $100,000), and (2) the reduction in the investment account for the dividends received, $12,000 ($40,000 × 30%). The entries are

	(1)		
Dec. 31	Equity Investments—Beck Common	30,000	
	Revenue from Investment in Beck Company		30,000
	(To record 30% equity in Beck's 2001 net earnings)		

A	=	L	+	SE
+30,000				+30,000

	(2)		
Dec. 31	Cash	12,000	
	Equity Investments—Beck Common		12,000
	(To record dividends received)		

A	=	L	+	SE
+12,000				
-12,000				

[3]Conversely, the investor increases (debits) a loss account and decreases (credits) the investment account for its share of the investee's net loss.

After the transactions for the year are posted, the investment and revenue accounts are as shown in Illustration 12-4.

Illustration 12-4
Investment and revenue accounts after posting

Equity Investments—Beck Common			
Jan. 1	120,000	Dec. 31	**12,000**
Dec. 31	**30,000**		
Dec. 31 Bal.	138,000		

Revenue from Investment in Beck Company			
		Dec. 31	**30,000**

During the year, the investment account has increased by $18,000 ($138,000 – $120,000). This $18,000 is Milar's 30% equity in the $60,000 increase in Beck's retained earnings ($100,000 – $40,000). In addition, Milar reports $30,000 of revenue from its investment, which is 30% of Beck's net earnings of $100,000. Note that the difference between reported earnings under the cost method and reported earnings under the equity method can be significant. For example, Milar would report only $12,000 of dividend revenue (30% × $40,000) if the cost method were used.

HOLDINGS OF MORE THAN 50%

STUDY OBJECTIVE 4
Describe the purpose and usefulness of consolidated financial statements.

A company that owns more than 50% of the common shares of another entity is known as the **parent company**. The entity whose shares are owned by the parent company is called the **subsidiary (affiliated) company**. Because of its share ownership, the parent company has a **controlling interest** in the subsidiary company. Voting control can also occur with share ownership of less than 50%, depending on how widely dispersed the share ownership is, and other factors mentioned previously.

When a company controls another company, **consolidated financial statements** are usually prepared. Consolidated financial statements present the assets and liabilities controlled by the parent company and the collective profitability of the subsidiary companies. They are prepared **in addition to** the financial statements for each of the individual parent and subsidiary companies. For example, Vivendi purchased the remaining 51% of its entertainment arm, Canal+, that it didn't already own at the same time it acquired Seagram. It uses the equity method to account for its investments in each of Canal+ and Seagram on its own individual statements. But, for external reporting, Vivendi Universal would consolidate Canal+'s and Seagram's results with its own. Under this approach, the individual assets and liabilities of Canal+ and Seagram would be included with those of Vivendi.

Helpful Hint From the viewpoint of the shareholders of the parent company, if the parent (A) has three wholly owned subsidiaries (B, C, and D), there are four separate legal entities but only one economic entity.

Consolidated statements are especially useful to the shareholders, board of directors, and management of the parent company. Moreover, consolidated statements inform creditors, prospective investors, and regulatory agencies as to the magnitude and scope of operations of the companies under common control. For example, regulators and the courts used the consolidated statements of Microsoft to determine that a breakup of Microsoft was in the public interest. Listed here are three companies that prepare consolidated statements and some of the companies they own.

Hudson's Bay Co.	Canadian Pacific Ltd.	Cara Operations Limited
Zellers Inc.	Canadian Pacific Hotels & Resorts Inc.	Swiss Chalet / Harvey's
Kmart Canada Co.	Canadian Pacific Railway Co.	The Second Cup Ltd.
	CP Ships Inc.	Kelsey's International Inc.
	Fairmont Hotels & Resorts Inc.	The Spectra Group of Great Restaurants Inc.
	Delta Hotels Ltd.	Beaver Foods Limited
	PanCanadian Petroleum Ltd.	Summit Food Service Distributors Inc.

Consolidation is a complex topic which is usually dealt with in advanced accounting courses.

BUSINESS INSIGHT

International Perspective

Paris-based Vivendi has nearly 50 subsidiary companies and affiliates. Some of its more significant acquisitions include Seagram (owner of Universal Music Group and Universal Studios), French pay-TV provider Canal+, telecom provider Cegetel, Internet provider AOL France, and media giant Havas. In addition to using these companies to provide telecommunications, Internet, and media services, Vivendi also provides water and wastewater services to 80 million customers worldwide. It became the largest water company in the world when it bought USFilter, the largest water company in the U.S., and expanded its environmental services portfolio with the acquisition of U.S. waste management company Superior Services.

BEFORE YOU GO ON . . .

Review It

1. What are the accounting entries for investments in common shares with ownership of less than 20%?
2. What entries are made under the equity method when (a) the investor receives a cash dividend from the investee and (b) the investee reports net earnings for the year?
3. What is the purpose of consolidated financial statements?

Do It

These are two independent situations:

1. Rho Jean Inc. acquired 5% of the 400,000 common shares of Stillwater Corp. at a total cost of $6 per share on May 18, 2001. On August 30, Stillwater declared and paid a $75,000 dividend. On December 31, Stillwater reported net earnings of $244,000 for the year.
2. Debbie, Inc., obtained significant influence over North Sails by buying 40% of North Sails's 60,000 outstanding common shares at a cost of $12 per share on January 1, 2001. On April 15, North Sails declared and paid a cash dividend of $45,000. On December 31, North Sails reported net earnings of $120,000 for the year.

Prepare all necessary journal entries for 2001 for (a) Rho Jean Inc. and (b) Debbie, Inc.

Reasoning: When an investor owns less than 20% of the common shares of another corporation, it is presumed that the investor has relatively little influence over the investee. As a result, the investee's net earnings are not considered a proper basis for recognizing earnings from the investor's investment. For investments of more than 20%, significant influence is presumed, and the investor's share of the net earnings of the investee should therefore be recorded. Note that even if the cost method is used, the account Equity Investments is still used to indicate that these are investments in equity securities, rather than debt securities.

Solution:

(a) Cost Method

Date	Account Titles and Explanation	Debit	Credit
May 18	Equity Investments (20,000 × $6)— Stillwater Common	120,000	
	Cash		120,000
	(To record purchase of 20,000 [5% × 400,000] Stillwater shares)		
Aug. 30	Cash	3,750	
	Dividend Revenue ($75,000 × 5%)		3,750
	(To record receipt of cash dividend)		

(b) Equity Method

Date	Account Titles and Explanation	Debit	Credit
Jan. 1	Equity Investments—North Sails Common (24,000 × $12)	288,000	
	Cash		288,000
	(To record purchase of 24,000 [40% × 60,000] North Sails shares)		
Apr. 15	Cash	18,000	
	Equity Investments—North Sails Common ($45,000 × 40%)		18,000
	(To record receipt of cash dividend)		
Dec. 31	Equity Investments—North Sails Common ($120,000 × 40%)	48,000	
	Revenue from Investment		48,000
	(To record 40% equity in North Sails's net earnings)		

STUDY OBJECTIVE 5

Distinguish between short-term and long-term investments.

Short- and Long-Term Investments

In addition to being classified as debt or equity investments, investments are also categorized as short-term or long-term investments.

SHORT-TERM INVESTMENTS

Alternate Terminology *Short-term investments* are also called *marketable securities* or *temporary investments.*

Short-term investments ordinarily consist of money market instruments, debt securities (government and corporate bonds), and equity securities (preferred and common shares). However, in order to be classified as a short-term investment, these investments must be (1) **readily marketable** and (2) **intended to be converted into cash** within the next year or operating cycle, whichever is longer. Investments that do not meet **both criteria** are classified as **long-term investments**.

Readily Marketable

An investment is "readily marketable" if it can be easily sold whenever the need for cash arises. Money market instruments meet this criterion, as they can be sold readily to other investors. Shares and bonds traded on organized securities markets, such as the Toronto Stock Exchange, are readily marketable because they can be bought and sold daily. In contrast, there may be only a limited market for the securities issued by small corporations and no market for the securities of a privately held company.

Intent to Convert

"Intent to convert" means that management intends to sell the investment within the next year or operating cycle, whichever is longer. Generally, this criterion is satisfied if the investment is considered a resource to be used whenever the need for cash arises. For example, a ski resort may invest idle cash during the summer months and intend to sell the securities to buy supplies and equipment shortly before the next winter season. This investment is considered temporary even if lack of snow cancels the next ski season and eliminates the need to convert the securities into cash as intended.

LONG-TERM INVESTMENTS

Long-term investments can also consist of debt securities (government and corporate bonds) and equity securities (preferred and common shares), among other items. To determine whether a debt or equity security is short-term or long-term, we test the investment against the short-term investment criteria. Investments that do not meet *both* short-term investment criteria—readily marketable and intent to convert—are **long-term investments**.

Valuation and Reporting of Investments

STUDY OBJECTIVE 6

Indicate how debt and equity investments are valued and reported in the financial statements.

The value of debt and equity investments may fluctuate greatly during the time they are held. The Scotia Capital Markets Universe Bond Index and the Toronto Stock Exchange (TSE) 300 Composite Index are examples of two indices which track the volatile nature of debt and share prices. These indices, based on Canadian bond and share prices, may drop drastically with unfavourable economic developments and may jump dramatically with favourable economic events. In light of such price fluctuations, how should investments be valued at the balance sheet date?

Valuation could be at cost, at market value, or at the lower of cost and market value. **Fair market value** is the amount for which a security could be sold in a normal market. However, many believe that, unless a security is going to be sold soon, the fair market value is not relevant because the price of the security will likely change again. **Conservatism** resolves this issue by requiring the application of the **lower of cost and market (LCM)** rule.

International Note

The oldest and most widely quoted stock market index in the U.S. is the Dow Jones. In Britain, it is the FT-SE; in Germany, the DAX; and in Japan, the Nikkei.

You were first introduced to the lower of cost and market rule in Chapter 9, with respect to inventories. Just as inventories have a relevant market value, so too do investments. If the market value of the investments falls below their cost, this potential loss should be recognized at the earliest possible time to minimize any negative impact on decision-makers. Application of the LCM rules varies depending upon whether the investment is short-term or long-term.

SHORT-TERM INVESTMENTS

To illustrate the valuation of short-term debt and equity investments, assume that on December 31, 2001, Plano Corporation has the following costs and market values:

Investments	Cost	Market Value	LCM Value
Bell Canada bonds	$ 50,000	$ 48,000	($2,000)
Nexfor shares	90,000	91,000	1,000
Total	$140,000	$139,000	($1,000)

The LCM rule is normally applied to the total portfolio and not to individual investments. Applying LCM individually results in an overly conservative valuation with what is already a conservative rule. Remember that while conservatism allows losses to be recognized in advance of realization, gains are not.

A	=	L	+	SE
-1,000				-1,000

Dec. 31	Loss on Decline in Value of Investment	1,000	
	Allowance to Reduce Cost to Market Value		1,000
	(To record loss in value on short-term investments)		

The decline in value from cost to market is reported as a loss on the statement of earnings (usually in the other expenses and losses section) because of the likelihood that the securities will be sold at market value since they are a short-term investment. A valuation allowance account, Allowance to Reduce Cost to Market Value, is used to record the difference between the cost and market value of the securities. The use of this **contra asset** account, Allowance to Reduce Cost to Market Value, enables the company to maintain a record of the investment cost. Actual cost is needed to determine the gain or loss realized when the securities are sold. The allowance account balance is deducted from the cost of the investments to arrive at the lower of cost and market valuation reported on the balance sheet for the short-term investments.

The allowance account is carried forward into future accounting periods, in a manner similar to the Allowance for Doubtful Accounts, which offsets Accounts Receivable. No entries are made to the Allowance to Reduce Cost to Market Value account during the period. At the end of each reporting period, the balance in the account is adjusted to the difference between cost and market value. If the market value recovers above the cost, the allowance account can be adjusted to a zero balance. The valuation allowance should never have a debit balance; this would result in the recognition of an unrealized gain.

LONG-TERM INVESTMENTS

Helpful Hint Note that while an allowance is used to record declines in market value below cost in the *total portfolio of short-term* investments, *individual long-term* investments are directly written down (but only if the decline is permanent).

Because long-term investments have longer maturities than short-term investments, **their carrying values should not be adjusted to reflect short-term fluctuations in market values.** If cost exceeds market and the decline is considered permanent, the investment must be reduced to its market value. This value becomes the investment's new cost base. Any write-down to market value is directly credited to the investment account, as no subsequent recovery in value is anticipated.

To illustrate, assume that Hébert Corporation purchased 10,000 shares of Bre-X Minerals Ltd. at a cost of $20 per share, as a long-term investment. These shares are now worthless. The adjusting entry for Hébert to record the realized loss of $200,000 is as follows:

Dec. 31	Loss on Decline in Value of Investment
	  Equity Investment—Bre-X Minerals Shares
	    (To record loss in value on
	    long-term investment in Bre-X shares)
		200,000	200,000	A = L + SE
				-200,000 -200,000

EVALUATING INVESTMENT PORTFOLIO PERFORMANCE

The potential for manipulation in valuing and reporting investments is readily apparent. Companies can easily "window dress" their reported earnings results—that is, make net earnings look better or worse than they really are. Refer back to the values of Plano Corporation's short-term investments. Assume Plano has a large net earnings amount this year and wants to minimize demands from shareholders for more dividends, or from employees for increased wages. It could simply choose to sell those investments that have losses (Bell Canada bonds) before the year end. This would have the effect of reducing earnings by \$2,000, compared to the \$1,000 LCM loss that would be recorded if Plano retained all of its investments.

Another way that earnings manipulation can occur is by altering a company's classification of investments as short-term or long-term. That is, if the investment portfolio contains some investments whose market value is greater than cost, and some whose market value is less than cost, classifying them as short-term allows increases to be offset against decreases, as only the net cost and net market values are taken into consideration when applying the LCM rule. One can see that companies could have an incentive to classify their investments as short-term rather than long-term depending on the investment's performance.

Alternatively, if the investments are classified as long-term, companies can potentially defer recognition of losses by simply assuming that the criterion of a permanent decline is not met. Clearly, it is important to consider the impact of the timing of actual and potential losses on current and future earnings when evaluating the performance of a company's investment portfolio.

DECISION TOOLKIT

Decision Checkpoints	Info Needed for Decision	Tool to Use for Decision	How to Evaluate Results
Is the company window dressing its results by manipulating its investment portfolio?	Balance of gains and losses; classification of investments	A company can window dress by selling winners and holding losers to increase reported earnings, or do the opposite to reduce reported earnings. Misclassification of investments as short-term or long-term allows companies to "time" (advance or defer) the recognition of losses.	Window dressing and misclassification are not easy to spot: it is difficult for an outsider to determine why companies choose to sell or hold a security, or classify it as they do. A user should evaluate a company's earnings as reported, including any gains and losses, to see total potential variation.

BEFORE YOU GO ON . . .

Review It

1. What are the proper valuation and reporting for short-term and long-term investments?
2. How might a company window dress its reported earnings?

BALANCE SHEET PRESENTATION OF INVESTMENTS

For balance sheet presentation, investments must be classified as either short-term or long-term.

Short-Term Investments

Because of their high liquidity, short-term investments are listed immediately below cash in the current asset section of the balance sheet or are directly combined with cash. Short-term investments are reported on the balance sheet at the lower of cost and market value. Because of the importance of market value to the reader of the financial statements, the market value is also disclosed, either in parentheses or in a note.

Long-Term Investments

Long-term investments are generally reported in a separate section of the balance sheet immediately below Current Assets.

Seagram's short- and long-term investments are reported as shown in the following extract from its balance sheet, before its merger with Vivendi:

Illustration 12-5
Presentation of investments

THE SEAGRAM COMPANY LTD.
Balance Sheet (Partial)
Fiscal Years Ended June 30
(U.S. dollars in millions)

	1999	1998
ASSETS		
Cash and cash equivalents	$1,533	$1,174
Receivables, net of allowance	2,985	2,155
Inventories	2,627	2,555
Other current assets	1,736	1,087
Total current assets	8,881	6,971
Investments	5,663	4,971

Seagram called its short-term investments "cash equivalents" and discloses in its notes that these include time deposits and highly liquid investments with original maturities of three months or less. In its note about its long-term investments, Seagram disclosed which of the company's investments were accounted for using the equity method and which were accounted for using the cost method.

STATEMENT OF EARNINGS PRESENTATION

Gains and losses on investments must be presented in the financial statements. In the statement of earnings, gains and losses, as well as interest and dividend revenue, are reported in the non-operating section, normally under the categories listed in Illustration 12-6.

Illustration 12-6
Non-operating items related to investments

Other Revenue and Gains	Other Expenses and Losses
Interest Revenue	Loss on Sale of Investments
Dividend Revenue	Loss on Decline in Value of Investment
Gain on Sale of Investments	

COMPLETE BALANCE SHEET

Many sections of classified balance sheets have been presented in this and preceding chapters. The balance sheet in Illustration 12-7 (on the next page) includes such topics from previous chapters as the issuance of common shares, restrictions on retained earnings, and issuance of long-term bonds. From this chapter, the statement includes (highlighted in red) short-term and long-term investments. Illustration 12-7 also includes a long-term investment reported at equity, descriptive notations within the statement, such as the basis for valuing merchandise, and two notes to the statement.

Illustration 12-7
Balance sheet

PACE CORPORATION
Balance Sheet
December 31, 2001

Assets			
Current assets			
Cash			$ 21,000
Short-term investments, at lower of cost and market (market $75,000)			**60,000**
Accounts receivable		$ 84,000	
Less: Allowance for doubtful accounts		4,000	80,000
Merchandise inventory, at FIFO cost			130,000
Prepaid insurance			23,000
Total current assets			314,000
Investments			
Equity investments in shares of less than 20% owned companies, at cost		**$150,000**	
Equity investment in shares of greater than 20% owned companies, at equity		**150,000**	
Total investments			300,000
Capital assets (Note 1)			
Land		$ 200,000	
Buildings	$800,000		
Less: Accumulated amortization	200,000	600,000	
Equipment	$180,000		
Less: Accumulated amortization	54,000	126,000	
Goodwill		170,000	
Total capital assets			1,096,000
Total assets			$1,710,000
Liabilities and Shareholders' Equity			
Current liabilities			
Accounts payable			$ 185,000
Bond interest payable			10,000
Income taxes payable			60,000
Total current liabilities			255,000
Long-term liabilities			
Bonds payable, 10%, due 2010		$ 300,000	
Less: Discount on bonds		10,000	
Total long-term liabilities			290,000
Total liabilities			545,000
Shareholders' equity			
Share capital			
Common shares, no par value, 200,000 shares authorized, 80,000 shares issued and outstanding		$ 900,000	
Retained earnings (Note 2)		265,000	
Total shareholders' equity			1,165,000
Total liabilities and shareholders' equity			$1,710,000

Note 1. Buildings and goodwill are amortized by the straight-line method over 40 years. Equipment is amortized using the declining balance method, at a 20% rate.
Note 2. Retained earnings of $100,000 is restricted for plant expansion.

BEFORE YOU GO ON . . .

Review It

1. Explain where short- and long-term investments are reported on a balance sheet.
2. Where are gains and losses from securities reported?
3. What do Loblaw's short-term investments consist of? Are they carried at cost, market, or LCM? Does Loblaw have any long-term investments? The answers to these questions are provided at the end of this chapter

Loblaws
A passion for food... *and a lot more!*

USING THE DECISION TOOLKIT

The Royal Bank provides financial services throughout Canada as well as in 35 other countries. It is Canada's largest money manager and owns the largest and most profitable investment dealer, RBC Dominion Securities. The Bank manages a loan portfolio in excess of $165 billion. In addition to a loan portfolio, the bank also has significant debt and equity investments. The nature of these investments varies from short-term to long-term. The following selected facts are from the Royal Bank's 1998 annual report.

ROYAL BANK OF CANADA
Consolidated Balance Sheet (Partial)
As at October 31
(in millions of dollars)

Assets	1998	1997
Short-term deposits with other banks	$ 15,113	$ 20,316
Securities	41,399	33,037
Loans	165,254	156,267

Other relevant information includes the following:

1. The maturity dates of the bank's securities range from under one year to over 10 years.
2. Within the bank's securities, there are investment account securities, trading account securities, and other types of securities. Investment account securities are purchased with the original intention to hold the securities to maturity, or until market conditions render alternative investments more attractive. The carrying value of the investment account securities was $12,093 million at the end of fiscal 1998; their estimated market value, $12,199 million. Trading account securities are purchased for resale over a short period of time. These securities are stated at estimated current market value.
3. The bank uses the equity method "to account for investments in associated corporations, which are corporations in which the bank holds at least a 20% interest but does not exercise control."
4. Its consolidated financial statements include the assets and liabilities and the results of operations of all subsidiaries.

Instructions

1. Why do you suppose the Royal Bank purchases investments rather than only make loans? Why does it purchase investments that vary in terms of both their maturities and their type (debt versus equity)?

2. Why do you think the Royal Bank would keep short-term deposits with other banks?
3. At what value should the bank report its investment account securities? Its trading account securities?
4. The bank uses the equity method to account for certain investments. Explain the impact the use of this method has on the recognition of earnings for the bank.
5. At the end of fiscal 1998, Royal Bank owns 100% of the voting shares of all of its subsidiaries except two. It owns 80% of RBC Dominion Securities Limited and 75% of the Finance Corporation of Bahamas Limited. Should the bank include the accounts of RBC Dominion and the Finance Corporation in its consolidated financial statements? Explain why or why not.

Solution

1. Although banks are primarily in the business of lending money, they also need to balance their portfolio by investing in other assets. For example, a bank may have excess cash that it has not yet loaned, which it wants to invest in very short-term liquid assets. Or, it may purchase investments for short-term speculation, because it believes these investments will appreciate in value. Banks also attempt to match their investments to produce cash inflows in accordance with the likely cash outflows needed for loans, debt repayments, and the like.
2. The Royal Bank keeps short-term deposits with other banks, such as the Bank of Canada, to ensure liquidity. In fact, the *Bank Act* requires maintenance of a certain margin of short-term deposits in case of a run on cash, such as was the case with the Y2K fears on December 31, 1999.
3. The bank should report its investment account securities at cost, which in this case is $12,093 million. Because these are long-term investments, they should be carried at cost unless there is a permanent decline in market value. The bank's trading account securities would also normally be carried at the lower of cost or market. However, since the securities will be sold in the near future, their market value is more relevant to the bank. For most corporations, this is not in accordance with generally accepted accounting principles.
4. Use of the equity method means that the bank records its proportionate share of investment earnings (or loss) when the investee declares its earnings (or loss). Because the bank can exert significant influence over the affairs of the investee, it is not appropriate to wait until the earnings are distributed as dividends to recognize earnings.
5. The bank should include in its consolidated financial statements the financial statements of all of its subsidiaries that it controls. This would include RBC Dominion and the Finance Corporation, as the bank owns more than 50% of each company.

Summary of Study Objectives

1 ***Identify the reasons corporations invest in debt and equity securities.*** Corporations invest for three common reasons: (1) they have excess cash either because of their operating cycle or because of economic swings; (2) they view investments as a significant revenue source; (3) they have strategic goals such as gaining control of a competitor or moving into a new line of business.

2 ***Explain the accounting for debt investments.*** Entries for investments in debt securities are required when (1) the bonds are purchased, (2) interest is received or accrued, and (3) the bonds are sold.

❸ ***Explain the accounting for equity investments.*** Entries for investments in shares are required when (1) the shares are purchased, (2) dividends are received, and (3) shares are sold. When the investor company is not able to exert significant influence (ownership usually < 20%) over the operating and financial policies of the investee company, the cost method should be used. When significant influence exists (ownership usually > 20%), the equity method should be used. When control is exercised (ownership usually > 50%), consolidated financial statements should be prepared for financial reporting purposes.

❹ ***Describe the purpose and usefulness of consolidated financial statements.*** When a company controls the voting shares of another company, consolidated financial statements are usually prepared. These statements are especially useful to the shareholders, board of directors, and management of the parent company.

❺ ***Distinguish between short-term and long-term investments.*** Short-term investments are securities held by a company that are readily marketable and intended to be converted to cash within the next year or operating cycle, whichever is longer. Investments that do not meet both criteria are classified as long-term investments.

❻ ***Indicate how debt and equity investments are valued and reported in the financial statements.*** Temporary investments in debt and equity securities are valued at the lower of cost and market, with market values separately disclosed. Long-term investments are valued at cost. If market value is anticipated to be less than cost on a permanent basis, the investment should be written down to market, which now becomes its new cost base.

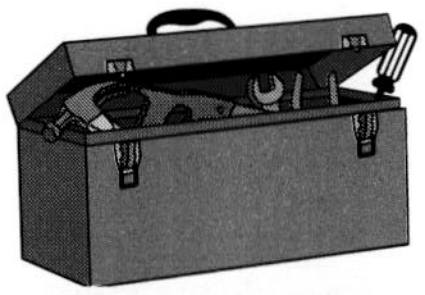

Decision Toolkit—A Summary

Decision Checkpoints	Info Needed for Decision	Tool to Use Decision	How to Evaluate Results
Is the company window dressing its results by manipulating its investment portfolio?	Balance of gains and losses; classification of investments	A company can window dress by selling winners and holding losers to increase reported earnings, or do the opposite to reduce reported earnings. Misclassification of investments as short-term or long-term allows companies to "time" (advance or defer) the recognition of losses.	Window dressing and misclassification are not easy to spot: it is difficult for an outsider to determine why companies choose to sell or hold a security, or classify it as they do. A user should evaluate a company's earnings as reported, including any gains and losses, to see total potential variation.

Glossary

Consolidated financial statements Financial statements that present the assets and liabilities controlled by the parent company and the collective profitability of the affiliated companies. (p. 652)

Controlling interest Ownership of more than 50% of the common shares of another entity. (p. 652)

Cost method An accounting method in which the investment in shares is recorded at cost and revenue is recognized only when cash dividends are received. (p. 650)

Debt investments Investments in money market instruments, and government and corporation bonds. (p. 647)

Equity investments Investments in the share capital of corporations. (p. 649)

Equity method An accounting method in which the investment in common shares is initially recorded at cost, and the investment account is then adjusted annually to show the investor's equity in the investee. (p. 651)

Fair market value Amount for which a security could be sold in a normal market. (p. 655)

Long-term investments Investments that are not readily marketable or that management does not intend to convert into cash within the next year or operating cycle, whichever is longer. (p. 655)

Lower of cost and market (LCM) A conservative rule that states that investments must be carried at the lower of their cost and market value. (p. 655)

Parent company A company that owns more than 50% of the common shares of another entity. (p. 652)

Short-term investments Investments that are readily marketable and intended to be converted into cash within the next year or operating cycle, whichever is longer. (p. 654)

Subsidiary (affiliated) company A company in which another company controls (usually owns more than 50%) its common shares. (p. 652)

DEMONSTRATION PROBLEM

In its first year of operations, DeMarco Company Ltd. had these selected transactions in short-term equity investments:

June 1	Purchased for cash 600 Sanburg common shares at $24 per share plus $300 of brokerage fees.
July 1	Purchased for cash 800 Cey common shares at $33 per share plus $600 of brokerage fees.
Sept. 1	Received a $1 per share cash dividend from Cey Corporation.
Nov. 1	Sold 200 Sanburg common shares for cash at $27 per share less $150 of brokerage fees.
Dec. 15	Received a $0.50 per share cash dividend on Sanburg common shares.

Instructions

(a) Journalize the transactions, assuming DeMarco uses the cost method to account for these transactions.

(b) Prepare the adjusting entry at December 31 to report the securities at their lower of cost and market value. At December 31, the fair market values per share were Sanburg, $25, and Cey, $30.

Solution to Demonstration Problem

(a)	June 1	Equity Investments—Sanburg Common	14,700	
		Cash [(600 × $24) + $300]		14,700
		(To record purchase of 600 Sanburg common shares)		
	July 1	Equity Investments—Cey Common	27,000	
		Cash [(800 × $33) + $600]		27,000
		(To record purchase of 800 Cey common shares)		
	Sept. 1	Cash	800	
		Dividend Revenue		800
		(To record receipt of $1 per share cash dividend from Cey)		
	Nov. 1	Cash [(200 × $27) − $150]	5,250	
		Equity Investments—Sanburg Common (200 ÷ 600 × $14,700)		4,900
		Gain on Sale of Equity Investments		350
		(To record sale of 200 Sanburg common shares)		
	Dec. 15	Cash [(600 − 200) × $0.50]	200	
		Dividend Revenue		200
		(To record receipt of $0.50 per share dividend from Sanburg)		
(b)	Dec. 31	Loss on Decline in Value of Short-Term Investments	2,800	
		Allowance to Reduce Cost to Market Value		2,800
		(To record loss on short-term securities)		

Investment	Cost	Fair Market Value	Gain (Loss)
Sanburg common shares	$ 9,800	$10,000	$ 200
Cey common shares	27,000	24,000	(3,000)
Total	$36,800	$34,000	($2,800)

Problem-Solving Strategies

1. Cost includes the price paid plus brokerage fees.
2. Gain or loss on sales is determined by the difference between net selling price and the cost of the securities.
3. The adjustment to LCM is based on the total difference between cost and fair market value of the securities.

SELF-STUDY QUESTIONS

Answers are at the end of the chapter.

(SO 2) 1. Debt investments are initially recorded at:
(a) cost.
(b) cost plus accrued interest.
(c) fair value.
(d) None of the above

(SO 2) 2. Hanes Company Ltd. sells debt investments costing $26,000 for $28,000 plus accrued interest that has been recorded. In journalizing the sale, credits are:
(a) Debt Investments and Loss on Sale of Debt Investments.
(b) Debt Investments, Gain on Sale of Debt Investments, and Bond Interest Receivable.
(c) Equity Investments and Bond Interest Receivable.
(d) The correct answer is not given.

(SO 3) 3. Pryor Company Ltd. receives net proceeds of $42,000 on the sale of equity investments that cost $39,500. This transaction will result in reporting in the statement of earnings a:
(a) loss of $2,500 under Other Expenses and Losses.
(b) loss of $2,500 under Operating Expenses.
(c) gain of $2,500 under Other Revenues and Gains.
(d) gain of $2,500 under Operating Revenues.

(SO 3) 4. The equity method of accounting for long-term investments in shares should be used when the investor has significant influence over an investee and owns:
(a) more than 20% of the investee's common shares.
(b) 20% or more of the investee's bonds.
(c) more than 50% of the investee's common shares.
(d) less than 20% of the investee's common shares.

(SO 4) 5. Which of these statements is *not* true?
Consolidated financial statements are useful to:
(a) determine the profitability of specific subsidiaries.
(b) determine the collective profitability of enterprises under common control.
(c) determine the breadth of a parent company's operations.
(d) determine the full extent of collective obligations of enterprises under common control.

6. Short-term investments must be readily marketable and be expected to be sold within: (SO 5)
(a) three months from the date of purchase.
(b) the next year or operating cycle, whichever is shorter.
(c) the next year or operating cycle, whichever is longer.
(d) the operating cycle.

7. At the end of the first year of operations, the total cost of the short-term investment portfolio is $120,000 and the total fair market value is $115,000. What should the financial statements show? (SO 6)
(a) An increase of an asset of $5,000 and a gain of $5,000
(b) A reduction of an asset of $5,000 and an unrealized loss of $5,000 in the shareholders' equity section
(c) A reduction of an asset of $5,000 in the current asset section and a loss of $5,000 under other expenses and losses
(d) No reduction and no loss

8. In the balance sheet, the Allowance to Reduce Cost to Market Value is reported as a: (SO 6)
(a) contra asset account.
(b) contra shareholders' equity account.
(c) loss in the statement of earnings.
(d) loss in the retained earnings statement.

9. If a company wants to increase its reported income by manipulating its investment accounts, which should it do? (SO 6)
(a) Sell its "winner" securities and hold its "loser" securities
(b) Hold its "winner" securities and sell its "loser" securities
(c) Reclassify its profitable short-term investments as long-term investments
(d) Reclassify its unprofitable long-term long-term investments as short-term investments

QUESTIONS

(SO 1) 1. What are the reasons that corporations invest in securities?

(SO 2) 2. (a) What is the cost of an investment in bonds?
(b) When is interest on bonds recorded?

(SO 2) 3. Ann Adler is confused about losses and gains on the sale of debt investments. Explain these issues to Ann:
(a) How the gain or loss is calculated
(b) The statement presentation of gains and losses

4. Clio Company Ltd. sells Cross bonds that cost $40,000 for $45,000, including $3,000 of accrued interest. In recording the sale, Clio books a $5,000 gain. Is this correct? Explain. (SO 2)

(SO 3) 5. What is the cost of an investment in shares?

(SO 3) 6. To acquire Mega Corporation shares, Duran Corp. pays $65,000 in cash plus $1,500, broker's fees. What entry should be made for this investment, assuming the shares are readily marketable?

(SO 3) 7. (a) When should a long-term investment in common shares be accounted for by the equity method?
(b) When is revenue recognized under the equity method?

(SO 3) 8. Malon Corporation uses the equity method to account for its ownership of 35% of the common shares of Flynn Packing. During 2001, Flynn reports net earnings of $80,000 and declares and pays cash dividends of $10,000. What recognition should Malon Corporation give to these events?

(SO 3) 9. What constitutes "significant influence"?

(SO 3) 10. Distinguish between the cost and equity methods of accounting for investments in common shares.

(SO 4) 11. What are consolidated financial statements?

(SO 5) 12. Kirk Wholesale Supply Ltd. owns shares in **Corel Corporation**, which it intends to hold indefinitely because of some negative tax consequences if it sold. Should the investment in Corel be classified as a short-term investment? Why?

13. What are the valuation guidelines for investments at the balance sheet date? (SO 6)

14. Wendy Walner is the controller of G-Products, Inc. At December 31, the company's investments in short-term securities cost $74,000 and have a fair market value of $70,000. Indicate how Wendy would report these data in the financial statements prepared on December 31. (SO 6)

15. Using the data in question 14, how would Wendy report these data if the investment were long-term and the decline was thought to be temporary? (SO 6)

16. Reo Company's investments in short-term securities at December 31 show a total cost of $192,000 and total fair market value of $140,000. Prepare the adjusting entry. (SO 6)

17. Using the data in question 16, prepare the adjusting entry assuming the securities are classified as long-term and the decline is expected to be a permanent one. (SO 6)

18. What is the proper statement presentation of the account Loss on Decline in Value of Investment? (SO 6)

19. What purposes are served by reporting the Allowance to Reduce Cost to Market Value as a contra asset in the balance sheet? (SO 6)

Brief Exercises

Journalize entries for debt investments. (SO 2)

BE12-1 Phelps Corporation purchased debt investments for $41,500 on January 1, 2001. On July 1, 2001, Phelps received cash interest of $2,075. Journalize the purchase and the receipt of interest. Assume no interest has been accrued.

Journalize entries for issue of debt. (SO 2)

BE12-2 For the data presented in BE12-1, prepare the journal entries to record the issue of debt and receipt of interest on the books of the investee (issuer). Assume that the 10-year, 5% bonds were issued at their face value of $41,500. You may find it helpful to refer to Chapter 10 where the entries on the books of the issuer were first illustrated.

Journalize entries for equity investments. (SO 3)

BE12-3 On August 1, McLain Company Ltd. buys 1,000 ABC common shares for $35,000 cash plus brokerage fees of $600. On December 1, the equity investments are sold for $38,000 cash. Journalize the purchase and sale of the common shares.

Journalize transactions under the equity method. (SO 3)

BE12-4 Harmon Company owns 30% of Hook Company. For the current year, Hook reports net earnings of $150,000 and declares and pays a $50,000 cash dividend. Record Harmon's equity in Hook's net earnings and the receipt of dividends from Hook. How much revenue was reported by Harmon?

Journalize transactions under the cost method. (SO 3)

BE12-5 For the data presented in BE12-4, assume that Harmon owns only 10% of Hook Company. Prepare the required journal entries to record Harmon's investment earnings. How much revenue was reported by Harmon? Explain why this differs from the answer obtained in BE12-4.

Prepare LCM entry for short-term investment. (SO 6)

BE12-6 Cost and fair market value data for the short-term securities of Michele Company Ltd. at December 31, 2001, are $62,000 and $59,000, respectively. Prepare the adjusting entry to record the securities at the lower of cost and market value.

Indicate statement presentation using fair market value. (SO 6)

BE12-7 For the data presented in BE12-6, show the financial statement presentation of the short-term investment and related accounts.

Prepare LCM entry for long-term investment. (SO 6)

BE12-8 In its first year of operations, Duggen Corporation holds equity securities costing $72,000 as a long-term investment. At December 31, 2001, the fair market value of the securities is $65,000. Prepare the adjusting entry to record the securities at fair market value assuming the decline is a permanent one.

Indicate statement presentation using fair market value.
(SO 6)

BE12-9 For the data presented in BE12-8, show the financial statement presentation of the long-term investment and related accounts.

Prepare investments section of the balance sheet.
(SO 6)

BE12-10 Saber Corporation has these long-term investments: common shares of Sword Co. (10% ownership), cost $108,000, fair market value $113,000; and common shares of Epee Inc. (30% ownership), cost $210,000, equity $250,000. Prepare the investments section of the balance sheet.

EXERCISES

Journalize debt investment transactions, and accrue interest.
(SO 2)

E12-1 Piper Corporation had these transactions pertaining to debt investments:

Jan.	1	Purchased 60 $1,000, 10% Harris Co. bonds for $60,000 cash plus brokerage fees of $900. Interest is payable semi-annually on July 1 and January 1.
July	1	Received semi-annual interest on Harris Co. bonds.
	1	Sold 30 Harris Co. bonds for $32,000 less $400 of brokerage fees.

Instructions
(a) Journalize the transactions.
(b) Prepare the adjusting entry for the accrual of interest at December 31.

Journalize transactions for investments in shares.
(SO 3)

E12-2 McCormick Inc. had these transactions pertaining to investments in common shares:

Jan.	1	Purchased 1,000 Starr Corporation common shares (5%) for $70,000 cash plus a $1,400 broker's commission.
July	1	Received a cash dividend of $9 per share.
Dec.	1	Sold 500 Starr Corporation common shares for $37,000 cash less an $800 broker's commission.
	31	Received a cash dividend of $9 per share.

Instructions
Journalize the transactions.

Journalize and post transactions under the equity method.
(SO 3)

E12-3 On January 1, Ranier Corporation purchased a 25% equity investment in Bellingham Corporation for $150,000. At December 31, Bellingham declared and paid a $60,000 cash dividend and reported net earnings of $200,000.

Instructions
(a) Journalize the transactions.
(b) Determine the amount to be reported as an investment in Bellingham shares at December 31.

Journalize entries under the cost and equity methods.
(SO 3)

E12-4 These are two independent situations:

1. Karen Cosmetics Ltd. acquired 10% of the 200,000 common shares of Bell Fashion Ltd. at a total cost of $12 per share on March 18, 2001. On June 30, Bell declared and paid a $75,000 dividend. On December 31, Bell reported net earnings of $122,000 for the year. At December 31, the market price of Bell Fashion was $15 per share. The shares are classified as short-term.
2. Barb, Inc. obtained significant influence over Diner Corporation by buying 30% of Diner's 30,000 outstanding common shares at a cost of $9 per share on January 1, 2001. On June 15, Diner declared and paid a cash dividend of $35,000. On December 31, Diner reported net earnings of $80,000 for the year.

Instructions
Prepare all the necessary journal entries for 2001 for (a) Karen Cosmetics Ltd. and (b) Barb, Inc.

Record acquisition and explain the accounting for a consolidation.
(SO 3, 4)

E12-5 In February 1998, **Zellers** acquired all of the outstanding shares of **Kmart Canada Co.**, a discount department store chain. The total cost of the acquisition was $421,794,000.

Instructions

(a) Prepare the journal entry to record Zellers' acquisition of Kmart, assuming that the purchase amount was paid in cash. What entry should Kmart make?
(b) What method should Zellers use to account for its investment in Kmart?
(c) Which company is the parent company and which company the subsidiary company?
(d) Kmart's financial results have been included in Zellers' results in the company's consolidated statements. Zellers' results have been included in the Hudson Bay Company's consolidated statements. Explain why these results are consolidated in each company's statements for reporting purposes.

Journalize equity investment transactions, and explain statement of earnings presentation.
(SO 3, 6)

E12-6 Malea Company Ltd. had these transactions pertaining to equity investments:

Feb. 1	Purchased 800 ABC common shares (2%) for $8,200 cash plus brokerage fees of $200.
July 1	Received cash dividends of $1 per share on ABC common shares.
Sept. 1	Sold 300 ABC common shares for $4,000 less brokerage fees of $100.
Dec. 1	Received cash dividends of $1 per share on ABC common shares.

Instructions

(a) Journalize the transactions.
(b) Explain how dividend revenue and the gain (loss) on sale should be reported in the statement of earnings.

Prepare adjusting entry to reflect LCM, and indicate statement presentation.
(SO 6)

E12-7 At December 31, 2001, the short-term investments for Nielson, Inc., are as follows:

Security	Cost	Fair Market Value
A	$17,500	$15,000
B	12,500	14,000
C	23,000	21,000
Total	$53,000	$50,000

Instructions

(a) Prepare the adjusting entry at December 31, 2001, to report the securities at the lower of cost and market value.
(b) Show the balance sheet and statement of earnings presentation at December 31, 2001.

Prepare adjusting entry to record fair market value, and indicate statement presentation.
(SO 6)

E12-8 Data for investments in shares classified as short-term investments are presented in E12-7. Assume instead that the investments are classified as long-term with the same cost and fair market value.

Instructions

(a) Prepare the adjusting entry at December 31, 2001, to report the securities at the lower cost and market value, assuming that any declines in value are permanent.
(b) Show the statement presentation at December 31, 2001.
(c) J. Arnet, a member of the board of directors, does not understand why a loss is recorded when nothing has been sold. Write a letter to Ms. Arnet explaining the reporting and the purposes it serves.

Prepare adjusting entries for fair market value, and indicate statement presentation for two classes of securities.
(SO 6)

E12-9 Felipe Company Ltd. has these data at December 31, 2001:

Securities	Cost	Fair Market Value
Short-term	$120,000	$100,000
Long-term	100,000	90,000

Additional information: (1) In previous periods, the market value of the short-term investment was always higher than its cost. (2) The decline in the market value of the long-term investment is considered permanent.

Instructions

(a) Prepare the adjusting entries to report each class of securities appropriately.
(b) Indicate the statement presentation of each class of securities and the related loss accounts.

Problems: Set A

Prepare bond entries for investor and investee.
(SO 2)

P12-1A CASB is establishing a new business venture in western Canada. In order to secure necessary start-up capital, it has issued 10-year 8% bonds which pay interest semi-annually on June 30 and December 31. On January 1, 2001, Densmore Consulting Ltd. paid $96,000 for CASB bonds with a face value of $100,000. On January 1, 2002, Densmore Consulting sold its CASB bonds to a third party for $99,000. CASB has a December 31 year end and uses the straight-line method of amortization. Densmore Consulting has an October 31 year end.

Instructions

(a) Prepare all required entries for the investor—Densmore Consulting. (Hint: Record Debt Investment at $96,000. For simplicity, ignore any premium or discount on the books of the investor. Bond investments do not record any premium or discount separately as is the case for bond liabilities.)

(b) Prepare all required entries for the investee (issuer)—CASB. You may find it helpful to refer to Chapter 10 where the entries on the books of the issuer were first illustrated.

(c) Comment on the differences in recording that you observe between the investor and the investee.

Journalize transactions, and show financial statement presentation.
(SO 2, 6)

P12-2A The following Lund Corporation transactions related to long-term bonds:

2001

Jan.	1	Purchased $50,000 RAM Corporation 10% bonds for $50,000.
July	1	Received interest on RAM bonds.
Dec.	31	Accrued interest on RAM bonds.

2002

Jan.	1	Received interest on RAM bonds.
	1	Sold $25,000 of RAM bonds for $27,500.
July	1	Received interest on RAM bonds.

Instructions

(a) Journalize the transactions.

(b) Assume that the fair market value of the bonds at December 31, 2001, was $47,000. These bonds are classified as long-term investments. Prepare the adjusting entry to record these bonds at the appropriate value, assuming any decline in market value is temporary.

(c) Show the balance sheet presentation of the bonds and interest receivable at December 31, 2001.

(d) Identify the statement of earnings accounts involved, and give the statement classification of each account.

Journalize investment transactions, prepare adjusting entry, and show financial statement presentation.
(SO 2, 3, 6)

P12-3A In January 2001, the management of Reed Company, Ltd. concludes that it has sufficient cash to purchase some short-term investments in debt and equity securities. During the year, these transactions occurred:

Feb.	1	Purchased 800 IBF common shares for $32,000 plus brokerage fees of $800.
Mar.	1	Purchased 500 RST common shares for $15,000 plus brokerage fees of $500.
Apr.	1	Purchased 60 $1,000, 12% CRT bonds for $60,000 plus $1,200 of brokerage fees. Interest is payable semi-annually on April 1 and October 1.
July	1	Received a cash dividend of $0.60 per share on the IBF common shares.
Aug.	1	Sold 200 IBF common shares at $42 per share less brokerage fees of $350.
Sept.	1	Received $1 per share cash dividend on the RST common shares.
Oct.	1	Received the semi-annual interest on the CRT bonds.
	1	Sold the CRT bonds for $63,000 less $1,000 of brokerage fees.

At December 31, the fair market values of the IBF and RST common shares were $39 and $30 per share, respectively.

Instructions

(a) Journalize the transactions and post to the accounts Debt Investments and Equity Investments. (Use the T account form.)
(b) Prepare the adjusting entry at December 31, 2001, to report the investments at the lower of cost and market value.
(c) Show the balance sheet presentation of investment securities at December 31, 2001.
(d) Identify the statement accounts and give the statement classification of each account.

Prepare entries under the cost and equity methods, and prepare a memorandum.
(SO 3)

P12-4A Cardinal Concrete Corp. acquired 20% of the outstanding common shares of Edra Inc. on January 1, 2001, by paying $1,200,000 for 50,000 shares. Edra declared and paid an $0.80 per share cash dividend on June 30 and again on December 31, 2001. Edra reported net earnings of $700,000 for the year.

Instructions

(a) Prepare the journal entries for Cardinal Concrete for 2001, assuming Cardinal cannot exercise significant influence over Edra. (Use the cost method.)
(b) Prepare the journal entries for Cardinal Concrete for 2001, assuming Cardinal can exercise significant influence over Edra. (Use the equity method.)
(c) The board of directors of Cardinal Concrete is confused about the differences between the cost and equity methods. Prepare a memorandum for the board that explains each method and shows in tabular form the account balances under each method at December 31, 2001.

Prepare entries for investor under the cost and equity methods.
(SO 3, 4 6)

P12-5A Sub Corporation has 200,000 no par value common shares outstanding. On January 10, 2002, Par Company purchased a block of these shares in the open market at $20 cash per share. At the end of 2002, Sub Corporation reported net earnings of $210,000 and declared and paid a $0.50 per share dividend.

This problem assumes three independent situations related to the accounting for the purchase of the block of shares by Par Company.

Situation A: Par Company purchased 30,000 shares of Sub common.
Situation B: Par Company purchased 60,000 shares of Sub common.
Situation C: Par Company purchased all 200,000 shares of Sub common.

Instructions

(a) For each situation, identify the accounting method that should be used by Par Company to account for its investment.
(b) For each situation, prepare the journal entries for Par Company for the year ended December 31, 2002, to record all transactions related to the investment.
(c) Compare Par's non-consolidated balance sheet and statement of earnings accounts related to these investments at year end for each situation.
(d) In Situation C, what kind of financial statements should be prepared to report the operations of Par and Sub? Whose name will be on the financial statements?

Record equity transactions for investor and investee.
(SO 3, 6)

P12-6A The following transactions occurred during the year ended November 30, 2002.

Dec. 1, 2001	Mountain View Corp. purchased 20,000 shares on the open market, representing a 40% interest in Lakeside Corp. for $10 cash per share.
Dec. 31, 2001	Lakeside paid a $0.25 per share dividend.
Nov. 30, 2002	Lakeside reported net earnings of $50,000.

Instructions

(a) Prepare all journal entries to record these transactions on (1) Mountain View's books and (2) Lakeside's books.
(b) Show the presentation of the equity investment for Mountain View on its November 30, 2002, balance sheet.

Journalize short-term share transactions, and show balance sheet presentation.
(SO 3, 6)

P12-7A Here is Hi-Tech Company's portfolio of short-term investments at December 31, 2000:

	Cost
500 shares of Awixa Corporation common shares	$26,000
700 shares of HAL Corporation common shares	42,000
400 shares of Renda Corporation preferred shares	16,800

On December 31, the total cost of the portfolio equalled the total fair market value. Hi-Tech had these transactions related to the securities during 2001:

Jan.	7	Sold 500 Awixa Corporation common shares at $56 per share less brokerage fees of $700.
	10	Purchased 200 of Mintor Corporation's $70 common shares at $78 per share plus brokerage fees of $240.
	26	Received a cash dividend of $1.15 per share on HAL Corporation common shares.
Feb.	2	Received cash dividends of $0.40 per share on Renda Corporation preferred shares.
	10	Sold all 400 Renda Corporation preferred shares at $28 per share less brokerage fees of $180.
July	1	Received a cash dividend of $1 per share on HAL Corporation common shares.
Sept.	1	Purchased an additional 400 shares of the $70 common shares of Mintor Corporation at $82 per share plus brokerage fees of $400.
Dec.	15	Received a cash dividend of $1.50 per share on Mintor Corporation common shares.

At December 31, 2001, the fair market values of the securities were:

HAL Corporation common shares	$64 per share
Mintor Corporation common shares	$70 per share

Hi-Tech uses separate account titles for each investment, such as "Investment in HAL Corporation Common Shares."

Instructions

(a) Prepare journal entries to record the transactions.
(b) Post to the investment accounts. (Use T accounts.)
(c) Prepare the adjusting entry at December 31, 2001, to report the portfolio at the lower of cost and market value.
(d) Show the balance sheet presentation at December 31, 2001.

Journalize transactions, prepare adjusting entry for long-term equity investments, and show balance sheet presentation.
(SO 3, 6)

P12-8A On December 31, 2000, Harmony Associates owned the following securities that are held as long-term investments:

Common Shares	Shares	Cost
A Co.	1,000	$50,000
B Co.	6,000	36,000
C Co.	1,200	24,000

On this date, the total fair market value of the securities was equal to their cost. The securities are not held for influence or control over the investees. In 2001, these transactions occurred:

July	1	Received a $1 per share semi-annual cash dividend on B Co. common shares.
Aug.	1	Received a $0.50 per share cash dividend on A Co. common shares.
Sept.	1	Sold 500 B Co. common shares for cash at $8 per share less brokerage fees of $100.
Oct.	1	Sold 400 A Co. common shares for cash at $54 per share less brokerage fees of $600.
Nov.	1	Received a $1 per share cash dividend on C Co. common shares.
Dec.	15	Received a $0.50 per share cash dividend on A Co. common shares.
	31	Received a $1 per share semi-annual cash dividend on B Co. common shares.

At December 31, the fair market values per share of the common shares were A Co., $47, B Co., $6, and C Co., $18.

Instructions

(a) Journalize the transactions for 2001 and post to the account Equity Investments. (Use the T account form.)
(b) Prepare the adjusting entry at December 31, 2001, to show the securities at the lower of cost and market value, assuming any declines are permanent.
(c) Show the balance sheet presentation of the investments at December 31, 2001.

Analyse information related to the cost and equity methods.
(SO 3, 6)

P12-9A On January 1, 2000, Landriault Ltée. purchased a 30% (300,000 of 1,000,000 shares outstanding) equity interest in Groth Inc.'s common shares for $7,500,000. On December 31, 2002, the Equity Investment (in Groth's Common Shares) account was reported on Landriault's balance sheet at $10,750,000. Over the last three years, Groth had paid a constant annual cash dividend of $500,000 ($0.50 per share).

Instructions

(a) Determine the total earnings of Groth Inc. during the period January 1, 2000, through December 31, 2002.
(b) If Landriault had accounted for its investment in Groth using the cost method rather than the equity method, what would the balance in its Equity Investment account be at December 31, 2002?

Determine valuation of equity investments.
(SO 3, 6)

P12-10A On January 1, 2000, Sturge Enterprises Inc. held the following investments:

X corporation: 1,500 shares @ $11 each
Y Corporation: 2,000 shares @ $8 each

During the year, Sturge made the following purchases:

X corporation: 1,500 shares @ $10 each
X corporation: 1,000 shares @ $8 each
X corporation: 1,000 shares @ $7 each
Y corporation: 500 shares @ $9 each
Z corporation: 3,000 shares @ $12 each

The market values of the various securities at year end were as follows:

X Corporation: $6
Y Corporation: $10
Z Corporation: $12

Any declines in market value are considered to be temporary.

Instructions

(a) Calculate the cost of Sturge Enterprises' equity investment portfolio at December 31, 2000.
(b) Calculate the market value of Sturge Enterprises' equity investment portfolio at December 31, 2000.
(c) If Sturge Enterprises considers its entire portfolio to be a short-term investment, what loss should be recorded on the statement of earnings?
(d) If Sturge Enterprises decides to classify the X Corporation shares as a long-term investment and the Y Corporation and Z Corporation shares as short-term investments, what would be the impact on the statement of earnings?

Classify accounts on balance sheet.
(SO 6)

P12-11A You are provided with the following accounts of New Bay Inc. as of December 31, 2002.

Accounts payable	$ 35,000
Accounts receivable	65,000
Accumulated amortization, computers	8,000
Accumulated amortization, equipment	6,000
Allowance for doubtful accounts	10,000
Bonds payable, 8%, due 2012	250,000
Cash	2,000
Common shares, 10,000 no par value shares	100,000
Computers	12,000
Debt investment (Aliant Inc. bonds)	180,000

Discount on bonds payable	18,000
Equipment	22,000
Equity investment (Hemosol Inc. common shares), at equity	50,000
Income taxes payable	12,000
Merchandise inventory	37,000
Retained earnings	53,000
Salaries payable	8,000
Short-term investments, at cost (market $25,000)	16,000

Instructions

Indicate where each of the above accounts would be classified on New Bay's balance sheet at December 31, 2002.

Prepare a balance sheet. (SO 6)

P12-12A The following data, presented in alphabetical order, are taken from the records of Bansal Corporation:

Accounts payable	$ 240,000
Accounts receivable	110,000
Accumulated amortization—buildings	180,000
Accumulated amortization—equipment	52,000
Allowance for doubtful accounts	6,000
Allowance to reduce cost to market value	15,000
Bond investments	360,000
Bonds payable (10%, due 2012)	400,000
Buildings	900,000
Cash	92,000
Common shares (no par value; 500,000 shares authorized, 300,000 shares issued)	1,500,000
Discount on bonds payable	20,000
Dividends payable	50,000
Equipment	275,000
Equity investment (in Abitibi Inc. shares [30% ownership]), at equity	240,000
Goodwill, net of amortization	200,000
Income taxes payable	120,000
Land	500,000
Merchandise inventory	170,000
Notes payable (due 2003)	70,000
Prepaid insurance	16,000
Retained earnings	450,000
Short-term investments, at cost	200,000

Instructions

Prepare a balance sheet at December 31, 2002.

PROBLEMS: SET B

Prepare bond entries for investor and investee. Show balance sheet presentation. (SO 2, 6)

P12-1B The following bond transactions occurred during the year ended February 1, 2002, for the University of New Brunswick (UNB) and Otutye Ltd.

Feb. 1, 2001	UNB sold $3 million of 8%, five-year bonds at 103 to Otutye Ltd. The bonds were dated February 1, 2001, with interest payable semi-annually each August 1 and February 1. The University's and Otutye's year ends are also February 1.
Aug. 1, 2001	Paid the semi-annual interest on the bonds. The University uses the straight-line method of amortizing any bond discount or premium.
Feb. 1, 2002	Semi-annual interest payment date.

Aug. 1, 2002

1. Semi-annual interest payment date.
2. After paying the semi-annual interest on the bonds on this date, UNB decided to repurchase the bonds and retire them. UNB repurchased all $3 million of the bonds from Otutye at a cash price of $3.1 million.

Instructions

(a) Prepare journal entries for UNB (investee/issuer) to record the above bond transactions. You may find it helpful to review entries for bond liabilities in Chapter 10.
(b) Show how the bond liability would be presented on UNB's February 1, 2002, balance sheet, immediately after the second semi-annual interest payment date.
(c) Prepare journal entries for Otutye Ltd. (investor) to record the above bond transactions.
(d) Show how the debt investment would be presented on Otutye's February 1, 2002, balance sheet.
(e) The Comptroller of UNB, Larry Guitard, is discussing the advantages and disadvantages of the straight-line and effective-interest methods of bond amortization with his office staff. What do you think he is saying?

P12-2B The following Givarz Corporation transactions related to long-term bonds:

Journalize transactions, and show financial statement presentation.
(SO 2, 6)

2001

Jan.	1	Purchased $100,000 of Leslye Corporation 9% bonds for $100,000.
July	1	Received interest on Leslye bonds.
Dec.	31	Accrued interest on Leslye bonds.

2002

Jan.	1	Received interest on Leslye bonds.
	1	Sold $25,000 of Leslye bonds for $30,500.
July	1	Received interest on Leslye bonds.

Instructions

(a) Journalize the transactions.
(b) Assume that the fair market value of the bonds at December 31, 2001, was $97,000. Prepare the adjusting entry to record these bonds at the lower of cost and market value, assuming that any decline in market value is temporary.
(c) Show the balance sheet presentation of the bonds and interest receivable at December 31, 2001, and indicate where any gain or loss is reported in the financial statements.

P12-3B In January 2001, the management of Mead Company Ltd. concludes that it has sufficient cash to permit some short-term investments in debt and equity securities. During the year, these transactions occurred:

Journalize investment transactions, prepare adjusting entry, and show financial statement presentation.
(SO 2, 3, 6)

Feb.	1	Purchased 600 CBF common shares for $31,800 plus brokerage fees of $600.
Mar.	1	Purchased 800 RSD common shares for $20,000 plus brokerage fees of $400.
Apr.	1	Purchased 50 $1,000, 12% MRT bonds for $50,000 plus $1,000 of brokerage fees. Interest is payable semi-annually on April 1 and October 1.
July	1	Received a cash dividend of $0.60 per share on the CBF common shares.
Aug.	1	Sold 200 CBF common shares at $56 per share less brokerage fees of $200.
Sept.	1	Received a $1 per share cash dividend on the RSD common shares.
Oct.	1	Received the semi-annual interest on the MRT bonds.
	1	Sold the MRT bonds for $51,000 less $1,000 of brokerage fees.

At December 31, the fair market values of the CBF and RSD common shares were $55 and $24 per share, respectively.

Instructions

(a) Journalize the transactions and post to the accounts Debt Investments and Equity Investments. (Use the T account form.)
(b) Prepare the adjusting entry at December 31, 2001, to report the investment securities at the lower of cost and market.
(c) Show the balance sheet presentation of investment securities at December 31, 2001.
(d) Identify the statement of earnings accounts and give the statement classification of each account.

Prepare entries under the cost and equity methods, and tabulate differences.
(SO 3)

P12-4B DFM Services Ltd. acquired 30% of the outstanding common shares of BNA Company Ltd. on January 1, 2001, by paying $800,000 for 40,000 shares. BNA declared and paid $0.20 per share cash dividends on March 15, June 15, September 15, and December 15, 2001. BNA reported net earnings of $350,000 for the year.

Instructions

(a) Prepare the journal entries for DFM Services for 2001, assuming DFM cannot exercise significant influence over BNA. (Use the cost method.)
(b) Prepare the journal entries for DFM Services for 2001, assuming DFM can exercise significant influence over BNA. (Use the equity method.)
(c) In tabular form, indicate the investment and statement of earnings account balances at December 31, 2001, under each method of accounting.

Prepare entries for investor under the cost and equity methods.
(SO 3, 4, 6)

P12-5B McReynolds Mariners has 150,000 no par value common shares outstanding and a fiscal year which begins on October 1. On October 1, 2001, LeTourneau Enterprises purchases 30% of the outstanding common shares of McReynolds Mariners from another shareholder for $40 per share. LeTourneau intends to hold the shares as a long-term investment. On December 31, 2001, McReynolds Mariners issues a 4% common stock dividend when the shares are trading for $42 per share. On May 31, 2002, McReynolds Mariners pays a cash dividend of $2.00 per share to common shareholders. McReynolds Mariners' net earnings for the year ended September 30, 2002, was $350,000. The market value of each share of McReynolds Mariners at September 30, 2002, was $50.

Instructions

(a) Prepare all entries for LeTourneau Enterprises for the year ended September 30, 2002, assuming that it exercises significant influence over McReynolds Mariners.
(b) Prepare all entries for LeTourneau Enterprises for the year ended September 30, 2002, assuming that it is unable to exercise significant influence over McReynolds Mariners.
(c) Compare the balance sheet and statement of earnings accounts of LeTourneau Enterprises at September 30, 2002, under the two assumptions.
(d) If LeTourneau had purchased 100% of McReynolds's common shares, what method of accounting for this investment would LeTourneau use? What kind of financial statements should it issue? Whose name would be on the financial statements—LeTourneau's, McReynolds's, or both names?

Record equity transactions for investor and investee.
(SO 3, 6)

P12-6B Outer Cove Outfitters Ltd. operates an adventure tourism operation in Atlantic Canada. The company's shareholders' equity section at the beginning of the current fiscal year was as follows:

OUTER COVE OUTFITTERS LTD.
Balance Sheet
May 1, 2002

Shareholders' Equity:	
Common shares, no par value; authorized 50,000 shares; issued and outstanding, 30,000 shares	$600,000
Retained earnings	325,000
Total shareholders' equity	$925,000

Listed below are selected transactions that occurred during the year:

1. On May 1, Outer Cove Outfitters sold 20,000 shares to Sam Cumby for $25 per share. The total number of shares issued and outstanding is now 50,000. Sam is not able to exercise significant influence over Outer Cove Outfitters and intends to hold the investment for the long term.
2. On September 1, Outer Cove Outfitters issued a 5% common stock dividend. The market value of the common shares on that date was $28 per share.
3. On November 1, Outer Cove Outfitters paid a $0.50 per share cash dividend.
4. Outer Cove Outfitters recorded net earnings of $200,000 for the year.
5. The market value of Outer Cove Outfitters' common shares on April 30, 2003, was $33 per share.

Instructions

(a) Prepare all journal entries for Outer Cove Outfitters and for Sam Cumby.
(b) Show the balance sheet presentation for Outer Cove Outfitters and for Sam Cumby.

Journalize equity transactions and show statement presentation.
(SO 3, 6)

P12-7B The following data are in Big Head Todd Corporation's portfolio of short-term securities at December 31, 2000:

	Cost
500 shares of Aglar Corporation common shares	$26,000
700 shares of BAL Corporation common shares	42,000
400 shares of Hicks Corporation preferred shares	16,800

On December 31, the total cost of the portfolio equalled total fair market value. Big Head Todd had the following transactions related to the securities during 2001:

Jan. 7 Sold 500 Aglar Corporation common shares at $56 per share less brokerage fees of $700.
10 Purchased 200 $70 common shares of Miley Corporation at $78 per share, plus brokerage fees of $240.
26 Received a cash dividend of $1.15 per share on BAL Corporation common shares.
Feb. 2 Received cash dividends of $0.40 per share on Hicks Corporation preferred shares.
10 Sold all 400 Hicks Corporation preferred shares at $30.00 per share less brokerage fees of $180.
Sept. 1 Purchased an additional 400 the $70 common shares of Miley Corporation at $82 per share, plus brokerage fees of $400.
Dec. 15 Received a cash dividend of $1.50 per share on Miley Corporation common shares.

At December 31, 2001, the fair market values of the securities were:

BAL Corporation common shares	$64 per share
Miley Corporation common shares	$72 per share

Big Head Todd Company uses separate account titles for each investment, such as "Investment in BAL Corporation Common Shares."

Instructions

(a) Prepare journal entries to record the transactions.
(b) Post to the investment accounts. (Use T accounts.)
(c) Prepare the adjusting entry at December 31, 2001, to report the portfolio at the lower of cost and market value.
(d) Show the balance sheet presentation at December 31, 2001.

Journalize transactions, prepare adjusting entry for equity investments, and show balance sheet presentation.
(SO 3, 6)

P12-8B On December 31, 2000, Koo Associates Ltd. owned the following securities that are held as long-term investments. The securities are not held for influence or control over the investee.

Common Shares	Number of Shares	Cost
X Co.	2,000	$90,000
Y Co.	5,000	45,000
Z Co.	2,000	30,000

On this date, the total fair market value of the securities was equal to their cost. In 2001, these transactions occurred:

July 1 Received a $1 per share semi-annual cash dividend on Y Co. common shares.
Aug. 1 Received a $0.50 per share cash dividend on X Co. common shares.
Sept. 1 Sold 700 Y Co. common shares for cash at $8 per share less brokerage fees of $200.
Oct. 1 Sold 600 X Co. common shares for cash at $54 per share less brokerage fees of $500.
Nov. 1 Received a $1 per share cash dividend on Z Co. common shares.
Dec. 15 Received a $0.50 per share cash dividend on X Co. common shares.
31 Received a $1 per share semi-annual cash dividend on Y Co. common shares.

At December 31, the fair market values per share of the common shares were X Co., $48, Y Co., $8, and Z Co., $17.

Instructions

(a) Journalize the transactions for 2001 and post to the account Equity Investments. (Use the T account form.)
(b) Prepare the adjusting entry at December 31, 2001, to show the securities at the lower of cost and market. Any declines are considered to be permanent.
(c) Show the balance sheet presentation of the equity investments at December 31, 2001.

Analyse information related to the cost and equity methods.
(SO 3, 6)

P12-9B You are presented with the following selected information for the Khalil Travel Agency:

KHALIL TRAVEL AGENCY LTD.
Balance Sheet
December 31, 2001

Shareholders' Equity:	
Common shares, 180,000 no par value shares issued and outstanding	$ 900,000
Retained earnings	300,000
Total shareholders' equity	$1,200,000

On July 1, 2001, Gord Stewart purchased shares of the Khalil Travel Agency when the shares were trading at $15 per share. The market value of each share of Khalil Travel Agency at December 31, 2001, was $18.

Gord intends to hold these shares as a long-term investment. Gord Stewart's bookkeeper prepared an unadjusted trial balance as at December 31, 2001, under the assumption that Gord could not exercise significant influence over Khalil. Accordingly, the bookkeeper presented the following information:

GORD STEWART
Balance Sheet
December 31, 2001

Long-term investment:	
Investment in shares of Khalil Travel Agency (market value $648,000)	$540,000

GORD STEWART
Statement of Earnings
For the Year Ending December 31, 2001

Dividend revenue from investment in shares of Khalil Travel Agency	$72,000

Instructions

(a) How many shares of the Khalil Travel Agency did Gord Stewart purchase? What percentage of the shares of Khalil does Gord own?
(b) What was the cash dividend paid per share of Khalil Travel Agency?
(c) Gord informs his bookkeeper that he is able to exercise significant influence over Khalil Travel Agency and tells him to change the method of accounting for the investment. The bookkeeper says that this is good as the investment will now be carried on Gord's balance sheet at $558,000 at December 31, 2001. Assuming that earnings occur evenly throughout the year, what were the net earnings of the Khalil Travel Agency for the year ended December 31, 2001?
(d) Assuming that Gord Stewart is able to exercise significant influence over the Khalil Travel Agency, what amount will Gord report on his statement of earnings for 2001?

P12-10B The following table summarizes information about the short- and long-term investment portfolio of Daoust Corporation at year-end.

Determine valuation of investments.
(SO 3, 6)

Short-Term Investments	Quantity Purchased	Cost/Security	Market Value/Security
T-Bills	10,000	$ 1	$ 1
Nortel Networks	5,000	75	167
Microsoft	5,000	120	60
Laidlaw	1,000	5	1
Long-Term Investments			
Government of Canada bonds	1,000	100	140
CIBC bonds	2,000	98	100

Instructions

(a) At what value should the short-term investment portfolio be reported at year end? The long term investment portfolio?

(b) Prepare any required adjusting entries to apply the lower of cost and market rule at year end.

(c) The president of Daoust Corporation is speculating about holding Microsoft and Laidlaw for the long term, rather than the short term. She doesn't believe there is any point in selling these shares in the near term until their values recover. What impact would it have on Daoust's statement of earnings if the Microsoft and Laidlaw shares were classified as long-term investments and the declines in market values were assumed to be due to temporary considerations? If the declines in market values were assumed to be permanent? What advice can you offer the president about this situation?

P12-11B You are provided with the following selected accounts of Lenarduzzi Corporation:

Classify accounts on financial statements.
(SO 6)

Bonds payable, 6%, due 2008	$ 200,000
Common shares, no par value, 200,000 shares authorized, 100,000 shares issued	500,000
Dividends	25,000
Dividend revenue	90,000
Equity investments, at cost	100,000
Equity investments, at equity	500,000
Gain on sale of investments	15,000
Goodwill	48,000
Interest revenue	23,000
Loss on decline in value of investment	2,000
Premium on bonds payable	5,000
Retained earnings	2,500,000
Short-term debt investment (CIBC bonds), at cost (market $155,000)	132,000
Short-term equity investment (Bell Canada International preferred shares), at market (cost $65,000)	59,000

Instructions

Indicate where each of the above accounts would be classified on Lenarduzzi's year-end financial statements.

P12-12B The following data, presented in alphabetical order, are taken from the records of Alameda Corporation:

Prepare a balance sheet.
(SO 6)

Accounts payable	$ 250,000
Accounts receivable	120,000
Accumulated amortization—building	180,000
Accumulated amortization—equipment	52,000
Allowance for doubtful accounts	6,000
Allowance to reduce cost to market	8,000
Bond investments	150,000

Bonds payable (10%, due 2010)	500,000
Buildings	950,000
Cash	92,000
Common shares (no par value; 500,000 shares authorized, 150,000 shares issued)	1,584,000
Dividends payable	80,000
Equipment	275,000
Equity investment (Dodge common shares [10% ownership]), at cost	278,000
Equity investment (Huston common shares [30% ownership]), at equity	230,000
Goodwill, net of accumulated amortization	200,000
Income taxes payable	120,000
Land	500,000
Merchandise inventory	170,000
Notes payable (due 2003)	70,000
Premium on bonds payable	40,000
Prepaid insurance	16,000
Retained earnings	271,000
Short-term equity investment, at cost	180,000

The equity investment in Dodge common shares is considered a short-term investment.

Instructions

Prepare a balance sheet at December 31, 2002.

BROADENING YOUR PERSPECTIVE

Financial Reporting and Analysis

FINANCIAL REPORTING PROBLEM: *Loblaw Companies Limited*

BYP12-1 The annual report of **Loblaw** is presented in Appendix A.

Instructions

(a) What information about investments is reported in the consolidated balance sheet?

(b) Based on the information in Note 5 for Loblaw's financial statements, how much interest income was earned on short-term investments in 1999? 1998?

(c) On December 10, 1998, Loblaw purchased 98% of the common shares of Provigo. What method of accounting should Loblaw use to account for this purchase on its non-consolidated financial statements? How did Loblaw report this purchase on its consolidated financial statements?

(d) Note 1 to the financial statements identifies Loblaw's effective interest in the voting equity share capital of its subsidiaries. What is this percentage? Using other information provided in the annual report, identify any three of Loblaw's subsidiary companies.

COMPARATIVE ANALYSIS PROBLEM: *Loblaw and Sobeys*

BYP12-2 The financial statements of **Sobeys Inc.** are presented in Appendix B, following the financial statements for **Loblaw** in Appendix A.

Instructions

Compare the investing activities sections of the statements of cash flows of the two companies for 1999 and 1998. What conclusions concerning the nature of investment activity can be drawn from these data?

RESEARCH CASE

BYP12-3 The January 9, 1999, issue of *The Economist* includes an article entitled, "How to Make Mergers Work." A merger results in the business combination of two or more companies.

Instructions

Read the article and answer these questions:

(a) What percentage of mergers actually added value to the combined firm? Which investors tend to gain from the merger, and which tend to lose?

(b) The article suggests that mergers in the past tended to be undertaken to create diversified conglomerates, but that mergers today tend to be defensive in nature. Give motivations for defensive mergers and examples of industries where they have taken place.

(c) What are some reasons that mergers often fail?

(d) What are some methods for increasing the likelihood of success?

INTERPRETING FINANCIAL STATEMENTS

BYP12-4 Shock waves rippled through nationalistic Canadians at the thought that a forestry icon, **MacMillan Bloedel Limited**, could be sold to the world's largest integrated forest products company. That is indeed what happened when **Weyerhaeuser Company Limited** paid $3.5 billion in 1999 to purchase MacMillan Bloedel. The annual cost savings of the combined companies, estimated to be at least US$150 million, are driving future profit growth. Weyerhaeuser is now the world's largest private owner of softwood timber, with about 33.5 million acres in Canada and 5.7 million acres in the southern U.S. and the Pacific Northwest.

Weyerhaeuser uses the equity method to account for its investment in MacMillan Bloedel and consolidates the results for reporting purposes.

Instructions

(a) Prepare the journal entries (if any) that Weyerhaeuser made to record the following assumed transactions related to its acquisition of 100% of MacMillan Bloedel's common shares:
   1. MacMillan Bloedel is acquired for \$3.5 billion. Assume this payment was made in cash.
   2. MacMillan Bloedel reports net earnings of \$42 million.
   3. MacMillan Bloedel declares dividends of \$43 million.

(b) Explain why Weyerhaeuser would account for its equity investment in MacMillan Bloedel using the equity method of accounting on its non-consolidated statements, but combine both companies' operations on consolidated statements.

A GLOBAL FOCUS

BYP12-5 **Xerox Corporation** has a 50% investment interest in a joint venture with the Japanese corporation Fuji, called **Fuji Xerox**. Xerox accounts for this investment using the equity method. The following additional information regarding this investment was taken from Xerox's 1998 annual report (in millions of US\$):

Investment in Fuji Xerox per balance sheet	\$ 1,354
Xerox's equity in Fuji Xerox net earnings	108
Xerox total assets	30,024
Xerox total liabilities	25,167
Fuji Xerox total assets	6,279
Fuji Xerox total liabilities	3,757

Instructions

(a) What alternative approaches are available for accounting for long-term equity investments? Discuss whether Xerox is correct in using the equity method to account for this investment.

(b) Under the equity method, how does Xerox report its investment in Fuji Xerox? If Xerox controlled Fuji Xerox, it would have to prepare consolidated financial statements. Discuss how this would change Xerox's financial statements. That is, in what way and how much would assets and liabilities change?

(c) The use of 50% joint ventures is becoming a fairly common practice. Why might companies like Xerox and Fuji prefer to participate in a joint venture rather than own a majority share?

BYP12-6 **SPS Technologies, Inc.** was formed in 1903 as Standard Pressed Steel. Today, the company is engaged in the design, manufacture, and marketing of high-strength mechanical fasteners, superalloys, and magnetic materials for the aerospace, automotive, and off-highway industries. The company has facilities in Canada, the United Kingdom, the United States, Ireland, Australia, China, Spain, Brazil, Mexico, and India.

The following note to the financial statements appeared in a recent SPS annual report:

SPS TECHNOLOGIES

SPS TECHNOLOGIES, INC.
Notes to the Financial Statements

Investments in Affiliates

As of December 31, 1999, the Company's investments in affiliates consist of a 22.05 percent interest in Precision Fasteners Limited (PFL), Bombay, India, and a 55 percent interest in Shanghai SPS Biao Wu Fasteners Co. Ltd. (SSBW), Shanghai, China. ... The Company is not able to exercise effective control over the operations [of SSBW]. The Company received \$99 of dividends from affiliates in 1997. No dividends were received in 1999 and 1998. Retained earnings of 1999, 1998, and 1997 included undistributed earnings (loss) of affiliates ... of \$(657), \$1,081, and \$3,161, respectively.

Instructions

(a) Do the investments in these two companies represent short- or long-term investments? Are these investments in the shares or bonds of these companies?
(b) The ownership percentages in these companies vary. Based on the information given, which accounting method seems appropriate for each company? What other information would you like to have before deciding how to account for each investment?
(c) Why do SPS's retained earnings include its affiliates' undistributed earnings (losses)?
(d) If SPS was able to exercise control over the operations of SSBW, what would change in its reporting?

FINANCIAL ANALYSIS ON THE WEB

BYP12-7 The Ontario Securities Commission (OSC) is the regulatory agency of Canada's largest capital market. Its job is to administer and enforce securities legislation in the province of Ontario. The OSC site provides useful information for investors.

www.wiley.com/canada/kimmel

Instructions

Specific requirements of this web case can be found on the Kimmel website.

BYP12-8 The Investor Learning Centre is an independent, not-for-profit organization, created by the Canadian Securities Institute, the country's recognized authority in investment education. We will now explore the glossary of this site to learn commonly used investment terms.

Instructions

Specific requirements of this web case can be found on the Kimmel website.

Critical Thinking

COLLABORATIVE LEARNING ACTIVITY

BYP12-9 At the beginning of the question and answer portion of the annual shareholders' meeting of Revell Corporation, shareholder Carol Finstrom asks, "Why did management sell the holdings in AHM Company at a loss when this company was very profitable during the period its shares were held by Revell?"

Since President Larry Wisdom has just concluded his speech on the recent success and bright future of Revell, he is taken aback by this question and responds, "I remember we paid $1,100,000 for those shares some years ago, and I am sure we sold the shares at a much higher price. You must be mistaken."

Finstrom retorts, "Well, right here in note number 7 to the annual report, it shows that 240,000 shares, a 30% interest in AHM, were sold on the last day of the year. Also, it states that AHM earned $550,000 this year and paid out $150,000 in cash dividends. Further, a summary statement indicates that in past years, while Revell held AHM shares, AHM earned $1,240,000 and paid out $440,000 in dividends. Finally, the statement of earnings for this year shows a loss on the sale of AHM shares of $180,000. So, I doubt that I am mistaken."

Red-faced, President Wisdom turns to you.

Instructions

With the class divided into groups, help out President Wisdom: what dollar amount did Revell receive upon the sale of the AHM shares? Explain why both Finstrom and Wisdom are correct.

COMMUNICATION ACTIVITY

BYP12-10 Chapperal Corporation has purchased two securities for its portfolio. The first is an equity investment in Sting Ray Corporation, one of its suppliers. Chapperal purchased 10% of Sting Ray with the intention of holding it for a number of years but has no intention of purchasing more shares. The second investment is a purchase of debt securities. Chapperal purchased the debt securities because its analysts believe that changes in market interest rates will cause these securities to increase in value in a short period of time. Chapperal intends to sell the securities as soon as they have increased in value.

Instructions

Write a memo to Gil Stiles, the chief financial officer, explaining how to account for each of these investments and the implications for reported earnings from this accounting treatment.

ETHICS CASE

BYP12-11 Kreiter Financial Services Company holds a large portfolio of debt and equity securities as an investment. The total fair market value of the portfolio at December 31, 2001, is lower than total cost, with some securities having increased in value and others having decreased. Vicki Lemke, the financial vice-president, and Ula Greenwood, the controller, are in the process of classifying for the first time the securities in the portfolio.

Lemke suggests classifying the securities that have increased in value as short-term securities in order to increase net earnings for the year. She wants to classify the securities that have decreased in value as long-term securities so that the temporary decreases in value will not affect the 2001 net earnings.

Greenwood disagrees. She recommends classifying the securities that have decreased in value as short-term securities and those that have increased in value as long-term securities. Greenwood argues that the company is having a good earnings year and that recognizing the losses now will help to smooth earnings for this year. Moreover, for future years, when the company may not be as profitable, the company will have built-in gains.

Instructions

(a) Will classifying the securities as Lemke and Greenwood suggest actually affect earnings as each says it will?
(b) Is there anything unethical in what Lemke and Greenwood propose? Who are the stakeholders affected by their proposals?
(c) Assume that Lemke and Greenwood classify the portfolio properly. Now, at year end, Lemke proposes to sell the securities that will increase net earnings for 2001, and Greenwood proposes to sell the securities that will decrease net earnings for 2001. Is this unethical?

Answers to Self-Study Questions

1. a   2. b   3. c   4. a   5. a   6. c   7. c   8. a   9. c

Answer to Loblaw Review It Question 3

Loblaw's short-term investments are detailed in Note 5. They consist of U.S. government securities, commercial paper, bank deposits, and repurchase agreements. They are carried at the lower of cost or quoted market value. Loblaw has long-term investments in franchised stores.

CHAPTER 13

Statement of Cash Flows

STUDY OBJECTIVES

After studying this chapter, you should be able to:

1. Indicate the primary purpose of the statement of cash flows.
2. Distinguish among operating, investing, and financing activities.
3. Explain the impact of the product life cycle on a company's cash flows.
4. Prepare a statement of cash flows using one of two approaches: (a) the indirect method or (b) the direct method.
5. Use the statement of cash flows to evaluate a company.

"I've Got $10 Billion Dollars Burning a Hole in My Pocket!"

Things move fast in the high technology sector. Very fast. The business story of the turn-of-the-millennium period is surely the explosion of activity in areas such as software, Internet-based services, and high-speed communications. Everyone knows stories of software companies started in basements that were sold for millions in a year, and of young entrepreneurs who become dot.com millionaires on the day of their initial public offerings. More established businesses are in an acquisition fever, announcing new mergers or takeovers almost faster than they can be reported. Wireless communications companies double their subscriber base every three to six months.

In this environment, companies must be ready to respond to changes quickly in order to survive and thrive. They need to produce new products and expand to new markets continually. To do this takes cash—lots and lots of cash. Keeping lots of cash available is a real challenge for a young company. It requires great cash management and careful attention to cash flow.

One technique for cash management that is common in young high-tech companies is paying employees in part through stock options. This frees up cash for business activities, especially in the crucial early phase of the company. And employees like it because the options become valuable if the company does well and its share price increases.

Microsoft, at 25 years of age the great-granddaddy of the software industry, was a pioneer of this and other cash management strategies. By some estimates, more than 1,000 Microsoft employees became millionaires through stock options in the first 20 years of the company's operations.

The story of Microsoft's phenomenal growth—how it was founded in 1975 by Bill Gates and, by 2000, had grown so large and powerful that a U.S. judge ordered it to be broken up—is well-known. But the numbers are nonetheless startling. Seattle-based Microsoft's 1999 statement of cash flows reported cash provided by operating activities in excess of US$10

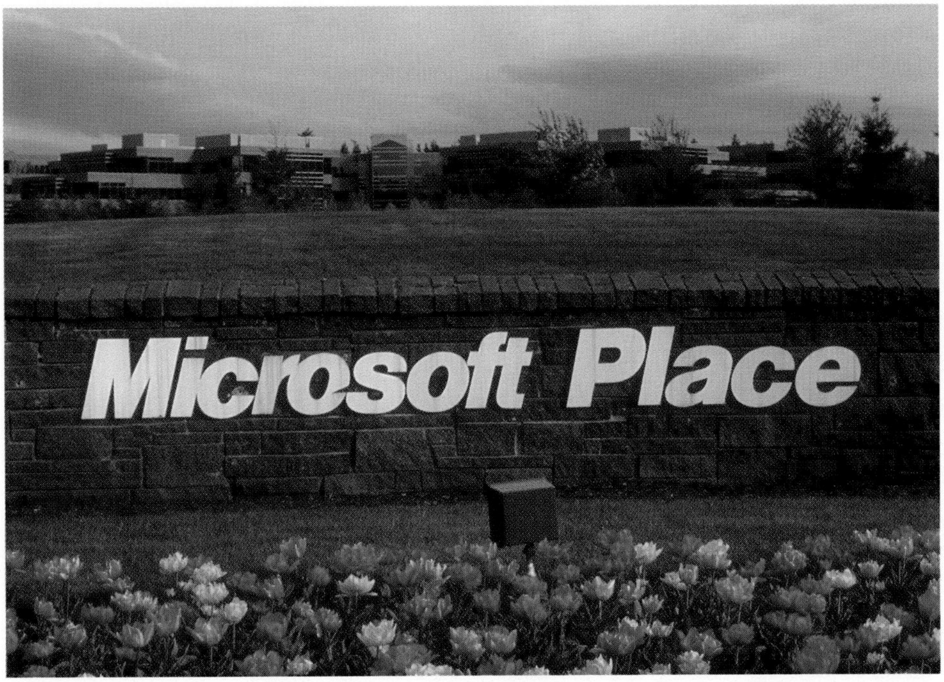

On the World Wide Web
Corel Corporation:
http://www.corel.ca
Microsoft Corporation:
http://www.microsoft.com

billion. Its cash flow per share, $1.96, is double the industry average, and more than its earnings per share of $1.59. Its cash and short-term investments amounted to nearly US$5 billion on its balance sheet at its fiscal year end of June 30, 1999.

That kind of money is astounding, even in this big-money sector. As a comparison, consider Corel Corporation. Based in Ottawa, Corel is an internationally recognized developer of graphics and business applications, such as CorelDRAW and WordPerfect. Founded in 1985 by Dr. Michael Cowpland, Corel is younger than Microsoft by 10 years—eons in the computing world. Cowpland may not be the worldwide household name that Bill Gates is, but Corel is certainly a major player. It generated cash from operations of US$9.9 million for the year ending November 30, 1999, down from a high of US$55 million in 1997. This is still only a drop in the bucket compared with Microsoft's billions.

It is impossible to predict what the future will hold for either of these companies. What effect will the *Antitrust Act* decision have on Microsoft, and on the industry as a whole? How will Corel's recent forays into products associated with the Linux operating system, long touted by many experts as a superior product to the ubiquitous Windows, pan out over time? And, what impact will Corel's and Microsoft's recent strategic alliance for the development, testing, and marketing of products related to Microsoft's .NET platform have on the fortunes of both companies?

Cash management is sure to continue to be an important factor for both companies, as for their ever-growing list of upstart competitors. Beyond that, anything is possible in this sector, where change is the only constant. After all, who could've predicted in 1975 that 19-year-old Bill Gates would become the world's best-known billionaire?

The balance sheet, statement of earnings, and statement of retained earnings do not always show the whole picture of the financial condition of a company or institution. In fact, looking at these three financial statements of some well-known companies, a thoughtful investor might ask questions like these: How did Andrés Wines pay cash dividends in a year in which it had no cash, only bank indebtedness? How did the Student Centre of McGill University purchase more than $97,000 of capital assets in a year in which it reported a loss of $114,000? How did the companies that were involved in the 600 acquisitions mentioned in Chapter 12 finance these deals, worth $60 billion? Answers to these and similar questions can be found in this chapter, which presents the statement of cash flows.

The content and organization of this chapter are as follows:

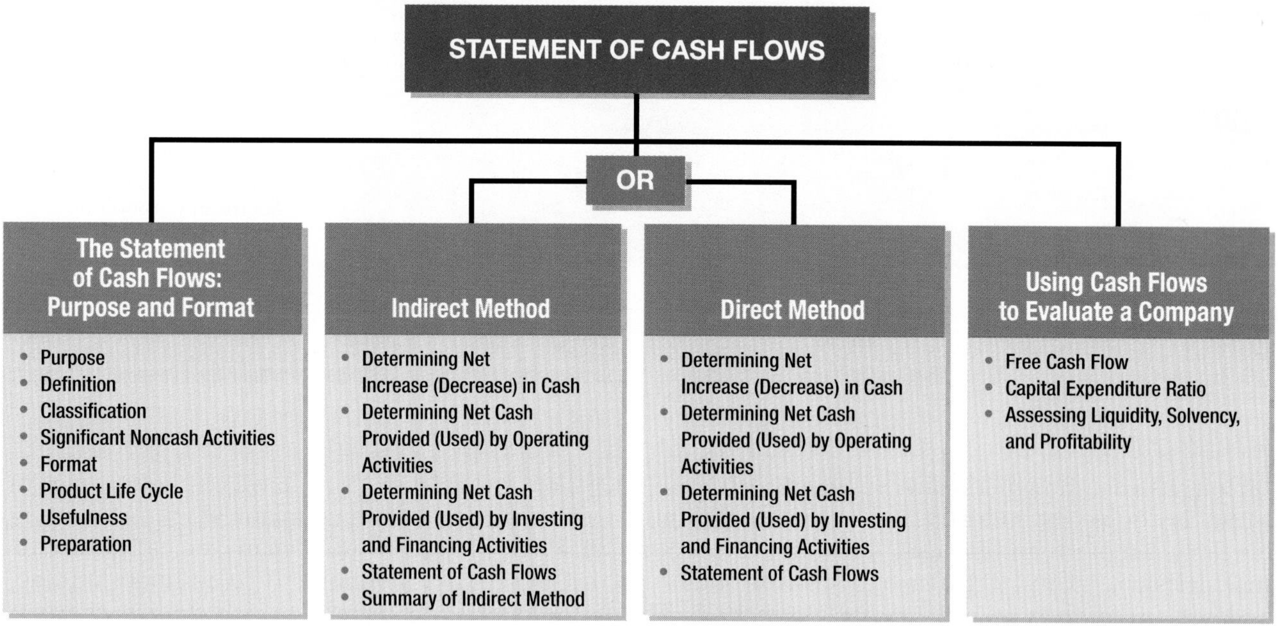

The Statement of Cash Flows: Purpose and Format

The basic financial statements we have presented so far provide only limited information about a company's cash flows (cash receipts and cash payments). For example, comparative balance sheets show the increase in capital assets during the year, but they do not show how the additions were financed or paid for. The statement of earnings shows net earnings, but it does not indicate the amount of cash generated by operating activities. Similarly, the statement of retained earnings shows cash dividends declared but not the cash dividends paid during the year. None of these statements presents a detailed summary of the **net change in cash** as a result of operating, investing, and financing activities during the period.

PURPOSE OF THE STATEMENT OF CASH FLOWS

The primary purpose of the **statement of cash flows** is to provide information about cash receipts, cash payments, and the net change in cash resulting from the operating, investing, and financing activities of a company during the period. These cash activities are reported in a format that reconciles the beginning and ending cash balances.

STUDY OBJECTIVE 1

Indicate the primary purpose of the statement of cash flows.

Reporting the causes of changes in cash is useful because investors, creditors, and other interested parties want to know what is happening to a company's most liquid resource, its cash. As the opening story about Microsoft and Corel demonstrates, to understand a company's financial position, it is essential to understand its cash flows. The statement of cash flows provides answers to these important questions about an enterprise:

Where did the cash come from during the period?
What was the cash used for during the period?
What was the change in the cash balance during the period?

The answers provide important clues about whether dynamic companies like Microsoft and Corel will be able to continue to thrive and invest in new opportunities. The statement of cash flows also provides clues about whether a struggling company will survive or perish.

DEFINITION OF CASH

The statement of cash flows is often prepared using **cash and cash equivalents** as its basis. Cash equivalents are short-term, highly liquid investments that are readily convertible to cash within a very short period of time. Generally, only investments due within three months qualify with this definition. Sometimes short-term or demand loans are also deducted from this amount. Because of the varying definitions of "cash" that can be used in this statement, companies must clearly define *cash equivalents* when they are included.

CLASSIFICATION OF CASH FLOWS

The statement of cash flows classifies cash receipts and cash payments into operating, investing, and financing activities. Transactions within each activity are as follows:

STUDY OBJECTIVE 2

Distinguish among operating, investing, and financing activities.

1. **Operating activities** include the cash effects of transactions that create revenues and expenses and thus enter into the determination of net earnings.
2. **Investing activities** include (a) purchasing and disposing of investments and productive capital assets using cash and (b) lending money and collecting the loans.
3. **Financing activities** include (a) obtaining cash from issuing debt and repaying the amounts borrowed and (b) obtaining cash from shareholders and paying them dividends.

Operating activities is the most important category, because it shows the cash provided or used by company operations. Ultimately, a company must generate cash from its operating activities in order to continue as a going concern and to expand. Illustration 13-1 lists typical cash receipts and cash payments within each of the three activities.

As you can see, some cash flows relating to investing or financing activities are classified as operating activities. For example, receipts of investment revenue (interest and dividends) and payments of interest to lenders are classified as operating activities because these items are reported in the statement of earnings.

Note that, generally, **(1) operating activities involve income determination (statement of earnings) items, (2) investing activities involve cash flows resulting from changes in long-term asset items, and (3) financing activities involve cash flows resulting from changes in long-term liability and shareholders' equity items.**

Illustration 13-1 Typical cash receipts and payments classified by activity

Types of Cash Inflows and Outflows

Operating activities

Cash inflows:
- From sale of goods or services
- From interest received and dividends received

Cash outflows:
- To suppliers for inventory
- To employees for services
- To government for taxes
- To lenders for interest
- To others for expenses

Investing activities

Cash inflows:
- From sale of capital assets
- From sale of investments (debt or equity securities of other entities)
- From collection of principal on loans to other entities

Cash outflows:
- To purchase capital assets
- To purchase investments (debt or equity securities of other entities)
- To make loans to other entities

Financing activities

Cash inflows:
- From issuance of equity securities (company's own shares)
- From issuance of debt (bonds and notes)

Cash outflows:
- To shareholders as dividends
- To redeem long-term debt or reacquire share capital

Helpful Hint Operating activities generally relate to changes in current assets and current long-term liabilities. Investing activities generally relate to changes in long-term assets. Financing activities relate to changes in noncurrent liabilities and shareholders' equity accounts.

SIGNIFICANT NONCASH ACTIVITIES

Not all of a company's significant activities involve cash. Here are three examples of significant noncash activities:

1. Issuance of common shares to purchase assets
2. Conversion of bonds into common shares
3. Issuance of debt to purchase assets

Significant financing and investing activities that do not affect cash are not reported in the body of the statement of cash flows. However, these activities are reported in a note to the financial statements.

The reporting of these activities in a note satisfies the **full disclosure principle**, because it identifies significant noncash investing and financing activities of the company.

FORMAT OF THE STATEMENT OF CASH FLOWS

The three activities—operating, investing, and financing—plus the significant noncash investing and financing activities make up the general format of the statement of cash flows. A widely used form of the statement of cash flows is shown in Illustration 13-2.

Illustration 13-2 Format of statement of cash flows

COMPANY NAME Statement of Cash Flows Period Covered		
Cash flows from operating activities		
(List of individual inflows and outflows)	XX	
Net cash provided (used) by operating activities		XXX
Cash flows from investing activities		
(List of individual inflows and outflows)	XX	
Net cash provided (used) by investing activities		XXX
Cash flows from financing activities		
(List of individual inflows and outflows)	XX	
Net cash provided (used) by financing activities		XXX
Net increase (decrease) in cash		XXX
Cash at beginning of period		XXX
Cash at end of period		XXX
Note x: Noncash investing and financing activities		
(List of individual noncash transactions)		XXX

Alternative Terminology The *statement of cash* flows is also commonly known as the *statement of changes in financial position.*

As illustrated, the section of cash flows from operating activities always appears first, followed by the investing activities and financing activities sections. Also, **the individual inflows and outflows from investing and financing activities are reported separately**. The cash outflow for the purchase of capital assets is reported separately from the cash inflow from the sale of capital assets. Similarly, the cash inflow from the issuance of debt securities is reported separately from the cash outflow for the retirement of debt. If a company did not report the inflows and outflows separately, it would obscure the investing and financing activities of the enterprise and thus make it more difficult for the user to assess future cash flows.

The reported operating, investing, and financing activities result in net cash either **provided or used** by each activity. The net cash provided or used by each activity is totalled to show the net increase (decrease) in cash for the period. The net increase (decrease) in cash for the period is then added to or subtracted from the beginning-of-period cash balance to obtain the end-of-period cash balance. The end-of-period cash balance should agree with the cash balance reported on the balance sheet. Finally, any significant noncash investing and financing activities are reported in a note to the statement.

BUSINESS INSIGHT

Investor Perspective

Net earnings are not the same as net cash generated by operating activities. The differences are illustrated by the following results from recent annual reports for the same fiscal year ($ in millions):

Company	Net Earnings	Net Cash Provided by Operating Activities
Canadian Tire Corporation Limited	$167.0	$ 313.1
Dylex Ltd.	19.9	36.5
Hudson's Bay Company	(39.7)	(157.5)
Mark's Work Wearhouse Ltd.	5.8	15.8
Reitmans (Canada) Limited	12.4	25.9
Sears Canada Inc.	146.4	224.1

Note the wide disparity among these companies that were all engaged in similar types of retail merchandising.

BEFORE YOU GO ON . . .

Review It

1. What is the primary purpose of a statement of cash flows?
2 What are cash equivalents?
3. What are the major classifications of cash flows on the statement of cash flows?
4. What are some examples of significant noncash activities?

THE PRODUCT LIFE CYCLE

STUDY OBJECTIVE 3

Explain the impact of the product life cycle on a company's cash flows.

All products go through a series of phases called the **product life cycle**. The phases (in order of their occurrence) are often referred to as the **introductory phase**, **growth phase**, **maturity phase**, and **decline phase**. The introductory phase occurs at the beginning of a company's life, when the company is purchasing assets and beginning to produce and sell product. During the growth phase, the company is striving to expand its production and sales. In the maturity phase, sales and production level off. And during the decline phase, sales of the product fall due to a weakening in consumer demand.

If a company had only one product and that product was, for example, nearing the end of its saleable life, we would say that the company was in the decline phase. Companies generally have more than one product, however, and not all of a company's products are in the same phase of the product life cycle at the same time. We can still characterize a company as being in one of the four phases because the majority of its products are in a particular phase.

Illustration 13-3 shows that the phase a company is in affects its cash flows. In the **introductory phase**, we expect that the company will be spending considerable amounts to purchase productive assets, but it will not be generating positive cash from operating activities. That is, cash used in operating activities will exceed cash generated by operating activities during the introductory phase. To support its asset purchases, the company will have to issue equity or securities. Thus, during the introductory phase, we expect cash from operating activities to be negative, cash from investing to be negative, and cash from financing to be positive.

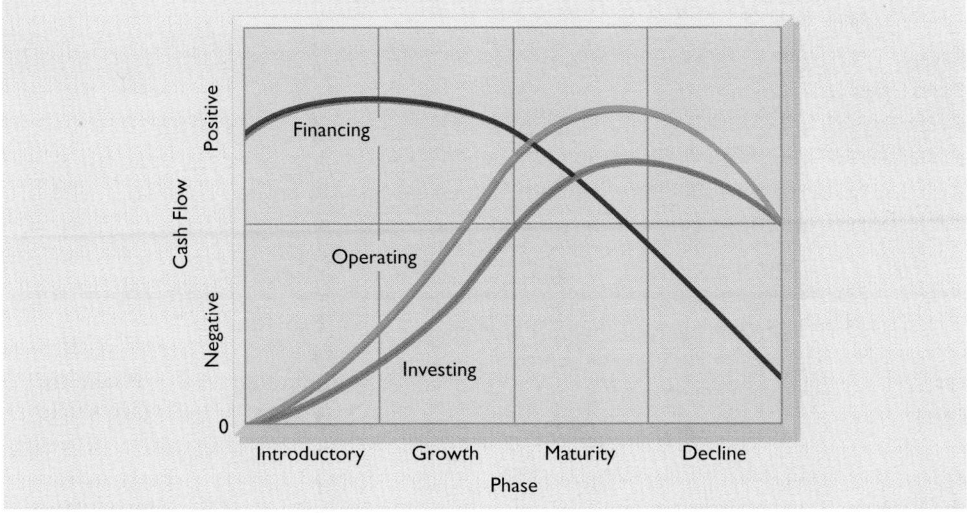

Illustration 13-3 Impact of product life cycle on cash flows

During the **growth phase**, we expect to see the company start to generate small amounts of cash from operating activities. Cash from operating activities will be less than net earnings during this phase. One reason net earnings will exceed cash flow from operating activities during this period is explained by the difference between the cash paid for inventory and the amount expensed as cost of goods sold. Since sales are projected to be increasing, the size of inventory purchases must increase. Thus, less inventory will be expensed on an accrual basis than purchased on a cash basis in the growth phase. Also, collections on accounts receivable will lag behind sales. Because sales are growing, accrual sales during a period will exceed cash collections during that period. Cash needed for asset acquisitions will continue to exceed cash provided by operating activities, requiring that the company make up the deficiency by issuing new debt. Thus, the company continues to show negative cash from investing and positive cash from financing in the growth phase.

During the **maturity phase**, cash from operating activities and net earnings are approximately the same. Cash generated from operating activities exceeds investing needs. Thus, in the maturity phase the company can actually start to retire debt or buy back shares.

Finally, during the **decline phase**, cash from operating activities decreases. Cash from investing might actually become positive as the firm sells off excess assets. Cash from financing may be negative as the company buys back shares and retires debt.

Consider Microsoft. During its early years, it had significant product development costs with little revenue. Microsoft was lucky in that its agreement with IBM to provide the operating system for IBM PCs gave it an early steady source of cash to support growth. As noted earlier, one way it conserved cash was to pay employees with stock options rather than cash. Today, Microsoft could best be characterized as being between the growth and maturity phases. It continues to spend considerable amounts on research and development and investment in new assets. For the last three years its cash from operating activities has exceeded its net earnings. Also, cash from operating activities for the most recent year exceeded cash used for investing. Common shares repurchased exceeded common shares issued over the last three years. For Microsoft, as for any large company, the challenge is to maintain its growth. This may prove difficult as Microsoft has been ordered by a U.S. District Court to break into two separate entries—an applications and Internet focused company and a Windows operating system company. In the software industry, where products become obsolete very quickly, the challenge is particularly great.

BUSINESS INSIGHT

Investor Perspective

Listed here are the net earnings, and cash from operating, investing, and financing activities during a recent year for some well-known companies. The final column suggests their likely phase in the life cycle based on these figures.

Company ($ in millions)	Net Earnings	Cash Provided (Used) by Operating Activities	Cash Provided (Used) by Investing Activities	Cash Provided (Used) by Financing Activities	Likely Phase in Life Cycle
CanWest Global Communications Corp.	$200.1	$140.5	($135.5)	$(52.3)	Early maturity
Chapters Online Inc.	(11.7)	(6.5)	(1.3)	4.3	Introductory
Corel Corporation	(30.4)	14.4	(10.1)	(10.4)	Growth
Hudson's Bay Company	(39.7)	157.5	(719.2)	454.8	Maturity
Loews Cineplex Entertainment Corporation	(62.1)	30.8	28.7	(58.7)	Late growth
T. Eaton Company Limited	(72.0)	(126.7)	(95.3)	72.5	Decline

USEFULNESS OF THE STATEMENT OF CASH FLOWS

Many investors believe that "Cash is cash and everything else is accounting." Cash flow is less susceptible to management manipulation and fraud than traditional accounting measures such as net earnings. Although we suggest that reliance on cash flows to the exclusion of accrual accounting is inappropriate, comparing cash from operating activities to net earnings can reveal important information about the "quality" of reported net earnings—that is, the extent to which net earnings provide a good measure of actual performance.

The information in a statement of cash flows should help investors, creditors, and others evaluate these aspects of the firm's financial position:

1. **The company's ability to generate future cash flows.** By examining relationships between cash provided by operating activities and increases or decreases in cash, investors and others can predict the amounts, timing, and uncertainty of future cash flows better than with accrual-based data.
2. **The company's ability to pay dividends and meet obligations.** Simply put, if a company does not have adequate cash, it cannot pay employees, settle debts, or pay dividends. Employees, creditors, shareholders, and customers should be particularly interested in this statement because it shows the flows of cash in a business.
3. **The reasons for the difference between net earnings and net cash provided (used) by operating activities**. Net earnings are important because they provide information on the success or failure of a business enterprise. However, some analysts are critical of accrual-based net earnings because they require many estimates. As a result, the reliability of net earnings is often challenged. Such is not the case with cash. Many financial statement users investigate the reasons for the difference between net earnings and net cash provided by operating activities. Then they can assess for themselves the reliability of the earnings number.

Helpful Hint Earnings from operating activities and cash flow from operating activities are different. Earnings from operating activities are based on accrual accounting; cash flow from operating activities is prepared on a cash basis.

4. **The investing and financing transactions during the period.** By examining a company's investing activities and financing activities, a financial statement reader can better understand *why* assets and liabilities increased or decreased during the period.

In summary, the information in the statement of cash flows is useful in answering the following questions:

How did cash increase when there was a net loss for the period?
How were the proceeds of the bond issue used?
How was the expansion in the plant and equipment financed?
Why were dividends not increased?
How was the retirement of debt accomplished?
How much money was borrowed during the year?
Is cash flow greater or less than net earnings?

BUSINESS INSIGHT

Investor Perspective

Many analysts from investment houses say that they are using cash flow figures instead of, or in addition, to net earnings because they have lost faith in accrual accounting numbers. They suggest that accrual-based net earnings is losing its usefulness because companies take advantage of accrual accounting rules to report net earnings figures that meet management's goals. Evidence of this shift toward cash flows is found in the fact that 72% of brokerage firm reports now use a cash flow earnings multiple. An increasing number of companies report a cash earnings number as supplemental information in their annual report.

Source: Elizabeth MacDonald "Analysts Increasingly Favor Using Cash Flow Over Reported Earnings in Stock Valuations," *Wall Street Journal*, April 1, 1999, C1.

PREPARING THE STATEMENT OF CASH FLOWS

STUDY OBJECTIVE 4

Prepare a statement of cash flows using one of two approaches: (a) the indirect method or (b) the direct method.

The statement of cash flows is prepared differently from the other basic financial statements. First, it is not prepared from an adjusted trial balance. Because the statement requires detailed information concerning the changes in account balances that occurred between two periods of time, an adjusted trial balance does not provide the data necessary for the statement. Second, the statement of cash flows deals with cash receipts and payments. As a result, **the accrual concept is not used in the preparation of a statement of cash flows**.

The information to prepare this statement usually comes from three sources:

1. **Comparative balance sheet.** Information in this statement indicates the amount of the changes in assets, liabilities, and shareholders' equity from the beginning to the end of the period.
2. **Current statement of earnings.** Information in this statement helps the reader determine the amount of cash provided or used by operating activities during the period.
3. **Additional information.** Additional information includes transaction data that are needed to determine how cash was provided or used during the period.

Preparing the statement of cash flows from these data sources involves the three major steps explained in Illustration 13-4. First, to see where you are headed, start by identifying the change in cash during the period. Has cash increased or decreased during the year? Second, determine the net cash provided (used) by operating activities. Third, determine the net cash provided (used) by investing and financing activities.

Illustration 13-4 Three major steps in preparing the statement of cash flows

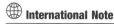

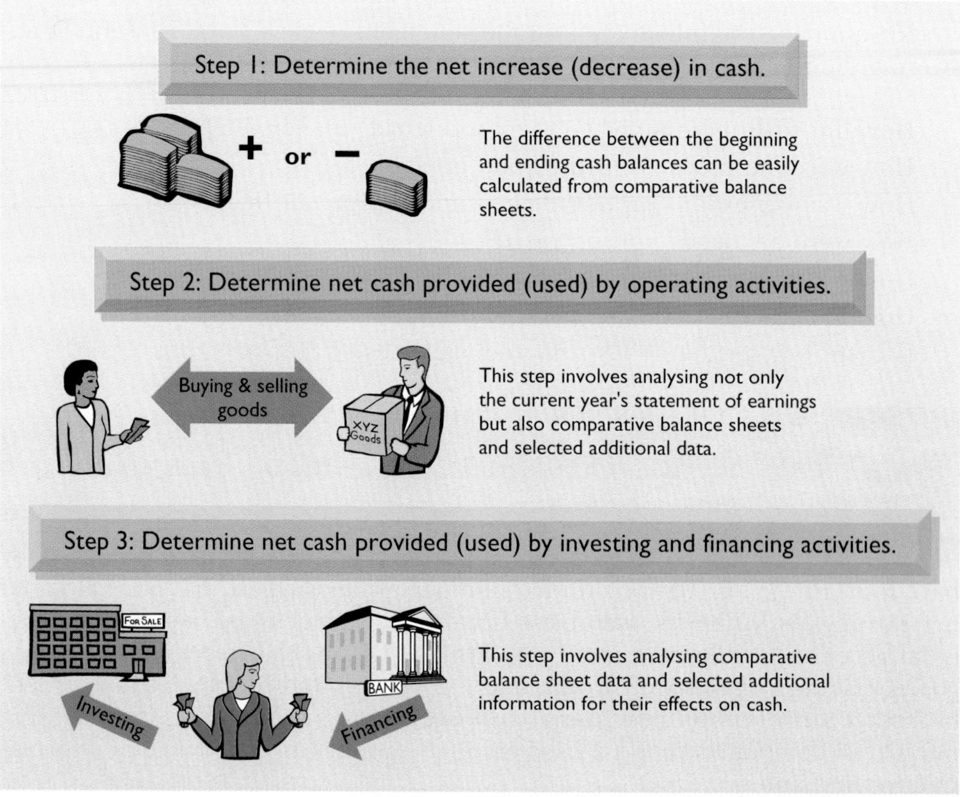

Indirect and Direct Methods

In order to determine the cash provided (used) by operating activities, **net earnings must be converted from an accrual basis to a cash basis**. This conversion may be done by either of two methods: indirect or direct. **Both methods arrive at the same total amount** for "Net cash provided (used) by operating activities," but they differ in disclosing the items that make up the total amount. Note that the two different methods affect only the operating activities section. The investing activities and financing activities sections **are not affected by the choice of method**.

International Note

International accounting requirements are quite similar with regard to the cash flow statement. But there are some interesting exceptions. In Japan, operating and investing activities are combined. In Australia, the direct method is mandatory. In Spain, the indirect method is mandatory. Also, in a number of European countries, a cash flow statement is not required at all, although in practice most publicly traded companies provide one.

The indirect method is used extensively in practice. Companies favour the indirect method for three reasons: (1) it is easier to prepare, (2) it focuses on the differences between net earnings and net cash flow from operating activities, and (3) it tends to reveal less company information to competitors.

Others, however, favour the direct method. This method is more consistent with the objective of a statement of cash flows because it shows operating cash receipts and payments. The CICA has expressed a preference for the direct method but allows the use of either method.

On the following pages, in two separate sections, we describe the use of the two methods. Section 1 illustrates the indirect method, and Section 2 illustrates the direct method. These sections are independent of each other. When you have finished the section(s) assigned by your instructor, turn to the next topic on page 721—"Using Cash Flows to Evaluate a Company."

BEFORE YOU GO ON . . .

Review It

1. What are the phases of the product life cycle, and how do they affect the statement of cash flows?
2. Based on its statement of cash flows, in what stage of the product life cycle is Loblaw? The answer to this question is provided at the end of this chapter.
3. Why is the statement of cash flows useful? What key information does it convey?
4. What are the three major steps in the preparation of a statement of cash flows?

Loblaws
A passion for food... *and a lot more!*

Do It

During the first week of its existence, Plano Molding Corp. had these transactions:

1. Issued 100,000 no par value common shares for $800,000 cash.
2. Borrowed $200,000 from the HSBC Bank, signing a five-year note bearing 8% interest.
3. Purchased two semi-trailer trucks for $170,000 cash.
4. Paid employees $12,000 for salaries and wages.
5. Collected $20,000 cash for services rendered.

Classify each of these transactions by type of cash flow activity.

Reasoning: All cash flows are classified into three activities for purposes of reporting cash inflows and outflows: operating activities, investing activities, and financing activities. Operating activities include the cash effects of transactions that create revenues and expenses and thus enter into the determination of net earnings. Investing activities include (a) purchasing and disposing of investments and productive capital assets using cash and (b) lending money and collecting the loans. Financing activities include (a) obtaining cash from issuing debt and repaying the amounts borrowed and (b) obtaining cash from shareholders and providing them with a return on their investment.

Solution:

1. Financing activity
2. Financing activity
3. Investing activity
4. Operating activity
5. Operating activity

SECTION 1

STATEMENT OF CASH FLOWS—INDIRECT METHOD

To explain and illustrate the indirect method, we will use the transactions of a service company, Computer Services Company Limited, for two years: 2000 and 2001. Annual statements of cash flows will be prepared. Basic transactions will be used in the first year with additional transactions in the second year.

STUDY OBJECTIVE 4a

Prepare a statement of cash flows using the indirect method.

FIRST YEAR OF OPERATIONS—2000

Computer Services Company Limited started on January 1, 2000, when it issued 50,000 no par value common shares for $50,000 cash. The company rented its office space and furniture and performed consulting services throughout the first year. The comparative balance sheet for the beginning and end of 2000, showing increases and decreases, appears in Illustration 13-5.

Illustration 13-5 Comparative balance sheet for 2000, with increases and decreases

COMPUTER SERVICES COMPANY LIMITED
Comparative Balance Sheet
December 31

Assets	Dec. 31, 2000	Jan. 1, 2000	Change Increase/Decrease
Cash	$34,000	$0	$34,000 increase
Accounts receivable	30,000	0	30,000 increase
Equipment	10,000	0	10,000 increase
Total	$74,000	$0	
Liabilities and Shareholders' Equity			
Accounts payable	$ 4,000	$0	$ 4,000 increase
Common shares	50,000	0	50,000 increase
Retained earnings	20,000	0	20,000 increase
Total	$74,000	$0	

Helpful Hint Note that although each of the balance sheet items increased, their individual effects are not the same. Some of these increases are cash inflows, and some are cash outflows.

The statement of earnings and additional information for Computer Services Company are shown in Illustration 13-6.

Illustration 13-6 Statement of earnings and additional information for 2000

COMPUTER SERVICES COMPANY LIMITED
Statement of Earnings
For the Year Ended December 31, 2000

Revenues	$85,000
Operating expenses	40,000
Earnings before income taxes	45,000
Income tax expense	10,000
Net earnings	$35,000

Additional information:
(a) A dividend of $15,000 was declared and paid during the year.
(b) The equipment was purchased at the end of 2000. No amortization was taken in 2000.

Helpful Hint You may wish to immediately insert into the statement of cash flows the beginning and ending cash balances and the increase (decrease) in cash necessitated by these balances. The net increase (decrease) is the target amount. The net cash flows from the three activities must equal the target amount.

DETERMINING THE NET INCREASE (DECREASE) IN CASH (STEP 1)

To prepare a statement of cash flows, the first step is to **determine the net increase or decrease in cash**. This is a simple calculation. For example, Computer Services Company had no cash on hand at the beginning of 2000, but had $34,000 on hand at the end of the year. Thus, the change in cash for 2000 was an increase of $34,000.

DETERMINING NET CASH PROVIDED (USED) BY OPERATING ACTIVITIES (STEP 2)

To determine net cash provided (or used if negative) by operating activities under the indirect method, **net earnings are adjusted for items that did not affect cash**. A useful starting point in determining net cash provided by operating activities is to understand **why** net earnings must be converted. Under generally accepted accounting principles, most companies use the accrual basis of accounting. As you have learned, this basis requires that revenue be recorded when earned and that expenses be recorded when incurred. Earned revenues may include credit sales that have not been collected in cash, and expenses incurred may include costs that have not been paid in cash. Under the accrual basis of accounting, net earnings do not indicate the net cash provided by operating activities. Therefore, under the indirect method, net earnings must be adjusted to convert certain items to the cash basis.

The **indirect method** (or reconciliation method) starts with net earnings and converts them to net cash provided by operating activities. In other words, **the indirect method adjusts net earnings for items that affected reported net earnings but did not affect cash**, as shown in Illustration 13-7. That is, noncash charges in the statement of earnings are added back to net earnings and noncash credits are deducted to arrive at net cash provided by operating activities.

A useful starting point in identifying the adjustments to net earnings are the current asset and current liability accounts other than cash. Those accounts—receivables, payables, prepayments, and inventories—should be analysed for their effects on cash. We will now do this for various accounts.

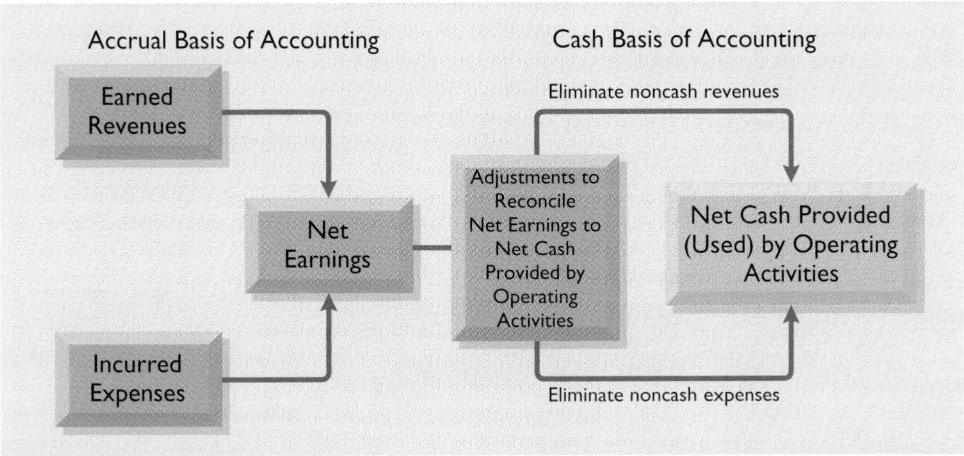

Illustration 13-7 Net earnings versus net cash provided by operating activities

Increase in Accounts Receivable. When accounts receivable increase during the year, revenues on an accrual basis are higher than revenues on a cash basis. In other words, operating activities of the period lead to revenues, **but not all of these revenues result in an increase in cash**. Some of the revenues result in an increase in accounts receivable.

For example, Computer Services Company, in its first year of operations, had revenues of $85,000 but collected only $55,000 in cash. On an accrual basis, revenue was $85,000. On a cash basis, we would record only the $55,000 received during the period. To convert net earnings to net cash provided by operating activities, the increase of $30,000 in the Accounts Receivable account must be deducted from net earnings.

The calculation is as follows:

Net earnings (from revenues)	$85,000	Accrual-based earnings
Deduct: Increase in accounts receivable	30,000	
Cash provided (used) by operating activities (cash receipts from customers)	$55,000	Cash-based earnings

The T account analysis in Illustration 13-8 can also be used to derive cash receipts from customers.

Illustration 13-8 Analysis of accounts receivable

Helpful Hint The T account shows that revenue less increase in receivables equals cash receipts. ($85,000 − $30,000 = $55,000).

ACCOUNTS RECEIVABLE				
Jan. 1	Balance	0	Receipts from customers	55,000
	Revenues	85,000		
Dec. 31	Balance	30,000		

Increase in Inventories. Computer Services Company is a service company, not a merchandising company, and has no merchandise inventory. If a merchandising company was preparing a statement of cash flows using the indirect method, any increase in the Merchandise Inventory account balance would be deducted from net earnings, in a manner similar to the increase in the Accounts Receivable account explained above. Conversely, a decrease in the Merchandise Inventory account balance would result in an addition to net earnings.

The Merchandise Inventory account is increased by the cost of goods purchased and decreased by the cost of goods sold. If the account balance shows a net increase over the year, the cost of goods purchased is greater than the cost of goods sold expense recorded on the statement of earnings. Consequently, any increase in the account balance would be deducted from the statement of earnings, and a decrease added, to adjust cost of goods sold to reflect the actual cost of purchases made during the year. The analysis of accounts payable—shown in the next section—completes the analysis by converting the cost of goods purchased from an accrual basis to a cash basis.

Increase in Accounts Payable. In the first year, Computer Services Company's operating expenses incurred on account were credited to Accounts Payable. When accounts payable increase during the year, operating expenses on an accrual basis are higher than they are on a cash basis. For Computer Services Company, operating expenses reported in the statement of earnings were $40,000. However, since Accounts Payable increased $4,000, only $36,000 ($40,000 − $4,000) of the expenses were paid in cash. To convert net earnings to net cash provided by operating activities, the increase of $4,000 in Accounts Payable must be added to net earnings as follows:

Net earnings (from operating expenses)	($40,000)	Accrual-based earnings
Add: Increase in accounts payable	4,000	
Cash provided (used) by operating activities (payments to creditors)	($36,000)	Cash-based earnings

The T account analysis in Illustration 13-9 also indicates that payments to creditors are less than operating expenses.

Illustration 13-9 Analysis of accounts payable

Helpful Hint The T account shows that operating expenses less increase in accounts payable equals payments to creditors. ($40,000 − $4,000 = $36,000).

ACCOUNTS PAYABLE				
Payments to creditors	36,000	Jan. 1	Balance	0
			Operating expenses	40,000
		Dec. 31	Balance	4,000

For Computer Services Company, the changes in Accounts Receivable and Accounts Payable were the only changes in current asset and current liability accounts. This means that any other revenues or expenses reported in the statement of earnings were received or paid in cash. Thus, Computer Services Company's income tax expense of $10,000 was paid in cash, and no adjustment of net earnings is necessary.

The operating activities section of the statement of cash flows for Computer Services Company is shown in Illustration 13-10.

COMPUTER SERVICES COMPANY LIMITED
Statement of Cash Flows—Indirect Method (Partial)
For the Year Ended December 31, 2000

Cash flows from operating activities		
Net earnings		$35,000
Adjustments to reconcile net earnings to net cash provided by operating activities:		
Increase in accounts receivable	($30,000)	
Increase in accounts payable	4,000	(26,000)
Net cash provided by operating activities		$ 9,000

Illustration 13-10 Operating activities section for 2000—indirect method

Helpful Hint Whether the indirect or direct method (Section 2) is used, net cash provided by operating activities will be the same.

DETERMINING NET CASH PROVIDED (USED) BY INVESTING AND FINANCING ACTIVITIES (STEP 3)

The third and final step in preparing the statement of cash flows begins with a study of the balance sheet to determine changes in noncurrent accounts. The changes in each noncurrent account are then analysed using selected transaction data to determine the effect, if any, the changes had on cash.

For Computer Services Company, the three noncurrent accounts are Equipment, Common Shares, and Retained Earnings, and all three have increased during the year. What caused these increases? No transaction data are given for the increases in Equipment of $10,000 and Common Shares of $50,000. When other explanations are lacking, we assume that any differences involve cash. Thus, the increase in Equipment is assumed to be a purchase of equipment for $10,000 cash. This purchase is reported as a cash outflow in the investing activities section. The increase in Common Shares is assumed to result from the issuance of common shares for $50,000 cash. It is reported as an inflow of cash in the financing activities section of the statement of cash flows. In doing your homework, assume that **any unexplained differences in noncurrent accounts involve cash**.

The reasons for the net increase of $20,000 in the Retained Earnings account are determined by analysis. First, net earnings increased retained earnings by $35,000. Second, the additional information provided at the bottom of the statement of earnings in Illustration 13-6 indicates that a cash dividend of $15,000 was declared and paid. The $35,000 increase due to net earnings is reported in the operating activities section. The cash dividend paid is reported in the financing activities section.

This analysis can also be made directly from the Retained Earnings account

Illustration 13-11 Analysis of retained earnings

RETAINED EARNINGS					
Dec. 31	**Cash dividend**	**15,000**	Jan. 1	Balance	0
			Dec. 31	**Net earnings**	**35,000**
			Dec. 31	Balance	20,000

in the ledger of Computer Services Company as shown in Illustration 13-11.

The $20,000 increase in Retained Earnings in 2000 is a *net* change. When a net change in a noncurrent balance sheet account has occurred during the year, it is generally necessary to report the causes of the net change separately in the statement of cash flows.

STATEMENT OF CASH FLOWS—2000

Having completed the three steps, we can prepare the statement of cash flows by the indirect method. The statement starts with the operating activities section, followed by the investing activities section, and ends with the financing activities section. The 2000 statement of cash flows for Computer Services Company is shown in Illustration 13-12.

Illustration 13-12 Statement of cash flows for 2000—indirect method

COMPUTER SERVICES COMPANY LIMITED
Statement of Cash Flows—Indirect Method
For the Year Ended December 31, 2000

Cash flows from operating activities		
Net earnings		$35,000
Adjustments to reconcile net earnings to net cash provided by operating activities:		
Increase in accounts receivable	($30,000)	
Increase in accounts payable	4,000	(26,000)
Net cash provided by operating activities		9,000
Cash flows from investing activities		
Purchase of equipment	($10,000)	
Net cash used by investing activities		(10,000)
Cash flows from financing activities		
Issuance of common shares	$50,000	
Payment of cash dividends	(15,000)	
Net cash provided by financing activities		35,000
Net increase in cash		34,000
Cash at beginning of period		—
Cash at end of period		$34,000

Computer Services Company's statement of cash flows for 2000 shows that operating activities **provided** $9,000 cash; investing activities **used** $10,000 cash; and financing activities **provided** $35,000 cash. The increase in cash of $34,000 reported in the statement of cash flows agrees with the increase of $34,000 shown as the change in the Cash account in the comparative balance sheet.

SECOND YEAR OF OPERATIONS—2001

Presented in Illustrations 13-13 and 13-14 is information related to the second year of operations for Computer Services Company.

Illustration 13-13 Comparative balance sheet for 2001, with increases and decreases

COMPUTER SERVICES COMPANY LIMITED
Comparative Balance Sheet
December 31

Assets	2001	2000	Change Increase/Decrease
Cash	$ 56,000	$34,000	$ 22,000 increase
Accounts receivable	20,000	30,000	10,000 decrease
Prepaid expenses	4,000	0	4,000 increase
Land	130,000	0	130,000 increase
Building	160,000	0	160,000 increase
Accumulated amortization—building	(11,000)	0	11,000 increase
Equipment	27,000	10,000	17,000 increase
Accumulated amortization—equipment	(3,000)	0	3,000 increase
Total	$383,000	$74,000	
Liabilities and Shareholders' Equity			
Accounts payable	$ 59,000	$ 4,000	$ 55,000 increase
Bonds payable	130,000	0	130,000 increase
Common shares	50,000	50,000	0
Retained earnings	144,000	20,000	124,000 increase
Total	$383,000	$74,000	

Illustration 13-14 Statement of earnings and additional information for 2001

COMPUTER SERVICES COMPANY LIMITED
Statement of Earnings
For the Year Ended December 31, 2001

Revenues		$507,000
Operating expenses (excluding amortization)	$261,000	
Amortization expense	15,000	
Loss on sale of equipment	3,000	279,000
Earnings from operations		228,000
Income tax expense		89,000
Net earnings		$139,000

Additional information:
(a) In 2001, the company declared and paid a $15,000 cash dividend.
(b) The company obtained land through the issuance of $130,000 of long-term bonds.
(c) An office building costing $160,000 was purchased for cash; equipment costing $25,000 was also purchased for cash.
(d) During 2001, the company sold equipment with a book value of $7,000 (cost of $8,000 less accumulated amortization of $1,000) for $4,000 cash.

DETERMINING THE NET INCREASE (DECREASE) IN CASH (STEP 1)

To prepare a statement of cash flows from this information, the first step is to **determine the net increase or decrease in cash**. As indicated from the information presented, cash increased by $22,000 ($56,000 – $34,000).

DETERMINING NET CASH PROVIDED (USED) BY OPERATING ACTIVITIES (STEP 2)

As in step 2 in 2000, net earnings on an accrual basis must be adjusted to arrive at net cash provided (used) by operating activities. Explanations for the adjustments to net earnings for Computer Services Company in 2001 are as follows:

Decrease in Accounts Receivable. Accounts receivable decrease during the period because cash receipts are higher than revenues reported on an accrual basis. To convert net earnings to net cash provided by operating activities, the decrease of $10,000 in the Accounts Receivable account must be added to net earnings.

Increase in Prepaid Expenses. Prepaid expenses increase during a period when cash paid for expenses is greater than expenses reported on an accrual basis. For Computer Services Company, cash payments have been made in the current period, but expenses (as charges to the statement of earnings) have been deferred to future periods. To convert net earnings to net cash provided by operating activities, the increase of $4,000 in the Prepaid Expenses account must be deducted from net earnings. An increase in prepaid expenses results in a decrease in cash during the period.

Increase in Accounts Payable. Like the increase in 2000, the 2001 increase of $55,000 in Accounts Payable must be added to net earnings to arrive at net cash provided by operating activities.

Helpful Hint Amortization is similar to any other expense in that it reduces net earnings. It differs in that it does not involve a current cash outflow; that is why it must be added back to net earnings to arrive at cash provided by operating activities.

Amortization Expense. During 2001, Computer Services Company reported amortization expense of $15,000. Of this amount, $11,000 related to the building and $4,000 to the equipment. These two amounts were determined by analysing the accumulated amortization accounts as follows:

Increase in Accumulated Amortization—Building. As shown in Illustration 13-13, this accumulated amortization increased by $11,000. This change represents the amortization expense on the building for the year. **Because amortization expense is a noncash charge, it is added back to net earnings** in order to arrive at net cash provided by operating activities.

Increase in Accumulated Amortization—Equipment. The increase in the Accumulated Amortization—Equipment account was $3,000. This amount does not represent the total amortization expense for the year, though, because the additional information indicates that this account was decreased (debited $1,000) as a result of the sale of some equipment. Thus, amortization expense for 2001 was $4,000 ($3,000 + $1,000). This amount is **added to net earnings** to determine net cash provided by operating activities. The T account in Illustration 13-15 provides information about the changes that occurred in this account in 2001.

Illustration 13-15 Analysis of accumulated amortization—equipment

ACCUMULATED AMORTIZATION—EQUIPMENT				
Accumulated amortization on equipment sold	1,000	Jan. 1	Balance	0
			Amortization expense	**4,000**
		Dec. 31	Balance	3,000

Amortization expense of $11,000 on the building plus amortization expense of $4,000 on the equipment equals the amortization expense of $15,000 reported on the statement of earnings.

Other charges to expense **that do not require the use of cash**, such as the amortization of bond discounts (added to net earnings) or premiums (deducted from net earnings), are treated in the same manner as amortization of capital assets. Amortization and similar noncash charges are frequently listed in the statement of cash flows as the first adjustments to net earnings.

Loss on Sale of Equipment. On the statement of earnings, Computer Services Company reported a $3,000 loss on the sale of equipment (book value of $7,000 less cash proceeds of $4,000). The loss reduced net earnings but **did not reduce cash**. Thus, the loss is **added to net earnings** in determining net cash provided by operating activities.[1]

As a result of the previous adjustments, net cash provided by operating activities is $218,000, as calculated in Illustration 13-16.

Illustration 13-16 Operating activities section for 2001—indirect method

COMPUTER SERVICES COMPANY
Statement of Cash Flows—Indirect Method (Partial)
For the Year Ended December 31, 2001

Cash flows from operating activities		
Net earnings		$ 139,000
Adjustments to reconcile net earnings to net cash provided by operating activities:		
Amortization expense	$15,000	
Loss on sale of equipment	3,000	
Decrease in accounts receivable	10,000	
Increase in prepaid expenses	(4,000)	
Increase in accounts payable	55,000	79,000
Net cash provided by operating activities		$218,000

Helpful Hint By custom we use the label "amortization expense," even though the expense causes an *increase* in accumulated amortization and could also be described as an "increase in accumulated amortization."

DETERMINING NET CASH PROVIDED (USED) BY INVESTING AND FINANCING ACTIVITIES (STEP 3)

After the determination of net cash provided by operating activities, the final step involves analysing the remaining changes in balance sheet accounts to determine net cash provided/used by investing and financing activities.

Increase in Land. As indicated from the change in the Land account, land worth $130,000 was purchased through the issuance of long-term bonds. Although the issuance of bonds payable for land has no effect on cash, it is a significant noncash investing and financing activity that merits disclosure. As indicated earlier, these activities are disclosed in a note to the statement of cash flows.

Increase in Building. As indicated in the additional information, an office building was acquired using cash of $160,000. This transaction is a cash outflow reported in the investing activities section.

Increase in Equipment. The equipment account increased by $17,000. Based on the additional information, this was a net increase that resulted from two transactions: (1) a purchase of equipment for $25,000 and (2) the sale of equipment costing $8,000 for $4,000 cash proceeds.

The T account in Illustration 13-17 shows the reasons for the change in this account during the year.

[1] If a gain on sale occurs, the treatment the opposite: to allow a gain to flow through to net cash provided by operating activities would be double-counting the gain—once in net earnings and again in the investing activities section as part of the cash proceeds from sale. As a result, a gain is deducted from net earnings in reporting net cash provided by operating activities.

Illustration 13-17
Analysis of equipment

EQUIPMENT				
Jan. 1	Balance	10,000	Cost of equipment sold	8,000
	Purchase of equipment	25,000		
Dec. 31	Balance	27,000		

These transactions are classified as investing activities. Each transaction should be reported separately. Thus, the purchase of equipment should be reported as an outflow of cash for $25,000, and the sale should be reported as an inflow of cash for $4,000. Note that it is the *cash flow* that is important here, not the cost or book value of the equipment.

Helpful Hint When shares or bonds are issued for cash, it is the amount of the issuance price (proceeds) that appears on the statement of cash flows as a financing inflow—rather than the legal value of the shares or face value of the bonds.

Increase in Bonds Payable. The Bonds Payable account increased by $130,000. As shown in the additional information, land was acquired through the issuance of these bonds. As indicated earlier, this noncash transaction is reported in a note to the statement.

Helpful Hint It is the *payment* of dividends, not the declaration, that appears on the statement of cash flows.

Increase in Retained Earnings. Retained Earnings increased by $124,000 during the year. This increase can be explained by two factors: (1) net earnings of $139,000 increased Retained Earnings and (2) dividends of $15,000 decreased Retained Earnings. Net earnings are converted to net cash provided by operating activities in the operating activities section. Payment of the dividends is a **cash outflow that is reported as a financing activity**.

STATEMENT OF CASH FLOWS—2001

Combining the previous items, we obtain a statement of cash flows for 2001 for Computer Services Company as presented in Illustration 13-18.

Illustration 13-18 Statement of cash flows for 2001—indirect method

Helpful Hint Note that in the investing and financing activities sections, positive numbers indicate cash inflows (receipts) and negative numbers indicate cash outflows (payments).

COMPUTER SERVICES COMPANY LIMITED
Statement of Cash Flows—Indirect Method
For the Year Ended December 31, 2001

Cash flows from operating activities		
Net earnings		$139,000
Adjustments to reconcile net earnings to net cash provided by operating activities:		
Amortization expense	$ 15,000	
Loss on sale of equipment	3,000	
Decrease in accounts receivable	10,000	
Increase in prepaid expenses	(4,000)	
Increase in accounts payable	55,000	79,000
Net cash provided by operating activities		218,000
Cash flows from investing activities		
Purchase of building	($160,000)	
Purchase of equipment	(25,000)	
Sale of equipment	4,000	
Net cash used by investing activities		(181,000)
Cash flows from financing activities		
Payment of cash dividends	($15,000)	
Net cash used by financing activities		(15,000)
Net increase in cash		22,000
Cash at beginning of period		34,000
Cash at end of period		$ 56,000
Note X: Noncash investing and financing activities		
Issuance of bonds payable to purchase land		$130,000

Summary of Conversion to Net Cash Provided by Operating Activities—Indirect Method

As shown in the previous illustrations, the statement of cash flows prepared by the indirect method starts with net earnings and adds or deducts items not affecting cash, to arrive at net cash provided by operating activities. The additions and deductions consist of (1) changes in specific noncash current assets and current liabilities and (2) noncash charges reported in the statement of earnings. A summary of the adjustments for the changes in the account balances of the noncash current assets and current liabilities is provided in Illustration 13-19.

Illustration 13-19
Adjustments for current assets and current liabilities

	Adjustments to Convert Net Earnings to Net Cash Provided by Operating Activities	
Change in Current Asset Account Balance	**Add to Net Earnings**	**Deduct from Net Earnings**
Accounts receivable	Decrease	Increase
Inventory	Decrease	Increase
Prepaid expenses	Decrease	Increase
Other current assets	Decrease	Increase
Change in Current Liability Account Balance		
Accounts payable	Increase	Decrease
Accrued expenses payable	Increase	Decrease
Other current liabilities	Increase	Decrease

Adjustments for the noncash items reported in the statement of earnings are made as shown in Illustration 13-20.

Illustration 13-20
Adjustments for noncash charges

Noncash Items on Statement of Earnings	Adjustments to Convert Net Earnings to Net Cash Provided by Operating Activities
Amortization of capital assets expense	Add
Loss on sale of asset	Add
Gain on sale of asset	Deduct

BEFORE YOU GO ON . . .

Review It

1. What is the format of the operating activities section of the statement of cash flows using the indirect method?
2. Where is amortization expense shown on a statement of cash flows using the indirect method?
3. Where are significant noncash investing and financing activities shown in the statement of cash flows? Give some examples.

Do It

The following information relates to Reynolds Company Inc., a merchandising company. Use it to prepare a statement of cash flows using the indirect method.

REYNOLDS COMPANY INC.
Comparative Balance Sheet
December 31

Assets	2001	2000	Change Increase/Decrease
Cash	$ 54,000	$ 37,000	$ 17,000 increase
Accounts receivable	68,000	26,000	42,000 increase
Inventories	54,000	—	54,000 increase
Prepaid expenses	4,000	6,000	2,000 decrease
Land	45,000	70,000	25,000 decrease
Buildings	200,000	200,000	0
Accumulated amortization—buildings	(21,000)	(11,000)	10,000 increase
Equipment	193,000	68,000	125,000 increase
Accumulated amortization—equipment	(28,000)	(10,000)	18,000 increase
Total	$569,000	$386,000	
Liabilities and Shareholders' Equity			
Accounts payable	$ 23,000	$ 40,000	$ 17,000 decrease
Accrued expenses payable	10,000	–	10,000 increase
Bonds payable	110,000	150,000	40,000 decrease
Common shares	220,000	60,000	160,000 increase
Retained earnings	206,000	136,000	70,000 increase
Total	$569,000	$386,000	

REYNOLDS COMPANY INC.
Statement of Earnings
For the Year Ended December 31, 2001

Revenues		$890,000
Cost of goods sold	$465,000	
Operating expenses	221,000	
Interest expense	12,000	
Loss on sale of equipment	2,000	700,000
Earnings from operations		190,000
Income tax expense		65,000
Net earnings		$125,000

Additional information:

(a) Operating expenses include amortization expense of $33,000.
(b) Land was sold at its book value for cash.
(c) Cash dividends of $55,000 were declared and paid in 2001.
(d) Interest expense of $12,000 was paid in cash.
(e) Equipment with a cost of $166,000 was purchased for cash. Equipment with a cost of $41,000 and a book value of $36,000 was sold for $34,000 cash.
(f) Bonds of $10,000 were redeemed at their book value for cash; bonds of $30,000 were converted into common shares.
(g) Common shares of $130,000 were issued for cash.
(h) Accounts payable pertain to merchandise suppliers.

Reasoning: The balance sheet and the statement of earnings are prepared from an adjusted trial balance of the general ledger. The statement of cash flows is prepared from an analysis of the content in the statement of earnings and changes in the balance sheet.

Solution:

REYNOLDS COMPANY INC.
Statement of Cash Flows—Indirect Method
For the Year Ended December 31, 2001

Cash flows from operating activities		
Net earnings		$125,000
Adjustments to reconcile net earnings to net cash provided by operating activities:		
Amortization expense	$ 33,000	
Increase in accounts receivable	(42,000)	
Increase in inventories	(54,000)	
Decrease in prepaid expenses	2,000	
Decrease in accounts payable	(17,000)	
Increase in accrued expenses payable	10,000	
Loss on sale of equipment	2,000	(66,000)
Net cash provided by operating activities		59,000
Cash flows from investing activities		
Sale of land	$ 25,000	
Sale of equipment	34,000	
Purchase of equipment	(166,000)	
Net cash used by investing activities		(107,000)
Cash flows from financing activities		
Redemption of bonds	($ 10,000)	
Sale of common shares	130,000	
Payment of dividends	(55,000)	
Net cash provided by financing activities		65,000
Net increase in cash		17,000
Cash at beginning of period		37,000
Cash at end of period		$ 54,000
Note X: Noncash investing and financing activities		
Conversion of bonds into common shares		$ 30,000

Helpful Hint To prepare the statement of cash flows,

1. Determine the net increase (decrease) in cash.
2. Determine net cash provided (used) by operating activities. Remember that operating activities generally relate to changes in noncash current assets and current liabilities.
3. Determine net cash provided (used) by investing and financing activities. Remember that investing activities generally relate to changes in noncurrent assets. Financing activities generally relate to changes in noncurrent liabilities and shareholders' equity accounts.

Note: This concludes Section 1 on the preparation of the statement of cash flows using the indirect method. Unless your instructor assigns Section 2, you should turn to the concluding section of the chapter, "Using Cash Flows to Evaluate a Company," on page 721.

SECTION 2

STATEMENT OF CASH FLOWS—DIRECT METHOD

To explain and illustrate the direct method, we will use the transactions of a merchandising company, Jiang Company Limited, for two years: 2000 and 2001. Annual statements of cash flows, will be prepared. Basic transactions will be used in the first year with additional transactions in the second year.

FIRST YEAR OF OPERATIONS—2000

STUDY OBJECTIVE 4b

Prepare a statement of cash flows using the direct method.

Jiang Company began business on January 1, 2000, when it issued 300,000 no par value common shares for $300,000 cash. The company rented office and sales space along with equipment. The comparative balance sheet at the beginning and end of 2000 and the changes in each account are shown in Illustration 13-21. The statement of earnings and additional information for Jiang Company are shown in Illustration 13-22.

Illustration 13-21 Comparative balance sheet for 2000, with increases and decreases

JIANG COMPANY LIMITED
Comparative Balance Sheet
December 31

Assets	Dec. 31, 2000	Jan. 1, 2000	Change Increase/Decrease
Cash	$159,000	$0	$159,000 increase
Accounts receivable	15,000	0	15,000 increase
Inventory	160,000	0	160,000 increase
Prepaid expenses	8,000	0	8,000 increase
Land	80,000	0	80,000 increase
Total	$422,000	$0	
Liabilities and Shareholders' Equity			
Accounts payable	$ 60,000	$0	$ 60,000 increase
Accrued expenses payable	20,000	0	20,000 increase
Common shares	300,000	0	300,000 increase
Retained earnings	42,000	0	42,000 increase
Total	$422,000	$0	

Illustration 13-22 Statement of earnings and additional information for 2000

JIANG COMPANY LIMITED
Statement of Earnings
For the Year Ended December 31, 2000

Revenues from sales	$780,000
Cost of goods sold	450,000
Gross profit	330,000
Operating expenses	170,000
Earnings before income taxes	160,000
Income tax expense	48,000
Net earnings	$112,000

Additional information:
(a) Dividends of $70,000 were declared and paid in cash.
(b) The accounts payable increase resulted from the purchase of merchandise.

The three steps cited in Illustration 13-4 for preparing the statement of cash flows are used in the direct method.

DETERMINING THE NET INCREASE (DECREASE) IN CASH (STEP 1)

The comparative balance sheet for Jiang Company shows a zero cash balance at January 1, 2000, and a cash balance of $159,000 at December 31, 2000. Therefore, the change in cash for 2000 was a net increase of $159,000.

DETERMINING NET CASH PROVIDED (USED) BY OPERATING ACTIVITIES (STEP 2)

Under the **direct method**, net cash provided by operating activities is calculated by **adjusting each item in the statement of earnings** from the accrual basis to the cash basis. To simplify and condense the operating activities section, **only major classes of operating cash receipts and cash payments are reported**. The difference between these major classes of cash receipts and cash payments is the net cash provided by operating activities, as shown in Illustration 13-23.

Illustration 13-23 Major classes of cash receipts and payments

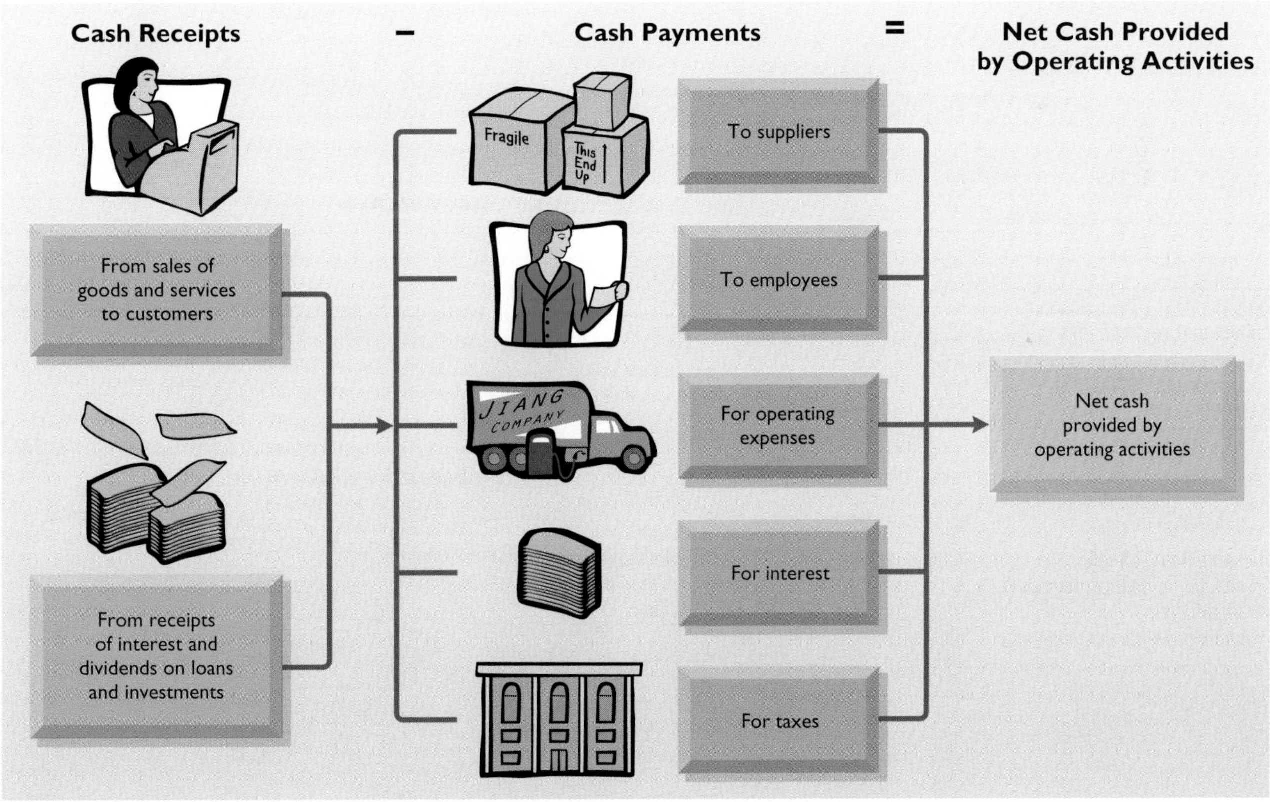

An efficient way to apply the direct method is to analyse the revenues and expenses reported in the statement of earnings in the order in which they are listed, and to then determine cash receipts and cash payments related to these revenues and expenses. The direct method adjustments for Jiang Company in 2000 to determine net cash provided by operating activities are presented in the following sections.

Cash Receipts from Customers. The statement of earnings for Jiang Company reported revenues from customers of $780,000. To determine cash receipts from customers, it is necessary to consider the change in accounts receivable during the year. When accounts receivable increase during the year, revenues on an accrual basis are higher than cash receipts from customers. In other words, operations have led to increased revenues, but not all of these revenues resulted in cash receipts. To determine the amount of cash receipts, the increase in accounts receivable is deducted from sales revenues. Conversely, a decrease in accounts receivable is added to sales revenues because cash receipts from customers then exceed sales revenues.

For Jiang Company, accounts receivable increased by $15,000. Thus, cash receipts from customers were $765,000, as follows:

Revenues from sales	$ 780,000
Deduct: Increase in accounts receivable	15,000
Cash receipts from customers	**$765,000**

Cash receipts from customers may also be determined from an analysis of the Accounts Receivable account, as shown in Illustration 13-24.

Illustration 13-24 Analysis of accounts receivable

ACCOUNTS RECEIVABLE

Jan. 1 Balance	0	**Receipts from customers**	**765,000**
Revenues from sales	780,000		
Dec. 31 Balance	15,000		

Helpful Hint The T account shows that revenue less increase in receivables equals cash receipts. ($780,000 − $15,000 = $765,000).

The relationships among cash receipts from customers, revenues from sales, and changes in accounts receivable are shown in Illustration 13-25.

Illustration 13-25 Formula to calculate cash receipts from customers—direct method

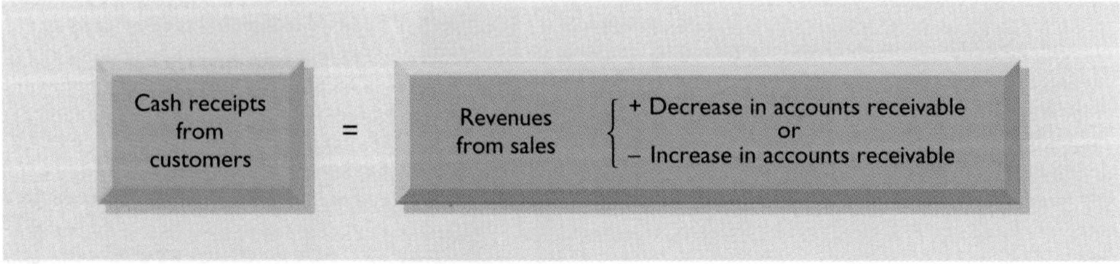

Cash Payments to Suppliers. Jiang Company reported cost of goods sold on its statement of earnings of $450,000. To determine cash payments to suppliers, it is first necessary to find purchases for the year. To find purchases, cost of goods sold is adjusted for the change in inventory. When inventory increases during the year, it means that purchases this year exceed cost of goods sold. As a result, the increase in inventory is added to cost of goods sold to arrive at purchases.

In 2000, Jiang Company's inventory increased by $160,000. Purchases, therefore, are calculated as shown.

Cost of goods sold	$ 450,000
Add: Increase in inventory	160,000
Purchases	**$610,000**

After purchases are calculated, cash payments to suppliers are determined by adjusting purchases for the change in accounts payable (this assumes that only purchases of inventory on account are recorded in the Accounts Payable account). When accounts payable increase during the year, purchases on an accrual basis are higher than they are on a cash basis. As a result, an increase in accounts payable is deducted from purchases to arrive at cash payments to suppliers. Conversely, a decrease in accounts payable is added to purchases, because cash payments to suppliers exceed purchases. Cash payments to suppliers were $550,000:

Purchases	$ 610,000
Deduct: Increase in accounts payable	60,000
Cash payments to suppliers	**$550,000**

Cash payments to suppliers may also be determined from an analysis of the Accounts Payable account, as shown in Illustration 13-26.

Illustration 13-26 Analysis of accounts payable

ACCOUNTS PAYABLE					
Payments to suppliers	**550,000**	Jan.	1	Balance	0
				Purchases	610,000
		Dec.	31	Balance	60,000

Helpful Hint The T account shows that purchases less increase in accounts payable equals payments to suppliers. ($610,000 − $60,000 = $550,000).

The relationship between cash payments to suppliers, cost of goods sold, changes in inventory, and changes in account payable is shown in the formula in Illustration 13-27.

Illustration 13-27 Formula to calculate cash payments to suppliers—direct method

Cash payments to suppliers = Cost of goods sold { + Increase in inventory or − Decrease in inventory } { + Decrease in accounts payable or − Increase in accounts payable }

Cash Payments for Operating Expenses. Operating expenses of $170,000 were reported on Jiang Company's statement of earnings. To determine the cash paid for operating expenses, this amount must be adjusted for any changes in prepaid expenses and accrued expenses payable (where operating expenses incurred on account were recorded). For example, since the Prepaid Expenses account increased by $8,000 during the year, cash paid for operating expenses was $8,000 higher than operating expenses reported on the statement of earnings. To convert operating expenses to cash payments for operating expenses, the increase of $8,000 must be added to operating expenses. Conversely, if prepaid expenses decrease during the year, the decrease must be deducted from operating expenses.

Operating expenses must also be adjusted for changes in accrued expenses payable. When accrued expenses payable increase during the year, operating expenses on an accrual basis are higher than they are on a cash basis. As a result, an increase in accrued expenses payable is deducted from operating expenses to arrive at cash payments for operating expenses. Conversely, a decrease in accrued expenses payable is added to operating expenses, because cash payments exceed operating expenses.

Jiang Company's cash payments for operating expenses were $158,000, calculated as shown:

Operating expenses	$ 170,000
Add: Increase in prepaid expenses	8,000
Deduct: Increase in accrued expenses payable	20,000
Cash payments for operating expenses	**$158,000**

The relationships among cash payments for operating expenses, changes in prepaid expenses, and changes in accrued expenses payable are shown in the formula in Illustration 13-28.

Illustration 13-28 Formula to calculate cash payments for operating expenses—direct method

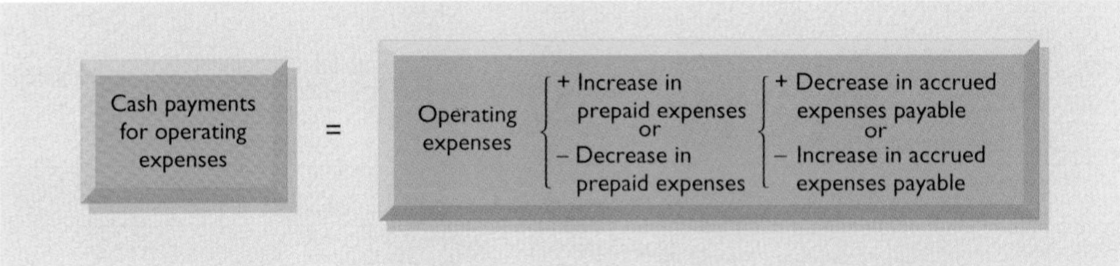

Cash Payments for Interest and Income Taxes. Jiang Company has no interest expense. The statement of earnings for Jiang Company shows income tax expense of $48,000. This amount equals the cash paid because the comparative balance sheet indicates no income taxes payable at either the beginning or end of the year. If Jiang needed to determine the cash paid for income taxes (or interest), assuming a payable account existed, it would simply adjust the expense for any decrease (+) or increase (–) in the payable account.

All of the revenues and expenses in the 2000 statement of earnings have now been adjusted to a cash basis. The operating activities section of the statement of cash flows is presented in Illustration 13-29.

Illustration 13-29 Operating activities section—direct method

Helpful Hint Whether the indirect (Section 1) or direct method is used, net cash provided by operating activities will be the same.

JIANG COMPANY LIMITED
Statement of Cash Flows—Direct Method (Partial)
For the Year Ended December 31, 2000

Cash flows from operating activities		
Cash receipts from customers		$765,000
Cash payments:		
To suppliers	$550,000	
For operating expenses	158,000	
For income taxes	48,000	756,000
Net cash provided by operating activities		$ 9,000

DETERMINING NET CASH PROVIDED (USED) BY INVESTING AND FINANCING ACTIVITIES (STEP 3)

Preparing the investing and financing activities sections of the statement of cash flows begins with a determination of the changes in noncurrent accounts reported in the comparative balance sheet. The change in each account is then analysed using the additional information to determine the effect, if any, the change had on cash.

Increase in Land. No additional information is given for the increase in Land. In such a case, you should assume that the increase affected cash. You should make the same assumption in doing assignments when the cause of a change in a noncurrent account is not explained. The purchase of land is an investing activity. Thus, an outflow of cash of $80,000 for the purchase of land should be reported in the investing activities section.

Increase in Common Shares. As indicated earlier, 300,000 no par value shares were sold for $300,000 cash. The issuance of common shares is a financing activity. Thus, a cash inflow of $300,000 from the issuance of common shares is reported in the financing activities section.

Increase in Retained Earnings. For the Retained Earnings account, the reasons for the net increase of $42,000 are determined by analysis. First, net earnings increased retained earnings by $112,000. The adjustment of accrual-based revenues and expenses to arrive at net cash provided by operating activities was done in step 2 earlier. Second, the additional information indicates that a cash dividend of $70,000 was declared and paid. The cash dividend paid is reported as an outflow of cash in the financing activities section.

Helpful Hint It is the *payment* of dividends, not the declaration, that appears on the cash flow statement.

This analysis can also be made directly from the Retained Earnings account in the ledger of Jiang Company, as shown in Illustration 13-30.

Illustration 13-30 Analysis of retained earnings

RETAINED EARNINGS					
Dec. 31	**Cash dividend**	**70,000**	Jan. 1	Balance	0
			Dec. 31	**Net earnings**	**112,000**
			Dec. 31	Balance	42,000

The $42,000 increase in Retained Earnings in 2000 is a net change. When a net change in a noncurrent balance sheet account has occurred during the year, it is generally necessary to report the individual items that cause the net change.

STATEMENT OF CASH FLOWS—2000

The statement of cash flows can now be prepared. The operating activities section is reported first, followed by the investing and financing activities sections. The statement of cash flows for Jiang Company for 2000 is presented in Illustration 13-31.

The statement of cash flows shows that operating activities **provided** $9,000 of the net increase in cash of $159,000. Financing activities **provided** $230,000 of cash, and investing activities **used** $80,000 of cash. The net increase in cash for the year of $159,000 agrees with the $159,000 increase in cash reported in the comparative balance sheet.

Illustration 13-31
Statement of cash flows for 2000—direct method

JIANG COMPANY LIMITED
Statement of Cash Flows—Direct Method
For the Year Ended December 31, 2000

Cash flows from operating activities		
Cash receipts from customers		$765,000
Cash payments:		
To suppliers	$550,000	
For operating expenses	158,000	
For income taxes	48,000	756,000
Net cash provided by operating activities		9,000
Cash flows from investing activities		
Purchase of land	($80,000)	
Net cash used by investing activities		(80,000)
Cash flows from financing activities		
Issuance of common stock	$300,000	
Payment of cash dividend	(70,000)	
Net cash provided by financing activities		230,000
Net increase in cash		159,000
Cash at beginning of period		—
Cash at end of period		$159,000

Helpful Hint Note that in the investing and financing activities sections, positive numbers indicate cash inflows (receipts) and negative numbers indicate cash outflows (payments).

Second Year of Operations—2001

Illustrations 13-32 and 13-33 present the comparative balance sheet, the statement of earnings, and additional information pertaining to the second year of operations for Jiang Company.

Illustration 13-32 Comparative balance sheet for 2001, with increases and decreases

JIANG COMPANY LIMITED
Comparative Balance Sheet
December 31

Assets	2001	2000	Change Increase/Decrease
Cash	$191,000	$159,000	$ 32,000 increase
Accounts receivable	12,000	15,000	3,000 decrease
Inventory	130,000	160,000	30,000 decrease
Prepaid expenses	6,000	8,000	2,000 decrease
Land	180,000	80,000	100,000 increase
Equipment	160,000	0	160,000 increase
Accumulated amortization—equipment	(16,000)	0	16,000 increase
Total	$663,000	$422,000	
Liabilities and Shareholders' Equity			
Accounts payable	$ 52,000	$ 60,000	$ 8,000 decrease
Accrued expenses payable	15,000	20,000	5,000 decrease
Income taxes payable	12,000	0	12,000 increase
Bonds payable	90,000	0	90,000 increase
Common shares	400,000	300,000	100,000 increase
Retained earnings	94,000	42,000	52,000 increase
Total	$663,000	$422,000	

Illustration 13-33
Statement of earnings and additional information for 2001

JIANG COMPANY LIMITED
Statement of Earnings
For the Year Ended December 31, 2001

Revenues from sales		$975,000
Cost of goods sold	$660,000	
Operating expenses (excluding amortization)	176,000	
Amortization expense	18,000	
Loss on sale of store equipment	1,000	855,000
Earnings before income taxes		120,000
Income tax expense		36,000
Net earnings		$ 84,000

Additional information:
(a) In 2001, the company declared and paid a $32,000 cash dividend.
(b) Bonds were issued at face value for $90,000 in cash.
(c) Equipment costing $180,000 was purchased for cash.
(d) Equipment costing $20,000 was sold for $17,000 cash when the book value of the equipment was $18,000.
(e) Common shares of $100,000 were issued to acquire land.

DETERMINING THE NET INCREASE (DECREASE) IN CASH (STEP 1)

The comparative balance sheet shows a beginning cash balance of $159,000 and an ending cash balance of $191,000. Thus, there was a net increase in cash in 2001 of $32,000.

DETERMINING NET CASH PROVIDED (USED) BY OPERATING ACTIVITIES (STEP 2)

Cash Receipts from Customers. Revenues from sales were $975,000. Since accounts receivable decreased by $3,000, cash receipts from customers were greater than sales revenues. Cash receipts from customers were $978,000, calculated as shown:

Revenues from sales	$ 975,000
Add: Decrease in accounts receivable	3,000
Cash receipts from customers	**$978,000**

Cash Payments to Suppliers. The calculations for the conversion of cost of goods sold to purchases, and of purchases to cash payments to suppliers, are similar to those made in 2000. For 2001, purchases are calculated using cost of goods sold of $660,000 from the statement of earnings and the decrease in inventory of $30,000 from the comparative balance sheet. Purchases of $630,000 are then adjusted by the decrease in accounts payable of $8,000. Cash payments to suppliers were $638,000:

Cost of goods sold	$ 660,000
Deduct: Decrease in inventory	30,000
Purchases	630,000
Add: Decrease in accounts payable	8,000
Cash payments to suppliers	**$638,000**

Cash Payments for Operating Expenses. Operating expenses (exclusive of amortization expense) for 2001 were reported at $176,000. This amount is adjusted for changes in prepaid expenses and accrued expenses payable to arrive at cash payments for operating expenses.

As indicated from the comparative balance sheet, prepaid expenses decreased by $2,000 during the year. This means that $2,000 was allocated to operating expenses (thereby increasing operating expenses), but cash payments did not increase by that amount. To arrive at cash payments for operating expenses, the decrease in prepaid expenses is deducted from operating expenses.

Accrued expenses payable decreased by $5,000 during the period. As a result, cash payments were higher by $5,000 than the amount reported for operating expenses. The decrease in accrued expenses payable is added to operating expenses. Cash payments for operating expenses were $179,000, calculated as shown:

Operating expenses, exclusive of amortization	$ 176,000
Deduct: Decrease in prepaid expenses	2,000
Add: Decrease in accrued expenses payable	5,000
Cash payments for operating expenses	**$179,000**

Amortization Expense and Loss on Sale of Equipment. Operating expenses are shown exclusive of amortization. Amortization expense in 2001 was $18,000. Amortization expense is not shown on a statement of cash flows under the direct method because it is a noncash charge. If the amount for operating expenses includes amortization expense, operating expenses must be reduced by the amount of amortization to determine cash payments for operating expenses.

The loss on sale of store equipment of $1,000 is also a noncash charge. The loss on sale of equipment reduces net earnings, but it does not reduce cash. Thus, the loss on sale of equipment is not reported on a statement of cash flows prepared using the direct method.

Cash Payments for Interest and Income Taxes. Once again, Jiang had no interest payments. Income tax expense reported on the statement of earnings was $36,000. Income taxes payable, however, increased by $12,000, which means that $12,000 of the income taxes have not been paid. As a result, income taxes paid were less than income taxes reported on the statement of earnings. Cash payments for income taxes were therefore $24,000, as shown:

Income tax expense	$ 36,000
Deduct: Increase in income taxes payable	12,000
Cash payments for income taxes	**$24,000**

The relationships among cash payments for income taxes, income tax expense, and changes in income taxes payable are shown in the formula in Illustration 13-34.

Cash payments for income taxes = Income tax expense { + Decrease in income taxes payable or − Increase in income taxes payable

Illustration 13-34 Formula to calculate cash payments for income taxes—direct method

DETERMINING NET CASH PROVIDED (USED) BY INVESTING AND FINANCING ACTIVITIES (STEP 3)

Increase in Land. Land increased by $100,000. The additional information indicates that common shares were issued to purchase the land. Although the issuance of common shares for land has no effect on cash, it is a **significant noncash investing and financing transaction**. This transaction requires disclosure in a note to the statement of cash flows.

Increase in Equipment. The comparative balance sheet shows that the Equipment account increased by $160,000 in 2001. The additional information in Illustration 13-33 indicates that the increase resulted from two investing transactions: (1) equipment costing $180,000 was purchased for cash, and (2) equipment costing $20,000 was sold for $17,000 cash when its book value was $18,000. The relevant data for the statement of cash flows are the cash paid for the purchase and the cash proceeds from the sale. For Jiang Company, the investing activities section will show purchase of equipment, $180,000, as an outflow of cash, and sale of equipment, $17,000, as an inflow of cash. The two amounts **should not be netted; both flows should be shown**.

The analysis of the changes in equipment should include the related Accumulated Amortization account. These two accounts for Jiang Company are shown in Illustration 13-35.

EQUIPMENT

Jan. 1	Balance	0	Cost of equipment sold	20,000
	Cash purchase	180,000		
Dec. 31	Balance	160,000		

ACCUMULATED AMORTIZATION—EQUIPMENT

Sale of equipment	2,000	Jan. 1	Balance	0
			Amortization expense	18,000
		Dec. 31	Balance	16,000

Illustration 13-35 Analysis of equipment and related accumulated amortization

Increase in Bonds Payable. Bonds Payable increased by $90,000. The additional information in Illustration 13-33 indicates that bonds with a face value of $90,000 were issued for $90,000 cash. The issuance of bonds is a financing activity. For Jiang Company, there is an inflow of cash of $90,000 from the issuance of bonds payable.

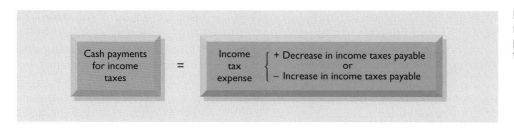

Increase in Common Shares. The Common Shares account increased by $100,000. As indicated in the additional information, land was acquired by issuing common shares. This transaction is a **significant noncash investing and financing transaction** that should be reported in a note to the statement.

Increase in Retained Earnings. The net increase in Retained Earnings of $52,000 resulted from net earnings of $84,000 and the declaration and payment of a cash dividend of $32,000. **Net earnings are not reported in the statement of cash flows under the direct method.** Cash dividends paid of $32,000 are reported in the financing activities section as an outflow of cash.

STATEMENT OF CASH FLOWS—2001

The statement of cash flows for Jiang Company is shown in Illustration 13-36.

Illustration 13-36 Statement of cash flows for 2001—direct method

JIANG COMPANY LIMITED
Statement of Cash Flows—Direct Method
For the Year Ended December 31, 2001

Cash flows from operating activities		
Cash receipts from customers		$978,000
Cash payments:		
To suppliers	$638,000	
For operating expenses	179,000	
For income taxes	24,000	841,000
Net cash provided by operating activities		137,000
Cash flows from investing activities		
Purchase of equipment	($180,000)	
Sale of equipment	17,000	
Net cash used by investing activities		(163,000)
Cash flows from financing activities		
Issuance of bonds payable	$ 90,000	
Payment of cash dividends	(32,000)	
Net cash provided by financing activities		58,000
Net increase in cash		32,000
Cash at beginning of period		159,000
Cash at end of period		$191,000
Note X: Noncash investing and financing activities		
Issuance of common shares to purchase land		$100,000

BEFORE YOU GO ON . . .

Review It

1. What is the format of the operating activities section of the statement of cash flows using the direct method?
2. Where is amortization expense shown on a statement of cash flows using the direct method?
3. Where are significant noncash investing and financing activities shown on the financial statements? Give some examples.

Do It

The following information relates to Reynolds Company Inc., a merchandising company. Use it to prepare a statement of cash flows using the direct method.

REYNOLDS COMPANY INC.
Comparative Balance Sheet
December 31

Assets	2001	2000	Change Increase/Decrease
Cash	$ 54,000	$ 37,000	$ 17,000 increase
Accounts receivable	68,000	26,000	42,000 increase
Inventories	54,000	—	54,000 increase
Prepaid expenses	4,000	6,000	2,000 decrease
Land	45,000	70,000	25,000 decrease
Buildings	200,000	200,000	0
Accumulated amortization—buildings	(21,000)	(11,000)	10,000 increase
Equipment	193,000	68,000	125,000 increase
Accumulated amortization—equipment	(28,000)	(10,000)	18,000 increase
Total	$569,000	$386,000	
Liabilities and Shareholders' Equity			
Accounts payable	$ 23,000	$ 40,000	$ 17,000 decrease
Accrued expenses payable	10,000	—	10,000 increase
Bonds payable	110,000	150,000	40,000 decrease
Common shares	220,000	60,000	160,000 increase
Retained earnings	206,000	136,000	70,000 increase
Total	$569,000	$386,000	

REYNOLDS COMPANY INC.
Statement of Earnings
For the Year Ended December 31, 2001

Revenues		$890,000
Cost of goods sold	$465,000	
Operating expenses	221,000	
Interest expense	12,000	
Loss on sale of equipment	2,000	700,000
Earnings from operations		190,000
Income tax expense		65,000
Net earnings		$125,000

Additional information:

(a) Operating expenses include amortization expense of $33,000 and charges from prepaid expenses of $2,000.
(b) Land was sold at its book value for cash.
(c) Cash dividends of $55,000 were declared and paid in 2001.
(d) Interest expense of $12,000 was paid in cash.
(e) Equipment with a cost of $166,000 was purchased for cash. Equipment with a cost of $41,000 and a book value of $36,000 was sold for $34,000 cash.
(f) Bonds of $10,000 were redeemed at their book value for cash; bonds of $30,000 were converted into common shares.
(g) Common shares of $130,000 were issued for cash.
(h) Accounts payable pertain to merchandise suppliers.

Reasoning: The direct method reports cash receipts less cash payments to arrive at net cash provided by operating activities.

Solution:

REYNOLDS COMPANY INC.
Statement of Cash Flows—Direct Method
For the Year Ended December 31, 2001

Cash flows from operating activities		
Cash receipts from customers		$848,000[a]
Cash payments:		
To suppliers	$536,000[b]	
For operating expenses	176,000[c]	
For interest expense	12,000	
For income taxes	65,000	789,000
Net cash provided by operating activities		59,000
Cash flows from investing activities		
Sale of land	$ 25,000	
Sale of equipment	34,000	
Purchase of equipment	(166,000)	
Net cash used by investing activities		(107,000)
Cash flows from financing activities		
Redemption of bonds	($ 10,000)	
Sale of common shares	130,000	
Payment of dividends	(55,000)	
Net cash provided by financing activities		65,000
Net increase in cash		17,000
Cash at beginning of period		37,000
Cash at end of period		$ 54,000
Note X: Noncash investing and financing activities		
Conversion of bonds into common shares		$ 30,000

Calculations:
[a]$848,000 = $890,000 − $42,000
[b]$536,000 = $465,000 + $54,000 + $17,000
[c]$176,000 = $221,000 − $33,000 − $2,000 − $10,000

Helpful Hint To prepare the statement of cash flows,

1. Determine the net increase (decrease) in cash.
2. Determine net cash provided (used) by operating activities. Remember that operating activities report cash receipts and payments for the statement of earnings. Accrual-based amounts are adjusted for changes in noncash current assets and current liabilities to arrive at cash-based amounts.
3. Determine net cash provided (used) by investing and financing activities. Remember that investing activities generally relate to changes in noncurrent assets. Financing activities generally relate to changes in noncurrent liabilities and shareholders' equity accounts.

Note: This concludes Section 2 on the preparation of the statement of cash flows using the direct method. You should now turn to the next—and concluding—section of the chapter, "Using Cash Flows to Evaluate a Company."

USING CASH FLOWS TO EVALUATE A COMPANY

Traditionally, the ratios most commonly used by investors and creditors have been based on accrual accounting. In previous chapters, we introduced same cash-based ratios that are gaining increased acceptance among analysts. In this section, we review some of those measures and introduce some new ones.

STUDY OBJECTIVE 5

Use the statement of cash flows to evaluate a company.

FREE CASH FLOW

In the statement of cash flows, cash provided by operating activities is supposed to indicate the cash-generating capability of the company. Analysts have noted, however, that **cash provided by operating activities fails to take into account that a company must invest in new capital assets** just to maintain its current level of operations. It also must at least **maintain dividends at current levels** to satisfy investors. As discussed in Chapter 7, **free cash flow** is the term used to describe the cash remaining from operating activities after adjustment for capital expenditures and dividends.

Consider the following example. Suppose that MPC produces and sells 10,000 personal computers this year. It reports cash provided by operating activities of $100,000. In order to maintain production at 10,000 computers, MPC then invests $15,000 in equipment. It also chooses to pay $5,000 in dividends. Its free cash flow was $80,000 ($100,000 − $15,000 − $5,000). The company could use this $80,000 either to purchase new capital assets to expand the business or to pay an $80,000 dividend.

Illustration 13-37 provides basic information excerpted from the 1999 statement of cash flows of Microsoft Corporation.

Illustration 13-37
Microsoft cash flow information

MICROSOFT CORPORATION
Statement of Cash Flows (Partial)
June 30, 1999
(millions of US$)

Cash provided by operating activities		$10,030
Cash flows from investing activities		
Additions to property and equipment	($ 583)	
Purchase of investments	(36,441)	
Sale of investments	(25,833)	
Cash used by investing activities		(11,191)
Cash paid for dividends on preferred shares		(28)

Free cash flow is often calculated with the formula applied to Microsoft in Illustration 13-38. Alternative definitions also exist.

Illustration 13-38
Free cash flow

FREE CASH FLOW	=	CASH PROVIDED BY OPERATING ACTIVITIES	−	CAPITAL EXPENDITURES	−	DIVIDENDS PAID
$9,419	=	$10,030	−	$583	−	$28

$9,419 million is a tremendous amount of cash generated by Microsoft in a single year. It is available for the acquisition of new assets, the retirement of debt or equity securities, the payment of dividends, or fighting the antitrust decision.

Software company Corel Corporation is one of Microsoft's competitors on some products (e.g., WordPerfect and Word) and its partner on others (e.g., Microsoft .NET). Like Microsoft, Corel's success depends on continuing to improve its existing products while developing new products to keep pace with rapid changes in technology. Corel's free cash flow for 1999 was a negative value of $9.2 million. While its cash flow from operating activities was a positive $9.9 million, capital expenditures of $19.1 million resulted in a negative cash flow for 1999. These expenditures were primarily to acquire capital equipment, products, and technology. They were financed partially by cash, and the remainder by issuing common shares. So, while Microsoft still has cash available for future acquisitions (including investment in Corel), divestures, or other purposes, Corel has utilized its cash capacity to date.

DECISION TOOLKIT

Decision Checkpoints	Info Needed for Decision	Tool to Use for Decision	How to Evaluate Results
How much cash did the company generate to either expand operations or pay dividends?	Cash provided by operating activities, cash spent on capital assets, and cash dividends. (Ideally, the measure would use cash spent to maintain the current level of operations, but that is rarely available.)	Free cash flow = Cash provided by operating activities − Capital expenditures − Dividends paid	Significant free cash flow indicates greater potential to finance new investment and pay additional dividends.

BUSINESS INSIGHT

Investor Perspective

Managers in some industries have long suggested that accrual-based income measures understate the true long-term potential of their companies because of excessive amortization charges. For example, cable companies frequently stated that, once they had installed a cable, it would require minimal maintenance and would guarantee the company returns for a long time to come. As a consequence, cable companies, which reported strong operating cash flows but low net earnings, had high share prices because investors focused more on their cash flows from operating activities than on their net earnings. A *Wall Street Journal* article suggests, however, that investors have grown impatient with the cable companies and have lost faith in cash flow from operating activities as an indicator of cable company performance. As it turns out, cable companies have had to make many expensive upgrades to previously installed cable systems. After cable share prices fell dramatically, cable industry analysts emphasized that either free cash flow or net earnings was a better indicator of a cable TV company's long-term potential than cash provided by operating activities.

Source: Susan Pulliam and Mark Robichaux, "Heard on the Street: Cash Flow Stops Propping Cable Stock," *Wall Street Journal,* January 9, 1997, C1.

CAPITAL EXPENDITURE RATIO

Capital expenditures are purchases of capital assets. In addition to free cash flows, another indicator of a company's ability to generate sufficient cash to finance new fixed assets is the **capital expenditure ratio**: cash provided by operating activities divided by capital expenditures. This measure is similar to free cash flow, except that free cash flow reveals the amount of cash available for discretionary use by management. The capital expenditure ratio provides a *relative measure* of cash provided by operating activities compared to cash used for the purchase of productive assets. Using the Microsoft information in Illustration 13-37, we can calculate its capital expenditure ratio as shown in Illustration 13-39.

$$\text{CAPITAL EXPENDITURE RATIO} = \frac{\text{CASH PROVIDED BY OPERATING ACTIVITIES}}{\text{CAPITAL EXPENDITURES}}$$

(millions of US$)	Microsoft	Corel
	$\frac{\$10,030}{\$583} = 17.2$ times	$= (0.5)$ times

Illustration 13-39 Capital expenditure ratio for Microsoft and Corel

Microsoft's ratio of 17.2 times suggests that it could have spent 17 times more on capital assets than it did *without requiring any additional outside financing*. In comparison, Corel's capital expenditure ratio for 1999 was a negative 0.5 times. This provides additional evidence of Microsoft's superior cash-generating capability. It is important to note that this ratio will vary across industries depending on the capital intensity of the industry. That is, we would expect a manufacturing company to have a lower ratio (because by necessity it has higher capital expenditures) than a software company, which spends less of its money on capital assets and more of its money on "intellectual" capital.

DECISION TOOLKIT

Decision Checkpoints	Info Needed for Decision	Tool to Use for Decision	How to Evaluate Results
Can the company finance its capital expenditures with cash provided by operating activities?	Cash provided by operating activities and cash spent on capital assets (capital expenditures)	$\text{Capital expenditure ratio} = \frac{\text{Cash provided by operating activities}}{\text{Capital expenditures}}$	A high value indicates no need for outside financing. It may indicate that the company is in the mature or declining phase of the product life cycle.

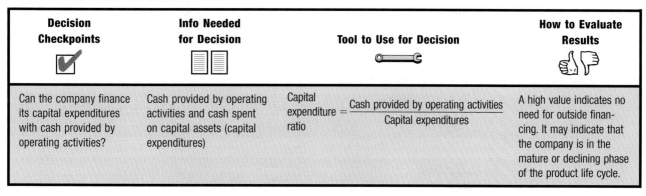

ASSESSING LIQUIDITY, SOLVENCY, AND PROFITABILITY USING CASH FLOWS

Previous chapters have presented ratios used to analyse a company's liquidity, solvency, and profitability. Those ratios used accrual-based numbers from the statement of earnings and balance sheet. In this section, we focus on ratios that are *cash-based* rather than accrual-based. That is, instead of using numbers from the statement of earnings, these ratios use numbers from the statement of cash flows.

As discussed earlier, many analysts are critical of accrual-based numbers, because they feel that the adjustment process allows too much management discretion. These analysts like to supplement accrual-based analysis with measures that use the cash flow statement. One disadvantage of these measures is that, unlike the more commonly employed accrual-based measures, there are no readily available industry averages for comparison. In the following discussion, we use cash flow–based ratios to analyse Microsoft. In addition to the cash flow information provided in Illustration 13-37, we need the following information related to Microsoft:

(millions of US$)	1999	1998
Current assets	$20,233	$15,889
Total assets	37,156	22,357
Current liabilities	8,718	5,730
Total liabilities	8,718	5,730
Sales	19,747	14,484
Net earnings	7,785	4,490

Liquidity

"Liquidity" is the ability of a business to meet its immediate obligations. You learned that one measure of liquidity is the current ratio: current assets divided by current liabilities. A disadvantage of the current ratio is that it uses year-end balances of current asset and current liability accounts, and these year-end balances may not be representative of the company's position during most of the year.

A ratio that partially corrects this problem is the **cash current debt coverage ratio**: cash provided by operating activities divided by average current liabilities. Because cash provided by operating activities involves the entire year rather than a balance at one point in time, it is often considered a better representation of liquidity on the average day. The ratio is shown in Illustration 13-40, with the ratio calculated for Microsoft Corporation and comparative numbers given for Corel. We have also provided each company's current ratio for comparison.

Illustration 13-40 Cash current cash debt coverage ratio

$$\text{CASH CURRENT DEBT COVERAGE RATIO} = \frac{\text{CASH PROVIDED BY OPERATING ACTIVITIES}}{\text{AVERAGE CURRENT LIABILITIES}}$$

(millions of US$)	Cash current debt coverage ratio	Current ratio
Microsoft	$\frac{\$10,030}{(\$8,718 + \$5,730)/2} = 1.39$ times	2.32:1
Corel	0.11 times	1.25:1

Microsoft's net cash provided by operating activities is nearly 1.4 times its average current liabilities. Corel's ratio of 0.11 times is substantially lower than that of Microsoft. Keep in mind that Microsoft's cash position is extraordinary. For example, many companies now have current ratios in the range of 1.0. By this standard, Corel's current ratio of 1.25:1 is respectable, but Microsoft's current ratio of 2.32:1 is very strong.

DECISION TOOLKIT

Decision Checkpoints	Info Needed for Decision	Tool to Use for Decision	How to Evaluate Results
Is the company generating sufficient cash provided by operating activities to meet its current obligations?	Cash provided by operating activities and average current liabilities	Cash current debt coverage ratio = $\frac{\text{Cash provided by operating activities}}{\text{Average current liabilities}}$	A high value suggests good liquidity. Since the numerator contains a "flow" measure, it provides a good supplement to the current ratio.

Solvency

"Solvency" is the ability of a company to survive over the long term. A measure of solvency that uses cash figures is the **cash total debt coverage ratio**: the ratio of cash provided by operating activities to total debt as represented by average total liabilities. This ratio indicates a company's ability to repay its liabilities from cash generated from operating activities—that is, without having to liquidate productive assets such as property, plant, and equipment. The cash total debt coverage ratios for Microsoft and Corel for 1999 are given in Illustration 13-41. The debt to total assets ratios for each company are also provided for comparison.

Illustration 13-41 Cash total debt coverage ratio

$$\text{CASH TOTAL DEBT COVERAGE RATIO} = \frac{\text{CASH PROVIDED BY OPERATING ACTIVITIES}}{\text{AVERAGE TOTAL LIABILITIES}}$$

(millions of US$)	Cash total debt coverage ratio	Debt to total assets ratio
Microsoft	$\frac{\$10,030}{}$ = 1.39 times	23%
Corel	0.11 times	58%

Microsoft has no long-term obligations. Its cash total debt coverage ratio is identical to its cash current debt coverage ratio. Obviously, Microsoft is very solvent. On the other hand, Corel has significant debt, and its cash total debt coverage ratio suggests that its long-term financial health needs much closer monitoring than that of Microsoft.

DECISION TOOLKIT

Decision Checkpoints	Info Needed for Decision	Tool to Use for Decision	How to Evaluate Results
Is the company generating sufficient cash provided by operating activities to meet its long-term obligations?	Cash provided by operating activities and average total liabilities	Cash total debt coverage ratio $= \frac{\text{Cash provided by operating activities}}{\text{Average total liabilities}}$	A high value suggests the company is solvent; that is, it will meet its obligations in the long term.

Profitability

"Profitability" refers to a company's ability to generate a reasonable return. Earlier chapters introduced accrual-based ratios that measure profitability, such as gross profit rate, profit margin, and return on assets. In measures of profitability, the potential differences between cash accounting and accrual accounting are most pronounced. Although some differences are expected, because of the difference in the timing of revenue and expense recognition under cash versus accrual accounting, significant differences should be investigated. A cash-based measure of performance is the cash return on sales ratio.

The **cash return on sales ratio** is cash provided by operating activities divided by net sales. This ratio indicates the company's ability to turn sales into dollars. A low cash return on sales ratio should be investigated because it might indicate that the company is recognizing sales that are not really sales—that is, sales it will never collect. The cash return on sales ratios for Microsoft and Corel for 1999 are presented in Illustration 13-42. The profit margin ratio is also presented for comparison.

Illustration 13-42 Cash return on sales ratio

$$\text{CASH RETURN ON SALES RATIO} = \frac{\text{CASH PROVIDED BY OPERATING ACTIVITIES}}{\text{NET SALES}}$$

(millions of US$)	Cash return on sales ratio	Profit margin ratio
Microsoft	$\frac{\$10,030}{\$19,747} = 51\%$	39%
Corel	4%	(7)%

Corel's cash return on sales ratio of 4% is substantially less than Microsoft's at 51%. The cash return on sales ratio of Microsoft exceeds its profit margin. This is the result of timing differences between cash-basis and accrual-basis accounting. This may suggest that the company employs conservative accounting practices that result in lower reported net earnings. Corel, on the other hand, may be employing more aggressive accounting practices. In fact, 1999 is the first year Corel has reported a profit since 1996, when it acquired WordPerfect, the word processing competitor to Microsoft's Word. Corel is trying to turn around its fortunes by eliminating nonstrategic units, slashing expenditures and jobs, combining facilities, and limiting marketing and product development. Corel is also hoping that enthusiastic support for the Linux operating system will result in improved profitability.

DECISION TOOLKIT

Decision Checkpoints	Info Needed for Decision	Tool to Use for Decision	How to Evaluate Results
Are differences between cash and accrual accounting reasonable?	Cash provided by operating activities, sales, and profit margin ratio	$\text{Cash return on sales ratio} = \dfrac{\text{Cash provided by operating activities}}{\text{Net sales}}$	The cash return on sales ratio should be compared to the profit margin ratio, and significant differences over a series of years should be investigated.

BUSINESS INSIGHT

Management Perspective

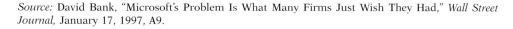

A *Wall Street Journal* article noted that while Microsoft's cash position is enviable, it does present some challenges. Management can't find enough ways to spend the cash. For example, unlike computer chip manufacturer Intel Corporation (another huge generator of cash), Microsoft has few manufacturing costs, so it cannot spend huge sums on new capital assets. Microsoft's management would like to purchase other major software companies, but the federal government won't let it, for fear that it will reduce competition. Instead, Microsoft is constrained to purchase small software makers with promising new products. Ironically, even this does not use much of its cash because, first of all, the companies are small, and second, the owners of these small companies prefer to be paid with Microsoft shares rather than cash.

Microsoft's huge holdings of liquid assets could eventually hurt its share performance. Liquid assets typically provide about a 5% return, whereas Microsoft investors are accustomed to 30% returns. If Microsoft's performance starts to decline because it can't find enough good investment projects, it should distribute cash to its common shareholders in the form of dividends. One big problem: Bill Gates owns roughly 20% of Microsoft, and the last thing he wants to do is pay personal income tax on billions of dollars of dividend income. In the early years, Microsoft did not pay dividends because it wanted to conserve cash. Today it is drowning in cash but still doesn't pay a dividend on its common shares.

Source: David Bank, "Microsoft's Problem Is What Many Firms Just Wish They Had," *Wall Street Journal,* January 17, 1997, A9.

BEFORE YOU GO ON . . .

Review It

1. What is the difference between cash from operating activities and free cash flow?
2. What does it mean if a company has negative free cash flow?
3. Why might an analyst want to supplement accrual-based ratios with cash-based ratios? What are some cash-based ratios?

USING THE DECISION TOOLKIT

Rogers Communications Inc. is Canada's number 1 cable company. Rogers' hybrid fibre-coaxial network is one of the most advanced in North America. The company also operates wireless communications systems and a multimedia group which includes radio and television broadcasting and the publication of magazines and newspapers. Shaw Communications Inc. is also one of Canada's top cable companies, whose core business is providing broadband cable television and Internet services.

The defining feature of today's cable and telecommunications market is change spurred by technological advances and deregulation. Consequently, one particular characteristic of this industry is the heavy investment required in capital assets. It is therefore important to examine various cash-based measures for Rogers and Shaw.

Instructions

Calculate the following cash-based measures for Rogers for 1998, and compare them with those provided here for Shaw:

1. Free cash flow
2. Capital expenditure ratio
3. Cash current debt coverage ratio
4. Cash total debt coverage ratio
5. Cash return on sales ratio

Selected financial statement data for Rogers, and comparative data for Shaw, follow.

ROGERS COMMUNICATIONS INC.
Consolidated Balance Sheets
As at December 31
(in thousands of dollars)

	1998	1997
Assets		
Current assets	$ 506,416	$ 454,929
Noncurrent assets	5,878,437	5,692,086
Total assets	$6,384,853	$6,147,015
Liabilities and Shareholders' Equity		
Current liabilities	$1,059,897	$ 856,586
Long-term liabilities	5,366,481	5,807,852
Total liabilities	6,426,378	6,664,438
Shareholders' equity	(41,525)	(517,423)
Total liabilities and shareholders' equity	$6,384,853	$6,147,015

ROGERS COMMUNICATIONS INC.
Consolidated Statements of Income
For the Years Ended December 31
(in thousands of dollars)

	1998	1997
Revenue	$2,839,229	$2,695,322
Expenses	2,204,460	3,234,777
Net income (loss)	$ 634,769	($ 539,455)

ROGERS COMMUNICATIONS INC.
Consolidated Statements of Changes in Financial Position
For the Years Ended December 31
(in thousands of dollars)

	1998	1997
Funds provided by operating activities	$ 331,060	$ 263,227
Funds provided (used) by financing activities	(671,824)	433,048
Funds provided (used) by investing activities	350,680	(1,018,260)
Increase (decrease) in funds	$ 9,916	($ 321,985)

Funds are defined as cash and short-term deposits less bank advances. Cash spent on capital assets in 1998 was $658,479. Cash paid for dividends was $29,955.

Here are the comparative data for Shaw (also in thousands):

1. Free cash flow	($124,658)
2. Capital expenditures ratio	0.70 times
3. Cash current debt coverage ratio	0.71 times
4. Cash total debt coverage ratio	0.12 times
5. Cash return on sales ratio	30.3%

SHAW

Solution

1. Rogers' free cash flow is actually not free at all. It is a negative $357,374 ($331,060 – $658,479 – $29,955). Shaw's is also a negative $124,658. In both companies, capital investments exceed their cash flow from operating activities. Therefore, both need to seek external financing to pay for these acquisitions. Rogers' total liabilities exceed its total assets on its balance sheet. It has been working to repay its debt, as is evident from the negative financing section of its statement of changes in financial position (statement of cash flows). In addition, Rogers has been financing its capital expenditures primarily by selling other assets and investments (see the positive investing activities section of the statement of changes in financial position). For example, in 1998 Rogers sold telecommunications subsidiary Rogers Telecom in order to raise cash to pay down debt.
2. Rogers' capital expenditure ratio is 0.50 times ($331,060 ÷ $658,479) and Shaw's is 0.70 times. This is a useful supplement to the free cash flow measure. It shows that Rogers only generates enough cash from operating activities to finance half of its capital expenditures. Shaw does better,

generating 70% of its capital expenditure financing through operating activities. The cable industry is very capital intensive, so it is not surprising that these measures are well below those of Microsoft and Corel.

3. The cash current debt coverage ratio for Rogers is calculated as: $331,060 ÷ [($1,059,897 + $856,586)/2] = 0.35 times

   Compared to Shaw, whose value is 0.71 times, Rogers is not generating enough cash to meet its current obligations. In anticipation of deregulation allowing telephone companies to compete with cable operations, Rogers has been upgrading its cable network to handle two-way interaction and has been developing Cantel. But these improvements have been expensive, and the company has been struggling for several years.

4. The cash total debt coverage ratio for Rogers is calculated as: $331,060 ÷ [($6,426,378 + $6,664,438)/2] = 0.05 times

   Once again, Rogers cannot generate enough cash from operating activities to finance its short-term liabilities, much less its long-term or total liabilities. Neither company—Shaw's value is 0.12 times—is doing well in this regard.

5. The cash return on sales ratio for Rogers is 11.7%: ($331,060 ÷ $2,839,229). This is much less than Shaw's at 30.3%. Shaw is far more successful than Rogers in generating cash flow from operating activities.

SUMMARY OF STUDY OBJECTIVES

1 *Indicate the primary purpose of the statement of cash flows.* The statement of cash flows provides information about the cash receipts and cash payments of an entity during a period. A secondary objective is to provide information about the operating, investing, and financing activities of the entity during the period.

2 *Distinguish among operating, investing, and financing activities.* Operating activities include the cash effects of transactions that enter into the determination of net earnings. Investing activities involve cash flows resulting from changes in investments and long-term asset items. Financing activities involve cash flows resulting from changes in long-term liability and shareholders' equity items.

3 *Explain the impact of the product life cycle on a company's cash flows.* During the introductory stage, cash provided by operating activities and cash from investing are negative, whereas cash from financing activities is positive. During the growth stage, cash provided by operating activities becomes positive. During the maturity stage, cash provided by operating activities exceeds investing needs, so the company begins to retire debt. During the decline stage, cash provided by operating activities is reduced, cash from investing activities becomes positive, and cash from financing activities becomes more negative.

4a *Prepare a statement of cash flows using the indirect method.* The preparation of a statement of cash flows involves three major steps: (a) determine the net increase or decrease in cash, (b) determine net cash provided (used) by operating activities, and (c) determine net cash provided (used) by investing and financing activities. Under the indirect method, accrual-basis net earnings are adjusted to net cash provided by operating activities.

4b *Prepare a statement of cash flows using the direct method.* The preparation of the statement of cash flows involves three major steps: (a) determine the net increase or decrease in cash, (b) determine net cash provided (used) by operating activities, and (c) determine net cash provided (used) by investing and financing activities. The direct method reports cash receipts less cash payments to arrive at net cash provided by operating activities.

5 *Use the statement of cash flows to evaluate a company.* A number of measures can be derived by using information from the statement of cash flows and other required financial statements. Free cash flow indicates the amount of cash a company generated during the current year that is available for the payment of dividends or for expansion. The capital expenditure ratio, cash provided by operating activities divided by capital expenditures, complements free cash flow by giving a relative indicator of the sufficiency of cash from operating activities to fund capital expenditures. Liquidity can be measured with the cash current debt coverage ratio (cash provided by operating activities divided by average current liabilities). Solvency can be measured by the cash total debt coverage ratio (cash provided by operating activities divided by average total liabilities). Profitability can be measured by the cash return on sales ratio (cash provided by operating activities divided by sales).

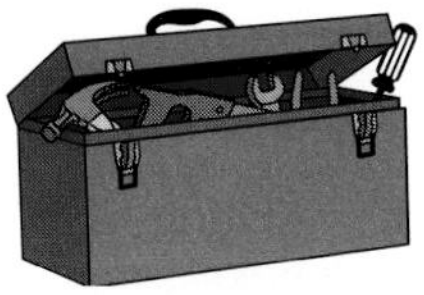

Decision Toolkit—A Summary

Decision Checkpoints	Info Needed for Decision	Tool to Use for Decision	How to Evaluate Results
How much cash did the company generate to either expand operations or pay dividends?	Cash provided by operating activities, cash spent on fixed assets, and cash dividends. (Ideally, the measure would use cash spent to maintain the current level of operations, but that is rarely available.)	Free cash flow = Cash provided by operating activities − Capital expenditures − Dividends paid	Significant free cash flow indicates greater potential to finance new investment and pay additional dividends
Can the company finance its capital expenditures with cash provided by operating activities?	Cash provided by operating activities and cash spent on capital assets (capital expenditures)	Capital expenditure ratio = $\frac{\text{Cash provided by operating activities}}{\text{Capital expenditures}}$	A high value indicates no need for outside financing. It may indicate that the company is in the mature or declining phase of the product life cycle.
Is the company generating sufficient cash provided by operating activities to meet its current obligations?	Cash provided by operating activities and average current liabilities	Cash current debt coverage ratio = $\frac{\text{Cash provided by operating activities}}{\text{Average current liabilities}}$	A high value suggests good liquidity. Since the numerator contains a "flow" measure, it provides a good supplement to the current ratio.
Is the company generating sufficient cash provided by operating activities to meet its long-term obligations?	Cash provided by operating activities and average total liabilities	Cash total debt coverage ratio = $\frac{\text{Cash provided by operating activities}}{\text{Average total liabilities}}$	A high value suggests the company is solvent; that is, it will meet its obligations in the long term.
Are differences between cash and accrual accounting reasonable?	Cash provided by operating activities, sales, and profit margin ratio	Cash return on sales ratio = $\frac{\text{Cash provided by operating activities}}{\text{Net sales}}$	The cash return on sales ratio should be compared to the profit margin ratio, and significant differences over a series of years should be investigated.

Glossary

Capital expenditure ratio A cash-based ratio that indicates the extent to which cash provided by operating activities was sufficient to fund capital expenditure (capital asset) purchases during the year. (p. 723)

Cash current debt coverage ratio A cash-based ratio used to evaluate liquidity, calculated as net cash provided by operating activities divided by average current liabilities. (p. 724)

Cash return on sales ratio A cash-based ratio used to evaluate profitability by dividing net cash provided by operating activities by sales. (p. 726)

Cash total debt coverage ratio A cash-based ratio used to evaluate solvency, calculated as net cash provided by operating activities divided by average total liabilities. (p. 725)

Direct method A method of determining net cash provided by operating activities by adjusting each item in the statement of earnings from the accrual basis to the cash basis. (p. 709)

Financing activities Cash flow activities that include (a) obtaining cash from issuing debt and repaying the amounts borrowed and (b) obtaining cash from shareholders and providing them with a return on their investment. (p. 687)

Free cash flow Cash provided by operating activities less a charge for dividends and capital expenditures. (p. 721)

Indirect method A method of preparing a statement of cash flows in which net earnings are adjusted for items that do not affect cash, to determine net cash provided by operating activities. (p. 697)

Investing activities Cash flow activities that include (a) purchasing and disposing of investments and productive long-lived assets using cash and (b) lending money and collecting on those loans. (p. 687)

Operating activities Cash flow activities that include the cash effects of transactions which create revenues and expenses and thus enter into the determination of net earnings. (p. 687)

Statement of cash flows A basic financial statement that provides information about the cash receipts and cash payments of an entity during a period, classified as operating, investing, and financing activities, in a format that reconciles the beginning and ending cash balances. (p. 687)

Demonstration Problem

The statement of earnings for Kosinski Manufacturing Company Inc. contains the following condensed information:

KOSINSKI MANUFACTURING COMPANY INC.
Statement of Earnings
For the Year Ended December 31, 2001

Revenues		$6,583,000
Operating expenses, excluding amortization	$4,920,000	
Amortization expense	880,000	5,800,000
Earnings before income taxes		783,000
Income tax expense		353,000
Net earnings		$ 430,000

Included in operating expenses is a $24,000 loss resulting from the sale of machinery for $270,000 cash. Machinery was purchased at a cost of $750,000. The following current asset and current liability balances are reported on Kosinski's comparative balance sheet at December 31:

	2001	2000	Increase (Decrease)
Cash	$672,000	$130,000	$542,000
Accounts receivable	775,000	610,000	165,000
Inventories	834,000	867,000	(33,000)
Accounts payable	521,000	501,000	20,000

Income tax expense of $353,000 represents the amount paid in 2001. Dividends declared and paid in 2001 totalled $200,000.

Instructions

(a) Prepare the statement of cash flows using the indirect method.
(b) Prepare the statement of cash flows using the direct method.

Problem-Solving Strategy

This demonstration problem illustrates both the direct and indirect methods using the same basic data. Note the similarities and the differences between the two methods. Both methods report the same information in the investing and financing activities sections. The cash flow from operating activities section reports different information, but the amount—net cash provided by operating activities—is the same for both methods.

Solution to Demonstration Problem

(a)

KOSINSKI MANUFACTURING COMPANY INC.
Statement of Cash Flows—Indirect Method
For the Year Ended December 31, 2001

Cash flows from operating activities		
Net earnings		$ 430,000
Adjustments to reconcile net earnings to net cash provided by operating activities:		
Amortization expense	$ 880,000	
Loss on sale of machinery	24,000	
Increase in accounts receivable	(165,000)	
Decrease in inventories	33,000	
Increase in accounts payable	20,000	792,000
Net cash provided by operating activities		1,222,000

Cash flows from investing activities		
Sale of machinery	$ 270,000	
Purchase of machinery	(750,000)	
Net cash used by investing activities		(480,000)
Cash flows from financing activities		
Payment of cash dividends	($200,000)	
Net cash used by financing activities		(200,000)
Net increase in cash		542,000
Cash at beginning of period		130,000
Cash at end of period		$ 672,000

(b)

KOSINSKI MANUFACTURING COMPANY INC.
Statement of Cash Flows—Direct Method
For the Year Ended December 31, 2001

Cash flows from operating activities		
Cash collections from customers		$ 6,418,000*
Cash payments for operating expenses		(4,843,000)**
Cash payment for income taxes		(353,000)
Net cash provided by operating activities		1,222,000
Cash flows from investing activities		
Sale of machinery	$ 270,000	
Purchase of machinery	(750,000)	
Net cash used by investing activities		(480,000)
Cash flows from financing activities		
Payment of cash dividends	($ 200,000)	
Net cash used by financing activities		(200,000)
Net increase in cash		542,000
Cash at beginning of period		130,000
Cash at end of period		$ 672,000

Direct Method Calculations:

*Calculation of cash collections from customers:	
Revenues per the statement of earnings	$ 6,583,000
Deduct: Increase in accounts receivable	165,000
Cash collections from customers	$ 6,418,000
**Calculation of cash payments for operating expenses:	
Operating expenses per the statement of earnings	$ 4,920,000
Deduct: Loss on sale of machinery	24,000
Deduct: Decrease in inventories	33,000
Deduct: Increase in accounts payable	20,000
Cash payments for operating expenses	$ 4,843,000

Self-Study Questions

Answers are at the end of the chapter.

(SO 1) 1. Which of the following is *incorrect* about the statement of cash flows?
(a) It is a fourth basic financial statement.
(b) It provides information about an entity's cash receipts and cash payments during a period.
(c) It reconciles the ending cash account balance to the balance per the bank statement.

(d) It provides information about the operating, investing, and financing activities of the business.

(SO 2) 2. The statement of cash flows classifies cash receipts and cash payments by these activities:
(a) operating and non-operating.
(b) investing, financing, and operating.
(c) financing, operating, and non-operating.
(d) investing, financing, and non-operating.

(SO 2) 3. Which is an example of a cash flow from an operating activity?
(a) Payment of cash to lenders for interest
(b) Receipt of cash from the sale of share capital
(c) Payment of cash dividends to the company's shareholders
(d) None of the above

(SO 2) 4. Which is an example of a cash flow from an investing activity?
(a) Receipt of cash from the issuance of bonds payable
(b) Payment of cash to repurchase outstanding share capital
(c) Receipt of cash from the sale of equipment
(d) Payment of cash to suppliers for inventory

(SO 2) 5. Cash dividends paid to shareholders are classified on the statement of cash flows as:
(a) operating activities.
(b) investing activities.
(c) financing activities.
(d) a note to the financial statements.

(SO 2) 6. Which is an example of a cash flow from a financing activity?
(a) Receipt of cash from sale of land
(b) Issuance of debt for cash
(c) Purchase of equipment for cash
(d) None of the above

(SO 2) 7. Which of the following is *incorrect* about the statement of cash flows?
(a) The direct method may be used to report cash provided by operating activities.
(b) The statement shows the cash provided (used) by three categories of activity.
(c) The operating section is the last section of the statement.
(d) The indirect method may be used to report cash provided by operating activities.

(SO 3) 8. During the introductory phase of a company's life cycle, one would normally expect to see:
(a) negative cash from operating activities, negative cash from investing activities, and positive cash from financing activities.
(b) negative cash from operating activities, positive cash from investing activities, and positive cash from financing activities.
(c) positive cash from operating activities, negative cash from investing activities, and negative cash from financing activities.
(d) positive cash from operating activities, negative cash from investing activities, and positive cash from financing activities.

Questions 9 and 10 apply only to the indirect method.

9. Net earnings are $132,000, accounts payable increased by $10,000 during the year, inventory decreased by $6,000 during the year, and accounts receivable increased by $12,000 during the year. Under the indirect method, what is net cash provided by operating activities? (SO 4a)
(a) $102,000 (c) $124,000
(b) $112,000 (d) $136,000

10. Noncash items that are added back to net earnings in determining cash provided by operating activities under the indirect method do *not* include: (SO 4a)
(a) amortization expense—capital assets.
(b) amortization of bond discount.
(c) gain on sale of equipment.
(d) loss on sale of equipment.

Questions 11 and 12 apply only to the direct method.

11. The beginning balance in accounts receivable is $44,000, the ending balance is $42,000, and sales during the period are $129,000. What are cash receipts from customers? (SO 4b)
(a) $127,000 (c) $131,000
(b) $129,000 (d) $141,000

12. Which of the following items is reported in the operating activities section of a statement of cash flows prepared by the direct method? (SO 4b)
(a) Loss on sale of building
(b) Increase in accounts receivable
(c) Amortization expense
(d) Cash payments to suppliers

13. The statement of cash flows should *not* be used to evaluate an entity's ability to: (SO 5)
(a) produce net earnings.
(b) generate future cash flows.
(c) pay dividends.
(d) meet obligations.

14. Free cash flow provides an indication of a company's ability to: (SO 5)
(a) generate net earnings.
(b) generate cash to pay dividends.
(c) generate cash to invest in new capital expenditures.
(d) both (b) and (c).

15. Which of the following ratios provides a useful comparison to the profit margin ratio? (SO 5)
(a) Capital expenditure ratio
(b) Cash return on sales ratio
(c) Cash total debt coverage ratio
(d) Cash current debt coverage ratio

Questions

(SO 1) 1. (a) What is a statement of cash flows?
(b) Alice Weiseman maintains that the statement of cash flows is an optional financial statement. Do you agree? Explain.

(SO 1) 2. What questions about cash are answered by the statement of cash flows?

(SO 1) 3. What are cash equivalents? Why might the statement of cash flows be prepared to explain the increase (decrease) in cash and cash equivalents rather than just cash?

(SO 1) 4. Why is the statement of cash flows useful?

(SO 2) 5. Distinguish among the three activities reported in the statement of cash flows.

(SO 2) 6. (a) What are the major sources (inflows) of cash in a statement of cash flows?
(b) What are the major uses (outflows) of cash?

(SO 2) 7. Why is it important to disclose certain noncash transactions? How should they be disclosed?

(SO 2) 8. Wilma Flintstone and Barny Kublestone were discussing the format of the statement of cash flows of Rock Candy Co. A note to Rock Candy's statement of cash flows was entitled "Noncash investing and financing activities." Give three examples of significant noncash transactions that would be reported in this note.

(SO 2) 9. When the total cash inflows exceed the total cash outflows in the statement of cash flows, how and where is this excess identified?

(SO 2) 10. During 2001, Carson Corporation converted $1,700,000 of its total $2,000,000 of bonds payable into common shares. Indicate how the transaction would be reported on a statement of cash flows, if at all.

(SO 3) 11.
(a) What are the phases of the product life cycle?
(b) What effect does each phase have on the numbers reported in a statement of cash flows?

(SO 4) 12. Why is it necessary to use comparative balance sheets, a current statement of earnings, and certain transaction data in preparing a statement of cash flows?

13. Contrast the advantages and disadvantages of the direct and indirect methods of preparing the statement of cash flows. Are both methods acceptable? Which method is preferred by the CICA? Which method is more popular? (SO 4)

14. Describe the indirect method for determining net cash provided (used) by operating activities. (SO 4a)

15. Why is it necessary to convert accrual-based net earnings to cash-based earnings when preparing a statement of cash flows? (SO 4a)

16. The president of Aerosmith Inc. is puzzled. During the last year, the company experienced a net loss of $800,000, yet its cash increased by $300,000 during the same period of time. Explain to the president how this could occur. (SO 4a)

17. Identify five items that are adjustments to convert net earnings to net cash provided by operating activities under the indirect method. (SO 4a)

18. Why and how is amortization expense reported in a statement of cash flows prepared using the indirect method? (SO 4a)

19. Describe the direct method for determining net cash provided by operating activities. (SO 4b)

20. Give the formulas under the direct method for calculating (a) cash receipts from customers and (b) cash payments to suppliers. (SO 4b)

21. Crawford Inc. reported sales of $2 million for 2001. Accounts receivable decreased by $100,000 and accounts payable increased by $300,000. Calculate cash receipts from customers, assuming that the receivable and payable transactions related to operating activities. (SO 4b)

22. In the direct method, why is amortization expense not reported in the cash flows from operating activities section? (SO 4b)

23. Give an example of one accrual-based ratio and one cash-based ratio to measure these characteristics of a company: (SO 5)
(a) Liquidity
(b) Solvency
(c) Profitability

Brief Exercises

BE13-1 Each of these items must be considered in preparing a statement of cash flows for Murphy Corp. for the year ended December 31, 2001. For each item, state how it should be shown in the statement of cash flows for 2001.

Indicate statement presentation of selected transactions. (SO 2)

(a) Issued bonds for $200,000 cash.
(b) Purchased equipment for $150,000 cash.
(c) Sold land costing $20,000 for $20,000 cash.
(d) Declared and paid a $50,000 cash dividend.

Classify items by activities.
(SO 2)

BE13-2 Classify each item as an operating, investing, or financing activity. Assume all items involve cash unless there is information to the contrary.

(a) Purchase of equipment
(b) Sale of building
(c) Redemption of bonds
(d) Amortization
(e) Payment of dividends
(f) Issuance of share capital

Identify financing activity transactions.
(SO 2)

BE13-3 The following T account is a summary of the cash account of Baker Company Ltd.:

Cash (Summary Form)

Balance, Jan. 1	8,000		
Receipts from customers	364,000	Payments for goods	200,000
Dividends on equity investments	6,000	Payments for operating expenses	140,000
Proceeds from sale of equipment	36,000	Interest paid	10,000
Proceeds from issuance of		Taxes paid	8,000
bonds payable	100,000	Dividends paid	40,000
Balance, Dec. 31	116,000		

What amount of net cash provided (used) by financing activities should be reported in the statement of cash flows?

Answer questions related to the phases of product life cycle.
(SO 3)

BE13-4

(a) Why is cash from operating activities likely to be lower than reported net earnings during the growth phase?
(b) Why is cash from investing often positive during the late maturity phase and during the decline phase?

Determine cash received from sale of equipment.
(SO 4)

BE13-5 The T accounts for the Equipment and related Accumulated Amortization account for Trevis Company Ltd. at the end of 2001 are shown here:

Equipment

Beg. bal.	80,000	Disposals	22,000
Acquisitions	41,600		
End. bal.	99,600		

Accumulated Amortization

Disposals	5,500	Beg. bal.	44,500
		Amort.	12,000
		End. bal.	51,000

In addition, Trevis Company's statement of earnings reported a loss on the sale of equipment of $6,700. What amount was reported on the statement of cash flows as "cash flow provided by sale of equipment"?

Calculate cash provided by operating activities—indirect method.
(SO 4a)

BE13-6 Crystal, Inc. reported net earnings of $2.5 million in 2001. Amortization for the year was $260,000, accounts receivable decreased by $350,000, and accounts payable decreased by $310,000. Calculate net cash provided by operating activities using the indirect approach.

Calculate cash provided by operating activities—indirect method.
(SO 4a)

BE13-7 The net earnings for Sterling Engineering Co. for 2001 was $280,000. For 2001, amortization on capital assets was $60,000, and the company incurred a loss on sale of capital assets of $9,000. Calculate net cash provided by operating activities under the indirect method.

Calculate cash provided by operating activities—indirect method.
(SO 4a)

BE13-8 The comparative balance sheet for Rolex Corporation shows these changes in noncash current asset accounts: accounts receivable decrease, $80,000, prepaid expenses increase, $12,000, and inventories increase, $30,000. Calculate net cash provided by operating activities using the indirect method assuming that net earnings are $200,000.

Calculate cash payments for income taxes—indirect method.
(SO 4a)

BE13-9 Depeche Corporation reported income tax expense of $70,000 on its 2001 statement of earnings, and income taxes payable of $12,000 at December 31, 2000, and $9,000 at December 31, 2001. What amount of cash payments were made for income taxes during 2001?

Calculate receipts from customers—direct method.
(SO 4b)

BE13-10 Idol Corporation has accounts receivable of $14,000 at January 1, 2001, and of $24,000 at December 31, 2001. Sales revenues were $480,000 for the year 2001. What is the amount of cash receipts from customers in 2001?

BE13-11 Excel Corporation reports operating expenses of $90,000 excluding amortization expense of $15,000 for 2001. During the year prepaid expenses decreased by $6,600 and accrued expenses payable increased by $4,400. Calculate the cash payments for operating expenses in 2001.

Calculate cash payments for operating expenses—direct method.
(SO 4b)

BE13-12 Jain Corporation reported cash provided by operating activities of $300,000, cash used by investing activities of $250,000, and cash provided by financing activities of $70,000. In addition, cash spent for capital assets during the period was $200,000. Average current liabilities were $150,000 and average total liabilities were $225,000. No dividends were paid. Calculate these values:
(a) Free cash flow
(b) Capital expenditure ratio
(c) Cash current debt coverage ratio

Calculate cash-based ratios.
(SO 5)

BE13-13 **Alliance Atlantis Communications Inc.** reported a 30% increase in cash flow for its first quarter of 1999–2000. It attributes this increase in cash flow to the overwhelming success of its movie *Austin Powers: The Spy Who Shagged Me.* To date, the film has earned more than $20 million in Canadian box office sales. Alliance reported cash provided by operating activities of $234,983,000 and revenues of $163,309,000. An amount of $258,000 was paid for preferred dividends. Cash spent on capital asset additions during the quarter was $4,318,000. Calculate these values:
(a) Free cash flow
(b) Capital expenditure ratio
(c) Cash return on sales

Calculate cash-based ratios.
(SO 5)

EXERCISES

E13-1 Li Eng Corporation had these transactions during 2001:
(a) Purchased a machine for $30,000, giving a long-term note in exchange.
(b) Issued $50,000 of no par value common shares for cash.
(c) Collected $16,000 of accounts receivable.
(d) Declared and paid a cash dividend of $25,000.
(e) Sold a long-term investment with a cost of $15,000 for $15,000 cash.
(f) Issued $200,000 of no par value common shares upon conversion of bonds having a face value of $200,000.
(g) Paid $18,000 on accounts payable.

Classify transactions by type of activity.
(SO 2)

Instructions
Analyse the transactions and indicate whether each transaction resulted in a cash flow provided (used) by operating activities, investing activities, financing activities, or non-cash investing and financing activities.

E13-2 An analysis of comparative balance sheets, the current year's statement of earnings, and the general ledger accounts of Brosnan Corp. uncovered the following items. Assume all items involve cash unless there is information to the contrary.
(a) Purchase of land
(b) Payment of dividends
(c) Sale of building at book value
(d) Exchange of land for patent
(e) Amortization
(f) Redemption of bonds
(g) Receipt of interest on notes receivable
(h) Issuance of share capital
(i) Amortization of patent
(j) Issuance of bonds for land
(k) Payment of interest on notes payable
(l) Conversion of bonds into common shares
(m) Loss on sale of land
(n) Receipt of dividends on equity investment

Classify transactions by type of activity.
(SO 2)

Instructions

Indicate how each item should be classified in the statement of cash flows using these four major classifications: operating activity (specify indirect or direct method), investing activity, financing activity, and noncash investing or financing activity.

Identify phases of product life cycle.
(SO 3)

E13-3 The information in the table is from the statement of cash flows for a company at four different points in time (A, B, C, and D). Negative values are presented in parentheses.

	Point in Time			
	A	**B**	**C**	**D**
Cash provided by operating activities	$100,000	$ 30,000	$ (60,000)	$ (10,000)
Cash provided by investing activities	30,000	25,000	(100,000)	(40,000)
Cash provided by financing activities	(50,000)	(110,000)	70,000	120,000
Net earnings	100,000	10,000	(40,000)	(5,000)

Instructions

For each point in time, state whether the company is most likely characterized as being in the introductory phase, growth phase, maturity phase, or decline phase. In each case, explain your choice.

Prepare the operating activities section—indirect method.
(SO 4a)

E13-4 Pesci Company Ltd. reported net earnings of $195,000 for 2001. Pesci also reported amortization expense of $35,000 and a loss of $5,000 on the sale of equipment. The comparative balance sheet shows an increase in accounts receivable of $15,000 for the year, an $8,000 increase in accounts payable, and a $4,000 decrease in prepaid expenses.

Instructions

Prepare the operating activities section of the statement of cash flows for 2001. Use the indirect method.

Prepare the operating activities section—indirect method.
(SO 4a)

E13-5 The current sections of Barth Inc.'s balance sheets at December 31, 2000 and 2001, are presented here:

	2001	**2000**
Current assets		
Cash	$105,000	$ 99,000
Accounts receivable	110,000	89,000
Inventory	171,000	186,000
Prepaid expenses	27,000	32,000
Total current assets	$413,000	$406,000
Current liabilities		
Accrued expenses payable	$ 15,000	$ 5,000
Accounts payable	85,000	92,000
Total current liabilities	$100,000	$ 97,000

Barth's net earnings for 2001 were $122,000. Amortization expense was $24,000.

Instructions

Prepare the net cash provided by operating activities section of Barth Inc.'s statement of cash flows for the year ended December 31, 2001, using the indirect method.

Prepare partial statement of cash flows—indirect method.
(SO 4a)

E13-6 These three accounts appear in the general ledger of Dupré Corp. during 2001:

Equipment

Date		Debit	Credit	Balance
Jan. 1	Balance			160,000
July 31	Purchase of equipment	70,000		230,000
Sept. 2	Cost of equipment constructed	53,000		283,000
Nov. 10	Cost of equipment sold		45,000	238,000

Accumulated Amortization—Equipment

Date		Debit	Credit	Balance
Jan. 1	Balance			71,000
Nov. 10	Accumulated amortization on equipment sold	30,000		41,000
Dec. 31	Amortization for year		24,000	65,000

Retained Earnings

Date		Debit	Credit	Balance
Jan. 1	Balance			105,000
Aug. 23	Dividends (cash)	14,000		91,000
Dec. 31	Net earnings		47,000	138,000

Instructions

From the postings in the accounts, indicate how the information is reported on a statement of cash flows using the indirect method. The loss on sale of equipment was $6,000.

Prepare a statement of cash flows—indirect method—and calculate cash-based ratios.
(SO 4a, 5)

E13-7 Here is a comparative balance sheet for Winfrey Company Ltd.:

WINFREY COMPANY LTD.
Comparative Balance Sheet
December 31

Assets	2001	2000
Cash	$ 63,000	$ 22,000
Accounts receivable	85,000	76,000
Inventories	180,000	189,000
Land	75,000	100,000
Equipment	260,000	200,000
Accumulated amortization	(66,000)	(42,000)
Total	$597,000	$545,000
Liabilities and Shareholders' Equity		
Accounts payable	$ 34,000	$ 47,000
Bonds payable	150,000	200,000
Common shares	214,000	164,000
Retained earnings	199,000	134,000
Total	$597,000	$545,000

Additional information:

1. Net earnings for 2001 were $105,000.
2. Cash dividends of $40,000 were declared and paid.
3. Bonds payable amounting to $50,000 were redeemed for $50,000 cash.
4. Common shares were issued for $50,000 cash.
5. Sales for 2001 were $978,000.

Instructions

(a) Prepare a statement of cash flows for 2001 using the indirect method.
(b) Calculate these cash-based ratios:
  1. Cash current debt coverage
  2. Cash return on sales
  3. Cash total debt coverage

Calculate cash provided by operating activities—direct method.
(SO 4b)

E13-8 McGillis Company Ltd. completed its first year of operations on December 31, 2001. Its initial statement of earnings showed that McGillis had revenues of $157,000 and operating expenses of $78,000. Accounts receivable and accounts payable at year end were $42,000 and $33,000, respectively. Assume that accounts payable related to operating expenses. Ignore income taxes.

Instructions

Calculate net cash provided by operating activities using the direct method.

Calculate cash payments—direct method.
(SO 4b)

E13-9 The statement of earnings for Garcia Company Inc. shows cost of goods sold, $355,000, and operating expenses (exclusive of amortization), $230,000. The comparative balance sheet for the year shows that inventory increased $6,000, prepaid expenses decreased $6,000, accounts payable (merchandise suppliers) decreased $8,000, and accrued expenses payable increased $8,000.

Instructions

Using the direct method, calculate (a) cash payments to suppliers and (b) cash payments for operating expenses.

Calculate cash flow from operating activities—direct method.
(SO 4b)

E13-10 The 2001 accounting records of Flypaper Airlines Inc. reveal these transactions and events:

Payment of interest	$ 6,000	Collection of accounts receivable	$180,000
Cash sales	48,000	Payment of salaries and wages	68,000
Receipt of dividend revenue	14,000	Amortization expense	16,000
Payment of income taxes	16,000	Proceeds from sale of aircraft	812,000
Net earnings	38,000	Purchase of equipment for cash	22,000
Payment of accounts payable for merchandise	90,000	Loss on sale of aircraft	3,000
		Payment of dividends	14,000
Payment for land	74,000	Payment of operating expenses	20,000

Instructions

Prepare the cash flows from operating activities section using the direct method. (Not all of the items will be used.)

Calculate cash flows—direct method.
(SO 4b)

E13-11 The following information is taken from the 2001 general ledger of Robinson Company Limited:

Rent	Rent expense	$ 31,000
	Prepaid rent, January 1	5,900
	Prepaid rent, December 31	3,000
Salaries	Salaries expense	$ 54,000
	Salaries payable, January 1	5,000
	Salaries payable, December 31	8,000
Sales	Revenue from sales	$180,000
	Accounts receivable, January 1	12,000
	Accounts receivable, December 31	9,000

Instructions

In each case, calculate the amount that should be reported in the operating activities section of the statement of cash flows under the direct method.

Compare two companies by using cash-based ratios.
(SO 5)

E13-12 Information for two companies in the same industry, Rita Corporation and Les Corporation, is presented here:

	Rita Corporation	Les Corporation
Cash provided by operating activities	$200,000	$200,000
Average current liabilities	50,000	100,000
Average total liabilities	200,000	250,000
Net earnings	200,000	200,000
Sales	400,000	800,000

Instructions

Using the cash-based ratios presented in this chapter, compare the (a) liquidity, (b) solvency, and (c) profitability of the two companies.

Compare two companies by using cash-based ratios.
(SO 5)

E13-13 Presented here is 1998 information for **PepsiCo, Inc.** and **Coca-Cola Company**:

(millions of US$)	PepsiCo	Coca-Cola
Cash provided by operating activities	$ 3,211	$ 3,433
Average current liabilities	6,085	6,175
Average total liabilities	14,712	10,175
Net earnings	1,993	3,533
Sales	22,348	18,813

Instructions

Using the cash-based ratios presented in this chapter, compare the (a) liquidity, (b) solvency, and (c) profitability of the two companies.

PROBLEMS: SET A

P13-1A You are provided with the following transactions that took place during a recent fiscal year:

Distinguish among operating, investing, and financing activities.
(SO 2)

	Transaction	Classification	Cash Inflow or Outflow?
(a)	Recorded amortization expense on the capital assets.		
(b)	Removed, from the accounting records, accumulated amortization on capital assets that were sold during the year.		
(c)	Incurred a loss on sale of capital assets.		
(d)	Acquired a building by paying 10% in cash and signing a mortgage payable for the balance.		
(e)	Made principal repayments on the mortgage.		
(f)	Issued common shares.		
(g)	Purchased shares of another company to be held as a long-term equity investment.		
(h)	Paid dividends to common shareholders.		
(i)	Sold inventory on credit. The company uses a perpetual inventory system.		
(j)	Purchased inventory on credit.		
(k)	Paid wages owing to employees.		

Instructions

Complete the table indicating whether each item (1) should be classified as an operating (O) activity, investing (I) activity, financing (F) activity, or as a noncash (NC) transaction, and (2) represents a cash inflow or cash outflow. If the transaction does not affect the statement or notes in any way, state that there is no effect.

P13-2A The following selected account balances relate to the capital asset accounts of Trudeau Inc. at year end:

Determine cash flow effects of changes in capital asset accounts.
(SO 4)

	2002	2001
Accumulated amortization—buildings	$337,500	$300,000
Accumulated amortization—equipment	144,000	96,000
Amortization expense	101,500	85,500
Buildings	750,000	750,000
Equipment	300,000	240,000
Land	100,000	70,000
Loss on sale of equipment	1,000	0

Additional information:

1. Trudeau purchased $80,000 of equipment and $30,000 of land for cash in 2002.
2. Trudeau also sold equipment in 2002.

Instructions

(a) Determine the amounts of any cash inflows or outflows related to the capital asset accounts in 2002.

(b) Indicate where each of the cash inflows or outflows identified in (a) would be classified on the statement of cash flows.

Prepare the operating activities section—indirect method.
(SO 4a)

P13-3A The statement of earnings of Breckenridge Company Ltd. is presented here:

BRECKENRIDGE COMPANY LTD.
Statement of Earnings
For the Year Ended November 30, 2001

Sales		$6,900,000
Cost of goods sold		
Beginning inventory	$1,900,000	
Purchases	4,400,000	
Goods available for sale	6,300,000	
Ending inventory	1,600,000	
Total cost of goods sold		4,700,000
Gross profit		2,200,000
Operating expenses		
Selling expenses	$ 450,000	
Administrative expenses	700,000	1,150,000
Earnings before income taxes		1,050,000
Income tax expense		350,000
Net earnings		$ 700,000

Additional information:

1. Accounts receivable decreased by $300,000 during the year.
2. Prepaid expenses increased by $150,000 during the year.
3. Accounts payable to suppliers of merchandise decreased by $300,000 during the year.
4. Accrued expenses payable decreased by $100,000 during the year.
5. Income tax payable increased by $20,000 during the year.
6. Administrative expenses include amortization expense of $60,000.

Instructions

Prepare the operating activities section of the statement of cash flows for the year ended November 30, 2001, for Breckenridge Company, using the indirect method.

Prepare the operating activities section—indirect method.
(SO 4a)

P13-4A Data for Vail Company Limited are presented in P13-9A.

Instructions

Prepare the operating activities section of the statement of cash flows using the indirect method.

Prepare a statement of cash flows—indirect method.
(SO 4a)

P13-5A Condensed financial data of Galenti, Inc. follow.

GALENTI, INC.
Comparative Balance Sheet
December 31

Assets	2001	2000
Cash	$ 97,800	$ 38,400
Accounts receivable	90,800	33,000
Inventories	112,500	102,850
Prepaid expenses	18,400	16,000
Investments	108,000	94,000
Capital assets	270,000	242,500
Accumulated amortization	(50,000)	(52,000)
Total	$647,500	$474,750
Liabilities and Shareholders' Equity		
Accounts payable	$ 92,000	$ 67,300
Accrued expenses payable	16,500	17,000
Bonds payable	85,000	110,000
Common shares	220,000	175,000
Retained earnings	234,000	105,450
Total	$647,500	$474,750

GALENTI, INC.
Statement of Earnings Data
For the Year Ended December 31, 2001

Sales		$342,780
Less:		
Cost of goods sold	$115,460	
Operating expenses, excluding amortization	12,410	
Amortization expense	46,500	
Income taxes	7,280	
Interest expense	2,730	
Loss on sale of capital assets	7,500	191,880
Net earnings		$150,900

Additional information:

1. New capital assets costing $85,000 were purchased for cash during the year.
2. Old capital assets having an original cost of $57,500 were sold for $1,500 cash.
3. Bonds matured and were paid off at face value for cash.
4. A cash dividend of $22,350 was declared and paid during the year.

Instructions

Prepare a statement of cash flows using the indirect method.

P13-6A This comparative balance sheet is for Cousin Tommy's Toy Company Ltd. as at December 31:

Prepare a statement of cash flows—indirect method.
(SO 4a)

COUSIN TOMMY'S TOY COMPANY LTD.
Comparative Balance Sheet
December 31

Assets	2001	2000
Cash	$ 41,000	$ 45,000
Accounts receivable	47,500	52,000
Inventory	151,450	142,000
Prepaid expenses	16,780	21,000
Land	100,000	130,000
Equipment	228,000	155,000
Accumulated amortization—equipment	(45,000)	(35,000)
Building	200,000	200,000
Accumulated amortization—building	(60,000)	(40,000)
Total	$679,730	$670,000
Liabilities and Shareholders' Equity		
Accounts payable	$ 43,730	$ 40,000
Bonds payable	250,000	300,000
Common shares	200,000	150,000
Retained earnings	186,000	180,000
Total	$679,730	$670,000

Additional information:

1. Operating expenses include amortization expense of $42,000 and charges from prepaid expenses of $4,220.
2. Land was sold for cash at book value.
3. Cash dividends of $32,000 were paid.
4. Net earnings for 2001 was $38,000.
5. Equipment was purchased for $95,000 cash. In addition, equipment costing $22,000 with a book value of $10,000 was sold for $8,100 cash.
6. Bonds were converted at face value by issuing 50,000 no par value common shares.

Instructions

Prepare a statement of cash flows for the year ended December 31, 2001, using the indirect method.

Prepare a statement of cash flows—indirect method—and calculate cash-based ratios.
(SO 4a, 5)

P13-7A These are the financial statements of Swayze Company, Inc.:

SWAYZE COMPANY, INC.
Comparative Balance Sheet
December 31

Assets	2001	2000
Cash	$ 29,000	$ 13,000
Accounts receivable	28,000	14,000
Merchandise inventory	25,000	35,000
Capital assets	60,000	78,000
Accumulated amortization	(20,000)	(24,000)
Total	$122,000	$116,000
Liabilities and Shareholders' Equity		
Accounts payable	$ 29,000	$ 23,000
Income taxes payable	5,000	8,000
Bonds payable	27,000	33,000
Common shares	18,000	14,000
Retained earnings	43,000	38,000
Total	$122,000	$116,000

SWAYZE COMPANY, INC.
Statement of Earnings
For the Year Ended December 31, 2001

Sales		$220,000
Cost of goods sold		180,000
Gross profit		40,000
Selling expenses	$18,000	
Administrative expenses	6,000	24,000
Earnings from operations		16,000
Interest expense		2,000
Earnings before income taxes		14,000
Income tax expense		4,000
Net earnings		$ 10,000

The following additional data were provided:
1. Dividends declared and paid were $5,000.
2. During the year, equipment was sold for $8,500 cash. This equipment originally cost $18,000 and had a book value of $8,500 at the time of sale.
3. All amortization expense is in the selling expense category.
4. All sales and purchases are on account.

Instructions

(a) Prepare a statement of cash flows using the indirect method.
(b) Calculate these cash-based measures:
   1. Cash current debt coverage ratio
   2. Cash return on sales ratio
   3. Cash total debt coverage ratio
   4. Free cash flow

Prepare the operating activities section—direct method.
(SO 4b)

P13-8A Data for Breckenridge Company are presented in P13-3A.

Instructions

Prepare the operating activities section of the statement of cash flows using the direct method.

P13-9A Vail Company's statement of earnings contained the condensed information below:

Prepare the operating activities section—direct method.
(SO 4b)

VAIL COMPANY LIMITED
Statement of Earnings
For the Year Ended December 31, 2001

Revenues		$840,000
Operating expenses, excluding amortization	$624,000	
Amortization expense	60,000	
Loss on sale of equipment	26,000	710,000
Earnings before income taxes		130,000
Income tax expense		40,000
Net earnings		$ 90,000

Vail's balance sheet contained these comparative data at December 31:

	2001	2000
Accounts receivable	$47,000	$55,000
Accounts payable	41,000	33,000
Income taxes payable	4,000	9,000

Accounts payable pertain to operating expenses.

Instructions
Prepare the operating activities section of the statement of cash flows using the direct method.

P13-10A Data for Galenti, Inc. are presented in P13-5A. Further analysis reveals that accounts payable pertain to merchandise creditors.

Prepare a statement of cash flows—direct method.
(SO 4b)

Instructions
Prepare a statement of cash flows for Galenti, Inc. using the direct method.

P13-11A You are provided with the following transactions for Great Big Sea Inc. during the year ended July 31, 2001:

Prepare a statement of earnings and a statement of cash flows—direct method.
(SO 4b)

1. Sold 1,000 no par value common shares for $75 each.
2. Purchased recording equipment by signing a $200,000, 10% note payable.
3. Recorded amortization for the year on the recording equipment assuming a four-year life, zero residual value, and use of the straight-line method of amortization.
4. Recorded amount owing for interest on the note payable. Interest is owing for the full year.
5. Paid the amount of interest owing plus $15,000 on the principal of the note.
6. Purchased an inventory of CDs on credit. The invoice was for $75,000.
7. Sold CDs to customers for $200,000. Immediately collected $150,000 from the customers, with the balance on credit.
8. The cost of the CDs that were sold was $42,000.
9. Collected another $8,000 from the customers.
10. Sold a piece of equipment with a cost of $10,000 and accumulated amortization of $2,500 for $6,000. Collected the full $6,000 immediately.

Instructions
(a) Prepare a statement of earnings and a statement of cash flows, using the direct method, for Great Big Sea Inc. for the year ended July 31, 2001. (You may ignore income taxes.)
(b) Compare the results of the accrual-based statement and the cash-based statement. Which do you think is more useful to decision-makers?

P13-12A Data for Swayze Company, Inc. are presented in P13-7A. Further analysis reveals the following:

Prepare a statement of cash flows—direct method. Calculate cash-based ratios.
(SO 4b, 5)

1. Accounts payable pertain to merchandise suppliers.
2. All operating expenses except for amortization were paid in cash.

Instructions

(a) Prepare a statement of cash flows for Swayze Company using the direct method.

(b) Calculate these cash-based measures:
1. Cash current debt coverage ratio
2. Cash return on sales ratio
3. Cash total debt coverage ratio
4. Free cash flow

Identify the impact of transactions on ratios.
(SO 5)

P13-13A You are provided with the following transactions that took place during the year.

Transactions	Free Cash Flow ($125,000)	Capital Expenditure Ratio (7x)	Cash Current Debt Coverage Ratio (0.5x)	Cash Total Debt Coverage Ratio (0.3x)	Cash Return on Sales Ratio (30%)
(a) Recorded credit sales, $2,500.					
(b) Collected $1,500 owing from customers.					
(c) Paid amount owing to suppliers, $2,750.					
(d) Recorded sales returns of $500 and credited the customer's account.					
(e) Purchased new equipment, $5,000; signed a long-term note payable for the cost of the equipment.					
(f) Purchased a patent and paid $15,000 cash for the asset.					

Instructions

For each transaction listed above, indicate whether it will increase (I), decrease (D), or have no effect (NE) on the ratios.

Discuss cash position.
(SO 5)

P13-14A **Sleeman Breweries Ltd.** is the largest craft brewer in Canada and the country's leading brewer of premium beers. In 1998, Sleeman purchased the Upper Canada Brewery Company and West Coast Beverages Distributors for $25 million.

The 1998 balance sheet of Sleeman Breweries showed current assets of $24 million and current liabilities of $25 million, including a bank overdraft (negative cash balance) of close to $3 million. On a more positive note, Sleeman nearly doubled its earnings in 1998, from $4 million in 1997 to $7 million in 1998. In addition, its statement of cash flows indicates that Sleeman generated $7 million of cash from operating activities in 1998.

Instructions

(a) Do you believe that Sleeman's creditors should be worried about the bank overdraft? Explain why or why not.

(b) If you were a creditor of Sleeman, and noted that it did not have enough current assets to cover its current liabilities, what additional information might you request to help you assess the company's solvency?

(c) Why do you think Sleeman generated $6.9 million cash from operating activities but has no cash?

Problems: Set B

P13-1B You are provided with the following transactions that took place during a recent fiscal year:

Distinguish among operating, investing, and financing activities. (SO 2)

	Transaction	Classification	Cash Inflow or Outflow?
(a)	Recorded amortization expense on the capital assets.		
(b)	Recorded interest expense amortizing a bond discount.		
(c)	Recorded cash proceeds for a sale of capital assets.		
(d)	Acquired land by issuing common shares.		
(e)	Paid a cash dividend to preferred shareholders.		
(f)	Distributed a stock dividend to common shareholders.		
(g)	Recorded cash sales.		
(h)	Recorded sales on account.		
(i)	Purchased inventory for cash.		
(j)	Purchased inventory on account.		
(k)	Paid income taxes.		

Instructions

Complete the table indicating whether each item (1) should be classified as an operating (O) activity, investing (I) activity, financing (F) activity, or as a noncash (NC) transaction, and (2) represents a cash inflow or cash outflow. If the transaction does not affect the statement or notes in any way, state that there is no effect.

P13-2B The following selected account balances relate to the shareholders' equity accounts of Wood Corp. at year end:

Determine cash flow effects of changes in equity accounts. (SO 4)

	2002	2001
Common shares, 10,500 and 10,000 shares, respectively, for 2002 and 2001	$160,000	$140,000
Cash dividends	10,000	10,000
Preferred shares, 5,000 shares	125,000	125,000
Stock dividends	10,500	0
Retained earnings	300,000	240,000

Instructions

(a) What was the amount of net earnings reported by Wood Corp. in 2002?

(b) Determine the amounts of any cash inflows or outflows related to the share capital and dividend accounts in 2002.

(c) Indicate where each of the cash inflows or outflows identified in (b) would be classified on the statement of cash flows.

Prepare the operating activities section—indirect method.
(SO 4a)

P13-3B The statement of earnings of Maria Company Ltd. is presented here:

MARIA COMPANY LTD.
Statement of Earnings
For the Year Ended December 31, 2001

Sales		$7,100,000
Cost of goods sold		5,210,000
Gross profit		1,890,000
Operating expenses		
Selling expenses	$400,000	
Administrative expenses	525,000	
Amortization expense	105,000	1,030,000
Earnings before income taxes		860,000
Income tax expense		300,000
Net earnings		$ 560,000

Additional information:

1. Accounts receivable increased by $510,000 during the year.
2. Prepaid expenses decreased by $170,000 during the year.
3. Inventory increased by $220,000 during the year.
4. Accounts payable to merchandise suppliers increased by $50,000 during the year.
5. Accrued expenses payable decreased by $180,000 during the year.
6. Income taxes payable decreased by $28,000 during the year.

Instructions

Prepare the operating activities section of the statement of cash flows for the year ended December 31, 2001, for Maria Company using the indirect method.

Prepare the operating activities section—indirect method.
(SO 4a)

P13-4B Data for Hanalei International Inc. are presented in P13-9B.

Instructions

Prepare the operating activities section of the statement of cash flows using the indirect method.

Prepare a statement of cash flows—indirect method.
(SO 4a)

P13-5B Condensed financial data of Norway Company, Inc. follow:

NORWAY COMPANY, INC.
Comparative Balance Sheet
December 31

Assets	2001	2000
Cash	$ 96,700	$ 47,250
Accounts receivable	86,800	57,000
Inventories	121,900	102,650
Investments	84,500	87,000
Capital assets	250,000	205,000
Accumulated amortization	(49,500)	(40,000)
Total	$590,400	$458,900
Liabilities and Shareholders' Equity		
Accounts payable	$ 52,700	$ 48,280
Accrued expenses payable	12,100	18,830
Bonds payable	100,000	70,000
Common shares	250,000	200,000
Retained earnings	175,600	121,790
Total	$590,400	$458,900

NORWAY COMPANY, INC.
Statement of Earnings Data
For the Year Ended December 31, 2001

Sales		$297,500
Gain on sale of capital assets		8,750
		306,250
Less:		
Cost of goods sold	$99,460	
Operating expenses	14,670	
Amortization expense	49,700	
Income taxes	7,270	
Interest expense	2,940	174,040
Net earnings		$132,210

Additional information:

1. New capital assets costing $92,000 were purchased for cash during the year.
2. Investments were sold at cost.
3. Capital assets costing $47,000 were sold for $15,550, resulting in a gain of $8,750.
4. A cash dividend of $78,400 was declared and paid during the year.

Instructions

Prepare a statement of cash flows using the indirect method.

Prepare a statement of cash flows—indirect method. (SO 4a)

P13-6B Presented here is the comparative balance sheet for Cortina Company Limited at December 31:

CORTINA COMPANY LIMITED
Comparative Balance Sheet
December 31

Assets	2001	2000
Cash	$ 40,000	$ 57,000
Accounts receivable	77,000	64,000
Inventory	132,000	140,000
Prepaid expenses	12,140	16,540
Land	125,000	150,000
Equipment	200,000	175,000
Accumulated amortization—equipment	(60,000)	(42,000)
Building	250,000	250,000
Accumulated amortization—building	(75,000)	(50,000)
Total	$701,140	$760,540
Liabilities and Shareholders' Equity		
Accounts payable	$ 33,000	$ 45,000
Bonds payable	235,000	265,000
Common shares	280,000	250,000
Retained earnings	153,140	200,540
Total	$701,140	$760,540

Additional information:

1. Operating expenses include amortization expense of $70,000 and charges from prepaid expenses of $4,400.
2. Land was sold for cash at cost.
3. Cash dividends of $74,290 were paid.
4. Net earnings for 2001 was $26,890.
5. Equipment was purchased for $65,000 cash. In addition, equipment costing $40,000 with a book value of $13,000 was sold for $14,000 cash.
6. Bonds were converted at face value by issuing 30,000 shares of no par value common shares.

Instructions

Prepare a statement of cash flows for 2001 using the indirect method.

Prepare a statement of cash flows—indirect method, and calculate cash-based ratios.
(SO 4a, 5)

P13-7B Here are the financial statements of Seymor Company Limited:

SEYMOR COMPANY LIMITED
Comparative Balance Sheet
December 31

Assets		2001		2000
Cash		$ 26,000		$ 13,000
Accounts receivable		18,000		14,000
Merchandise inventory		38,000		35,000
Capital assets	$70,000		$78,000	
Less accumulated amortization	(30,000)	40,000	(24,000)	54,000
Total		$122,000		$116,000
Liabilities and Shareholders' Equity				
Accounts payable		$ 29,000		$ 33,000
Income taxes payable		15,000		20,000
Bonds payable		20,000		10,000
Common shares		25,000		25,000
Retained earnings		33,000		28,000
Total		$122,000		$116,000

SEYMOR COMPANY LIMITED
Statement of Earnings
For the Year Ended December 31, 2001

Sales		$240,000
Cost of goods sold		180,000
Gross profit		60,000
Selling expenses	$28,000	
Administrative expenses	6,000	34,000
Earnings from operations		26,000
Interest expense		2,000
Earnings before income taxes		24,000
Income tax expense		7,000
Net earnings		$ 17,000

The following additional data were provided:

1. Dividends of $12,000 were declared and paid.
2. During the year, equipment was sold for $10,000 cash. This equipment originally cost $15,000 and had a book value of $10,000 at the time of sale.
3. Additional equipment was purchased for cash. No other capital asset transactions occured.
4. All amortization expense is in the selling expense category.
5. All sales and purchases are on account.

Instructions

(a) Prepare a statement of cash flows using the indirect method.
(b) Calculate these cash-based measures:
   1. Cash current debt coverage ratio
   2. Cash return on sales ratio
   3. Cash total debt coverage ratio
   4. Free cash flow

Prepare the operating activities section—direct method.
(SO 4b)

P13-8B Data for Maria Company are presented in P13-3B.

Instructions

Prepare the operating activities section of the statement of cash flows using the direct method.

Prepare the operating activities section—direct method.

(SO 4b)

P13-9B The statement of earnings of Hanalei International Inc. reported the following condensed information:

HANALEI INTERNATIONAL INC.
Statement of Earnings
For the Year Ended December 31, 2001

Revenues	$430,000
Operating expenses	280,000
Earnings from operations	150,000
Income tax expense	47,000
Net earnings	$103,000

Hanalei's balance sheet contained these comparative data at December 31:

	2001	2000
Accounts receivable	$50,000	$40,000
Accounts payable	30,000	41,000
Income taxes payable	6,000	4,000

Hanalei has no amortizable assets. Accounts payable pertain to operating expenses.

Instructions

Prepare the operating activities section of the statement of cash flows using the direct method.

Prepare a statement of cash flows—direct method.

(SO 4b)

P13-10B Data for Norway Company, Inc. are presented in P13-5B. Further analysis reveals that accounts payable pertain to merchandise creditors.

Instructions

Prepare a statement of cash flows for Norway Company using the direct method.

Prepare a statement of earnings and a statement of cash flows—direct method.

(SO 4b)

P13-11B DesRoches Inc. incorporated a repair business on January 1, 2002, by selling common shares for $5,000. On the same day, it borrowed $15,000 from a local bank, at a 10% interest rate. Principal and interest are repayable in full in two years. DesRoches rented space on January 5, paying rent in advance for three months—January, February, and March—at the rate of $800 a month. The company also purchased insurance, effective January 1, for a 12-month period, paying $1,200 in cash.

The company rented repair and office equipment, on January 1, for $500 a month. It paid January's rent and hope to be able to purchase this equipment at a later date when its cash flow improves.

In January, the company purchased $1,000 of supplies on account. The cost of the supplies remaining at the end of the month was $400. Cash paid on accounts payable during the month totalled $800. During the month, the company provided repair services of $2,500 for cash, and $5,000 on account. Cash collected from customers during January was $2,200. Other operating expenses paid during the month totalled $2,000. Unpaid salaries at the end of the month were $500.

Instructions

(a) Prepare a statement of earnings and a statement of cash flows, using the direct method, for DesRoches Inc. for the month ended January 31, 2002. (You may ignore income taxes.)

(b) Compare the results of the accrual-based statement and the cash-based statement. Which do you think is more useful to decision-makers?

Prepare a statement of cash flows—direct method. Calculate cash-based ratios.

(SO 4b, 5)

P13-12B Data for the Seymor Company Limited are presented in P13-7B. Further analysis reveals the following:

1. Accounts payable pertain to merchandise creditors.
2. All operating expenses except for amortization are paid in cash.

Instructions

(a) Prepare a statement of cash flows using the direct method.
(b) Calculate these cash-basis measures:
   1. Cash current debt coverage ratio
   2. Cash return on sales ratio
   3. Cash total debt coverage ratio
   4. Free cash flow

Identify the impact of transactions on ratios.
(SO 5)

P13-13B You are provided with the following transactions that took place during the year:

Transactions	Free Cash Flow ($125,00)	Capital Expenditure Ratio (7x)	Cash Current Debt Coverage Ratio (0.5x)	Cash Total Debt Coverage Ratio (0.3x)	Cash Return on Sales Ratio (30%)
(a) Recorded cash sales, $8,000.					
(b) Purchased inventory for $1,500 cash.					
(c) Purchased new equipment, $10,000; signed a short-term note payable for the cost of the equipment.					
(d) Paid a $20,000 cash dividend to common shareholders.					
(e) Acquired a building for $750,000, by signing a mortgage payable for $450,000 and issuing common shares for the balance.					
(f) Made a principal payment on the mortgage currently due, $45,000.					

Instructions

For each transaction listed above, indicate whether it will increase (I), decrease (D), or have no effect (NE) on the ratios.

Discuss cash position.
(SO 5)

P13-14B MP3.com, Inc. offers about 250,000 songs from 40,000 artists for free downloading from its Internet site.

The company reported $21.9 million (all figures in U.S. dollars) in revenues in 1999, a one-year growth of 1,785%! Its 1999 balance sheet shows current assets of $442.5 million and current liabilities of $54.3 million. Although it generated an operating cash flow of $29.6 million, it has reported a net loss of $42.5 million.

In spite of a troubling lawsuit where MP3.com has been found guilty of copyright violations, its share price has recently rebounded by 20% as it works to settle this lawsuit. Potential damages from this suit could cost MP3.com as much as $250 million.

Instructions

(a) Explain how MP3.com can generate a positive cash flow from operating activities but still report a net loss.
(b) How is it possible that MP3.com has such a large growth in revenue and still reports a net loss?
(c) If you were an investor in MP3.com's shares, would you be worried about its lack of profitability? Explain why or why not.

BROADENING YOUR PERSPECTIVE

FINANCIAL REPORTING AND ANALYSIS

FINANCIAL REPORTING PROBLEM: *Loblaw Companies Limited*

Instructions

BYP13-1 Refer to the annual report of **Loblaw** presented in Appendix A to answer the following questions:

Instructions

(a) How does Loblaw define "cash" for the purpose of its cash flow statement?
(b) Does Loblaw use the indirect or direct method to prepare its statement of cash flows? How can you tell?
(c) What was the amount of increase or decrease in cash for the year ended January 1, 2000? For the year ended January 2, 1999?
(d) What was the amount of net cash flows from operating activities for the year ended January 1, 2000? For the year ended January 2, 1999? What were the primary causes of any significant changes in cash provided (used) by operating activities between 1999 and 1998?
(e) From your analysis of the 1999 statement of cash flows, what were the significant investing activities? Financing activities?
(f) Did Loblaw report any significant noncash investing and financing activities?
(g) Identify any cash-based ratios reported by Loblaw in its 11-year summary.

COMPARATIVE ANALYSIS PROBLEM: *Loblaw and Sobeys*

BYP13-2 The financial statements of **Sobeys, Inc.** are presented in Appendix B, following the financial statements for **Loblaw** in Appendix A.

Instructions

(a) Based on the information in the financial statements, calculate these 1999 ratios for each company:
  1. Cash current debt coverage
  2. Cash return on sales
  3. Cash total debt coverage
(b) What conclusions concerning the management of cash can be drawn from these data?

RESEARCH CASE

BYP13-3 The March 1998 issue of *CAmagazine* includes an article by John Sloan entitled "Going With The Flow." This article discusses new reporting requirements instituted in 1998 for cash flow statements.

Instructions

Read the article and answer these questions:

(a) Changes to the reporting requirements for statements of cash flows have brought Canadian standards for the statement more in line with the standards of other countries. Which country's standards for statements of cash flows are we now harmonized with? What was the rationale behind this move?
(b) A number of changes are apparent in the new statement of cash flows. Identify the nature of the change with respect to each of the following items:
  1. The heading of the statement
  2. Treatment of noncash transactions
  3. Definition of cash and cash equivalents
  4. Direct versus indirect method

INTERPRETING FINANCIAL STATEMENTS

BYP13-4 Mattel Inc. makes toys—some very famous toys—in seven different countries. Among these are Barbie, Fisher-Price, Disney toys, and Hot Wheels cars. In 1998, the company had a disappointing year. A review of the company's balance sheet reveals that its cash dropped from $694.9 million to $212.4 million. This drop of $482.5 million represented a 69% decrease in cash. The following additional information was also available from Mattel's financial statements:

(in thousands)	**1998**	**1997**
Cash	$ 212,454	$ 694,947
Accounts receivable, net	983,050	1,091,416
Inventories	584,358	428,844
Prepaid expenses and other current assets	277,948	246,529
Total current assets	2,057,810	2,461,736
Total current liabilities	1,317,211	1,173,424
Cash provided (used) by operating activities	547,501	481,854
Cash provided (used) by investing activities	(1,052,435)	(205,964)
Cash provided (used) by financing activities	(24,343)	(116,228)

Instructions

(a) Discuss whether Mattel has suffered a significant reduction in its liquidity as a result of this decline in cash on hand. Use the current ratio and the cash current debt coverage ratio to support your position. (Note: Current liabilities at December 31, 1996 were $960,400.)

(b) Using the data provided, explain why cash declined, and discuss whether this should be a concern to the company and its investors.

The incredible early growth of <www.chapters.ca> has put fear into the hearts of traditional booksellers. **Chapters Online Inc.**'s share price has soared to surprising levels, despite the fact that the company has not yet reported any profit, reaching $19.50 at the end of its third quarter. During the quarter, ending January 1, 2000, Chapters On-line reported a 2,019% increase in its revenues since it began. The following financial information is taken from the second quarterly report of Chapters Online:

CHAPTERS ONLINE INC.
Quarterly Report
39 weeks ended January 1, 2000

Cash used by operating activities	($17,348,872)
Cash used by investing activities	(7,216,399)
Cash provided by financing activities	75,605,999
Cash, end of period	$51,040,730
Capital expenditures	$(7,216,399)
Dividends paid	0
Revenue	22,238,257
Net loss	(25,749,171)

Instructions

(a) Use the information provided in Chapters Online's statement of cash flows to explain what stage in its product life cycle Chapters Online is currently in.

(b) Calculate free cash flow and the capital expenditure ratio for Chapters Online for the 39 weeks ended January 1, 2000, and discuss its ability to finance expansion from internally generated cash. Thus far, Chapters Online has avoided purchasing large warehouses. Instead, it has used those of others. It is possible, however, that in order to increase customer satisfaction, the company may have to build its own warehouses. If this happens, how might your impression of its ability to finance expansion change?

(c) Calculate Chapters Online's cash return on sales and profit margin ratios.

(d) Discuss any potential implications of Chapters Online's cash used by operating activities and its net loss.
(e) Based on your findings in parts (a) to (d), can you conclude whether or not Chapters Online's high share price is justified at January 1, 2000? What has happened to Chapters Online's share price subsequently?

A GLOBAL FOCUS

BYP13-6 The statement of cash flows has become a commonly provided financial statement by companies throughout the world. It is interesting to note, however, that its format does vary across countries. The following statement of cash flows is from the 1998 financial statements of French building materials manufacturer **Saint-Gobain Group**

SAINT-GOBAIN GROUP
Consolidated Statements of Cash Flows
December 31

(in millions of euro)	1998	1997
Cash flow from operating activities		
Net operating income	€ 1,096	€ 920
Profit on sale of non-current assets	(394)	(307)
Depreciation and amortization	1,136	1,037
Dividends from associated companies	74	43
Sources from operations	1,912	1,693
(Increase) decrease in stocks	(174)	(41)
(Increase) decrease in trade accounts receivable	(59)	(241)
Increase (decrease) in trade accounts payable	79	79
Changes in income taxes payable and deferred taxes	14	3
Changes in provisions	(48)	4
Cash provided by operating activities	**1,724**	**1,497**
Cash flow from investing activities		
Acquisition of fixed assets	(1,288)	(1,353)
Investments in consolidated companies	(1,349)	(850)
Investments in unconsolidated companies	(382)	(244)
Total expenditure on fixed assets and investments	(3,019)	(2,447)
Cash (debt) acquired	(19)	(17)
Acquisition of treasury stock	(344)	(3)
Disposal of fixed and intangible assets	25	55
Disposal of investments	1,107	814
(Cash) debt disposed of	3	(125)
(Increase) decrease in deferred charges and other intangible assets	(68)	(48)
(Increase) decrease in deposits, long term receivables	9	31
(Increase) decrease in receivables related to investing activities	(124)	37
Cash used for investing activities	**(2,430)**	**(1,703)**
Cash flow from financing activities		
Issue of share capital	105	265
Minority interests in share capital increases of subsidiaries	4	4
(Decrease) increase in long term debt	132	541
Dividends paid	(248)	(82)
Dividends paid to minority shareholders of consolidated subsidiaries	(44)	(82)
Cash provided by (used for) financing activities	**(51)**	**507**
Net effect of exchange rate fluctuations on cash and cash equivalents	(9)	(39)
Increase (decrease) in cash and cash equivalents (net)	(766)	262
Net cash and cash equivalents at the beginning of the year	(92)	(354)
Net cash and cash equivalents at the end of the year	€ **(858)**	€ **(92)**

Instructions

(a) What similarities to Canadian statements of cash flows do you notice in terms of general format, as well as terminology?
(b) What differences do you notice in terms of general format, as well as terminology?
(c) Using the data provided in the statement of cash flows, calculate (1) free cash flow and (2) capital expenditure ratio. Does the difference in the format of the statement or the terminology complicate your efforts to calculate these measures?

FINANCIAL ANALYSIS ON THE WEB

BYP13-7 The software industry presents some unique challenges regarding cash flow. The industry is highly competitive, with a practice of providing free, or heavily discounted, products as a market-entry technique. This case reviews the sources and uses of cash flows of a major company in the software industry. The changing share price of this company is evaluated against its cash and earnings (loss) position, and other relevant cash-based ratios.

Instructions

Specific requirements of this web case can be found on the Kimmel website.

CRITICAL THINKING

COLLABORATIVE LEARNING ACTIVITY

BYP13-8 Greg Rhoda and Debra Sondgeroth are examining the following statement of cash flows for Tuktoyaktuk Trading Company Limited for the year ended January 31, 2001:

TUKTOYAKTUK TRADING COMPANY LIMITED
Statement of Cash Flows
For the Year Ended January 31, 2001

Sources of cash	
From sales of merchandise	$370,000
From sale of share capital	420,000
From sale of investment (purchased below)	80,000
From amortization	55,000
From issuance of note for truck	20,000
From interest on investments	6,000
Total sources of cash	951,000
Uses of cash	
For purchase of fixtures and equipment	340,000
For merchandise purchased for resale	258,000
For operating expenses (including amortization)	170,000
For purchase of investment	75,000
For purchase of truck by issuance of note	20,000
For interest on note payable	3,000
Total uses of cash	866,000
Net increase in cash	$ 85,000

Greg claims that Tuktoyaktuk's statement of cash flows is an excellent portrayal of a superb first year, with cash increasing $85,000. Debra replies that it was not a superb first year—but, rather, that the year was an operating failure, that the statement is presented incorrectly, and that $85,000 is not the actual increase in cash. The cash balance at the beginning of the year was $140,000.

Instructions

With the class organized into groups, answer the following questions:

(a) With whom do you agree, Greg or Debra? Explain your position.

(b) Using the data provided, prepare a statement of cash flows in proper form using the *indirect* method. The only noncash items in the statement of earnings are amortization and the gain from the sale of the investment.
(c) Prepare a statement of cash flows in proper form using the *direct* method.
(d) Would you recommend the payment of a dividend this year?

COMMUNICATION ACTIVITY

BYP13-9 Arnold Byte, the owner-president of Computer Services Corporation, is unfamiliar with the statement of cash flows that you, as his accountant, prepared. He asks for further explanations.

Instructions
Write him a brief memo explaining the form and content of the statement of cash flows.

ETHICS CASE

BYP13-10 Paradis Corporation is a medium-sized wholesaler of automotive parts. It has 10 shareholders who have been paid a total of $1 million in cash dividends for eight consecutive years. The board of directors' policy requires that in order for this dividend to be declared, net cash provided by operating activities as reported in the current year's statement of cash flows must exceed $1 million. The job of president and CEO Phil Monat is secure so long as Phil produces annual operating cash flows to support the usual dividend.

At the end of the current year, controller Rick Rodgers presents president Monat with some disappointing news. The net cash provided by operating activities is calculated by the indirect method to be only $970,000. The president says to Rick, "We must get that amount above $1 million. Isn't there some way to increase operating cash flow by another $30,000?" Rick answers, "These figures were prepared by my assistant. I'll go back to my office and see what I can do." The president replies, "I know you won't let me down, Rick."

Upon close scrutiny of the statement of cash flows, Rick concludes that he can get the operating cash flows above $1 million by reclassifying a $60,000, two-year note payable listed in the financing activities section as "Proceeds from bank loan—$60,000." He will report the note instead as "Increase in payables—$60,000" and treat it as an adjustment of net earnings in the operating activities section. He returns to the president, saying, "You can tell the board to declare their usual dividend. Our net cash flow provided by operating activities is $1,030,000." "Good man, Rick! I knew I could count on you," exults the president.

Instructions
(a) Who are the stakeholders in this situation?
(b) Was there anything unethical about the president's actions? Was there anything unethical about the controller's actions?
(c) Are the board members or anyone else likely to discover the misclassification?

Answers to Self-Study Questions
1. c 2. b 3. a 4. c 5. c 6. b 7. c 8. a 9. d 10. c 11. c
12. d 13. a 14. d 15. b

Answer to Loblaw Review Question 2
Loblaw has a positive cash flow from operating activities that exceeds net earnings. Its cash outflows for investing activities are significant, and exceed cash provided from operating activities. It has a negative cash flow from financing activities, indicating that it is repaying debt and retiring shares faster than it is issuing new debt and equity. Therefore, Loblaw appears to be in the late growth or early maturity phase.

Loblaws
A passion for food... *and a lot more!*

CHAPTER 14

Financial Analysis: The Big Picture

STUDY OBJECTIVES

After studying this chapter, you should be able to:

1. Understand the concept of earning power and indicate how irregular items are presented.
2. Discuss the need for comparative analysis and identify the tools of financial statement analysis.
3. Explain and apply horizontal analysis.
4. Explain and apply vertical analysis.
5. Identify and calculate ratios, describe their purpose, and use them to analyse a firm's liquidity, solvency, and profitability.
6. Discuss the limitations of financial statement analysis.

Wearhouse's Annual Report Hits the Mark

The annual report," a recent Canadian Institute of Chartered Accountants (CICA) document points out, "is a signal about the company for the entire year. You only get one shot." Mark's Work Wearhouse Ltd. has hit the bullseye three times in a row, garnering the Award of Excellence from the CICA for its annual reports published in January of 1997, 1998, and 1999.

Mark's Work Wearhouse, the largest specialty men's retailer in Canada, has 153 stores across the country, including Work World, L'Équipeur, and Dockers. Its focus is on providing apparel and footwear for customers who typically do not wear a suit and tie to work.

The judges for the Award of Excellence called Mark's Work Wearhouse's 1999 annual report "a model of excellence," and "ground-breaking." It includes all the standard features of an annual report, such as financial information for the year, information about the company's directors, and a message from the president. But it also gives readers much more: a quick overview of the company, a general discussion of the current North American retail environment, a review of the company's corporate goals and strategic plan, an 11-year financial review, forecasts for the coming years, and, most significantly, a *frank* "post mortem" on the previous year's forecasts.

Frankness, in fact, is the norm throughout Mark's Work Wearhouse annual reports. Some companies are tempted to use these reports to present a falsely optimistic picture, making good indicators sound more important than they are and hiding bad news in vague language. Mark's has opted to be clear and straightforward with shareholders, presenting information in a manner that is upbeat, while being clear and honest about the difficulties the firm has faced.

Its 2000 report, for example, states right on page 1, "The fall season of 1999 has been described as the most disruptive time period that anyone can remember. For our Company, there were two major influences—the effects of the bankruptcy of Eaton's and, once again, a winter season that was mild and late in arriving."

On the World Wide Web
Mark's Work Wearhouse Ltd.
http://www.marks.com

Further on, there is a lengthy section of no-nonsense, in-depth management discussion and analysis. And the human resources section gives remarkably frank and detailed information about the business objectives of each senior officer and whether or not they were met.

Format and presentation can also, of course, make a big difference in the accessibility of a report. Mark's document is an 80-page booklet illustrated with quality photos, charts, and graphics, all laid out with an eye for attractiveness and ease of reading. Financial information is provided first as highlights up front, then in more detail later on. Basic corporate information, such as contact numbers and the date of the annual meeting, is on the inside back cover. The report even includes a glossary of terms.

The annual report is the single most important document a public company produces, a tool that gives shareholders—as well as creditors, regulators, potential investors, and others—the information they need to make useful decisions about the company.

Mark's commitment to excellence in its annual report is evidence of a more general commitment to its shareholders. The company has also been honoured more than once by the investment community with the Grand Prix Best Overall Investor Relations Award for its communications and relations with shareholders.

PREVIEW OF CHAPTER 14

An important lesson can be learned from Mark's Work Wearhouse: Effective communication is the key to understanding. By now you have learned a significant amount about financial reporting by Canadian corporations. Using some of the basic decision tools presented in this book, you can perform a rudimentary analysis of any company and draw basic conclusions about its financial health. Although it would not be wise for you to bet your life savings on a company's shares relying solely on your current level of knowledge, we strongly encourage you to practise your new skills wherever possible. Only with practice will you improve your ability to interpret financial numbers.

Before unleashing you on the world of high finance, we will expose you to a few more important concepts and techniques, and provide you with one last comprehensive review of corporate financial statements. We use all of the decision tools presented in this text to analyse a stellar example of financial reporting—Mark's Work Wearhouse Ltd.

The content and organization of this chapter are as follows:

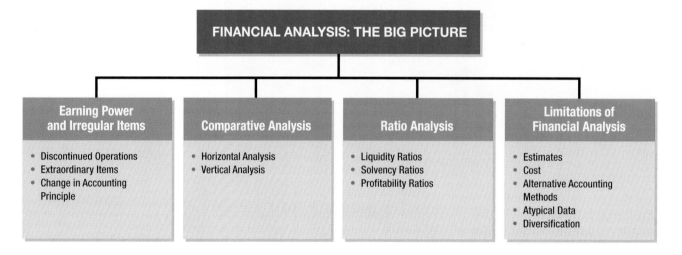

FINANCIAL ANALYSIS: THE BIG PICTURE

Earning Power and Irregular Items
- Discontinued Operations
- Extraordinary Items
- Change in Accounting Principle

Comparative Analysis
- Horizontal Analysis
- Vertical Analysis

Ratio Analysis
- Liquidity Ratios
- Solvency Ratios
- Profitability Ratios

Limitations of Financial Analysis
- Estimates
- Cost
- Alternative Accounting Methods
- Atypical Data
- Diversification

EARNING POWER AND IRREGULAR ITEMS

STUDY OBJECTIVE 1

Understand the concept of earning power and indicate how irregular items are presented.

Ultimately, the value of a company is a function of its future cash flows. When analysts use this year's or past years' net earnings to estimate future cash flows, they must make sure that the net earnings do not include irregular revenues, expenses, gains, or losses. Net earnings adjusted for irregular items are referred to as **earning power**. **Earning power is the most likely level of income to be obtained in the future**—that is, to the extent the year's net earnings are a good predictor of future years' net earnings. Earning power differs from actual net earnings by the amount of irregular revenues, expenses, gains, and losses included in the year's net earnings.

Users are interested in earning power because it helps them derive an estimate of future earnings without the "noise" of irregular items. For example, suppose Rye Corporation reports that this year's net earnings are $500,000, but included in that amount is a once-in-a-lifetime gain of $400,000. In estimating next year's net earnings for Rye Corporation, we would likely ignore this $400,000 gain and estimate that next year's net earnings will be in the neighbourhood of $100,000. That is, based on this year's results, the company's earning power is roughly $100,000. Therefore, identifying irregular items is important if you are going to use reported earnings to estimate a company's value.

To help determine earning power (or regular income), irregular items are identified by type on the statement of earnings. Two types of irregular items are reported:

1. Discontinued operations
2. Extraordinary items

Another type of irregular item, one that affects prior period earnings, is a change in accounting principle. Since prior period earnings are affected, a change in accounting principle is reported on the statement of retained earnings, rather than on the current period statement of earnings.

All these irregular items are reported net of income taxes; that is, the applicable income tax expense or tax savings is shown for earnings before income taxes and for each of the irregular items. The general concept is "Let the tax follow earnings or loss."

DISCONTINUED OPERATIONS

Discontinued operations refers to the disposal of a significant segment of a business, such as the elimination of a major class of customers or an entire activity. For example, the sale by Imasco Limited of its food service businessess (Fast Food Merchandisers, Inc., Hardee's Food Systems, Inc., and its Roy Rogers restaurants) was reported as discontinued operations. The phasing out of a model or part of a line of business, however, is *not* considered to be a disposal of a segment.

When the disposal of a significant segment occurs, the statement of earnings should report both earnings from continuing operations and earnings (or loss) from discontinued operations. **The earnings (loss) from discontinued operations consist of the earnings (loss) from operations and the gain (loss) on disposal of the segment.**

To illustrate, assume that Rozek Inc. has revenues of $2.5 million and expenses of $1.7 million from continuing operations in 2001. The company therefore has earnings before income taxes of $800,000 ($2,500,000 − $1,700,000). During 2001, the company discontinues and sells its unprofitable chemical division. The loss in 2001 from chemical operations (net of $60,000 taxes) is $140,000, and the loss on disposal of the chemical division (net of $30,000 taxes) is $70,000. With an assumed 30% tax rate on earnings before income taxes, the statement of earnings appears in Illustration 14-1.

Illustration 14-1 Statement presentation of discontinued operations

ROZEK INC.
Statement of Earnings (Partial)
For the Year Ended December 31, 2001

Earnings before income taxes		$800,000
Income tax expense		240,000
Earnings from continuing operations		560,000
Discontinued operations		
Loss from operations of chemical division, net of $60,000 income tax savings	**$140,000**	
Loss from disposal of chemical division, net of $30,000 income tax savings	**70,000**	**(210,000)**
Net earnings		$350,000

Note that the caption "Earnings from continuing operations" is used and the section "Discontinued operations" is added. **Within the new section, both**

the operating loss and the loss on disposal are reported net of applicable income taxes. This presentation clearly indicates the separate effects of continuing operations and discontinued operations on net earnings.

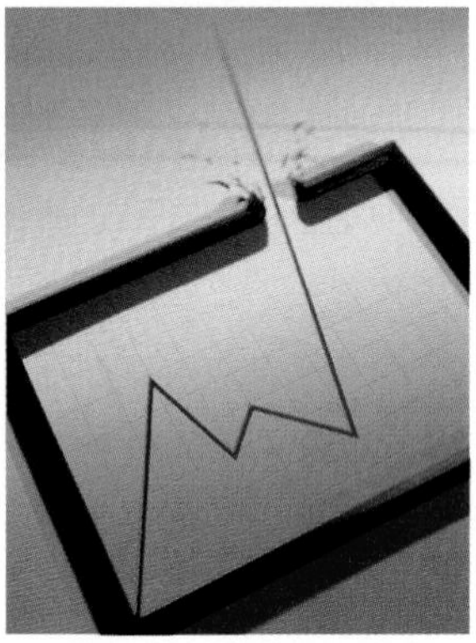

BUSINESS INSIGHT

Investor Perspective

The Toronto-Dominion Bank reported a phenomenal $3 billion of net earnings in fiscal 1999, the largest on record by a Canadian bank. However, at least half of these earnings came from one-time items resulting from the sale of discontinued businesses. Only one Canadian company (BCE) has earned more than the TD—it also did it with the help of one-time gains. The biggest "pure"—without any irregular items—profit in this country's corporate history was reported by the Royal Bank in 1998 in the amount of $1.8 billion.

Source: Richard Blackwell, "TD Rakes in $3-Billion Profit," *The Globe and Mail*, November 19, 1999, A1.

DECISION TOOLKIT

Decision Checkpoints	Info Needed for Decision	Tool to Use for Decision	How to Evaluate Results
Has the company sold any major lines of business?	Discontinued operations section of statement of earnings	Anything reported in this section indicates that the company has discontinued a major line of business.	If a major business line has been discontinued, its results in the current period should not be included in estimates of future net earnings.

EXTRAORDINARY ITEMS

Extraordinary items are events and transactions that meet these three conditions:

1. **They are not expected to occur frequently.**
2. **They are not typical of normal business activities.**
3. **They are not subject to management's discretion.**

To be regarded as infrequent, the event or transaction should be unlikely to happen again in the foreseeable future. To be considered atypical, the item should be unusual and only incidentally related to the customary activities of the entity. To be judged outside of management's discretion, the item should not depend primarily on decisions or determinations by management, including owners' directives.

All three criteria must be evaluated in terms of the environment in which the entity operates. Thus, Alcan Aluminium Limited reported the government cancellation of a contract to supply power to B.C. Hydro as an extraordinary item because the event was infrequent, unusual, and not determined by management. In contrast, Canada West Tree Fruits Ltd. of the Okanagan Valley does not report frost damage to its fruit crop as an extraordinary item because frost damage is not viewed as infrequent there.

In reality, extraordinary items are rare. *Financial Reporting in Canada* notes that only four companies, of the 200 surveyed, reported an extraordinary item in 1998. Illustration 14-2 shows the appropriate classification of extraordinary and ordinary items.

Extraordinary items		**Ordinary items**	
1. Effects of major casualties (acts of God), if rare in the area.	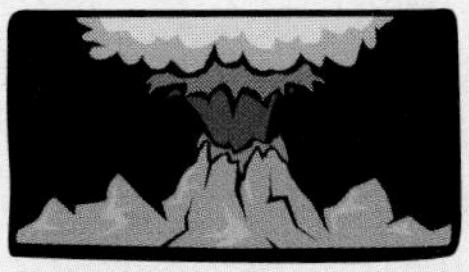	1. Effects of major casualties (acts of God), not uncommon in the area.	
2. Expropriation (takeover) of property by a foreign government.		2. Write-down of inventories or write-off of receivables.	
3. Effects of a newly enacted law or regulation, such as a condemnation action.		3. Losses attributable to labour strikes.	
		4. Gains or losses from sales of capital assets.	

Illustration 14-2 Classification of extraordinary and ordinary items

Extraordinary items are reported net of taxes in a separate section of the statement of operations immediately below discontinued operations. To illustrate, assume that in 2001 a revolutionary foreign government expropriates property held as an investment by Rozek Inc. If the loss is $70,000 before applicable income taxes of $21,000, the statement of earnings presentation will show a deduction of $49,000, as in Illustration 14-3.

Helpful Hint Ordinary gains and losses are reported at pre-tax amounts in arriving at earnings before income taxes.

Illustration 14-3 Statement presentation of extraordinary items

ROZEK INC.
Statement of Earnings (Partial)
For the Year Ended December 31, 2001

Earnings before income taxes		$800,000
Income tax expense		240,000
Earnings from continuing operations		560,000
Discontinued operations		
Loss from operations of chemical division, net of $60,000 income tax savings	$140,000	
Loss from disposal of chemical division, net of $30,000 income tax savings	70,000	(210,000)
Earnings before extraordinary item		350,000
Extraordinary item		
Expropriation of investment, net of $21,000 income tax savings		**(49,000)**
Net earnings		$301,000

As illustrated, the caption "Earnings before extraordinary item" is added immediately before the listing of extraordinary items. This presentation clearly indicates the effect of the extraordinary item on net earnings. If there were no discontinued operations, the third line of the statement of earnings in Illustration 14-3 would be "Earnings before extraordinary item."

If a transaction or event meets one, but not all, of the criteria for an extraordinary item, it should be reported in a separate line item in the upper half of the statement of earnings, rather than be reported in the bottom half as an extraordinary item. Usually, these items are reported under either "Other revenues and gains" or "Other expenses and losses" at their gross amount (not net of tax). This is true, for example, of gains (losses) resulting from the sale of capital assets, as explained in Chapter 9.

Mark's Work Wearhouse did not report any extraordinary items in its 1999 statement of earnings. It did, however, incur significant costs from closing two pilot test stores in the U.S. marketplace. The costs associated with the closure of the U.S. pilot stores did not meet the criteria for discontinued items, since the closure was not a separate activity from the company's continuing operations. Instead, Mark's Work Wearhouse reported these costs separate from its other expenses on the 1999 statement of earnings, immediately preceding earnings before income taxes. This presentation suggests that charges such as these occur infrequently. In analysing Mark's Work Wearhouse's results, we must decide whether to use its earnings as reported, or instead to assume that these charges are, in fact, not representative of the company's future earning power. If we assume they are not representative of the company's earning power, we would eliminate them from (add them back to) net earnings (after consideration of their income tax impact) to estimate next year's earnings.

DECISION TOOLKIT

Decision Checkpoints	Info Needed for Decision	Tool to Use for Decision	How to Evaluate Results
Has the company experienced any extraordinary events or transactions?	Extraordinary item section of statement of earnings	Anything reported in this section indicates that the company experienced an event that was infrequent, unusual, and not influenced by management.	These items should usually be ignored in estimating future net earnings.

CHANGE IN ACCOUNTING PRINCIPLE

Alternative Terminology *Accounting principles* are also known as *accounting policies.*

For ease of comparison, financial statements are expected to be prepared on a basis **consistent** with that used for the preceding period. That is, where a choice of accounting principles is available, the principle chosen should be applied consistently from period to period. A **change in accounting principle** occurs when the principle used in the current year is different from the one used in the preceding year. A change is permitted when management can show that there has been a change in the reporting circumstances and that the new principle is preferable to the old principle.

A change in accounting principle affects reporting in these four ways:

1. The new principle should be used for reporting the results of operations of the current year.
2. The cumulative effect of the change in accounting principle should be reported (net of tax) as an adjustment to opening retained earnings.
3. All prior period financial statements should be restated to facilitate comparison.
4. The effects of the change should be detailed and disclosed in a note.

Examples of a change in accounting principle include a change in amortization methods (such as declining-balance to straight-line) and a change in inventory costing methods (such as FIFO to average cost). The effect of a change in an accounting principle on prior period earnings can be significant. When BCE Inc. changed the way it calculated amortization expense in response to regulatory changes, it reported a decrease in retained earnings of $2.9 billion.

We will use our earlier illustration of Rozek Inc. to illustrate how changes in accounting principles are reported. Assume that at the beginning of 2001, Rozek changes from the straight-line method to the declining-balance method of amortization for equipment which had been purchased on January 1, 1998. The cumulative effect on prior year statements of earnings (for 1998 to 2001) is to increase amortization expense and decrease earnings before income taxes by $24,000. If the company had a 30% tax rate, the net of tax effect of the change on prior period net earnings would be $16,800 ($24,000 − $7,200 [$24,000 × 30%] income tax savings).

The presentation of this change in the statement of retained earnings is shown in Illustration 14-4. The opening retained earnings balance is assumed to be $500,000.

Illustration 14-4 Statement presentation of a change in accounting principle

ROZEK INC.
Statement of Retained Earnings (Partial)
For the Year Ended December 31, 2001

Retained earnings, January 1, 2001, as previously reported	$500,000
Deduct: Cumulative effect on prior years of change in amortization method, net of $7,200 income tax savings	(16,800)
Retained earnings, January 1, 2001, as adjusted	483,200
Add: Net earnings	301,000
Retained earnings, December 31, 2001	$784,200

A financial statement from any prior year which is presented for comparative purposes would be restated using the declining-balance method of amortization. Rozek's statement of earnings will also show amortization expense for the current year on a declining-balance basis (i.e., using the new method of amortization). Accumulated amortization on the balance sheet will be calculated as though declining-balance had always been used. An appropriately cross-referenced note to the statements should detail the impact of the change and the fact that prior years' statements have been restated.

Mark's Work Wearhouse reported a change in accounting policy in fiscal 1999. This change resulted from the adoption of a new method of accounting for future income taxes. Although Mark's Work Wearhouse details the effects of this change in a note to its financial statements, it reported that "no adjustments were required to January 25, 1997, opening retained earnings or to the total income tax expenses in each of the periods ended January 25, 1997, and January 31, 1998, as changes to the total income tax expense were not material." Note that the company references the opening *1997* balance rather than the 1999 balance of retained earnings. Mark's Work Wearhouse reports three comparative years in its 1999 financial statements, and the 1997 figure is the earliest opening retained earnings reported. If the effect of the change in accounting principle had been material, it is this earliest reported opening balance that would be adjusted for the cumulative impact of the change.

DECISION TOOLKIT

Decision Checkpoints	Info Needed for Decision	Tool to Use for Decision	How to Evaluate Results
Has the company changed any of its accounting principles?	Cumulative effect of change in accounting principle in statement of retained earnings	Anything reported in this manner indicates that the company has changed an accounting principle during the current year.	Fiinancial statements are restated using new principle for comparability.

BEFORE YOU GO ON . . .

Review It

1. What is earning power?
2. What irregular items affect the statement of earnings? What effect do they have on the estimation of future earnings and future cash flows?
3. What irregular item affects the statement of retained earnings? What impact does this item have on the comparability of prior period earnings?
4. Does Loblaw report any irregular items in 1999? The answer to this question is provided at the end of this chapter.

Loblaws
A passion for food... *and a lot more!*

COMPARATIVE ANALYSIS

STUDY OBJECTIVE 2

Discuss the need for comparative analysis and identify the tools of financial statement analysis.

Any item reported in a financial statement has significance: its inclusion indicates its existence and amount at a given time. For example, when Mark's Work Wearhouse reports $11,749 thousand on its balance sheet as cash, we know that Mark's Work Wearhouse did have cash and that the amount was $11,749 thousand. But whether that represents an increase over prior years, or whether it is adequate in relation to the company's needs, cannot be determined from the amount alone. The amount must be compared with other financial data to provide more information.

Throughout this book, we have relied on three types of comparisons to improve the decision usefulness of financial information:

1. **Intracompany basis**. Comparisons within a company are often useful to detect changes in financial relationships and significant trends. For example, a comparison of Mark's Work Wearhouse's current year's cash amount with the prior year's cash amount shows either an increase or a decrease. Likewise, a comparison of Mark's Work Wearhouse's year-end cash amount with the amount of its total assets at year end shows the proportion of total assets in the form of cash.
2. **Intercompany basis**. Comparisons with other companies provide insight into a company's competitive position. For example, Mark's Work Wearhouse's total sales for the year can be compared with the total sales of its competitors in the retail apparel industry.
3. **Industry averages**. Comparisons with industry averages provide information about a company's relative position within the industry. For example, Mark's Work Wearhouse's financial data can be compared with the averages for its industry compiled by financial ratings organizations such as Dun & Bradstreet, the *Financial Post*, and Statistics Canada.

Three basic tools are used in financial statement analysis to highlight the significance of financial statement data:

1. Horizontal analysis
2. Vertical analysis
3. Ratio analysis

In previous chapters, we relied primarily on ratio analysis, supplemented with some basic horizontal and vertical analysis. In the remainder of this section, we introduce more formal forms of horizontal and vertical analysis. A detailed review of ratio analysis then follows.

HORIZONTAL ANALYSIS

STUDY OBJECTIVE 3

Explain and apply horizontal analysis.

Horizontal analysis is a technique for evaluating a series of financial statement data over a period of time. Its purpose is to determine the increase or decrease that has taken place, expressed as either an amount or a percentage.

As an example, here are the recent net corporate sales figures (in thousands) of Mark's Work Wearhouse:

52 weeks ended January 25, 1997	53 weeks ended January 31, 1998	52 weeks ended January 30, 1999
$220,902	$252,016	$283,401

Alternative Terminology *Horizontal analysis* is also often referred to as *trend analysis.*

If we assume that 1997 is the base year, we can measure all percentage increases or decreases from this base period amount with the formula shown in Illustration 14-5.

$$\text{Change Since Base Period} = \frac{\text{Current-Year Amount} - \text{Base-Year Amount}}{\text{Base-Year Amount}}$$

Illustration 14-5
Horizontal analysis of changes since base period

We can, for example, determine that net sales for Mark's Work Wearhouse increased approximately 14% [($252,016 − $220,902) ÷ $220,902] from 1997 to 1998. Similarly, we can also determine that net sales increased 28% [($283,401 − $220,902) ÷ $220,902] from 1997 to 1999. Alternatively, we can express current year sales as a percentage of the base period. To do so, we would divide the current year amount by the base year amount. The percentage of the base period for each of three years, assuming 1997 as the base period, is shown for net sales in Illustration 14-6.

MARK'S WORK WEARHOUSE LTD.
Net Sales
Base Period 1997
(in thousands)

1997	1998	1999
$220,902	$252,016	$283,401
100%	114%	128%

Illustration 14-6
Horizontal analysis of net sales

To further illustrate horizontal analysis, we will use the financial statements of Mark's Work Wearhouse. Condensed balance sheets for 1998 and 1999, showing dollar and percentage changes, are presented in Illustration 14-7.

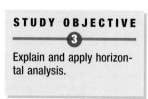

Illustration 14-7
Horizontal analysis of a balance sheet

Mark's Work Wearhouse

Helpful Hint It is difficult to comprehend the significance of a change when only the dollar amount of change is examined. When the change is expressed in percentage form, it is easier to grasp its true magnitude.

MARK'S WORK WEARHOUSE LTD.
Condensed Balance Sheets
January 30
(in thousands)

			Increase (Decrease) During 1999	
	1999	1998	Amount	Percent
Assets				
Current assets	$ 96,360	$ 75,810	$20,550	27.1%
Capital assets (net)	32,244	27,267	4,977	18.3
Other assets	4,388	2,540	1,848	72.8
Total assets	$132,992	$105,617	$27,375	25.9
Liabilities and Shareholders' Equity				
Current liabilities	$ 56,525	$ 44,397	$12,128	27.3
Long-term liabilities	23,161	14,474	8,687	60.0
Total liabilities	79,686	58,871	20,815	35.4
Shareholders' equity	53,306	46,746	6,560	14.0
Total liabilities and shareholders' equity	$132,992	$105,617	$27,375	25.9

The comparative balance sheet shows that a number of changes occurred in Mark's Work Wearhouse's financial position from 1998 to 1999. In the assets section, current assets increased by $20,550 thousand, or 27.1% ($20,550 ÷ $75,810), capital assets (net) increased by $4,977 thousand, or 18.3%, and other assets increased 72.8%. The large increase in current assets was mainly due to increases in merchandise inventories, resulting from the net addition of 38 corporate stores in 1999. The large increase in other assets was mostly from goodwill on franchise store purchases and increases in future income tax assets resulting from the change in accounting principle.

In the liabilities section, current liabilities increased by $12,128 thousand, or 27.3%, primarily due to the increase in accounts payable from the increased inventory purchases. Long-term liabilities increased by $8,687 thousand, or 60%, mainly to fund the purchase of new corporate stores. In the shareholders' equity section, we find that equity increased 14.0%. This suggests that the company expanded its asset base during 1999 and financed most of the expansion by incurring additional long-term debt.

Presented in Illustration 14-8 is a two-year comparative statement of earnings for Mark's Work Wearhouse, for 1998 and 1999, in a condensed format.

Illustration 14-8
Horizontal analysis of a statement of earnings

MARK'S WORK WEARHOUSE LTD.
Condensed Statements of Earnings
52 Weeks Ended January 30
(in thousands)

			Increase (Decrease) During 1999	
	1999	1998	Amount	Percent
Sales	$283,401	$252,016	$31,385	12.5%
Cost of sales	169,163	149,923	19,240	12.8
Gross margin	114,238	102,093	12,145	11.9
Front-line expenses	78,086	66,712	11,374	17.0
Back-line expenses	22,195	22,977	(782)	(3.4)
Earnings before provision for closure of U.S. pilot stores and income taxes	13,957	12,404	1,553	12.5
Provision for closure of U.S. pilot stores	2,961	—	2,961	n/a
Earnings before income taxes	10,996	12,404	(1,408)	(11.4)
Income taxes	5,244	5,853	(609)	(10.4)
Net earnings	$ 5,752	$ 6,551	$ (799)	(12.2)

Helpful Hint Note that, in a horizontal analysis, while the amount column is additive (the total is a decrease of $799 thousand), the percentage column is not additive (12.2% is **not** a total).

Horizontal analysis of the statements of earnings shows that sales increased by $31,385 thousand, or 12.5% ($31,385 ÷ $252,016). This increase is noteworthy when compared to a year of modest retail sales growth in Canada. Cost of sales kept pace with the increase in sales, with an increase of 12.8%. Overall, gross margin increased 11.9%. Front-line expenses increased over the prior year by $11,374 thousand, or 17.0%—Mark's Work Wearhouse classifies all expenses resulting from direct contact with customers as front-line expenses. Other companies normally call these types of expenses selling expenses. The purchase and conversion of 31 franchise stores to corporate stores drove the front-line increase due to increased staff and occupancy costs for the expanded retail square footage. In addition, advertising costs also increased within this category by $1.3 million, as Christmas season television spots were added to Mark's Work Wearhouse's advertising campaign. Back-line expenses—better known as administrative expenses—incurred to support store operations decreased 3.4%. Overall, earnings before provision for closure of the U.S. pilot stores and income taxes increased 12.5%. The 12.2% decline in net earnings can be attributed almost entirely to the provision for closure of the two U.S. pilot stores.

Helpful Hint When using horizontal analysis, both dollar amount changes and percentage changes need to be examined. It is not necessarily bad if a company's earnings are growing at a declining rate. The **amount** of increase may be the same as or more than the base year, but the **percentage** change may be less because the base is greater each year.

The measurement of changes from period to period in percentages is relatively straightforward and quite useful. However, the calculations can be affected by complications. If an item has no value in a base year or preceding year and a value in the next year, no percentage change can be determined. For example, no percentage could be calculated for the "Provision for closure of U.S. pilot stores" category in Mark's Work Wearhouse's condensed statement of earnings. And, if a negative amount appears in the base or preceding period, and a positive amount in the following year, or vice versa, no percentage change can be calculated.

Other factors reduce the value of performing a horizontal analysis on the statement of cash flows. We haven't provided a horizontal analysis of Mark's Work Wearhouse's statements of cash flows as it is not as useful as horizontal analyses performed on the balance sheet and statement of earnings. The amounts presented in the statement of cash flows (except in the operating activities section) detail the changes between two periods (opening and ending balance sheets), and percentage changes of changes are not very meaningful.

DECISION TOOLKIT

Decision Checkpoints	Info Needed for Decision	Tool to Use for Decision	How to Evaluate Results
How do the company's financial position and operating results compare with those of previous periods?	Statement of earnings and balance sheet	Comparative financial statements should be prepared over at least two years, with the first year reported as the base year. Changes in each line item relative to the base year should be presented both by amount and by percentage. This is called horizontal analysis.	A significant change should be investigated to determine the reason for the change.

VERTICAL ANALYSIS

STUDY OBJECTIVE 4

Explain and apply vertical analysis.

Vertical analysis is a technique for evaluating financial statement data that expresses each item in a financial statement as a percentage of a base amount. For example, on a balance sheet we might say that current assets are 22% of total assets (total assets being the base amount). Or, on a statement of earnings we might say that selling expenses are 16% of net sales (net sales being the base amount).

Alternative Terminology *Vertical analysis* is sometimes referred to as *common-size analysis.*

Presented in Illustration 14-9 is the comparative balance sheet of Mark's Work Wearhouse for 1998 and 1999, analysed vertically. The base for the asset items is **total assets**, and the base for the liability and shareholders' equity items is **total liabilities and shareholders' equity**.

Illustration 14-9 Vertical analysis of a balance sheet

Mark's Work Wearhouse

MARK'S WORK WEARHOUSE LTD.
Condensed Balance Sheets
January 30
(in millions)

	1999		1998	
Assets	Amount	Percent	Amount	Percent
Current assets	$ 96,360	**72.5%**	$ 75,810	**71.8%**
Capital assets (net)	32,244	**24.2**	27,267	**25.8**
Other assets	4,388	**3.3**	2,540	**2.4**
Total assets	$132,992	**100.0%**	$105,617	**100.0%**
Liabilities and Shareholders' Equity				
Current liabilities	$ 56,525	**42.5%**	$ 44,397	**42.0%**
Long-term liabilities	23,161	**17.4**	14,474	**13.7**
Total liabilities	79,686	**59.9**	58,871	**55.7**
Shareholders' equity	53,306	**40.1**	46,746	**44.3**
Total liabilities and shareholders' equity	$132,992	**100.0%**	$105,617	**100.0%**

In this case, even though capital assets increased by $4,977 thousand from 1998 to 1999 (see Illustration 14-7), they decreased from 25.8% to 24.2% of total assets. Also, even though long-term liabilities increased 60.0% from 1998 to 1999, they are only 17.4% of total liabilities and shareholders' equity. Total liabilities have increased from 55.7% to 59.9% of total liabilities and shareholders' equity. This switch to a higher percentage of debt financing has two causes. First, current assets increased, requiring a corresponding increase in current liabilities. Secondly, shareholders' equity, although increasing 14.0% over the two years, decreased as a proportion of total liabilities and shareholders' equity. Thus, the company shifted toward a heavier reliance on debt financing both by using more short-term debt and by reducing the amount of equity.

Vertical analysis of the comparative statements of earnings of Mark's Work Wearhouse, shown in Illustration 14-10, reveals that cost of sales as a percentage of sales increased very slightly, from 59.5% to 59.7%, with a corresponding decline in gross margin (profit) percentage. Costs rose as a result of slightly higher markdowns and shrinkage experienced by the company in 1999. Markdowns were required because the warm winter weather in 1999 contributed to poorer than expected sales performance of gloves, hats, and other winter apparel.

Illustration 14-10
Vertical analysis of a statement of earnings

Mark's Work Wearhouse

MARK'S WORK WEARHOUSE LTD.
Condensed Statement of Earnings
52 Weeks Ended January 30
(in thousands)

	1999		1998	
	Amount	Percent	Amount	Percent
Sales	$283,401	100.0%	$252,016	100.0%
Cost of sales	169,163	59.7	149,923	59.5
Gross margin	114,238	40.3	102,093	40.5
Front-line expenses	78,086	27.6	66,712	26.5
Back-line expenses	22,195	7.8	22,977	9.1
Earnings before provision for closure of U.S. pilot stores and income taxes	13,957	4.9	12,404	4.9
Provision for closure of U.S. pilot stores	2,961	1.0	—	—
Earnings before income taxes	10,996	3.9	12,404	4.9
Income taxes	5,244	1.9	5,853	2.3
Net earnings	$ 5,752	2.0%	$ 6,551	2.6%

Consistent with our horizontal analysis findings, front-line expenses rose 1.1% as a percentage of sales, from 26.5% to 27.6%. Back-line expenses declined from 9.1% to 7.8% of sales. Earnings before the nonrecurring item and income taxes stay consistent as a percentage of sales, at 4.9%. As noted, because these nonrecurring charges are difficult to interpret, this is likely a more relevant figure for analysis than the 0.6% (2.6% − 2.0%) decline noted in net earnings.

An associated benefit of vertical analysis is that it enables you to compare companies of different sizes. For example, one of Mark's Work Wearhouse's main competitors is a much larger company—The Gap, Inc. The Gap operates nearly 2,600 casual clothing stores in Canada, France, Germany, Japan, the UK, and the U.S. Although not incorporated in Canada, the Gap is a closer competitor to Mark's Work Wearhouse than any Canadian company. Mark's Work Wearhouse notes in its annual report that competition is "fierce as department stores, discount department stores, other discount stores, unisex stores and men's specialty stores battle for market share within this market sector," and "many of these stores are now large U.S.-based retailers." Using vertical analysis, we can make a more meaningful comparison of the condensed statements of earnings of Mark's Work Wearhouse and The Gap, as shown in Illustration 14-11.

Illustration 14-11 Intercompany comparison by vertical analysis

Mark's Work Wearhouse

CONDENSED STATEMENT OF EARNINGS
52 Weeks Ended January 30,1999
(in thousands)

	Mark's Work Wearhouse Ltd.		The Gap, Inc.	
	Amount	Percent	Amount	Percent
Sales	$283,401	**100.0%**	$9,054,462	**100.0%**
Cost of sales	169,163	**59.7**	4,658,520	**51.4**
Gross margin	114,238	**40.3**	4,395,942	**48.6**
Operating expenses	100,281	**35.4**	3,076,680	**34.0**
Earnings before provision for closure of U.S. pilot stores and income taxes	13,957	**4.9**	1,319,262	**14.6**
Provision for closure of U.S. pilot stores	2,961	**1.0**	—	—
Earnings before income taxes	10,996	**3.9**	1,319,262	**14.6**
Income taxes	5,244	**1.9**	494,723	**5.5**
Net earnings	$ 5,752	**2.0%**	$ 824,539	**9.1%**

Although The Gap's sales are 32 times as large as Mark's Work Wearhouse's sales, and are reported in U.S. dollars, vertical analysis eliminates these differences. The Gap outperforms Mark's Work Wearhouse on its earnings from continuing operations (before provision for closure of U.S. pilot stores and income taxes), reporting earnings of 14.6% of sales, compared to 4.9% for Mark's Work Wearhouse. The difference can be attributed primarily to The Gap's relative superiority in using its size to reduce its cost of sales and operations.

Both Mark's Work Wearhouse and The Gap include horizontal and vertical analysis in their annual reports. The Gap even goes so far as to report its statement of earnings using both dollar amounts and vertical percentages.

Although vertical analysis can also be performed on the statement of cash flows, this is seldom done. The value of this statement comes from the analysis it allows of where cash came from and what it was used for, not from the preparation of percentage comparisons of these changes against a base amount.

DECISION TOOLKIT

Decision Checkpoints	Info Needed for Decision	Tool to Use for Decision	How to Evaluate Results
How do the relationships between items in this year's financial statements compare with last year's relationships or those of competitors?	Statement of earnings and balance sheet	Each line item on the statement of earnings should be presented as a percentage of net sales, and each line item on the balance sheet should be presented as a percentage of total assets (total liabilities and shareholders' equity). These percentages should be investigated for differences, either across years in the same company, or in the same year across different companies. This is called vertical analysis.	Any difference, either across years or between companies, should be investigated to determine the cause.

BEFORE YOU GO ON...

Review It

1. What different bases can be used to compare financial information?
2. What is horizontal analysis?
3. What is vertical analysis?

Ratio Analysis

STUDY OBJECTIVE 5

Identify and calculate ratios, describe their purpose, and use them to analyse a firm's liquidity, solvency, and profitability.

In previous chapters, we presented many ratios used for evaluating the financial health and performance of a company. In this section, we provide a comprehensive review of those ratios and discuss some important relationships among them. Since earlier chapters demonstrated the calculation of each of these ratios, in this chapter, we instead focus on their interpretation. Page references to prior discussions are provided if you feel you need to review any individual ratios.

For analysis of the primary financial statements, ratios can be classified into three types:

1. **Liquidity ratios**: measures of the short-term ability of the enterprise to pay its maturing obligations and to meet unexpected needs for cash
2. **Solvency ratios**: measures of the ability of the enterprise to survive over a long period of time
3. **Profitability ratios**: measures of the earnings or operating success of an enterprise for a given period of time

As a tool of analysis, ratios can provide clues to underlying conditions that may not be apparent from an inspection of the individual components of a particular ratio. But a single ratio by itself is not very meaningful. Accordingly, in this discussion, we use the following comparisons:

1. **Intracompany comparisons** covering two years for Mark's Work Wearhouse Ltd. (using condensed comparative financial information from Illustrations 14-9 and 14-10)
2. **Intercompany comparisons** using The Gap Inc. as one of Mark's Work Wearhouse's principal competitors
3. **Industry average comparisons** for apparel retailers and comparisons with other sources (For some of the ratios that we use, industry comparisons are not available. These are denoted "n/a.")

LIQUIDITY RATIOS

Liquidity ratios measure the short-term ability of an enterprise to pay its maturing obligations and to meet unexpected needs for cash. Short-term creditors, such as bankers and suppliers, are particularly interested in assessing liquidity. The measures that can be used to determine the enterprise's short-term debt-paying ability are working capital, the current ratio, the acid-test ratio, the cash current debt coverage ratio, the credit risk ratio, the receivables turnover ratio, the average collection period, the inventory turnover ratio, and days in inventory.

Working Capital

Working capital is the difference between current assets and current liabilities. It is one measure of liquidity. However, as we learned in Chapter 2, the current ratio, which expresses current assets and current liabilities as a ratio rather than as an amount, is a more useful indicator of liquidity. Consequently, we will not illustrate working capital again here, but focus instead on the current ratio.

Current Ratio

The **current ratio** expresses the relationship of current assets to current liabilities, calculated by dividing current assets by current liabilities. It is widely used for evaluating a company's liquidity and short-term debt-paying ability. The 1999 and 1998 current ratios for Mark's Work Wearhouse and comparative data are shown in Illustration 14-12.

Ratio	Formula	Indicates	Mark's Work Wearhouse 1999	Mark's Work Wearhouse 1998	The Gap 1999	Industry 1999	Page in book
Current ratio	$\dfrac{\text{Current assets}}{\text{Current liabilities}}$	Short-term debt-paying ability	1.70	1.71	1.21	1.80	70

Illustration 14-12
Current ratio

What does the measure actually mean? The 1999 ratio of 1.70 means that for every dollar of current liabilities, Mark's Work Wearhouse has \$1.70 of current assets. We sometimes state such ratios as 1.70:1 to reinforce this interpretation. Mark's Work Wearhouse's current ratio—and therefore its liquidity—remained relatively consistent in 1999 but was below the industry average. However, it exceeded the current ratio of The Gap and of Mark's Work Wearhouse's own financial goal "to maintain a current ratio of not less than 1.50:1."

The current ratio is only one measure of liquidity. As it does not take into account the composition of current assets, a satisfactory current ratio could conceal the fact that a portion of current assets may be tied up in slow-moving inventory. Thus, the current ratio does not take into account the fact that a dollar of cash is more readily available to pay the bills than is a dollar's worth of slow-moving inventory. This weakness is addressed by the next ratio.

BUSINESS INSIGHT
Investor Perspective

The apparent simplicity of the current ratio can have real-world limitations, because adding equal amounts to both the numerator and the denominator causes the ratio to decrease. Assume, for example, that a company has \$2,000,000 of current assets and \$1,000,000 of current liabilities; its current ratio is 2:1. If it purchases \$1,000,000 of inventory on account, it will have \$3,000,000 of current assets and \$2,000,000 of current liabilities; its current ratio decreases to 1.5:1. If, instead, the company pays off \$500,000 of its current liabilities, it will have \$1,500,000 of current assets and \$500,000 of current liabilities; its current ratio increases to 3:1. Thus, any trend analysis should be done with care, as the ratio is susceptible to quick changes and is easily influenced by management.

Acid-Test Ratio

The **acid-test** or **quick ratio** is a measure of a company's immediate short-term liquidity. It is calculated by dividing the sum of cash, short-term investments, and net receivables by current liabilities. Thus, it is an important complement to the current ratio. Note that it does not include inventory or prepaid expenses. Cash, short-term investments, and net receivables are much more liquid than inventory and prepaid expenses. The inventory may not be readily saleable, and the prepaid expenses may not be transferable to others. The acid-test ratio for Mark's Work Wearhouse is shown in Illustration 14-13.

Illustration 14-13
Acid-test ratio

Ratio	Formula	Indicates	Mark's Work Wearhouse 1999	Mark's Work Wearhouse 1998	The Gap 1999	Industry 1999	Page in book
Acid-test or quick ratio	$\dfrac{\text{Cash} + \text{Short-term investments} + \text{Net receivables}}{\text{Current liabilities}}$	Immediate short-term liquidity	0.28	0.29	0.20	0.40	530

Like the current ratio, the acid-test ratio remained relatively consistent in 1999 but was lower than the industry ratio. However, when compared with The Gap's of 0.20:1, Mark's Work Wearhouse's acid-test ratio seems more than adequate.

Cash Current Debt Coverage Ratio

A disadvantage of the current and acid-test ratios is that they use year-end balances of current asset and current liability accounts. These year-end balances may not be representative of the company's position during most of the year. A ratio that partially corrects for this problem is the ratio of cash provided by operating activities to average current liabilities, called the **cash current debt coverage ratio**. Because it uses cash provided by operating activities rather than a balance at one point in time, it may provide a better representation of liquidity. Mark's Work Wearhouse's cash current debt coverage ratio is shown in Illustration 14-14.

Illustration 14-14
Cash current debt coverage ratio

Ratio	Formula	Indicates	Mark's Work Wearhouse 1999	Mark's Work Wearhouse 1998	The Gap 1999	Industry 1999	Page in book
Cash current debt coverage ratio	Cash provided by operating activities / Average current liabilities	Short-term debt-paying ability (cash basis)	0.14	(0.13)	1.10	n/a	74, 724

Mark's Work Wearhouse's cash from operating activities was a net inflow of $6.9 million in 1999, compared to a net outflow of $6.0 million in 1998. The cash outflow was caused primarily by increased merchandise inventories needed for acquisitions made during the year. Mark's Work Wearhouse's cash inflow in 1999, and its cash current debt coverage ratio, improved over 1998. Is the coverage adequate? Probably not. It is less than a commonly accepted threshold of 0.40, and substantially less than The Gap's. No industry comparison is available.

Credit Risk Ratio

The **credit risk ratio** indicates a company's overall credit risk. It is useful in monitoring the quality of receivables. Mark's Work Wearhouse's credit risk ratio can be calculated for its receivables from franchise (Mark's and Work World) stores, as shown in Illustration 14-15.

Illustration 14-15
Credit risk ratio

Ratio	Formula	Indicates	Mark's Work Wearhouse 1999	Mark's Work Wearhouse 1998	The Gap 1999	Industry 1999	Page in book
Credit risk ratio	Allowance for doubtful accounts / Accounts receivable	Overall credit risk	21.9	31.7	n/a	n/a	427

Mark's Work Wearhouse's credit risk ratio has declined in 1999, suggesting that Mark's overall credit risk is decreasing. Mark's Work Wearhouse comments on the concentration of credit risk in its annual report, stating that "there are no individually significant clients who could create a credit risk to the Company in its operated stores." The Gap does not have *any* receivables so the credit risk ratio cannot be calculated.

Receivables Turnover Ratio

Liquidity may be measured by how quickly certain assets can be converted to cash. Low values of the previous ratios can sometimes be compensated for if some of the company's current assets are highly liquid. How liquid, for example, are the receivables? The ratio used to assess the liquidity of the receivables is the **receivables turnover ratio**, which measures the number of times, on average, receivables are collected during the period. The receivables turnover ratio is calculated by dividing net credit sales (net sales less cash sales) by average net receivables during the year. The receivables turnover ratio for Mark's Work Wearhouse is shown in Illustration 14-16.

Illustration 14-16
Receivables turnover ratio

Ratio	Formula	Indicates	Mark's Work Wearhouse 1999	Mark's Work Wearhouse 1998	The Gap 1999	Industry 1999	Page in book
Receivables turnover ratio	$\frac{\text{Net credit sales}}{\text{Average net receivables}}$	Liquidity of receivables	21.8	20.2	n/a	48.1	429

Since companies don't normally disclose the proportions of their sales that were made for cash and for credit, we normally assume that all sales are credit sales. The receivables turnover ratio for Mark's Work Wearhouse improved in 1999, although it remained substantially below the industry average. It is normal for companies in this industry to have a high turnover ratio, since, in reality, few sales are made on account. As noted earlier, The Gap does not have any receivables, so there is no receivables turnover ratio available for it.

BUSINESS INSIGHT

Investor Perspective

In some cases, the receivables turnover ratio may be misleading. Some companies, especially large retail chains, issue their own credit cards. They encourage customers to use these cards, and they slow their collections in order to earn a healthy return on the outstanding receivables in the form of interest at rates of 18% to 22%. In general, however, the faster the turnover, the greater the reliance that can be placed on the current and acid-test ratios for assessing liquidity.

Average Collection Period

A popular variant of the receivables turnover ratio converts it into an **average collection period** in days. This is done by dividing the receivables turnover ratio into 365 days. The average collection period for Mark's Work Wearhouse is shown in Illustration 14-17.

Illustration 14-17
Average collection period

Ratio	Formula	Indicates	Mark's Work Wearhouse 1999	Mark's Work Wearhouse 1998	The Gap 1999	Industry 1999	Page in book
Average collection period	$\frac{\text{365 days}}{\text{Receivables turnover ratio}}$	Liquidity of receivables and collection success	16.7	18.1	n/a	7.6	429

Mark's Work Wearhouse's 1999 receivables turnover of 21.8 times is divided into 365 days to obtain approximately 17 (16.7) days. This means that the average collection period for receivables is 17 days or approximately two-and-a-half weeks. Analysts frequently use the average collection period to assess the effectiveness of a company's credit and collection policies. The general rule is that the collection period should not greatly exceed the credit term period (i.e., the time allowed for payment). It is interesting to note that the industry's average collection period is significantly shorter than that of Mark's Work Wearhouse. The shorter period may be due to more aggressive collection practices, but it is more likely due to a difference in credit terms granted. Others in the industry might be granting more generous discounts for early payment than Mark's Work Wearhouse.

Inventory Turnover Ratio

The **inventory turnover ratio** measures the number of times on average the inventory is sold during the period. Its purpose is to measure the liquidity of the inventory. The inventory turnover ratio is calculated by dividing the cost of goods sold by the average inventory during the period. Unless seasonal factors are significant, average inventory can be calculated from the beginning and ending inventory balances. Mark's Work Wearhouse's inventory turnover ratio is shown in Illustration 14-18.

Illustration 14-18
Inventory turnover ratio

Ratio	Formula	Indicates	Mark's Work Wearhouse 1999	Mark's Work Wearhouse 1998	The Gap 1999	Industry 1999	Page in book
Inventory turnover ratio	$\frac{\text{Cost of goods sold}}{\text{Average inventory}}$	Liquidity of inventory	1.9	2.2	4.3	3.6	309

Mark's Work Wearhouse's inventory turnover ratio declined in 1999. The turnover of 1.9 is much less than the industry average of 3.6 and The Gap's average of 4.3. It is also less than the financial goal Mark's Work Wearhouse set for itself of 2.4. Generally, the faster the inventory turnover, the less cash there is tied up in inventory and the less chance there is of inventory becoming obsolete. Because of these concerns, Mark's Work Wearhouse had to mark down some of its winter inventory after the warmest winter in 140 years. Of course, a downside of high inventory turnover is that the company can run out of inventory when it is needed.

Mark's Work Wearhouse notes in its annual report that its turnover ratio is somewhat misleading as many of its corporate stores were acquired late in the year, and the ratio applies to only a small portion of the year. The company maintains that "while it will continue to monitor inventory turnover and exert extra effort to improve in this area, it will do so carefully in the Mark's Division, because today's consumers, subject to increasing time pressures, expect that destination stores will always be in 'in stock' for them whenever they find the time to shop."

Days in Inventory

A variant of the inventory turnover ratio is the **days in inventory**, which measures the average number of days it takes to sell the inventory. The average days in inventory for Mark's Work Wearhouse is shown in Illustration 14-19.

Illustration 14-19
Average days in inventory

Ratio	Formula	Indicates	Mark's Work Wearhouse 1999	Mark's Work Wearhouse 1998	The Gap 1999	Industry 1999	Page in book
Days in inventory	$\frac{\text{365 days}}{\text{Inventory turnover ratio}}$	Liquidity of inventory and inventory management	192.1	165.9	84.9	101.4	309

Mark's Work Wearhouse's 1999 inventory turnover ratio of 1.9 divided into 365 is approximately 192 days. An average selling time of 192 days is higher than the industry average and significantly higher than that of The Gap. Some of this difference might be explained by differences in product lines across the two companies, although in many ways the types of products of these two companies are quite similar.

Inventory turnover ratios vary considerably among industries. For example, grocery store chains have a turnover of 8 times and an average selling period of 46 days. In contrast, jewellery stores have an average turnover of 1.7 times and an average selling period of 215 days. Within a company, there may even be significant differences in inventory turnover among different types of products. Thus, in a grocery store the turnover of perishable items such as produce, meats, and dairy products is faster than the turnover of soaps and detergents.

SOLVENCY RATIOS

Solvency ratios measure the ability of an enterprise to survive over a long period of time. Long-term creditors and shareholders are interested in a company's long-run solvency, particularly its ability to pay interest as it comes due and to repay the face value of debt at maturity. The debt to total assets ratio, times interest earned ratio, cash interest coverage ratio, and cash total debt coverage ratio provide information about debt-paying ability. In addition, free cash flow and the capital expenditure ratio provide information about the company's solvency and its ability to pay additional dividends or invest in new projects.

Debt to Total Assets Ratio

The **debt to total assets ratio** measures the percentage of the total assets provided by creditors. It is calculated by dividing total liabilities (both current and long-term) by total assets. This ratio indicates the degree of financial leveraging; it thus provides some indication of the company's ability to withstand losses without hurting the interests of its creditors. The higher the percentage of debt to total assets, the greater the risk that the company may be unable to meet its maturing obligations. The lower the ratio, the more equity "buffer" there is available to creditors if the company becomes insolvent. So, from the creditors' point of view, a low ratio of debt to total assets is desirable. Mark's Work Wearhouse's debt to total assets ratio is shown in Illustration 14-20.

Illustration 14-20 Debt to total assets ratio

Ratio	Formula	Indicates	Mark's Work Wearhouse 1999	Mark's Work Wearhouse 1998	The Gap 1999	Industry 1999	Page in book
Debt to total assets ratio	$\frac{\text{Total liabilities}}{\text{Total assets}}$	Percentage of total assets provided by creditors	0.60	0.56	0.21	0.26	71, 548

Mark's Work Wearhouse's 1999 ratio of 0.60 means that creditors have provided financing sufficient to cover 60% of the company's total assets. Mark's Work Wearhouse's 60% is significantly above The Gap's debt to total assets ratio of 21% and the industry average of 0.26. Mark's Work Wearhouse's solvency declined during the year. In that time, the company's use of short- and long-term debt financing increased to finance both the purchase and working capital requirements of store acquisitions.

The adequacy of this ratio is often judged in light of the company's earnings. Generally, companies with relatively stable earnings, such as public utilities, have higher debt to total assets ratios than cyclical companies with widely fluctuating earnings, such as many high-tech companies.

Another ratio with a similar meaning is the **debt to equity ratio.** It shows the relative use of borrowed funds compared with resources invested by the owners. Because this ratio can be calculated in several ways, care should be taken when making comparisons. Debt may be defined to include only the noncurrent portion of liabilities, and intangible assets may be excluded from shareholders' equity (which would then equal tangible net worth). If debt and shareholders' equity are defined to include all liabilities and all equity, then when the debt to total assets ratio equals 50%, the debt to equity ratio is 1:1 (because total liabilities plus shareholders' equity equals total assets). Using this definition, Mark's Work Wearhouse's debt to equity ratio for 1999 is 1.5:1 ($79,686 ÷ $53,306). This means that Mark's has financed its operations with 1.5 times as much debt as equity.

Times Interest Earned Ratio

The **times interest earned ratio** (also called interest coverage) indicates the company's ability to meet interest payments as they come due. It is calculated by dividing earnings before interest expense and income taxes by interest expense. Note that this ratio uses earnings before interest expense and income taxes (EBIT) because this amount represents what is available to cover interest. Mark's Work Wearhouse's times interest earned ratio is shown in Illustration 14-21.

Illustration 14-21 Times interest earned ratio

Ratio	Formula	Indicates	Mark's Work Wearhouse 1999	Mark's Work Wearhouse 1998	The Gap 1999	Industry 1999	Page in book
Times interest earned ratio	Earnings before interest expense and income tax expense (EBIT) / Interest expense	Ability to meet interest payments as they come due	5.1	6.3	70.4	19.1	548

For Mark's Work Wearhouse, the 1999 coverage was 5.1 times, which indicates that earnings before interest and taxes were 5.1 times the amount need for interest expense. This earnings figure excluded the nonrecurring provision for the closure of the U.S. pilot stores. If that figure is included, then Mark's Work Wearhouse's interest coverage ratio declines to 4.3 in 1999. This was substantially less than the industry average, and far from The Gap's astronomical ratio of 70.4 times. As Mark's Work Wearhouse's reliance on debt increases, its ability to cover the interest payments on this debt also declines. Yet, the times interest earned ratio is still positive, indicating that the company is still able to service its debt.

Cash Interest Coverage Ratio

The times interest earned ratio is based on earnings before interest and taxes, which do not necessarily indicate whether the company has the cash available to pay the interest. By also deducting amortization from EBIT, we can substitute a cash-basis measure of solvency, known as the **cash interest coverage ratio**. The cash interest coverage ratio is calculated by dividing earnings before interest expense, income tax expense, and (depreciation and) amortization expense (EBITDA) by interest expense. Mark's Work Wearhouse's cash interest coverage ratio is shown in Illustration 14-22.

Illustration 14-22 Cash interest coverage ratio

Ratio	Formula	Indicates	Mark's Work Wearhouse 1999	Mark's Work Wearhouse 1998	The Gap 1999	Industry 1999	Page in book
Cash interest coverage ratio	Earnings before interest expense, income tax expense, and amortization expense (EBITDA) / Interest expense	Cash flow available to cover interest payments	6.7	9.4	122.0	n/a	548

Mark's Work Wearhouse's cash interest coverage ratio of 6.7 times is stronger than its times interest earned or interest coverage ratio of 5.1 times, which includes the noncash amortization charge. In both cases, while still indicating a positive amount to cover interest payments, Mark's Work Wearhouse's coverage is declining and is nowhere near as strong as The Gap's coverage.

Cash Total Debt Coverage Ratio

The ratio of cash provided by operating activities to average total liabilities, called the **cash total debt coverage ratio**, is a cash-based measure of solvency. This ratio indicates a company's ability to repay its liabilities from cash generated from operating activities, thus without having to liquidate the assets used in its operations. Illustration 14-23 shows Mark's Work Wearhouse's cash total debt coverage ratio.

Illustration 14-23 Cash total debt coverage ratio

Ratio	Formula	Indicates	Mark's Work Wearhouse 1999	Mark's Work Wearhouse 1998	The Gap 1999	Industry 1999	Page in book
Cash total debt coverage ratio	Cash provided by operating activities / Average total liabilities	Long-term debt-paying ability (cash basis)	0.10	(0.10)	0.67	n/a	74, 725

An industry ratio for this measure is not available, but Mark's Work Wearhouse's 0.10 did improve (from negative to positive!) from 1998 to 1999 for reasons discussed under the cash current debt coverage ratio. One way of interpreting the cash total debt coverage ratio is to say that cash generated from one year of operating activities would be sufficient to pay off 10% of Mark's Work Wearhouse's total liabilities. If 10% of this year's liabilities were retired each year, it would take 10 years to retire all debt, whereas it would take The Gap less than two years to do so. A general rule of thumb is that a measure above 0.25 is acceptable.

Free Cash Flow

One indication of a company's solvency, as well as of its ability to pay additional dividends or expand operations, is the amount of excess cash it generates after investing to maintain its current productive capacity and after paying current dividends. This amount is referred to as **free cash flow**. For example, if you generate $100,000 of cash from operating activities but you spend $30,000 to maintain and replace your productive facilities at their current levels and pay $10,000 in dividends, you have $60,000 to use either to expand operations or to pay additional dividends.

Mark's Work Wearhouse's free cash flow is shown in Illustration 14-24.

Illustration 14-24 Free cash flow

Ratio	Formula	Indicates	Mark's Work Wearhouse 1999	Mark's Work Wearhouse 1998	The Gap 1999	Industry 1999	Page in book
Free cash flow	Cash provided by operating activities − Capital expenditures − Dividends paid	Cash available for paying more dividends or expanding operations	(in millions) ($3.6)	($7.1)	(in millions) $519.7	n/a	373, 721

Although Mark's Work Wearhouse's free cash flow has improved considerably from 1998 to 1999, The Gap's sheer size and global coverage allow it to generate cash at a much faster rate than Mark's Work Wearhouse's Canadian operations can.

Capital Expenditure Ratio

In addition to free cash flow, another indicator of a company's ability to generate sufficient cash to finance new capital assets is the **capital expenditure ratio**: cash provided by operating activities divided by capital expenditures. This measure is similar to free cash flow, except that free cash flow indicates the amount of cash available for the purchase of capital assets *in the future*, while the capital expenditure ratio measures the cash provided by operating activities compared to cash used for the purchase of capital assets *in the current period*.

Illustration 14-25
Capital expenditure ratio

Ratio	Formula	Indicates	Mark's Work Wearhouse 1999	Mark's Work Wearhouse 1998	The Gap 1999	Industry 1999	Page in book
Capital expenditure ratio	Cash provided by operating activities / Capital expenditures	Ability to generate sufficient cash to finance new capital assets	2.2	(6.9)	1.7	n/a	723

Mark's Work Wearhouse's capital expenditure ratio is 2.2 times in 1999, compared to a negative result produced in 1998 due to cash used (rather than provided) by operating activities. Mark's ratio suggests it could have purchased 2.2 times the capital assets it did in 1999 *without requiring any additional outside financing*. The Gap's capital expenditure ratio is 1.7 times, and there is no industry ratio available.

PROFITABILITY RATIOS

Profitability ratios measure the earnings or operating success of an enterprise for a given period of time. A company's earnings, or lack of them, affect its ability to obtain debt and equity financing, its liquidity position, and its ability to grow. As a consequence, creditors and investors alike are interested in evaluating profitability. Profitability is frequently used as the ultimate test of management's operating effectiveness. Some commonly used measures of profitability are discussed in the following pages.

Average Useful Life of Capital Assets

The **average useful life of capital assets** for a company can be estimated by dividing the average cost of capital assets by the amortization expense. The average useful life of Mark's Work Wearhouse's capital assets is shown in Illustration 14-26.

Illustration 14-26
Average useful life of capital assets

Ratio	Formula	Indicates	Mark's Work Wearhouse 1999	Mark's Work Wearhouse 1998	The Gap 1999	Industry 1999	Page in book
Average useful life of capital assets	Average cost of capital assets / Amortization expense	Average useful life of capital assets	5.3	4.8	8.3	n/a	480

The average useful life of Mark's capital assets is just over five years in 1999, up slightly from 1998. This increase is likely attributable to the corporate stores acquired. Mark's capital assets are not as old as The Gap's, which average just over eight years old. There is no average age available for the industry.

The Gap does not report the useful lives over which it is amortizing its capital assets. It is in cases such as these that the calculation of the average useful life is necessary. Mark's, however, does report the useful lives over which it is amortizing its capital assets: buildings over 15 years; furniture, fixtures, and equipment over five years; and leasehold improvements, computer equipment, and software over their lease terms, which are not specified. Given this information, our estimate of the average useful life of capital assets in total does not appear to be unreasonable.

Average Age of Capital Assets

The **average age of capital assets** can be approximated by dividing accumulated amortization by amortization expense. The average age of Mark's Work Wearhouse's capital assets is shown in Illustration 14-27.

Illustration 14-27
Average age of capital assets

Ratio	Formula	Indicates	Mark's Work Wearhouse 1999	Mark's Work Wearhouse 1998	The Gap 1999	Industry 1999	Page in book
Average age of capital assets	Accumulated amortization / Amortization expense	Average age of capital assets	3.1	2.7	3.4	n/a	481

Mark's Work Wearhouse's capital assets are, on average, three years old. This does not necessarily mean that they are three years old; it could just mean that Mark's purchased them used and has *owned* them for three years. Mark's average is comparable with The Gap's. With a five-year useful life (see Illustration 14-26), this means that Mark's may have to replace these assets in the next two years.

Return on Common Shareholders' Equity Ratio

A widely used measure of profitability from the common shareholder's viewpoint is the **return on common shareholders' equity ratio**. This ratio shows how many dollars of net earnings were earned for each dollar invested by the owners. It is calculated by dividing net earnings minus any preferred share dividends—that is, earnings available to common shareholders—by average common shareholders' equity. The return on common shareholders' equity for Mark's Work Wearhouse is shown in Illustration 14-28.

Illustration 14-28
Return on common shareholders' equity ratio

Ratio	Formula	Indicates	Mark's Work Wearhouse 1999	Mark's Work Wearhouse 1998	The Gap 1999	Industry 1999	Page in book
Return on common shareholders' equity ratio	Earnings available to common shareholders / Average common shareholders' equity	Profitability of common shareholders' investment	0.17	0.16	0.53	0.24	614

Mark's Work Wearhouse's return (excluding the nonrecurring item) on common shareholder's equity improved slightly in 1999, and is not all that far from the industry ratio of 24%. However, it is substantially below The Gap's return of 53%. Remember though, that The Gap's earnings are 95 times those of Mark's Work Wearhouse, and its shareholders' equity 30 times as large.

The return on common shareholders' equity is influenced by other measures of profitability. The relationships among these measures are very important, as understanding them can help management determine where to focus its efforts to improve profitability. Illustration 14-29 diagrams these relationships. Our discussion of the next few profitability ratios is structured around this diagram.

Illustration 14-29
Relationships among profitability measures

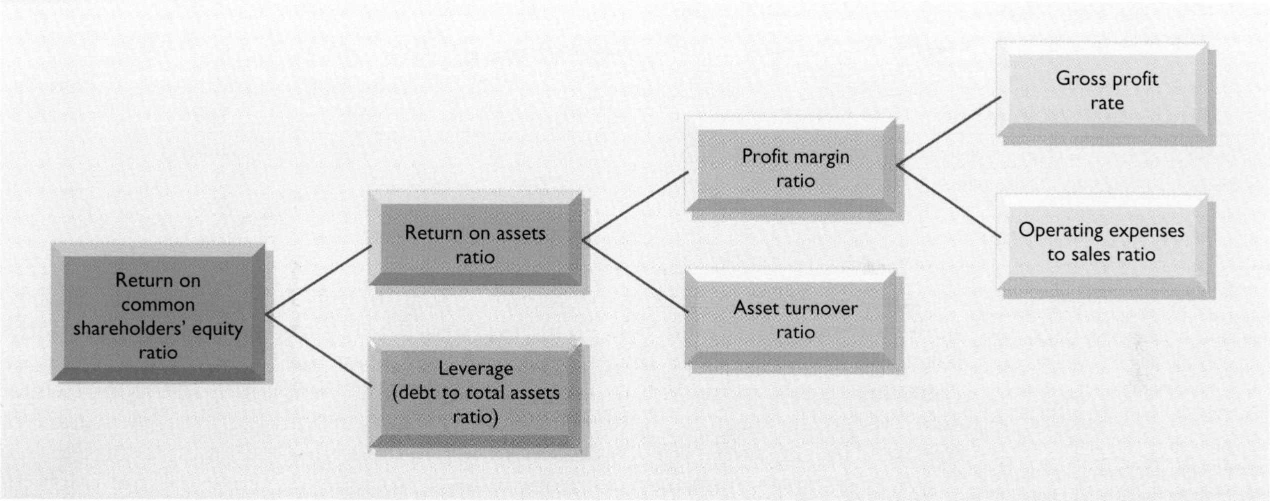

Return on Assets Ratio

The return on common shareholders' equity ratio is affected by two factors: the **return on assets ratio** and the degree of leverage. The return on assets ratio measures the overall profitability of assets in terms of the income earned on each dollar invested in assets. It is calculated by dividing net earnings by average total assets. Mark's Work Wearhouse's return on assets ratio is shown in Illustration 14-30.

Illustration 14-30
Return on assets ratio

Ratio	Formula	Indicates	Mark's Work Wearhouse 1999	Mark's Work Wearhouse 1998	The Gap 1999	Industry 1999	Page in book
Return on assets ratio	$\frac{\text{Net earnings}}{\text{Average total assets}}$	Overall profitability of assets	0.07	0.07	0.22	0.12	66

Mark's Work Wearhouse has a 7% return on assets in both 1999 and 1998. This rate remains below that of the industry and The Gap.

Note that Mark's Work Wearhouse's rate of return on shareholders' equity (17%) is substantially higher than its rate of return on assets (7%). The reason is that Mark's Work Wearhouse has made effective use of **leverage. Leveraging** or **trading on the equity** at a gain means that the company has borrowed money at a lower rate of interest than the rate of return it earns on the assets it purchased with the borrowed funds. Leverage enables management to use money supplied by non-owners to increase the return to owners.

A comparison of the rate of return on assets with the rate of interest paid for borrowed money indicates the profitability of trading on the equity. If you borrow money at 8% and your rate of return on assets is 11%, you are trading on the equity at a gain. Note, however, that trading on the equity is a two-way street: for example, if you borrow money at 11% and earn only 8% on it, you are trading on the equity at a loss.

Profit Margin Ratio

The return on assets ratio is affected by two factors, the first of which is the profit margin ratio. The **profit margin ratio**, or rate of return on sales, is a measure of the percentage of each dollar of sales that results in net earnings. It is calculated by dividing net earnings by net sales for the period. Mark's Work Wearhouse's profit margin ratio is shown in Illustration 14-31.

Illustration 14-31 Profit margin ratio

Ratio	Formula	Indicates	Mark's Work Wearhouse 1999	Mark's Work Wearhouse 1998	The Gap 1999	Industry 1999	Page in book
Profit margin ratio	Net earnings / Net sales	Net earnings generated by each dollar of sales	0.03	0.03	0.09	0.06	67

Mark's Work Wearhouse experienced a 3% profit margin, which, exclusive of the nonrecurring item, exceeded its financial goal of 2%. It is also noteworthy that Mark's sales and earnings before the provision for closure of the U.S. pilot stores and income taxes grew from 1998 to 1999 (see Illustration 14-10), in a very poor "winter year." Its profit margin is, however, low in comparison with the industry average of 6% and The Gap's 9%. This could be due to the different product lines carried.

Average profit margins vary from industry to industry. High-volume (high inventory turnover) enterprises, such as grocery stores and pharmacy chains, generally have low profit margins, whereas low-volume enterprises, such as jewellery stores and airplane manufacturers, have high profit margins.

Asset Turnover Ratio

The other factor that affects the return on assets ratio is the asset turnover ratio. The **asset turnover ratio** measures how efficiently a company uses its assets to generate sales. It is determined by dividing net sales by average total assets for the period. The resulting number shows the dollars of sales produced by each dollar invested in assets. Illustration 14-32 shows the asset turnover ratio for Mark's Work Wearhouse.

Illustration 14-32 Asset turnover ratio

Ratio	Formula	Indicates	Mark's Work Wearhouse 1999	Mark's Work Wearhouse 1998	The Gap 1999	Industry 1999	Page in book
Asset turnover ratio	Net sales / Average total assets	How efficiently assets are used to generate sales	2.4	2.5	2.6	2.3	482

The asset turnover ratio shows that Mark's Work Wearhouse generated sales of $2.40 in 1999 for each dollar it had invested in assets. Although the ratio declined a bit from 1998 to 1999, it is better than the industry average and quite close to the much larger Gap's. This is remarkable given the other performance measures we've compared. Mark's Work Wearhouse, despite its smaller size or perhaps because of it, utilizes its assets very efficiently.

Asset turnover ratios vary considerably among industries. The average asset turnover for utility companies is 0.45, for example, while the grocery store industry has an average asset turnover of 3.49.

In summary, Mark's Work Wearhouse's return on assets ratio remained unchanged from 1998 to 1999 at 7%. However, underlying this apparent stability was an increased profitability on each dollar of sales, as measured by the profit margin ratio (2.6% to 3.1%, both rounded to 0.03 in Illustration 14-31) which, however, is offset by a decline in the sales-generating efficiency of its assets, as measured by the asset turnover ratio. The combined effects of profit margin and asset turnover on return on assets for Mark's Work Wearhouse can be analysed as shown in Illustration 14-33.

Illustration 14-33
Composition of return on assets ratio

Ratios:	Profit Margin: Net Earnings / Net Sales	×	Asset Turnover: Net Sales / Average Total Assets	=	Return on Assets: Net Earnings / Average Total Assets
Mark's Work Wearhouse					
1999	3.1%	×	2.4 times	=	7.4% (rounded to 7%)
1998	2.6%	×	2.5 times	=	6.5% (rounded to 7%)

Gross Profit Rate

Two factors strongly influence the profit margin ratio. One is the gross profit rate. The **gross profit rate** is determined by dividing gross profit (net sales less cost of goods sold) by net sales. This rate indicates a company's ability to maintain an adequate selling price above its cost of goods sold. As an industry becomes more competitive, this ratio declines. For example, in the early years of the personal computer industry, gross profit rates were quite high. Today, because of increased competition and a belief that most brands of personal computers are similar in quality, gross profit rates have become thin. Gross profit rates should be closely monitored over time. Illustration 14-34 shows Mark's Work Wearhouse's gross profit rate.

Much can be learned about Mark's Work Wearhouse's gross profit by reading its annual report. The company details each component which affects its gross profit. While not as good as The Gap's gross profit rate, Mark's Work Wearhouse's is slightly better than that of the industry. The company is justifiably proud of its performance, noting in its annual report: "Despite a very weak Canadian dollar against the U.S. dollar, an extremely competitive environment as the department stores try to change their blends to a higher apparel component and discount food and hard goods retailers try to make inroads in selected entry-level apparel commodities, the Company managed to maintain its gross margin rate in its Mark's Division." The gross profit rate dropped only two-tenths of a point from 40.5% (rounded to 0.41 in Illustration 14-34) in fiscal 1998 to 40.3% (rounded to 0.40 in Illustration 14-34) in 1999.

Illustration 14-34
Gross profit rate

Ratio	Formula	Indicates	Mark's Work Wearhouse 1999	Mark's Work Wearhouse 1998	The Gap 1999	Industry 1999	Page in book
Gross profit rate	Gross profit / Net sales	Margin between selling price and cost of goods sold	0.40	0.41	0.49	0.39	254

Operating Expenses to Sales Ratio

This is the other factor that directly affects the profit margin ratio. Management can influence a company's profitability by maintaining adequate prices, cutting expenses, or both. The **operating expenses to sales ratio** measures the costs incurred to support each dollar of sales. It is calculated by dividing operating expenses (selling and administrative expenses) by net sales. The operating expenses to sales ratio for Mark's Work Wearhouse is shown in Illustration 14-35.

Illustration 14-35 Operating expenses to sales ratio

Ratio	Formula	Indicates	Mark's Work Wearhouse 1999	Mark's Work Wearhouse 1998	The Gap 1999	Industry 1999	Page in book
Operating expenses to sales ratio	$\frac{\text{Operating expenses}}{\text{Net sales}}$	The costs incurred to support each dollar of sales	0.35	0.36	0.34	n/a	256

During recent years, the financial press has frequently carried stories about the retail industry's efforts to "restructure" operations and cut expenses. Mark's Work Wearhouse obviously did so from 1998 to 1999. The impact is apparent in its operating expense ratio of 35%, relatively consistent with that of its very large rival, The Gap.

Cash Return on Sales Ratio

The profit margin ratio discussed earlier is an accrual-based ratio using net earnings as a numerator. The cash-based counterpart to that ratio is the **cash return on sales ratio**, which uses cash provided by operating activities as the numerator and net sales as the denominator. The difference between these two ratios relates to the differences between accrual accounting and cash-based accounting, such as differences in the timing of revenue and expense recognition. The cash return on sales ratio for Mark's Work Wearhouse is shown in Illustration 14-36.

Illustration 14-36 Cash return on sales ratio

Ratio	Formula	Indicates	Mark's Work Wearhouse 1999	Mark's Work Wearhouse 1998	The Gap 1999	Industry 1999	Page in book
Cash return on sales ratio	$\frac{\text{Cash provided by operating activities}}{\text{Net sales}}$	Net cash flow generated by each dollar of sales	0.02	0.02	0.15	n/a	726

Earnings Per Share (EPS)

Shareholders usually think in terms of the number of shares they own or plan to buy or sell. Expressing net earnings earned on a per share basis provides a useful perspective for determining profitability. **Earnings per share** is a measure of the net earnings earned on each common share. It is calculated by dividing net earnings by the weighted average number of common shares outstanding during the year. When we use "earnings per share," it refers to the amount of net earnings applicable to each *common* share. Therefore, when we calculate earnings per share, if there are preferred dividends declared for the period, they must be deducted from net earnings to arrive at earnings available to the common shareholders. Mark's Work Wearhouse's earnings per share is shown in Illustration 14-37.

Ratio	Formula	Indicates	Mark's Work Wearhouse 1999	Mark's Work Wearhouse 1998	The Gap 1999	Industry 1999	Page in book
Earnings per share (EPS)	Earnings available to common shareholders / Average number of common shares outstanding	Net earnings earned on each common share	$0.27	$0.24	$1.43	n/a	613

Illustration 14-37
Earnings per share

Note that no industry average is presented in Illustration 14-37. Industry data for earnings per share are not reported, and in fact the Mark's Work Wearhouse and The Gap EPS ratio should not be compared. Such comparisons are not meaningful because of the wide variations in the number of shares outstanding among companies. Mark's Work Wearhouse's earnings per share (exclusive of nonrecurring items) increased three cents per share in 1999. This represents a 12.5% increase over the 1998 EPS of $0.24.

Book Value Per Share

Book value per share is common shareholders' equity, expressed on a per-share basis. It represents **the equity a common shareholder has in the net assets of the corporation** from owning a share. Since net assets (assets less liabilities) equal shareholders' equity, book value is calculated by dividing shareholders' equity by the number of common shares outstanding.

When a corporation has more than one class of shares, the calculation of book value is a little more complicated. Since preferred shares have a claim on net assets over common shareholders, the preferred shareholders' legal capital must be deducted from total shareholders' equity to determine the shareholders' equity that belongs to the common shareholders.

Mark's Work Wearhouse's book value per common share is shown in Illustration 14-38.

Illustration 14-38
Book value per share

Ratio	Formula	Indicates	Mark's Work Wearhouse 1999	Mark's Work Wearhouse 1998	The Gap 1999	Industry 1999	Page in book
Book value share	Common shareholder's equity / Number of common shares outstanding	Equity per common share	$1.91	$1.71	$2.94	$4.75	787

Book value per share seldom, if ever, equals market value. Book value is based on recorded historical costs. Market value reflects the subjective judgements of shareholders and prospective investors about the company's potential for future earnings and growth. The correlation between book value and market value per share is often remote. However, comparing book value to market value can help discover if there are unrecorded or undervalued assets (or conversely, overvalued assets). Mark's Work Wearhouse's market value per share is nearly twice its book value. The Gap's market value per share is nearly 13 times its book value. Both companies' book values are less than the industry.

Cash Flow Per Share

Cash flow is an important measure of performance for companies. **Cash flow per share** is calculated by dividing cash flow from all (operating, investing, and financing) activities by the weighted average number of common shares outstanding. This is exactly how earnings per share are calculated, except that cash flow replaces net earnings. As with earnings per share, if there are any preferred dividends, they must also be deducted to arrive at the cash flow available to the common shareholders.

Mark's Work Wearhouse's cash flow per share is shown in Illustration 14-39.

Illustration 14-39
Cash flow per share

Ratio	Formula	Indicates	Mark's Work Wearhouse 1999	Mark's Work Wearhouse 1998	The Gap 1999	Industry 1999	Page in book
Cash flow per share	Net cash flow from all activities / Average number of common shares outstanding	Cash flow per common share	\$0.09	(\$0.42)	\$1.95	\$1.85	788

Mark's cash flow per share is one-third its reported earnings per share of \$0.27. The Gap's cash flow per share exceeds its earnings per share. It is interesting to compare cash flow per share to earnings per share. Neither statistic on its own provides sufficient information for decision makers. However, taken together, earnings and cash flow provide two significant pieces of information needed to predict a company's future viability.

Because of the importance of the statement of cash flows to a wide variety of users, many have recommended that the statement of cash flows include **cash flow per share** data, much as the statement of earnings includes **earnings per share** data. Although the CICA does not require the inclusion of cash flow per share data in the statement of cash flows, companies often include the ratio in their annual reports.

Price-Earnings Ratio

The **price-earnings ratio** is an oft-quoted statistic that measures the ratio of the market price of each common share to the earnings per share. The price-earnings (P-E) ratio is a reflection of investors' assessments of a company's future earnings. It is calculated by dividing the market price per share by earnings per share. Mark's Work Wearhouse's price-earnings ratio is shown in Illustration 14-40.

Illustration 14-40
Price-earnings ratio

Ratio	Formula	Indicates	Mark's Work Wearhouse 1999	Mark's Work Wearhouse 1998	The Gap 1999	Industry 1999	Page in book
Price-earnings ratio	Share price / Earnings per share	Relationship between market price per share and earnings per share	12.0	15.4	26.2	23.6	613

At the end of fiscal 1999 and 1998, the market price of Mark's Work Wearhouse's shares was \$3.25 and \$3.70, respectively. The Gap's shares were selling for US\$37.42 at the end of 1999. Over 50% of Mark's Work Wearhouse's common shares are closely held. This makes it impossible for an outsider to acquire a majority of the shares without the consent of management and other insiders. However, it also means that the shares are not very liquid.

In 1999, each common share of Mark's Work Wearhouse's sold for 12 times the amount that was earned on each share. Mark's Work Wearhouse's 1999 price-earnings ratio is lower than the previous year, and significantly lower than both the industry average and the price-earnings ratio of The Gap. These higher P-E ratios suggest that the market is more optimistic about The Gap and other companies in the industry than Mark's Work Wearhouse. However, it might also signal that their shares are overpriced. The average price-earnings ratio for the shares that constitute the Standard and Poor's Composite 500 Company Index in 1999 was an unusually high 36 times.

BUSINESS INSIGHT

Investor Perspective

The price-earnings ratio is a user-friendly yardstick that even a novice investor can use to help gauge whether a share is outrageously pricey or sitting in the bargain bin. If a company's shares have great prospects for growth, a high P-E multiple may be justified—because the company will earn more and because investors will be willing to pay more for those earnings. Take Research in Motion Limited, located in Waterloo, Ontario, a maker of *Blackberry*, a wireless e-mail pager. *Blackberry* won the 2000 *PC World* World Class Award for Best Wireless Communication Device. Research in Motion's shares traded at a P-E multiple of 966 in early 2000, indicating investors' cheery optimism about the company's future.

High multiples, however, can also mean high risk. To determine when to "buy" or "sell" at a certain price, many investors study a company's P-E ratio over time. If the highs and lows of a particular share's P-E ratio remain constant over several stock market cycles, then the highs and lows can indicate selling and buying points for the shares. Studying the P-E ratios of competitor companies and the industry index can also put the movements into perspective.

Source: Carolyn Leitch, "Taking the Measure of a Stock's Value," *Globe and Mail*, April 1, 2000, N5.

Payout Ratio

The **payout ratio** measures the percentage of earnings distributed in the form of cash dividends. It is calculated by dividing cash dividends declared on common shares by net earnings. Companies that have high growth rates are characterized by low payout ratios, because they reinvest most of their net earnings in the business. The payout ratio for Mark's Work Wearhouse is shown in Illustration 14-41.

Illustration 14-41
Payout ratio

Ratio	Formula	Indicates:	Mark's Work Wearhouse 1999	1998	The Gap 1999	Industry 1999	Page in book
Payout ratio	Cash dividends / Net earnings	Percentage of earnings distributed in the form of cash dividends	n/a	n/a	0.09	0.13	611

Mark's Work Wearhouse does not pay dividends on its common shares. The Gap's payout ratio of 9% is relatively low, compared to that of the industry at 13%. Growth is a priority for both companies, whence the low or non-existent payout ratios.

Management has some control over the amount of dividends paid each year, and companies are generally reluctant to reduce a dividend below the amount paid in a previous year. Therefore, the payout ratio will actually increase if a company's net earnings decline but the company keeps its total dividend payment the same. Of course, unless the company returns to its previous level of profitability, maintaining this higher dividend payout ratio is probably not possible over the long run.

BUSINESS INSIGHT

Management Perspective

Generally, companies with stable earnings have high payout ratios. For example, BCE has an 81% payout ratio. Conversely, companies that are expanding rapidly, such as Alliance Atlantic Communications and Corel, have never paid a cash dividend.

Dividend Yield

Another measure, the **dividend yield**, supplements the payout ratio. The dividend yield reports the rate of return an investor earned from dividends during the year. It is calculated by dividing cash dividends per share declared to common shareholders by the share price at the end of the year. The dividend yield for Mark's Work Wearhouse is shown in Illustration 14-42.

Illustration 14-42 Dividend yield

Ratio	Formula	Indicates	Mark's Work Wearhouse 1999	Mark's Work Wearhouse 1998	The Gap 1999	Industry 1999	Page in book
Dividend yield	Cash dividends per common share / Year-end share price	Rate of return earned from dividends	n/a	n/a	0.002	n/a	611

Mark's Work Wearhouse did not pay any dividends to its common shareholders, but The Gap's common shareholders received eight cents a share. The industry average was a 14-cent dividend per share. The Gap's shareholders received a 0.2% rate of return on their share investment. As with the payout ratio, companies that have high growth rates, such as The Gap, can also be expected to have low dividend yields. A dividend yield is not available for the industry as closing share prices aren't comparable.

To conclude and summarize our analysis of Mark's Work Wearhouse's financial health, we can say that its honest and open reporting style lends confidence to its future. Its current liquidity appears strong, although the management of its merchandise inventories in the future (and management's hopes for a cold winter!) require further attention. Cash generated from operating activities, while improving, is still below the average for the industry. Mark's Work Wearhouse's solvency is also not as strong as the industry's. Creditors will no doubt carefully watch the results of the corporate restructuring and the associated debt requirements in the future. Mark's Work Wearhouse's operations are profitable in a competitive environment. Mark's is extremely efficient in capitalizing on its earning power and utilizing its assets effectively. Although investment interest is somewhat limited by the number of available Mark's Work Wearhouse shares, investors remain confident about Mark's future profitability, as its earnings per share (before irregular items) rise, and so are still willing to pay a reasonable multiple of earnings for these shares. A caveat to keep in mind, however, is that our interpretation was based on earnings before discontinued items. The impact of the closure of the two U.S. pilot stores will be watched closely by investors and creditors alike in the future.

A summary of the ratios discussed in the chapter is presented in Illustration 14-43, including the formula and purpose or use of each ratio.

Illustration 14-43
Summary of liquidity, profitability, and solvency ratios

RATIO **Liquidity Ratios**	**FORMULA**	**PURPOSE OR USE**
Working capital	Current assets − Current liabilities	Measures short-term debt-paying ability
Current ratio	$\frac{\text{Current assets}}{\text{Current liabilities}}$	Measures short-term debt-paying ability
Acid test or quick ratio	$\frac{\text{Cash + Short-term investments + Net receivables}}{\text{Current liabilities}}$	Measures immediate short-term liquidity
Cash current debt coverage ratio	$\frac{\text{Cash provided by operating activities}}{\text{Average current liabilities}}$	Measures short-term debt-paying ability (cash basis)
Credit risk ratio	$\frac{\text{Allowance for doubtful accounts}}{\text{Accounts receivable}}$	Measures overall credit risk
Receivables turnover ratio	$\frac{\text{Net credit sales}}{\text{Average net receivables}}$	Measures liquidity of receivables
Average collection period	$\frac{\text{365 days}}{\text{Receivables turnover ratio}}$	Measures number of days receivables are outstanding
Inventory turnover ratio	$\frac{\text{Cost of goods sold}}{\text{Average inventory}}$	Measures liquidity of inventory
Days in inventory	$\frac{\text{365 days}}{\text{Inventory turnover ratio}}$	Measures number of days inventory is on hand
Solvency Ratios		
Debt to total assets ratio	$\frac{\text{Total liabilities}}{\text{Total assets}}$	Measures percentage of total assets provided by creditors
Times interest earned ratio	$\frac{\text{Earnings before interest expense and income tax expense (EBIT)}}{\text{Interest expense}}$	Measures ability to meet interest payments as they come due
Cash interest coverage ratio	$\frac{\text{Earnings before interest expense, income tax expense, and amortization expense (EBITDA)}}{\text{Interest expense}}$	Measures ability to meet interest payments as they come due
Cash total debt coverage ratio	$\frac{\text{Cash provided by operating activities}}{\text{Average total liabilities}}$	Measures long-term debt-paying ability (cash basis)

Free cash flow	Cash provided by operating activities − Capital expenditures − Dividends paid	Measures cash available for paying more dividends or expanding operations
Capital expenditure ratio	$\dfrac{\text{Cash provided by operating activities}}{\text{Capital expenditures}}$	Measures ability to generate sufficient cash to finance new capital assets
Profitability Ratios		
Average useful life of capital assets	$\dfrac{\text{Average cost of capital assets}}{\text{Amortization expense}}$	Measures average useful life of capital assets
Average age of capital assets	$\dfrac{\text{Accumulated amortization}}{\text{Amortization expense}}$	Measures average age of capital assets
Return on common shareholders' equity ratio	$\dfrac{\text{Earnings available to common shareholders}}{\text{Average common shareholders' equity}}$	Measures profitability of shareholders' investment
Return on assets ratio	$\dfrac{\text{Net earnings}}{\text{Average total assets}}$	Measures overall profitability of assets
Profit margin ratio	$\dfrac{\text{Net earnings}}{\text{Net sales}}$	Measures net earnings generated by each dollar of sales
Asset turnover ratio	$\dfrac{\text{Net sales}}{\text{Average total assets}}$	Measures how efficiently assets are used to generate sales
Gross profit rate	$\dfrac{\text{Gross profit}}{\text{Net sales}}$	Measures margin between selling price and cost of goods sold
Operating expenses to sales ratio	$\dfrac{\text{Operating expenses}}{\text{Net sales}}$	Measures the cost incurred to support each dollar of sales
Cash return on sales ratio	$\dfrac{\text{Cash provided by operating activities}}{\text{Net sales}}$	Measures the net cash flow generated by each dollar of sales
Earnings per share	$\dfrac{\text{Earnings available to common shareholders}}{\text{Average number of common shares outstanding}}$	Measures net earnings earned on each common share
Book value per share	$\dfrac{\text{Common shareholders' equity}}{\text{Number of common shares outstanding}}$	Measures the equity (net assets) per common share
Cash flow per share	$\dfrac{\text{Net cash flow from all activities}}{\text{Average number of common shares outstanding}}$	Measures the net cash flow per common share
Price-earnings ratio	$\dfrac{\text{Share price}}{\text{Earnings per share}}$	Measures relationship between market price per share and earnings per share
Payout ratio	$\dfrac{\text{Cash dividends}}{\text{Net earnings}}$	Measures percentage of earnings distributed in the form of cash dividends
Dividend yield	$\dfrac{\text{Cash dividends per common share}}{\text{Year-end share price}}$	Measures rate of return earned from dividends

BEFORE YOU GO ON...

Review It

1. What are liquidity ratios? Explain working capital, the current ratio, acid-test ratio, cash current debt coverage ratio, credit risk ratio, receivables turnover ratio, average collection period, inventory turnover ratio, and days in inventory.
2. What are solvency ratios? Explain the debt to total assets ratio, times interest earned ratio, cash interest coverage ratio, cash total debt coverage ratio, free cash flow, and the capital expenditure ratio.
3. What are profitability ratios? Explain average useful life, average age, the return on common shareholders' equity ratio, return on assets ratio, profit margin, asset turnover ratio, gross profit rate, operating expenses to sales ratio, cash return on sales ratio, earnings per share, book value per share, cash flow per share, price-earnings ratio, payout ratio, and dividend yield.

Limitations of Financial Analysis

STUDY OBJECTIVE 6

Discuss the limitations of financial statement analysis.

Significant business decisions are frequently made using one or more of the three analytical tools presented in this chapter: horizontal, vertical, and ratio analyses. You should be aware of some of the limitations of these tools and of the financial statements on which they are based.

ESTIMATES

Financial statements contain numerous estimates. Estimates are used, for example, in determining the allowance for uncollectible receivables, periodic amortization, the costs of warranties, and contingent losses. To the extent that estimates are inaccurate, the financial ratios and percentages are also inaccurate.

COST

Traditional financial statements are based on cost and are not adjusted for price-level changes. Comparisons of unadjusted financial data from different periods may be rendered invalid by significant inflation or deflation. For example, a three-year comparison of Mark's Work Wearhouse's revenues shows a growth of 28%. But if, for example, the general price level also increased by 3%, the company's real growth would be 25%. Also, some capital assets might be many years old. The historical cost at which they are shown on the balance sheet may be lower than what they could currently be sold for.

ALTERNATIVE ACCOUNTING METHODS

Variations among companies in the application of generally accepted accounting principles may hamper comparability. For example, The Gap uses the FIFO method of inventory costing, while Mark's Work Wearhouse uses an average costing (retail) method. Depending on the timing and cost of their merchandise purchases, their current and inventory turnover ratios may not be comparable. In addition to differences in inventory costing methods, differences can also exist in reporting other items, such as amortization.

As well, in an increasing number of industries, competition is global. To evaluate a firm's standing, an investor must make comparisons to firms from other countries just as we did by comparing Canadian-based Mark's Work Wearhouse with the globally oriented Gap. Although differences in accounting methods might be detectable from reading the notes to the financial statements, adjusting the financial data to compensate for different methods is difficult, if not impossible, in some cases.

ATYPICAL DATA

Fiscal year-end data may not be typical of a company's financial condition during the year. Companies frequently establish a fiscal year end that coincides with the low point in their operating activity or inventory levels. Therefore, certain account balances (for cash, receivables, payables, and inventories) may not be representative of the balances in the accounts during the year.

DIVERSIFICATION

Diversification in Canadian industry also limits the usefulness of financial analysis. Many firms today are so diversified that they cannot be classified by industry. The Irving Group of Companies includes holdings that range from forest operations, including pulp, tissue, and news print mills, to Canada's largest oil refinery and Irving Mainway stores. The manufactured products are transported by Irving-owned companies producing ships, trucks, and rail cars. As a consequence, deciding what industry a company is in is actually one of the main challenges to arriving at an effective evaluation of its results.

Other companies may appear to be comparable but are not. The Gap, Inc. includes Gap, GapKids, Banana Republic, and Old Navy. The Gap's product line is not exactly the same as Mark's Work Wearhouse's, but is more comparable than that of other companies included in the retail apparel industry classification, such as Sears. Sears sells many other products—furniture, appliances, automotive parts, and hardware—besides casual clothing and footwear.

When companies have significant operations in different lines of business, they are required to report additional disclosures in a **segmental data** note to their financial statements. Segmental data include all of the following by business segment: total sales, total identifiable assets, operating profit, amortization expense, and capital expenditures. Many analysts say that the segmental information is the most important data in the financial statements, because, without it, a comparison of diversified companies is very difficult.

BUSINESS INSIGHT

Investor Perspective

Many people would argue that non-financial performance measures are more important than financial measures in assessing success. Financial measures can evaluate only past performance; non-financial measures may be better predictors of future performance. Non-financial performance measures include factors such as customer service, customer satisfaction, and market performance. Knowledge resources also contribute to a firm's success. These include innovation, information systems, employee satisfaction and abilities, and company and product reputation.

DECISION TOOLKIT

Decision Checkpoints	Info Needed for Decision	Tool to Use for Decision	How to Evaluate Results
Are efforts to evaluate the company significantly hampered by any of the common limitations of financial analysis?	Financial statements as well as a general understanding of the company and its business	The primary limitations of financial analysis are estimates, cost, alternative accounting methods, atypical data, and diversification.	If any of these factors is significant, the analysis should be relied upon with caution.

BEFORE YOU GO ON...

Review It

1. What are some of the limitations of financial analysis?
2. What are the required disclosures in segmental data notes?

USING THE DECISION TOOLKIT

When analysing a company, you should always investigate an extended period of time in order to determine whether the condition and performance of the company are changing. The condensed financial statements of Mark's Work Wearhouse Company for 1997 and 1996 follow, and supplement the data presented earlier in the chapter for 1999 and 1998:

MARK'S WORK WEARHOUSE LTD.
Condensed Balance Sheets
January 25 and 27
(in thousands)

Assets	1997	1996
Current assets		
Cash and short-term investments	$11,749	$ 85
Accounts receivable	12,284	10,828
Merchandise inventories	44,040	44,619
Other current assets	2,304	1,569
Total current assets	70,377	57,101
Capital assets (net)	21,976	11,993
Other assets	793	1,963
Total assets	$93,146	$71,057
Liabilities and Shareholders' Equity		
Current liabilities	$42,154	$32,769
Long-term liabilities	14,108	6,134
Total liabilities	56,262	38,903
Shareholders' equity—common	36,884	32,154
Total liabilities and shareholders' equity	$93,146	$71,057

MARK'S WORK WEARHOUSE LTD.
Condensed Statements of Earnings
52 Weeks Ended January 25 and 27
(in thousands)

	1997	1996
Sales	$220,902	$198,262
Cost of sales	136,933	124,781
Gross profit	83,969	73,481
Front-line expenses	59,218	50,138
Back-line expenses	16,441	16,969
Earnings before income taxes	8,310	6,374
Income taxes	4,387	3,257
Net earnings	$ 3,923	$ 3,117

Additional Information:

1. Interest expense was $1,849 thousand in 1997; $1,672 thousand in 1996.
2. Cash flow generated from operating activities in 1997 was $13,863 thousand; in 1996, $1,683 thousand.
3. Cash paid for capital assets was $5,998 thousand in 1997; $7,290 thousand in 1996.

Instructions

Calculate the following ratios for Mark's Work Wearhouse for 1997 and 1996, and comment on each, relative to the amounts reported in the chapter for 1999 and 1998.

1. Liquidity:
   (a) Current ratio
   (b) Cash current debt coverage ratio (Current liabilities on January 28, 1995, were $31,217 thousand.)
   (b) Inventory turnover ratio (Merchandise inventory on January 28, 1995, was $36,788 thousand.)
2. Solvency:
   (a) Debt to total assets ratio
   (b) Times interest earned ratio
   (c) Free cash flow
3. Profitability:
   (a) Return on common shareholders' equity ratio (Shareholders' equity on January 28, 1995, was $28,922 thousand.)
   (b) Return on assets ratio (Total assets on January 28, 1995, were $64,541 thousand.)
   (c) Profit margin ratio

Solution

1. Liquidity:
   (a) Current ratio

$$1997\text{:}\quad \frac{\$70,377}{\$42,154} = 1.67\text{:}1$$

$$1996\text{:}\quad \frac{\$57,101}{\$32,769} = 1.74\text{:}1$$

(b) Cash current debt coverage ratio

1997: $\dfrac{\$13,863}{(\$42,154 + \$32,769)/2} = 0.37$

1996: $\dfrac{\$1,683}{(\$32,769 + \$31,217)/2} = 0.05$

(c) Inventory turnover ratio

1997: $\dfrac{\$136,933}{(\$44,040 + \$44,619)/2} = 3.1 \text{ times}$

1996: $\dfrac{\$124,781}{(\$44,619 + \$36,788)/2} = 3.1 \text{ times}$

Mark's Work Wearhouse's liquidity, as measured by the current ratio, declined in 1997. However, as we noted in the chapter, it returned to the 1.7 range in 1998 and 1999. Its cash current debt coverage ratio was obviously strong in 1997, before the decline in cash in 1998 and 1999 took place. This provided Mark's Work Wearhouse with a sufficient liquidity base to be able to survive a lower than normal cash flow in subsequent years. Mark's Work Wearhouse's inventory turnover ratio, constant in 1996 and 1997, has since declined progressively.

2. Solvency:

(a) Debt to total assets ratio

1997: $\dfrac{\$52,262}{\$93,146} = 56\%$

1996: $\dfrac{\$38,903}{\$71,057} = 55\%$

(b) Times interest earned ratio

1997: $\dfrac{\$3,923 + \$4,387 + \$1,849}{\$1,849} = 5.5 \text{ times}$

1996: $\dfrac{\$3,117 + \$3,257 + \$1,672}{\$1,672} = 4.8 \text{ times}$

(c) Free cash flow

1997: \$13,863 − \$5,998 = \$7,865 (in thousands)

1996: \$1,683 − \$7,290 = (\$5,607) (in thousands)

Mark's Work Wearhouse's solvency, as measured by the debt to total assets ratio, was relatively consistent from 1996 through 1998, rising slightly in 1999. Between 1996 and 1998, its times interest earned ratio improved. This improvement, and the relatively consistent debt to assets ratio, gives us confidence that Mark's Work Wearhouse's solvency levels are not unusual, but instead about the normal measure. It is apparent that Mark's Work Wearhouse can meet its debt payments when due. Mark's Work Wearhouse's free cash flow appears to jump up and down throughout the years, depending on the acquisitions and restructuring Mark's is undergoing. In 1996, Mark's Work Wearhouse purchased Work World.

3. Profitability

(a) Return on common shareholders' equity ratio

1997: $\dfrac{\$3,923}{(\$36,884 + \$32,154)/2} = 11.4\%$

1996: $\dfrac{\$3{,}117}{(\$32{,}154 + \$28{,}922)/2} = 10.2\%$

(b) Return on assets ratio

1997: $\dfrac{\$3{,}923}{(\$93{,}146 + \$71{,}057)/2} = 4.8\%$

1996: $\dfrac{\$3{,}117}{(\$71{,}057 + \$64{,}541)/2} = 4.6\%$

(c) Profit margin ratio

1997: $\dfrac{\$3{,}923}{\$220{,}902} = 1.8\%$

1996: $\dfrac{\$3{,}117}{\$198{,}262} = 1.6\%$

Mark's Work Wearhouse's return on common shareholders' equity has improved since 1996, as have its return on assets and profit margin ratios. Mark's Work Wearhouse's profitability in the subsequent years of 1998 and 1999 appears to be even stronger than we recognized earlier in our chapter discussion.

Summary of Study Objectives

1 ***Understand the concept of earning power and indicate how irregular items are presented.*** Earning power refers to a company's ability to sustain its profits from operations. Irregular items—discontinued operations and extraordinary items—are presented on the statement of earnings, net of tax, below "Earnings from continuing operations" to highlight their infrequent nature. A third type of irregular item—the cumulative effect on prior periods' earnings of a change in accounting principle—is presented on the statement of retained earnings, net of tax, as an adjustment to opening retained earnings. For comparability, all prior periods' financial statements presented are restated using the new principle.

2 ***Discuss the need for comparative analysis and identify the tools of financial statement analysis.*** Comparative analysis is performed to evaluate a company's liquidity, profitability, and solvency. Comparisons can detect changes in financial relationships and significant trends, and provide insight into a company's competitiveness and relative position in its industry. Financial statements may be analysed horizontally, vertically, and with ratios.

3 ***Explain and apply horizontal analysis.*** Horizontal analysis is a technique for evaluating a series of data over a period of time to determine the increase or decrease that has taken place, expressed as either an amount or a percentage.

4 ***Explain and apply vertical analysis.*** Vertical analysis is a technique that expresses each item in a financial statement as a percentage of a relevant total or base amount.

5 ***Identify and calculate ratios, describe their purpose, and use them to analyse a company's liquidity, solvency, and profitability.*** Financial ratios are provided in Illustrations 14-12 through 14-19 (liquidity), Illustrations 14-20 through 14-25 (solvency), and Illustrations 14-26 through 14-42 (profitability).

6 ***Discuss the limitations of financial statement analysis.*** The usefulness of analytical tools is limited by the use of estimates, the cost basis, the application of alternative accounting methods, atypical data at year end, and the diversification of companies.

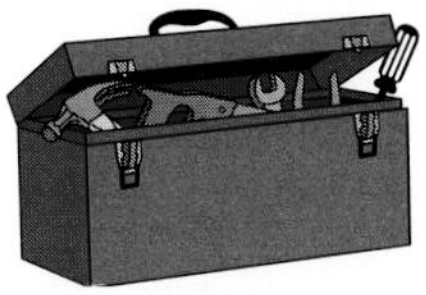

Decision Toolkit—A Summary

Decision Checkpoints	Info Needed for Decision	Tool to Use for Decision	How to Evaluate Results
Has the company sold any major lines of business?	Discontinued operations section of statement of earnings	Anything reported in this section indicates that the company has discontinued a major line of business.	If a major business line has been discontinued, its results in the current period should not be included in estimates of future net earnings.
Has the company experienced any extraordinary events or transactions?	Extraordinary item section of statement of earnings	Anything reported in this section indicates that the company experienced an event that was infrequent, unusual, and not determined by management.	These items should usually be ignored in estimating future net earnings.
Has the company changed any of its accounting principles?	Cumulative effect of change in accounting principle in statement of retained earnings	Anything reported in this section indicates that the company has changed an accounting principle during the current year.	Financial statements are restated using new principle for comparability.
How do the company's financial position and operating results compare with those of previous periods?	Statement of earnings and balance sheet	Comparative financial statements should be prepared over at least two years, with the first year reported as the base year. Changes in each line item relative to the base year should be presented both by amount and by percentage. This is called horizontal analysis.	A significant change should be investigated to determine the reason for the change.
How do the relationships between items in this year's financial statements compare with last year's relationships or those of competitors?	Statement of earnings and balance sheet	Each line item on the statement of earnings should be presented as a percentage of net sales, and each line item on the balance sheet should be presented as a percentage of total assets (total liabilities and shareholders' equity). These percentages should be investigated for differences, either across years in the same company, or in the same year across different companies. This is called vertical analysis.	Any difference, either across years or between companies, should be investigated to determine the cause.
Are efforts to evaluate the company significantly hampered by any of the common limitations of financial analysis?	Financial statements as well as a general understanding of the company and its business	The primary limitations of financial analysis are estimates, cost, alternative accounting methods, atypical data, and diversification.	If any of these factors is significant, the analysis should be relied upon with caution.

GLOSSARY

Acid-test (quick) ratio A measure of a company's immediate short-term liquidity, calculated as the sum of cash, short-term investments, and net receivables divided by current liabilities. (p. 774)

Asset turnover ratio A measure of how efficiently a company uses its assets to generate sales, calculated as net sales divided by average total assets. (p. 784)

Average age of capital assets A measure of the age of a company's capital assets, calculated as accumulated amortization divided by amortization expense. (p. 782)

Average collection period The average number of days that receivables are outstanding, calculated as receivables turnover divided into 365 days. (p. 776)

Average useful life of capital assets A comparative measure of capital assets, calculated as the average cost of capital assets divided by amortization expense. (p. 781)

Book value per share The equity a common shareholder has in the net assets of the corporation from owning one share, calculated by dividing the common shareholders' equity by the number of common shares. (p. 787)

Capital expenditure ratio A cash-based ratio that indicates the extent to which cash provided by operating activities was sufficient to fund capital asset expenditures during the year. (p. 780)

Cash current debt coverage ratio A cash-based measure of short-term debt-paying ability, calculated as cash provided by operating activities divided by average current liabilities. (p. 775)

Cash flow per share The cash flow produced by each common share, calculated by dividing cash provided by all (operating, investing, and financing activities) by the weighted average number of common shares. (p. 788)

Cash interest coverage ratio A measure of a company's solvency, indicating cash available to repay annual interest obligations, calculated by dividing earnings before interest expense, income tax expense, and amortization expense (EBITDA) by interest expense. (p. 779)

Cash return on sales ratio The cash-based measure of net earnings generated by each dollar of sales, calculated as cash from operating activities divided by net sales. (p. 786)

Cash total debt coverage ratio A cash-based measure used to evaluate solvency, calculated as cash from operating activities divided by average total liabilities. (p. 779)

Change in accounting principle Use of an accounting principle in the current year different from the one used in the preceding year. (p. 764)

Credit risk ratio A measure of the risk that a company's customers may not pay their accounts, calculated as Allowance for Doubtful Accounts divided by Accounts Receivable. (p. 775)

Current ratio A measure that expresses the relationship of current assets to current liabilities, calculated as current assets divided by current liabilities. (p. 773)

Days in inventory A measure of the average number of days it takes to sell the inventory, calculated as inventory turnover divided into 365 days. (p. 777)

Debt to total assets ratio A measure of the percentage of total assets provided by creditors, calculated as total debt divided by total assets. (p. 778)

Discontinued operations The disposal of a significant segment of a business. (p. 761)

Dividend yield A measure of the rate of return an investor earned from dividends during the year. (p. 790)

Earning power The most likely level of income to be obtained in the future. It is determined by adjusting net income for irregular items. (p. 760)

Earnings per share The net earnings earned by each common share, calculated as net earnings divided by the weighted average common shares outstanding. (p. 786)

Extraordinary items Events and transactions that meet these three conditions: they are (1) infrequent in occurrence, (2) unusual in nature, and (3) not the result of a management determination. (p. 762)

Free cash flow The amount of cash from operating activities after adjusting for capital expenditures and cash dividends paid. (p. 780)

Gross profit rate An indicator of a company's ability to maintain an adequate selling price above its cost of goods sold, calculated as gross profit divided by net sales. (p. 785)

Horizontal analysis A technique for evaluating a series of financial statement data over a period of time to determine the increase (decrease) that has taken place, expressed as either an amount or a percentage. (p. 767)

Inventory turnover ratio A measure of the liquidity of inventory, calculated as cost of goods sold divided by average inventory. (p. 777)

Leveraging (trading on the equity) Borrowing money at a lower rate of interest than can be earned by using the borrowed money; also referred to as "trading on the equity." (p. 783)

Liquidity ratios Measures of the short-term ability of an enterprise to pay its maturing obligations and to meet unexpected needs for cash. (p. 773)

Operating expenses to sales ratio A measure of the costs incurred to support each dollar of sales, calculated as operating expenses divided by net sales. (p. 786)

Payout ratio A measure of the percentage of earnings distributed in the form of cash dividends, calculated as cash dividends divided by net earnings. (p. 789)

Price-earnings ratio A comparison of the market price of each common share to the earnings per share, calculated as the market price of the shares divided by earnings per share. (p. 788)

Profit margin ratio A measure of the net earnings generated by each dollar of sales, calculated as net earnings divided by net sales. (p. 784)

Profitability ratios Measures of the earnings or operating success of an enterprise for a given period of time. (p. 773)

Receivables turnover ratio A measure of the liquidity of receivables, calculated as net credit sales divided by average net receivables. (p. 776)

Return on assets ratio An overall measure of profitability, calculated as net earnings divided by average total assets. (p. 783)

Return on common shareholders' equity ratio A measure of the dollars of net earnings earned for each dollar invested by the owners, calculated as earnings available to common shareholders divided by average common shareholders' equity. (p. 782)

Segmental data A required note disclosure for diversified companies in which the company reports the following for each major business segment: sales, operating profit, identifiable assets, amortization expense, and capital expenditures. (p. 794)

Solvency ratios Measures of the ability of the enterprise to survive over a long period of time. (p. 773)

Times interest earned ratio A measure of a company's ability to meet interest payments as they come due, calculated as earnings before interest expense and income taxes (EBIT) divided by interest expense. (p. 779)

Vertical analysis A technique for evaluating financial statement data that expresses each item in a financial statement as a percentage of a base amount. (p. 770)

Working capital The difference between the amounts of current assets and current liabilities. (p. 773)

Demonstration Problem

The events and transactions of Dever Corporation for the year ending December 31, 2001, resulted in these data:

Cost of goods sold	$2,600,000
Net sales	4,400,000
Other expenses and losses	9,600
Other revenues and gains	5,600
Selling and administrative expenses	1,100,000
Earnings from operations of plastics division (discontinued operations)	70,000
Gain on sale of plastics division (discontinued operations)	500,000
Loss from flood disaster (extraordinary loss)	600,000
Cumulative effect of changing from straight-line amortization to double declining-balance (increase in amortization expense)	300,000
Retained earnings, Jan. 1	3,926,000

Analysis reveals the following:

1. All items are before the applicable income tax rate of 30%.
2. The plastics division was sold on July 1.
3. All operating data for the plastics division have been segregated.
4. No dividends were declared in 2001.

Instructions

Prepare statements of earnings and retained earnings for the year.

Solution to Demonstration Problem

DEVER CORPORATION
Statement of Earnings
For the Year Ended December 31, 2001

Net sales		$4,400,000
Cost of goods sold		2,600,000
Gross profit		1,800,000
Selling and administrative expenses		1,100,000
Earnings from operations		700,000
Other revenues and gains	$ 5,600	
Other expenses and losses	(9,600)	(4,000)
Earnings before income taxes		696,000
Income tax expense ($696,000 × 30%)		208,800
Earnings from continuing operations		487,200
Discontinued operations		
Earnings from operations of plastics division, net of $21,000 income taxes ($70,000 × 30%)	$ 49,000	
Gain on sale of plastics division, net of $150,000 income taxes ($500,000 × 30%)	350,000	399,000
Earnings before extraordinary item		886,200
Extraordinary item		
Flood loss, net of income tax savings of $180,000 ($600,000 × 30%)		(420,000)
Net earnings		$ 466,200

DEVER CORPORATION
Statement of Retained Earnings
For the Year Ended December 31, 2001

Retained earnings, January 1	$3,926,000
Cumulative effect on prior years of change in amortization method, net of $90,000 income tax savings ($300,000 × 30%)	(210,000)
Retained earnings, January 1, as restated	3,716,000
Add: Net earnings	466,200
Retained earnings, December 31	$4,182,200

Self-Study Questions

Answers are at the end of the chapter.

All of the Self-Study Questions in this chapter employ decision tools.

(SO 1) 1. In reporting discontinued operations, a special section in the statement of earnings should show:
(a) gains and losses on the disposal of the discontinued segment.
(b) gains and losses from operations of the discontinued segment.
(c) neither (a) nor (b).
(d) both (a) and (b).

(SO 1) 2. The Candy Stick Corporation has net earnings of $225,000, and a pre-tax extraordinary loss of $100,000. If the income tax rate is 25% on all items, the statement of earnings should show earnings before extraordinary items, and extraordinary items, respectively, of:
(a) $325,000 and ($100,000).
(b) $325,000 and ($75,000).
(c) $300,000 and ($100,000).
(d) $300,000 and ($75,000).

(SO 2) 3. Comparisons of data within a company are an example of the following comparative basis:
(a) industry averages.
(b) intracompany.
(c) intercompany.
(d) both (b) and (c).

(SO 3) 4. In horizontal analysis, each item is expressed as a percentage of the:
(a) net earnings amount.
(b) shareholders' equity amount.
(c) total assets amount.
(d) base-year amount.

(SO 3) 5. Leland Corporation reported net sales of $300,000, $330,000, and $360,000 in the years 1999, 2000, and 2001, respectively. If 1999 is the base year, what is the trend percentage for 2001?
(a) 77%.
(b) 108%.
(c) 120%.
(d) 130%.

(SO 4) 6. In vertical analysis, the base amount for amortization expense is generally:
(a) net sales.
(b) amortization expense in a previous year.
(c) gross profit.
(d) capital assets.

7. The following schedule is a display of what type of analysis? (SO 4)

	Amount	**Percent**
Current assets	$200,000	25%
Capital assets	600,000	75%
Total assets	$800,000	100%

(a) Horizontal analysis
(b) Differential analysis
(c) Vertical analysis
(d) Ratio analysis

8. Which measure is an evaluation of a firm's ability to pay current liabilities? (SO 5)
(a) Working capital
(b) Acid-test ratio
(c) Current ratio
(d) All of the above

9. Which measure is useful for evaluating efficiency in managing inventories? (SO 5)
(a) Inventory turnover ratio
(b) Days in inventory
(c) Both (a) and (b)
(d) None of the above

10. Which of these is *not* a liquidity ratio? (SO 5)
(a) Current ratio
(b) Asset turnover ratio
(c) Inventory turnover ratio
(d) Receivables turnover ratio

11. DuPlessis Corporation reported net earnings, $24,000; net sales, $400,000; and average assets, $600,000, for 2001. What is the 2001 profit margin? (SO 5)
(a) 6%
(b) 12%
(c) 40%
(d) 200%

12. Which of the following is generally *not* considered to be a limitation of financial analysis? (SO 6)
(a) Use of ratio analysis
(b) Use of estimates
(c) Use of cost
(d) Use of alternative accounting methods

QUESTIONS

All of the Questions in this chapter employ decision tools.

(SO 1) 1. Explain earning power. What relationship does this concept have to the treatment of irregular items on the statement of earnings?

(SO 1) 2. Indicate which of the following items would be reported as an extraordinary item on Fine & Fancy Food Corporation's statement of earnings.
   (a) Loss from damages caused by a volcano eruption
   (b) Loss from the sale of short-term investments
   (c) Loss attributable to a labour strike
   (d) Loss caused when Canadian Food Inspection Agency prohibited the manufacture and sale of a product line
   (e) Loss of inventory from flood damage for a warehouse located on a flood plain that floods every five to 10 years
   (f) Loss on the write-down of outdated inventory
   (g) Loss from a foreign government's expropriation of a production facility
   (h) Loss from damage to a warehouse from a minor earthquake

(SO 1) 3. Iron Ingots Inc. reported earnings per share of $3.26 for 2000 and had no extraordinary items. In 2001, earnings per share on earnings before extraordinary items was $2.99, and earnings per share on net earnings was $3.49. Do you consider this trend to be favourable? Why or why not?

(SO 1) 4. Rodger Robotics Inc. has been in operation for three years. All of its manufacturing equipment, which has a useful life of 10 to 12 years, has been amortized on a straight-line basis. During the fourth year, Rodger Robotics changes to an accelerated amortization method for all of its equipment.
   (a) Will Rodger Robotics likely record a positive or negative effect due to this change?
   (b) How will this change be reported?

(SO 2) 5. (a) Distinguish among the following bases of comparison: intracompany, industry averages, and intercompany.
   (b) Give the principal value of using each of the three bases of comparison.

(SO 3, 4) 6. Two popular methods of financial statement analysis are horizontal analysis and vertical analysis. Explain the difference between these two methods.

(SO 3, 4) 7. (a) If Roe Company had net earnings of $540,000 in 2000, and it experienced a 24.5% increase in net earnings for 2001, what are its net earnings for 2001?
   (b) If six cents of every dollar of Roe's revenue in 2000 is net earnings, what is the dollar amount of 2000 revenue?

(SO 5) 8. (a) Tia Kim believes that the analysis of financial statements is directed at two characteristics of a company: liquidity and profitability. Is Tia correct? Explain.
   (b) Are short-term creditors, long-term creditors, and shareholders primarily interested in the same characteristics of a company? Explain.

9. Name the major ratios which are useful in assessing (a) liquidity and (b) solvency. (SO 5)

10. Tony Robins is puzzled. His company had a profit margin of 10% in 2001. He feels that this is an indication that the company is doing well. Joan Graham, his accountant, says that more information is needed to determine the company's financial well-being. Who is correct? Why? (SO 5)

11. What does each of the following types of ratios measure? (SO 5)
   (a) Liquidity ratios
   (b) Solvency ratios
   (c) Profitability ratios

12. What is the difference between the current ratio and the acid-test ratio? The times interest earned ratio and the cash interest coverage ratio? (SO 5)

13. Gerry Bullock Company Ltd., a retail store, has a receivables turnover ratio of 4.5 times. The industry average is 12.5 times. Does Bullock have a collection problem with its receivables or is it an outstanding success? (SO 5)

14. Which ratios should be used to help answer each of these questions? (SO 5)
   (a) How efficient is a company in using its assets to produce sales?
   (b) How near to sale is the inventory on hand?
   (c) How many dollars of net earnings were earned for each dollar invested by the owners?
   (d) How able is a company to meet interest charges as they fall due?

15. Recently, the price-earnings ratio of **Future Shop Ltd.** was 80.0, and the price-earnings ratio of **Corel Corporation** was 56.7. Which company did the stock market likely favour? Explain. (SO 5)

16. (a) What is the formula for calculating the payout ratio? (SO 5)
   (b) Do you expect this ratio to be high or low for a growth company?

17. Holding all other factors constant, indicate whether each of the following changes generally signals good or bad news about a company: (SO 5)
   (a) Increase in profit margin ratio
   (b) Decrease in inventory turnover ratio
   (c) Increase in current ratio
   (d) Decrease in earnings per share
   (e) Increase in price-earnings ratio
   (f) Increase in debt to total assets ratio
   (g) Decrease in cash interest coverage ratio

18. The return on assets for Windsor Corporation is 7.6%. During the same year, Windsor's return on common shareholders' equity is 12.8%. What is the explanation for the difference in the two rates? (SO 5)

(SO 5) 19. Which two ratios do you think should be of greatest interest in each of the following cases?
(a) A pension fund considering the purchase of 20-year bonds
(b) A bank contemplating a short-term loan
(c) A common shareholder

(SO 5) 20. (a) What is meant by "trading on the equity"?
(b) How would you determine the profitability of trading on the equity?

(SO 5) 21. Khris Inc. has net earnings of $270,000, an average of 50,000 common shares outstanding, and preferred dividends for the period of $40,000. What is Khris's earnings per common share? Phil Remmers, the president of Khris Inc., believes that the computed EPS of the company is high. Comment.

22. Identify and briefly explain the limitations of financial analysis. (SO 6)

23. Explain how the choice of one of the following accounting methods over the other raises or lowers a company's net earnings during a period of continuing inflation. (SO 6)
(a) Use of FIFO instead of average cost for inventory costing
(b) Use of a six-year life for machinery instead of a nine-year life
(c) Use of straight-line amortization instead of accelerated declining-balance amortization

BRIEF EXERCISES

All of the Brief Exercises in this chapter employ decision tools.

Prepare a discontinued operations section of a statement of earnings. (SO 1)

BE14-1 On June 30, Osborn Corporation discontinued its operations in Mexico. During the year, the operating loss was $400,000 before taxes. On September 1, Osborn disposed of the Mexican facility at a pretax loss of $150,000. The applicable tax rate is 30%. Show the discontinued operations section of Osborn's statement of earnings.

Prepare a corrected statement of earnings with an extraordinary item. (SO 1)

BE14-2 An inexperienced accountant for Lima Corporation showed the following in Lima's 2001 statement of earnings: Earnings before income taxes, $300,000; Income tax expense, $72,000; Extraordinary loss from flood (before taxes), $60,000; and Net earnings, $168,000. The extraordinary loss and taxable earnings are both subject to a 30% tax rate. Prepare a corrected statement of earnings beginning with "Earnings before income taxes."

Prepare a change in accounting principles section of a statement of retained earnings. (SO 1)

BE14-3 On January 1, 2001, Shirli Inc. changed from the straight-line method of amortization to the declining-balance method. The cumulative effect of the change was to increase the prior years' amortization by $40,000 and 2001 amortization by $8,000. Show how the change in accounting principle would be presented in the 2001 statement of retained earnings, assuming the tax rate is 30% and opening retained earnings, $350,000.

Prepare horizontal analysis. (SO 3)

BE14-4 Using these data from the comparative balance sheet of Rioux Company Ltd., perform a horizontal analysis.

	December 31, 2001	December 31, 2000
Accounts receivable	$ 600,000	$ 400,000
Inventory	780,000	600,000
Total assets	3,220,000	2,800,000

Calculate percentage of change. (SO 3)

BE14-5 Net earnings were $500,000 in 1999, $420,000 in 2000, and $504,000 in 2001. What is the percentage of change from (a) 1999 to 2000 and (b) 2000 to 2001? Is the overall change an increase or a decrease?

Calculate net earnings. (SO 3)

BE14-6 If Cavalier Company Ltd. had net earnings of $672,300 in 2001, and it experienced a 25% increase in net earnings over 2000, what were its 2000 net earnings?

Calculate change in net earnings.
(SO 3)

BE14-7 Horizontal analysis (trend analysis) percentages for Tilden Company Ltd.'s sales, cost of goods sold, and expenses are listed here:

Horizontal Analysis	2001	2000	1999
Sales	96.2%	106.8%	100.0%
Cost of goods sold	102.0	97.0	100.0
Expenses	110.6	95.4	100.0

Explain whether Tilden's net earnings increased, decreased, or remained unchanged over the three-year period.

Prepare vertical analysis.
(SO 4)

BE14-8 Using the data presented in BE14-4 for Rioux Company Ltd., perform a vertical analysis.

Calculate change in net earnings.
(SO 4)

BE14-9 Vertical analysis (common-size) percentages for Waubons Company's sales, cost of goods sold, and expenses are listed here:

Vertical Analysis	2001	2000	1999
Sales	100.0%	100.0%	100.0%
Cost of goods sold	59.2	62.4	64.5
Expenses	25.0	26.6	29.5

Did Waubons' net earnings as a percentage of sales increase, decrease, or remain unchanged over the three-year period? Provide numerical support for your answer.

Calculate liquidity ratios.
(SO 5)

BE14-10 **The Arctic Group Inc.**, based in Alberta, operates in the packaged ice industry. Selected condensed financial data are taken from a recent balance sheet:

THE ARCTIC GROUP INC.
Balance Sheet (Partial)
December 31, 1998

Current assets	
Cash and term deposits	$ 4,437,979
Cash held in trust	435,130
Accounts receivable	4,151,555
Inventories	1,557,166
Prepaid expenses and deferred charges	249,289
Total current assets	10,831,119
Total current liabilities	11,643,174

What are its (a) current ratio and (b) acid-test ratio?

Evaluate collection of accounts receivable.
(SO 5)

BE14-11 The following data are taken from the quarterly report of **Maple Leaf Foods Inc.**:

MAPLE LEAF FOODS INC.
As at September 30
(in thousands)

	1999	1998	1997
Accounts receivable	$ 209,890	$ 205,641	$ 319,587
Sales (assume on account)*	2,631,748	2,398,635	2,735,735

*Assume terms for all sales are 1/10, n/45.

Calculate, for 1999 and 1998, (a) the receivables turnover ratio and (b) the average collection period. What conclusions about the management of accounts receivable can be drawn from these data?

Evaluate management of inventory.
(SO 5)

BE14-12 The following data were taken from the statement of earnings of Shumway Company Ltd.:

	2001	2000
Sales revenue	$6,420,000	$6,240,000
Beginning inventory	980,000	837,000
Purchases	4,640,000	4,661,000
Ending inventory	1,020,000	980,000

For each year, calculate (a) the inventory turnover ratio and (b) the days in inventory. What conclusions concerning the management of the inventory can be drawn from these data?

Calculate profitability ratios. (SO 5)

BE14-13 **Staples, Inc.** is a large supplier of office products in Canada, the U.S., the UK, Germany, the Netherlands, and Portugal. The company had net earnings of $185.3 million and net revenue of $7,213 million in 1998. Its total assets were $2,639 million at the beginning of the year and $3,179 million at the end of the year. What are Staples, Inc.'s (a) asset turnover ratio and (b) profit margin ratio? (Round to two decimals.)

Calculate profitability ratios. (SO 5)

BE14-14 Haymark Products Company has shareholders' equity of $400,000 and net earnings of $50,000. It has a payout ratio of 20% and a rate of return on assets of 16%. How much did Haymark Products pay in cash dividends, and what were its average assets?

Calculate cash-based liquidity, profitability, and solvency ratios. (SO 5)

BE14-15 **The Topps Company, Inc.** is a trading card company, whose products (including Star Wars and Pokémon cards) are sold in more than 50 countries. Selected data taken from the 1998 financial statements are as follows ($ in thousands):

Net sales for 1998	$229,414
Current liabilities, January 1, 1998	80,964
Current liabilities, December 31, 1998	68,619
Net cash provided by operating activities	29,522
Total liabilities, January 1, 1998	86,858
Total liabilities, December 31, 1998	116,797

Calculate these ratios at December 31, 1998: (a) cash current debt coverage ratio, (b) cash return on sales ratio, and (c) cash total debt coverage ratio.

EXERCISES

All of the Exercises in this chapter employ decision tools.

Prepare the irregular items portion of a statement of earnings. (SO 1)

E14-1 The Davis Company Ltd. has earnings from continuing operations of $240,000 for the year ended December 31, 2001. It also has the following items (before considering income taxes): (1) an extraordinary fire loss of $60,000, (2) a gain of $40,000 from the discontinuance of a division, which includes a $110,000 gain from the operation of the division and a $70,000 loss on its disposal, and (3) a cumulative change in accounting principle that resulted in an increase in the prior years' amortization of $30,000. Assume all items are subject to income taxes at a 30% tax rate.

Instructions

Prepare Davis Company's statement of earnings for 2001, beginning with "Earnings from continuing operations."

Evaluate the effects of irregular items. (SO 1, 5)

E14-2 *The Financial Post* routinely publishes summaries of quarterly and annual earnings reports in a feature called "Earnings Summary." A typical report looks like the following one for **Alliance Atlantis Communications Inc.**:

ALLIANCE ATLANTIS (AACb/TSE)

	Current	**Yr. Ago**	**%chg**
		Sept. 30-2nd Q	
Revenue (000s)	190,300	131,000	45
Net income (000s)	9,200	(42,500)	
EPS	0.33	(2.55)	
Cash Flow (000s)	157,900	108,800	45
		6 mos.	
Revenue (000s)	353,600	211,600	67
Net income (000s)	16,400	(38,300)	
EPS	0.57	(2.34)	
Cash flow (000s)	287,900	172,400	67

Alliance Atlantis's net income for the latest six months included a $2.5 million gain on the sale of an investment. Net income for the year-ago quarter and six months included $81.4 million of merger and restructuring expenses.

The letters in parentheses following the company name indicate the company's share symbol and the exchange on which Alliance Atlantis Communications Inc.'s Class B shares are traded—in this case, the Toronto Stock Exchange.

The first section reports results for the second quarter ended September 30, 1999, compared to the second quarter ended September 30, 1998. The second section reports results for the six months to date, compared to the six months ended a year before, September 30, 1998.

Instructions

(a) Why did the *Financial Post* list the gain on the sale of the investment, and the merger and restructuring expenses separately?

(b) By what percentage did Alliance Atlantis Communications' revenue and cash flow improve in the quarter ended September 30, 1999, compared to the previous year? Show how the percentage changes were calculated.

(c) Did Alliance Atlantis Communications have a loss in any quarter of 1999? Of 1998?

(d) As an investor, what numbers should you use to determine Alliance Atlantis's profit margin ratio? Calculate the six-month profit margin ratio for 1999 and 1998, using the numbers that you consider most useful. Explain your decision.

(e) What was the approximate average number of shares outstanding in 1999? Did this number of outstanding shares change from September 30, 1998, to September 30, 1999?

Prepare horizontal analysis. (SO 3)

E14-3 Here is financial information for Merchandise Inc.:

	December 31, 2001	December 31, 2000
Current assets	$120,000	$100,000
Capital assets (net)	400,000	330,000
Current liabilities	91,000	70,000
Long-term liabilities	144,000	95,000
Common shares	150,000	115,000
Retained earnings	135,000	150,000

Instructions

Prepare a schedule showing a horizontal analysis for 2001 using 2000 as the base year.

Prepare vertical analysis. (SO 4)

E14-4 Operating data for Fleetwood Corporation are presented here:

	2001	2000
Sales	$800,000	$600,000
Cost of goods sold	472,000	390,000
Selling expenses	120,000	72,000
Administrative expenses	80,000	54,000
Income tax expense	38,400	25,200
Net earnings	$ 89,600	$ 58,800

Instructions

Prepare a schedule showing a vertical analysis for 2001 and 2000.

Prepare horizontal and vertical analyses. (SO 3, 4)

E14-5 Here are the comparative statements of earnings of Olympic Corporation:

OLYMPIC CORPORATION
Comparative Statements of Earnings
For the Years Ended December 31

	2001	2000
Net sales	$550,000	$550,000
Cost of goods sold	440,000	450,000
Gross profit	110,000	100,000
Operating expenses	57,200	54,000
Net earnings	$ 52,800	$ 46,000

Instructions

(a) Prepare a horizontal analysis of the statement of earnings data for Olympic Corporation using 2000 as a base. (Show the amounts for increases or decreases.)

(b) Prepare a vertical analysis of the statement of earnings data for Olympic Corporation for both years.

E14-6 The condensed comparative balance sheets of the **Mountain Equipment Co-operative**, an outdoor equipment supplier, are presented here:

Prepare horizontal and vertical analyses. (SO 3, 4)

MOUNTAIN EQUIPMENT CO-OPERATIVE
Comparative Balance Sheets
December 31
(in thousands)

	1998	1997
Assets		
Current assets	$29,931	$29,910
Investment and advances	288	251
Capital assets	22,864	16,878
Total assets	$53,083	$47,039
Liabilities and Members' Equity		
Current liabilities	$9,735	$13,576
Long-term liabilities	9,045	3,370
Total liabilities	18,780	16,946
Members' equity	34,303	30,093
Total liabilities and members' equity	$53,083	$47,039

Instructions

(a) Prepare a horizontal analysis of the balance sheet data for Mountain Equipment Co-op using 1997 as a base. Show the amount of any increase or decrease, as well.

(b) Prepare a vertical analysis of the balance sheet data for Mountain Equipment Co-op for 1998 and 1997, using total assets as your base.

(c) Comment on any significant changes from 1997 to 1998.

E14-7 The **Student's Society of McGill University (SSMU)** had the following selected financial statement data as at May 31, for 1999 and 1998.

Calculate liquidity ratios and compare results. (SO 5)

	1999	1998
Current assets		
Cash	$ 427,801	$ 936,163
Short-term investments	697,327	213,630
Accounts receivable	169,318	154,275
Inventories	33,569	38,968
Prepaid expenses	86,452	61,810
Total current assets	1,414,467	1,404,846
Total current liabilities	1,051,765	974,019
Revenue	2,442,890	2,483,212
Cash provided from operating activities	118,687	527,200

Instructions

(a) Calculate SSMU's current ratio, acid-test ratio, cash current debt coverage ratio, receivables turnover ratio, and average collection period for 1999. Use total revenue as a substitute for credit sales in the receivables turnover ratio.

(b) Comment on SSMU's liquidity.

E14-8 Firpo Incorporated had the following transactions involving current assets and current liabilities during February 2001:

Perform current and acid-test ratio analysis. (SO 5)

Feb. 3 Collected accounts receivable of $15,000.
7 Purchased equipment for $25,000 cash.
11 Paid $3,000 for a three-year insurance policy.
14 Paid accounts payable of $14,000.
18 Declared cash dividends, $6,000.

Additional information:

1. As at February 1, 2001, current assets were $140,000 and current liabilities were $50,000.
2. As at February 1, 2001, current assets included $15,000 of inventory and $5,000 of prepaid expenses.

Instructions

(a) Calculate the current ratio as at the beginning of the month and after each transaction.
(b) Calculate the acid-test ratio as at the beginning of the month and after each transaction.

Calculate selected ratios. (SO 5)

E14-9 Georgette Company Ltd. has these comparative balance sheet data:

GEORGETTE COMPANY
Balance Sheets
December 31

	2001	2000
Cash	$ 20,000	$ 30,000
Receivables (net)	65,000	60,000
Inventories	60,000	50,000
Capital assets (net)	200,000	180,000
	$345,000	$320,000
Accounts payable	$ 50,000	$ 60,000
Mortgage payable (15%)	100,000	100,000
Common shares	140,000	120,000
Retained earnings	55,000	40,000
	$345,000	$320,000

Additional information for 2001:

1. Net earnings was $25,000.
2. Sales on account were $420,000. Sales returns and allowances amounted to $20,000.
3. Cost of goods sold was $198,000.
4. Net cash provided by operating activities was $44,000.
5. Capital expenditures were $20,000.

Instructions

Calculate the following ratios at December 31, 2001:

(a) current
(b) acid-test
(c) receivables turnover
(d) average collection period
(e) inventory turnover
(f) days in inventory
(g) cash return on sales
(h) cash total debt coverage
(i) cash current debt coverage
(j) capital expenditure ratio

Calculate selected ratios. (SO 5)

E14-10 Selected comparative statement data of Canada's number one bookseller, **Chapters Inc.**, are presented here (in thousands):

	1998	1997
Revenue	$577,880	$456,611
Cost of product, purchasing, selling, and administration	536,580	423,707
Interest expense	3,785	2,627
Net earnings	10,301	8,420
Accounts receivable	7,636	6,117
Inventories	224,606	142,103
Total assets	345,485	219,410
Total common shareholders' equity	115,222	104,433
Cash provided by operating activities	6,265	16,815

Instructions
Calculate the following ratios for 1998:

(a) profit margin	(d) return on common shareholders' equity
(b) asset turnover	(e) cash return on sales
(c) return on assets	(f) gross profit rate

Determine effect on selected ratios.
(SO 5)

E14-11 Mahat Corporation started the year with the following ratios:

Current ratio	1.5:1
Cash current debt coverage ratio	40%
Debt to total assets ratio	30%
Return on assets	20%
Cash interest coverage ratio	5 times
Credit risk ratio	5%

Instructions
Determine the effect each of the following later transactions by Mahat had on these ratios. Indicate whether the transaction causes each ratio to improve (I) or deteriorate (D), or if the transaction has no effect (NE).

(a) Mahat purchased merchandise inventory on account from a supplier. Mahat uses a perpetual inventory system.
(b) The company paid cash on an account payable.
(c) Mahat sold merchandise on account to a customer.
(d) The customer paid its account.
(e) Mahat purchased capital assets, issuing a long-term note payable in payment.

Calculate selected ratios.
(SO 5)

E14-12 Here is the statement of earnings for Jean LeFay, Inc:

JEAN LEFAY, INC.
Statement of Earnings
For the Year Ended December 31, 2001

Sales	$400,000
Cost of goods sold	230,000
Gross profit	170,000
Expenses (including $35,000 of amortization, $20,000 of interest and $24,000 of income taxes)	100,000
Net earnings	$ 70,000

Additional information:
1. There were 30,000 common shares outstanding at January 1, 2001. On July 1, 2001, 10,000 more shares were issued.
2. The market price of Jean LeFay, Inc. shares was $15 in 2001.
3. Cash dividends of $21,000 were paid, $5,000 of which were to preferred shareholders.
4. Cash provided by operating activities was $98,000.

Instructions
Calculate the following measures for 2001:

(a) earnings per share	(d) times interest earned ratio
(b) price-earnings ratio	(e) cash interest coverage ratio
(c) payout ratio	(f) cash return on sales ratio

Calculate amounts from ratios.
(SO 5)

E14-13 Shaker Corporation experienced a fire on December 31, 2001, in which its financial records were partially destroyed. It has been able to salvage some of the records and has ascertained the following balances:

	December 31, 2001	December 31, 2000
Cash	$ 30,000	$ 10,000
Receivables (net)	72,500	126,000
Inventory	200,000	180,000
Accounts payable	50,000	10,000
Notes payable	30,000	20,000
Common shares	400,000	400,000
Retained earnings	113,500	101,000

Additional information:

1. The inventory turnover is 3.6 times.
2. The return on common shareholders' equity is 22%.
3. The receivables turnover is 9.4 times.
4. The return on assets is 16%.
5. Total assets at December 31, 2000, were $605,000.

Instructions

Calculate the following for Shaker Corporation:

(a) cost of goods sold for 2001
(b) net sales for 2001
(c) net earnings for 2001
(d) total assets at December 31, 2001

Problems: Set A

All of the Problems in this chapter employ decision tools.

Prepare horizontal analysis and answer questions.
(SO 3)

P14-1A Brampton-based **Nortel Networks Corporation**, formerly known as Northern Telecom, has had significant growth through acquisitions over the last two decades. And, in spite of recent losses, investors believe Nortel's future potential to be very strong. The following selected information is available for the three most recent years of this maker of telecommunication products:

NORTEL NETWORKS CORPORATION
Statements of Operations
Years Ended December 31
(in millions of U.S. dollars, except for per share data)

	1999	1998	1997
Revenues	$22,217	$17,575	$15,449
Cost of revenues	12,597	10,050	9,111
Gross profit	9,620	7,525	6,338
Selling, general, and administrative expenses	4,102	3,093	2,714
Research and development expense	2,908	2,453	2,147
Interest expense	172	232	169
Other expenses	1,912	1,683	41
Total expenses	9,094	7,461	5,071
Earnings before income taxes	526	64	1,267
Income tax	696	601	438
Net earnings (loss)	$ (170)	$ (537)	$ 829
Earnings (loss) per share	$ (0.07)	$ (0.25)	$ 0.39
Market price per share	$145.85	$ 38.30	$ 31.79

NORTEL NETWORKS CORPORATION
Balance Sheets (Partial)
December 31
(in millions of U.S. dollars)

	1999	1998	1997
Current assets	$13,068	$10,317	$ 8,547
Total assets	22,597	19,732	12,554
Current liabilities	7,790	5,893	4,883
Long-term liabilities	2,289	2,274	2,261
Preferred shares	609	609	609
Common shares	10,077	8,553	1,609
Retained earnings	2,156	2,568	3,514

Instructions

(a) Prepare a horizontal analysis (dollar value and percentage changes) for Nortel.
(b) What components found in Nortel's balance sheet and statement of earnings have been the primary drivers of its rapid growth?
(c) How has Nortel been primarily financing its growth?

Prepare vertical analysis and comment on profitability.
(SO 4, 5)

P14-2A Here are comparative statement data for Chen Company and Couric Company, two competitors. All balance sheet data are as at December 31, 2001, and December 31, 2000.

	CHEN COMPANY		COURIC COMPANY	
	2001	2000	2001	2000
Net sales	$1,549,035		$339,038	
Cost of goods sold	1,080,490		238,006	
Operating expenses	302,275		79,000	
Interest expense	6,800		1,252	
Income tax expense	47,840		7,740	
Current assets	325,975	$312,410	83,336	$ 79,467
Capital assets (net)	521,310	500,000	139,728	125,812
Current liabilities	66,325	75,815	35,348	30,281
Long-term liabilities	108,500	90,000	29,620	25,000
Common shares	500,000	500,000	120,000	120,000
Retained earnings	172,460	146,595	38,096	29,998

Instructions

(a) Prepare a vertical analysis of the 2001 statement of earnings data for Chen Company and Couric Company.
(b) Comment on the relative profitability of the companies by calculating the return on assets and the return on common shareholders' equity ratios for both companies.

Calculate ratios from balance sheet and statement of earnings.
(SO 5)

P14-3A The comparative statements of Johnson Company Ltd. are presented here:

JOHNSON COMPANY LTD.
Statements of Earnings
For the Years Ended December 31

	2001	2000
Net sales	$1,818,500	$1,750,500
Cost of goods sold	1,005,500	996,000
Gross profit	813,000	754,500
Selling and administrative expenses (including amortization expense of $62,000 and $52,000 for 2001 and 2000, respectively)	506,000	479,000
Earnings from operations	307,000	275,500
Other expenses and losses		
Interest expense	18,000	19,000
Earnings before income taxes	289,000	256,500
Income tax expense	86,700	77,000
Net earnings	$ 202,300	$ 179,500

JOHNSON COMPANY LTD.
Balance Sheets
December 31

	2001	2000
Assets		
Current assets		
Cash	$ 60,100	$ 64,200
Short-term investments	54,000	50,000
Accounts receivable (net of allowance for doubtful accounts of $5,000 and $5,300, respectively)	107,800	102,800
Inventory	123,000	115,500
Total current assets	344,900	332,500
Capital assets (net)	625,300	520,300
Total assets	$970,200	$852,800
Liabilities and Shareholders' Equity		
Current liabilities		
Accounts payable	$150,000	$145,400
Income taxes payable	43,500	42,000
Total current liabilities	193,500	187,400
Bonds payable	210,000	200,000
Total liabilities	403,500	387,400
Shareholders' equity		
Common shares (60,000 shares)	300,000	300,000
Retained earnings	266,700	165,400
Total shareholders' equity	566,700	465,400
Total liabilities and shareholders' equity	$970,200	$852,800

All sales were on account. Net cash provided by operating activities for 2001 was $280,000.

Instructions
Calculate the following ratios for 2001:
(a) earnings per share
(b) return on common shareholders' equity
(c) return on assets
(d) working capital

(e) current ratio
(f) acid-test
(g) credit risk ratio
(h) receivables turnover
(i) average collection period
(j) inventory turnover
(k) days in inventory
(l) times interest earned
(m) asset turnover
(n) debt to total assets
(o) cash current debt coverage
(p) cash return on sales
(q) cash total debt coverage
(r) cash interest coverage

Perform ratio analysis; comment on results.
(SO 5)

P14-4A Condensed balance sheet and statement of earnings data for Pitka Corporation are presented here:

PITKA CORPORATION
Balance Sheets
December 31

	2001	2000	1999
Cash	$ 25,000	$ 20,000	$ 18,000
Receivables (net)	50,000	45,000	48,000
Other current assets	90,000	85,000	64,000
Investments	75,000	70,000	45,000
Plant and equipment (net)	400,000	370,000	358,000
	$640,000	$590,000	$533,000
Current liabilities	$ 75,000	$ 80,000	$ 70,000
Long-term debt	80,000	85,000	50,000
Common shares	340,000	300,000	300,000
Retained earnings	145,000	125,000	113,000
	$640,000	$590,000	$533,000

PITKA CORPORATION
Statements of Earnings
For the Years Ended December 31

	2001	2000
Sales	$740,000	$700,000
Less: Sales returns and allowances	40,000	50,000
Net sales	700,000	650,000
Cost of goods sold	420,000	400,000
Gross profit	280,000	250,000
Operating expenses (including income taxes)	236,000	218,000
Net earnings	$ 44,000	$ 32,000

Additional information:

1. The market price of Pitka's common shares were $4.00, $5.00, and $7.95 for 1999, 2000, and 2001, respectively.
2. All dividends were paid in cash. (Hint: Analyse retained earnings to calculate dividends.)
3. On July 1, 2000, 4,000 common shares were issued, bringing the total number of outstanding shares to 34,000.

Instructions

(a) Calculate the following ratios for 2000 and 2001:
1. profit margin
2. gross profit
3. asset turnover
4. earnings per share
5. price-earnings
6. payout
7. debt to total assets
8. dividend yield

(b) Based on the ratios calculated, discuss briefly the improvement or lack thereof in the financial position and operating results from 2000 to 2001 for Pitka Corporation.

Calculate ratios; comment on overall liquidity and profitability.
(SO 5)

P14-5A This financial information is for Caroline Company Ltd.:

CAROLINE COMPANY LTD.
Balance Sheets
December 31

	2001	2000
Assets		
Cash	$ 70,000	$ 65,000
Short-term investments	45,000	40,000
Receivables (net of allowance for doubtful accounts of $5,000 and $4,000, respectively)	94,000	90,000
Inventories	230,000	125,000
Prepaid expenses	25,000	23,000
Land	130,000	130,000
Building and equipment (net of accumulated amortization of $75,000 and $60,000, respectively)	290,000	175,000
Total assets	$884,000	$648,000
Liabilities and Shareholders' Equity		
Notes payable	$200,000	$100,000
Accounts payable	45,000	42,000
Accrued liabilities	40,000	40,000
Bonds payable, due 2003	250,000	150,000
Common shares	200,000	200,000
Retained earnings	149,000	116,000
Total liabilities and shareholders' equity	$884,000	$648,000

CAROLINE COMPANY LTD.
Statements of Earnings
For the Years Ended December 31

	2001	2000
Sales	$850,000	$790,000
Cost of goods sold	620,000	575,000
Gross profit	230,000	215,000
Operating expenses (including amortization expense of $15,000 and $11,000, respectively)	194,000	180,000
Net earnings	$ 36,000	$ 35,000

Additional information:

1. Inventory at the beginning of 2000 was $115,000.
2. Receivables at the beginning of 2000 were $88,000.
3. Total assets at the beginning of 2000 were $630,000.
4. No common share transactions occurred during 2000 or 2001.
5. All sales were on account.

Instructions

(a) Indicate, by using ratios, the change in liquidity and profitability of Caroline Company from 2000 to 2001. (Note: Not all profitability ratios can be calculated.)

(b) On the following page are three independent situations and a ratio that may be affected. For each situation, calculate the affected ratio (1) as at December 31, 2001, and (2) as at December 31, 2002. Net earnings for 2002 were $40,000. Total assets on December 31, 2002, were $900,000.

Situation	Ratio
1. 18,000 common shares were sold at par on July 1, 2002.	Return on common shareholders' equity
2. All of the notes payable were paid in 2002.	Debt to total assets
3. The market price of common shares was $9 and $12.80 on December 31, 2001 and 2002, respectively.	Price-earnings

P14-6A **Future Shop** sells computers, office equipment, and other electronic products in more than 90 stores throughout Canada. **InterTan** owns 1,500 Radio Shack and Tandy stores in Canada, Australia, and the UK. Selected financial data of these two close competitors are presented here (in millions) for a recent year:

Calculate selected ratios, and compare liquidity, profitability, and solvency for two companies.
(SO 5)

	FUTURE SHOP LTD.	INTERTAN, INC.
	Statement of Earnings Data for Year	
Sales	$1,960.3	$500.1
Cost of sales	1,546.7	280.9
Gross profit	413.6	219.2
Selling, general, administrative, and other expenses	432.5	180.7
Interest expense	—	3.3
Unusual item	83.8	35.1
Total expenses	516.3	219.1
Earnings (loss) before income taxes	(102.7)	0.1
Income tax recovery (expense)	20.5	(24.7)
Net earnings (loss)	$ (82.2)	$ (24.6)
	Balance Sheet Data (End of Year)	
Current assets	$221.3	$174.0
Capital and other assets	117.2	24.3
Total assets	$338.5	$198.3
Current liabilities	$253.9	$ 77.0
Long-term liabilities	28.3	10.5
Total liabilities	282.2	87.5
Shareholders' equity	56.3	110.8
Total liabilities and shareholders' equity	$338.5	$198.3
	Other Data	
Average net accounts receivables	$ 20.1	$ 9.1
Average inventories	207.4	130.1
Average total assets	389.9	210.9
Average total shareholders' equity	73.1	98.4
Net cash provided (used) by operating activities	(49.2)	25.9

The unusual items related to the closure of Future Shop's U.S. operations and InterTan's UK operations in fiscal 1999.

Instructions

(a) For each company, calculate the following ratios. Industry averages are provided in parentheses following each ratio, where available.

1. current (1.58:1)
2. receivables turnover (28.1×)
3. average collection period (13 days)
4. inventory turnover (4.9×)
5. days in inventory (74 days)
6. profit margin (1.5%)
7. asset turnover (3.2×)
8. return on assets (4.7%)
9. return on common shareholders' equity (11.5%)
10. debt to total assets (61%)
11. times interest earned (6.9×)
12. cash current debt coverage (n/a)
13. cash return on sales (n/a)
14. cash total debt coverage (n/a)

(b) Compare the liquidity, solvency, and profitability of the two companies.

Calculate numerous ratios.
(SO 5)

P14-7A The comparative statements of National Drug Company Ltd. are as follows:

NATIONAL DRUG COMPANY LTD.
Statements of Earnings
For the Years Ended March 31

	2002	2001
Net sales (all on account)	$650,000	$550,000
Expenses		
Cost of goods sold	435,000	374,000
Selling and administrative expenses	88,800	86,800
Amortization expense	42,000	38,000
Interest expense	6,200	5,000
Total expenses	572,000	503,800
Earnings before income taxes	78,000	46,200
Income tax expense	22,000	15,000
Net earnings	$ 56,000	$ 31,200

NATIONAL DRUG COMPANY LTD.
Balance Sheets
March 31

Assets	2002	2001
Current assets		
Cash	$27,000	$18,000
Short-term investments	24,000	15,000
Accounts receivable (net)	98,000	74,000
Inventory	88,000	70,000
Total current assets	237,000	177,000
Capital assets (net)	429,000	383,000
Total assets	$666,000	$560,000
Liabilities and Shareholders' Equity		
Current liabilities		
Accounts payable	$118,000	$110,000
Income taxes payable	29,000	20,000
Total current liabilities	147,000	130,000
Long-term liabilities		
Bonds payable	140,000	80,000
Total liabilities	287,000	210,000
Shareholders' equity		
Common shares (30,000 shares)	150,000	150,000
Retained earnings	229,000	200,000
Total shareholders' equity	379,000	350,000
Total liabilities and shareholders' equity	$666,000	$560,000

Additional data:

1. The common shares recently sold at $18.50 per share.
2. The net cash provided by operating activities during 2002 was $49,000.
3. The net cash used by all the activities in 2002 was $9,000.

Instructions

Calculate the following ratios for 2002:

(a) current ratio
(b) acid-test
(c) cash current debt coverage
(d) collection period
(e) days in inventory
(f) profit margin
(g) cash return on sales ratio
(h) asset turnover
(i) return on assets
(j) return on common shareholders' equity
(k) book value per share
(l) cash flow per share
(m) earnings per share
(n) price-earnings
(o) payout ratio
(p) debt to total assets
(q) times interest earned
(r) cash total debt coverage
(s) cash interest coverage

Determine effect of discontinued operations on ratios.
(SO 1, 5)

P14-8A Toronto-based **Cott Corporation** reported the following discontinued items in its financial statements after disposing of its food business:

COTT CORPORATION
Discontinued Items
(in millions of U.S. dollars)

	1999 (January 1, 2000)	1998 (January 2, 1999)	1997 (January 31, 1998)
Sales—discontinued operations	$14.4	$28.5	$28.5
Income (loss) from discontinued operations	(0.8)	(3.8)	(5.1)
Current assets—discontinued operations		12.0	12.5
Current liabilities—discontinued operations	1.0	5.7	2.1

Other selected information, which *includes* the effects of the above discontinued operations, follows:

	1999	1998	1997
Sales	$990.8	$958.5	$1,047.8
Net income (loss)	18.5	(109.5)	(4.7)
Total current assets	171.9	249.4	365.9
Total assets	589.6	699.2	861.5
Total current liabilities	109.2	172.2	194.6
Total liabilities	447.3	577.2	630.6

Instructions

(a) Calculate the following ratios both including and excluding the effects of the discontinued operations for 1999 and 1998:
1. current ratio
2. debt to total assets ratio
3. return on assets ratio
4. profit margin ratio
5. asset turnover ratio

(b) Comment on your results. Which ratio calculations—including or excluding the effects of the discontinued operations—are most useful for investors?

Prepare ratio analysis to compare two companies, one on the verge of bankruptcy.
(SO 5)

P14-9A You are presented with the following comparative financial information for two Canadian retailers whose identities have been disguised. At the end of the current year, one of these retailers was liquidated and purchased by another retailer (Company C).

	COMPANY A Balance Sheet (thousands of dollars)		COMPANY B Balance Sheet (thousands of dollars)	
	current year	prior year	current year	prior year
Assets				
Cash and short-term investments	$ 21,964	$ 32,407	$ 7,514	$ 91,167
Credit card receivables	718,686	644,963	—	—
Other accounts receivable	169,738	181,873	56,737	28,063
Merchandise inventory	1,655,618	1,416,595	350,619	272,536
Other current assets	122,062	94,166	469,557	—
Total current assets	2,688,068	2,370,004	884,427	391,766
Capital and other assets	1,915,994	1,510,189	200,337	1,252,510
Total assets	$4,604,062	$3,880,193	$1,084,764	$1,644,276
Liabilities and Shareholders' Equity				
Total current liabilities	$1,230,902	$ 869,039	$ 837,780	$ 441,145
Total long-term liabilities	1,314,884	1,300,991	116,139	976,426
Total liabilities	2,545,786	2,170,030	953,919	1,417,571
Total shareholders' equity	2,058,276	1,170,163	130,845	226,705
Total liabilities and shareholders' equity	$4,604,062	$3,340,193	$1,084,764	$1,644,276

	Statement of Earnings For the Year Ended (in thousands)		Statement of Earnings For the Year Ended (in thousands)	
	current year	prior year	current year	prior year
Revenue (all on credit)	$7,074,978	$6,446,652	$1,688,200	$1,666,534
Earnings (loss) before interest, unusual items, and taxes	$ 187,209	$ 19,908	$ (108,643)	$ (92,472)
Interest expense	(97,171)	(88,315)	(17,279)	(20,693)
Unusual items	—	(243,000)	(124,543)	(80,361)
Income tax (expense) recovery	(50,361)	41,674	(83,170)	23,364
Net earnings (loss) from continuing operations	$ 39,677	$ (269,733)	$ (333,635)	$ (170,162)

Instructions

(a) Prepare the following ratios for each of Company A and Company B for the current year:
1. current ratio
2. acid-test ratio
3. receivables turnover ratio
4. average collection period
5. debt to total assets ratio
6. return on assets ratio
7. asset turnover ratio (current year only)

(b) Which company do you think is in financial trouble? Provide support for your conclusion.

P14-10A Future Shop Ltd. is a Canadian retailer of appliances and electronic devices such as computers and stereos. Its financial statements are presented below. **Circuit City Stores Inc.** in the United States has three operating segments: Circuit City retails similar products to Future Shop; Divx sells encrypted DVDs; CarMax is a retailer of automobiles. Circuit City Stores' financial statements are also presented below. They are prepared in accordance with U.S. generally accepted accounting principles and recorded in U.S. dollars.

Calculate and compare ratios for a Canadian retailer and its American counterpart.
(SO 5)

	CIRCUIT CITY STORES INC. Statement of Earnings For the Year Ended (in thousands of U.S. dollars)		FUTURE SHOP LTD. Statement of Earnings For the Year Ended (in thousands of dollars)	
	February 28, 1999	February 28, 1998	April 3, 1999	March 31, 1998
Sales	$10,804,447	$8,870,797	$1,960,274	$1,760,160
Cost of sales	8,359,428	6,827,133	1,546,723	1,370,773
Gross profit	2,445,019	2,043,664	413,551	389,387
Selling, general and administrative expenses	2,186,177	1,848,559	432,444	386,080
Unusual items	—	—	83,830	—
Interest expense	28,319	26,861	—	—
Total expenses	2,214,496	1,875,420	516,274	386,080
Earnings (loss) before income taxes	230,523	168,244	(102,723)	3,307
Income tax (expense) recovery	(87,599)	(63,933)	20,478	654
Net earnings (loss)	$ 142,924	$ 104,311	$ (82,245)	$ 3,961

	CIRCUIT CITY STORES INC. Balance Sheet (in thousands of U.S. dollars)		FUTURE SHOP LTD. Balance Sheet (in thousands of dollars)	
	February 28, 1999	February 28, 1998	April 3, 1999	March 31, 1998
Assets				
Current assets				
Cash and short-term investments	$ 265,880	$ 116,612	—	$ 58,945
Cash held in escrow			$ 20,251	
Accounts receivable	574,316	598,035	25,099	15,121
Inventory	1,517,675	1,410,545	160,092	254,690
Prepaid expenses and other current assets	36,644	21,157	1,544	1,634
Future income taxes	—	—	14,343	2,648
Total current assets	2,394,515	2,146,349	221,329	333,038
Capital and other assets	1,050,751	1,085,352	117,187	108,269
Total assets	$3,445,266	$3,231,701	$338,516	$441,307
Liabilites and Shareholders' Equity				
Total current liabilities	$ 963,805	$ 905,826	$253,878	$314,318
Total long-term liabilities	576,331	595,836	28,309	37,123
Total liabilities	1,540,136	1,501,662	282,187	351,441
Total shareholders' equity	1,905,130	1,730,039	56,329	89,866
Total liabilities and shareholders' equity	$3,445,266	$3,231,701	$338,516	$441,307

Instructions

(a) Based on the information provided, calculate relevant ratios, and assess the liquidity, solvency, and profitability for 1999 for Circuit City Stores Inc. and Future Shop Ltd.

(b) What other information might help you make a more meaningful comparison between Future Shop and the operations of its American counterpart?

Interpret company and industry ratios.
(SO 5)

P14-11A Nextec Corp. has been in business for five years. Nextec now has plans to create a new software package intended to allow users with limited computer knowledge to easily navigate the Internet by using their television sets and a control box that plugs into the cable jack.

You are the loan officer at a Canadian chartered bank. The manager has asked you to analyse Nextec's financial statements and recommend whether or not the bank should lend Nextec additional funds for the project, based on its historical financial statements. Comparative financial statements follow:

NEXTEC CORP.
Balance Sheet
March 31

Assets	2002	2001
Cash	$ 45,000	$ —
Accounts Receivable	510,000	470,000
Inventory	50,000	40,000
Prepaid Expenses	5,000	10,000
Patents	40,000	—
Accumulated Amortization	(2,000)	—
	$648,000	$520,000
Liabilities and Shareholders' Equity		
Bank Overdraft	$ —	$ 20,000
Accounts Payable	50,000	60,000
Current Portion of Long-Term Debt	60,000	50,000
Long-Term Debt	100,000	160,000
Common Shares	100,000	100,000
Retained Earnings	338,000	130,000
	$648,000	$520,000

NEXTEC CORP.
Statement of Earnings
For the Year Ended March 31

	2002	2001
Sales (all on credit)	$1,600,000	$1,400,000
Cost of Sales	300,000	200,000
Gross Profit	1,300,000	1,200,000
Operating Expenses		
Salaries	870,000	940,000
Office	20,000	20,000
Rent	40,000	40,000
Interest	20,000	30,000
Amortization Expense	2,000	—
	952,000	1,030,000
Earnings Before Taxes	348,000	170,000
Income Taxes (40%)	139,200	68,000
Net Earnings	$ 208,800	$ 102,000

Selected comparative ratios and industry averages follow:

	2002	2001	Industry Average
Current ratio	5.5 to 1	4 to 1	2 to 1
Collection period	112 days	120 days	45 days
Inventory turnover	6.7×	5.7×	5×
Return on shareholders' equity	63%	44%	40%
Debt to total assets	32%	56%	50%
Average age of capital assets	1 year	n/a	3 years

Instructions

(a) Indicate whether the 2002 ratios presented above are favourable or unfavourable compared to the industry average.
(b) Based on a comparison of Nextec Corp.'s ratios with the industry average, identify *one* significant area that Nextec Corp. must improve and what it should do to improve it.
(c) The President of Nextec Corp. estimates that the company needs $1,000,000 to ensure the new software project's success. Based on the ratios given, and the financial statements presented, determine whether or not you would lend $1,000,000 to Nextec Corp. Explain your decision.
(d) Identify one additional thing Nextec could do (other than borrow) to raise the money it needs.
(e) In addition to the financial statements of Nextec Corp., list two other non-financial factors that should be considered when evaluating Nextec Corp.

P14-12A Presented here are an incomplete statement of earnings and an incomplete comparative balance sheet for Schwenke Corporation:

Calculate missing information given a set of ratios.
(SO 5)

SCHWENKE CORPORATION
Statement of Earnings
For the Year Ended December 31, 2002

Sales	$ (a)
Cost of goods sold	(b)
Gross profit	(c)
Operating expenses	221,000
Earnings from operations	(d)
Interest expense	12,000
Earnings before income taxes	(e)
Income tax expense (36.3%)	(f)
Net earnings	$125,000

SCHWENKE CORPORATION
Balance Sheet
December 31, 2002

Assets	
Current assets	
Cash	$ 54,000
Accounts receivable (net)	(g)
Inventory	(h)
Total current assets	(i)
Capital assets (net)	(j)
Total assets	$ (k)
Liabilities	
Current liabilities	$ (l)
Long-term liabilities	110,000
Total liabilities	(m)
Shareholders' Equity	
Common shares	220,000
Retained earnings	206,000
Total shareholders' equity	426,000
Total liabilities and shareholders' equity	$ (n)

Additional information:

1. The profit margin is 14%.
2. The gross profit percentage is 48%.
3. The asset turnover ratio is 1.6.
4. The current ratio is 5.5:1.
5. The acid-test ratio is 3.7:1.

Instructions

Calculate the missing information using the ratios. Round your answers to the nearest thousand dollars. Use ending balances instead of average balances, where averages are required for ratio calculations. Show your calculations. (Hint: Start with one ratio and derive as much information as possible from it before trying another ratio.)

Assess the impact of transactions on ratios.
(SO 5)

P14-13A You are provided with the following information for Konotopsky Venture Inc.

Transactions	Current ratio (1.5:1)	Receivables turnover ratio (15x)	Inventory turnover ratio (5x)	Debt to total assets ratio (25%)	Times interest earned ratio (20x)	Return on assets ratio (10%)
(a) Issued 10-year, 9% bonds, payable at their $500,000 face value to finance a capital asset expansion.						
(b) Recorded and paid $22,500 of interest expense on bonds payable.						
(c) Issued preferred shares for $10,000 cash.						
(d) Paid $400 of cash dividends to preferred shareholders.						
(e) Purchased inventory on credit, $1,500. (Perpetual system)						
(f) Sold inventory purchased in the previous transaction. (Deal only with the entry that affects cost of goods sold.)						
(g) Recorded the credit sale related to the previous transaction, $2,500.						
(h) Collected the proceeds from the sale in the previous transaction.						

Instructions

Indicate whether the above transactions will increase (I), decrease (D), or have no effect (NE) on each of the ratios presented.

P14-14A Fly-by-Night Inc. is in its first year of operations. Obtaining financing has been difficult. The president of the company is debating the selection of generally accepted accounting principles. She would like you to advise her of the impact that selected accounting policies will have on various ratios.

Assess the impact of acccounting policy choices on ratios.
(SO 5)

Policy choice	Current ratio (1.5:1)	Gross profit rate (40%)	Earnings per share ($1.50)	Debt to total assets ratio (25%)	Times interest earned ratio (20x)	Return on assets ratio (10%)
(a) It is a period of inflation and the president would like to use the FIFO inventory cost flow method instead of average cost.						
(b) The company is considering using double declining-balance amortization, which will produce a higher expense than other methods.						
(c) The company is considering using the effective-interest method of amortizing a bond premium, rather than the straight-line method. This will result in more interest expense this year than had the straight-line method been used.						
(d) The company is leasing automobiles and is setting up the lease as a capital lease. Its interest expense and amortization expense under the capital lease will be higher this year than the rent expense would be under an operating lease.						

Instructions
Indicate whether the above policy choices will increase (I), decrease (D), or have no effect (NE) on each of the ratios presented.

PROBLEMS: SET B

All of the Problems in this chapter employ decision tools.

Perform horizontal analysis before and after extraordinary item.
(SO 1, 3)

P14-1B **Aliant Inc.** is a new growth company, which was formed by combining Bruncor, Island Telecom Inc., Maritime Telegraph and Telephone Company, and NewTel Enterprises Limited. You are provided with the following information taken from Aliant Inc.'s 1999 annual report:

ALIANT INC.
Statements of Earnings
(in thousands)

	1999	1998	1997	1996	1995	1994
Total operating revenues*	$2,026,338	$1,723,772	$1,610,079	$1,373,906	$1,284,990	$1,228,870
Total operating expenses*	(1,570,506)	(1,313,135)	(1,227,564)	(1,014,498)	(970,648)	(892,870)
Restructuring costs	(78,000)	—	—	—	—	—
Other income	27,506	9,901	2,173	6,487	10,284	22,512
Interest charges	(122,734)	(108,036)	(109,659)	(121,829)	(131,297)	(123,164)
Income taxes	(134,374)	(140,793)	(128,545)	(116,432)	(95,151)	(103,257)
Net earnings before extraordinary item	148,230	171,709	146,484	127,634	98,178	132,091
Extraordinary item	—	—	(344,335)	—	—	—
Net earnings (loss)	$ 148,230	$ 171,709	$ (197,851)	$ 127,634	$ 98,178	$ 132,091

* Revenues and expenses for 1997 and later years have been restated to report gross revenues from settlements and contribution. Consequently, revenue and expense growth in 1997 is distorted.

ALIANT INC.
Balance Sheet (selected items)
(in thousands)

	1999	1998	1997	1996	1995	1994
Total assets	$2,874,956	$2,676,991	$2,461,326	$3,096,036	$3,116,147	$2,346,963
Shareholders' equity	1,105,800	1,041,616	941,596	1,268,529	1,222,506	1,199,815
Long-term debt, including current portion	1,187,573	1,107,546	1,023,448	1,014,177	1,139,873	1,072,760

Instructions

(a) Prepare a horizontal analysis (dollar value and percentage changes) for Aliant Inc. You may exclude the following from your analysis: restructuring costs, other income, income taxes, and extraordinary items. Comment on the horizontal analysis.

(b) In 1997, Aliant recorded an extraordinary loss on its statement of earnings which also resulted in an increase in accumulated amortization. Perform a horizontal analysis for earnings before extraordinary items and for total assets as if the extra charge to accumulated amortization in 1997 had never been recorded.

P14-2B Here are comparative statement data for Breau Company Ltd. and Shields Company Ltd., two competitors. All balance sheet data are as at December 31, 2001, and December 31, 2000.

Prepare vertical analysis and comment on profitability.
(SO 4, 5)

	BREAU COMPANY LTD.		SHIELDS COMPANY LTD.	
	2001	2000	2001	2000
Net sales	$250,000		$1,200,000	
Cost of goods sold	160,000		720,000	
Operating expenses	51,000		252,000	
Interest expense	3,000		10,000	
Income tax expense	11,000		65,000	
Current assets	130,000	$110,000	700,000	$650,000
Capital assets (net)	305,000	270,000	800,000	750,000
Current liabilities	60,000	52,000	250,000	275,000
Long-term liabilities	50,000	68,000	200,000	150,000
Common shares	260,000	210,000	750,000	700,000
Retained earnings	65,000	50,000	300,000	275,000

Instructions

(a) Prepare a vertical analysis of the 2001 statement of earnings data for Breau Company and Shields Company.

(b) Comment on the relative profitability of the companies by calculating the return on assets and the return on common shareholders' equity ratios for both companies.

P14-3B The comparative statements of Marti Rosen Company Inc. are presented here:

Calculate ratios from balance sheet and statement of earnings.
(SO 5)

MARTI ROSEN COMPANY INC.
Statements of Earnings
For the Years Ended December 31

	2001	2000
Net sales	$660,000	$624,000
Cost of goods sold	440,000	405,600
Gross profit	220,000	218,400
Selling and administrative expense (including $46,000 and $45,000 of amortization for 2001 and 2002, respectively)	143,880	149,760
Earnings from operations	76,120	68,640
Other expenses and losses		
Interest expense	7,920	7,200
Earnings before income taxes	68,200	61,440
Income tax expense	25,300	24,000
Net earnings	$ 42,900	$ 37,440

MARTI ROSEN COMPANY INC.
Balance Sheets
December 31

Assets	2001	2000
Current assets		
Cash	$ 23,100	$ 21,600
Short-term investments	34,800	33,000
Accounts receivable (net)	106,200	93,800
Inventory	72,400	64,000
Total current assets	236,500	212,400
Capital assets (net of accumulated amortization of $321,000 and $275,000, respectively)	465,300	459,600
Total assets	$701,800	$672,000
Liabilities and Shareholders' Equity		
Current liabilities		
Accounts payable	$134,200	$132,000
Income taxes payable	25,300	24,000
Total current liabilities	159,500	156,000
Bonds payable	132,000	120,000
Total liabilities	291,500	276,000
Shareholders' equity		
Common shares (15,000 shares)	150,000	150,000
Retained earnings	260,300	246,000
Total shareholders' equity	410,300	396,000
Total liabilities and shareholders' equity	$701,800	$672,000

All sales were on account. Net cash provided by operating activities was $36,000.

Instructions

Calculate the following ratios for 2001:

(a) earnings per share
(b) return on common shareholders' equity
(c) return on assets
(d) current
(e) acid-test
(f) receivables turnover
(g) average collection period
(h) inventory turnover
(i) days in inventory
(j) times interest earned
(k) asset turnover
(l) debt to total assets
(m) cash current debt coverage
(n) cash return on sales
(o) cash total debt coverage
(p) cash interest coverage
(q) capital expenditure
(r) average useful life of capital assets

Perform ratio analysis; comment on results. (SO 5)

P14-4B Here are condensed balance sheets and statement of earnings data for Colinas Corporation:

COLINAS CORPORATION
Balance Sheets
December 31

	2001	2000	1999
Cash	$ 40,000	$ 24,000	$ 20,000
Receivables (net)	70,000	45,000	48,000
Other current assets	80,000	75,000	62,000
Investments	90,000	70,000	50,000
Capital assets (net)	450,000	400,000	360,000
	$730,000	$614,000	$540,000
Current liabilities	$ 98,000	$ 75,000	$ 70,000
Long-term debt	97,000	75,000	65,000
Common shares	400,000	340,000	300,000
Retained earnings	135,000	124,000	105,000
	$730,000	$614,000	$540,000

COLINAS CORPORATION
Statements of Earnings
For the Years Ended December 31

	2001	2000
Sales	$700,000	$750,000
Less: Sales returns and allowances	40,000	50,000
Net sales	660,000	700,000
Cost of goods sold	420,000	400,000
Gross profit	240,000	300,000
Operating expenses (including income taxes)	194,000	237,000
Net earnings	$ 46,000	$ 63,000

Additional information:

1. The market price of Colinas's common shares was $5.00, $4.50, and $2.30 for 1999, 2000, and 2001, respectively.
2. All dividends were paid in cash. (Hint: Analyse retained earnings to determine dividends.)
3. On July 1, 2000, 4,000 common shares were issued, and on July 1, 2001, 6,000 shares were issued. 40,000 shares are outstanding at the end of 2001.

Instructions

(a) Calculate the following ratios for 2000 and 2001:

1. profit margin
2. gross profit rate
3. asset turnover
4. earnings per share
5. price-earnings
6. payout
7. debt to total assets
8. dividend yield

(b) Based on the ratios calculated, briefly discuss the improvement or lack thereof in the financial position and operating results from 2000 to 2001 of Colinas Corporation.

P14-5B Financial information for Star Track Company Ltd. is presented here:

Calculate ratios; comment on overall liquidity and profitability.
(SO 5)

STAR TRACK COMPANY LTD.
Balance Sheets
December 31

	2001	2000
Assets		
Cash	$ 50,000	$ 42,000
Short-term investments	80,000	100,000
Receivables (net of allowance for doubtful accounts of $5,000 and $4,000, respectively)	100,000	87,000
Inventories	440,000	400,000
Prepaid expenses	25,000	31,000
Land	75,000	75,000
Building and equipment (net)	570,000	500,000
Total assets	$1,340,000	$1,235,000
Liabilities and Shareholders' Equity		
Notes payable	$ 125,000	$ 125,000
Accounts payable	160,000	140,000
Accrued liabilities	50,000	50,000
Bonds payable, due 2003	200,000	200,000
Common shares (100,000 shares)	500,000	500,000
Retained earnings	305,000	220,000
Total liabilities and shareholders' equity	$1,340,000	$1,235,000

STAR TRACK COMPANY LTD.
Statements of Earnings
For the Years Ended December 31

	2001	2000
Sales	$1,000,000	$940,000
Cost of goods sold	650,000	635,000
Gross profit	350,000	305,000
Operating expenses	235,000	215,000
Net earnings	$ 115,000	$ 90,000

Additional information:
1. Inventory at the beginning of 2000 was $350,000
2. Receivables at the beginning of 2000 were $80,000.
3. Total assets at the beginning of 2000 were $1,175,000.
4. Current liabilities at the beginning of 2000 were $300,000.
5. Total shareholders' equity at the beginning of 2000 was $740,000.
6. No common share transactions occurred during 2000 or 2001.
7. All sales were on account.
8. Cash provided by operating activities was $80,000 in 2001, and $65,000 in 2000.

Instructions

(a) Indicate, by using ratios, the change in liquidity and profitability of Star Track Company from 2000 to 2001. (Note: Not all profitability ratios can be calculated.)

(b) Given below are three independent situations and a ratio that may be affected. For each situation, calculate the affected ratio (1) as at December 31, 2001, and (2) as at December 31, 2002. Net earnings for 2002 were $125,000. Total assets on December 31, 2002, were $1,500,000.

Situation	Ratio
1. 65,000 common shares were sold on July 1, 2002.	Earnings per share
2. All of the notes payable were paid in 2002.	Debt to total assets
3. The market price of common shares on December 31, 2002, was $6.25. The market price on December 31, 2001, was $5.	Price-earnings

Complete selected ratios, and compare liquidity, profitability, and solvency for two companies.

(SO 5)

P14-6B **Inco Limited** is the western world's top producer of nickel, and also mines and processes other precious minerals and metals throughout the world. **Falconbridge Limited** is also one of the world's leading producers of nickel, among other metals and minerals. Both companies are headquartered in Toronto. Selected financial data of these two close competitors are presented here (in millions) for a recent year:

	INCO LIMITED	FALCONBRIDGE LIMITED
Statement of Earnings Data for the Year		
Net sales	$1,766	$1,674
Cost of sales and operating expenses	1,735	1,359
Selling, general, and administrative expenses	96	86
Interest expense	86	54
Other expenses	55	250
Earnings (loss) before income taxes	(206)	(75)
Income and mining tax recovery	94	39
Earnings (loss) from continuing operations	(112)	(36)
Earnings from discontinued operations	36	—
Net earnings (loss)	$ (76)	$ (36)
Earnings (loss) per share	$(0.63)	$(0.24)
Balance Sheet Data End of Year		
Current assets		
Cash and cash equivalents	$ 82	$ 100
Accounts receivable	256	294
Inventories	473	372
Other current assets	63	—
Total current assets	874	766
Capital and other assets	6,468	4,033
Total assets	$7,342	$4,799
Current liabilities	$ 560	$ 340
Long-term liabilities	2,424	2,141
Total liabilities	2,984	2,481
Shareholders' equity	4,358	2,318
Total liabilities and shareholders' equity	$7,342	$4,799
Other Data		
Average net accounts receivable	$ 323.5	$ 336.7
Average inventories	634.5	349.0
Average total assets	7,557.0	4,556.3
Average total shareholders' equity	4,414.5	2,319.0
Net cash provided (used) by operating activities	174.0	176.9
Capital expenditures	437.0	647.3
Dividends paid	44.0	76.7

Instructions

(a) Calculate liquidity, solvency, and profitability ratios, as appropriate, for each company.

(b) Calculate the liquidity, solvency, and profitability of each company compared to its competitor and the industry. Selected industry averages are available for the following ratios:

Current ratio	1.67
Acid-test ratio	0.7
Receivables turnover	9.7×
Inventory turnover	4.1×
Times interest earned	1.8×
Capital expenditure ratio	40%
Profit margin	1.73%
Return on assets	1.1%
Earnings per share	$0.16

Calculate numerous ratios.
(SO 5)

P14-7B The comparative statements of Ultra Vision Company Ltd. are presented here:

ULTRA VISION COMPANY LTD.
Statements of Earnings
For the Years Ended December 31

	2001	2000
Net sales (all on account)	$600,000	$520,000
Expenses		
Cost of goods sold	415,000	354,000
Selling and administrative expense (including amortization expense of $43,000 and $39,000 for 2000 and 2001, respectively)	120,800	114,800
Interest expense	7,200	6,000
Income tax expense	18,000	14,000
Total expenses	561,000	488,800
Net earnings	$ 39,000	$ 31,200

ULTRA VISION COMPANY LTD.
Balance Sheets
December 31

	2001	2000
Assets		
Current assets		
Cash	$ 21,000	$ 18,000
Short-term investments	18,000	15,000
Accounts receivable (net)	92,000	74,000
Inventory	84,000	70,000
Total current assets	215,000	177,000
Capital assets (net)	423,000	383,000
Total assets	$638,000	$560,000
Liabilities and Shareholders' Equity		
Current liabilities		
Accounts payable	$112,000	$110,000
Income taxes payable	23,000	20,000
Total current liabilities	135,000	130,000
Long-term liabilities		
Bonds payable	130,000	80,000
Total liabilities	265,000	210,000
Shareholders' equity		
Common shares (30,000 shares)	150,000	150,000
Retained earnings	223,000	200,000
Total shareholders' equity	373,000	350,000
Total liabilities and shareholders' equity	$638,000	$560,000

Additional data: The common shares recently sold at $19.50 per share.

Instructions

Calculate the following ratios for 2001:

(a) current
(b) acid-test
(c) receivables turnover
(d) average collection period
(e) inventory turnover
(f) days in inventory
(g) profit margin
(h) asset turnover
(i) return on assets
(j) return on common shareholders' equity
(k) earnings per share
(l) price-earnings
(m) payout
(n) debt to total assets
(o) times interest earned
(p) cash interest coverage

P14-8B You are presented with the following selected information from the **T. Eaton Company Limited**'s balance sheet:

Determine effect of discontinued operations on ratios. (SO 1, 5)

T. EATON COMPANY LIMTED
Balance Sheet
(thousands of dollars)

	January 31, 1998	January 25, 1997
Continuing operations:		
Accounts receivable	$ 56,737	$ 28,063
Total current assets	884,427	391,766
Total current liabilities	837,780	441,145
Discontinued operations:		
Accounts receivable	453,637	557,314
Other current assets	15,920	18,213
Total discontinued operations in current assets	469,557	575,527
Long-term assets of real estate operations	38,628	272,943
Borrowings	411,701	515,927
Other current liabilities	12,717	18,434
Total discontinued operations in current liabilities	424,418	534,361
Long-term liabilities of real estate operations	40,257	212,740

Instructions

(a) Calculate the following ratios for Eaton's for 1998, first using only the results from continuing operations, then including the results from discontinued operations. Revenue from credit sales was $1,688,200 for the year ended January 31, 1998.
  1. current ratio
  2. receivables turnover ratio
  3. average collection period of receivables

(b) Which ratios are of more relevance to investors? Would your answer change if you learned that Eaton's was liquidated at the end of 1999 and purchased by Sears?

P14-9B You are presented with the following comparative financial information for two Canadian airline companies whose identities have been disguised. One of these companies is in financial trouble and was acquired by another airline company (Company C) at the end of the current year.

Prepare ratio analysis to compare two companies, one on the verge of bankruptcy. (SO 5)

	COMPANY A Balance Sheet (millions of dollars)		COMPANY B Balance Sheet (millions of dollars)	
	current year	prior year	current year	prior year
Assets				
Cash and short-term investments	$ 302.4	$ 193.9	$ 50.7	$ 13.5
Accounts receivable	267.7	221.9	5.2	5.2
Materials and supplies	123.3	138.5	0.5	0.5
Other current assets	53.0	38.4	4.1	3.5
Total current assets	746.4	592.7	60.5	22.7
Capital and other assets	1,352.2	1,318.5	126.1	85.5
Total assets	$2,098.6	$1,911.2	$186.6	$108.2
Liabilities and Shareholders' Equity				
Total current liabilities	$ 953.6	$ 877.1	$ 49.9	$ 29.0
Total long-term liabilities	1,304.8	1,057.3	42.2	29.9
Total liabilities	2,258.4	1,934.4	92.1	58.9
Total shareholders' equity	(159.8)	(23.2)	94.5	49.3
Total liabilities and shareholders' equity	$2,098.6	$1,911.2	$186.6	$108.2

	Statement of Earnings For the Year Ended (in thousands)		Statement of Earnings For the Year Ended (in thousands)	
	current year	prior year	current year	prior year
Operating revenues (assume all on credit)	$3,171.3	$3,077.5	$203.6	$125.4
Operating expenses	3,193.1	2,980.4	173.1	112.3
Operating income (loss)	(21.8)	97.1	30.5	13.1
Non-operating expenses	113.5	89.9	1.2	0.7
Earnings (loss) before income taxes	(135.3)	7.2	29.3	12.4
Income tax expense	2.3	1.8	13.5	5.9
Net earnings (loss)	$ (137.6)	$ 5.4	$ 15.8	$ 6.5

Instructions

(a) Prepare the following ratios for each of Company A and Company B for the current year:
1. current ratio
2. acid-test ratio
3. receivables turnover ratio
4. average collection period
5. debt to total assets ratio
6. return on assets ratio
7. operating expenses to sales ratio
8. assset turnover ratio

(b) Which company do you think is in financial trouble? Provide support for your conclusion.

Calculate and compare ratios for a Canadian steel producer and its American counterpart.
(SO 5)

P14-10B IPSCO Inc. is one of Canada's major steel companies, headquartered in Regina. Its annual steel-making capacity is 1 million tons of steel in Canada, and 2.5 million tons in the U.S. **Bethlehem Steel Corporation** is a leading U.S. steel producer and one of IPSCO's competitors. Selected financial data for the two companies follows (both in millions of U.S. dollars):

	IPSCO	BETHLEHEM STEEL
	Earnings Data for the Year Ended December 31, 1999	
Sales	$ 808.3	$3,914.8
Cost of sales	615.8	3,966.3
Selling, research, and administration	75.8	127.1
Interest expense	19.1	43.6
Earnings (loss) before income taxes	97.6	(222.2)
Income tax (expense) recovery	(23.3)	39.0
Net earnings (loss)	$ 74.3	$ (183.2)
	Balance Sheet Data as at December 31, 1999	
Current assets	$ 479.2	$1,209.4
Capital and other assets	993.8	4,326.8
Total assets	$1,473.0	$5,536.2
Current liabilities	$ 196.7	$1,033.4
Long-term liabilities	396.4	3,225.7
Total liabilities	593.1	4,259.1
Shareholders' equity	879.9	1,277.1
Total liabilities and shareholders' equity	$1,473.0	$5,536.2

	Other Data	
Average net receivables	$ 100.8	$ 271.1
Average inventory	188.5	952.7
Average total assets	1,367.9	5,578.8
Average current liabilities	160.9	1,009.3
Average total liabilities	532.4	4,195.6
Average shareholders' equity	835.5	1,383.3
Cash provided by operating activities	55.5	226.6

	Selected Industry Averages
Asset turnover	0.8
Average collection period	53 days
Current ratio	1.8
Gross profit rate	18.4%
Inventory turnover	4.8x
Profit margin ratio	2.6%
Return on assets ratio	2.0%
Return on common shareholders' equity	5.2%
Times interest earned	2.5

Instructions

Based on the information provided, calculate relevant ratios, and assess the liquidity, solvency, and profitability, for 1999, for IPSCO and Bethlehem Steel compared to each other and the industry.

Interpret company and industry ratios.
(SO 5, 6)

P14-11B Selected ratios for two companies operating in the beverage industry follow, in alphabetical order, for the year ended December 31, 1999. Industry ratios, where available, have also been included ("n/a" indicates that the ratio was not available).

Ratio	Refresh Corp.	Taste.Com	Industry
Acid-test (quick) ratio	0.4 to 1.0	0.7 to 1.0	0.4 to 1.0
Asset turnover	1.0 times	1.0 times	0.9 times
Cash flow per share	$1.56	$2.12	$1.87
Cash total debt coverage	32%	20%	n/a
Current ratio	0.6 to 1.0	1.1 to 1.0	0.8 to 1.0
Credit risk ratio	5.1%	7.2%	6.5%
Debt to total assets	56%	72%	n/a
Earnings per share	$0.98	$1.37	$1.08
Gross profit rate	73.8%	60.0%	57.7%
Inventory turnover	5.8 times	9.9 times	8.3 times
Price-earnings	50.3 times	24.3 times	32.2 times
Profit margin	12.3%	11.2%	8.1%
Receivables turnover	11.4 times	9.8 times	9.3 times
Return on assets	11.2%	9.3%	7.2%
Return on common shareholders' equity	25.7%	29.8%	26.4%
Times interest earned	15.3 times	7.9 times	5.3 times

Instructions

Answer the following questions, citing relevant ratios to justify your answer:

(a) Which company appears to be the most liquid?

(b) As a potential investor, are you concerned with the debt levels of either company?
(c) Which company is the most profitable?
(d) One should always be cautious in interpreting ratios. Identify any *two* facts that you should keep in mind about the limitations of ratio analysis as you interpret the ratios in this question.

Calculate missing information given a set of ratios. (SO 5)

P14-12B Presented here are an incomplete statement of earnings and an incomplete comparative balance sheet of Vienna Corporation:

VIENNA CORPORATION
Statement of Earnings
For the Year ended December 31, 2002

Sales	$11,000,000
Cost of goods sold	(a)
Gross profit	(b)
Operating expenses	1,665,000
Earnings from operations	(c)
Interest expense	(d)
Earnings before income taxes	(e)
Income tax expense	560,000
Net earnings	$ (f)

VIENNA CORPORATION
Balance Sheet
December 31, 2002

	2002	2001
Assets		
Current assets		
Cash	$ 450,000	$ 375,000
Accounts receivable (net)	(g)	950,000
Inventory	(h)	1,720,000
Total current assets	(i)	3,045,000
Capital assets (net)	4,620,000	3,955,000
Total assets	$ (j)	$7,000,000
Liabilities		
Current liabilities	$ (k)	$ 825,000
Long-term liabilities	(l)	2,800,000
Total liabilities	(m)	3,625,000
Shareholders' Equity		
Common shares	3,000,000	3,000,000
Retained earnings	400,000	375,000
Total shareholders' equity	3,400,000	3,375,000
Total liabilities and shareholders' equity	$ (n)	$7,000,000

Additional information:
1. The receivables turnover for 2002 is 10 times.
2. All sales are on account.
3. The gross profit rate is 36.73%.
4. The profit margin for 2002 is 14.5%.
5. Return on assets is 22%.
6. The current ratio on December 31, 2002, is 3:1.
7. The inventory turnover for 2002 is 6.444 times.

Instructions
Calculate the missing information using the ratios. Round your answers to the nearest thousand dollars. Use ending balances instead of average balances where averages are required for ratio calculations. Show your calculations. (Hint: Start with one ratio and derive as much information as possible from it before trying another ratio. You will not be able to calculate the missing amounts in the same sequence as they are presented above.)

P14-13B You are provided with the following information for Harrington Inc:

Assess the impact of transactions on ratios. (SO 5)

Transactions	Current ratio (1.5:1)	Debt to total assets ratio (25%)	Cash total debt coverage ratio (25%)	Cash interest coverage ratio (10x)	Return on assets ratio (10%)	Asset turnover ratio (3x)
(a) Issued 10-year, 9% bonds, payable at their $500,000 face value, to purchase $500,000 of capital assets.						
(b) Recorded and paid $22,500 of interest expense on bonds payable.						
(c) Recorded net earnings of $100,000.						
(d) Paid $4,000 of cash dividends to preferred shareholders.						
(e) Incurred operating expenses on credit, $1,500.						
(f) Billed for services rendered, $25,000.						
(g) Collected the accounts receivable in the previous transaction.						

Instructions

Indicate whether the above transactions will increase (I), decrease (D), or have no effect (NE) on each of the ratios presented.

P14-14B The president of Dot.Com is debating the selection of generally accepted accounting principles. She would like you to advise her of the impact that selected accounting policies will have on various ratios.

Assess the impact of accounting policy choices on ratios. (SO 5)

Policy choice	Current ratio (1.5:1)	Gross profit rate (40%)	Earnings per share ($1.50)	Debt to total assets ratio (25%)	Times interest earned ratio (20x)	Return on total assets ratio (10%)
(a) It is a period of deflation and the president would like to use the average inventory cost flow method instead of FIFO.						
(b) The company is considering using straight-line						

amortization which will produce a lower expense than other methods.

(c) The company is considering using the effective-interest method of amortizing a bond discount, rather than the straight-line method. This will result in less interest expense this year than had the straight-line method been used.

(d) The company is leasing equipment and is setting up the lease as an operating lease. Its rent expense under an operating lease will be lower than interest and amortization expenses under a capital lease.

Instructions

Indicate whether the above policy choices will increase (I), decrease (D), or have no effect (NE) on each of the ratios presented.

BROADENING YOUR PERSPECTIVE

FINANCIAL REPORTING AND ANALYSIS

FINANCIAL REPORTING PROBLEM: *Loblaw Companies Limited*

Loblaws
A passion for food... *and a lot more!*

BYP14-1 You are considering investing in **Loblaw Companies Limited**'s common shares. Before doing so, you wish to analyse the company further. Excerpts from the annual report of Loblaw are presented in Appendix A of this textbook.

Instructions

(a) Prepare an 11-year horizontal trend analysis, using 1989 as the base year of (1) sales and (2) operating income. Comment on the significance of the trend results.

(b) For 1999, calculate the debt to total assets ratio. Find the times interest earned (called interest coverage) ratio, and the cash total debt coverage ratio (called cash flows from operating activities to total debt and debt equivalents) presented in Loblaw's 11-year summary of financial ratios. How would you evaluate Loblaw's long-run solvency?

(c) For 1999, calculate the profit margin ratio and the asset turnover ratio. Find the return on assets ratio (called return on average total assets), return on common shareholders' equity (called return on average common equity), and the price-earnings ratio presented in Loblaw's 11-year summary of financial ratios. How would you evaluate Loblaw's profitability?

(d) What information not included in the annual report may also be useful to you in making a decision about Loblaw's?

COMPARATIVE ANALYSIS PROBLEM: *Loblaw and Sobeys*

BYP14-2 The financial statements of **Sobeys Inc.** are presented in Appendix B, following the financial statements for **Loblaw Companies Limited** in Appendix A.

Loblaws
A passion for food... *and a lot more!*

Sobeys

Instructions

(a) Based on the information in the financial statements, determine each of the following for each company:
   1. The percentage increase in sales and in net earnings from 1998 to 1999.
   2. The percentage increase in total assets and in total shareholders' equity from 1998 to 1999.
   3. The earnings per share for each of these two years.

(b) What conclusions concerning the two companies can be drawn from these data?

RESEARCH CASES

BYP14-3 The chapter stresses the importance of comparing an individual company's financial ratios to industry norms. Published industry averages include Dun & Bradstreet Canada's *Key Business Ratios* and Statistics Canada's *Financial Performance Indices for Canadian Business*. These publications include vertical analysis financial statements and various ratios.

Obtain the most recent edition of industry averages available in your library and locate the financial statements of Sears Canada Inc. [Note that these indices are normally a few years old before they become accessible to libraries.]

Instructions

(a) Prepare a vertical analysis balance sheet and statement of earnings for Sears.
(b) Calculate the ratios for Sears that are presented in the merchandising–department store industry category. [Note that the specific ratio definitions used in calculating industry ratios should be described in the material.]
(c) Use your answers from parts (a) and (b) to compare Sears to the appropriate industry data. How does Sears compare to its competitors?

BYP14-4 The "Mastering Management" supplement to *The Financial Post* of February 1/3, 1997, includes an article by Marshall W. Meyer entitled, "The Secrets That Lay Behind Improved Corporate Performance." This article discusses the differences between financial and non-financial measures, noting that financial performance cannot be sustained unless the non-financial underpinnings are measured as well.

Instructions

Read the article and answer the following questions:

(a) What are some examples of non-financial underpinnings of financial performance that should be measured?
(b) Identify two differences between financial and non-financial measures.
(c) Are non-financial measures subject to accounting standards?
(d) Does the author believe that financial measures predict future performance well? Explain why or why not.
(e) What two financial and two non-financial measures were used by a global electronics manufacturer to measure performance? Are there benefits in combining non-financial and financial measures?

INTERPRETING FINANCIAL STATEMENTS

BYP14-5 The Coca-Cola Company and **PepsiCo, Inc.** provide refreshments to every corner of the world. Selected data from the 1998 consolidated financial statements for The Coca-Cola Company and for PepsiCo, Inc., are presented here (in millions):

	Coca-Cola	PepsiCo
Total current assets (including cash, accounts receivable, and short-term investments totalling $3,473 for Coke and $2,847 for Pepsi)	$ 6,380	$ 4,362
Total current liabilities	8,640	7,914
Net sales	18,813	22,348
Cost of goods sold	5,562	9,330
Net income	3,533	1,993
Average receivables for the year	1,653	2,302
Average inventories for the year	925	874
Average total assets	18,013	21,381
Average common shareholders' equity	7,839	6,669
Average current liabilities	8,010	6,086
Average total liabilities	10,225	14,712
Total assets	19,145	22,660
Total liabilities	10,742	16,259
Income taxes	1,665	270
Interest expense	277	395
Cash provided by operating activities	3,433	3,211

Instructions

(a) Calculate the following liquidity ratios for 1998 for Coca-Cola and PepsiCo and comment on the relative liquidity of the two competitors:
1. current ratio
2. acid-test
3. receivables turnover
4. average collection period
5. inventory turnover
6. days in inventory
7. cash current debt coverage

(b) Calculate the following solvency ratios for the two companies and comment on the relative solvency of the two competitors:
1. debt to total assets ratio
2. times interest earned
3. cash total debt coverage ratio

(c) Calculate the following profitability ratios for the two companies and comment on the relative profitability of the two competitors:
1. profit margin
2. cash return on sales
3. asset turnover
4. return on assets
5. return on common shareholders' equity

A GLOBAL FOCUS

BYP14-6 The use of railroad transportation has changed dramatically around the world. Attitudes toward railroads and railroad usage differ across countries. In England, the railroads were run by the government until recently. Five years ago, **Railtrack Group PLC** became a publicly traded company. In 1998, **Canadian National Railway** merged with Illinois Central to create a truly North American railroad. The following data were taken from the financial statements for the 1998 fiscal years of each company (ended March 31, 1999, and December 31, 1998, respectively).

	Railtrack Group (pounds in millions)		Canadian National (dollars in millions)	
Financial Highlights	**1998**	**1997**	**1998**	**1997**
Cash and short-term investments	£ 380	£ 26	$ 263	$ 365
Accounts receivable	434	402	404	681
Total current assets	909	521	1,050	1,549
Total assets	7,095	5,760	10,864	7,075
Current liabilities	1,128	1,209	1,392	1,205
Total liabilities	3,882	2,888	6,573	3,658
Total shareholders' equity	3,213	2,872	4,291	3,417
Revenues	2,573		4,144	
Operating expenses	2,102		3,897	
Interest expense	93		244	
Income tax expense	3		(6)	
Net earnings	425		109	
Cash provided by operating activities	988		953	
Capital expenditures	1,275		404	
Dividends paid	42		99	

Where available, industry averages for the North American railroad industry are shown in parentheses next to each ratio below. Industry averages are not available for the UK railroad industry.

Instructions

(a) Calculate the following liquidity ratios for 1998 and discuss the relative liquidity of the two companies and of the railroad industry:
  1. current (0.72)
  2. acid-test (0.5)
  3. cash current debt coverage (n/a)
  4. receivables turnover (10.1×)

(b) Calculate the following solvency ratios for 1998 and discuss the relative solvency of the two companies and of the railroad industry:
  1. debt to total assets (n/a)
  2. times interest earned (2.9×)
  3. cash total debt coverage (n/a)
  4. free cash flow (n/a)
  5. capital expenditure ratio (n/a)

(c) Calculate the following profitability ratios for 1998 and discuss the relative profitability of the two companies and of the railroad industry:
  1. asset turnover (0.4×)
  2. profit margin (6.74%)
  3. return on assets (2.9%)
  4. return on common shareholders' equity (n/a)

(d) What factors might contribute to the differences that you found?

FINANCIAL ANALYSIS ON THE WEB

BYP14-7 The purpose and content of the management discussion and analysis (MD&A) section of an annual report is reviewed. The MD&A is then used to evaluate The Second Cup Ltd.'s corporate performance.

Instructions

Specific requirements of this web case can be found on the Kimmel website.

BYP14-8 Comparative data and industry data are employed to evaluate the performance and financial position of two integrated oil and gas companies, Petro-Canada and Suncore Energy, Inc.

Instructions

Specific requirements of this web case can be found on the Kimmel website.

Critical Thinking

COLLABORATIVE LEARNING ACTIVITY

BYP14-9 You are a loan officer for the bank in Hamilton, Ontario. Ted Worth, president of T. Worth Corporation, has just left your office. He is interested in an eight-year loan to expand the company's operations. The borrowed funds would be used to purchase new equipment. As evidence of the company's credit-worthiness, Worth provided you with the following facts:

	2001	2000
Current ratio	3.1	2.1
Acid-test ratio	0.8	1.4
Asset turnover ratio	2.8	2.2
Cash total debt coverage ratio	0.1	0.2
Net earnings	Up 32%	Down 8%
Earnings per share	$3.30	$2.50

Ted Worth is a very insistent (some would say pushy) man. When you told him that you would need additional information before making your decision, he acted offended, and said, "What more could you possibly want to know?" You responded that, at a minimum, you would need complete, audited financial statements.

Instructions

(a) Explain why you would want the financial statements to be audited.
(b) Discuss the implications of the ratios provided for the lending decision you are to make. That is, does the information paint a favourable picture? Are these ratios relevant to the decision?
(c) List three other ratios that you would want to calculate for this company, and explain why you would use each.
(d) What are the limitations of ratio analysis for credit and investing decisions?

COMMUNICATION ACTIVITY

BYP14-10 L.R. Stanton is the chief executive officer of Hi-Tech Electronics. Stanton is an expert engineer but a novice in accounting. Stanton asks you, as an accounting major, to explain (a) the bases for comparison in analysing Hi-Tech's financial statements and (b) the limitations, if any, of financial statement analysis.

Instructions

Write a memo to L.R. Stanton that explains the bases for comparison and the limitations of financial statement analysis.

ETHICS CASE

BYP14-11 Vern Fairly, president of Fairly Industries, wishes to issue a press release to bolster his company's image and maybe even its share price, which has been gradually falling. As controller, you have been asked to provide a list of 20 financial ratios along with some other operating statistics relative to Fairly Industries' first-quarter financials and operations.

Two days after you provide the ratios and data requested, you are asked by Roberta Saint-Onge, the public relations director of Fairly, to prove the accuracy of the financial and operating data contained in the press release written by the president and edited by Roberta. In the news release, the president highlights the sales increase of 25% over last year's first quarter and the positive change in the current ratio from 1.5:1 last year to 3:1 this year. He also emphasizes that production was up 50% over the prior year's first quarter. You note that the release contains only positive or improved ratios and none of the negative or deteriorated ratios. For instance, is there no mention of the fact that the debt to total assets ratio has increased from 35% to 55%, that inventories are up 89%, and that although the current ratio improved, the acid-test ratio fell from 1:1 to 0.5:1. Nor is there any mention that the reported profit for the quarter would have been a loss had the estimated lives of Fairly's plant and machinery not been increased by 30%. Roberta emphasized, "The Prez wants this release by early this afternoon."

Instructions

(a) Who are the stakeholders in this situation?
(b) Is there anything unethical in president Fairly's actions?
(c) Should you as controller remain silent? Does Roberta have any responsibility?

Answers to Self-Study Questions

1. d 2. d 3. b 4. d 5. c 6. a 7. c 8. d 9. c
10. b 11. a 12. a

Answer to Loblaw Review It Question 4

Loblaw did not report any discontinued or extraordinary items on its statement of earnings in 1999. Nor did it report any changes in accounting principle on its 1999 statement of retained earnings.

APPENDIX A

Specimen Financial Statements: Loblaw Companies Limited

On the World Wide Web
Loblaw Companies Limited
http://www.loblaw.com

The Annual Report

Once each year, public corporations issue an **annual report.** This report communicates financial information to shareholders and other interested parties. It summarizes the company's operating results and financial position in audited financial statements and other supplementary information.

Most annual reports are attractive, effectively designed communication vehicles. They not only give readers financial information, but also more qualitative information such as the company's strategic vision, its goals and objectives, and its plans for the future. Annual reports also usually include information about how the company is governed and its assumed social responsibilities, and details about its products, people, and geographic areas of operation. While qualitative information provides a useful context for the understanding and interpretation of the financial information, the basic function of every annual report is to report financial information.

The following items are traditionally included in corporate annual reports:

Financial Highlights
Report to Shareholders
Management Discussion and Analysis
Financial Statement Package
- Management's Statement of Responsibility
- Auditors' Report
- Financial Statements
  - Statements of Earnings
  - Statements of Retained Earnings
  - Balance Sheets
  - Statements of Cash Flows
  - Notes to the Financial Statements

Supplementary Financial Information
- Eleven-Year Summary

In this appendix, we illustrate current financial reporting with a comprehensive set of corporate financial statements. These statements have been prepared in accordance with generally accepted accounting principles and audited by an independent chartered accounting firm. We are grateful for permission to use the actual financial statements and other accompanying financial information from the annual report of Canada's largest food distributor, Loblaw Companies Limited.

Let's turn now to selected excerpts from the Loblaw Companies Limited 1999 annual report.

Financial Highlights

The financial highlights section is usually presented inside the front cover or on the first page of the annual report. This section generally reports the total or per share amounts for selected financial items of the current year and one or more previous years. Financial items typically presented include sales, operating income, net earnings (or loss), cash flows from operating activities, capital investment, earnings (or loss) per share, the dividend rate, and the market value of the company's shares at the end of the year. The financial highlights section from Loblaw's 1999 annual report is shown on the following page:

Financial Highlights

52 Weeks Ended January 1, 2000
($ millions)

		1999	*1998*
Sales and Earnings	Sales	**18,783**	12,497
	Trading profit (EBITDA)	**1,084**	712
	Operating income	**811**	529
	Interest expense	**112**	68
	Net earnings	**376**	261
Cash Flow	Cash flows from operating activities before acquisition restructuring and other charges	**791**	530
	Capital investment	**802**	599
Per Common Share ($)	Earnings before goodwill charges	**1.52**	1.06
	Net earnings	**1.37**	1.06
	Cash flows from operating activities before acquisition restructuring and other charges	**2.88**	2.15
	Dividend rate (period end)	**.24**	.20
	Book value	**10.56**	9.46
	Market value (period end)	**35.25**	37.40
Financial Ratios	Returns on sales		
	Trading profit (EBITDA)	**5.8%**	5.7%
	Operating income	**4.3%**	4.2%
	Net earnings	**2.0%**	2.1%
	Return on average total assets (1)	**11.9%**	10.9%
	Return on average common shareholders' equity (1)	**13.7%**	12.8%
	Interest coverage on total debt (2)	**7.2:1**	7.8:1
	Total debt (2) to shareholders' equity (1)	**.69:1**	.71:1

(1) Ratios are computed as follows:
Return on average total assets – operating income divided by average total assets excluding cash and short term investments.
Return on average common shareholders' equity – net earnings before extraordinary items less preferred dividends divided by average common shareholders' equity.
Total debt to shareholders' equity – total debt divided by total shareholders' equity.
(2) Total debt is defined as total debt less cash and short term investments.
(3) Certain prior period's information was reclassified to conform with the current period's presentation.

Net Earnings, Earnings before Goodwill Charges and Dividend Rate per Common Share
($)

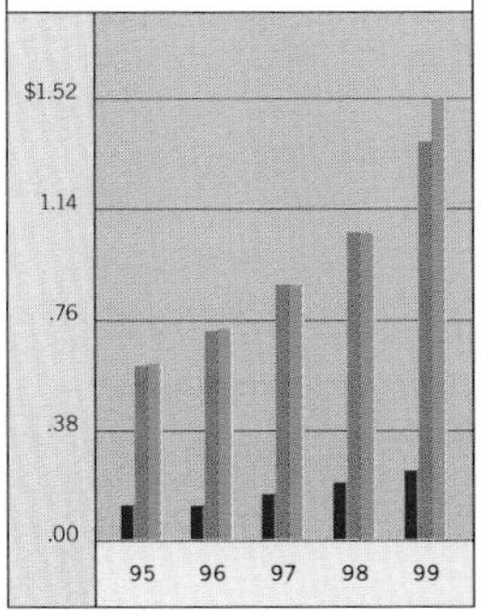

Dividend Rate per Common Share (period end)
Net Earnings per Common Share
Earnings before Goodwill Charges per Common Share

Return on Average Common Shareholders' Equity

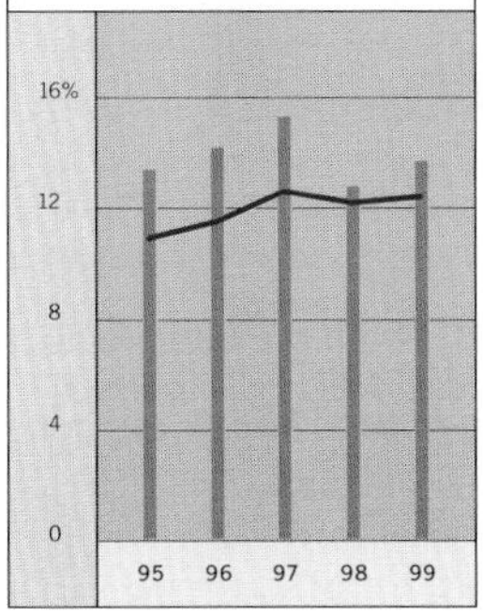

Return on Average Common Shareholders' Equity
Five Year Average Return

Total Return on $100 Investment
(includes dividend reinvestment)
($)

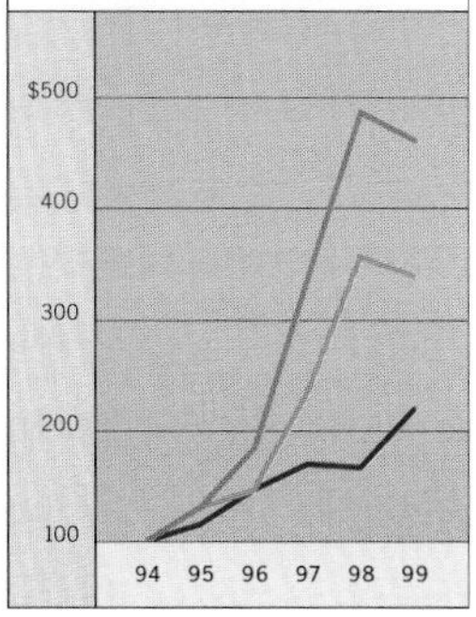

Loblaw Companies Limited
TSE Food Stores Index
TSE 300 Index

Report to Shareholders

Report to Shareholders

Nearly every annual report contains a report or letter to the shareholders from the Chair of the Board of Directors (also called the Chief Executive Officer), or the President (also called the Chief Operating Officer), or both. This letter typically discusses the company's accomplishments during the past year and highlights significant events such as acquisitions, new products, operating achievements, business philosophy, changes in officers or directors, financing commitments, expansion plans, and future prospects. The report to the shareholders of Loblaw Companies Limited, signed by Galen Weston, Chair, and Richard Currie, President, is shown below:

1999 was a fitting end to the most commercially successful decade in this Company's history.

W. GALEN WESTON
Chairman

RICHARD J. CURRIE
President

The year 1999 was a particularly strong one in every respect for Loblaw Companies. In other writings, we have referred to it as a "spectacular" year, which we believe does not overstate either the results or the accomplishments. It was a fitting end to the most commercially successful decade in this Company's history.

Sales increased by $6.3 billion or 50% to $18.8 billion. The late 1998 acquisitions of Provigo, with its leading market share in Quebec, and Agora Foods which, by year end earned us the leading market share in Atlantic Canada, added $5.1 billion of the increase. Equally important was the existing base business sales increase of $1.2 billion or 10% in 1999. In the first year of this decade, Loblaw's Canadian sales were $7.1 billion. We ended the decade almost 3 times larger than we started, which represents average annual growth of 11% for the past 10 years. All regions of business continue to enjoy healthy growth from a combination of new store activity and an average 4% same-store sales growth in 1999. With food inflation running less than 2%, our real growth has been considerable.

Operating income reached an all-time high of $811 million in 1999, a $282 million or 53% improvement over the $529 million earned last year. Return on sales improved to 4.3% from 4.2% in 1998. Provigo and Agora contributed solidly during their first full year as part of Loblaw Companies. Some redefining

Earnings per common share have now increased an average of 25% per year over the past 7 years.

and restructuring of those operations occurred in 1999, providing the synergy benefits that we anticipated in the first year. The amount of effort to merge these businesses into the Loblaw operations in 1999 was enormous. For it to be done while maintaining a very strong earnings growth rate in Loblaw was very rewarding.

Loblaw started the 90s with Canadian operating income of $184 million, yielding a 2.6% return on sales. So, while sales increased strongly over the period, earnings improved at almost twice that rate, with average annual growth of about 18% for the past 10 years resulting in the 1999 return on sales of 4.3%.

Earnings per common share for 1999 increased 29% to $1.37 from last year's $1.06 and have now increased an average of 18% each year for the past 10 years and 25% per year over the past 7 years. The price of a Loblaw common share sextupled over the decade.

The fundamental operating principle of Loblaw Companies is to concentrate on food retailing while providing our customers in each community with the best in one-stop shopping for everyday household needs. Our new stores reflect that principle with new departments, new services and new shopping excitement as Loblaw strives to be a small but regular part of Canadian life every day. Whether the day involves shopping for groceries, dropping off the dry cleaning or film, buying clothes for the kids, checking out the latest in natural vitamins and health foods while waiting for the pharmacist to fill your prescription or just picking up tonight's already prepared hot dinner, Loblaw wants to be there.

No longer just a grocery store, Loblaw, through its many regional banners and formats, now offers a truly unique, enjoyable and convenient shopping experience.

No longer just a grocery store, Loblaw, through its many regional banners and formats, now offers a truly unique, enjoyable and convenient shopping experience under one roof. In support of this strategy in 1999, over $800 million was invested in new stores, new departments and to revitalize and standardize information systems. The capital investment program will continue its relentless pace in 2000.

Our private brands provide a unique opportunity for our customers. *no name* started a revolution in the 70s with good quality, value products that provide a lower cost alternative to the national brands. *President's Choice* has come to stand for unique or premium quality products with exceptional value and is one of the most recognized and trusted names in Canada according to recent surveys. Following our fundamental operating principle, we have taken the strength of the *President's Choice* name and extended our offering into financial services. *President's Choice Financial* services offer the convenience of regular banking services through the Internet, the telephone and conveniently located automated banking machines and kiosks in our stores. *President's Choice Financial* services feature high interest rate bank accounts, no fee banking, low interest rate loans, mortgages and debit cards. Each financial product also offers *PC* points that are redeemable for free groceries and other store products. We are now in a successful test mode of a credit card offering. There is enormous untapped value in the *President's Choice* brand and we will continue to explore opportunities for extending this brand to provide our customers with new and valued products and services to be even more a part of Canadian life every day.

The outlook for Loblaw Companies in 2000 and beyond is very positive. It has the number one market share position in Canada by a wide margin and it possesses strong operating momentum, driven by a seasoned, skilled and relatively young management team. The Company is proud of the contribution it has made and continues to make to the Canadian economy, particularly in supporting small Canadian businesses and being a responsible employer of over 108,000 Canadians. We continue to enjoy good relationships with our 85,000 unionized employees and value our coordinated efforts to find ways to balance the needs of the business with those of our employees. Loblaw Companies in the past decade has created more unionized jobs than any Canadian company or any company operating in Canada. But non-traditional, non-unionized competitors, as they increasingly move into food retailing, continue to be a threat to this Company and its employees. In our important year 2000 union negotiations, we will be looking for creative ways to continue to provide job growth for Canadians and job security for our employees.

The outlook for 2000 and beyond is very positive – Loblaw has the number one market share position in Canada and it possesses strong operating momentum.

Last year's Annual Report stated that 1998 had been an "exceptional" year and the year 1999 earlier in this Report was called a "spectacular" year. These are not idle adjectives. The energy expended and the quality of work produced by your management and employees on behalf of shareholders in 1999 was truly remarkable. They have our gratitude and respect.

W. Galen Weston (signed)
Chairman

Richard J. Currie (signed)
President

MANAGEMENT DISCUSSION AND ANALYSIS

Management Discussion and Analysis

In this portion of the annual report, management analyses the operating results presented in the financial statements. In addition, they usually shed light on their competition, market position, and market share. The majority of the annual report is based on historical information, which is often dated by the time the reader receives it. This section attempts to be more forward-looking—including a management discussion about the future directions and prospects of the company. Ideally, management's comments should be expressed in a frank and forthright manner with no subterfuge or bias.

Net earnings per share rose to $1.37 in 1999, a 29% increase over 1998.

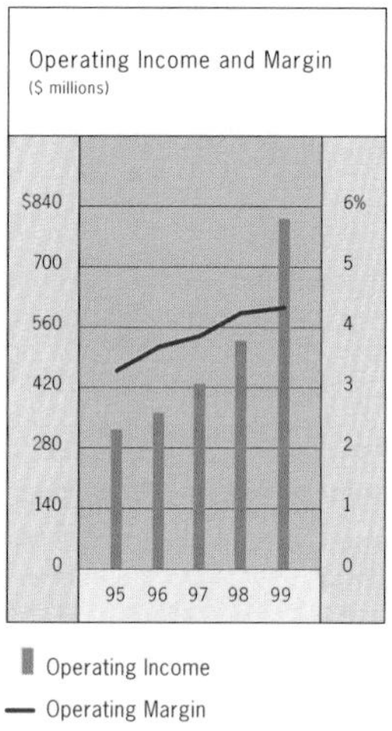

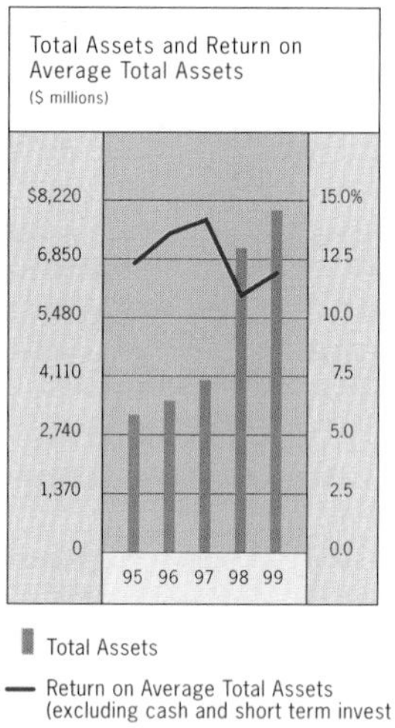

Highlights

- 29% increase in net earnings per common share to $1.37 from last year's $1.06.
- 43% increase in earnings before goodwill charges per common share to $1.52 from last year's $1.06.
- 50% sales growth to $18.8 billion – 10% sales growth in the base business and 40% growth attributable to the 1998 Provigo and Agora fourth quarter acquisitions.
- Operating margin improved to 4.3% from 4.2% in 1998.
- Capital investment program of $802 million compared to $599 million in 1998.
- Cash flows from operating activities before acquisition restructuring and other charges increased to $791 million from $530 million in 1998.
- .69:1 debt/equity ratio compared to .71:1 in 1998.
- 56 new corporate and franchised stores opened adding approximately 1 million square feet of selling space, net of closures.
- 154 President's Choice Financial services pavilions opened and 233 automated banking machines installed by the end of 1999.

Net earnings per common share improved 29% to $1.37 from the $1.06 earned in 1998. Earnings before goodwill charges per common share increased 43% to $1.52 from the $1.06 earned in 1998. Sales increased 50% or $6.3 billion over last year to $18.8 billion. The base Loblaw business grew by 10% with an additional 40% growth attributable to the fourth quarter 1998 Provigo and Agora acquisitions.

Operating income improved to $811 million, a 53% increase over the $529 million earned in 1998. The operating margin (operating income divided by sales) improved to 4.3% from 4.2% in 1998 and the trading margin (EBITDA divided by sales) strengthened to 5.8% from 5.7% in 1998. This represents the seventh consecutive year of improved returns on sales.

Interest expense increased 65% to $112 million from $68 million in 1998. The increase resulted from higher net average borrowing levels due to the full year impact of the 1998 acquisitions, together with a capital investment program of $802 million, partially offset by the effect of interest income in connection with an income tax refund.

The effective income tax rate decreased to 42.7% (40.1% excluding the impact of non-deductible goodwill charges) from 43.1% in 1998.

Results of Operations

Sales

Sales of the base business in 1999 grew by 10% and the acquisitions contributed an additional 40% increase in sales. The sales growth is attributable to same-store sales growth of over 4% and the results of increased average store square footage from new stores opened as part of the capital investment program. In both 1999 and 1998, price inflation was not a significant factor in the sales growth.

During the third quarter of 1999, the Company completed the sale of 44 stores, principally Loeb in Ontario, as part of the Provigo transaction. The applicable 1999 and 1998 sales and earnings from these stores were excluded from the Company's reported results. The remaining Ontario stores acquired in the Provigo acquisition were converted to existing Loblaw banners and programs during the year.

Operating Results

($ millions)	1999	Change	1998
Sales	**$18,783**	50%	$12,497
Operating income	**$ 811**	53%	$ 529
Operating margin	**4.3%**		4.2%
Trading profit (EBITDA)	**$ 1,084**	52%	$ 712
Trading margin	**5.8%**		5.7%

Several of our President's Choice products are fine examples of Old World tradition, offering homestyle flavour and old-fashioned value with New World convenience.

The 1999 corporate and franchised store capital investment program increased the weighted average net square footage by 5% compared to a net 10% increase in the base business weighted average square footage in 1998. The weighted average square footage change in corporate and franchised stores includes the impact of store openings and closures throughout the year.

Over the past three years, the Company's $1.9 billion capital investment program significantly expanded the store network and strengthened the existing store base through renovation, expansion and/or replacement. Some of these new, larger stores were replacements for older, smaller, less efficient stores that did not offer the broad range of products and services that today's shopper demands. During 1999, 56 (1998 – 65) new corporate and franchised stores were opened and 96 (1998 – 38) underwent major renovation or minor expansion. New stores include major expansions to existing locations, which is consistent with the definition used by the Food Marketing Institute. In 1999, the average store size increased 8% to 41,900 square feet for corporate stores and 15% to 22,100 square feet for franchised stores, many of which are located in smaller cities and towns in rural areas. The store investment activity benefited all banners to varying degrees.

In 2000, the Company plans to open, expand or remodel over 100 corporate and franchised stores throughout Canada with a similar geographic investment pattern to that of the last several years with the exception of increased investment in Quebec. This will result in an expected net increase of 3 million square feet or an 8% net increase, which is expected to generate additional sales growth.

Operating Income

Operating income grew by $282 million or 53% to $811 million in 1999 following a 24% increase in 1998. Operating margin improved to 4.3% from 4.2% in 1998, while trading margin increased to 5.8% from 5.7% in 1998. The positive impact on operating margins resulted from continued focus on cost control, rationalization and centralization of similar functions, the integration of Provigo and Agora and from higher volumes leveraging off fixed costs. Gross margins (cost of sales divided by sales) improved slightly from a combination of reduced product costs and improved product mix by selling a different mix of products with a proportionately higher

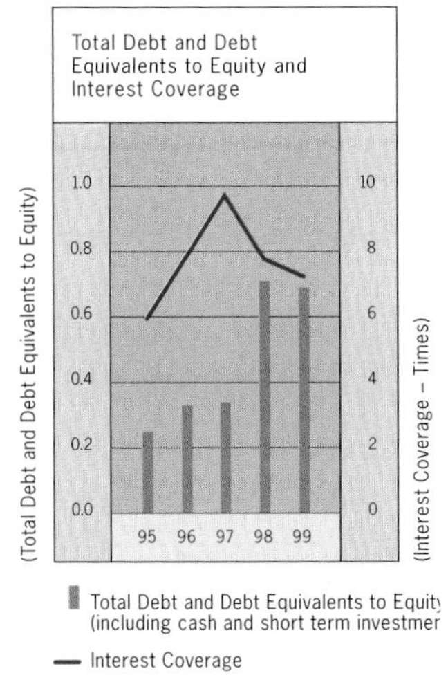

margin than in prior years even though some individual product margins may have actually decreased compared to last year.

During the second quarter of 1999, the Company completed the Provigo valuation analysis and recorded the purchase equation, including goodwill of $1.6 billion upon acquisition. The resultant statement of earnings impact of all components of the purchase equation was recorded retroactively to the beginning of the year.

In 2000, operating income growth is expected to be similar to that achieved over the past several years excluding the impact of Provigo and Agora 1999 results. Growth will be supported by the maturing of stores opened during the past couple of years, the integration and development of the Provigo and Agora businesses and the significant capital investment program in stores and support services.

Interest and Income Taxes

Interest expense increased $44 million or 65% in 1999 following a $24 million increase in 1998. The increase resulted primarily from an increase in average net borrowing levels, which was due to the full year impact of the 1998 fourth quarter acquisitions of Provigo and Agora, together with a capital investment program of $802 million, partially offset by the positive effect of interest income in connection with an income tax refund. The positive impact of interest rate derivatives, as discussed in Note 9 to the financial statements, was offset in 1999 by the negative impact of currency derivatives. In 2000, total interest expense is expected to increase as a result of higher borrowing levels and the 1999 inclusion of interest income in connection with an income tax refund. Capital investment should be funded, for the most part, from cash flows from operating activities in 2000.

The effective income tax rate decreased in 1999 to 42.7% (40.1% excluding the impact of non-deductible goodwill charges) compared to 43.1% in 1998. The decrease was a result of higher Quebec income taxed at a lower effective rate and higher non-taxable amounts offset by non-deductible goodwill charges. In 2000, the tax rate is expected to be similar to 1999.

Capital Resources and Liquidity

The Company maintained a sound financial position in 1999 and this position is expected to continue in 2000. The total debt to equity ratio, including cash and short term investments, improved to .69:1 in 1999 from .71:1 in 1998. The improvement in the ratio was a result of the increase in shareholders' equity from net earnings retained in the business being in excess of the increase in the Company's debt level. For the eleventh consecutive year, the ratio remains well within the Company's internal guideline of a less than 1:1 ratio.

The 2000 ratio is expected to be relatively consistent with 1999 as the one-time charges to retained earnings as the Company implements the new Canadian Institute of Chartered Accountants (CICA) accounting requirements for the measurement of employee future benefits (including pension and other retirement and post-employment benefits) and future income taxes will be offset by net earnings retained in the business. During the first quarter of 2000, the expected decrease to retained earnings (net of income tax) is approximately $130 million and $19 million related to the change in measurement of employee future benefits and future income taxes respectively.

The 1999 interest coverage declined to 7.2 times from 7.8 times in 1998, which reflects the full year interest impact from higher debt levels as a result of the 1998 fourth quarter acquisitions of Provigo and Agora.

The 1999 capital investment program reached a record high of $802 million. This was a $203 million increase over 1998 reflecting the Company's ongoing commitment to invest in growth across Canada including new stores, expansions and significant remodeling and refurbishing. At year end 1999, projects-in-progress, which the Company has effectively committed to complete, total approximately $115 million of the 2000 estimated capital investment of $900 million.

Cash flows from operating activities before acquisition restructuring and other charges increased to $791 million from $530 million in 1998 mainly reflecting improved operating income.

Short term liquidity is provided by a combination of internally generated cash flow, net cash, short term investments and access to the commercial paper market. During the first quarter of 1999, the Company increased its commercial paper program from $500 million to $800 million. This program continues to be rated A-1 and R-1 (low) by the Canadian Bond Rating Service (CBRS) and the Dominion Bond Rating Service (DBRS) respectively. The Company's commercial paper program is supported

Major Cash Flow Components

($ millions)	1999	Change	1998
Capital investment	**$ 802**	34%	$ 599
Business acquisitions	**$ 14**		$ 941
Business disposition	**$ 161**		
Cash flows from operating activities before acquisition restructuring and other charges	**$ 791**	49%	$ 530
Cash flows (used in) from financing activities	**$ (70)**		$ 775

by lines of credit extended by several banks totaling $920 million. Commercial paper is used primarily for short term financing requirements.

Longer term capital resources are provided by direct access to capital markets. The Company's and Provigo Inc.'s debentures and notes are rated A (High) by CBRS and A (high) by DBRS. The Company accesses longer term capital markets through its Medium Term Note (MTN) program. The Company files an MTN shelf prospectus to issue, over a 2 year term, up to a specified principal amount of unsecured debt obligations with maturities of not less than one year. During the first quarter of 1998, the Company filed a shelf prospectus to issue up to $500 million of MTN. In 1998, the Company issued $200 million of MTN and during the first quarter of 1999, the Company issued the remaining $300 million of MTN related to the 1998 shelf prospectus. In the first quarter of 1999, the Company filed another shelf prospectus to issue up to $500 million of MTN. During the first quarter of 1999, the Company issued $300 million of MTN related to the 1999 shelf prospectus. The proceeds from the $600 million of MTN issued in the first quarter of 1999 were used to repay $472 million of the $771 million unsecured credit facility used in the acquisition of Provigo. The issue of $600 million of MTN improved the Company's 1999 working capital position. During the first quarter of 2000, the Company issued the remaining $200 million of MTN related to the 1999 shelf prospectus.

Our first dry cleaner opened in 1994 in Toronto. Since that time, this unique, convenient service has been added to over 70 locations across Canada.

During the first quarter of 2000, the Company announced its intention to redeem its $100 million 5.39% Notes in accordance with their terms. In addition, during the second quarter of 2000, the Company plans to file a shelf prospectus to issue up to $1.0 billion of MTN. This prospectus will cover the Company's funding and refinancing needs for a 2 year period from the filing date.

In 1998, the $75 million Series 6, 9.75% debentures and the $16 million First Preferred Shares, Second Series debt equivalents were redeemed according to their terms.

Financial instruments are used to manage the effective interest rate on total debt including underlying commercial paper and short term investments. The Company maintains treasury centres, which operate under Company approved policies and guidelines covering funding, investing, foreign exchange and interest rate management.

The Company expects to meet its 2000 cash requirements through a combination of internally generated funds, its $800 million commercial paper program and by drawing on the available MTN facility.

President's Choice GREEN paper towels and GREEN bathroom tissue, made from 100% recycled paper with a minimum of 100% post-consumer waste, are just two of our successful environment-friendly products.

The 1999 year end weighted average interest rate on fixed rate long term debt (excluding capital lease obligations included in other long term debt) was 7.7% as compared to 8.4% last year. The MTN issues in 1998 and 1999 reduced the 1999 weighted average interest rate. The weighted average term to maturity, measured both on the basis of maturity date and on the earlier of maturity or first retraction date, was 20 years for each at the end of 1999 compared to 19 years for each at the end of 1998. The increase in the term to maturity was due to the longer term MTN issued in 1998 and 1999.

Common shareholders' equity reached $2.9 billion in 1999, an increase of $309 million over 1998 mainly from $292 million of the current year's net earnings retained in the business. During 1999, the Company purchased 630,200 of its common shares for $22 million pursuant to Normal Course Issuer Bids. The Company's dividend policy is to declare dividends equal to approximately 20 to 25% of the prior year's normalized net earnings per common share giving consideration to the year end cash position, future cash flow requirements and investment opportunities.

Subsequent to period end, the Company announced that it amended its Normal Course Issuer Bid (NCIB) currently in place and set to expire on March 21, 2000 to allow the Company to enter into equity derivatives including forward contracts with respect to its common shares under the NCIB. In addition, the Company intends to renew its NCIB to purchase on The Toronto Stock Exchange or enter into equity derivatives including forward contracts to purchase up to 5% of its common shares outstanding. The Company, in accordance with the rules and by-laws of The Toronto Stock Exchange, may purchase its shares at the then market prices of such common shares.

Accounting Policy Changes Subsequent to 1999

The CICA has issued two accounting standards, Section 3465 "Income Taxes" and Section 3461 "Employee Future Benefits", effective for fiscal years beginning on or after January 1, 2000.

Section 3465 will change the Company's method of accounting for income taxes from the deferred method to the asset and liability method. Under the asset and liability method, future income taxes are recognized for the temporary differences between the tax and accounting bases of the Company's assets and liabilities based on income tax rates and income tax laws that are expected to apply in the periods in

Full service floral departments are now standard attractions in our new large stores after their impressive debut in 1984. Our seasonal garden centres lead the industry with innovative products.

which the differences are expected to affect income. Adoption of this new standard is not expected to have a material effect on the Company's financial statements.

Section 3461 requires employee future benefits, including pension and other retirement and post-employment benefits, to be measured using market interest rates on high quality debt instruments instead of management's best estimate of the effect of future events. As employee future benefits include other retirement and post-employment benefits, the Company must change the method of accounting for these benefits from the cash basis to the accrual basis as described above. The annual benefit expense will depend on a number of variables that are market driven and outside the control of the Company. These variables include future medical inflation rates, health care cost trend rates, benefit plan changes and interest rates.

The Company intends to adopt both standards retroactively without restatement of prior periods. Therefore, in the first quarter of fiscal 2000, the cumulative effect of initial adoption will be reported as a decrease to retained earnings of approximately $19 million and $130 million (net of income tax of $100 million) for Sections 3465 and 3461 respectively.

Risk and Risk Management

The Company successfully competes in the Canadian food distribution industry. Its operating philosophy is indicative of its long term objectives of security and growth. The Company employs various strategies, which may carry some short term risk, in order to achieve these objectives and to minimize the impact of perceived threats related to competitive erosion and loss of cost advantage.

Strategies employed by the Company include the utilization and refinement of a variety of store formats, banners and sizes in order to appeal to the changing demographics of various markets. By developing and operating new departments and services that complement the traditional supermarket, the Company competes effectively and efficiently in an evolving market where non-traditional food retailers continue to increase their offering of products typically associated with supermarkets. The Company follows a strategy of enhancing profitability on a market-by-market basis by selecting a store format, size and banner that is the best fit for each market. By operating across Canada through corporate, franchised and associated stores and by servicing independent accounts, the Company strategically minimizes and balances its exposure to regional and industry economic risk.

The Company maintains a significant portfolio of owned sites and, whenever practical, follows the strategy of purchasing sites for future store locations. This enhances the Company's operating flexibility and also allows it to benefit from any long term property value appreciation. A significant competitive advantage the Company has developed is its powerful controlled label products such as *President's Choice*, *no name*, *Club Pack*, *GREEN*, *TOO GOOD TO BE TRUE* and *EXACT*, which enhance customer loyalty by providing overall superior value and provide some protection against national brand pricing strategies.

Corporate Stores
Owned vs. Leased
(thousands of sq. ft.)

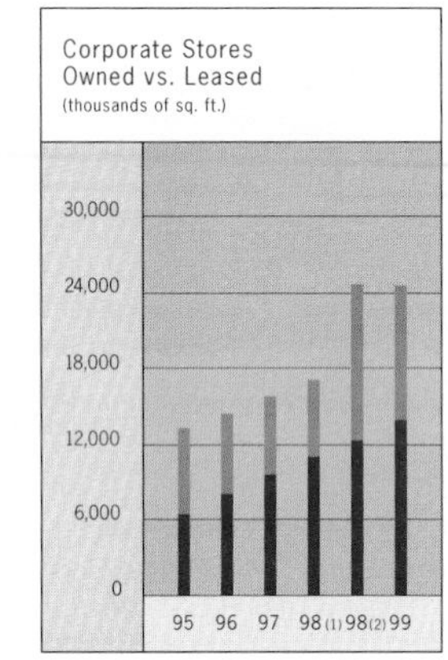

■ Owned ■ Leased

(1) Excluding acquisitions
(2) Including acquisitions, excluding 1999 dis

The Company will enter new markets and will review acquisitions when the opportunities arise. Such was the case in late 1998 with the Provigo and Agora acquisitions. The Company will also exit a particular market and reallocate assets elsewhere when there is a strategic advantage to do so. The success of these strategies depends to a large extent on the financial strength of the Company and the strategic deployment of the Company's financial resources. The Company maintains a strong balance sheet in order to minimize its vulnerability to short term earnings pressure and to provide a stable base for long term growth.

Low cost, non-union competitors are a threat to the Company's cost structure. The Company is willing to accept the short term costs of labour disruption in order to achieve competitive labour costs for the longer term, which helps to ensure long term sustainable sales and earnings growth. In 2000, 57 labour agreements affecting approximately 34,000 employees will be negotiated with the single largest agreement covering approximately 15,000 employees. Management's objective is to continue to negotiate longer term contracts to provide a more stable labour environment. The Company has good relations with its employees and unions and, although possible, no labour disruption is anticipated.

Since opening our first KIDZ KLŌZ department in 1995, we have grown to over 74 locations. Quality children's clothing provides excellent value in support of a convenient one-stop shop for everyday household needs.

The Company self-insures its own risks to an appropriate level and limits its exposure through the purchase of excess insurance from financially stable insurance companies. The Company has comprehensive loss prevention programs in place and actively manages its claims handling and litigation processes to reduce the risk it retains.

The Company endeavours to be a socially and environmentally responsible company and recognizes that the competitive pressures for economic growth and cost efficiency must be integrated with environmental stewardship and ecological considerations. Environmental committees throughout the Company meet regularly to monitor and enforce the maintenance of responsible business operations. This includes conducting environmental audits of warehouses, stores, equipment and gas stations and implementing packaging, waste reduction and recycling programs.

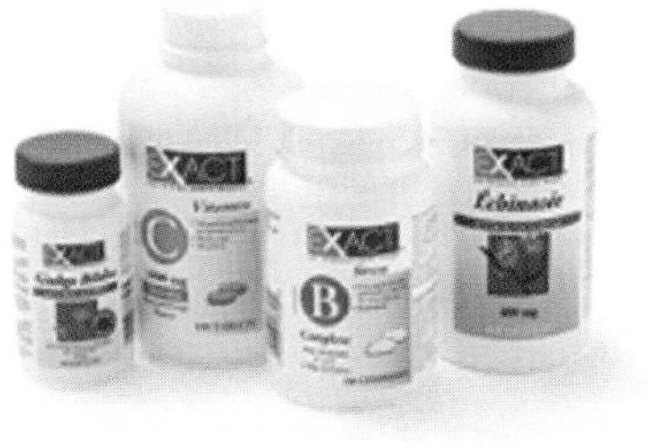

Our 269 in-store pharmacies are the smart alternative to the traditional drug store for health and beauty care needs. Our EXACT vitamins and herbal-based products provide exceptional value at a reasonable price.

Year 2000

The Company has been addressing the year 2000 challenge for several years. Systems development to modernize and enhance systems is an ongoing investment process in the Company. This development investment had the added benefit, in many instances, of ensuring year 2000 compliance. In 1999, the Company completed and tested its systems modifications and replacements ensuring its readiness for the year 2000.

As the change in date has occurred, the Company believes that it adequately addressed the risks posed by the year 2000 issue and as a result the year 2000 issue has had no material or adverse effect on operations, earnings and financial condition.

Outlook

Continued capital investment in stores and support services as well as the potential to leverage our product reputation and capabilities into other retail fields makes us optimistic that the year 2000 and future sales and earnings growth rates will be similar to those achieved over the past decade while maintaining a strong balance sheet and substantial cash flow.

Financial Statement Package

MANAGEMENT'S STATEMENT OF RESPONSIBILITY

An important element in corporate annual reports is a statement made by management about its role in, and responsibility for, the accuracy and integrity of the financial statements. In Loblaw's "Management's Statement of Responsibility," the President, Executive Vice President, and Senior Vice President and Controller, on behalf of management, do the following: (1) assume primary responsibility for the financial statements and the related notes, (2) outline and assess the company's internal control system, (3) declare that the financial statements have been prepared in conformity with generally accepted accounting principles, and (4) comment on the audit and the composition and role of the Audit Committee of the Board of Directors. Loblaw's management statement is presented below:

Management's Statement of Responsibility

Management is responsible for the preparation and presentation of the consolidated financial statements and all other information in the Annual Report. This responsibility includes the selection and consistent application of appropriate accounting principles and methods in addition to making the judgements and estimates necessary to prepare the consolidated financial statements in accordance with Canadian generally accepted accounting principles. It also includes ensuring that the other financial information presented elsewhere in the Annual Report is consistent with the consolidated financial statements.

To provide reasonable assurance that assets are safeguarded and that relevant and reliable financial information is being produced, management maintains a system of internal controls. Internal auditors, who are employees of the Company, review and evaluate internal controls on management's behalf, coordinating this work with the independent auditor. The consolidated financial statements have been audited by the independent auditor, KPMG llp , whose report follows.

The Board of Directors, acting through an Audit Committee which is comprised solely of directors who are not employees of the Company, is responsible for determining that management fulfills its responsibilities in the preparation of the consolidated financial statements and the financial control of operations. The Audit Committee recommends the independent auditor for appointment by the shareholders. It meets regularly with financial management, internal auditors and the independent auditor to discuss internal controls, auditing matters and financial reporting issues. The independent auditor and internal auditors have unrestricted access to the Audit Committee. The Audit Committee reviews the consolidated financial statements and the Management Discussion and Analysis prior to the Board of Directors approving them for inclusion in the Annual Report.

Richard J. Currie (signed)
President

Donald G. Reid (signed)
Executive Vice President

Stephen A. Smith (signed)
Senior Vice President, Controller

Toronto, Canada March 3, 2000

AUDITORS' REPORT

All publicly held corporations, as well as many other enterprises and organizations (both profit and not-for-profit, large and small), engage the services of independent professional accountants for the purpose of obtaining an objective, expert report on their financial statements. Based on a comprehensive examination of the company's accounting system, records, and financial statements, the external auditors issue the auditors' report.

The standard auditors' report consists of three paragraphs: (1) an introductory paragraph, (2) a scope paragraph, and (3) the opinion paragraph. In the **introductory paragraph**, the auditors identify who and what was audited and indicate the responsibilities of management and the auditors relative to the financial statements. In the **scope paragraph**, the auditors state that the audit was conducted in accordance with generally accepted auditing standards and discuss the nature and limitations of the audit. In the **opinion paragraph**, the auditors express an informed opinion as to (1) the fairness of the financial statements and (2) their conformity with generally accepted accounting principles. The auditors' report of KPMG, Chartered Accountants, addressed to the shareholders of Loblaw Companies Limited, is shown below:

Auditor's Report

To the Shareholders of Loblaw Companies Limited:

We have audited the consolidated balance sheets of Loblaw Companies Limited as at January 1, 2000 and January 2, 1999 and the consolidated statements of earnings, retained earnings and cash flow for the 52 week periods then ended. These consolidated financial statements are the responsibility of the Company's management. Our responsibility is to express an opinion on these consolidated financial statements based on our audits.

We conducted our audits in accordance with Canadian generally accepted auditing standards. Those standards require that we plan and perform an audit to obtain reasonable assurance whether the consolidated financial statements are free of material misstatement. An audit includes examining, on a test basis, evidence supporting the amounts and disclosures in the consolidated financial statements. An audit also includes assessing the accounting principles used and significant estimates made by management, as well as evaluating the overall consolidated financial statement presentation.

In our opinion, these consolidated financial statements present fairly, in all material respects, the financial position of the Company as at January 1, 2000 and January 2, 1999 and the results of its operations and its cash flow for the periods then ended in accordance with Canadian generally accepted accounting principles.

KPMG (signed)
Chartered Accountants

Toronto, Canada March 3, 2000

The auditors' report issued on Loblaw's financial statements is **unqualified** or **clean**—that is, it contains no qualifications or exceptions. In other words, the auditors conformed completely with generally accepted auditing standards in performing the audit, and the financial statements conformed in all material respects with generally accepted accounting principles.

When the financial statements do not conform with generally accepted accounting principles or the scope of the audit has been restricted, the auditors must issue a **qualified** opinion and describe the exception. If the lack of conformity with GAAP is sufficiently material, the auditors are compelled to issue an **adverse** opinion or denial. An adverse opinion means that the financial statements do not fairly present the company's financial condition and/or the results of the company's operations at the dates and for the periods reported.

Companies strive to obtain an unqualified auditors' report. Hence, rarely are you likely to encounter anything other than this type of opinion on the financial statements.

MANAGEMENT'S STATEMENT OF RESPONSIBILITY

The standard set of financial statements consists of: (1) a comparative balance sheet for two years, (2) a comparative statement of earnings for two years, (3) a comparative statement of retained earnings (sometimes combined with the statement of earnings) for two years, (4) a comparative statement of cash flow for two years, and (5) a set of accompanying notes that are considered an integral part of the financial statements. Some companies, such as Loblaw, present the statement of earnings first. Companies may also present comparative figures for three years instead of two. The auditors' report covers all of the financial statements and accompanying notes.

The financial statements and accompanying notes for Loblaw for the fiscal years 1999 and 1998 appear on the following pages. They are **consolidated financial statements,** which means that the statements include the financial results of all of its stores and operations, combined as though they were one entity.

Consolidated Statements of Earnings

52 Weeks Ended January 1, 2000
($ millions)

		1999	1998
Sales		**$18,783**	$12,497
Operating Expenses	Cost of sales, selling and administrative expenses	**17,699**	11,785
	Depreciation	**273**	183
		17,972	11,968
Operating Income		**811**	529
Interest Expense (Income)	Long term	**139**	96
	Other	**(27)**	(28)
		112	68
Earnings Before Income Taxes		**699**	461
Income Taxes (note 4)		**280**	199
Earnings Before Goodwill Charges		**419**	262
Goodwill Charges (note 1)		**43**	1
Net Earnings for the Period		**$ 376**	$ 261
Per Common Share ($)	Earnings before goodwill charges	**$ 1.52**	$ 1.06
	Net earnings	**$ 1.37**	$ 1.06

Consolidated Statements of Retained Earnings

52 Weeks Ended January 1, 2000
($ millions)

		1999	1998
Retained Earnings, Beginning of Period		**$ 1,429**	$ 1,221
	Net earnings for the period	**376**	261
	Premium on common shares purchased for cancellation (note 8)	**(20)**	(2)
	Stock option plan cash payments, net of tax (note 1)	**(3)**	
		1,782	1,480
	Dividends declared		
	Preferred shares		1
	Common shares, per share – 22¢ (1998 – 20¢)	**61**	50
		61	51
Retained Earnings, End of Period		**$ 1,721**	$ 1,429

See accompanying notes to consolidated financial statements.

Consolidated Balance Sheets

As at January 1, 2000
($ millions)

		1999	1998
Assets			
Current Assets	Cash (note 5)	$ 481	$ 624
	Short term investments (note 5)	245	48
	Accounts receivable	325	345
	Inventories	1,222	1,141
	Prepaid expenses and other assets	50	84
	Taxes recoverable	92	7
		2,415	2,249
Franchise Investments and Other Receivables		160	134
Fixed Assets (note 6)		3,549	3,194
Goodwill (note 2)		1,685	1,363
Other Assets		170	165
		$7,979	$7,105
Liabilities			
Current Liabilities	Bank indebtedness (note 5)	$ 296	$ 135
	Commercial paper (note 5)	428	231
	Accounts payable and accrued liabilities	2,066	1,806
	Short term bank loans (note 2)		770
	Long term debt due within one year (note 7)	22	14
		2,812	2,956
Long Term Debt (note 7)		1,979	1,364
Other Liabilities		171	68
Deferred Income Taxes		113	122
		5,075	4,510
Shareholders' Equity			
Share Capital (note 8)		1,183	1,166
Retained Earnings		1,721	1,429
		2,904	2,595
		$7,979	$7,105

See accompanying notes to consolidated financial statements.

Approved by the Board

W. Galen Weston (signed)
Director

Richard J. Currie (signed)
Director

Consolidated Cash Flow Statements

52 Weeks Ended January 1, 2000
($ millions)

		1999	1998
Operations	Net earnings	**$ 376**	$ 261
	Depreciation and amortization	**317**	185
	Loss (gain) on fixed asset sales	**6**	(3)
	Deferred income taxes	**53**	26
	Other	**2**	(4)
		754	465
	Changes in non-cash working capital	**37**	65
Cash Flows from Operating Activities before the following:		**791**	530
	Acquisition restructuring and other charges	**(135)**	
Cash Flows from Operating Activities		**656**	530
Investment	Fixed asset purchases	**(802)**	(599)
	Short term investments (note 5)	**(197)**	54
	Proceeds from fixed asset sales	**21**	17
	Business acquisitions (note 2)	**(14)**	(941)
	Business disposition (note 2)	**161**	
	(Increase) decrease in franchise investments and other receivables	**(27)**	13
	Net (increase) decrease in other items	**(32)**	66
Cash Flows used in Investing Activities		**(890)**	(1,390)
Financing	Short term bank loans (note 2)	**(770)**	767
	Commercial paper (note 5)	**197**	(31)
	Long term debt (note 7)		
	– Issued	**602**	200
	– Retired	**(14)**	(110)
	Share capital (note 8)		
	– Issued	**3**	22
	– Retired	**(22)**	(22)
	Dividends	**(61)**	(51)
	Other	**(5)**	
Cash Flows (used in) from Financing Activities		**(70)**	775
Decrease in Cash		**(304)**	(85)
Cash at Beginning of Period		**489**	574
Cash at End of Period		**$ 185**	$ 489
Cash position:	Cash	**$ 185**	$ 489
	Short term investments	**245**	48
	Commercial paper	**(428)**	(231)
	Cash position	**$ 2**	$ 306
Other cash flow information:	Net interest paid	**$ 114**	$ 70
	Net income taxes paid	**$ 200**	$ 186

Cash is defined as cash net of bank indebtedness.
Cash position is defined as cash and short term investments net of bank indebtedness and commercial paper.
See accompanying notes to consolidated financial statements.

Notes to Consolidated Financial Statements

52 Weeks Ended January 1, 2000
($ millions except Share Capital)

1. Summary of Significant Accounting Policies

The consolidated financial statements have been prepared in accordance with Canadian generally accepted accounting principles.

Basis of Consolidation The consolidated financial statements include the accounts of the Company and its subsidiaries. The Company's effective interest in the voting equity share capital of its subsidiaries is 100%.

Revenue Recognition Sales include revenues from consumers through corporate stores operated by the Company and sales to and service fees from franchised stores, associated stores and independent accounts but exclude inter-company sales.

Cash Offsetting Cash balances, for which the Company has the ability to and intent of offset, are used to reduce reported bank indebtedness.

Inventories Retail store inventories are stated at the lower of cost and net realizable value less normal profit margin. Wholesale inventories are stated at the lower of cost and net realizable value. Cost is determined substantially using the first-in, first-out method.

Fixed Assets Fixed assets are stated at cost including capitalized interest. Depreciation is recorded principally on a straight-line basis to amortize the cost of these assets over their estimated useful lives. Estimated useful lives range from 20 to 40 years for buildings and 3 to 10 years for equipment and fixtures. Leasehold improvements are depreciated over the lesser of the applicable useful life and term of the lease.

Goodwill Goodwill represents the excess of the purchase price of the business acquired over the fair value of the underlying net tangible assets acquired at the date of acquisition. Goodwill is amortized on a straight-line basis over the estimated life of the benefit determined for each acquisition. The weighted average remaining amortization period is 39 years. Any permanent impairment in value, based on projected cash flows, is written off against net earnings. Goodwill charges are net of income tax recovery of $1 (1998 – $1).

Translation of Foreign Currencies Assets and liabilities denominated in foreign currencies are translated at the exchange rates in effect at each period end date. The resulting exchange gains or losses are included in the current period's net earnings. Revenues and expenses denominated in foreign currencies are translated at the average exchange rates for the period.

Financial Derivatives The Company uses interest rate derivatives and currency derivatives to manage its exposure to fluctuations in exchange rates and interest rates. The income or expense arising from these derivatives is included in interest expense. Unrealized gains or losses on currency derivatives are offset by unrealized gains or losses on the Company's foreign currency net assets. The net exchange difference is recorded in the income statement.

Post-Retirement Benefits and Pensions The cost of post-retirement health, insurance and other benefits, excluding pensions, is expensed when paid. Defined benefit pension expense is accrued as earned.

Stock Option Plan The Company has an employee stock option plan as described in Note 8. Consideration paid by employees on the exercise of a stock option is credited to share capital. For those employees electing to receive the cash differential, the excess of the market price of the shares at the date of exercise over the specified stock option price, together with the related taxes of $2 in 1999, are charged to retained earnings.

Use of Estimates The preparation of the consolidated financial statements in conformity with Canadian generally accepted accounting principles requires management to make estimates and assumptions that affect the amounts reported in the consolidated financial statements and accompanying notes. These estimates are based on management's best knowledge of current events and actions that the Company may undertake in the future.

Comparative Figures Certain prior period's information was reclassified to conform with the current period's presentation.

Notes to Consolidated Financial Statements

2. Business Acquisitions and Disposition

Provigo Inc. On January 18, 1999, the Company purchased the remaining 2% of Provigo Inc.'s ("Provigo") common shares, pursuant to which the Company issued 525,841 common shares (including 64 common fractional shares which were subsequently cancelled) valued at $16 and paid $14 in cash. On December 10, 1998, the Company purchased 98% of Provigo's common shares, pursuant to which the Company issued 28,715,059 common shares valued at $890, paid $771 in cash and assumed net bank indebtedness of $89. The $771 cash consideration was financed by way of a 364 day unsecured credit facility that was repaid during 1999. In total, the Company issued 29,240,900 common shares valued at $906, paid cash of $785 and assumed net bank indebtedness of $89 to acquire Provigo.

The Provigo acquisition was accounted for using the purchase method. During the second quarter of 1999, the Company completed the Provigo valuation analysis and recorded the purchase equation including goodwill of $1.6 billion. Since December 10, 1998, 100% of Provigo's results of operations have been included in the Company's consolidated financial statements excluding the results of certain stores, principally 44 Loeb stores. In 1999, the Company sold these 44 stores for proceeds of $161 representing fair value. This sale transaction was recorded as part of the Provigo purchase equation.

The goodwill arising on this transaction is being amortized over 40 years. Details of the purchase equation including total consideration paid and net assets acquired at their fair values are summarized below:

Fixed Assets	$ 553
Other Assets (including Provigo net bank indebtedness of $89)	435
Liabilities (including Provigo long term debt)	(1,087)
Net assets including acquisition restructuring and other charges acquired	(99)
Goodwill	1,643
	1,544
Less non-cash consideration:	
Common shares issued	(906)
Acquisition costs	(14)
Net cash paid (cash paid of $785 less proceeds on disposition of $161)	624
Net bank indebtedness assumed	89
Cash consideration	$ 713

Agora Foods On November 30, 1998, the Company purchased Agora Foods, the Atlantic Canada food distribution operations of Oshawa Foods, for cash paid of $81 resulting in goodwill of $49. This acquisition was accounted for using the purchase method. The fair value of the acquired working capital including other assets was $4 and of the acquired fixed assets was $28. The fair value of the net assets acquired and the results of operations have been included in the Company's consolidated financial statements from the date of acquisition. The goodwill arising on this transaction is being amortized over 40 years.

3. Pensions

The Company maintains defined benefit pension plans. Current actuarial estimates indicate that the Company's registered defined benefit pension plans have a present value of accrued pension benefits of $560 (1998 – $544) and a market-related value of pension fund assets of $738 (1998 – $679). As at period end, prepaid pension costs of $147 (1998 – $97) relating to these plans are included in other assets.

Notes to Consolidated Financial Statements

4. Income Taxes

The Company's effective income tax rate is made up as follows:

	1999	1998
Combined basic Canadian federal and provincial income tax rate	42.5%	44.5%
Net decrease resulting from:		
Operating in countries with lower effective tax rates	(1.2)	(.7)
Non-taxable amounts including capital gains/losses	(1.1)	(.1)
Other	(.1)	(.6)
Effective income tax rate before goodwill charges	40.1	43.1
Non-deductible goodwill charges	2.6	
Effective income tax rate	42.7%	43.1%

5. Cash, Short Term Investments, Bank Indebtedness and Commercial Paper

Cash, short term investments, bank indebtedness and the Company's commercial paper program form an integral part of the Company's cash management. The Company has $714 (1998 – $672) in cash and short term investments held by its wholly owned non-Canadian subsidiaries which are carried at the lower of cost or quoted market value. The $35 (1998 – $33) income from these investments is included as a reduction of other interest expense. Cash of $481 (1998 – $624) consists of cash and short term investments with a maturity from the period end date of less than 90 days. Short term investments of $245 (1998 – $48) consist primarily of United States government securities, commercial paper, bank deposits and repurchase agreements with a maturity from the period end date of greater than 90 days.

At period end 1999, the Company has a net loan payable to the Company's majority shareholder, George Weston Limited and one of its subsidiaries, of $136 (1998 – $24) included in bank indebtedness. The interest rates were set at market at the time of the transactions and is included in other interest expense.

6. Fixed Assets

	1999			1998		
	Cost	Accumulated Depreciation	Net Book Value	Cost	Accumulated Depreciation	Net Book Value
Properties held for development	$ 246		$ 246	$ 164		$ 164
Properties under development	114		114	150		150
Land	687		687	603		603
Buildings	1,713	$ 367	1,346	1,488	$ 311	1,177
Equipment and fixtures	1,660	885	775	1,451	714	737
Leasehold improvements	510	160	350	447	124	323
	4,930	1,412	3,518	4,303	1,149	3,154
Capital leases – buildings and equipment	85	54	31	86	46	40
	$5,015	$1,466	$3,549	$4,389	$1,195	$3,194

Interest capitalized to fixed assets during the year is $17 (1998 – $13).

Notes to Consolidated Financial Statements

7. Long Term Debt

	1999	1998
Loblaw Companies Limited Debentures		
Series 5, 10%, due 2006, retractable annually commencing 1996, redeemable in 2001	**$ 50**	$ 50
Series 8, 10%, due 2007, redeemable in 2002	**61**	61
Provigo Inc. Debentures		
Series 1991, 11.25%, due 2001	**100**	100
Series 1996, 8.7%, due 2006	**125**	125
Series 1997, 6.35%, due 2004	**100**	100
Other	**32**	
Loblaw Companies Limited Notes		
11.4%, due 2031 – principal	**151**	151
– effect of coupon repurchase	**11**	15
8.75%, due 2033	**200**	200
7.34%, due 2001	**100**	100
5.39% to 2000 and 7.91% thereafter, due 2007, redeemable in 2000	**100**	100
6.65%, due 2027	**100**	100
6.45%, due 2028	**200**	200
5.75%, due 2009	**125**	
6.50%, due 2029	**175**	
6.00%, due 2014	**100**	
6.45%, due 2039	**200**	
Other at a weighted average interest rate of 11.6%, due 2000 to 2039	**71**	76
Total long term debt	**2,001**	1,378
Less due within one year	**22**	14
	$1,979	$1,364

The 5 year schedule of repayment of long term debt based on the earlier of maturity or first retraction date, excluding the Series 5 debentures which may be renewed depending on market conditions at the time of renewal, is as follows: 2000 – $22; 2001 – $214; 2002 – $12; 2003 – $4; 2004 – $102. Subsequent to period end 1999, the Company announced its intention to redeem its $100 5.39% Notes in accordance with their terms.

Loblaw Companies Limited Debentures The interest rate on the Series 5 debentures was reset in 1999 at 10%. Current intentions are to reset the interest rate on the Series 5 debentures in 2000 to encourage renewal. Accordingly, the Series 5 debentures are excluded from the amount due within one year.

Provigo Inc. Debentures – Other The $32 represents the unamortized portion of the adjustment to fair value the Provigo Inc. debentures. This adjustment was recorded as part of the Provigo purchase equation and calculated using the Company's average credit spread applicable to the remaining life of the Provigo debentures. The adjustment is being amortized over the remaining term of the Provigo Inc. debentures.

In 1998, the First Preferred Shares, Second Series debt equivalents were redeemed according to their terms at $70 dollars each and the $75 Series 6, 9.75% debentures were redeemed.

Subsequent to period end 1999, the Company issued $200 of Notes with an interest rate of 6.95%, due 2005 and plans to file a shelf prospectus to issue up to $1.0 billion of Medium Term Notes covering a 2 year period from the filing date.

Notes to Consolidated Financial Statements

8. Share Capital ($)

	Number of Shares Issued		Share Capital ($ millions)	
	1999	1998	1999	1998
Common shares issued	**274,910,365**	274,423,338	**$1,183**	$1,166
Weighted average common shares outstanding	**275,076,485**	246,571,823		

Share Description Common shares (authorized – unlimited). In the first quarter of 1999, the Company purchased the remaining 2% of Provigo's common shares by issuing 525,841 common shares (including 64 common fractional shares which were subsequently cancelled) valued at $16 million. In 1998 pursuant to the Provigo acquisition, the Company issued 28,715,059 common shares valued at $890 million (see Note 2).

In 1998, the First Preferred Shares, First Series were redeemed according to their terms at $50 each.

Stock Option Plan The Company maintains a stock option plan for certain employees. Under the plan, the Company may grant options for up to 12 million common shares. Stock options have up to a 7 year term, are exercisable at the designated common share price and vest 20% cumulatively on each anniversary date of the grant after the first anniversary. Employees granted stock options during or after 1997 may elect to acquire common shares at the price specified in the terms of the option or may elect to receive cash equal to the excess of the market price at the date of exercise over the specified option price. In 1999, the Company issued 591,450 common shares (1998 – 2,987,421) for cash consideration of $3 million (1998 – $22 million) on the exercise of employee stock options and share appreciation value, net of tax, of $3 million (1998 – $.3 million) was paid out on 138,635 common shares (1998 – 29,018). A summary of the status of the Company's stock option plan and activity during the periods is presented below:

	1999		1998	
	Options (number of shares)	Weighted Avg. Exercise Price/Share	Options (number of shares)	Weighted Avg. Exercise Price/Share
Outstanding options, beginning of period	**4,452,882**	**$13.542**	6,656,965	$ 8.491
Granted	**162,480**	**$35.600**	1,175,000	$24.500
Exercised	**(730,085)**	**$ 9.538**	(3,016,439)	$ 7.159
Forfeited/Cancelled	**(87,205)**	**$14.107**	(362,644)	$ 9.419
Outstanding options, end of period	**3,798,072**	**$15.243**	4,452,882	$13.542
Options exercisable, end of period	**2,092,118**	**$ 9.952**	2,421,281	$ 8.072

The following table summarizes information about the Company's stock options outstanding at January 1, 2000:

	Outstanding Stock Options			Exercisable Stock Options	
Range of Exercise Prices	Number of Options Outstanding	Weighted Avg. Remaining Contractual Life (years)	Weighted Avg. Exercise Price/Share	Number of Exercisable Options	Weighted Avg. Exercise Price/Share
$ 7.792 – $14.250	2,572,992	2	$10.143	1,938,302	$ 8.798
$24.500 – $35.600	1,225,080	5	$25.954	153,816	$24.500

The exercise of stock options would not materially dilute net earnings per common share.

Notes to Consolidated Financial Statements

Normal Course Issuer Bid (NCIB) During 1999, the Company purchased 630,200 (1998 – 60,000) of its common shares for $22 million (1998 – $2 million) pursuant to Normal Course Issuer Bids.

Subsequent to period end, the Company announced that it amended its NCIB currently in place and set to expire on March 21, 2000 to allow the Company to enter into equity derivatives including forward contracts with respect to its common shares under the NCIB. In addition, the Company intends to renew its NCIB to purchase on The Toronto Stock Exchange or enter into equity derivatives including forward contracts to purchase up to 5% of its common shares outstanding. The Company, in accordance with the rules and by-laws of The Toronto Stock Exchange, may purchase its shares at the then market prices of such common shares.

9. Financial Instruments

Currency Derivatives The Company has entered into currency derivatives to exchange an amount of $841 Canadian dollar debt for United States dollar debt. The derivatives are a hedge against exchange rate fluctuations on United States dollar net assets, principally short term investments. The derivatives mature as follows: 2000 – $119; 2001 – $85; 2002 – $90; 2003 – $49 and thereafter to 2009 – $498. Currency adjustments receivable or payable arising from the derivatives may be settled in cash on maturity or the term may be extended. As at period end, a currency adjustment of $58 (1998 – $58) was included in other liabilities.

Interest Rate Derivatives The Company has entered into interest rate derivative agreements converting a net notional $217 of 7.8% fixed rate debt into floating rate debt. The net maturities are as follows: 2000 – $177; 2002 – $59; 2003 – $98; 2004 – $58 and thereafter to 2013 – $(175).

Counterparty Risk Changes in the underlying exchange rates and interest rates of the Company's currency and interest rate derivatives will result in market gains and losses. Furthermore, the Company may be exposed to losses should any counterparty to its derivative contracts fail to fulfill its obligations. The Company has sought to minimize potential counterparty losses by transacting with counterparties that have a minimum A rating and placing risk adjusted limits on its exposure to any single counterparty. The Company has implemented internal policies, controls and reporting processes permitting ongoing assessment and corrective action respecting its derivative activity. In addition, principal amounts on currency derivatives are netted by agreement and there is no exposure to loss of the notional principal amounts on the interest rate derivatives.

Fair Value of Financial Instruments The fair value of a financial instrument is the estimated amount that the Company would receive or pay to terminate the contracts at the reporting date. The following methods and assumptions were used to estimate the fair value of each type of financial instrument by reference to various market value data and other valuation techniques as appropriate.

The fair values of cash, short term investments, accounts receivable, bank indebtedness, commercial paper, accounts payable, accrued liabilities and short term bank loans approximate their carrying values given their short term maturities.

The fair values of long term debt issues are estimated based on the discounted cash payments of the debt at the Company's estimated incremental borrowing rates for debt of the same remaining maturities.

The fair values of interest rate derivatives are estimated by discounting cash payments of the derivatives at market derivative rates for derivatives of the same remaining maturities.

		1999		1998
	Carrying Value	Estimated Fair Value	Carrying Value	Estimated Fair Value
Long term debt	**$2,001**	**$1,988**	$1,378	$1,599
Interest rate derivatives net asset		**$ 9**		$ 3

Notes to Consolidated Financial Statements

10. Other Information

Segmented Information The Company's only reportable operating segment is food distribution. All sales to external parties are generated in Canada and all fixed assets and goodwill are attributable to Canadian operations.

Contingent Liabilities and Commitments The Company and its subsidiaries are involved in various claims and litigation arising out of the ordinary course and conduct of its business. Although such matters cannot be predicted with certainty, management does not consider the Company's exposure to such litigation to be material to these consolidated financial statements.

Commitments for net operating lease payments total $1.4 billion ($1.6 billion gross net of $173 of expected sub-lease income). Net payments for each of the next 5 years and thereafter are as follows: 2000 – $163; 2001 – $140; 2002 – $131; 2003 – $128; 2004 – $125 and thereafter to 2056 – $755. Gross rentals under leases assigned at the time of sale of United States divisions and the sale of 44 Loeb stores for which the Company is contingently liable amount to $259.

In connection with the purchase of Provigo, the Company has committed to support Quebec small business and farming communities as follows: for a period of 7 years commencing 1999 and, subject to business dispositions, the aggregate amount of goods and services purchased from Quebec suppliers in the ordinary course of business will not fall below those of 1998. The Company fulfilled its commitment in 1999.

Related Party Transactions The Company's majority shareholder, George Weston Limited, and its subsidiaries are related parties. It is the Company's policy to conduct all transactions and settle balances with related parties on normal trade terms. Total purchases from related companies represent about 3% of cost of sales, selling and administrative expenses.

Pursuant to an investment management agreement, the Company, through a wholly owned non-Canadian subsidiary, manages certain United States cash and short term investments on behalf of wholly owned non-Canadian subsidiaries of George Weston Limited. Management fees are based on market rates and have been included in interest expense.

In 1998, the Company sold its investment in a subsidiary to George Weston Limited at fair value resulting in inter-company investment holdings. There is no financial statement impact to either company. In addition, the Company sold its investment in another subsidiary to George Weston Limited for fair value.

SUPPLEMENTARY FINANCIAL INFORMATION

In addition to the financial statements and the accompanying notes, supplementary financial information typically includes a multiple-year summary of related financial data. Other financial information, including quarterly results and shareholder or investor information, is also often presented.

ELEVEN-YEAR SUMMARY

Usually presented in close proximity to the audited financial statements is a five- or ten-year summary of selected financial data. From such a summary, one can determine trends and growth patterns over a fairly long period of time. Loblaw presented the following eleven-year summary that includes operating results, financial position data, and selected financial ratios.

Eleven Year Summary

($ millions)	1999	1998	1997	1996	1995	1994	1993	1992	1991	1990	1989
Sales and Earnings											
Sales	**18,783**	12,497	11,008	9,848	9,854	10,000	9,356	9,262	8,533	8,417	7,934
Trading profit (EBITDA)	**1,084**	712	573	481	449	410	326	313	328	324	295
Operating income	**811**	529	428	361	322	274	203	197	223	220	195
Interest expense	**112**	68	44	46	54	63	54	62	63	71	91
Net earnings	**376**	261	213	174	147	126	90	76	99	89	59
Financial Position											
Working capital	**(397)**	(707)	202	154	179	29	148	145	262	50	34
Fixed assets	**3,549**	3,194	2,093	1,738	1,491	1,603	1,414	1,231	1,115	1,078	1,044
Goodwill	**1,685**	1,363	38	40	42	44	49	52	54	58	70
Total assets	**7,979**	7,105	4,013	3,531	3,197	3,042	2,743	2,504	2,362	2,282	2,040
Total debt (1)	**1,999**	1,842	513	435	287	525	506	426	397	536	619
Total shareholders' equity	**2,904**	2,595	1,495	1,311	1,160	1,105	985	916	884	718	652
Cash Flow											
Cash flows from operating activities before acquisition restructuring and other charges	**791**	530	426	262	270	328	279	269	215	242	220
Capital investment	**802**	599	517	389	302	339	315	198	159	171	166

(1) Total debt is defined as total debt and debt equivalents less cash and short term investments.

(2) Cash flows from operating activities before acquisition restructuring and other charges per common share is after preferred dividends.

(3) Ratios are computed as follows:
Return on average total assets – operating income divided by average total assets excluding cash and short term investments.
Return on average common shareholders' equity – net earnings before extraordinary items less preferred dividends divided by average common share capital, retained earnings, foreign currency translation adjustment and the applicable portion of contributed surplus.
Total debt to shareholders' equity – total debt divided by total shareholders' equity.

(4) Certain prior periods' information was reclassified to conform with the current period's presentation.

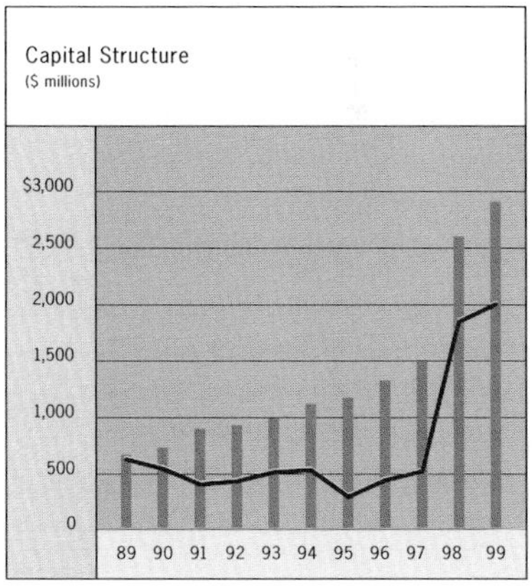

Total Shareholders' Equity
— Total Debt

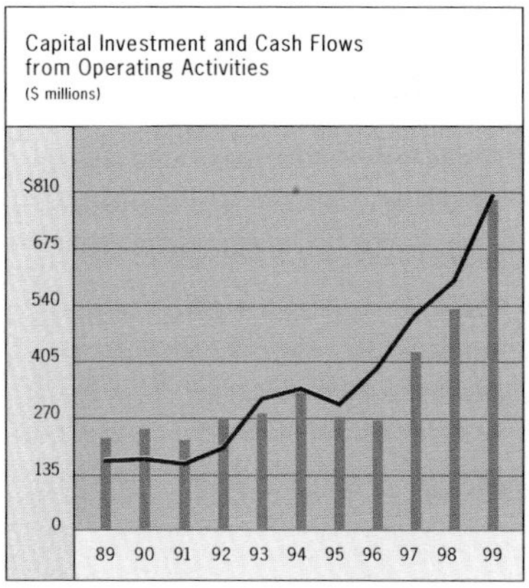

Cash Flows from Operating Activities before Acquisition Restructuring and Other Charges
— Capital Investment

Eleven Year Summary

	1999	1998	1997	1996	1995	1994	1993	1992	1991	1990	1989
Per Common Share ($)											
Earnings before goodwill charges	**1.52**	1.06	.88	.73	.61	.50	.37	.30	.40	.39	.28
Net earnings	**1.37**	1.06	.88	.72	.60	.50	.36	.29	.39	.37	.27
Dividend rate (period end)	**.24**	.20	.16	.12	.12	.09	.08	.08	.08	.07	.07
Cash flows from operating activities before acquisition restructuring and other charges (2)	**2.88**	2.15	1.76	1.08	1.12	1.35	1.15	1.11	.90	1.07	1.01
Capital investment	**2.92**	2.43	2.14	1.62	1.25	1.41	1.34	.83	.70	.79	.77
Book value	**10.56**	9.46	6.08	5.35	4.74	4.27	3.79	3.52	3.17	2.66	2.37
Market value (period end)	**35.25**	37.40	26.00	14.25	10.29	7.96	7.63	6.50	5.75	6.13	4.83
Financial Ratios											
Returns on sales (%)											
Trading profit (EBITDA)	**5.8**	5.7	5.2	4.9	4.6	4.1	3.5	3.4	3.8	3.8	3.7
Operating income	**4.3**	4.2	3.9	3.7	3.3	2.7	2.2	2.1	2.6	2.6	2.5
Net earnings	**2.0**	2.1	1.9	1.8	1.5	1.3	1.0	.8	1.2	1.1	.7
Return on average total assets (%) (3)	**11.9**	10.9	14.2	13.6	12.3	10.6	8.6	9.0	10.5	10.5	9.8
Return on average common shareholders' equity (%) (3)	**13.7**	12.8	15.3	14.2	13.4	12.5	9.7	8.8	13.4	14.6	11.7
Interest coverage on total debt (1)	**7.2**	7.8	9.7	7.9	6.0	4.3	3.7	3.1	3.5	3.0	2.1
Total debt (1) to shareholders' equity (3)	**.69**	.71	.34	.33	.25	.48	.51	.46	.45	.75	.95
Cash flows from operating activities before acquisition restructuring and other charges to total debt (1)	**.40**	.29	.83	.60	.94	.62	.58	.63	.54	.45	.35
Price/net earnings ratio (period end)	**25.8**	35.3	29.6	19.8	17.2	15.9	21.2	22.4	14.7	16.6	17.9
Market/book ratio (period end)	**3.3**	4.0	4.3	2.7	2.2	1.9	2.0	1.9	1.8	2.3	2.0

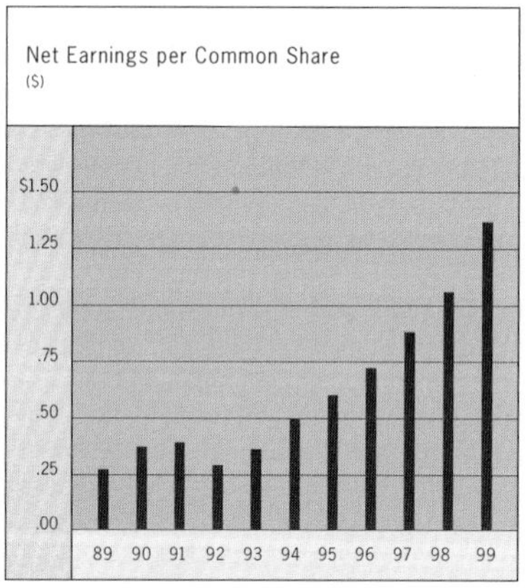

Net Earnings per Common Share

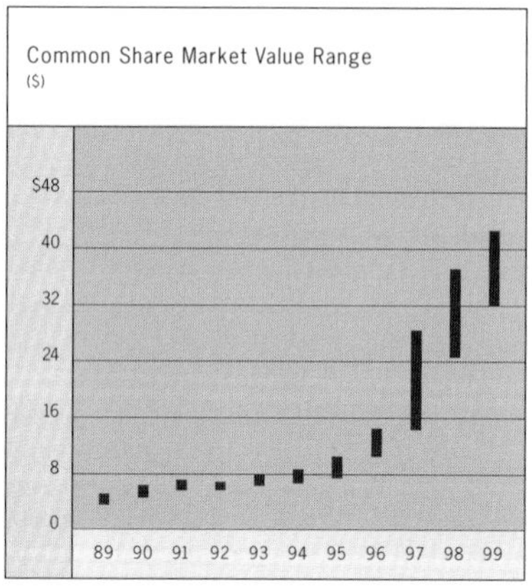

Market Value per Common Share

APPENDIX B

Specimen Financial Statements: Sobeys Inc.

On the World Wide Web
Sobeys Inc.
http://www.sobeys.com

Selected excerpts from the annual report of Canada's second largest food distributor, Sobeys Inc., are included in this appendix as an illustration of current financial reporting. We thank Sobeys for allowing us to present its financial statements and other accompanying financial information for your use throughout this textbook.

Financial Review

Management's Discussion and Analysis

Sobeys Inc. This section of the report provides management's discussion and analysis of the current financial condition of Sobeys Inc. ("Sobeys" or "the Company") and its financial performance for the year ended May 1, 1999. As part of this discussion, we assess the outlook of each business segment, the current financial condition of the Company, and the impact of risks. This discussion should be read in conjunction with the consolidated financial statements, including the notes that accompany them found on pages 23 to 33.

The fiscal 1999 financial performance of Sobeys (including results of operations, sales, operating income and net earnings) includes the results of 22 weeks of The Oshawa Group Limited ("Oshawa") operations and are therefore not directly comparable to the prior year.

Management's Discussion and Analysis continued

SALES
($ billions)

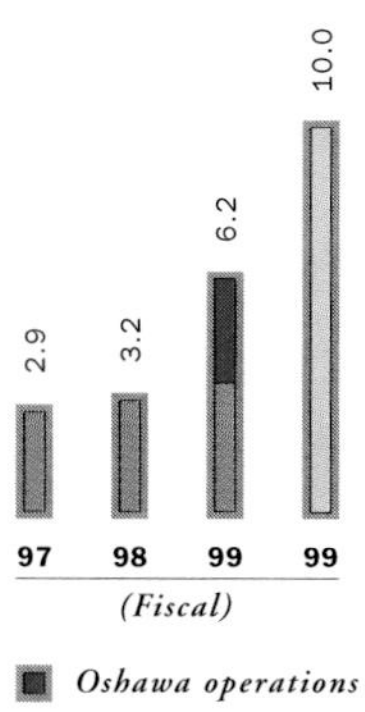

On a proforma basis, the combined Sobeys/ Oshawa business would generate $10.0 billion in annual sales for fiscal 1999.

Business strategy

Sobeys is the second largest food distributor in Canada in terms of sales, number of supermarkets and geographic presence, and the country's only national foodservice distributor.

The Company's goal is to exceed our customers expectations by operating the best Food Distribution and Foodservice businesses in Canada – to be market driven, focused on superior execution, and supported by effective operations.

Prior to its acquisition of Oshawa in December 1998, Sobeys pursued growth outside its core Atlantic Canadian market, principally in Quebec and Ontario, for many years through small acquisitions and internal expansion. By the end of the Company's fiscal 1998, in fact, more than 30% of the Company's food distribution revenues were derived outside Atlantic Canada.

With the establishment of Sobeys Canada Inc. (subsequently renamed Sobeys Inc.) on October 27, 1998, and the offers by Sobeys to purchase all of the issued shares of Oshawa in November 1998, the stage was set for the Company's growth and diversification on a much larger scale.

In December 1998, Sobeys acquired the voting and non-voting shares of Oshawa for approximately $1.5 billion (as explained in note 2 of the financial statements). At that time, Sobeys became a public company with 62% ownership by Empire Company Limited. The Oshawa acquisition will provide the geographic scope, range of store formats, product diversity and complementary competencies to enable Sobeys to serve its customers better and compete more effectively with larger players in central and western Canada. As a national player, the Company should benefit in the years ahead from revenue diversification and increased financial strength and added financial flexibility. This acquisition is also expected to enhance the Company's position relative to the ongoing consolidation taking place in the North American food distribution industry.

The acquisition of Oshawa was accounted for using the purchase method, as explained in note 2 of the financial statements. This has resulted in the inclusion of 22 weeks of Oshawa's results from the date of the acquisition.

Results of operations

During fiscal 1999, Sobeys Inc. opened or replaced 8 new Sobeys banner stores, and 7 new IGA banner stores. An additional 10 Sobeys banner stores and 15 IGA banner stores were renovated or expanded. As a result, at the end of fiscal 1999, the Company operated 1,392 stores comprised of 443 corporate stores and 949 franchised stores, 28 distribution centres and 31 Foodservice operations. The acquisition of Oshawa, which added 9.5 million retail square feet, combined with the new stores opened during the year and the renovation of existing stores, resulted in the Company's total retail selling area increasing to 14.1 million square feet, from 4.3 million square feet in fiscal 1998, a 228% increase in net retail selling area.

Sales

Sales for the combined Food Distribution and Foodservice businesses totaled $6.23 billion in fiscal 1999, a 98% increase over last year. The majority of this increase is due to the inclusion of 22 weeks of Oshawa's operations (which increased sales by 88% or $2.8 billion). For this 22 week period, Oshawa's sales increased 5.4% over the same period last year. On a comparable basis, excluding 22 weeks of Oshawa results, total sales increased by 9.1% for fiscal 1999. On a proforma basis, the inclusion of Oshawa's operations for a full year would generate $10.0 billion in annual sales for the Company in fiscal 1999.

Management's Discussion and Analysis continued

($ millions)	F99	F98
Sales		
Food Distribution	$ 5,173.5	$ 2,747.3
Foodservice	1,058.3	407.8
	$ 6,231.8	$ 3,155.1
Operating Income		
Food Distribution	$ 95.6	$ 46.2
Foodservice	16.1	13.9
	$ 111.7	$ 60.1

OPERATING INCOME
Fiscal 1999
($111.7 million)

85.6% *Food Distribution*
14.4% *Foodservice*

Operating income

Before a restructuring charge of $85.1 million, operating income (EBIT or earnings before interest and taxes) increased 86%, reaching $111.7 million in fiscal 1999. This increase was primarily the result of increased sales volume from the Oshawa acquisition. The Company recorded an operating income margin (EBIT/Sales) of 1.79% and a trading margin (EBITDA/Sales – or earnings before interest, taxes, depreciation and amortization divided by sales) of 3.10% in fiscal 1999, compared to an operating income margin of 1.91% and a trading margin of 3.35% earned in the prior year. Included in this year's results is a 22 week contribution from Oshawa, which produced a 1.73% operating income margin and a 2.76% trading margin over the period.

Depreciation and amortization expense

Depreciation and amortization expense increased by 80% to reach $81.8 million in fiscal 1999. Expressed as a percentage of sales, depreciation and amortization expense dropped to 1.31% in fiscal 1999, compared with 1.44% in fiscal 1998. The reasons for the dollar increase in depreciation and amortization expense are: (i) the inclusion of Oshawa's results for the 22 weeks ended May 1, 1999, which added $26.3 million to depreciation expense; (ii) goodwill increased by $736 million as a result of the Oshawa acquisition, increasing amortization by $8.0 million from the prior year; and (iii) Sobey's capital expenditure program totaling $265.8 million, which added $2.1 million to depreciation expense. The previous factors are expected to add $41.4 million to depreciation and amortization expense in fiscal 2000.

Financing costs

Financing costs amounted to $46.3 million in fiscal 1999, a $35.5 million increase from the $10.8 million recorded last year. Interest on long term debt increased $30.4 million over last year. Interest on short term debt, net of interest income, increased by $5.1 million from the prior year. The increase in interest expense from fiscal 1998 is primarily as a result of the increased debt required to finance the acquisition of Oshawa. Sobeys is committed to a debt reduction program that will lower the cost of borrowing as further explained in the debt section of this analysis.

Net earnings

Net loss for the 1999 fiscal year amounted to $8.1 million ($0.22 loss per share), a $45.4 million decrease in earnings from the $37.3 million recorded in fiscal 1998. Excluding the after tax restructuring charge of $47.1 million, net earnings increased 4.6% to $39.1 million or $1.07 per share. Net earnings are forecast to increase in fiscal 2000, primarily as a result of the $35 million pre-tax savings expected to be realized from the successful integration of the former Sobeys and Oshawa businesses.

Segmented results

Sobeys operates principally in two business segments: (i) Food Distribution, consisting of 83% of Sobeys total fiscal 1999 sales and 86% of its total operating income, and (ii) Foodservice, consisting of 17% of total fiscal 1999 sales and 14% of its operating income. The Food Distribution segment consists of the distribution of food products throughout all provinces. The Foodservice segment also distributes foodservice products to customers in all provinces of Canada.

Food Distribution

Sales

Food Distribution sales grew by $2.43 billion or 88% to reach $5.17 billion in fiscal 1999. $2.18 billion of the increase resulted from the inclusion of Oshawa results for the 22 weeks since the acquisition while 8.8% growth in the former Sobeys operation added $250 million. Same-store sales for all banners increased by 2.9%. After adjusting for the effects of food price inflation of 1.3%, real same store sales for all banners increased by 1.6%. The Company's fiscal 1999 Food Distribution sales are not directly comparable to fiscal 1998, as a result of the inclusion of Oshawa sales for 22 weeks in fiscal 1999. For this 22 week period, Oshawa's Food Distribution sales increased 5.2% over the same period last year. On a comparable basis, after excluding the impact of the 22 weeks of Oshawa's results, total sales increased 5.7% from fiscal 1998.

SALES
FOOD DISTRIBUTION
($ billions)

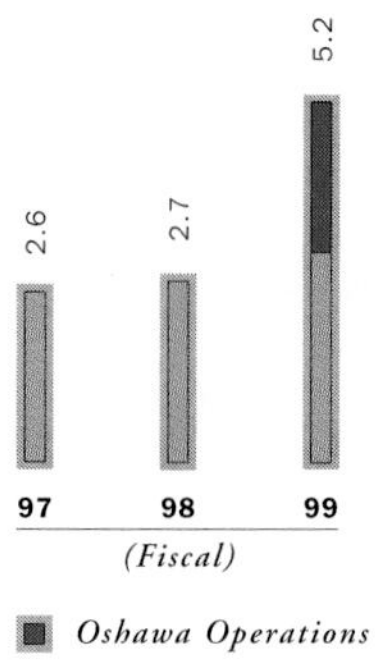

The inclusion of 22 weeks of Oshawa results added $2.2 billion to Food Distribution sales in fiscal 1999.

Same store sales	Before inflation	Adjusted for 1.3% food inflation
All banners	2.9%	1.6%
Sobeys store banner	3.9%	2.6%
IGA store banner	2.7%	1.4%

This growth was supported by $265.8 million in combined capital expenditures, including an increase in total retail store square footage of 268,000. The Oshawa acquisition also added 9.5 million retail square feet and $94.9 million in additional capital expenditures since the acquisition.

During fiscal 1999, as part of its sales growth initiatives, the Company continued to enhance its "Club Sobeys" loyalty program. This program rewards customers with additional discounts on selected featured items as well as Club points that can be redeemed for future grocery purchases. The Company intends to expand the "Club Sobeys" concept, eventually making this benefit available across the IGA network. Increased use of the "Club Sobeys" loyalty database to support targeted marketing efforts is considered important to the Company maintaining and enhancing its customer base.

The acquisition of Oshawa added 109 corporate stores and 838 franchised stores, significantly expanding the Company's base in Quebec and Ontario as well as creating a presence in western Canada. As of the end of fiscal 1999, the Company has a total of 1,392 stores, comprised of 443 corporate stores and 949 franchised stores. The Company's stores now operate under 12 corporate and franchised retail banners including "IGA," "Sobeys," "Foodland," "Price Chopper," "Boni Choix," "Knechtel," "Price Check Foods," "Lofood Stores," "Needs," "Green Gables," "Food Town," and "Lawtons Drugs." In total the Oshawa acquisition tripled the number of corporate and franchised stores. The acquired corporate stores average 26,100 square feet in size whereas the average size of the acquired franchised stores is 12,300 square feet.

OPERATING INCOME
($ millions)

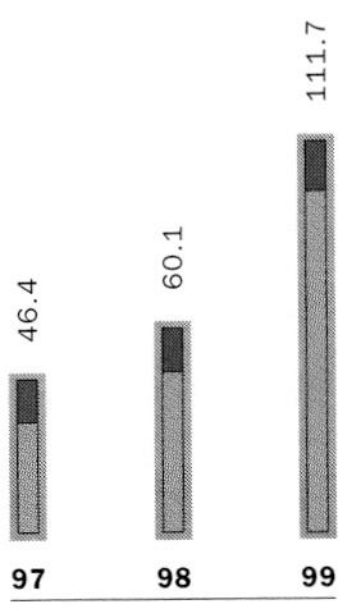

(Fiscal)

Food Distribution
Foodservice

After the inclusion of 22 weeks of Oshawa results in fiscal 1999, operating income grew by 86%.

Banners	Corporate stores	Franchised stores	Totals
IGA	64	504	568
Sobeys	114	–	114
Foodland	4	111	115
Price Chopper	41	–	41
Knechtel	2	79	81
Price Check	25	–	25
Lawtons	60	6	66
Food Town	–	109	109
Lofood	11	1	12
Needs & Green Gables	118	1	119
Boni Choix	2	121	123
Other banners	2	17	19
Totals	443	949	1,392

The Company's retail capital expenditure program in fiscal 2000 includes plans to increase the total combined retail square footage by 8.5%, resulting in over 15 million retail square feet. By the end of fiscal 2000 the distribution of retail square footage by region is expected to be: Atlantic Canada 17.8%, Quebec 29.6%, Ontario 34.2%, and Western Canada 18.4%.

Operating income
In fiscal 1999, Food Distribution operating income (EBIT) was 1.85% of sales or $95.6 million compared with 1.68% or $46.2 million in fiscal 1998. The bulk of this percentage increase is attributable to a continued focus on reduction of operating expenses. In addition, operating income was positively affected by continued expansion of the Company's private label sales.

Foodservice

Sales
Foodservice sales for fiscal 1999 amounted to $1.06 billion, an increase of 159% over last year. Inclusion of the results of Oshawa for 22 weeks added $606 million or 93% of the $651 million increase. For this 22 week period, Oshawa Foodservice sales increased 6.2% over the same period last year. After excluding 22 weeks of the Oshawa operations, total sales increased by 11% for fiscal 1999 due to growth in each of the geographic areas served by the former Sobeys businesses.

SALES
FOODSERVICE
($ millions)

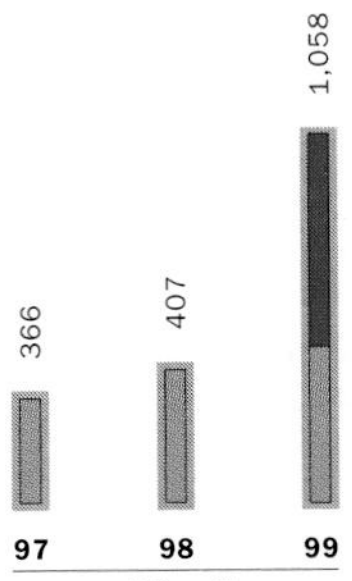

(Fiscal)

Oshawa Operations

The inclusion of 22 weeks of Oshawa results added $606 million to Foodservice sales in fiscal 1999.

Operating income
In fiscal 1999, Foodservice operating income (EBIT) was 1.52% of sales compared with 3.42% in fiscal 1998. The Company's fiscal 1999 operating income is not comparable to fiscal 1998 due to the inclusion of: (i) 22 weeks of Oshawa's operations for the current year and (ii) profit from internal supply arrangements in the prior year. The impact of the Oshawa acquisition accounted for 1.38 percentage points of this change whereas the former Sobeys business accounted for 0.52 percentage points of the difference. Traditional internal supply arrangements with the Food Distribution operations have been realigned and after reflecting the national scope of the Foodservice business, fiscal 2000 operating income is budgeted to reach 1.80% of sales.

Liquidity and capital resources
Cash provided by operating activities was $260.0 million in fiscal 1999, compared with $91.7 million last year. The increase in fiscal 1999 was primarily due to the Oshawa acquisition.

Cash flows used in investing activities increased to $1.53 billion in fiscal 1999, compared with $79.8 million in fiscal 1998. The increase in investing activities over the prior year was primarily due to the acquisition of Oshawa.

TOTAL ASSETS
($ millions)

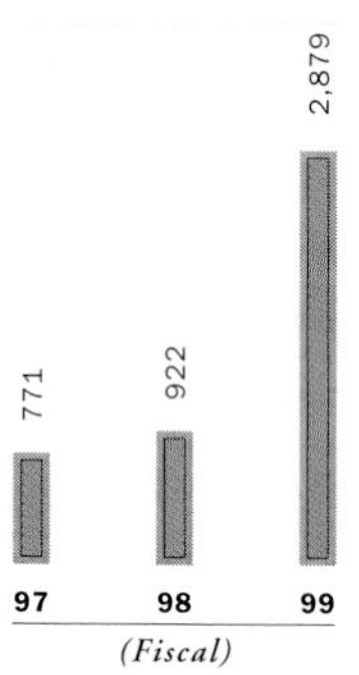

Total assets tripled in fiscal 1999 primarily as a result of the Oshawa acquisition.

CAPITAL SPENDING
($ millions)

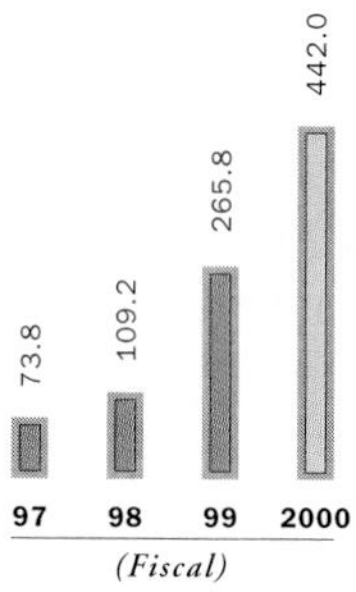

With the inclusion of 52 weeks of Oshawa, capital spending is expected to increase to $442 million ($150 million in Sobeys direct capital expenditures and $292 million in franchisee and third party financing).

Other capital expenditures (net of disposals) increased by $115.1 million in fiscal 1999 to reach $196.6 million. The Company equipped a total of 15 new stores and renovated 10 existing stores while 11 new stores and 15 renovated stores were added as a result of the Oshawa acquisition. In total, the Company opened 26 new and renovated 25 stores in fiscal 1999.

The Company plans to continue its growth plan, which focuses on a combination of new store openings and renovations, as well as growth through acquisitions as appropriate. The Company expects to open 53 new stores, replace 18 older stores and renovate approximately 237 stores in fiscal 2000. Capital project activity for fiscal 2000 is expected to total $442 million, supported by $292 million in franchise and third party lease financing and $150 million in Sobeys direct capital expenditures. Capital activity includes approximately $125 million on new and replacement store construction, $118 million on renovations and over $146 million on warehouse related expenditures. The balance of the capital budget is earmarked for information technology and minor store expenditures.

Cash flows provided by financing activities increased to $1.3 billion in fiscal 1999, compared to cash flow used for financing of $15.2 million in fiscal 1998. The increase in fiscal 1999 was primarily the result of the issue of $913.7 million in long term debt and $404.3 million in common shares to finance the Oshawa acquisition.

The Company plans to finance capital spending for fiscal 2000 through funds from operations, existing bank credit lines, franchisee third party leases, and operating leases. At year-end, the Company maintained bank credit facilities in excess of borrowings of $178 million.

Debt

The Oshawa acquisition and capital expenditure program necessitated substantial increases in debt levels over last year. Short term debt, comprised of bank loans and bankers' acceptances, increased $32.0 million to reach $122.5 million at year-end. Long term debt, comprised of $800 million in seven year non-revolving term debt and $173.9 million of other long term debt, as described in note 6 of the financial statements, increased $832.7 million over fiscal 1998.

Sixty percent of the bank credit long term debt is scheduled to be repaid over the next seven years. Realization of forecast earnings improvement coupled with this long term debt repayment schedule is expected to improve the financial condition of the Company. Existing credit facilities include an annual ratio test which grants a 37.5 basis point reduction in the interest rate charged on the debt for each five percentage point decline in the debt-to-capital ratio. Debt is prepayable at anytime without penalty. Planned debt repayments will positively impact net income through significantly reduced interest expense.

Risk and risk management

The most significant operating risk affecting the Company is the potential for reduced revenues and declining profit margins as a result of intense competition given the mature structure of the Canadian food distribution industry. To mitigate this risk, the Company's strategy is to be geographically diversified with a national presence, to be market-driven, to be focused on superior execution and to be supported by cost effective operations. The Company is committed to tailoring its offerings to meet changing customer needs as well as providing consumers with greater value and product diversity.

Sobeys has two significant national operations in the food industry, Food Distribution (corporate and franchise) and Foodservice which provides a measure of diversification and balance of earnings should competition in a particular region or sector intensify or the economies of a region or sector change.

The recent acquisition of Oshawa has presented Sobeys with many integration challenges and opportunities. Management believes that the planned integration savings from the combination of the two companies of $35 million in fiscal 2000 and an additional $35 million in fiscal 2001 will be realized.

In addition, Sobeys have adopted a number of key financial policies to manage financial risk. For example: in the ordinary course of managing its debt, the Company has entered into various interest rate and currency swaps, which are not reflected on the balance sheet. As explained in note 6 of the financial statements, the effect of these interest rate swaps is to fix the rate the Company pays on $800 million of debt.

Sobeys is self-insured for limited risks while maintaining comprehensive loss prevention and management programs to mitigate retained risks. The range of non-insured related risk exposure is not anticipated to be material to the overall operations of the Company.

Management's Discussion and Analysis continued

The Company completes an ongoing comprehensive environmental compliance report and is not aware of any significant environmental liabilities.

As explained in note 2 to the financial statements, as a result of the Oshawa acquisition the Company's foodservice operations in Atlantic Canada and a small number of food stores in Quebec and Ontario are currently under review by the Competition Bureau. The Company anticipates no material loss of business will occur upon completion of this review.

Certain forward-looking statements are included in this annual report relating to capital expenditures, cost reduction, operating improvements and year 2000 compliance. Such statements are subject to inherent uncertainties and risks, including but not limited to: business and economic conditions generally in the Company's operating regions; pricing pressures and other competitive factors; results of the Company's ongoing efforts to reduce costs; the ability to integrate the newly acquired Oshawa operations; and the availability and terms of financing. Consequently, actual results and events may vary significantly from those included in or contemplated or implied by such statements.

Year 2000

The Company has been evaluating its information technology and other systems and equipment to identify and adjust date sensitive systems for year 2000 compliance. A year 2000 project team has been created and is lead by staff from the Company's information technology department as well as representatives from other areas of the Company. The year 2000 team has developed a four-phase plan to effectively resolve any year 2000 issues. These phases consist of assessment, remediation, testing and implementation.

The assessment, remediation and testing phases are complete with final implementation in all divisions scheduled by the end of calendar 1999. Sobeys has undertaken a complete system review as part of its strategy to address year 2000 issues.

The total cost of implementing the information technology plans, including year 2000 compliance, is not expected to have a material impact on the financial condition of the Company.

The Company cannot assure with absolute certainty that there will not be an adverse impact on operations if third parties do not appropriately address their year 2000 issues in a timely manner.

Although the Company does not believe the actual impact of any system failures related to the century change will be material, various contingency plans have been developed with critical suppliers to ensure the timely delivery of inventory and prepare for normal business activities following the century change. These plans include alternate means of communication with suppliers, manual operation of certain systems, as well as the implementation of contingency ordering procedures. Under the terms of these ordering procedures, critical suppliers will provide inventory to the Company based on historical ordering patterns. These suppliers will also substitute products and adjust inventory levels of substitute items based on the availability of certain products. The Company will continue to develop and finalize the implementation of its contingency plans with third parties throughout 1999.

The Company's response to year 2000 issues is believed adequate to mitigate all known material risks related to the century change. However, due to inherent uncertainties surrounding these issues, Sobeys is unable to rule out any material adverse year 2000-related impact on the operations, earnings and financial condition of the Company.

Outlook

As a result of the addition of Oshawa, management expects to achieve significant economies of scale. The Company believes that this acquisition will generate increased savings through synergies in purchasing, administration and technology, and by streamlining our capital expenditures. Important benefits are also expected from identifying and sharing best practices across the new Company. Sobeys' integration model was based on the achievement of $70 million in annual pretax synergies within a two year period, $35 million of which will be generated during our first full year of operation commencing May 2, 1999.

The Canadian grocery distribution industry operates under a mature market structure. Competition is intense, however there are currently no major price wars, as large players concentrate on integration issues and food price inflation is low. Sobeys' focus in this environment is to: (i) emphasize the effective integration of its operations and acquisitions, (ii) reduce product and operational costs (iii) prudently rationalize its' banners, (iv) concentrate on improving distribution network efficiencies, and (v) enhance the Company's banner positioning.

The opportunities associated with the planned successful integration of the Sobeys and Oshawa businesses are meaningful. Accordingly we look for continued growth in earnings in future years.

Financial Statements

Management's Responsibility for Financial Reporting

Preparation of the consolidated financial statements accompanying this annual report and the presentation of all other information in the report is the responsibility of management. The financial statements have been prepared in accordance with appropriate and generally accepted accounting principles and reflect management's best estimates and judgements. All other financial information in the report is consistent with that contained in the financial statements.

The Board of Directors, through its Audit Committee, oversees management in carrying out its responsibilities for financial reporting and systems of internal control. The Audit Committee, which is chaired by and includes a majority of non-management directors, meets regularly with financial management and external auditors to satisfy itself as to the reliability and integrity of financial information and the safeguarding of assets. The Audit Committee reports its findings to the Board of Directors for consideration in approving the annual financial statements to be issued to shareholders. The external auditors have full and free access to the Audit Committee.

Douglas B. Stewart
Vice-Chairman and
Chief Executive Officer
June 22, 1999

Allan D. Rowe
Executive Vice President and
Chief Financial Officer
June 22, 1999

Auditors' Report

To the Shareholders of Sobeys Inc.

We have audited the consolidated balance sheets of Sobeys Inc. as at May 1, 1999, May 2, 1998 and May 3, 1997, and the consolidated statements of earnings, retained earnings, and changes in financial position for the years then ended. These financial statements are the responsibility of the company's management. Our responsibility is to express an opinion on these financial statements based on our audits.

We conducted our audits in accordance with generally accepted auditing standards. Those standards require that we plan and perform an audit to obtain reasonable assurance whether the financial statements are free of material misstatement. An audit includes examining, on a test basis, evidence supporting the amounts and disclosures in the financial statements. An audit also includes assessing the accounting principles used and significant estimates made by management, as well as evaluating the overall financial statement presentation.

In our opinion, these consolidated financial statements present fairly, in all material respects, the financial position of the company as at May 1, 1999, May 2, 1998 and May 3, 1997, and the results of its operations and the changes in its financial position for the years then ended in accordance with generally accepted accounting principles.

New Glasgow, Nova Scotia
June 14, 1999

Grant Thornton
Chartered Accountants

Consolidated Balance Sheet

(in thousands) May 1	1999	1998	1997
ASSETS			
Current			
Cash	$ 71,133	$ 27,176	$ 30,413
Marketable securities, at cost (quoted market value $5,445; 1998 $316,095; 1997 $215,635)	4,546	315,205	215,205
Receivables	394,323	77,289	65,562
Income taxes recoverable	9,623	–	–
Inventories	462,122	190,289	183,314
Prepaid expenses	31,284	8,446	8,454
Due from parent company	–	9,950	12,462
	973,031	628,355	515,410
Investments and advances (Note 3)	144,633	9,853	9,758
Property and equipment (Note 4)	868,942	273,069	235,220
Goodwill (less accumulated amortization of $18,850)	734,335	4,676	5,308
Deferred income taxes	87,413	6,960	4,831
Deferred costs	70,463	–	–
	$ 2,878,817	$ 922,913	$ 770,527
LIABILITIES			
Current			
Bank loans (Note 5)	$ 7,485	$ –	$ –
Bankers' acceptances (Note 5)	115,000	40,500	37,500
Commercial paper	–	50,000	48,000
Accounts payable and accrued charges	1,013,017	292,531	265,040
Income taxes payable	–	5,467	3,145
Long term debt due within one year	74,031	7,953	8,088
Due to parent company	–	200,000	100,000
	1,209,533	596,451	461,773
Long term debt (Note 6)	899,874	133,277	140,356
Minority interest	–	–	171
Deferred revenue (Note 1)	19,421	–	–
	2,128,828	729,728	602,300
SHAREHOLDERS' EQUITY			
Capital stock (Note 7)	647,207	66,801	66,801
Deferred foreign exchange translation gain (loss)	(230)	1,368	756
Retained earnings	103,012	125,016	100,670
	749,989	193,185	168,227
	$ 2,878,817	$ 922,913	$ 770,527

See accompanying notes to the consolidated financial statements.

On Behalf of the Board

Director

Director

Consolidated Statement of Retained Earnings

(in thousands) Year Ended May 1	1999	1998	1997
Balance, beginning of year	$ 125,016	$ 100,670	$ 86,278
Net earnings (loss)	(8,074)	37,339	26,870
	116,942	138,009	113,148
Dividends paid	13,930	12,993	12,478
Balance, end of year	$ 103,012	$ 125,016	$ 100,670

See accompanying notes to the consolidated financial statements.

Consolidated Statement of Earnings

(in thousands) Year Ended May 1	1999	1998	1997
Sales	$ 6,231,838	$ 3,155,084	$ 2,947,574
Cost of sales, selling and administrative expenses	6,038,344	3,049,530	2,858,182
Depreciation and amortization	81,817	45,408	42,963
Operating income	111,677	60,146	46,429
Interest expense			
Long term debt	46,104	15,749	17,433
Short term debt	197	(4,918)	(5,402)
	46,301	10,831	12,031
	65,376	49,315	34,398
Restructuring and integration charge (Note 8)	(85,143)	–	–
Operating earnings (loss) before the following items	(19,767)	49,315	34,398
Investment income	1,074	4,409	2,031
Minority interest (expense)	–	(10)	(7)
	(18,693)	53,714	36,422
Income taxes (recovery) (Note 9)			
Restructuring and integration charge	(38,017)	–	–
Other operations	27,398	16,375	9,552
	(10,619)	16,375	9,552
Net earnings (loss)	$ (8,074)	$ 37,339	$ 26,870
Earnings per share (Note 10)	$ (0.22)	$ 1.65	$ 1.19

See accompanying notes to the consolidated financial statements.

Consolidated Statement of Changes in Financial Position

(in thousands) Year Ended May 1	1999	1998	1997
Cash provided by (used for) operations			
Net earnings (loss)	$ (8,074)	$ 37,339	$ 26,870
Items not affecting cash (Note 11)	83,010	43,271	41,835
Restructuring and integration charge net of income taxes of $38,017	47,126	–	–
Operating cash flow before restructuring and integration charge	122,062	80,610	68,705
Restructuring and integration charge (Note 8)	(85,143)	–	–
Operating cash flow	36,919	80,610	68,705
Net change in other current items	223,031	11,119	14,041
Total cash provided by operations	259,950	91,729	82,746
Cash provided by (used for) financing			
Bank loans	7,485	–	(16,403)
Bankers' acceptances	74,500	3,000	(1,975)
Commercial paper	(50,000)	2,000	8,000
Issue of long term debt	913,656	597	–
Repayment of long term debt	(214,032)	(7,811)	(11,967)
Issue of capital stock	580,406	–	–
Receipt of deferred revenue	13,200	–	–
Payment of dividends	(13,930)	(12,993)	(12,478)
Total cash provided by (used for) financing	1,311,285	(15,207)	(34,823)
Total cash available	1,571,235	76,522	47,923
Cash used for (provided by) investments			
Property, equipment and other assets	265,839	109,197	73,838
Proceeds on disposal of fixed assets	(69,213)	(27,672)	(22,640)
Long term investments and advances	4,755	(7)	412
Increase in deferred costs	27,736	–	–
Marketable securities	(38,222)	–	–
Business acquisitions, net of cash acquired	1,461,945	1,176	15,279
Decrease (increase) in deferred foreign currency translation gains	(612)	(594)	(388)
Parent company preference shares and note receivable (Note 12)	(124,950)	(2,512)	(30,116)
Buy-out of minority interest	–	171	–
Total cash used	1,527,278	79,759	36,385
Increase (decrease) in cash	43,957	(3,237)	11,538
Cash, beginning of year	27,176	30,413	18,875
Cash, end of year	$ 71,133	$ 27,176	$ 30,413
Operating cash flow before restructuring and integration charge per share (Note 10)	$ 3.34	$ 3.56	$ 3.03

See accompanying notes to the consolidated financial statements.

Notes to the Consolidated Financial Statements

May 1, 1999
All notes in thousands except share capital

1. Accounting policies

Principles of consolidation

These consolidated financial statements include the accounts of the Company and all subsidiary companies. Marketable securities are accounted for on the cost basis.

Depreciation

Depreciation is recorded on a straight line basis over the estimated useful lives of the assets as follows:

Equipment and vehicles	3 – 10 years
Buildings	15 – 40 years
Leasehold improvements	7 – 10 years

Inventories

Warehouse inventories are valued at the lower of cost and net realizable value with cost being determined on a first-in, first-out basis. Retail inventories are valued at the lower of cost and net realizable value less normal profit margins as determined by the retail method of inventory valuation.

Leases

Leases meeting certain criteria are accounted for as capital leases. The imputed interest is charged against income and the capitalized value is depreciated on a straight line basis over its estimated useful life. Obligations under capital leases are reduced by rental payments net of imputed interest. All other leases are accounted for as operating leases with rental payments being expensed as incurred.

Goodwill

Goodwill represents the cost of investments in subsidiary companies in excess of fair value of the underlying assets at date of acquisition. Goodwill is amortized on a straight line basis over its estimated life of 40 years.

The Company evaluates the carrying value of goodwill by considering whether the amortization of the goodwill balance over its remaining life can be recovered through undiscounted future operating cash flows of the acquired operation(s).

Interest capitalization

Interest related to the period of construction is capitalized as part of the cost of the related building. The amount of interest capitalized to construction in progress in the current year was $391; 1998 $327; 1997 $392.

Deferred revenue

Deferred revenue consists of a long term purchase agreement and rental revenue arising from the sale of subsidiaries. Deferred revenue is being taken into income over the term of the related agreement and leases.

Foreign currency

Assets and liabilities of self-sustaining foreign investments are translated at exchange rates prevailing at the balance sheet date. The revenues and expenses of the foreign operations are translated at average exchange rates prevailing during the year. The gains and losses on translation are deferred and included as a separate component of shareholders' equity titled "deferred foreign exchange translation gain/loss."

Development and store opening expenses

Development and opening expenses of new stores and store conversions are written off during the first year of operation.

Information systems development costs

Costs directly attributable to the development of core information system projects are capitalized and amortized over their estimated useful life of seven years. As at May 1, 1999 these costs were included in fixed assets in the amount of $47.3 million. This project began in 1998 and no amortization has been recorded to date. The new system will be fully operational in May 2000 at which time amortization will occur.

Accounting estimates

The preparation of consolidated financial statements in conformity with generally accepted accounting principles requires management to make estimates and assumptions that affect the amounts reported in the consolidated financial statements and accompanying notes. These estimates are based on management's best knowledge of current events and actions that the Company may undertake in the future.

Notes to the Consolidated Financial Statements

2. Business acquisition

Sobeys Inc. ("Sobeys"), formerly Sobeys Canada Inc., was incorporated on October 27, 1998 as a wholly owned subsidiary of Empro Holdings Limited ("Empro"), an indirect wholly owned subsidiary of Empire Company Limited. On November 2, 1998 Sobeys acquired all the issued and outstanding shares of Sobeys Capital Inc. ("Sobeys Capital") from Empro for consideration of 22,646,500 common shares. This acquisition has been accounted for as a continuity of interests and is treated in a manner similar to a pooling of interest. At the date of the combination, Sobeys had nominal assets and net book value, while Sobeys Capital had total assets of $980 million, total liabilities of $773 million and a net book value of $207 million.

On November 2, 1998 Sobeys acquired 972,700 Class "A" non-voting shares of The Oshawa Group Limited ("Oshawa") from Empro for $24 million, representing the carrying value of the shares held by Empro.

During the period from December 1, 1998 to January 25, 1999, Sobeys acquired all the remaining issued and outstanding Class "A" shares and all the issued and outstanding common shares of Oshawa, for combined consideration of cash of $1.1 billion and 21,252,502 common shares valued at $380 million. This acquisition has been accounted for by the purchase method under which the results from operations of Oshawa, since the date of acquisition, have been included in Sobeys financial statements. Details of the acquisition are as follows:

Fair value of identifiable assets acquired	$ 1,494,543
Less identifiable liabilities assumed	713,044
Fair value of identifiable net assets acquired	781,499
Goodwill	736,208
Total purchase consideration	$ 1,517,707
Consideration representing:	
Cash	$ 1,113,413
Common shares	404,294
	$ 1,517,707

Certain aspects of the Company's acquisition of Oshawa are currently under review by the Competition Bureau. Specific foodservice operations in the Maritimes and a small number of food stores in local Ontario and Quebec markets are being examined. The Company anticipates that no material loss of business will occur upon completion of the review. If necessary, any gain or loss arising from a possible Competition Bureau ruling, will be reflected as an adjustment to the purchase price allocation.

3. Investments and advances

	1999	1998	1997
Loans receivable	$ 92,479	$ 9,439	$ 9,220
Mortgages receivable	51,640	–	–
Other	514	414	538
	$ 144,633	$ 9,853	$ 9,758

Loans receivable

Loans receivable represent long term financing to certain retail associates. These loans are primarily secured by inventory, fixtures and equipment, bear interest at rates which fluctuate with prime and have repayment terms up to ten years. The carrying amount of the loans receivable approximates fair value based on the variable interest rates charged on the loans and the operating relationship of the associates with the Company.

Mortgages receivable

The majority of the mortgages receivable balance relates to the sale of 24 retail properties by The Oshawa Group in calendar 1997. These mortgages of $50,300 are for a term of 3 years and bear interest at 5.25%. Principal repayment is due on maturity.

The loans and mortgages receivable are net of a current portion of $14,010.

4. Property and equipment

	1999			1998			1997
	Cost	Accumulated Depreciation	Net Book Value	Cost	Accumulated Depreciation	Net Book Value	Net Book Value
Land	$ 93,308	$ –	$ 93,308	$ 8,588	$ –	$ 8,588	$ 8,339
Land held for development	60,151	–	60,151	35,784	–	35,784	23,446
Construction in progress	21,340	–	21,340	13,475	–	13,475	9,399
Buildings	310,863	88,463	222,400	87,951	30,418	57,533	58,366
Information system development costs	47,290	–	47,290	10,270	–	10,270	–
Equipment	998,705	655,695	343,010	376,588	243,135	133,453	123,066
Leasehold improvements	171,300	94,164	77,136	30,311	17,148	13,163	12,028
Assets under capital leases	7,189	2,882	4,307	3,784	2,981	803	576
	$1,710,146	$ 841,204	$ 868,942	$ 566,751	$ 293,682	$ 273,069	$ 235,220

5. Bank loans and bankers' acceptances

Under the terms of a credit agreement entered into between the Company and a banking syndicate arranged by the Bank of Nova Scotia, a revolving term credit facility was established. This facility will expire on December 8, 1999, however various provisions of the agreement provide the Company with the ability to extend the facility for a minimum period of two years.

Interest is payable on this facility at rates which fluctuate with changes in the prime rate.

As security for this facility and the secured bank loans provided under the credit agreement, the Company has provided a fixed and floating charge over all assets, subject to permitted encumbrances, a general assignment of book debts and the assignment of proceeds of insurance policies.

6. Long term debt

	1999	1998	1997
First mortgage loans, average interest rate 10.0%, due 1999 – 2016	$ 33,931	$ 23,899	$ 25,430
Secured bank loans, average interest rate 8.2%, due Dec. 9, 2005	800,000	–	–
Debentures, average interest rate 10.9%, due 2003 – 2013	109,338	115,900	121,675
Notes payable and other debt at interest rates fluctuating with the prime rate	17,529	425	558
	960,798	140,224	147,663
Capital lease obligations, due 1999 – 2003, net of imputed interest	13,107	1,006	781
	973,905	141,230	148,444
Less amount due within one year	74,031	7,953	8,088
	$ 899,874	$ 133,277	$ 140,356

Notes to the Consolidated Financial Statements

6. Long term debt (continued)

The Company has fixed the interest rate on $204.4 million of its long term debt at 8.4% for 3 years and has fixed the interest rate on $595.6 million of its long term debt at 8.2% for 7 years by utilizing interest exchange agreements.

Long term debt is secured by land and buildings, specific charges on certain assets and additional security as described in Note 5. Debt retirement payments and capital lease obligations in each of the next five fiscal years are:

	Long term debt	Capital leases
2000	$ 71,497	$ 2,534
2001	67,884	2,559
2002	98,250	2,271
2003	97,886	1,170
2004	105,799	1,023

Operating leases

The net aggregate, annual, minimum rent payable under operating leases is approximately $119,681 ($180,693 gross less of expected sub-lease income of $61,012).

7. Capital stock

	Number of shares
Authorized	
During the year the Company created the following authorized capital:	
Preferred shares, par value of $25 each, issuable in series as a class	500,000,000
Preferred shares, without par value, issuable in series as a class	500,000,000
Common shares, without par value	500,000,000
1998 and 1997	
Preferred shares par value of $10 each, non-cumulative, redeemable, issuable in series as a class	905,681
Common shares, without par value	1,000,000
Common shares, par value of $100 each	667,997

Issued and outstanding

	Number of shares			Capital stock (in thousands)		
	1999	1998	1997	1999	1998	1997
Common shares, without par value	55,596,617	–	–	$ 647,207	$ –	$ –
Common shares, without par value	–	207	207	–	1	1
Common shares, par value of $100 each	–	667,997	667,997	–	66,800	66,800
Total capital stock				$ 647,207	$ 66,801	$ 66,801

Comparative figures for 1998 and 1997 represent the authorized and issued and outstanding amounts for Sobeys Capital Inc.

During the year the Company issued the following common shares:

a) 22,646,500 to a subsidiary of Empire Company Limited (parent company) in exchange for common shares of Sobeys Capital Inc., of which $68,835,000 was allocated to share capital.

b) 21,252,502 as partial consideration for common shares of The Oshawa Group Limited of which $379,888,473 was allocated to share capital.

c) 1,959,004 to a subsidiary of Empire (parent company) for common shares of The Oshawa Group of which $24,405,626 was allocated to share capital.

d) 9,738,610 to a subsidiary of Empire (parent company) for cash consideration of $174,077,673.

8. Restructuring and integration charge

Subsequent to the acquisition of The Oshawa Group Limited on November 30, 1998, the Company commenced a comprehensive review of its strategic direction, facilities and staffing levels of all operations of the combined organizations. This integration initiative was undertaken to create

8. Restructuring and integration charge (continued)

operating efficiencies, cost savings and revenue enhancement opportunities. This project, which was substantially complete in April 1999, brought together the operating groups of both business units and generated a new business plan for the future. In connection with the integration initiative, the Company recorded a $85.1 million charge ($47.1 million after tax) in the fourth quarter for restructuring and integration. The amount remaining in liabilities as at May 1, 1999 is $69.2 million.

Foodservice Segment

$45.2 million of the restructuring and integration charge relates to the Foodservice segment and involves the rationalization of operations and modernization of the distribution supply network. These activities are scheduled to commence late in 1999 and continue until early 2001. The charge to exit these activities is comprised of severance and other obligations to employees, lease commitments for closed locations and other charges.

Food Distribution Segment

The remaining charge of $39.9 million relates to the Food Distribution segment. The rationalization of Ontario operations accounts for the majority of this charge. It includes severance and other obligations to employees and other charges resulting from the closure of 17 smaller marginal stores in Ontario, the franchising of 56 corporate owned stores and the streamlining of certain department operations in Ontario. Substantially all of these activities are scheduled to commence in early fiscal 2000 and be completed by year end. The remaining charge for the Food Distribution segment includes severance and other costs associated with the roll out of Sobeys' common information systems across acquired business units. Systems implementation is scheduled to commence in early 2000 and end in mid 2001.

9. Income taxes

The effective rate of corporate income taxes varies from statutory rates as a result of the receipt of intercorporate dividends, the amortization of goodwill being non-deductible for income tax purposes and the large corporation tax of $1,285 (1998 $383; 1997 $399).

10. Earnings and cash flow per share

Earnings and cash flow per share amounts are calculated on the weighted average number of shares outstanding (1999 – 36,518,471; 1998 and 1997 – 22,646,500 representing the shares exchanged in 1999 as described in Note 2).

	1999	1998	1997
Earnings before restructuring and integration charge	$ 39,052	$ 37,339	$ 26,870
Restructuring and integration charge net of income taxes of $38,017	(47,126)	–	–
Net earnings (loss)	$ (8,074)	$ 37,339	$ 26,870
Earnings per share is comprised of the following:			
Earnings before restructuring and integration charge	$ 1.07	$ 1.65	$ 1.19
Restructuring and integration charge net of income taxes	(1.29)	–	–
Net earnings (loss)	$ (0.22)	$ 1.65	$ 1.19

11. Items not affecting cash

	1999	1998	1997
Depreciation and amortization	$ 81,817	$ 45,408	$ 42,963
Deferred income taxes	(7,584)	(2,129)	(951)
Gain (loss) on disposal of assets	(2,191)	(8)	(177)
Writedown of fixed assets	10,300	–	–
Amortization of deferred items	668	–	–
	$ 83,010	$ 43,271	$ 41,835

Notes to the Consolidated Financial Statements

12. Related party transactions

The Company leased certain real property from related parties during the year. The aggregate net payments under these leases amounted to approximately $45,535 (1998 $39,880; 1997 $39,795). The Company was charged expenses of $60 (1998 $80; 1997 $80) by related parties. The Company had sales to related parties of $671 (1998 $846; 1997 $8,411) and made purchases of $767 (1998 $716; 1997 $717) from related parties.

On November 30, 1998, prior to Sobeys acquisition of 100% of the capital stock of The Oshawa Group Limited, $315,000 of preferred shares of the parent company (Empire) were redeemed, $9,950 due from parent company was repaid and $200,000 due to parent company was repaid.

For 1997 and 1998, these intercompany investments (preferred shares and note receivable) have been shown as "other assets" in the "identifiable assets" section of Note 15.

Interest expense paid on the due to parent company was $6,627 in 1999 (1998 $6,946; 1997 $5,087).

Interest income received on the due from parent company was $501 in 1999 (1998 $1,027; 1997 $1,262).

13. Financial instruments

Foreign exchange contracts

The Company utilizes financial instruments which are not reflected on the balance sheet to reduce foreign exchange risks on its U.S. long term debt. At May 1, 1999, $194.9 million U.S. was covered by such instruments with $43.2 million U.S. maturing in 2002 and $151.7 million U.S. maturing in 2005.

The fair value of the foreign exchange agreements represents the amount the Company would pay or receive to terminate the agreements. At May 1, 1999, the estimated payment on termination is $11.0 million U.S. based on market conditions.

All the financial instrument contracts are with Canadian Schedule 1 Banks thereby controlling the Company's credit risk exposure.

Other financial instruments

The book value of cash, receivables, income taxes recoverable, bank loans, bankers' acceptances and accounts payable and accrued charges approximate fair values at May 1, 1999. The fair value of marketable securities is $5.45 million.

The total fair value of long term debt is estimated to be $999.4 million. The fair value of variable rate long term debt is assumed to approximate its carrying amount. The fair value of other long term debt has been estimated by discounting future cash flows at a rate currently offered for debt of similar maturities and credit quality.

14. Contingent liabilities

Uncertainty due to the year 2000 issue

The year 2000 issue arises because many computerized systems use two digits rather than four to identify a year. Date-sensitive systems may recognize the year 2000 as 1900 or some other date, resulting in errors when information using year 2000 dates is processed. In addition, similar problems may arise in some systems which use certain dates in 1999 to represent something other than a date. The effects of the year 2000 issue may be experienced before, on, or after January 1, 2000, and, if not addressed, the impact on operations and financial reporting may range form minor errors to significant systems failure which could affect an entity's ability to conduct normal business operations. It is not possible to be certain that all aspects of the year 2000 issue affecting the entity, including those related to the efforts of customers, suppliers or other third parties, will be resolved.

Guarantees and commitments

The Company has undertaken to provide cash to meet any obligations which Sobey Leased Properties Limited (a wholly owned subsidiary of Empire Company Limited) is unable or fails to meet until all of its debentures have been paid in full in accordance with their terms. Any deficiency payment made by the Company will be by purchase of fully-paid non-assessable 5% redeemable, non-voting preference shares of that company. The aggregated outstanding principal amounts of these debentures at May 1, 1999 is $48,770.

At May 1, 1999 the Company was contingently liable for letters of credit issued in the aggregate amount of $18,000.

15. Segmented information

	1999	1998	1997
Sales			
Food Distribution	$ 5,173,516	$ 2,747,308	$ 2,581,361
Foodservice	1,058,322	407,776	366,213
	6,231,838	3,155,084	2,947,574
Operating income			
Food Distribution	95,559	46,217	32,084
Foodservice	16,118	13,929	14,345
	111,677	60,146	46,429
Identifiable assets			
Food Distribution	1,766,838	513,906	465,210
Foodservice	377,644	79,381	72,547
Other (Note 12)		324,950	227,462
Goodwill	734,335	4,676	5,308
	2,878,817	922,913	770,527
Depreciation and amortization			
Food Distribution	73,299	42,206	39,368
Foodservice	8,518	3,202	3,595
	81,817	45,408	42,963
Capital expenditures			
Food Distribution	249,159	105,575	71,697
Foodservice	16,680	3,622	2,141
	$ 265,839	$ 109,197	$ 73,838

The Company operates principally in two business segments, Food Distribution and Foodservice. The Food Distribution segment consists of the distribution of food products throughout all provinces of Canada. The Foodservice segment also distributes foodservice products to customers throughout Canada.

16. Pension plan

The Company maintains a defined contribution plan and a number of defined benefit pension plans. Current actuarial estimates indicate the pension benefits under the defined benefit plan at May 1, 1999 are $165,624 and the pension fund assets, using the moving average market value are $169,926.

17. Subsequent events

Immediately following the year end, the two operating subsidiary companies amalgamated. Subsequently, the Company changed its name to Sobeys Inc.

18. Comparative figures

Comparative figures have been reclassified, where necessary, to reflect the current year's presentation.

APPENDIX C

Time Value of Money

STUDY OBJECTIVES

After studying this appendix, you should be able to:

1. Distinguish between simple and compound interest.
2. Solve for future value of a single amount.
3. Solve for future value of an annuity.
4. Identify the variables fundamental to solving present value problems.
5. Solve for present value of a single amount.
6. Solve for present value of an annuity.
7. Calculate the present value of notes and bonds.

Would you rather receive $1,000 today or a year from now? You should prefer to receive the $1,000 today because you can invest the $1,000 and earn interest on it. As a result, you will have more than $1,000 a year from now. What this example illustrates is the concept of the **time value of money**. Everyone prefers to receive money today rather than in the future because of the interest factor.

NATURE OF INTEREST

Interest is payment for the use of another person's money. It is the difference between the amount borrowed or invested (called the **principal**) and the amount repaid or collected. The amount of interest to be paid or collected is usually stated as a rate over a specific period of time. The rate of interest is normally stated as an annual rate.

The amount of interest involved in any financing transaction is based on three elements:

1. **Principal (*p*):** The original amount borrowed or invested.
2. **Interest Rate (*i*):** An annual percentage of the principal.
3. **Time (*n*):** The number of years that the principal is borrowed or invested.

SIMPLE INTEREST

STUDY OBJECTIVE 1

Distinguish between simple and compound interest.

Simple interest is calculated on the principal amount only. It is the return on the principal for one period. Simple interest is usually expressed as shown in Illustration C-1.

Illustration C-1 Interest calculation

Interest = Principal (p) × Rate (i) × Time (n)

For example, if you borrowed $5,000 for two years at a simple interest rate of 12% annually, you would pay $1,200 in total interest calculated as follows:

$$\begin{aligned}\text{Interest} &= p \times i \times n \\ &= \$5{,}000 \times 0.12 \times 2 \\ &= \$1{,}200\end{aligned}$$

COMPOUND INTEREST

Compound interest is calculated on principal **and** on any interest earned that has not been paid or withdrawn. It is the return on (or growth of) the principal for two or more time periods. Compounding calculates interest not only on the principal but also on the interest earned to date on that principal, assuming the interest is left on deposit.

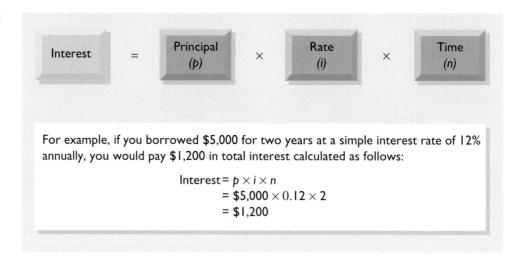

To illustrate the difference between simple and compound interest, assume that you deposit $1,000 in the Caisse Populaire, where it will earn simple interest of 9% per year. You deposit another $1,000 in Citizens Bank, where it will earn interest of 9% per year compounded annually. Assume that in both cases you will not withdraw any interest until three years from the date of deposit. The calculation of interest to be received and the accumulated year-end balances are indicated in Illustration C-2.

Illustration C-2 Simple versus compound interest

Caisse Populaire

Simple Interest Calculation	Simple Interest	Accumulated Year-end Balance
Year 1 $1,000.00 × 9%	$ 90.00	$1,090.00
Year 2 $1,000.00 × 9%	90.00	$1,180.00
Year 3 $1,000.00 × 9%	90.00	$1,270.00
	$ 270.00	

Citizens Bank

Compound Interest Calculation	Compound Interest	Accumulated Year-end Balance
Year 1 $1,000.00 × 9%	$ 90.00	$1,090.00
Year 2 $1,090.00 × 9%	98.10	$1,188.10
Year 3 $1,188.10 × 9%	106.93	$1,295.03
	$ 295.03	

$25.03 Difference

Note in Illustration C-2 that simple interest uses the initial principal of $1,000 to calculate the interest in all three years. Compound interest uses the accumulated balance (principal plus interest to date) at each year end to calculate interest in the succeeding year—which explains why your compound interest account is larger.

Obviously, if you had a choice between investing your money at simple interest or at compound interest, you would choose compound interest, all other things—especially risk—being equal. In the example, compounding provides $25.03 of additional interest income. For practical purposes compounding assumes that unpaid interest earned becomes a part of the principal, and the accumulated balance at the end of each year becomes the new principal on which interest is earned during the next year.

As can be seen in Illustration C-2, you should invest your money at Citizens Bank, which compounds interest annually. Compound interest is used in most business situations. Simple interest is generally applicable only to short-term situations of one year or less.

SECTION 1

FUTURE VALUE CONCEPTS

FUTURE VALUE OF A SINGLE AMOUNT

STUDY OBJECTIVE 2

Solve for future value of a single amount.

The **future value of a single amount** is the value at a future date of a given amount invested assuming compound interest. For example, in Illustration C-2, $1,295.03 is the future value of the $1,000 at the end of three years. The $1,295.03 could be determined more easily by using the following formula:

$$FV = p \times (1 + i)^n$$

Where:

FV = Future value of a single amount
p = Principal (or present value)
i = Interest rate for one period
n = Number of periods

The $1,295.03 is calculated as follows:

$$\begin{aligned} FV &= p \times (1 + i)^n \\ &= \$1{,}000 \times (1 + i)^3 \\ &= \$1{,}000 \times 1.29503 \\ &= \$1{,}295.03 \end{aligned}$$

The 1.29503 is calculated by multiplying $(1.09 \times 1.09 \times 1.09 = 1.29503)$. The amounts in this example can be depicted in the time diagram shown in Illustration C-3.

Illustration C-3 Time diagram

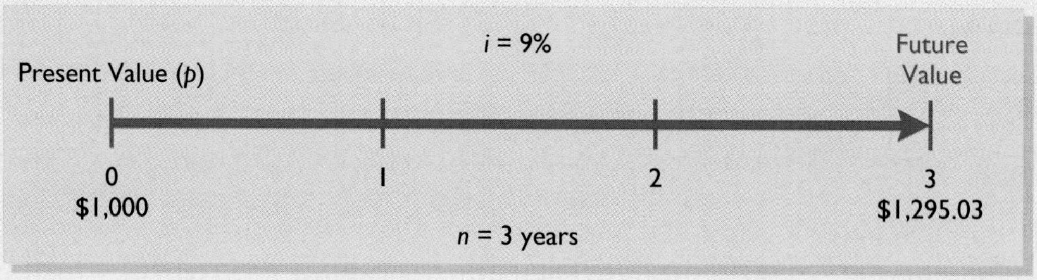

Another method that may be used to calculate the future value of a single amount involves the use of a compound interest table. This table shows the future value of 1 for n periods. Table 1 is such a table.

TABLE 1 Future Value of 1 ($FV = p \times (1 + i)^n$)

(n) Periods	4%	5%	6%	8%	9%	10%	11%	12%	15%
1	1.04000	1.05000	1.06000	1.08000	1.09000	1.10000	1.11000	1.12000	1.15000
2	1.08160	1.10250	1.12360	1.16640	1.18810	1.21000	1.23210	1.25440	1.32250
3	1.12486	1.15763	1.19102	1.25971	1.29503	1.33100	1.36763	1.40493	1.52088
4	1.16986	1.21551	1.26248	1.36049	1.41158	1.46410	1.51807	1.57352	1.74901
5	1.21665	1.27628	1.33823	1.46933	1.53862	1.61051	1.68506	1.76234	2.01136
6	1.26532	1.34010	1.41852	1.58687	1.67710	1.77156	1.87041	1.97382	2.31306
7	1.31593	1.40710	1.50363	1.71382	1.82804	1.94872	2.07616	2.21068	2.66002
8	1.36857	1.47746	1.59385	1.85093	1.99256	2.14359	2.30454	2.47596	3.05902
9	1.42331	1.55133	1.68948	1.99900	2.17189	2.35795	2.55803	2.77308	3.51788
10	1.48024	1.62889	1.79085	2.15892	2.36736	2.59374	2.83942	3.10585	4.04556
11	1.53945	1.71034	1.89830	2.33164	2.58043	2.85312	3.15176	3.47855	4.65239
12	1.60103	1.79586	2.01220	2.51817	2.81267	3.13843	3.49845	3.89598	5.35025
13	1.66507	1.88565	2.13293	2.71962	3.06581	3.45227	3.88328	4.36349	6.15279
14	1.73168	1.97993	2.26090	2.93719	3.34173	3.79750	4.31044	4.88711	7.07571
15	1.80094	2.07893	2.39656	3.17217	3.64248	4.17725	4.78459	5.47357	8.13706
16	1.87298	2.18287	2.54035	3.42594	3.97031	4.59497	5.31089	6.13039	9.35762
17	1.94790	2.29202	2.69277	3.70002	4.32763	5.05447	5.89509	6.86604	10.76126
18	2.02582	2.40662	2.85434	3.99602	4.71712	5.55992	6.54355	7.68997	12.37545
19	2.10685	2.52695	3.02560	4.31570	5.14166	6.11591	7.26334	8.61276	14.23177
20	2.19112	2.65330	3.20714	4.66096	5.60441	6.72750	8.06231	9.64629	16.36654

In Table 1, n is the number of compounding periods. The percentages are the periodic interest rates, and the five-decimal-place numbers in the respective columns are the future value of 1 factors. In using Table 1, the principal amount is multiplied by the future value factor for the specified number of periods and interest rate. For example, the future value factor for two periods at 9% is 1.18810. Multiplying this factor by $1,000 equals $1,188.10, which is the accumulated balance at the end of year 2 in the Citizens Bank example in Illustration C-2. The $1,295.03 accumulated balance at the end of the third year can be calculated from Table 1 by multiplying the future value factor for three periods (1.29503) by the $1,000.

The demonstration problem in Illustration C-4 shows how to use Table 1.

Illustration C-4
Demonstration problem—using Table 1 for *FV* of 1

John and Mary Rich invested $20,000 in a savings account paying 6% interest at the time their son, Mike, was born. The money is to be used by Mike for his education. On his 18th birthday, Mike withdraws the money from his savings account. How much did Mike withdraw from his account?

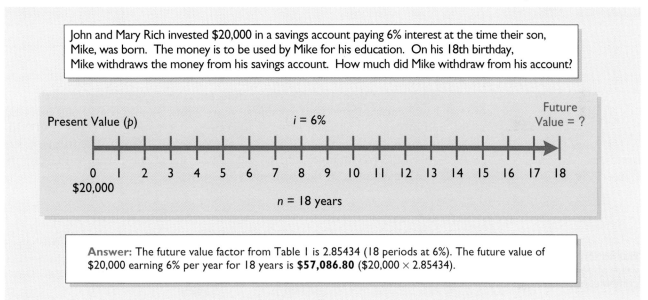

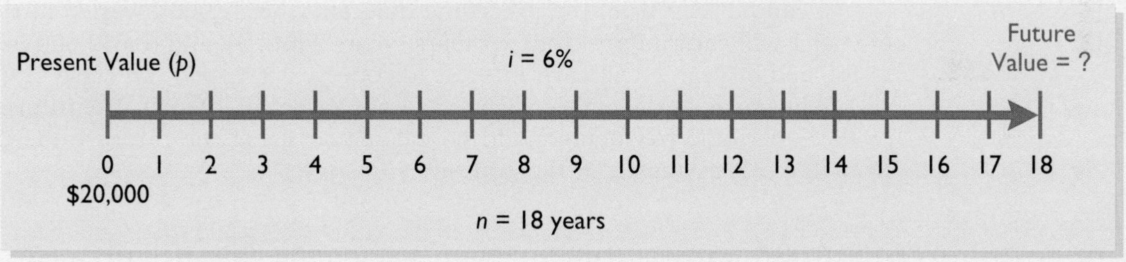

Answer: The future value factor from Table 1 is 2.85434 (18 periods at 6%). The future value of $20,000 earning 6% per year for 18 years is **$57,086.80** ($20,000 × 2.85434).

Future Value of an Annuity

STUDY OBJECTIVE 3
Solve for future value of an annuity.

The preceding discussion involved the accumulation of only a single principal sum. Individuals and businesses frequently encounter situations in which a series of equal dollar amounts are to be paid or received periodically, such as loans or lease (rental) contracts. Such payments or receipts of equal dollar amounts are referred to as an **annuity**. The **future value of an annuity** is the sum of all the payments (receipts) plus the accumulated compound interest on them. In calculating the future value of an annuity, it is necessary to know (1) the interest rate, (2) the number of compounding periods, and (3) the amount of the periodic payments or receipts.

To illustrate the calculation of the future value of an annuity, assume that you invest $2,000 at the end of each year for three years at 5% interest compounded annually. This situation is depicted in the time diagram in Illustration C-5.

Illustration C-5 Time diagram for a three-year annuity

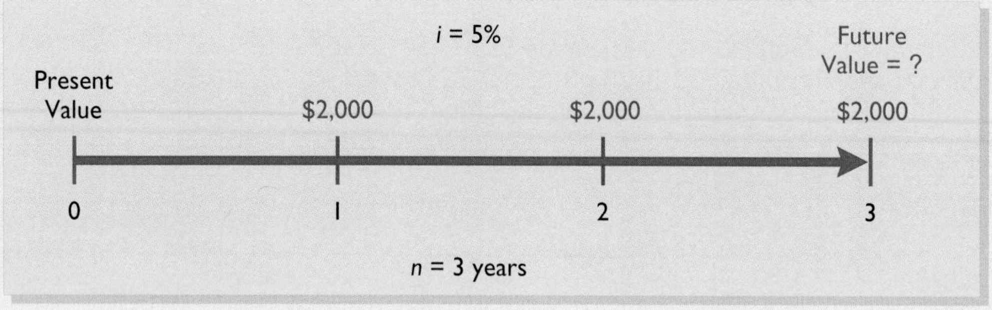

As can be seen from the preceding diagram, the $2,000 invested at the end of year 1 will earn interest for two years (years 2 and 3), and the $2,000 invested at the end of year 2 will earn interest for one year (year 3). The last $2,000 investment (made at the end of year 3) will not earn any interest. The future value of these periodic payments could be calculated using the future value factors from Table 1, as shown in Illustration C-6.

Illustration C-6 Future value of periodic payment computation

Year Invested	Amount Invested	×	Future Value of 1 Factor at 5%	=	Future Value
1	$2,000	×	1.10250		$2,205
2	$2,000	×	1.05000		2,100
3	$2,000	×	1.00000		2,000
			3.15250		$6,305

The first $2,000 investment is multiplied by the future value factor for two periods (1.1025) because two years' interest will accumulate on it (in years 2 and 3). The second $2,000 investment will earn only one year's interest (in year 3) and therefore is multiplied by the future value factor for one year (1.0500). The final $2,000 investment is made at the end of the third year and will not earn any interest. Consequently, the future value of the last $2,000 invested is only $2,000 since it does not accumulate any interest.

This method of calculation is required when the periodic payments or receipts are not equal in each period. However, when the periodic payments (receipts) are the same in each period, the future value can be calculated by using a future value of an annuity of 1 table. Table 2 is such a table.

TABLE 2 Future Value of an Annuity of 1 ($FV = p \times (((1 + i)^n - I) \div i)$)

(*n*) Periods	4%	5%	6%	8%	9%	10%	11%	12%	15%
1	1.00000	1.00000	1.00000	1.00000	1.00000	1.00000	1.00000	1.00000	1.00000
2	2.04000	2.05000	2.06000	2.08000	2.09000	2.10000	2.11000	2.12000	2.15000
3	3.12160	3.15250	3.18360	3.24640	3.27810	3.31000	3.34210	3.37440	3.47250
4	4.24646	4.31012	4.37462	4.50611	4.57313	4.64100	4.70973	4.77933	4.99338
5	5.41632	5.52563	5.63709	5.86660	5.98471	6.10510	6.22780	6.35285	6.74238
6	6.63298	6.80191	6.97533	7.33593	7.52334	7.71561	7.91286	8.11519	8.75374
7	7.89829	8.14201	8.39384	8.92280	9.20044	9.48717	9.78327	10.08901	11.06680
8	9.21423	9.54911	9.89747	10.63663	11.02847	11.43589	11.85943	12.29969	13.72682
9	10.58280	11.02656	11.49132	12.48756	13.02104	13.57948	14.16397	14.77566	16.78584
10	12.00611	12.57789	13.18079	14.48656	15.19293	15.93742	16.72201	17.54874	20.30372
11	13.48635	14.20679	14.97164	16.64549	17.56029	18.53117	19.56143	20.65458	24.34928
12	15.02581	15.91713	16.86994	18.97713	20.14072	21.38428	22.71319	24.13313	29.00167
13	16.62684	17.71298	18.88214	21.49530	22.95339	24.52271	26.21164	28.02911	34.35192
14	18.29191	19.59863	21.01507	24.21492	26.01919	27.97498	30.09492	32.39260	40.50471
15	20.02359	21.57856	23.27597	27.15211	29.36092	31.77248	34.40536	37.27971	47.58041
16	21.82453	23.65749	25.67253	30.32428	33.00340	35.94973	39.18995	42.75328	55.71747
17	23.69751	25.84037	28.21288	33.75023	36.97351	40.54470	44.50084	48.88367	65.07509
18	25.64541	28.13238	30.90565	37.45024	41.30134	45.59917	50.39593	55.74971	75.83636
19	27.67123	30.53900	33.75999	41.44626	46.01846	51.15909	56.93949	63.43968	88.21181
20	29.77808	33.06595	36.78559	45.76196	51.16012	57.27500	64.20283	72.05244	102.44358

Table 2 shows the future value of 1 to be received periodically for a given number of periods. From Table 2 it can be seen that the future value of an annuity of 1 factor for 3 periods at 5% is 3.15250. The future value factor is the total of the three individual future value factors as shown in Illustration C-6. Multiplying this amount by the annual investment of $2,000 produces a future value of $6,305.

The demonstration problem in Illustration C-7 (at the top of the next page) shows how to use Table 2.

Illustration C-7
Demonstration problem—using Table 2 for *FV* of an annuity of 1

Jean and Andrée Lévesque's daughter, Céline, has just started high school. They decide to start a university fund for her. They will invest $2,500 in a savings account at the end of each year she is in high school (four payments total). The account will earn 6% interest compounded annually. How much will be in the fund at the time Céline graduates from high school?

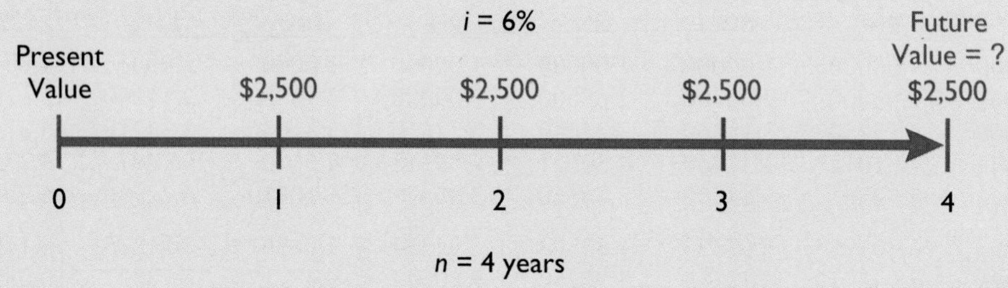

Answer: The future value factor from Table 2 is 4.37462 (four periods at 6%). The future value of $2,500 invested each year for four years at 6% interest is **$10,936.55** ($2,500 × 4.37462).

SECTION 2

PRESENT VALUE CONCEPTS

PRESENT VALUE VARIABLES

STUDY OBJECTIVE 4

Identify the variables fundamental to solving present value problems.

The **present value**, like the future value, is based on three variables: (1) the dollar amount to be received (future amount), (2) the length of time until the amount is received (number of periods), and (3) the interest rate (the discount rate). The process of determining the present value is referred to as **discounting the future amount**.

In this textbook, present value calculations are used in measuring several items. For example, in Chapter 10, to determine the market price of a bond, the present value of the principal and interest payments is calculated. In addition, the determination of the amount to be reported for notes payable and lease liability involves present value computations.

Present Value of a Single Amount

To illustrate present value concepts, assume that you are willing to invest a sum of money that will yield \$1,000 at the end of one year. In other words, what amount would you need to invest today to have \$1,000 one year from now? If you want a 10% rate of return, the investment or present value is \$909.09 (\$1,000 ÷ 1.10). The calculation of this amount is shown in Illustration C-8.

STUDY OBJECTIVE 5

Solve for present value of a single amount.

$$\text{Present Value} = \text{Future Value} \div (1 + i)^n$$
$$PV = FV \div (1 + 10\%)^1$$
$$PV = \$1{,}000 \div 1.10$$
$$PV = \$909.09$$

Illustration C-8 Present value calculation—\$1,000 discounted at 10% for one year

The future amount (\$1,000), the discount rate (10%), and the number of periods (1) are known. The variables in this situation can be depicted in the time diagram in Illustration C-9.

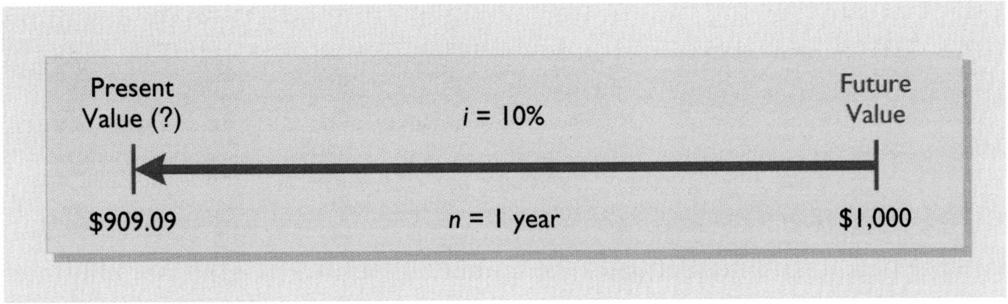

Illustration C-9 Finding present value if discounted for one period

If the single amount of \$1,000 is to be received **in two years** and discounted at 10% [$PV = \$1{,}000 \div (1 + 10\%)^2$], its present value is \$826.45 [(\$1,000 ÷ 1.10) ÷ 1.10]. This is depicted in Illustration C-10.

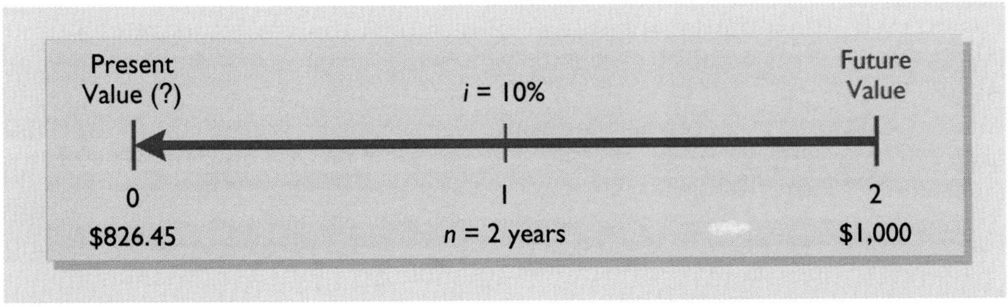

Illustration C-10 Finding present value if discounted for two periods

The present value of 1 may also be determined through tables that show the present value of 1 for *n* periods. In Table 3 on the following page, *n* is the number of discounting periods involved. The percentages are the periodic interest rates or discount rates, and the five-decimal-place numbers in the respective columns are the present value of 1 factors.

TABLE 3 Present Value of 1 ($PV = FV \div (1 + i)^n$)

(n) Periods	4%	5%	6%	8%	9%	10%	11%	12%	15%
1	.96154	.95238	.94340	.92593	.91743	.90909	.90090	.89286	.86957
2	.92456	.90703	.89000	.85734	.84168	.82645	.81162	.79719	.75614
3	.88900	.86384	.83962	.79383	.77218	.75131	.73119	.71178	.65752
4	.85480	.82270	.79209	.73503	.70843	.68301	.65873	.63552	.57175
5	.82193	.78353	.74726	.68058	.64993	.62092	.59345	.56743	.49718
6	.79031	.74622	.70496	.63017	.59627	.56447	.53464	.50663	.43233
7	.75992	.71068	.66506	.58349	.54703	.51316	.48166	.45235	.37594
8	.73069	.67684	.62741	.54027	.50187	.46651	.43393	.40388	.32690
9	.70259	.64461	.59190	.50025	.46043	.42410	.39092	.36061	.28426
10	.67556	.61391	.55839	.46319	.42241	.38554	.35218	.32197	.24718
11	.64958	.58468	.52679	.42888	.38753	.35049	.31728	.28748	.21494
12	.62460	.55684	.49697	.39711	.35553	.31863	.28584	.25668	.18691
13	.60057	.53032	.46884	.36770	.32618	.28966	.25751	.22917	.16253
14	.57748	.50507	.44230	.34046	.29925	.26333	.23199	.20462	.14133
15	.55526	.48102	.41727	.31524	.27454	.23939	.20900	.18270	.12289
16	.53391	.45811	.39365	.29189	.25187	.21763	.18829	.16312	.10686
17	.51337	.43630	.37136	.27027	.23107	.19784	.16963	.14564	.09293
18	.49363	.41552	.35034	.25025	.21199	.17986	.15282	.13004	.08081
19	.47464	.39573	.33051	.23171	.19449	.16351	.13768	.11611	.07027
20	.45639	.37689	.31180	.21455	.17843	.14864	.12403	.10367	.06110

When Table 3 is used, the future value is multiplied by the present value factor specified at the intersection of the number of periods and the discount rate. For example, the present value factor for one period at a discount rate of 10% is 0.90909, which equals the \$909.09 (\$1,000 × 0.90909) calculated in Illustration C-8. For two periods at a discount rate of 10%, the present value factor is 0.82645, which equals the \$826.45 (\$1,000 × 0.82645) calculated previously.

Note that a higher discount rate produces a smaller present value. For example, using a 15% discount rate, the present value of \$1,000 due one year from now is \$869.57 versus \$909.09 at 10%. It should also be recognized that the further removed from the present the future value is, the smaller the present value. For example, using the same discount rate of 10%, the present value of \$1,000 due in **five years** is \$620.92 versus the present value of \$1,000 due in **one year** is \$909.09.

The following two demonstration problems (Illustrations C-11, C-12) illustrate how to use Table 3.

Illustration C-11
Demonstration problem—using Table 3 for *PV* of 1

Suppose you have a winning lottery ticket and Lotto 6/49 gives you the option of taking $10,000 three years from now or taking the present value of $10,000 now. Lotto 6/49 uses an 8% rate in discounting. How much will you receive if you accept your winnings now?

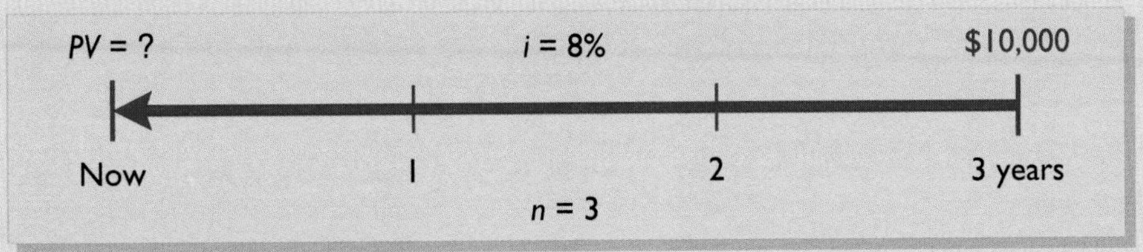

Answer: The present value factor from Table 3 is 0.79383 (three periods at 8%). The present value of $10,000 to be received in three years discounted at 8% is **$7,938.30** ($10,000 × 0.79383).

Illustration C-12
Demonstration problem—using Table 3 for *PV* of 1

Determine the amount you must deposit now in your SUPER savings account, paying 9% interest, in order to accumulate $5,000 for a down payment four years from now on a new Chevy Blazer.

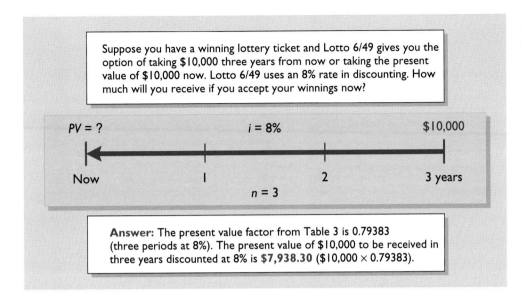

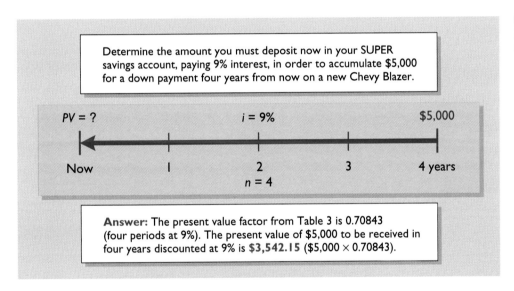

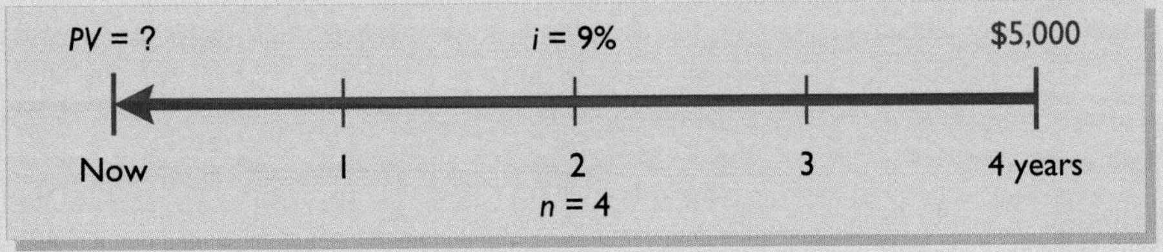

Answer: The present value factor from Table 3 is 0.70843 (four periods at 9%). The present value of $5,000 to be received in four years discounted at 9% is **$3,542.15** ($5,000 × 0.70843).

Present Value of an Annuity

STUDY OBJECTIVE 6
Solve for present value of an annuity.

The preceding discussion involved the discounting of only a single future amount. Businesses and individuals frequently engage in transactions in which a series of equal dollar amounts are to be received or paid periodically. Examples of a series of periodic receipts or payments are loan agreements, instalment sales, mortgage notes, lease (rental) contracts, and pension obligations. These series of periodic receipts or payments are called **annuities**. In calculating the **present value of an annuity**, it is necessary to know (1) the discount rate, (2) the number of discount periods, and (3) the amount of the periodic receipts or payments. To illustrate the calculation of the present value of an annuity, assume that you will receive $1,000 cash annually for three years at a time when the discount rate is 10%. This situation is depicted in the time diagram in Illustration C-13.

Illustration C-13 Time diagram for a three-year annuity

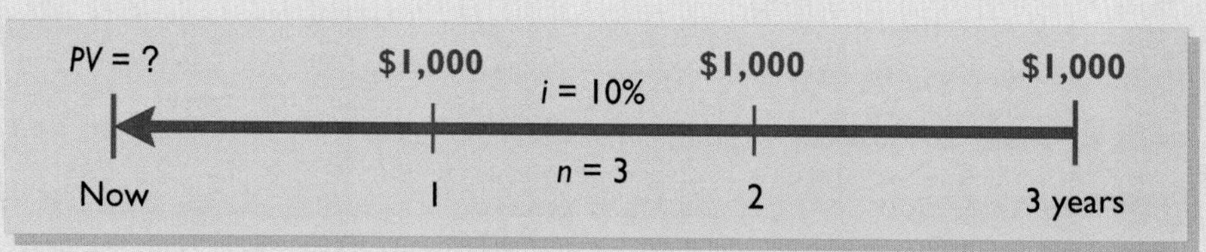

The present value in this situation may be calculated as shown in Illustration C-14.

Illustration C-14 Present value of a series of future amounts calculation

Future Amount	×	Present Value of 1 Factor at 10%	=	Present Value
$1,000 (One year away)		0.90909		$ 909.09
1,000 (Two years away)		0.82645		826.45
1,000 (Three years away)		0.75132		751.32
		2.48686		$2,486.86

This method of calculation is required when the periodic cash flows are not uniform in each period. When the future receipts are the same in each period, there are two other ways to calculate present value. First, the annual cash flow can be multiplied by the sum of the three present value factors. In the previous example, $1,000 × 2.48686 equals $2,486.86. Second, annuity tables may be used. As illustrated in Table 4 below, these tables show the present value of 1 to be received periodically for a given number of periods.

TABLE 4 Present Value of an Annuity of 1 ($PV = (1 - (1 \div (1 + i)^n)) \div i$)

(n) Periods	4%	5%	6%	8%	9%	10%	11%	12%	15%
1	0.96154	0.95238	0.94340	0.92593	0.91743	0.90909	0.90090	0.89286	0 .86957
2	1.88609	1.85941	1.83339	1.78326	1.75911	1.73554	1.71252	1.69005	1.62571
3	2.77509	2.72325	2.67301	2.57710	2.53129	2.48685	2.44371	2.40183	2.28323
4	3.62990	3.54595	3.46511	3.31213	3.23972	3.16987	3.10245	3.03735	2.85498
5	4.45182	4.32948	4.21236	3.99271	3.88965	3.79079	3.69590	3.60478	3.35216
6	5.24214	5.07569	4.91732	4.62288	4.48592	4.35526	4.23054	4.11141	3.78448
7	6.00205	5.78637	5.58238	5.20637	5.03295	4.86842	4.71220	4.56376	4.16042
8	6.73274	6.46321	6.20979	5.74664	5.53482	5.33493	5.14612	4.96764	4.48732
9	7.43533	7.10782	6.80169	6.24689	5.99525	5.75902	5.53705	5.32825	4.77158
10	8.11090	7.72173	7.36009	6.71008	6.41766	6.14457	5.88923	5.65022	5.01877
11	8.76048	8.30641	7.88687	7.13896	6.80519	6.49506	6.20652	5.93770	5.23371
12	9.38507	8.86325	8.38384	7.53608	7.16073	6.81369	6.49236	6.19437	5.42062
13	9.98565	9.39357	8.85268	7.90378	7.48690	7.10336	6.74987	6.42355	5.58315
14	10.56312	9.89864	9.29498	8.24424	7.78615	7.36669	6.98187	6.62817	5.72448
15	11.11839	10.37966	9.71225	8.55948	8.06069	7.60608	7.19087	6.81086	5.84737
16	11.65230	10.83777	10.10590	8.85137	8.31256	7.82371	7.37916	6.97399	5.95423
17	12.16567	11.27407	10.47726	9.12164	8.54363	8.02155	7.54879	7.11963	6.04716
18	12.65930	11.68959	10.82760	9.37189	8.75563	8.20141	7.70162	7.24967	6.12797
19	13.13394	12.08532	11.15812	9.60360	8.95011	8.36492	7.83929	7.36578	6.19823
20	13.59033	12.46221	11.46992	9.81815	9.12855	8.51356	7.96333	7.46944	6.25933

From Table 4 it can be seen that the present value of an annuity of 1 factor for three periods at 10% is 2.48685.[1] This present value factor is the total of the three individual present value factors, as shown in Illustration C-14. Applying this amount to the annual cash flow of $1,000 produces a present value of $2,486.85.

The following demonstration problem (Illustration C-15) illustrates how to use Table 4.

Illustration C-15
Demonstration problem—using Table 4 for *PV* of an annuity of 1

Kildare Corporation has just signed a capital lease contract for equipment that requires rental payments of $6,000 each, to be paid at the end of each of the next five years. The appropriate discount rate is 12%. What is the present value of the rental payments—that is, the amount used to capitalize the leased equipment?

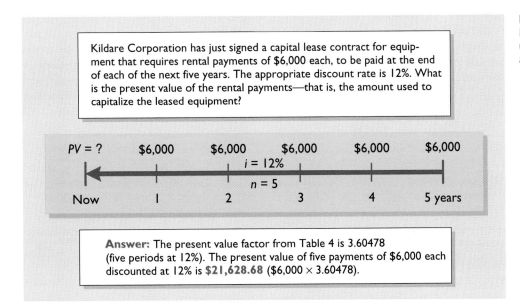

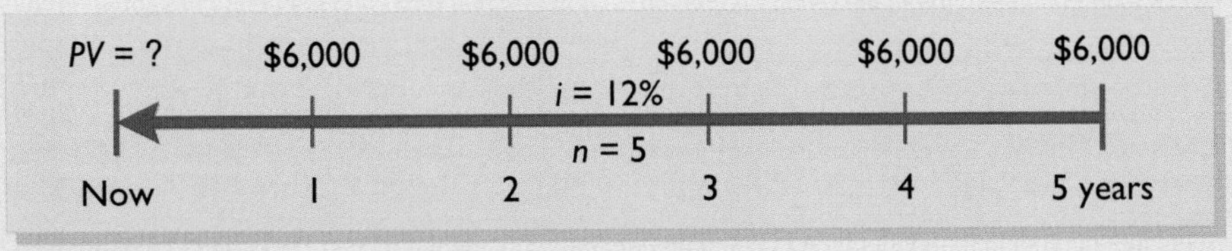

Answer: The present value factor from Table 4 is 3.60478 (five periods at 12%). The present value of five payments of $6,000 each discounted at 12% is **$21,628.68** ($6,000 × 3.60478).

TIME PERIODS AND DISCOUNTING

In the preceding calculations, the discounting has been done on an annual basis using an annual interest rate. Discounting may also be done over shorter periods of time such as monthly, quarterly, or semiannually. When the time frame is less than one year, it is necessary to convert the annual interest rate to the applicable time frame. Assume, for example, that the investor in Illustration C-14 received $500 **semiannually** for three years instead of $1,000 annually. In this case, the number of periods becomes 6 (3 × 2), the semiannual discount rate is 5% (10% × 6/12 mos.). The present value factor from Table 4 is 5.07569, and the present value of the future cash flows is $2,537.85 (5.07569 × $500). This amount is slightly higher than the $2,486.86 calculated in Illustration C-14 because interest is calculated twice during the same year. Therefore interest is earned on the first half year's interest.

CALCULATING THE PRESENT VALUE OF A LONG-TERM NOTE OR BOND

STUDY OBJECTIVE 7
Calculate the present value of notes and bonds.

The present value (or market price) of a long-term note or bond is a function of three variables: (1) the payment amounts, (2) the length of time until the amounts are paid, and (3) the discount rate. Our illustration uses a five-year bond issue.

[1]The difference of 0.00001 between 2.48686 and 2.48685 is due to rounding.

The first variable (dollars to be paid) is made up of two elements: (1) a series of interest payments (an annuity) and (2) the principal amount (a single sum). To calculate the present value of the bond, both the interest payments and the principal amount must be discounted—two different calculations.

When the investor's discount rate is equal to the bond's contractual interest rate, the present value of the bonds will equal the face value of the bonds. To illustrate, assume a bond issue of 10%, five-year bonds with a face value of $100,000 with interest payable **semiannually** on January 1 and July 1. If the discount rate is the same as the contractual rate, the bonds will sell at face value. In this case, the investor will receive (1) $100,000 at maturity and (2) a series of ten $5,000 interest payments ($100,000 × 10% × 6/12 mos.) over the term of the bonds. The length of time is expressed in terms of interest periods, in this case, 10, and the discount rate per semiannual interest period, 5%. The following time diagram (Illustration C-16) depicts the variables involved in this discounting situation.

Illustration C-16 Time diagram for present value of a 10%, five-year bond paying interest semiannually

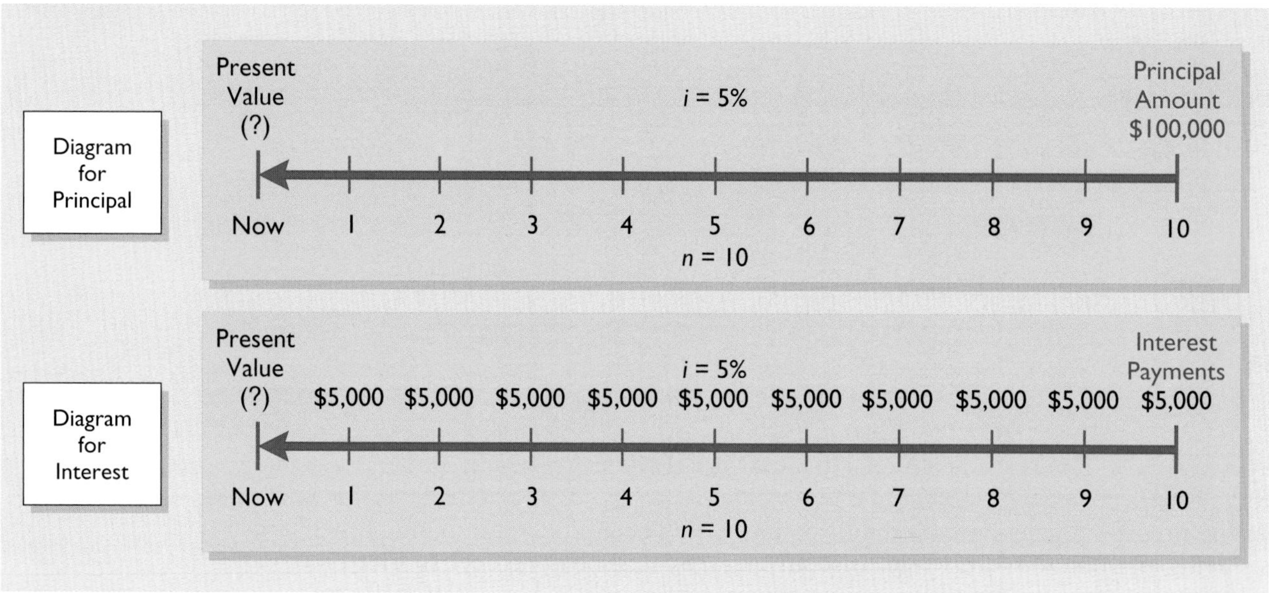

The calculation of the present value of these bonds is shown in Illustration C-17.

Illustration C-17 Present value of principal and interest (face value)

10% Contractual Rate—10% Discount Rate	
Present value of principal to be received at maturity	
$100,000 × *PV* of 1 due in 10 periods at 5%	
$100,000 × 0.61391 (Table 3)	$ 61,391
Present value of interest to be received periodically over the term of the bonds	
$5,000 × *PV* of 1 due periodically for 10 periods at 5%	
$5,000 × 7.72173 (Table 4)	38,609
Present value of bonds	**$100,000**

Now assume that the investor's required rate of return is 12%, not 10%. The future amounts are again $100,000 and $5,000, respectively, but now a discount rate of 6% (12% × 6/12 mos.) must be used. The present value of the bonds is $92,639, as calculated in Illustration C-18.

10% Contractual Rate—12% Discount Rate	
Present value of principal to be received at maturity	
$100,000 × 0.55839 (Table 3)	$ 55,839
Present value of interest to be received periodically over the term of the bonds	
$5,000 × 7.36009 (Table 4)	36,800
Present value of bonds	**$92,639**

Illustration C-18
Present value of principal and interest (discount)

Conversely, if the discount rate is 8% and the contractual rate is 10%, the present value of the bonds is $108,111, calculated as shown in Illustration C-19.

10% Contractual Rate—8% Discount Rate	
Present value of principal to be received at maturity	
$100,000 × 0.67556 (Table 3)	$ 67,556
Present value of interest to be received periodically over the term of the bonds	
$5,000 × 8.11090 (Table 4)	40,555
Present value of bonds	**$108,111**

Illustration C-19
Present value of principal and interest (premium)

The above discussion relied on present value tables in solving present value problems. Electronic hand-held calculators may also be used to calculate present values without the use of these tables. Many calculators, especially the "business" calculators, have present value (*PV*) and future value (*FV*) functions. They allow you to calculate present or future values by inputting the proper amount, discount rate, and periods, and pressing the *PV* or *FV* key. Most computer spreadsheets and programs also have built-in formulas to perform present and future value functions given the basic information of the situation.

Summary of Study Objectives

1 ***Distinguish between simple and compound interest.*** Simple interest is calculated on the principal only while compound interest is calculated on the principal and any interest earned that has not been withdrawn.

2 ***Solve for future value of a single amount.*** Prepare a time diagram of the problem. Identify the principal amount, the number of compounding periods, and the interest rate. Using the future value of 1 table, multiply the principal amount by the future value factor specified at the intersection of the number of periods and the interest rate.

3 ***Solve for future value of an annuity.*** Prepare a time diagram of the problem. Identify the amount of the periodic payments, the number of compounding periods, and the interest rate. Using the future value of an annuity of 1 table, multiply the amount of the payments by the future value factor specified at the intersection of the number of periods and the interest rate.

4 ***Identify the variables fundamental to solving present value problems.*** The following three variables are fundamental to solving present value problems: (1) the future amount, (2) the number of periods, and (3) the interest rate (the discount rate).

5 ***Solve for present value of a single amount.*** Prepare a time diagram of the problem. Identify the future amount, the number of discounting periods, and the discount (interest) rate. Using the present value of 1 table, multiply the future amount by the present value factor specified at the intersection of the number of periods and the discount rate.

6 ***Solve for present value of an annuity.*** Prepare a time diagram of the problem. Identify the future amounts (annuities), the number of discounting periods, and the discount (interest) rate. Using the present value of an annuity of 1 table, multiply the amount of the annuity by the present value factor specified at the intersection of the number of periods and the interest rate.

7 ***Calculate the present value of notes and bonds.*** Determine the present value of the principal amount: Multiply the principal amount (a single future amount) by the present value factor (from the present value of 1 table) intersecting at the number of periods (number of interest payments) and the discount rate. Determine the present value of the series of interest payments: Multiply the amount of the interest payment by the present value factor (from the present value of an annuity of 1 table) intersecting at the number of periods (number of interest payments) and the discount rate. Add the present value of the principal amount to the present value of the interest payments to arrive at the present value of the note or bond.

GLOSSARY

Annuity A series of equal dollar amounts to be paid or received periodically. (p. C-5)

Compound interest The interest calculated on the principal and any interest earned that has not been paid or received. (p. C-2)

Discounting the future amount(s) The process of determining present value. (p. C-8)

Future value of a single amount The value at a future date of a given amount invested, assuming compound interest. (p. C-3)

Future value of an annuity The sum of all the payments or receipts plus the accumulated compound interest on them. (p. C-5)

Interest Payment for the use of another's money. (p. C-2)

Present value The value now of a given amount to be invested or received in the future, assuming compound interest. (p. C-8)

Present value of an annuity A series of future receipts or payments discounted to their value now, assuming compound interest. (p. C-11)

Principal The amount borrowed or invested. (p. C-2)

Simple interest The interest calculated on the principal only. (p. C-2)

BRIEF EXERCISES (USE TABLES TO SOLVE EXERCISES)

Calculate the future value of a single amount.
(SO 1, 2)

BEC-1 Don Smith invested $5,000 at 8% annual interest, and left the money invested without withdrawing any of the interest for 12 years. At the end of the 12 years, Don withdrew the accumulated amount of money. (a) What amount did Don withdraw, assuming the investment earns simple interest? (b) What amount did Don withdraw, assuming the investment earns interest compounded annually?

Calculate the future value of a single amount.
(SO 2)

BEC-2 Porter Company Limited signed a lease for an office building for a period of eight years. Under the lease agreement, a security deposit of $10,000 is made. The deposit will be returned at the expiration of the lease with interest compounded at 6% per year. What amount will Porter receive at the time the lease expires?

Calculate the future value of a single amount.
(SO 2)

BEC-3 Ron Watson borrowed $20,000 on July 1, 1999. This amount plus accrued interest at 9% compounded annually is to be repaid on July 1, 2004. How much will Ron have to repay on July 1, 2004?

Use future value tables.
(SO 2, 3)

BEC-4 For each of the following cases, indicate (a) to what interest rate columns and (b) to what number of periods you would refer in looking up the future value factor.

1. In Table 1 (future value of 1):

	Annual Rate	Number of Years Invested	Compounded
Case A	6%	5	Annually
Case B	5%	3	Semiannually

2. In Table 2 (future value of an annuity of 1):

	Annual Rate	Number of Years Invested	Compounded
Case A	5%	10	Annually
Case B	4%	6	Semiannually

BEC-5 David and Kathy Hatcher invested $7,000 in a savings account paying 8% annual interest when their daughter, Sue, was born. They also deposited $1,000 on each of her birthdays until she was 18 (including her 18th birthday). How much was in the savings account on her 18th birthday (after the last deposit)?

Calculate the future value of a single amount and of an annuity.
(SO 2, 3)

BEC-6 Gordon Company Ltd. issued $1,000,000 of 10-year bonds and agreed to make annual deposits of $60,000. The deposits are made at the end of each year into an account paying 5% annual interest. What amount will be in the account at the end of 10 years?

Calculate the future value of an annuity.
(SO 3)

BEC-7 Smolinski Company Ltd. is considering an investment which will return a lump sum of $500,000 five years from now. What amount should Smolinski Company pay for this investment to earn a 12% return?

Calculate the present value of a single amount investment.
(SO 5)

BEC-8 Pizzeria Company Inc. earns 15% on an investment that will return $875,000 eight years from now. What is the amount Pizzeria should invest now to earn this rate of return?

Calculate the present value of a single amount investment.
(SO 5)

BEC-9 Ramos Limited is considering purchasing equipment. The equipment will produce the following cash flows: Year 1, $35,000; Year 2, $45,000; Year 3, $55,000. Ramos requires a minimum rate of return of 15%. What is the maximum price Ramos should pay for this equipment?

Calculate the maximum price to pay for a machine.
(SO 5)

BEC-10 If Kerry Rodriguez invests $2,090 now and she will receive $10,000 at the end of 15 years, what annual rate of interest will Kerry earn on her investment? [Hint: Use Table 3.]

Calculate the interest rate on a single amount.
(SO 5)

BEC-11 Maloney Cork has been offered the opportunity of investing $43,233 now. The investment will earn 15% per year and at the end of that time will return Maloney $100,000. How many years must Maloney wait to receive $100,000? [Hint: Use Table 3.]

Calculate the number of periods of a single amount.
(SO 5)

BEC-12 For each of the following cases, indicate (a) to what interest rate columns and (b) to what number of periods you would refer in looking up the discount rate.

Use present value tables.
(SO 5, 6)

1. In Table 3 (present value of 1):

	Annual Rate	Number of Years Involved	Discounts per Year
Case A	12%	6	Annually
Case B	10%	15	Annually
Case C	8%	8	Semiannually

2. In Table 4 (present value of an annuity of 1):

	Annual Rate	Number of Years Involved	Number of Payments Involved	Frequency of Payments
Case A	12%	20	20	Annually
Case B	10%	5	5	Annually
Case C	8%	4	8	Semiannually

BEC-13 (a) What is the present value of $10,000 due eight periods from now, discounted at 10%?
(b) What is the present value of $10,000 to be received at the end of each of six periods, discounted at 8%?

Determine present values.
(SO 5, 6)

BEC-14 Kilarny Corporation is considering investing in an annuity contract that will return $25,000 annually at the end of each year for 15 years. What amount should Kilarny Company pay for this investment if it earns a 6% return?

Calculate the present value of an annuity investment.
(SO 6)

BEC-15 Zarita Enterprises earns 9% on an investment that pays back $110,000 at the end of each of the next six years. What is the amount Zarita Enterprises invested to earn the 9% rate of return?

Calculate the present value of an annuity investment.
(SO 6)

BEC-16 Barney Googal owns a garage and is contemplating purchasing a tire retreading machine for $16,100. After estimating costs and revenues, Barney projects a net cash flow from the retreading machine of $2,690 annually for eight years. Barney hopes to earn a return of 11% on such investments. What is the present value of the retreading operation? Should Barney Googal purchase the retreading machine?

Calculate the present value of a machine for purposes of making a purchase decision.
(SO 6)

Calculate the interest rate on an annuity.
(SO 6)

BEC-17 Annie Dublin made an investment of $9,818.15. From this investment, she will receive $1,000 annually for the next 20 years starting one year from now. What rate of interest will Annie's investment be earning for her? [Hint: Use Table 4.]

Calculate the number of periods of an annuity.
(SO 6)

BEC-18 Andy Sainz invests $7,786.15 now for a series of $1,000 annual returns beginning one year from now. Andy will earn a return of 9% on the initial investment. How many annual payments of $1,000 will Andy receive? [Hint: Use Table 4.]

Calculate the present value of bonds.
(SO 7)

BEC-19 The CrossCountry Railway Co. is about to issue $100,000 of 10-year bonds paying a 11% interest rate, with interest payable semiannually. The discount rate for such securities is 8%. How much can CrossCountry Railway expect to receive from the sale of these bonds?

Calculate the present value of bonds.
(SO 7)

BEC-20 Assume the same information as BEC-19 except that the discount rate was 12% instead of 8%. In this case, how much can CrossCountry Railway expect to receive from the sale of these bonds?

Calculate the present value of a note.
(SO 7)

BEC-21 Caledonian Corporation receives a $50,000,six-year note bearing interest of 8% (paid annually) from a customer at a time when the discount rate is 9%. What is the present value of the note received by Caledonian?

Calculate the present value of bonds.
(SO 7)

BEC-22 Galway Bay Enterprises issued 9%, eight-year, $2,000,000 par value bonds that pay interest semiannually on October 1 and April 1. The bonds are dated April 1, 2001, and are issued on that date. The discount rate of interest for such bonds on April 1, 2001, is 12%. What cash proceeds did Galway Bay receive from issuance of the bonds?

Calculate the present value of a note.
(SO 7)

BEC-23 Hung-Chao Yu Inc. issues a 10%, five-year mortgage note on January 1, 2001 to obtain financing for new equipment. Land is used as collateral for the note. The terms provide for semiannual instalment payments, of $112,825. What were the cash proceeds received from the issuance of the note?

FINANCIAL ANALYSIS ON THE WEB

www.wiley.com/canada/kimmel

BYPC-1 This case illustrates the time value of money. If you want to see how long it will take to reach your financial goals, try using the "Investing for Kids Java Goals Calculator." Don't be put off by the title, it's an interesting site.

Instructions

Specific requirements of this web case can be found on the Kimmel website.

COMPANY INDEX

WE WANT TO HEAR FROM YOU!

By sharing your opinions about Financial Accounting, you will help us ensure that you are getting the most value for your textbook dollars. After you have used the book for a while, please fill out this form. Fold, tape, and mail it, or fax us toll free at 1(800)565-6802! This questionnaire is also available on our website at: www.wiley.com/canada/kimmel

Course name: ____________________ School name: ____________________

Your name: ____________________ Instructor's Name: ____________________

1) Did you purchase this book (check all that apply):

❑ From your campus bookstore

❑ From a bookstore off-campus

❑ New ❑ Used ❑ For yourself

❑ For yourself and at least one other student

2) Was this text available at the bookstore when you needed it:

❑ Yes ❑ No

3) How far along are you in this course (put an X where you are now)?

❑ __________ ❑ __________ ❑

Beginning Midway Completed

4) How much of this text have you used (put an X where appropriate)?

❑ __________ ❑ __________ ❑

Skimmed Read half Read entire book

5) Have you read the introductory material (i.e., the preface)?

❑ Yes ❑ No ❑ Parts of it

6) Even if you have only skimmed this text, please rate the following features:

Features:	Very valuable/effective	Somewhat valuable/effective	Not valuable/effective
Value as a reference			
Readability			
Design			
Study & review material			
Problems & cases			
Relevant examples			
Overall perception			

7) What do you like most about this book?

____

____

____

What do you like least?

____

____

____

8) May we quote you? Yes______ No_______

If you would like to receive information on other Wiley business books, please fill in the following information:

Mailing address:____

(Street) (Apt. #)

____

(City) (Province) (Postal Code)

9) At the end of the semester, what do you intend to do with this text?

❑ Keep it ❑ Sell it ❑ Unsure

Thank you for your time and feedback!

WILEY
Publishers Since 1807

(fold here)

MAIL POSTE
Canada Post Corporation / Société canadienne des postes
Postage paid / Port payé
if mailed in Canada / si posté au Canada
Business Reply / Réponse d'affaires
0108529899 01

0108529899-M9W1L1-BR01

COLLEGE DIVISION
JOHN WILEY & SONS CANADA LTD
22 WORCESTER RD
PO BOX 56213 STN BRM B
TORONTO ON M7Y 9C1